Election Law

Election Law

Cases and Materials
FOURTH EDITION

Daniel Hays Lowenstein
PROFESSOR OF LAW
UNIVERSITY OF CALIFORNIA, LOS ANGELES
SCHOOL OF LAW

Richard L. Hasen
WILLIAM H. HANNON DISTINGUISHED PROFESSOR OF LAW
LOYOLA LAW SCHOOL
LOS ANGELES, CALIFORNIA

Daniel P. Tokaji
ASSOCIATE PROFESSOR OF LAW
THE OHIO STATE UNIVERSITY
MICHAEL E. MORITZ COLLEGE OF LAW

CAROLINA ACADEMIC PRESS
Durham, North Carolina

ISBN 10: 1-59460-542-4
ISBN 13: 978-1-59460-542-0
Library of Congress Control Number: 2008930708

Carolina Academic Press
700 Kent Street
Durham, North Carolina 27701
Telephone (919) 489-7486
Fax (919) 493-5668
www.cap-press.com

Printed in the United States of America

For
Sharon
Aaron
Nathan
—D.H.L.

For
Lori
Deborah
Shana
Jared
—R.H.

For
Renuka
—D.T

To the memory of
our friend and colleague,
Gary Schwartz
—D.H.L. and R.H.

Summary of Contents

Contents

Introduction to the Fourth Edition

We do not believe the federal prohibition on age discrimination in employment applies to casebook editors, but a few years ago our senior editor, Lowenstein, advised our then junior editor, Hasen, that there would be no need to research that question, because the Fourth Edition would be Lowenstein's last. It seemed prudent, then, to bring on a new editor, ready to serve as Lowenstein's replacement. Lowenstein and Hasen were extremely pleased when Daniel P. Tokaji of the Moritz College of Law at the Ohio State University agreed to take on the role. He joins us as co-editor of this Fourth Edition.

Lowenstein claims the privilege of adding a personal note in this and the following two paragraphs.[a] I began making election law my principal academic specialty in 1980, at which time I believe I was the only law professor in America to do so. Roy Schotland of Georgetown doubled the field the following year, and our number grew slowly through the 1980s. Around the beginning of the 1990s it began to grow faster, and that trend has continued to the present day. If you believe in straight-line extrapolation, in twenty years about 98 percent of American law professors will be specializing in election law.

From early on, I knew that a good casebook would be beneficial for the field, but I hoped someone else would produce one. Finally, more than a decade after I began teaching the subject, and prompted and encouraged by a number of friends, especially Bruce Cain, I set myself to the task. Had I known of its onerousness from the start, I probably would never have begun. But Keith Sipe and the entire staff at Carolina Academic Press made the project as easy for me as they could, and since the book has been in print I have been gratified by the encouragement and constructive criticism I have received from students and colleagues who have used the book.

A couple of years after the book first appeared, I had the great good fortune of being able to recruit Rick Hasen to join me as co-editor, first of the annual supplements and then of the Second and Third Editions. Those who have been using the book from the start do not need to be told how much Hasen's participation improved the book. Now good fortune has struck again, with the addition of Dan Tokaji. A part of me is in this book, and I cannot imagine a better set of hands within which to leave it than those belonging to Hasen and Tokaji. I believe it is a strength of the book that the co-editors disagree among ourselves on substantive issues but see eye to eye on pedagogy and what a casebook should be. We want this book to train lawyers who may practice in election law, but even more we want to provoke thought about the growing interactions between the legal and elec-

---

a. Hasen reserves the right of rebuttal to appear in the Introduction to the Fifth Edition of the book. He has much to say about how much Lowenstein is responsible for the creation of this field (and some of it is even printable in a family publication!).

toral systems. We want the book to have a distinctive and sometimes even idiosyncratic voice, but not to be a vehicle for proselytizing. We want conservatives and liberals, reformers and traditionalists, and Republicans and Democrats all to be comfortable with this book. Then again, at times we want them all to be uncomfortable.

With respect to the Fourth Edition, we are proud to have achieved at least one goal. The volume you are holding is thinner than its predecessor, by about 77 pages. This despite the fact that since the Third Edition the Voting Rights Act has been renewed and the Supreme Court has decided a number of significant election law cases in a variety of fields, including campaign finance, redistricting, political parties, and election administration. Aside from the addition of this new material, we have made other changes, including a significant revamping of the campaign finance chapters, expanded coverage of the political science literature on campaigns in Chapter 11, expanded coverage of election administration in Chapter 7, and addition of a new section in Chapter 8 (on ballot propositions), discussing the vexing question of how strictly election law ground rules should be enforced against participants.

Those who are deeply learned in logic will have deduced that if the size of the book has been reduced and significant amounts of new material have been added, then some material must have been cut. We hope that the cuts make the book more streamlined and usable. But if you are an instructor who is regretting the loss of some of your favorite cases, take consolation in the fact that the same is true of some of ours.

Acknowledgments

Another addition is the Appendix on election law research, written by Sarah Sampson, of the Georgetown Law Library. We thank Ms. Sampson for her generous contribution and we hope our readers find it useful. In addition to the acknowledgements contained in the introductions to the first three editions, we wish to add our thanks to the following able research assistants: Alex Chen, Danielle De Smeth, Amanda Dittmar, Melissa Eakin, Natalie Heaton, John Khosravi, Ben Kington, Hal Melom, Jonathan Miles, Kristine Noyes, and Damion Robinson.

Introduction to the Third Edition

The first edition of this book was published in 1995 and the second edition in 2001. The Voting Rights Act is scheduled to come up for renewal in 2007, and we supposed that would be a good year if a third edition was warranted by sufficient interest in the book.

But as admirers of Scottish poetry are well aware, plans of mice and men, however well-laid, are apt to go agley, and the same applies to the plans of casebook authors. In 2002, Congress passed the Bipartisan Campaign Reform Act, the most important revision of federal election campaign law since 1974, and in December, 2003, the Supreme Court upheld most of the BCRA's provisions in *McConnell v. Federal Election Commission*. In addition, there have been important developments in redistricting law since our second edition, especially the Supreme Court's revisiting the question of partisan gerrymandering in *Vieth v. Jubelirer*. We reluctantly concluded that to attempt to deal with these developments in supplements would be too cumbersome.

This third edition is not a comprehensive revision. Indeed, if it were software we would probably call it Version 2.1. We have thoroughly revised the later chapters on campaign finance and made significant revisions to the redistricting chapters. Some other chapters, such as the one on ballot measures, have also been overhauled. But many chapters are virtually unchanged. We still intend to prepare a more thorough revision in 2007, and will welcome comments and suggestions by students, instructors, and others who use the book.

In the Introduction to the second edition, we mentioned two then-new resources in our field. One was the Election-Law Listserver, a forum for exchange of information and debate on developments in election law. If you'd like to subscribe, you may do so at <http://majordomo.lls.edu/cgi-bin/lwgate/ELECTION-LAW_GL>. The other was the inauguration of the quarterly *Election Law Journal*, published by Mary Ann Liebert, Inc., and edited by the two of us, assisted by attorney Sam Hirsch and an outstanding Editorial Advisory Board. As this is written, ELJ is completing its third volume. For information, visit <http://www.liebertpub.com/elj/>. Or flip through some copies in your local law library. If the *Election Law Journal* is not there, the librarian will no doubt appreciate being advised of this deficiency.

Election law has not been immune to the recent "blogging" phenomenon. One blog that is perhaps occasionally eccentric but always well-informed is owned and operated by Rick Hasen, who recused himself from participation in this paragraph. Hasen imaginatively entitled his blog "Election Law." Visit him at <http://electionlawblog.org>.

Other blogs of interest include Robert Bauer's blog on campaign finance issues <http://moresoftmoneyhardlaw.com>, Ed Still's "Votelaw" blog <http://www.votelaw.com/blog>, and Dan Tokaji's blog on voting technology issues <http://equalvote.

blogspot.com>. These and other election law resources are linked on the right side of the "Election Law" blog.

Acknowledgments

To our cumulative list of acknowledgments we add the name of Richard Ellis, a political scientist who, having been good enough to write an essay on pluralism for our first chapter, which we carry over from the second edition, for this edition has—together with his publisher, the University Press of Kansas—kindly permitted us to reprint a chapter from his book on initiatives. In addition we thank the students who have assisted us on the supplements since the second edition or worked directly on the third edition: Landon Bailey, Peter Bartle, Justin Bowen, Grant Davis Denny, Nicole Drey, Amber Star Healy, Michael Kovaleski, Tamara McCrossen, Matt Richardson, Eugene Rome, and Jesse Saivar.

Daniel Hays Lowenstein
Richard L. Hasen

Los Angeles
June 2004

Introduction to
the Second Edition

The introduction to the first edition of this book (reprinted below) stated that "election law has not been a subject in the university." Much has changed in the last six years. Election law is a course that now is taught in a large number of universities, is the subject of regular symposia in law reviews and, with the controversy over the 2000 presidential election, had its fifteen minutes as a subject of popular interest as well.

Those readers who have a strong interest in the field should note two developments. First, in January 1996, the election-law "listserver" was born. A listserver is an e-mail system by which any member of the group can post a message that is simultaneously delivered to all other members of the group. The election-law listserver is devoted to discussion of current developments in election law as well as related research and pedagogical issues. If you would like further information, point your web browser to <majordomo.lls.edu/cgi-bin/lwgate/ELECTION-LAW_GL>.

Second, the editors of this casebook have agreed to serve as editors of a new quarterly, peer-reviewed scholarly publication, the *Election Law Journal*. More information about the journal is available at <www.liebertpub.com/elj>.

Changes in the Second Edition

Although instructors who have used the first edition will find much here left intact, the book does make some significant changes. Some chapters were added simply to keep up with issues that have arisen in the last six years, such as the explosion of soft money and issue advocacy (see Chapter 18). Other chapters were added to expand coverage of the book, such as in the area of campaigns (Chapter 11) and campaign finance disclosure (Chapter 21). Of course, no book on election law in 2001 would be complete without a discussion of the 2000 presidential election controversy. Chapter 3 and Part III of Chapter 4 tackle issues related to the Florida recount. Finally, we have dropped some cases and added others as appropriate. Users of the second edition who wish to copy portions of deleted material from the first edition for classroom use have permission to do so.

Acknowledgments

We appreciate the helpful comments and suggestions from a number of our colleagues including Heather Gerken, Craig Holman, Antoinette Sedillo Lopez, Lance Olson, Nathaniel Persily, Melissa Saunders, Roy Schotland, David Schultz, Eugene Volokh, and Adam Winkler. The book would not have been possible without the generous support of our deans, David Burcham of Loyola Law School and Jonathan Varat of UCLA.

We gratefully acknowledge the research assistance of Michael Sweet, who helped with the 1996 supplement, Susan Bang and Mark Burnstein (1997), Beth Correia and Matthew Gorman (1998), Julie Caron Remer and Timothy Tozer (1999), and Greg Grossman (2000). We also thank Sofya Bendersky, Meghan Crowley, Caroline Djang, and Denise Waller for help on the second edition. The staffs of the Loyola and UCLA law libraries have been tremendously helpful to us as well.

We also thank Karen Mathews, Ann Palmer, Thelma Wong Terre and the faculty support staffs at Loyola and UCLA for exemplary administrative support, Tim Heindl for computer support, and the folks at Carolina Academic Press for putting it all together.

Hasen thanks his wife Lori Klein for judicious advice, patience, love, and support, especially when preparing the book seemed like caring for an additional child.

Since the first edition of this book was published, Lowenstein's sons, Aaron and Nathan, have (unexpectedly) grown up, and both are working in political jobs—Aaron for a city council member in New York City, Nathan as a redistricting analyst in California. Though they apparently have failed to learn from the error of their father's ways, their conscientiousness and sense of high purpose entitles them to be added to the list of family members mentioned in the previous introduction, from whom Lowenstein has received guidance.

Daniel Hays Lowenstein
Richard L. Hasen

Los Angeles
June 2001

Introduction to the First Edition

This book is based on the proposition that elections are important and that the structure and rules that govern them deserve the attention of citizens in general and of scholars and legal professionals in particular.

As the American university is constituted, election law falls at junctures formed by other subjects. This has not been an advantage, because junctures—these junctures, at least—have been peripheries. Most legal scholars who have considered election law issues have done so in pursuance of a different subject, most commonly constitutional law. In political science, election law falls at the juncture of two subdisciplines, American politics and public law. Most political scientists who specialize in American politics have no particular interest in law. Most political scientists who specialize in public law have no particular interest in electoral politics.

So election law has not been a subject in the university. But the confrontation of electoral politics and legal regulation has been pervasive and consequential in the past three or four decades. That election law has not been a subject is the university's loss and the university's failure.

Election law *has* been a growing subject in courtrooms, legislative chambers and political headquarters. One consequence has been increased work for lawyers. To prepare for such work is one good reason for law students to study election law. This book attempts to assist students in that preparation, but not in what might be termed a nuts-and-bolts fashion. There are some nuts and some bolts in this book (certainly the former!), but they are not presented exhaustively or systematically. Lawyers who need technical information about the Federal Election Campaign Act or the Voting Rights Act can find it easily enough. Indeed, details learned in law school are likely to have changed by the time the student is ready to apply them.

What distinguishes an outstanding legal professional from an ordinary one in the field of election law is the ability to understand the details of legal regulations as they affect and at least aspire to benefit the democratic political system. The sometimes mindless actions of election authorities (see *Barker v. Wisconsin Ethics Board* in Chapter 13 for one example[a]) provide evidence that not all lawyers practicing election law have an adequate sense of their mission or the ability to carry it out. One goal of this book is to provide stimuli to law students that may help them develop this sense and this ability.

---

a. This case has been demoted to a note case on page 939 in the third edition.

The broader purposes of the book go beyond professional preparation. Study of and debate over democratic institutions are activities that enrich our lives as citizens and that enhance our ability to serve the society in which we live.

The book is interdisciplinary. Not because of a general belief in interdisciplinary studies, but because study of a subject at the juncture of other subjects must be interdisciplinary.

More concretely, the book assumes that lawyers and political scientists have much to learn from each other about election law. The lawyers, judges, and legal scholars who believe they have proved a point because they have shown that a given cause *could* have a given effect are neither imaginary nor extinct. Neither are the political scientists who conclude their rigorous empirical studies with casual and sometimes foolish assertions of their normative or policy implications.

Lawyers can benefit from exposure to the empiricism of political science. Political scientists can benefit from more focused attention on the legal questions to which their empirical studies may be relevant. Legal questions, after all, are normative questions of a particularly concrete and immediate nature.

Conventions Used in This Book

In the interest of saving the publisher's space and the reader's time, most of the materials reprinted in this book have been significantly edited. Insertions are indicated with brackets. Deletions are indicated with brackets or ellipses. However, footnotes have been deleted and citations have been deleted or altered without signalling. Sometimes, formatting of the original sources has been revised. For example, I do not follow the Supreme Court's practice of surrounding indented quotes with quotation marks. For purposes of serious research, the reader should consult the original sources.

Footnotes that are signalled with a number are from the original work and retain the numbers that they have in the original. Footnotes signalled with a letter are mine.

Opinions differ on the extent to which law school casebooks should contain references to the scholarly literature. The interdisciplinary nature of this book has persuaded me that heavy annotations are appropriate. Very few readers of this book — whether instructors, students, or general readers — will have a strong background on all the subjects presented. The references are intended to facilitate further reading on matters of interest and to provide a head start on research projects. They are not intended to be intimidating, and I hope they will not have that effect.

Although the references are extensive, they are not remotely exhaustive. In most cases they should be sufficient to get you into the literature that interests you.

Acknowledgments

This book was conceived more than a decade ago over breakfast with Andy Schepard at a long-since defunct restaurant in Westwood. Andy and I decided that there ought to be an election law textbook and that we should compile it. Shortly thereafter, circumstances enticed Andy into other enterprises, a misfortune for which there is some consolation in the thought that election law's loss has been family law's gain. This would have been a better book if Andy had been able to stay with it. Only a few of his words remain (primarily in Chapter 7[b]), but I like to believe that some traces of Andy's energy, enthusiasm, and incisiveness have continued to animate the project.

Steve Ansolabehere, Bruce Cain, Morgan Kousser, and Ray Wolfinger read portions of the manuscript of this book and gave me helpful suggestions.

Aside from judicial decisions, this book draws primarily on academic materials. Nevertheless, I hope there are some politics in the book. If so, and if the politics make any sense, it is only because my activities in and around politics have allowed me to be associated with people of extraordinary talent and understanding. This group has included Howard Berman, Michael Berman, Jerry Brown, Carl D'Agostino, Doug Faigin, Jean-Marc Hamel, Pierre-Marc Johnson. André Larocque, Tom Quinn, Tony Quinn, Keiko Shimabukuro, Jonathan Steinberg, Bob Stern, and Henry Waxman.

I have been equally fortunate in academic associates. Marlene Nicholson and John Shockley deserve very special mention. Through their participation in the Law and the Political Process Study Group, as well as through their writings, they have done as much as anyone to earn recognition for election law as an academic subject in its own right. Others who have been particularly consistent sources of stimulation and support include David Adamany, Steve Ansolabehere, Bruce Cain, Mike Fitts, Steve Gottlieb, Bernie Grofman, Morgan Kousser, Jerry López, Mark Rush, Gary Schwartz, Steve Shiffrin, and, recently, three of my younger colleagues, George Brown, Dan Bussel and Eugene Volokh.

I thank Deans Bill Warren and Susan Prager individually for the tangible and intangible assistance they have provided and also as surrogates for the entire UCLA Law School Faculty. One could not hope for a more supportive group of colleagues. Similarly, I should like to express my appreciation to Joel Aberbach. Kathy Bawn, Shanto Iyengar, and John Petrocik for their friendship and assistance, but also as representatives of their colleagues in the very strong UCLA Political Science Department.

Many groups of UCLA students have struggled with these materials in versions even cruder than the present published version. Each group has helped me understand the subject better. Particular mention should be made of the many able research assistants who have worked with me. Those who worked most directly on this book were Don Deyo, Todd Schwartz, Michael Sweet, and Stacy Weinstein.

There is no need to thank Myra Saunders and the UCLA Law Library staff. Their invariable helpfulness and friendliness, and the miraculously speedy retrievals that they produce upon demand are things we have learned to take for granted at the law school.

But I do need to thank the clerical assistants who have worked with me over the years. Karen Mathews played this role down the home stretch, and she was almost too good to be true.

Keith Sipe, Mayapriya Long, Andrew Wilson, and the other folks at Carolina Academic Press are patience incarnate.

Although I have not attempted to conceal my own views on the subjects treated in this book, I have tried to assure that the book is not a brief for those or any other views. But I hope the book is animated by a respect for truth and a regard for the public good. My

---

b. This chapter is now Chapter 9 in the fourth edition. — Eds.

parents taught me this aspiration, and their teaching has been reinforced by the example set by my wife, my sister and a gaggle of cousins, aunts, uncles, and in-laws.

Everyone I have mentioned has left a mark on this book.

Daniel Hays Lowenstein

Los Angeles
May, 1995

Copyright Acknowledgments

Election Law

Chapter 1

Introductory Readings

It has been said, "there is no democratic theory—there are only democratic theories."[a] Probably most such theories would include at least two fundamental concepts, however differently they may be defined and combined: first, that certain basic rights or liberties should be guaranteed to each individual, and second, that each individual should have an equal opportunity to participate in the making of public policy so that each individual's interests will be served.[b]

In this book, our primary concern will be with how the laws governing elections further (or hinder) the attainment of these democratic goals. Our emphasis will be on statutes that have been enacted and legal doctrines that have been developed, primarily since the early 1960s, with the intention of reforming the political system in the direction of greater equality. Among the most important of these developments are the adoption of the one person, one vote rule by the Supreme Court; the adoption and amendment by Congress of the Voting Rights Act; the adoption by Congress and state legislatures of campaign finance regulations; and, more recently, the widespread adoption of legislative term limits and of various reforms in election administration.

Some of our attention will be on constitutional law, which may be an instrument of reform, as in the case of the one person, one vote rule, or may be an impediment to some proposed reforms, as in the case of campaign finance regulation. (The word "reform," as used throughout this book, is likely to be a source of controversy. Probably a good working definition of "reform" is a proposed or actual change that at least some people claim will be for the better.) The constitutional issues we will be considering often reflect the tensions long recognized between the twin goals of liberty and equality, or between either of these goals and the need for honest, workable and efficient processes.

Most of the book deals with elections, the most fundamental mechanism for achieving equality in a democracy. The book also will consider some of the influences most likely to affect political equality that are brought to bear on public officials. Throughout the book we shall be alert to empirical findings of social scientists that cast light on the likely consequences of reforms that have been enacted or proposed.

I. Factions and the Public Interest

We begin with a sampling of theoretical writings on the relationship between majorities and minorities, between public and private interests, and between citizens and rep-

---

a. Robert A. Dahl, A PREFACE TO DEMOCRATIC THEORY 1 (1956). See also J. Roland Pennock, DEMOCRATIC THEORY xiii (1979).

b. See, e.g., John Rawls, A THEORY OF JUSTICE 60–65 (1971).

resentatives. It should be apparent that even if the entire book were devoted to these theoretical questions we could do little more than introduce them. Nevertheless, this chapter will help give us a broader framework against which to consider the legal and empirical materials that follow.

The first selection is an essay by James Madison that is possibly the most influential work of political theory ever written by an American. THE FEDERALIST PAPERS were a series of essays by Madison, John Jay, and Alexander Hamilton in which they attempted to persuade the citizens of New York that the new constitution, proposed by the convention that met in Philadelphia in 1787, should be ratified. In the tenth essay in the series, Madison addresses the dangers that are posed for a republic by the existence of "factions." If you substitute "special interest group" for Madison's word "faction," you may be surprised at how contemporary are the issues Madison struggles with.

James Madison, THE FEDERALIST PAPERS, No. 10
(Clinton Rossiter, ed., 1961)

Among the numerous advantages promised by a well-constructed Union, none deserves to be more accurately developed than its tendency to break and control the violence of faction. The friend of popular governments never finds himself so much alarmed for their character and fate, as when he contemplates their propensity to this dangerous vice. He will not fail, therefore, to set a due value on any plan which, without violating the principles to which he is attached, provides a proper cure for it. The instability, injustice, and confusion introduced into the public councils, have, in truth, been the mortal diseases under which popular governments have everywhere perished, as they continue to be the favorite and fruitful topics from which the adversaries to liberty derive their most specious declamations. The valuable improvements made by the American constitutions on the popular models, both ancient and modern, cannot certainly be too much admired; but it would be an unwarrantable partiality to contend that they have as effectually obviated the danger on this side, as was wished and expected. Complaints are everywhere heard from our most considerate and virtuous citizens, equally the friends of public and private faith and of public and personal liberty, that our governments are too unstable, that the public good is disregarded in the conflicts of rival parties, and that measures are too often decided, not according to the rules of justice and the rights of the minor party, but by the superior force of an interested and overbearing majority. However anxiously we may wish that these complaints had no foundation, the evidence of known facts will not permit us to deny that they are in some degree true. It will be found, indeed, on a candid review of our situation, that some of the distresses under which we labor have been erroneously charged on the operation of our governments; but it will be found, at the same time, that other causes will not alone account for many of our heaviest misfortunes; and, particularly, for that prevailing and increasing distrust of public engagements and alarm for private rights which are echoed from one end of the continent to the other. These must be chiefly, if not wholly, effects of the unsteadiness and injustice with which a factious spirit has tainted our public administration.

By a faction, I understand a number of citizens, whether amounting to a majority or minority of the whole, who are united and actuated by some common impulse of passion, or of interest, adverse to the rights of other citizens, or to the permanent and aggregate interests of the community.

There are two methods of curing the mischiefs of faction: the one, by removing its causes; the other, by controlling its effects.

There are again two methods of removing the causes of faction: the one, by destroying the liberty which is essential to its existence; the other, by giving to every citizen the same opinions, the same passions, and the same interests.

It could never be more truly said than of the first remedy that it was worse than the disease. Liberty is to faction what air is to fire, an aliment without which it instantly expires. But it could not be less folly to abolish liberty, which is essential to political life, because it nourishes faction than it would be to wish the annihilation of air, which is essential to animal life, because it imparts to fire its destructive agency.

The second expedient is as impracticable as the first would be unwise. As long as the reason of man continues fallible, and he is at liberty to exercise it, different opinions will be formed. As long as the connection subsists between his reason and his self-love, his opinions and his passions will have a reciprocal influence on each other; and the former will be objects to which the latter will attach themselves. The diversity in the faculties of men, from which the rights of property originate, is not less an insuperable obstacle to a uniformity of interests. The protection of these faculties is the first object of government. From the protection of different and unequal faculties of acquiring property, the possession of different degrees and kinds of property immediately results; and from the influence of these on the sentiments and views of the respective proprietors ensues a division of the society into different interests and parties.

The latent causes of faction are thus sown in the nature of man; and we see them everywhere brought into different degrees of activity, according to the different circumstances of civil society. A zeal for different opinions concerning religion, concerning government, and many other points, as well of speculation as of practice; an attachment to different leaders ambitiously contending for pre-eminence and power; or to persons of other descriptions whose fortunes have been interesting to the human passions, have, in turn, divided mankind into parties, inflamed them with mutual animosity, and rendered them much more disposed to vex and oppress each other than to co-operate for their common good. So strong is this propensity of mankind to fall into mutual animosities that where no substantial occasion presents itself the most frivolous and fanciful distinctions have been sufficient to kindle their unfriendly passions and excite their most violent conflicts. But the most common and durable source of factions has been the various and unequal distribution of property. Those who hold and those who are without property have ever formed distinct interests in society. Those who are creditors, and those who are debtors, fall under a like discrimination. A landed interest, a manufacturing interest, a mercantile interest, a moneyed interest, with many lesser interests, grow up of necessity in civilized nations, and divide them into different classes, actuated by different sentiments and views. The regulation of these various and interfering interests forms the principal task of modern legislation and involves the spirit of party and faction in the necessary and ordinary operations of the government.

No man is allowed to be a judge in his own cause, because his interest would certainly bias his judgment, and, not improbably, corrupt his integrity. With equal, nay with greater reason, a body of men are unfit to be both judges and parties at the same time; yet what are many of the most important acts of legislation but so many judicial determinations, not indeed concerning the rights of single persons, but concerning the rights of large bodies of citizens? And what are the different classes of legislators but advocates and parties to the causes which they determine? Is a law proposed concerning private debts? It is a question to which the creditors are parties on one side and the debtors on the other. Justice ought to hold the balance between them. Yet the parties are, and must be, themselves the judges; and the most numerous party, or in other words, the most powerful faction must be expected to prevail. Shall domestic manufacturers be encouraged, and in what degree, by restrictions on foreign manufacturers? are questions which would be differently decided by the landed and the manufacturing classes, and probably by neither with a sole regard to justice and the public good. The apportionment of taxes on the various descriptions of property is an act which seems to require the most exact impartiality; yet there is, perhaps, no legislative act in which greater opportunity and temptation are given to a predominant party to trample on the rules of justice. Every shilling with which they overburden the inferior number is a shilling saved to their own pockets.

It is in vain to say that enlightened statesmen will be able to adjust these clashing interests and render them all subservient to the public good. Enlightened statesmen will not always be at the helm. Nor, in many cases, can such an adjustment be made at all without taking into view indirect and remote considerations, which will rarely prevail over the immediate interest which one party may find in disregarding the rights of another or the good of the whole.

The inference to which we are brought is that the *causes* of faction cannot be removed and that relief is only to be sought in the means of controlling its *effects*.

If a faction consists of less than a majority, relief is supplied by the republican principle, which enables the majority to defeat its sinister views by regular vote. It may clog the administration, it may convulse the society; but it will be unable to execute and mask its violence under the forms of the Constitution. When a majority is included in a faction, the form of popular government, on the other hand, enables it to sacrifice to its ruling passion or interest both the public good and the rights of other citizens. To secure the public good and private rights against the danger of such a faction, and at the same time to preserve the spirit and the form of popular government, is then the great object to which our inquiries are directed. Let me add that it is the great desideratum by which this form of government can be rescued from the opprobrium under which it has so long labored and be recommended to the esteem and adoption of mankind.

By what means is this object attainable? Evidently by one of two only. Either the existence of the same passion or interest in a majority at the same time must be prevented, or the majority, having such coexistent passion or interest, must be rendered, by their number and local situation, unable to concert and carry into effect schemes of oppression. If the impulse and the opportunity be suffered to coincide, we well know that neither moral nor religious motives can be relied on as an adequate control. They are not found to be such on the injustice and violence of individuals, and lose their efficacy in proportion to the number combined together, that is, in proportion as their efficacy becomes needful.

From this view of the subject it may be concluded that a pure democracy, by which I mean a society consisting of a small number of citizens, who assemble and administer the government in person, can admit of no cure for the mischiefs of faction. A common passion or interest will, in almost every case, be felt by a majority of the whole; a communication and concert results from the form of government itself; and there is nothing to check the inducements to sacrifice the weaker party or an obnoxious individual. Hence it is that such democracies have ever been spectacles of turbulence and contention; have ever been found incompatible with personal security or the rights of property; and have in general been as short in their lives as they have been violent in their deaths. Theoretic politicians, who have patronized this species of government, have erroneously supposed that by reducing mankind to a perfect equality in their political rights, they would at the same time be perfectly equalized and assimilated in their possessions, their opinions, and their passions.

A republic, by which I mean a government in which the scheme of representation takes place, opens a different prospect and promises the cure for which we are seeking. Let us examine the points in which it varies from pure democracy, and we shall comprehend both the nature of the cure and the efficacy which it must derive from the Union.

The two great points of difference between a democracy and a republic are: first, the delegation of the government, in the latter, to a small number of citizens elected by the rest; secondly, the greater number of citizens and greater sphere of country over which the latter may be extended.

The effect of the first difference is, on the one hand, to refine and enlarge the public views by passing them through the medium of a chosen body of citizens, whose wisdom may best discern the true interest of their country and whose patriotism and love of justice will be least likely to sacrifice it to temporary or partial considerations. Under such a regulation it may well happen that the public voice, pronounced by the representatives of the people, will be more consonant to the public good than if pronounced by the people themselves, convened for the purpose. On the other hand, the effect may be inverted. Men of factious tempers, of local prejudices, or of sinister designs, may, by intrigue, by corruption, or by other means, first obtain the suffrages, and then betray the interests of the people. The question resulting is, whether small or extensive republics are most favorable to the election of proper guardians of the public weal; and it is clearly decided in favor of the latter by two obvious considerations:

In the first place it is to be remarked that however small the republic may be the representatives must be raised to a certain number in order to guard against the cabals of a few; and that however large it may be they must be limited to a certain number in order to guard against the confusion of a multitude. Hence, the number of representatives in the two cases not being in proportion to that of the constituents, and being proportionally greater in the small republic, it follows that if the proportion of fit characters be not less in the large than in the small republic, the former will present a greater option, and consequently a greater probability of a fit choice.

In the next place, as each representative will be chosen by a greater number of citizens in the large than in the small republic, it will be more difficult for unworthy candidates to practice with success the vicious arts by which elections are too often carried; and the suffrages of the people being more free, will be more likely to center on men who possess the most attractive merit and the most diffusive and established characters.

It must be confessed that in this, as in most other cases, there is a mean, on both sides of which inconveniencies will be found to lie. By enlarging too much the number of electors, you render the representative too little acquainted with all their local circumstances and lesser interests; as by reducing it too much, you render him unduly attached to these, and too little fit to comprehend and pursue great and national objects. The federal Constitution forms a happy combination in this respect; the great and aggregate interests being referred to the national, the local and particular to the State legislatures.

The other point of difference is the greater number of citizens and extent of territory which may be brought within the compass of republican than of democratic government; and it is this circumstance principally which renders factious combinations less to be dreaded in the former than in the latter. The smaller the society, the fewer probably will be the distinct parties and interests composing it; the fewer the distinct parties and interests, the more frequently will a majority be found of the same party; and the smaller the number of individuals composing a majority, and the smaller the compass within which they are placed, the more easily will they concert and execute their plans of oppression. Extend the sphere and you take in a greater variety of parties and interests; you make it less probable that a majority of the whole will have a common motive to invade the rights of other citizens; or if such a common motive exists, it will be more difficult for all who feel it to discover their own strength and to act in unison with each other. Besides other impediments, it may be remarked that, where there is a consciousness of unjust or dishonorable purposes, communication is always checked by distrust in proportion to the number whose concurrence is necessary.

Hence, it clearly appears that the same advantage which a republic has over a democracy in controlling the effects of faction is enjoyed by a large over a small republic—is enjoyed by the Union over the States composing it. Does this advantage consist in the substitution of representatives whose enlightened views and virtuous sentiments render them superior to local prejudices and schemes of injustice? It will not be denied that the representation of the Union will be most likely to possess these requisite endowments. Does it consist in the greater security afforded by a greater variety of parties, against the event of any one party being able to outnumber and oppress the rest? In an equal degree does the increased variety of parties comprised within the Union increase this security. Does it, in fine, consist in the greater obstacles opposed to the concert and accomplishment of the secret wishes of an unjust and interested majority? Here again the extent of the Union gives it the most palpable advantage.

The influence of factious leaders may kindle a flame within their particular States but will be unable to spread a general conflagration through the other States. A religious sect may degenerate into a political faction in a part of the Confederacy; but the variety of sects dispersed over the entire face of it must secure the national councils against any danger from that source. A rage for paper money, for an abolition of debts, for an equal division of property, or for any other improper or wicked project, will be less apt to pervade the whole body of the Union than a particular member of it, in the same proportion as such a malady is more likely to taint a particular county or district than an entire State.

In the extent and proper structure of the Union, therefore, we behold a republican remedy for the diseases most incident to republican government. And according to the degree of pleasure and pride we feel in being republicans ought to be our zeal in cherishing the spirit and supporting the character of federalists.

Notes and Questions

1. Consider carefully Madison's definition of the term "faction" in the second paragraph of *Federalist No. 10*. Does this definition enable you to identify those groups Madison would regard as factions and those he would not? Is it necessary, for Madison's purposes, to be able to identify particular groups as factions? Which terms in Madison's definition, if any, seem subject to differing interpretations? How would you interpret those terms? Do you think you can improve on Madison's definition?

2. Peter H. Schuck, *Against (And For) Madison: An Essay in Praise of Factions*, 15 YALE LAW & POLICY REVIEW 553, 555–557 (1997), argues that to be useful in current times, Madison's definition of "faction" must be modified:

Madison asserts the objectivity of the public interest ("the permanent and aggregate interest of the community")—a conception that stands above and apart from any special interest or from any combination of such interests—including those of a majority. Such a transcendent conception, of course was hardly Madison's invention. In one form or another, it had constituted a convention of most political philosophy stretching back through the writings of Rousseau, Aquinas, Aristotle, and Plato....

[O]ne of the most significant innovations of liberal political theory, especially of the American variety, is its challenge to the Madisonian conception of the public interest. Much of modern liberalism has repudiated this conception in favor of one defined in terms of process values and political participation through group activity. This procedural notion of the public interest is the dominant one today, essentially accepted even by progressives and social democrats on the left and by market and libertarian conservatives on the right....

To understand the role of special interest groups in the American polity today, then, we must define faction in a way that does not depend—as Madison's definition manifestly does—on a transcendent conception of the public interest that no longer elicits strong defense or justification, even from those who most vehemently condemn pluralism's processes and policies. All definitions of "special" interests can be criticized for being under-inclusive, arbitrary, or subjective. To characterize any interest as "general," to assert that its goals correspond with those of the community at large, is not simply a presumptuous claim but also inevitably a form of approbation. To characterize an interest as "special," in contrast, is to ascribe to it a partial, parochial, or narrowly self-interested quality; in common parlance this label is almost always deprecatory.

If Schuck correctly describes the dominant view among contemporary theorists as rejecting substantive conceptions of the public interest in favor of procedural ones, are the theorists correct? Consider the proposition that economic prosperity consistent with environmental protection is in the public interest. Or that citizens should have the right to speak freely and exercise religion as (and if) they choose. Or that bribery in the conduct of government should be minimized. Is there any significant body of opinion that disagrees that such goals are in the public interest or that citizens ought to have such rights? Theorists might respond that such substantive conceptions of the public interest are too general, that as soon as we begin to address the tradeoffs—for example, between economic prosperity and environmental protection, or the limits to such rights as freedom of speech and freedom of religion, or the determination of what is a bribe—consensus will disappear. But is it any different with process issues? Everyone might favor a campaign finance system that assures electoral competition, minimizes corruption and maximizes freedom to engage in political activity, but would there be more agreement on the tradeoffs between these goals than on the tradeoffs between economic growth and environmental protection? For a negative answer, see Daniel H. Lowenstein, *Political Reform Is Political*, in THE U.S. HOUSE OF REPRESENTATIVES: REFORM OR REBUILD 194, 195–200 (Joseph F. Zimmerman and Wilma Rule, eds., 2000).

3. Madison says it is the "diversity in the faculties of men, from which the rights of property originate.... The protection of these faculties is the first object of government." In making this statement, was Madison speaking for a faction? Whether or not he was, the approval of the federal constitutional system advocated by Madison was certain to benefit some groups and harm others. As Justice Felix Frankfurter observed,

Hardly any distribution of political authority that could be assailed as rendering government non-republican would fail ... to operate to the prejudice of some groups, and to the advantage of others, within the body politic.... No shift of power but works a corresponding shift in influence among the groups composing a society.

Baker v. Carr, 369 U.S. 186, 266, 299 (1962) (dissenting opinion).

Throughout this book, we shall see changes in the political system being proposed, opposed, adopted or rejected in legislatures, courts and administrative agencies. The reformers, their opponents, and the decision-makers normally justify their positions by reference to the public interest and democratic principles. In addition to these considerations, bear in mind which interest groups will gain and which will lose from the actual or proposed changes. Does the question of who will gain and who will lose affect what interests line up on each side and the eventual outcome? Should it? Suppose it is shown that a proposed law will benefit a particular group—incumbent legislators, for example, or labor unions, or law students. Would that be a legitimate argument against the proposal?

4. According to Madison, factions can consist of a majority or a minority of the population, but only a majority faction is likely to have its way under a republican constitution. Why? Many contemporary reformers, both conservative and liberal, believe minority interests too often can veto or bring about changes in a manner contrary to the public interest and opposed by the majority. Are these reformers wrong? Was Madison wrong? Have conditions changed in relevant ways since Madison's time? What conditions?

5. In *Federalist No. 10* Madison points to a sharp contrast between a democracy and a republic. The differences are "the delegation of the government, in the latter, to a small number of citizens elected by the rest; secondly, the greater number of citizens and greater sphere of country over which the latter may be extended." One conclusion that some have drawn is that the initiative process, which we examine in Chapter 8, is anti-republican because it bypasses the representative legislature. But that conclusion emphasizes Madison's first difference at the expense of the second. Morton White, PHILOSOPHY, *THE FEDERALIST*, AND THE CONSTITUTION 137–38 (1987), summarizes his reading of Madison on this point as follows:

> [T]he small population of a pure democracy—its first fundamental feature— makes it very likely that a pure democracy will contain a small-numbered majority which has a factious *motive*. And the fact that the citizens of a pure democracy must assemble and administer the government in person—the second fundamental feature of a pure democracy—makes it likely that a factious majority in a pure democracy will have an *opportunity* to "concert and execute their plans of oppression." Finally, according to Madison, if a small-numbered majority has both a factious motive and an opportunity to act, it will in all likelihood invade the rights of others or act against the common good....

On White's reading of Madison, is it correct to conclude that the initiative process is anti-republican?

6. Concern that majorities will tyrannize over minorities in a democracy has continued. John C. Calhoun, in another classic of American political theory, *A Disquisition on Government* (published posthumously in 1853) claimed that Madison's solution to the problem of faction was insufficient to protect minorities. Calhoun proposed instead a requirement that the government act with the approval of a "concurrent majority," meaning that all major interests must concur. Beginning with a similar impulse, a more recent influential book argued that, in principle, unanimous consent should be required for government action, but that since the cost of obtaining unanimity on any specific pro-

posal would be prohibitive, the unanimity requirement should be applied only to the adoption of a constitution, which would permit day-to-day decisions to be made with less than unanimous approval. James M. Buchanan & Gordon Tullock, THE CALCULUS OF CONSENT (1962). For a cogent criticism of the ethical desirability of a unanimity rule, see Douglas W. Rae, *The Limits of Consensual Decision*, 69 AMERICAN POLITICAL SCIENCE REVIEW 1270 (1975).

7. How persuasive do you find Madison's arguments for larger legislative districts? Do you think his views would be the same if he were writing under modern conditions?

II. Citizens and Representatives

The next selection is a speech by Edmund Burke, one of the great British statesmen of the late eighteenth century. Burke had just been elected to the House of Commons from Bristol, and was addressing his constituents in 1774. His speech followed the other person who had been elected from Bristol at the same time as Burke. The other candidate had expressed views favorable to "instructions," by which was meant the practice of constituents binding their representative to vote on legislative matters in accordance with the opinion of the constituents. Burke's response is the centerpiece for what has become one of the leading debates in democratic theory.

Edmund Burke, SPEECH TO THE ELECTORS OF BRISTOL
1 Burke's Works 442, 446–48 (1854)

GENTLEMEN, ...

I am sorry I cannot conclude without saying a word on a topic touched upon by my worthy colleague....

He tells you that "the topic of instructions has occasioned much altercation and uneasiness in this city;" and he expresses himself (if I understand him rightly) in favour of the coercive authority of such instructions.

Certainly, gentlemen, it ought to be the happiness and glory of a representative to live in the strictest union, the closest correspondence, and the most unreserved communication with his constituents. Their wishes ought to have great weight with him; their opinion, high respect; their business, unremitted attention. It is his duty to sacrifice his repose, his pleasures, his satisfactions, to theirs; and above all, ever, and in all cases, to prefer their interest to his own. But his unbiassed opinion, his mature judgment, his enlightened conscience, he ought not to sacrifice to you, to any man, or any set of men living. These he does not derive from your pleasure; no, nor from the law and the constitution. They are a trust from Providence, for the abuse of which he is deeply answerable. Your representative owes you, not his industry only, but his judgment; and he betrays, instead of serving you, if he sacrifices it to your opinion.

My worthy colleague says, his will ought to be subservient to yours. If that be all, the thing is innocent. If government were a matter of will upon any side, yours, without question, ought to be superior. But government and legislation are matters of reason and judgment, and not of inclination; and what sort of reason is that, in which the determination precedes the discussion; in which one set of men deliberate, and another decide;

and where those who form the conclusion are perhaps three hundred miles distant from those who hear the arguments?

To deliver an opinion, is the right of all men; that of constituents is a weighty and respectable opinion, which a representative ought always to rejoice to hear; and which he ought always most seriously to consider. But *authoritative* instructions; *mandates* issued, which the member is bound blindly and implicitly to obey, to vote, and to argue for, though contrary to the clearest conviction of his judgment and conscience, — these are things utterly unknown to the laws of this land, and which arise from a fundamental mistake of the whole order and tenor of our constitution.

Parliament is not a *congress* of ambassadors from different and hostile interests; which interests each must maintain, as an agent and advocate, against other agents and advocates; but parliament is a *deliberative* assembly of *one* nation, with *one* interest, that of the whole; where, not local purposes, not local prejudices, ought to guide, but the general good, resulting from the general reason of the whole. You choose a member indeed; but when you have chosen him, he is not member of Bristol, but he is a member of *parliament*. If the local constituent should have an interest, or should form an hasty opinion, evidently opposite to the real good of the rest of the community, the member for that place ought to be as far, as any other, from any endeavour to give it effect. I beg pardon for saying so much on this subject. I have been unwillingly drawn into it; but I shall ever use a respectful frankness of communication with you. Your faithful friend, your devoted servant, I shall be to the end of my life: a flatterer you do not wish for. On this point of instructions, however, I think it scarcely possible we ever can have any sort of difference. Perhaps I may give you too much, rather than too little, trouble.

Notes and Questions

1. Would Madison have agreed with Burke?

2. Is Burke's argument undercut by modern communications, which make the debate on public issues accessible to each representative's constituents?

3. When Burke spoke, the British Parliament included so-called "pocket boroughs," districts with little or no population whose Member could in effect be chosen by a wealthy landlord or nobleman. Some of these seats in Parliament were for sale, but others would be awarded to leaders of the parliamentary faction favored by the individual who controlled the district. Accordingly, Burke was assured of being returned to Parliament even if, as occurred in 1780, he failed to win reelection from Bristol.

Is Burke's view of the proper conduct of a legislative representative realistic under modern American conditions? Is it consistent with democratic principles? What changes— in our electoral system, in our attitudes toward elective office, or otherwise—would be necessary to induce modern legislators to act consistently with Burke's views?

4. A 19th-century Englishman, W.S. Gilbert, expressed a different view of the "M.P.'s" (i.e., Member of Parliament's, or legislator's) role:

> When in that House M.P.'s divide,
> If they've a brain and cerebellum, too,
> They've got to leave that brain outside,
> And vote just as their leaders tell 'em to.
> But then the prospect of a lot

> Of dull M.P.'s in close proximity,
> All thinking for themselves, is what
> No man can face with equanimity.

Gilbert & Sullivan, Iolanthe, Act II.

Notice that the system described by Gilbert and still prevailing in Britain and to varying degrees in many other democracies is different from either of the alternatives considered by Burke. Instead of following his or her own judgment or the views of his or her constituents, the representative is bound by the dictates of the party leadership. Would Burke approve? Would you?

5. Burke's speech provides the leading text for one of the longest-running debates in democratic theory. An excellent modern commentary may be found in Hanna Pitkin, The Concept of Representation (1967).

A great deal of empirical research in the United States has attempted to discern the influences that affect legislative behavior. One of the many leading works is John W. Kingdon, Congressmen's Voting Decisions (3d ed., 1989). See also R. Douglas Arnold, *Can Inattentive Citizens Control Their Elected Representatives?* in Congress Reconsidered 401 (Lawrence C. Dodd & Bruce I. Oppenheimer, eds., 5th ed., 1993).

6. Would you favor a system in which measures could be put on the ballot by petition to permit voters to inform their legislators how the voters think a public policy question should be resolved? If so, should the result be binding on legislators or only advisory? How broadly would you define the scope of public policy questions that could be put before the voters in this manner. For example, would the question whether individual human life begins at (a) conception; (b) viability; (c) birth; or (d) a different biological stage be permissible for the ballot? See *New England Christian Action Council v. Secretary of the Commonwealth*, 532 N.E.2d 40 (Mass. 1989).

7. In the late 1990s, proponents of term limits sponsored initiatives instructing members of Congress to vote for an amendment to the Constitution establishing congressional term limits. Those candidates who failed to sign a pledge supporting the particular term limit specified in the Amendment would have the words "DECLINED TO PLEDGE TO SUPPORT TERM LIMITS" printed next to their names on the ballot. Those Congressional incumbents who failed to support the measure in Congress were branded as having "DISREGARDED VOTERS' INSTRUCTION ON TERM LIMITS."

In *Cook v. Gralike*, 531 U.S. 510 (2001), the Supreme Court struck down a Missouri initiative along these lines. The Court first held that Missouri failed to demonstrate "that either the people or the States had a right to give legally binding, *i.e.,* nonadvisory, instructions to their representatives..., much less that such a right would apply to federal representatives." The Court further held that even assuming a state had such a power, it could not use ballots for congressional elections as a means of giving its instructions binding force.

What would be the harm of the Missouri initiative? The Court wrote that "it seems clear that the adverse labels handicap candidates at the most crucial stage in the election process—the instant before the vote is cast." If voters have a preference for term limits, and the initiative provides additional information about term limits, is the "handicap" unfair? See Elizabeth Garrett, *The Law and Economics of "Informed Voter" Ballot Notations*, 85 Virginia Law Review 1533 (1999). According to the Court in *Cook*, how competent are voters to make decisions about candidates at the time they cast their ballots? See James A. Gardner, *Neutralizing the Incompetent Voter: A Comment on* Cook v. Gralike, 1 Election Law Journal 49 (2002).

8. Burke's speech is most often recalled in connection with the question whether representatives should act on their own or their constituents' views, when the two conflict. A related and equally important question addressed in the speech that should not be overlooked is how the representative should balance the interests of his or her constituency with those of the nation as a whole. What values are served by a district orientation on the part of representatives? Is excessive parochialism inevitable in a district-based democratic system? Is a strong party system along the lines described by W.S. Gilbert likely to be beneficial in accomplishing a balance between local and nationwide interests? For the suggestion that strong presidential leadership may offset the parochialism of Congress, see Michael Fitts & Robert Inman, *Controlling Congress: Presidential Influence in Domestic Fiscal Policy*, 80 GEORGETOWN LAW JOURNAL 1737 (1992).

III. Pluralism and Progressivism

A contemporary school of thought whose proponents claim to be the heirs of James Madison is known as "pluralism." The following essay describes the intellectual history of pluralism, several of its variants, and some of the criticisms that have been levelled at it.

Richard J. Ellis, *Pluralism*[c]

The concept of "pluralism" is usually associated with post-war American behavioral political science, but pluralism's roots extend back to the early twentieth century, and are as much European as American. The Englishman Harold Laski introduced the term "pluralism" into political science in a number of essays he published mostly while teaching at Harvard University between 1916 and 1920.

Laski and other English pluralists sought to vindicate the rights and autonomy of associations by challenging the modern doctrine of an unlimited and unitary state sovereignty. Sovereignty was a myth. The world, Neville Figgis explained, is "not, as a fact, composed of a few vast unities known as States, set over against crowds of isolated individuals." Rather each society "is a society of societies, each and all with rights, liberty and life of their own."[1] The history of societies, Laski agreed, showed repeatedly that organized groups, even unpopular ones like militant female suffragists, striking miners, or conscientious objectors, imposed limits on the allegedly sovereign state, forcing public officials to adopt policies to which they were opposed.[2]

Although pluralists frequently appealed to "the real facts of human society"[3] their challenge to what they termed "the monistic theory of the state" was more normative than empirical, though typically the "is" and the "ought" were woven seamlessly together. In arguing that "the state is only one among many forms of human association,"[4] for instance, Laski meant not only to highlight the empirical fact of the social and political importance of associations and groups, but also, and more importantly, to advance a radically anti-statist normative vision. For the young Laski, the state was owed no more loyalty

---

c. We are grateful to Professor Ellis for preparing this essay for this volume.
1. Cited in David Nicholls, THE PLURALIST STATE 140 (1975).
2. Harold J. Laski, STUDIES IN THE PROBLEM OF SOVEREIGNTY 12 (1917).
3. Nicholls, *supra*, at 141.
4. STUDIES at 65.

than other groups; each group, including the state, deserved only the loyalty it earned "by virtue of its achievement."[5]

Not all pluralists shared Laski's anarchic and syndicalist sympathies. Others, like Figgis and Barker, allowed that the state had an important role to play in regulating conflict between associations and thus in creating the political conditions necessary for associations to pursue their own ends. But the main objective of the English pluralists was to help the groups they cared most deeply about, which for Figgis, for example, meant religious associations but for Laski and others meant labor and the trade unions. And herein lies an explanation for English pluralism's precipitous decline in the 1920s. For pluralists failed to persuade others, or even eventually themselves, that pluralism was the most effective means to help the groups they wanted to assist. Laski himself gradually abandoned or watered down his pluralist ideas, because along with the rest of the left he came to believe, particularly after the Great Crash of 1929, that labor had more to gain from an active, even paternal state than from a minimal, pluralist state.

Ironically, at the same time that English pluralism as a normative vision and intellectual force was in decline, the empirical study of organized groups was gaining ground in American universities. The American political scientists believed, with Arthur Bentley, that there was too much moralizing about the evils of special interest groups and too little objective empirical description and analysis of group behavior in the political process. By 1950, when David Truman's landmark book, *The Governmental Process*, was published, the discipline was relatively rich in empirical studies of interest group influence. Though the term "pluralism" was rarely if ever used, political scientists were beginning to speak of the "group basis of politics"[6] or the "group theory of politics." Truman and others had helped to revive interest in Bentley who, in his 1908 book, *The Process of Government*, had argued that groups, not laws, institutions or constitutions, were the essential "raw materials" of government. Truman followed Bentley in trying to understand the governmental process by treating groups, specifically interest groups, as "a primary unit of analysis."[7] Over the next decade this increasingly influential mode of analysis would become known by advocates and even more frequently by detractors as "analytical pluralism" or simply "pluralism."

Critics were quick to charge pluralists with believing that groups were all that mattered, often pointing to Bentley's remark that "when the groups are adequately stated, everything is stated."[8] But most of those tagged as pluralists, including most especially Truman, never maintained anything so implausible. Pluralists looked to groups as "*a major explanatory variable*,"[9] but explicitly rejected the notion that government officials passively registered or mirrored the sum total of organized group preferences. The relative importance of groups and government officials in the shaping of policy, Truman emphasized, was an empirical question, not one to be settled by "preassigning weights and roles."[10] Analytic pluralists, to be sure, generally avoided using the term, "the state," but this was not because their explanations were "society-centered" or because they believed government officials lacked autonomy or importance vis-à-vis societal groups. Rather it was because they doubted, for epistemological as well as empirical reasons, that the myr-

5. Harold J. Laski, THE FOUNDATIONS OF SOVEREIGNTY AND OTHER ESSAYS 170 (1917).
6. Earl Latham, THE GROUP BASIS OF POLITICS (1952).
7. David Truman, THE GOVERNMENTAL PROCESS: POLITICAL INTERESTS AND PUBLIC OPINION xix (2d ed. 1971 [1951]).
8. Arthur F. Bentley, THE PROCESS OF GOVERNMENT 209 (1967 [1908]).
9. Truman, *supra*, at xxii (emphasis added).
10. *Id.* at xxv.

iad institutions and officials of government, particularly in the United States, were coherent enough to warrant a locution that treated the government as a unitary actor with a single will. The same doubts fed pluralists' skepticism of concepts like "the public interest" or "the will of the people," since society no less than the state was a complex mix of rival interests and objectives. In this respect, the modern American pluralists were kindred spirits of the early twentieth century English pluralists.

Another strain in criticism of American pluralism objected not to its focus on societal groups but to its portrayal of the distribution of power within the United States as dispersed. Pluralists, it was claimed, slighted the severe inequalities in resources and power in American society, and mistakenly believed that the system was self-correcting, that the mobilization of one group would necessarily lead to the mobilization of an equal and opposite countervailing pressure. Pluralists were also said to believe that all important or legitimate interests and opinions were represented within the political system, or even that all groups had substantially equal access to the policy-making process. As the ideological dust kicked up in the 1960s has slowly settled, scholars have begun to recognize that few if any of those scholars commonly described as pluralists harbored such naive views of the political process.[11] The important question, in any event, is not whether it is possible to find someone myopic enough to believe that all groups have equal or nearly equal power, but whether pluralists are logically committed to these propositions. How widely dispersed power is within any given policy domain or in any given place or time is an empirical question that cannot be settled by methodological or theoretical fiat. Nor can it be satisfactorily answered without a comparative perspective: the same distribution of power may be reasonably characterized as either concentrated or dispersed depending on one's comparative referent or on one's normative benchmark. There is no inherent reason that an empirical commitment to the study of interest groups ala Truman need predispose the analyst to find any given distribution of political power. Nor need a normative commitment to pluralism, understood as wide dispersion of political influence and power, necessarily predispose one to find pluralism as a socio-political fact in any given setting.

The term "pluralist" is a particularly confusing label because it is often applied to those who conclude that power in a given locale is dispersed rather than concentrated. Pluralism can be a useful term to describe either an empirical reality—one in which there is, for example, widespread dispersal of power, and bargaining rather than hierarchical decision-making—or a normative commitment to such dispersed power, but it does not help to call those scholars who find dispersed power "pluralists." When Robert Dahl[12] finds a pattern of dispersed influence in contemporary New Haven politics that no more makes him a pluralist than his discovery of concentrated oligarchic power in early New Haven makes him an elitist.

Dahl remains the archetypal pluralist in the minds of many, even though he is not a group theorist on the model of Bentley and Truman. Whether or not Dahl counts as a pluralist, he is certainly among the keenest students of the dilemmas of pluralism. Dahl maintained that it was one thing to recognize (as Laski did) that government officials often could not "enforce decisions by unilateral, hierarchical means" but must often bargain with powerful and autonomous groups to negotiate "temporary armistices,"[13] but it

---

11. Martin J. Smith, *Pluralism, Reformed Pluralism and Neopluralism: The Role of Pressure Groups in Policy-making*, 38 POLITICAL STUDIES 302–22 (1990).

12. Robert A. Dahl, WHO GOVERNS? DEMOCRACY AND POWER IN AN AMERICAN CITY (1961).

13. Robert A. Dahl and Charles Lindblom, POLITICS, ECONOMICS AND WELFARE 498 (1953).

was "quite another to turn this social fact into a prescription of the desirable, and to argue in effect that politicians should not even attempt to exercise 'the last say,' but should turn that power over to national organizations bargaining among themselves."[14] The fundamental dilemma of a pluralist democracy, in Dahl's view, is that autonomous associations, groups, or organizations are highly desirable and yet also capable of great harms if not controlled by a central authority.[15]

Why is pluralism desirable? Advocates of pluralism see autonomous organizations fulfilling a variety of beneficial purposes. Some emphasize pluralism's role in facilitating individual development and self-expression[16] while others emphasize the importance of groups in integrating the individual into society.[17] Associations are also seen as seedbeds of civic virtue, an enabling environment in which citizens learn the habits of self-government.[18] A different emphasis is evident among those who stress pluralism's defensive political function, as an organizational counterweight to the coercive powers of the central government.[19]

Pluralism may be essential to the functioning of large-scale democracies but that does not mean, as Dahl emphasizes, that pluralism is without disadvantages. To begin with, group leaders may dominate or oppress group members, particularly where the costs of exit from a group are high. Less ominously, the group's elites may fail to represent the opinions of its membership—the elites may be more conservative or more radical, more compromising or more confrontational, than the membership.

A second problem with organizational pluralism is that all groups are not created equal: organized interests, all other things being equal, have an advantage over unorganized interests, and some interests are easier to organize than other interests.[20] Autonomy for the lambs may well mean a quick dinner for the wolves. It is the weaker groups, as Schattschneider argued, who generally have the greatest interest in "enlarging the scope of conflict" by appealing to public authority and thereby modifying the imbalance in private power relations.[21] Recognition that group autonomy may serve the interests of the most powerful groups is a powerful argument against the radically anti-statist vision of the English pluralists, but not nearly so troubling to the pluralist vision of post-war American political scientists, most of whom were New Deal Democrats. The problems of group autonomy are real, but they need to be counterbalanced with an appreciation for the limits of central control. Absent the articulation of group preferences and mobilization of group interests, a central political authority would define who was a group and what were legitimate interests. Without group pressures, the state would find it difficult if not impossible to gauge the intensity with which preferences were held. If group autonomy without central control is bad for the lambs, central control without group autonomy is no better.

---

14. *Id.* at 507.
15. Robert A. Dahl, Dilemmas of Pluralist Democracy: Autonomy vs. Control (1982).
16. Nancy L. Rosenblum, Membership and Morals: The Personal Uses of Pluralism in America (1998).
17. Robert A. Nisbet, The Twilight of Authority (1975).
18. Robert D. Putnam, Bowling Alone: The Collapse and Revival of American Community (2000).
19. Judith N. Shklar, *The Liberalism of Fear*, in Liberalism and the Moral Life (Nancy Rosenblum, ed., 1989).
20. Mancur Olson, Jr., The Logic of Collective Action (1965).
21. E.E. Schattschneider, The Semisovereign People (1960).

Other critics worry that even if all groups were equal, pluralism might, in Dahl's words, "deform civic consciousness" by fostering particularistic or short-run demands at the expense of a broader common good or long-run social needs.[22] Whether civic consciousness is higher or the common good is more closely attended to in those countries or policy domains where interest groups are less prevalent or less assertive is an empirical question, the answer to which is far from self-evident. A related concern is that private associations may be given essentially public functions, thereby removing or reducing democratic control over governmental decisions. One manifestation of this problem is European-style corporatism, in which bargains are worked out between peak associations representing labor, business and farmers. In the United States, the problem of alienating democratic control may take the form of powerful groups capitalizing on the fragmentation of the system by "capturing" governmental officials in a specialized policy domain.[23] Dispersed power is not inconsistent with groups monopolizing power in specialized segments of the political system. Again the extent to which this accurately describes policy-making in any given system or policy domain is an empirical question.

Among the most common criticisms of pluralism is that it was little more than an apologia for American or, alternatively, Western democracy. Whether or not those who were associated with pluralist ideas were satisfied with the state of democracy in America or Western Europe, pluralism as a normative vision is not inherently conservative. In much of the non-Western world, for example, even the most modest pluralist ideas pose a subversive challenge to entrenched state power and economic privilege. In 1968 Henry Kariel wrote an obituary for pluralism, which, he said, "as an ideology ... only lingers quietly as a submerged, inarticulate ingredient of Western liberalism"[24] Over three decades later it would appear that reports of pluralism's decline let alone its death have been greatly exaggerated. Particularly as a normative vision, as an antidote to plebiscitary democracy and to centralized state control, political pluralism has shown renewed appeal and relevance across the globe.

Notes and Questions

1. Was James Madison a pluralist?

2. Robert Dahl, mentioned by Ellis, placed great emphasis on the concept of "intensity," the strength of an individual's or group's support or opposition to a government policy. Dahl maintained that the best protection for minority groups against tyranny by majorities lay not in constitutional safeguards but in the operation of the political system along pluralist lines. The idea was that groups whose freedoms or vital interests were threatened by a proposed policy would feel the most intensely about the issue. That intensity would be reflected in increased political activity. "All other things being equal," Dahl concluded, "the outcome of a policy decision will be determined by the relative intensity of preference among the members of a group."

---

22. DILEMMAS at 43.
23. Grant McConnell, PRIVATE POWER AND AMERICAN DEMOCRACY (1966); Theodore J. Lowi, THE END OF LIBERALISM (1969).
24. Henry S. Kariel, *Pluralism*, in INTERNATIONAL ENCYCLOPEDIA OF THE SOCIAL SCIENCES 168 (David L. Sills, ed., 1968).

Dahl also asserted that "intensity is almost a modern psychological version of natural rights." Would Madison agree? Do you? How, if at all, would Madison's definition of "faction" be affected if the term "intense preferences" were substituted for "rights"?

3. One influential criticism of pluralism mentioned briefly by Ellis is based on the problem of the "free rider." According to this line of thought, a government policy beneficial to a number of people is a "collective good" for that group. That is, either the policy will be adopted and benefit all members of the group, or it will not be adopted and none of the members will benefit. An obvious example is governmental protection of air quality. There is no way for individuals to obtain the benefit of cleaner air for themselves without obtaining it for everyone. If a lot of organizing activity and substantial resources are needed to obtain the benefit, the free rider analysis yields the paradoxical result that a small group may be better situated than a large group. Each member of the small group, perhaps a concentrated industry, will regard its own contribution to the collective effort as crucial, and therefore will be motivated to contribute. But members of a large group, such as consumers, individual taxpayers, or small businesspersons, may be motivated to take a free ride. That is, each such individual will reason that his or her own contribution is such a minute percentage of the whole that the overall success of the effort will not be affected. "Better to take a free ride," individuals might reason. "If others contribute, I will benefit from the favored policy and be even better off because I will have saved the time or money I declined to contribute. If others also opt for a free ride none of us will get the government policy we want, but at least I will save by not contributing to a losing effort."

The classic work on the free rider problem is Mancur Olson, THE LOGIC OF COLLECTIVE ACTION (1965).

4. Although Ellis criticizes use of the word "pluralism" to refer to a descriptive theory of politics, nevertheless the term is commonly used for that purpose. On the other hand, critics have attacked pluralism less for its description of government policy as the outcome of the struggle of interest groups than for its normative conclusion that this outcome is satisfactory. Are the struggles over reform of the political system, with which much of this book deals, the practical counterpart of the theoretical debate over pluralism? For one view, see J. Skelly Wright, *Politics and the Constitution: Is Money Speech?*, 85 YALE LAW JOURNAL 1001 (1976).

5. During the 1950s pluralism was probably the dominant normative theory in American political science. Criticisms that were developed in the 1960s, including the free rider problem and the criticisms described by Ellis, have had their effect. Nevertheless, it is probably still true that the majority of political scientists and many journalists, judges, and people active in electoral politics are greatly influenced by the pluralist outlook, and by related theories centered around political parties, described in Chapter 9.

As Ellis mentions, many of the normative criticisms of pluralism are based on concerns about arguably unjust differences in the power and influence of various groups. One early version of this criticism was probably unfair to pluralism. During the 1950s, the most flagrant instance of inequality in the United States was the disfranchisement and subjugation of African-Americans in the South. Pluralism, however, assumes basic political rights for all such as freedom of speech, freedom of association, and the right to vote. Therefore, the subjugation of southern blacks was not a failure of pluralism but a failure to implement pluralism.

Pluralism could not evade responsibility so easily for other possible inequalities. The free rider problem and other theoretical issues—for example, the view that dispersed groups can be satisfied with symbolic gestures, while concentrated groups with lobbyists in Washington or the state capitol demand substantive benefits[d]—suggested that broadly based interests would face an unequal struggle against concentrated interests, especially economic interests. These criticisms of pluralism suggested that interests such as the natural environment, consumers, women's groups, small businesses, general taxpayers, and low income people would suffer and corporate interests as well as those of well-organized labor unions would have unfair advantages. The criticisms have undeniable force. Yet history, as she often does, played an ironic game with the critics of pluralism. Just as these criticisms were being forcefully articulated, American society saw the emergence of a potent "public interest" movement. Environmental organizations such as the Sierra Club, the Natural Resources Defense Council, and the Environmental Defense Fund, women's groups such as the National Organization for Women, political reform organizations such as Common Cause, and even more specialized groups such as Americans for Nonsmokers' Rights not only were able to enlist large numbers of members, but won major political successes.

6. As Ellis' essay suggests, much of the development and criticism of American pluralist thought occurred in the 1950s and 1960s. The story did not end there, as Andrew S. McFarland, NEOPLURALISM (2004) demonstrates in a very useful review and interpretation of subsequent research. McFarland groups critics such as Mancur Olson, Jr., E.E. Schattschneider, and Grant McConnell as "multiple-elite theorists," because they claimed on various grounds that a pluralist system would be dominated by relatively few "elites," though they conceded that different individuals would have influence in different policy sectors. McFarland writes, at 9–10:

> But by 1980, the new multiple-elite theory was being overturned. Later researchers studying questions of power, policymaking, and interest groups usually found well-organized representation of interest groups on two or more sides of an issue, a finding repeated more than a dozen times. The frequency of such findings contradicted multiple-elite theory. The research finding of a number of well-organized groups wielding power in public policy areas might be termed *neopluralism*; it is different from the original pluralist theory, in that it recognizes that subgovernments sometimes exist and that Olson's logic of collective action has a major impact.
>
> [Next came] research explaining why interest groups exist when we would not expect them to exist, according to Olson's theory. [Researchers pointed to] the existence of …"interest group sustainers." These included patrons, such as government, foundations, or wealthy persons who give resources to a group. Another interest group sustainer is a policy network, a communications network of persons concerned with policymaking in some area who have high personal stakes in a policy for occupational or other reasons and therefore participate in policymaking. A third interest group sustainer is social movements, which motivate persons to form groups in a way not explainable by Olson.

7. Although pluralism remains an important strain in popular political thought in America, the dominant strain probably is a conception most often associated with the Progressive movement of the early twentieth century but extending back to Thomas Jefferson and beyond. In what we shall call the *progressivist* view, the individual citizen is taken as the unit of analysis, in contrast to the pluralists' concentration on groups. Citizens are thought of as rational, reasonably well-informed, concerned about public issues, and desirous of re-

---

d. See Murray J. Edelman, THE SYMBOLIC USES OF POLITICS (1964).

solving issues in accord with the common good. Their political beliefs are not entirely dominated by the particular interests of groups to which they belong. Candidates for office compete by debating the substance of issues in the manner befitting a rational, informed, public spirited and actively involved audience. Once elected, representatives act pretty much like the voters who elected them. That is, they consider each issue of public policy individually, voting in accordance with their informed, rational sense of what is in the public interest.

Probably very few people past junior high school age believe that American democracy actually operates in this manner most of the time.[e] Nevertheless, popular progressivist thinking holds up something like this as the ideal. Social prejudice and selfish pursuit of economic and political interests will constantly cause departures from the ideal, but the progressivist goal is to cultivate civic virtue in the individual and design institutions to minimize these departures.

8. This book focuses on pluralism, political party theories, and progressivism rather than on any of a number of other academic theories—such as feminism, critical race studies, or law and economics—because most courts and other political actors have tended to view the field through these lenses. However, students and instructors with an interest in other academic perspectives will find grist for their theoretical mills in the issues dealt with in this book. Two additional academic theories, one related to pluralism and one related to progressivism, bear mentioning here because they have appeared in numerous scholarly articles (and occasional court cases) discussing election law:

Public Choice Theory. Public choice theory, which applies economic models of rational[f] decisionmaking to issues of political science, is closely related to the pluralist conception of politics. Public choice theory assumes that politicians rationally seek to maximize the chances of reelection and individuals rationally seek government action furthering self-interested goals. Like progressivism, it begins at the level of the individual, but like pluralism, it believes that much political action occurs when individuals organize for group action. If truth be known, we have already smuggled in a central concept of public choice theory, that of the free rider: In the struggle among interest groups, small, cohesive groups enjoy disproportionate influence over the political process.

Public choice theory also has a normative component that focuses on how to make the political process "efficient," that is, maximizing social wealth without regard to its distribution. In other words, public choice theorists care about the size of the pie, not how large a piece each person gets. But in the interest group struggle, inefficiency is a common problem:

> When interest groups use their political capital to secure goods from the state, they engage in "rent seeking." Rent seeking occurs when resources are used in order to capture a monopoly right instead of being put to a productive use. For example, when firms compete for the exclusive control of a local cable television franchise, they use their resources lobbying the local regulatory board, instead of investing those resources productively. Like these potential cable franchisees, organized interest groups expend their resources competing for political favors, such as tax breaks or subsidies, instead of putting them to some productive use. Rent seeking is … inefficient because it leads to an overall decline in social wealth....

---

e. Perhaps contemporary young people, who draw their edification from the likes of "South Park" and the "Daily Show," are likely to be more rather than less cynical than the general population.

f. By "rational," public choice theorists do not mean "sensible." Rather, they mean that an individual makes choices in accord with a consistent set of preferences: thus, if one prefers liver to ice cream for dessert, one rationally chooses liver when offered the choice of liver or ice cream for dessert.

Richard L. Hasen, *Clipping Coupons for Democracy: An Egalitarian/Public Choice Defense of Campaign Finance Vouchers*, 84 California Law Review 1, 9–11 (1996). Thus, under the normative public choice vision, election laws should be written to make it more difficult for groups to engage in socially wasteful rent seeking. How does that differ from the normative vision of pluralists? Of progressives?

For an introduction to the use of public choice theory in law, see Daniel A. Farber and Philip P. Frickey, Law and Public Choice: A Critical Introduction (1991). The use of economic models to explain politics has become very popular in the political science literature as well, where it is commonly referred to as "rational choice theory." For a book-length critique of rational choice theory, see Donald P. Green and Ian Shapiro, Pathologies of Rational Choice Theory: A Critique of Applications in Political Science (1994). For defenses by a number of rational choice theorists, see The Rational Choice Controversy: Economic Models of Politics Reconsidered (Jeffrey Friedman ed., 1996).

Civic Republicanism. Civic republicanism does not necessarily reject pluralism as an accurate description of the current American political system. Like progressivism, however, civic republicanism argues for a politics aimed at promoting the common good. It rejects the normative notion that politics should be merely about structuring interest group competition. Where civic republicanism differs from progressivism is in civic republicanism's special emphasis on facilitating *deliberation* among legislators:

> Many republican conceptions treat politics as above all deliberative; and deliberation is to cover ends as well as means.... [T]he belief in political deliberation is a distinctly American contribution to republican thought. The function of politics, on this view, is not simply to implement existing private preferences. Political actors are not supposed to come to the process with pre-selected interests that operate as exogenous variables. The purpose of politics is not to aggregate private preferences, or to achieve an equilibrium among contending social forces. The republican belief in deliberation counsels political actors to achieve a measure of critical distance from prevailing desires and practices, subjecting these desires and practices to scrutiny and review.

> To say this is not to suggest that deliberation calls for some standard entirely external to private beliefs and values (as if such a thing could be imagined). The republican position is instead that existing desires should be revisable in light of collective discussion and debate, bringing to bear alternative perspectives and additional information. Thus, for example, republicans will attempt to design political institutions that promote discussion and debate among the citizenry; they will be hostile to systems that promote lawmaking as "deals" or bargains among self-interested private groups; they may well attempt to insulate political actors from private pressure; and they may also favor judicial review designed to promote political deliberation and perhaps to invalidate laws when deliberation has not occurred.

> ... The antonym of deliberation is the imposition of outcomes by self-interested and politically powerful private groups; republicans emphasize that deliberative processes are often undermined by intimidation, strategic and manipulative behavior, collective action problems, adaptive preferences, or—most generally—disparities in political influence. The requirement of deliberation is designed to ensure that political outcomes will be supported by reference to a consensus (or at least broad agreement) among political equals.

Cass R. Sunstein, *Beyond the Republican Revival*, 97 Yale Law Journal 1539, 1548–50 (1988). As Sunstein suggests, civic republicans place an emphasis on political equality:

"Political equality, in republican terms, is understood as a requirement that all individuals and groups have access to the political process; large disparities in political influence are disfavored." Id. at 1552.

Assuming that "insulat[ing] political actors from private pressure" is indeed possible, is it desirable? How would a believer in strong political parties respond? Consider Michael A. Fitts, *Look Before You Leap: Some Cautionary Notes on Civic Republicanism*, 97 YALE LAW JOURNAL 1651, 1657 (1988):

> According to the political science literature, insulation of individual government actors and dispersion of government power is a serious *problem* in government, both as an impediment to effective and coordinated action and as a system that facilitates the influence and power of concentrated and wealthier special interest groups. Political parties, which seek to overcome those discrete sources of influence, are thus "the special form of political organization adapted to the mobilization of the majority."
>
> Not surprisingly, the political party literature views political dialogue and ideological politics, especially in the extreme, more skeptically. According to Sunstein, modern civic republicanism envisions rational dialogue as a "Rawlsian ideal"—by leading participants to "think from the point of view of everyone," a type of consensus is often achieved. Much of the political science literature suggests, however, that ideological debate—discussing public problems in terms of fundamental questions and beliefs—can sometimes create and exacerbate divisions and disputes in a public political context. Deep moral discussion can thus *undermine* the ability to reach consensus, and take action.

For an elaboration on these themes, see Michael A. Fitts, *The Vices of Virtue: A Political Party Perspective on Civic Virtue Reforms of the Legislative Process*, 136 UNIVERSITY OF PENNSYLVANIA LAW REVIEW 1567 (1988).

IV. Electoral Process and Democracy

This book deals with controversies over election procedures and regulations. How important are such questions to the functioning of a democracy? The following short excerpt may help to keep our subject in proper perspective. Is it a challenge to the very idea of this course and this book?

Irving Kristol, REFLECTIONS OF A NEOCONSERVATIVE
50–51 (1983)

Though the phrase "the quality of life" trips easily from so many lips these days, it tends to be one of those clichés with many trivial meanings and no large, serious one. Sometimes it merely refers to such externals as the enjoyment of cleaner air, cleaner water, cleaner streets. At other times it refers to the merely private enjoyment of music, painting, or literature. Rarely does it have anything to do with the way the citizen in a democracy views himself—his obligations, his intentions, his ultimate self-definition.

Instead, what I would call the "managerial" conception of democracy is the predominant opinion among political scientists, sociologists, and economists, and has, through the untiring efforts of these scholars, become the conventional journalistic opinion as well. The root idea behind this managerial conception is that democracy is a "political system" (as they say) which can be adequately defined in terms of—can be fully reduced to—its mechanical arrangements. Democracy is then seen as a set of rules and procedures, and *nothing but* a set of rules and procedures, whereby majority rule and minority rights are reconciled into a state of equilibrium. If everyone follows these rules and procedures, then a democracy is in working order. I think this is a fair description of the democratic idea that currently prevails in academia. One can also fairly say that it is now the liberal idea of democracy par excellence.

I cannot help but feel that there is something ridiculous about being this kind of a democrat, and I must further confess to having a sneaking sympathy for those of our young radicals who also find it ridiculous. The absurdity is the absurdity of idolatry—of taking the symbolic for the real, the means for the end. The purpose of democracy cannot possibly be the endless functioning of its own political machinery. The purpose of any political regime is to achieve some version of the good life and the good society. It is not at all difficult to imagine a perfectly functioning democracy which answers all questions except one—namely, why should anyone of intelligence and spirit care a fig for it?

There is, however, an older idea of democracy—one which was fairly common until about the beginning of this century—for which the conception of the quality of public life is absolutely crucial. This idea starts from the proposition that democracy is a form of self-government, and that if you want it to be a meritorious polity, you have to care about what kind of people govern it. Indeed, it puts the matter more strongly and declares that if you want self-government, you are only entitled to it if that "self" is worthy of governing. There is no inherent right to self-government if it means that such government is vicious, mean, squalid, and debased. Only a dogmatist and a fanatic, an idolater of democratic machinery, could approve of self-government under such conditions.

And because the desirability of self-government depends on the character of the people who govern, the older idea of democracy was very solicitous of the condition of this character. It was solicitous of the individual self, and felt an obligation to educate it into what used to be called "republican virtue." And it was solicitous of that collective self which we call public opinion and which, in a democracy, governs us collectively. Perhaps in some respects it was nervously oversolicitous—that would not be surprising. But the main thing is that it cared, cared not merely about the machinery of democracy but about the quality of life that this machinery might generate.

Notes and Questions

1. You have chosen to enroll in or teach a course, or read a book, devoted to the "set of rules and procedures," the "mechanical arrangements," that govern a democracy. We have chosen to compile such a book. Can you defend yourselves and us against the charge that each of us is "a dogmatist and a fanatic, an idolater of democratic machinery?"

2. For better or for worse, the field of election law has grown dramatically over the last few decades and the growth seems to be accelerating.[g] No doubt some of that growth reflects the attention that the United States Supreme Court has paid to the topic in recent decades. According to one study, from the period 1901–1960, the Court decided an average of 10.3 election law cases per decade with a written opinion. From 1961–2000, that

---

g. For an overview of the field by numerous prominent scholars, see the symposium, *Election Law as Its Own Field of Study*, 32 LOYOLA OF LOS ANGELES LAW REVIEW 1095 (1999).

figure jumped to 60 per decade. The trend also appears when one considers the percentage of election law cases on the Supreme Court's docket. In the earlier period, election law cases made up 0.7% of the cases the Court decided by written opinion; in the latter period, that percentage increased seven and one-half times to an average 5.3% of cases. Richard L. Hasen, THE SUPREME COURT AND ELECTION LAW, JUDGING EQUALITY FROM *BAKER V. CARR* TO *BUSH V. GORE* 1–2 (2003).

Chapter 2

The Right to Vote

If the election mechanism is at the heart of any democracy, then the right to vote in elections is a central democratic right and the act of voting is the most elemental form of democratic participation. The simplest and most natural place to begin our study of election law is thus with the right to vote itself. Who is entitled to the franchise? And when should courts interfere with a state's decision to limit the franchise to particular groups? The remaining chapters in this book will consider the electoral system within which the right to vote is located.

For two centuries the history of the United States (and of much of the rest of the world) has usually been in the direction of allowing more people to vote in more elections that increasingly have controlled the most important aspects of government policymaking. The suffrage was limited in important ways when the United States Constitution was adopted. Property qualifications, denial of the vote to racial groups (African Americans and Native Americans), and restriction of the vote to men were the most important departures from universal suffrage. In the course of American history, each of these restrictions on the right to vote and numerous others have been eliminated. In Part I of this chapter, we shall provide a brief overview of this history.

Whether we are more impressed with the progress that these developments reflect or with the unfortunate fact that they were necessary in the first place, we should not assume that the direction of change has always been toward extension of the franchise. As we shall see, the late nineteenth and early twentieth centuries comprised a cruelly regressive period during which the hard-won right for African Americans to vote in the southern states was taken away for all practical purposes. That right was finally restored in the mid-twentieth century. Another group, resident aliens, was permitted to vote in many states during much of the nineteenth century. That extension of the franchise was revoked around the turn of the century and, with minor exceptions, has not been restored. The constitutionality of denying the vote to aliens is considered later in this Chapter.

In Part II of this Chapter, we consider the role of courts in policing legislative limits on the franchise. May a state limit voting to those who (1) pay a poll tax; (2) are literate; (3) are residents; (4) are non-felons; or (5) are citizens? In recent years, the courts have read the U.S. Constitution to prohibit some, but not all, of these limits on the franchise. Which voter qualifications, if any, should be a matter of legislative prerogative? We then turn to a related question: once a state grants the right to vote to a particular group in general elections, may it limit the franchise in particular *types* of elections, such as school board elections?

Whether people actually vote after they are granted the right to do so may seem more a question for political scientists and party activists than for students of the law. However, voting procedures that are either fixed by law or amenable to legal reform may affect turnout, and the distinction between procedural barriers and the denial of the right to vote is not a sharp one. During the post-Reconstruction period, the Fifteenth Amendment precluded white southern Democrats from overtly denying the vote to African Americans. Instead, they relied on a variety of devices that made voting so difficult that the practical effect was almost as great as a denial of the right to vote. No such extreme restrictions are in effect today in the United States, but various requirements for voting, especially the requirement that individuals take the initiative to register if they wish to be eligible to vote, may be significant causes of low turnout in American elections, compared to those in other industrialized democracies. Chapter 7 looks at registration rules, and related election administration issues.

Most people nowadays agree that the right to vote should be nearly universal, but that has not always been the case.[a] Opponents of extending the franchise have argued at various times that the masses would so misuse the vote that, far from being benefited, their lot would be worsened; that mass suffrage would be futile, for power would always remain in an elite class; and that even if extension of the right to vote furthered the goal of political equality, this would be more than offset by harmful effects on other values, such as liberty.

Although no one seriously proposes cutting back the right to vote in major ways, past criticisms of universal suffrage cannot all be dismissed as insincere or lacking in substance. Similar arguments are heard today in opposition to proposals to make voting easier. Jonah Goldberg argues: "[V]oting should be harder, not easier—for everybody.... If you are having an intelligent conversation with somebody, is it enriched if a mob of uninformed louts, never mind ex-cons and rapists, barges in? People who want to make voting easier are in effect saying that those who previously didn't care or know enough about the country to vote are exactly the kind of voters this country needs now." Jonah Goldberg, The *Cellblock Voting Bloc*, Los Angeles Times, Mar. 8, 2005, at B11. Lurking behind these and many of the legal and policy disputes reviewed in this book is the question whether democracy should be thought of as competition among interests or as a deliberative process seeking the common good. Measures that some have believed would improve the deliberative quality of democracy—restricting the vote to property-owners or to people who can read and write, or requiring would-be voters to take the time to register and thereby demonstrate a sense of the responsibilities of a citizen—have appeared to others as self-interested devices to enhance the political power of the well-off. For example, is the 18-year-old age requirement for voting a desirable assurance of maturity in public decision-making, or is it a device for reinforcing adult society's strict control over younger teenagers?

I. A Brief History of the Right to Vote in the United States

A. The Extension of the Suffrage

1. The Attainment of White Male Suffrage

The American colonies inherited property qualifications for voting that had been established in England at least as early as the fifteenth century. In addition, British law ex-

---

a. Albert O. Hirschman, The Rhetoric of Reaction (1991), provides a lively account of the history of conservative arguments against the extension of the franchise over a period of two centuries. He concludes that the arguments have tended to reflect dogmatic assumptions that could be and have been levied against virtually all proposed social, economic, and political reforms, but that these assumptions often have little empirical grounding. In a concluding chapter, Hirschman finds that liberal reformers tend to rely on a set of similarly dogmatic opposing assumptions.

cluded women, Catholics, Jews, aliens, and servants from the franchise. However, because of cheap land and lax administration, suffrage was far more widespread in practice in the colonies during the eighteenth century than in England.

Although estimates of the percentage of people who were eligible to vote during the colonial and revolutionary periods are uncertain, it appears that at least half the white adult males could vote before the Revolution in all states, and that in some states at least three-quarters and perhaps nearly 100 percent could vote. Because of cheap land and scarce labor, most white men who could not meet the property qualifications during their youth could do so by the time they had attained middle age.

The fact that the property qualifications were not extremely restrictive in practice was one reason that their imposition did not become a major point of contention during the period leading up to the Revolution. Another reason was that the restrictions sometimes were not enforced or were easily evaded, especially when political contests were highly competitive and individuals therefore had the greatest incentive to vote. In addition to these practical considerations, there was no ideological consensus during the eighteenth century in favor of universal white male suffrage. Before the Revolution, the prevailing political theory was influenced by Aristotle's idea of balanced government, which held that tyranny would result if either the monarchical, the aristocratic, or the democratic principle dominated the others. Finally, in the absence of a secret ballot, voting by tenants, employees, or paupers was regarded as likely to lead to corruption or coercion, with a consequent magnification of influence by the wealthy.

The Constitution of the United States did not purport to regulate the franchise. The only federal officials chosen by direct election under the original Constitution were the members of the House of Representatives, and Article I, §2 of the Constitution said that "the Electors in each State shall have the Qualifications requisite for Electors of the most numerous Branch of the State Legislature."[b] What those qualifications were to be was entirely up to the states. Nor was there any impetus in the direction of universal suffrage from the federal government. The Northwest Ordinance and other laws governing territories imposed landowning requirements for voting. Difficulties with land titles and other practical problems quickly made property requirements a dead letter in much of the west, however.

With the arrival of the nineteenth century, the idea of universal white manhood suffrage became ascendant. The Aristotelian view was opposed by a Puritan belief that for purposes of secular politics, people should be treated as if they were equal and, increasingly, by natural rights theories of political equality.

Religious tests for voting and exclusion on the basis of status as a servant or employee (but not as a slave) were largely eliminated by the end of the revolutionary period. With one significant exception (Rhode Island, discussed below), property qualifications more or less petered out over the three-quarters of a century following the Revolution. In many places, the payment of a tax was permitted as an alternative to satisfying the property qualifications. Although the poll tax later became a prominent device for *denying* the vote to blacks and poor whites in the South, in the eighteenth century it was a liberalizing device that opened the franchise to persons whose wealth did not take the form of land. Similarly, service in the militia was increasingly accepted as an alternative to owning land or paying taxes, thereby extending the right to vote to a higher percentage of young men.

---

b. The Seventeenth Amendment, providing for direct election of Senators, contains a virtually identical clause.

During the Jeffersonian period, several states adopted universal white male suffrage or regulations that came very close. The trend continued throughout the first half of the nineteenth century, though at a very uneven pace in different states. Often the movement toward extension of the franchise was pushed forward by party competition, as each party sought to benefit by extending the franchise to new groups of voters who would, it was hoped, reward the party with their votes. The movement also benefited from less savory considerations, such as the contention in Virginia and North Carolina that universal white male suffrage was needed to assure unity among whites in the event of a slave rebellion. Despite this argument, these two states were among the last to adopt universal white male suffrage, in the 1850s.

The only truly dramatic event in the early extension of suffrage occurred in Rhode Island. In that state during the Jeffersonian period, the property qualifications did not prevent most adult males from voting, so there was no strong pressure to eliminate them. After the War of 1812, as industry began to develop and cities to grow, it became apparent that the non-landowning working class would be composed of immigrants, largely Catholic. Resistance to suffrage reform became strong in rural areas, where Protestant farmers had no desire to share political power with these newcomers. Pressure for a liberalized franchise grew, but was stoutly resisted by the rural interests who controlled the state government.

In 1841, a group called the Rhode Island Suffrage Association, under the leadership of Thomas Dorr, called for a constitutional convention, delegates to which would be elected by universal white male suffrage. Dorr's convention competed with a constitutional convention sponsored by the official state government. The official convention's Charter retained property qualifications, and for a time it appeared that popular support for Dorr might result in the overthrow of the Charter government. However, the national government under President John Tyler supported the Charter government, and the following year the constitution was liberalized to allow native-born citizens the right to qualify to vote with personal rather than real property. Dorr was forced to flee from Rhode Island, which for many years continued to discriminate between native-born and naturalized citizens, but whose new constitution was, in one important respect, more liberal than Dorr's, in that it permitted African Americans to vote.

By the time of the Civil War, adult white male suffrage was the rule in most of the states, with relatively minor exceptions. Although limited voting by women had been permitted in New Jersey until 1807, the almost universal rule restricted voting to men. For African Americans, there had actually been a regression since the colonial period, when a number of states, north and south, had permitted voting by free blacks. By 1860, most states restricted voting to whites, with most of the exceptions located in New England.[c]

2. The Fifteenth Amendment and Its Betrayal

As the Civil War ended, black suffrage not only was the exception rather than the rule in the North, but also was unpopular, as evidenced by its defeat in several (though not all) referendums that occurred in the 1860s. Accordingly, in 1865 and 1866, the Republicans, uncertain of their electoral prospects, did little to promote voting rights for African Americans. The Fourteenth Amendment, proposed in 1866 and ratified in 1868, made

---

c. There was also a regression in the first half of the nineteenth century in the number of states permitting aliens to vote. The history of voting by aliens is sketched briefly in Note 3 following *Skafte v. Rorex, infra* at page 51.

African Americans citizens and guaranteed "equal protection of the laws." It did not, however, expressly prohibit voting discrimination, though it did reduce the representation in Congress of states that denied voting rights to male inhabitants 21 and over. In 1866, the congressional Republicans won a landslide victory and thus felt safe in ordering black suffrage in areas where doing so would not arouse opposition in their northern constituencies. In 1867, blacks were given the franchise in the District of Columbia and in federal territories. The Reconstruction Act of 1867 required that blacks be allowed to vote in southern states as a condition of readmission.

By 1868, the Democrats were resurgent and although Ulysses Grant, the Republican candidate, was elected in 1868, the margin was perilously close in many northern states. Republicans also began to fear that some black voters in the South were in danger of being won over by the Democrats. The Republicans responded to these concerns by rushing the Fifteenth Amendment through the lame duck session of Congress in January and February, 1869. This was accomplished with some difficulty, and the final version of the Fifteenth Amendment was something of a compromise, falling short of the hopes of some that the federal Constitution would impose universal adult male suffrage or bar literacy and property tests. As adopted, the Fifteenth Amendment reads as follows:

> Section 1. The right of citizens of the United States to vote shall not be denied or abridged by the United States or by any State on account of race, color, or previous condition of servitude.

> Section 2. The Congress shall have power to enforce this article by appropriate legislation.

Ratification by the requisite number of states was completed within thirteen months, but only after considerable uncertainty. Ratification was assisted by legislation requiring Georgia, Mississippi, Texas, and Virginia to ratify the Fifteenth Amendment as a condition of readmission to the Union.

One impetus for the Fifteenth Amendment was the principled view of many that it was wrong to deny the vote on grounds of race, especially to a group whose vulnerability as recently emancipated slaves made the protection accorded by the right to vote particularly important. Section 2 provided express authority for legislation to safeguard their voting rights, an opportunity of which Congress availed itself through several laws enacted in succeeding years. Perhaps even greater impetus for the Fifteenth Amendment came from the desire of the Republican Party for electoral advantage. Black voters in many northern states, though few in number, could be expected to reinforce shaky Republican majorities, while the gratitude of African Americans in north and south would strengthen their voting loyalty to the GOP. The Fifteenth Amendment also benefitted northern Republicans by ending a potentially divisive debate. Once black voting was a fait accompli, Democrats could no longer exploit the *threat* of black voting as a way of appealing to white voters. It would thus be a mistake to assume that the Fifteenth Amendment was aimed primarily at the south. In the southern states, extension of the vote to blacks had been accomplished by military reconstruction and by the constitutions of the states that had already been readmitted.

The Fifteenth Amendment had the dual purpose of enfranchising African Americans in the northern states and reinforcing the right to vote in the south. The first purpose was successfully accomplished and, for a while, the second was accomplished too. African Americans did not only vote but were also elected to office in substantial numbers, with over 300 elected from southern states by 1872. But despite the Fifteenth Amendment, a disastrous retrenchment was to occur in the South.

The year 1877, when Union soldiers were removed from the South as part of the settlement of the disputed presidential election of 1876, is often given as the end of Reconstruction. It is easy to imagine that from 1877 on, the Solid South system—an almost
exclusively white electorate, ubiquitous control by the Democratic Party, and low voter
turnout—was firmly entrenched. In reality, it took thirty years of concentrated effort to
accomplish this result. The driving forces were racism, partisanship, and class politics.

Partisan political competition was a reality in the South until nearly the end of the
nineteenth century. It is true that the Democrats carried every southern state in presidential elections from 1880 on, but the vote was not always lopsided, and state and local
races were often more competitive. Republicans or the candidates of a variety of third
parties occasionally won statewide elections and often mounted a serious threat. Although
the number of southern black legislators began to decline in the 1870s, some continued
to serve through the 1890s.

White support for disfranchisement of African Americans came primarily from "black
belt counties" (those with especially large African American populations) and from wealthier areas. Typical leaders in the disfranchisement movement were wealthy, well-educated,
and from established families. White opposition to disfranchisement came mostly from
poorer and predominantly white areas, and from members of the Republican and other
opposition parties. Their opposition to disfranchisement may have been motivated by
principle, but it certainly was motivated by recognition that their partisan and class interests had no hope of success without the support of black voters. Blacks themselves actively resisted disfranchisement in both judicial and political arenas, though ultimately without
success.

Roughly speaking, in the 1870s and 1880s, southern Democrats often relied on violence and fraud to gain or consolidate control of state legislatures. Violence was often ineffective. The use of fraud was more successful, but it created the danger that it would trigger
a new round of federal intervention. Accordingly, in the 1880s and 1890s, southern Democratic legislatures adopted laws making it more difficult for blacks (and often poor
whites) to vote. Finally, in the 1890s and the 1900s, constitutional conventions were summoned. The discriminatory laws that had already been passed helped to assure that these
conventions would be dominated overwhelmingly by Democrats. The new constitutions
that emerged entrenched even stronger discrimination devices.

The following is a description of some of the leading devices that were adopted in the
southern states during this period, together with a brief indication of their subsequent
history:

> **Secret Ballots:** Although ostensibly introduced as a good government device
> to reduce voter corruption and preserve the integrity of the ballot box, the se-
> cret ballot was also favored in the South (and perhaps in the North as well) as a
> device to prevent illiterates from voting. In the South, this had a detrimental ef-
> fect on blacks, who had been denied education as slaves and subjected to infe-
> rior education after the Civil War. Furthermore, election officials could
> discriminatorily provide assistance to white voters who needed it, while denying
> assistance to black voters. In South Carolina and Florida, the "eight-box" device
> was used, to similar effect. Voters had to place separate ballots for different of-
> fices in separate ballot boxes, and ballots placed in the wrong box were not
> counted. Precinct officials gave no assistance to illiterate blacks, and the boxes could
> be moved around frequently during the day of the election, to confound any
> outside person who might seek to instruct black voters on which box was which.

Currently, most Americans are sufficiently literate that the secret ballot is not a major barrier to voting. Furthermore, the 1982 amendments to the Voting Rights Act mandate that any voter who needs assistance because of blindness, disability or illiteracy is entitled to receive it from a person of the voter's choice.[d]

The adoption of the secret ballot may have reduced turnout by as many as seven percentage points, but this effect was no greater in the south than in the rest of the country. See Jac C. Heckelman, *The effect of the secret ballot on voter turnout rates*, 82 PUBLIC CHOICE 107 (1995). Heckelman argues that the effect on turnout was not primarily caused by deterrence of voting by illiterates. He contends that party symbols that were usually placed on ballots made it possible for illiterates to vote when they were permitted to do so. Furthermore, literacy tests were a much more direct and potent way of preventing voting by illiterates. Rather, Heckelman contends that bribery of voters, a common practice in the nineteenth century, became impractical once a state adopted the secret ballot, because there was no way of assuring that the voter had voted as desired. The elimination of bribery also eliminated the incentive for some people to vote.

Poll Tax: Georgia adopted a poll tax in 1877. Other southern states did not follow suit until the 1890s, but by 1904 all the former states of the Confederacy had adopted a poll tax. The poll tax was justified by its proponents as a device to disenfranchise blacks, but it also had the effect, and probably the intent, of lowering white turnout. The poll tax was a particularly severe obstacle to voting in some states, which required an individual to pay not only the current year's tax but also unpaid taxes from previous years.

The 24th Amendment, added to the Constitution in 1964, banned poll taxes in federal elections. Two years later, the Supreme Court in *Harper v. Virginia Board of Elections*, 383 U.S. 663 (1966), ruled that the use of the poll tax in any election violated the Equal Protection Clause. We consider *Harper* in Part II of this Chapter.

Literacy Tests: Literacy tests were among the most important devices adopted at the disfranchisement conventions in the decades before and after the turn of the century. They were often accompanied by escape provisions, the best known of which was the "grandfather clause," which waived the literacy test for persons who were eligible to vote or whose ancestors were eligible to vote on a date prior to the initial enfranchisement of African Americans. Grandfather clauses were declared unconstitutional in *Guinn v. United States*, 238 U.S. 347 (1915), but the literacy tests could be and were administered in a discriminatory manner against blacks. By the 1950s and early 1960s, discriminatory literacy tests were the most important devices for restricting voting by African Americans in the South.

In *Lassiter v. Northampton County Board of Elections*, 360 U.S. 45 (1959), the Supreme Court held that a literacy test, fairly applied, did not violate the Equal Protection Clause. Literacy tests in the South often were *not* fairly applied, but proving discrimination on a case-by-case basis was a laborious chore. The Voting Rights Act of 1965 banned literacy tests in most of the Deep South. In *South Carolina v. Katzenbach*, 383 U.S. 301 (1966), the Supreme Court held that the literacy test ban was a permissible exercise of Congress' power to enforce the Fifteenth Amendment, despite the fact that the literacy test itself was not uncon-

---

d. Voting Rights Act §208, 42 U.S.C. §1973aa-6.

stitutional. In the 1970 amendments to the Voting Rights Act, Congress extended the literacy test ban to the entire country, but only until 1975.[e] In 1975 the ban was made permanent. See 42 U.S.C. §1973b(e)(2).

White Primary: Democratic primaries were held in some local elections in the South beginning in the 1870s as a device to coopt opposition or to assure a unified party vote. Apparently the first statewide primary held anywhere in the country was held in Louisiana in 1892, to prevent an intra-party division over the state lottery from leading to a Republican or Populist victory. Black voting in Democratic primaries was sometimes permitted until around the turn of the century, and was not much of an issue. Until the 1930s, the overwhelming majority of African Americans wanted to vote *against* the Democrats in the South, not to vote in their primaries. However, once interparty opposition was essentially eliminated, the white primary helped preserve the Democratic monopoly and provided an extra barrier against effective participation by black voters.

The elimination of the white primary was a major objective of civil rights litigation from the 1920s until success was finally achieved in the 1940s. The *White Primary Cases* are described in Chapter 9, in connection with the constitutional status of political parties.

The end result of this process was the elimination of partisan competition in the South during the first half of the twentieth century, drastically low rates of black registration and voting, and turnout even among whites that was much lower than in the rest of the country. The absence of partisan competition reduced the incentive to vote. Furthermore, a number of the discriminatory devices, though ostensibly aimed solely at African Americans, could be and sometimes were turned against poor white voters when it was necessary to protect the political control of the dominant groups.

3. Votes for Women

Enactment of the constitutional amendment guaranteeing the vote to racial minorities was accomplished relatively quickly, but the Fifteenth Amendment marked only the beginning of the long struggle to make suffrage for blacks a permanent reality. The struggle for the enfranchisement of women was similarly long, but the sequence was the opposite. The adoption of the Nineteenth Amendment took more than three-quarters of a century, but once it was accomplished, the struggle was over.

The beginning of the American women's rights movement is commonly dated from an 1848 meeting in Seneca Falls, New York, led by Elizabeth Cady Stanton and Lucretia Mott. The demand for the right to vote contained in the Declaration of Sentiments adopted at Seneca Falls was regarded as particularly radical. The founders of the women's movement were abolitionists, and their call for the right to vote was motivated in part by the desire to win the right to participate more effectively in the movement to end slavery. Leaders of the movement, including Lucy Stone and Susan B. Anthony, worked actively to support the Union cause during the Civil War. Many of them were disillusioned when, after the war, the Republican Party pushed for votes for blacks but not for women. Efforts to obtain judicial relief failed when the Supreme Court ruled that the Fourteenth Amendment did not prevent denying women the right to vote. *Minor v. Happersett*, 88 U.S. 162 (1875).

---

e. The Supreme Court upheld the nationwide literacy test ban in *Oregon v. Mitchell*, 400 U.S. 112 (1970).

In 1890, two women's suffrage groups merged to form the National American Woman Suffrage Association ("NAWSA"). By this time several states allowed women to vote in school or municipal elections and, in 1890, Wyoming was admitted as the first state to allow full woman suffrage. Colorado, Utah, and Idaho followed suit by 1896, but it was not until 1910 that Washington became the next state to do so. After 1910, several more states joined the fold, and New York's doing so in 1917 became the turning point in the effort to obtain women's suffrage nationwide. By that time, enough representatives had voting female constituents to provide impetus to the approval by Congress of the Nineteenth Amendment in 1919. The amendment was ratified by the 36th state and became part of the Constitution in August, 1920.

In the 1890s, arguments for women's suffrage were cast largely in terms of equality and individual rights. However, around the turn of the century, the appeal of arguments based on the principle of universal suffrage diminished, as opposition to voting by immigrant groups in the North and blacks in the South mounted. One of the leading arguments made against suffrage for women was that it would give more influence to "the poor, the ignorant, and the immoral," groups who were often assumed to be identical by proponents of this viewpoint.

The leaders of the women's suffrage movement were mainly white, native-born, middle-class women who were by no means immune to the prejudices that characterized their period. Accordingly, arguments for women's suffrage shifted from arguments based on equality and the principle of universal suffrage to arguments based on reforms that women would favor and help to bring about, particularly prohibition of alcoholic beverages and a variety of reforms espoused by the Progressive movement.

In contrast to the highly partisan politics that led first to the granting of the franchise to blacks and then to the denial of it to blacks in the South, party played a much smaller role in the struggle for women's suffrage. The NAWSA was consistently nonpartisan. Indeed, many of its members shared the general anti-party views common among Progressive reformers. It is true that as a general rule, Republican legislators were more likely to support women's suffrage than Democrats, at least in part because women were expected to support prohibition, a cause supported by more Republicans than Democrats. A group known as the Women's Party, smaller and more militant than the NAWSA, in 1914 and 1916 urged women in states where they could vote to oppose Democrats because of President Wilson's lack of leadership in support of women's suffrage. However, there is little evidence that such campaigning was effective. As the inevitability of nationwide women's suffrage began to be clear, representatives of both parties joined the bandwagon so as not to provoke opposition from the new class of voters.

Contemporaries expected that voting by women would boost two political causes: peace and prohibition. Whether this would have occurred is hard to say, because World War I ended and the prohibition amendment (the Eighteenth) was enacted before women's suffrage was accomplished. As Aileen S. Kraditor, a historian of the women's suffrage movement, has written:

> The addition of women to the electorate has not significantly altered American voting patterns as the suffragists predicted it would.[f] But it would not be correct for that reason to deny that an enormous change took place with the en-

f. Kraditor was writing in 1965. Beginning in the 1980s political analysts have sometimes observed a "gender gap," consisting of somewhat greater support for Democrats by women and Republicans by men.

actment of the Nineteenth Amendment. Even those many suffragists who wanted the vote primarily to enact reforms became suffragists partly because of the intense shame they felt at being thought unfit to help govern their country. When they acquired that right they felt a new pride in American democracy and a new respect for themselves.[g]

4. *The Reenfranchisement of African Americans in the South*

In 1910, when racial segregation and disfranchisement of blacks were firmly established in the South and when belief in racial equality was at a low point throughout the nation, blacks and whites who retained a commitment to civil rights formed the National Association for the Advancement of Colored People. Reenfranchisement was one of the NAACP's major goals, and litigation was one of its major weapons.

The NAACP's most important litigation campaign relating to voting rights was a sustained attack on the white primary. The key victory, in *Smith v. Allwright*, 321 U.S. 649 (1944), was largely responsible for an increase in black registration in the South from an estimated 250,000 in 1940, to as many as 775,000 in 1947.

A second disfranchisement device, the poll tax, was vulnerable to political attack because it prevented some whites as well as blacks from voting and was sometimes associated with corrupt political machines, which would pay the poll tax for voters expected to be reliable machine supporters. The poll tax was repealed in North Carolina in 1920, and in five other states, Florida, Georgia, Louisiana, South Carolina, and Tennessee, between 1937 and the mid-1950s.

In addition to attacks on legal impediments to registering, action to encourage registration of blacks began in earnest after World War II. In Mississippi, returning African American veterans led registration efforts, and although these did not achieve great numerical success, Mississippi's discriminatory practices received nationwide exposure during a Senate investigation into the Democratic senatorial primary of 1946. The NAACP and a variety of voter leagues and other civil rights organizations conducted intense registration drives.

These legal and political efforts were by no means without effect. By the mid-1950s, over a million African Americans were registered in the South, representing 20 to 25 percent of the voting age black population, as compared with about 5 percent before *Smith v. Allwright*. However, the gains were concentrated in the upper South and the largest cities of the deep South. In 24 deep South black belt counties, not a single African American was registered at the end of 1952. Literacy tests and often flagrantly discriminatory administration of the registration system, supplemented by violence and economic retaliation sometimes directed against African Americans who sought to register, blocked further progress. It became the consensus among voting rights supporters that federal action would be necessary.

Voting rights legislation was passed by Congress in 1957 and 1960, and there were relatively minor voting provisions in the Civil Rights Act of 1964. The general thrust of these

---

g. Aileen S. Kraditor, THE IDEAS OF THE WOMAN SUFFRAGE MOVEMENT, 1890–1920 263–64 (1965). See also Adam Winkler, *A Revolution Too Soon: Woman Suffragists and the "Living Constitution,"* 76 NEW YORK UNIVERSITY LAW REVIEW 1456 (2001).

laws was to enable the Justice Department and private citizens to bring actions in federal courts to enforce nondiscriminatory voting procedures. It would be an exaggeration to say that these reforms were a failure. By 1964, an estimated 38 percent of southern voting age blacks were registered, a significant increase from a decade before. The 1957 and 1960 civil rights laws contributed to this progress, which also was prompted by intensified registration drives conducted by the NAACP and newer organizations such as the Student Non-violent Coordinating Committee, the Congress of Racial Equality, and the Southern Christian Leadership Conference. Still, the laws that had been passed were not sufficient to bring about equal access to the ballot box throughout the South. The key flaw was that the burden of initiating litigation was on the Justice Department or on voting rights proponents. Case-by-case litigation was slow and costly.[h]

Events in Selma, Alabama, in 1965, led the voting rights issue to a climax. Martin Luther King, who had recently been awarded the Nobel Peace Prize, led a series of voting rights demonstrations in Selma. 2,000 demonstrators, including King, were arrested. King later met with President Lyndon Johnson, who agreed to seek legislation prohibiting literacy tests and eliminating local officials' discretion by imposing federal registrars where necessary. On March 7, 1965, demonstrators marching from Selma to Montgomery were beaten by state troopers and county police. A week later, in a dramatic address to Congress, President Johnson employed the civil rights slogan, "We shall overcome," in demanding strong voting rights legislation. In August, he was able to sign the Voting Rights Act of 1965 into law.[i]

Sections 2 and 3 of the Act were permanent additions to law and generally applicable. Section 2 essentially restated the Fifteenth Amendment, barring states and localities from employing voting mechanisms that would deny or abridge on account of race or color the right of American citizens to vote. Section 3 further strengthened the remedies in suits brought by the Justice Department to enforce the Fifteenth Amendment. Although Section 2 was later to become, in an amended form, a key provision of the Act, in 1965 Sections 2 and 3 were regarded as relatively unimportant.

The provisions that were dramatically new and that would make the Fifteenth Amendment a reality were in Sections 4 through 9, which were to be in effect only for five years and were applicable only in states or localities that in 1964 used a literacy or other test as a condition for registering or voting and in which less than half the voting age population voted in the 1964 presidential election. As a practical matter, the areas "covered" by the Act were Alabama, Georgia, Louisiana, Mississippi, South Carolina, Virginia, and large parts of North Carolina.

Section 4 of the act prohibited the use of literacy tests and other tests or devices in covered areas. Sections 6 through 8 authorized the federal government, under specified circumstances but without the need for judicial proceedings, to appoint federal registrars and election observers, to assure nondiscriminatory election administration. To prevent states from devising new means of disfranchisement, Section 5 required covered states

---

h. Nevertheless, litigation has continued to be a significant device for those seeking to protect or extend the franchise to minority group members. See Peyton McCrary, *Bringing Equality to Power: How the Federal Courts Transformed the Electoral Structure of Southern Politics, 1960–1990*, 5 UNIVERSITY OF PENNSYLVANIA JOURNAL OF CONSTITUTIONAL LAW 665 (2003).

i. 42 U.S.C. §1973 et seq. Provisions of the Voting Rights Act are commonly referred to by the Act's internal section numbers rather than by their codification in the United States Code, and that practice will be followed henceforth in this volume.

and localities to submit changes in "any voting qualification or prerequisite to voting, or standard, practice or procedure with respect to voting" to either the attorney general or to the U.S. District Court for the District of Columbia for "preclearance." No such change could be implemented without preclearance, but if preclearance were denied by the attorney general, it could be sought judicially.

The Voting Rights Act proved to be one of the most successful civil rights measures in American history. In the words of one leading student of the Act:

> In Mississippi, that stronghold within a stronghold, black voter registration increased from 6.7 percent before the act to 59.8 in 1967. The act simply overwhelmed the major bulwarks of the disfranchising system. In the seven states originally covered, black registration increased from 29.3 percent in March 1965 to 56.6 percent in 1971–72; the gap between black and white registration rates narrowed from 44.1 percentage points to 11.2.[j]

The great effect that reenfranchisement of African Americans has had on southern politics is manifested in many ways. One of the most dramatic is the change in the way in which southern politicians seek electoral support. A well known example is George Wallace, who in the 1960s had been a national symbol of racial segregation, but who in 1982 was elected governor of Alabama only because his changed attitudes permitted him to carry the black vote by an overwhelming majority against a Republican opponent.

The fact that the major provisions of the Act were temporary has turned out to be an advantage to proponents of minority voting rights rather than a hindrance, for each time the Act has been scheduled to expire it has not only been renewed, but strengthening or broadening amendments have been added. For example, in 1970, the coverage formula was updated to refer to the 1968 rather than the 1964 presidential election, thereby considerably expanding the covered areas. In addition, the 1970 amendments made the ban on literacy tests nationwide for a five-year period.

The Act was again renewed and amended in 1975. The nationwide ban on literacy tests was made permanent, and plaintiffs were given new advantages in litigation brought under the Act, including the possibility of being awarded attorneys' fees. The most important of the 1975 amendments extended the protection of the Act beyond racial minorities to specified language minorities — Asian Americans, Native Americans, Alaskan natives, and persons of Spanish heritage. Concomitantly, coverage was extended to three new states, Alaska, Arizona, and Texas, and portions of many other states around the country. Congress renewed the Act once again in 1982, giving it considerably more teeth. Additionally, Congress expanded the coverage of one portion of the Act, requiring bilingual voting assistance in specified areas, in 1992.

The most recent extension and amendment of the Voting Rights Act occurred in 2006, with the language provisions set to expire in 2031 and section 5 preclearance in 2032. The most significant change was to impose a higher standard for preclearance, one that focuses on racial minorities' opportunity to elect their preferred candidate of choice. The latest amendment did not change the formula for coverage, and that has led to litigation claiming the law is unconstitutional as exceeding congressional power to enforce the Fourteenth and Fifteenth Amendments. We consider the 1982 and 2006 amendments in Chapter 5.

---

j. Chandler Davidson, *The Voting Rights Act: A Brief History*, in Controversies in Minority Voting 7, 21 (1992).

5. *Additional Extensions of the Franchise*

The elimination of property qualifications and of racial and gender discrimination have been the most important extensions of the franchise in American history, but by no means the only ones. A few additional ones are worthy of brief consideration, some of which we will revisit in Chapter 7.

Age: Until 1970, most states set the minimum voting age at 21. The 1970 amendments to the Voting Rights Act prohibited states from setting a minimum voting age above 18. In *Oregon v. Mitchell*, 400 U.S. 112 (1970), four justices believed Congress had no power under the Constitution to set a voting age, but four justices believed Congress was acting within its power to enforce the Fourteenth Amendment. The remaining member of the Court, Justice Black, believed Congress had the power to set the voting age for federal elections but not state and local elections. The problem with this interpretation was that it disregarded the Constitution's text. Article I, §2 and the Seventeenth Amendment prescribe that the qualifications for congressional electors are to be the same as the qualifications for electors for the most numerous branch of the state legislature. Justice Black's view nevertheless prevailed, because there were five justices who believed Congress could set the voting age in federal elections and there were five who believed Congress could not set the voting age for state and local elections. The anomaly was eliminated in 1971 by adoption of the 26th Amendment, which prohibits a state from setting a voting age above 18.

Durational residency: Prior to 1972, states commonly denied the right to vote to persons who had recently moved into the state. Typically, a residency period of one year was required. Because of the high rate of transiency in the United States, lengthy durational residency requirements prevented significant numbers of people from voting. However, the Supreme Court struck down a Tennessee requirement of one year's residency in the state and three months' residency in the county, observing that "30 days appears to be an ample period of time for the State to complete whatever administrative tasks are necessary to prevent fraud." *Dunn v. Blumstein*, 405 U.S. 330, 348 (1972). Despite this statement, the next year the Court upheld Arizona's 50-day durational residence requirement, *Marston v. Lewis*, 410 U.S. 679 (1973), and Georgia's 50-day pre-election cut-off for registering to vote, *Burns v. Fortson*, 410 U.S. 686 (1973).

The registration cut-off is distinct from, though related to, the durational residence requirement. Long-time residents of the state who satisfy the durational residence requirement will be barred from voting if they miss the registration cut-off. The difference between a 50-day and a 30-day residency requirement is not particularly great, because it affects only people who move into the jurisdiction within a twenty-day period. The same 20-day difference in the registration cut-off may have a much more substantial effect on turnout, because the closer to the election, the more likely people are to have developed an interest in the campaign that generates an incentive to register. We explore the legal significance of this and other election administration rules affecting turnout in Chapter 7.

Marston and *Burns* notwithstanding, nearly all states have 30-day residency requirements and registration cut-offs or less. An important reason for this near-uniformity is that Section 202 of the Voting Rights Act, added in 1970, sets a maximum 30-day residence and registration period for voting in presidential elections. States that might otherwise prefer longer than a 30-day period no doubt would find it more trouble than it is worth to retain one deadline for presidential registration and another for all other elections. Section 202 also requires states to provide absentee ballots for presidential voting to voters who will be out of the state on election day, and it permits voters who move during the thirty days before a presidential election to vote for president in their old state of residence.

Notes and Questions

1. *Bibliographical Note*: An excellent overview of the history of the franchise in America is provided in J. Morgan Kousser, *Suffrage*, in 3 ENCYCLOPEDIA OF AMERICAN POLITICAL HISTORY 1236 (Jack P. Greene, ed., 1984). The above account has drawn primarily on Kousser's essay and on the following sources: Chandler Davidson, *The Voting Rights Act: A Brief History*, in CONTROVERSIES IN MINORITY VOTING 7–51 (Bernard Grofman and Chandler Davidson, eds., 1992); William Gillette, THE RIGHT TO VOTE: POLITICS AND THE PASSAGE OF THE FIFTEENTH AMENDMENT (1965); Alexander Keyssar, THE RIGHT TO VOTE: THE CONTESTED HISTORY OF DEMOCRACY IN THE UNITED STATES (2000); J. Morgan Kousser, THE SHAPING OF SOUTHERN POLITICS: SUFFRAGE RESTRICTION AND THE ESTABLISHMENT OF THE ONE-PARTY SOUTH, 1880–1910 (1974); Aileen S. Kraditor, THE IDEAS OF THE WOMAN SUFFRAGE MOVEMENT, 1890–1920 (1965); Steven F. Lawson, BLACK BALLOTS: VOTING RIGHTS IN THE SOUTH, 1944–1969 (1976); and Chilton Williamson, AMERICAN SUFFRAGE: FROM PROPERTY TO DEMOCRACY, 1760–1860 (1960). For a recent overview, see Pamela S. Karlan, *Ballots and Bullets: The Exceptional History of the Right to Vote*, 71 UNIVERSITY OF CINCINNATI LAW REVIEW 1345 (2003).

2. This section has dealt with the broadening of categories of people who are generally eligible to vote. It is worth noticing, in passing, that the scope of the right to vote also has expanded enormously. When the Constitution was adopted, only one chamber—the House of Representatives—of one of the three branches of government was subject to direct popular control. By 1800, the selection of electors for president and vice-president became, in reality, a process of popular election in most states. In 1913, the Seventeenth Amendment made the Senate subject to popular elections as well.

State governments may have been more democratically controlled from the start than the federal government, but the domain of popular elections has expanded even further at the state level. All state legislative chambers are chosen in direct elections, as are governors and, in most states, other executive officials such as attorneys general and treasurers. In many states, judges are elected. In 1818, Connecticut adopted a constitution providing that future constitutional amendments would be subject to popular approval. Today, every state but Delaware subjects constitutional amendments to an election, and most states submit bond measures or other types of special legislation to popular approval as well. Since early in the twentieth century, about half the states have employed the initiative and referendum devices to permit a vote of the people on particular legislative proposals.

II. Court Review of State Limitations on the Franchise

Harper v. Virginia State Board of Elections
383 U.S. 663 (1966)

Mr. Justice DOUGLAS delivered the opinion of the Court.

These are suits by Virginia residents to have declared unconstitutional Virginia's poll tax.[1] The three-judge District Court, feeling bound by our decision in *Breedlove v. Sut-*

---

1. Section 173 of Virginia's Constitution directs the General Assembly to levy an annual poll tax not exceeding $1.50 on every resident of the State 21 years of age and over (with exceptions not relevant here). One dollar of the tax is to be used by state officials 'exclusively in aid of the public free

tles, 302 U.S. 277 [1937], dismissed the complaint. The cases came here on appeal and we noted probable jurisdiction.

While the right to vote in federal elections is conferred by Art. I, §2, of the Constitution (*United States v. Classic*, 313 U.S. 299, 314–315 [1941]), the right to vote in state elections is nowhere expressly mentioned. It is argued that the right to vote in state elections is implicit, particularly by reason of the First Amendment and that it may not constitutionally be conditioned upon the payment of a tax or fee. We do not stop to canvass the relation between voting and political expression. For it is enough to say that once the franchise is granted to the electorate, lines may not be drawn which are inconsistent with the Equal Protection Clause of the Fourteenth Amendment. That is to say, the right of suffrage "is subject to the imposition of state standards which are not discriminatory and which do not contravene any restriction that Congress, acting pursuant to its constitutional powers, has imposed." *Lassiter v. Northampton County Board of Elections*, 360 U.S. 45, 51 [1959]. We were speaking there of a state literacy test which we sustained, warning that the result would be different if a literacy test, fair on its face, were used to discriminate against a class.[3]

But the *Lassiter* case does not govern the result here, because, unlike a poll tax, the 'ability to read and write * * * has some relation to standards designed to promote intelligent use of the ballot.' *Lassiter*.

We conclude that a State violates the Equal Protection Clause of the Fourteenth Amendment whenever it makes the affluence of the voter or payment of any fee an electoral standard. Voter qualifications have no relation to wealth nor to paying or not paying this or any other tax.[4] Our cases demonstrate that the Equal Protection Clause of the Fourteenth Amendment restrains the States from fixing voter qualifications which invidiously discriminate. Thus without questioning the power of a State to impose reasonable residence restrictions on the availability of the ballot, we held in *Carrington v. Rash*, 380 U.S. 89 [1965], that a State may not deny the opportunity to vote to a bona fide resident merely because he is a member of the armed services. "By forbidding a soldier ever to controvert the presumption of non-residence, the Texas Constitution imposes an invidious discrimination in violation of the Fourteenth Amendment." Previously we had said that neither home-site nor occupation "affords a permissible basis for distinguishing between qualified voters within the State." *Gray v. Sanders*, 372 U.S. 368 [1963]. We think the same must be true of requirements of wealth or affluence or payment of a fee.

---

schools' and the remainder is to be returned to the counties for general purposes. Section 18 of the Constitution includes payment of poll taxes as a precondition for voting. Section 20 provides that a person must 'personally' pay all state poll taxes for the three years preceding the year in which he applies for registration. By §21 the poll tax must be paid at least six months prior to the election in which the voter seeks to vote. Since the time for election of state officials varies, the six months' deadline will vary, election from election. The poll tax is often assessed along with the personal property tax. Those who do not pay a personal property tax are not assessed for a poll tax, it being their responsibility to take the initiative and request to be assessed. Enforcement of poll taxes takes the form of disenfranchisement of those who do not pay, §22 of the Virginia Constitution providing that collection of delinquent poll taxes for a particular year may not be enforced by legal proceedings until the tax for that year has become three years delinquent.

3. We recently held in *Louisiana v. United States*, 380 U.S. 145 [1965], that a literacy test which gave voting registrars "a virtually uncontrolled discretion as to who should vote and who should not" had been used to deter Negroes from voting and accordingly we struck it down. While the "Virginia poll tax was born of a desire to disenfranchise the Negro" (*Harman v. Forssenius*, 380 U.S. 528, 543 [1965]), we do not stop to determine whether on this record the Virginia tax in its modern setting serves the same end.

4. Only a handful of States today condition the franchise on the payment of a poll tax....

Long ago in *Yick Wo v. Hopkins*, 118 U.S. 356 [1886] the Court referred to "the political franchise of voting" as a "fundamental political right, because [it is] preservative of all rights." Recently in *Reynolds v. Sims* [377 U.S. 533 (1964)], we said, "Undoubtedly, the right of suffrage is a fundamental matter in a free and democratic society. Especially since the right to exercise the franchise in a free and unimpaired manner is preservative of other basic civil and political rights, any alleged infringement of the right of citizens to vote must be carefully and meticulously scrutinized." There we were considering charges that voters in one part of the State had greater representation per person in the State Legislature than voters in another part of the State. We concluded:

> A citizen, a qualified voter, is no more nor no less so because he lives in the city or on the farm. This is the clear and strong command of our Constitution's Equal Protection Clause. This is an essential part of the concept of a government of laws and not men. This is at the heart of Lincoln's vision of "government of the people, by the people, (and) for the people." The Equal Protection Clause demands no less than substantially equal state legislative representation for all citizens, of all places as well as of all races.

We say the same whether the citizen, otherwise qualified to vote, has $1.50 in his pocket or nothing at all, pays the fee or fails to pay it. The principle that denies the State the right to dilute a citizen's vote on account of his economic status or other such factors by analogy bars a system which excludes those unable to pay a fee to vote or who fail to pay.

It is argued that a State may exact fees from citizens for many different kinds of licenses; that if it can demand from all an equal fee for a driver's license, it can demand from all an equal poll tax for voting. But we must remember that the interest of the State, when it comes to voting, is limited to the power to fix qualifications. Wealth, like race, creed, or color, is not germane to one's ability to participate intelligently in the electoral process. Lines drawn on the basis of wealth or property, like those of race are traditionally disfavored. To introduce wealth or payment of a fee as a measure of a voter's qualifications is to introduce a capricious or irrelevant factor. The degree of the discrimination is irrelevant. In this context—that is, as a condition of obtaining a ballot—the requirement of fee paying causes an "invidious" discrimination that runs afoul of the Equal Protection Clause. Levy "by the poll," as stated in *Breedlove* is an old familiar form of taxation; and we say nothing to impair its validity so long as it is not made a condition to the exercise of the franchise. *Breedlove* sanctioned its use as "a prerequisite of voting." To that extent the Breedlove case is overruled.

We agree, of course, with Mr. Justice Holmes that the Due Process Clause of the Fourteenth Amendment "does not enact Mr. Herbert Spencer's Social Statics" (*Lochner v. People of State of New York*, 198 U.S. 45 [1905]). Likewise, the Equal Protection Clause is not shackled to the political theory of a particular era. In determining what lines are unconstitutionally discriminatory, we have never been confined to historic notions of equality, any more than we have restricted due process to a fixed catalogue of what was at a given time deemed to be the limits of fundamental rights. Notions of what constitutes equal treatment for purposes of the Equal Protection Clause do change. This Court in 1896 held that laws providing for separate public facilities for white and Negro citizens did not deprive the latter of the equal protection and treatment that the Fourteenth Amendment commands. *Plessy v. Ferguson*, 163 U.S. 537 [1896]. Seven of the eight Justices then sitting subscribed to the Court's opinion, thus joining in expressions of what constituted unequal and discriminatory treatment that sound strange to a contemporary ear. When, in 1954—more than a half-century later—we repudiated the "separate-but-equal" doctrine of *Plessy* as respects public education we stated: "In approaching this problem, we cannot turn the clock back to 1868 when the Amendment was adopted, or even to 1896 when *Plessy v. Ferguson* was written." *Brown v. Board of Education*, 347 U.S. 483, 492 [1954].

In a recent searching re-examination of the Equal Protection Clause, we held, as already noted, that "the opportunity for equal participation by all voters in the election of state legislators" is required. *Reynolds*. We decline to qualify that principle by sustaining this poll tax. Our conclusion, like that in *Reynolds v. Sims*, is founded not on what we think governmental policy should be, but on what the Equal Protection Clause requires.

We have long been mindful that where fundamental rights and liberties are asserted under the Equal Protection Clause, classifications which might invade or restrain them must be closely scrutinized and carefully confined. Those principles apply here. For to repeat, wealth or fee paying has, in our view, no relation to voting qualifications; the right to vote is too precious, too fundamental to be so burdened or conditioned.

Reversed.

Mr. Justice BLACK, dissenting.

... It should be pointed out at once that the Court's decision is to no extent based on a finding that the Virginia law as written or as applied is being used as a device or mechanism to deny Negro citizens of Virginia the right to vote on account of their color. Apparently the Court agrees with the District Court below and with my Brothers HARLAN and STEWART that this record would not support any finding that the Virginia poll tax law the Court invalidates has any such effect. If the record could support a finding that the law as written or applied has such an effect, the law would of course be unconstitutional as a violation of the Fourteenth and Fifteenth Amendments and also 42 U.S.C. s 1971(a).... What the Court does hold is that the Equal Protection Clause necessarily bars all States from making payment of a state tax, any tax, a prerequisite to voting.

[I] think the interpretation that this Court gave the Equal Protection Clause in *Breedlove* was correct. The mere fact that a law results in treating some groups differently from others does not, of course, automatically amount to a violation of the Equal Protection Clause. To bar a State from drawing any distinctions in the application of its laws would practically paralyze the regulatory power of legislative bodies. Consequently "The constitutional command for a state to afford 'equal protection of the laws' sets a goal not attainable by the invention and application of a precise formula." Voting laws are no exception to this principle. All voting laws treat some persons differently from others in some respects. Some bar a person from voting who is under 21 years of age; others bar those under 18. Some bar convicted felons or the insane, and some have attached a freehold or other property qualification for voting. The *Breedlove* case upheld a poll tax which was imposed on men but was not equally imposed on women and minors, and the Court today does not overrule that part of *Breedlove* which approved those discriminatory provisions. And in *Lassiter*, this Court held that State laws which disqualified the illiterate from voting did not violate the Equal Protection Clause. From these cases and all the others decided by this Court interpreting the Equal Protection Clause, it is clear that some discriminatory voting qualifications can be imposed without violating the Equal Protection Clause....

Mr. Justice HARLAN, whom Mr. Justice STEWART joins, dissenting.

The final demise of state poll taxes, already totally proscribed by the Twenty-Fourth Amendment with respect to federal elections and abolished by the States themselves in all but four States with respect to state elections, is perhaps in itself not of great moment. But that fact that the coup de grace has been administered by this Court instead of being left to the affected States or to the federal political process should be a matter of continuing concern to all interested in maintaining the proper role of this tribunal under our scheme of government....

Property qualifications and poll taxes have been a traditional part of our political structure. In the Colonies the franchise was generally a restricted one. Over the years, these and other restrictions were gradually lifted, primarily because popular theories of political representation had changed. Often restrictions were lifted only after wide public debate. The issue of woman suffrage, for example, raised question of family relationships, of participation in public affairs, of the very nature of the type of society in which Americans wished to live; eventually a consensus was reached, which culminated in the Nineteenth Amendment no more than 45 years ago.

Similarly with property qualifications, it is only by fiat that it can be said, especially in the context of American history, that there can be no rational debate as to their advisability. Most of the early Colonies had them; many of the States have had them during much of their histories; and, whether one agrees or not, arguments have been and still can be made in favor of them. For example, it is certainly a rational argument that payment of some minimal poll tax promotes civic responsibility, weeding out those who do not care enough about public affairs to pay $1.50 or thereabouts a year for the exercise of the franchise. It is also arguable, indeed it was probably accepted as sound political theory by a large percentage of Americans through most of our history, that people with some property have a deeper stake in community affairs, and are consequently more responsible, more educated, more knowledgeable, more worthy of confidence, than those without means, and that the community and Nation would be better managed if the franchise were restricted to such citizens. Nondiscriminatory and fairly applied literacy tests, upheld by this Court in *Lassiter*, find justification on very similar grounds.

These viewpoints, to be sure, ring hollow on most contemporary ears. Their lack of acceptance today is evidenced by the fact that nearly all of the States, left to their own devices, have eliminated property or poll-tax qualifications; by the cognate fact that Congress and three-quarters of the States quickly ratified the Twenty-Fourth Amendment; and by the fact that rules such as the "pauper exclusion" in Virginia law, have never been enforced.

Property and poll-tax qualifications, very simply, are not in accord with current egalitarian notions of how a modern democracy should be organized. It is of course entirely fitting that legislatures should modify the law to reflect such changes in popular attitudes. However, it is all wrong, in my view, for the Court to adopt the political doctrines popularly accepted at a particular moment of our history and to declare all others to be irrational and invidious, barring them from the range of choice by reasonably minded people acting through the political process. It was not too long ago that Mr. Justice Holmes felt impelled to remind the Court that the Due Process Clause of the Fourteenth Amendment does not enact the laissez-faire theory of society, *Lochner*. The times have changed, and perhaps it is appropriate to observe that neither does the Equal Protection Clause of that Amendment rigidly impose upon America an ideology of unrestrained egalitarianism....

Notes and Questions

1. *The Equal Protection Clause:* In a number of the cases in this book, persons claim that an election regulation, such as the denial of the right to vote challenged in *Harper*, violates the Equal Protection Clause. That clause appears in Section 1 of the Fourteenth Amendment, which reads in part as follows:

No State shall make or enforce any law which shall abridge the privileges or immunities of citizens of the United States; nor shall any state deprive any person of life, liberty, or property, without due process of law; *nor deny to any person within its jurisdiction the equal protection of the laws.* [Emphasis added.]

There is no occasion here to consider in depth the intricacies of equal protection doctrine, but the following very simplified summary should assist persons who have never studied constitutional law to understand the equal protection cases contained in this book.

Although the phrase "equal protection of the laws" might seem to suggest that the clause is more concerned with the enforcement of laws than with their content, the overwhelming majority of controversies under the Equal Protection Clause arise because of attacks on classifications that are explicitly or implicitly written into statutes. However, as the Supreme Court has often recognized, almost all legislation classifies people and thus treats them differently. Persons who engage in certain economic transactions are subjected to different forms of taxation and regulation than persons who engage in different types of transactions. Persons convicted of engaging in certain forms of conduct are punished by the criminal law while others who refrain from such conduct are not. And so on.

Because the Supreme Court has not wanted the Equal Protection Clause to be a means of voiding virtually all legislation, it has said that only "invidious" distinctions are prohibited. Since World War II, and especially as constitutional law developed in the 1960s with cases like *Harper,* the Court's determination of what distinctions are invidious has tended to depend on the nature of the classification and on the nature of the benefit or penalty that is contingent on the classification.

Certain types of classifications are regarded as "suspect." Classifications drawn according to race or national origin are examples. When a law draws a suspect classification, the Court will subject it to "strict scrutiny" under the Equal Protection Clause. It will be struck down unless the law is shown to be "narrowly tailored" to promote a "compelling state interest." (Strict scrutiny that requires narrow tailoring to a compelling state interest is not limited to equal protection cases. In this book we shall see essentially the same concept applied in many cases arising under the First Amendment.)

Even if the classification drawn by a statute is not suspect, it will still be subject to strict scrutiny if the classification burdens or denies a "fundamental right" for some people while not burdening or denying the rights of others. As we shall see, one of the fundamental rights that triggers strict scrutiny under the Equal Protection Clause has been the right to vote. The *Harper* opinion does not use the term "strict scrutiny" in reaching its result, describing the Virginia poll tax as "irrational," although it does say that classifications burdening fundamental rights like voting "must be closely scrutinized and carefully confined." Later, the Supreme Court adopted strict scrutiny terminology in many of its right to vote cases, saying that laws infringing on the fundamental right to vote must be narrowly tailored to serve a compelling interest.

If the classification being challenged is not suspect and does not burden a fundamental right, then it will not be subjected to strict scrutiny. Instead, it will be upheld so long as it has a rational basis.[k] This is usually a standard that statutes can meet, since

---

k. In some cases the Court engages in "intermediate scrutiny," which is not as severe as "strict scrutiny" but not as lax as the "rational basis" test. For example, different statutory treatment of men and women receives intermediate scrutiny. *See Craig v. Boren,* 429 U.S. 190 (1976). By and large, the equal protection cases contained in this book do not raise questions of intermediate scrutiny. However, in *Anderson v. Celebrezze,* discussed in Chapter 10, the Supreme Court articulated a comparable, "flexible" standard to be used in some election law cases.

the Court will accept any legitimate interest the statute may be intended to further. The Court will not even require a showing that a statute actually accomplishes its purposes, so long as the legislature could have believed it would. Although there are exceptions, some of which we shall encounter in this book, statutes that are subjected to strict scrutiny usually are struck down, and those that are tested for a rational basis usually are upheld.

2. At issue in *Harper* is whether the Equal Protection Clause bars the use of a poll tax (which the Court assumes was not administered as a means to discriminate against African-American voters). How should the Court decide whether the Equal Protection Clause bars the use of a poll tax? Should it defer to the practice of most states? What if such practices change over time, as was the case with the poll tax? By the time the Court decided *Harper*, all but four states had eliminated poll taxes for voting in state elections. Is that an argument for or against the Supreme Court's decision in this case to bar the practice in the four outlier states?

3. Both the majority and dissenters in *Harper* appear to agree that a fairly-applied literacy test would not violate the Equal Protection Clause under the authority of the 1959 *Lassiter* case. (Recall from Part I of this chapter that Congress has banned the use of literacy tests under the Voting Rights Act. But that is a statute that—in theory—Congress could repeal at any time.) If the constitutional question ever arose again, should *Lassiter* be overruled? Are *Lassiter* and *Harper* inconsistent? *Compare* Richard H. Pildes, *Why Rights Are Not Trumps: Social Meanings, Expressive Harms, and Constitutionalism*, 27 Journal of Legal Studies 725, 746 (1998) (no) with Richard L. Hasen, *Bad Legislative Intent*, 2006 Wisconsin Law Review 843, 878–879 (yes).

In *United States v. Carolene Products*, 304 U.S. 144, 152 n.4 (1938), the Supreme Court made a celebrated statement regarding its function of reviewing the constitutionality of state and federal laws, especially under broadly worded constitutional guarantees such as "due process of law" and "equal protection of the laws." The Court explained that ordinarily, legislatures would be given broad leeway to enact laws deemed to be in the public interest. Legislatures were more likely than courts to be aware of the varied consequences of legislative policies, and interest groups were presumably capable of defending themselves against unjustifiably harsh policies by exercising their political rights. In the famous footnote 4, however, the Court mentioned several possible exceptions to this generally deferential approach, one of which was "whether legislation which restricts those political processes which can ordinarily be expected to bring about repeal of undesirable legislation [might] be subjected to more exacting judicial scrutiny under the general prohibitions of the Fourteenth Amendment than are most other types of legislation." Surely the most basic process that might be used by a group seeking repeal of undesirable legislation is their right to vote. Does that fact justify the Court's decision in *Harper*? If so, what of the Court's decision in *Lassiter* upholding a literacy test?

4. *The Secret Drafting History of* Harper. Consider the following history gleaned from the files of deceased Supreme Court Justices and recounted in Richard L. Hasen, The Supreme Court and Election Law: Judging Equality from Baker v. Carr to Bush v. Gore 37–38 (2003):

> Although *Harper* ... stated its principles as self-evident, the result in the 6–3 case reversing the lower court was hardly inevitable. The case began as a proposed a 6–3 *per curiam* summary affirmance (that is, without a written opinion) of the lower court decision upholding the poll tax. Justice Goldberg, joined by Chief Justice Warren and Justice Douglas, circulated a proposed dissent. Relying on *Reynolds, Gray,* and *Carrington*, along with the Virginia poll tax's legislative

history evincing intent to discriminate against both African-Americans and poor whites, Justice Goldberg would have held that "no reasonable state interest is served by barring from voting those citizens who desire to vote but who lack the requisite funds."

Justice Goldberg sought to explain the limits of the equal protection principle that would bar the use of a poll tax in elections:

> The application of these principles obviously does not mean that Government — State or Federal — must equalize all economic inequalities among citizens. Nor does it mean that the Government cannot impose burdens or exactions which by reason of economic circumstances fall more heavily upon some than others. Nor however desirable it may be as a matter of social and legislative policy, does it require the State affirmatively to provide relief for all the incidents of poverty. The Constitution does not command absolute equality in all areas. It does mean, however, that a State may not frustrate or burden the exercise of the basic and precious right to vote by imposing substantial obstacles upon that exercise by a class of citizens not justified by any legitimate state interest. In particular it means that with respect to the fundamental right to vote, a reverse means test cannot be applied. A classification based upon financial means embodied in a voting statute is inherently not "reasonable in light of ... [the statute's] purpose."

Justice Goldberg further rejected the long American history of tolerance for property qualifications and poll taxes as irrelevant for contemporary application of constitutional principles. "[W]e must consider voting rights in light of their full development, their 'present place in American life throughout the nation,' cf. *Brown v. Board of Education*, and our present conception of the meaning and application of the Equal Protection Clause."

Only one day after Justice Goldberg's dissent circulated, Justice Black circulated a memorandum to the other Justices asking that the case be put for a full hearing. Justice Black perhaps expected from the initial 6–3 vote for summary affirmance that the case would lead to a similar 6–3 vote on an opinion affirming the validity of the poll tax and distinguishing the cases cited by Justice Goldberg. If so, his expectations were dashed, because Justices Brennan, Clark, and White changed positions. Justice Black ultimately issued a dissent arguing the question of poll taxes should be left to the states unless Congress wanted to use its enforcement powers to ban the practice.

What, if anything, does this history tell you about how the Supreme Court Justices create election law precedents? About how they *should* do so? Consider HASEN, *supra*, at 157–58:

> The Constitution was not amended in 1965; three Justices simply changed their minds about its meaning. Justice Black in his *Harper* dissent protested that the Court had overruled prior precedent "not by using its limited power to interpret the original meaning of the Equal Protection Clause, but by giving that clause a new meaning which it believes represents a better governmental policy." Two days before the opinion issued, Justice Douglas added a sentence to the *Harper* majority opinion responding to Justice Black's point: "Our conclusion, like that in *Reynolds v. Sims*, is founded not on what we think governmental policy should be, but on what the Equal Protection Clause requires."

If the history of the Court's political equality jurisprudence ... shows anything, it shows that there has been no distinction between the Justices' views of
the meaning of the Equal Protection Clause and what the Constitution requires.
As has often been remarked, the Supreme Court is not final because it is right;
it is right because it is final. At least in the area of political equality, there is little question the Justices of the Warren Court (like the Justices of the Burger and
Rehnquist Court that followed) have "made it up" as they have gone along, even
if the Justices, like Justice Douglas, have perceived a need to profess Blackstonean
notions of "discovering the law" to preserve their legitimacy.

5. If you were a *legislator* rather than a *judge*, would you support the imposition of literacy tests or poll taxes (assuming the Constitution did not bar such limits)? Why or why
not? What about limiting the franchise on the basis of (1) citizenship; (2) residency; or
(3) non-felon status? We consider some of these additional restrictions below.

Skafte v. Rorex
191 Colo. 399, 553 P.2d 830 (1976),
appeal dismissed, 430 U.S. 961 (1977)

PRINGLE, Chief Justice.

[Appellant Skafte, a permanent resident alien, was denied the right to register to vote
in school elections and then challenged the constitutionality of a Colorado statute permitting only United States citizens to vote. The District Court ruled that the statute was
valid, and the Colorado Supreme Court affirmed on the grounds stated in this opinion.]

I.

The appellant asserts that the statutes prohibiting permanent resident aliens from voting in school elections violate the Equal Protection Clause.

A.

At the outset, the registrar contends that the Equal Protection Clause has no application to the issue in this case. For this proposition, she relies on section 2 of the Fourteenth Amendment. Section 2 provides, in part:

> [W]hen the right to vote at any election for the choice of electors for President
> and Vice President of the United States, Representatives in Congress, the Execu-
> tive and Judicial officers of a State, or the members of the Legislature thereof, is
> denied to any of the male inhabitants of such state, being twenty-one years of age,
> *and citizens of the United States,* or in any way abridged, except for participation in
> rebellion or other crime, the basis of representation therein shall be reduced in the
> proportion which the number of such male citizens shall bear to the whole num-
> ber of male citizens twenty-one years of age in such State. [Emphasis supplied.]

The registrar argues that section 2 makes the Equal Protection Clause of the Fourteenth Amendment inapplicable to this case, since the specific wording of the section
shows that those adopting the Fourteenth Amendment considered citizenship a valid classification in legislation dealing with the franchise. We do not agree with this contention.

Local school elections are not contained in the types of elections expressly listed in
section 2. Moreover, the implicit sanction of a citizenship requirement contained in section 2 for the elections there listed does not warrant a conclusion that the Equal Protec-

tion Clause is inapplicable in the instant case. Indeed, the United States Supreme Court has rejected the general proposition that section 2 was intended to supplant the Equal Protection Clause in the area of voting rights. *Richardson v. Ramirez*, 418 U.S. 24 (1974); *Reynolds v. Sims*, 377 U.S. 533 (1964).

Nevertheless, we do believe that section 2 is helpful in deciding the constitutional questions raised in this appeal. The section demonstrates, as an historical matter, that the requirement of citizenship to exercise the franchise was assumed to be a valid one at the time the Fourteenth Amendment was adopted. Hence in deciding the constitutional issues in this case, we are mindful of the language of section 2.

B.

The appellant asserts that the alienage classification created here requires strict judicial scrutiny. The United States Supreme Court has consistently used language suggesting that citizenship with respect to the franchise is not a suspect classification and that therefore the compelling interest test does not apply. See *Hill v. Stone*, 421 U.S. 289 (1975); *Sugarman v. Dougall*, 413 U.S. 634 (1973); *Kramer v. Union Free School District No. 15*, 395 U.S. 621 (1969) [*infra*].

C.

We hold that the state's citizenship requirements for a school district election do not contravene the Equal Protection Clause of the Fourteenth Amendment. The state has a rational interest in limiting participation in government to those persons within the political community. Aliens are not a part of the political community.

The United States Supreme Court has recognized a state's valid interest in establishing a government and in limiting participation in that government to those within the concept of a political community. *Sugarman*, 413 U.S. at 642. The Supreme Court has noted that "alienage itself is a factor that reasonably could be employed in defining 'political community.'" *Sugarman, supra*, at 649. Indeed, the Court has further stated that "implicit in many of this Court's voting rights decisions is the notion that citizenship is a permissible criterion for limiting such rights." *Sugarman, supra*, at 649.

The appellant contends that this justification satisfies the Equal Protection requirement only as it pertains to voting in *general* elections. He contends, however, that a school election is a "special interest" election, and therefore the proposition that a citizenship requirement is valid for general elections does not apply.

We believe that a school election is an election which falls within the class of cases prohibiting aliens from voting contemplated by the Supreme Court in *Sugarman*. We point out that school districts are governmental entities.... Further, in *Kramer v. Union Free School District No. 15, supra*, the Supreme Court indicated that school elections are elections involving participation by the political community.

Moreover, voting in school elections involves participation in the decision making process of the polity, a factor which indicates the "general" nature of such elections. It is in fact a determination of participation or not in the government policymaking process which often has been crucial in deciding cases contesting alienage classifications. The Supreme Court in *In Re Griffiths*, 413 U.S. 717 (1973), held unconstitutional a requirement that bar examinees be citizens. The court noted that the acts of a lawyer "hardly involve matters of state policy" and that the status of holding a license to practice law does not "place one so close to the core of the political process as to make him a formulator of government policy." 413 U.S. at 729 (footnote omitted).

The administration of school districts, however, does involve ... matters of "state policy" and entails the formulation of such policy. Therefore, voting in school elections constitutes participation in the government policy-making process.

[The court stated that the denial of suffrage to resident aliens "is properly tailored to the state's interest," citing an earlier decision upholding the exclusion of aliens from juries on the ground that aliens as a group did not owe allegiance to the United States. Although many aliens do in fact hold such allegiance, the court said there was no test short of citizenship that would distinguish those who did from those who did not.]

Thus, we conclude that the State has shown a reasonable basis justifying the classification here challenged. Consequently, the citizenship requirement in school elections does not deprive the appellant of equal protection of the laws.

[In Part II, the court rejected appellant's argument that the prohibition against voting by resident aliens created an unconstitutional "conclusive presumption." In Part III, it rejected the assertion that the prohibition was an interference with Congress' power to regulate immigration and naturalization.]

The judgment is affirmed.

Notes and Questions

1. *The Equal Protection Clause and Alienage.* In cases such as *Sugarman*, cited in *Skafte*, the Supreme Court has treated most laws discriminating against aliens as "suspect," but has made an exception for laws restricting the ability of non-citizens to participate in government. It was because of this exception that the denial of suffrage to non-citizens was not regarded as a suspect classification in *Skafte*. But even assuming there was no suspect classification, should the court have applied strict scrutiny on the ground that the fundamental right to vote was granted to some (citizens) and denied to others (resident aliens)? For a strong argument to this effect, see Gerald M. Rosberg, *Aliens and Equal Protection: Why Not the Right to Vote?*, 75 MICHIGAN LAW REVIEW 1092, 1106–09 (1977).

2. What state interests might justify the denial of the right to vote to aliens? Rosberg, *supra*, considers a number of possible state interests, including that aliens may have less of a stake in the outcome of elections than citizens; that aliens are likely to lack the information and understanding of politics needed to vote intelligently; and that aliens may have less of a commitment to the well-being of the United States and its states and localities than citizens. Rosberg argues that none of these alleged interests holds much water, though he acknowledges that some of them may be plausible enough to pass a rational basis test.

Rosberg's unstated assumption is that denial of suffrage to aliens must serve some instrumental purpose of the state. Unquestionably, the right to vote serves instrumental purposes for individuals and groups, namely protecting their interests that are affected by public policy decisions. If that is the primary reason for the importance of the right to vote, then the denial of the suffrage to aliens in the absence of a strong instrumental purpose served by that denial may be quite troubling. In *Skafte*, the court justifies the denial as a limitation of the vote to "persons within the political community." Is this an instrumental purpose? Is the right to vote important not only as a means of protecting the rights and interests of individuals and groups but as a means for a community as a whole to define and govern itself? If so, is it legitimate for the community to protect its own self-definition by determining which individuals will be deemed members of the community and therefore entitled to participate in its self-government? These general questions are discussed in Frank I. Michelman, *Conceptions of Democ-*

racy in American Constitutional Argument: Voting Rights, 41 FLORIDA LAW REVIEW 443 (1989).

Sanford Levinson, *Suffrage and Community: Who Should Vote?*, 41 FLORIDA LAW REVIEW 545, 557 (1989), doubts whether denial of the vote to noncitizens can be justified under a conception of voting either as an instrumental means of protecting individual interests or as an expression of the "shared values" embodied in a community:

> If we asked persons only five yes-or-no questions to figure out their basic values, would citizenship be one of them? If the answer is "no," because a person's citizenship conveys too little relevant information, then we might ask why something as important as the vote is based on citizenship, even within a communalist perspective.

> [A] conception of citizenship as a surrogate for shared interests is a fatally underinclusive category because the universe of people whose interests are vitally affected by any given election is far larger than the universe of those who are allowed to participate ... If we view citizenship as a surrogate for shared values, then it may be grossly overinclusive: the set of people sharing the (proper) values may be far smaller than the set of people designated as citizens. Noncitizens also may share what are thought to be the requisite values.

3. According to Rosberg, *supra*, 75 MICHIGAN LAW REVIEW at 1094–1100, alien voting was fairly widespread at the end of the eighteenth century, but in the first half of the nineteenth there was a trend toward making citizenship a requirement for voting. This trend was reversed after the Civil War, and by the end of the nineteenth century, about half the states had had some experience with alien suffrage. Starting in the 1890s, a reaction set in, which received additional impetus from the assassination of President McKinley in 1901 by an immigrant and from World War I. The last state to repeal alien suffrage was Arkansas in 1926. More recently, aliens have been permitted to vote in decentralized school elections in Chicago and New York City, and several towns in Maryland have permitted aliens to vote in municipal elections.

If, as *Skafte* holds, resident aliens do not have a constitutional right to vote, is it an unconstitutional abridgement of citizens' right to vote if aliens are given the suffrage? In Germany, where immigration has been a controversial political issue, the Federal Constitutional Court has so ruled. See Gerald L. Neuman, *"We Are the People": Alien Suffrage in German and American Perspective*, 13 MICHIGAN JOURNAL OF INTERNATIONAL LAW 259, 283–87 (1992). Neuman acknowledges that from a communitarian perspective a plausible case could be made that permitting aliens to vote is unconstitutional in the United States, but he concludes that American courts would be unlikely to intervene because

> Popular sovereignty in the United States has been a flexible notion, which has not restricted political power by a rigid definition of the 'People,' and certainly not by the legal category of national citizenship.

Id. at 324.

4. The authors of a study of political participation by Latinos have proposed an innovative form of voting by resident aliens:

> [We advocate] a modified form of the current effort to make noncitizens eligible to vote. We would add two twists. First, we would allow noncitizens to vote only for the five-year period during which they are statutorily ineligible to naturalize. Under this system, recently immigrated permanent residents would

be able to obtain a five-year voter registration card.... After the five years, they would no longer be eligible for permanent resident voting privileges, but would be able to naturalize.... Although the authors of this discussion do not fully agree on whether voting should be limited to local elections (de la Garza) or should include all elections (DeSipio), we both advocate the extension of noncitizen voting privileges to local elections at a minimum.

The second twist is that naturalization applicants who can show that they voted in most primary and general elections during the five-year period of noncitizen voter registration would be exempt from the naturalization exam. The exam is designed to test good citizenship through indirect measures such as knowledge of American history and civics. We propose that voting is an equally good measure of commitment to and understanding of the American system.

Rodolfo O. de la Garza & Louis DeSipio, *Save the Baby, Change the Bathwater, and Scrub the Tub: Latino Electoral Participation After Seventeen Years of Voting Rights Act Coverage*, 71 Texas Law Review 1479, 1522–23 (1993).

5. The *Skafte* opinion refers to *Richardson v. Ramirez*, 418 U.S. 24, 41–56 (1974), in which the Supreme Court upheld provisions of the California Constitution denying the vote to persons who had been convicted of felonies, even after they had finished their sentences and paroles. The Court relied primarily on Section 2 of the Fourteenth Amendment:

Representatives shall be apportioned among the several States according to their respective numbers, counting the whole number of persons in each State, excluding Indians not taxed. But when the right to vote at any election for the choice of electors for President and Vice President of the United States, Representatives in Congress, the Executive and Judicial officers of a State, or the members of the Legislature thereof, is denied to any of the male inhabitants of such State, being twenty-one years of age, *and citizens of the United States*, or in any way abridged, *except for participation in rebellion, or other crime*, the basis of representation therein shall be reduced in the proportion which the number of such male citizens shall bear to the whole number of male citizens twenty-one years of age in such State. [Emphasis added.]

Section 2 thus imposes a sanction consisting of reduced representation in the House of Representatives upon a state that denies suffrage to its inhabitants, but specifies a number of grounds upon which suffrage may be denied that are exempt from the sanction. One of these exempt grounds for denial of suffrage is participation in rebellion or other crime. In *Richardson*, Justice Rehnquist wrote for the majority that Section 1 of the Fourteenth Amendment, which contains the Equal Protection Clause, "in dealing with voting rights as it does, could not have meant to bar outright a form of disenfranchisement which was expressly exempted from the less drastic sanction of reduced representation which §2 imposed for other forms of disenfranchisement." 418 U.S. at 55. Note that the sanction in Section 2 also is inapplicable when a state denies the franchise to noncitizens. Why did the *Skafte* court not regard *Richardson* as dispositive? Should it have? See Rosberg, *supra*, 75 Michigan Law Review at 1102–04.

Richardson v. Ramirez has come in for severe criticism from some scholars. See Laurence H. Tribe, American Constitutional Law 1094 (2d ed. 1988); David L. Shapiro, *Mr. Justice Rehnquist: A Preliminary View*, 90 Harvard Law Review 293, 302–04 (1976). For an argument that the Fifteenth Amendment repealed Section 2 of the Fourteenth Amendment, and therefore that *Richardson* erred in concluding that felon disenfranchisement is constitutionally authorized, see Gabriel J. Chin, *Reconstruction, Felon Disenfranchisement, and the Right to Vote: Did the Fifteenth Amendment Repeal Section 2 of the Fourteenth Amendment?*, 92 Georgetown Law Journal 249 (2004).

Under some state constitutions, the franchise is denied to those who have been convicted of crimes of "moral turpitude." Under such a provision, should the vote be denied to an individual who has been found to be a habitual violator of the statute prohibiting drunk driving? See *Jarrard v. Clayton County Board of Registrars*, 425 S.E.2d 874 (Ga. 1993).

6. Jamin B. Raskin, *Legal Aliens, Local Citizens: The Historical, Constitutional and Theoretical Meanings of Alien Suffrage*, 141 UNIVERSITY OF PENNSYLVANIA LAW REVIEW 1391, 1417–41 (1993), maintains that extending the franchise to resident aliens is neither prohibited nor required by the Constitution. Doctrinally, he bases his disagreement with Rosberg's view that the vote is constitutionally required on Section 2 of the 14th Amendment and *Richardson*. He adds an additional and broader point:

> [E]ven if we follow the doctrinal somersaults required to arrive at Rosberg's position, his argument is not wholly persuasive as a description, historical or normative, of how the franchise expands in the American polity. None of the principal excluded national groups who gained access to the ballot in American history did so by way of judicial action through the Equal Protection Clause. Rather, they fought their way in through political agitation. This history encloses an important democratic logic: it is the standing citizenry, after hearing and debating appeals from the voteless, that must extend rights of political membership to disenfranchised outsiders seeking entry and equality.

Id. at 1431–32.

7. The hottest current controversy over extension of the franchise concerns voting by convicted felons. In 2002, the Supreme Court of Canada, by a 5–4 decision, ruled that incarcerated felons have a right to vote under the Canadian Charter of Rights and Freedoms, adopted in 2000. The chief justice wrote:

> The government's novel theory that would permit elected representatives to disenfranchise a segment of the population[l] finds no place in a democracy built upon principles of inclusiveness, equality, and citizen participation. That not all self-proclaimed democracies adhere to this conclusion says little about what the Canadian vision of democracy embodied in the Charter permits. Moreover, the argument that only those who respect the law should participate in the political process cannot be accepted. Denial of the right to vote on the basis of attributed moral unworthiness is inconsistent with the respect for the dignity of every person that lies at the heart of Canadian democracy and the Charter.[m]

Denial of the franchise to currently incarcerated felons is almost universal in the United States,[n] which is apparently a "self-proclaimed" democracy according to the Canadian Supreme Court. Nor does that seem likely to change much in the immedi-

---

l. If the Canadian Supreme Court regards this as a *novel* theory, it apparently has never heard of the eighteenth, nineteenth, and twentieth centuries. — EDS.

m. Sauvé v. Canada (Chief Electoral Officer), [2002] 3 S.C.R. 519, 522 (Can.). For background, see John C. Courtney, ELECTIONS 36–39 (2004).

n. The exceptions are Maine and Vermont. See Rosanna M. Taormina, Comment, *Defying One-Person, One-Vote: Prisoners and the "Usual Residence" Principle*, 152 UNIVERSITY OF PENNSYLVANIA LAW REVIEW 431, 460 (2003) (appendix).

ate future. But felons who have completed their punishments (including parole or probation) are denied the franchise in about a third of the states. Strenuous efforts to end this denial are under way. Litigation is one form of these efforts. *Richardson* seems to suggest that the denial is consistent with the Constitution. Nevertheless, the Ninth Circuit refused to dismiss statutory *and* constitutional claims for voting rights brought by former felons. *Farrakhan v. Washington*, 338 F.3d 1009 (9th Cir. 2003). An *en banc* panel declined, by a 6–5 vote, to rehear the *Farrakhan* decision. Judge Kozinski published an opinion for the dissenters. 359 F.3d 1116 (9th Cir. 2004). The Second Circuit reached a contrary opinion when it dismissed a Voting Rights Act claim brought by an incarcerated felon. *Muntaqim v. Coombe*, 366 F.3d 102 (2nd Cir. 2004). The Eleventh Circuit reached a similar result. *Johnson v. Governor of Florida*, 405 F.3d 1214 (11th Cir. 2005) (*en banc*).

The fact that the claimant was still incarcerated was not central to *Muntaqim*'s reasoning. The court gave this summary of its reason for rejecting the claim:

> The application of the Voting Rights Act to felon disenfranchisement statutes such as that of New York would infringe upon the states' well-established discretion to deprive felons of the right to vote. Because the Supreme Court has instructed us that statutes should not be construed to alter the constitutional balance between the states and the federal government unless Congress makes its intent to do so unmistakably clear, we will not construe the Voting Rights Act to extend to New York's felon disenfranchisement statute.

The issue takes on heightened salience because a disproportionate number of incarcerated and former felons are blacks and Hispanics. Thus, the plaintiff in *Muntaqim* alleged that "although blacks and Hispanics constitute less than thirty percent of the voting-age population in New York State, they make up over eighty percent of the inmates in the state prison system."

The Supreme Court denied certiorari in *Farrakhan*, *Muntaqim*, and *Johnson*. After the Supreme Court denied certiorari, the Second Circuit granted en banc review in *Muntaqim*, consolidated it with another case, and reaffirmed the panel's earlier ruling that the Voting Rights Act does not preclude felon disfranchisement. *Hayden v. Pataki*, 449 F.3d 305 (2d Cir. 2006). That still leaves a split in the circuits by reason of the Ninth Circuit's decision in *Farrakhan*. Additional proceedings are under way in other circuits. It seems likely the Supreme Court will need to address the merits of the issue sooner or later.

A number of states in the 2000s have relaxed their felon disenfranchisement laws without litigation. Reenfranchisement could have partisan political implications, as it is widely believed that ex-felons are more likely to vote for Democrats than Republicans. Somewhat surprisingly, then, Florida's Republican governor has worked hard to restore the voting rights of thousands of ex-felons. *See* Emily Bazelon, *The Secret Weapon of 2008: Felons Are Getting the Vote Back — and Republicans Aren't Stopping Them*, SLATE, April 27, 2007, <http://www.slate.com/id/2165134>. A listing of the policies of each state on voting by felons may be found in Jeff Manza & Christopher Uggen, *Punishment and Democracy: Disenfranchisement of Nonincarcerated Felons in the United States*, 2 PERSPECTIVES ON POLITICS 491, at 494 (2004); *see also* Jeff Manza & Christopher Uggen, LOCKED OUT: FELON DISENFRANCHISEMENT AND AMERICAN DEMOCRACY (2006).

8. *Residency*. As we have seen, though voting is a fundamental right which often triggers strict scrutiny, strict scrutiny does not apply to discrimination in voting on the basis

of citizenship or felon-status. The same is true of discrimination against non-residents. Though the Supreme Court has held it unconstitutional to discriminate against *residents* of a jurisdiction whose residence began after they had joined the military, *see Carrington v. Rash*, 380 U.S. 89 (1965), discrimination against non-residents is generally constitutionally permissible under rational basis review. In *Holt Civic Club v. City of Tuscaloosa*, 439 U.S. 60 (1978) plaintiffs lived within the "police jurisdiction" of Tuscaloosa, Alabama which consisted of the area outside but within three miles of the city limits. Under Alabama law, city criminal ordinances were applicable and the jurisdiction of the municipal courts extended to the police jurisdiction. In addition, businesses located within the police jurisdiction had to pay a license tax half the amount they would be required to pay if they were within the city. However, the city's power of zoning, eminent domain, and ad valorem taxation did not extend to the police jurisdiction. The Supreme Court majority rejected plaintiffs' claim they were denied equal protection because they were denied the vote in Tuscaloosa city elections:

> Appellants' argument that extraterritorial extension of municipal powers requires concomitant extraterritorial extension of the franchise proves too much. The imaginary line defining a city's corporate limits cannot corral the influence of municipal actions. A city's decisions inescapably affect individuals living immediately outside its borders. The granting of building permits for high rise apartments, industrial plants, and the like on the city's fringe unavoidably contributes to problems of traffic congestion, school districting, and law enforcement immediately outside the city. A rate change in the city's sales or ad valorem tax could well have a significant impact on retailers and property values in areas bordering the city. The condemnation of real property on the city's edge for construction of a municipal garbage dump or waste treatment plant would have obvious implications for neighboring nonresidents. Indeed, the indirect extraterritorial effects of many purely internal municipal actions could conceivably have a heavier impact on surrounding environs than the direct regulation contemplated by Alabama's police jurisdiction statutes. Yet no one would suggest that nonresidents likely to be affected by this sort of municipal action have a constitutional right to participate in the political processes bringing it about. And unless one adopts the idea that the Austinian notion of sovereignty, which is presumably embodied to some extent in the authority of a city over a police jurisdiction, distinguishes the direct effects of limited municipal powers over police jurisdiction residents from the indirect though equally dramatic extraterritorial effects of purely internal municipal actions, it makes little sense to say that one requires extension of the franchise while the other does not.

The dissenters in *Holt* did not disagree with the majority that a jurisdiction could deny the vote to non-residents. Instead, Justice Brennan, writing for the dissenters, argued that the majority impermissibly allowed the jurisdiction to define "residency" too narrowly:

> The criterion of geographical residency is thus entirely arbitrary when applied to this case. It fails to explain why, consistently with the Equal Protection Clause, the "government unit" which may exclude from the franchise those who reside outside of its geographical boundaries should be composed of the city of Tuscaloosa rather than of the city together with its police jurisdiction. It irrationally distinguishes between two classes of citizens, each with equal claim to residency (insofar as that can be determined by domicile or intention or other similar criteria), and each governed by the city of Tuscaloosa in the place of their residency.

The Court argues, however, that if the franchise were extended to residents of the city's police jurisdiction, the franchise must similarly be extended to all those indirectly affected by the city's actions. This is a simple non sequitur. There is a crystal-clear distinction between those who reside in Tuscaloosa's police juris-diction, and who are therefore subject to that city's police and sanitary ordi-nances, licensing fees, and the jurisdiction of its municipal court, and those who reside in neither the city nor its police jurisdiction, and who are thus merely af-fected by the indirect impact of the city's decisions. This distinction is recog-nized in Alabama law, and is consistent with, if not mandated by, the very conception of a political community underlying constitutional recognition of bona fide residency requirements.

Should restrictions based on citizenship, residency, and non-felon status be subject to a more permissive constitutional standard than other restrictions? What about laws prohibiting minors from voting? Does the 26th Amendment's prohibition on denying voting rights to those *over* eighteen imply that voting discrimination against those *under* eighteen is permissible?

9. Once a state grants the right to vote to adult, citizen, resident non-felons, may a state limit the franchise in *particular elections*, such as school board elections, to a sub-set of otherwise eligible voters? Consider the next case.

Kramer v. Union Free School District No. 15
395 U.S. 621 (1969)

Mr. Chief Justice WARREN delivered the opinion of the Court.

In this case we are called on to determine whether §2012 of the New York Education Law is constitutional. The legislation provides that in certain New York school districts residents who are otherwise eligible to vote in state and federal elections may vote in the school district election only if they (1) own (or lease) taxable real property within the district, or (2) are parents (or have custody of) children enrolled in the local public schools. Appellant, a bachelor who neither owns nor leases taxable real property, filed suit in federal court claiming that §2012 denied him equal protection of the laws in vio-lation of the Fourteenth Amendment....

I.

[In school] districts such as the one involved in this case, which are primarily rural and suburban, the school board is elected at an annual meeting of qualified school dis-trict voters ...

Appellant is a 31-year-old college-educated stockbroker who lives in his parents' home in the Union Free School District No. 15, a district to which §2012 applies. He is a citi-zen of the United States and has voted in federal and state elections since 1959. However, since he has no children and neither owns nor leases taxable real property, appellant's at-tempts to register for and vote in the local school district elections have been unsuccess-ful....

II.

At the outset, it is important to note what is *not* at issue in this case. The requirements of §2012 that school district voters must (1) be citizens of the United States, (2) be bona fide residents of the school district, and (3) be at least 21 years of age are not challenged....

The sole issue in this case is whether the *additional* requirements of §2012 — requirements which prohibit some district residents who are otherwise qualified by age and citizenship from participating in district meetings and school board elections — violate the Fourteenth Amendment's command that no State shall deny persons equal protection of the laws.

"In determining whether or not a state law violates the Equal Protection Clause, we must consider the facts and circumstances behind the law, the interests which the State claims to be protecting, and the interests of those who are disadvantaged by the classification." *Williams v. Rhodes*, 393 U.S. 23, 30 (1968). And, in this case, we must give the statute a close and exacting examination. "[S]ince the right to exercise the franchise in a free and unimpaired manner is preservative of other basic civil and political rights, any alleged infringement of the right of citizens to vote must be carefully and meticulously scrutinized." *Reynolds v. Sims*, [*infra*]. This careful examination is necessary because statutes distributing the franchise constitute the foundation of our representative society. Any unjustified discrimination in determining who may participate in political affairs or in the selection of public officials undermines the legitimacy of representative government.

Thus, state apportionment statutes, which may *dilute* the effectiveness of some citizens' votes, receive close scrutiny from this Court. *Reynolds*. No less rigid an examination is applicable to statutes *denying* the franchise to citizens who are otherwise qualified by residence and age. Statutes granting the franchise to residents on a selective basis always pose the danger of denying some citizens any effective voice in the governmental affairs which substantially affect their lives. Therefore, if a challenged state statute grants the right to vote to some bona fide residents of requisite age and citizenship and denies the franchise to others, the Court must determine whether the exclusions are necessary to promote a compelling state interest.

And, for these reasons, the deference usually given to the judgment of legislators does not extend to decisions concerning which resident citizens may participate in the election of legislators and other public officials. Those decisions must be carefully scrutinized by the Court to determine whether each resident citizen has, as far as is possible, an equal voice in the selections. Accordingly, when we are reviewing statutes which deny some residents the right to vote, the general presumption of constitutionality afforded state statutes and the traditional approval given state classifications if the Court can conceive of a "rational basis" for the distinctions made are not applicable. The presumption of constitutionality and the approval given "rational" classifications in other types of enactments are based on an assumption that the institutions of state government are structured so as to represent fairly all the people. However, when the challenge to the statute is in effect a challenge of this basic assumption, the assumption can no longer serve as the basis for presuming constitutionality. And, the assumption is no less under attack because the legislature which decides who may participate at the various levels of political choice is fairly elected. Legislation which delegates decision making to bodies elected by only a portion of those eligible to vote for the legislature can cause unfair representation. Such legislation can exclude a minority of voters from any voice in the decisions just as effectively as if the decisions were made by legislators the minority had no voice in selecting....

Nor is the need for close judicial examination affected because the district meetings and the school board do not have "general" legislative powers. Our exacting examination is not necessitated by the subject of the election; rather, it is required because some resident citizens are permitted to participate and some are not....

III.

Besides appellant and others who similarly live in their parents' homes, the statute also disenfranchises the following persons (unless they are parents or guardians of children enrolled in the district public school): senior citizens and others living with children or relatives; clergy, military personnel, and others who live on tax-exempt property; boarders and lodgers; parents who neither own nor lease qualifying property and whose children are too young to attend school; parents who neither own nor lease qualifying property and whose children attend private schools.

Appellant asserts that excluding him from participation in the district elections denies him equal protection of the laws. He contends that he and others of his class are substantially interested in and significantly affected by the school meeting decisions. All members of the community have an interest in the quality and structure of public education, appellant says, and he urges that "the decisions taken by local boards ... may have grave consequences to the entire population." Appellant also argues that the level of property taxation affects him, even though he does not own property, as property tax levels affect the price of goods and services in the community.

We turn therefore to question whether the exclusion is necessary to promote a compelling state interest. First appellees argue that the State has a legitimate interest in limiting the franchise in school district elections to "members of the community of interest"— those "primarily interested in such elections." Second, appellees urge that the State may reasonably and permissibly conclude that "property taxpayers" (including lessees of taxable property who share the tax burden through rent payments) and parents of the children enrolled in the district's schools are those "primarily interested" in school affairs.

We do not understand appellees to argue that the State is attempting to limit the franchise to those "subjectively concerned" about school matters. Rather, they appear to argue that the State's legitimate interest is in restricting a voice in school matters to those "directly affected" by such decisions. The State apparently reasons that since the schools are financed in part by local property taxes, persons whose out-of-pocket expenses are "directly" affected by property tax changes should be allowed to vote. Similarly, parents of children in school are thought to have a "direct" stake in school affairs and are given a vote.

Appellees argue that it is necessary to limit the franchise to those "primarily interested" in school affairs because "the ever increasing complexity of the many interacting phases of the school system and structure make it extremely difficult for the electorate fully to understand the whys and wherefores of the detailed operations of the school system." Appellees say that many communications of school boards and school administrations are sent home to the parents through the district pupils and are "not broadcast to the general public"; thus, nonparents will be less informed than parents. Further, appellees argue, those who are assessed for local property taxes (either directly or indirectly through rent) will have enough of an interest "through the burden on their pocketbooks, to acquire such information as they may need."

We need express no opinion as to whether the State in some circumstances might limit the exercise of the franchise to those "primarily interested" or "primarily affected." Of course, we therefore do not reach the issue of whether these particular elections are of the type in which the franchise may be so limited. For, assuming, *arguendo*, that New York legitimately might limit the franchise in these school district elections to those "primarily interested in school affairs," close scrutiny of the §2012 classifications demonstrates that they do not accomplish this purpose with sufficient precision to justify denying appellant the franchise.

Whether classifications allegedly limiting the franchise to those resident citizens "primarily interested" deny those excluded equal protection of the laws depends, *inter alia*, on whether all those excluded are in fact substantially less interested or affected than those the statute includes. In other words, the classifications must be tailored so that the exclusion of appellant and members of his class is necessary to achieve the articulated state goal. Section 2012 does not meet the exacting standard of precision we require of statutes which selectively distribute the franchise. The classifications in §2012 permit inclusion of many persons who have, at best, a remote and indirect interest, in school affairs and, on the other hand, exclude others who have a distinct and direct interest in the school meeting decisions.[15]

Nor do appellees offer any justification for the exclusion of seemingly interested and informed residents—other than to argue that the §2012 classifications include those "whom the State could understandably deem to be the most intimately interested in actions taken by the school board," and urge that "the task of ... balancing the interest of the community in the maintenance of orderly school district elections against the interest of any individual in voting in such elections should clearly remain with the Legislature." But the issue is not whether the legislative judgments are rational. A more exacting standard obtains. The issue is whether the §2012 requirements do in fact sufficiently further a compelling state interest to justify denying the franchise to appellant and members of his class. The requirements of §2012 are not sufficiently tailored to limiting the franchise to those "primarily interested" in school affairs to justify the denial of the franchise to appellant and members of his class.

Mr. Justice STEWART, with whom Mr. Justice BLACK, and Mr. Justice HARLAN join, dissenting.

In *Lassiter*, this Court upheld against constitutional attack a literacy requirement, applicable to voters in all state and federal elections, imposed by the State of North Carolina. Writing for a unanimous Court, Mr. Justice Douglas said:

> The States have long been held to have broad powers to determine the conditions under which the right of suffrage may be exercised, absent of course the discrimination which the Constitution condemns.

Believing that the appellant in this case is not the victim of any "discrimination which the Constitution condemns," I would affirm the judgment of the District Court....

Although at times variously phrased, the traditional test of a statute's validity under the Equal Protection Clause is a familiar one: a legislative classification is invalid only "if it rest[s] on grounds wholly irrelevant to achievement of the regulation's objectives." It was under just such a test that the literacy requirement involved in *Lassiter* was upheld. The premise of our decision in that case was that a State may constitutionally impose upon its citizens voting requirements reasonably "designed to promote intelligent use of the ballot." A similar premise underlies the proposition, consistently endorsed by this Court, that a State may exclude nonresidents from participation in its elections. Such residence requirements, designed to help ensure that voters have a substantial stake in the outcome of elections and an opportunity to become familiar with the candidates and issues voted upon, are entirely permissible exercises of state authority. Indeed, the appellant explic-

---

15. For example, appellant resides with his parents in the school district, pays state and federal taxes and is interested in and affected by school board decisions; however, he has no vote. On the other hand, an uninterested unemployed young man who pays no state or federal taxes, but who rents an apartment in the district, can participate in the election.

itly concedes, as he must, the validity of voting requirements relating to residence, literacy, and age. Yet he argues—and the Court accepts the argument—that the voting qualifications involved here somehow have a different constitutional status. I am unable to see the distinction.

Clearly a State may reasonably assume that its residents have a greater stake in the outcome of elections held within its boundaries than do other persons. Likewise, it is entirely rational for a state legislature to suppose that residents, being generally better informed regarding state affairs than are nonresidents, will be more likely than nonresidents to vote responsibly. And the same may be said of legislative assumptions regarding the electoral competence of adults and literate persons on the one hand, and of minors and illiterates on the other. It is clear, of course, that lines thus drawn can not infallibly perform their intended legislative function. Just as "[i]lliterate people may be intelligent voters," nonresidents or minors might also in some instances be interested, informed, and intelligent participants in the electoral process. Persons who commute across a state line to work may well have a great stake in the affairs of the State in which they are employed; some college students under 21 may be both better informed and more passionately interested in political affairs than many adults. But such discrepancies are the inevitable concomitant of the line drawing that is essential to law making. So long as the classification is rationally related to a permissible legislative end, therefore—as are residence, literacy, and age requirements imposed with respect to voting—there is no denial of equal protection.

Thus judged, the statutory classification involved here seems to me clearly to be valid. New York has made the judgment that local educational policy is best left to those persons who have certain direct and definable interests in that policy: those who are either immediately involved as parents of school children or who, as owners or lessees of taxable property, are burdened with the local cost of funding school district operations. True, persons outside those classes may be genuinely interested in the conduct of a school district's business—just as commuters from New Jersey may be genuinely interested in the outcome of a New York City election. But unless this Court is to claim a monopoly of wisdom regarding the sound operation of school systems in the 50 States, I see no way to justify the conclusion that the legislative classification involved here is not rationally related to a legitimate legislative purpose....

With good reason, the Court does not really argue the contrary. Instead, it strikes down New York's statute by asserting that the traditional equal protection standard is inapt in this case, and that a considerably stricter standard—under which classifications relating to "the franchise" are to be subjected to "exacting judicial scrutiny"—should be applied. But the asserted justification for applying such a standard cannot withstand analysis.

The Court is quite explicit in explaining why it believes this statute should be given "close scrutiny":

> The presumption of constitutionality and the approval given "rational" classifications in other types of enactments are based on an assumption that the institutions of state government are structured so as to represent fairly all the people. However, when the challenge to the statute is in effect a challenge of this basic assumption, the assumption can no longer serve as the basis for presuming constitutionality.

I am at a loss to understand how such reasoning is at all relevant to the present case. The voting qualifications at issue have been promulgated, not by Union Free School District No. 15, but by the New York State Legislature, and the appellant is of course fully able to participate in the election of representatives in that body. There is simply no claim whatever here that the state government is not "structured so as to represent fairly all the people," including the appellant.

In any event, it seems to me that under *any* equal protection standard, short of a doctrinaire insistence that universal suffrage is somehow mandated by the Constitution, the appellant's claim must be rejected. First of all, it must be emphasized—despite the Court's undifferentiated references to what it terms "the franchise"—that we are dealing here, not with a general election, but with a limited, special-purpose election. The appellant is eligible to vote in all state, local, and federal elections in which general governmental policy is determined. He is fully able, therefore, to participate not only in the processes by which the requirements for school district voting may be changed, but also in those by which the levels of state and federal financial assistance to the District are determined. He clearly is not locked into any self-perpetuating status of exclusion from the electoral process....

Notes and Questions

1. The argument of the school district was that the franchise may be limited to those with an "interest" in decisions of the district, in the sense of being "directly affected" by the decisions as opposed to being "subjectively concerned." In which of these senses is the Court using the term in the next-to-last paragraph of the majority opinion?

2. In footnote 15, the Court describes a hypothetical individual with supposedly less of a stake in school district elections than Kramer, but who is eligible to vote because he is a tenant. Is the Court correct in assuming that a person who is a tenant is unaffected by fiscal decisions of the school district? Compare *City of Phoenix v. Kolodziejski*, 399 U.S. 204, 210 (1970), in which the Court wrote:

> Property taxes may be paid initially by property owners, but a significant part of the ultimate burden of each year's tax on rental property will very likely be borne by the tenant rather than the landlord since ... the landlord will treat the property tax as a business expense and normally will be able to pass all or a large part of this cost on to the tenants in the form of higher rent.

3. (a) Suppose Paula is a 31-year-old who resides with her parents just outside the boundaries of District No. 15. She does most of her shopping in the district and has recently completed a doctoral dissertation on the operations of District No. 15. Will the Court order the District to let her vote in District elections? Would it make any difference if she owns commercial property in the District and runs a business there, and if her school-age children reside with her former husband within the District and attend the public schools? See *Hill v. Stone*, 421 U.S. 289, 302, 306 (1975) (Rehnquist, J., dissenting); *Reeder v. Bd. of Supervisors of Elections*, 305 A.2d 132 (Md. 1973). See also *Millis v. Bd. of Cy. Com'rs. of Larimer Cy.*, 626 P.2d 652 (Colo., 1981) (fact that in-state nonresidents of a district were allowed to vote did not preclude the district from denying the vote to out-of-staters).

(b) Would it make any difference if Paula is African American and proves that the District boundaries were drawn to exclude her neighborhood because most of the residents are African-American? Cf. *Gomillion v. Lightfoot*, 364 U.S. 339 (1960). Because of a belief that voters in her neighborhood would tend to vote in a particular manner, *e.g.*, for higher (or lower) school budgets? Cf. *Carrington v. Rash*, 380 U.S. 89, 94 (1965).

(c) Suppose the New York statute were amended to permit non-residents who own property subject to property taxation in the District to vote in school board elections. Would the Court hold that the votes of residents had been diluted unconstitutionally?

See *Spahos v. Mayor and Councilmen of Savannah Beach*, 207 F.Supp 688 (S.D.Ga. 1962), aff'd. per curiam 371 U.S. 206 (1962); *Brown v. Bd. of Com'rs. of Chattanooga*, 722 F.Supp. 380, 397–400 (M.D.Tenn. 1989).

Permitting nonresident landowners to vote in Town elections was upheld in *May v. Town of Mountain Village*, 132 F.3d 576 (10th Cir. 1997), cert. denied 524 U.S. 938 (1998). However, extraterritorial voting was struck down as an unconstitutional dilution of residents' votes in *Board of County Commissioners of Shelby County v. Burson*, 121 F.3d 244 (6th Cir. 1997), cert. denied sub nom. *Walkup v. Board of Commissioners of Shelby County*, 522 U.S. 1113 (1998). In that case, Shelby County was divided into two school districts, one consisting of the city of Memphis (Memphis City Schools) and the other consisting of the rest of the county (Shelby County School District). The members of the latter district were regarded as county officials, which meant that under the Tennessee constitution, all residents of the county, including residents of Memphis, were permitted to vote for them. The Sixth Circuit did not regard this extraterritorial voting as per se unconstitutional, but struck it down after considering a number of factors, including that Memphis made up about three-fourths of the county population.

4. In WIT v. BERMAN, 306 F.3d 1256 (2nd Cir. 2002), plaintiffs divided their time between living in New York City and living in houses in the Hamptons at the far end of Long Island. They voted in their Long Island communities. Had they not done so, they would have been eligible to vote in New York City. The Second Circuit rejected a claim that their being denied the vote in New York City violated the Equal Protection Clause. Judge Winter pointed out that residence for voting purposes is closely tied to the legal concept of domicile, which is premised on the idea that one may be domiciled at only one place at a given time. Judge Winter continued:

> At first blush, it may seem that domicile plays such a key role because it is a close proxy for determining the election district in which a voter has the greatest stake in the outcome of elections. This is an oversimplification, however.
>
> Particularly in modern times, domicile is very often a poor proxy for a voter's stake in electoral outcomes because many of an individual voter's varied interests are affected by outcomes in elections in which they do not vote. Some, or even many, voters may reasonably perceive that their primary political concerns are affected more by outcomes in elections in which they do not vote than by outcomes in elections in which they do vote. There are endless examples of the bad fit between domicile and a voter's interest in electoral outcomes. For example, a person who works in a factory, or owns one, located in a municipality other than where the person lives, has interests in that municipality's tax, traffic, law enforcement, and other policies....
>
> However, while one may mount ethereal arguments against the single-domicile-registration rule, the administrative problems that interests-based rules would cause for thousands of registrars of voters render those rules virtually unthinkable. Voter registration is generally a nondiscretionary function of local government carried out by low level officials. Absent meaningful guidance, some registrars (even in the same precinct) would use a "whatever-you-say" approach, others will adopt a "show-me-beyond-a-reasonable-doubt" stance, while yet others will resort to *ad hoc, ad hominem,* or whimsical standards.
>
> Given the need for workable standards, determination of where one may vote based on interests in electoral outcomes is not a manageable rule. Honoring the desires of voters to vote in other districts based on their expression of subjective

interests in the political decisions of those other districts would essentially lead to a "vote-in-however-many-districts-you-please" rule. Such a rule would be truly chaotic, save for the small measure of order that corruption would bring to it. An objective test of voter interests is equally unworkable. At the very least, it would involve an ever-changing analysis by registrars of the merits of political issues—e.g., does an employee of a firm in one city who lives in another have a sufficient interest in the traffic and tax policies of the former to vote there, or is there sufficiently harmful acid rain in Vermont as a result of loose environmental standards in Ohio to justify a Vermonter voting in Ohio—and would also be chaotic.

Domicile as a rule may have its philosophical defects, therefore, but it has enormous practical advantages over the alternatives. It almost always insures that a voter has *some* stake in the electoral outcome in the domiciliary district and almost always does not involve large numbers of disputes over where one may vote. The domicile rule informs would-be voters where they may vote, a vital function that encourages registration and voting. Moreover, it gives voters the notice required for the enforcement of criminal laws against individuals voting in places where they are not eligible....

To be sure, domicile as a test entails administrative difficulties at the margins. The domicile of students is an example. So too is the registration of the homeless. However, these difficulties are slight compared to those that abandonment of the domicile rule and its one domicile/one electoral district restriction might entail.

5. Would it be desirable to eliminate all voter qualifications, including age, residency, and citizenship, on the theory that only those who have a genuine (subjective) interest would bother to vote in any given election? Should such an approach be constitutionally required? See Rex E. Lee, *Mr. Herbert Spencer and the Bachelor Stockbroker: Kramer v. Union Free School District No. 15*, 15 ARIZONA LAW REVIEW 457, 468 (1973).

6. The majority in *Kramer* argues that the usual presumption of constitutionality assumes that everyone is represented in the governmental process that leads to the policy in question. Therefore, the presumption of constitutionality should not apply in a case where the complainant is denied the right to vote. Justice Stewart rebuts this contention by pointing out that the voting restriction was enacted by the New York State Legislature, in which Kramer was fully represented. Are you persuaded by Justice Stewart's argument? Would Justice Stewart's position be undermined if it can be shown that as a practical matter, Kramer's chances of getting the legislature to change the rules regarding school district voting were nil? See Mark Tushnet, *Darkness on the Edge of Town: The Contributions of John Hart Ely to Constitutional Theory*, 89 YALE LAW JOURNAL 1037, 1048–51 (1980).

7. In a 9–0 decision issued the same day as *Kramer*, the Court in *Cipriano v. City of Houma*, 395 U.S. 701 (1969), struck down a Louisiana statute which permitted only property owners to vote in elections to approve *revenue* bond issues for municipally-owned utilities. The next term a 5–3 majority reached the same conclusion in a case involving Arizona provisions which gave only property owners the right to vote in elections to approve *general obligation* bonds. *City of Phoenix v. Kolodziejski*, 399 U.S. 204 (1970).

When a government issues bonds, it borrows money from the purchasers of the bonds. In the case of revenue bonds, the loans will be repaid only from revenues of the project (for example, a municipal parking garage) for which the bonds are issued. General obligation bonds give the bondholders a right to be repaid from the jurisdiction's general revenues and are backed by the full faith and credit of the jurisdiction. Can you see why some justices concurred in *Cipriano* but dissented in *Kolodziejski?*

8. In *Lockport v. Citizens for Community Action*, 430 U.S. 259 (1977), the Court upheld a New York statute that required for approval of a county charter revision a majority vote of *both* city residents *and* non-city residents. Under the statute a revision was defeated although it received a majority of all votes, because a majority of non-city residents voted no. The Court distinguished *Kramer*, *Cipriano*, and *Kolodziejski*, saying that here the discrepant effects on city and non-city voters justified the discrimination.

9. Despite the holding of *Kramer*, we shall see in the next Chapter that the Supreme Court has permitted states to deny the franchise in certain "special purpose districts" such as water storage districts and to weight those votes unequally. Before turning to that material, we begin with the permissibility of unequally weighted votes in congressional, state, and local elections.

Chapter 3

Representation

In Chapter 2 we saw that the United States Constitution does not directly grant the right to vote to individuals but that numerous amendments to the Constitution have barred denying the franchise on a variety of grounds and that the right to vote has been further extended by statutes and by court decisions. In this chapter and the three that follow, the right to vote is considered in its relationship to the system of representation of which it is a part.

Cases involving the equal *weighting* of votes have had both practical and theoretical importance. In *Reynolds v. Sims* the Supreme Court imposed the "one person, one vote" standard and thereby required the restructuring of at least one house of the state legislature in nearly every state. Although we shall limit ourselves to relatively brief excerpts from *Reynolds* and its companion cases, the reader should not draw the inference that it is an unimportant case. To the contrary, most people would list it as one of the landmark decisions in Supreme Court history. The excerpts we shall consider express conflicting theoretical perspectives with which Chief Justice Warren and Justice Stewart addressed the question of "malapportionment" (i.e., unequally populated legislative districts). The reason for not dwelling on the many issues and sub-issues making up the malapportionment debate is that *Reynolds* has been so successful that these issues, though still of intellectual interest, are no longer alive as a practical matter. The desire to extend *Reynolds* in different directions has generated many additional issues, and these will provide the focus of our study.

Following our consideration of *Reynolds*, we proceed to extension of the one person, one vote rule to local government. When this was accomplished in *Avery v. Midland County*, the theoretical issues began to resemble those in the *Kramer* line of cases, which we considered in Chapter 2. The two lines converged in *Salyer Land Co. v. Tulare Lake Basin Water Storage District* and *Ball v. James*. Voting schemes in which only property owners could vote and votes were weighted on a one dollar (or one acre), one vote basis were upheld by the Supreme Court in the case of local districts with specialized functions. Although these cases have had relatively small practical importance, they bring into question the nature of representation and its relation to interest group influence and political power. Among other issues, they raise the question whether government must always represent an undifferentiated public interest or, alternatively, it may represent specialized constituencies without losing its "public" character.

I. The Right to an Equally Weighted Vote

It has long been recognized that severe population disparity between different districts which elect representatives to a legislative or other governmental assembly creates a serious theoretical and practical inequality between voters in the respective districts. *E.g.*,

John Locke, Two Treatises on Government 390–91 (Peter Laslett, ed., 2d ed., 1964). Yet until the 1960s, the Supreme Court refused to rule on matters of legislative apportionment, regarding them as nonjusticiable political questions. See *Colegrove v. Green*, 328 U.S. 549 (1946) (Frankfurter, J., plurality opinion).

Two landmark cases in the 1960s dramatically changed the Court's disposition toward legislative apportionment. The first, *Baker v. Carr*, 369 U.S. 186 (1962), held that challenges to malapportioned districts under the Equal Protection Clause *were* justiciable in federal courts, but did not decide whether such districts were in fact unconstitutional. "Malapportionment" is the term commonly used to describe a districting plan whose districts are improperly unequal in population. A district is described as "underrepresented" if its population is greater than the mean, and as "overrepresented" if its population is less than the mean.[a]

The second landmark case, *Reynolds v. Sims*, 377 U.S. 533 (1964), was presaged by *Gray v. Sanders*, 372 U.S. 368 (1963), striking down unequal weighting of votes within a single constituency, and by *Wesberry v. Sanders*, 376 U.S. 1 (1964), requiring that Congressional districts be drawn on an equal population basis. *Gray* prevented states from using a system analogous to the electoral college in electing statewide officials and did not involve the more common question of a multi-member governmental body.[b] *Wesberry* was not decided under the Equal Protection Clause but under Article I, §§2 and 4 of the Constitution, and was thus applicable only to the United States House of Representatives. The constitutional requirements that would be applicable to the state legislatures and to elected local government bodies remained undecided—but not for long.

In *Reynolds v. Sims*, Alabama voters challenged unequally populated state legislative districts as violative of the Equal Protection Clause. The Supreme Court struck down the Alabama legislative districts and, in companion cases decided on the same day, struck down state legislative districts in New York, Maryland, Virginia, Delaware, and Colorado. In these cases, the Court required that seats in both houses of a bicameral state legislature be apportioned on a substantially equal population basis—in short, "one person, one vote." Following are excerpts from Chief Justice Warren's opinion for the Court in *Reynolds*, and from Justice Stewart's dissent in the Colorado case.

Reynolds v. Sims

377 U.S. 533 (1964)

MR. CHIEF JUSTICE WARREN delivered the opinion of the Court....

III.

A predominant consideration in determining whether a State's legislative apportionment scheme constitutes an invidious discrimination violative of rights asserted under the Equal Protection Clause is that the rights allegedly impaired are individual and personal in nature. As stated by the Court in *United States v. Bathgate*, 246 U.S. 220, 227, "[t]he right to vote is personal...." While the result of a court decision in a state legislative ap-

a. Baker v. Carr: *A Commemorative Symposium*, 80 North Carolina Law Review 1103 (2002) marked the 40th anniversary of the celebrated case. Contributions are by Guy-Uriel E. Charles; Robert L. Pushaw, Jr.; Mark Tushnet; James A. Gardner; Sanford Levinson; Nathaniel A. Persily, Thad Kousser & Patrick Egan; Heather K. Gerken; Luis Fuentes-Rohwer; Richard L. Hasen; and Roy A. Schotland.

b. Is the electoral college, which is used to elect the President of the United States, itself unconstitutional? Not according to *New v. Ashcroft*, 293 F.Supp.2d 256 (E.D.N.Y. 2003).

portionment controversy may be to require the restructuring of the geographical distribution of seats in a state legislature, the judicial focus must be concentrated upon ascertaining whether there has been any discrimination against certain of the State's citizens which constitutes an impermissible impairment of their constitutionally protected right to vote.... Undoubtedly, the right of suffrage is a fundamental matter in a free and democratic society. Especially since the right to exercise the franchise in a free and unimpaired manner is preservative of other basic civil and political rights, any alleged infringement of the right of citizens to vote must be carefully and meticulously scrutinized....

Legislators represent people, not trees or acres. Legislators are elected by voters, not farms or cities or economic interests. As long as ours is a representative form of government, and our legislatures are those instruments of government elected directly by and directly representative of the people, the right to elect legislators in a free and unimpaired fashion is a bedrock of our political system. It could hardly be gainsaid that a constitutional claim had been asserted by an allegation that certain otherwise qualified voters had been entirely prohibited from voting for members of their state legislature. And, if a State should provide that the votes of citizens in one part of the State should be given two times, or five times, or 10 times the weight of votes of citizens in another part of the State, it could hardly be contended that the right to vote of those residing in the disfavored areas had not been effectively diluted. It would appear extraordinary to suggest that a State could be constitutionally permitted to enact a law providing that certain of the State's voters could vote two, five, or 10 times for their legislative representatives, while voters living elsewhere could vote only once. And it is inconceivable that a state law to the effect that, in counting votes for legislators, the votes of citizens in one part of the State would be multiplied by two, five, or 10, while the votes of persons in another area would be counted only at face value, could be constitutionally sustainable. Of course, the effect of state legislative districting schemes which give the same number of representatives to unequal numbers of constituents is identical. Overweighting and overvaluation of the votes of those living here has the certain effect of dilution and undervaluation of the votes of those living there. The resulting discrimination against those individual voters living in disfavored areas is easily demonstrable mathematically. Their right to vote is simply not the same right to vote as that of those living in a favored part of the State. Two, five, or 10 of them must vote before the effect of their voting is equivalent to that of their favored neighbor. Weighting the votes of citizens differently, by any method or means, merely because of where they happen to reside, hardly seems justifiable. One must be ever aware that the Constitution forbids "sophisticated as well as simpleminded modes of discrimination." ...

State legislatures are, historically, the fountainhead of representative government in this country.... But representative government is in essence self-government through the medium of elected representatives of the people, and each and every citizen has an inalienable right to full and effective participation in the political processes of his State's legislative bodies. Most citizens can achieve this participation only as qualified voters through the election of legislators to represent them. Full and effective participation by all citizens in state government requires, therefore, that each citizen have an equally effective voice in the election of members of his state legislature. Modern and viable state government needs, and the Constitution demands, no less.

Logically, in a society ostensibly grounded on representative government, it would seem reasonable that a majority of the people of a State could elect a majority of that State's legislators. To conclude differently, and to sanction minority control of state legislative bodies, would appear to deny majority rights in a way that far surpasses any possible denial of minority rights that might otherwise be thought to result. Since legislatures are responsible for enacting laws by which all citizens are to be governed, they should be bodies which are collectively responsive to the popular will. And the concept of equal protection has been traditionally viewed as requiring the uniform treatment of persons standing in the same relation to the governmental action questioned or challenged. With respect to the allocation of legislative representation, all voters, as citizens of a State, stand in the same relation regardless of where they live. Any suggested criteria for the differentiation of citizens are insufficient to justify any discrimination, as to the weight of their votes, unless relevant to the permissible purposes of legislative apportionment. Since the achieving of fair and effective representation for all citizens is concededly the basic aim of legislative apportionment, we conclude that the Equal Protection Clause guarantees the opportunity for equal participation by all voters in the election of state legislators. Diluting the weight of votes because of place of residence impairs basic constitutional rights under the Fourteenth Amendment just as much as invidious discriminations based upon factors such as race or economic status. Our constitutional system amply provides for the protection of minorities by means other than giving them majority control of state legislatures. And the democratic ideals of equality and majority rule, which have served this Nation so well in the past, are hardly of any less significance for the present and the future.

We are told that the matter of apportioning representation in a state legislature is a complex and many-faceted one. We are advised that States can rationally consider factors other than population in apportioning legislative representation. We are admonished not to restrict the power of the States to impose differing views as to political philosophy on their citizens. We are cautioned about the dangers of entering into political thickets and mathematical quagmires. Our answer is this: a denial of constitutionally protected rights demands judicial protection; our oath and our office require no less of us. . . .

To the extent that a citizen's right to vote is debased, he is that much less a citizen. The fact that an individual lives here or there is not a legitimate reason for overweighting or diluting the efficacy of his vote. The complexions of societies and civilizations change, often with amazing rapidity. A nation once primarily rural in character becomes predominantly urban. Representation schemes once fair and equitable become archaic and outdated. But the basic principle of representative government remains, and must remain, unchanged—the weight of a citizen's vote cannot be made to depend on where he lives. Population is, of necessity, the starting point for consideration and the controlling criterion for judgment in legislative apportionment controversies. A citizen, a qualified voter, is no more nor no less so because he lives in the city or on the farm. This is the clear and strong command of our Constitution's Equal Protection Clause. This is an essential part of the concept of a government of laws and not men. This is at the heart of Lincoln's vision of "government of the people, by the people, [and] for the people." The Equal Protection Clause demands no less than substantially equal state legislative representation for all citizens, of all places as well as of all races.

Lucas v. 44th General Assembly of Colorado
377 U.S. 713, 744 (1964)

MR. JUSTICE STEWART, whom MR. JUSTICE CLARK joins, dissenting.

It is important to make clear at the outset what these cases are not about. They have nothing to do with the denial or impairment of any person's right to vote. Nobody's right to vote has been denied. Nobody's right to vote has been restricted. Nobody has been deprived of the right to have his vote counted. The voting right cases which the Court cites are, therefore, completely wide of the mark. Secondly, these cases have nothing to do with the "weighting" or "diluting" of votes cast within any electoral unit. The rule of *Gray v. Sanders* is, therefore, completely without relevance here....

The question involved here in these cases is quite a different one. Simply stated, the question is to what degree, if at all, the Equal Protection Clause of the Fourteenth Amendment limits each sovereign State's freedom to establish appropriate electoral constituencies from which representatives to the State's bicameral legislative assembly are to be chosen. The Court's answer is a blunt one, and, I think, woefully wrong. The Equal Protection Clause, says the Court, "requires that the seats in both houses of a bicameral state legislature must be apportioned on a population basis."

After searching carefully through the Court's opinions..., I have been able to find but two reasons offered in support of this rule. First, says the Court, it is "established that the fundamental principle of representative government in this country is one of equal representation for equal numbers of people...." With all respect, I think that this is not correct, simply as a matter of fact. It has been unanswerably demonstrated before now that this "was not the colonial system, it was not the system chosen for the national government by the Constitution, it was not the system exclusively or even predominantly practiced by the States at the time of adoption of the Fourteenth Amendment, it is not predominantly practiced by the States today."[6] Secondly, says the Court, unless legislative districts are equal in population, voters in the more populous districts will suffer a "debasement" amounting to a constitutional injury. As the Court explains it, "To the extent that a citizen's right to vote is debased, he is that much less a citizen." We are not told how or why the vote of a person in a more populated legislative district is "debased," or how or why he is less a citizen, nor is the proposition self-evident. I find it impossible to understand how or why a voter in California, for instance, either feels or is less a citizen than a voter in Nevada, simply because, despite their population disparities, each of those States is represented by two United States Senators.

To put the matter plainly, there is nothing in all the history of this Court's decisions which supports this constitutional rule. The Court's draconian pronouncement, which makes unconstitutional the legislatures of most of the 50 States, finds no support in the words of the Constitution, in any prior decision of this Court, or in the 175-year political history of our Federal Union. With all respect, I am convinced these decisions mark a long step backward into that unhappy era when a majority of the members of this Court were thought by many to have convinced themselves and each other that the demands of the Constitution were to be measured not by what it says, but by their own notions of wise political theory. The rule announced today is at odds with long-established principles of constitutional adjudication under the Equal Protection Clause, and it stifles values of local individuality and initiative vital to the character of the Federal Union which it was the genius of our Constitution to create.

I.

What the Court has done is to convert a particular political philosophy into a constitutional rule, binding upon each of the 50 States, from Maine to Hawaii, from Alaska to Texas, without regard and without respect for the many individualized and differentiated

---

[6]. *Baker v. Carr*, 369 U.S. at 301 (Frankfurter, J., dissenting).

characteristics of each State, characteristics stemming from each State's distinct history, distinct geography, distinct distribution of population, and distinct political heritage. My own understanding of the various theories of representative government is that no one theory has ever commanded unanimous assent among political scientists, historians, or others who have considered the problem. But even if it were thought that the rule announced today by the Court is, as a matter of political theory, the most desirable general rule which can be devised as a basis for the make-up of the representative assembly of a typical State, I could not join in the fabrication of a constitutional mandate which imports and forever freezes one theory of political thought into our Constitution, and forever denies to every State any opportunity for enlightened and progressive innovation in the design of its democratic institutions, so as to accommodate within a system of representative government the interests and aspiration of diverse groups of people, without subjecting any group or class to absolute domination by a geographically concentrated or highly organized majority.

Representative government is a process of accommodating group interests through democratic institutional arrangements. Its function is to channel the numerous opinions, interests, and abilities of the people of a State into the making of the State's public policy. Appropriate legislative apportionment, therefore, should ideally be designed to insure effective representation in the State's legislature, in cooperation with other organs of political power, of the various groups and interests making up the electorate. In practice, of course, this ideal is approximated in the particular apportionment system of any State by a realistic accommodation of the diverse and often conflicting political forces operating within the State.

I do not pretend to any specialized knowledge of the myriad of individual characteristics of the several States, beyond the records in the cases before us today. But I do know enough to be aware that a system of legislative apportionment which might be best for South Dakota, might be unwise for Hawaii with its many islands, or Michigan with its Northern Peninsula. I do know enough to realize that Montana with its vast distances is not Rhode Island with its heavy concentrations of people. I do know enough to be aware of the great variations among the several States in their historic manner of distributing legislative power—of the Governors' Councils in New England, of the broad powers of initiative and referendum retained in some States by the people, of the legislative power which some States give to their Governors, by the right of veto or otherwise, of the widely autonomous home rule which many States give to their cities. The Court today declines to give any recognition to these considerations and countless others, tangible and intangible, in holding unconstitutional the particular systems of legislative apportionment which these States have chosen. Instead, the Court says that the requirements of the Equal Protection Clause can be met in any State only by the uncritical, simplistic, and heavy-handed application of sixth-grade arithmetic.

But legislators do not represent faceless numbers. They represent people, or, more accurately, a majority of the voters in their districts—people with identifiable needs and interests which require legislative representation, and which can often be related to the geographical areas in which these people live. The very fact of geographic districting, the constitutional validity of which the Court does not question, carries with it an acceptance of the idea of legislative representation of regional needs and interests. Yet if geographical residence is irrelevant, as the Court suggests, and the goal is solely that of equally "weighted" votes, I do not understand why the Court's constitutional rule does not require the abolition of districts and the holding of all elections at large.

The fact is, of course, that population factors must often to some degree be subordinated in devising a legislative apportionment plan which is to achieve the important goal of ensuring a fair, effective, and balanced representation of the regional, social, and economic interests within a State. And the further fact is that throughout our history the apportionments of State Legislatures have reflected the strongly felt American tradition that the public interest is composed of many diverse interests, and that in the long run it can better be expressed by a medley of component voices than by the majority's monolithic command. What constitutes a rational plan reasonably designed to achieve this objective will vary from State to State, since each State is unique, in terms of topography, geography, demography, history, heterogeneity and concentration of population, variety of social and economic interests, and in the operation and interrelation of its political institutions. But so long as a State's apportionment plan reasonably achieves, in the light of the State's own characteristics, effective and balanced representation of all substantial interests, without sacrificing the principle of effective majority rule, that plan cannot be considered irrational.

Notes and Questions

1. Not surprisingly, *Baker*, *Reynolds*, and the other redistricting cases prompted a flood of commentary. Among the better writings in the 1960s were Carl A. Auerbach, *The Reapportionment Cases: One Person, One Vote—One Vote, One Value*, 1964 SUPREME COURT REVIEW 1 (1964), and Phil C. Neal, *Baker v. Carr: Politics in Search of Law*, 1962 SUPREME COURT REVIEW 252 (1962). A prolific and highly regarded commentator on the redistricting cases was the late Robert G. Dixon, whose views in the 1960s were synthesized in his book, DEMOCRATIC REPRESENTATION: REAPPORTIONMENT IN LAW AND POLITICS (1968). Later commentary may be found in two excellent anthologies, REAPPORTIONMENT IN THE 1970's (Nelson W. Polsby, ed., 1971), and REPRESENTATION AND REDISTRICTING ISSUES (Bernard Grofman et al., eds., 1982).

2. Chief Justice Warren emphasizes that individuals and not economic or geographic interests elect representatives, whereas Justice Stewart sees the process as an accommodation of group interests. Do they differ in their views as to how the political system in fact operates, or as to how it ought to operate? Are their views on this point inconsistent with one another? What difference, if any, does it make whether we think of elected officials as representing individuals or groups?

3. Whose position, as between Chief Justice Warren and Justice Stewart, would be preferred by James Madison? By a pluralist? In A PREFACE TO DEMOCRATIC THEORY (1956), Robert A. Dahl emphasized that the minority should prevail over the majority when and only when its preference is more intense than the majority's.

Some writers in the pluralist tradition have sharply criticized the one person, one vote rule. Bruce E. Cain, *Election Law as a Field: A Political Scientist's Perspective*, 32 LOYOLA OF LOS ANGELES LAW REVIEW 1105, 1109 (1999), acknowledges that most political scientists probably support the one person, one vote rule, but regards *Reynolds* as a setback to Madisonian theory, whose

> basic premise was that the popular will was best checked by institutions that were insulated from public opinion, similar to courts, or by the competition between representatives from various types of constituencies. The *Reynolds* cases elevated majoritarian principles over the prudentially cautious design of the Founding Fathers. Skepticism about the public whim has given way to reverence for the majority will.

Another pluralist, John Moeller, *The Supreme Court's Quest for Fair Politics*, 1 Constitutional Commentary 203, 213 (1984), writes:

> The solution the courts have imposed ignores our Madisonian political tradition. Most Americans identify with one or more groups, and those groups, representing varying constituencies, compete with each other for advantage. One consequence of Madisonian politics is an inherent tension in the scheme of representation. It calls for majoritarian government, which requires that most of the time most of the people will rule. But it also calls for reflective representation, which means that the institutions will "reflect the people in all their diversity, so that all the people may feel that their particular interests and even prejudices ... were brought to bear on the decision-making process."

See also Alexander M. Bickel, The Supreme Court and the Idea of Progress 108–13 (1978). But consider Daniel Hays Lowenstein, *The Supreme Court Has No Theory of Politics—And Be Thankful for Small Favors*, in The U.S. Supreme Court and the Electoral Process 245, 251 (David K. Ryden, ed., 2000):

> Some pluralist writers have been critical of the Supreme Court's ruling in *Reynolds*. Although this criticism may not be surprising in light of Chief Justice Warren's progressivist reasoning, it is misplaced. These writers have viewed the Court in *Reynolds* as detaching the Madisonian system of countervailing groups and factions from redistricting. Despite *Reynolds'* progressivist foundation, however, there was no good reason to suppose *a priori* that the "one person, one vote" rule's constraint on redistricting would fundamentally alter the pluralist process of negotiation and compromise that characterizes legislative redistricting.

4. In the 1950s and 1960s, many people hoped or feared that if the Supreme Court imposed an equal population requirement on state legislative districts and, to a lesser extent, on congressional districts, the result would be a major shift in policy toward liberalism and a major partisan shift in favor of the Democrats. The reason was that the overrepresented rural areas tended to be far more conservative and Republican than the underrepresented urban areas. No such massive shift took place. In retrospect the reason is clear. Had *Reynolds* been decided twenty or so years earlier, the shift might have occurred, but by 1964 the growth of suburbs, which at that time tended to be conservative and Republican, had about equalled the earlier growth of cities. Did *Reynolds* have any systematic and major policy consequences at all? Many people have found it difficult to believe that it did not, but social scientists generally have found weak effects at most. See, for example, Timothy G. O'Rourke, The Impact of Reapportionment 119–145 (1980). Many such studies looked for changes in policy direction caused by redistricting, such as an increase in overall state spending or spending in particular policy sectors. A more recent study focused on the geographic distribution of spending and found dramatic changes in favor of the counties that gained representation as a result of redistricting. See Stephen Ansolabehere, Alan Gerber and James M. Snyder, Jr., *Equal Votes, Equal Money: Court-Ordered Redistricting and the Distribution of Public Expenditures in the American States*, 96 American Political Science Review 767 (2002).

5. Whether or not districts are equal in population, they are likely to group together those interests that are geographically concentrated (e.g., farmers, poor people in cities, some racial and ethnic groups), but not groups that are dispersed (e.g., dentists, veterans, other racial and ethnic groups). Is a group better off politically if it is concentrated or dispersed? What would be the consequences of significantly increasing or decreasing the extent to which constituencies consist of single interest groups? See generally James M. Buchanan & Gordon Tullock, The Calculus of Consent 217–20 (1962).

6. The phrase "fair and effective representation," appearing in the next-to-last paragraph of Part III of Chief Justice Warren's opinion in *Reynolds*, has been repeated innumerable times. What does "fair and effective representation" mean as it is used in that passage? What facts would suggest a lack of fair and effective representation? Does Chief Justice Warren say there is a constitutional right to fair and effective representation? If so, is such a right enforceable? By whom? If Chief Justice Warren did not say there is a constitutional right to fair and effective representation, should he have? For discussion of some of these questions, see Daniel Hays Lowenstein, *Bandemer's Gap: Gerrymandering and Equal Protection*, in POLITICAL GERRYMANDERING AND THE COURTS 70–73 (Bernard Grofman, ed., 1990).

7. In *Reynolds*, the Court speaks indifferently of districts with equal population and with equal numbers of voters. The number of actual voters changes enough from election to election that it would be difficult to draw district lines to equalize the number of votes, but the theoretical argument is sometimes made that a measure closer to actual voters than population should be used. See, *e.g.*, *Garza v. County of Los Angeles*, 918 F.2d 763, 778, 779–86 (9th Cir. 1990) (Kozinski, J., concurring and dissenting in part), cert. denied 498 U.S. 1028 (1991). Although the Supreme Court has upheld redistricting on a basis other than population, it has stated a preference for equal population, see *Burns v. Richardson*, 384 U.S. 73 (1966), and population is nearly the universal basis for districting in the United States. Scot A. Reader, *One Person, One Vote Revisited: Choosing a Population Basis to Form Political Districts*, 17 HARVARD JOURNAL OF LAW & PUBLIC POLICY 521 (1994), argues that the logic of *Reynolds* and subsequent cases ought to require equal numbers of voters rather than equal population, but he is skeptical that the Constitution ought to be so interpreted.

If population is to be the basis of representation, should we go a step further and allow eligible voters to cast votes on behalf of residents who are not voters? Robert W. Bennett, *Should Parents Be Given Extra Votes on Account of their Children? Toward a Conversational Understanding of American Democracy*, 94 NORTHWESTERN UNIVERSITY LAW REVIEW 503 (2000), has discussed a proposal to give parents extra votes on account of their minor children.[c]

8. One issue left open by *Reynolds* was precisely how equal the population of districts must be. In *Swann v. Adams*, 385 U.S. 440 (1967), the Court struck down a Florida legislative apportionment when the largest deviation from the mean population for any one district was 18 percent and the ratios of the largest to the smallest district in each house were, respectively, 1.41 to 1 and 1.30 to 1. The Court said such discrepancies could not be upheld without a showing of some rational basis, which could not include "deference to area and economic or other group interests." In subsequent cases the Court was willing to find that adherence to municipal boundaries can in some circumstances justify moderate deviation from exact equality (up to at least about 17%) in state and local districting. See *Abate v. Mundt*, 403 U.S. 182 (1971); *Mahan v. Howell*, 410 U.S. 315 (1973); *Voinovich v. Quilter*, 507 U.S. 146, 161 (1993). Small deviations (up to 10%) at the state level require no justification at all. *Gaffney v. Cummings*, 412 U.S. 735 (1973).

---

c. One editor of this volume, who has three school-age children, regards this as a proposal well worth considering. Another, whose children are grown, dismisses it out of hand. The third, who recently got married, is undecided. — EDS.

At least, this is how most practitioners interpreted *Gaffney*. In *Daly v. Hunt*, 93 F.3d 1212, 1220 (4th Cir. 1996), the court stated that a maximum population deviation under ten percent "does not completely insulate" a districting plan from attack. If the plan is under the ten percent threshold it is presumed to be valid, but can be overturned if it is shown to be the result of "arbitrariness or discrimination" or was not the result of an "honest and good faith effort to construct districts ... as nearly of equal population as is practicable" (quoting *Roman v. Sincock*, 377 U.S. 695 (1964) and *Reynolds*). In *Daly*, the legislature had considered a plan with a maximum deviation of 1.55%, but the maximum deviation in the plan finally adopted was 8.33%. Is that fact sufficient for the plaintiffs to overcome the presumption of validity? See also *Gaffney*. What if population deviations close to but not exceeding ten percent systematically favor one region of a state over another (and, not coincidentally, one party over the other)? Compare *Larios v. Cox*, 300 F.Supp.2d 1320 (N.D.Ga. 2004) (striking down a Georgia legislative plan), with *Rodriguez v. Pataki*, 308 F.Supp.2d 346 (S.D.N.Y. 2004) (upholding a New York state senate plan).

The Supreme Court summarily affirmed the Georgia decision, *Larios v. Cox*, 542 U.S. 947 (2004). While not affirming the lower court's reasoning, the summary affirmence presumably decides that a plan within the 10% threshold can violate the one person, one vote rule. Justice Stevens, concurring, and Justice Scalia, dissenting, filed separate opinions. Most lower courts seem to be interpreting the Supreme Court's action in *Cox* as meaning that a maximum population deviation under ten percent places the burden of proof on the plaintiff to show arbitrariness or discrimination, but does not create a safe harbor. For example, in *Moore v. Itawamba County*, 431 F.3d 257 (5th Cir. 2005), the Fifth Circuit disapproved the District Judge's treatment of a maximum deviation of 9.38 percent as a safe harbor. "The formulaic threshold is not an absolute determinant. Rather, it effectively allocates the burden of proof." Following that principle, the court found allegations that overpopulating the western districts discriminated against the west side of the county insufficient to withstand summary judgment dismissing the claim.

If the ten percent threshold allows for some degree of scrutiny of plans that are within it, is the presumption of invalidity for plans with more than a ten percent deviation also flexible? What if the population of the jurisdiction is very small and spread over a large area? See *Frank v. Forest County*, 336 F.3d 570 (7th Cir. 2003).

Of course, state law may impose population standards more strict than those imposed by the federal Constitution. See, *e.g.*, *Fay v. St. Louis County Board of Commissioners*, 674 N.W.2d 433 (Minn.App. 2004).

9. In the case of congressional districting, which under *Wesberry v. Sanders* is governed by Art. I, §2 and not by the Equal Protection Clause, the Court has not tolerated any avoidable deviation from mathematical equality. *Kirkpatrick v. Preisler*, 394 U.S. 526 (1969); *White v. Weiser*, 412 U.S. 783 (1973).

Neither Art. I, §2, which governs elections for the House of Representatives, nor the Equal Protection Clause contains an explicit requirement of "one person, one vote," much less an indication of how equal the districts must be. Accordingly, many commentators have been unimpressed with the Court's reliance on the two constitutional provisions as an explanation for the dramatically different population standards the Court has imposed. A different justification is proposed by Charles Black, *Representation in Law and Equity*, 10 Nomos: Representation 131 (1968). Black, a proponent of "structural interpretation" of the Constitution, argues that the federal government's greater interest in federal elections justifies a stricter standard of population equality for congressional elections than for state and local elections, in which the federal government has less interest. However, a political scientist finds it perverse to give state legislators greater leeway when they design their own districts than when they define those of the members of the House of Representatives. See James L. McDowell, *"One Person, One Vote" and the Decline of Community*, 23 LEGAL STUDIES FORUM 131, 138 (1999).

The Supreme Court's latest word on these questions (other than the summary affirmance in *Larios*) is contained in two 5–4 decisions handed down on the same day in 1983. In *Karcher v. Daggett*, 462 U.S. 725 (1983), the Court struck down a New Jersey congressional districting plan on population grounds, when the population difference between the largest and smallest districts amounted to 0.6984 percent. Relying on *Kirkpatrick*, the Court refused to set any percentage below which population inequality in Congressional districts would be regarded as de minimis. In *Brown v. Thomson*, 462 U.S. 835 (1983), a case whose unusual factual and procedural background may or may not prevent it from having important precedential effect, the Court validated a Wyoming state legislative plan in which the maximum population deviation amounted to 89 percent.

Justice Sandra Day O'Connor, concurring in *Brown v. Thomson*, commented: "As a Member of the majority in both cases, I feel compelled to explain the reasons for my joinder in these apparently divergent decisions." 462 U.S. at 848. Readers are invited to search through Justice O'Connor's opinion and all the other opinions delivered that day in search of a satisfactory explanation.

10. Though *Wesberry* and *Reynolds* were fiercely controversial when they were decided, the one person, one vote standard has become widely accepted in the United States. For that reason, and because legislative bodies do not wish to jeopardize their districting plans by straying too near the boundaries of the equal population standards that have been staked out by the Supreme Court, serious challenges to legislative districts on grounds of population have become relatively unusual.

When such cases are brought, the plaintiffs usually have concerns other than population equality. *Larios*, in which Republicans opposed a plan adopted by Georgia Democrats, is one example. Another occurred this decade in Pennsylvania. As mentioned above, in *Karcher* the Court refused to set a level below which any population inequality in a congressional plan would be regarded as *de minimis*. Does that mean *any* inequality, no matter how trivial, constitutes a prima facie constitutional violation? Apparently so, according to *Vieth v. Pennsylvania*, 195 F.Supp.2d 672 (M.D.Pa. 2002). In that case, Democrats successfully challenged a Republican-drawn plan, whose maximum population deviation consisted of nineteen people. The largest district had a population of 646,380 while the population of the smallest district was 646,361.[d] The laugh was on the Democrats, because the court permitted the legislature to make politically insignificant changes to correct the (so-called) population disparity. The Democrats also pressed a challenge to the plan as a partisan gerrymander, which was their real concern. As we shall see in Chapter 6, that claim was decided (against the Democrats) by a closely divided Supreme Court in 2004.

---

d. These figures are taken from an earlier decision in the same litigation, *Vieth v. Pennsylvania*, 188 F.Supp.2d 532, 535 (M.D.Pa. 2002).

In *Graham v. Thornburgh*, 207 F.Supp.2d 1280 (D.Kans. 2002), the court upheld a congressional plan with a maximum deviation of 33 people. It was shown that the legislature could have adopted a plan with perfect equality (defined as permitting a deviation of one person, because the number of districts in the state did not divide equally into the total population), which put the burden on the state to show that the deviation was justifiable. However, the court believed the plan was reasonably designed to meet a set of criteria the legislature had established, especially in light of the small size of the deviation. The existence of alternative plans that achieved perfect equality was not decisive when those plans were not demonstrably superior when measured against the legislature's stated criteria.

Even before the Pennsylvania decision striking down a plan because of a maximum population deviation of nineteen people, many drafters of congressional districting plans were reducing the deviations in their plans to the absolute minimum. Given that after the Supreme Court's summary affirmance in *Larios v. Cox*, lower courts have been unwilling to recognize a maximum deviation under ten percent as a safe harbor for state and local plans, it is likely that in the decade following the 2010 census, state and local as well as congressional redistricters seek to reduce deviations to the absolute minimum of one person. Is any purpose served by such judicial zeal?

11. Compliance with the equal protection requirement, however strict or lax the requirement may be, is based on the census, which is performed each decade in the year ending in zero. The census is used for many purposes, but its basis is Article I, section 2, of the Constitution, which calls for an "actual enumeration" of the population of each state, "in such manner" as Congress may direct. Article I, section 2, calls for members of the House of Representatives and also direct taxes to be apportioned on the basis of the census. For reasons unrelated to the subject matter of this book, the direct taxation provision has become a dead letter, so that reapportionment is the only constitutionally stated purpose for the census that has any practical importance. As Peter Skerry, COUNTING ON THE CENSUS? RACE, GROUP IDENTITY, AND THE EVASION OF POLITICS (2000), explains, the use of the census for apportionment created an incentive for states to seek to maximize their counted population in the census, while its use for direct taxation gave the states an incentive to try to minimize their counted population. Consistent with the goal of James Madison and many of the other framers to create offsetting political pressures within the federal system as a way of preventing abuses, states would be restrained in their efforts to influence the census, because whether they sought to increase or lower their own population counts, what they stood to gain in one area they would lose in the other. That balance has been upset by the practical elimination of the direct taxation function, so that states now have an unmixed incentive to increase their relative share of the nation's population as counted by the census. That incentive is supplemented by additional statutory incentives pointing in the same direction. The failure of the original constitutional plan to create offsetting pressures no doubt accounts in part for the contentiousness of politics surrounding the census.

Article I, section 2, states that *apportionment* of the House of Representatives — that is, allocation of House seats among the states — will be based on the census. As a result of *Wesberry* and *Reynolds*, the census must also be used for *districting* — that is, establishing the boundaries of districts within which members of the House, state legislatures, and other governmental bodies are elected. In addition, the census is the basis for distribution of grants and other benefits in numerous federal programs, as well as for an immense variety of publicly and privately sponsored research.

Over the past couple of decades, the question of whether statistical sampling can and should be used has become a contentious partisan issue. It is generally conceded that the method that has been used in the recent past — a mail survey, followed by personal visits to households that do not respond — results in a significant undercount. Furthermore, the persons missed by the census are not a random sample of the public. In particular, the size of the undercount is considerably larger among certain racial and ethnic groups than among the population at large. Sampling, i.e., statistically based extrapolation from the people who are actually counted, would yield a more accurate total population figure than the methods that have been used in the past.

Without much controversy since at least the 1950s, the Census Bureau has used various forms of sampling to produce demographic, social, and economic data of various sorts. The proposal to extend the use of sampling has provoked considerable argument along two lines of cleavage. The first divides states and municipalities that stand to gain in relative population from sampling and those that stand to lose in relative population. Roughly, jurisdictions such as California and Texas with large immigrant populations are in the former category, and many midwestern and southern states are in the latter. Because allocations under many federal programs are based either on total population or population of ethnic, income, or other groups that are likely to be disproportionately undercounted, these jurisdictions stand to gain or lose substantial amounts in federal grants and subsidies.

However, the dispute between states and municipalities has been overshadowed, politically, by the dispute between the parties. The most heavily undercounted groups tend to be disproportionately Democratic in their voting behavior. It is not surprising that with almost one voice Democrats have favored sampling and Republicans have opposed it.[e] Some of the most vituperative budget battles of the 1990s turned on efforts by the Clinton administration to implement sampling in the 2000 census and by the Republican Congress to prevent it.

Part of the Republican strategy was to object to sampling as either unconstitutional, because it is not an "actual enumeration," or violative of 13 U.S.C. §195, a section of the Census Act that reads, "Except for the determination of population for purposes of apportionment of Representatives in Congress among the several States, the Secretary [of Commerce] shall, if he considers it feasible, authorize the use of the statistical method known as 'sampling' in carrying out the provisions of this title." The Clinton administration argued that the exception in the first clause of Section 195 meant simply that the Secretary of Commerce was not *required* to use sampling for purposes of apportionment. A five-member majority of the Supreme Court rejected this view and ruled that sampling *could not* be used for apportionment. *Department of Commerce v. United States House of Representatives*, 525 U.S. 316 (1999).

---

e. Skerry, *supra*, argues that both parties are mistaken to view the issue in such strong partisan terms. He argues that by even the largest estimates the population differences between a "headcount" census and an "adjusted" census will be small in percentage terms, and that a much more important factor is which party, if either, controls the drawing of district lines in a state. Both of these points are correct, but they do not negate the parties' belief that the headcount is better for the Republicans while the adjusted census would be better for the Democrats. If the Democrats draw the lines, they would be able to create smaller districts that are safely Democratic, giving them more leeway to put the "saved" Democratic voters into neighboring districts, if the adjusted census were used. Similarly, if Republicans draw the lines, they would be able to make safe Democratic districts larger, thereby "using up" more Democratic voters, if the headcount is used. Skerry's argument supports the view that the partisan importance of the question has often been exaggerated, but not that the question has no predictable partisan consequences at all.

Although the Republicans thus won the battle in the Supreme Court, the war probably would have continued had a Democratic president been elected in 2000. The partisan consequences of apportionment of House seats among the states are less significant than the districting that would occur within the states. The *Department of Commerce* decision did nothing to resolve which population figures should be used for the latter purpose. Had the Commerce Department issued adjusted figures and done so early enough for use in redistricting, the battle would have shifted to state legislatures to decide which figures should be used — and, undoubtedly to courts, as inevitable law suits charged that the wrong figures were used. For discussion of some of the legal problems that would have arisen, see Nathaniel Persily, *Color by Numbers: Race, Redistricting, and the 2000 Census*, 85 Minnesota Law Review 899, 902–925 (2001). Not surprisingly, the Department of Commerce under Republican President George W. Bush did not do so.

Although the political debate on the census issue is saturated with partisanship, there are strong policy considerations on both sides of the argument. As was mentioned above, the use of sampling would generate a more accurate population total and would reduce or eliminate inequity resulting from undercounts of varying margins among different population groups. On the other hand, when it comes to the methodological details, the use of statistical sampling techniques is as much an art as a science and may be subject to abusive manipulation when it occurs in such a politically charged context. Furthermore, though statistical techniques would generate more accurate results in the aggregate, the more local the analysis, the less accurate would be the sampling techniques. Yet, for purposes of legislative districting and allocating some federal grants, local rather than aggregate numbers are most relevant. Skerry, *supra*, is highly skeptical of the use of sampling. Unfortunately, there is no similarly accessible and comprehensive statement of the opposing view. However, for one brief summary of arguments in favor of sampling, see Stephen E. Fienberg, *The New York City Census Adjustment Trial: Witness for the Plaintiffs*, 34 Jurimetrics 65 (1993). Many of Skerry's arguments are criticized by Nathaniel Persily, *The Right to Be Counted*, 53 Stanford Law Review 1077 (2001).

12. Other questions left open by *Reynolds v. Sims* included whether and to what extent its doctrine was applicable to local government. Consider the following cases, and observe the degree to which the argument over extending *Reynolds* parallels the arguments in the *Kramer* line of cases, reviewed in Chapter 2. In the cases in Part II of this chapter, the *Kramer* and *Reynolds* lines will converge.

Avery v. Midland County
390 U.S. 474 (1968)

Mr. Justice WHITE delivered the opinion of the Court.

[Petitioner challenged electoral districts of drastically unequal population, asserting that the one person, one vote rule should be applied to the Midland County, Texas, Commissioners Court, the governing body of the county.]

Midland County has a population of about 70,000. The Commissioners Court is composed of five members. One, the County Judge, is elected at large from the entire county, and in practice casts a vote only to break a tie. The other four are Commissioners chosen from districts. The population of those districts, according to the 1963 estimates that were relied upon when this case was tried, was respectively 67,906; 852; 414; and 828. This vast imbalance resulted from placing in a single district virtually the entire city of Midland, Midland County's only urban center, in which 95% of the county's population resides.

The Commissioners Court is assigned by the Texas Constitution and by various statutory enactments with a variety of functions. According to the commentary to Vernon's Texas Statutes, the court:

> is the general governing body of the county. It establishes a courthouse and jail, appoints numerous minor officials such as the county health officer, fills vacancies in the county offices, lets contracts in the name of the county, builds roads and bridges, administers the county's public welfare services, performs numerous duties in regard to elections, sets the county tax rate, issues bonds, adopts the county budget, and serves as a board of equalization for tax assessments.

The court is also authorized, among other responsibilities, to build and run a hospital, an airport, and libraries. It fixes boundaries of school districts within the county, may establish a regional public housing authority, and determines the districts for election of its own members....

In *Reynolds v. Sims*, the Equal Protection Clause was applied to the apportionment of state legislatures. Every qualified resident, *Reynolds* determined, has the right to a ballot for election of state legislators of equal weight to the vote of every other resident, and that right is infringed when legislators are elected from districts of substantially unequal population. The question now before us is whether the Fourteenth Amendment likewise forbids the election of local government officials from districts of disparate population. As has almost every court which has addressed itself to this question, we hold that it does.

When the State apportions its legislature, it must have due regard for the Equal Protection Clause. Similarly, when the State delegates lawmaking power to local government and provides for the election of local officials from districts specified by statute, ordinance, or local charter, it must insure that those qualified to vote have the right to an equally effective voice in the election process. If voters residing in oversize districts are denied their constitutional right to participate in the election of state legislators, precisely the same kind of deprivation occurs when the members of a city council, school board, or county governing board are elected from districts of substantially unequal population. If the five senators representing a city in the state legislature may not be elected from districts ranging in size from 50,000 to 500,000, neither is it permissible to elect the members of the city council from those same districts. In either case, the votes of some residents have greater weight than those of others; in both cases the equal protection of the laws has been denied.

That the state legislature may itself be properly apportioned does not exempt subdivisions from the Fourteenth Amendment. While state legislatures exercise extensive power over their constituents and over the various units of local government, the States universally leave much policy and decisionmaking to their governmental subdivisions. Legislators enact many laws but do not attempt to reach those countless matters of local concern necessarily left wholly or partly to those who govern at the local level. What is more, in providing for the governments of their cities, counties, towns, and districts, the States characteristically provide for representative government—for decisionmaking at the local level by representatives elected by the people And, not infrequently, the delegation of power to local units is contained in constitutional provisions for local home rule which are immune from legislative interference. In a word, institutions of local government have always been a major aspect of our system, and their responsible and responsive operation is today of increasing importance to the quality of life of more and more of our citizens. We therefore see little difference, in terms of the application of the Equal Protection Clause and of the principles of *Reynolds v. Sims*, between the exercise of state power through legislatures and its exercise by elected officials in the cities, towns, and counties.[6]

We are urged to permit unequal districts for the Midland County Commissioners Court on the ground that the court's functions are not sufficiently "legislative." The parties have devoted much effort to urging that alternative labels — "administrative" versus "legislative" — be applied to the Commissioners Court. As the brief description of the court's functions above amply demonstrates, this unit of local government cannot easily be classified in the neat categories favored by civics texts. The Texas commissioners courts are assigned some tasks which would normally be thought of as "legislative," others typically assigned to "executive" or "administrative" departments, and still others which are "judicial." In this regard Midland County's Commissioners Court is representative of most of the general governing bodies of American cities, counties, towns, and villages. One knowledgeable commentator has written of "the states' varied, pragmatic approach in establishing government." That approach has produced a staggering number of governmental units — the preliminary calculation by the Bureau of the Census for 1967 is that there are 81,304 "units of government" in the United States — and an even more staggering diversity. Nonetheless, while special-purpose organizations abound and in many States the allocation of functions among units results in instances of overlap and vacuum, virtually every American lives within what he and his neighbors regard as a unit of local government with general responsibility and power for local affairs. In many cases citizens reside within and are subject to two such governments, a city and a county.

The Midland County Commissioners Court is such a unit. While the Texas Supreme Court found that the Commissioners Court's legislative functions are "negligible," the court does have power to make a large number of decisions having a broad range of impacts on all the citizens of the county. It sets a tax rate, equalizes assessments, and issues bonds. It then prepares and adopts a budget for allocating the county's funds, and is given by statute a wide range of discretion in choosing the subjects on which to spend. In adopting the budget the court makes both long-term judgments about the way Midland County should develop — whether industry should be solicited, roads improved, recreation facilities built, and land set aside for schools — and immediate choices among competing needs.

The Texas Supreme Court concluded that the work actually done by the Commissioners Court "disproportionately concern[s] the rural areas." Were the Commissioners Court a special-purpose unit of government assigned the performance of functions affecting definable groups of constituents more than other constituents, we would have to confront the question whether such a body may be apportioned in ways which give greater influence to the citizens most affected by the organization's functions. That question, however, is not presented by this case, for while Midland County authorities may concentrate their attention on rural roads, the relevant fact is that the powers of the Commissioners Court include the authority to make a substantial number of decisions that affect all citizens, whether they reside inside or outside the city limits of Midland. The Commissioners maintain buildings, administer welfare services, and determine school districts both inside and outside the city. The taxes imposed by the court fall equally on all

---

6. Inequitable apportionment of local governing bodies offends the Constitution even if adopted by a properly apportioned legislature representing the majority of the State's citizens. The majority of a State — by constitutional provision, by referendum, or through accurately apportioned representatives — can no more place a minority in oversize districts without depriving that minority of equal protection of the laws than they can deprive the minority of the ballot altogether, or impose upon them a tax rate in excess of that to be paid by equally situated members of the majority....

property in the county. Indeed, it may not be mere coincidence that a body apportioned with three of its four voting members chosen by residents of the rural area surrounding the city devotes most of its attention to the problems of that area, while paying for its expenditures with a tax imposed equally on city residents and those who live outside the city. And we might point out that a decision not to exercise a function within the court's power—a decision, for example, not to build an airport or a library, or not to participate in the federal food stamp program—is just as much a decision affecting all citizens of the county as an affirmative decision....

This Court is aware of the immense pressures facing units of local government, and of the greatly varying problems with which they must deal. The Constitution does not require that a uniform straitjacket bind citizens in devising mechanisms of local government suitable for local needs and efficient in solving local problems. Last Term, for example, the Court upheld a procedure for choosing a school board that placed the selection with school boards of component districts even though the component boards had equal votes and served unequal populations. *Sailors v. Board of Education of Kent County*, 387 U.S. 105 (1967). The Court rested on the administrative nature of the area school board's functions and the essentially appointive form of the scheme employed. In *Dusch v. Davis*, 387 U.S. 112 (1967), the Court permitted Virginia Beach to choose its legislative body by a scheme that included at-large voting for candidates, some of whom had to be residents of particular districts, even though the residence districts varied widely in population....

Mr. Justice HARLAN, dissenting.

... The argument most generally heard for justifying the entry of the federal courts into the field of state legislative apportionment is that since state legislatures had widely failed to correct serious malapportionments in their own structure, and since no other means of redress had proved available through the political process, this Court was entitled to step into the picture. While I continue to reject that thesis as furnishing an excuse for the federal judiciary's straying outside its proper constitutional role, and while I continue to believe that it bodes ill for the country and the entire federal judicial system if this Court does not firmly set its face against this loose and short-sighted point of view, the important thing for present purposes is that no such justification can be brought to bear in this instance.

No claim is made in this case that avenues of political redress are not open to correct any malapportionment in elective local governmental units, and it is difficult to envisage how such a situation could arise. Local governments are creatures of the States, and they may be reformed either by the state legislatures, which are now required to be apportioned according to *Reynolds*, or by amendment of state constitutions. In these circumstances, the argument of practical necessity has no force. The Court, then, should withhold its hand until such a supposed necessity does arise, before intruding itself into the business of restructuring local governments across the country....

The present case affords one example of why the "one man, one vote" rule is especially inappropriate for local governmental units. The Texas Supreme Court held as a matter of Texas law:

> Theoretically, the commissioners court is the governing body of the county and the commissioners represent all the residents, both urban and rural, of the county. But developments during the years have greatly narrowed the scope of the functions of the commissioners court and limited its major responsibilities to the nonurban areas of the county. It has come to pass that the city government ... is the major concern of the city dwellers and the administration of the affairs of the county is the major concern of the rural dwellers.

Despite the specialized role of the commissioners court, the majority has undertaken to bring it within the ambit of *Reynolds* simply by classifying it as "a unit of local government with general responsibility and power for local affairs." Although this approach is intended to afford "equal protection" to all voters in Midland County, it would seem that it in fact discriminates against the county's rural inhabitants. The commissioners court, as found by the Texas Supreme Court, performs more functions in the area of the county outside Midland City than it does within the city limits. Therefore, each rural resident has a greater interest in its activities than each city dweller. Yet under the majority's formula the urban residents are to have a dominant voice in the county government, precisely proportional to their numbers, and little or no allowance may be made for the greater stake of the rural inhabitants in the county government.

This problem is not a trivial one and is not confined to Midland County. It stems from the fact that local governments, unlike state governments, are often specialized in function. Application of the *Reynolds* rule to such local governments prevents the adoption of apportionments which take into account the effect of this specialization, and therefore may result in a denial of equal treatment to those upon whom the exercise of the special powers has unequal impact. Under today's decision, the only apparent alternative is to classify the governmental unit as other than "general" in power and responsibility, thereby, presumably, avoiding application of the *Reynolds* rule....

A common pattern of development in the Nation's urban areas has been for the less affluent citizens to migrate to or remain within the central city, while the more wealthy move to the suburbs and come into the city only to work. The result has been to impose a relatively heavier tax burden upon city taxpayers and to fragmentize governmental services in the metropolitan area. An oft-proposed solution to these problems has been the institution of an integrated government encompassing the entire metropolitan area. In many instances, the suburbs may be included in such a metropolitan unit only by majority vote of the voters in each suburb. As a practical matter the suburbanites often will be reluctant to join the metropolitan government unless they receive a share in the government proportional to the benefits they bring with them and not merely to their numbers. The city dwellers may be ready to concede this much, in return for the ability to tax the suburbs. Under the majority's pronouncements, however, this rational compromise would be forbidden: the metropolitan government must be apportioned solely on the basis of population if it is a "general" government....

Mr. Justice FORTAS, dissenting.

I submit that the problem presented by many, perhaps most, county governments (and by Midland County in particular) is precisely the same as those arising from special-purpose units. The functions of many county governing boards, no less than the governing bodies of special-purpose units, have only slight impact on some of their constituents and a vast and direct impact on others. They affect different citizens residing within their geographical jurisdictions in drastically different ways.

Study of county government leaves one with two clear impressions: that the variations from unit to unit are great; and that the role and structure of county government are currently in a state of flux. County governments differ in every significant way: number of constituents, area governed, number of competing or overlapping government units within the county, form, and means of selection of the governing board, services provided, the number and functions of independent county officials, and sources of revenue.

Some generalizations can be made about county governments. First, most counties today perform certain basic functions delegated by the State: assessment of property, collection of property taxes, recording of deeds and other documents, maintenance of rural roads, poor relief, law enforcement, and the administration of electoral and judicial functions. Some counties have begun to do more, especially by the assumption of municipal and policy-making functions. But most counties still act largely as administrative instrumentalities of the State.

Second, "[t]he absence of a single chief executive and diffusion of responsibility among numerous independently elected officials are general characteristics of county government in the United States." Those who have written on the subject have invariably pointed to the extensive powers exercised within the geographical region of the county by officials elected on a countywide basis and by special districts organized to perform specific tasks. Often these independent officials and organs perform crucial functions of great importance to all the people within the county.

These generalizations apply with particular force in this case. The population of Midland County is chiefly in a single urban area. That urban area has its own municipal government which, because of home rule, has relative autonomy and authority to deal with urban problems. In contrast, the Midland County government, like county governments generally, acts primarily as an administrative arm of the State. It provides a convenient agency for the State to collect taxes, hold elections, administer judicial and peace-keeping functions, improve roads, and perform other functions which are the ordinary duties of the State. The powers of the Commissioners Court, which is the governing body of Midland County, are strictly limited by statute and constitutional provision. Although a mere listing of these authorizing statutes and constitutional provisions would seem to indicate that the Commissioners Court has significant and general power, this impression is somewhat illusory because very often the provisions which grant the power also circumscribe its exercise with detailed limitations.

For example, the petitioner cites [provisions] granting the Commissioners Court authority to levy taxes. Yet, at the time this suit was tried, ... no county could levy a tax in excess of 80 cents on $100 property valuation. And ... that 80 cents [was allocated] among the four "constitutional purposes" ... (not more than 25 cents for general county purposes, not more than 15 cents for the jury fund, not more than 15 cents for roads and bridges, and not more than 25 cents for permanent improvements).

Another example is the authority to issue bonds. It is true, as the majority notes, that the Commissioners Court does have this authority. Yet ... a detailed code [regulates] how and for what purposes bonds may be issued. Significantly, ... county bonds "shall never be issued for any purpose" unless the bond issue has been submitted to the qualified property-taxpaying voters of the county.

More important than the statutory and constitutional limitations, the limited power and function of the Commissioners Court are reflected in what it actually does. The record and briefs do not give a complete picture of the workings of the Commissioners Court. But it is apparent that the Commissioners are primarily concerned with rural affairs, and more particularly with rural roads....

Substance, not shibboleth, should govern in this admittedly complex and subtle area; and the substance is that the geographical extent of the Commissioners Court is of very limited meaning. Midland County's Commissioners Court has its primary focus in nonurban areas and upon the nonurban people. True, the county's revenues come largely from the City of Midland. But the Commissioners Court fixes the tax rate subject to the specific limitations provided by the legislature. It must spend tax revenues in the categories and percentages which the legislature fixes. Taxes are assessed and collected, not by it,

but by an official elected on a countywide basis. It is quite likely that if the city dwellers
were given control of the Commissioners Court, they would reduce the load because it
is spent primarily in the rural area. This is a state matter. If the State Legislature, in which
presumably the city dwellers are fairly represented (*Reynolds v. Sims*), wishes to reduce the
load, it may do so. But unless we are ready to adopt the position that the Federal Constitution forbids a State from taxing city dwellers to aid their rural neighbors, the fact
that city dwellers pay most taxes should not determine the composition of the county
governing body. We should not use tax impact as the sole or controlling basis for vote
distribution. It is merely one in a number of factors, including the functional impact of
the county government, which should be taken into account in determining whether a particular voting arrangement results in reasonable recognition of the rights and interests of
citizens. Certainly, neither tax impact nor the relatively few services rendered within the
City of Midland should compel the State to vest practically all voting power in the city residents to the virtual denial of a voice to those who are dependent on the county government for roads, welfare, and other essential services.

Texas should have a chance to devise a scheme which, within wide tolerance, eliminates
the gross underrepresentation of the city, but at the same time provides an adequate, effective voice for the nonurban, as well as the urban, areas and peoples.

[Justice STEWART also dissented.]

Notes and Questions

1. In *Board of Estimate v. Morris*, 489 U.S. 688 (1989), the Court struck down the system for selecting the membership of the New York City Board of Estimate, which had
significant budgetary and other fiscal authority. Three members of the Board, who cast
two votes each, were the mayor and two other officials who were elected citywide. The remaining members were the five borough presidents, each of whom was elected within
his or her respective borough. The populations of the boroughs were unequal by a big margin. How can *Morris* be distinguished from *Sailors v. Board of Education*, described in
the majority opinion in *Avery*?

Should the fact that the members who were elected citywide could control the Board
on most issues have led the *Morris* Court to uphold the Board's structure? Justice White,
writing for the Court, responded as follows:

> The city ... erroneously implies that the Board's composition survives constitu-
> tional challenge because the citywide members cast a 6–5 majority of board votes
> and hence are in position to control the outcome of board actions. The at-large
> members, however, as the courts below observed, often do not vote together;
> and when they do not, the outcome is determined by the votes of the borough
> presidents, each having one vote. Two citywide members, with the help of the
> presidents of the two least populous boroughs, the Bronx and Staten Island, will
> prevail over a disagreeing coalition of the third citywide member and the pres-
> idents of the three boroughs that contain a large majority of the city's popula-
> tion. Furthermore, because the Mayor has no vote on budget issues, the citywide
> members alone cannot control board budgetary decisions.

If the Mayor were permitted to vote on budgetary issues and if evidence showed that the
citywide members of the Board usually voted as a bloc, would the result in *Morris* be different?

In some states, especially in the South, all state legislators elected from a county are formally or informally constituted as the "delegation" from that county. As a practical mat-

ter, these delegations are often given virtually complete control over legislation affecting that county. Because of the need to comply with one person, one vote, the delegation may consist of a mixture of representatives whose districts are entirely or only partially within the county. See generally Binny Miller, *Who Shall Rule and Govern? Local Legislative Delegations, Racial Politics, and the Voting Rights Act*, 102 YALE LAW JOURNAL 105 (1992). Suppose a county contains two legislative districts entirely within the county and one-tenth of an additional district. Could residents of the fully contained districts challenge the make-up of the county's delegation on the ground that in-county residents of the fractional district have ten times more voting power on the delegation than members of the fully contained districts? See *Vander Linden v. Hodges*, 193 F.3d 268 (4th Cir. 1999).

2. Do you agree with the *Sailors* exception to the one person, one vote rule for "appointed" bodies? How would you determine if a body is "appointive" or "elective"?

Consider *Cunningham v. Municipality of Metropolitan Seattle*, 751 F.Supp. 885 (W.D.Wash. 1990). The Municipality of Metropolitan Seattle ("Metro") was created to control water pollution in King County, Washington. The 42 members of its governing council were chosen by various methods. 24 were county or city elected officials who automatically became members of the Metro Council. Most of the rest were also elected local officials who did not automatically become members upon election but were chosen by the bodies on which they sat. For example, in a number of cities the mayor and city council selected a representative to the Metro Council from their own number. The *Cunningham* court was willing to assume that those who did not become members of the council automatically on election to their local office could be considered "appointive" rather than "elective." Nevertheless, the court found that the council as a whole was an elective body, because a majority of its members were elective. Since the one person, one vote standard was not satisfied, the Metro Council structure was declared unconstitutional.

The *Cunningham* approach could lead to some odd results. In *Cunningham*, all the members of the Seattle city council were members of the Metro Council, and therefore were regarded as elective rather than appointive members. This fact was decisive, because if the Seattle delegation had been appointive, so would a majority of the Metro Council, so that the council would have been treated as appointive under the *Cunningham* approach. The legislature could have avoided the constitutional violation by reducing the Seattle delegation, thus requiring appointment of some percentage of the Seattle city council members, in which case a majority of the Metro Council would have been appointive. Suppose Seattle voters had been underrepresented on the council, despite the entire city council sitting as Metro Council members.[f] In that hypothetical situation, the *Cunningham* court's approach apparently would have permitted the legislature to remedy the problem by aggravating Seattle's underrepresentation!

Does *Cunningham* lend credence to Justice Harlan's concern, expressed in his *Avery* dissent, that application of the one person, one vote rule to local government would discourage the formation of metropolitan government entities like Metro? The *Cunningham* court stated, without citing evidentiary support, that "[t]here is no reason to believe that the vigorous governments and citizens of this region will fail to make Metro a continuing success if a change in the method of selecting its council is required to meet constitutional standards." 751 F.Supp. at 889.

3. The Supreme Court affirmed summarily (i.e., without hearing oral argument or issuing an opinion) a lower-court decision upholding the election of justices to the Louisiana

---

f. In the actual *Cunningham* case, Seattle was overrepresented.

Supreme Court from unequally populated districts. *Wells v. Edwards*, 409 U.S. 1095 (1973). Justices White, Douglas, and Marshall dissented.

4. In *Hadley v. Junior College District*, 397 U.S. 50 (1970), the Court imposed the one person, one vote doctrine on a consolidated junior college district. The Court said constitutional distinctions could not "be drawn on the basis of the purpose of the election.... While there are differences in the powers of different officials, the crucial consideration is the right of each qualified voter to participate on an equal footing in the election process." 397 U.S. at 55. The Court went on to say that if the purpose of the election were determinative courts would have to distinguish between various elections. The Court could not "readily perceive judicially manageable standards to aid in such a task." However, the Court also said:

> It is of course possible that there might be some case in which a State elects certain functionaries whose duties are so far removed from normal governmental activities and so disproportionately affect different groups that a popular election in compliance with *Reynolds*, ... might not be required.

Id. at 56. Is this last quotation from *Hadley* consistent with the earlier two?

Was the result in *Wells v. Edwards*, Note 3, *supra*, consistent with *Hadley*? Did "judicially manageable standards" for distinguishing elections that are subject to the one person-one vote requirement from those that are not emerge in the *Salyer Land* and *Ball* cases, reprinted below?

II. Voting, Representation, and "Special-Purpose" Elections

Salyer Land Co. v. Tulare Lake Basin Water Storage District
410 U.S. 719 (1973)

Mr. Justice REHNQUIST delivered the opinion of the Court.

... We are here presented with the issue expressly reserved in *Avery*:

> Were the [county's governing body] a special-purpose unit of government assigned the performance of functions affecting definable groups of constituents more than other constituents, we would have to confront the question whether such a body may be apportioned in ways which give greater influence to the citizens most affected by the organization's functions.

The particular type of local government unit whose organization is challenged on constitutional grounds in this case is a water storage district, organized pursuant to the California Water Storage District Act....

Appellee district consists of 193,000 acres of intensively cultivated, highly fertile farm land located in the Tulare Lake Basin. Its population consists of 77 persons, including 18 children, most of whom are employees of one or another of the four corporations that farm 85% of the land in the district.

Such districts are authorized to plan projects and execute approved projects "for the acquisition, appropriation, diversion, storage, conservation, and distribution of water...." Incidental to this general power, districts may "acquire, improve, and operate" any necessary works for the storage and distribution of water as well as any drainage or reclamation works connected therewith, and the generation and distribution of hydroelectric power may be provided for. They may fix tolls and charges for the use of water and collect them from all persons receiving the benefit of the water or other services in proportion to the services rendered. The costs of the projects are assessed against district land in accordance with the benefits accruing to each tract held in separate ownership. And land that is not benefited may be withdrawn from the district on petition.

Governance of the districts is undertaken by a board of directors. Each director is elected from one of the divisions within the district, and each must take an official oath and execute a bond....

It is the voter qualification for such elections that appellants claim invidiously discriminates against them and persons similarly situated. Appellants are landowners, a landowner-lessee, and residents within the area included in the appellee's water storage district.... They allege that [the procedures for electing board members] unconstitutionally deny to them the equal protection of the laws guaranteed by the Fourteenth Amendment, in that only landowners are permitted to vote in water storage district general elections, and votes in those elections are apportioned according to the assessed valuation of the land....

I

It is first argued that [California Water Code] §41000, limiting the vote to district landowners, is unconstitutional since nonlandowning residents have as much interest in the operations of a district as landowners who may or may not be residents. Particularly, it is pointed out that the homes of residents may be damaged by floods within the district's boundaries, and that floods may, as with appellant Ellison, cause them to lose their jobs. Support for this position is said to come from the recent decisions of this Court striking down various state laws that limited voting to landowners, *Kolodziejski*, *Cipriano*, and *Kramer*....

Cipriano and *Phoenix* involved application of the "one person, one vote" principle to residents of units of local governments exercising general governmental power, as that term was defined in *Avery*. *Kramer* and *Hadley* extended the "one person, one vote" principle to school districts exercising powers which,

> while not fully as broad as those of the Midland County Commissioners, certainly show that the trustees perform important governmental functions within the districts, and we think these powers are general enough and have sufficient impact throughout the district to justify the conclusion that the principle which we applied in *Avery* should also be applied here. [*Hadley*.]

But the Court was also careful to state that:

> It is of course possible that there might be some case in which a State elects certain functionaries whose duties are so far removed from normal governmental activities and so disproportionately affect different groups that a popular election in compliance with *Reynolds* might not be required, but certainly we see nothing in the present case that indicates that the activities of these trustees fit in that category. Education has traditionally been a vital governmental function and these trustees, whose election the State has opened to all qualified voters, are governmental officials in every relevant sense of that term.

We conclude that the appellee water storage district, by reason of its special limited purpose and of the disproportionate effect of its activities on landowners as a group, is the sort of exception to the rule laid down in *Reynolds* which the quoted language from *Hadley* and the decision in *Avery* contemplated.

The appellee district in this case, although vested with some typical governmental powers,[7] has relatively limited authority. Its primary purpose, indeed the reason for its existence, is to provide for the acquisition, storage, and distribution of water for farming in the Tulare Lake Basin.[8] It provides no other general public services such as schools, housing, transportation, utilities, roads, or anything else of the type ordinarily financed by a municipal body. There are no towns, shops, hospitals, or other facilities designed to improve the quality of life within the district boundaries, and it does not have a fire department, police, buses, or trains.

Not only does the district not exercise what might be thought of as "normal governmental" authority, but its actions disproportionately affect landowners. All of the costs of district projects are assessed against land by assessors in proportion to the benefits received. Likewise, charges for services rendered are collectible from persons receiving their benefit in proportion to the services. When such persons are delinquent in payment, just as in the case of delinquency in payments of assessments, such charges become a lien on the land. In short, there is no way that the economic burdens of district operations can fall on residents *qua* residents, and the operations of the districts primarily affect the land within their boundaries.

Under these circumstances, it is quite understandable that the statutory framework for election of directors of the appellee focuses on the land benefited, rather than on people as such. California has not opened the franchise to all residents, as Missouri had in *Hadley*, nor to all residents with some exceptions, as New York had in *Kramer*. The franchise is extended to landowners, whether they reside in the district or out of it, and indeed whether or not they are natural persons who would be entitled to vote in a more traditional political election. Appellants do not challenge the enfranchisement of nonresident landowners or of corporate landowners for purposes of election of the directors of appellee. Thus, to sustain their contention that all residents of the district must be accorded a vote would not result merely in the striking down of an exclusion from what was otherwise a delineated class, but would instead engraft onto the statutory scheme a wholly new class of voters in addition to those enfranchised by the statute.

We hold, therefore, that the popular election requirements enunciated by *Reynolds* and succeeding cases are inapplicable to elections such as the general election of appellee Water Storage District.

II

Even though appellants derive no benefit from the *Reynolds* and *Kramer* lines of cases, they are, of course, entitled to have their equal protection claim assessed to determine whether the State's decision to deny the franchise to residents of the district while granting it to landowners was "wholly irrelevant to achievement of the regulation's objectives."

---

7. The board has the power to employ and discharge persons on a regular staff and to contract for the construction of district projects. It can condemn private property for use in such projects and may cooperate (including contract) with other agencies, state and federal. Both general obligation bonds and interest-bearing warrants may be authorized.

8. Appellants strongly urge that districts have the power to, and do, engage in flood control activities. The interest of such activities to residents is said to be obvious since houses may be destroyed and as in the case of appellant Ellison, jobs may disappear. But Calif. Water Code §43151 provides that any agreement entered into with the State or the United States must be "for a purpose appertaining to or beneficial to the project of the district...." And the statute which assertedly gives support to the flood control activities, simply states that a district "may cooperate and contract with the state ... or the United States" for the purpose of "flood control." Thus, any flood control activities are incident to the exercise of the district's primary functions of water storage and distribution.

No doubt residents within the district may be affected by its activities. But this argument proves too much. Since assessments imposed by the district become a cost of doing business for those who farm within it, and that cost must ultimately be passed along to the consumers of the produce, food shoppers in far away metropolitan areas are to some extent likewise "affected" by the activities of the district. Constitutional adjudication cannot rest on any such "house that Jack built" foundation, however. The California Legislature could quite reasonably have concluded that the number of landowners and owners of sufficient amounts of acreage whose consent was necessary to organize the district would not have subjected their land to the lien of its possibly very substantial assessments unless they had a dominant voice in its control. Since the subjection of the owners' lands to such liens was the basis by which the district was to obtain financing, the proposed district had as a practical matter to attract landowner support. Nor, since assessments against landowners were to be the sole means by which the expenses of the district were to be paid, could it be said to be unfair or inequitable to repose the franchise in landowners but not residents. Landowners as a class were to bear the entire burden of the district's costs, and the State could rationally conclude that they, to the exclusion of residents, should be charged with responsibility for its operation. We conclude, therefore, that nothing in the Equal Protection Clause precluded California from limiting the voting for directors of appellee district by totally excluding those who merely reside within the district.

III

Appellants assert that even if residents may be excluded from the vote, lessees who farm the land have interests that are indistinguishable from those of the landowners. Like landowners, they take an interest in increasing the available water for farming and, because the costs of district projects may be passed on to them either by express agreement or by increased rentals, they have an equal interest in the costs.

Lessees undoubtedly do have an interest in the activities of appellee district analogous to that of landowners in many respects. But in the type of special district we now have before us, the question for our determination is not whether or not we would have lumped them together had we been enacting the statute in question, but instead whether "if any state of facts reasonably may be conceived to justify" California's decision to deny the franchise to lessees while granting it to landowners.

The term "lessees" may embrace the holders of a wide spectrum of leasehold interests in land, from the month-to-month tenant holding under an oral lease, on the one hand, to the long-term lessee holding under a carefully negotiated written lease, on the other. The system which permitted a lessee for a very short term to vote might easily lend itself to manipulation on the part of large landowners because of the ease with which such landowners could create short-term interests on the part of loyal employees. And, even apart from the fear of such manipulation, California may well have felt that landowners would be unwilling to join in the forming of a water storage district if short-term lessees whose fortunes were not in the long run tied to the land were to have a major vote in the affairs of the district.

The administration of a voting system which allowed short-term lessees to vote could also pose significant difficulties. Apparently, assessment rolls as well as state and federal land lists are used by election boards in determining the qualifications of the voters. Such lists, obviously, would not ordinarily disclose either long- or short-term leaseholds....

Finally, we note that California has not left the lessee without remedy for his disenfranchised state. Sections 41002 and 41005 of the California Water Code provide for voting in the general election by proxy. To the extent that a lessee entering into a lease of substantial duration, thereby likening his status more to that of a landowner, feels that the right to vote in the election of directors of the district is of sufficient import to him, he may bargain for that right at the time he negotiates his lease. And the longer the term of the lease, and the more the interest of the lessee becomes akin to that of the landowner, presumably the more willing the lessor will be to assign his right. Just as the lessee may by contract be required to reimburse the lessor for the district assessments so he may by contract acquire the right to vote for district directors.

Under these circumstances, the exclusion of lessees from voting in general elections for the directors of the district does not violate the Equal Protection Clause.

IV

The last claim by appellants is that §41001, which weights the vote according to assessed valuation of the land, is unconstitutional. They point to the fact that several of the smaller landowners have only one vote per person whereas the J. G. Boswell Company has 37,825 votes, and they place reliance on the various decisions of this Court holding that wealth has no relation to resident-voter qualifications and that equality of voting power may not be evaded. See, *e.g.*, *Gray*; *Harper*.

Appellants' argument ignores the realities of water storage district operation. Since its formation in 1926, appellee district has put into operation four multimillion-dollar projects. The last project involved the construction of two laterals from the Basin to the California State Aqueduct at a capital cost of about $2,500,000. Three small landowners having land aggregating somewhat under four acres with an assessed valuation of under $100 were given one vote each in the special election held for the approval of the project. The J. G. Boswell Company, which owns 61,665.54 acres with an assessed valuation of $3,782,220 was entitled to cast 37,825 votes in the election. By the same token, however, the assessment commissioners determined that the benefits of the project would be uniform as to all of the acres affected, and assessed the project equally as to all acreage. Each acre has to bear $13.26 of cost and the three small landowners, therefore, must pay a total of $46, whereas the company must pay $817,685 for its part.[10] Thus, as the District Court found, "the benefits and burdens to each landowner ... are in proportion to the assessed value of the land." We cannot say that the California legislative decision to permit voting in the same proportion is not rationally based.

Accordingly, we ... hold that the voter qualification statutes for California water storage district elections are rationally based, and therefore do not violate the Equal Protection Clause.

Mr. Justice DOUGLAS, with whom Mr. Justice BRENNAN and Mr. Justice MARSHALL concur, dissenting.

The vices of this case are fourfold.

First. Lessees of farmlands, though residents of the district, are not given the franchise.

---

10. [S]mall landowners are protected from crippling assessments resulting from district projects by the dual vote which must be taken in order to approve a project. Not only must a majority of the votes be cast for approval, but also a majority of the voters must approve. In this case, about 189 landowners constitute a majority and 189 of the smallest landowners in the district have only 2.34% of the land.

Second. Residents who own no agricultural lands but live in the district and face all the perils of flood which the district is supposed to control are disfranchised.

Third. Only agricultural landowners are entitled to vote and their vote is weighted, one vote for each one hundred dollars of assessed valuation....

Fourth. The corporate voter is put in the saddle.

There are 189 landowners who own up to 80 acres each. These 189 represent 2.34% of the agricultural acreage of the district. There are 193,000 acres in the district. Petitioner Salyer Land Co. is one large operator, West Lake Farms and South Lake Farms are also large operators. The largest is J. G. Boswell Co. These four farm almost 85% of all the land in the district. Of these, J. G. Boswell Co. commands the greatest number of votes, 37,825, which are enough to give it a majority of the board of directors. As a result, it is permanently in the saddle. Almost all of the 77 residents of the district are disfranchised. The hold of J. G. Boswell Co. is so strong that there has been no election since 1947, making little point of the provision in §41300 of the California Water Code for an election every other year.

The result has been calamitous to some who, though landless, have even more to fear from floods than the ephemeral corporation.

I

... Assuming, *arguendo*, that a State may, in some circumstances, limit the franchise to that portion of the electorate "primarily affected" by the outcome of an election, *Kramer*, the limitation may only be upheld if it is demonstrated that "all those excluded are in fact substantially less interested or affected than those the [franchise] includes." *Ibid.* The majority concludes that "there is no way that the economic burdens of district operations can fall on residents *qua* residents, and the operations of the districts primarily affect the land within their boundaries."

But, with all respect, that is a great distortion. In these arid areas of our Nation a water district seeks water in time of drought and fights it in time of flood. One of the functions of water districts in California is to manage flood control. That is general California statutory policy. It is expressly stated in the Water Code that governs water districts. The California Supreme Court ruled some years back that flood control and irrigation are different but complementary aspects of one problem.

From its inception in 1926, this district has had repeated flood control problems. Four rivers, Kings, Kern, Tule, and Kaweah, enter Tulare Lake Basin. South of Tulare Lake Basin is Buena Vista Lake. In the past, Buena Vista has been used to protect Tulare Lake Basin by storing Kern River water in the former. That is how Tulare Lake Basin was protected from menacing floods in 1952. But that was not done in the great 1969 flood, the result being that 88,000 of the 193,000 acres in respondent district were flooded. The board of the respondent district — dominated by the big landowner J. G. Boswell Co. — voted 6–4 to table the motion that would put into operation the machinery to divert the flood waters to the Buena Vista Lake. The reason is that J. G. Boswell Co. had a long-term agricultural lease in the Buena Vista Lake Basin and flooding it would have interfered with the planting, growing, and harvesting of crops the next season.

The result was that water in the Tulare Lake Basin rose to 192.5 USGS datum. Ellison, one of the appellants who lives in the district, is not an agricultural landowner. But his residence was 15 1/2 feet below the water level of the crest of the flood in 1969.

The appellee district has large levees; and if they are broken, damage to houses and loss of life are imminent.

Landowners — large or small, resident or nonresident, lessees or landlords, share-croppers or owners — all should have a say. But irrigation, water storage, the building of levees, and flood control, implicate the entire community. All residents of the district must be granted the franchise.

This case, as I will discuss below, involves the performance of vital and important governmental functions by water districts clothed with much of the paraphernalia of government. The weighting of votes according to one's wealth is hostile to our system of government. As a nonlandowning bachelor was held to be entitled to vote on matters affecting education, *Kramer*, so all the prospective victims of mismanaged flood control projects should be entitled to vote in water district elections, whether they be resident nonlandowners, resident or nonresident lessees, and whether they own 10 acres or 10,000 acres. Moreover, their votes should be equal regardless of the value of their holdings, for when it comes to performance of governmental functions all enter the polls on an equal basis.

The majority, however, would distinguish the water storage district from "units of local government having general governmental powers over the entire geographic area served by the body," *Avery*, and fit this case within the exception contemplated for "a special-purpose unit of government assigned the performance of functions affecting definable groups of constituents more than other constituents." *Id.* The Avery test was significantly liberalized in *Hadley.* ... We said,

> [S]ince the [junior college] trustees can levy and collect taxes, issue bonds with certain restrictions, hire and fire teachers, make contracts, collect fees, supervise and discipline students, pass on petitions to annex school districts, acquire property by condemnation, and in general manage the operations of the junior college, their powers are equivalent, for apportionment purposes, to those exercised by the county commissioners in *Avery.* ... [T]hese powers, while not fully as broad as those of the Midland County Commissioners, certainly show that the trustees *perform important governmental functions* ... and have *sufficient impact throughout the district* to justify the conclusion that the principle which we applied in *Avery* should also be applied here. (Emphasis added.)

Measured by the *Hadley* test, the Tulare Lake Basin Water Storage District surely performs "important governmental functions" which "have sufficient impact throughout the district" to justify the application of the *Avery* principle.

Water storage districts in California are classified as irrigation, reclamation, or drainage districts. Such state agencies "are considered exclusively governmental," and their property is "held only for governmental purpose," not in the "proprietary sense." They are a "public entity," just as "any other political subdivision." That is made explicit in various ways. The Water Code of California states that "[a]ll waters and water rights" of the State "within the district are given, dedicated, and set apart for the uses and purposes of the district." Directors of the district are "public officers of the state." The district possesses the power of eminent domain. Its works may not be taxed. It carries a governmental immunity against suit. A district has powers that relate to irrigation, storage of water, drainage, flood control, and generation of hydroelectric energy.

Whatever may be the parameters of the exception alluded to in *Avery* and *Hadley*, I cannot conclude that this water storage district escapes the constitutional restraints relative to a franchise within a governmental unit.

II

When we decided *Reynolds* and discussed the problems of malapportionment we thought and talked about people—of population, of the constitutional right of "qualified citizens to vote," of "the right of suffrage," of the comparison of "one man's vote" to that of another man's vote....

It is indeed grotesque to think of corporations voting within the framework of political representation of people. Corporations were held to be "persons" for purposes both of the Due Process Clause of the Fourteenth Amendment and of the Equal Protection Clause. Yet, it is unthinkable in terms of the American tradition that corporations should be admitted to the franchise. Could a State allot voting rights to its corporations, weighting each vote according to the wealth of the corporation? Or could it follow the rule of one corporation, one vote?

It would be a radical and revolutionary step to take, as it would change our whole concept of the franchise. California takes part of that step here by allowing corporations to vote in these water district matters that entail performance of vital governmental functions. One corporation can outvote 77 individuals in this district. Four corporations can exercise these governmental powers as they choose, leaving every individual inhabitant with a weak, ineffective voice. The result is a corporate political kingdom undreamed of by those who wrote our Constitution.

Notes and Questions

1. The majority notes that voting by corporations and non-resident landowners was not challenged. Why do you think this was the case? Would appellants have strengthened or weakened their chances of winning if they had urged that only residents should be permitted to vote?

2. Is Part II of Justice Douglas' dissenting opinion consistent with Part I?

3. California Elections Code §18521 provides in part:

A person shall not ... receive, agree, or contract for ... any money ... or other valuable consideration ... because he ... :

(a) Voted, agreed to vote, refrained from voting, or agreed to refrain from voting for any particular person....

This section is not expressly applicable to water storage district elections, which are governed by the Water Code. Would such a provision be desirable from the majority's point of view? From Justice Douglas' point of view? From your point of view?

4. Mary is employed by Boswell and has been elected to one of the Water Storage District board seats controlled by Boswell. She asks you for legal advice prior to the vote on whether to divert the flood waters to Buena Vista Lake under circumstances identical to those described by Justice Douglas. Boswell has instructed Mary to vote against diversion. She believes the residents of the district would benefit from diversion and that the benefits of diversion to other companies with land in the district would be even greater than the very substantial costs diversion will impose on Boswell. How would you advise Mary?

5. Suppose it were the case that diversion of flood waters would benefit Salyer Land but harm Boswell, and that the benefit to Salyer Land would be greater than the loss to Boswell. Would it be proper for Salyer Land to pay Boswell to instruct its representatives on the board to vote for diversion?

6. Is *Salyer* consistent with the Court's earlier decisions? Consider Richard Briffault, *Who Rules at Home? One Person/One Vote and Local Governments*, 60 UNIVERSITY OF CHICAGO LAW REVIEW 339, 361–62 (1993):

> The Court in *Salyer* was markedly more deferential to state determinations concerning local arrangements and much less protective of the interest of local residents in voting in local elections than it had been previously. The Court predicated the exception from the model of local democratic government on the "special limited purpose" of the water storage district and the "disproportionate effect of its activities on landowners." But neither "special limited purpose," nor "disproportionate effect" was adequately defined.
>
> From the perspective of residents dependent on the district's water, it is not obvious that water storage is a more limited function than a junior college. Indeed, comparing governmental functions is just the sort of standardless exercise that *Hadley* had warned against in refusing to hinge the standard of review on the "importance" of an office. Furthermore, although the California water storage district legislation established a fairly tight nexus linking receipt of water, assessment for water project costs, and the local vote, the Court did not explain how the water district arrangement differed from the service-payment-franchise relationship in *Kramer*. Much as nonparents and nontaxpayers may be affected by the operations of a local school board, water storage district residents as well as landowners may be affected by district actions.

7. Would it be unconstitutional if only owners of land in the district were eligible for election to the board? In Missouri, the state constitution provided for appointment of a board to recommend to the voters a plan of local government reorganization for the St. Louis area. Membership on this board was limited to landowners. In *Quinn v. Millsap*, 491 U.S. 95 (1989), the Court struck down this requirement as a denial of equal protection to non-landowners who were denied the right to serve. *Salyer Land* and *Ball v. James*, *infra*, were distinguished on the ground that the St. Louis government reorganization plan was not as directly connected to landownership as the water operations of the districts in *Salyer* and *Ball*.

Suppose that landownership within the Tulare Lake Basin Water Storage District were a qualification for service on the board of directors and that this qualification were challenged by Boswell on the ground that none of the persons it wished to "elect" to the board owned land in the district. What result?

8. In BALL v. JAMES, 451 U.S. 355 (1981), the Court rejected a challenge to the one acre, one vote system used to elect the board of the Salt River Project Agricultural Improvement and Power District, which stored and delivered water to landowners in a large part of central Arizona. The district had begun as a private association of farmers in the late 19th century, though it had received federal assistance since 1903. In 1906, it began supporting its water operations by generating and selling hydroelectric power. It converted into a public district under Arizona law to obtain relief from financial difficulties during the Depression. By converting, the District's bonds became exempt from federal taxation. However, the conversion was not accomplished until the Arizona statutes were amended to permit the acreage-based voting system.

By the time of this law suit, the district included almost half Arizona's population and provided electric power to a large part of Phoenix and other cities. Furthermore, although the landowner-voters who received subsidized water were theoretically subject to assessments on their land to support the district, since 1951 no assessments had been needed because of the revenues from the sale of electricity. Excerpts from Justice Stewart's opinion for the Court follow:

"First, the District simply does not exercise the sort of governmental powers that invoke the strict demands of *Reynolds*. The District cannot impose ad valorem property taxes or sales taxes. It cannot enact any laws governing the conduct of citizens, nor does it administer such normal functions of government as the maintenance of streets, the operation of schools, or sanitation, health, or welfare services.

"Second..., the District's water functions, which constitute the primary and originating purpose of the District, are relatively narrow. The District and Association do not own, sell, or buy water, nor do they control the use of any water they have delivered. The District simply stores water behind its dams, conserves it from loss, and delivers it through project canals.... [A]ll water delivered by the Salt River District, like the water delivered by the Tulare Lake Basin Water Storage District, is distributed according to land ownership, and the District does not and cannot control the use to which the landowners who are entitled to the water choose to put it. As repeatedly recognized by the Arizona courts, though the state legislature has allowed water districts to become nominal public entities in order to obtain inexpensive bond financing, the districts remain essentially business enterprises, created by and chiefly benefiting a specific group of landowners. As in *Salyer*, the nominal public character of such an entity cannot transform it into the type of governmental body for which the Fourteenth Amendment demands a one-person, one-vote system of election.

"Finally, neither the existence nor size of the District's power business affects the legality of its property-based voting scheme. [T]he provision of electricity is not a traditional element of governmental sovereignty, and so is not in itself the sort of general or important governmental function that would make the government provider subject to the doctrine of the *Reynolds* case. In any event, since the electric power functions were stipulated to be incidental to the water functions which are the District's primary purpose, they cannot change the character of that enterprise. The Arizona Legislature permitted the District to generate and sell electricity to subsidize the water operations which were the beneficiaries intended by the statute. A key part of the *Salyer* decision was that the voting scheme for a public entity like a water district may constitutionally reflect the narrow primary purpose for which the district is created. In this case, the parties have stipulated that the primary legislative purpose of the District is to store, conserve, and deliver water for use by District landowners, that the sole legislative reason for making water projects public entities was to enable them to raise revenue through interest-free bonds, and that the development and sale of electric power was undertaken not for the primary purpose of providing electricity to the public, but 'to support the primary irrigation functions by supplying power for reclamation uses and by providing revenues which could be applied to increase the amount and reduce the cost of water to Association subscribed lands.'

"... [N]o matter how great the number of nonvoting residents buying electricity from the District, the relationship between them and the District's power operations is essentially that between consumers and a business enterprise from which they buy. Nothing in the *Avery*, *Hadley*, or *Salyer* cases suggests that the volume of business or the breadth of economic effect of a venture undertaken by a government entity as an incident of its narrow and primary governmental public function can, of its own weight, subject the entity to the one-person, one-vote requirements of the *Reynolds* case.

"The functions of the Salt River District are therefore of the narrow, special sort which justifies a departure from the popular-election requirement of the *Reynolds* case. And as in *Salyer*, an aspect of that limited purpose is the disproportionate relationship the District's functions bear to the specific class of people whom the system makes eligible to vote. The voting landowners are the only residents of the District whose lands are subject to liens to secure District bonds. Only these landowners are subject to the acreage-based taxing power of the District, and voting landowners are the only residents who have ever committed capital to the District through stock assessments charged by the Association.[19] The *Salyer* opinion did not say that the selected class of voters for a special public entity must be the only parties at all affected by the operations of the entity, or that their entire economic well-being must depend on that entity. Rather, the question was whether the effect of the entity's operations on them was disproportionately greater than the effect on those seeking the vote.

"As in the *Salyer* case, we conclude that the voting scheme for the District is constitutional because it bears a reasonable relationship to its statutory objectives. Here, according to the stipulation of the parties, the subscriptions of land which made the Association and then the District possible might well have never occurred had not the subscribing landowners been assured a special voice in the conduct of the District's business. Therefore, as in *Salyer*, the State could rationally limit the vote to landowners. Moreover, Arizona could rationally make the weight of their vote dependent upon the number of acres they own, since that number reasonably reflects the relative risks they incurred as landowners and the distribution of the benefits and the burdens of the District's water operations."

Justice Powell, who joined in the majority opinion, wrote a separate concurrence emphasizing that the district's electoral system was controlled by the state legislature, which of course was elected on a one person, one vote basis. Justice White wrote a dissenting opinion, joined by Brennan, Marshall, and Blackmun.

(a) Is mosquito abatement a "normal" function of government or a "traditional element of government sovereignty"? Running a library? Operation of day care centers? How would you decide? Would the "normality" of such government activities be relevant to deciding whether single purpose districts to carry them out are subject to the one person-one vote rule? Should it be?

(b) Suppose the Salt River District began to operate a garbage disposal service, at a profit, to help finance its water distribution services. The majority lists sanitation services as a "normal" government function, but in many places this function has been handed over to private enterprise. Would the result in *Ball v. James* be affected?

Consider Briffault, *supra*, 60 UNIVERSITY OF CHICAGO LAW REVIEW at 374–75:

> [It is not] obvious why "sanitation, health, or welfare services" are more normal functions of government than the storage and distribution of water. There are more than 3,000 local governments specially created to address water management functions. How can a governmental activity so widespread not be a normal function of government? It may be that the existence of private providers of water undercuts the appreciation of the extent of public water storage and distribution activity, but surely the determination of whether a public service is a normal function of government cannot turn on the absence of private sector

---

19. The Court of Appeals found it significant that 98% of the District's revenues come from sales of electricity, and only 2% from charges assessed for water deliveries. This fact in no way affects the constitutionality of the voting scheme. When the consumers of electricity supply those power revenues, they are simply buying electricity; they are neither committing capital to the District nor committing any of their property as security for the credit of the District.

alternatives, lest the role of private security forces, private carting services, and private schools undermine the "governmentalness" of the traditional governmental functions concerning public safety, sanitation, and primary education.

(c) A big city school district sets up a local school council for each of the more than 500 schools in the district. The main functions served by each council are to select the principal for the school and approve a plan for spending money appropriated to the school by the citywide board of education. Each council consists of the principal, two teachers, six parents of children in the school and two residents of the area served by the school. The latter eight members are elected by the residents. Are these elections subject to the one person, one vote rule? Judge Posner gave the following reasons for answering this question in the negative in *Pittman v. Chicago Board of Education*, 64 F.3d 1098 (7th Cir. 1995), cert. denied 517 U.S. 1243 (1996):

> The line between a general-purpose governmental body and a special-purpose ... one is wavering and indistinct. We are not even certain that it is the correct line. [Judge Posner concedes that the Chicago local school councils involved the same governmental function, education, as was involved in *Kramer* and *Hadley*.] But there is an important distinction between *Kramer* and *Hadley* on the one hand and our case on the other hand. The school board in *Kramer* and the board of trustees of the junior college district in *Hadley* had the power to tax. The local school councils in our case do not. Taxation without representation is abhorrent to Americans, but these local school councils have no power to tax directly and they also have no power to tax indirectly, for they do not have the power to raise revenues through the sale of bonds or to increase the total spending on the schools. [T]he writ of each [council] runs no farther than a single school. Basically they select a principal and determine school expenditures but within budgetary limits set by the board of education. They have less power than the board of trustees of a private school.

> We are mindful that in neither *Kramer* nor *Hadley* did the Supreme Court single out the power to tax as critical to the decision; and when it came to distinguish these cases in the later irrigation-district decisions the basis for distinction that the Court offered was that nowadays education unlike irrigation is regarded as a vital government function—a point that had been stressed in *Hadley* itself. But the point has to be considered in context. The boards involved in *Kramer* and *Hadley* were the governing bodies of the schools and colleges, respectively, in the districts.... The governing body of the public schools of Chicago is the Board of Education of the City of Chicago, not these local councils. Vital public education may be, but these councils, unlike the boards in *Kramer* and *Hadley*, do not control it. The interest of the public at large in the councils is therefore attenuated.

9. In William H. Riker, *Democracy and Representation: A Reconciliation of Ball v. James and Reynolds v. Sims*, 1 SUPREME COURT ECONOMIC REVIEW 39 (1982), a well-known political scientist and public choice theorist first argued (controversially) that *Reynolds* and the other one person-one vote cases had very little effect on policies pursued by the state legislatures. He then wrote:

> [M]y generalization about this line of cases from *Reynolds* to *Ball* is that, if the elimination of trivial (in terms of public policy) restrictions on voting [i.e., the *Reynolds* rule applied to state legislatures] did not hurt anyone, then the Court proceeded with the elimination; but when the elimination came to mean an ar-

bitrary transfer of significant rights in and values of property [i.e., when one person-one vote was proposed in the circumstances of *Ball*], the Court refused to continue the process.

Id. at 59. Professor Riker approved of *Ball v. James*. Laurence Tribe has written of *Ball* and *Salyer Land* that they rest "on the most problematic of foundations," but his explanation of the cases—that "the Burger Court was evidently unwilling to divest wealthy landowners of the political power they wielded by virtue of their land-holdings"—is not very different from Riker's explanation of *Ball*. Laurence H. Tribe, AMERICAN CONSTITUTIONAL LAW 1088, 1670 (2nd ed., 1988).

10. The majority and the dissent in *Ball* differed over the significance of the fact that the state legislature, in which the appellees were represented, had control over the structure of the Salt River District. Was the dissent correct in arguing that this fact is no more relevant here than in the earlier cases in which the Court extended one person-one vote to local government entities? If so, could it be that the earlier cases and not *Ball v. James* were wrongly decided? What arguments can you make on both sides of this question? See Alexander Bickel, THE SUPREME COURT AND THE IDEA OF PROGRESS 152–56 (1978). Is the question related in any way to the debate between the pluralists and their critics, referred to in Chapter 1? For a broad theoretical framework that may be relevant, see Frank Michelman, *Political Markets and Community Self-Determination: Competing Judicial Models for Local Government Legitimacy*, 53 INDIANA LAW JOURNAL 145 (1977–78). Several cases, including *Salyer* and *Ball*, are analyzed in terms of Michelman's framework in Phillip S. Althoff & William H. Greig, *The United States Supreme Court on Rights and/or Participation: The "Deviant" Voting and Redistricting Cases*, 13 JOURNAL OF CONTEMPORARY LAW 31 (1987).

Michelman himself addressed *Ball* in a later article, finding the decision more consistent with a communitarian conception of government than with a pluralist, interest-based conception. From a pluralist standpoint, it is hard to justify the exclusion of the consumers of electricity, who are so obviously interested in the affairs of the district. But, Michelman continues:

> What might begin to explain (if not justify) the majority's conclusion, and its accompanying rhetoric of denial that the Salt River District constituted a government in the full sense, is the thought that instrumental protection of extra-political interests neither exhausts the value of a voting right to its holder nor alone suffices to explain the first-magnitude status of such rights in the constitutional firmament. For insofar as rights of admission to political participation were esteemed on constitutive, perhaps in addition to instrumental grounds, the Salt River District and its ilk—unlike the cities in *Cipriano* and *Kolodziejski* and the school district in *Kramer*—might easily have been perceived as *fora non conveniens* for the realization of the self-constitutive values of citizenship. Apparently required for such realization is participation in the affairs of a "political community." Perhaps the majority Justices doubted ... that the Salt River District, given its history and the accompanying understandings about its place in the lives of the people, defined or constituted any such thing.

Frank I. Michelman, *Conceptions of Democracy in American Constitutional Argument: Voting Rights*, 41 FLORIDA LAW REVIEW 443, 469 (1989).

11. Another line of cases has been compared with the *Kramer-Avery-Salyer-Ball* line. In *Carrington v. Rash*, 380 U.S. 89 (1965), the Court struck down a Texas prohibition on voting by members of the Armed Services whose Texas residence began after they had

joined the military. Likewise, in *Evans v. Cornman*, 398 U.S. 419 (1970), the Court struck down Maryland's denial of the vote to persons who resided on the grounds of the National Institutes of Health, a federal enclave located within Maryland.

In *Holt Civic Club v. City of Tuscaloosa*, 439 U.S. 60 (1978), discussed in Chapter 2 at page 55, plaintiffs lived within the "police jurisdiction" of Tuscaloosa, Alabama, which consisted of the area outside but within three miles of the city limits. Under Alabama law, city criminal ordinances were applicable and the jurisdiction of the municipal courts extended to the police jurisdiction. In addition, businesses located within the police jurisdiction had to pay a license tax half the amount they would be required to pay if they were within the city. However, the city's powers of zoning, eminent domain, and ad valorem taxation did not extend to the police jurisdiction. The Supreme Court majority rejected plaintiffs' claim that they were denied equal protection because they were denied the vote in Tuscaloosa city elections.

Melvyn R. Durschlag, in *Salyer, Ball, and Holt: Reappraising the Right to Vote in Terms of Political 'Interest' and Vote Dilution*, 33 CASE WESTERN RESERVE LAW REVIEW 1 (1982), argues that in cases where Group A lacks a sufficient "interest" in the matters voted upon, it would dilute unconstitutionally the votes of Group B, which does have such an interest, to extend the franchise to Group A. He therefore contends that in all the cases we have been considering, constitutional problems are presented whether the franchise is extended or contracted. The decisive consideration, in his view, is whether the powers of the public entity are such that it can directly redistribute wealth to or from the group in question. Applying his standard, Professor Durschlag concludes that *Salyer* was correctly decided, but that *Ball* and *Holt* were in error.

12. A simpler view, rejected by Professor Durschlag, would place great importance on the nominal boundaries of the public entity under state law. It might be presumed that these boundaries reflect the "community" that makes up the entity, without regard to anyone's "interests." On this view, *Holt* would have been rightly decided, but *Salyer* and *Ball* would have been in error.

Perhaps such a view can be justified on grounds offered by James A. Gardner, in *Liberty, Community and the Constitutional Structure of Political Influence: A Reconsideration of the Right to Vote*, 145 UNIVERSITY OF PENNSYLVANIA LAW REVIEW 893 (1997). Gardner argues that writers such as Durschlag err when they seek to explain voting decisions in terms of "interests." Gardner acknowledges that much of the rhetoric in Supreme Court decisions gives the impression that the Court protects the right to vote in order to permit individuals and groups to defend their interests. Nevertheless, Gardner contends that the results over a broad range of cases are more consistent with a right to vote that is grounded not on protection of interests, but on a right not to be excluded from a practice that symbolizes full membership in the political community. For example, Gardner writes:

> Compared to the plaintiffs in *Holt*, the plaintiff in *Kramer* had a far less plausible claim that his inability to vote impaired in any significant way his ability to protect his rights and liberties from government infringement....

> What really bothered [Kramer], it seems, was the *fact* of his exclusion, not the *result* of it. "All members of the community," he flatly asserted, "have an interest in the quality and structure of public education." Nor was there any evidence that the plaintiff or any other excluded individuals had ever actually been harmed by a decision of a school board. Under the circumstances, the interest claimed by the plaintiff seems to arise less in virtue of any impact on actual individuals like him than in virtue of community membership itself; the interest,

in other words, is definitional—it defines who is and who is not a member of the community....

The contrast with *Holt* is instructive. Both Kramer and the Holt residents were represented only virtually on the pertinent municipal councils because they could not vote. Moreover, the school board had much less power to harm Kramer than Tuscaloosa had to harm the citizens of Holt. The Holt residents, however, by living in the suburbs, had voluntarily excluded themselves from the municipal political community and thus were confined to basing their voting-rights claim on the need to protect their interests from infringement by a government in which they were unrepresented.

Suppose you are counsel representing plaintiffs before the Supreme Court in a case challenging an alleged denial or infringement of the right to vote, in which you could plausibly argue either that your clients are being excluded symbolically from the political community or that their ability to use the vote to defend their political interests is being impaired. If Gardner is correct that the Court's language in voting cases tends to emphasize interest-protection but that it is exclusion from the political community that drives results, which theory would you emphasize the most in your briefs and in your oral argument?

13. Can the *Salyer-Ball* exception be used to limit the right to vote to a group defined by race? The Supreme Court answered that question in the negative in *Rice v. Cayetano*, 528 U.S. 495 (2000). In that case, a Hawaiian agency called the Office of Hawaiian Affairs (OHA) administered programs intended to benefit "native Hawaiians," defined as individuals at least half descended from the original Hawaiians who lived there prior to 1778 when Europeans first visited the islands, and "Hawaiians," defined as those who were at all descended from the original pre-1778 Hawaiians. The plaintiff in *Rice v. Cayetano* did not challenge the limitation of the benefits of the programs to native Hawaiians and Hawaiians. Rather, he challenged a provision of the state constitution permitting only native Hawaiians and Hawaiians to vote for members of the OHA.

The Court held in a 7–2 decision that the restriction violated the Fifteenth Amendment. Justice Kennedy, writing for five members of the Court, rejected the state's contention that the voting restriction could be upheld under the *Salyer-Ball* exception because of the limited purposes of the OHA: "The question before us is not the one-person, one-vote requirement of the Fourteenth Amendment, but the race neutrality command of the Fifteenth Amendment. Our special purpose district cases have not suggested that compliance with the one-person, one-vote rule of the Fourteenth Amendment somehow excuses compliance with the Fifteenth Amendment. We reject that argument here."

In response to the state's claim that the voting restriction was justified because the OHA members could be likened to fiduciaries of a trust and the eligible voters to beneficiaries, Justice Kennedy made these broader comments regarding the Fifteenth Amendment:

> There is no room under the Amendment for the concept that the right to vote in a particular election can be allocated based on race. Race cannot qualify some and disqualify others from full participation in our democracy. All citizens, regardless of race, have an interest in selecting officials who make policies on their behalf, even if those policies will affect some groups more than others. Under the Fifteenth Amendment voters are treated not as members of a distinct race but as members of the whole citizenry. Hawaii may not assume, based on race, that petitioner or any other of its citizens will not cast a principled vote. To accept the position advanced by the State would give rise to the same indignities, and the same resulting tensions and animosities, the Amendment was designed to eliminate.

For commentary on the case, see Ellen D. Katz, *Race and the Right to Vote after* Rice v. Cayetano, 99 MICHIGAN LAW REVIEW 491 (2000).

Section 1 of the Fifteenth Amendment provides as follows: "The right of citizens of the United States to vote shall not be denied or abridged by the United States or by any State on account of race, color, or previous condition of servitude." Under the *Fourteenth* Amendment, if a classification is based on race or abridges some group's right to vote, the classification may nevertheless be upheld if it is necessary to further a compelling state interest. Plainly, any classification that denies or abridges the right of a citizen to vote on account of race or color and therefore comes within the *Fifteenth* Amendment is based on race *and* results in an abridgement of the right to vote. Nevertheless, under Fourteenth Amendment doctrine, the state still has the opportunity to defend the classification under the strict scrutiny test. Under the Fifteenth Amendment, can the restriction be upheld if it satisfies strict scrutiny? The Ninth Circuit upheld the Hawaiian voting restriction that the Supreme Court later struck down in *Rice v. Cayetano*. Does the Fifteenth Amendment leave any room for such a result?

14. *POSTSCRIPT*:

> CORCORAN, Calif.—The Boswells and the Salyers, two of the richest and most powerful farming families in America, have ended decades of rivalry and rancor over their San Joaquin Valley empires with a huge land deal in which one colossus will swallow the other.
>
> Fred Salyer, 72, has agreed to sell his cotton and grain empire—about 25,000 acres of fertile San Joaquin Valley soil—to J.G. Boswell for tens of millions of dollars, according to business associates and employees....

Mark Arax, "2 Farm Giants End Decades of Rivalry With Land Deal," *Los Angeles Times*, February 10, 1995, p. A1, col. 5.[g]

---

g. The Boswell saga may be pondered in depth in Mark Arax and Rick Wartzman, THE KING OF CALIFORNIA: J.G. BOSWELL AND THE MAKING OF A SECRET AMERICAN EMPIRE (2003).

Chapter 4

Districting Criteria

Reynolds v. Sims and the other redistricting cases established that districts must be approximately or precisely equal in population. Consistent with that constraint, there remain an almost infinite number of ways in which district lines can be drawn, and the differences between them may have notable political consequences.[a] In this chapter, we shall consider redistricting criteria that some have proposed as desirable. In Chapter 5 we shall consider claims that districting plans and other electoral arrangements dilute the votes of racial, ethnic, and language minorities, or that undue reliance on race and ethnicity may render a districting plan unconstitutional. In Chapter 6 we shall consider partisan aspects of redistricting.

To illustrate the dramatically different political consequences that can be caused by redistricting plans with equally populated districts, consider a simplified hypothetical jurisdiction with 300 residents, all voters, and with three legislative districts. 160 residents always vote Democratic, and 140 always vote Republican. Consider the makeup of the legislature under each of the following plans, each of which complies perfectly with the one person, one vote rule.

Plan 1:

	Democrats	Republicans
District 1	90	10
District 2	35	65
District 3	35	65

Plan 2:

	Democrats	Republicans
District 1	60	40
District 2	60	40
District 3	40	60

Under Plan 1 the Republicans will control the legislature, whereas under Plan 2 the Democrats will prevail. It is not obvious, even in principle, what is the most just or most democratic basis on which to draw district lines. For example, in our hypothetical case it might be assumed that Plan 2 is preferable because it assures that the Democrats, who are in the majority, will control the legislature. But suppose District 1 in Plan 1 (which votes 90–10 Democratic) consists of a predominantly African-American, low-income central city area, and Districts 2 and 3 in that plan consist of predominantly white, middle-class suburbs with a modest Republican majority distributed fairly evenly throughout the two districts. Plan 1 might then be preferred by some, since it assures effective representation to the central city residents, who comprise a substantial minority with distinctive political needs. It also creates districts containing "communities of interest," favored by some.

---

a. For a thoughtful discussion of the political consequences of redistricting and the political environment within which redistricting plans are enacted, see Bruce E. Cain, The Reapportionment Puzzle (1984).

Perhaps a third possibility exists. District 1 of Plan 1 might be preserved to assure a district in which African-American voters can select a candidate of their choice, but the other two districts might be rearranged so that the Democrats, with a majority of the total vote, would be assured a majority of the seats.

Plan 3:

	Democrats	Republicans
District 1	90	10
District 2	10	90
District 3	60	40

Suppose that in order to create the outcome in Plan 3, it is necessary that Districts 2 and 3 consist of fantastic shapes that divide numerous suburban cities between the two districts. Which of the three plans do you think is best? Which is worst? Of course, any real-life redistricting situation involves a vastly more complicated set of choices between large numbers of political and interest group concerns.

The legislature (or in some states an administrative agency) must adopt a new plan at least after each decennial federal census. Whatever criteria one thinks *should* be employed in drawing district lines, few would deny that most often in legislatures two important criteria in fact have been the political well-being of the incumbents and of the controlling party. To control the process when redistricting is carried out by the legislature, a party must have either a majority in both houses and the governorship or a sufficient majority in both houses to override a gubernatorial veto. Following the 2000 census, a third criterion became important in legislatures that are now subject to term limits in many states. Members of those legislatures often are less concerned with their current districts than with congressional or other districts they can run in when they are "termed out."

The criteria for redistricting can come up in judicial proceedings in three different settings. In the first, the state has adopted a plan that the court finds insufficient under the population standards or on some other ground. In this situation, courts have been directed not to disturb the state's plan more than necessary to bring it into compliance with the one person, one vote rule, at least where the state's plan is only slightly deficient and can be corrected with a few minor changes. *White v. Weiser*, 412 U.S. 783, 794–97 (1973). See also *Upham v. Seamon*, 456 U.S. 37 (1982), which reached a similar result where certain lines in a redistricting plan were disapproved by the Attorney General under Section 5 of the Voting Rights Act. The United States District Court could adjust the lines in question but had no basis for modifying other parts of the statutory plan.

Second, the state may have failed to adopt any plan, or one that even approximates population equality. In this case the court will have to devise its own plan. The Supreme Court has given little guidance, except to state that the lower courts should avoid both multimember districts and minor population discrepancies, even where they would be upheld in a legislatively-adopted plan. *Chapman v. Meier*, 420 U.S. 1 (1975).[b] In *Legislature v. Reinecke, infra,* we shall examine the criteria that the California Supreme Court used for devising a plan when it was placed in this situation in 1973 (and again in 1992).

---

b. Plans devised by federal courts are not subject to preclearance under Section 5 of the Voting Rights Act. However, if the plan approved by a court was submitted to it by a legislative agency, then preclearance is required if the jurisdiction is "covered" by Section 5. *McDaniel v. Sanchez*, 452 U.S. 130 (1981). For analysis and criticism of *McDaniel*, see Katharine Inglis Butler, *Reapportionment, the Courts and the Voting Rights Act: A Resegregation of the Political Process?*, 56 UNIVERSITY OF COLORADO LAW REVIEW 1, 42–55, 71–78 (1984). Preclearance is required for a plan formulated by a state court in a jurisdiction covered by Section 5 of the Voting Rights Act.

Finally, the court may be faced with a plan adopted by the state that satisfies the one person, one vote rule but that is challenged as unconstitutional because it is unfair to some group within the electorate. Although the Supreme Court has never held that compliance with one person, one vote assures satisfaction of the Equal Protection Clause, it has set a very high standard for plaintiffs challenging districting schemes on non-population grounds under the Constitution. *Gaffney v. Cummings*, 412 U.S. 735, 751–54 (1973). In Chapter 6, we shall consider how the courts have responded to attacks on districting plans on the ground that they are partisan gerrymanders. In Chapter 5, we shall consider claims by racial, ethnic, and language minorities that their votes are diluted by districting plans or other electoral mechanisms. As we shall see, the 1982 amendments to the Voting Rights Act provide a strong basis for many such claims.

The differences among these three settings in which courts consider redistricting plans and the different standards applicable in each are often overlooked, sometimes by lawyers who should know better. We hope readers of this book will avoid this error.

Aside from population equality, many criteria have been proposed for legislative districting. Most of them have been controversial. One set of criteria was authoritatively adopted in California in 1973, after a lengthy struggle between a Democratic legislature and Republican Governor Ronald Reagan resulted in a failure to adopt a redistricting plan. See *Legislature v. Reinecke*, 9 Cal.3d 166, 107 Cal. Rptr. 18, 107 P.2d 626 (1973). The following is a portion of the report of the Special Masters, whose recommended districts were adopted with minor changes by the state Supreme Court and governed California elections through the 1980 election. *Legislature v. Reinecke*, 10 Cal.3d 396, 110 Cal. Rptr. 718, 516 P.2d 6 (1973).[c] Consider carefully those criteria the Masters adopt and those they reject. Do you agree with their choice of criteria to guide a court that is forced to create a districting plan? Do you think any or all of these criteria should be constitutionally mandatory for legislatures that adopt districting plans? Whether or not they are required constitutionally, do you believe these criteria embody the public interest and that a legislature that fails to follow them may justly be criticized? Would you want to add additional criteria that were not considered by the Special Masters, for any of these purposes?

Legislature v. Reinecke
10 Cal.3d 396, 110 Cal.Rptr. 718, 516 P.2d 6 (1973)

APPENDIX
REPORT AND RECOMMENDATIONS OF SPECIAL MASTERS ON
REAPPORTIONMENT

The Special Masters appointed by the Court in these cases were directed as follows:

"The Masters shall hold public hearings to permit the presentation of evidence and argument with respect to the possible criteria of reapportionment and of proposed plans to carry out such criteria.

"Following such hearings the Masters shall recommend to the Court for possible adoption reapportionment plans which shall provide for 43 single member congressional dis-

---

c. Following the 1990 census, California again had a Democratic legislature and a Republican governor (Pete Wilson), with the result, again, that the California Supreme Court had to design redistricting plans. The court instructed its masters to use the same criteria that were described by the masters in 1973. See *Wilson v. Eu*, 1 Cal.4th 707, 4 Cal.Rptr. 379, 823 P.2d 545 (1992).

tricts, 40 single member Senate districts and 80 single member Assembly districts. The Masters shall set forth the criteria underlying the plans they recommend for adoption and the reasons for their recommendations." ...

The oral and written presentations covered a wide range of subjects, some relevant to the issues at hand and others irrelevant or beyond the scope of the Court's directive to the Masters....

The most frequently voiced objection to all plans recommended by the Legislature, including the reapportionment plan for the Senate that the Governor found tolerable, was that those plans were designed primarily to favor incumbents and to obtain partisan advantage for one or the other of the major political parties. It was evident that there was widespread public cynicism about the political process, and it was frequently stated that the Masters were in a singularly advantageous position unavailable to legislators, who cannot escape the inevitable force of self-interest. Many who appeared expressed the belief that any plans promulgated by the Court or by the Masters would be less incumbent-oriented or politically motivated than the plans recommended by the Legislature or others with special interests in reapportionment.

After the hearings began, the Legislature passed and the Governor vetoed Senate Bill 195, which contained congressional and legislative reapportionment plans. Both houses of the Legislature and 41 members of the congressional delegation urged that the plans set forth in Senate Bill 195 should be recommended to the Court because those plans represent reapportionments most nearly approximating appropriate political solutions. The Senate in particular urged that its plan contained in the bill should be recommended on the ground that the Governor had indicated that he would have approved that plan had it been presented to him in a separate bill. Certain minority assemblymen urged that as much of the assembly plan as did not meet with the Governor's disapproval be recommended, and they offered modifications of the rest of that plan designed to meet the Governor's objections. Similarly, 41 members of Congress offered modifications of the congressional plan contained in Senate Bill 195 to meet the Governor's objections. Underlying all of these proposals was the basic premise that "reapportionment is primarily a matter for the legislative branch of the government to resolve," and the recently reiterated position of the United States Supreme Court that political solutions to reapportionment problems are not only entirely proper but indeed inevitable. *Gaffney v. Cummings*, 412 U.S. 735 (1973); *White v. Weiser*, 412 U.S 783 (1973).

Unlike the situation in the *Gaffney* and *White* cases, however, in these proceedings there are no duly enacted political solutions to be recommended to the Court but only "plans that are at best truncated products of the legislative process." Accordingly, in making their recommendations to the Court the Masters cannot escape the political thicket by seeking a compromise between legislative and gubernatorial views, a compromise that the Legislature and the Governor were unable to achieve. It is therefore concluded that the plans contained in Senate Bill 195 and in the proposed modifications thereof mentioned above cannot properly command any preferential consideration but must be measured for recommendation or rejection in whole or in part by the following criteria that the Masters determine to be appropriate for reapportionment. All other plans submitted by individuals or groups must likewise be measured by the objective criteria deemed to be appropriate.

CRITERIA FOR REAPPORTIONMENT

Having considered the oral and written presentations, pertinent provisions of the Constitution of the United States and the Constitution and Statutes of California, the case law expressed in judicial decisions, and authoritative sources in the field of political science, the following are recommended as the criteria to be used in formulating plans for reapportionment of legislative districts in California:

1. As required by the federal Constitution, the districts in each plan should be numerically equal in population as nearly as practicable, with strict equality in the case of congressional districts and reasonable equality in the case of state legislative districts. The population of Senate and assembly districts should be within 1% of the ideal except in unusual circumstances, and in no event should a deviation greater than 2% be permitted.

Although a greater percentage variation has been permitted in the reapportionment plans of other states, the populations of districts in such states were relatively small. Legislative districts in California are large, so that even a 1% or 2% variance in population affects a large number of persons. The variance in the number of persons more directly relates to the practical attainment of numerical equality than does a percentage figure, and districts can be formulated in California pursuant to other criteria recommended without deviating from the ideal by more than 1%, except in unusual circumstances.

2. The territory included within a district should be contiguous and compact, taking into account the availability and facility of transportation and communication between the people in a proposed district, between the people and candidates in the district, and between the people and their elected representatives.

3. Counties and cities within a proposed district should be maintained intact, insofar as practicable.

4. The integrity of California's basic geographical regions (coastal, mountain, desert, central valley and intermediate valley regions) should be preserved insofar as practicable.

5. The social and economic interests common to the population of an area which are probable subjects of legislative action, generally termed a "community of interests" should be considered in determining whether the area should be included within or excluded from a proposed district in order that all of the citizens of the district might be represented reasonably, fairly and effectively. Examples of such interests, among others, are those common to an urban area, a rural area, an industrial area or an agricultural area, and those common to areas in which the people share similar living standards, use the same transportation facilities, have similar work opportunities, or have access to the same media of communication relevant to the election process.

Most of the people making oral or written presentations urged consideration of the foregoing criteria in formulating proposed reapportionment plans. Many presentations were made urging adherence to the criteria of maintaining the integrity of counties and cities, and deploring needless division thereof in the formation of districts. It is clear that in many situations county and city boundaries define political, economic and social boundaries of population groups. Furthermore, organizations with legitimate political concerns are constituted along local political subdivision lines. Therefore, unnecessary division of counties and cities in reapportionment districting should be avoided.

6. State senatorial districts should be formed by combining adjacent assembly districts, and, to the degree practicable, assembly district boundaries should be used as congressional district boundaries.

Cogent reasons exist for the formation of senate districts from assembly districts. If assembly districts are formed logically and in compliance with the criteria recommended herein, then senate districts created by combining such districts are also likely to comply. This is particularly so if such an eventual pairing is kept in mind when forming the various legislative districts. The resulting legislative districts will be more comprehensible to the electorate and the task of administering elections would be considerably simplified, thus saving money and insuring greater accuracy.

Similarly, use of assembly district boundaries to the degree feasible in formation of congressional districts will promote all of these advantages. Obviously, it is impossible to make all congressional district lines congruent with assembly district lines, since there are 43 congressional districts and 80 assembly districts, but in larger counties it is possible to use common boundaries in a substantial number of instances.

7. The basis for reapportionment should be the 1970 census. In counties for which the U.S. Census Bureau has established census tracts, such tracts should be used as the basic unit for district formation, with division of such tracts being made only when necessary for population equality or to improve substantially compliance with other recommended criteria.

Census tracts are the basic unit used by the Census Bureau for measuring the characteristics of the population. Tracts average approximately 4,000 persons in size, and an effort has been made by the Census Bureau to make them homogeneous as to social characteristics and to use prominent natural or manmade geographical features as boundaries. Thus, following, rather than disregarding, census tracts will aid in establishing natural, well defined legislative districts and will aid in obtaining valid pertinent socio-economic data about such districts.[8]

The use of whole census tracts makes it difficult to comply literally with another recommended criterion, that of maintaining the integrity of city boundaries. Some cities have exceedingly irregular boundaries with an odd assortment of "fingers" and "peninsulas" jutting out from the basic part of the city. In many such cases, the boundaries as of the date of the census do not reflect the present boundaries or what they are likely to be during the balance of the decade. Often census tract boundaries do not correspond exactly with the boundaries of such cities. In such instances, census tract boundaries which preserve the bulk of the city in one district have been followed even though it resulted in trimming off small peninsulas or other such extensions of territory. This has been done only where the population affected was relatively small.

As to all of the recommended criteria, their applicability, priority and scope, other than population equality, depend on circumstances indigenous to the area under consideration. To the extent required by the federal Constitution, population equality controls.

CONSIDERATION OF PLANS SUBMITTED BY THE LEGISLATURE AND OTHERS

As has been noted before, legislative plans for reapportionment, passed by the Legislature but vetoed by the Governor, were submitted for consideration. In addition, various individual legislators, local governmental groups and private groups or individuals submitted plans for reapportioning all or a portion of the state.

The plans submitted by the Legislature cannot be recommended for adoption.

The assembly plan and the congressional plan needlessly depart from the criteria of compactness and maintenance of county line and city line integrity. A cursory examination of the assembly plan reveals numerous peculiarly shaped districts that very frequently cut

---

8. Moreover, the population data available on the computer used by the Masters was on a census tract basis.... [Because of improved technology, it is now nearly as simple to use census units below the level of tracts, the smallest of which are usually called blocks.—Eds.]

city and county lines, often linking distant population areas together while disregarding more proximate populations that could have been included. Governor Reagan's veto message cites many examples of particularly objectionable districts which are not compact and which needlessly cut city and county lines.

Like the assembly plan, the congressional plan contained in Senate Bill 195 violates the recommended criteria of compactness and respect for city and county lines. Some districts contain appendages linking distant population areas while frequently cutting city and county lines. Again, the Governor's veto message cites specific examples of the most objectionable districts. 41 members of the congressional delegation have also submitted a plan which they refer to as a "modification" of Senate Bill 195. While this plan does modify the congressional plan approved by the Legislature, and improves upon it in a number of aspects by cutting fewer county lines and city lines and increasing compactness, it was not passed by the Legislature and does not reflect the Legislature's approval of the modification. Furthermore, the Legislature is responsible for enacting a reapportionment plan, and this responsibility cannot be assumed by the congressional delegation.

Special consideration was given to the senate plan because the Governor has indicated that he deems it acceptable and would have approved it had it been presented to him in a separate bill. The plan, however, needlessly departs from the recommended criteria of reasonable population equality, compactness and respect for county and city lines.

Furthermore, the senate plan raises grave constitutional questions involving population deviations and dilutions of voting strength of black and Spanish-surnamed persons. It is true that *Mahan v. Howell* upheld a population variance of 16.4% in a legislative redistricting plan where that variance was justified by a consistently applied state policy of preserving county lines. Nevertheless, the senate plan, which has a population variance of 16.5%, with 21 of the 40 districts deviating by more than 5% from the ideal, does not appear to meet the constitutional requirements implicit in *Mahan v. Howell* and in *White v. Regester*, 412 U.S. 755 (1973). The senate plan cannot be justified under *White* because it has substantially greater population variances than were allowed in *White*. Even under *Mahan* the plan is suspect because of the absence of a rationally and consistently applied state policy such as preservation of county lines. While the Senate claims to have employed criteria such as county and city line preservation and community of interest recognition, it has not done so. The districts in the plan unnecessarily split cities and counties, often combine whole or partial counties across mountain ranges or bodies of water and disregard travel patterns, geography, common economic activities and other "community of interest" indicators.

There is also evidence that the senate plan dilutes the voting strength of blacks and persons of Spanish-surname by dividing homogeneous ethnic groups into a number of districts or by "packing" too many members of an ethnic group into a single district. Despite assertions that the senate plan was not deliberately designed to discriminate or foster racialism, the Masters are persuaded that the senate plan is constitutionally suspect and should not be recommended to the Court.

Finally, the Masters have concluded that the factor of overriding importance in each plan in Senate Bill 195 was the goal of incumbent reelection. While protection of incumbents may be desirable to assure a core of experienced legislators, the objective of reapportionment should not be the political survival or comfort of those already in office.[16] It is best if an incumbent's continuation in office depended upon effectiveness and

---

16. A plan that seriously jeopardizes most incumbents would not necessarily be in the public interest, but the advantage enjoyed by incumbents accruing from their former service and from name

responsiveness to constituents rather than upon the design of district boundaries. Extensive changes in constituencies necessitated by decennial redistricting are bound to affect most incumbents, who naturally value stability and predictability, and any reapportionment plan will make it necessary for some to work harder to become known to constituents.

All of the other reapportionment plans submitted have been carefully considered by the Masters. It is recognized that for each legislative body there are many potential plans that may pass constitutional muster and reflect roughly comparable apportionment wisdom. With one exception, the plans presented for statewide redistricting dealt only with one legislative body. Since one recommended criterion calls for an integrated approach to formation of assembly, senate and congressional districts, no plan for either house of the Legislature or for Congress was a particularly suitable vehicle for complying with this criterion. Further, lurking within proposed statewide plans may be dubious political considerations or implications that are not readily apparent and which may be difficult to detect and evaluate. Because of these and other problems no statewide plan submitted for adoption is recommended. Several such plans contained valuable suggestions for resolving specific problems and all plans submitted were considered carefully in connection with the preparation of the recommendations.

Proposed plans that have been presented dealing with specific limited areas of the state have also been carefully considered. Proper weight was given to the reasons underlying such proposals. However, innumerable districts ideal for particular communities can be constructed if each is considered in isolation but when the entire state is divided into a specified number of districts, that which may appear ideal for one place or another must be subordinated to the goal of fair and reasonable reapportionment of the whole state. That is the goal sought and upon which the recommendations to the Court are based.[18]

PLANS RECOMMENDED FOR ADOPTION

Having concluded that plans presented either by the Legislature or others should not be recommended for adoption, the Masters formulated original plans in accordance with the criteria recommended herein....

In formulating these plans the Masters were aware of the observations of the United States Supreme Court that "Districting inevitably has sharp political impact and inevitably political decisions must be made by those charged with the task," *Weiser*, and that "Politics and political considerations are inseparable from districting and apportionment," and districting without regard for political impact "may produce, whether intended or not, the most grossly gerrymandered results." *Gaffney*. It is also true that political fairness is an appropriate goal of reapportionment, *Gaffney*, and that there are legitimate interests to be served by allowing incumbents and their constituents to maintain existing relationships and in affording incumbents fair opportunities to seek reelection. Accordingly, it was deemed appropriate to consider whether the recommended plans are politically fair and whether they needlessly prejudice the legitimate interests of incumbents and their constituents.

---

recognition makes it highly unlikely that most would be in serious jeopardy solely because of redistricting.

18. Any person with even a passing acquaintance with reapportionment becomes aware of what is known as the "ripple effect," whereby the casting of one district on the water produces ripples felt throughout the state. If uncontrolled, this effect may result in the initial choice of a perfect district in one place leading to intolerably imperfect districts elsewhere.

Testing for political fairness is at best an imprecise endeavor. Techniques employed in other states and mentioned in some decisions are not practical in California where there have been major population shifts and where traditionally and historically voters have demonstrated more political independence than voters elsewhere. However, with general measuring devices such as party registration and such electoral data as [are] available it should be possible to detect a redistricting plan likely to produce a manifestly unfair political result. On the basis of such testing it appears that the proposed and recommended plans are neither politically unfair nor unfair to incumbents, but may result in fewer "safe seats" and more "competitive seats."

Political science literature suggests that the most effective means of avoiding the creation of constituencies that unduly favor one of the political parties is to create an appropriate number of competitive districts. The typical legislative approach is to maximize safe seats for both parties. Ideal districting should accommodate shifting political trends, allowing electoral majorities to be represented by legislative majorities. The central rationale of two party politics is that it offers voters alternative choices of candidates and programs. According to democratic theory, parties should contest for public support through electoral mechanisms that translate predominant public opinion into public policy. This involves the ability of popularly elected majorities to govern, while insuring the representation of the minority party, temporarily out of power, as a check on a usually transitory majority party.

The Masters are aware that there are instances where the places of residence of some incumbents under the recommended plans will not be located within the districts they formerly represented in large part and it will be necessary for them to change their residences if they wish to seek reelection in the areas encompassed within their former districts. This is because the increase in population and shift in the centers of population have caused a change in the size and configuration of districts. It is an unfortunate but necessary result that population shifts and adherence to objective criteria bring about inconvenience to some incumbents in order that the citizens generally may benefit.

If it turns out that the new district lines are not announced by the Court in time for incumbent legislators and other candidates to select a residence and become an elector in a district "for one year ... immediately preceding" the election (Cal.Const., Art. IV, sec. 2, subd. (c)), it is recommended that the Court give consideration to an interpretation that the cited section is inapplicable to such tardily formed districts so as to permit candidates to file for election if they are residents of the district at the time of filing and otherwise comply with election law requirements.

Notes and Questions

1. In 1980, article 21 was added to the California Constitution requiring that districting at the state level be performed in conformance with the following standards:

(a) Each member of the Senate, Assembly, Congress, and the Board of Equalization shall be elected from a single-member district.[d]

(b) The population of all districts of a particular type shall be reasonably equal.

---

d. In the past, a few states have used multi-member districts for the election of members of Congress. Currently, states are required by 2 U.S.C. §2c to use single-member districts for the House of Representatives.

(c) Every district shall be contiguous.

(d) Districts of each type shall be numbered consecutively commencing at the northern boundary of the state and ending at the southern boundary.

(e) The geographical integrity of any city, county, or city and county, or of any geographical region shall be respected to the extent possible without violating the requirements of any other subdivision of this section.

In what ways does article 21 follow the Masters' criteria? In what ways do they differ? Are there criteria missing from the Masters' report and from article 21 that you believe should be considered? Are the criteria of article 21 sufficient to satisfy federal statutory and constitutional requirements?

2. Many states have constitutional provisions setting forth redistricting criteria, comparable to those in California's Article 21, though the content of the criteria varies widely from state to state. When a districting plan is adopted legislatively, state courts often tend to apply state criteria in a permissive manner. For example, in *Kilbury v. Franklin County Board of Commissioners*, 90 P.3d 1071 (Wash. 2004) (en banc), the court applied a state requirement that districts be "as compact as possible" by asking whether the plan was adopted arbitrarily or capriciously.

In Idaho, two legislative plans adopted by a redistricting commission were found to be unconstitutional on population grounds. A third plan was held to satisfy the population requirements but was attacked for a district unnecessarily made up of portions of two counties. The state constitution required that districts not be so formed if "ideal district size may be achieved by internal division of the county." The Idaho Supreme Court upheld the plan, saying "[w]e simply cannot micromanage all the difficult steps the Commission must take in performing the high-wire act that is legislative district drawing. Rather, we must constrain our focus to determining whether the split was done to effectuate an improper purpose or whether it dilutes the right to vote." *Bonneville County v. Ysursa*, 129 P.3d 1213 (Idaho 2005). In *Ysursa*, the only way to have avoided the split in question may well have been to split one or more other districts among counties. But if the commission split a district in a manner that was not dilutive and not improperly motivated but that nevertheless was not needed to attain equal population, what justification would there be under the Idaho constitution to uphold the split?

A similar question can be posed regarding a provision in the Rhode Island constitution requiring that districts be "as compact in territory as possible." In *Parella v. Montalbano*, 899 A.2d 1226 (R.I. 2006), the Rhode Island Supreme Court upheld a plan against a compactness challenge, reaffirming an earlier statement that the Constitution is "clearly intended to leave the [L]egislature with a wide discretion as to the territorial structuring of the electoral districts." Is that a correct reading of the compactness clause? It is perhaps worth noting that the legislature was undoubtedly under political stress when it adopted the plan in question, as it was the first redistricting following a constitutional amendment cutting the membership of the legislature by a fourth.

3. As the California Masters indicated, the Supreme Court has taken the position that redistricting is a political process and that federal courts therefore should interfere as little as possible with plans enacted under state law, except as necessary to conform to federal constitutional and statutory requirements. However, the Masters refused to give any preferred consideration to Senate Bill 195, which had been passed by both houses of the legislature but vetoed by the governor.

Under similar circumstances, most federal courts have at least been willing to give "careful consideration" to a vetoed legislative plan, but without necessarily giving it preferred consideration over plans that may be submitted by other parties. *Carstens v. Lamm*, 543 F.Supp. 68, 78–9 (D. Colo. 1982); *O'Sullivan v. Brier*, 540 F.Supp. 1200, 1202 (D.Kans. 1982). Other federal courts have been more deferential to plans that made it part of the way through the legislative process. One such court stated it could not "simply embrace" the plan that went furthest through the process, but indicated that it would try to incorporate in its own plan features common to those plans that came closest to being enacted. *Shayer v. Kirkpatrick*, 541 F.Supp. 922, 932 (W.D.Mo. 1982). In *Donnelly v. Meskill*, 345 F.Supp. 962, 964 (D.Conn. 1972), the fact that one of the plans submitted to the court was similar to a vetoed plan passed by both houses of the legislature "tip[ped] the scales" in favor of that plan. In *Skolnick v. State Electoral Board*, 336 F.Supp. 839, 846 (N.D.Ill. 1971), the court adopted a plan in part because it received "overwhelming approval" in the lower house of the Illinois legislature, although it was never voted upon in the upper house.

If the Supreme Court's premise is accepted that in districting cases, courts should defer as much as possible to the political process, does this militate for or against deference to plans that have made it part but not all the way through the state's legislative process? Should it matter how far through the process the plan went? Whether the plan received bipartisan support or was supported only by one party? What the reasons were for the plan's failure to be enacted? How well the plan comports with constitutional and statutory requirements and with other public interest criteria? Which criteria?

4. Many state constitutions allow the *referendum*, which is a procedure whereby bills enacted by the legislature and signed by the governor (or receiving enough legislative votes to override the governor's veto) may be submitted to voter approval. In California, a referendum petition that receives signatures of five percent of the electorate within ninety days after enactment of a bill is sufficient to submit the bill to the voters under art. II, §§9 and 10 of the California Constitution. If the bill is approved by the voters it goes into effect the day after the election. If the voters reject it, it does not go into effect at all.

In 1981, the California legislature, controlled by Democrats, passed redistricting bills that were signed by Democratic Governor Jerry Brown. Republicans successfully circulated referendum petitions objecting to the bills, which thus could not go into effect, if at all, until the day after the election. However, the referendum elections were to be held at the 1982 primary, by which time districts were needed so that congressional and state legislative candidates could be nominated.

Under these circumstances, should a court, in deciding on districts to govern the 1982 elections, defer to the plan adopted by the legislature and signed by the governor? What arguments can you make in support of deference to the legislative plan to distinguish the cases where the legislature has passed a plan that has been vetoed by the governor? How can you respond to these arguments, and thereby oppose judicial deference to the legislative plan? See *Assembly v. Deukmejian*, 30 Cal.3d 638, 180 Cal.Rptr. 297, 639 P.2d 939 (1982).

5. Granted that federal courts have been instructed by the Supreme Court to defer to state political determinations on redistricting, so long as these are consistent with federal constitutional and statutory requirements, should federal courts also defer to state *judicial* determinations? Since *Reynolds*, the preponderance of redistricting litigation has occurred in federal rather than state courts.[e] Nevertheless, state courts are equally

---

e. California has been a conspicuous exception. The districting plans for the 1970s and the 1990s were formulated by the California Supreme Court.

empowered and obligated to enforce federal law. In *Scott v. Germano*, 381 U.S. 407 (1965), the Supreme Court stated that federal courts should defer to state courts when parallel redistricting cases were pending in both. In the years that followed, this instruction may often have been overlooked or honored in the breach. However, *Germano* was strongly reaffirmed by a unanimous Court in *Growe v. Emison*, 507 U.S. 25, 32–37 (1993).

We have seen that in many situations, especially when the legislative process has broken down, a court has considerable discretion to shape a redistricting plan as it sees fit. Many litigants in redistricting controversies believe that the exercise of this discretion tends to be influenced by foreseeable partisan or other political predilections on the part of judges. Does *Growe* encourage recourse to the state judiciary by litigants who believe they have a sympathetic majority on the state supreme court? If so, is this a good thing?

In *Smith v. Clark*, 189 F.Supp.2d 503 (S.D.Miss. 2002), and subsequent orders in the same case reported in the same volume of F.Supp.2d at pages 529 and 548, a three-judge District Court enjoined the state from implementing a congressional districting plan that had been adopted by a state court after the Mississippi legislature failed to adopt a plan following the 2000 census. The *state* court action had been brought by Democratic plaintiffs, who intervened in the *federal* action that was initiated by Republican plaintiffs. The plan adopted by the state court was drawn by the Democratic plaintiffs in that action. The federal court rejected the plan offered to it by the Republican plaintiffs, but the Republicans did not object to the plan the federal court adopted. The Democrats did object.

The three-judge court gave three reasons for rejecting the state court's plan, notwithstanding the Supreme Court's decisions in *Scott v. Germano* and *Growe v. Emison*. First, the state court plan was adopted by a single judge after being drafted by a partisan group of plaintiffs, and therefore could not be said to reflect state policy. Second, it had not been precleared under Section 5 of the Voting Rights Act. Third, the state court was not authorized to adopt a plan by the Mississippi legislature, which had the exclusive power to redistrict (aside from Congress) under Article I, Section 4 of the Constitution.

In *Branch v. Smith*, 538 U.S. 254 (2003), the Supreme Court, relying on the second of these reasons, affirmed the displacement of the state court's plan with the District Court's plan.[f] Does this decision reflect a retreat from the *Scott-Growe* protection of state autonomy? Recall that plans drawn by a state court in a covered jurisdiction, but not plans drawn by a federal court, are subject to preclearance. For analysis of the issues in *Branch*, written before the Supreme Court ruled, see Jonathan H. Steinberg & Aimee Dudovitz, Branch v. Smith—*Election Law Federalism After* Bush v. Gore: *Are State Courts Unconstitutional Interlopers in Congressional Redistricting?*, 2 ELECTION LAW JOURNAL 91 (2003).

---

f. The Court ignored the District Court's first reason and pointedly declined to affirm the third.

Chapter 5

Minority Vote Dilution

Equal treatment of racial, ethnic, and language minorities is a criterion for redistricting that has loomed so large that we must devote a long chapter to it. Other representational arrangements besides districting—especially the selection of officials in at-large elections or from multi-member districts—have also been challenged as discriminating against minority groups. In this chapter we shall consider such questions as well.

As we shall see, most of the litigation on race in redistricting has occurred under the Voting Rights Act, first enacted in 1965 and later amended on several occasions. Our attention will be concentrated mainly on two sections of the Voting Rights Act, Sections 2 and 5. We shall also take notice of some decisions in the 1990s, in which the Supreme Court placed some limits on the use of race in redistricting.

I. Beyond the Right to Cast a Ballot

In Chapter 2, we saw that the Voting Rights Act of 1965 had the dramatic effect of breaking down the barriers that prevented African Americans from voting in the deep South. In the "covered" states of Alabama, Georgia, Louisiana, Mississippi, South Carolina, Virginia, and much of North Carolina, the most important provisions that accomplished this result were the temporary ban on literacy tests (later made permanent and extended to the entire country), the appointment of federal registrars where necessary, and the "preclearance" requirement in Section 5. Preclearance meant that when a covered jurisdiction adopted or changed any "voting qualification or prerequisite to voting, or standard, practice, or procedure with respect to voting," the change could not go into effect until it had been approved by either the attorney general (who, as a practical matter, receives virtually all preclearance requests) or the U.S. District Court for the District of Columbia.[a]

No one doubted that the immediate and primary purpose of the 1965 act was to assure the right to vote to African Americans, nor that the Act was spectacularly successful in accomplishing this goal. A much more controversial question was whether the act extended to a situation in which blacks were able to vote, but by chance or design the system of representation had the effect of minimizing the influence of their votes.

---

a. As was mentioned in Chapter 2, amendments to the Voting Rights Act since 1965 have added three states—Alaska, Arizona, and Texas—and portions of several additional states, including New York and California, to the list of covered jurisdictions. When a state such as New York or California adopts a change in electoral procedures of the sort covered by Section 5, the changes must be precleared before they can be implemented in the parts of the state that are covered by the Act. *Lopez v. Monterey County*, 525 U.S. 266 (1999).

This important question reached the Supreme Court in 1969, in four separate cases consolidated in the following decision.

Allen v. State Board of Elections
393 U.S. 544 (1969)

MR. CHIEF JUSTICE WARREN delivered the opinion of the Court....

In these four cases, the States have passed new laws or issued new regulations. The central issue is whether these provisions fall within the prohibition of §5 that prevents the enforcement of [changes in voting qualifications and procedures] unless the State first complies with one of the section's approval procedures.

[In the first and most important of the cases, Mississippi amended its statutes to permit county boards of supervisors to change election procedures so that board members would be elected at-large (i.e., each member would be elected by the entire county) rather than from districts. In the second case, a Mississippi statute changed the office of county superintendent of education in eleven specified counties from elective to appointive. In the third case, Mississippi changed the requirements for independent candidates in general elections. In the fourth case, Virginia changed procedures for assisting illiterate voters who sought to vote for write-in candidates.]

[W]e turn to a consideration of whether these state enactments are subject to the approval requirements of §5. These requirements apply to "any voting qualification or prerequisite to voting, or standard, practice, or procedure with respect to voting...." The Act further provides that the term "voting" "shall include all action necessary to make a vote effective in any primary, special, or general election, including, but not limited to, registration, listing ... or other action required by law prerequisite to voting, casting a ballot, and having such ballot counted properly and included in the appropriate totals of votes cast with respect to candidates for public or party office and propositions for which votes are received in an election." §14(c)(1). Appellees in the Mississippi cases maintain that §5 covers only those state enactments which prescribe who may register to vote. While accepting that the Act is broad enough to insure that the votes of all citizens should be cast, appellees urge that §5 does not cover state rules relating to the qualification of candidates or to state decisions as to which offices shall be elective....

We must reject a narrow construction that appellees would give to §5. The Voting Rights Act was aimed at the subtle, as well as the obvious, state regulations which have the effect of denying citizens their right to vote because of their race. Moreover, compatible with the decisions of this Court, the Act gives a broad interpretation to the right to vote, recognizing that voting includes "all action necessary to make a vote effective." We are convinced that in passing the Voting Rights Act, Congress intended that state enactments such as those involved in the instant cases be subject to the §5 approval requirements.

[The Court's review of the legislative history is omitted.]

The weight of the legislative history and an analysis of the basic purposes of the Act indicate that the enactment in each of these cases constitutes a "voting qualification or prerequisite to voting, or standard, practice, or procedure with respect to voting" within the meaning of §5.

[The first of the four cases] involves a change from district to at-large voting for county supervisors. The right to vote can be affected by a dilution of voting power as well as by an absolute prohibition on casting a ballot. See *Reynolds*. Voters who are members of a racial minority might well be in the majority in one district, but in a decided minority in the county as a whole. This type of change could therefore nullify their ability to elect the candidate of their choice just as would prohibiting some of them from voting.

In [the second case] an important county officer in certain counties was made appointive instead of elective. The power of a citizen's vote is affected by this amendment; after the change, he is prohibited from electing an officer formerly subject to the approval of the voters. Such a change could be made either with or without a discriminatory purpose or effect; however, the purpose of §5 was to submit such changes to scrutiny.

The changes in [the third case] appear aimed at increasing the difficulty for an independent candidate to gain a position on the general election ballot. These changes might also undermine the effectiveness of voters who wish to elect independent candidates....

The [last case involves] new procedures for casting write-in votes. As in all these cases, we do not consider whether this change has a discriminatory purpose or effect. It is clear, however, that the new procedure with respect to voting is different from the procedure in effect when the State became subject to the Act; therefore, the enactment must meet the approval requirements of §5 in order to be enforceable....

All four cases are remanded to the District Courts with instructions to issue injunctions restraining the further enforcement of the enactments until such time as the States adequately demonstrate compliance with §5....

MR. JUSTICE HARLAN, concurring in part and dissenting in part.

[T]he Court's construction ignores the structure of the complex regulatory scheme created by the Voting Rights Act. The Court's opinion assumes that §5 may be considered apart from the rest of the Act. In fact, however, the provision is clearly designed to march in lock-step with §4 — the two sections cannot be understood apart from one another. Section 4 is one of the Act's central provisions, suspending the operation of all literacy tests and similar "devices" for at least five years in States whose low voter turnout indicated that these "tests" and "devices" had been used to exclude Negroes from the suffrage in the past. Section 5, moreover, reveals that it was not designed to implement new substantive policies but that it was structured to assure the effectiveness of the dramatic step that Congress had taken in §4. The federal approval procedure found in §5 only applies to those States whose literacy tests or similar "devices" have been suspended by §4. As soon as the State regains the right to apply a literacy test or similar "device" under §4, it also escapes the commands of §5....

As soon as it is recognized that §5 was designed solely to implement the policies of §4, it becomes apparent that the Court's decision today permits the tail to wag the dog. For the Court has now construed §5 to require a revolutionary innovation in American government that goes far beyond that which was accomplished by §4. The fourth section of the Act had the profoundly important purpose of permitting the Negro people to gain access to the voting booths of the South once and for all. But the action taken by Congress in §4 proceeded on the premise that once Negroes had gained free access to the ballot box, state governments would then be suitably responsive to their voice, and federal intervention would not be justified. In moving against "tests and devices" in §4, Congress moved only against those techniques that prevented Negroes from voting at all. Congress did not attempt to restructure state governments. The Court now reads §5, however, as vastly increasing the sphere of federal intervention beyond that contemplated by §4, despite the fact that the two provisions were designed simply to interlock. The District Court for the District of Columbia is no longer limited to examining any new state statute that may tend to deny Negroes their right to vote, as the "tests and devices" suspended by §4 had done. The decision today also requires the special District Court to determine whether various systems of representation favor or disfavor the Negro voter—an area well beyond the scope of §4.... Moreover, it is not clear to me how a court would go about deciding whether an at-large system is to be preferred over a district system. Under one system, Negroes have *some* influence in the election of *all* officers; under the other, minority groups have *more* influence in the selection of *fewer* officers. If courts cannot intelligently compare such alternatives, it should not be readily inferred that Congress has required them to undertake the task....

Section 5, then, should properly be read to require federal approval only of those state laws that change either voter qualifications or the manner in which elections are conducted. This does not mean, however, that the District Courts in the four cases before us were right in unanimously concluding that the Voting Rights Act did not apply. Rather, it seems to me that only the judgment in [the first case] should be affirmed, as that case involves a state statute which simply gives each county the right to elect its Board of Supervisors on an at-large basis.

[Justice Harlan concluded that in the remaining three cases the changes were within §5, as he interpreted it. Justices Marshall and Douglas joined Justice Harlan in dissenting on a remedial question, the discussion of which is omitted in the above excerpts. Justice Black dissented from the Court's entire decision because he believed §5 was unconstitutional.]

Notes and Questions

1. Whether Congress contemplated in 1965 that Section 5 would extend to structural aspects of elections beyond the right to vote itself remains a controversial issue. However, its primary interest is historical. Most people would agree that Congress' extensions and amendments of the Voting Rights Act in 1970, 1975, 1982, and 2006, without inserting language seeking to overrule *Allen*, constitute a ratification of that decision. That view is not held universally, however, and was challenged by Justice Thomas in his concurring opinion in *Holder v. Hall*, portions of which are reprinted later in this chapter.

2. Challenges to at-large electoral systems in local jurisdictions have been the most common type of case brought under the Voting Rights Act since the 1970s, but the logic of *Allen* extended to other aspects of the electoral system. The Court recognized this in *Perkins v. Matthews*, 400 U.S. 379 (1971), holding that annexations of new areas into cities were subject to preclearance, because the new voters added to the city could affect the voting power of prior residents, including protected minority groups; and in *Georgia v. United States*, 411 U.S. 526 (1973), holding that the adoption of legislative districting plans were subject to preclearance.

These decisions had a big practical impact. See, *e.g.*, Chandler Davidson, *The Voting Rights Act: A Brief History*, in Controversies in Minority Voting 7, 28–29 (1992):

> Until *Allen*, section 5 had been little used. The Justice Department, in the three and one-half years between passage of the act and the *Allen* decision, had objected to only six proposed changes in election procedure in covered jurisdictions, and none of these concerned vote dilution. In the three and one-half years following *Allen*, there were 118 objections, of which 88 involved dilution schemes. These included attempts to replace single-member district systems with multi-member ones, to replace plurality rules by majority-vote requirements, to create numbered-place systems and staggered terms, and to annex disproportionately

white suburbs. A tally at the end of 1989 revealed that 2,335 proposed changes had been objected to under section 5. The great majority of objections involved proposals that would have diluted the votes of racial groups or language minorities. Had it not been for section 5 and the *Allen* decision, almost all the proposals would have become law. Moreover, white officials in the South would surely have implemented a much larger number of dilutionary changes had there been no section 5 to deter them.

At the same time, the *percentage* of preclearance requests that have been denied has been small, well under two percent of the total. See Timothy G. O'Rourke, *The 1982 Amendments and the Voting Rights Paradox*, in *id.*, 85, 85–87.

3. Alert readers of our indispensable footnotes will recall from Chapter 4 (footnote b) that redistricting plans formulated by state courts are subject to Section 5 preclearance. Do other state court decisions that change election laws also require preclearance before they can be put into effect? Generally yes, but not always, as became clear from *Riley v. Kennedy*, 128 S.Ct. 1970 (2008). Vacancies on city councils in Alabama were filled by gubernatorial appointments. The legislature passed a "local law," which was precleared, calling for special elections to fill such vacancies, but only for the city of Mobile. The Supreme Court of Alabama eventually determined that the local law violated the state constitution. In the meantime, however, a lower state court had upheld the statute and a vacancy on the Mobile city council had been filled by a special election. The state supreme court's decision had the effect of restoring gubernatorial appointments to fill vacancies. The question for the Supreme Court in *Riley* was whether under these circumstances the special election system was in "force or effect" within the meaning of Section 5. If it was, then the state supreme court decision switching back to gubernatorial appointments would have to be precleared. But Justice Ginsburg, writing for a 7–2 majority, held that it was not. One reason, she said, was that otherwise an erroneous decision by a lower state court could have the practical effect of binding the whole state to a law that, according to the state supreme court, was invalid. Justices Stevens and Souter dissented.

4. As has been pointed out by Katharine Inglis Butler, *Reapportionment, the Courts, and the Voting Rights Act: A Resegregation of the Political Process?*, 56 UNIVERSITY OF COLORADO LAW REVIEW 1, 28–29 (1984), preclearance decisions of the Attorney General are often final, as a practical matter.

> The Attorney General's decision to deny preclearance is not subject to judicial review and can be overturned only through a burdensome declaratory judgment action in the District of Columbia District Court—a remedy not often pursued. The vast majority of election law changes are submitted by local political subdivisions, e.g., counties, cities, and school boards. Many cannot afford the declaratory judgment action, and for most others, challenging the Attorney General's objection is not worth the effort. Thus, virtually all submissions are made initially to the Attorney General, and few of his decisions are ever challenged. Consequently, many of the Attorney General's substantive preclearance standards have never been subjected to judicial scrutiny.

Suppose that a jurisdiction seeks preclearance for a districting plan in the District of Columbia District Court and that the Attorney General, appearing in the case, makes no objection to the plan. Intervenors, however, contend that the plan violates Section 5 and that preclearance should therefore be denied. The Attorney General's approval would have been final if the jurisdiction had sought it. Is the Attorney General's assent to the plan binding on the District Court? See *Georgia v. Ashcroft*, 195 F.Supp.2d 25 (D.D.C. 2002).

As we shall see later in this chapter, the District Court's ruling was vacated and remanded on other grounds.

5. One three-judge federal court expressed strong disapproval of the procedures the Justice Department used in preclearing a congressional districting plan for Georgia in 1991 and 1992:

> One of the "third party" redistricting proposals submitted to the legislature in 1991 would later earn the ominous moniker, "the max-black plan." That plan, created by Ms. Kathleen Wilde, then an attorney with the American Civil Liberties Union and in her capacity as advocate for the Black Caucus of the Georgia General Assembly, provided for three "majority-minority" congressional districts in Georgia....
>
> During the redistricting process, Ms. Wilde was in constant contact with both Keith Borders and Thomas Armstrong, the DOJ line attorneys overseeing preclearance of Georgia's redistricting efforts. There were countless communications, including notes, maps, and charts, by phone, mail and facsimile, between Wilde and the DOJ team; those transactions signified close cooperation between Wilde and DOJ during the preclearance process. The Court was presented with a sampling of these communiques, and we find them disturbing.
>
> It is obvious from a review of the materials that Ms. Wilde's relationship with the DOJ Voting Section was informal and familiar; the dynamics were that of peers working together, not of an advocate submitting proposals to higher authorities. DOJ was more accessible—and amenable—to the opinions of the ACLU than to those of the Attorney General of the State of Georgia. It is clear from our proceedings that Ms. Wilde discussed with DOJ lawyers the smallest details of her plan, constantly sending revisions, updates, and data throughout the period from October, 1991 to April, 1992; she occasionally sent documents to DOJ lawyers "per your request." Ms. Wilde worked with DOJ in other ways: During the reapportionment process for Georgia's House districts, DOJ attorney Nancy Sardison told Mark Cohen, the Senior Assistant Attorney General for Georgia, to meet with Ms. Wilde to revise a majority-black House district. Mr. Cohen had presumptuously thought the district satisfactory, but was dutifully informed by Ms. Sardison that Ms. Wilde was "still having some problems with it." Contrary to Mr. Armstrong's claims at trial, the max-black proposal was not merely "one of the alternatives [DOJ] considered," and Ms. Wilde was not simply one of various advocates. Her work was of particular importance to DOJ lawyers, whose criteria for and opinions of Georgia's submissions were greatly influenced by Ms. Wilde and her agenda....
>
> During our hearings it became clear that the Department of Justice had cultivated a number of partisan "informants" within the ranks of the Georgia legislature, including at least one State Senator—a congressional candidate no less—and an aide to [the] Lieutenant Governor.... DOJ regularly received from them information on the General Assembly's redistricting sessions.... DOJ used that information even to question the integrity of State legislators who could not know their accusers....
>
> It is unclear whether DOJ's maximization policy was driven more by Ms. Wilde's advocacy or DOJ's own misguided reading of the Voting Rights Act. This much, however, is clear: the close working relationship between Ms. Wilde and the Voting Section, the repetition of Ms. Wilde's ideas in [objection letters sent

by the Assistant Attorney General for Civil Rights], and the slow convergence of size and shape between the max-black plan and the plan DOJ finally precleared, bespeak a direct link between the max-black plan formulated by the ACLU and the preclearance requirements imposed by DOJ.

Succinctly put, the considerable influence of ACLU advocacy on the voting rights decisions of the United States Attorney General is an embarrassment.

Johnson v. Miller, 864 F.Supp. 1354, 1360–68 (S.D.Ga. 1994), aff'd., *Miller v. Johnson*, 515 U.S. 900 (1995). The court's description of the preclearance process in the Georgia case may or may not be a fair one, and to the extent it is accurate it may or may not be representative of the process in other cases. To the extent that it is accurate and representative, are you as troubled by it as the court was? Presumably, interested groups play an influential role in the implementation of policy throughout the federal government. Is such influence less appropriate in the implementation of the Voting Rights Act than in other policy areas? Is it relevant to these questions that Ms. Wilde was employed by a non-profit organization and was representing members of one of the groups the Voting Rights Act is intended to protect?

However these questions may be answered, it is clear that voting rights activists did not represent the only outside influence on the Justice Department. As John Dunne, the Assistant Attorney General for Civil Rights under the George Bush administration in the early 1990s testified in the *Miller* litigation:

You know, I can't tell you that I was sort of like a monk hidden away in a monastery with only the most pure of intentions. I am a Republican. I was part of a Republican administration. And to tell you that at no moment during the … discharge of my responsibilities, was I totally immune or insensitive to political consideration, I don't think would justify anybody's belief.

Quoted in Charles S. Bullock III, *Winners and Losers in the Latest Round of Redistricting*, 44 EMORY LAW JOURNAL 943, 948 (1995).

II. Applying Section 5

Allen and the subsequent reenactments of the Voting Rights Act firmly established the principle that the act extends to electoral mechanisms that affect the ability of minority voters as a group to make their votes count. However, the establishment of this principle did not, by itself, provide answers to questions raised by Justice Harlan in his *Allen* dissent regarding how the attorney general and the courts should decide which electoral procedures impermissibly discriminate against minority groups.

The Supreme Court addressed these issues in 1976 in *Beer v. United States*, reprinted below. In that case, the Court established "nonretrogression" as the standard for applying Section 5. This principle declared that a districting plan should be precleared by the Justice Department unless it appeared that under the new plan, fewer districts would be subject to electoral control by a protected minority group than under the plan that was being replaced. The Justice Department later took the view that under certain circumstances, preclearance could be denied even in the absence of retrogression. As we shall see, the Supreme Court has generally rejected that view. But the meaning of retrogression has continued to be a controversial issue, most recently addressed in the 2006 amendments to the Voting Rights Act.

Beer v. United States

425 U.S. 130 (1976)

Mr. Justice STEWART delivered the opinion of the Court....

The city of New Orleans brought this suit under §5 seeking a judgment declaring that a reapportionment of New Orleans' councilmanic districts did not have the purpose or effect of denying or abridging the right to vote on account of race or color. The District Court entered a judgment of dismissal, holding that the new reapportionment plan would have the effect of abridging the voting rights of New Orleans' Negro citizens....

I

New Orleans is a city of almost 600,000 people. Some 55% of that population is white and the remaining 45% is Negro. Some 65% of the registered voters are white, and the remaining 35% are Negro.[4] In 1954, New Orleans adopted a mayor-council form of government. Since that time the municipal charter has provided that the city council is to consist of seven members, one to be elected from each of five councilmanic districts, and two to be elected by the voters of the city at large. The 1954 charter also requires an adjustment of the boundaries of the five single-member councilmanic districts following each decennial census to reflect population shifts among the districts.

In 1961, the city council redistricted the city based on the 1960 census figures. That reapportionment plan established four districts that stretched from the edge of Lake Pontchartrain on the north side of the city to the Mississippi River on the city's south side. The fifth district was wedge shaped and encompassed the city's downtown area. In one of these councilmanic districts, Negroes constituted a majority of the population, but only about half of the registered voters. In the other four districts white voters clearly outnumbered Negro voters. No Negro was elected to the New Orleans City Council during the decade from 1960 to 1970.

After receipt of the 1970 census figures the city council adopted a reapportionment plan (Plan I) that continued the basic north-to-south pattern of councilmanic districts combined with a wedge-shaped, downtown district. Under Plan I Negroes constituted a majority of the population in two districts, but they did not make up a majority of registered voters in any district. The largest percentage of Negro voters in a single district under Plan I was 45.2%. When the city submitted Plan I to the Attorney General pursuant to §5, he objected to it, stating that it appeared to "dilute black voting strength by combining a number of black voters with a larger number of white voters in each of the five districts." He also expressed the view that "the district lines (were not) drawn as they (were) because of any compelling governmental need" and that the district lines did "not reflect numeric population configurations or considerations of district compactness or regularity of shape."

Even before the Attorney General objected to Plan I, the city authorities had commenced work on a second plan—Plan II. That plan followed the general north-to-south districting pattern common to the 1961 apportionment and Plan I. It produced Negro population majorities in two districts and a Negro voter majority (52.6%) in one district.

---

4. The difference in the two figures is due in part to the fact that proportionately more whites of voting age are registered to vote than are Negroes and in part to the fact that the age structures of the white and Negro populations of New Orleans differ significantly—72.3% of the white population is of voting age, but only 57.1% of the Negro population is of voting age.

When Plan II was submitted to the Attorney General, he posed the same objections to it that he had raised to Plan I. In addition, he noted that "the predominantly black neighborhoods in the city are located generally in an east to west progression," and pointed out that the use of north-to-south districts in such a situation almost inevitably would have the effect of diluting the maximum potential impact of the Negro vote. Following the rejection by the Attorney General of Plan II, the city brought this declaratory judgment action in the United States District Court for the District of Columbia....

II

A

The appellants urge, and the United States on reargument of this case has conceded, that the District Court was mistaken in holding that Plan II could be rejected under §5 solely because it did not eliminate the two at-large councilmanic seats that had existed since 1954. The appellants and the United States are correct in their interpretation of the statute in this regard.

The language of §5 clearly provides that it applies only to proposed changes in voting procedures.... The ordinance that adopted Plan II made no reference to the at-large councilmanic seats. Indeed, since those seats had been established in 1954 by the city charter, an ordinance could not have altered them; any change in the charter would have required approval by the city's voters. The at-large seats, having existed without change since 1954, were not subject to review in this proceeding under §5.

B

The principal argument made by the appellants in this Court is that the District Court erred in concluding that the makeup of the five geographic councilmanic districts under Plan II would have the effect of abridging voting rights on account of race or color. In evaluating this claim it is important to note at the outset that the question is not one of constitutional law, but of statutory construction. A determination of when a legislative reapportionment has "the effect of denying or abridging the right to vote on account of race or color," must depend, therefore, upon the intent of Congress in enacting the Voting Rights Act and specifically §5.

The legislative history reveals that the basic purpose of Congress in enacting the Voting Rights Act was "to rid the country of racial discrimination in voting." *South Carolina v. Katzenbach*. Section 5 was intended to play an important role in achieving that goal:

> Section 5 was a response to a common practice in some jurisdictions of staying one step ahead of the federal courts by passing new discriminatory voting laws as soon as the old ones had been struck down. That practice had been possible because each new law remained in effect until the Justice Department or private plaintiffs were able to sustain the burden of proving that the new law, too, was discriminatory.... Congress therefore decided, as the Supreme Court held it could, "to shift the advantage of time and inertia from the perpetrators of the evil to its victim," by "freezing election procedures in the covered areas unless the changes can be shown to be nondiscriminatory." H.R.Rep.No. 94-196, pp. 57–58.

By prohibiting the enforcement of a voting-procedure change until it has been demonstrated to the United States Department of Justice or to a three-judge federal court that the change does not have a discriminatory effect, Congress desired to prevent States from "undo(ing) or defeat(ing) the rights recently won" by Negroes. H.R.Rep.No.91-397, p. 8. Section 5 was intended "to insure that (the gains thus far achieved in minority political participation) shall not be destroyed through new (discriminatory) procedures and techniques." S.Rep.No.94-295, p. 19.

When it adopted a 7-year extension of the Voting Rights Act in 1975, Congress explicitly stated that "the standard (under §5) can only be fully satisfied by determining on the basis of the facts found by the Attorney General (or the District Court) to be true whether the ability of minority groups to participate in the political process and to elect their choices to office is *augmented, diminished, or not affected* by the change affecting voting...." H.R.Rep.No.94-196, p. 60 (emphasis added). In other words the purpose of §5 has always been to insure that no voting-procedure changes would be made that would lead to a retrogression in the position of racial minorities with respect to their effective exercise of the electoral franchise.

It is thus apparent that a legislative reapportionment that enhances the position of racial minorities with respect to their effective exercise of the electoral franchise can hardly have the "effect" of diluting or abridging the right to vote on account of race within the meaning of §5. We conclude, therefore, that such an ameliorative new legislative apportionment cannot violate §5 unless the new apportionment itself so discriminates on the basis of race or color as to violate the Constitution.

The application of this standard to the facts of the present case is straightforward. Under the apportionment of 1961 none of the five councilmanic districts had a clear Negro majority of registered voters, and no Negro has been elected to the New Orleans City Council while that apportionment system has been in effect. Under Plan II, by contrast, Negroes will constitute a majority of the population in two of the five districts and a clear majority of the registered voters in one of them. Thus, there is every reason to predict, upon the District Court's hypothesis of bloc voting, that at least one and perhaps two Negroes may well be elected to the council under Plan II. It was therefore error for the District Court to conclude that Plan II "will ... have the effect of denying or abridging the right to vote on account of race or color" within the meaning of §5 of the Voting Rights Act.

It is possible that a legislative reapportionment could be a substantial improvement over its predecessor in terms of lessening racial discrimination, and yet nonetheless continue so to discriminate on the basis of race or color as to be unconstitutional. The United States has made no claim that Plan II suffers from any such disability, nor could it rationally do so....

Accordingly, the judgment of the District Court is vacated, and the case is remanded to that court for further proceedings consistent with this opinion.

It is so ordered.

Mr. Justice STEVENS took no part in the consideration or decision of this case.

Mr. Justice WHITE, dissenting.

With Mr. Justice MARSHALL, I cannot agree that §5 of the Voting Rights Act of 1965 reaches only those changes in election procedures that are more burdensome to the complaining minority than pre-existing procedures. As I understand §5, the validity of *any* procedural change otherwise within the reach of the section must be determined under the statutory standard whether the proposed legislation has the purpose or effect of abridging or denying the right to vote based on race or color.

This statutory standard is to be applied here in light of the District Court's findings, which are supported by the evidence and are not now questioned by the Court. The findings were that the nominating process in New Orleans' councilmanic elections is subject to majority vote and "anti-single-shot" rules and that there is a history of bloc racial voting in New Orleans, the predictable result being that no Negro candidate will win in any district in which his race is in the minority. In my view, where these facts exist, combined with a segregated residential pattern, §5 is not satisfied unless, to the extent practicable, the new electoral districts afford the Negro minority the opportunity to achieve legislative representation roughly proportional to the Negro population in the community. Here, with a seven-member city council, the black minority constituting approximately 45% of the population of New Orleans, would be entitled under §5, as I construe it, to the opportunity of electing at least three city councilmen more than provided by the plan at issue here.

Bloc racial voting is an unfortunate phenomenon, but we are repeatedly faced with the findings of knowledgeable district courts that it is a fact of life. Where it exists, most often the result is that neither white nor black can be elected from a district in which his race is in the minority. As I see it, Congress has the power to minimize the effects of racial voting, particularly where it occurs in the context of other electoral rules operating to muffle the political potential of the minority. I am also satisfied that §5 was aimed at this end, among others, and should be so construed and applied....

Applying §5 in this way would at times require the drawing of district lines based on race; but Congress has this power where deliberate discrimination at the polls and the relevant electoral laws and customs have effectively foreclosed Negroes from enjoying a modicum of fair representation in the city council or other legislative body....

Mr. Justice MARSHALL, with whom Mr. Justice BRENNAN joins, dissenting.

... While we have settled the contours of §5's jurisdiction..., we have yet to devote much attention to defining §5's substantive force within those bounds. Thus, we are faced today for the first time with the question of §5's substantive application to a redistricting plan. Essentially, we must answer one question: When does a redistricting plan have the effect of "abridging" the right to vote on account of race or color?

The Court never answers this question. Instead, it produces a convoluted construction of the statute that transforms the single question suggested by §5 into three questions, and then provides precious little guidance in answering any of them. Under the Court's reading of §5, we cannot reach the abridgment question unless we have first determined that a proposed redistricting plan would "lead to a retrogression in the position of racial minorities" in comparison to their position under the existing plan. The Court's conclusion that §5 demands this preliminary inquiry is simply wrong; it finds no support in the language of the statute and disserves the legislative purposes behind §5....

The legislative history of the Voting Rights Act makes clear, and the Court assiduously ignores, that §5 was designed to preclude new districting plans that "perpetuate discrimination," to prevent covered jurisdictions from "circumventing the guarantees of the 15th amendment" by switching to new, and discriminatory, districting plans the moment litigants appear on the verge of having an existing one declared unconstitutional, and promptly to end discrimination in voting by pressuring covered jurisdictions to remove all vestiges of discrimination from their enactments before submitting them for preclearance. None of these purposes is furthered by an inquiry into whether a proposed districting plan is "ameliorative" or "retrogressive." Indeed, the statement of these purposes is alone sufficient to demonstrate the error of the Court's construction.

All the purposes of the statute are met, however, by the inquiry §5's language plainly contemplates: whether, in absolute terms, the covered jurisdiction can show that its proposed plan meets the constitutional standard.[b] Because it is consistent with both the statutory language and the legislative purposes, this is the proper construction of the provision. Thus, it is the effect of the plan itself, rather than the effect of the change in plans, that should be at issue in a §5 proceeding....

[W]e have ... acknowledged that a showing of less than proportional representation of Negroes by Negro-elected representatives is not alone sufficient to prove unconstitutional dilution:

> To sustain such claims (of dilution), it is not enough that the racial group allegedly discriminated against has not had legislative seats in proportion to its voting potential. The plaintiffs' burden is to produce evidence to support findings that the political processes leading to nomination and election were not equally open to participation by the group in question — that its members had less opportunity than did other residents in the district to participate in the political processes and to elect legislators of their choice. *White v. Regester.*

It is this constitutionally based concept of dilution that we have held to govern in §5 proceedings. The concept may be readily transferred to the §5 context simply by adjusting for the shifted burden of proof. Thus, if the proposed redistricting plan underrepresents minority group members, the burden is on the covered jurisdiction to show that "the political processes leading to nomination and election were ... equally open to participation by the group in question." If the jurisdiction cannot make such a showing, then the proposed plan must be rejected, unless compelling reasons for its adoption can be demonstrated.

Application of these standards to the case before us is straightforward. Preliminarily, while I agree with the Court that the two at-large seats on the New Orleans City Council are not themselves before the Court for approval and cannot serve as an independent basis for the rejection of Plan II, I do not think Plan II should be assessed without regard to the seven-member council it is designed to fill. Proportional representation of Negroes among the five district seats on the council does not assure Negroes proportional representation on the entire council when, as the District Court found, the two at-large seats will be occupied by white-elected members....

Thus the District Court correctly began by considering the seven-member council and a districting plan that, given New Orleans' long history of racial bloc voting, allows Negroes the expectation of no more than one seat (14% of the council), if that, in a city with a 34.5% Negro voting population. Manifestly, the plan serves to underrepresent the Negro voting population. The District Court then, properly, turned to consider whether Negroes are excluded from full participation in the political processes in New Orleans. The court found considerable evidence of both past and present exclusion, none of which is seriously contested here.

[T]he city has failed to show an acceptable justification for the racially dilutive effect of Plan II. Accordingly, the District Court correctly concluded that appellants failed to demonstrate that Plan II would not have the effect of abridging the right to vote on account of race....

---

b. In an earlier footnote, omitted here, Justice Marshall had written, insofar "as redistricting legislation is concerned..., I believe a showing of purpose or of effect is alone sufficient to demonstrate unconstitutionality...." As we shall see in the next section, the Supreme Court later held, contrary to Justice Marshall's view, that a showing of discriminatory effect was insufficient to establish a constitutional violation without a showing of discriminatory purpose. — EDS.

Notes and Questions

1. Many voting rights activists were dissatisfied with the nonretrogression principle, because they believed it provided no relief to protected groups if they had been treated unfairly all along. In most jurisdictions as of the 1970s there were few and often no congressional, state or local districts in which African-Americans predominated. During the redistricting of the 1980s and, especially, the 1990s, those in charge of redistricting often felt legal and sometimes political pressure to create additional "majority-minority districts." As a result, *reducing* the number of majority-minority districts often was not even possible and almost never was likely as a practical matter. Whatever could be said for or against *Beer* as a matter of statutory construction, for practical purposes the decision seemed to make Section 5 marginal at best to the redistricting process. As we shall see, in the post-1990 redistricting round, the Justice Department found reason to believe that it was not necessarily limited by the *Beer* nonretrogression rule. But through the 1980s, most proceedings under the Voting Rights Act relating to redistricting arose under Section 2, which we shall consider in the next section.

2. Justice Stewart gives various reasons for his conclusion that only retrogressive changes justify denial of preclearance under Section 5, but his opinion contains almost no discussion of what is meant by retrogression. Preclearance of the New Orleans redistricting plan had been denied on the ground that it should have contained more districts in which blacks were a majority of registered voters. Once having interpreted Section 5 as embodying the nonretrogression rule, in a single conclusory paragraph Justice Stewart could reach the "straightforward" conclusion that New Orleans, which increased the number of such districts from none to one, was entitled to preclearance.

Justice Stewart's "straightforward" conclusion glossed over difficult questions about what should be regarded as retrogression. Concentrating blacks into two districts so that they made up the majority of the population in both and the majority of registered voters in one meant that the percentage of blacks in the remaining three districts was much lower than it could have been if the black population had been more evenly divided among the five districts. Was there a reason why *that* did not constitute retrogression, other than the fact that all the participants in the controversy—the Justice Department, voting rights activists, and the city itself—proceeded on the opposite theory? The Court's failure to address this fundamental theoretical question—is a minority group better off controlling the highest possible number of districts or having a substantial presence in all or most districts?—has not itself been a great practical problem, because the same answer that was assumed in *Beer* continued to be assumed throughout the subsequent history of the Voting Rights Act,[c] at least until *Georgia v. Ashcroft*, discussed below. Nor, for the reason given in Note 1, has the Court been required to say much on more subtle questions about what constitutes retrogression. That began to change in the post-2000 redistricting, however. In future decades, the nonretrogression rule figures to have new teeth and its application promises to be more complex than at any previous time.

The reason nonretrogression is developing new teeth is that the factors mentioned in Note 1 no longer apply. In the post-1990 round, majority-minority districts were created at all levels of government in unprecedented numbers. At least the theoretical possibility

---

c. In *Thornburg v. Gingles*, reprinted in the next section, the Court gave a much more thorough analysis of the concepts underlying Section 2 of the Voting Rights Act, and much of what was said in that opinion also can explain why majority-minority districts should be favored under Section 5, so that a reduction in the number of such districts would constitute retrogression.

of retrogression now exists in many places where it did not exist before. Furthermore, there is reason to believe that in the absence of Section 5, there could be significant pressure for retrogression in some places.

One reason is that under the racial gerrymandering cases considered later in this chapter, overly aggressive efforts to create majority-minority districts may be held to violate the Constitution. This in itself may not create much pressure for retrogressive plans, especially since majority-minority districts that are necessary to comply with Section 5 are unlikely to be held unconstitutional, at least under current doctrine. However, a majority-minority district drawn in a particular manner to serve other political interests may be constitutionally vulnerable. If, in order to maintain the existing number of majority-minority districts, legislators have to sacrifice other interests or risk having the entire plan being declared unconstitutional, they might feel temptation to reduce the number of majority-minority districts. This is one situation in which the new teeth of the nonretrogression rule would be felt, because if the legislators succumb to the temptation, they probably will be unable to win preclearance for their plan.

A second reason is that in some places, the percentage of African-Americans in the population has decreased. Suppose that after the 1990 census blacks made up 40 percent of the population of a city and that in the subsequent redistricting, they constituted a majority in two of the five city council districts. Suppose that because of migration patterns, the 2000 census shows blacks making up only 25 percent of the city. It might be difficult for political or geographical reasons to draw a new plan in which blacks continue to be a majority in two districts. Would it be retrogression in the new plan if blacks are the majority in only one district?

In fact, when that situation occurs it is likely to present an even more complicated political and legal problem than the above paragraph suggests, because the most likely reason blacks have declined as a percentage of the population in many American metropolitan areas—including some covered by Section 5—is that they have been replaced by Hispanics, another protected minority group under the Voting Rights Act. Notes 3 and 4 below explore some of the complexities that can arise in redistricting when three racial or ethnic groups are significantly represented in the population.

In 2001, the Justice Department adopted regulations setting forth, among other things, how it would approach the question of retrogression in preclearance proceedings. 66 Fed.Reg. 5411-14, available at http://www.usdoj.gov/crt/voting/sec_5/fedregvoting.htm. The Department's general approach is described in the regulations as follows:

> A proposed plan is retrogressive under the Section 5 "effect" prong if its net effect would be to reduce minority voters' "effective exercise of the electoral franchise" when compared with the benchmark plan [which is usually the plan in effect when the new redistricting plan is adopted.] *See Beer.* The effective exercise of the electoral franchise usually is assessed in redistricting submissions in terms of the opportunity for minority voters to elect candidates of their choice. The presence of racially polarized voting is an important factor considered by the Department of Justice in assessing minority voting strength. A proposed redistricting plan ordinarily will occasion an objection by the Department of Justice if the plan reduces minority voting strength relative to the benchmark plan and a fairly-drawn alternative plan could ameliorate or prevent that retrogression.

3. Suppose there is an area of 500 voters that must be divided into five legislative districts of 100 voters each. Racially, the voters break down as follows: 280 white, 150 African-American, and 70 Latino. The old plan, which must be replaced because of a new census,

consists of five districts. For simplification, we begin with the assumption that each of the old districts has a white majority, so that retrogression is not possible. Initially the legislature enacts Plan I. However, in response to pressure from African-American organizations, Plan I is repealed, and Plan II is adopted. The racial composition of the districts under the two plans is as follows:[d]

Plan I

	Dist. 1	Dist. 2	Dist. 3	Dist. 4	Dist. 5
White	65	65	65	70	15
African-American	30	30	30	30	30
Latino	5	5	5	0	55

Plan II

	Dist. 1	Dist. 2	Dist. 3	Dist. 4	Dist. 5
White	80	80	80	20	20
African-American	10	10	10	60	60
Latino	10	10	10	20	20

What result if Latino voters sue to have Plan I restored, on the ground that Plan II dilutes Latino votes? Will these plaintiffs have a better chance if, instead of seeking to restore Plan I, they ask the court to impose a new plan, Plan III, whose districts' racial compositions are as follows?

Plan III

	Dist. 1	Dist. 2	Dist. 3	Dist. 4	Dist. 5
White	90	90	35	30	35
African-American	10	10	60	60	10
Latino	0	0	5	10	55

Would the white voters have a constitutional objection if Plan III is adopted? Would your answer be affected if it were shown that white voters in this area nearly always vote for Republican candidates and African-American and Latino voters nearly always vote for Democrats?

Because we have assumed up to now that the old plan contains no majority-minority districts, we have eliminated the possibility of retrogression. The legal claims referred to above would have to be brought either under the Constitution or Section 2 of the Voting Rights Act, possibilities explored in the next section. Now let us reintroduce the possibility of retrogression by assuming that Plan II was adopted in 2001, creating three majority white-Anglo districts and two majority-African-American districts. Now assume that the 2010 census shows that the white-Anglo population has declined to 260, the black population has declined to 120, and the Latino population has grown to 120. The incumbent members, three of whom are white-Anglo and two of whom are African-American, propose an incumbent-protection plan, Plan IV.

Plan IV

	Dist. 1	Dist. 2	Dist. 3	Dist. 4	Dist. 5
White	70	70	80	20	20
African-American	5	0	0	60	55
Latino	25	30	20	20	25

---

d. For purposes of simplification, we make the unrealistic assumption that all residents are voters. Thus, each of the plans perfectly satisfies the one person, one vote rule.

An organization representing Latinos comes forward with Plan V. If it is adopted, would it be precleared under Section 5 of the Voting Rights Act?

Plan V

	Dist. 1	Dist. 2	Dist. 3	Dist. 4	Dist. 5
White	70	70	90	20	10
African-American	15	15	10	20	60
Latino	15	15	0	60	30

4. *United Jewish Organizations v. Carey*, 430 U.S. 144 (1977), described in Part IV of this chapter, arose when Hasidic Jews objected to being divided into two districts to facilitate creation of majority-minority districts for blacks and Puerto Ricans. The existence of possible conflicts between groups, whether between nonwhites and a subgroup of whites or between two racial or ethnic minorities, has caused some commentators to express skepticism of the vote dilution principle. See Hugh Davis Graham, *Voting Rights and the American Regulatory State*, in Controversies in Minority Voting, *supra*, at 177, 193–94:

> Although statutory language continues to disclaim any goal of proportional representation for protected minorities, enforcement practices tend to affirm it. Hispanic immigrants are protected, but Russian immigrants are not. Minority rights leaders claim a right to vote for candidates of their "first choice," but it is not clear from what principle this right derives, or how it is defined, or whether nonminority voters (or women) also possess it. Protected classes are given rights to nondilution, but other voters, including women and many minorities, possess no such rights.
>
> Indeed the theory of nondilution is so tactically selective that it risks incoherence as a general proposition. It does not apply to women, whose history of political discrimination and electoral underrepresentation equals and arguably exceeds that of blacks and Hispanics. Furthermore, it is not clear upon what principle the right of nondilution rests. If redistricting in contiguous neighborhoods of black and Hispanic voters brings competing claims to protection against nondilution in newly drawn districts, as is increasingly likely between blacks and Hispanics in Miami, Houston, and Los Angeles, then whose claims should be vindicated and why? Will blacks, as the target beneficiaries of the Voting Rights Act during its first decade, have a superior claim to nondilution in the coming electoral clashes with neighboring Hispanics? Upon what principles are federal judges to award nondilution preference?

Others continue to regard the existence of legal protection against minority vote dilution as essential so long as bloc-voting white majorities can nullify the votes of racial or language minorities. For example, one such writer acknowledges that the idea of "more-or-less permanent, racially defined factions locked in electoral battle over the spoils of the political system runs contrary to a number of currently fashionable theories of politics." Samuel Issacharoff, *Polarized Voting and the Political Process: The Transformation of Voting Rights Jurisprudence*, 90 Michigan Law Review 1833, 1872 (1992). Nevertheless, he defends judicial remedies against vote dilution in these terms:

> The focus on racially polarized voting patterns forced the judiciary to confront the actual operation of challenged electoral systems in order to identify precisely the discriminatory mechanisms that frustrated minority political aspirations. By redirecting focus to the bloc voting practices of majority white com-

munities and the resulting exclusion of minority-supported candidates from public office, the new voting rights jurisprudence identified two fundamental distortions in the electoral arena. First, electoral systems that fail to curb the deleterious consequences of racial bloc voting reward a racially defined majority faction with disproportionate political power and, consequently, with disproportionate access to the goods and services distributed through the legislative process. Second, the emergence of a racially defined majority faction compounds the potential for continued social and economic subordination of historically disadvantaged minorities.

Id. at 1836–37.

5. Through the 1990s round of redistricting it was widely believed that even in the absence of actual or intended retrogression, preclearance could be denied if a plan was intentionally discriminatory against a protected minority group. The Supreme Court decided otherwise in *Reno v. Bossier Parish School Board*, 528 U.S. 320 (2000) (*Bossier Parish II*).[e] The 2006 renewal of the Voting Rights Act added a new paragraph to Section 5 to nullify *Bossier Parish II* by restoring the "discriminatory purpose" standard that was in place and administered until 2000. One study found that "by the 1990s, the purpose prong of section 5 had become the dominant legal basis for [preclearance] objections. As a result, the jurisprudential change likely to have the greatest impact on the incidence of objections by the late 1990s was to eliminate the purpose prong or section 5. that is, in effect, what the majority opinion in Bossier II accomplished." Peyton McCrary, Christopher Seaman, & Richard Valelly, *The Law of Preclearance: Enforcing Section 5*, in David Epstein et al., eds., THE FUTURE OF THE VOTING RIGHTS ACT 20, 29 (2006). That is why historian Morgan Kousser called the nullification of *Bossier Parish II* the "most important part" of the 2006 amendments. J. Morgan Kousser, *The Strange, Ironic Career of Section 5 of the Voting Rights Act, 1965–2007*, 86 TEXAS LAW REVIEW 667, 754 (2008).

6. In *Georgia v. Ashcroft*, 195 F.Supp.2d 25 (D.D.C. 2002), a three-judge District Court refused to grant preclearance to a state Senate plan adopted by the Georgia legislature. In *Georgia*, the courts were spared the possible problem of competing minority groups, because the only large minority group in question was African Americans. The legislature's plan preserved about the same number of majority-minority districts as the previous Georgia Senate plan but reduced the black population of a few of the districts to very close to 50 percent. According to the District Court, the mere fact that the number of majority-minority districts arguably had been maintained or even increased was not sufficient to warrant preclearance, but neither would a finding that the number had been reduced be sufficient reason for denying preclearance.[f]

---

e. This case is known as *Bossier Parish II*. We shall encounter *Bossier Parish I* in the next section.

f. There was some question as to exactly how many majority-minority districts were in the plan. The court regarded black voting age population as a percentage of total voting age population ("BVAP" and "VAP" in the parlance of redistricters) as more relevant than total population figures. But Georgia and the Justice Department offered different figures for BVAP, depending on how one counts individuals who identify themselves as both black and of some other racial or ethnic group on the census form. The court also considered the percentage of blacks among registered voters. There were thus three percentages of blacks that could be considered. These percentages varied by only small margins, but the legislature had drawn some of the districts so close to 50–50 that the different methods led to slightly different results on the total of majority-minority districts. As is explained in the text, the court did not regard the number of majority-minority districts as dispositive. Therefore the court was not called upon to endorse one method over the others.

> While courts have frequently considered the number of "majority-minority" districts as indicative of minority voting strength, the parties in this matter apparently agree that Section 5 is not an absolute mandate for maintenance of such districts. This agreement is entirely proper.

Instead, the court said a fact-intensive inquiry was required, centering on the extent of polarized voting.

The state presented expert testimony that given voting patterns in Georgia, a congressional district in which 44.3 percent of the voting age population was black had a 50 percent chance of electing the candidate preferred by black voters. The districts giving rise to contention were districts in which the black voting age population of the district (BVAP) was reduced to about 50 percent, meaning that blacks had more than an even chance of electing the candidate of their choice according to the state's expert. The state argued that so long as the number of such districts is not reduced from the number in the benchmark plan, the plan should be precleared. The court rejected this argument on the ground that the test under Section 5 is not whether a minority group has a sufficient number of "equal opportunity" districts, but whether the new plan reduces the minority group's electoral strength. If the level of racially polarized voting is such that even at 50 percent of BVAP, blacks are less likely to elect the candidate of their choice than at the higher levels of BVAP in the benchmark plan, then preclearance should be denied.

The court acknowledged that the great majority of blacks in the legislature had voted for the plan. While it conceded that this support was strong evidence that the plan had no retrogressive *intent*, black legislative support was less probative that the plan had no retrogressive *effect*. But why would the blacks in the legislature support a plan that the court found to have a retrogressive effect? The answer is that the plan was intended to strengthen the Democrats' chances of maintaining control of the state Senate. All the black members of the legislature were Democrats, and their committee chairmanships and other leadership positions depended on maintaining their party's majority. They were therefore willing to strengthen Democratic prospects in adjacent districts by moving some black voters into those districts, even at the cost of slightly increasing black legislators' electoral jeopardy in a few instances. The court acknowledged this motivation, but said that "it does not follow that anything that is good for the Democratic Party is good for African-American voters—at least within the context of this court's Section 5 inquiry."

Does application of the Voting Rights Act in this manner promote the Act's purposes? In the following decision, a 5–4 majority on the Supreme Court overruled the District Court on the merits. Is the Supreme Court's approach more in accord with the Act's purposes? (Hint: These are not intended as rhetorical questions.)

As we shall see, when the Voting Rights Act was renewed in 2006, one of the most significant amendments to the law was intended precisely to overrule *Georgia v. Ashcroft*. But we need to know something about the decision to understand what came to be known as the "*Georgia v. Ashcroft* fix."[g]

---

g. However, because the 2006 amendments deprive the decision of authoritativeness, we have edited it more severely than we otherwise would have done, particularly with respect to the specifics of the Georgia plan.

Georgia v. Ashcroft

539 U.S. 461 (2003)

Justice O'CONNOR delivered the opinion of the Court.

In this case, we decide whether Georgia's State Senate redistricting plan should have been precleared under §5 of the Voting Rights Act of 1965.... We therefore must decide whether Georgia's State Senate redistricting plan is retrogressive as compared to its previous, benchmark districting plan.

I

A

[Preclearance problems, litigation, and legislative action caused Georgia to use several different redistricting plans during the 1990s. The final plan for the State Senate was adopted by the legislature in 1997. That plan] drew 56 districts, 11 of them with a total black population of over 50%, and 10 of them with a black voting age population of over 50%. The 2000 census revealed that these numbers had increased so that 13 districts had a black population of at least 50%, with the black voting age population exceeding 50% in 12 of those districts. After the 2000 census, the Georgia General Assembly began the process of redistricting the Senate once again. No party contests that a substantial majority of black voters in Georgia vote Democratic, or that all elected black representatives in the General Assembly are Democrats. The goal of the Democratic leadership—black and white—was to maintain the number of majority-minority districts and also increase the number of Democratic Senate seats.... The Vice Chairman of the Senate Reapportionment Committee, Senator Robert Brown..., who is black, ... believed when he designed the Senate plan that as the black voting age population in a district increased beyond what was necessary, it would "pus[h] the whole thing more towards [the] Republican[s]." And "correspondingly," Senator Brown stated, "the more you diminish the power of African-Americans overall." ... The plan as designed by Senator Brown's committee kept true to the dual goals of maintaining at least as many majority-minority districts while also attempting to increase Democratic strength in the Senate. Part of the Democrats' strategy was not only to maintain the number of majority-minority districts, but to increase the number of so-called "influence" districts, where black voters would be able to exert a significant—if not decisive—force in the election process.... According to the 2000 census, as compared to the benchmark plan, the new plan reduced by five the number of districts with a black voting age population in excess of 60%. Yet it increased the number of majority-black voting age population districts by one, and it increased the number of districts with a black voting age population of between 25% and 50% by four....

The Senate adopted its new districting plan on August 10, 2001, by a vote of 29 to 26. Ten of the eleven black Senators voted for the plan. The Georgia House of Representatives passed the Senate plan by a vote of 101 to 71. Thirty-three of the thirty-four black Representatives voted for the plan. No Republican in either the House or the Senate voted for the plan, making the votes of the black legislators necessary for passage. The Governor signed the Senate plan into law on August 24, 2001, and Georgia subsequently sought to obtain preclearance.

B

... Georgia, which bears the burden of proof in this action, see *Pleasant Grove v. United States*, 479 U.S. 462 (1987), attempted to prove that its Senate plan was not retrogressive either in intent or in effect. [The Attorney General opposed preclearance, objecting in particular to Districts 2, 12 and 26. In these districts, the black voting age population (BVAP), dropped respectively from 60.58% to 50.31%, 55.34% to 50.66%, and 62.45% to 50.80%. In each of these districts, the percentage of black registered voters dropped to just under 50%. The three-judge District Court denied preclearance.]

After the District Court refused to preclear the plan, Georgia enacted another plan, largely similar to the one at issue here, except that it added black voters to Districts 2, 12, and 26. The District Court precleared this plan. No party has contested the propriety of the District Court's preclearance of the Senate plan as amended. Georgia asserts that it will use the plan as originally enacted if it receives preclearance.

We noted probable jurisdiction to consider whether the District Court should have precleared the plan as originally enacted by Georgia in 2001, and now vacate the judgment below....

III
... B

Georgia argues that ... its State Senate plan should be precleared because it does not lead to "a retrogression in the position of racial minorities with respect to their effective exercise of the electoral franchise." *Beer.*

While we have never determined the meaning of "effective exercise of the electoral franchise," this case requires us to do so in some detail. First, the United States and the District Court correctly acknowledge that in examining whether the new plan is retrogressive, the inquiry must encompass the entire statewide plan as a whole. Thus, while the diminution of a minority group's effective exercise of the electoral franchise in one or two districts may be sufficient to show a violation of §5, it is only sufficient if the covered jurisdiction cannot show that the gains in the plan as a whole offset the loss in a particular district.

Second, any assessment of the retrogression of a minority group's effective exercise of the electoral franchise depends on an examination of all the relevant circumstances, such as the ability of minority voters to elect their candidate of choice, the extent of the minority group's opportunity to participate in the political process, and the feasibility of creating a nonretrogressive plan. See, *e.g., Johnson v. De Grandy,* 512 U.S. 997 (1994); *Richmond v. United States,* 422 U.S. 358 (1975); *Thornburg v. Gingles,* 478 U.S. 30 (1986) (O'CONNOR, J., concurring in judgment)....

In assessing the totality of the circumstances, a court should not focus solely on the comparative ability of a minority group to elect a candidate of its choice. While this factor is an important one in the §5 retrogression inquiry, it cannot be dispositive or exclusive. The standard in §5 is simple—whether the new plan "would lead to a retrogression in the position of racial minorities with respect to their effective exercise of the electoral franchise." *Beer.*

The ability of minority voters to elect a candidate of their choice is important but often complex in practice to determine. In order to maximize the electoral success of a minority group, a State may choose to create a certain number of "safe" districts, in which it is highly likely that minority voters will be able to elect the candidate of their choice. See *Thornburg* (O'CONNOR, J., concurring in judgment). Alternatively, a State may choose to create a greater number of districts in which it is likely—although perhaps not quite as likely as under the benchmark plan—that minority voters will be able to elect candidates of their choice. Section 5 does not dictate that a State must pick one of these methods of redistricting over another. Either option "will present the minority group with its own array of electoral risks and benefits,' and presents "hard choices about what would truly 'maximize' minority electoral success." *Thornburg* (O'CONNOR, J., concurring in judgment). On one hand, a smaller number of safe majority-minority districts may virtually guarantee the election of a minority group's preferred candidate in those districts. Yet even if this concentration of minority voters in a few districts does not constitute the unlawful packing of minority voters, see *Voinovich v. Quilter*, 507 U.S. 146 (1993), such a plan risks isolating minority voters from the rest of the state, and risks narrowing political influence to only a fraction of political districts. And while such districts may result in more "descriptive representation" because the representatives of choice are more likely to mirror the race of the majority of voters in that district, the representation may be limited to fewer areas.

On the other hand, spreading out minority voters over a greater number of districts creates more districts in which minority voters may have the opportunity to elect a candidate of their choice. Such a strategy has the potential to increase "substantive representation" in more districts, by creating coalitions of voters who together will help to achieve the electoral aspirations of the minority group. See *id.* It also, however, creates the risk that the minority group's preferred candidate may lose. Yet as we stated in *Johnson v. De Grandy*:

> [T]here are communities in which minority citizens are able to form coalitions with voters from other racial and ethnic groups, having no need to be a majority within a single district in order to elect candidates of their choice. Those candidates may not represent perfection to every minority voter, but minority voters are not immune from the obligation to pull, haul, and trade to find common political ground, the virtue of which is not to be slighted in applying a statute meant to hasten the waning of racism in American politics.

Section 5 gives States the flexibility to choose one theory of effective representation over the other.

In addition to the comparative ability of a minority group to elect a candidate of its choice, the other highly relevant factor in a retrogression inquiry is the extent to which a new plan changes the minority group's opportunity to participate in the political process.... Thus, a court must examine whether a new plan adds or subtracts "influence districts"—where minority voters may not be able to elect a candidate of choice but can play a substantial, if not decisive, role in the electoral process. In assessing the comparative weight of these influence districts, it is important to consider "the likelihood that candidates elected without decisive minority support would be willing to take the minority's interests into account." *Thornburg* (O'CONNOR, J., concurring in judgment). In fact, various studies have suggested that the most effective way to maximize minority voting strength may be to create more influence or coalitional districts. Section 5 leaves room for States to use these types of influence and coalitional districts. Indeed, the State's choice ultimately may rest on a political choice of whether substantive or descriptive representation is preferable. The State may choose, consistent with §5, that it is better to risk having fewer minority representatives in order to achieve greater overall representation of a minority group by increasing the number of representatives sympathetic to the interests of minority voters.

In addition to influence districts, one other method of assessing the minority group's opportunity to participate in the political process is to examine the comparative position of legislative leadership, influence, and power for representatives of the benchmark majority-minority districts. A legislator, no less than a voter, is "not immune from the obligation to pull, haul, and trade to find common political ground." *Johnson v. De Grandy.* Indeed, in a representative democracy, the very purpose of voting is to delegate to chosen representatives the power to make and pass laws. The ability to exert more control over that process is at the core of exercising political power. A lawmaker with more legislative influence has more potential to set the agenda, to participate in closed-door meetings, to negotiate from a stronger position, and to shake hands on a deal. Maintaining or increasing legislative positions of power for minority voters' representatives of choice, while not dispositive by itself, can show the lack of retrogressive effect under §5.

And it is also significant, though not dispositive, whether the representatives elected from the very districts created and protected by the Voting Rights Act support the new districting plan. The District Court held that the support of legislators from benchmark majority-minority districts may show retrogressive purpose, but it is not relevant in assessing retrogressive effect. But we think this evidence is also relevant for retrogressive effect....

C

The District Court failed to consider all the relevant factors when it examined whether Georgia's Senate plan resulted in a retrogression of black voters' effective exercise of the electoral franchise....

In the face of Georgia's evidence that the Senate plan as a whole is not retrogressive, the United States introduced nothing apart from the evidence that it would be more difficult for minority voters to elect their candidate of choice in Districts 2, 12, and 26. As the District Court stated, the United States did not introduce any evidence to rebut Georgia's evidence that the increase in black voting age population in the other districts offsets any decrease in black voting age population in the three contested districts....

The testimony from those who designed the Senate plan confirms what the statistics suggest — that Georgia's goal was to "unpack" the minority voters from a few districts to increase blacks' effective exercise of the electoral franchise in more districts. Other evidence supports the implausibility of finding retrogression here. An examination of black voters' opportunities to participate in the political process shows, if anything, an increase in the effective exercise of the electoral franchise. It certainly does not indicate retrogression. The 34 districts in the proposed plan with a black voting age population of above 20% consist almost entirely of districts that have an overall percentage of Democratic votes of above 50%.... These statistics make it more likely as a matter of fact that black voters will constitute an effective voting bloc, even if they cannot always elect the candidate of their choice. These statistics also buttress the testimony of the designers of the plan such as Senator Brown, who stated that the goal of the plan was to maintain or increase black voting strength and relatedly to increase the prospects of Democratic victory.

The testimony of Congressman John Lewis is not so easily dismissed. Congressman Lewis is not a member of the State Senate and thus has less at stake personally in the outcome of this litigation. Congressman Lewis testified that "giving real power to black voters comes from the kind of redistricting efforts the State of Georgia has made," and that the Senate plan "will give real meaning to voting for African Americans" because "you have a greater chance of putting in office people that are going to be responsive." Section 5 gives States the flexibility to implement the type of plan that Georgia has submitted for preclearance — a plan that increases the number of districts with a majority-black voting age population, even if it means that in some of those districts, minority voters will face a somewhat reduced opportunity to elect a candidate of their choice.

The dissent's analysis presumes that we are deciding that Georgia's Senate plan is not retrogressive. To the contrary, we hold only that the District Court did not engage in the correct retrogression analysis because it focused too heavily on the ability of the minority group to elect a candidate of its choice in the majority-minority districts. While the District Court engaged in a thorough analysis of the issue, we must remand the case for the District Court to examine the facts using the standard that we announce today. We leave it for the District Court to determine whether Georgia has indeed met its burden of proof....

IV

The District Court is in a better position to reweigh all the facts in the record in the first instance in light of our explication of retrogression. The judgment of the District Court for the District of Columbia, accordingly, is vacated, and the case is remanded for further proceedings consistent with this opinion.

It is so ordered.

[Short concurring opinions by Justices Kennedy and Thomas are omitted.]

Justice SOUTER, with whom Justice STEVENS, Justice GINSBURG, and Justice BREYER join, dissenting....

I agree with the Court that reducing the number of majority-minority districts within a State would not necessarily amount to retrogression barring preclearance under §5 of the Voting Rights Act of 1965. The prudential objective of §5 is hardly betrayed if a State can show that a new districting plan shifts from supermajority districts, in which minorities can elect their candidates of choice by their own voting power, to coalition districts, in which minorities are in fact shown to have a similar opportunity when joined by predictably supportive nonminority voters. Before a State shifts from majority-minority to coalition districts, however, the State bears the burden of proving that nonminority voters will reliably vote along with the minority. It must show not merely that minority voters in new districts may have some influence, but that minority voters will have effective influence translatable into probable election results comparable to what they enjoyed under the existing district scheme. And to demonstrate this, a State must do more than produce reports of minority voting age percentages; it must show that the probable voting behavior of nonminority voters will make coalitions with minorities a real prospect. If the State's evidence fails to convince a factfinder that high racial polarization in voting is unlikely, or that high white crossover voting is likely, or that other political and demographic facts point to probable minority effectiveness, a reduction in supermajority districts must be treated as potentially and fatally retrogressive, the burden of persuasion always being on the State.

The District Court majority perfectly well understood all this and committed no error. Error enters this case here in this Court, whose majority unmoors §5 from any practical and administrable conception of minority influence that would rule out retrogression in a transition from majority-minority districts, and mistakes the significance of the evidence supporting the District Court's decision....

The Court holds that a State can carry its burden to show a nonretrogressive degree of minority "influence" by demonstrating that "'candidates elected without decisive minority support would be willing to take the minority's interests into account.'" But this cannot be right.

The history of §5 demonstrates that it addresses changes in state law intended to perpetuate the exclusion of minority voters from the exercise of political power. When this Court held that a State must show that any change in voting procedure is free of retrogression it meant that changes must not leave minority voters with less chance to be effective in electing preferred candidates than they were before the change.... In addressing the burden to show no retrogression, therefore, "influence" must mean an opportunity to exercise power effectively....

The power to elect a candidate of choice has been forgotten; voting power has been forgotten. It is very hard to see anything left of the standard of nonretrogression.... Indeed, to see the trouble ahead, one need only ask how on the Court's new understanding, state legislators or federal preclearance reviewers under §5 are supposed to identify or measure the degree of influence necessary to avoid the retrogression the Court nominally retains as the §5 touchstone. Is the test purely *ad hominem*, looking merely to the apparent sentiments of incumbents who might run in the new districts? Would it be enough for a State to show that an incumbent had previously promised to consider minority interests before voting on legislative measures? Whatever one looks to, however, how does one put a value on influence that falls short of decisive influence through coalition? Nondecisive influence is worth less than majority-minority control, but how much less? Would two influence districts offset the loss of one majority-minority district? Would it take three? Or four? The Court gives no guidance for measuring influence that falls short of the voting strength of a coalition member, let alone a majority of minority voters. Nor do I see how the Court could possibly give any such guidance. The Court's "influence" is simply not functional in the political and judicial worlds....

Identical problems of comparability and administrability count at least as much against the Court's further gloss on nonretrogression, in its novel holding that a State may trade off minority voters' ability to elect a candidate of their choice against their ability to exert some undefined degree of influence over a candidate likely to occupy a position of official legislative power. The Court implies that one majority-minority district in which minority voters could elect a legislative leader could replace a larger number of majority-minority districts with ordinary candidates, without retrogression of overall minority voting strength. Under this approach to §5, a State may value minority votes in a district in which a potential committee chairman might be elected differently from minority votes in a district with ordinary candidates.

It is impossible to believe that Congress could ever have imagined §5 preclearance actually turning on any such distinctions. In any event, if the Court is going to allow a State to weigh minority votes by the ambitiousness of candidates the votes might be cast for, it is hard to see any stopping point. I suppose the Court would not go so far as to give extra points to an incumbent with the charisma to attract a legislative following, but would it value all committee chairmen equally? (The committee chairmen certainly would not.) And what about a legislator with a network of influence that has made him a proven dealmaker? Thus, again, the problem of measurement: is a shift from 10 majority-minority districts to 8 offset by a good chance that one of the 8 may elect a new Speaker of the House?

[Justice Souter's analysis of the evidence is omitted.]

Section 5, after all, was not enacted to address abstractions. It was enacted "to shift the advantage of time and inertia from the perpetrators of the evil to its victim," *Beer....* Section 5 can only be addressed, and the burden to prove no retrogression can only be carried, with evidence of how particular populations of voters will probably act in the circumstances in which they live. The State has the burden to convince on the basis of such evidence. The District Court considered such evidence: it received testimony, decided what it was worth, and concluded as the trier of fact that the State had failed to carry its burden. There was no error, and I respectfully dissent.

Notes and Questions

1. For a study of the interaction of legal and political science issues raised in *Georgia v. Ashcroft*, see Richard H. Pildes, *Is Voting-Rights Law Now at War with Itself? Social Science and Voting Rights in the 2000s*, 80 NORTH CAROLINA LAW REVIEW 1517 (2002).

2. The majority in *Georgia v. Ashcroft* writes: "The standard in §5 is simple — whether the new plan 'would lead to a retrogression in the position of racial minorities with respect to their effective exercise of the electoral franchise.'" Simple? According to the majority, what is a "retrogression"? Does that differ from the standard set forth in *Beer*? How is the Court's conception of retrogression different from the dissent's? For suggestions of how the concepts in Justice O'Connor's opinion for the Court might have been implemented, see David T. Canon, *Renewing the Voting Rights Act: Retrogression, Influence, and the "Georgia v. Ashcroft Fix,"* 7 ELECTION LAW JOURNAL 1 (2008).

3. Who benefited from this decision? One beneficiary might have been the Democrats, who could spread Democratic voters more reliably across a larger number of districts. The dissenters are concerned that in the longer run, "§5 will simply drop out as a safeguard against the 'unremitting and ingenious defiance of the Constitution' that required the procedure of preclearance in the first place." Was the dissenters' concern warranted? Given Congress' "*Georgia v. Ashcroft* fix," that must remain a hypothetical question.

The Democrats controlled both houses of the Georgia Legislature when the plan under challenge in *Georgia v. Ashcroft* was adopted. In the first election under the plan, the Republicans won control of the Senate. In 2004, the first election after *Georgia v. Ashcroft*, the Republicans enlarged their lead in the Senate and won control of the House. Despite these election results, the plan might still have benefited the Democrats, but not enough for them to withstand the Republican tide. For analysis of Republican gains in state and local elections throughout the South during that period, see David Lublin, THE REPUBLICAN SOUTH: DEMOCRATIZATION AND PARTISAN CHANGE (2004).

Presumably the African-American members of the Senate lost considerable influence by reason of the shift in partisan control. Do the election results that actually occurred under the plan affect your assessment of the Court's decision? More generally, it is inevitable that some rules of election law will turn out to benefit one party or the other under particular circumstances. But is it appropriate for a factor in any legal standard to be satisfied *because* a particular party is favored? Can that consequence be escaped if the goal of the statute is to enhance the political power of a minority group that overwhelmingly supports a particular party?

4. Dating from the 1982 amendments, Section 5 and related provisions of the Voting Rights Act were set to expire in 2007. Rather than wait until then, the 109th Congress (2005–06) set out to renew ahead of schedule. As Shakespeare said of true love, the course of important legislation never did run smooth, and VRA renewal was no exception. Congressional action seemed possible in the fall of 2005 but was derailed by Hurricane Katrina. It seemed likely again in late spring of 2006, but was derailed when a group of House Republicans proposed modifying or deleting Section 203, which requires voting materials to appear in foreign languages under specified circumstances.[h] Other proposals insisted that the formula for determining which jurisdictions are "cov-

---

h. Section 203 is described in Chapter 7. For a surprising application of Section 203 in California, which may have fueled congressional concern about the section, see Note 12 at the end of Chapter 8.

ered" under Section 4 and therefore subject to Section 5 preclearance should be changed or updated and that the "bail out" requirements for a covered jurisdiction to free itself should be eased. Although these controversies temporarily stalled the legislation, the proposed changes were finally rejected and the legislation passed in July, 2006. Congress, which lags behind major league sports in selling names to corporate sponsors, entitled its law the Fannie Lou Hamer, Rosa Parks, and Coretta Scott King Voting Rights Act Reauthorization Act and Amendment Acts of 2006, but it is known to its friends for short as the Voting Rights Act Reauthorization Act, (VRARA), or simply as the 2006 amendments. For excellent accounts of its history, see J. Morgan Kousser, *The Strange, Ironic Career of Section 5 of the Voting Rights Act, 1965–2005*, 86 Texas Law Review 668 (2008); Nathaniel Persily, *The Promise and Pitfalls of the New Voting Rights Act*, 117 Yale Law Journal 174 (2007); James Thomas Tucker, *The Politics of Persuasion: Passage of the Voting Rights Act Reauthorization Act of 2006*, 33 Journal of Legislation 205 (2007).

Although the proposed amendments just mentioned were defeated, the new legislation does contain some changes to the Voting Rights Act. The most important of these changes were intended to nullify the Supreme Court's rulings in *Georgia v. Ashcroft* and, as we have seen, *Bossier Parish II*.

5. The "*Georgia v. Ashcroft* fix" appears in a new paragraph added to Section 5, as follows:

(b) Any voting qualification or prerequisite to voting, or standard, practice, or procedure with respect to voting that has the purpose of or will have the effect of diminishing the ability of any citizens of the United States on account of race or color, or in contravention of the guarantees [protecting language minorities], to elect their preferred candidates of choice denies or abridges the right to vote within the meaning of subsection (a) of this section.

An additional new paragraph (d) specifies that "[t]he purpose of subsection (b) of this section is to protect the ability of such citizens to elect their preferred candidates of choice."

The main purpose of these changes to Section 5 was to change the law to what Congress perceived it to have been before *Georgia v. Ashcroft*. Thus, the House Report accompanying the renewal legislation stated:

[L]eaving the *Georgia* standard in place would encourage States to spread minority voters under the guise of "influence" and would effectively shut minority voters out of the political process. In essence, the Committee heard that Section 5, if left uncorrected, would now allow "States to turn black and other minority voters into second class voters who can influence elections of white candidates, but who cannot elect their preferred candidates, including candidates of their own race." This is *clearly not* the outcome that Congress intended the Voting Rights Act and Section 5 to have on minority voters. [House Report at 70.][i]

The House Report, at 71, stated the legislation's intent as follows:

This change is intended to restore Section 5 and the effect prong to the standard of analysis set forth by this Committee during its examination of Section 5 in 1975, such that a change should be denied preclearance under Section 5 if it diminishes the ability of minority groups to elect their candidates of choice. Such was the standard of analysis articulated by the Supreme Court in *Beer v. United*

---

i. The House Report can be found at http://judiciary.house.gov/media/pdfs/109-478.pdf.

States, the retrogression standard of analysis on which the Court, the Department of Justice, and minority voters relied for 30 years, and the standard the Committee seeks to restore. Voting changes that leave a minority group less able to elect a preferred candidate of choice, either directly or when coalesced with other voters, cannot be precleared under Section 5. Furthermore, by adding the adjective "preferred" before "candidate," the Committee makes clear that the purpose of Section 5 is to protect the electoral power of minority groups to elect candidates that the minority community desires to be their elected representative.

Is it clear how the new Section 5 will be applied? According to one scholar who testified before the Senate Judiciary Committee:

> There are three points that all supporters of this revised standard agree upon concerning its meaning. First, the standard does not freeze in place minority percentages in districts for the 25 year tenure of this reauthorization. Second, the standard does not place special emphasis on majority-minority districts — that is, districts in which minorities comprise 50 percent of the voting age population (VAP), citizen voting age population (CVAP), or registered voter population. Third, the standard prevents retrogression by way of overconcentration, as well as underconcentration.

Supplemental Testimony of Nathaniel Persily to Senate Judiciary Committee, available at <http://electionlawblog.org/archives/persily-answers.pdf>. Beyond these points of agreement, Persily suggests that "preclearance determinations will depend on context-specific inquiries according to a number of factors," including the extent of racial polarization, incumbency, turnout rates, and the potential for coalitions between the minority group and majority voters or between different minority groups.

For extensive commentary on the questions raised by the *Georgia v. Ashcroft* fix, see Nathaniel Persily, *Promises and Pitfalls, supra*, at 216–51.

6. Among the interesting features of the politics of the 2006 amendments were the divisions of opinion among scholars who in the past had been staunch supporters of the Voting Rights Act. There were some in this group who had serious doubts about whether Section 5, especially in its more rigid form as represented by the lower court decision in *Georgia v. Aschroft* and in VRARA in the form of the *Georgia v. Ashcroft* fix, might be doing more harm than good. They worried that rigid application could impede the ability of black and white politicians in the covered states to work together in coalitions. For one expression of this view, see Samuel Issacharoff, *Is Section 5 of the Voting Rights Act a Victim of Its Own Success?*, 104 COLUMBIA LAW REVIEW 1710 (2004). For an opposing view, see Michael J. Pitts, *Let's Not Call the Whole Thing Off Just Yet: A Response to Samuel Issacharoff's Suggestion to Scuttle Section 5 of the Voting Rights Act*, 84 NEBRASKA LAW REVIEW 605 (2005). A related perspective is that dramatic changes in the environment in which the Voting Rights Act operates called for a serious reconsideration of what form of regulation is best suited to present circumstances. Richard H. Pildes, *Political Avoidance, Constitutional Theory, and the VRA*, 117 YALE LAW JOURNAL POCKET PART 148, 149–50 (2007), criticizes Congress for not engaging in such a reconsideration:

> [I]t is useful to begin with the context of the VRA today, then turn to the legislative process itself and the political economy that drove it. First, on context: when Congress last revisited the VRA in 1982, there were few black elected officials; virtually no Republican Party at the state and local levels in much of the South; voting was extremely polarized along racial lines; and the central institutional devices that occupied Congress's attention were multimember and at-large elec-

tion structures that contributed to the virtual absence of black political representation. In the last twenty-five years, all of these elements have changed, some in ways easily visible, some in ways experts recognize. There is now robust two-party competition in the South; a significant cohort of black elected officials now exists at all levels and in most states with significant minority populations, with black elected state legislators making up thirty-one to forty-five percent of *all* Democratic state legislators in the Deep South states of Alabama, Florida, Georgia, Louisiana, Mississippi, and South Carolina; the VRA must be applied in today's multiethnic America, not the biracial context of the South of decades past; and racially polarized voting has declined somewhat....

The effects these changes ought to have on the structure of the VRA are, of course, much debated, but the fact of change since 1982 is not. Yet the VRA that emerged from Congress in 2006 reflects not a single one of these changes in any way. Though there are as many judicial findings of VRA section 2 violations since 1990 in Pennsylvania as in South Carolina, for example, section 5 continues to cover the latter and not the former. The regionally specific areas of the country singled out for special coverage are neither expanded nor contracted from what they have been since 1982 (indeed, the structure of coverage goes back even earlier).

7. The other reason for some usual supporters of strong voting rights legislation having reservations was their fear that the renewed Section 5 might be declared unconstitutional. Congress may act only pursuant to a power granted to it by the Constitution. In *South Carolina v. Katzenbach*, 383 U.S. 301 (1966), the Supreme Court, over the dissent of Justice Black, upheld the original preclearance provisions of Section 5 as a valid exercise of Congressional power to "enforce" the Fifteenth Amendment. In doing so, the Court acknowledged Section 5's serious inroads on state prerogatives. Those inroads were justified because of the long-standing and flagrant unwillingness of southern states to enforce the Fourteenth and Fifteenth Amendments' guarantees against denial of the right to vote on grounds of race. One concern is whether the same inroads are justified under contemporary conditions.

Furthermore, in recent years, the Supreme Court has undergone a "federalism revolution." It has read congressional power over the states much more narrowly than it had in cases such as *South Carolina v. Katzenbach*. In a line of cases beginning with *City of Boerne v. Flores*, 521 U.S. 507 (1997), the Court has scrutinized with varying degrees of care congressional actions against the state ostensibly taken under its power to enforce the Fourteenth Amendment. In *Boerne*, the Court explained that Congress' power under Section 5 of the Fourteenth Amendment is limited: "Congress does not enforce a constitutional right by changing what the right is. It has been given the power 'to enforce,' not the power to determine what constitutes a constitutional violation." The Court further explained that "[t]here must be a congruence and proportionality between the injury to be prevented or remedied and the means adopted to that end."

Two more recent cases, *Nevada Department of Human Resources v. Hibbs*, 538 U.S. 721 (2003), and *Tennessee v. Lane* 541 U.S. 506 (2004), appear to have given Congress more leeway. Nevertheless, some scholars urged Congress to extend Section 5 for five or seven years instead of the 25 that Congress actually settled on, to ease the ability of covered jurisdictions to "bail out" of coverage, and make other changes that might improve the chances of the renewed preclearance requirement being upheld as constitutional. Indeed, some thought the *Georgia v. Aschroft* fix, by removing a degree of flexibility, would increase the chances that Section 5 will be struck down. We offer no predictions. For the view that the amended Section 5 is constitutional, see, Pamela S. Karlan, *Section 5 Squared: Con-*

gressional Power to Extend and Amend the Voting Rights Act, 44 Houston Law Review 1 (2007). For a more cautious evaluation, see Richard L. Hasen, *Congressional Power to Renew the Preclearance Provisions of the Voting Rights Act after* Tennessee v. Lane, 66 Ohio State Law Journal 177 (2005). One conundrum affecting the constitutional analysis of the Section 5 renewal is that it is hard to know whether an absence of discriminatory measures affecting voting in the covered jurisdictions is the result of changed attitudes or because discriminatory measures have been prevented by Section 5. Ellen D. Katz, *Congressional Power to Extend Preclearance: A Response to Professor Karlan*, 44 Houston Law Review 33 (2007), suggests that because of this problem, the salience of race in politics, evidenced by various phenomena including polarized voting, should count as showing the need for federal regulation, in contrast to the cases requiring evidence of discrimination by states to support new regulations.

As this book was in press, a lower court upheld the constitutionality of the amended Section 5 in *Northwest Austin Municipal Utility District Number One (NAMUDNO) v. Mukasey*, ___ F. Supp. 2d. ___, 2008 WL 2221034 (D.D.C. 2008).

III. Applying Section 2

From the standpoint of a minority group protected by the Voting Rights Act, Section 5 has two important advantages. The state or locality must take the initiative to get preclearance, and the state or locality also has the burden of showing that there is no violation of Section 5. However, Section 5 also has important limitations. First, it comes into play only when the state or locality wishes to change its electoral system in some way. That is an unimportant point for purposes of redistricting, because the one person, one vote rule forces a change every decade, but for other possibly objectionable features of the electoral system, the jurisdiction can avoid Section 5 by preserving the *status quo*. Second, Section 5 applies only to "covered" jurisdictions. Third, as we have just seen, the substantive standard under Section 5 is nonretrogression. And fourth, the group cannot initiate a proceeding but depends on the Justice Department or the District Court to deny preclearance.

When voting rights plaintiffs wish to challenge a districting plan or other feature of a state or locality's electoral system, they can do so under the Constitution or Section 2 of the Voting Rights Act. Until Section 2 was amended in 1982, it was regarded as duplicative of the Constitution.

Probably the greatest number of actions brought by voting rights plaintiffs have been challenges to either at-large elections or multi-member districts. At-large elections occur, usually at the local level, when each office is voted upon throughout the jurisdiction, rather than the jurisdiction being divided into districts. Election of officers such as governors and mayors who do not sit in collegial bodies are almost inevitably at-large. The controversy arises when members of a collegial body, such as a city council, are elected at-large. In the United States, at-large elections usually are run according to one of two methods. In the first, there is a separate jurisdiction-wide election for each seat.[j] In the second, all candidates for office run against each other, each voter may cast a number of

---

j. Sometimes this system includes "residential districts." The overall jurisdiction is divided into districts, and candidates for a given seat must reside within the corresponding district. However, the candidates are elected by voters throughout the jurisdiction

votes equal to the number of offices to be filled, and the top vote-getters are elected. For example, in an election to fill three seats on a city council, all voters in the city could vote for up to three candidates, and the top three candidates would be elected. In multi-member districts, which often occur in state legislative elections as well as some local elections,[k] more than one member but fewer than all the members of a collegial body are elected from the same district.

The controversy over multi-member districts and at-large districts stems from the fact that they often result in preventing the election of representatives of a minority group or faction that might be able to elect some representatives in single-member districts. At-large elections sometimes are defended on the ground that the representatives are more likely to serve the community as a whole rather than the parochial interests of a particular locality. A similar defense of multi-member districts can be made, but is more attenuated. Indeed, it has been contended that the inconsistent use of multi-member districts "is almost surely a discriminatory practice." Charles Backstrom et al., *Establishing a Statewide Effects Baseline*, in Political Gerrymandering and the Courts 145, 152 (B. Grofman, ed., 1990).

What standard should be applicable when minority plaintiffs claim their votes are diluted by a districting plan, at-large voting, or some other feature of the system of representation? In early cases brought under the Constitution and Section 2, the courts required plaintiffs to show that the representational system, considered under the totality of circumstances, served "to cancel out or minimize the voting strength of racial groups." *White v. Regester*, 412 U.S. 755, 765 (1973).[l] On its face, the standard looks hard to meet, but plaintiffs enjoyed excellent success, for two reasons. First, many of the cases were brought in the southern states that were still temporally close to the days of segregation and disfranchisement. Second, most of the cases challenged at-large elections at the local level, which led to permanent hundred-percent white membership on local councils and boards, even in jurisdictions with substantial minority populations.

The Court disturbed this state of affairs in *City of Mobile v. Bolden*, 446 U.S. 55 (1980), requiring a showing that a representational system challenged under either the Fifteenth Amendment or section 2 was intentionally discriminatory. *Mobile* was widely regarded as a great setback by civil rights activists. Whether it was as much of a setback as they thought became doubtful in light of *Rogers v. Lodge*, 458 U.S. 613 (1982), in which an at-large system was struck down on the basis of an "intent" analysis that bore a strong resemblance to the old totality of circumstances approach. In any event, by that time the activists had already persuaded Congress to amend Section 2 to prohibit a voting procedure that "*results* in a denial or abridgement" of the right to vote, regardless of intent. The amended Section 2 included the phrase "totality of circumstances," taken from the court decisions of the 1970s, and also listed as an abridgement of the right to vote a racial or language group's having "less opportunity than other members of the electorate ... to elect representatives of their choice."

The complete text of the amended Section 2 appears in *Thornburg v. Gingles*, which follows. *Gingles* was the first case to construe the amended Section 2 and remains a foun-

---

k. In the past, elections for the House of Representatives occasionally were conducted in multi-member districts. Currently, federal law requires single-member districts. 2 U.S.C. §2c.

l. The other leading cases were *Whitcomb v. Chavis*, 403 U.S. 124 (1971), and *Zimmer v. McKeithen*, 485 F.2d 1297 (5th Cir. 1973), *aff'd sub nom. East Carroll Parish School Board v. Marshall*, 424 U.S. 636 (1976) (per curiam).

dational case for voting rights law. As we shall see, instead of interpreting the amendments as effecting a return to the pre-*Mobile* totality of circumstances test, the *Gingles* majority attempted to make the application of Section 2 more precise.

Thornburg v. Gingles
478 U.S. 30 (1986)

Justice BRENNAN announced the judgment of the Court and delivered the opinion of the Court with respect to Parts I, II, III-A, III-B, IV-A, and V, and an opinion with respect to Part III-C, in which Justice MARSHALL, Justice BLACKMUN, and Justice STEVENS join, and an opinion with respect to Part IV-B, in which Justice WHITE joins.

This case requires that we construe for the first time §2 of the Voting Rights Act of 1965, as amended June 29, 1982. The specific question to be decided is whether the three-judge District Court, convened in the Eastern District of North Carolina..., correctly held that the use in a legislative redistricting plan of multimember districts in five North Carolina legislative districts violated §2 by impairing the opportunity of black voters "to participate in the political process and to elect representatives of their choice." §2(b).

I
BACKGROUND

In April 1982, the North Carolina General Assembly enacted a legislative redistricting plan for the State's Senate and House of Representatives. Appellees, black citizens of North Carolina who are registered to vote, challenged seven districts, one single-member and six multimember districts, alleging that the redistricting scheme impaired black citizens' ability to elect representatives of their choice in violation of the Fourteenth and Fifteenth Amendments to the United States Constitution and of §2 of the Voting Rights Act.

After appellees brought suit, but before trial, Congress amended §2. The amendment was largely a response to this Court's plurality opinion in *Mobile v. Bolden*, 446 U.S. 55 (1980), which had declared that, in order to establish a violation either of §2 or of the Fourteenth or Fifteenth Amendments, minority voters must prove that a contested electoral mechanism was intentionally adopted or maintained by state officials for a discriminatory purpose. Congress substantially revised §2 to make clear that a violation could be proved by showing discriminatory effect alone and to establish as the relevant legal standard the "results test," applied by this Court in *White v. Regester*.

Section 2, as amended, reads as follows:

(a) No voting qualification or prerequisite to voting or standard, practice, or procedure shall be imposed or applied by any State or political subdivision in a manner which results in a denial or abridgement of the right of any citizen of the United States to vote on account of race or color, or in contravention of the guarantees set forth in section 4(f)(2),[m] as provided in subsection (b).

(b) A violation of subsection (a) is established if, based on the totality of circumstances, it is shown that the political processes leading to nomination or election in the State or political subdivision are not equally open to participation

---

m. Section 4(f)(2), added to the act in 1975, extends coverage to members of specified language minorities. — EDS.

by members of a class of citizens protected by subsection (a) in that its members have less opportunity than other members of the electorate to participate in the political process and to elect representatives of their choice. The extent to which members of a protected class have been elected to office in the State or political subdivision is one circumstance which may be considered: *Provided*, That nothing in this section establishes a right to have members of a protected class elected in numbers equal to their proportion in the population.

The Senate Judiciary Committee majority Report accompanying the bill that amended §2, elaborates on the circumstances that might be probative of a §2 violation, noting the following "typical factors":[4]

1. the extent of any history of official discrimination in the state or political subdivision that touched the right of the members of the minority group to register, to vote, or otherwise to participate in the democratic process;

2. the extent to which voting in the elections of the state or political subdivision is racially polarized;

3. the extent to which the state or political subdivision has used unusually large election districts, majority vote requirements, anti-single shot provisions, or other voting practices or procedures that may enhance the opportunity for discrimination against the minority group;

4. if there is a candidate slating process, whether the members of the minority group have been denied access to that process;

5. the extent to which members of the minority group in the state or political subdivision bear the effects of discrimination in such areas as education, employment and health, which hinder their ability to participate effectively in the political process;

6. whether political campaigns have been characterized by overt or subtle racial appeals;

7. the extent to which members of the minority group have been elected to public office in the jurisdiction.

Additional factors that in some cases have had probative value as part of plaintiffs' evidence to establish a violation are:

whether there is a significant lack of responsiveness on the part of elected officials to the particularized needs of the members of the minority group.

whether the policy underlying the state or political subdivision's use of such voting qualification, prerequisite to voting, or standard, practice or procedure is tenuous.

The District Court applied the "totality of the circumstances" test set forth in §2(b) to appellees' statutory claim, and, relying principally on the factors outlined in the Senate Report, held that the redistricting scheme violated §2 because it resulted in the dilution of black citizens' votes in all seven disputed districts. In light of this conclusion, the court did not reach appellees' constitutional claims.

---

4. These factors were derived from the analytical framework of *White v. Regester*, as refined and developed by the lower courts, in particular by the Fifth Circuit in *Zimmer v. McKeithen*, 485 F.2d 1297 (1973) (en banc), aff'd *sub nom. East Carroll Parish School Board v. Marshall*, 424 U.S. 636 (1976) (per curiam). [Because of this derivation, these "totality of circumstances" factors are often referred to as *Zimmer* factors in Voting Rights Act cases and commentary.—EDS.]

[At this point, Justice Brennan summarizes the findings of the District Court to the effect that most of the factors set forth in the Senate Report were present to a significant extent in the relevant North Carolina districts.]

Based on these findings, the court declared the contested portions of the 1982 redistricting plan violative of §2 and enjoined appellants from conducting elections pursuant to those portions of the plan. Appellants, the Attorney General of North Carolina and others, took a direct appeal to this Court ... with respect to five of the multimember districts—House Districts 21, 23, 36, and 39, and Senate District 22.... We ... now affirm with respect to all of the districts except House District 23. With regard to District 23, the judgment of the District Court is reversed.

II
SECTION 2 AND VOTE DILUTION THROUGH USE OF MULTIMEMBER DISTRICTS

An understanding both of §2 and of the way in which multimember districts can operate to impair blacks' ability to elect representatives of their choice is prerequisite to an evaluation of appellants' contentions. First, then, we review amended §2 and its legislative history in some detail. Second, we explain the theoretical basis for appellees' claim of vote dilution.

A
SECTION 2 AND ITS LEGISLATIVE HISTORY

... The Senate Report which accompanied the 1982 amendments elaborates on the nature of §2 violations and on the proof required to establish these violations. First and foremost, the ... intent test was repudiated for three principal reasons—it is "unnecessarily divisive because it involves charges of racism on the part of individual officials or entire communities," it places an "inordinately difficult" burden of proof on plaintiffs, and it "asks the wrong question." The "right" question, as the Report emphasizes repeatedly, is whether "as a result of the challenged practice or structure plaintiffs do not have an equal opportunity to participate in the political processes and to elect candidates of their choice."[9]

In order to answer this question, a court must assess the impact of the contested structure or practice on minority electoral opportunities "on the basis of objective factors." [Here, Justice Brennan summarizes the factors from the Senate Report, quoted above.] The Report stresses, however, that this list of typical factors is neither comprehensive nor exclusive. While the enumerated factors will often be pertinent to certain types of §2 violations, particularly to vote dilution claims, other factors may also be relevant and may be considered. Furthermore, the Senate Committee observed that "there is no requirement that any particular number of factors be proved, or that a majority of them point one way or the other." Rather, the Committee determined that "the question whether the political processes are 'equally open' depends upon a searching practical evaluation of the 'past and present reality,'" and on a "functional" view of the political process.

Although the Senate Report espouses a flexible, fact-intensive test for §2 violations, it limits the circumstances under which §2 violations may be proved in three ways. First, electoral devices, such as at-large elections, may not be considered *per se* violative of §2. Plaintiffs must demonstrate that, under the totality of the circumstances, the devices result in unequal access to the electoral process. Second, the conjunction of an allegedly

---

9. The Senate Committee found that "voting practices and procedures that have discriminatory results perpetuate the effects of past purposeful discrimination."

dilutive electoral mechanism and the lack of proportional representation alone does not establish a violation. Third, the results test does not assume the existence of racial bloc voting; plaintiffs must prove it.

B

VOTE DILUTION THROUGH THE USE OF MULTIMEMBER DISTRICTS

Appellees contend that the legislative decision to employ multimember, rather than single-member, districts in the contested jurisdictions dilutes their votes by submerging them in a white majority,[11] thus impairing their ability to elect representatives of their choice.[12]

The essence of a §2 claim is that a certain electoral law, practice, or structure interacts with social and historical conditions to cause an inequality in the opportunities enjoyed by black and white voters to elect their preferred representatives. This Court has long recognized that multimember districts and at-large voting schemes may "'operate to minimize or cancel out the voting strength of racial [minorities in] the voting population.'"[13] *Burns v. Richardson*, 384 U.S. 73, 83 (1966) (quoting *Fortson v. Dorsey*, 379 U.S. 433, 439 (1965)). The theoretical basis for this type of impairment is that where minority and majority voters consistently prefer different candidates, the majority, by virtue of its numerical superiority, will regularly defeat the choices of minority voters.[14] Multimember districts and at-large election schemes, however, are not *per se* violative of minority voters' rights. Minority voters who contend that the multimember form of districting violates §2 must prove that the use of a multimember electoral structure operates to minimize or cancel out their ability to elect their preferred candidates.

While many or all of the factors listed in the Senate Report may be relevant to a claim of vote dilution through submergence in multimember districts, unless there is

---

11. Dilution of racial minority group voting strength may be caused by the dispersal of blacks into districts in which they constitute an ineffective minority of voters or from the concentration of blacks into districts where they constitute an excessive majority.

12. The claim we address in this opinion is one in which the plaintiffs alleged and attempted to prove that their ability to elect the representatives of their choice was impaired by the selection of a multimember electoral structure. We have no occasion to consider whether §2 permits, and if it does, what standards should pertain to, a claim brought by a minority group, that is not sufficiently large and compact to constitute a majority in a single-member district, alleging that the use of a multimember district impairs its ability to influence elections. [For a recent case discussing the issue, see *Metts v. Murphy*, 363 F.3d 8 (1st Cir. 2004) (en banc). The question may be resolved in *Bartlett v. Strickland*, a case pending before the Supreme Court and discussed in the notes following this case.—Eds.]

We note also that we have no occasion to consider whether the standards we apply to respondents' claim that multimember districts operate to dilute the vote of geographically cohesive minority groups, that are large enough to constitute majorities in single-member districts and that are contained within the boundaries of the challenged multimember districts, are fully pertinent to other sorts of vote dilution claims, such as a claim alleging that the splitting of a large and geographically cohesive minority between two or more multimember or single-member districts resulted in the dilution of the minority vote.

13. Commentators are in widespread agreement with this conclusion. [Justice Brennan cites several secondary authorities. Readers seeking references to the pre-*Gingles* literature on vote dilution will find copious references in this footnote and elsewhere in Justice Brennan's opinion.—Eds.].

14. Not only does "[v]oting along racial lines" deprive minority voters of their preferred representative in these circumstances, it also "allows those elected to ignore [minority] interests without fear of political consequences," *Rogers v. Lodge*, leaving the minority effectively unrepresented.

a conjunction of the following circumstances, the use of multimember districts generally will not impede the ability of minority voters to elect representatives of their choice. Stated succinctly, a bloc voting majority must usually be able to defeat candidates supported by a politically cohesive, geographically insular minority group. These circumstances are necessary preconditions for multimember districts to operate to impair minority voters' ability to elect representatives of their choice for the following reasons. First, the minority group must be able to demonstrate that it is sufficiently large and geographically compact to constitute a majority in a single-member district.[16] If it is not, as would be the case in a substantially integrated district, the multi-member form of the district cannot be responsible for minority voters' inability to elect its candidates. Second, the minority group must be able to show that it is politically cohesive. If the minority group is not politically cohesive, it cannot be said that the selection of a multimember electoral structure thwarts distinctive minority group interests. Third, the minority must be able to demonstrate that the white majority votes sufficiently as a bloc to enable it — in the absence of special circumstances, such as the minority candidate running unopposed — usually to defeat the minority's preferred candidate. In establishing this last circumstance, the minority group demonstrates that submergence in a white multimember district impedes its ability to elect its chosen representatives.

Finally, we observe that the usual predictability of the majority's success distinguishes structural dilution from the mere loss of an occasional election. Cf. *Bandemer*.

III
RACIALLY POLARIZED VOTING

Having stated the general legal principles relevant to claims that §2 has been violated through the use of multimember districts, we turn to the arguments of appellants and of the United States as *amicus curiae* addressing racially polarized voting....

A
THE DISTRICT COURT'S TREATMENT OF RACIALLY POLARIZED VOTING

... The District Court found that blacks and whites generally preferred different candidates and, on that basis, found voting in the districts to be racially correlated....[n]

The court then considered the relevance to the existence of legally significant white bloc voting of the fact that black candidates have won some elections. It determined that in most instances, special circumstances, such as incumbency and lack of opposition, rather than a diminution in usually severe white bloc voting, accounted for these candidates' success. The court also suggested that black voters' reliance on bullet voting was a significant factor in their successful efforts to elect candidates of their choice....

---

16. In this case appellees allege that within each contested multimember district there exists a minority group that is sufficiently large and compact to constitute a single-member district. In a different kind of case, for example a gerrymander case, plaintiffs might allege that the minority group that is sufficiently large and compact to constitute a single-member district has been split between two or more multimember or single-member districts, with the effect of diluting the potential strength of the minority vote.

n. For a description of the statistical techniques employed by the District Court to reach this conclusion and approved by the Supreme Court, see Bernard Grofman, Lisa Handley & Richard G. Niemi, MINORITY REPRESENTATION AND THE QUEST FOR VOTING EQUALITY 82–108 (1992). — EDS.

B
THE DEGREE OF BLOC VOTING THAT IS LEGALLY SIGNIFICANT UNDER §2 ...

2
The Standard for Legally Significant Racial Bloc Voting

The purpose of inquiring into the existence of racially polarized voting is twofold: to ascertain whether minority group members constitute a politically cohesive unit and to determine whether whites vote sufficiently as a bloc usually to defeat the minority's preferred candidates. Thus, the question whether a given district experiences legally significant racially polarized voting requires discrete inquiries into minority and white voting practices. A showing that a significant number of minority group members usually vote for the same candidates is one way of proving the political cohesiveness necessary to a vote dilution claim and, consequently, establishes minority bloc voting within the context of §2. And, in general, a white bloc vote that normally will defeat the combined strength of minority support plus white "crossover" votes rises to the level of legally significant white bloc voting. The amount of white bloc voting that can generally "minimize or cancel" black voters' ability to elect representatives of their choice, however, will vary from district to district according to a number of factors, including the nature of the allegedly dilutive electoral mechanism; the presence or absence of other potentially dilutive electoral devices, such as majority vote requirements, designated posts, and prohibitions against bullet voting; the percentage of registered voters in the district who are members of the minority group; the size of the district; and, in multimember districts, the number of seats open and the number of candidates in the field.

Because loss of political power through vote dilution is distinct from the mere inability to win a particular election, a pattern of racial bloc voting that extends over a period of time is more probative of a claim that a district experiences legally significant polarization than are the results of a single election.... Also for this reason, in a district where elections are shown usually to be polarized, the fact that racially polarized voting is not present in one or a few individual elections does not necessarily negate the conclusion that the district experiences legally significant bloc voting. Furthermore, the success of a minority candidate in a particular election does not necessarily prove that the district did not experience polarized voting in that election; special circumstances, such as the absence of an opponent, incumbency, or the utilization of bullet voting, may explain minority electoral success in a polarized contest.[o]

As must be apparent, the degree of racial bloc voting that is cognizable as an element of a §2 vote dilution claim will vary according to a variety of factual circumstances. Consequently, there is no simple doctrinal test for the existence of legally significant racial bloc voting. However, the foregoing general principles should provide courts with substantial guidance in determining whether evidence that black and white voters generally prefer different candidates rises to the level of legal significance under §2....

---

o. Suppose the elections used by the plaintiffs to show the *presence* of racially polarized voting involve challengers from a racial or language minority who are defeated by white anglo incumbents. Can the defendants point to incumbency as a "special circumstance" to defeat what otherwise would be evidence establishing racially polarized voting? See *Nipper v. Smith*, 1 F.3d 1171, 1180–82 (11th Cir. 1993).—Eds.

Cᴘ
EVIDENCE OF RACIALLY POLARIZED VOTING

1
Appellants' Argument

North Carolina and the United States also contest the evidence upon which the District Court relied in finding that voting patterns in the challenged districts were racially polarized. They argue that the term "racially polarized voting" must, as a matter of law, refer to voting patterns for which the *principal cause* is race. They contend that the District Court utilized a legally incorrect definition of racially polarized voting by relying on bivariate statistical analyses which merely demonstrated a correlation between the race of the voter and the level of voter support for certain candidates, but which did not prove that race was the primary determinant of voters' choices. According to appellants and the United States, only multiple regression analysis, which can take account of other variables which might also explain voters' choices, such as "party affiliation, age, religion, income[,] incumbency, education, campaign expenditures," "media use measured by cost, ... name, identification, or distance that a candidate lived from a particular precinct," can prove that race was the primary determinant of voter behavior.

[W]e disagree: For purposes of §2, the legal concept of racially polarized voting incorporates neither causation nor intent. It means simply that the race of voters correlates with the selection of a certain candidate or candidates; that is, it refers to the situation where different races (or minority language groups) vote in blocs for different candidates. As we demonstrate below, appellants' theory of racially polarized voting would thwart the goals Congress sought to achieve when it amended §2 and would prevent courts from performing the "functional" analysis of the political process and the "searching practical evaluation of the 'past and present reality'" mandated by the Senate Report.

2
Causation Irrelevant to Section 2 Inquiry

The first reason we reject appellants' argument that racially polarized voting refers to voting patterns that are in some way *caused by race*, rather than to voting patterns that are merely *correlated with the race of the voter*, is that the reasons black and white voters vote differently have no relevance to the central inquiry of §2. By contrast, the correlation between race of voter and the selection of certain candidates is crucial to that inquiry.

Both §2 itself and the Senate Report make clear that the critical question in a §2 claim is whether the use of a contested electoral practice or structure results in members of a protected group having less opportunity than other members of the electorate to participate in the political process and to elect representatives of their choice. As we explained [above], multimember districts may impair the ability of blacks to elect representatives of their choice where blacks vote sufficiently as a bloc as to be able to elect their preferred candidates in a black majority, single-member district and where a white majority votes sufficiently as a bloc usually to defeat the candidates chosen by blacks. It is the *difference* between the choices made by blacks and whites—not the reasons for that difference—that results in blacks having less opportunity than whites to elect their preferred representatives. Consequently,

---

p. Recall that this section is joined by only four justices: Brennan, Marshall, Blackmun, and Stevens. — Eᴅs.

we conclude that under the "results test" of §2, only the correlation between race of voter and selection of certain candidates, not the causes of the correlation, matters.

The irrelevance to a §2 inquiry of the reasons why black and white voters vote differently supports, by itself, our rejection of appellants' theory of racially polarized voting. However, their theory contains other equally serious flaws that merit further attention. As we demonstrate below, the addition of irrelevant variables distorts the equation and yields results that are indisputably incorrect under §2 and the Senate Report.

3
Race of Voter as Primary Determinant of Voter Behavior

Appellants and the United States contend that the legal concept of "racially polarized voting" refers not to voting patterns that are merely *correlated with the voter's race*, but to voting patterns that are *determined primarily by the voter's race*, rather than by the voter's other socioeconomic characteristics.

The first problem with this argument is that it ignores the fact that members of geographically insular racial and ethnic groups frequently share socioeconomic characteristics, such as income level, employment status, amount of education, housing and other living conditions, religion, language, and so forth.... Where such characteristics are shared, race or ethnic group not only denotes color or place of origin, it also functions as a shorthand notation for common social and economic characteristics. Appellants' definition of racially polarized voting is even more pernicious where shared characteristics are causally related to race or ethnicity. The opportunity to achieve high employment status and income, for example, is often influenced by the presence or absence of racial or ethnic discrimination. A definition of racially polarized voting which holds that black bloc voting does not exist when black voters' choice of certain candidates is most strongly influenced by the fact that the voters have low incomes and menial jobs—when the reason most of those voters have menial jobs and low incomes is attributable to past or present racial discrimination—runs counter to the Senate Report's instruction to conduct a searching and practical evaluation of past and present reality and interferes with the purpose of the Voting Rights Act to eliminate the negative effects of past discrimination on the electoral opportunities of minorities....

4
Race of Candidate as Primary Determinant of Voter Behavior

North Carolina's and the United States' suggestion that racially polarized voting means that voters select or reject candidates *principally* on the basis of the *candidate's race* is also misplaced.

First, both the language of §2 and a functional understanding of the phenomenon of vote dilution mandate the conclusion that the race of the candidate *per se* is irrelevant to racial bloc voting analysis. Section 2(b) states that a violation is established if it can be shown that members of a protected minority group "have less opportunity than other members of the electorate to ... elect representatives *of their choice*." (Emphasis added.) Because both minority and majority voters often select members of their own race as their preferred representatives, it will frequently be the case that a black candidate is the choice of blacks, while a white candidate is the choice of whites. Indeed, the facts of this case illustrate that tendency—blacks preferred black candidates, whites preferred white candidates. Thus, as a matter of convenience, we and the District Court may refer to the preferred representative of black voters as the "black candidate" and to the preferred representative of white voters as the "white candidate." Nonetheless, the fact that race of voter and race of candidate is often correlated is not directly pertinent to a §2 inquiry. Under §2, it is the status of the candidate as the chosen representative of a particular racial group, not the race of the candidate, that is important....

5
Racial Animosity as Primary Determinant of Voter Behavior

Finally, we reject the suggestion that racially polarized voting refers only to white bloc voting which is caused by white voters' *racial hostility* toward black candidates. To accept this theory would frustrate the goals Congress sought to achieve by repudiating the intent test of *Mobile v. Bolden,* and would prevent minority voters who have clearly been denied an opportunity to elect representatives of their choice from establishing a critical element of a vote dilution claim....

The grave threat to racial progress and harmony which Congress perceived from requiring proof that racism caused the adoption or maintenance of a challenged electoral mechanism is present to a much greater degree in the proposed requirement that plaintiffs demonstrate that racial animosity determined white voting patterns. Under the old intent test, plaintiffs might succeed by proving only that a limited number of elected officials were racist; under the new intent test plaintiffs would be required to prove that most of the white community is racist in order to obtain judicial relief. It is difficult to imagine a more racially divisive requirement.

A second reason Congress rejected the old intent test was that in most cases it placed an "inordinately difficult burden" on §2 plaintiffs. The new intent test would be equally, if not more, burdensome....

6
Summary

In sum, we would hold that the legal concept of racially polarized voting, as it relates to claims of vote dilution, refers only to the existence of a correlation between the race of voters and the selection of certain candidates. Plaintiffs need not prove causation or intent in order to prove a prima facie case of racial bloc voting and defendants may not rebut that case with evidence of causation or intent.

IV
THE LEGAL SIGNIFICANCE OF SOME BLACK CANDIDATES' SUCCESS
A[q]

North Carolina and the United States maintain that the District Court failed to accord the proper weight to the success of some black candidates in the challenged districts. Black residents of these districts, they point out, achieved improved representation in the 1982 General Assembly election. They also note that blacks in House District 23 have enjoyed proportional representation consistently since 1973 and that blacks in the other districts have occasionally enjoyed nearly proportional representation. [A]ppellants and the United States contend that if a racial minority gains proportional or nearly proportional representation in a single election, that fact alone precludes, as a matter of law, finding a §2 violation.

Section 2(b) provides that "[t]he extent to which members of a protected class have been elected to office ... is one circumstance which may be considered." The Senate Commit-

---

q. In this section, Justice Brennan speaks for the Court. —EDS.

tee Report also identifies the extent to which minority candidates have succeeded as a pertinent factor. However, the Senate Report expressly states that "the election of a few minority candidates does not 'necessarily foreclose the possibility of dilution of the black vote,'" noting that if it did, "the possibility exists that the majority citizens might evade [§2] by manipulating the election of a 'safe' minority candidate." ... Thus, the language of §2 and its legislative history plainly demonstrate that proof that some minority candidates have been elected does not foreclose a §2 claim.

[T]he District Court could appropriately take account of the circumstances surrounding recent black electoral success in deciding its significance to appellees' claim. In particular..., the court could properly notice the fact that black electoral success increased markedly in the 1982 election—an election that occurred after the instant lawsuit had been filed—and could properly consider to what extent "the pendency of this very litigation [might have] worked a one-time advantage for black candidates in the form of unusual organized political support by white leaders concerned to forestall single-member districting."

Nothing in the statute or its legislative history prohibited the court from viewing with some caution black candidates' success in the 1982 election, and from deciding on the basis of all the relevant circumstances to accord greater weight to blacks' relative lack of success over the course of several recent elections. Consequently, we hold that the District Court did not err, as a matter of law, in refusing to treat the fact that some black candidates have succeeded as dispositive of appellees' §2 claim. Where multimember districting generally works to dilute the minority vote, it cannot be defended on the ground that it sporadically and serendipitously benefits minority voters.

B^r

The District Court did err, however, in ignoring the significance of the *sustained* success black voters have experienced in House District 23. In that district, the last six elections have resulted in proportional representation for black residents. This persistent proportional representation is inconsistent with appellees' allegation that the ability of black voters in District 23 to elect representatives of their choice is not equal to that enjoyed by the white majority.

In some situations, it may be possible for §2 plaintiffs to demonstrate that such sustained success does not accurately reflect the minority group's ability to elect its preferred representatives, but appellees have not done so here. Appellees presented evidence relating to black electoral success in the last three elections; they failed utterly, though, to offer any explanation for the success of black candidates in the previous three elections.[s] Consequently, we believe that the District Court erred, as a matter of law, in ignoring the sustained success black voters have enjoyed in House District 23, and would reverse with respect to that District.

---

r. This section is joined only by Justices Brennan and White. However, as may be seen below in Part IV of the O'Connor concurring opinion, four additional justices reached a similar conclusion.— EDS.

s. This assertion has been criticized on the ground that the Court "did not discuss the fact that in District 23 black voters had to employ 'bullet voting' to elect the black candidate and thus forfeited their chance to influence which whites would be elected. Nor did the Court address the evidence that the black who was elected was actually chosen by the white voters and had to 'sail trim' his legislative positions accordingly." Lani Guinier, *Groups, Representation, and Race-Conscious Districting: A Case of the Emperor's Clothes*, 71 TEXAS LAW REVIEW 1589, 1636–37 (1993).—EDS.

V[t]
ULTIMATE DETERMINATION OF VOTE DILUTION

Finally, appellants and the United States dispute the District Court's ultimate conclusion that the multimember districting scheme at issue in this case deprived black voters of an equal opportunity to participate in the political process and to elect representatives of their choice.

A

[The Court concluded that the District Court's findings of vote dilution should be affirmed if not clearly erroneous.]

B

The District Court in this case carefully considered the totality of the circumstances and found that in each district racially polarized voting; the legacy of official discrimination in voting matters, education, housing, employment, and health services; and the persistence of campaign appeals to racial prejudice acted in concert with the multimember districting scheme to impair the ability of geographically insular and politically cohesive groups of black voters to participate equally in the political process and to elect candidates of their choice. It found that the success a few black candidates have enjoyed in these districts is too recent, too limited, and, with regard to the 1982 elections, perhaps too aberrational, to disprove its conclusion. Excepting House District 23, with respect to which the District Court committed legal error, we affirm the District Court's judgment....

The judgment of the District Court is

Affirmed in part and reversed in part.

Justice WHITE, concurring.

I join Parts I, II, III-A, III-B, IV-A, and V of the Court's opinion and agree with Justice BRENNAN's opinion as to Part IV-B. I disagree with Part III-C of Justice BRENNAN's opinion.

Justice BRENNAN states in Part III-C that the crucial factor in identifying polarized voting is the race of the voter and that the race of the candidate is irrelevant. Under this test, there is polarized voting if the majority of white voters vote for different candidates than the majority of the blacks, regardless of the race of the candidates. I do not agree. Suppose an eight-member multimember district that is 60% white and 40% black, the blacks being geographically located so that two safe black single-member districts could be drawn. Suppose further that there are six white and two black Democrats running against six white and two black Republicans. Under Justice BRENNAN's test, there would be polarized voting and a likely §2 violation if all the Republicans, including the two blacks, are elected, and 80% of the blacks in the predominantly black areas vote Democratic. I take it that there would also be a violation in a single-member district that is 60% black, but enough of the blacks vote with the whites to elect a black candidate who is not the choice of the majority of black voters. This is interest-group politics rather than a rule hedging against racial discrimination. I doubt that this is what Congress had in mind in amending §2 as it did, and it seems quite at odds with the discussion in *Whitcomb v. Chavis*....

---

t. In Part V, Justice Brennan speaks for the Court. — EDS.

Justice O'CONNOR, with whom THE CHIEF JUSTICE, Justice POWELL, and Justice REHNQUIST join, concurring in the judgment.

… In construing this compromise legislation, we must make every effort to be faithful to the balance Congress struck. This is not an easy task. We know that Congress intended to allow vote dilution claims to be brought under §2, but we also know that Congress did not intend to create a right to proportional representation for minority voters. There is an inherent tension between what Congress wished to do and what it wished to avoid, because any theory of vote dilution must necessarily rely to some extent on a measure of minority voting strength that makes some reference to the proportion between the minority group and the electorate at large. In addition, several important aspects of the "results" test had received little attention in this Court's cases or in the decisions of the Courts of Appeals employing that test on which Congress also relied. Specifically, the legal meaning to be given to the concepts of "racial bloc voting" and "minority voting strength" had been left largely unaddressed by the courts when §2 was amended.

The Court attempts to resolve all these difficulties today. First, the Court supplies definitions of racial bloc voting and minority voting strength that will apparently be applicable in all cases and that will dictate the structure of vote dilution litigation. Second, the Court adopts a test, based on the level of minority electoral success, for determining when an electoral scheme has sufficiently diminished minority voting strength to constitute vote dilution. Third, although the Court does not acknowledge it expressly, the combination of the Court's definition of minority voting strength and its test for vote dilution results in the creation of a right to a form of proportional representation in favor of all geographically and politically cohesive minority groups that are large enough to constitute majorities if concentrated within one or more single-member districts. In so doing, the Court has disregarded the balance struck by Congress in amending §2 and has failed to apply the results test as described by this Court in *Whitcomb* and *White*.

I

… Although §2 does not speak in terms of "vote dilution," I agree with the Court that proof of vote dilution can establish a violation of §2 as amended. The phrase "vote dilution," in the legal sense, simply refers to the impermissible discriminatory effect that a multimember or other districting plan has when it operates "to cancel out or minimize the voting strength of racial groups." *White*. This definition, however, conceals some very formidable difficulties. Is the "voting strength" of a racial group to be assessed solely with reference to its prospects for electoral success, or should courts look at other avenues of political influence open to the racial group? Insofar as minority voting strength is assessed with reference to electoral success, how should undiluted minority voting strength be measured? How much of an impairment of minority voting strength is necessary to prove a violation of §2? What constitutes racial bloc voting and how is it proved? What weight is to be given to evidence of actual electoral success by minority candidates in the face of evidence of racial bloc voting?

The Court resolves the first question summarily: minority voting strength is to be assessed solely in terms of the minority group's ability to elect candidates it prefers. Under this approach, the essence of a vote dilution claim is that the State has created single-member or multimember districts that unacceptably impair the minority group's ability to elect the candidates its members prefer.

In order to evaluate a claim that a particular multimember district or single-member district has diluted the minority group's voting strength to a degree that violates §2, however, it is also necessary to construct a measure of "undiluted" minority voting strength.... Put simply, in order to decide whether an electoral system has made it harder for minority voters to elect the candidates they prefer, a court must have an idea in mind of how hard it "should" be for minority voters to elect their preferred candidates under an acceptable system.

Several possible measures of "undiluted" minority voting strength suggest themselves. First, a court could simply use proportionality as its guide.... Second, a court could posit some alternative districting plan as a "normal" or "fair" electoral scheme and attempt to calculate how many candidates preferred by the minority group would probably be elected under that scheme. There are ... a variety of ways in which even single-member districts could be drawn, and each will present the minority group with its own array of electoral risks and benefits; the court might, therefore, consider a range of acceptable plans in attempting to estimate "undiluted" minority voting strength by this method. Third, the court could attempt to arrive at a plan that would maximize feasible minority electoral success, and use this degree of predicted success as its measure of "undiluted" minority voting strength. If a court were to employ this third alternative, it would often face hard choices about what would truly "maximize" minority electoral success. An example is [a scenario] in which a minority group could be concentrated in one completely safe district or divided among two districts in each of which its members would constitute a somewhat precarious majority.

The Court today has adopted a variant of the third approach, to wit, undiluted minority voting strength means the maximum feasible minority voting strength....

The Court's definition of the elements of a vote dilution claim is simple and invariable: a court should calculate minority voting strength by assuming that the minority group is concentrated in a single-member district in which it constitutes a voting majority. Where the minority group is not large enough, geographically concentrated enough, or politically cohesive enough for this to be possible, the minority group's claim fails. Where the minority group meets these requirements, the representatives that it could elect in the hypothetical district or districts in which it constitutes a majority will serve as the measure of its undiluted voting strength. Whatever plan the State actually adopts must be assessed in terms of the effect it has on this undiluted voting strength. If this is indeed the single, universal standard for evaluating undiluted minority voting strength for vote dilution purposes, the standard is applicable whether what is challenged is a multimember district or a particular single-member districting scheme....

The Court's statement of the elements of a vote dilution claim also supplies an answer to another question posed above: *how much* of an impairment of undiluted minority voting strength is necessary to prove vote dilution. The Court requires the minority group that satisfies the threshold requirements of size and cohesiveness to prove that it will *usually* be unable to elect as many representatives of its choice under the challenged districting scheme as its undiluted voting strength would permit....

This measure of vote dilution, taken in conjunction with the Court's standard for measuring undiluted minority voting strength, creates what amounts to a right to *usual, roughly* proportional representation on the part of sizable, compact, cohesive minority groups....

As shaped by the Court today, then, the basic contours of a vote dilution claim require no reference to most of the "*Zimmer* factors" that were developed by the Fifth Circuit to implement *White*'s results test and which were highlighted in the Senate Report. If a minority group is politically and geographically cohesive and large enough to constitute a voting majority in one or more single-member districts, then unless white voters usually support the minority's preferred candidates in sufficient numbers to enable the minority group to elect as many of those candidates as it could elect in such hypothetical districts, it will routinely follow that a vote dilution claim can be made out, and the multimember district will be invalidated....

II

In my view, the Court's test for measuring minority voting strength and its test for vote dilution, operating in tandem, come closer to an absolute requirement of proportional representation than Congress intended when it codified the results test in §2....

In my view, we should refrain from deciding in this case whether a court must invariably posit as its measure of "undiluted" minority voting strength single-member districts in which minority group members constitute a majority. There is substantial doubt that Congress intended "undiluted minority voting strength" to mean "maximum feasible minority voting strength." Even if that is the appropriate definition in some circumstances, there is no indication that Congress intended to mandate a single, universally applicable standard for measuring undiluted minority voting strength, regardless of local conditions and regardless of the extent of past discrimination against minority voters in a particular State or political subdivision. Since appellants have not raised the issue, I would assume that what the District Court did here was permissible under §2, and leave open the broader question whether §2 *requires* this approach.

[T]he District Court concluded that there was a severe diminution in the prospects for black electoral success in each of the challenged districts, as compared to single-member districts in which blacks could constitute a majority, and that this severe diminution was in large part attributable to the interaction of the multimember form of the district with persistent racial bloc voting on the part of the white majorities in those districts. But the District Court's extensive opinion clearly relies as well on a variety of the other *Zimmer* factors....

In enacting §2, Congress codified the "results" test this Court had employed, as an interpretation of the Fourteenth Amendment, in *White* and *Whitcomb*.... In my view, therefore, it is to *Whitcomb* and *White* that we should look in the first instance in determining how great an impairment of minority voting strength is required to establish vote dilution in violation of §2.

The "results" test as reflected in *Whitcomb* and *White* requires an inquiry into the extent of the minority group's opportunities to participate in the political processes. While electoral success is a central part of the vote dilution inquiry, *White* held that to prove vote dilution, "it is not enough that the racial group allegedly discriminated against has not had legislative seats in proportion to its voting potential," and *Whitcomb* flatly rejected the proposition that "any group with distinctive interests must be represented in legislative halls if it is numerous enough to command at least one seat and represents a majority living in an area sufficiently compact to constitute a single member district." To the contrary, the results test as described in *White* requires plaintiffs to establish "that the political processes leading to nomination and election were not equally open to participation by the group in question—that its members had less opportunity than did other residents in the district to participate in the political processes and to elect legislators of their choice." ...

[A] court should consider all relevant factors bearing on whether the minority group has "less opportunity than other members of the electorate to participate in the political process and to elect representatives of their choice." The court should not focus solely on the minority group's ability to elect representatives of its choice....

III

... Insofar as statistical evidence of divergent racial voting patterns is admitted solely to establish that the minority group is politically cohesive and to assess its prospects for electoral success, I agree [with the plurality in Part II-C of the Brennan opinion] that defendants cannot rebut this showing by offering evidence that the divergent racial voting patterns may be explained in part by causes other than race, such as an underlying divergence in the interests of minority and white voters. I do not agree, however, that such evidence can never affect the overall vote dilution inquiry. Evidence that a candidate preferred by the minority group in a particular election was rejected by white voters for reasons other than those which made that candidate the preferred choice of the minority group would seem clearly relevant in answering the question whether bloc voting by white voters will consistently defeat minority candidates. Such evidence would suggest that another candidate, equally preferred by the minority group, might be able to attract greater white support in future elections.

I believe Congress also intended that explanations of the reasons why white voters rejected minority candidates would be probative of the likelihood that candidates elected without decisive minority support would be willing to take the minority's interests into account. In a community that is polarized along racial lines, racial hostility may bar these and other indirect avenues of political influence to a much greater extent than in a community where racial animosity is absent although the interests of racial groups diverge.... Similarly, I agree with Justice WHITE that Justice BRENNAN's conclusion that the race of the candidate is always irrelevant in identifying racially polarized voting conflicts with *Whitcomb* and is not necessary to the disposition of this case.

IV

[Though her specific analysis of some of the North Carolina multimember districts diverges in detail from Brennan's, Justice O'Connor agrees with Brennan and White that the history of black success in District 23 required reversal, but not in the other districts.]

V

... Compromise is essential to much if not most major federal legislation, and confidence that the federal courts will enforce such compromises is indispensable to their creation. I believe that the Court today strikes a different balance than Congress intended to when it codified the results test and disclaimed any right to proportional representation under §2. For that reason, I join the Court's judgment but not its opinion.

Justice STEVENS, with whom Justice MARSHALL and Justice BLACKMUN join, concurring in part and dissenting in part.

In my opinion, the findings of the District Court ... adequately support the District Court's judgment concerning House District 23 as well as the balance of that judgment.

Notes and Questions

1. The effects of the Voting Rights Act on the number of minority elected officials has been as dramatic as its effect on voting by African Americans in the southern states.

> The number of black elected officials increased from fewer than 100 in 1965
> in the seven originally targeted states to 3,265 in 1989. In 1989 blacks in these states

comprised 9.8 percent of all elected officials as compared with about 23 percent of the voting-age population. While no estimates for Hispanic officeholders in 1965 are available, their number in six states with especially large Hispanic concentrations—Arizona, California, Florida, New Mexico, New York, and Texas—increased from 1,280 in 1973 to 3,592 in 1990. Hispanic officials thus constitute about 4 percent of the elected officials in those states, as compared with the Hispanic voting-age population of approximately 17 percent.[u]

Some of this increase may have been a simple consequence of the right to vote and have occurred before the 1982 amendments. However, it seems clear that the 1982 amendments stimulated the growth.

Thornburg v. Gingles answered some of the questions that were being presented to the courts, but it left many questions unresolved and undoubtedly opened some new ones. The following notes survey some of the questions that have been raised in post-*Thornburg* litigation. The notes also summarize some of the viewpoints that have been expressed in the heated post-*Thornburg* public debate on race-conscious districting.

2. *Section 2 and Section 5*. Prior to the 1982 amendments, Section 2 had little independent significance, as it was regarded as largely a restatement of the 15th Amendment. Particularly after the Supreme Court's decision in *Bolden* gave a narrow construction to both the 15th Amendment and Section 2 as they applied to districting questions, most controversies under the Voting Rights Act arose under Section 5. As we have seen, the primary guide to application of Section 5 was the nonretrogression principle, set forth by the Supreme Court in *Beer*.

Did the 1982 amendments and their interpretation by the Supreme Court in *Thornburg* affect Section 5? If Section 5 were still governed solely by the nonretrogression principle, then many changes in electoral procedures might be entitled to preclearance under Section 5 but be vulnerable to attack under Section 2. To avoid this anomaly, the Justice Department adopted a regulation saying it would withhold pre-clearance if necessary "to prevent a clear violation of Section 2." For commentary, see Drew S. Days III, *Section 5 and the Role of the Justice Department*, in CONTROVERSIES IN MINORITY VOTING 52, 57 (Bernard Grofman & Chandler Davidson, eds., 1992) (CONTROVERSIES).

In *Reno v. Bossier Parish School Board* (*Bossier Parish I*), 520 U.S. 471 (1997), the Supreme Court ruled that the regulation was invalid. Writing for a majority, Justice O'Connor said:

> ... §5, we have held, is designed to combat only those effects that are retrogressive. To adopt appellants' position, we would have to call into question more than 20 years of precedent interpreting §5. This we decline to do. Section 5 already imposes upon a covered jurisdiction the difficult burden of proving the *absence* of discriminatory purpose and effect. To require a jurisdiction to litigate whether its proposed redistricting plan also has a dilutive "result" before it can implement that plan—even if the Attorney General bears the burden of proving that "result"—is to increase further the serious federalism costs already implicated by §5.

3. *Totality of Circumstances*. Does the three-pronged test adopted in *Thornburg* effectively displace the "totality of circumstances" test (whose components are also referred

to as the *Zimmer* or Senate Report factors)? If plaintiffs satisfy the three-pronged test, may a court nevertheless decide for the defendant on the basis of the totality of the circumstances? Alternatively, may a court rely on the totality of the circumstances to rule in favor of plaintiffs who are unable to satisfy the three-pronged test?

The Supreme Court answered the second of these questions in the affirmative in *Johnson v. De Grandy*, 512 U.S. 997, 1011 (1994):

> [I]f *Gingles* so clearly identified the three [prongs] as generally necessary to prove a §2 claim, it just as clearly declined to hold them sufficient in combination.... This was true not only because bloc voting was a matter of degree, with a variable legal significance depending on other facts, but also because the ultimate conclusions about equality or inequality of opportunity were intended by Congress to be judgments resting on comprehensive, not limited canvassing of relevant facts. Lack of electoral success is evidence of vote dilution, but courts must also examine other evidence in the totality of circumstances, including the extent of the opportunities minority voters enjoy to participate in the political processes.

See *Jenkins v. Manning*, 116 F.3d 685 (3d Cir. 1997), a case that, according to the court, fell into "that category of unusual cases where the *Gingles* factors are proved, but under the totality of circumstances, no section 2 violation is established."

4. *The* Gingles *Test — Compactness*. The *Gingles* majority identified three "necessary preconditions" that plaintiffs must establish to show that multimember districts violate Section 2:

> First, the minority group must be able to demonstrate that it is sufficiently large and geographically compact to constitute a majority in a single-member district.... Second, the minority group must be able to show that it is politically cohesive.... Third, the minority must be able to demonstrate that the white majority votes sufficiently as a bloc to enable it ... usually to defeat the minority's preferred candidate.

Early decisions after *Gingles* did not treat the requirement that minority voters reside in a geographically compact area as a major obstacle to a Section 2 claim. Thus, writing in 1992, Grofman et al. reported that

> lower courts have, almost without exception, interpreted [the compactness portion] of the first prong to mean only contiguity.... Thus, the courts have tended not to separate the question of geographic compactness from the question of whether the minority group is numerous enough to constitute a majority; if the plaintiffs are able to draw a (contiguous) plan in which they comprise a majority in at least one district, then they have met the first prong, regardless of the shape of the district.

Bernard Grofman, Lisa Handley & Richard G. Niemi, Minority Representation and the Quest for Voting Equality 54–60 (1992) (Minority Representation). However, in later decisions, the compactness requirement has been a more serious hurdle for Section 2 plaintiffs. For a review of the case law, see Richard H. Pildes & Richard G. Niemi, *Expressive Harms, "Bizarre Districts," and Voting Rights: Evaluating Election-District Appearances After Shaw v. Reno*, 92 Michigan Law Review 483, 532–36 (1993). As we shall see in Part IV, the Supreme Court ruled in *Shaw v. Reno* that in some circumstances, the drawing of non-compact districts for the purpose of increasing minority representation may be unconstitutional. The "compactness" portion of the first prong is therefore an important issue in contemporary Section 2 litigation.

How should the population be counted to determine whether the minority group in question can constitute a majority of a compact district? Should total population, voting age population (VAP), or citizen voting age population (CVAP, pronounced see-vap by aficionados) be used? When Latinos are in question, significant percentages are often recent immigrants, so that the Latino percentage of citizens is likely to be substantially below their percentage of the total population or voting age population.[v] For this reason, a three-judge District Court reviewing a Section 2 challenge by Latino voters to a California congressional and state Senate district regarded CVAP as the most relevant figure. *Cano v. Davis*, 211 F.Supp.2d 1208 (C.D. Cal. 2002).

5. *Influence Districts.* Is the requirement that the minority group be large enough to constitute a majority in a single-member district necessary for a Section 2 claim? Apparently so, according to Justice Brennan's statement of the first "prong." But consider note 12, in which he says *Gingles* is an action based on a minority group's inability to *elect* representatives of their choice, and that therefore the Court is not deciding if there could be an action in which the ability to *influence* elections is sought. Could the first *Gingles* prong be applicable in such an action? If not, are there any other differences between the two types of action? If there are no other differences, what is the point of distinguishing the two types and establishing the ability of the group to elect a candidate as a requirement for one type but not the other?

Should there be an ability-to-elect requirement? Yes, according to two authors whose writings appear to have influenced the *Gingles* majority:

> Black voters are injured by at-large elections only if the election returns show that districted elections satisfying the one person, one vote rule would likely have required a more favorable result. To demonstrate this, the black voters must be residentially concentrated enough and politically cohesive enough that a putative districting plan would contain majority-black districts whose clear electoral choices were in fact defeated by at-large voting. If blacks' residences are substantially integrated throughout the jurisdiction, even if they vote as a bloc for unsuccessful candidates, the at-large district can't be blamed for their defeat.

James Blacksher & Larry Menefee, *At-Large Elections and One Person, One Vote: The Search for the Meaning of Racial Vote Dilution*, in Minority Vote Dilution 203, 233–34 (Chandler Davidson, ed., 1989) (orig. pub. 1984). Compare Kathryn Abrams, *"Raising Politics Up": Minority Political Participation and Section 2 of the Voting Rights Act*, 63 N.Y.U. Law Review 449, 466–67 (1988):

> The emphasis on quantifiability implicit in the *Gingles* standard obscures the fact that elections are rarely won by a single voting group, and that electoral influence is often a crucial step on the path to electoral victory.

For better or for worse, and despite the Supreme Court's disclaimer in note 12 of *Gingles*, lower courts were unreceptive to claims by minority groups that Section 2 requires the drawing of influence districts where possible. See, e.g., *McNeil v. Springfield Park District*, 851 F.2d 937, 947 (7th Cir. 1988), cert. denied 490 U.S. 1031 (1989):

> Courts might be flooded by the most marginal Section 2 claims if plaintiffs had to show only that an electoral practice or procedure weakened their ability

---

v. The same could also be true if the plaintiff group consisted of Asian-Americans. However, concentrations of Asian-American populations large enough to be a majority in a legislative district are still relatively rare.

to influence elections. While Congress intended to make it easier for minorities to show that their vote has been diluted, it presumably did not intend to require courts to entertain claims by a tiny segment of a multi-member district's population that the group's inescapably minimal influence has been impaired by the electoral arrangements.

Did *Georgia v. Ashcroft*'s recognition of possible advantages to minorities of interracial coalitions suggest that Section 2 should now be construed to require the creation of influence districts when possible? In *League of United Latin American Citizens v. Perry*, 548 U.S. 399 (2006), decided shortly before Congress' enactment of the *Georgia v. Ashcroft* fix described above in Part II, Justice Kennedy, joined by Chief Justice Roberts and Justice Alito, strongly rejected the argument that *Georgia* required the creation of influence districts under Section 2. In discussing whether the district court erred in rejecting the an influence district claim to challenge the modification of Texas' 24th Congressional District, formerly held by white Democrat Martin Frost, Justice Kennedy wrote:

> That African-Americans had influence in the district, does not suffice to state a §2 claim in these cases. The opportunity "to elect representatives of their choice" requires more than the ability to influence the outcome between some candidates, none of whom is their candidate of choice. There is no doubt African-Americans preferred Martin Frost to the Republicans who opposed him. The fact that African-Americans preferred Frost to some others does not, however, make him their candidate of choice. Accordingly, the ability to aid in Frost's election does not make the old District 24 an African-American opportunity district for purposes of §2. If §2 were interpreted to protect this kind of influence, it would unnecessarily infuse race into virtually every redistricting, raising serious constitutional questions.

> Appellants respond by pointing to *Georgia v. Ashcroft*, where the Court held that the presence of influence districts is a relevant consideration under §5 of the Voting Rights Act. The inquiry under §2, however, concerns the opportunity "to elect representatives of their choice," not whether a change has the purpose or effect of "denying or abridging the right to vote." *Ashcroft* recognized the differences between these tests, and concluded that the ability of racial groups to elect candidates of their choice is only one factor under §5. So while the presence of districts "where minority voters may not be able to elect a candidate of choice but can play a substantial, if not decisive, role in the electoral process" is relevant to the §5 analysis, the lack of such districts cannot establish a §2 violation. The failure to create an influence district in these cases thus does not run afoul of §2 of the Voting Rights Act.

Justices Thomas and Scalia, who concurred separately in *LULAC*, more strongly rejected plaintiffs' voting rights claims, apparently making a Court majority rejecting a reading of Section 2 to require the creation of influence districts following *Georgia*.

If *Georgia v. Ashcroft*, which highlighted the virtues of influence districts, did not support the claim that such districts may be required by Section 2, it might be supposed that Congress' disapproval of *Georgia* in the 2006 amendments would bury influence district claims even deeper. But perhaps not. The Court, in its 2008–09 term, will review a case, *Pender County v. Bartlett*, 649 S.E.2d 364 (2007), cert. granted *sub nom. Bartlett v. Strickland*, 128 S. Ct. 1648 (2008), in which the issue is presented, though in a somewhat unusual manner. The North Carolina Constitution requires that a whole county be contained in a single legislative district if possible, consistent with federal population and voting rights requirements. Pender County contained 61 percent of the population needed for a House district and an adjacent county, New Hanover, contained 239 percent of that population. Thus, it should have been possible to create two districts entirely within New Hanover, with a third district consisting of all of Pender and the remainder of New Hanover. However, in the belief that it was required by Section 2 to create an African American influence district, the North Carolina legislature divided Pender between two districts, each of which also included a portion of New Hanover. The North Carolina Supreme Court ruled that Section 2 does not require influence districts and therefore found there was no justification for departing from the state constitutional requirement that all of Pender be included within one district.

6. *Political Cohesiveness.* The second *Gingles* prong requires the plaintiff minority group to show that it is "politically cohesive." Does this mean anything more than that the members of the group tend to vote as a bloc, in a manner distinct from the majority? Most lower courts have regarded evidence of bloc voting by the minority group as sufficient to satisfy the second prong. E.g., *Gomez v. City of Watsonville*, 863 F.2d 1407, 1414–16 (9th Cir. 1988), cert. denied 489 U.S. 1080 (1989).

The factual determination whether the minority group has voted cohesively requires complex statistical techniques that need not be reviewed here. For a thorough discussion, see MINORITY REPRESENTATION, at 82–108. One basic issue is which past elections should be chosen for analysis of voting patterns. For example, can the plaintiffs rely on bloc voting in "exogenous" elections, i.e., elections held in jurisdictions that include but are larger than the jurisdiction in question? See, e.g., *Westwego Citizens for Better Government v. City of Westwego*, 872 F.2d 1201, 1207–10 (5th Cir. 1989) (holding that plaintiffs challenging at-large elections for the Board of Aldermen in a small city could rely on voting patterns within the city in statewide and parishwide elections).

Although polarized voting is usually demonstrated by statistical analysis of voting patterns, in *Cottier v. City of Martin*, 445 F.3d 1113 (8th Cir. 2006), a ruling that no violation of Section 2 had occurred was overruled in part because the District Court failed to give adequate weight to exit polls suggesting polarized voting.

7. *Majority Bloc Voting.* The third *Gingles* prong is that the white majority must usually vote as a bloc for candidates different from those supported by minority voters. How one-sided does the white majority's voting need to be? If white voters typically oppose candidates supported by most African-Americans by a 60–40 majority, is that sufficient? It appears from Justice Brennan's discussion that there is no particular percentage that must be exceeded to constitute bloc voting. Rather, the one-sided voting must be sufficient "usually to defeat the minority's preferred candidate." Thus, the degree of bloc voting that is necessary to establish a Section 2 violation would depend on the relative size and political cohesiveness of the minority electorate. See generally MINORITY REPRESENTATION, at 73.

Another issue related to the third prong is whether it matters *why* a white majority votes as a bloc to a degree sufficient to defeat candidates preferred by the minority group. Can the defendant jurisdiction defend on the ground that the bloc voting is attributable to causes—such as political party or ideology—other than race?[w] A number of lower courts have held that it is the fact of polarized voting along racial lines and not the reasons for that polarized voting that is of legal significance. See MINORITY REPRESENTA-

---

w. For statisticians, the issue is whether to use a bivariate analysis (considering only race as an independent variable) or a multivariate analysis (considering a variety of independent variables).

TION, at 74–75. However, the opposite conclusion was reached in *League of United Latin American Citizens v. Clements*, 999 F.2d 831, 850 (5th Cir. 1993), cert. denied 510 U.S. 1071 (1994), in which the defendants contended

> that the district court erred in refusing to consider the nonracial causes of voting preferences they offered at trial. Unless the tendency among minorities and whites to support different candidates, and the accompanying losses by minority groups at the polls, are somehow tied to race, defendants argue, plaintiffs' attempt to establish legally significant white bloc voting, and thus their vote dilution claim under §2, must fail. When the record indisputably proves that partisan affiliation, not race, best explains the divergent voting patterns among minority and white citizens in the contested counties, defendants conclude, the district court's judgment must be reversed.
>
> We agree. The scope of the Voting Rights Act is indeed quite broad, but its rigorous protections, as the text of §2 suggests, extend only to defeats experienced by voters "on account of race or color." Without an inquiry into the circumstances underlying unfavorable election returns, courts lack the tools to discern results that are in any sense "discriminatory," and any distinction between deprivation and mere losses at the polls becomes untenable. In holding that the failure of minority-preferred candidates to receive support from a majority of whites on a regular basis, without more, sufficed to prove legally significant racial bloc voting, the district court loosed §2 from its racial tether and fused illegal vote dilution and political defeat.

Is this ruling consistent with *Gingles*? Two judges argued at considerable length for a similar conclusion in *Nipper v. Smith*, 39 F.3d 1494, 1514–27 (11th Cir. 1994) (en banc), cert. denied 514 U.S. 1083 (1995). Two judges vigorously disagreed. Id. at 1547, 1548–56.

As a practical matter, polarized voting often presents difficult questions of proof, but in many of the Voting Rights Act cases in previous decades, it probably was strongly present. Now polarized voting may be less pervasive, especially in cases involving plaintiff groups other than blacks. Thus, in *Cano v. Davis*, 211 F.Supp.2d 1208 (C.D.Cal. 2002), the court granted summary judgment against a Section 2 challenge to California districts brought by Latinos, largely for that reason:

> It is certainly not our view that racial discrimination no longer affects our political institutions or motivates any portion of the electorate of Los Angeles County. Still, the election returns offered by both sets of litigants reveal that in Los Angeles County, whites and other non-Latinos are currently far more willing to support Latino candidates for office than in the past. In short, at the outset of the 21st century, the data in the record before us paints [*sic*] a far more encouraging picture of racial voting attitudes than did the data in [a Los Angeles case from the 1980s].

It is perhaps noteworthy that the three-judge panel in *Cano* was made up of judges all generally regarded as liberal. On the consequences of declining polarized voting, see Note, *The Future of Majority-Minority Districts in Light of Declining Racially Polarized Voting*, 116 HARVARD LAW REVIEW 2208 (2003).

8. *Are There Only Two Prongs? Only One?* The second and third *Gingles* prongs can easily be conflated and can be described jointly as a single requirement of "polarized voting." Is it possible to go further and consider the first prong — the requirement of a minority community large enough to constitute a majority in one single-member district — together with the polarized voting requirement as part of a single test. J. Morgan Kousser, *Beyond Gingles: Influence Districts and the Pragmatic Tradition in Voting Rights Law*, 27 UNIVER-

SITY OF SAN FRANCISCO LAW REVIEW 551 (1993), argues that it is not only possible to do so, but necessary in order to give full meaning to Section 2. He also argues that a unified understanding of the *Gingles* test can help dissolve some of the controversy over influence districts (see Note 5 above). It is worth considering Kousser's analysis at some length.

> As has often been noted, the term "majority" [in the first *Gingles* prong] by itself conceals problems: Does it mean a majority of the total population? Of the voting age population? Of voting age citizens? Of registered voters? Of those who actually turn out to vote? What is the legal or logical basis for choosing one of these definitions?[x]
>
> Without minimizing these difficulties, the first *Gingles* prong is more logically understood when it is combined with the other two, that is, with variations in the cohesiveness of both majority and minority group voters over a series of different elections. Considered as one coherent standard, the *Gingles* test is not an abstract, mechanical criterion, but necessarily a flexible, practical one. As minority group cohesiveness increases and majority group cohesiveness declines, the level of minority group concentration necessary to elect the choice of that group declines, and vice versa. No single point of concentration which is much less than 100% guarantees minority or majority voters an ability to elect. No fixed, situation-free definition of a "majority" or "political majority" is possible.

Id. at 562–63. Kousser gives a number of illustrations. For example, if a minority group made up half the voters in a district and if 70% of white voters supported candidate *A*, while 60% of the minority voters supported candidate *B*, then *B* would lose with 45% of the total vote. However, if the minority group constituted only 30% of the voters, *B* could win with a 55% vote total if only 60% of white voters supported *A* while 90% of minority voters supported *B*. Indeed, minority voters could make up as little as 10% of the electorate and *B* could still win with a 51% vote total if white voters supported *A* by only 52% while minority voters supported *B* by 80%.

Kousser continues:

> As a matter of logic, the statement in the lower court opinion in *Gingles* that "no aggregation of less than 50% of an area's voting age population can possibly constitute an effective voting majority" is simply false. [Furthermore], there is no bright line, to use legal terminology, or no "natural cutting-point," to adopt the jargon of social science, to differentiate "control districts" from "influence districts." Fifty percent of the voters is no magic number, nor is forty or thirty or twenty or even ten. The outcome, even in [the above] very simple example[s], depends on the relative cohesion of the two groups, and not just their proportions of the electorate. If the example were complicated in an attempt to mimic the real world—including differential registration and turnout rates, different age structures, more than two ethnic groups, and variations in cohesion rates in different elections—the results would be even less determi-

---

x. There is considerable case law on these questions that Kousser raises. See, e.g., *Brewer v. Ham*, 876 F.2d 448, 452 (5th Cir. 1989) (voting age population, not total population, should be used); *Romero v. City of Pomona* 883 F.2d 1418, 1425–26 (9th Cir. 1989) (eligible voters, not total population, should be used). See generally Kimball Brace et al., *Minority Voting Equality: The 65 Percent Rule in Theory and Practice*, 10 LAW & POLICY 43 (1988).—EDS.

y. As Kousser later points out, another factor that can have a large effect on the ability of the minority group to elect the candidates of its choice is the party structure:

> In partisan contests, the proportion of the dominant minority group necessary to have

nant.[y] If the point of the *Gingles* standard is to assure that members of minority groups have a fair opportunity to elect candidates of their choice, and if it is outcomes, not just demographic goals that matter, then it is not a mechanical set of criteria.

Id. at 565. Finally, Kousser attempts to defend his proposed contextual method of applying Section 2:

> Those who favor a bright line standard to create heavily minority districts err for the same reason as those who oppose any judicial or administrative intervention in matters of electoral structure at all. Both treat racism or racial discrimination as categorical, rather than as interval-level variables. But the history of inter-ethnic attitudes and behavior in the United States and elsewhere shows that racism or ethnocentrism is not like a simple light switch, either off or on, but like a more sophisticated dimmer switch. Proponents of control districts think that in the vast majority of places, the racist light is still completely on: their opponents, that it is usually completely off. Racism has faded markedly, but by no means totally, in the United States since the 1940s. Promoting judicial and administrative procedures that require practical, particularized appraisals and remedies that include districts in which minorities will enjoy various degrees of influence recognizes that racism is a variable phenomenon and treats it with a measured and serious response.

Id. at 587.

Whether or not you agree with Kousser's interpretation of *Gingles*, how would you resolve this problem? A rural county in a southern state has a population approximately 60% African American and 40% white. The five members of the County Board of Supervisors are elected at large. Because the turnout of African American voters has been slightly lower than whites, the electorate in recent county elections has been about 55% African American and 45% white. In several recent elections a white candidate has run against an African American candidate. About 80% of the African American voters have voted for the African American candidates, while about 95% of the white voters have voted for the white candidates. The result in every case has been a victory for the white candidate, usually with an overall total of 53–55%. If African American voters claim that Section 2 has been violated and seek as a remedy the creation of districts, at least three of which will have "safe" African American majorities, how would you rule? Cf. *Smith v. Brunswick County, Virginia, Board of Supervisors*, 984 F.2d 1393 (4th Cir. 1993).

As Kousser emphasizes, the question of how large a percentage a minority group must be in a district for that group to elect or have a fair opportunity to elect their preferred candidates is an empirical question. It is a question that has received considerable study. In the 1970s and 1980s, courts and voting rights activists tended to assume that the minority group's percentage of the population had to be a large supermajority, and the figure of 65 percent was often used in litigation. Later, the 65 percent figure was rejected by most if not all courts and scholars. One important study limited to African Americans found:

> a high probability of effectively controlling the district might well be lower than in nonpartisan elections, because a percentage well below 50% of the voters could comprise a majority of the dominant political party. In such an instance, the crucial question would be the likely extent of white or other group defection from minority-endorsed party nominees in the general election.

Kousser, *supra* at 578. —Eds.

It is rarely necessary for minority voters to be a clear majority within a district to have a good chance of electing a minority representative, and the 65% rule enforced by the courts certainly seems excessive. By the same token, black candidates seem to have a fair chance of winning election, even in districts with a white majority ...

Charles Cameron, David Epstein & Sharyn O'Halloran, *Do Majority-Minority Districts Maximize Substantive Black Representation in Congress?*, 90 AMERICAN POLITICAL SCIENCE REVIEW 794, 804 (1996). These authors found that all else being equal, there would be a 50 percent chance in the south of electing a black representative in a congressional district with a 40 percent black population. In the northwest, the figure would be 47 percent. In the northeast it would be 28 percent. Id. at 805.[z] Another study found that in the case of Hispanics, the percentage of the population must be considered in conjunction with the percentage of the Hispanics who have lived in the United States at least five years. On average, a district with a 55 percent Hispanic population has an 84 percent chance of electing a Hispanic representative. See David Lublin, THE PARADOX OF REPRESENTATION: RACIAL GERRYMANDERING AND MINORITY INTERESTS IN CONGRESS 54 (1997). More recent researchers have taken into account a range of factors that can influence the chances of minority group voters being able to elect the candidates of their choice, including not only the minority percentage of the district population and the voting cohesiveness of both the minority and white voters, but many other factors, including the effects of primaries in partisan elections. See Bernard Grofman, Lisa Handley & David Lublin, *Drawing Effective Minority Districts: A Conceptual Framework and Some Empirical Evidence*, 79 NORTH CAROLINA LAW REVIEW 1383 (2001).

In *Cano v. Davis*, 211 F.Supp.2d 1208 (C.D. Cal. 2002), Latino plaintiffs challenging California congressional and state Senate districts under Section 2 presented expert testimony that the crucial factor determining Latinos' ability to elect candidates of their choice is the percentage of Latino voters in a Democratic primary. Although not reaching the issue, the *Cano* court expressed skepticism of this approach as a means of deciding the first prong of *Gingles*, saying (in footnote 28) that reliance on Democratic Party registration figures is "a measure that is unprecedented in redistricting law and that raises difficult analytical questions, particularly in view of the existence of a number of Latino Republican office-holders in California, and of recent efforts by the California Republican Party to increase its share of the Latino vote and registration."

9."*Rainbow Coalitions.*" Suppose there is no single minority community that is large enough to satisfy the first *Gingles* prong, but that two such communities—African-Americans and Latinos, for example, or Latinos and Asian-Americans—would together be large enough, if combined in a district. Is the first prong satisfied?

Most courts that have considered this question have admitted the possibility that a "rainbow coalition" can establish a Section 2 claim, but only if the component minorities can show that they in fact constitute an electoral coalition. See, e.g., *Nixon v. Kent County*, 34 F.3d 369 (6th Cir. 1994); *Brewer v. Ham*, 876 F.2d 448, 454 (5th Cir. 1989); *Romero v.*

---

z. This aspect of their study is criticized by David Lublin, *Racial Redistricting and African-American Representation: A Critique of "Do Majority-Minority Districts Maximize Substantive Black Representation in Congress?"*, 93 AMERICAN POLITICAL SCIENCE REVIEW 183 (1999). Lublin believes minorities ordinarily need a majority of a district's population to elect candidates of their choice. For a response, see David Epstein & Sharyn O'Halloran, *A Social Science Approach to Race, Redistricting, and Representation*, 93 AMERICAN POLITICAL SCIENCE REVIEW 187 (1999).

City of Pomona, 883 F.2d 1418, 1426–27 (9th Cir. 1989). The Supreme Court conditionally endorsed this approach in *Growe v. Emison*, 507 U.S. 25, 41 (1993):

> Assuming (without deciding) that it was permissible for the District Court to combine distinct ethnic and language minority groups for purposes of assessing compliance with §2, when dilution of the power of such an agglomerated political bloc is the basis for an alleged violation, proof of minority political cohesion is all the more essential.

10. *Intent.* The 1982 amendments to Section 2 were largely motivated to avoid the intent requirement that had been imposed in *Bolden* for both constitutional and statutory claims. Although intent has not been an issue in most of the Voting Rights Act litigation since that time, it has not become irrelevant. *Garza v. County of Los Angeles*, 918 F.2d 763 (9th Cir. 1990), held that if plaintiffs can show discriminatory intent, they may be able to establish a Section 2 violation even if their showing in other respects falls short of the *Gingles* requirements.

In *Garza*, the single-member districts for the Los Angeles County Board of Supervisors were found to violate Section 2. The trial court's finding of intent, affirmed by the Court of Appeals, was based in large part on the expert testimony of an historian, J. Morgan Kousser, to the effect that over a long period supervisorial district lines had been adjusted to divide growing Latino areas in order to protect white incumbents. The substance of Kousser's testimony, together with his suggestions on how the presence or absence of discriminatory intent in redistricting can be determined, is set forth in J. Morgan Kousser, *How to Determine Intent: Lessons from L.A.*, 7 JOURNAL OF LAW & POLITICS 591 (1991).

In *Cano*, in addition to their conventional *Gingles* claim, Latino plaintiffs also contended that the California legislature had intentionally limited the Latino population of a congressional and state Senate district in Los Angeles. The plaintiffs thus argued that under *Garza*, they were entitled to relief even if they could not meet the three prongs required by *Gingles*. The court declined to find legally cognizable intentional discrimination:

> Plaintiffs admit that they do not allege that defendants were motivated by racial hostility. Nor do they suggest that there was any desire to effectuate invidious racial discrimination generally. Although we assume, for summary judgment purposes, the truth of plaintiffs' intent evidence, and of their charge that the legislature sought to limit the number of Latino voters in the two districts at issue, given the background and record of California's 2001 redistricting, the evidence does not support an inference that the legislature intended to marginalize a racial group politically through invidious discrimination, or invidiously to maintain a system that perpetuates racial discrimination. Thus the intent appears not to be of the type that the Supreme Court held necessary for an intentional vote dilution claim in *Bolden*, *Rogers*, and *Bandemer*. Leaving aside plaintiffs' proffers, the other evidence as to intent reflects a complex set of legislative motivations that comprehended several goals, including protecting incumbents, ensuring adequate representation for Latinos and other minority groups through the establishment of majority-minority districts such as [a new district elsewhere], and advancing partisan interests. Given the facts and circumstances in the record before us, including (1) the use of traditional districting principles to establish the districts in question, (2) the absence of any legal necessity to create another new majority-minority Congressional district in addition to the one being newly-created in the redistricting statute, and (3) the high degree of Latino representation and participation in the redistricting process, we strongly doubt

that the 2001 redistricting statute was a "purposeful device to further racial discrimination," in whole or in part. *Bolden.*

11. *Single-Member Districts.* Does the *Gingles* analysis apply to claims that single-member district plans dilute the votes of a protected minority? Footnote 12 of the *Gingles* opinion expressly leaves this question open. However, if *Gingles* does *not* apply to single-member districts, then apparently it would be possible for a jurisdiction to violate Section 2 by creating a multi-member district in an area where at least one majority-minority district could have been created, but to avoid violating Section 2 by creating single-member districts *without* creating any such majority-minority district. It is difficult to see how such an interpretation could be regarded as consistent.

Although *Growe v. Emison*, 570 U.S. 25, 39–40 (1993), raised some doubt on this point, in *Johnson v. De Grandy*, 512 U.S. 997, 1006 (1994), the Court seemed to apply the *Gingles* test to single-member districts, subject to the proviso that "the *Gingles* factors cannot be applied mechanically and without regard to the nature of the claim," quoting from *Voinovich v. Quilter*, 507 U.S. 146 (1993). In *De Grandy*, the trial court had struck down district lines for the Florida House of Representatives in the Miami area because additional compact districts in which Latinos would have comprised the majority could have been drawn. The Supreme Court reversed, regarding it as decisive under the circumstances of the case that the percentage of Miami Latino-majority districts in the plan was proportional to the percentage of Latino population in Miami. However, the Supreme Court refused to declare that a state's creation of a proportional number of majority-minority districts would provide a "safe harbor" that would assure compliance with Section 2 by a single-member district plan.

12. *Judges.* Does the anti-dilution provision of Section 2 apply to the election of judges? That is, are judges "representatives" within the meaning of Section 2's assurance of equal opportunity for protected groups "to elect representatives of their choice"? The Supreme Court answered these questions in the affirmative by a 6–3 majority in *Chisom v. Roemer*, 501 U.S. 380 (1991). The majority opinion by Justice Stevens emphasized that the Court was ruling on the scope of the coverage of Section 2 and was not addressing "the elements that must be proved to establish a violation of the Act or the remedy that might be appropriate to redress a violation if proved."

In *Houston Lawyers' Association v. Attorney General of Texas*, 501 U.S. 419 (1991), a companion case to *Chisom*, Justice Stevens wrote for the majority that "we believe that the State's interest in maintaining an electoral system—in this case, Texas' interest in maintaining the link between a district judge's jurisdiction and the area of residency of his or her voters—is a legitimate factor to be considered by courts among the 'totality of circumstances' in determining whether a §2 violation has occurred." Is a county-wide or other at-large system of electing judges violative of Section 2 if plaintiffs prove the presence of polarized voting that prevents a protected minority from electing judges of their choice? See *League of United Latin American Citizens v. Clements*, 999 F.2d 831, 868–76 (5th Cir. 1993), cert. denied 510 U.S. 1071 (1994); *Nipper v. Smith*, 39 F.3d 1494 (11th Cir. 1994), cert. denied 514 U.S. 1083 (1995).

Between 1965, when the Voting Rights Act was enacted, and 1991, when *Chisom* was decided, it was assumed in many places that the Act did not apply to judicial elections. As a result, many changes in the procedures for such elections in covered jurisdictions were never submitted for preclearance. *Chisom* made it apparent that the failure to obtain preclearance violates Section 5. The usual remedy for a Section 5 violation is a restoration of the system that prevailed before the change requiring preclearance was made.

However, changes that occurred as many as thirty years ago in judicial elections often were part of broader changes in the structure of the judiciary, so that restoring the pre-change system would be impractical. For a vivid example of the difficulties and complexities that may arise in such a situation, see *Lopez v. Monterey County*, 519 U.S. 9 (1996).[a]

13. *Small Boards and Sole Officeholders.* Suppose in a municipality with a three-member elected governing body, there is a minority community that is too small to satisfy the first *Gingles* prong but would be large enough if the governing body were expanded to five members. Does the failure to expand violate Section 2? Similarly, does a municipality violate Section 2 by electing a single individual to carry out functions that could be carried out by an elected board on which minorities could expect representation? (We shall refer to such individuals as "sole officeholders." Though our locution is hardly mellifluous, the more common "single-member officers" is inaccurate. The officeholder is not a "member" of any body.)

A divided Supreme Court answered these questions in the negative in *Holder v. Hall*, 512 U.S. 874 (1994). Justice Kennedy, writing for himself, Chief Justice Rehnquist and Justice O'Connor, reasoned from the premise that any claim of vote dilution implies some non-dilutive benchmark against which the challenged system can be measured.

> [T]he search for a benchmark is quite problematic when a §2 dilution challenge is brought to the size of a government body. There is no principled reason why one size should be picked over another as the benchmark for comparison. Respondents here argue that we should compare Bleckley County's sole commissioner system to a hypothetical five-member commission in order to determine whether the current system is dilutive. [Several reasons had been advanced for selecting a five-member body for comparison, including that a Georgia statute authorized counties to replace single commissioners with five-member commissions and that Bleckley County itself had recently switched from a single superintendent of education to a five-member school board.]
>
> That Bleckley County was authorized by the State to expand its commission, and that it adopted a five-member school board, are ... irrelevant considerations in the dilution inquiry. At most, those facts indicate that Bleckley County could change the size of its commission with minimal disruption. But the county's failure to do so says nothing about the effects the sole commissioner system has on the voting power of Bleckley County's citizens. Surely a minority group's voting strength would be no more or less diluted had the State not authorized the county to alter the size of its commission, or had the county not enlarged its school board. One gets the sense that respondents and the United States have chosen a benchmark for the sake of having a benchmark. But it is one thing to say that a benchmark can be found, quite another to give a convincing reason for finding it in the first place.

Justice Thomas, joined by Justice Scalia, concurred in the judgment but selected *Holder* for the statement of much broader views, as we shall see shortly. Four justices dissented.

Holder was consistent with earlier decisions by lower courts upholding sole officeholders against Section 2 challenges. One such decision, *Butts v. City of New York*, 779 F.2d 141 (2d Cir. 1985), cert. denied 478 U.S. 1021 (1986), was particularly disfavored by

---

a. The *Lopez* case revisited the Supreme Court in *Lopez v. Monterey County*, 525 U.S. 266 (1999). The result was a remand, meaning that the difficulties and complexities had to go through at least one more round of litigation.

some voting rights advocates, because it upheld not only a sole office but a provision for a run-off primary if no candidate received more than 40 percent in the initial primary. Critics argued that "a majority-vote requirement has the effect of creating a *de facto* 'white primary': In the first election, white party members choose among the white candidates, and in the runoff they unite behind the surviving white candidate." Pamela S. Karlan, *Undoing the Right Thing: Single-Member Offices and the Voting Rights Act*, 77 VIRGINIA LAW REVIEW 1, 26–27 (1991). More generally, Karlan concluded that "the single-member office doctrine expresses a deeply felt, if unconscious, need to maintain white political control in the guise of protecting democratic values." *Id.* at 41. Thus, she argued that courts have been willing to implement Section 2 to facilitate election of minority-group members to multi-member bodies where a white majority will retain control, but that they are reluctant to enforce Section 2 when doing so might result in governing authority being vested entirely in a non-white representative. Is Karlan's criticism applicable to *Holder v. Hall*?

14. *Consent Decrees and Standing.* Often, Section 2 litigation is settled in the form of a consent decree. This is an agreement, ratified by the court, setting forth steps that will be taken to remedy violations alleged in the law suit. Note that the effect of a consent decree is that the governmental entity will act contrary to its own or the state's legally established procedures, without those procedures having been found by the court to be violative of the Voting Rights Act. Once new procedures have been implemented, those elected under the new procedures are more likely to want to preserve them than to rally behind the former procedures. What if citizens believe they are entitled to elections run under the duly established procedures? Do they have legal recourse?

Litigation in the 1980s resulted in a consent decree revising certain Alabama county election procedures. Chilton County agreed to expand its County Commission from four to seven members, to institute a form of proportional representation known as cumulative voting, and to make other changes. In the following decade, *Holder v. Hall* and decisions of the 11th Circuit made it highly questionable at best whether these remedies could be imposed under Section 2. But the county, whose commissioners held their seats under the revised procedures, declined to seek dissolution or modification of the consent decree. Voters in the county sought to intervene in the dormant litigation of the 1980s in order to challenge the consent decree. In *Dillard v. Chilton County Commission*, 495 F.3d 1324 (11th Cir. 2007), the 11th Circuit held that they lacked standing to do so.

15. Gingles *and Proportional Representation.* Is *Gingles* sound as statutory interpretation? In particular, is it consistent with the proviso in Section 2 that proportional representation is not required? Justice O'Connor, concurring in *Gingles*, thought not. The same conclusion is reached by Daniel D. Polsby & Robert D. Popper, *Ugly: An Inquiry Into the Problem of Racial Gerrymandering Under the Voting Rights Act*, 92 MICHIGAN LAW REVIEW 652, 657–59 (1993).

16. *Is* Gingles *a Dead End?* A vigorous theoretical and political debate rages around Section 2 and the legal assault on dilution of the votes of racial, ethnic, and language minority group members. This chapter cannot hope to do justice to that debate, but at least one portion of it can be examined by considering three divergent responses to Karlan's point described above, that in many situations, precisely because such groups *are* minorities, *Gingles*-type anti-dilutive measures will be unable to prevent white majorities from controlling government policy.

(a) *The view that* Gingles *does not go far enough.* One view is most famously set forth in the writings of Lani Guinier. Guinier contends that the *Gingles* anti-dilution frame-

work represents the "second generation" of the voting rights movement, the first generation having been the successful fight for the basic right to vote in the 1960s.

> On the assumption that racial bloc voting by a white electoral majority will in-
> variably result in the defeat of black representatives, second-generation voting rights
> litigants seek to integrate the legislature primarily through the subdivision of
> predominantly white electorates into single-member districts. The second-gen-
> eration remedial agenda is premised on the notion that black representatives,
> elected from majority-black subdistricts and electorally accountable only to black
> voters, will represent those voters' concerns from their newly established leg-
> islative seats. Once integrated, legislative bodies will deliberate more effectively
> and will be "legitimated" as a result of their more inclusive character.

Lani Guinier, *No Two Seats: The Elusive Quest for Political Equality*, 77 VIRGINIA LAW RE-
VIEW 1413, 1415 (1991). Guinier does not doubt the value of the "authentic black representation" that the "second generation" has sought, with considerable success, to accomplish:

> Authenticity reflects the group consciousness, group history, and group per-
> spective of a disadvantaged and stigmatized minority. Authenticity recognizes
> that black voters are a discrete "social group" with a distinctive voice.... [A]uthen-
> tic representation also facilitates black voter mobilization, participation, and
> confidence in the process of self-government.

Lani Guinier, *The Triumph of Tokenism: The Voting Rights Act and the Theory of Black
Electoral Success*, 89 MICHIGAN LAW REVIEW 1077, 1108 (1991).

Nevertheless, Guinier believes that the "black electoral success theory" underlying
the second-generation efforts inevitably will fail to accomplish the idealistic goals of
the Voting Rights Act, because of its acceptance of districting as the central mechanism
of representation.

> I conclude that the districting model, at least at the local county and munic-
> ipal level, fails to achieve the political equality and political empowerment ob-
> jectives of the Voting Rights Act, although it permits physical access to the
> representative body for minority representatives. First, districting ignores the
> role of prejudice at the legislative level. Even though such prejudice remains a per-
> vasive problem, the districting model defends majoritarian principles without
> constraining representatives of the majority to represent, reflect, or accommo-
> date minority interests within local legislative decisionmaking. Second, district-
> ing uses a delegate model of representation but fails to ensure substantive
> accountability to constituents' policy preferences, not just service needs. Third,
> by focusing on geographic, rather than political, interests, districting depresses
> the level of political competition and discourages the interactive political orga-
> nization necessary to mobilize voters to participate meaningfully throughout the
> political process. In this way, districting fails to realize the moral proposition
> implicit in the statute's political equality and political empowerment norms that
> each citizen should have the same chance as every other citizen to influence leg-
> islative outcomes.

No Two Seats, at 1433. Thus, Guinier believes the "black electoral success theory" needs
to be supplemented by her own theory of "proportionate interest representation."

> Proportionate interest representation disavows the pluralist conception of
> fairness, which falsely assumes equal bargaining power simply based on access,
> or numerically proportionate electoral success for all groups. Fairness and re-

sponsiveness should be related objectives. Yet, in a racially polarized environment, some systems may be procedurally fair but fundamentally unresponsive. For example, while improving the prospects of black electoral success, black single-member districts may undermine the possibility of effecting true policy change. In a system shaped by irrational, majority prejudice, remedial mechanisms that eliminate pure majority rule and enforce principles of interest proportionality may provide better proxies for political fairness.

Triumph of Tokenism, at 1136–37.

The realization of proportionate interest representation would require basic changes in both the electoral and legislative systems. Guinier summarizes her arguments for electoral change as follows:

Winner-take-all territorial districting imperfectly distributes representation based on group attributes and disproportionately rewards those who win the representational lottery. Territorial districting uses an aggregating rule that inevitably groups people by virtue of some set of externally observed characteristics such as geographic proximity or racial identity. In addition, the winner-take-all principle inevitably wastes some votes. The dominant group within the district gets all the power; the votes of supporters of nondominant groups or disaffected voters within the dominant group are wasted. Their votes lose significance because they are consistently cast for political losers.

The essential unfairness of districting is a result, therefore, of two assumptions: (1) that a majority of voters within a given geographic community can be configured to constitute a "group"; and (2) that incumbent politicians, federal courts, or some other independent set of actors can fairly determine which group to advantage by giving it all the power within the district. When either of these assumptions is not accurate, as is most often the case, the districting is necessarily unfair.

Another effect of these assumptions is gerrymandering, which results from the arbitrary allocation of disproportionate political power to one group. Districting breeds gerrymandering as a means of allocating group benefits; the operative principle is deciding whose votes get wasted. Whether it is racially or politically motivated, gerrymandering is the inevitable by-product of an electoral system that aggregates people by virtue of assumptions about their group characteristics and then inflates the winning group's power by allowing it to represent *all* voters in a regional unit.

Given a system of winner-take-all territorial districts and working within the limitations of this particular election method, the courts have sought to achieve political fairness for racial minorities. As a result, there is some truth to the assertion that minority groups, unlike other voters, enjoy a special representational relationship under the Voting Rights Act's 1982 amendments to remedy their continued exclusion from effective political participation in some jurisdictions. But the proper response is not to deny minority voters that protection. The answer should be to extend that special relationship to *all* voters by endorsing *the equal opportunity to vote for a winning candidate* as a universal principle of political fairness.

I use the term "one-vote, one-value" to describe the principle of political fairness that as many votes as possible should count in the election of representatives. One-vote, one-value is realized when everyone's vote counts for someone's election. The only system with the potential to realize this principle for *all* voters is one in which the unit of representation is political rather than regional, and the aggregating rule is proportionality rather than winner-take-all. Semiproportional systems, such as cumulative voting, can approximate the one-vote, one-value principle by minimizing the problem of wasted votes.

Lani Guinier, *Groups, Representation, and Race-Conscious Districting: A Case of the Emperor's Clothes*, 71 TEXAS LAW REVIEW 1589, 1592–94 (1993).

There is an extensive literature debating the pros and cons of the "semiproportional systems" that Guinier recommends. For a useful description of some of these systems by an articulate exponent of views similar to Guinier's, see Pamela S. Karlan, *Maps and Misreadings: The Role of Geographic Compactness in Racial Vote Dilution Litigation*, 24 HARVARD CIVIL RIGHTS-CIVIL LIBERTIES LAW REVIEW 173, 221–36 (1989). See also MINORITY REPRESENTATION 124–28. The voting rights debate over semiproportional systems is in turn part of a larger debate over the merits of proportional voting systems versus the single-member district system. Support for proportional systems appears to be widespread among legal scholars who study election law and has received strong support from at least a few political scientists. See, e.g., Douglas J. Amy, REAL CHOICES/NEW VOICES: THE CASE FOR PROPORTIONAL REPRESENTATION ELECTIONS IN THE UNITED STATES (1993); Richard L. Engstrom, *The Political Thicket, Electoral Reform, and Minority Voting Rights*, in Mark E. Rush & Richard L. Engstrom, FAIR AND EFFECTIVE REPRESENTATION? DEBATING ELECTORAL REFORM AND MINORITY RIGHTS 3 (2001). Probably the great majority of empirical political scientists who study American politics favor single-member districts, but not surprisingly, supporters of the *status quo* have tended not to participate as frequently in the debate. The debate in the United States has been largely one among theorists, but Great Britain has seen a more practical debate over proportional representation in recent years. Michael Pinto-Duschinsky, a British political scientist, has published two short but vigorous statements in defense of the single-member system: *Send the Rascals Packing: Defects of Proportional Representation and the Virtues of the Westminster Model*, 36 REPRESENTATION 117 (1999); *A Reply to the Critics*, 36 REPRESENTATION 148 (1999). For a skeptical but not entirely unfriendly evaluation of proportional representation, see Mark E. Rush, *The Hidden Costs of Electoral Reform*, in Rush & Engstrom, *supra*. See also Mark E. Rush, *Making the House More Representative: Hidden Costs and Unintended Consequences*, in Joseph F. Zimmerman & Wilma Rule, eds., THE U.S. HOUSE OF REPRESENTATIVES: REFORM OR REBUILD? 51 (2000); Daniel H. Lowenstein, *Political Reform Is Political*, in *id.*, at 194, 202–06.

To date, courts have not been inclined to order proportional or semiproportional devices of the sort favored by Guinier and Karlan as remedies for Section 2 violations. See, e.g., *Cane v. Worcester County*, 35 F.3d 921 (4th Cir. 1994), cert. denied *sub nom. Worcester County v. Cane*, 518 U.S. 1016 (1996), holding that it was an abuse of discretion for a United States District Court to impose cumulative voting as a remedy for a Section 2 violation without giving the county the opportunity to submit a single-member district plan. However, in at least a few places in Maryland and Alabama, cumulative voting has been instituted as a means of settling Voting Rights Act litigation. See *Maryland County to Use Cumulative Voting*, BALLOT ACCESS NEWS, May 3, 1994, at 1. In Section 2 challenges to at large elections for judges, two federal appellate courts have rejected remedies intended to bring about proportional representation. See *White v. Alabama*, 74 F.3d 1058 (11th Cir. 1996); *Cousin v. Sundquist*, 145 F.3d 818 (6th Cir. 1998), cert. denied, 525 U.S. 1138 (1999). Cumulative voting was imposed on a city and a park district as a remedy for a Section 2 violation in *McCoy v. Chicago Heights*, 6 F.Supp.2d 973 (N.D.Ill. 1998). That remedy was overruled in *Harper v. City of Chicago Heights*, 223 F.3d 593 (7th Cir. 2000), cert. denied,

531 U.S. 1150 (2001). In *Cottier v. City of Martin*, 475 F.Supp.2d 932 (D.S.Dak. 2007), the court found that extraordinary circumstances justified imposition of cumulative voting as a remedy. One of the circumstances was that native Americans were so evenly distributed throughout the jurisdiction that it would be impossible to create a single district that they could control. Under that circumstance, could the first prong of *Gingles* have been met?

Guinier's call for change in the legislative system is aimed primarily at local government and is necessitated by the existence of "deliberative gerrymandering."

> Although efforts to increase black representation have an independent value, prejudice may simply transfer the "gerrymandering" problem from the electorate to the legislature. Black electoral visibility is useless if district-based electoral arrangements gerrymander legislative decisionmaking and reproduce in the legislature a mirror image of a racially skewed electorate. With few exceptions, the litigation and activist strategy has thus far failed to anticipate the inevitable third-generation problem: the deliberative gerrymander.

Triumph of Tokenism, at 1126. Various remedial devices would be used against deliberative gerrymandering.

> Where majority representatives refuse to bargain with representatives of the minority, simple majority vote rules would be replaced. "A minority veto" for legislation of vital importance to minority interests would respond to evidence of gross "deliberative gerrymanders." Alternatively, depending on the proof of disproportionate majority power, plaintiffs might seek minority assent through other supermajority arrangements, concurrent legislative majorities, consociational arrangements, or rotation in office.

Id. at 1140.

The hopes of Guinier and others that the Voting Rights Act would be applied to legislative procedures received an apparently fatal blow in *Presley v. Etowah County Commission*, 502 U.S. 491 (1992), which held that changes in voting procedures of local governing bodies and in the powers of their members were not changes "with respect to voting" that required preclearance under Section 5. Justice Kennedy wrote for a six-member majority:

> Were we to accept the appellants' proffered reading of §5, we would work an unconstrained expansion of its coverage. Innumerable state and local enactments having nothing to do with voting affect the power of elected officials. When a state or local body adopts a new governmental program or modifies an existing one it will often be the case that it changes the powers of elected officials....

> Appellants and the United States fail to provide a workable standard for distinguishing between changes in the routine organization and functioning of government. Some standard is necessary, for in a real sense every decision taken by government implicates voting. This is but the felicitous consequence of democracy, in which power derives from the people. Yet no one would contend that when Congress enacted the Voting Rights Act it meant to subject all or even most decisions of government in covered jurisdictions to federal supervision. Rather, the Act by its terms covers any "voting qualification or prerequisite to voting, or standard, practice, or procedure with respect to voting."

Is the difficulty of finding a "workable standard" an adequate justification for interpreting the statute to provide no protection to minority groups at the legislative stage? Not according to Pamela S. Karlan, *The Rights to Vote: Some Pessimism About Formalism*, 71 TEXAS LAW REVIEW 1705, 1725–26 (1993):

[The proper adjudication of *Presley*] required an intimate, functional appraisal of political reality. If the Court were not forced to confront such fundamentally political and intractable claims, it would have every incentive to exclude them from its definition of voting.

The 1982 amendments to the Voting Rights Act, however, require precisely this form of judicial engagement. Congress has expressly directed courts to consider whether racial and ethnic minority groups have an equal opportunity "to *participate in the political process* and to elect representatives of their choice." And while the statute does not provide a clear benchmark for assessing aggregation claims, let alone governance issues, its "political process" language forces courts to address these question on the merits.[b]

Aside from the question of statutory interpretation and the difficulty, emphasized by Justice Kennedy, of fashioning a workable remedy, there is also the empirical question of whether the problem of "deliberative gerrymandering" is typically a serious one. It is possible to find particular instances in which minority members of legislative bodies have been deprived of the opportunity to exercise influence, and the *Presley* case itself included an especially flagrant example. But it is probably easier to cite counter-examples. For example, Willie Brown, an African-American, served as Speaker of the California Assembly from 1981 to 1995, longer than anyone else in history, and during that period wielded great power. The author of a systematic study of African American members of the House of Representatives in the 1990s found little indication of deliberative gerrymandering:

> The finding that racial legislation and bills that are sponsored by black members of Congress have a slight advantage in the legislative process surprised me as much as anything in this book. I expected that the evidence would support Guinier's argument that minorities have a tough time in majority-rule institutions. The majoritarian nature of the legislative process in the House is well established, and nothing in the black politics or congressional literature prepared me for this finding. I do not want to exaggerate the point. The [Congressional Black Caucus] clearly does not run the House—and did not even when the House was controlled by the Democrats. A relatively small faction of the work of the House touches on racial issues. However, when racial legislation does come up, it has as good a chance as any (and slightly better) of making its way through the legislative process.

David T. Canon, RACE, REDISTRICTING, AND REPRESENTATION: THE UNINTENDED CONSEQUENCES OF BLACK MAJORITY DISTRICTS 171–72 (1999).

(b) *The view that* Gingles *goes too far.* Soon after *Gingles* was issued, it received influential criticism in a book by Abigail M. Thernstrom, WHOSE VOTES COUNT? (1987).[c] Thernstrom reviews the history of the Voting Rights Act from its adoption through the 1982

---

b. More recently, Professor Karlan has claimed that *Presley* stands in tension with the Court's approach in *Georgia v. Ashcroft*, which "created an anomalous world in which changes that augment or preserve the political power of representatives elected from minority communities could be used to justify granting preclearance while changes that diminished that power could not be used to justify an objection." Pamela S. Karlan, *Section 5 Squared: Congressional Power to Extend and Amend the Voting Rights Act*, 44 HOUSTON LAW REVIEW 1, 10 (2007).

c. Thernstrom's book was controversial. For sharp criticism, see J. Morgan Kousser, *The Voting Rights Act and the Two Reconstructions*, in CONTROVERSIES 135, 166–76; Pamela S. Karlan & Peyton McCrary, *Without Fear and Without Research: Abigail Thernstrom on the Voting Rights Act*, 4 JOURNAL OF LAW & POLITICS 751 (1988).

amendments and the *Gingles* decision, and concludes that its original, widely-supported goals of extending the right to vote and eliminating abusive practices in the South were quietly transmuted into anticompetitive policies that enjoy little public support.

> [O]ur sensitivity to the special significance of black officeholding in the South, where blacks were disfranchised before 1965, has shaded into a belief in the entitlement of black and Hispanic candidates everywhere to extraordinary protection from white competition.

Id. at 235. Many of the criticisms of the race-conscious districting mandated by *Gingles* that have been advanced by Thernstrom and others are summarized in the concurring opinion of Justice Thomas in *Holder v. Hall*, reprinted below.

Some commentators who believe *Gingles* goes "too far" begin from the same recognition expressed by Lani Guinier that in a country in which minority groups are, after all, minorities, only so much can be accomplished by providing such groups with the opportunity to elect their own representatives. Thus, Carol Swain writes:

> When African Americans question the common strategy of drawing legislative districts with large black majorities, they are sometimes viewed by other blacks with suspicion and regarded as "enemies of the group." Yet the electoral demography of the United States favors such a policy. The statistics on the distribution and concentration of blacks in the population reveal a need to look beyond the creation of majority-black political units as a way to increase political representation of African Americans. Blacks have already made the most of their opportunities to elect black politicians in congressional districts with black majorities.... Some experts suggest that African Americans and Hispanics might be able to find twelve to fifteen new districts for themselves after the 1990s redistricting. Beyond that, and in years to come, we can expect severe limitations on what can be achieved by relying on the creation of black districts to ensure the election of black politicians.

Carol M. Swain, BLACK FACES, BLACK INTERESTS 200 (1993). Swain does not respond to these limitations by demanding institutional change to obtain what Guinier calls "proportionate interest representation." Instead, Swain believes minority groups should welcome districts in which they fall short of a majority but constitute a significant element. Swain argues that a strategy of coalition-building with progressive white voters and politicians offers the best hope for minority groups.

> Black districts with smaller percentages of black voters would give more African-American candidates an incentive to build multiracial coalitions. Lowering the threshold of black voters has other implications: blacks dispersed over more districts might encourage greater responsiveness from white elected officials. No politician can afford to concentrate on one racial or ethnic group to the exclusion of others. Most representatives know that ignoring a significant minority population can be political suicide, because an opponent can build a coalition of disaffected groups. Less overwhelmingly black districts would also undoubtedly make their own representatives feel less secure. Many of the representatives would become more attentive and vigilant, and therefore their constituents would profit.
>
> Much of the future growth of black substantive and descriptive representation will depend on coalition building with other racial and ethnic groups. The issue of biracial coalitions between whites and blacks has been intensely debated since the 1960s, when Stokely Carmichael and Charles V. Hamilton wrote their classic book on black power[, *Black Power: The Politics of Liberation in America*].

Carmichael and Hamilton warned against coalitions with whites until blacks had had the opportunity to develop independent bases of power that would allow them to be more than junior partners. Now, in the 1990s, it can be argued that the time has come.

Id. at 210–11.[d]

But has that time come, at least in the specific sense that minority group candidates can realistically hope to be elected in majority-white districts? Swain devotes much of her book to attempting to show that this question may be answered in the affirmative. The same answer is given by Timothy G. O'Rourke, *The 1982 Amendments and the Voting Rights Paradox*, in CONTROVERSIES, 85, 109:

> In Virginia, one of the half dozen southern states targeted by the 1965 act, minority candidates running at large have since the late 1960s regularly won seats on local councils. Fredericksburg and Roanoke—overwhelmingly white cities—have elected and reelected black mayors. Both parties have run black candidates for statewide office, and in recent years a black candidate has been elected lieutenant governor and then governor. These developments are most assuredly attributable to the Voting Rights Act. But they are not successes attributable to section 5 or section 2. Instead they are attributable to the gradual workings of the original law—the enrollment of minority voters, the large-scale entry of minority voters into the rank and file of the political parties, the entry of minority candidates into politics, and a growing receptiveness of a predominantly white electorate to minority candidates.

> Yet it is a measure of the fantastical quality of the contemporary discussions of voting rights law that such successes are so easily explained away.... [F]or instance, Laughlin McDonald dismisses L. Douglas Wilder's election of Virginia as exceptional and as an example of "racially polarized voting" (since Wilder received only two-fifths of the white vote). Such successes, of course, must be explained away to preserve the legal momentum for creating safe minority districts.

(c) *The view that* Gingles *is about right.* Despite the criticism it has received, the *Gingles* regime also has numerous defenders. Among the more prominent are Bernard Grofman, Lisa Handley & Richard G. Niemi, the authors of MINORITY REPRESENTATION, and we shall consider their views in some detail. Responding to the view of some critics that *Gingles* reflects a group-based theory of politics that is contrary to the idea of a "colorblind" society, they write:

> We would emphasize, first, that the rights provided by the act are contingent, appropriate only when a significant liability threshold has been met. Only when African-Americans or Hispanics are made a "permanent minority" as a result of racial bloc voting by the majority or by various practices and procedures is there intervention under the Voting Rights Act. Intervention in such circumstances is, we believe, in accord with the Madisonian tradition...,

---

d. See also Daniel A. Farber, *The Outmoded Debate Over Affirmative Action*, 82 CALIFORNIA LAW REVIEW 893, 926 (1994):

> To be effective, African American representatives must form coalitions with other minority and white legislators who share their interests. However, it may be difficult to develop coalitions if African Americans are realigned to form new majority-minority districts since the representatives from their former districts will have less motivation, based on present constituents, to consider African American interests. Whether the net result would be an increase in African American legislative power is unclear.

which condemns factions, even majority factions, and seeks to design constitutional rules that serve as safeguards against the pernicious consequences of such factionalism.

Because the rights are contingent, the applicability of Section 2 of the Voting Rights Act, like Section 5, is, in principle, "self-liquidating." ... Moreover, the three conditions — residential segregation sufficient to allow the drawing of districts in which minority group members are a majority, racially polarized voting, and a "usual" lack of minority electoral success — are conditions that few people wish to see perpetuated. Thus, if minority assimilation proceeds in such a fashion that residential segregation becomes a thing of the past, minority groups will be unable to launch successful voting rights suits. Or if voting in a jurisdiction is no longer polarized along racial or linguistic/ethnic lines — or even if it is, but the level of white crossover voting permits significant and repeated minority access — the Voting Rights Act will become a dead letter in that jurisdiction.

Second, though it is true that most other voting rights violations (e.g., of the one-person, one-vote standard) are customarily defined in terms of the violation of individual rights, clearly there are types of discrimination directed against individuals as a function of their status as members of a minority community. In such situations it seems foolish to think that liability and remedies cannot be race conscious. In the present context, because racially polarized voting is a prerequisite for a voting rights violation and residential segregation a prerequisite for submergence, it is not plausible to attempt only "color-blind" tests and solutions.

Furthermore, to argue that policies in the voting rights area must be free of all considerations of race and ethnicity is like blaming the messenger for the message.

MINORITY REPRESENTATION at 131–32. Grofman et al. acknowledge the force behind some of the complaints of critics as divergent as Guinier and Swain, but they do not regard those complaints as decisive.

To be sure, blacks have sometimes been elected in majority-white areas, but such situations are not that common, despite various well-publicized cases. And when they do occur, they can often be attributed to overwhelming support from black voters combined with limited support from Hispanics, Asians, or whites (e.g., the mayoral elections of David Dinkins in New York City and Harold Washington in Chicago, the gubernatorial election of Douglas Wilder in Virginia), or to plurality victories against a divided opposition (Wilder's initial legislative victory against a field of white candidates)....

In a similar vein, we agree with Swain that in the long run, major additional gains in black (or Hispanic) representation can come only by building coalitions that make possible the election of minority candidates from districts that are not majority or near majority minority, but we do not see this as a reason to stop trying to create black or Hispanic majority seats where there is evidence of vote dilution. We also differ with Swain and other scholars who look to multiracial coalition building as the primary direction for future black (or Hispanic) politics, so severe, in our perception, is the level of present-day racial polarization.

At the same time, we share with Swain and others the concern that there is only a limited prospect for further gains in African-American representation in

Congress or the state legislatures from the creation of additional majority-black districts. Patterns of black geographic distribution are such that only a relatively small number of additional black majority legislative and congressional seats can be created. Moreover, there are also limits to the foreseeable gains in black representation from further shifts from at-large to single-member district representation at the municipal level, although there are greater prospects for gains in black representation at the level of school boards. For Hispanics, however, there are still great gains in representation possible at the local level with the elimination of at-large city council and school board elections (e.g., in Texas and California), and further gains to be made in Congress and the state legislatures because of the dramatic increase in the Hispanic population over the last decade....

Although revisionist critics of the Voting Rights Act ... see it as accentuating the importance of racial and linguistic cleavages, we see it as forcing an assessment, on the basis of case-specific evidence, of the reality of those cleavages and an effort to give minorities a full opportunity to be part of the political process when those divisions are especially strong. Rather than fearing the election of minority candidates from largely minority constituencies, we ask whether we would really prefer the most likely alternative—the lack of minority electoral success still characteristic of majority-white jurisdictions in the South, especially those at the state legislative and congressional level. Whereas some revisionist critics see the success of the Voting Rights Act threatening our aspirations for a color-blind society, we see it as a necessary evil in a color-conscious world—admittedly the "politics of second best."

Yet our view of the "politics of second best" is ultimately an optimistic one. Though we may agree with Guinier that the increase in the number of black elected officials "has not visibly altered the disadvantaged socio-economic condition or social isolation of black voters" and that sustained black mobilization has not emerged despite some black electoral success, we would also say that too much is being expected of the franchise. Some suffragettes, it is said, thought that achieving the vote would bring an end to war. That they were wrong does not make us want to repeal the Nineteenth Amendment. Similarly, the fact that the rhetoric concerning what was to be expected from black enfranchisement now seems dramatically overstated ought not to lead us to dismiss the real gains that have resulted from that enfranchisement—the change, for example, from fewer than 1,500 elected officials in 1970 to over 7,300 in 1990....

Still another reason for optimism over a broad interpretation of the Voting Rights Act is that majority-minority districts are serving as a necessary "port of entry" for minorities into pluralist politics. The opportunity to hold office and to make a record while in office is perhaps the most important means whereby minority candidates can establish a reputation that will earn them considerable crossover support. Even Governor Wilder, one of the most celebrated examples of black success in a majority-white constituency, was initially elected in the state legislature as a plurality victor in a district with a significant black population and was reelected to the legislature from a district that had been reconfigured to have a clear black majority. As with whites/Anglos, success of minority politicians at one level can be parleyed into higher office. But the important difference is that minority politicians are often able to get started because of majority-minority districts.

Finally, we would emphasize that cross-racial coalitions may be easier to achieve at the level of political elites than at the mass level.... But of course, multiracial/ethnic elite interaction demands that minorities as well as majorities be elected in the first place....

We do not presume, of course, that racial prejudice vanishes within legislative halls. There are surely instances in which the influence of minority elected officials on outcomes appears to have been minimal.... But there is considerable evidence for political change and accomplishment, as well....

[A]t some point, we hope the argument will be correct that the act has outlived its usefulness and is no longer necessary. For now, however, we are convinced that by ensuring that the right to vote is not an empty ritual but that minorities will be involved in decision-making bodies as well as in campaigns, the Voting Rights Act serves to integrate minorities into the American political process and helps ameliorate the alienation that came from their previous exclusion. If that is so, the act will be seen as one of the most important and successful pieces of legislation of this century, and its broad interpretation one of the most important achievements of the courts.

MINORITY REPRESENTATION at 134–37.[e]

16. *Partisan Politics and Section 2.* The foregoing notes—and the following one—show that the demand of Section 2, as interpreted in *Gingles*, for race-conscious districting raises numerous legal, policy, and theoretical questions. It should not be imagined, however, that the public debate has been unaffected by partisan and other political concerns.

A majority-minority district will usually be an overwhelmingly Democratic district.[f] The concentration of Democrats in a number of such districts is likely to leave a disproportionate number of Republican voters in the rest of the state or jurisdiction. Given typical patterns of political geography in the United States, a districting plan that has a high number of majority-minority districts is likely to be one that benefits Republicans in the jurisdiction as a whole. For more detailed analysis and empirical confirmation, see Kimball Brace, Bernard Grofman & Lisa Handley, *Does Redistricting Aimed to Help Blacks Necessarily Help Republicans?*, 49 JOURNAL OF POLITICS 169 (1987).

Political partisans have not been oblivious to this phenomenon. In many instances, Democratic politicians have resisted the creation of majority-minority districts, especially white Democratic incumbents whose own electoral prospects may be adversely affected. Democrats may feel constrained to create majority-minority districts, whether because of the Voting Rights Act, a liberal ideology, or the need to respond to minority groups who make up an important part of the Democratic electoral coalition. In this case, Democrats are likely to draw odd-shaped districts to accommodate the need for majority-minority districts without the Democrats having to "pay" for them by a reduction of the total number of Democratic-leaning districts. It was just such efforts by Democrats in North Carolina that led to the controversy in *Shaw v. Reno*, featured later in this chapter.

---

e. Centrists such as Grofman and his co-authors have been criticized for not grounding their views more firmly in political theory. See Keith J. Bybee, MISTAKEN IDENTITY: THE SUPREME COURT AND THE POLITICS OF MINORITY REPRESENTATION 60–69 (1998). Some might take this as praise rather than criticism.

f. An exception is likely to be a Hispanic district in Florida. Cuban-Americans, unlike other Hispanics and African-Americans, have at times been predominantly Republican in their voting.

Republicans, despite an ideology that usually opposes compensatory race policies, often react very differently. As Carol Swain writes:

> Republican leaders have zealously urged the creation of the maximum number of "safe" black and Hispanic districts.... The Republican position on minority districts may seem surprising, given that Republicans have gained so much political mileage by opposing affirmative action quotas. Why would Republicans want more minority-elected officials, if most are likely to be Democrats? Why do Republicans care about the number and size of black districts?
>
> The answers would appear to be simple. It is in the Republican interest to want large black districts. To the extent that the black Democrats are concentrated in legislative districts, it is easier for Republican candidates to win more seats overall. The creation of a newly black district is likely to drain black voters from other districts, many of them represented by white Democrats. The more "lily-white" the districts so drained become, the easier it is for Republicans to win them. In short, by adopting such a redistricting strategy, Republicans give African Americans the opportunity to increase their descriptive representation but, quite possibly, at the expense of their substantive representation.

Swain, *supra*, at 205. Some writers believe Republican benefits from the Voting Rights Act can be even more far-reaching, because of heightened tensions within the Democratic coalition:

> Legislative districts were redrawn for the 1992 elections under circumstances that increasingly strained the fragile alliance between Hispanics and blacks. According to Raul Yzaguirre, president of the National Council of La Raza, relations between the two "have not been particularly wholesome or happy" in the past twenty years. Redistricting under these circumstances threatens to split the alliance and further fragment the Democratic coalition. Republicans, determined to accelerate this process, have pressed for strict voting rights enforcement with the zeal of new converts. Under these circumstances it is no surprise that tensions within the voting rights policy community should rise, especially at its Democratic core among party professionals, committee staff, and practitioner academics.

Hugh Davis Graham, *Voting Rights and the American Regulatory State*, in CONTROVERSIES 177, 195.

The partisan effects of creating majority-minority districts for African Americans are usually greater in the south than in the rest of the country. The reason is that in the rest of the country, blacks tend to live in urban centers, surrounded by other predominantly Democratic groups, such as Catholics, Hispanics, and Jews. Even if highly-Democratic blacks are concentrated in one or a few districts, the remaining districts are still likely to be safely Democratic. See David Lublin, THE PARADOX OF REPRESENTATION, *supra*, at 91–97. In the south, African American voters are more likely to be surrounded by Republicans. For this reason, state legislatures that were controlled by Democrats and were required by the Voting Rights Act in the 1990s to create additional majority-minority districts typically went to great lengths to do so in a manner that would not jeopardize white Democratic incumbents. To facilitate this goal, they often created majority-minority districts extremely irregular in shape. As we shall see, those districts became the subject of the Supreme Court's racial gerrymandering cases.

The dramatic Republican victory in the 1994 election sparked increased interest in the partisan consequences of majority-minority districts. Many journalistic commentaries identified the creation of majority-minority districts, especially in the South, as a cause of the

Republican gains in the House of Representatives. The question stirred considerable controversy among Democrats and liberals, as voting rights activists sought to avoid blame for what their side of the political spectrum viewed as a political disaster. David Lublin, who has studied the question carefully, estimates that taking into account the 1992 and 1994 elections, racially-motivated districting cost the Democrats between seven and eleven seats. *Id.* at 109–14.

Would African Americans be better off if they were more evenly divided among districts instead of being concentrated into a few districts that they can control? Recall that this was the question that the Supreme Court declined to address in *Beer*, when it simply assumed that a plan that concentrated high percentages of blacks into two out of five councilmanic districts could not be retrogressive compared to an earlier plan with a more even distribution. Cameron et al., *Do Majority-Minority Districts Maximize Substantive Black Representation in Congress?, supra,* studied empirically the relation between the percentage of African-Americans in a congressional district and the degree to which the representative of that district voted in the House in accord with the preferences of African-Americans. In general, they found that although black representatives were most likely to vote in accord with black voter preferences, the difference between white Republican representatives and white Democrats was much greater than the difference between white Democrats and black Democrats. This led them to the conclusion that electing more Democrats was much more beneficial to blacks—so far as winning House roll call votes is concerned—than electing more blacks. They summarized their findings as follows:

> First, a trade-off does exist between maximizing the number of black representatives in Congress and maximizing the number of votes in favor of minority-sponsored legislation. In particular, districting plans designed to maximize descriptive representation concentrate minority voters more than do plans designed to maximize substantive representation. Second, electoral effects dominate representation effects; that is, the largest effect from adding minority voters to a district comes not from influencing the actions of any given representative but from influencing the type of representative elected. [Finally], given recent electoral and roll-call voting patterns, the districting strategy that maximizes substantive minority representation varies by region. Outside the South, optimal districting schemes divide black voters as equally as possible across districts. Inside the South, substantive minority representation is maximized by creating concentrated minority districts with about 47% black voting-age population.

Id. at 795. The authors recognize that representatives serve other functions beyond casting roll call votes. Their findings by no means end the arguments, but the authors contend that the trade-offs implicit in creating or requiring majority-minority districts should be recognized:

> [A] trade-off between descriptive and substantive representation does exist: Districting schemes that maximize the number of minority representatives do not necessarily maximize substantive minority representation. In practice, policymakers must choose their objective function, be it to maximize black representation, maximize the number of black representatives, or some combination of these.

Id. at 808.

Partisanship provides a useful lens through which to evaluate three of the most-watched districting cases of the 2000s, in California, Georgia, and New Jersey. See

Cano v. Davis, supra; *Georgia v. Ashcroft, supra*; *Page v. Bartels*, 144 F.Supp.2d 346 (D.N.J. 2001).

In each of these states, the districting process was more or less controlled by the Democrats, though with variations from state to state. Democratic control was most straightforward in Georgia, where Democrats in the legislature enacted the plan over Republican opposition. The Democrats also controlled the legislature and the governorship in California, but the plan was adopted with bipartisan support. The reason was that the Democrats had done so well in congressional and state legislative elections up to and including 2000 that they were content to consolidate their gains, rather than try to take more seats away from the Republicans. For their part the Republicans supported the plan, in the belief that if they did not do so, the Democrats were likely to enact a plan that would be even worse for the Republicans. In New Jersey, the state legislature was redistricted by a commission, composed of five Democrats and five Republicans. The commission predictably deadlocked along partisan lines, in which event New Jersey law called for an 11th member to be appointed to the commission. The 11th member was Larry Bartels, a political scientist. Bartels sided with the Democrats.

The California plan was challenged by Latino plaintiffs. In Georgia and New Jersey, Republicans stood behind African-American plaintiffs. In each state, what gave rise to the controversy was that the plan reduced the minority population in certain districts, either to make the districts more comfortable for non-minority Democratic incumbents or to strengthen surrounding districts for the Democrats, at the cost of making the election of candidates favored by the minority groups in the challenged districts somewhat less certain than would have been the case if the minority populations had not been reduced.

In California and New Jersey, the plans were upheld. The final result in Georgia was the same, but in the District Court the state Senate plan was rejected. Though differences in the fact situations in each state and differences in the judges may have been part of the reason for the different outcomes in the lower courts, the main reason appears to be a legal one: Of the three states, only Georgia is subject to Section 5 of the Voting Rights Act, while in California and New Jersey, plaintiffs had to rely on Section 2.[g] The District Court in *Georgia v. Ashcroft* held that the reduction in black population constituted retrogression, whereas in California and New Jersey, equally or more consequential reductions in minority population survived attack under the *Gingles* test. Georgia is subject to Section 5 because of a past history of voting discrimination against blacks. Is that a good reason for inconsistent results in these states? In other words, one might believe that "friendly" reduction of minority percentages in selected districts for incumbent-protection or partisan purposes should be permitted, or one might believe it should be prohibited. But is the past discrimination in Georgia a good reason for prohibiting it there and permitting it in California and New Jersey?

Whether such concerns may have influenced the Supreme Court in *Georgia v. Ashcroft* is a matter of speculation. One thing is certain: *Georgia v. Ashcroft* represents a challenge to those who believe Supreme Court results in voting rights cases are driven by partisanship. The five conservative justices upheld a plan adopted by Democrats and supported by liberal black politicians. The four liberal justices would have furthered the interests of Republicans by striking down that plan.

---

g. A few counties in California are subject to Section 5, but in the case of a statewide redistricting plan, only the districts affecting the covered counties need to be precleared. The districts challenged in *Cano* were in Imperial, Los Angeles, and San Diego Counties, none of which is subject to Section 5.

For an interesting account of the New Jersey litigation written by one of the lawyers in the case, see Sam Hirsch, *Unpacking* Page v. Bartels: *A Fresh Redistricting Paradigm Emerges in New Jersey*, 1 ELECTION LAW JOURNAL 7 (2002).

17. *A Salvo from the Court's Conservatives.* We have seen that in *Holder v. Hall* the Court ruled that a Section 2 claim could not be based on a contention that a single official was elected rather than a multi-member body. The plurality opinion by Justice Kennedy and a concurring opinion by Justice O'Connor worked within the *Gingles* framework. Justice Thomas, joined by Justice Scalia, made up the remainder of the majority in *Holder*, but concurred on much broader grounds. As Justice Thomas wrote, "I would hold that the size of a governing body is not a 'standard, practice, or procedure' within the terms of the Act. In my view, however, the only principle limiting the scope of the terms 'standard, practice, or procedure' that can be derived from the text of the Act would exclude, not only the challenge to size advanced today, but also challenges to allegedly dilutive election methods that we have considered within the scope of the Act in the past."

As Justice Thomas recognized, his approach would require overruling *Gingles* and several subsequent cases. His concurring opinion in *Holder* consists primarily of two long parts. Part II could be described as the "statutory" or "legal" portion of his opinion, in which he attempts to show that his narrow reading of Section 2 is justified by normal procedures of statutory interpretation. Justice Harlan's dissenting opinion in *Allen* had demonstrated that it was at least plausible to believe that the similar language in Section 5 of the original Voting Rights Act did not include electoral systems that allegedly could dilute minority votes. However, in attempting to demonstrate that the current Section 2 is similarly limited, Justice Thomas faced the formidable challenge of the text and background of the 1982 amendments. Interested readers can consult Justice Thomas' full opinion and determine for themselves how successfully he fared against that challenge.

Reprinted below are substantial excerpts from Part I of Justice Thomas' opinion, in which he addresses many of the broader issues raised by the attempt to proscribe minority vote dilution. It may provide a suitably provocative note on which to conclude this section.

Holder v. Hall

512 U.S. 874 (1994) (concurring opinion)

Justice THOMAS, with whom Justice SCALIA joins, concurring in the judgment....

I

If one surveys the history of the Voting Rights Act, one can only be struck by the sea change that has occurred in the application and enforcement of the Act since it was passed in 1965. The statute was originally perceived as a remedial provision directed specifically at eradicating discriminatory practices that restricted blacks' ability to register and vote in the segregated South. Now, the Act has grown into something entirely different. In construing the Act to cover claims of vote dilution, we have converted the Act into a device for regulating, rationing, and apportioning political power among racial and ethnic groups. In the process, we have read the Act essentially as a grant of authority to the federal judiciary to develop theories on basic principles of representative government, for it is only a resort to political theory that can enable a court to determine which electoral systems provide the "fairest" levels of representation or the most "effective" or "undiluted" votes to minorities.

Before I turn to an analysis of the text of §2 to explain why, in my view, the terms of the statute do not authorize the project that we have undertaken in the name of the Act,

I intend first simply to describe the development of the basic contours of vote dilution actions under the Voting Rights Act. An examination of the current state of our decisions should make obvious a simple fact that for far too long has gone unmentioned: vote dilution cases have required the federal courts to make decisions based on highly political judgments—judgments that courts are inherently ill-equipped to make. A clear understanding of the destructive assumptions that have developed to guide vote dilution decisions and the role we have given the federal courts in redrawing the political landscape of the Nation should make clear the pressing need for us to reassess our interpretation of the Act.

A

As it was enforced in the years immediately following its enactment, the Voting Rights Act of 1965 was perceived primarily as legislation directed at eliminating literacy tests and similar devices that had been used to prevent black voter registration in the segregated South....

The Act was immediately and notably successful in removing barriers to registration and ensuring access to the ballot....

The Court's decision in *Allen*, however, marked a fundamental shift in the focal point of the Act.... The decision in *Allen* ... ensured that the terms "standard, practice, or procedure" would extend to encompass a wide array of electoral practices or voting systems that might be challenged for reducing the potential impact of minority votes.

As a consequence, *Allen* also ensured that courts would be required to confront a number of complex and essentially political questions in assessing claims of vote dilution under the Voting Rights Act. The central difficulty in any vote dilution case, of course, is determining a point of comparison against which dilution can be measured. As Justice Frankfurter observed several years before *Allen*, "[t]alk of 'debasement' or 'dilution' is circular talk. One cannot speak of 'debasement' or 'dilution' of the value of a vote until there is first defined a standard of reference as to what a vote should be worth." *Baker v. Carr* (Frankfurter, J., dissenting). But in setting the benchmark of what "undiluted" or fully "effective" voting strength should be, a court must necessarily make some judgments based purely on an assessment of principles of political theory. As Justice Harlan pointed out in his dissent in *Allen*, the Voting Rights Act supplies no rule for a court to rely upon in deciding, for example, whether a multimember at-large system of election is to be preferred to a single-member district system; that is, whether one provides a more "effective" vote than another.... The choice is inherently a political one, and depends upon the selection of a theory for defining the fully "effective" vote—at bottom, a theory for defining effective participation in representative government. In short, what a court is actually asked to do in a vote dilution case is "to choose among competing bases of representation—ultimately, really, among competing theories of political philosophy." *Baker* (Frankfurter, J., dissenting).

Perhaps the most prominent feature of the philosophy that has emerged in vote dilution decisions since *Allen* has been the Court's preference for single-member districting schemes, both as a benchmark for measuring undiluted minority voting strength and as a remedial mechanism for guaranteeing minorities undiluted voting power. Indeed, commentators surveying the history of voting rights litigation have concluded that it has been the objective of voting rights plaintiffs to use the Act to attack multimember districting schemes and to replace them with single-member districting systems drawn with majority-minority districts to ensure minority control of seats.

It should be apparent, however, that there is no principle inherent in our constitutional system, or even in the history of the Nation's electoral practices, that makes single-member districts the "proper" mechanism for electing representatives to governmental bodies or for giving "undiluted" effect to the votes of a numerical minority. On the contrary, from the earliest days of the Republic, multimember districts were a common feature of our political systems. The Framers left unanswered in the Constitution the question whether congressional delegations from the several States should be elected on a general ticket from each State as a whole or under a districting scheme and left that matter to be resolved by the States or by Congress. It was not until 1842 that Congress determined that Representatives should be elected from single-member districts in the States....

The obvious advantage the Court has perceived in single-member districts, of course, is their tendency to enhance the ability of any numerical minority in the electorate to gain control of seats in a representative body. But in choosing single-member districting as a benchmark electoral plan on that basis the Court has made a political decision and, indeed, a decision that itself depends on a prior political choice made in answer to Justice Harlan's question in *Allen*. Justice Harlan asked whether a group's votes should be considered to be more "effective" when they provide *influence* over a greater number of seats, or *control* over a lesser number of seats. In answering that query, the Court has determined that the purpose of the vote — or of the fully "effective" vote — is controlling seats. In other words, in an effort to develop standards for assessing claims of dilution, the Court has adopted the view that members of any numerically significant minority are denied a fully effective use of the franchise unless they are able to control seats in an elected body. Under this theory, votes that do not control a representative are essentially wasted; those who cast them go unrepresented and are just as surely disenfranchised as if they had been barred from registering. Such conclusions, of course, depend upon a certain theory of the "effective" vote, a theory that is not inherent in the concept of representative democracy itself.

In fact, it should be clear that the assumptions that have guided the Court reflect only one possible understanding of effective exercise of the franchise, an understanding based on the view that voters are "represented" only when they choose a delegate who will mirror their views in the legislative halls. But it is certainly possible to construct a theory of effective political participation that would accord greater importance to voters' ability to influence, rather than control, elections. And especially in a two-party system such as ours, the influence of a potential "swing" group of voters composing 10%–20% of the electorate in a given district can be considerable. Even such a focus on practical influence, however, is not a necessary component of the definition of the "effective" vote. Some conceptions of representative government may primarily emphasize the formal value of the vote as a mechanism for participation in the electoral process, whether it results in control of a seat or not. Under such a theory, minorities unable to control elected posts would not be considered essentially without a vote; rather, a vote duly cast and counted would be deemed just as "effective" as any other. If a minority group is unable to control seats, that result may plausibly be attributed to the inescapable fact that, in a majoritarian system, numerical minorities lose elections.

In short, there are undoubtedly an infinite number of theories of effective suffrage, representation, and the proper apportionment of political power in a representative democracy that could be drawn upon to answer the questions posed in *Allen*. I do not pretend to have provided the most sophisticated account of the various possibilities; but such matters of political theory are beyond the ordinary sphere of federal judges. And that is precisely the point. The matters the Court has set out to resolve in vote dilution cases are questions of political philosophy, not questions of law. As such, they are not readily subjected to any judicially manageable standards that can guide courts in attempting to select between competing theories.

But the political choices the Court has had to make do not end with the determination that the primary purpose of the "effective" vote is controlling seats or with the selection of single-member districting as the mechanism for providing that control. In one sense, these were not even the most critical decisions to be made in devising standards for assessing claims of dilution, for in itself, the selection of single-member districting as a benchmark election plan will tell a judge little about the number of minority districts to create. Single-member districting tells a court "how" members of a minority are to control seats, but not "how many" seats they should be allowed to control.

But "how many" is the critical issue. Once one accepts the proposition that the effectiveness of votes is measured in terms of the control of seats, the core of any vote dilution claim is an assertion that the group in question is unable to control the "proper" number of seats — that is, the number of seats that the minority's percentage of the population would enable it to control in the benchmark "fair" system. The claim is inherently based on ratios between the numbers of the minority in the population and the numbers of seats controlled. As Justice O'CONNOR has noted, "any theory of vote dilution must necessarily rely to some extent on a measure of minority voting strength that makes some reference to the proportion between the minority group and the electorate at large." *Gingles* (opinion concurring in judgment). As a result, only a mathematical calculation can answer the fundamental question posed by a claim of vote dilution. And once again, in selecting the proportion that will be used to define the undiluted strength of a minority — the ratio that will provide the principle for decision in a vote dilution case — a court must make a political choice.

The ratio for which this Court has opted, and thus the mathematical principle driving the results in our cases, is undoubtedly direct proportionality. Indeed, four Members of the Court candidly recognized in *Gingles* that the Court had adopted a rule of roughly proportional representation, at least to the extent proportionality was possible given the geographic dispersion of minority populations. (O'CONNOR, J., concurring in judgment). While in itself that choice may strike us intuitively as the fairest or most just rule to apply, opting for proportionality is still a political choice, not a result required by any principle of law.

B

The dabbling in political theory that dilution cases have prompted, however, is hardly the worst aspect of our vote dilution jurisprudence. Far more pernicious has been the Court's willingness to accept the one underlying premise that must inform every minority vote dilution claim: the assumption that the group asserting dilution is not merely a racial or ethnic group, but a group having distinct political interests as well. Of necessity, in resolving vote dilution actions we have given credence to the view that race defines political interest. We have acted on the implicit assumption that members of racial and ethnic groups must all think alike on important matters of public policy and must have their own "minority preferred" representatives holding seats in elected bodies if they are to be considered represented at all.

It is true that in *Gingles* we stated that whether a racial group is "politically cohesive" may not be assumed, but rather must be proved in each case. But the standards we have employed for determining political cohesion have proved so insubstantial that this "precondition" does not present much of a barrier to the assertion of vote dilution claims on behalf of any racial group.[h] Moreover, it provides no test — indeed, it is not designed to

---

h. Cf. *Citizens for a Better Gretna v. Gretna*, 834 F.2d 496, 501–02 (5th Cir. 1987) (emphasizing that political cohesion under *Gingles* can be shown where a "significant number" of minority voters prefer the same candidate, and suggesting that data showing that anywhere from 49% to 67% of the

provide a test—of whether race itself determines a distinctive political community of interest. According to the rule adopted in *Gingles*, plaintiffs must show simply that members of a racial group tend to prefer the same candidates. There is no set standard defining how strong the correlation must be, and an inquiry into the cause for the correlation (to determine, for example, whether it might be the product of similar socioeconomic interests rather than some other factor related to race) is unnecessary. Thus, whenever similarities in political preferences along racial lines exist, we proclaim that the cause of the correlation is irrelevant, but we effectively rely on the fact of the correlation to assume that racial groups have unique political interests.

As a result, *Gingles'* requirement of proof of political cohesiveness, as practically applied, has proved little different from a working assumption that racial groups can be conceived of largely as political interest groups. And operating under that assumption, we have assigned federal courts the task of ensuring that minorities are assured their "just" share of seats in elected bodies throughout the Nation.

To achieve that result through the currently fashionable mechanism of drawing majority-minority single-member districts, we have embarked upon what has been aptly characterized as a process of "creating racially 'safe boroughs.'" *United States v. Dallas County Comm'n*, 850 F.2d 1433, 1444 (11th Cir. 1988) (Hill, J., concurring specially), cert. denied, 490 U.S. 1030 (1989). We have involved the federal courts, and indeed the Nation, in the enterprise of systematically dividing the country into electoral districts along racial lines— an enterprise of segregating the races into political homelands that amounts, in truth, to nothing short of a system of "political apartheid." *Shaw*, [*infra*, Part IV]. Blacks are drawn into "black districts" and given "black representatives"; Hispanics are drawn into Hispanic districts and given "Hispanic representatives"; and so on. Worse still, it is not only the courts that have taken up this project. In response to judicial decisions and the promptings of the Justice Department, the States themselves, in an attempt to avoid costly and disruptive Voting Rights Act litigation, have begun to gerrymander electoral districts according to race. That practice now promises to embroil the courts in a lengthy process of attempting to undo, or at least to minimize, the damage wrought by the system we created. See, e.g., *Shaw*; *Hays v. Louisiana*, 839 F.Supp. 1188 (W.D.La.1993), vacated, 114 S.Ct. 2731.

The assumptions upon which our vote dilution decisions have been based should be repugnant to any nation that strives for the ideal of a color-blind Constitution. "The principle of equality is at war with the notion that District A must be represented by a Negro, as it is with the notion that District B must be represented by a Caucasian, District C by a Jew, District D by a Catholic, and so on." *Wright v. Rockefeller*, 376 U.S. 52, 66 (1964) (Douglas, J., dissenting). Despite Justice Douglas' warning sounded 30 years ago, our voting rights decisions are rapidly progressing towards a system that is indistinguishable in principle from a scheme under which members of different racial groups are divided into separate electoral registers and allocated a proportion of political power on the basis of race. Under our jurisprudence, rather than requiring registration on racial rolls and dividing power purely on a population basis, we have simply resorted to the somewhat less precise expedient of drawing geographic district lines to capture minority populations and to ensure the existence of the "appropriate" number of "safe minority seats."

That distinction in the practical implementation of the concept, of course, is immaterial. The basic premises underlying our system of safe minority districts and those be-

---

members of a minority group preferred the same candidate established cohesion), cert. denied, 492 U.S. 905 (1989).

hind the racial register are the same: that members of the racial group must think alike and that their interests are so distinct that the group must be provided a separate body of representatives in the legislature to voice its unique point of view. Such a "system, by whatever name it is called, is a divisive force in a community, emphasizing differences between candidates and voters that are irrelevant." *Id.* Justice Douglas correctly predicted the results of state sponsorship of such a theory of representation: "When racial or religious lines are drawn by the State, ... antagonisms that relate to race or to religion rather than to political issues are generated; communities seek not the best representative but the best racial or religious partisan." In short, few devices could be better designed to exacerbate racial tensions than the consciously segregated districting system currently being constructed in the name of the Voting Rights Act.

As a practical political matter, our drive to segregate political districts by race can only serve to deepen racial divisions by destroying any need for voters or candidates to build bridges between racial groups or to form voting coalitions. "Black-preferred" candidates are assured election in "safe black districts"; white-preferred candidates are assured election in "safe white districts." Neither group needs to draw on support from the other's constituency to win on election day.

[T]he system we have instituted affirmatively encourages a racially based understanding of the representative function. The clear premise of the system is that geographic districts are merely a device to be manipulated to establish "black representatives" whose real constituencies are defined, not in terms of the voters who populate their districts, but in terms of race. The "black representative's" function, in other words, is to represent the "black interest."

Perhaps not surprisingly, the United States has now adopted precisely this theory of racial group representation, as the arguments advanced in another case decided today, *Johnson v. De Grandy*, 512 U.S. 997 (1994), should show. The case involved a claim that an apportionment plan for the Florida Legislature should have provided another Hispanic district in Dade County. Florida responded to the claim of vote dilution by arguing that the plan already provided Dade County Hispanics with seats in proportion to their numbers. According to the Solicitor General, this claim of proportionality should have been evaluated, not merely on the basis of the population in the Dade County area where the racial gerrymandering was alleged to have occurred, but on a statewide basis. It did not matter, in the Solicitor General's view, that Hispanic populations elsewhere in the State could not meet the *Gingles* geographic compactness test and thus could not possibly have controlled districts of their own. After all, the Solicitor General reasoned, the Hispanic legislators elected from Hispanic districts in Dade County would represent, not just the interests of the Dade County Hispanics, but the interests of all the Hispanics in the State. As the argument shows, at least some careful observers have recognized the racial gerrymandering in our vote dilution cases for what it is: a slightly less precise mechanism than the racial register for allocating representation on the basis of race.

C

While the results we have already achieved under the Voting Rights Act might seem bad enough, we should recognize that our approach to splintering the electorate into racially designated single-member districts does not by any means mark a limit on the authority federal judges may wield to rework electoral systems under our Voting Rights Act jurisprudence. On the contrary, in relying on single-member districting schemes as a touchstone, our cases so far have been somewhat arbitrarily limited to addressing the interests of minority voters who are sufficiently geographically compact to form a majority in a single-member district. There is no reason *a priori*, however, that our focus should be so constrained. The decision to rely on single-member geographic districts as a mechanism for conducting elections is merely a political choice—and one that we might reconsider in the future. Indeed, it is a choice that has undoubtedly been influenced by the adversary process: in the cases that have come before us, plaintiffs have focused largely upon attacking multimember districts and have offered single-member schemes as the benchmark of an "undiluted" alternative.

But as the destructive effects of our current penchant for majority-minority districts become more apparent, courts will undoubtedly be called upon to reconsider adherence to geographic districting as a method for ensuring minority voting power. Already, some advocates have criticized the current strategy of creating majority-minority districts and have urged the adoption of other voting mechanisms—for example, cumulative voting or a system using transferable votes—that can produce proportional results without requiring division of the electorate into racially segregated districts. Cf., *e.g.*, [writings of Guinier, Karlan, and others].

Such changes may seem radical departures from the electoral systems with which we are most familiar. Indeed, they may be unwanted by the people in the several States who purposely have adopted districting systems in their electoral laws. But nothing in our present understanding of the Voting Rights Act places a principled limit on the authority of federal courts that would prevent them from instituting a system of cumulative voting as a remedy under §2, or even from establishing a more elaborate mechanism for securing proportional representation based on transferable votes. [G]eographic districting is not a requirement inherent in our political system. Rather, districting is merely another political choice made by the citizenry in the drafting of their state constitutions. Like other political choices concerning electoral systems and models of representation, it too is presumably subject to a judicial override if it comes into conflict with the theories of representation and effective voting that we may develop under the Voting Rights Act.

Indeed, the unvarnished truth is that all that is required for districting to fall out of favor is for Members of this Court to further develop their political thinking. We should not be surprised if voting rights advocates encourage us to "revive our political imagination," Guinier, and to consider "innovative and nontraditional remedies" for vote dilution, Karlan, for under our Voting Rights Act jurisprudence, it is only the limits on our "political imagination" that place restraints on the standards we may select for defining undiluted voting systems. Once we candidly recognize that geographic districting and other aspects of electoral systems that we have so far placed beyond question are merely political choices, those practices, too, may fall under suspicion of having a dilutive effect on minority voting strength. And when the time comes to put the question to the test, it may be difficult indeed for a Court that, under *Gingles*, has been bent on creating roughly proportional representation for geographically compact minorities to find a principled reason for holding that a geographically dispersed minority cannot challenge districting itself as a dilutive electoral practice. In principle, cumulative voting and other non-district-based methods of effecting proportional representation are simply more efficient and straightforward mechanisms for achieving what has already become our tacit objective: roughly proportional allocation of political power according to race....

D

Such is the current state of our understanding of the Voting Rights Act. That our reading of the Act has assigned the federal judiciary the task of making the decisions I have described above should suggest to the Members of this Court that something in our jurisprudence has gone awry. We would be mighty Platonic guardians indeed if Congress had granted us the authority to determine the best form of local government for every county, city, village, and town in America. But under our constitutional system, this Court is not a centralized politburo appointed for life to dictate to the provinces the "correct" theories of democratic representation, the "best" electoral systems for securing truly "representative" government, the "fairest" proportions of minority political influence, or, as respondents would have us hold today, the "proper" sizes for local governing bodies. We should be cautious in interpreting any Act of Congress to grant us power to make such determinations....

A full understanding of the authority that our current interpretation of the Voting Rights Act assigns to the federal courts, and of the destructive effects that our exercise of that authority is presently having upon our body politic, compels a single conclusion: a systematic reexamination of our interpretation of the Act is required.

II

... In my view, our current practice should not continue. Not for another Term, not until the next case, not for another day. The disastrous implications of the policies we have adopted under the Act are too grave; the dissembling in our approach to the Act too damaging to the credibility of the federal judiciary. The "inherent tension"—indeed, I would call it an irreconcilable conflict—between the standards we have adopted for evaluating vote dilution claims and the text of the Voting Rights Act [i.e., the proviso in Section 2 that proportional representation is not required,] would itself be sufficient in my view to warrant overruling the interpretation of §2 set out in *Gingles*. When that obvious conflict is combined with the destructive effects our expansive reading of the Act has had in involving the federal judiciary in the project of dividing the Nation into racially segregated electoral districts, I can see no reasonable alternative to abandoning our current unfortunate understanding of the Act....[i]

IV. Racial Gerrymandering

The Supreme Court decisions we review in this Part were among the most important and controversial of the 1990s. They came as a surprise. Going into the decade, the question of minority vote dilution and its remedies seemed to be predominantly a statutory one. *Bolden*, the 1982 amendments to Section 2, and *Gingles* combined to channel claims of minority vote dilution through the Voting Rights Act. As we shall see, decisions of legislatures to avoid dilution or of courts to remedy it seemed insulated from constitutional review. The Supreme Court altered this picture in 1993, when it issued the first of the racial gerrymandering decisions, *Shaw v. Reno*.

At the time, the racial gerrymandering doctrine seemed momentous. Many voting rights activists worried that their long efforts and the ground they had gained to control the consequences of polarized voting were doomed. Some conservatives hoped that federal intrusion into the ability of states and localities to structure their political processes as they wish would be sharply curtailed. The perspective of time suggests that both the

---

i. For a recent study supporting Justice Thomas' position, see Anthony A. Peacock, DECONSTRUCTING THE REPUBLIC: VOTING RIGHTS, THE SUPREME COURT, AND THE FOUNDERS' REPUBLICANISM RECONSIDERED (2008).

hopes and the fears were greatly exaggerated. The racial gerrymandering cases were a response to a particular set of circumstances that shaped redistricting in some states in the decade of the 1990s. In the 2000s, when those circumstances no longer prevailed, there were almost no successful racial gerrymandering cases at all. It is still necessary for the student of election law to be aware of the racial gerrymandering cases, partly because they are a significant part of the history of the subject that continues to shape the way government officials and lawyers think about redistricting, and partly because the cases have not been overruled and there is no telling when they might make a comeback, possibly in modified form. Indeed, as we shall see in Chapter 6, some justices on the Supreme Court have sought to import racial gerrymandering concepts into the law of partisan gerrymandering.

The majority in *Shaw v. Reno* relied on two earlier cases, *Gomillion v. Lightfoot* and *Wright v. Rockefeller*. The dissenters relied on a third case, *United Jewish Organizations v. Carey*, which they thought disposed of the issue. We shall preface our consideration of *Shaw* with brief descriptions of these three precedents.

In *Gomillion v. Lightfoot*, 364 U.S. 340 (1960), African Americans challenged an Alabama statute changing the boundaries of the City of Tuskegee. As Justice Frankfurter described the allegations,

> Prior to Act 140 the City of Tuskegee was square in shape; the Act transformed it into a strangely irregular twenty-eight-sided figure.... The essential inevitable effect of this redefinition of Tuskegee's boundaries is to remove from the city all save only four or five of its 400 Negro voters while not removing a single white voter or resident. The result of the Act is to deprive the Negro petitioners discriminatorily of the benefits of residence in Tuskegee, including, *inter alia*, the right to vote in municipal elections.

The Court ruled that Act 140 violated the Fifteenth Amendment.

Gomillion is often referred to as a districting case, but that is inaccurate. In a districting plan, voters who are excluded from one district, for whatever reason, do not lose their right to vote. They simply cast their votes in a different district. When voters are removed from a city, as was the case in *Gomillion*, they are no longer permitted to vote in city elections at all.

Against the argument of the city that the state legislature had unlimited power to change city boundaries, the Court held that the Fifteenth Amendment was violated because the true purpose and effect of the change was to deprive members of one race of their ability to vote:

> A statute which is alleged to have worked unconstitutional deprivations of petitioners' rights is not immune to attack simply because the mechanism employed by the legislature is a redefinition of municipal boundaries. [T]he Alabama Legislature has not merely redrawn the Tuskegee city limits with incidental inconvenience to the petitioners; it is more accurate to say that it has deprived the petitioners of the municipal franchise and consequent rights and to that end it has incidentally changed the city's boundaries. While in form this is merely an act redefining metes and bounds, if the allegations are established, the inescapable human effect of this essay in geometry and geography is to despoil colored citizens, and only colored citizens, of their theretofore enjoyed voting rights.

Wright v. Rockefeller, 376 U.S. 52 (1964), was a challenge to a New York congressional districting plan in which one Manhattan district, represented by black Representative Adam Clayton Powell, consisted of 86 percent blacks and Puerto Ricans, while in the other three Manhattan congressional districts blacks and Puerto Ricans made up 5, 28, and 29 percent of the population.[j] Plaintiffs alleged that the plan violated both the Fourteenth and the Fifteenth Amendments because it "separate[d] eligible voters by race and place of origin." Plaintiffs claimed that the plan discriminated against blacks and Puerto Ricans by excluding them from the district in which they made up 5 percent of the population. The Supreme Court held that the plaintiffs had failed to demonstrate that the districts were racially motivated and therefore did not address what the legal consequences of racial motivation would have been.

A New York districting plan was also the subject of *United Jewish Organizations v. Carey*, 430 U.S. 144 (1977), but in this case the plan was for the state legislature. The case was brought by Hasidic Jews, who made up an insular community in the Williamsburgh area of the borough of Brooklyn. In a plan adopted by the legislature in 1972, the Hasidic community was located in one senate district and one assembly district. However, Brooklyn was covered by the Voting Rights Act and therefore subject to Section 5 preclearance, which the Attorney General refused to provide. The Attorney General insisted that the percentage of nonwhites be increased in certain of the majority-minority districts that had been created by the first plan. In 1974 the legislature adopted a second plan to comply with the Attorney General's demands. The second plan split the Hasidic community into two senate and two assembly districts. Plaintiffs challenging the plan did not allege that the Hasidic community had a right, as a religious group, to favored treatment. To the contrary, they alleged that it was unconstitutional to base a districting plan on racial considerations, as had been done in the case of the 1974 plan.

Justice White wrote the lead opinion for the Supreme Court, setting forth two different reasons for rejecting plaintiffs' claim. In the aggregate, Justice White's opinion was joined by a majority. However, he was joined by only three other justices—Stevens, Brennan, and Blackmun—in one portion of his opinion, and by only two—Stevens and Rehnquist—in the other. Justice Stewart, joined by Justice Powell, concurred separately, and Chief Justice Burger dissented.[k] As described by Justice White, the plaintiffs offered four propositions in support of their claim:

> First, that whatever might be true in other contexts, the use of racial criteria in districting and apportionment is never permissible; second, that even if racial considerations may be used to redraw district lines in order to remedy the residual effects of past unconstitutional reapportionments, there are no findings here of prior discriminations that would require or justify as a remedy that white voters may be reassigned in order to increase the size of black majorities in certain districts; third, that the use of a "racial quota" in redistricting is never acceptable; and fourth, that even if the foregoing general propositions are infirm, what New York actually did in this case was unconstitutional, particularly in its use of a 65% nonwhite racial quota for certain districts.

Justice White said that the first three arguments were precluded by the Court's prior decisions (including *Beer*), upholding and construing the Voting Rights Act. It was in response to the fourth argument that the justices divided. In the portion of his opinion joined by Stevens, Brennan and Blackmun, Justice White stated that under *Beer*, the Attorney General would have been correct to withhold preclearance if the old legislative plan being replaced had more 65%-minority districts than were contained in the new plan. In that case, a new plan with fewer 65%-minority districts would have been a retrogressive plan.

---

j. Representative Powell intervened in the case to defend the congressional plan.

k. The remaining Justice, Marshall, did not participate.

Furthermore, there was no evidence in the record indicating how many 65%-minority districts were contained in the old plan. Therefore, the plaintiffs had failed to prove their case. This was a disingenuous argument. For reasons given earlier in this chapter, it was extremely unlikely that New York's 1972 plan reduced the number of 65%-minority districts. As Chief Justice Burger argued in his dissent, if the Court really were worried about that, it could have remanded and ordered the trial court to make the necessary findings. Nevertheless, the approach these four justices took had the effect of avoiding difficult issues.

In the portion of his opinion joined by Stevens and Rehnquist, Justice White took a more substantive approach. Furthermore, what he said in this portion of his opinion was similar to the position taken separately by Stewart and Powell, so that in effect it had majority support. Therefore, for purposes of the later debate in *Shaw*, it was the crucial portion of the *UJO* case. The basis for this portion of the opinion was that even assuming that Section 5 did not require creation of the 65%-minority districts, New York was still free to create them, so long as it did not violate the Fourteenth or Fifteenth Amendment. And it did not violate those amendments by consciously enhancing the representation of minority groups, because no racial slur or stigma was directed at whites, there was no canceling out of the voting strength of whites, and the plan as a whole did not underrepresent whites. In the passage that received the most attention in *Shaw*, Justice White wrote:

> New York's revision of certain district lines is little different in kind from the decision by a State in which a racial minority is unable to elect representatives from multimember districts to change to single-member districting for the purpose of increasing minority representation. This change might substantially increase minority representation at the expense of white voters, who previously elected all of the legislators but who with single-member districts could elect no more than their proportional share. If this intentional reduction of white voting power would be constitutionally permissible, as we think it would be, we think it is also permissible for a State, employing sound districting principles such as compactness and population equality, to attempt to prevent racial minorities from being repeatedly outvoted by creating districts that will afford fair representation to the members of those racial groups who are sufficiently numerous and whose residential patterns afford the opportunity of creating districts in which they will be in the majority.

These were the primary precedents that were debated in *Shaw v. Reno*. The political background to *Shaw* is described by Michael Barone & Grant Ujifusa, THE ALMANAC OF AMERICAN POLITICS 1994, at 942 (1993):

> North Carolina's robust growth in the 1980s gave it a new 12th congressional district in the 1990 Census, its first new seat in 60 years. It had one of the most turbulent districting processes in the nation, thanks to application of the Voting Rights Act, whose 1982 amendments were interpreted by the Justice Department as requiring the creation of not one but two black-majority districts in a state that had none before. Thus in December 1991 was struck down the first Democratic plan, which would have created a new black-majority 1st District in east Carolina, but would have left Charlie Rose's 7th District with a large number of blacks and created a Republican-leaning new seat in the central Piedmont.
>
> Republicans chortled, hoping for the creation of a black-Lumbee Indian majority district that would cost Rose his majority, but the last laugh was on them. Clever Democratic districters drew up a plan with a second black district consisting of a thin line of territory, in some places no wider than I-85, linking black precincts from Durham west to Charlotte; the new Republican 12th District dis-

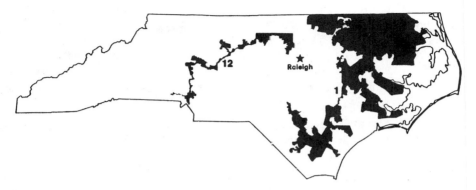

Source: CQ Press, CONGRESSIONAL DISTRICTS IN THE 1990S: A PORTRAIT OF AMERICA (1993). Reprinted by permission.

appeared, and the marginal 5th and 8th Districts were made more Democratic—pretty ingenious work. It violated the age-old principle of contiguity, but it was accepted by the Justice Department in 1992. Nevertheless, it was widely attacked for its extremely irregular district lines (its only competitor for this was Texas, a plan also drawn by Democrats to preserve their own seats while complying with the Voting Rights Act), and in June 1993, a case was pending in the U.S. Supreme Court on the future of the plan.

Shaw v. Reno

509 U.S. 630 (1993)

Justice O'CONNOR delivered the opinion of the Court.

This case involves two of the most complex and sensitive issues this Court has faced in recent years: the meaning of the constitutional "right" to vote, and the propriety of race-based state legislation designed to benefit members of historically disadvantaged racial minority groups. As a result of the 1990 census, North Carolina became entitled to a twelfth seat in the United States House of Representatives. The General Assembly enacted a reapportionment plan that included one majority-black congressional district. After the Attorney General of the United States objected to the plan pursuant to §5 of the Voting Rights Act of 1965, the General Assembly passed new legislation creating a second majority-black district. Appellants allege that the revised plan, which contains district boundary lines of dramatically irregular shape, constitutes an unconstitutional racial gerrymander. The question before us is whether appellants have stated a cognizable claim.

I

The voting age population of North Carolina is approximately 78% white, 20% black, and 1% Native American; the remaining 1% is predominantly Asian. The black population is relatively dispersed; blacks constitute a majority of the general population in only 5 of the State's 100 counties.... The largest concentrations of black citizens live in the Coastal Plain, primarily in the northern part. The General Assembly's first redistricting plan contained one majority-black district centered in that area of the State.

Forty of North Carolina's one hundred counties are covered by §5 of the Voting Rights Act of 1965....

The Attorney General ... interposed a formal objection to the General Assembly's plan. The Attorney General specifically objected to the configuration of boundary lines drawn in the south-central to southeastern region of the State. In the Attorney General's view, the General Assembly could have created a second majority-minority district "to give effect to black and Native American voting strength in this area" by using boundary lines "no more irregular than [those] found elsewhere in the proposed plan," but failed to do so for "pretextual reasons."

[T]he General Assembly enacted a revised redistricting plan that included a second majority-black district. The General Assembly located the second district not in the south-central to southeastern part of the State, but in the north-central region along Interstate 85.

The first of the two majority-black districts contained in the revised plan, District 1, is somewhat hook shaped. Centered in the northeast portion of the State, it moves southward until it tapers to a narrow band; then, with finger-like extensions, it reaches far into the southern-most part of the State near the South Carolina border. District 1 has been compared [by a judge in the lower court] to a "Rorschach ink-blot test," and [by the *Wall Street Journal* to] a "bug splattered on a windshield."

The second majority-black district, District 12, is even more unusually shaped. It is approximately 160 miles long and, for much of its length, no wider than the I-85 corridor. It winds in snake-like fashion through tobacco country, financial centers, and manufacturing areas "until it gobbles in enough enclaves of black neighborhoods." Northbound and southbound drivers on I-85 sometimes find themselves in separate districts in one county, only to "trade" districts when they enter the next county. Of the 10 counties through which District 12 passes, five are cut into three different districts; even towns are divided. At one point the district remains contiguous only because it intersects at a single point with two other districts before crossing over them. One state legislator has remarked that "[i]f you drove down the interstate with both car doors open, you'd kill most of the people in the district." ...

The Attorney General did not object to the General Assembly's revised plan. But numerous North Carolinians did. The North Carolina Republican Party and individual voters brought suit in Federal District Court alleging that the plan constituted an unconstitutional political gerrymander under *Davis v. Bandemer*. That claim was dismissed, see *Pope v. Blue*, 809 F.Supp. 392 (W.D.N.Car. 1992), and this Court summarily affirmed, 113 S.Ct. 30 (1992).

Shortly after the complaint in *Pope v. Blue* was filed, appellants instituted the present action ... Appellants alleged not that the revised plan constituted a political gerrymander, nor that it violated the "one person, one vote" principle, see *Reynolds*, but that the State had created an unconstitutional racial gerrymander. [The lower court dismissed the case, relying heavily on *United Jewish Organizations*. Plaintiffs appealed.]

II ... B

... Our focus is on appellants' claim that the State engaged in unconstitutional racial gerrymandering. That argument strikes a powerful historical chord: It is unsettling how closely the North Carolina plan resembles the most egregious racial gerrymanders of the past.

An understanding of the nature of appellants' claim is critical to our resolution of the case. In their complaint, appellants did not claim that the General Assembly's reapportionment plan unconstitutionally "diluted" white voting strength. They did not even claim to be white. Rather, appellants' complaint alleged that the deliberate segregation of voters into separate districts on the basis of race violated their constitutional right to participate in a "color-blind" electoral process.

Despite their invocation of the ideal of a "color-blind" Constitution, appellants appear to concede that race-conscious redistricting is not always unconstitutional. That concession is wise: This Court never has held that race-conscious state decisionmaking is impermissible in all circumstances. What appellants object to is redistricting legislation that is so extremely irregular on its face that it rationally can be viewed only as an effort to segregate the races for purposes of voting, without regard for traditional districting principles and without sufficiently compelling justification. For the reasons that follow, we conclude that appellants have stated a claim upon which relief can be granted under the Equal Protection Clause.

III
A

... Classifications of citizens solely on the basis of race "are by their very nature odious to a free people whose institutions are founded upon the doctrine of equality." *Hirabayashi v. United States*, 320 U.S. 81, 100 (1943).... Accordingly, we have held that the Fourteenth Amendment requires state legislation that expressly distinguishes among citizens because of their race to be narrowly tailored to further a compelling governmental interest. See, *e.g.*, *Wygant v. Jackson Bd. of Ed.*, 476 U.S. 267, 277–278 (1986) (plurality opinion).

These principles apply not only to legislation that contains explicit racial distinctions, but also to those "rare" statutes that, although race-neutral, are, on their face, "unexplainable on grounds other than race." *Arlington Heights v. Metropolitan Housing Development Corp.*, 429 U.S. 252, 266 (1977).

B

Appellants contend that redistricting legislation that is so bizarre on its face that it is "unexplainable on grounds other than race," *Arlington Heights, supra*, demands the same close scrutiny that we give other state laws that classify citizens by race. Our voting rights precedents support that conclusion.

... At issue in [*Wright v. Rockefeller*] were four districts contained in a New York apportionment statute. The plaintiffs alleged that the statute excluded nonwhites from one district and concentrated them in the other three. Every member of the Court assumed that the plaintiffs' allegation that the statute "segregate[d] eligible voters by race and place of origin" stated a constitutional claim. The Justices disagreed only as to whether the plaintiffs had carried their burden of proof at trial. The dissenters thought the unusual shape of the district lines could "be explained only in racial terms." The majority, however, accepted the District Court's finding that the plaintiffs had failed to establish that the districts were in fact drawn on racial lines. Although the boundary lines were somewhat irregular, the majority reasoned, they were not so bizarre as to permit of no other conclusion. Indeed, because most of the nonwhite voters lived together in one area, it would have been difficult to construct voting districts without concentrations of nonwhite voters.

Wright illustrates the difficulty of determining from the face of a single-member districting plan that it purposefully distinguishes between voters on the basis of race. A reapportionment statute typically does not classify persons at all; it classifies tracts of land, or addresses. Moreover, redistricting differs from other kinds of state decisionmaking in that the legislature always is aware of race when it draws district lines, just as it is aware of age, economic status, religious and political persuasion, and a variety of other demographic factors. That sort of race consciousness does not lead inevitably to impermissible race discrimination. As *Wright* demonstrates, when members of a racial group live together in one community, a reapportionment plan that concentrates members of the group in one district and excludes them from others may reflect wholly legitimate purposes. The district lines may be drawn, for example, to provide for compact districts of contiguous territory, or to maintain the integrity of political subdivisions.

The difficulty of proof, of course, does not mean that a racial gerrymander, once established, should receive less scrutiny under the Equal Protection Clause than other state legislation classifying citizens by race. Moreover, it seems clear to us that proof sometimes will not be difficult at all. In some exceptional cases, a reapportionment plan may be so highly irregular that, on its face, it rationally cannot be understood as anything other than an effort to "segregat[e] ... voters" on the basis of race. *Gomillion v. Lightfoot*, in which a tortured municipal boundary line was drawn to exclude black voters, was such a case. So, too, would be a case in which a State concentrated a dispersed minority population in a single district by disregarding traditional districting principles such as compactness, contiguity, and respect for political subdivisions. We emphasize that these criteria are important not because they are constitutionally required—they are not, cf. *Gaffney v. Cummings*, 412 U.S. 735, 752 n.18 (1973)—but because they are objective factors that may serve to defeat a claim that a district has been gerrymandered on racial lines....

Put differently, we believe that reapportionment is one area in which appearances do matter. A reapportionment plan that includes in one district individuals who belong to the same race, but who are otherwise widely separated by geographical and political boundaries, and who may have little in common with one another but the color of their skin, bears an uncomfortable resemblance to political apartheid. It reinforces the perception that members of the same racial group—regardless of their age, education, economic status, or the community in which they live—think alike, share the same political interests, and will prefer the same candidates at the polls. We have rejected such perceptions elsewhere as impermissible racial stereotypes. By perpetuating such notions, a racial gerrymander may exacerbate the very patterns of racial bloc voting that majority-minority districting is sometimes said to counteract.

The message that such districting sends to elected representatives is equally pernicious. When a district obviously is created solely to effectuate the perceived common interests of one racial group, elected officials are more likely to believe that their primary obligation is to represent only the members of that group, rather than their constituency as a whole. This is altogether antithetical to our system of representative democracy....

For these reasons, we conclude that a plaintiff challenging a reapportionment statute under the Equal Protection Clause may state a claim by alleging that the legislation, though race-neutral on its face, rationally cannot be understood as anything other than an effort to separate voters into different districts on the basis of race, and that the separation lacks sufficient justification. It is unnecessary for us to decide whether or how a reapportionment plan that, on its face, can be explained in nonracial terms successfully could be challenged. Thus, we express no view as to whether "the intentional creation of majority-minority districts, without more" always gives rise to an equal protection claim. *Post* (WHITE, J., dissenting). We hold only that, on the facts of this case, plaintiffs have stated a claim sufficient to defeat the state appellees' motion to dismiss.

C

The dissenters consider the circumstances of this case "functionally indistinguishable" from multimember districting and at-large voting systems, which are loosely described as "other varieties of gerrymandering." We have considered the constitutionality of these practices in other Fourteenth Amendment cases and have required plaintiffs to demonstrate that the challenged practice has the purpose and effect of diluting a racial group's voting strength. See, *e.g.*, *Rogers v. Lodge*; *Mobile v. Bolden*; *White v. Regester*; *Whitcomb v. Chavis*. At-large and multimember schemes, however, do not classify voters on the basis of race. Classifying citizens by race, as we have said, threatens special harms that are not present in our vote-dilution cases. It therefore warrants different analysis....

The dissenters make two other arguments that cannot be reconciled with our precedents. First, they suggest that a racial gerrymander of the sort alleged here is functionally equivalent to gerrymanders for nonracial purposes, such as political gerrymanders. This Court has held political gerrymanders to be justiciable under the Equal Protection Clause. See *Davis v. Bandemer*. But nothing in our case law compels the conclusion that racial and political gerrymanders are subject to precisely the same constitutional scrutiny. In fact, our country's long and persistent history of racial discrimination in voting—as well as our Fourteenth Amendment jurisprudence, which always has reserved the strictest scrutiny for discrimination on the basis of race—would seem to compel the opposite conclusion.

Second, Justice STEVENS argues that racial gerrymandering poses no constitutional difficulties when district lines are drawn to favor the minority, rather than the majority. We have made clear, however, that equal protection analysis "is not dependent on the race of those burdened or benefited by a particular classification." *Richmond v. J.A. Croson Co.*, 488 U.S. 469, 494 (plurality opinion). Indeed, racial classifications receive close scrutiny even when they may be said to burden or benefit the races equally.

Finally, nothing in the Court's highly fractured decision in *UJO*—on which the District Court almost exclusively relied, and which the dissenters evidently believe controls—forecloses the claim we recognize today. *UJO* concerned New York's revision of a reapportionment plan to include additional majority-minority districts in response to the Attorney General's denial of administrative preclearance under §5. In that regard, it closely resembles the present case. But the cases are critically different in another way. The plaintiffs in *UJO*—members of a Hasidic community split between two districts under New York's revised redistricting plan—did not allege that the plan, on its face, was so highly irregular that it rationally could be understood only as an effort to segregate voters by race. Indeed, the facts of the case would not have supported such a claim. Three Justices approved the New York statute, in part, precisely because it adhered to traditional districting principles:

> [W]e think it ... permissible for a State, *employing sound districting principles such as compactness and population equality,* to attempt to prevent racial minorities from being repeatedly outvoted by creating districts that will afford fair representation to the members of those racial groups who are sufficiently numerous *and whose residential patterns afford the opportunity* of creating districts in which they will be in the majority. ([O]pinion of WHITE, J., joined by STEVENS and REHNQUIST, JJ.).[1]

As a majority of the Justices construed the complaint, the *UJO* plaintiffs made a different claim: that the New York plan impermissibly "diluted" their voting strength. Five of the eight Justices who participated in the decision resolved the case under the framework the Court previously had adopted for vote-dilution cases. Three Justices rejected

---

1. The emphasis in this quotation is added by Justice O'Connor.

the plaintiffs' claim on the grounds that the New York statute "represented no racial slur or stigma with respect to whites or any other race" and left white voters with better than proportional representation. Two others concluded that the statute did not minimize or cancel out a minority group's voting strength and that the State's intent to comply with the Voting Rights Act, as interpreted by the Department of Justice, "foreclose[d] any finding that [the State] acted with the invidious purpose of discriminating against white voters." (Stewart, J., joined by Powell, J., concurring in judgment).

The District Court below relied on these portions of *UJO* to reject appellants' claim. In our view, the court used the wrong analysis. *UJO*'s framework simply does not apply where, as here, a reapportionment plan is alleged to be so irrational on its face that it immediately offends principles of racial equality. *UJO* set forth a standard under which white voters can establish unconstitutional vote dilution. But it did not purport to overrule *Gomillion* or *Wright*. Nothing in the decision precludes white voters (or voters of any other race) from bringing the analytically distinct claim that a reapportionment plan rationally cannot be understood as anything other than an effort to segregate citizens into separate voting districts on the basis of race without sufficient justification. Because appellants here stated such a claim, the District Court erred in dismissing their complaint.

IV

[T]he very reason that the Equal Protection Clause demands strict scrutiny of all racial classifications is because without it, a court cannot determine whether or not the discrimination truly is "benign." Thus, if appellants' allegations of a racial gerrymander are not contradicted on remand, the District Court must determine whether the General Assembly's reapportionment plan satisfies strict scrutiny. We therefore consider what that level of scrutiny requires in the reapportionment context.

The state appellees suggest that a covered jurisdiction may have a compelling interest in creating majority-minority districts in order to comply with the Voting Rights Act. The States certainly have a very strong interest in complying with federal antidiscrimination laws that are constitutionally valid as interpreted and as applied. But in the context of a Fourteenth Amendment challenge, courts must bear in mind the difference between what the law permits, and what it requires.

For example, on remand North Carolina might claim that it adopted the revised plan in order to comply with the §5 "nonretrogression" principle.... In *Beer*, we held that a reapportionment plan that created one majority-minority district where none existed before passed muster under §5 because it improved the position of racial minorities.

Although the Court concluded that the redistricting scheme at issue in *Beer* was nonretrogressive, it did not hold that the plan, for that reason, was immune from constitutional challenge. The Court expressly declined to reach that question. Indeed, the Voting Rights Act and our case law make clear that a reapportionment plan that satisfies §5 still may be enjoined as unconstitutional. See 42 U.S.C. §1973c (neither a declaratory judgment by the District Court for the District of Columbia nor preclearance by the Attorney General "shall bar a subsequent action to enjoin enforcement" of new voting practice); *Allen* (after preclearance, "private parties may enjoin the enforcement of the new enactment ... in traditional suits attacking its constitutionality"). Thus, we do not read *Beer* or any of our other §5 cases to give covered jurisdictions *carte blanche* to engage in racial gerrymandering in the name of nonretrogression. A reapportionment plan would not be narrowly tailored to the goal of avoiding retrogression if the State went beyond what was reasonably necessary to avoid retrogression. Our conclusion is supported by the plurality opinion in *UJO*, in which four Justices determined that New York's creation of additional majority-minority districts was constitutional because the plaintiffs had failed to demonstrate that the State "did more than the Attorney General was authorized to *require* it to do under the nonretrogression principle of *Beer*." ([O]pinion of WHITE, J., joined by BRENNAN, BLACKMUN, and STEVENS, JJ.) (emphasis added).

Before us, the state appellees contend that the General Assembly's revised plan was necessary not to prevent retrogression, but to avoid dilution of black voting strength in violation of §2, as construed in *Gingles*....

Appellants maintain that the General Assembly's revised plan could not have been required by §2. They contend that the State's black population is too dispersed to support two geographically compact majority-black districts, as the bizarre shape of District 12 demonstrates, and that there is no evidence of black political cohesion. They also contend that recent black electoral successes demonstrate the willingness of white voters in North Carolina to vote for black candidates. Appellants point out that blacks currently hold the positions of State Auditor, Speaker of the North Carolina House of Representatives, and chair of the North Carolina State Board of Elections. They also point out that in 1990 a black candidate defeated a white opponent in the Democratic Party run-off for a United States Senate seat before being defeated narrowly by the Republican incumbent in the general election. Appellants further argue that if §2 did require adoption of North Carolina's revised plan, §2 is to that extent unconstitutional. These arguments were not developed below, and the issues remain open for consideration on remand.

The state appellees alternatively argue that the General Assembly's plan advanced a compelling interest entirely distinct from the Voting Rights Act. We previously have recognized a significant state interest in eradicating the effects of past racial discrimination. But the State must have a "strong basis in evidence for [concluding] that remedial action [is] necessary." *Croson, supra*, 488 U.S., at 500.

... This question also need not be decided at this stage of the litigation....

V

Racial classifications of any sort pose the risk of lasting harm to our society. They reinforce the belief, held by too many for too much of our history, that individuals should be judged by the color of their skin. Racial classifications with respect to voting carry particular dangers. Racial gerrymandering, even for remedial purposes, may balkanize us into competing racial factions; it threatens to carry us further from the goal of a political system in which race no longer matters—a goal that the Fourteenth and Fifteenth Amendments embody, and to which the Nation continues to aspire. It is for these reasons that race-based districting by our state legislatures demands close judicial scrutiny.

In this case, the Attorney General suggested that North Carolina could have created a reasonably compact second majority-minority district in the south-central to southeastern part of the State. We express no view as to whether appellants successfully could have challenged such a district under the Fourteenth Amendment.... Today we hold only that appellants have stated a claim under the Equal Protection Clause by alleging that the North Carolina General Assembly adopted a reapportionment scheme so irrational on its face that it can be understood only as an effort to segregate voters into separate voting districts because of their race, and that the separation lacks sufficient justification. If the allegation of racial gerrymandering remains uncontradicted, the District Court further must determine whether the North Carolina plan is narrowly tailored to further a compelling governmental interest. Accordingly, we reverse the judgment of the District Court and remand the case for further proceedings consistent with this opinion.

It is so ordered.

Justice WHITE, with whom Justice BLACKMUN and Justice STEVENS join, dissenting.

The facts of this case mirror those presented in *UJO*, where the Court rejected a claim that creation of a majority-minority district violated the Constitution, either as a *per se* matter or in light of the circumstances leading to the creation of such a district. Of particular relevance, five of the Justices reasoned that members of the white majority could not plausibly argue that their influence over the political process had been unfairly cancelled, (opinion of WHITE, J., joined by REHNQUIST and STEVENS, JJ.), or that such had been the State's intent (Stewart, J., concurring in judgment, joined by Powell, J.). Accordingly, they held that plaintiffs were not entitled to relief under the Constitution's Equal Protection Clause. On the same reasoning, I would affirm the district court's dismissal of appellants' claim in this instance.

The Court today chooses not to overrule, but rather to sidestep, *UJO*. It does so by glossing over the striking similarities, focusing on surface differences, most notably the (admittedly unusual) shape of the newly created district, and imagining an entirely new cause of action. Because the holding is limited to such anomalous circumstances, it perhaps will not substantially hamper a State's legitimate efforts to redistrict in favor of racial minorities. Nonetheless, the notion that North Carolina's plan, under which whites remain a voting majority in a disproportionate number of congressional districts, and pursuant to which the State has sent its first black representatives since Reconstruction to the United States Congress, might have violated appellants' constitutional rights is both a fiction and a departure from settled equal protection principles. Seeing no good reason to engage in either, I dissent.

I

A

The grounds for my disagreement with the majority are simply stated: Appellants have not presented a cognizable claim, because they have not alleged a cognizable injury. To date, we have held that only two types of state voting practices could give rise to a constitutional claim. The first involves direct and outright deprivation of the right to vote, for example by means of a poll tax or literacy test. Plainly, this variety is not implicated by appellants' allegations and need not detain us further. The second type of unconstitutional practice is that which "affects the political strength of various groups," *Bolden* (STEVENS, J., concurring in judgment), in violation of the Equal Protection Clause. As for this latter category, we have insisted that members of the political or racial group demonstrate that the challenged action have the intent and effect of unduly diminishing their influence on the political process. Although this severe burden has limited the number of successful suits, it was adopted for sound reasons.

The central explanation has to do with the nature of the redistricting process. As the majority recognizes, "redistricting differs from other kinds of state decisionmaking in that the legislature always is aware of race when it draws district lines, just as it is aware of age, economic status, religious and political persuasion, and a variety of other demographic factors." "Being aware," in this context, is shorthand for "taking into account," and it hardly can be doubted that legislators routinely engage in the business of making electoral predictions based on group characteristics—racial, ethnic, and the like.... Because extirpating such considerations from the redistricting process is unrealistic, the Court has not invalidated all plans that consciously use race, but rather has looked at their impact.

Redistricting plans also reflect group interests and inevitably are conceived with partisan aims in mind. To allow judicial interference whenever this occurs would be to invite constant and unmanageable intrusion. Moreover, a group's power to affect the political process does not automatically dissipate by virtue of an electoral loss. Accordingly, we have asked that an identifiable group demonstrate more than mere lack of success at the polls to make out a successful gerrymandering claim. See, *e.g.*, *White v. Regester*; *Whitcomb v. Chavis*.

... Indeed, as a brief survey of decisions illustrates, the Court's gerrymandering cases all carry this theme—that it is not mere suffering at the polls but discrimination in the polity with which the Constitution is concerned....

To distinguish a claim that alleges that the redistricting scheme has discriminatory intent and effect from one that does not has nothing to do with dividing racial classifications between the "benign" and the malicious—an enterprise which, as the majority notes, the Court has treated with skepticism. Rather, the issue is whether the classification based on race discriminates against anyone by denying equal access to the political process....

B

The most compelling evidence of the Court's position prior to this day, for it is most directly on point, is *UJO*. The Court characterizes the decision as "highly fractured," but that should not detract attention from the rejection by a majority in *UJO* of the claim that the State's intentional creation of majority-minority districts transgressed constitutional norms. As stated above, five Justices were of the view that, absent any contention that the proposed plan was adopted with the intent, or had the effect, of unduly minimizing the white majority's voting strength, the Fourteenth Amendment was not implicated. Writing for three members of the Court, I justified this conclusion as follows:

> It is true that New York deliberately increased the nonwhite majorities in certain districts in order to enhance the opportunity for election of nonwhite representatives from those districts. Nevertheless, there was no fencing out of the white population from participation in the political processes of the county, and the plan did not minimize or unfairly cancel out white voting strength.

In a similar vein, Justice Stewart was joined by Justice Powell....

Under either formulation, it is irrefutable that appellants in this proceeding likewise have failed to state a claim. As was the case in New York, a number of North Carolina's political subdivisions have interfered with black citizens' meaningful exercise of the franchise, and are therefore subject to §§4 and 5 of the Voting Rights Act.... Like New York, North Carolina failed to prove to the Attorney General's satisfaction that its proposed redistricting had neither the purpose nor the effect of abridging the right to vote on account of race or color.... Finally, like New York, North Carolina reacted by modifying its plan and creating additional majority-minority districts.

In light of this background, it strains credulity to suggest that North Carolina's purpose in creating a second majority-minority district was to discriminate against members of the majority group by "impair[ing] or burden[ing their] opportunity ... to participate in the political process." [*UJO*] (Stewart, J., concurring in judgment). The State has made no mystery of its intent, which was to respond to the Attorney General's objections, by improving the minority group's prospects of electing a candidate of its choice. I doubt that this constitutes a discriminatory purpose as defined in the Court's equal protection cases—i.e., an intent to aggravate "the unequal distribution of electoral power." *Post* (STEVENS, J., dissenting). But even assuming that it does, there is no question that appellants have not alleged the requisite discriminatory effects. Whites constitute roughly 76 percent of the total population and 79 percent of the voting age population in North Carolina. Yet, under the State's plan, they still constitute a voting majority in 10 (or 83 percent) of the 12 congressional districts. Though they might be dissatisfied at the prospect of casting a vote for a losing candidate—a lot shared by many, including a disproportionate number of minority voters—surely they cannot complain of discriminatory treatment.

II

The majority attempts to distinguish *UJO* by imagining a heretofore unknown type of constitutional claim. In its words, "*UJO* set forth a standard under which white voters can establish unconstitutional vote dilution.... Nothing in the decision precludes white voters (or voters of any other race) from bringing the analytically distinct claim that a reapportionment plan rationally cannot be understood as anything other than an effort to segregate citizens into separate voting districts on the basis of race without sufficient justification." There is no support for this distinction in *UJO*, and no authority in the cases relied on by the Court either. More importantly, the majority's submission does not withstand analysis. The logic of its theory appears to be that race-conscious redistricting that "segregates" by drawing odd-shaped lines is qualitatively different from race-conscious redistricting that affects groups in some other way. The distinction is without foundation.

A

The essence of the majority's argument is that *UJO* dealt with a claim of vote dilution—which required a specific showing of harm—and that cases such as *Gomillion v. Lightfoot* and *Wright v. Rockefeller* dealt with claims of racial segregation—which did not. I read these decisions quite differently. Petitioners' claim in *UJO* was that the State had "violated the Fourteenth and Fifteenth Amendments by *deliberately revising its reapportionment plan along racial lines*" (emphasis added). They also stated: "Our argument is ... that the history of the area demonstrates that there could be—and in fact was— *no reason other than race* to divide the community at this time" (emphasis in original). Nor was it ever in doubt that "the State deliberately used race in a purposeful manner." In other words, the "analytically distinct claim" the majority discovers today was in plain view and did not carry the day for petitioners. The fact that a demonstration of discriminatory effect was required in that case was not a function of the kind of claim that was made. It was a function of the type of injury upon which the Court insisted.

Gomillion is consistent with this view. To begin, the Court's reliance on that case as the font of its novel type of claim is curious. Justice Frankfurter characterized the complaint as alleging a deprivation of the right to vote in violation of the *Fifteenth* Amendment. Regardless whether that description was accurate, it seriously deflates the precedential value which the majority seeks to ascribe to *Gomillion*: As I see it, the case cannot stand for the proposition that the intentional creation of majority-minority districts, without more, gives rise to an equal protection challenge under the Fourteenth Amendment. But even recast as a Fourteenth Amendment case, *Gomillion* does not assist the majority, for its focus was on the alleged *effect* of the city's action, which was to exclude black voters from the municipality of Tuskegee. As the Court noted, the "inevitable effect of this redefinition of Tuskegee's boundaries" was "to deprive the Negro petitioners discriminatorily of the benefits of residence in Tuskegee." ... In *Gomillion*, in short, the group that formed the majority at the state level purportedly set out to manipulate city boundaries in order to remove members of the minority, thereby denying them valuable municipal services. No analogous purpose or effect has been alleged in this case.

The only other case invoked by the majority is *Wright v. Rockefeller*.... The Court affirmed the District Court's dismissal of the complaint on the ground that plaintiffs had not met their burden of proving discriminatory intent. I fail to see how a decision based on a failure to establish discriminatory *intent* can support the inference that it is unnecessary to prove discriminatory *effect*.

Wright is relevant only to the extent that it illustrates a proposition with which I have no problem: That a complaint stating that a plan has carved out districts on the basis of race *can*, under certain circumstances, state a claim under the Fourteenth Amendment. To that end, however, there must be an allegation of discriminatory purpose and effect, for the constitutionality of a race-conscious redistricting plan depends on these twin elements. In *Wright*, for example, the facts might have supported the contention that the districts were intended to, and did in fact, shield the Seventeenth District from any minority influence and "pack" black and Puerto Rican voters in the Eighteenth, thereby invidiously minimizing their voting strength. In other words, the purposeful creation of a majority-minority district could have discriminatory effect if it is achieved by means of "packing" — i.e., over-concentration of minority voters. In the present case, the facts could sustain no such allegation.

B

Lacking support in any of the Court's precedents, the majority's novel type of claim also makes no sense. As I understand the theory that is put forth, a redistricting plan that uses race to "segregate" voters by drawing "uncouth" lines is harmful in a way that a plan that uses race to distribute voters differently is not, for the former "bears an uncomfortable resemblance to political apartheid." The distinction is untenable.

Racial gerrymanders come in various shades: At-large voting schemes; the fragmentation of a minority group among various districts "so that it is a majority in none," otherwise known as "cracking"; the "stacking" of "a large minority population concentration ... with a larger white population"; and, finally, the "concentration of [minority voters] into districts where they constitute an excessive majority," also called "packing." In each instance, race is consciously utilized by the legislature for electoral purposes; in each instance, we have put the plaintiff challenging the district lines to the burden of demonstrating that the plan was meant to, and did in fact, exclude an identifiable racial group from participation in the political process.

Not so, apparently, when the districting "segregates" by drawing odd-shaped lines.[7] In that case, we are told, such proof no longer is needed. Instead, it is the *State* that must rebut the allegation that race was taken into account, a fact that, together with the legislators' consideration of ethnic, religious, and other group characteristics, I had thought we practically took for granted. Part of the explanation for the majority's approach has to do, perhaps, with the emotions stirred by words such as "segregation" and "political apartheid." But their loose and imprecise use by today's majority has, I fear, led it astray.

---

7. I borrow the term "segregate" from the majority, but, given its historical connotation, believe that its use is ill-advised. Nor is it a particularly accurate description of what has occurred. The majority-minority district that is at the center of the controversy is, according to the State, 54.71% African-American. Even if racial distribution was a factor, no racial group can be said to have been "segregated" — i.e., "set apart" or "isolate[d]." Webster's Collegiate Dictionary 1063 (9th ed. 1983).

The consideration of race in "segregation" cases is no different than in other race-conscious districting; from the standpoint of the affected groups, moreover, the line-drawings all act in similar fashion. A plan that "segregates" being functionally indistinguishable from any of the other varieties of gerrymandering, we should be consistent in what we require from a claimant: Proof of discriminatory purpose and effect.

The other part of the majority's explanation of its holding is related to its simultaneous discomfort and fascination with irregularly shaped districts. Lack of compactness or contiguity, like uncouth district lines, certainly is a helpful indicator that some form of gerrymandering (racial or other) might have taken place and that "something may be amiss." Disregard for geographic divisions and compactness often goes hand in hand with partisan gerrymandering.

But while district irregularities may provide strong indicia of a potential gerrymander, they do no more than that. In particular, they have no bearing on whether the plan ultimately is found to violate the Constitution. Given two districts drawn on similar, race-based grounds, the one does not become more injurious than the other simply by virtue of being snake-like, at least so far as the Constitution is concerned and absent any evidence of differential racial impact. The majority's contrary view is perplexing in light of its concession that "compactness or attractiveness has never been held to constitute an independent federal constitutional requirement for state legislative districts." *Gaffney*. It is shortsighted as well, for a regularly shaped district can just as effectively effectuate racially discriminatory gerrymandering as an odd-shaped one. By focusing on looks rather than impact, the majority "immediately casts attention in the wrong direction — toward superficialities of shape and size, rather than toward the political realities of district composition." R. Dixon, Democratic Representation: Reapportionment in Law and Politics 459 (1968).

Limited by its own terms to cases involving unusually-shaped districts, the Court's approach nonetheless will unnecessarily hinder to some extent a State's voluntary effort to ensure a modicum of minority representation. This will be true in areas where the minority population is geographically dispersed. It also will be true where the minority population is not scattered but, for reasons unrelated to race — for example incumbency protection — the State would rather not create the majority-minority district in its most "obvious" location.[10] When, as is the case here, the creation of a majority-minority dis-

---

10. This appears to be what has occurred in this instance. In providing the reasons for the objection, the Attorney General noted that "[f]or the south-central to southeast area, there were several plans drawn providing for a second majority-minority congressional district" and that such a district would have been no more irregular than others in the State's plan. North Carolina's decision to create a majority-minority district can be explained as an attempt to meet this objection. Its decision not to create the more compact southern majority-minority district that was suggested, on the other hand, was more likely a result of partisan considerations. Indeed, in a suit brought prior to this one, different plaintiffs charged that District 12 was "grossly contorted" and had "no logical explanation other than incumbency protection and the enhancement of Democratic partisan interests.... The plan ... ignores the directive of the [Department of Justice] to create a minority district in the southeastern portion of North Carolina since any such district would jeopardize the reelection of ... the Democratic incumbent." With respect to this incident, one writer has observed that "understanding why the configurations are shaped as they are requires us to know at least as much about the interests of incumbent Democratic politicians, as it does knowledge of the Voting Rights Act." Grofman, *Would Vince Lombardi Have Been Right If He Had Said: "When It Comes to Redistricting, Race Isn't Everything, It's the Only Thing"?*, 14 Cardozo L.Rev. 1237, 1258 (1993). The District Court in *Pope* [*v. Blue*] dismissed appellants' claim, reasoning in part that "plaintiffs do not allege, nor can they, that the state's redistricting plan has caused them to be "shut out of the political process."

trict does not unfairly minimize the voting power of any other group, the Constitution does not justify, much less mandate, such obstruction....

III

Although I disagree with the holding that appellants' claim is cognizable, the Court's discussion of the level of scrutiny it requires warrants a few comments. I have no doubt that a State's compliance with the Voting Rights Act clearly constitutes a compelling interest. Cf. *UJO*. Here, the Attorney General objected to the State's plan on the ground that it failed to draw a second majority-minority district for what appeared to be pretextual reasons. Rather than challenge this conclusion, North Carolina chose to draw the second district. As *UJO* held, a State is entitled to take such action.

The Court, while seemingly agreeing with this position, warns that the State's redistricting effort must be "narrowly tailored" to further its interest in complying with the law. It is evident to me, however, that what North Carolina did was precisely tailored to meet the objection of the Attorney General to its prior plan. Hence, I see no need for a remand at all, even accepting the majority's basic approach to this case.

Furthermore, how it intends to manage this standard, I do not know. Is it more "narrowly tailored" to create an irregular majority-minority district as opposed to one that is compact but harms other State interests such as incumbency protection or the representation of rural interests? Of the following two options—creation of two minority influence districts or of a single majority-minority district—is one "narrowly tailored" and the other not? Once the Attorney General has found that a proposed redistricting change violates §5's nonretrogression principle in that it will abridge a racial minority's right to vote, does "narrow tailoring" mean that the most the State can do is preserve the *status quo*? Or can it maintain that change, while attempting to enhance minority voting power in some other manner? This small sample only begins to scratch the surface of the problems raised by the majority's test. But it suffices to illustrate the unworkability of a standard that is divorced from any measure of constitutional harm. In that, State efforts to remedy minority vote dilution are wholly unlike what typically has been labeled "affirmative action." To the extent that no other racial group is injured, remedying a Voting Rights Act violation does not involve preferential treatment. It involves, instead, an attempt to *equalize* treatment, and to provide minority voters with an effective voice in the political process. The Equal Protection Clause of the Constitution, surely, does not stand in the way.

IV

Since I do not agree that petitioners alleged an Equal Protection violation and because the Court of Appeals faithfully followed the Court's prior cases, I dissent and would affirm the judgment below.

[Separate dissenting opinions by Justices Blackmun, Stevens, and Souter are omitted.]

Notes and Questions

1. Do *Gomillion v. Lightfoot* and *Wright v. Rockefeller* support the majority's decision in *Shaw*? For a negative answer, see Richard Briffault, *Race and Representation After* Miller v. Johnson, 1995 University of Chicago Legal Forum 23, 36–37. Is the majority's decision inconsistent with *United Jewish Organizations v. Carey*?

2. A number of writers have criticized *Shaw*, but none more strongly than A. Leon Higginbotham, Jr., Gregory A. Clarick & Marcella David, *Shaw v. Reno: A Mirage of Good*

Intentions with Devastating Racial Consequences, 62 FORDHAM LAW REVIEW 1593, 1603 (1994):

> With plaintiffs' urging, the Court has created law that could make *Shaw v. Reno* equivalent for the civil rights jurisprudence of our generation to what *Plessy v. Ferguson* and *Dred Scott v. Sandford* were for prior generations.

Critics have questioned not only Justice O'Connor's constitutional doctrine, but her rhetoric.

> However race-conscious the General Assembly had been, and it concededly had drawn the plan with the intent to create two majority-black districts, it had not in fact segregated the races into separate districts. Consider the racial composition of the two districts in which the *Shaw* plaintiffs lived. House District 2's population was 76.23 percent white and 21.94 percent black; House District 12's population was 41.80 percent white and 56.63 percent black. To say that either district even remotely resembles "political apartheid"—especially given that House District 2, where a majority of the *Shaw* plaintiffs lived, was a nearly perfect mirror of the state's overall racial makeup—would be risible if it were not so pernicious.

Pamela S. Karlan, *All Over the Map: The Supreme Court's Voting Rights Trilogy,* 1993 SUPREME COURT REVIEW 245, 282. T. Alexander Aleinikoff & Samuel Issacharoff, *Race and Redistricting: Drawing Constitutional Lines After Shaw v. Reno,* 92 MICHIGAN LAW REVIEW 588, 612 (1993), add that "the pejorative characterization [i.e., "political apartheid"] equates the attempt to ensure representation of underrepresented minority groups with attempts to deny racially dominated groups a role in democratic governance."

Aleinikoff and Issacharoff also challenge a number of the assumptions that underlie Justice O'Connor's reasoning:

> We are also troubled by the casual empirical assumptions of the Court's analysis. What is the evidence that race-conscious districting exacerbates racial bloc voting, or that it sends a message to an elected representative that she need only represent members of her group? There is only rudimentary evidence of the relative quality of representation and responsiveness in racially drawn districts, none of which is referred to by the Court, and none of which supports the categorical assertion that representation from such districts is fundamentally different from that afforded other constituent groups who form a majority in a congressional district. The Court's description of democratic legitimacy also seems rather thin. It is certainly arguable that democratic processes are enhanced rather than degraded when previously excluded groups are able to elect representatives of their choice, even if those representatives primarily seek to further the interests of that constituency.

Id. at 612–13.

A few scholars have praised *Shaw.* James F. Blumstein, *Racial Gerrymandering and Vote Dilution:* Shaw v. Reno *in Doctrinal Context,* 26 RUTGERS LAW JOURNAL 517 (1995), argues that the Court rightly applied the paradigm of racial discrimination it had developed in other contexts to racial redistricting. Katharine Inglis Butler, *Affirmative Racial Gerrymandering: Fair Representation for Minorities or a Dangerous Recognition of Group Rights?,* 20 RUTGERS LAW JOURNAL 595 (1995), applauds *Shaw* as valuing individual rather than group-based rights while arguing that racial gerrymandering is neither required by the Voting Rights Act nor justified to remedy past discrimination. Melissa L. Saunders,

The Dirty Little Secrets of Shaw, 24 HARVARD JOURNAL OF LAW & PUBLIC POLICY 141 (2000), argues that the racial gerrymandering doctrine does not fulfill the goals favored by writers such as Blumstein and Butler.

3. Justice White dissents on the ground that plaintiffs did not allege a "cognizable injury." For a redistricting plan to create such an injury, he says, it must "have the intent and effect of unduly diminishing [plaintiffs'] influence on the political process." The majority responds that plaintiffs have raised a claim under the Equal Protection Clause that is "distinct" from vote dilution claims. What kind of claim is this? One explanation is suggested by Richard H. Pildes & Richard G. Niemi, *Expressive Harms, "Bizarre Districts," and Voting Rights: Evaluating Election-District Appearances After Shaw v. Reno*, 92 MICHIGAN LAW REVIEW 483, 506–09 (1993):

> One can only understand *Shaw*, we believe, in terms of a view that what we call *expressive* harms are constitutionally cognizable. An expressive harm is one that results from the ideas or attitudes expressed through a governmental action, rather than from the more tangible or material consequences the action brings about. On this view, the *meaning* of a governmental action is just as important as what that action *does*. Public policies can violate the Constitution not only because they bring about concrete costs, but because the very meaning they convey demonstrates inappropriate respect for relevant public values. On this unusual conception of constitutional harm, when a governmental action expresses disrespect for such values, it can violate the Constitution.
>
> [*Shaw*] becomes intelligible only if one recognizes that it rests on just this concern for expressive harms. *Shaw* validates such harms as constitutionally cognizable, along with more familiar, concrete, material injuries. Indeed, close attention to the language of Justice O'Connor's opinion reveals a constant struggle to articulate exactly these sorts of expressive harms. Thus, the opinion is laden with references to the social perceptions, the messages, and the governmental reinforcement of values that the Court believes North Carolina's districting scheme conveys. There is simply no way to make sense of these references, which give the opinion its character and are central to its holding, without recognizing that the decision is grounded in concern for expressive harms. This conception of constitutionally cognizable harms explains why the Court is adamant that "reapportionment is one area in which appearances do matter." If they do, it must be because, even apart from any concrete harm to individual voters, such appearances themselves express a value structure that offends constitutional principles.
>
> *Shaw* therefore rests on the principle that, when government appears to use race in the redistricting context in a way that subordinates all other relevant values, the state has impermissibly endorsed too dominant a role for race. The constitutional harm must lie in this endorsement itself: the very expression of this kind of value reductionism becomes the constitutional violation.

A variant of the expressive harm idea has been put forth by Melissa L. Saunders, *Reconsidering* Shaw: *The* Miranda *of Race-Conscious Districting*, 109 YALE LAW JOURNAL 1603 (2000), who argues *Shaw* is intended to protect residents of the race-based district, who may suffer stigma from being "placed in a district that everyone knows has been created for the special benefit of one racial group.... For members of the race for whose special benefit the district is being created, it is the implication that they need special help to win elections. For everyone else in the district … it is the implication that those responsible for drawing districts do not care about their political interests, whatever they are."

Expressive harm as a rationale for *Shaw* has not gone without criticism.

> Normatively, the expressive harm explanation is vulnerable to the charge that law based on "appearances" rather than reality can have no firm grounding and, more generally, conflicts with one of the great truths in the western tradition: that actions and understandings based on appearances rather than reality are morally and intellectually deficient. In addition, the empirical assumptions on which the expressive harm explanation is based are probably implausible and certainly undemonstrated.

Daniel Hays Lowenstein, *You Don't Have to Be Liberal to Hate the Racial Gerrymandering Cases*, 50 STANFORD LAW REVIEW 779, 797 (1998). On the last point, Pamela S. Karlan, *Just Politics? Five Not So Easy Pieces of the 1995 Term*, 34 HOUSTON LAW REVIEW 289 (1997), shows that in later racial gerrymandering cases decided in 1996, the Court ignored evidence that the types of expressive harm assumed to accompany racial gerrymandering were not actually occurring. She observes, "It seems to be enough that the Court has perceived a pernicious message, regardless of whether voters or elected representatives have received one."

4. Questions surrounding the concept of "expressive harm" were thrown into sharp relief in *Goosby v. Town Board of the Town of Hempstead*, 981 F.Supp. 751 (E.D.N.Y. 1997), cert. denied 528 U.S. 1138 (2000). After an at large system for electing the six-member Town Board was found to violate Section 2, defendants were ordered to propose a remedial plan. Defendants submitted, as their first choice, a plan consisting of one majority-minority single-member district and a second district consisting of the rest of the town, from which the remaining five members would be elected at large. As a fallback, defendants proposed a plan consisting of six single-member districts, one of which was a majority-minority district. The majority-minority district was identical in the two plans. The difference was whether the remainder of the Town, whose population was overwhelmingly white, would vote in one multi-member district or in separate single-member districts. The court rejected defendants' preferred plan and ordered into effect the single-member district plan.

On what grounds could the preferred plan be rejected? The court gave this explanation:

> It is difficult to conceive of a districting proposal that inflicts greater "expressive harm" than the one at issue here. The single-member district in the proposed two-district plan would of course be viewed as the seat reserved for African-Americans, while the other district would be viewed as the domain of the white voters. The separation of nearly all black citizens into one single-member district and nearly all whites into a large multi-member one "bears an uncomfortable resemblance to political apartheid." *Shaw I*. The plan also creates the risk of pitting the member of the Town Board from the "black district" against the five members elected from the "white district."

Certainly, the two-district plan would have called attention to the deliberately created majority-minority district. But unlike *Shaw I* and the subsequent racial gerrymandering cases, the reason is not because of any feature of that district that the court finds objectionable. To the contrary, the majority-minority district is precisely the type of district the court requires the Town to adopt, and is the same as in the plan the court approves. Is there any basis for limiting the Town's discretion to elect the remaining members of the Board as the Town chooses, in order to avoid calling attention to the majority-minority district that the court requires?

5. Pildes and Niemi's concept of expressive harm may provide one answer to an objection raised by Justice White and others against the analysis in *Shaw*, namely, that if neither race-conscious districting nor noncompact districts are unconstitutional in themselves, it is hard to see why they are unconstitutional in combination.

The concept of expressive harm, if accepted, may justify upholding the race-based district that is regularly shaped and therefore does not "express" a single-minded concern with race while striking down the race-based district that, in Justice O'Connor's words, is "so highly irregular that, on its face, it rationally cannot be understood as anything other than an effort to 'segregat[e] ... voters' on the basis of race."

However, this explanation underlines a different objection to *Shaw*, that it seems to be based on a false premise. Consider the background to the creation of the 12th congressional district, described in the ALMANAC OF AMERICAN POLITICS, quoted above prior to the *Shaw* decision. The race-based decision *whether* to create a second majority-minority district was imposed on North Carolina, but the decision *how* to create that district, by means of the extremely irregular shape, was determined by partisan political considerations. Thus, the assumption that race was solely responsible for the odd shape is incorrect. As Karlan, *All Over the Map*, *supra*, 1993 SUPREME COURT REVIEW at 283–84 writes:

> Even if political gerrymandering cannot serve as a justification for race-consciousness, proof that it played a role in the choice among configurations logically negates the first element of the plaintiffs' case, namely, showing that the legislation "rationally cannot be understood as anything other than an effort to separate voters." Given her endorsement of partisan gerrymandering in *Bandemer*, Justice O'Connor, at least, should be reluctant to strike down an apportionment whose irregular lines are the function of political, rather than racial, concerns.

6. Aleinikoff and Issacharoff, writing in 1993 in a passage quoted in Note 2 above, stated that only rudimentary evidence existed regarding the quality of representation in racially drawn districts. Much research has been performed on that subject since *Shaw*, most notably a study by David T. Canon, RACE, REDISTRICTING, AND REPRESENTATION: THE UNINTENDED CONSEQUENCES OF BLACK MAJORITY DISTRICTS (1999). In response to Justice O'Connor's statement in *Shaw* that officials elected from race-based districts "are more likely to believe that their primary obligation is to represent only the members of that group, rather than their constituency as a whole," Canon states:

> I regard Justice O'Connor's position as a testable proposition rather than an uncontroversial assumption. [I] will test this proposition by examining the nature of racial representation in the U.S. House of Representatives. My thesis is that the process of candidate emergence and political campaigns exerts a powerful influence on representation in black majority districts. I challenge the prevailing notion that there are monolithic black interests that could produce *a* "representative of their choice" in most districts. Instead, factions within the African-American community produce candidates with different ideological backgrounds and different visions of the representation of racial interests. One significant effect of this ideological diversity among black candidates is to give a centrist coalition of moderate white and black voters the power to elect the black candidate of *their* choice in many districts.

Id. at 2–3. Although both proponents and opponents of race-based districting tend to assume that black candidates in majority-black districts subscribe to the "politics of difference," Canon's study

> contradict[s] that common wisdom.... [M]any of the African-American politicians who were elected in the new districts embody the politics of commonality rather than the politics of difference. Furthermore, even those who *campaign* by appealing to black voters do, in fact, spend a substantial proportion of their time in Congress representing the interests of white and black voters alike.

Id. at 4. Canon refers to candidates espousing the politics of difference as traditional candidates and those espousing the politics of commonality as new-style candidates. He develops a "supply-side" theory to explain when traditional or new-style candidates are most likely to succeed in a majority-minority district.

> We argue that individual politicians acting in their own self-interest may tip the balance of power in black-majority districts to a cohesive minority comprised of black and white moderates who will elect black racial moderates or even white candidates. We find that the former outcome prevails in a majority of the new districts where biracial coalitions elect candidates who embody a politics of commonality rather than a politics of difference.... In a nutshell the supply-side theory argues that the type of racial representation provided in a district depends on the racial composition of the candidate pool in the Democratic primary. In most instances..., if only black candidates run, a new-style black candidate will win. If a white candidate and at least one traditional black candidate run, a traditional black candidate will win.

Id. at 94. He sets forth seven hypotheses that make up his theory, of which the last three constitute the core:

> 5. If a single black candidate runs, there is no clear theoretical expectation concerning the nature of the electoral coalition.
>
> 6. If a traditional black, a new-style black, and a white run in the same district, the traditional black will win the nomination if there is a runoff election. If there is no runoff, and the black vote is deeply split, the white could win; if not, the traditional black will win, as the moderate vote is split.
>
> 7. If a traditional black and a new-style black run in a district with a substantial bloc of white voters (at least 30 percent) and no white candidate runs, the new-style black will win the nomination with the support of a biracial coalition.

Id. at 127. Canon then tests his theory, and finds that it accounts for the "dramatic success of new-style congressional candidates." *Id.* at 137. He concludes:

> The conventional wisdom concerning the "apartheid" districts is clearly undermined by the biracial nature of a majority of the 1992 campaigns.... Of the sixteen new or substantially altered districts only four produced a winning candidate who campaigned on the politics of difference.

7. *Shaw* is undoubtedly regarded as a "conservative" decision. The five-member majority was composed of the justices generally regarded as conservatives, and the insistence on treating "benign" and malignant racial classifications as equally suspect is consistent with a prominent theme of contemporary conservatism. Nevertheless, *Shaw* is by no means a pure gain, measured by conservative values. One such value is the preservation of the role of the states in the federal structure. The Voting Rights Act in general, and amended Section 2 as interpreted in *Gingles* in particular, intrude into the crucial realm

of the state's freedom to structure its own political system.[m] Most Americans would now agree that the intrusion was justified by the overriding need to assure the extension of voting rights, though of course they disagree over the appropriate degree of that intrusion. The intrusion is limited, however, in the sense that so long as the state complies, it is otherwise free to structure its political system as it chooses.

Shaw changes the situation. Assuming that the Court is not inclined to declare the Voting Rights Act and its own handiwork in *Gingles* unconstitutional, the new situation is that race-based districting is *required* up to the point mandated by federal law, but sharply *restricted* beyond the federal mandate. Thus, the zone of state discretion with respect to one important factor in districting is narrowed. Furthermore, given Justice O'-Connor's willingness to assume that the odd shape of North Carolina's 12th Congressional District must "rationally" be explained as motivated solely by race in the face of a record suggesting that the odd shape resulted from the state's desire to accommodate its own political goals with federally-imposed racial requirements, *Shaw* threatens to restrict state autonomy over districting beyond questions of race.

Related to these questions of federalism is a possible conflict between *Shaw* and conservative ideas regarding the role of race and ethnicity in politics. Peter Skerry, MEXICAN AMERICANS: THE AMBIVALENT MINORITY 11–15 (1993), draws a distinction between what he labels "minority" and "ethnic" groups. The terms do not necessarily refer to different groups but to different conceptions of how the groups do or should operate within the political system and how the system does or should protect the groups' rights and interests. The term "minority," Skerry writes, "has come to denote ... a victimized racial claimant group." *Id.* at 11. In contrast, an ethnic group is not defined by societal oppression or discrimination, but by the group itself, whose members hold "a positive identification with [the group's] ethnic and cultural heritage." *Id.* at 15. Conservatives — though not only conservatives — find it desirable, to the maximum extent possible, for groups to achieve social justice and promote their interests by acting, in Skerry's terms, as "ethnic" rather than "minority" groups. Indeed, a major difference between conservatives and liberals on racial issues might be described as a difference over the degree to which the "minority" group conception is necessary for the accomplishment of social justice.

In the context of voting rights issues, the "minority" approach is to provide the groups in question with legal rights to prescribed forms of representation, supreme over the state's political determinations. The "ethnic" approach is for the groups to compete within the state's political process to achieve as best they can the forms of representation that they prefer. If, in the post-*Shaw* regime, Congress has free rein to guarantee representational preference to racial and language groups, but the groups are constitutionally barred from competing for additional favorable representation within the state political systems, then the Constitution will be enshrining the "minority" approach and banning the "ethnic" approach. This appears to be a perverse result, especially from a conservative perspective.

For an elaboration of these points, see Lowenstein, *supra*.

8. The majority in *Shaw* acknowledged that the plaintiffs were not alleging that their votes were diluted. The only harm they claimed to suffer was that the state had "segregate[d]

---

m. Admittedly, the congressional districts under challenge in *Shaw* are part of the national system of government, not that of the state, and the federalism concerns expressed in this Note are perhaps minimal. However, *Shaw* is equally applicable to districting at the state and local levels.

citizens into separate voting districts on the basis of race." It is at least plausible to suggest that the harm alleged is suffered by all citizens as citizens, not by particular citizens as individuals. When such generalized harms are alleged, the Court ordinarily begins with asking whether the plaintiffs have "standing" to assert the claim in a judicial proceeding. We shall not review the intricacies of the standing doctrine, which is complex and beyond the scope of this book, but it is striking that the issue of standing appears to have been overlooked by both the majority and the dissenters in *Shaw*. It was not overlooked by commentators, who pounced on the Court's oversight. See, e.g., Samuel Issacharoff & Thomas C. Goldstein, *Identifying the Harm in Racial Gerrymandering Claims*, 1 MICHIGAN JOURNAL OF RACE & LAW 47, 57 (1996); Frank R. Parker, *The Constitutionality of Racial Redistricting: A Critique of* Shaw v. Reno, 3 DISTRICT OF COLUMBIA LAW REVIEW 1, 9–22 (1995); Karlan, *All Over the Map, supra*, at 278–79.

In 1995, on the same day that the Court decided *Miller v. Johnson*, excerpted below, it addressed the standing issue in *Hays v. Louisiana*, 515 U.S. 737 (1995), in which it held that residents of the district being challenged have standing to bring a racial gerrymandering action. Commentators have struggled to find a rationale for this ruling. If the harm is the separation of racial groups into voting districts without regard to dilution of votes or other disadvantaging of one group or the other, why are those who fall on one side of the separation more aggrieved than those who fall on the other side? John Hart Ely, *Standing to Challenge Pro-Minority Gerrymanders*, 111 HARVARD LAW REVIEW 576 (1997), suggests that only residents of the district in question who are not members of the racial group for whose benefit the district was created should have standing. Samuel Issacharoff & Pamela S. Karlan, *Standing and Misunderstanding in Voting Rights Law*, 111 HARVARD LAW REVIEW 2276, 2278 (1997), argue that Ely's suggestion is inconsistent with the theory of the racial gerrymandering cause of action as the Supreme Court has articulated it. It might be added that Ely's suggestion is in tension with the empirical findings of David Canon, described in Note 6, to the effect that white voters usually have a significant voice in choosing and are well represented by representatives of majority-black districts.

Is the standing requirement of *Hays* applicable to plaintiffs challenging a plan as an unconstitutional partisan gerrymander? That question is considered by some members of the Supreme Court in *Vieth v. Jubelirer*, set forth in the next chapter.

9. Whatever values *Shaw* promoted and whatever the soundness of its analysis, the novelty of the decision posed a number of problems for its implementation. First and most basically, what must a plaintiff demonstrate to show a prima facie violation of the Equal Protection Clause under *Shaw*? The majority acknowledged that "race-conscious" districting is not always unconstitutional. Does "race-conscious" mean "race-motivated"? The Court also said that districting "unexplainable on grounds other than race" is prima facie unconstitutional. If a districting plan is at all race-motivated, does it not follow that it cannot be *entirely* explained on grounds other than race? Is that sufficient? Or does "unexplainable on grounds other than race" mean that a plan is prima facie unconstitutional only if nothing *other* than race enters into the explanation? That interpretation would be consistent with the majority's emphasis that race must be the only explanation for the district in question. Indeed, J. Morgan Kousser, Shaw v. Reno *and the Real World of Redistricting and Representation*, 26 RUTGERS LAW JOURNAL 625, 653–54 (1995), cited fifteen instances in which Justice O'Connor stated that race must be the sole reason for a district's shape. Another question was the significance of the irregular shape of a district. Justice O'Connor's opinion suggests that irregular shape is the sole basis for concluding that a district is "unexplainable on grounds other than race." She thus emphasized that the

cause of action depended on the racial basis of the plan being evident "on its face." And she expressly declined to decide whether a plan known to be racially based would give rise to a cause of action if the racial basis did not appear on the face of the plan.

One problem with the *Shaw* approach was that, as we have seen, it was well-known that in fact the irregular shape of the Twelfth Congressional District in North Carolina resulted from the state legislature's determination to comply with the Justice Department's insistence on a second majority-minority district at the expense of the Republicans rather than the Democrats. More generally, it is virtually impossible that race or any other single consideration could be the *sole* cause of a district's configuration, especially if the districting plan is enacted through a political process. The unrealistic but repeated reference to race as a sole cause undoubtedly reflected Justice O'Connor's awareness of the difficulty of answering this question: If a plan only partially explainable by race can be unconstitutional and yet race-conscious districting is not always unconstitutional, how can a line be drawn?

Together with what constitutes a prima facie violation, the other important question left open by *Shaw* was what compelling state interests could defend a plan shown to be prima facie unconstitutional. Of particular importance was whether compliance with the Voting Rights Act would count as a compelling state interest sufficient to vindicate a plan. Bear in mind that the plans attacked in cases that reached the Supreme Court were from states that were covered by the Voting Rights Act. Legislatures in these states knew that if they did not create a sufficient number of majority-minority districts to satisfy the Justice Department, their plans would not be precleared and could not be put into effect. Indeed, in North Carolina and Georgia, the challenged districts were drawn only after the Justice Department had rejected earlier plans that created only one majority-minority district in North Carolina and only two in Georgia. Furthermore, these and other states knew that in many instances they would be vulnerable to Section 2 actions unless they created new majority-minority districts. Would the desire to comply with Section 5 or Section 2 of the Voting Rights Act be a compelling state interest?

As you review the following materials, watch for the ways in which these questions were resolved by the majority in post-*Shaw* decisions. Did the members of the majority agree, and did clear answers emerge? What new questions arose?

Post-*Shaw* Decisions

After the 1990 census, Georgia's population entitled it to go from ten to eleven congressional districts. One of the ten old districts was a majority-minority district. The Georgia legislature (the General Assembly) passed and sought preclearance for a new plan containing two majority-minority districts and a third district in which African Americans made up 35 percent of the voting age population. Despite the increase from one majority-minority district to two and an absence of evidence of an intent to discriminate, preclearance was denied. A second plan was also rejected, as Justice Department lawyers pointed to a so-called "max-black" plan that had been developed by the American Civil Liberties Union, containing three majority-minority districts. The General Assembly then adopted a plan based on the ACLU proposal, containing three majority-minority districts. Black representatives were elected from each of the three majority-minority districts.

One of these, the Eleventh District, was challenged by five white residents of the district as an unconstitutional racial gerrymander. The Eleventh District was described by the *Almanac of American Politics*: "Geographically, it is a monstrosity, stretching from At-

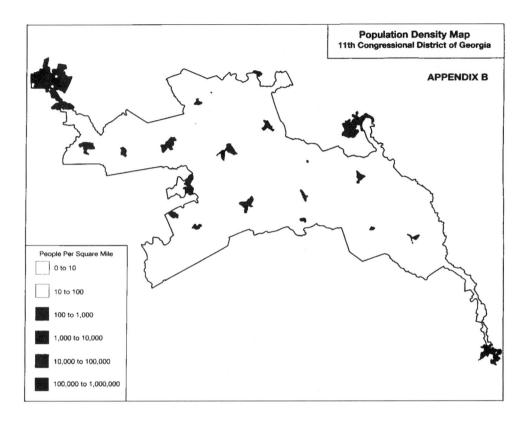

lanta to Savannah. Its core is the plantation country in the center of the state, lightly populated, but heavily black. It links by narrow corridors the black neighborhoods in Augusta, Savannah and southern DeKalb County." In MILLER v. JOHNSON, 515 U.S. 900
(1995) (from which the above characterizations are taken), the Supreme Court struck
down the Eleventh District as violative of the Equal Protection Clause.

The District Court had found and the state did not deny that "race was the predominant, overriding factor in drawing the Eleventh District." Rather, the state contended that
"regardless of the legislature's purposes, a plaintiff must demonstrate that a district's
shape is so bizarre that it is unexplainable other than on the basis of race." It may seem
to the uninitiated that the shape of the Georgia district is pretty bizarre, but veterans of
redistricting will see nothing unusual in the district's outline map. Comparison of the
Georgia district with the North Carolina district in *Shaw* or the Texas districts shown
later in this chapter will show that the Georgia Eleventh is pretty low down on the
bizarreness scale. What the District Court and the Supreme Court found remarkable
about the district was the enclosure of black neighborhoods in distant cities.

Justice Kennedy, writing for a majority that included Chief Justice Rehnquist and Justices O'Connor, Scalia, and Thomas, responded that the appellants' "conception of the constitutional violation misapprehends our holding in *Shaw.*"

> Our observation in *Shaw* of the consequences of racial stereotyping was not
> meant to suggest that a district must be bizarre on its face before there is a con-
> stitutional violation. Nor was our conclusion in *Shaw* that in certain instances a
> district's appearance (or, to be more precise, its appearance in combination with
> certain demographic evidence) can give rise to an equal protection claim a hold-

ing that bizarreness was a threshold showing, as appellants believe it to be. Our circumspect approach and narrow holding in *Shaw* did not erect an artificial rule barring accepted equal protection analysis in other redistricting cases. Shape is relevant not because bizarreness is a necessary element of the constitutional wrong or a threshold requirement of proof, but because it may be persuasive circumstantial evidence that race for its own sake, and not other districting principles, was the legislature's dominant and controlling rationale in drawing its district lines. The logical implication, as courts applying *Shaw* have recognized, is that parties may rely on evidence other than bizarreness to establish race-based districting.

... Appellants and some of their *amici* argue that the Equal Protection Clause's general proscription on race-based decisionmaking does not obtain in the districting context because redistricting by definition involves racial considerations. Underlying their argument are the very stereotypical assumptions the Equal Protection Clause forbids. It is true that redistricting in most cases will implicate a political calculus in which various interests compete for recognition, but it does not follow from this that individuals of the same race share a single political interest.... Nor can the argument that districting cases are excepted from standard equal protection precepts be resuscitated by *United Jewish Organizations of Williamsburgh, Inc. v. Carey* ... To the extent any of the opinions in that "highly fractured decision," *id.*, can be interpreted as suggesting that a State's assignment of voters on the basis of race would be subject to anything but our strictest scrutiny, those views ought not be deemed controlling....

Electoral districting is a most difficult subject for legislatures, and so the States must have discretion to exercise the political judgment necessary to balance competing interests. Although race-based decisionmaking is inherently suspect, until a claimant makes a showing sufficient to support that allegation the good faith of a state legislature must be presumed. The courts, in assessing the sufficiency of a challenge to a districting plan, must be sensitive to the complex interplay of forces that enter a legislature's redistricting calculus. Redistricting legislatures will, for example, almost always be aware of racial demographics; but it does not follow that race predominates in the redistricting process. *Shaw*. The distinction between being aware of racial considerations and being motivated by them may be difficult to make. This evidentiary difficulty, together with the sensitive nature of redistricting and the presumption of good faith that must be accorded legislative enactments, requires courts to exercise extraordinary caution in adjudicating claims that a state has drawn district lines on the basis of race. The plaintiff's burden is to show, either through circumstantial evidence of a district's shape and demographics or more direct evidence going to legislative purpose, that race was the predominant factor motivating the legislature's decision to place a significant number of voters within or without a particular district. To make this showing, a plaintiff must prove that the legislature subordinated traditional race-neutral districting principles, including but not limited to compactness, contiguity, respect for political subdivisions or communities defined by actual shared interests, to racial considerations. Where these or other race-neutral considerations are the basis for redistricting legislation, and are not subordinated to race, a state can "defeat a claim that a district has been gerrymandered on racial lines." *Shaw*.

[The District Court found] "it was 'exceedingly obvious' from the shape of the Eleventh District, together with the relevant racial demographics, that the drawing of narrow land bridges to incorporate within the District outlying appendages containing nearly 80% of the district's total black population was a deliberate attempt to bring black populations into the district. Although by comparison with other districts the geometric shape of the Eleventh District may not seem bizarre on its face, when its shape is considered in conjunction with its racial and population densities, the story of racial gerrymandering seen by the District Court becomes much clearer. [This evidence was confirmed by evidence that the Justice Department would accept "nothing less than abject surrender to its maximization agenda" and that the General Assembly "was driven by its overriding desire to comply."]

Race was, as the District Court found, the predominant, overriding factor explaining the General Assembly's decision to attach to the Eleventh District various appendages containing dense majority-black populations. As a result, Georgia's congressional redistricting plan cannot be upheld unless it satisfies strict scrutiny, our most rigorous and exacting standard of constitutional review.

... Whether or not in some cases compliance with the Voting Rights Act, standing alone, can provide a compelling interest independent of any interest in remedying past discrimination, it cannot do so here. As we suggested in *Shaw*, compliance with federal antidiscrimination laws cannot justify race-based districting where the challenged district was not reasonably necessary under a constitutional reading and application of those laws. The congressional plan challenged here was not required by the Voting Rights Act under a correct reading of the statute.

[It is] safe to say that the congressional plan enacted in the end was required in order to obtain preclearance. It does not follow, however, that the plan was required by the substantive provisions of the Voting Rights Act.

We do not accept the contention that the State has a compelling interest in complying with whatever preclearance mandates the Justice Department issues. When a state governmental entity seeks to justify race-based remedies to cure the effects of past discrimination, we do not accept the government's mere assertion that the remedial action is required. Rather, we insist on a strong basis in evidence of the harm being remedied. See, e.g., *Shaw.*... Our presumptive skepticism of all racial classifications prohibits us as well from accepting on its face the Justice Department's conclusion that racial districting is necessary under the Voting Rights Act. Where a State relies on the Department's determination that race-based districting is necessary to comply with the Voting Rights Act, the judiciary retains an independent obligation in adjudicating consequent equal protection challenges to ensure that the State's actions are narrowly tailored to achieve a compelling interest. Were we to accept the Justice Department's objection itself as a compelling interest adequate to insulate racial districting from constitutional review, we would be surrendering to the Executive Branch our role in enforcing the constitutional limits on race-based official action. We may not do so....

Georgia's drawing of the Eleventh District was not required under the Act because there was no reasonable basis to believe that Georgia's earlier enacted plans violated §5. Wherever a plan is "ameliorative," a term we have used to describe plans increasing the number of majority-minority districts, it "cannot violate §5 unless the new apportionment itself so discriminates on the basis of race or color as to violate the Constitution." *Beer.*... Acknowledging as much, the United States now relies on the fact that the Justice Department may object to a state proposal either on the ground that it has a prohibited purpose or a prohibited effect, see, e.g., *Pleasant Grove v. United States,* 479 U.S. 462, 469 (1987). The Government justifies its preclearance objections on the ground that the submitted plans violated §5's purpose element. The key to the Government's position, which is plain from its objection letters if not from its briefs to this Court, is and always has been that Georgia failed to proffer a nondiscriminatory purpose for its refusal in the first two submissions to take the steps necessary to create a third majority-minority district.

... The State's policy of adhering to other districting principles instead of creating as many majority-minority districts as possible does not support an inference that the plan "so discriminates on the basis of race or color as to violate the Constitution," *Beer,* and thus cannot provide any basis under §5 for the Justice Department's objection.

Instead of grounding its objections on evidence of a discriminatory purpose, it would appear the Government was driven by its policy of maximizing majority-black districts. Although the Government now disavows having had that policy and seems to concede its impropriety, the District Court's well-documented factual finding was that the Department did adopt a maximization policy and followed it in objecting to Georgia's first two plans....

Justice O'Connor wrote a short concurring opinion. Justices Ginsburg, joined by Justices Stevens, Breyer and Souter, dissented. Justice Stevens also wrote a dissenting opinion arguing that the plaintiffs lacked standing.

Notes and Questions

1. In contrast with *Shaw, Miller* appears to place less emphasis on the shape of a district as an element of the constitutional violation and more emphasis on the underlying racial motivation, with shape being significant primarily as an indicator of the existence of racial motivation. Briffault, *supra,* at 45, comments:

A doctrine based on appearances seems quite cynical. If appearance matters, it is presumably because a deeper value is offended by the appearance. If the value vindicated by *Shaw* is racial neutrality, then it is difficult to see why, given the Court's own principles, the concern with racially "segregated" districts should be cabined to irregularly shaped districts and not expanded to invalidate any intentional use of race in districting not narrowly tailored to remedy unconstitutional racial vote dilution. Although *Shaw* refused to go that far, *Miller v. Johnson* took a large step in that direction. Indeed, *Johnson* suggests that *Shaw*'s use of shape may have been just a way station on the road to a direct attack on the intentional use of race in the design of electoral systems.

One reason for the different approach in *Miller* may have been that Georgia's 11th Congressional District was not as irregularly shaped as the district in *Shaw.* However, later decisions suggest that the authors of the majority opinions in those two cases also may have made a difference, as Justice O'Connor continued to place considerable emphasis on the shape of districts while Justice Kennedy seems primarily concerned with motivation.

How does the shift in emphasis in *Miller* affect the *Shaw* majority's ground for distinguishing the racial gerrymandering cause of action from *United Jewish Organizations v. Carey?*

2. *Miller* requires a plaintiff to prove "that race was the *predominant* factor motivating the legislature's decision to place a significant number of voters within or without a particular district. To make this showing, a plaintiff must prove that the legislature subordinated traditional race-neutral districting principles, including but not limited to compactness, contiguity, respect for political subdivisions or communities defined by actual shared interests, to racial considerations" (emphasis added).

Many scholars have commented on the difficulty of attributing a predominant motive to a body as complex as a legislature engaged in as complex an enterprise as redistricting. See, e.g., Briffault, *supra*, at 50–52; Samuel Issacharoff, *The Constitutional Contours of Race and Politics*, 1995 SUPREME COURT REVIEW 45, 57–60; Pamela S. Karlan, *Still Hazy After All These Years: Voting Rights in the Post-*Shaw *Era*, 26 CUMBERLAND LAW REVIEW 287, 302–06 (1996). John Hart Ely, *Gerrymanders: The Good, the Bad, and the Ugly*, 50 STANFORD LAW REVIEW 607, 612 (1998), summarizes these views pithily:

> Drawing a voting district involves an infinity of choices, each of which is similarly likely to be influenced by a number of considerations. The boundaries zig and zag, shuck and jive, sidle like sidewinders. And each spasm has at least one story of its own: How in the name of heaven could one suppose the whole monstrosity to have a "dominant purpose," unless it's to accommodate as many little purposes as possible?

The "predominance" criterion has also been criticized as fundamentally misconceived in the context of a racial gerrymandering case:

> To ask whether one factor "predominates" over others is to imply that the districting process consists of a weighing or balancing of factors. But that is not what occurs with race in redistricting. Under the VRA, race is not a "factor" at all, but a prior requirement in a lexical ordering. In John Rawls' definition of a lexical (or serial) ordering:
>
> > This is an order which requires us to satisfy the first principle in the ordering before we can move on to the second, the second before we consider the third, and so on. A principle does not come into play until those previous to it are either fully met or do not apply. A serial ordering avoids, then, having to balance principles at all; those earlier in the ordering have an absolute weight, so to speak with respect to later ones, and hold without exception.
>
> A consideration that is lexically prior is a *privileged* consideration. It is a necessary precondition of what comes afterward, and aside from that, there is little that can be said about how it is "weighted" against the rest....
>
> Because the racial quotas imposed under the VRA were *privileged* considerations, debate over their "predominance" is inevitably uncertain and arbitrary. Although the majority and the dissenters in the racial gerrymandering cases debated numerous aspects of the complex factual records, there was no serious disagreement between them over what actually happened. In each case, the state was forced to create a minimum number of [majority-minority districts]. Subject to that constraint, the state produced its districting plan by a normal political process of competition and negotiation. The majority on the Court and the dissenters debated the artificial question of whether to characterize the privileged consideration as predominant, when they all knew that the privileged consideration was never balanced against other considerations at all.

Lowenstein, *supra*, at 806–07.

3. Notice that Justice Kennedy in *Miller* uses the term "predominant" in an unusual way. Ordinarily, one would not think a factor is predominant if it is less important than or subordinated to *any* other factor. However, Justice Kennedy says the plaintiff can prove predominance of race by showing that race was not subordinated to *certain* other factors, namely "traditional race-neutral districting principles, including but not limited to compactness, contiguity, and respect for political subdivisions or communities defined by actual share interests." If the only things legislatures ever considered in redistricting were race and what Justice Kennedy refers to as "traditional race-neutral districting principles," then his statement would make straightforward sense. In that case, race and traditional principles would interact like a seesaw—if the relative reliance on one goes up, the other goes down. But state legislators, left to their own devices, are likely to subordinate race *and* "traditional" districting principles to enhancing their own prospects for reelection or advancement, benefiting their party, and other political purposes. If the evidence shows that the legislature gave very little attention to traditional principles, some attention to race, and lots of attention to political goals, has the plaintiff proven a prima facie case under *Miller*?

* * *

In the next set of major racial gerrymandering decisions, the Court struck down congressional districts in Texas and North Carolina.

In the Texas case, BUSH v. VERA, 517 U.S. 952 (1996), the lead opinion was written by Justice O'Connor and joined by Chief Justice Rehnquist and Justice Kennedy. Three congressional districts were challenged: the 30th, a majority-black district in the Dallas area, and two districts in the Houston area, the 29th, which was majority-Hispanic, and the 18th, which was majority-black. All three were ruled unconstitutional by the Court. Here are excerpts from Justice O'Connor's opinion:

> The present case is a mixed motive case. The appellants concede that one of Texas' goals in creating the three districts at issue was to produce majority-minority districts, but they also cite evidence that other goals, particularly incum-

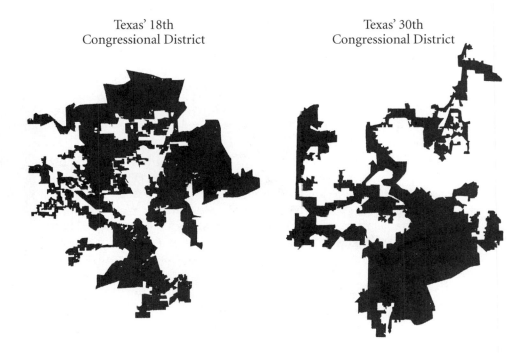

Texas' 18th
Congressional District

Texas' 30th
Congressional District

bency protection (including protection of "functional incumbents," i.e., sitting members of the Texas Legislature who had declared an intention to run for open congressional seats), also played a role in the drawing of the district lines. The record does not reflect a history of "*purely* race-based" districting revisions. Cf. *Miller* (emphasis added). A careful review is, therefore, necessary to determine whether these districts are subject to strict scrutiny. But review of the District Court's findings of primary fact and the record convinces us that the District Court's determination that race was the "predominant factor" in the drawing of each of the districts must be sustained.

Several factors other than race were at work in the drawing of the districts. Traditional districting criteria were not *entirely* neglected: Districts 18 and 29 maintain the integrity of county lines; each of the three districts takes its character from a principal city and the surrounding urban area; and none of the districts is as widely dispersed as the North Carolina district held unconstitutional in *Shaw II*. (These characteristics are, however, unremarkable in the context of large, densely populated urban counties.) More significantly, the District Court found that incumbency protection influenced the redistricting plan to an unprecedented extent.... And the appellants point to evidence that in many cases, race correlates strongly with manifestations of community of interest (for example, shared broadcast and print media, public transport infrastructure, and institutions such as schools and churches) and with the political data that is [*sic*] vital to incumbency protection efforts, raising the possibility that correlations between racial demographics and district lines may be explicable in terms of nonracial motivations....

Strict scrutiny would not be appropriate if race-neutral, traditional districting considerations predominated over racial ones. We have not subjected political gerrymandering to strict scrutiny. See *Bandemer*. And we have recognized incumbency protection, at least in the limited form of "avoiding contests between incumbent[s]," as a legitimate state goal. See *Karcher; White v. Weiser; Burns v. Richardson*. Because it is clear that race was not the only factor that motivated the legislature to draw irregular district lines, we must scrutinize each challenged district to determine whether the District Court's conclusion that race predominated over legitimate districting considerations, including incumbency, can be sustained. [Following lengthy discussion of the three districts, Justice O'Connor sustained the District Court's conclusion.]

Having concluded that strict scrutiny applies, we must determine whether the racial classifications embodied in any of the three districts are narrowly tailored to further a compelling state interest....

As we have done in each of our previous cases in which [the need to comply with Section 2] has been raised as a defense to charges of racial gerrymandering, we assume without deciding that compliance with the results test, as interpreted by our precedents, can be a compelling state interest. We also reaffirm that the "narrow tailoring" requirement of strict scrutiny allows the States a limited degree of leeway in furthering such interests. If the State has a "strong basis in evidence," *Shaw I*, for concluding that creation of a majority-minority district is reasonably necessary to comply with §2, and the districting that is based on race "substantially addresses the §2 violation," *Shaw II*, it satisfies strict scrutiny....

A §2 district that is *reasonably* compact and regular, taking into account traditional districting principles such as maintaining communities of interest and traditional boundaries, may pass strict scrutiny without having to defeat rival compact districts designed by plaintiffs' experts in endless "beauty contests."[n] ...

Strict scrutiny remains, nonetheless, strict. The State must have a "strong basis in evidence" for finding that the threshold conditions for §2 liability are present....

And, as we have noted above, the district drawn in order to satisfy §2 must not subordinate traditional districting principles to race substantially more than is "reasonably necessary" to avoid §2 liability. Districts 18, 29, and 30 fail to meet these requirements.

We assume, without deciding, that the State had a "strong basis in evidence" for finding the second and third threshold conditions for §2 liability to be present. We have, however, already found that all three districts are bizarrely shaped and far from compact, and that those characteristics are predominantly attributable to gerrymandering that was racially motivated and/or achieved by the use of race as a proxy.

These characteristics defeat any claim that the districts are narrowly tailored to serve the State's interest in avoiding liability under §2, because §2 does not require a State to create, on predominantly racial lines, a district that is not "reasonably compact." See *Johnson v. De Grandy*. If, because of the dispersion of the minority population, a reasonably compact majority-minority district cannot be created, §2 does not require a majority-minority district; if a reasonably compact district can be created, nothing in §2 requires the race-based creation of a district that is far from compact.

Appellants argue that bizarre shaping and non-compactness do not raise narrow tailoring concerns. Appellants Lawson et al. claim that under *Shaw I* and *Miller*, "[s]hape is relevant only as evidence of an improper motive." ...

These arguments cannot save the districts before us. The Lawson appellants misinterpret *Miller*: district shape is not irrelevant to the narrow tailoring inquiry. Our discussion in *Miller* served only to emphasize that the ultimate constitutional values at stake involve the harms caused by the use of unjustified racial classifications, and that bizarreness is not necessary to trigger strict scrutiny. Significant deviations from traditional districting principles, such as the bizarre shape and noncompactness demonstrated by the districts here, cause constitutional harm insofar as they convey the message that political identity is, or should be, predominantly racial....

[Justice O'Connor rejected the need to remedy past discrimination as a defense for the districts. She went on to reject the nonretrogression defense of the 18th congressional district under Section 5 of the Voting Rights Act, based on the fact that a black-majority district already existed in Houston.]

The judgment of the District Court is

Affirmed.

Although Justice O'Connor was the author of the plurality opinion from which the foregoing excerpts were taken, she also added a *concurring* opinion, in which she spoke

---

n. What is the basis in law for the requirement that the "§2 district" be "reasonably compact and regular"? — EDS.

for herself only. This opinion may have been the most significant of all the many opinions issued in the Texas and North Carolina cases, because in it Justice O'Connor stated firmly her view that to the extent a state does what is necessary to comply with the "results test" of Section 2 of the Voting Rights Act, it is exempt from a constitutional claim of racial gerrymandering. This point had been placed in doubt by Justice Kennedy's opinion for the Court in *Miller*, which said that the failure to demonstrate that its "black maximization" plan was required by Section 5 undermined Georgia's defense, "[w]hether or not in some cases compliance with the Voting Rights Act, standing alone, can provide a compelling interest independent of any interest in remedying past discrimination."

Justice O'Connor observed that in several cases the Supreme Court had interpreted and applied the results test, "assuming but never directly addressing its constitutionality." Accordingly, the Court "should allow States to assume the constitutionality" of Section 2, and it follows that "the States have a compelling interest in complying with the results test as this Court has interpreted it." Since the four justices who dissented from both the Texas and North Carolina decisions plainly agreed, there was at least a 5-member majority on the Court for the proposition that compliance with Section 2 is a compelling state interest, until and unless the Court declares the results test unconstitutional.

Justice Kennedy, who joined in the plurality opinion, also added his own personal statement. He referred to the plurality's statements "that strict scrutiny would not apply to all cases of intentional creation of majority-minority districts," saying that "I do not consider these dicta to commit me to any position on the question whether race is predominant whenever a State, in redistricting, foreordains that one race be the majority in a certain number of districts or in a certain part of the State." With respect to the state's reliance on the need to comply with Section 2 as a compelling state interest, Justice Kennedy wrote:

> While §2 does not require a noncompact majority-minority district, neither does it forbid it, provided that the rationale for creating it is proper in the first instance. Districts not drawn for impermissible reasons or according to impermissible criteria may take any shape, even a bizarre one. States are not prevented from taking into account race-neutral factors in drawing permissible majority-minority districts. If, however, the bizarre shape of the district is attributable to race-based districting unjustified by a compelling interest (*e.g.*, gratuitous race-based districting or use of race as a proxy for other interests), such districts may "cause constitutional harm insofar as they convey the message that political identity is, or should be, predominantly racial."

Is Justice Kennedy's separate opinion consistent with the plurality opinion's explanation of why the Texas districts were not "narrowly tailored" to comply with Section 2?

The remaining two votes to strike down the Texas districts were explained in a concurring opinion by Justice Thomas, joined by Justice Scalia:

> In my view, application of strict scrutiny in this case was never a close question. I cannot agree with Justice O'CONNOR's assertion that strict scrutiny is not invoked by the intentional creation of majority-minority districts. Though *Shaw I*[o] expressly reserved that question..., in *Miller* Georgia's concession that it intentionally created majority-minority districts was sufficient to show that race was a predominant, motivating factor in its redistricting.

---

o. Because the North Carolina case, discussed below, is named *Shaw v. Hunt, Shaw v. Reno* became known as *Shaw I*.

Strict scrutiny applies to all governmental classifications based on race, and we have expressly held that there is no exception for race-based redistricting. While we have recognized the evidentiary difficulty of proving that a redistricting plan is, in fact, a racial gerrymander, see *Miller*; *Shaw I*, we have never suggested that a racial gerrymander is subject to anything less than strict scrutiny....

I am willing to assume without deciding that the State has asserted a compelling state interest. Given that assumption, I agree that the State's redistricting attempts were not narrowly tailored to achieve its asserted interest. I concur in the judgment.

Does Justice Thomas' opinion imply that in his view, Sections 2 and 5 of the Voting Rights Act are unconstitutional insofar as they require states to create majority-minority districts or to avoid retrogression in the ability of racially defined groups to control or influence the election of representatives?

Strong dissenting opinions by Justices Stevens and Souter were each joined by Justices Ginsburg and Breyer.

The North Carolina case, SHAW v. HUNT, 517 U.S. 899 (1996) (*Shaw II*), was part of the same litigation as *Shaw v. Reno*. On remand, the District Court found that North Carolina's 12th congressional district, described in *Shaw I*, was constitutional. Chief Justice Rehnquist wrote an opinion for the Court overruling the District Court and striking down the 12th district.

The most significant portions of *Shaw II* were the discussions of the state's asserted compelling state interests as justifications for the district. In a footnote, the Court rejected the state's argument based on its desire to avoid litigation to overcome the Attorney General's refusal to grant preclearance and the possibility of litigation under Section 2. If the desire to avoid litigation against the Attorney General were a sufficient interest, then "*Miller* would have been wrongly decided because there the Court rejected the contention that complying with the Justice Department's preclearance objection could be a compelling interest. It necessarily follows that avoiding the litigation required to overcome the Department's objection could not be a compelling interest." The desire to avoid litigation under Section 2 "sweeps too broadly. We assume, *arguendo*, that a State may have a compelling interest in complying with the properly interpreted Voting Rights Act. But a State must also have a 'strong basis in evidence,' see *Shaw I* (quoting *Richmond v. J.A. Croson Co.*, 488 U.S. 469 (1989)), for believing that it is violating the Act. It has no such interest in avoiding meritless lawsuits."

In evaluating the Court's rejection of the state's interest in obtaining preclearance, it should be borne in mind that even if a state believes the Attorney General is acting unlawfully in refusing to preclear a districting plan, the state cannot implement the plan until preclearance is received. Under *Wesberry* and *Reynolds*, the state must adopt a new districting plan. If the Attorney General objects, the state's only two choices are to change its plans to satisfy the Attorney General's specifications or to seek preclearance in the United States District Court for the District of Columbia. However, in the case of redistricting plans, the latter is usually impractical, because it will be impossible to get a judgment in time for the first elections for which districts are required. Therefore, as a practical matter, if the state refuses to satisfy the Attorney General, it is likely to give up entirely its right to determine its own districts, which instead will be imposed by a court. See Katharine Inglis Butler, *Affirmative Racial Gerrymandering: Rhetoric and Reality*, 26 CUMBERLAND LAW REVIEW 313, 320 n.20 (1996), noting the "powerful incentive" to comply with the Justice Department's demands in order to avoid a court-drawn plan. To say that a state does not have a compelling interest in avoiding the cession of its districting power to judicial control would be remarkable. Yet the Court reaches that result in *Shaw II* by relying on *Miller*, when the point was never considered in *Miller*.

Aside from avoiding litigation, the Court also responded to the state's defense that District 12 was needed to avoid an actual violation of Section 2 of the Voting Rights Act:

> [A]ppellees contend, and the District Court found, that failure to enact a plan with a second majority-black district would have left the State vulnerable to a lawsuit under this section....
>
> We assume, *arguendo*, for the purpose of resolving this case, that compliance with §2 could be a compelling interest, and we likewise assume, *arguendo*, that the General Assembly believed a second majority-minority district was needed in order not to violate §2, and that the legislature at the time it acted had a strong basis in evidence to support that conclusion. We hold that even with the benefit of these assumptions, the North Carolina plan does not survive strict scrutiny because the remedy—the creation of District 12—is not narrowly tailored to the asserted end.
>
> ... Where, as here, we assume avoidance of §2 liability to be a compelling state interest, we think that the racial classification would have to realize that goal; the legislative action must, at a minimum, remedy the anticipated violation or achieve compliance to be narrowly tailored....
>
> Appellees do not defend District 12 by arguing that the district is geographically compact.... Rather they contend, and a majority of the District Court agreed, that once a legislature has a strong basis in evidence for concluding that a §2 violation exists in the State, it may draw a majority-minority district anywhere, even if the district is in no way coincident with the compact *Gingles* district, as long as racially polarized voting exists where the district is ultimately drawn.
>
> We find this position singularly unpersuasive. We do not see how a district so drawn would avoid §2 liability. If a §2 violation is proven for a particular area, it flows from the fact that individuals in this area "have less opportunity than other members of the electorate to participate in the political process and to elect representatives of their choice." The vote dilution injuries suffered by these persons are not remedied by creating a safe majority-black district somewhere else in the State. For example, if a geographically compact, cohesive minority population lives in south-central to southeastern North Carolina, as the Justice Department's objection letter suggested, District 12 which spans the Piedmont Crescent would not address that §2 violation. The black voters of the south-central to southeastern region would still be suffering precisely the same injury that they suffered before District 12 was drawn. District 12 would not address the professed interest of relieving the vote dilution, much less be narrowly tailored to accomplish the goal.
>
> Arguing, as appellees do and the District Court did, that the State may draw the district anywhere derives from a misconception of the vote-dilution claim. To accept that the district may be placed anywhere implies that the claim, and hence the coordinate right to an undiluted vote (to cast a ballot equal among voters), belongs to the minority as a group and not to its individual members. It does not....
>
> For the foregoing reasons, the judgment of the District Court is
>
> *Reversed.*

Justice Stevens, joined by Justices Ginsburg and Breyer, wrote a dissenting opinion. Justice Souter, also joined by Ginsburg and Breyer, dissented on the grounds stated in Souter's opinion in *Bush v. Vera*.

Notes and Questions

1. One criticism of the racial gerrymandering cases has centered on the majority's unrealistic characterization of the factors used by the state during the redistricting process. In *Shaw II*, the majority stated that "[r]ace was the criterion that, in the State's view, could not be compromised; respecting communities of interest and protecting Democratic incumbents came into play only after the race-based decision had been made." As we shall see, a different majority characterized the process in quite different terms in the later case of *Easley v. Cromartie*. The *Shaw II* characterization has received this criticism:

> Consider the statement that race "was the criterion that, *in the State's view*, could not be compromised." In the State's view? *Why* could race not be compromised, "in the State's view"? Because the members of the North Carolina legislature were driven by ideological fervor to create a second [majority-minority] district? Of course not. The legislature had already adopted a plan containing one [majority-minority district], but was forbidden to place it into effect by the Justice Department, which denied it preclearance. "Race was the criterion that, in the State's view, could not be compromised," for the excellent reason that the federal government *prohibited* the state from compromising the racial criterion. The *federal* government absolutely required North Carolina to redistrict, and the *federal* government absolutely prohibited North Carolina from redistricting without creating two [majority-minority districts]. That the racial criterion "could not be compromised" was not a question of "the State's view," but an objective circumstance imposed on North Carolina by the federal government.

Lowenstein, *supra*, at 804.

Another statement in *Shaw II*—that the supposition that a Section 2 remedial district "may be placed anywhere implies that the claim, and hence the coordinate right to an undiluted vote (to cast a ballot equal among voters), belongs to a minority as a group and not to its individual members. It does not."—has come in for criticism from Heather K. Gerken, *Understanding the Right to an Undiluted Vote*, 114 HARVARD LAW REVIEW 1663 (2001). Gerken argues that the right to an undiluted vote is a hybrid, neither entirely an individual nor entirely a group right. Or, more precisely, that it is an individual right but one which by its nature turns on the situation of the group as a whole rather than on any particular members of the group. Applying this concept, she finds the *Shaw II* Court's treatment of the Section 2 defense inadequate. See also Lowenstein, *supra*, at 821–22.

2. Are partisan politics playing a role in the racial gerrymandering litigation? Among Democrats, at least, it is not uncommon to hear charges that the Supreme Court and some lower courts are reaching results benefiting the Republican Party. The author of one study is skeptical of such charges.

> [I]f we take the cynical view of the intent behind [racially gerrymandered] districts, how should a rational, partisan Republican judicial appointee vote? Would it not be to uphold the districts in question, so as to effectuate the plans of the drafters? However the evidence on these questions plays out, it calls into further doubt the use of easy partisan stereotypes to label judges' decisions in voting rights cases.

Michael E. Solimine, *The Three-Judge District Court in Voting Rights Litigation*, 30 UNIVERSITY OF MICHIGAN JOURNAL OF LAW REFORM 79, 124–25 (1996). Solimine's study is limited to the lower court judges. A more detailed study that considers the racial gerrymandering cases in both the Supreme Court and the lower courts asserts that partisanship has been a pervasive consideration. See J. Morgan Kousser, COLORBLIND INJUSTICE: MINORITY VOTING RIGHTS AND THE UNDOING OF THE SECOND RECONSTRUCTION, Chapter 8 (1999).

3. Chief Justice Rehnquist, author of the Court's opinion in *Shaw II*, implies that a state would violate Section 2 when geography permits a compact majority-minority district in one area but the state, for political reasons, draws a non-compact majority-minority district elsewhere. Lowenstein, *supra*, questions whether in fact Rehnquist would actually have declared a plan violative under those circumstances.

The Chief Justice having gone to his eternal rest, we shall never know the answer to that question. But we do know that Justice Kennedy, together with the four liberal justices who dissented from all the Court's findings of unconstitutional racial gerrymanders, took Rehnquist at his word. As we shall see shortly, in the Court's most recent Section 2 decision, they relied on the pertinent passage from *Shaw II* as the basis for finding a violation of Section 2 in Texas' controversial mid-decade congressional plan.

* * *

Like some monster in a popular movie series, North Carolina's 12th District kept coming back. The legislature drew new lines in response to *Shaw II*, and the new district was challenged as a racial gerrymander. The District Court concluded that it was, and granted summary judgment for the plaintiffs. The Supreme Court reversed and ordered the District Court to hold a trial. *Hunt v. Cromartie*, 526 U.S. 541 (1999). It did, and again found the 12th District unconstitutional. The Supreme Court reversed in EASLEY v. CROMARTIE, 532 U.S. 234 (2001). Justice Breyer wrote for the majority, but the key vote was Justice O'Connor, who for the first time voted to uphold a plan against a racial gerrymandering challenge. All the other justices voted as they had in *Shaw I*, *Miller v. Johnson*, *Bush v. Vera*, and *Shaw II*.

As Justice Breyer said at the outset of his opinion, "The issue in this case is evidentiary." Acknowledging that the issue was whether the District Court had committed "clear error" in finding that the predominant reason for the new District 12 was race, Justice Breyer wrote:

> The critical District Court determination—the matter for which we remanded this litigation—consists of the finding that race *rather than* politics *predominantly* explains District 12's 1997 boundaries. That determination rests upon three findings (the district's shape, its splitting of towns and counties, and its high African-American voting population) that we previously found insufficient to support summary judgment. Given the undisputed evidence that racial identification is highly correlated with political affiliation in North Carolina, these facts in and of themselves cannot, as a matter of law, support the District Court's judgment. See *Vera* (O'CONNOR, J., principal opinion) ("If district lines merely correlate with race because they are drawn on the basis of political affiliation, which correlates with race, there is no racial classification to justify").
>
> [The District Court gave some additional reasons for its conclusion based on evidence presented at trial, but after extensive analysis Justice Breyer found the evidence insufficient.]
>
> We concede the record contains a modicum of evidence offering support for the District Court's conclusion.... The evidence taken together, however, does

not show that racial considerations predominated in the drawing of District 12's boundaries. That is because race in this case correlates closely with political behavior. The basic question is whether the legislature drew District 12's boundaries because of race *rather than* because of political behavior (coupled with traditional, nonracial districting considerations).... We can put the matter more generally as follows: In a case such as this one where majority-minority districts (or the approximate equivalent) are at issue and where racial identification correlates highly with political affiliation, the party attacking the legislatively drawn boundaries must show at the least that the legislature could have achieved its legitimate political objectives in alternative ways that are comparably consistent with traditional districting principles. That party must also show that those districting alternatives would have brought about significantly greater racial balance. Appellees failed to make any such showing here. We conclude that the District Court's contrary findings are clearly erroneous. Because of this disposition, we need not address appellants' alternative grounds for reversal.

The judgment of the District Court is

Reversed.

Justice Thomas, joined by Chief Justice Rehnquist and Justices Kennedy and Scalia, dissented on the ground that the findings of the District Court were not clearly erroneous.

Notes and Questions

1. For commentary on the decision, see Melissa L. Saunders, *A Cautionary Tale:* Hunt v. Cromartie *and the Next Generation of* Shaw *Litigation*, 1 ELECTION LAW JOURNAL 173 (2002). For a perspective on the case written before the Court's decision, see Guy-Uriel E. Charles and Luis Fuentes-Rohwer, *Challenges to Racial Redistricting in the New Millennium:* Hunt v. Cromartie *as a Case Study*, 58 WASHINGTON & LEE LAW REVIEW 227 (2001).

2. All the previous racial gerrymandering cases whose merits had been given more than summary attention by the Supreme Court had been decided in favor of the plaintiffs by a 5–4 vote, with the same five justices constituting the majority. Why did Justice O'Connor cast her deciding vote to uphold the plan in *Easley*? Are there factual differences that warrant a different result in *Easley* from the previous cases? The factual analyses are long and have not been set forth here, but we do not believe major factual differences are apparent to the naked eye. Except, perhaps, for this. The other racial gerrymandering cases that were resolved by the Court on the merits were attacks on majority-minority districts that were either required as a condition of preclearance or that the states could anticipate would be required for that purpose. As our notes to those cases have pointed out, the state legislatures set out to meet quotas for majority-minority districts because they had no choice. But after *Shaw II*, there was no realistic possibility that a chastened Justice Department would deny preclearance for failure to create a second majority-minority district. Thus, the legislature at least had the option of being motivated by other considerations than race, such as partisanship. But neither the majority opinion in *Easley* nor the dissent mentions this difference.

3. In the last paragraph of his opinion for the Court, Justice Breyer says that a plaintiff in a racial gerrymandering case must show, among other things, that an alternative plan could be devised that would bring about "significantly greater racial balance." What does he mean by racial balance? Is a district racially unbalanced if a majority of residents are African-American? Why? If so, is a district in which a majority of residents are white

racially unbalanced? Why not? What does racial balance have to do with the premises of the racial gerrymandering doctrine as set forth in *Shaw v. Reno* and the later cases?

4. In *Cano v. Davis*, 211 F.Supp.2d 1208 (C.D. Cal. 2002), *summarily aff'd.*, 537 U.S. 1100 (2003), Latino plaintiffs asserted a *Shaw* claim against two California congressional districts represented by white Democrats. The plaintiffs alleged that to protect these incumbents against potential Latino challengers in primaries, the legislature removed sufficient Latino precincts from their districts to assure that the Latino percentage of the population did not exceed a certain amount. The three-judge District Court rejected this claim on a summary judgment motion, stating that a legislatively-imposed ceiling on the percentage of Latino residents in a district might implicate a dilution claim but not the "analytically distinct" claim of racial gerrymandering. In footnote 9 of its opinion the court made clear that it was not holding that only white plaintiffs could bring *Shaw* claims, but went on to explain:

> [T]he rationale underlying *Shaw* is simply inapplicable to the districts at issue here. Plaintiffs' two *Shaw* claims are not addressed to the types of districts ordinarily at issue in the Supreme Court's racial gerrymandering cases. For one, these are not race-based districts that "balkanize us into competing racial factions" or deliberately segregate voters into separate racial enclaves. *Shaw I*. They cannot, under any fair reading, be characterized as "white districts" or "Caucasian districts." Nor are they districts that can only be reasonably understood to "belong" to one ethnic or racial group.
>
> To the contrary, the districts at issue here are diverse and multi-ethnic: each contains a variety of racial and ethnic groups; none unites any single group of individuals within its boundaries for the purpose of permitting that group to exercise hegemony. In fact, Latinos are the largest number of persons in any single racial or ethnic group in each district, and the number of whites in each case is substantially lower.

5. As of mid-2008, plaintiffs had won almost no racial gerrymandering claims this decade, whether of the "reverse" variety attempted in *Cano* or of the more conventional type.[p] Does this mean *Easley* made it much more difficult for plaintiffs to win these cases? A more likely explanation is that the racial gerrymandering cases of the 1990s represented a judicial reaction (perhaps a very ham-handed one) to the Justice Department's extremely aggressive application of Section 5 of the Voting Rights Act, which provoked some state legislatures to take liberties with district shapes beyond what they typically had done previously, in order to satisfy the Justice Department without abandoning their other political objectives. The chastisement the Court administered to the Justice Department in the 1990s was sufficient to prevent a repetition of these events in the 2000s and is likely to be sufficient for that purpose in future decades. If so, it is very likely that the racial gerrymandering doctrine will prove a swallow of a single summer, already obsolete. Indeed, in the second and third editions the editors of this volume, no less prone than the next person to get caught up in popular delusions, devoted a separate chapter to the racial gerrymandering cases. Check out the fifth edition for signs of further withering away! But for the time being, we think it is best for students of the subject to know something about this odd incident that helped to enliven the 1990s.

One reason is that the justices seem willing to draw on concepts from the racial gerrymandering cases when doing so suits their purposes. Some of the dissenters in *Vieth v.*

---

p. A rare exception is *Clark v. Putnam County*, 293 F.3d 1261 (11th Cir. 2002).

Jubelirer, a partisan gerrymandering case we shall consider in Chapter 6, though consistent dissenters in the racial gerrymandering cases, had no compunctions against trying (unsuccessfully, so far) to import racial gerrymandering doctrine into the law of partisan gerrymandering. Another example is the following case, the Supreme Court's most recent major pronouncement on Section 2 of the Voting Rights Act. We deferred it to the end of this chapter because, as will appear, doctrine from the racial gerrymandering cases makes an appearance.

* * *

In Texas the legislature was unable to agree on a congressional districting plan after the 2000 census, so a federal court adopted a plan (Plan 1151C). The Republicans, who took control of the legislature in 2002, adopted a new plan (Plan 1374C) that was challenged by Democrats. Their challenge to the plan as a whole as a partisan gerrymander, together with more background on the politics of the plan, is described in the next chapter. Two districts, numbered 23 and 24, were also challenged as violations of Section 2 of the Voting Rights Act.

Justice Kennedy wrote the lead opinion. In Part IV of his opinion, in which he was joined by Chief Justice Roberts and Justice Alito, the challenge to District 24 was rejected. District 24, located in Dallas, had long been represented by senior (and white) Democrat Martin Frost.[q] The Republican plan dismembered his district and he was not reelected in 2004. Plaintiffs conceded that District 24 had not been a majority-minority district under Plan 1151C. They contended that African-Americans were able to control the Democratic primary, which was tantamount to control of the Democratically-oriented district. Therefore, they contended that the dismemberment of the district violated Section 2. Kennedy, Roberts and Alito rejected this theory of liability. They were joined in the result by Justices Scalia and Thomas, who adhered to the views in Thomas' concurrence in *Holder v. Hall*.

Much more complicated was the Court's treatment of District 23 in Part III of Kennedy's opinion, in which he wrote for the Court, as he was joined by Justices Breyer, Ginsburg, Souter, and Stevens:

League of United Latin American Citizens v. Perry
548 U.S. 399 (2006)

JUSTICE KENNEDY announced the judgment of the Court and delivered the opinion of the Court with respect to [Part III]....

III.

... After the 2002 election, it became apparent that District 23 as then drawn had an increasingly powerful Latino population that threatened to oust the incumbent Republican, Henry Bonilla. Before the 2003 redistricting, the Latino share of the citizen voting-age population was 57.5%, and Bonilla's support among Latinos had dropped with each successive election since 1996. In 2002, Bonilla captured only 8% of the Latino vote and 51.5% of the overall vote. Faced with this loss of voter support, the legislature acted to protect Bonilla's incumbency by changing the lines—and hence the population mix—

---

q. Earlier in his opinion Justice Kennedy noted, perhaps with irony intended, that Frost was the mastermind of a plan adopted in 1991, regarded by Republicans as a Democratic gerrymander. The pro-Democratic results continued in 2002 under the court-drawn plan. Perhaps Justice Kennedy found it fitting that Rep. Frost, who had lived by the gerrymandering sword, should die by it.

of the district. To begin with, the new plan divided Webb County and the city of Laredo, on the Mexican border, that formed the county's population base. Webb County, which is 94% Latino, had previously rested entirely within District 23; under the new plan, nearly 100,000 people were shifted into neighboring District 28. The rest of the county, approximately 93,000 people, remained in District 23. To replace the numbers District 23 lost, the State added voters in counties comprising a largely Anglo, Republican area in central Texas. In the newly drawn district, the Latino share of the citizen voting-age population dropped to 46%, though the Latino share of the total voting-age population remained just over 50%.

These changes required adjustments elsewhere, of course, so the State inserted a third district between the two districts to the east of District 23, and extended all three of them farther north. New District 25 is a long, narrow strip that winds its way from McAllen and the Mexican border towns in the south to Austin, in the center of the State and 300 miles away. In between it includes seven full counties, but 77% of its population resides in split counties at the northern and southern ends. Of this 77%, roughly half reside in Hidalgo County, which includes McAllen, and half are in Travis County, which includes parts of Austin. The Latinos in District 25, comprising 55% of the district's citizen voting-age population, are also mostly divided between the two distant areas, north and south. The Latino communities at the opposite ends of District 25 have divergent "needs and interests," owing to "differences in socio-economic status, education, employment, health, and other characteristics."

The District Court summed up the purposes underlying the redistricting in south and west Texas: "The change to Congressional District 23 served the dual goal of increasing Republican seats in general and protecting Bonilla's incumbency in particular, with the additional political nuance that Bonilla would be reelected in a district that had a majority of Latino voting age population—although clearly not a majority of citizen voting age population and certainly not an effective voting majority." The goal in creating District 25 was just as clear: "[t]o avoid retrogression under § 5" of the Voting Rights Act given the reduced Latino voting strength in District 23.

A

The question we address is whether Plan 1374C violates § 2 of the Voting Rights Act....

B

Appellants argue that the changes to District 23 diluted the voting rights of Latinos who remain in the district. Specifically, the redrawing of lines in District 23 caused the Latino share of the citizen voting-age population to drop from 57.5% to 46%. The District Court recognized that "Latino voting strength in Congressional District 23 is, unquestionably, weakened under Plan 1374C." The question is whether this weakening amounts to vote dilution.

To begin the *Gingles* analysis, it is evident that the second and third *Gingles* preconditions—cohesion among the minority group and bloc voting among the majority population—are present in District 23. The District Court found "racially polarized voting" in south and west Texas, and indeed "throughout the State." ...

The first *Gingles* factor requires that a group be "sufficiently large and geographically compact to constitute a majority in a single-member district." Latinos in District 23 could have constituted a majority of the citizen voting-age population in the district, and in fact did so under Plan 1151C. Though it may be possible for a citizen voting-age majority to lack real electoral opportunity, the Latino majority in old District 23 did possess electoral opportunity protected by § 2.

While the District Court stated that District 23 had not been an effective opportunity district under Plan 1151C, it recognized the district was "moving in that direction." Indeed, by 2002 the Latino candidate of choice in District 23 won the majority of the district's votes in 13 out of 15 elections for statewide officeholders. And in the congressional race, Bonilla could not have prevailed without some Latino support, limited though it was. State legislators changed District 23 specifically because they worried that Latinos would vote Bonilla out of office.

Furthermore, to the extent the District Court suggested that District 23 was not a Latino opportunity district in 2002 simply because Bonilla prevailed, it was incorrect. The circumstance that a group does not win elections does not resolve the issue of vote dilution. We have said that "the ultimate right of § 2 is equality of opportunity, not a guarantee of electoral success for minority-preferred candidates of whatever race." *De Grandy*. In old District 23 the increase in Latino voter registration and overall population, the concomitant rise in Latino voting power in each successive election, the near-victory of the Latino candidate of choice in 2002, and the resulting threat to the Bonilla incumbency, were the very reasons that led the State to redraw the district lines. Since the redistricting prevented the immediate success of the emergent Latino majority in District 23, there was a denial of opportunity in the real sense of that term.

Plan 1374C's version of District 23, by contrast, "is unquestionably not a Latino opportunity district." Latinos, to be sure, are a bare majority of the voting-age population in new District 23, but only in a hollow sense, for the parties agree that the relevant numbers must include citizenship. This approach fits the language of § 2 because only eligible voters affect a group's opportunity to elect candidates. In sum, appellants have established that Latinos could have had an opportunity district in District 23 had its lines not been altered and that they do not have one now.

Considering the district in isolation, the three *Gingles* requirements are satisfied. The State argues, nonetheless, that it met its § 2 obligations by creating new District 25 as an offsetting opportunity district. It is true, of course, that "States retain broad discretion in drawing districts to comply with the mandate of § 2." *Shaw v. Hunt (Shaw II)*. This principle has limits, though. The Court has rejected the premise that a State can always make up for the less-than-equal opportunity of some individuals by providing greater opportunity to others. See *id.* ("The vote-dilution injuries suffered by these persons are not remedied by creating a safe majority-black district somewhere else in the State"). As set out below, these conflicting concerns are resolved by allowing the State to use one majority-minority district to compensate for the absence of another only when the racial group in each area had a § 2 right and both could not be accommodated.

As to the first *Gingles* requirement, it is not enough that appellants show the possibility of creating a majority-minority district that would include the Latinos in District 23. See *Shaw II* (rejecting the idea that "a § 2 plaintiff has the right to be placed in a majority-minority district once a violation of the statute is shown"). If the inclusion of the plaintiffs would necessitate the exclusion of others, then the State cannot be faulted for its choice. That is why, in the context of a challenge to the drawing of district lines, "the first *Gingles* condition requires the possibility of creating more than the existing number of reasonably compact districts with a sufficiently large minority population to elect candidates of its choice." *De Grandy*.

The District Court found that the current plan contains six Latino opportunity districts and that seven reasonably compact districts could not be drawn. Appellant GI Forum presented a plan with seven majority-Latino districts, but the District Court found these districts were not reasonably compact, in part because they took in "disparate and distant communities." While there was some evidence to the contrary, the court's resolution of the conflicting evidence was not clearly erroneous.

A problem remains, though, for the District Court failed to perform a comparable compactness inquiry for Plan 1374C as drawn. *De Grandy* requires a comparison between a challenger's proposal and the "existing number of reasonably compact districts." To be sure, § 2 does not forbid the creation of a noncompact majority-minority district. *Bush v. Vera* (Kennedy, J., concurring). The noncompact district cannot, however, remedy a violation elsewhere in the State. See *Shaw II* (unless "the district contains a 'geographically compact' population" of the racial group, "where that district sits, 'there neither has been a wrong nor can be a remedy'" (quoting *Growe*)). Simply put, the State's creation of an opportunity district for those without a § 2 right offers no excuse for its failure to provide an opportunity district for those with a § 2 right. And since there is no § 2 right to a district that is not reasonably compact, see *Abrams v. Johnson*, 521 U.S. 74, 91 (1997), the creation of a noncompact district does not compensate for the dismantling of a compact opportunity district.

THE CHIEF JUSTICE claims compactness should be only a factor in the analysis, but his approach comports neither with our precedents nor with the nature of the right established by § 2. *De Grandy* expressly stated that the first *Gingles* prong looks only to the number of "reasonably compact districts." *Shaw II*, moreover, refused to consider a noncompact district as a possible remedy for a § 2 violation....

Apart from its conflict with *De Grandy* and *Shaw II*, THE CHIEF JUSTICE's approach has the deficiency of creating a one-way rule whereby plaintiffs must show compactness but States need not (except, it seems, when using § 2 as a defense to an equal protection challenge). THE CHIEF JUSTICE appears to accept that a plaintiff, to make out a § 2 violation, must show he or she is part of a racial group that could form a majority in a reasonably compact district. If, however, a noncompact district cannot make up for the lack of a compact district, then this is equally true whether the plaintiff or the State proposes the noncompact district.

The District Court stated that Plan 1374C created "six *Gingles* Latino" districts, but it failed to decide whether District 25 was reasonably compact for § 2 purposes. It recognized there was a 300-mile gap between the Latino communities in District 25, and a similarly large gap between the needs and interests of the two groups. After making these observations, however, it did not make any finding about compactness. It ruled instead that, despite these concerns, District 25 would be an effective Latino opportunity district because the combined voting strength of both Latino groups would allow a Latino-preferred candidate to prevail in elections. The District Court's general finding of effectiveness cannot substitute for the lack of a finding on compactness, particularly because the District Court measured effectiveness simply by aggregating the voting strength of the two groups of Latinos. Under the District Court's approach, a district would satisfy § 2 no matter how noncompact it was, so long as all the members of a racial group, added together, could control election outcomes.

The District Court did evaluate compactness for the purpose of deciding whether race predominated in the drawing of district lines. The Latinos in the Rio Grande Valley and those in Central Texas, it found, are "disparate communities of interest," with "differences in socio-economic status, education, employment, health, and other characteristics." The court's conclusion that the relative smoothness of the district lines made the district compact, despite this combining of discrete communities of interest, is inapposite because the court analyzed the issue only for equal protection purposes. In the equal protection context, compactness focuses on the contours of district lines to determine whether race was the predominant factor in drawing those lines. See *Miller v. Johnson*. Under § 2, by contrast, the injury is vote dilution, so the compactness inquiry embraces different considerations. "The first *Gingles* condition refers to the compactness of the minority population, not to the compactness of the contested district." *Vera* (KENNEDY, J., concurring).

While no precise rule has emerged governing § 2 compactness, the "inquiry should take into account 'traditional districting principles such as maintaining communities of interest and traditional boundaries.'" *Abrams*. The recognition of nonracial communities of interest reflects the principle that a State may not "assum[e] from a group of voters' race that they 'think alike, share the same political interests, and will prefer the same candidates at the polls.'" *Miller*. In the absence of this prohibited assumption, there is no basis to believe a district that combines two far-flung segments of a racial group with disparate interests provides the opportunity that § 2 requires or that the first *Gingles* condition contemplates. "The purpose of the Voting Rights Act is to prevent discrimination in the exercise of the electoral franchise and to foster our transformation to a society that is no longer fixated on race." *Georgia v. Ashcroft*. We do a disservice to these important goals by failing to account for the differences between people of the same race.

While the District Court recognized the relevant differences, by not performing the compactness inquiry it failed to account for the significance of these differences under § 2. In these cases the District Court's findings regarding the different characteristics, needs, and interests of the Latino community near the Mexican border and the one in and around Austin are well supported and uncontested. Legitimate yet differing communities of interest should not be disregarded in the interest of race. The practical consequence of drawing a district to cover two distant, disparate communities is that one or both groups will be unable to achieve their political goals. Compactness is, therefore, about more than "style points," *post* (opinion of ROBERTS, C. J.); it is critical to advancing the ultimate purposes of § 2, ensuring minority groups equal "opportunity ... to participate in the political process and to elect representatives of their choice." 42 U.S.C. § 1973(b). (And if it were just about style points, it is difficult to understand why a plaintiff would have to propose a compact district to make out a § 2 claim.) As witnesses who know the south and west Texas culture and politics testified, the districting in Plan 1374C "could make it more difficult for thinly financed Latino-preferred candidates to achieve electoral success and to provide adequate and responsive representation once elected." We do not question the District Court's finding that the groups' combined voting strength would enable them to elect a candidate each prefers to the Anglos' candidate of choice. We also accept that in some cases members of a racial group in different areas—for example, rural and urban communities—could share similar interests and therefore form a compact district if the areas are in reasonably close proximity. See *Abrams* (BREYER, J., dissenting). When, however, the only common index is race and the result will be to cause internal friction, the State cannot make this a remedy for a § 2 violation elsewhere. We emphasize it is the enormous geographical distance separating the Austin and Mexican-border communities, coupled with the disparate needs and interests of these populations—not either factor alone—that renders District 25 noncompact for § 2 purposes. The mathematical possibility of a racial bloc does not make a district compact.

Since District 25 is not reasonably compact, Plan 1374C contains only five reasonably compact Latino opportunity districts. Plan 1151C, by contrast, created six such districts. The District Court did not find, and the State does not contend, that any of the Latino opportunity districts in Plan 1151C are noncompact. Contrary to THE CHIEF JUSTICE's suggestion, moreover, the Latino population in old District 23 is, for the most part, in closer geographic proximity than is the Latino population in new District 25. More importantly, there has been no contention that different pockets of the Latino population in old District 23 have divergent needs and interests, and it is clear that, as set out below, the Latino population of District 23 was split apart particularly because it was becoming so cohesive. The Latinos in District 23 had found an efficacious political identity, while this would be an entirely new and difficult undertaking for the Latinos in District 25, given their geographic and other differences.

Appellants have thus satisfied all three *Gingles* requirements as to District 23, and the creation of new District 25 does not remedy the problem.

C

We proceed now to the totality of the circumstances, and first to the proportionality inquiry, comparing the percentage of total districts that are Latino opportunity districts with the Latino share of the citizen voting-age population. As explained in *De Grandy,* proportionality is "a relevant fact in the totality of circumstances." It does not, however, act as a "safe harbor" for States in complying with §2. If proportionality could act as a safe harbor, it would ratify "an unexplored premise of highly suspect validity: that in any given voting jurisdiction…, the rights of some minority voters under §2 may be traded off against the rights of other members of the same minority class."

The State contends that proportionality should be decided on a regional basis, while appellants say their claim requires the Court to conduct a statewide analysis. In *De Grandy,* the plaintiffs "passed up the opportunity to frame their dilution claim in statewide terms." Based on the parties' apparent agreement that the proper frame of reference was the Dade County area, the Court used that area to decide proportionality. In these cases, on the other hand, appellants allege an "injury to African American and Hispanic voters throughout the State." The District Court, moreover, expressly considered the statewide proportionality argument. As a result, the question of the proper geographic scope for assessing proportionality now presents itself.

We conclude the answer in these cases is to look at proportionality statewide. The State contends that the seven districts in south and west Texas correctly delimit the boundaries for proportionality because that is the only area of the State where reasonably compact Latino opportunity districts can be drawn. This argument, however, misunderstands the role of proportionality. We have already determined, under the first *Gingles* factor, that another reasonably compact Latino district can be drawn. The question now is whether the absence of that additional district constitutes impermissible vote dilution. This inquiry requires an "'intensely local appraisal'" of the challenged district. *Gingles.* A local appraisal is necessary because the right to an undiluted vote does not belong to the "minority as a group," but rather to "its individual members." *Shaw II.* And a State may not trade off the rights of some members of a racial group against the rights of other members of that group. See *De Grandy.* The question is therefore not "whether line-drawing in the challenged area as a whole dilutes minority voting strength," *post* (opinion of ROBERTS, C. J.), but whether line-drawing dilutes the voting strength of the Latinos in District 23.

The role of proportionality is not to displace this local appraisal or to allow the State to trade off the rights of some against the rights of others. Instead, it provides some evidence of whether "the political processes leading to nomination or election in the State or political subdivision are not equally open to participation." 42 U.S.C. §1973(b). For this purpose, the State's seven-district area is arbitrary. It just as easily could have included six or eight districts. Appellants have alleged statewide vote dilution based on a statewide plan, so the electoral opportunities of Latinos across the State can bear on whether the lack of electoral opportunity for Latinos in District 23 is a consequence of

Plan 1374C's redrawing of lines or simply a consequence of the inevitable "win some, lose some" in a State with racial bloc voting. Indeed, several of the other factors in the totality of circumstances have been characterized with reference to the State as a whole. *Gingles* (listing Senate Report factors). Particularly given the presence of racially polarized voting—and the possible submergence of minority votes—throughout Texas, it makes sense to use the entire State in assessing proportionality.

Looking statewide, there are 32 congressional districts. The five reasonably compact Latino opportunity districts amount to roughly 16% of the total, while Latinos make up 22% of Texas' citizen voting-age population.... Latinos are, therefore, two districts shy of proportional representation. There is, of course, no "magic parameter," *De Grandy*, and "rough proportionality," *id.*, must allow for some deviations. We need not decide whether the two-district deficit in these cases weighs in favor of a §2 violation. Even if Plan 1374C's disproportionality were deemed insubstantial, that consideration would not overcome the other evidence of vote dilution for Latinos in District 23. "[T]he degree of probative value assigned to proportionality may vary with other facts," *id.*, and the other facts in these cases convince us that there is a §2 violation.

District 23's Latino voters were poised to elect their candidate of choice. They were becoming more politically active, with a marked and continuous rise in Spanish-surnamed voter registration. In successive elections Latinos were voting against Bonilla in greater numbers, and in 2002 they almost ousted him. Webb County in particular, with a 94% Latino population, spurred the incumbent's near defeat with dramatically increased turnout in 2002. In response to the growing participation that threatened Bonilla's incumbency, the State divided the cohesive Latino community in Webb County, moving about 100,000 Latinos to District 28, which was already a Latino opportunity district, and leaving the rest in a district where they now have little hope of electing their candidate of choice.

The changes to District 23 undermined the progress of a racial group that has been subject to significant voting-related discrimination and that was becoming increasingly politically active and cohesive. The District Court recognized "the long history of discrimination against Latinos and Blacks in Texas," and other courts have elaborated on this history with respect to electoral processes.... In addition, the "political, social, and economic legacy of past discrimination" for Latinos in Texas may well "hinder their ability to participate effectively in the political process," *Gingles* (citing Senate Report factors).

Against this background, the Latinos' diminishing electoral support for Bonilla indicates their belief he was "unresponsive to the particularized needs of the members of the minority group." *Ibid.* (same). In essence the State took away the Latinos' opportunity because Latinos were about to exercise it. This bears the mark of intentional discrimination that could give rise to an equal protection violation. Even if we accept the District Court's finding that the State's action was taken primarily for political, not racial, reasons, the redrawing of the district lines was damaging to the Latinos in District 23. The State not only made fruitless the Latinos' mobilization efforts but also acted against those Latinos who were becoming most politically active, dividing them with a district line through the middle of Laredo.

Furthermore, the reason for taking Latinos out of District 23, according to the District Court, was to protect Congressman Bonilla from a constituency that was increasingly voting against him. The Court has noted that incumbency protection can be a legitimate factor in districting, see *Karcher v. Daggett,* but experience teaches that incumbency protection can take various forms, not all of them in the interests of the constituents. If the justification for incumbency protection is to keep the constituency intact so the officeholder is accountable for promises made or broken, then the protection seems to accord with concern for the voters. If, on the other hand, incumbency protection means excluding some voters from the district simply because they are likely to vote against the officeholder, the change is to benefit the officeholder, not the voters. By purposely redrawing lines around those who opposed Bonilla, the state legislature took the latter course. This policy, whatever its validity in the realm of politics, cannot justify the effect on Latino voters. See *Gingles* (citing Senate Report factor of whether "the policy underlying" the State's action "is tenuous"). The policy becomes even more suspect when considered in light of evidence suggesting that the State intentionally drew District 23 to have a nominal Latino voting-age majority (without a citizen voting-age majority) for political reasons. This use of race to create the façade of a Latino district also weighs in favor of appellants' claim.

Contrary to THE CHIEF JUSTICE's suggestion that we are reducing the State's needed flexibility in complying with § 2, the problem here is entirely of the State's own making. The State chose to break apart a Latino opportunity district to protect the incumbent congressman from the growing dissatisfaction of the cohesive and politically active Latino community in the district. The State then purported to compensate for this harm by creating an entirely new district that combined two groups of Latinos, hundreds of miles apart, that represent different communities of interest. Under § 2, the State must be held accountable for the effect of these choices in denying equal opportunity to Latino voters. Notwithstanding these facts, THE CHIEF JUSTICE places great emphasis on the District Court's statement that "new District 25 is 'a more effective Latino opportunity district than Congressional District 23 had been.'" Even assuming this statement, expressed in the context of summarizing witnesses' testimony, qualifies as a finding of the District Court, two points make it of minimal relevance. First, as previously noted, the District Court measured the effectiveness of District 25 without accounting for the detrimental consequences of its compactness problems. Second, the District Court referred only to how effective District 23 "had been," not to how it would operate today, a significant distinction given the growing Latino political power in the district.

Based on the foregoing, the totality of the circumstances demonstrates a § 2 violation. Even assuming Plan 1374C provides something close to proportional representation for Latinos, its troubling blend of politics and race—and the resulting vote dilution of a group that was beginning to achieve § 2's goal of overcoming prior electoral discrimination—cannot be sustained....

JUSTICE SCALIA, with whom JUSTICE THOMAS joins....

II

I would dismiss appellants' vote-dilution claims premised on § 2 of the Voting Rights Act of 1965 for failure to state a claim, for the reasons set forth in JUSTICE THOMAS's opinion, which I joined, in *Holder v. Hall*. As THE CHIEF JUSTICE makes clear, the Court's § 2 jurisprudence continues to drift ever further from the Act's purpose of ensuring minority voters equal electoral opportunities....

CHIEF JUSTICE ROBERTS, with whom JUSTICE ALITO joins.[r] ...

I must ... dissent from Part III of the Court's opinion. According to the District Court's factual findings, the State's drawing of district lines in south and west Texas caused the area to move from five out of seven effective Latino opportunity congressional districts,

---

r. We give only the introduction to Chief Justice Roberts' argument on District 23. The formidable whole contests Justice Kennedy's opinion point by point and extends for 21 pages in the U.S. Reports.

with an additional district "moving" in that direction, to *six* out of seven effective Latino opportunity districts. The end result is that while Latinos make up 58% of the citizen voting age population in the area, they control 85% (six of seven) of the districts under the State's plan.

In the face of these findings, the majority nonetheless concludes that the State's plan somehow dilutes the voting strength of Latinos in violation of §2 of the Voting Rights Act. The majority reaches its surprising result because it finds that Latino voters in one of the State's Latino opportunity districts—District 25—are insufficiently compact, in that they consist of two different groups, one from around the Rio Grande and another from around Austin. According to the majority, this may make it more difficult for certain Latino-preferred candidates to be elected from that district—*even though Latino voters make up 55% of the citizen voting age population in the district and vote as a bloc.* The majority prefers old District 23, despite the District Court determination that new District 25 is "a more effective Latino opportunity district than Congressional District 23 had been." The District Court based that determination on a careful examination of regression analysis showing that "the Hispanic-preferred candidate [would win] *every* primary and general election examined in District 25," compared to the only partial success such candidates enjoyed in former District 23.

The majority dismisses the District Court's careful factfinding on the ground that the experienced judges did not properly consider whether District 25 was "compact" for purposes of §2. But the District Court opinion itself clearly demonstrates that the court carefully considered the compactness of the minority group in District 25, just as the majority says it should have. The District Court recognized the very features of District 25 highlighted by the majority and unambiguously concluded, under the totality of the circumstances, that the district was an effective Latino opportunity district, and that no violation of §2 in the area had been shown.

Unable to escape the District Court's factfinding, the majority is left in the awkward position of maintaining that its *theory* about compactness is more important under §2 than the actual prospects of electoral success for Latino-preferred candidates under a State's apportionment plan. And that theory is a novel one to boot. Never before has this or any other court struck down a State's redistricting plan under §2, on the ground that the plan achieves the maximum number of possible majority-minority districts, but loses on style points, in that the minority voters in one of those districts are not as "compact" as the minority voters would be in another district were the lines drawn differently. Such a basis for liability pushes voting rights litigation into a whole new area—an area far removed from the concern of the Voting Rights Act to ensure minority voters an equal opportunity "to elect representatives of their choice." 42 U.S.C. §1973(b)....

Notes and Questions

1. Does Justice Kennedy provide support for importing the standards of the racial gerrymandering cases into analysis of Section 2? Is doing so warranted by the language of Section 2? By the intent of the Congress that amended Section 2 in 1982? By precedent? On other grounds? Justice Kennedy appears to have regarded it as highly significant that the Texas Legislature went to great lengths to protect Representative Bonilla, who had very little electoral support from Hispanic voters in an area that was becoming increasingly Hispanic. How does that background fit into the Section 2 analysis, and how much weight should it be given?

2. Why do two of the three justices who consistently voted to strike down districts under the racial gerrymandering cases dissent from a holding based on importing the

racial gerrymandering standards into Section 2 analysis? Why do the four justices who consistently dissented in those racial gerrymandering cases all join Justice Kennedy's opinion?

3. Whatever one thinks of the result in *Georgia v. Ashcroft*, the facts of that case illustrate that minority legislators sometimes have goals in redistricting in addition to maximizing the number of majority-minority districts. In *LULAC*, the plan was drawn by a Republican legislature, in which the minority members — predominantly Democratic — presumably had little say. But *LULAC* will apply to redistricting plans drawn up by both parties. In a Democratic legislature containing minority legislators with considerable influence, *LULAC* may reduce these legislators' ability to obtain majority-minority districts configured in accord with their own goals. Is that consideration relevant to the Section 2 analysis?

Chapter 6

Partisan Gerrymandering

Concern in the United States over parties' use or abuse of redistricting for their own purposes is almost as old as the parties themselves. The first section of this chapter examines partisan gerrymandering as a political phenomenon and the second section considers efforts—mostly unsuccessful—to enlist the aid of the federal courts to combat gerrymanders.

I. Defining and Identifying Gerrymanders

Districting criteria may be proposed on the ground that they have intrinsic merit, or on the ground that they will help prevent "gerrymandering." Gerrymandering has received various definitions, which tend to fall into either of two categories. The first type of definition refers to plans drafted with an improper intent. The second consists of plans that have unfair effects. Consider the following:

> Those who favor judicial policing of gerrymandering are fond of quoting Chief Justice Warren's statement in *Reynolds v. Sims*, that "fair and effective representation for all citizens is concededly the basic aim of legislative apportionment." For such writers the "gerrymander" is the antithesis of "fair and effective representation," and their definitions of "gerrymander" tend to be just as broad and vague as Chief Justice Warren's phrase with which they are so enamored. Thus, they define "gerrymandering" as "dilut[ing] the voting strength" of groups of voters,[22] as "excessive manipulation" of the shapes of districts,[23] as creation of an "unjustifiable advantage" for one party over others,[24] as "discriminat[ion] against" one group compared to others,[25] or in more down-to-earth language, as "the dishing of one political party by another."[26]
>
> Now, it is hard to defend dilution of voting strength, manipulation (especially *excessive* manipulation), unjustifiable advantages, discrimination, and dish-

---

22. Richard L. Engstrom, *Post-Census Representational Districting: The Supreme Court, "One Person, One Vote," and the Gerrymandering Issue,* 7 SOUTHERN UNIVERSITY LAW REVIEW 173, 207 (1981).

23. Charles Backstrom, Leonard Robins & Scott Eller, *Issues in Gerrymandering: An Exploratory Measure of Partisan Gerrymandering Applied to Minnesota,* 62 MINNESOTA LAW REVIEW 1121, 1122 n.7 (1978); see also Robert Erikson, *Malapportionment, Gerrymandering and Party Fortunes in Congressional Elections,* 66 AMERICAN POLITICAL SCIENCE REVIEW 1234, 1237 (1972).

24. *Id.* at 1129.

25. Bernard Grofman & Howard A. Scarrow, *Current Issues in Reapportionment,* 4 LAW & POLICY QUARTERLY 435, 454 (1982).

26. David Mayhew, *Congressional Representation: Theory and Practice in Drawing the Districts,* in REAPPORTIONMENT IN THE 1970's 249, 274 (Nelson Polsby ed., 1971).

ing of political parties. On the other hand, voting strength cannot be characterized as diluted unless it can be compared to a level of strength that is agreed to be normal; the drawing of lines cannot be characterized as manipulative (in a pejorative sense) unless there is a method of drawing lines that is agreed to be nonmanipulative; an advantage cannot be characterized as unjustifiable unless there is an agreed-upon standard of justification and, equally importantly, a state of affairs cannot be characterized as an "advantage" unless there is an agreed-upon state of affairs regarded as neutral; a state of affairs agreed to be nondiscriminatory is necessary before we can say a group is discriminated against; and one person's dishing may be another's self-defense.

In short, definitions of "gerrymandering" of the sort just canvassed raise questions but do not answer them. The questions are: What, if anything, constitutes a "neutral" districting plan, and how can we recognize a neutral plan when we see one? To find concrete meanings for the various writers' conceptions of gerrymandering we must consider the specific criteria they have proposed for legislative districting. If those criteria cannot be demonstrated to be neutral and cannot be employed to distinguish neutral from nonneutral plans, they have no legitimate claim to the public interest label and they should not serve in court or elsewhere to identify gerrymanders.

Daniel H. Lowenstein & Jonathan Steinberg, *The Quest for Legislative Districting in the Public Interest: Elusive or Illusory?* 33 UCLA Law Review 1, 9–11 (1985).

Now consider the following rejoinder:

The fundamental premise on which Lowenstein and Steinberg build is that something cannot be constitutionally unfair, unequal, and wrong unless there is a standard or measure of what is fair, equal, and right. They believe, therefore, that once they have shown that there is no single, objective, neutral set of electoral district boundaries for a given state with a given geography and demography, they will have shown that courts should not concern themselves with the constitutionality of district boundaries.

The fundamental premise is not, however, jurisprudentially sound nor does it reflect the actual, historical behavior of the Supreme Court....

[J]udges, and indeed all those called upon to make ethical decisions, are often in a position to identify *a* wrong without being able to define *the* right.

Martin Shapiro, *Gerrymandering, Unfairness, and the Supreme Court*, 33 UCLA Law Review 227, 227–28 (1985).

Notes and Questions

1. In *Legislature v. Reinecke*, reprinted in Chapter 4, we considered the criteria used by special masters in crafting California's legislative districts in the 1970s. Most of the districting criteria put forth by the California Supreme Court's masters and contained in article 21 of the California Constitution are of the type known as "formal" criteria. These are criteria that look to the characteristics of individual districts, such as their shapes (compactness and contiguousness) and the areas and populations that they enclose (conformity to municipal boundaries, community of interest). Many reformers have favored a different type of criterion, sometimes referred to as "result-oriented." Result-oriented criteria take into account the expected political consequences of the districts. Examples

are that the districts should promote partisan competition, that they should (depending on the reformer) protect incumbents or avoid protection of incumbents, and that they should yield proportional results.

For a sampling of the extensive literature proposing various districting criteria, see Bruce Adams, *A Model State Reapportionment Statute Process: The Continuing Quest for Fair and Effective Representation*, 14 HARVARD JOURNAL OF LEGISLATION 825 (1977); Bernard Grofman, *Criteria for Districting: A Social Science Perspective*, 33 UCLA LAW REVIEW 77 (1985); Gordon E. Baker, *Judicial Determination of Political Gerrymandering: A "Totality of Circumstances" Approach*, 3 JOURNAL OF LAW & POLITICS 1 (1986). For a skeptical view of many of the proposed criteria, see Lowenstein & Steinberg, *supra*.

2. Of the "formal" criteria, the one most often pointed to, especially in popular debate, is compactness. For most people, the surest sign of a gerrymander is an oddly-shaped district. However, it is not easy to articulate persuasive reasons why a compact district is superior to a noncompact district. Skepticism of compactness as a criterion is cogently expressed in *Shaw v. Hunt*, 861 F.Supp. 408, 472 n.60 (E.D.N.C. 1994):

> [Districts'] perceived "ugliness"—their extreme irregularity of shape—is entirely a function of an artificial perspective unrelated to the common goings and comings of the citizen-voter. From the mapmaker's wholly imaginary vertical perspective at 1:25,000 or so range, a citizen may well find his district's one-dimensional, featureless shape aesthetically "bizarre," "grotesque," or "ugly." But back down at ground or eye-level, viewing things from his normal closely-bounded horizontal perspective, the irregularity of outline or exact volume of the district in which he resides is not a matter of any great practical consequence to his conduct as citizen-voter. In the earth-bound, horizontal workaday world of his political and other lives, it surely never occurs to him—until aroused to dislike something else about his district or his representative—that the lines that include him with others in a particular electoral district wander irregularly rather than evenly to enclose them. What happens is that after every re-drawing of the lines of any of the various overlapping electoral districts in which he resides, he learns quickly enough (if interested enough), either by official notice or unofficially, that he is now in the same or a new district that is identified by a number. He has no idea where exactly on the earth's surface the lines of the district—mostly invisible from this live perspective—run throughout their course. Nor does he need to know in order to conduct his political affairs effectively as a citizen of the district. In due course he learns that candidates A and B are contending for his vote, learns what he wants to about them, re-learns where his present voting location is, casts his vote, and thereafter has whatever contact he wants with his representative, completely unaffected either by where exactly his district boundaries lie, his lack of exact knowledge of their location, or by any "ugliness" that may from the mapmaker's perspective result from their irregular shape.

One response from defenders of the criterion is that compactness should be required, not because a compact district is necessarily inherently superior, but because compactness is a relatively objective criterion whose requirement, like that of equal population, will restrict the ability of line-drawers to gerrymander. For a forceful statement of this viewpoint, see Daniel D. Polsby & Robert D. Popper, *The Third Criterion: Compactness as a Procedural Safeguard Against Partisan Gerrymandering*, 9 YALE LAW & POLICY REVIEW 301 (1991). However, compactness as an inherently desirable attribute has had some defenders. Consider, for example, the following statement from *Prosser v. Elections Board*, 793 F.Supp. 859 (W.D.Wis. 1992) (three-judge court, per curiam):

> The objections to bizarre-looking reapportionment maps are not aesthetic (except for those who prefer Mondrian to Pollock). They are based on a recognition that representative democracy cannot be achieved merely by assuring population equality across districts. To be an effective representative, a legislator must represent a district that has a reasonable homogeneity of needs and interests; otherwise the policies he supports will not represent the preferences of most of his constituents. There is some although of course not a complete correlation between geographical propinquity and community of interests, and therefore compactness and contiguity are desirable features in a redistricting plan. Compactness and contiguity also reduce travel time and costs, and therefore make it easier for candidates for the legislature to campaign for office and once elected to maintain close and continuing contact with the people they represent. Viewing legislators as agents and the electorate as their principal, we can see that compactness and contiguity reduce the "agency costs" of representative democracy. But only up to a point, for the achievement of perfect contiguity and compactness would imply ruthless disregard for other elements of homogeneity; would require breaking up counties, towns, villages, wards, even neighborhoods. If compactness and contiguity are proxies for homogeneity of political interests, so is making district boundaries follow (so far as possible) rather than cross the boundaries of the other political subdivisions in the state.

Prosser differed from *Shaw v. Hunt*, in that in *Prosser*, as in *Legislature v. Reinecke*, the legislature had failed to adopt a districting plan and it was necessary for the court to do so. In *Shaw v. Hunt* (which, by the way, was overruled by the Supreme Court in 1996, as was described in Chapter 5), the court was considering a challenge to a legislatively adopted plan. Could this difference help explain the greater regard for compactness expressed in *Prosser*?

Another formal criterion that is usually much less controversial than compactness is contiguity. Although some state constitutions call for compact districts, more call for contiguity, which is ordinarily understood to be a requirement whether or not it is specified. "Contiguous" is usually understood to mean, in the words of one dictionary definition, "touching or connected throughout in an unbroken sequence." Questions about contiguity, so understood, typically arise when those drawing a plan choose or are required to cross a body of water. Crossing water is required in the case of an island. It will be accepted without question in many situations, such as crossing a river, which may be necessary, for example, to avoid dividing a city. But what about a district that crosses a bay or lake without including the land in between? For example, would a district be contiguous if it included parts of San Francisco and Oakland but excluded the land around the northern and southern ends of San Francisco Bay?

A different conception of contiguity was suggested in *Wilkins v. West*, 571 S.E.2d 100 (Va. 2002). The lower court had invalidated a plan, not simply because the district crossed water, but because there was no publicly available transportation between the parts of the district without going through another district. The Supreme Court of Virginia reversed, explaining its position as follows:

> While ease of travel within a district is a factor to consider when resolving issues of compactness and contiguity, resting the constitutional test of contiguity solely on physical access within the district imposes an artificial requirement which re-

flects neither the actual need of the residents of the district nor the panoply of factors which must be considered by the General Assembly in the design of a district. Short of an intervening land mass totally severing two sections of an electoral district, there is no *per se* test for the constitutional requirement of contiguity. Each district must be examined separately.

How would you advise the legislative leadership of Virginia regarding the requirement of contiguity in the state constitution?

3. The United States inherited from Britain the so-called Westminster system of elections, in which legislators are elected, usually one apiece, from geographically defined districts, with the candidate receiving the most votes declared the winner. This system may have been inevitable in the Colonial and Revolutionary periods, when neither full-fledged political parties nor modern devices of transportation and communication existed.[a] Since a separate winner-take-all election occurs in each district, when the elections are run along party lines there is no assurance that the statewide vote for a given party will be proportionate to the number of legislative seats it wins. For example, a minority party that is outvoted by a small margin in a large number of districts might win 45% of the vote and only win 30% of the seats. Very few democratic countries in the world other than those inheriting their political institutions from Great Britain use the Westminster system. To varying degrees, most systems used in other countries are more likely than the Westminster system to yield proportional results. For commentary on a variety of systems, see Choosing an Electoral System: Issues and Alternatives (Arend Lijphart & Bernard Grofman, eds., 1984).

Just as the one person, one vote rule provided a relatively simple and far-reaching solution to the complex difficulties that seemed to be created by *Baker v. Carr*'s decision that malapportionment questions are justiciable, some have urged that the constitutional solution to the gerrymandering problem should be a requirement of proportional representation. See Ronald Rogowski, *Representation in Political Theory and in Law*, 91 Ethics 395 (1981); John R. Low-Beer, Comment, *The Constitutional Imperative of Proportional Representation*, 94 Yale Law Journal 163 (1984). Others have seen the prospect that there is no stopping point short of proportional representation as a good reason for the courts to avoid the question of gerrymandering. See Martin Shapiro, *supra*, 33 UCLA Law Review at 252–56; Peter H. Schuck, *The Thickest Thicket: Partisan Gerrymandering and Judicial Regulation of Politics*, 87 Columbia Law Review 1325 (1987).

Most reformers, recognizing that it is difficult to assure proportional results so long as the Westminster system is in use, have sought anti-gerrymandering criteria that do not require proportionality. One such proposal is that "symmetry" be required rather than proportionality. Symmetry may be satisfied even if one party receives a disproportionately large number of seats, so long as any other party receiving the same percentage of the vote would have received the same disproportionately large number of seats. For example, if Republicans win 60% of the seats with only 52% of the statewide vote, the results would be symmetrical so long as the Democrats would also be likely to win 60% of the seats if they won 52% of the votes. See, e.g., Richard G. Niemi & John Deegan, Jr., *A Theory of Political Districting*, 72 American Political Science Review 1304 (1978). For criticism of symmetry as a criterion, see Lowenstein & Steinberg, *supra*, 33 UCLA

---

a. Aside from such practical considerations, the district representational system may also have origins in medieval notions of corporate and group representation. See Lani Guinier, *Groups, Representation, and Race-Conscious Districting: A Case of the Emperor's Clothes*, 71 Texas Law Review 1589, 1603–5 (1993).

Law Review at 55–60. And for a claim by two prominent political scientists that advanced statistical methods can solve some of symmetry's problems, see Bernard Grofman & Gary King, *The Future of Partisan Symmetry as a Judicial Test for Partisan Gerrymandering after* LULAC v. Perry, 6 Election Law Journal 2 (2007).

The question of proportional representation is placed in a theoretical and historical framework in Sanford Levinson, *Gerrymandering and the Brooding Omnipresence of Proportional Representation: Why Won't It Go Away?* 33 UCLA Law Review 257 (1985).

4. A party's "seats/votes" ratio is often used in discussions of districting, whether to test a plan against criteria such as proportionality or symmetry, or simply to see how well a party seems to be treated by a particular districting plan. Indeed, the ratio is commonly used as a rhetorical device in political debate, as a plan is shown to be a partisan gerrymander because a given party received only x percent of the seats when it received x plus y percent of the votes. The seats/votes ratio is certainly relevant to the evaluation of a districting plan, but it must be examined with caution, for a number of reasons. One is that American legislative elections are only partly conducted on a party basis. As we shall see in Chapter 9, American voters are often inclined to vote for the candidates they prefer, regardless of party. Thus, normally Republican voters might vote for Democratic state legislators because of the personalities and issues at stake between the candidates in particular districts. Mechanical application of a seats/votes ratio would imply that those voters wanted a Democratically controlled state legislature, which might not reflect their intent at all.

A second reason for caution in interpreting a seats/votes ratio is more technical. In *Reynolds v. Sims*, the Court spoke interchangeably about equal numbers of *people* in districts and equal numbers of *voters*. As we saw in Chapter 3, the Court prefers, and almost all jurisdictions use, population rather than number of voters. Although it might seem at first that there would be little difference between the two, in fact they can vary enormously. Some areas have much higher percentages of people not eligible to vote, especially because they are too young or are not citizens. Furthermore, as we shall see in Chapter 7, people of lower socioeconomic status are less likely to register and vote than those who are wealthier and, especially, better educated. By and large, lower income areas with a large immigrant population and with large families—the areas likely to have the lowest ratio of voters to population—are likely to be the most Democratic areas, while wealthier areas with few immigrants are more likely to be Republican. Comparison of two California congressional districts in the first election after the 2000 census shows how significant these disparities can be. In the 34th District, located in Los Angeles and containing the most heavily Latino population of any California district, a total of 65,824 votes were cast in the 2002 House race, which was won by Democrat Lucille Roybal-Allard. In the rural counties of the northeastern corner of California that make up the 4th District, 228,506 people voted in a House race won by Republican John Doolittle. Yet the populations of these districts, based on the 2000 census, were identical: 639,088 in each district.

This tendency for more voters in suburban areas is compounded by another phenomenon. Though districts are designed to be equal in population as of the time of the census, districts grow in population at different rates as the decade wears on. The most rapidly growing areas, typically characterized by new suburban development, are often populated disproportionately by Republicans. The most Democratic areas, in inner cities, typically have little growth, or may even be declining in population.[b] See generally Bruce Cain, The Reapportionment Puzzle 75–76 (1984).

---

b. This phenomenon gives the Democrats an advantage as a decade proceeds. However, it is offset by the imperfections in the census that were described in Chapter 3. Roughly speaking, it is prob-

A seats/votes ratio that does not take these circumstances into account may be misleading. For example, suppose a state is divided into three equally populated congressional districts, one with 200,000 voters, all of whom vote for the Republican candidate, and two with 100,000 voters, in each of which the Democratic candidate receives all of the votes. A naive seats/votes approach would find that the Republicans received only a third of the seats despite winning half of the votes. But the disparity results from the population-based districting rule, not from gerrymandering.

This distortion can easily be avoided, though the necessary adjustment is rarely made when seats/votes ratios are deployed in public discussion of redistricting. The usual method of computing a party's vote percentage is simply to add up the votes for the party's candidates in all the districts, and divide that total by the statewide total of votes cast for the major party candidates. The adjusted method is to calculate the party's vote percentage *within* each district, and then take the average of the party's district percentages. In the above example, Republicans received a third of the adjusted total (the average of 100%, 0%, and 0%), exactly the same as their percentage of the seats. See generally Graham Gudgin & P.J. Taylor, SEATS, VOTES, AND THE SPATIAL ORGANIZATION OF ELECTIONS 56–57 (1979).

5. Some supporters of reform propose modifying the procedures by which redistricting is done instead of or in addition to imposing substantive criteria. See Bruce E. Cain, THE REAPPORTIONMENT PUZZLE (1984). Some reform procedures are internal to the state legislatures, such as requirements for public hearings, provision of adequate staff and data to the minority party, or requirement of a legislative supermajority to pass a districting bill. The latter proposal would tend to give each of the major parties an effective veto in states with a fairly close partisan balance.

Alternatively, the districting power may be taken away from the legislature, usually in favor of a commission. The method of choosing members has varied in different proposals and, in some states, commissions actually created. A sharp distinction is sometimes drawn between "bipartisan" commissions, on which the assent of both major parties would be needed for adoption of a plan, and "nonpartisan" commissions, which are directed to adopt a plan either without regard to political consequences or that will be "neutral" politically. New Jersey's redistricting plan for the 2000s, which passed 6–5 by a bipartisan panel—thanks to a "nonpartisan" tie-breaker chosen by the state Supreme Court—was upheld against a Voting Rights Act challenge. See *Page v. Bartels,* 248 F.3d 175 (3rd Cir. 2001). The challenge was supported by Republicans who believed that the individual selected to be the tie-breaker, a well-regarded political scientist from Princeton, had Democratic leanings.

An unusual process has had considerable impact in Illinois. In that state, if the legislative process fails, redistricting is referred to a Legislative Redistricting Commission, which contains four Republicans and four Democrats. By a random drawing, one member of the commission is given a tie-breaking vote. In 1981, this lottery occurred, and the Democrats won. Under the resulting plan, the Democrats were able to control both houses of the legislature for the rest of the decade. In 1991, when the Republicans won the lottery, there arose "[u]nrestrained shouts of joy, seldom heard from the GOP side of the House during the last decade." A Republican leader predicted it was "reasonable to expect that the Senate will become Republican and that there will be [GOP] gains in the

---

ably fair to say that early in a decade, Democrats suffer from the census undercount, but that later in the decade Republicans lose by the delay until the next census for population growth in their strongest areas to be reflected in a districting plan.

House." Rick Pearson & Hugh Dellios, "Republicans hit jackpot in legislative remap," *Chicago Tribune*, September 6, 1991, at 1, col. 1. Both of these predictions came true and the Republicans maintained control of the Illinois Senate through the 2000 election, after which the legislature again had to be redistricted. In 2001, the tables turned again and the Democrats won the lottery. Republicans brought a constitutional challenge to the whole system (sour grapes?), but the lottery procedure was upheld against substantive due process and equal protection challenges in *Winters v. Illinois State Board of Elections*, 197 F.Supp.2d 1110 (N.D. Ill. 2001), *summarily aff'd.*, 535 U.S. 967 (2002). For an overview of practices and procedures followed in the states for drawing U.S. House districts, see David Butler & Bruce Cain, CONGRESSIONAL REDISTRICTING: COMPARATIVE AND THEORETICAL PERSPECTIVES 91–107 (1992).

6. A different kind of "procedural" change that is espoused by some is to entrust the districting process to the automatic processes of a computer. One possibility would be to program the computer to create equally populated districts in a random manner. A variation on this idea is to test the partisan consequences of a plan adopted by the legislature or some other institution by considering the probability of these consequences resulting from a randomly-devised plan. See Richard L. Engstrom, *The Supreme Court and Equipopulous Gerrymandering: A Remaining Obstacle in the Quest for Fair and Effective Representation*, 1976 ARIZONA STATE LAW JOURNAL 277, 314–18. Randomly-generated plans would be subject to the objection that they would preclude proponents of formal criteria such as those set forth in the California Masters' report from seeking assurance that their favored criteria would be reflected in the plan. Randomness as a method for creating districts or as a test against which a districting plan should be measured is subject to the further objection that there is no assurance that the results most likely to be generated in a random process are the fairest. See Lowenstein & Steinberg, *supra*, 33 UCLA LAW REVIEW, at 61–64.

The objections to randomness as a methodology or test for redistricting may be summarized in the idea that it would take the politics out of a decision that many people believe involves the kind of competing interests and values that should be resolved politically. One proposal that attempts to avoid this objection is to require that districts be drawn automatically by a computer but to allow the legislature to decide on any number of general criteria that should be built into the program that guides the computer.

> What is intriguing about computer technology is its ability to force decision-makers into the position of fully obligating themselves before the fact to a verifiable program explicitly stating the aims and objectives of redistricting.
>
> If the technology indeed existed to run multiattribute problems so as to achieve globally optimal solutions to the reapportionment puzzle, then the material basis for forcing legislators into an externally constrained precommitment strategy would be at hand. The courts could obligate states to reduce their reapportionment objectives to a computer program before the final census data became available and to live with the consequences of the computer-automated redistricting. The controlling computer algorithm would make explicit and obvious the policy choices of the states in ways that would allow courts to review reasonably and intelligently the relevant choices for unconstitutional attributes. Reapportionment decisions could then be challenged on the basis of the constitutional legitimacy of the considerations taken into account in the program, rather than the claimed unfairness of the electoral outcomes.

Samuel Issacharoff, *Judging Politics: The Elusive Quest for Judicial Review of Political Fairness*, 71 Texas Law Review 1643, 1699 (1993). One difficulty, which Issacharoff acknowledges, is that current and immediately foreseeable technology may not permit such an automated process that would take into account more than a very small number of criteria. But the difficulties may be more formidable than Issacharoff admits.

> Proponents of automation assume that despite current shortcomings, finding the optimal redistricting plan simply requires the development of faster computers. [T]his assumption is false—in general, redistricting is a far more difficult mathematical problem than has been recognized. In fact, the redistricting problem is so computationally complex that it is unlikely that any mere increase in the speed of computers will solve it.

Micah Altman, *The Computational Complexity of Automated Redistricting: Is Automation the Answer?* 23 RUTGERS COMPUTER & TECHNOLOGY LAW JOURNAL 81, 82 (1997). Altman adds:

> Practical computer methods capable of guaranteeing optimal districts do not exist, and probably never will. In the real world, automated redistricting proceeds through educated guesses at solutions and crude attempts to describe representational goals with mathematical formulas. As a consequence, automation may not eliminate the opportunity to manipulate politically, but instead shift that opportunity toward those groups that have access to the most extensive computing facilities and expertise. At the same time, automation shrouds the manipulation in the illusion of neutrality and behind a cloud of technical details. Even if computing resources are equal, districts can be politically influenced by the choice of how to characterize values and how to arrive at specific plans.

Id. at 136. Aside from Altman's objections, not everyone would agree with Issacharoff that the "politics" of districting consists of the adoption of general criteria that can be implemented mechanically. Instead, some would argue, the political process consists of accommodating different interests and values through a mixed process of electoral competition and negotiation. Such a process could be expected to reflect, to varying degrees, the different criteria that are espoused within the jurisdiction, but neither the process nor the outcome would be bound by any consistent ordering of such criteria.

7. That redistricting can have a dramatic and sometimes decisive effect on the electoral prospects of individual incumbents and other aspirants for legislative office is beyond question. Nor does anyone doubt that a party has at least the opportunity to enhance its prospects if it controls the redistricting process. However, the magnitude and durability of this partisan advantage are matters of controversy and uncertainty. Some studies have found surprisingly few partisan effects of districting, while others have found at least moderate gains in some but not all of the states in which gerrymanders are said to have occurred. Most of the studies that have found partisan gains have found them to be short-lived. For two studies that contain references to earlier research, see Peverill Squire, *The Partisan Consequences of Congressional Redistricting*, 23 AMERICAN POLITICS QUARTERLY 229 (1995); Harry Basehart & John Comer, *Redistricting and Incumbent Reelection Success in Five State Legislatures*, 23 AMERICAN POLITICS QUARTERLY 241 (1995).

Following the redistricting around the country in 2001 and 2002, many observers have called this the decade of "incumbent gerrymanders," referring to districting plans in which neither party obtains major gains but the incumbents of both parties have their districts strengthened. This is often an easy goal for a legislature to pursue: technically, because exchange of Republican areas for Democratic areas in adjacent districts can benefit the incumbents of both parties, and politically, because incumbents of both parties will find such an arrangement attractive. A good example is California. In the 1980s, when the Democrats controlled the legislature and the governorship, the partisan plans they passed, especially for the House of Representatives, led to a political and legal debate that lasted nearly the entire decade. The Democrats again controlled the legislature and the governorship in 2001–02, but passed a plan that drew wide support from Republican as well as Democratic legislators.

For a provocative exchange on how courts ought to regard incumbent gerrymanders, see Samuel Issacharoff, *Gerrymandering and Political Cartels*, 116 Harvard Law Review 593 (2002); Nathaniel Persily, *In Defense of Foxes Guarding Henhouses: The Case for Judicial Acquiescence to Incumbent-Protecting Gerrymanders*, 116 Harvard Law Review 649 (2002); Samuel Issacharoff, *Surreply: Why Elections?*, 116 Harvard Law Review 684 (2002). A lawyer who has represented the Democrats in numerous redistricting controversies this decade argues that although most states have indeed adopted incumbency oriented plans, four major states—Florida, Michigan, Ohio and Pennsylvania—adopted Republican gerrymanders, with the result that in the nation as a whole, the Republicans start off with a head start in the fierce competition to control the House of Representatives. Sam Hirsch, *The United States House of Unrepresentatives: What Went Wrong in the Latest Round of Congressional Redistricting*, 2 Election Law Journal 179 (2003). Hirsch calls for more aggressive judicial supervision of partisan gerrymanders, a subject considered in the next section. There is irony in such a prominent Democrat taking the position that his Republican counterparts were taking twenty years ago, when the shoe was on the other foot. For an argument against aggressive judicial intervention, see Luis Fuentes-Rohwer, *Doing Our Politics in Court: Gerrymandering, "Fair Representation" and an Exegesis Into the Judicial Role*, 78 Notre Dame Law Review 527 (2003).

II. Gerrymandering and the Constitution

In DAVIS v. BANDEMER, 478 U.S. 109 (1986), the Supreme Court considered whether, and under what circumstances, a partisan gerrymander violates the Equal Protection Clause. As we shall see, the Court revisited the question in the more recent case of *Vieth v. Jubelirer* and again in *LULAC v. Perry*. In none of these cases has there been a majority opinion on the merits.

Bandemer was an appeal by Democrats who objected to a Republican-passed plan to redistrict the Indiana state legislature. In the background were controversies over congressional redistricting, especially in California, where Republicans objected strenuously to a plan enacted by Democrats. National Republicans filed amicus briefs in *Bandemer* supporting the Indiana Democrats while California Democrats weighed in to support the Republican-adopted Indiana plan. Who says parties don't take a disinterested view of constitutional questions?

The Supreme Court divided into three groups in *Bandemer*. The largest group consisted of Justice White, who wrote the plurality opinion, and Justices Blackmun, Brennan, and Marshall. The first question was whether a claim that a partisan gerrymander violates the Equal Protection Clause is justiciable. Justice White answered that question in the affirmative, and on that issue he wrote for the Court, because he was joined by Justices Powell and Stevens. Justice O'Connor wrote an opinion, joined by Chief Justice Burger and Justice Rehnquist, that the question was nonjusticiable.

On the merits, White and the plurality found the Indiana plan constitutional. Stevens wrote a dissenting opinion, joined by Powell. The four members of the plurality and the three justices who thought the issue was nonjusticiable made up a majority to uphold the Indiana plan. Outside of Indiana, the question that drew most attention was what the constitutional criteria were for adjudicating partisan gerrymandering cases. Everyone agreed that in effect, White's opinion governed, but the proper interpretation of that opinion proved controversial. Here are excerpts:

[T]he appellees' claim, as we understand it, is that Democratic voters over the State as a whole, not Democratic voters in particular districts, have been subjected to unconstitutional discrimination. Although the statewide discrimination asserted here was allegedly accomplished through the manipulation of individual district lines, the focus of the equal protection inquiry is necessarily somewhat different from that involved in the review of individual districts.

[I]n order to succeed the Bandemer plaintffs were required to prove both intentional discrimination against an identifiable political group and an actual discriminatory effect on that group. See, *e.g., Mobile v. Bolden*, 446 U.S. 55 (1980). Further, we are confident that if the law challenged here had discriminatory effects on Democrats, this record would support a finding that the discrimination was intentional....

Indeed, quite aside from the anecdotal evidence, the shape of the House and Senate Districts, and the alleged disregard for political boundaries, we think it most likely that whenever a legislature redistricts, those responsible for the legislation will know the likely political composition of the new districts and will have a prediction as to whether a particular district is a safe one for a Democratic or Republican candidate or is a competitive district that either candidate might win....

As long as redistricting is done by a legislature, it should not be very difficult to prove that the likely political consequences of the reapportionment were intended.... The District Court held that because any apportionment scheme that purposely prevents proportional representation is unconstitutional, Democratic voters need only show that their proportionate voting influence has been adversely affected. Our cases, however, clearly foreclose any claim that the Constitution requires proportional representation or that legislatures in reapportioning must draw district lines to come as near as possible to allocating seats to the contending parties in proportion to what their anticipated statewide vote will be.

[T]he mere fact that a particular apportionment scheme makes it more difficult for a particular group in a particular district to elect the representatives of its choice does not render that scheme constitutionally infirm. [T]he power to influence the political process is not limited to winning elections. An individual or a group of individuals who votes for a losing candidate is usually deemed to be adequately represented by the winning candidate and to have as much opportunity to influence that candidate as other voters in the district. We cannot presume in such a situation, without actual proof to the contrary, that the candidate elected will entirely ignore the interests of those voters. This is true even in a safe district where the losing group loses election after election. Thus, a group's electoral power is not unconstitutionally diminished by the simple fact of an apportionment scheme that makes winning elections more difficult, and a failure of proportional representation alone does not constitute impermissible discrimination under the Equal Protection Clause.

As with individual districts, where unconstitutional vote dilution is alleged in the form of statewide political gerrymandering, the mere lack of proportional representation will not be sufficient to prove unconstitutional discrimination. Again, without specific supporting evidence, a court cannot presume in such a case that those who are elected will disregard the disproportionately underrepresented group. Rather, unconstitutional discrimination occurs only when the electoral system is arranged in a manner that will consistently degrade a voter's or a group of voters' influence on the political process as a whole.

Although this is a somewhat different formulation than we have previously used in describing unconstitutional vote dilution in an individual district, the focus of both of these inquiries is essentially the same. [In a footnote, Justice White made it clear he was referring to and relying on racial districting cases.] In both contexts, the question is whether a particular group has been unconstitutionally denied its chance to effectively influence the political process. In a challenge to an individual district, this inquiry focuses on the opportunity of members of the group to participate in party deliberations in the slating and nomination of candidates, their opportunity to register and vote, and hence their chance to directly influence the election returns and to secure the attention of the winning candidate. Statewide, however, the inquiry centers on the voters' direct or indirect influence on the elections of the state legislature as a whole. And, as in individual district cases, an equal protection violation may be found only where the electoral system substantially disadvantages certain voters in their opportunity to influence the political process effectively. In this context, such a finding of unconstitutionality must be supported by evidence of continued frustration of the will of a majority of the voters or effective denial to a minority of voters of a fair chance to influence the political process.

Based on these views, we would reject the District Court's apparent holding that *any* interference with an opportunity to elect a representative of one's choice would be sufficient to allege or make out an equal protection violation, unless justified by some acceptable state interest that the State would be required to demonstrate. In addition to being contrary to the above-described conception of an unconstitutional political gerrymander, such a low threshold for legal action would invite attack on all or almost all reapportionment statutes. District-based elections hardly ever produce a perfect fit between votes and representation.

Justice White went on to enumerate several of the deficiencies in the evidence presented by the Democratic plaintiffs, given the standards that he had set forth. One statement in that portion of his opinion elicited considerable comment: "Relying on a single election to prove unconstitutional discrimination is unsatisfactory."

Notes and Questions

1. What is the nature of the inequality or discrimination that Justice White holds could violate the Equal Protection Clause? Is it an inequality in the weighting of votes? If so, why are most of the precedents to which Justice White refers race discrimination cases rather than the non-racial right to vote cases such as *Reynolds, Kramer,* and their progeny?

2. Justice O'Connor said in her opinion concurring in the result that Justice White calls for "at least some use of simple proportionality as the standard for measuring the normal representational entitlement of a political party." Do you agree? Some commentators predicted that a *de facto* requirement of proportional representation would be the likely outcome of the *Bandemer* decision. See Peter H. Schuck, *The Thickest Thicket: Par-*

tisan Gerrymandering and Judicial Regulation of Politics, 87 Columbia Law Review 1325 (1987).

3. Justice White's opinion prompted divergent interpretations. Perhaps the most common was that the opinion contains inadequate standards and thus provides little or no guidance to lower courts.

> Neither Justice White's nor Justice Powell's approach to the question of partisan apportionment gives any real guidance to lower courts forced to adjudicate this issue; thus, Justice O'Connor's apprehension that courts will resort to a standard of rough proportional representation appears well-founded.... Of course, the results that *Bandemer* will spawn remain uncertain, but the Court may well come to regret involving the judiciary so deeply in this delicate political sphere.

Laurence H. Tribe, American Constitutional Law 1083–84 (2d ed. 1988).

A second interpretation was based on one of the defects Justice White identified in the plaintiffs' showing:

> Disproportionality remains the underlying test of constitutionality; the plurality merely adds the requirement that any such disproportion obtain over the long term, not just in a single election. This added requirement, in turn, creates practical difficulties. Lacking prescience, and recognizing that political winds may shift in unpredictable directions, courts adjudicating political gerrymandering claims will need to consider the results of two or more elections before finding consistent degradation. In combination with the inherent delays of litigation, the amount of time needed for such evidence to accrue may preclude relief for any given gerrymander before the next decennial apportionment.

Note, *The Supreme Court, 1985 Term*, 100 Harvard Law Review 100, 161 (1986). However, that interpretation appears to be inconsistent with footnote 17 to Justice White's opinion (not reprinted above) that Justice Powell "incorrectly asserts that more than one election must pass before a successful racial or political gerrymandering claim may be brought.... *Projected* election results based on district boundaries and past voting patterns may certainly support this type of claim, even where *no* election has yet been held under the challenged districting."

Another interpretation maintained that the standard for partisan gerrymandering established in *Bandemer* was one of degree.

> [T]here *is* a clear and manageable standard in *Davis v. Bandemer*—one offered in the plurality opinion. Under it, for partisan gerrymandering to be unlawful, it must be (1) intentional, (2) severe, and (3) predictably nontransient in its effects.
>
> ... The Supreme Court plurality in *Bandemer* was walking a tightrope. It wanted to set standards high enough to strongly discourage frivolous suits but low enough so that the most egregious partisan gerrymanders could be overturned by the courts. In my view the Supreme Court has succeeded admirably in that balancing act.

Bernard Grofman, *Toward a Coherent Theory of Gerrymandering: Bandemer and Thornburg*, in Political Gerrymandering and the Courts 29, 30–31 (Bernard Grofman, ed., 1990).

Yet another proposed interpretation maintained that the gerrymandering claim recognized in *Bandemer* will rarely be available to the major political parties, because it is not gerrymandering per se that is prohibited, but gerrymandering aimed at groups that need particular protection under the Fourteenth Amendment.

A gerrymandering claim brought by a group not constituted by race or by some other classification that has been recognized as "suspect" for equal protection purposes must demonstrate that the group is the victim of pervasive discrimination in the political process to such a degree that it is reasonable to suppose a districting plan contrary to their interests is the result of prejudice and an animus well beyond the usual bounds of political opposition in our system.

There is one other possibility. If a case should arise in which a partisan gerrymander between established political parties should be so effective as to virtually guarantee a minority group permanent dominance over state government, comparable to the situation that existed in *Baker v. Carr* and some of the other malapportionment cases, that might be unconstitutional as well. It [was] not necessary [in *Bandemer*] to determine whether gerrymandering really is a powerful enough tool to produce such a result, nor to decide exactly what the theory supporting judicial intervention in such a case would be.

Daniel Lowenstein, *Bandemer's Gap: Gerrymandering and Equal Protection*, in POLITICAL GERRYMANDERING AND THE COURTS 64, 89–90 (Bernard Grofman, ed., 1990). Dean Alfange, *Gerrymandering and the Constitution: Into the Thorns of the Thicket at Last*, 1986 SUPREME COURT REVIEW 175, reaches a somewhat similar conclusion, but is highly critical of the *Bandemer* decision thus interpreted.

Some impetus was given to the last of these interpretations when it was adopted by a federal court rejecting a challenge to the congressional districting plan in California. The Supreme Court summarily affirmed the lower court's action. *Badham v. Eu*, 488 U.S. 1024 (1989). This action validated the result, but did not necessarily commit the Supreme Court to the lower court's reasoning.

4. Were the standards of *Davis v. Bandemer* applicable when a court was not reviewing the constitutionality of a plan but instead was required to create a plan of its own, or choose among plans tendered to it, because the legislature had failed to adopt a plan? Consider the following, from *Prosser v. Elections Board*, 793 F.Supp. 859 (W.D.Wis. 1992) (three-judge court, per curiam):

> [I]f we were reviewing an enacted plan we would pay little heed to cries of gerrymandering, because every reapportionment plan has some political effect, and so could be denounced as "gerrymandering" committed by the party that had pressed for its enactment. But we are not reviewing an enacted plan. An enacted plan would have the virtue of political legitimacy. We are comparing submitted plans with a view to picking the one (or devising our own) most consistent with judicial neutrality. Judges should not select a plan that seeks partisan advantage—that seeks to change the ground rules so that one party can do better than it would do under a plan drawn up by persons having no political agenda— even if they would not be entitled to invalidate an enacted plan that did so.

5. Challenges based on *Bandemer* met with little success. See *Fund for Accurate & Informed Representation v. Weprin*, 796 F.Supp. 662, 668–69 (N.D.N.Y.), *aff'd mem.* 506 U.S. 1017 (1992); *Illinois Legislative Redistricting Commission v. LaPaille*, 782 F.Supp. 1272, 1275–76 (N.D.Ill. 1991); *Republican Party of Virginia v. Wilder*, 774 F.Supp. 400, 403–6 (W.D.Va. 1991). Justice Scalia's plurality opinion in *Vieth v. Jubelirer* lists many more examples in his footnote 6, which we have omitted below.

6. In *Republican Party of North Carolina v. Martin*, 980 F.2d 943 (4th Cir. 1992), reh. denied 991 F.2d 1202 (1993), cert. denied 510 U.S. 828 (1993), plaintiffs challenged the

system of electing superior court judges in North Carolina. Nominees were selected in partisan primaries in the judicial districts in question, but the party nominees then ran against each other in statewide elections. Although some judicial districts had majorities of Republican voters or were competitive between Democratic and Republican voters, the statewide electorate was perceived to be safely Democratic in low level elections. Under this system, only one Republican superior court judge had been elected in North Carolina since 1900. Does the system deny equal protection to Republican voters? The court thought *Davis v. Bandemer* was controlling. Do you agree?

Vieth v. Jubelirer
541 U.S. 267 (2004)

Justice SCALIA announced the judgment of the Court and delivered an opinion, in which THE CHIEF JUSTICE, Justice O'CONNOR, and Justice THOMAS join.

Plaintiffs-appellants ... challenge a map drawn by the Pennsylvania General Assembly establishing districts for the election of congressional Representatives, on the ground that the districting constitutes an unconstitutional political gerrymander.[1] In *Davis v. Bandemer*, 478 U.S. 109 (1986), this Court held that political gerrymandering claims are justiciable, but could not agree upon a standard to adjudicate them. The present appeal presents the questions whether our decision in *Bandemer* was in error, and, if not, what the standard should be.

I

The facts, as alleged by the plaintiffs, are as follows. The population figures derived from the 2000 census showed that Pennsylvania was entitled to only 19 Representatives in Congress, a decrease in 2 from the Commonwealth's previous delegation. Pennsylvania's General Assembly took up the task of drawing a new districting map. At the time, the Republican party controlled a majority of both state Houses and held the Governor's office. Prominent national figures in the Republican Party pressured the General Assembly to adopt a partisan redistricting plan as a punitive measure against Democrats for having enacted pro-Democrat redistricting plans elsewhere. The Republican members of Pennsylvania's House and Senate worked together on such a plan. On January 3, 2002, the General Assembly passed its plan, which was signed into law by Governor Schweiker as Act 1.

Plaintiffs, registered Democrats who vote in Pennsylvania, brought suit in the United States District Court for the Middle District of Pennsylvania, seeking to enjoin implementation of Act 1.... The complaint alleged, among other things, that the legislation created malapportioned districts ... and that it constituted a political gerrymander, in violation of Article I and the Equal Protection Clause of the Fourteenth Amendment. With regard to the latter contention, the complaint alleged that the districts created by Act 1 were "meandering and irregular," and "ignor[ed] all traditional redistricting criteria, including the preservation of local government boundaries, solely for the sake of partisan advantage."

[The District Court ruled in favor of the plaintiffs on the population (malapportionment) claim, with negligible political consequences, as is described in Chapter 3. The District Court dismissed the partisan gerrymandering claim. Plaintiffs appealed to the Supreme Court.]

---

1. The term "political gerrymander" has been defined as "[t]he practice of dividing a geographical area into electoral districts, often of highly irregular shape, to give one political party an unfair advantage by diluting the opposition's voting strength." Black's Law Dictionary 696 (7th ed.1999).

II

Political gerrymanders are not new to the American scene. [Justice Scalia gives some examples from the colonial period.] The political gerrymander remained alive and well (though not yet known by that name) at the time of the framing. There were allegations that Patrick Henry attempted (unsuccessfully) to gerrymander James Madison out of the First Congress. And in 1812, of course, there occurred the notoriously outrageous political districting in Massachusetts that gave the gerrymander its name—an amalgam of the names of Massachusetts Governor Elbridge Gerry and the creature ("salamander") which the outline of an election district he was credited with forming was thought to resemble. "By 1840 the gerrymander was a recognized force in party politics and was generally attempted in all legislation enacted for the formation of election districts. It was generally conceded that each party would attempt to gain power which was not proportionate to its numerical strength." E. Griffith, The Rise and Development of the Gerrymander 123 (1974).

It is significant that the Framers provided a remedy for such practices in the Constitution. Article 1, §4, while leaving in state legislatures the initial power to draw districts for federal elections, permitted Congress to "make or alter" those districts if it wished.[3] Many objected to the congressional oversight established by this provision. In the course of the debates in the Constitutional Convention, Charles Pinckney and John Rutledge moved to strike the relevant language. James Madison responded in defense of the provision that Congress must be given the power to check partisan manipulation of the election process by the States:

> Whenever the State Legislatures had a favorite measure to carry, they would take care so to mould their regulations as to favor the candidates they wished to succeed. Besides, the inequality of the Representation in the Legislatures of particular States, would produce a like inequality in their representation in the Natl. Legislature, as it was presumable that the Counties having the power in the former case would secure it to themselves in the latter. What danger could there be in giving a controuling power to the Natl. Legislature?

Although the motion of Pinckney and Rutledge failed, opposition to the "make or alter" provision of Article I, §4—and the defense that it was needed to prevent political gerrymandering—continued to be voiced in the state ratifying debates.... The power bestowed on Congress to regulate elections, and in particular to restrain the practice of political gerrymandering, has not lain dormant. In the Apportionment Act of 1842, Congress provided that Representatives must be elected from single-member districts "composed of contiguous territory." See Griffith 12 (noting that the law was "an attempt to forbid the practice of the gerrymander"). Congress again imposed these requirements in the Apportionment Act of 1862, and in 1872 further required that districts "contai[n] as nearly as practicable an equal number of inhabitants." In the Apportionment Act of 1901, Congress imposed a compactness requirement. The requirements of contiguity, compactness, and equality of population were repeated in the 1911 apportionment legislation but were not thereafter continued. Today, only the single-member-district-requirement remains. See 2 U.S.C. §2c. Recent history, however, attests to Congress's awareness of the sort of districting practices appellants protest, and of its power under Article I, §4 to control them. Since 1980, no fewer than five bills have been introduced to regulate gerrymandering in congressional districting. Eighteen years ago, we held

---

3. Article I, §4, provides as follows:

The Times, Places and Manner of holding Elections for Senators and Representatives, shall be prescribed in each State by the Legislature thereof; but the Congress may at any time by Law make or alter such Regulations, except as to the Places of chusing Senators.

that the Equal Protection Clause grants judges the power — and duty — to control political gerrymandering, see *Davis v. Bandemer*. It is to consideration of this precedent that we now turn.

III

As Chief Justice Marshall proclaimed two centuries ago, "[i]t is emphatically the province and duty of the judicial department to say what the law is." *Marbury v. Madison,* 1 Cranch 137, 177 (1803). Sometimes, however, the law is that the judicial department has no business entertaining the claim of unlawfulness — because the question is entrusted to one of the political branches or involves no judicially enforceable rights. See, *e.g., Nixon v. United States,* 506 U.S. 224 (1993) (challenge to procedures used in Senate impeachment proceedings); *Pacific States Telephone & Telegraph Co. v. Oregon,* 223 U.S. 118 (1912) (claims arising under the Guaranty Clause of Article IV, §4). Such questions are said to be "nonjusticiable," or "political questions."

In *Baker v. Carr,* 369 U.S. 186 (1962), we set forth six independent tests for the existence of a political question:

> [1] a textually demonstrable constitutional commitment of the issue to a coordinate political department; or [2] a lack of judicially discoverable and manageable standards for resolving it; or [3] the impossibility of deciding without an initial policy determination of a kind clearly for nonjudicial discretion; or [4] the impossibility of a court's undertaking independent resolution without expressing lack of the respect due coordinate branches of the government; or [5] an unusual need for unquestioning adherence to a political decision already made; or [6] the potentiality of embarrassment from multifarious pronouncements by various departments on one question.

These tests are probably listed in descending order of both importance and certainty. The second is at issue here, and there is no doubt of its validity. "The judicial Power" created by Article III, §1, of the Constitution is not *whatever* judges choose to do, see *Valley Forge Christian College v. Americans United for Separation of Church and State, Inc.,* 454 U.S. 464 (1982), or even *whatever* Congress chooses to assign them, see *Lujan v. Defenders of Wildlife,* 504 U.S. 555, 576–577 (1992); *Chicago & Southern Air Lines, Inc. v. Waterman S.S. Corp.,* 333 U.S. 103, 110–114 (1948). It is the power to act in the manner traditional for English and American courts. One of the most obvious limitations imposed by that requirement is that judicial action must be governed by *standard, by rule.* Laws promulgated by the Legislative Branch can be inconsistent, illogical, and ad hoc; law pronounced by the courts must be principled, rational, and based upon reasoned distinctions.

Over the dissent of three Justices, the Court held in *Davis v. Bandemer* that, since it was "not persuaded that there are no judicially discernible and manageable standards by which political gerrymander cases are to be decided," such cases *were* justiciable. The clumsy shifting of the burden of proof for the premise (the Court was "not persuaded" that standards do not exist, rather than "persuaded" that they do) was necessitated by the uncomfortable fact that the six-Justice majority could not discern what the judicially discernable standards might be. There was no majority on that point. Four of the Justices finding justiciability believed that the standard was one thing (plurality opinion of White, J., joined by Brennan, Marshall, and Blackmun, J.); two believed it was something else (Powell, J., joined by STEVENS, J., concurring in part and dissenting in part). The lower courts have lived with that assurance of a standard (or more precisely, lack of assurance that there is no standard), coupled with that inability to specify a standard, for the past

18 years. In that time, they have considered numerous political gerrymandering claims; this Court has never revisited the unanswered question of what standard governs.

Nor can it be said that the lower courts have, over 18 years, succeeded in shaping the standard that this Court was initially unable to enunciate. They have simply applied the standard set forth in *Bandemer's* four-Justice plurality opinion. This might be thought to prove that the four-Justice plurality standard has met the test of time—but for the fact that its application has almost invariably produced the same result (except for the incurring of attorney's fees) as would have obtained if the question were nonjusticiable: judicial intervention has been refused. As one commentary has put it, "[t]hroughout its subsequent history, *Bandemer* has served almost exclusively as an invitation to litigation without much prospect of redress." S. Issacharoff, P. Karlan, & R. Pildes, The Law of Democracy 886 (rev.2d ed.2002). The one case in which relief was provided (and merely preliminary relief, at that) did *not* involve the drawing of district lines;[5] in *all* of the cases we are aware of involving that most common form of political gerrymandering, relief was denied. [In a footnote, Justice Scalia lists twenty lower court decisions in which this occurred.] Moreover, although the case in which relief was provided seemingly involved the *ne plus ultra* of partisan manipulation, see n. 5, *supra,* we would be at a loss to explain why the *Bandemer* line should have been drawn just there, and should not have embraced several districting plans that were upheld despite allegations of extreme partisan discrimination, bizarrely shaped districts, and disproportionate results. See, *e.g., Session v. Perry,* 298 F.Supp.2d 451 (E.D.Tex.2004) *(per curiam); O'Lear v. Miller,* 222 F.Supp.2d 850 (E.D.Mich.), summarily aff'd, 537 U.S. 997 (2002); *Badham v. Eu,* 694 F.Supp. 664, 670 (N.D.Cal.1988), summarily aff'd, 488 U.S. 1024 (1989). To think that this lower-court jurisprudence has brought forth "judicially discernible and manageable standards" would be fantasy.

Eighteen years of judicial effort with virtually nothing to show for it justify us in revisiting the question whether the standard promised by *Bandemer* exists. As the following discussion reveals, no judicially discernible and manageable standards for adjudicating political gerrymandering claims have emerged. Lacking them, we must conclude that political gerrymandering claims are nonjusticiable and that *Bandemer* was wrongly decided.

A

We begin our review of possible standards with that proposed by Justice White's plurality opinion in *Bandemer* because, as the narrowest ground for our decision in that case, it has been the standard employed by the lower courts. The plurality concluded that a political gerrymandering claim could succeed only where plaintiffs showed "both intentional discrimination against an identifiable political group and an actual discriminatory effect on that group." As to the intent element, the plurality acknowledged that "[a]s long as redistricting is done by a legislature, it should not be very difficult to prove that the likely political consequences of the reapportionment were intended." However, the effects prong was significantly harder to satisfy. Relief could not be based merely upon the fact that a group of persons banded together for political purposes had failed to achieve representation commensurate with its numbers, or that the apportionment scheme made its winning of elections more difficult. Rather, it would have to be shown that, taking into

---

5. See *Republican Party of North Carolina v. Martin. Martin* dealt with North Carolina's system of electing superior court judges statewide, a system that had resulted in the election of only a single Republican judge since 1900. Later developments in the case are described in n. 8, *infra.* [Additional information on *Martin* is contained in Note 6 preceding this case.—EDS.]

account a variety of historic factors and projected election results, the group had been "denied its chance to effectively influence the political process" as a whole, which could be achieved even without electing a candidate. It would not be enough to establish, for example, that Democrats had been "placed in a district with a supermajority of other Democratic voters" or that the district "departs from pre-existing political boundaries." Rather, in a challenge to an individual district the inquiry would focus "on the opportunity of members of the group to participate in party deliberations in the slating and nomination of candidates, their opportunity to register and vote, and hence their chance to directly influence the election returns and to secure the attention of the winning candidate." A statewide challenge, by contrast, would involve an analysis of "the voters' direct *or indirect* influence on the elections of the state legislature as a whole" (emphasis added). With what has proved to be a gross understatement, the plurality acknowledged this was "of necessity a difficult inquiry." In her *Bandemer* concurrence, Justice O'CONNOR predicted that the plurality's standard "will over time either prove unmanageable and arbitrary or else evolve towards some loose form of proportionality." A similar prediction of unmanageability was expressed in Justice Powell's opinion, making it the prognostication of a majority of the Court. That prognostication has been amply fulfilled.

In the lower courts, the legacy of the plurality's test is one long record of puzzlement and consternation.... The test has been criticized for its indeterminacy by a host of academic commentators. See, *e.g.,* L. Tribe, American Constitutional Law §13-9, p. 1083 (2d ed. 1988) ("Neither Justice White's nor Justice Powell's approach to the question of partisan apportionment gives any real guidance to lower courts forced to adjudicate this issue ..."); Still, Hunting of the Gerrymander, 38 UCLA L.Rev. 1019, 1020 (1991) (noting that the plurality opinion has "confounded legislators, practitioners, and academics alike"); Schuck, The Thickest Thicket: Partisan Gerrymandering and Judicial Regulation of Politics, 87 Colum. L.Rev. 1325, 1365 (1987) (noting that the *Bandemer* plurality's standard requires judgments that are "largely subjective and beg questions that lie at the heart of political competition in a democracy"); Issacharoff, Judging Politics: The Elusive Quest for Judicial Review of Political Fairness, 71 Texas L.Rev. 1643, 1671 (1993) ("*Bandemer* begot only confusion"); Grofman, An Expert Witness Perspective on Continuing and Emerging Voting Rights Controversies, 21 Stetson L.Rev. 783, 816 (1992) ("[A]s far as I am aware I am one of only two people who believe that *Bandemer* makes sense. Moreover, the other person, Daniel Lowenstein, has a diametrically opposed view as to *what* the plurality opinion means").[c] Because this standard was misguided when proposed, has not been improved in subsequent application, and is not even defended before us today by the appellants, we decline to affirm it as a constitutional requirement.

B

Appellants take a run at enunciating their own workable standard based on Article I, §2, and the Equal Protection Clause. We consider it at length not only because it reflects the litigant's view as to the best that can be derived from 18 years of experience, but also because it shares many features with other proposed standards, so that what is said of it may be said of them as well. Appellants' proposed standard retains the two-pronged framework of the *Bandemer* plurality—intent plus effect—but modifies the type of showing sufficient to satisfy each.

---

c. Might not the Court have bothered to inquire whether either of those interpretations of *Bandemer* actually did make sense of it? One of the editors of this volume believes that one of the interpretations did! —EDS.

To satisfy appellants' intent standard, a plaintiff must "show that the mapmakers acted with a *predominant intent* to achieve partisan advantage," which can be shown "by direct evidence or by circumstantial evidence that other neutral and legitimate redistricting criteria were subordinated to the goal of achieving partisan advantage." As compared with the *Bandemer* plurality's test of mere intent to disadvantage the plaintiff's group, this proposal seemingly makes the standard more difficult to meet—but only at the expense of making the standard more indeterminate.

"Predominant intent" to disadvantage the plaintiff political group refers to the relative importance of that goal as compared with all the other goals that the map seeks to pursue—contiguity of districts, compactness of districts, observance of the lines of political subdivision, protection of incumbents of all parties, cohesion of natural racial and ethnic neighborhoods, compliance with requirements of the Voting Rights Act of 1965 regarding racial distribution, etc. Appellants contend that their intent test *must* be discernible and manageable because it has been borrowed from our racial gerrymandering cases. See *Miller; Shaw v. Reno*. To begin with, in a very important respect that is not so. In the racial gerrymandering context, the predominant intent test has been applied to the challenged district in which the plaintiffs voted. See *Miller, United States v. Hays*. Here, however, appellants do not assert that an apportionment fails their intent test if any single district does so. Since "it would be quixotic to attempt to bar state legislatures from considering politics as they redraw district lines," appellants propose a test that is satisfied only when "partisan advantage was the predominant motivation *behind the entire statewide plan*." Vague as the "predominant motivation" test might be when used to evaluate single districts, it all but evaporates when applied statewide. Does it mean, for instance, that partisan intent must outweigh all other goals—contiguity, compactness, preservation of neighborhoods, etc.—*statewide*? And how is the statewide "outweighing" to be determined? If three-fifths of the map's districts forgo the pursuit of partisan ends in favor of strictly observing political-subdivision lines, and only two-fifths ignore those lines to disadvantage the plaintiffs, is the observance of political subdivisions the "predominant" goal between those two? We are sure appellants do not think so.

Even within the narrower compass of challenges to a single district, applying a "predominant intent" test to *racial* gerrymandering is easier and less disruptive. The Constitution clearly contemplates districting by political entities, see Article I, §4, and unsurprisingly that turns out to be root-and-branch a matter of politics. By contrast, the purpose of segregating voters on the basis of race is not a lawful one, and is much more rarely encountered. Determining whether the shape of a particular district is so substantially affected by the presence of a rare and constitutionally suspect motive as to invalidate it is quite different from determining whether it is so substantially affected by the excess of an ordinary and lawful motive as to invalidate it. Moreover, the fact that partisan districting is a lawful and common practice means that there is almost *always* room for an election-impeding lawsuit contending that partisan advantage was the predominant motivation; not so for claims of racial gerrymandering. Finally, courts might be justified in accepting a modest degree of unmanageability to enforce a constitutional command which (like the Fourteenth Amendment obligation to refrain from racial discrimination) is clear; whereas they are not justified in inferring a judicially enforceable constitutional obligation (the obligation not to apply *too much* partisanship in districting) which is both dubious and severely unmanageable. For these reasons, to the extent that our racial gerrymandering cases represent a model of discernible and manageable standards, they provide no comfort here.

The effects prong of appellants' proposal replaces the *Bandemer* plurality's vague test of "denied its chance to effectively influence the political process" with criteria that are seemingly more specific. The requisite effect is established when "(1) the plaintiffs show that the districts systematically 'pack' and 'crack' the rival party's voters, *and* (2) the court's examination of the 'totality of circumstances' confirms that the map can thwart the plaintiffs' ability to translate a majority of votes into a majority of seats." This test is loosely based on our cases applying §2 of the Voting Rights Act. see, *e.g.*, *Johnson v. De Grandy*. But a person's politics is rarely as readily discernible—and *never* as permanently discernible—as a person's race. Political affiliation is not an immutable characteristic, but may shift from one election to the next; and even within a given election, not all voters follow the party line. We dare say (and hope) that the political party which puts forward an utterly incompetent candidate will lose even in its registration stronghold. These facts make it impossible to assess the effects of partisan gerrymandering, to fashion a standard for evaluating a violation, and finally to craft a remedy.[8]

Assuming, however, that the effects of partisan gerrymandering can be determined, appellants' test would invalidate the districting only when it prevents a majority of the electorate from electing a majority of representatives. Before considering whether this particular standard is judicially manageable we question whether it is judicially discernible in the sense of being relevant to some constitutional violation. Deny it as appellants may (and do), this standard rests upon the principle that groups (or at least political-action groups) have a right to proportional representation. But the Constitution contains no such principle. It guarantees equal protection of the law to persons, not equal representation in government to equivalently sized groups. It nowhere says that farmers or urban dwellers, Christian fundamentalists or Jews, Republicans or Democrats, must be accorded political strength proportionate to their numbers.[9]

Even if the standard were relevant, however, it is not judicially manageable. To begin with, how is a party's majority status to be established? Appellants propose using the results of statewide races as the benchmark of party support. But as their own complaint describes, in the 2000 Pennsylvania statewide elections some Republicans won and some Democrats won. Moreover, to think that majority status in statewide races establishes majority status for district contests, one would have to believe that the only factor determining voting behavior at all levels is political affiliation. That is assuredly not true. As one law review comment has put it:

---

8. A delicious illustration of this is the one case we have found—alluded to above—that provided relief under *Bandemer*. See n. 5, *supra*. In *Republican Party of North Carolina v. Hunt*, 1996 WL 60439 (C.A.4, Feb.12, 1996) *(per curiam)* (unpublished) judgt. order reported at 77 F.3d 470, the district court, after a trial with no less than 311 stipulations by the parties, 132 witness statements, approximately 300 exhibits, and 2 days of oral argument, concluded that North Carolina's system of electing superior court judges on a statewide basis "had resulted in Republican candidates experiencing a consistent and pervasive lack of success and exclusion from the electoral process as a whole and that these effects were likely to continue unabated into the future." In the elections for superior court judges conducted just *five days* after this pronouncement, "every Republican candidate standing for the office of superior court judge was victorious at the state level," a result which the Fourth Circuit thought (with good reason) "directly at odds with the recent prediction by the district court," causing it to remand the case for reconsideration.

9. The Constitution also does not share appellants' alarm at the asserted tendency of partisan gerrymandering to create more partisan representatives. Assuming that assertion to be true, the Constitution does not answer the question whether it is better for Democratic voters to have their State's congressional delegation include 10 wishy-washy Democrats (because Democratic voters are "effectively" distributed so as to constitute bare majorities in many districts), or 5 hardcore Democrats (because Democratic voters are tightly packed in a few districts). Choosing the former "dilutes" the vote of the radical Democrat; choosing the latter does the same to the moderate. Neither Article I, §2, nor the Equal Protection Clause takes sides in this dispute.

There is no statewide vote in this country for the House of Representatives or the state legislature. Rather, there are separate elections between separate candidates in separate districts, and that is all there is. If the districts change, the candidates change, their strengths and weaknesses change, their campaigns change, their ability to raise money changes, the issues change—everything changes. Political parties do not compete for the highest statewide vote totals or the highest mean district vote percentages: They compete for specific seats.

Lowenstein & Steinberg, The Quest for Legislative Districting in the Public Interest: Elusive or Illusory, 33 UCLA L.Rev. 1, 59–60 (1985). See also Schuck, Partisan Gerrymandering: A Political Problem Without Judicial Solution, in Political Gerrymandering and the Courts 240, 241 (B. Grofman ed.1990).

But if we could identify a majority party, we would find it impossible to assure that that party wins a majority of seats—unless we radically revise the States' traditional structure for elections. In any winner-take-all district system, there can be no guarantee, no matter how the district lines are drawn, that a majority of party votes statewide will produce a majority of seats for that party. The point is proved by the 2000 congressional elections in Pennsylvania, which, according to appellants' own pleadings, were conducted under a judicially drawn district map "free from partisan gerrymandering." On this "neutral playing fiel[d]," the Democrats' statewide majority of the major-party vote (50.6%) translated into a minority of seats (10, versus 11 for the Republicans). Whether by reason of partisan districting or not, party constituents may always wind up "packed" in some districts and "cracked" throughout others. Consider, for example, a legislature that draws district lines with no objectives in mind except compactness and respect for the lines of political subdivisions. Under that system, political groups that tend to cluster (as is the case with Democratic voters in cities) would be systematically affected by what might be called a "natural" packing effect. Our one-person, one-vote cases, see *Reynolds v. Sims*; *Wesberry v. Sanders,* have no bearing upon this question, neither in principle nor in practicality. Not in principle, because to say that each individual must have an equal say in the selection of representatives, and hence that a majority of individuals must have a majority say, is not at all to say that each discernable group, whether farmers or urban dwellers or political parties, must have representation equivalent to its numbers. And not in practicality, because the easily administrable standard of population equality adopted by *Wesberry* and *Reynolds* enables judges to decide whether a violation has occurred (and to remedy it) essentially on the basis of three readily determined factors—where the plaintiff lives, how many voters are in his district, and how many voters are in other districts; whereas requiring judges to decide whether a districting system will produce a statewide majority for a majority party casts them forth upon a sea of imponderables, and asks them to make determinations that not even election experts can agree upon.

For these reasons, we find appellants' proposed standards neither discernible nor manageable.

C

For many of the same reasons, we also reject the standard suggested by Justice Powell in *Bandemer.* He agreed with the plurality that a plaintiff should show intent and effect, but believed that the ultimate inquiry ought to focus on whether district boundaries had been drawn solely for partisan ends to the exclusion of "all other neutral factors relevant to the fairness of redistricting." Under that inquiry, the courts should consider numerous factors, though "[n]o one factor should be dispositive." The most important would be "the shapes of voting districts and adherence to established political subdivision boundaries." "Other relevant considerations include the nature of the legislative procedures by which the apportionment law was adopted and legislative history reflecting contemporaneous legislative goals." These factors, which "bear directly on the fairness of a redistricting plan," combined with "evidence concerning population disparities and statistics tending to show vote dilution," make out a claim of unconstitutional partisan gerrymandering. While Justice Powell rightly criticized the *Bandemer* plurality for failing to suggest a constitutionally based, judicially manageable standard, the standard proposed in his opinion also falls short of the mark. It is essentially a totality-of-the-circumstances analysis, where all conceivable factors, none of which is dispositive, are weighed with an eye to ascertaining whether the particular gerrymander has gone too far — or, in Justice Powell's terminology, whether it is not "fair." "Fairness" does not seem to us a judicially manageable standard. Fairness is compatible with noncontiguous districts, it is compatible with districts that straddle political subdivisions, and it is compatible with a party's not winning the number of seats that mirrors the proportion of its vote. Some criterion more solid and more demonstrably met than that seems to us necessary to enable the state legislatures to discern the limits of their districting discretion, to meaningfully constrain the discretion of the courts, and to win public acceptance for the courts' intrusion into a process that is the very foundation of democratic decisionmaking.

IV

We turn next to consideration of the standards proposed by today's dissenters. We preface it with the observation that the mere fact that these four dissenters come up with three different standards — all of them different from the two proposed in *Bandemer* and the one proposed here by appellants — goes a long way to establishing that there is no constitutionally discernible standard.

[The dissenting opinions by Justices Stevens, Souter, and Breyer are long. Below we provide only brief excerpts in which each of the dissenters sets forth the standard he would apply. Following each of those excerpts we provide a brief excerpt from Justice Scalia's response.

Part V of Justice Scalia's opinion is a response to Justice Kennedy, the concurring justice. For the convenience of the reader, we set forth that portion of Justice Scalia's opinion following Justice Kennedy's opinion.]

VI

We conclude that neither Article I, §2, nor the Equal Protection Clause, nor (what appellants only fleetingly invoke) Article I, §4, provides a judicially enforceable limit on the political considerations that the States and Congress may take into account when districting.

Considerations of *stare decisis* do not compel us to allow *Bandemer* to stand. That case involved an interpretation of the Constitution, and the claims of *stare decisis* are at their weakest in that field, where our mistakes cannot be corrected by Congress. They are doubly weak in *Bandemer* because the majority's inability to enunciate the judicially discernible and manageable standard that it thought existed (or did not think did not exist) presaged the need for reconsideration in light of subsequent experience. And they are triply weak because it is hard to imagine how any action taken in reliance upon *Bandemer* could conceivably be frustrated — except the bringing of lawsuits, which is not the sort of primary conduct that is relevant.

While we do not lightly overturn one of our own holdings, "when governing decisions are unworkable or are badly reasoned, 'this Court has never felt constrained to follow precedent.'" Eighteen years of essentially pointless litigation have persuaded us that *Ban-*

demer is incapable of principled application. We would therefore overrule that case, and decline to adjudicate these political gerrymandering claims.

The judgment of the District Court is affirmed.

It is so ordered.

Justice KENNEDY, concurring in the judgment.

A decision ordering the correction of all election district lines drawn for partisan reasons would commit federal and state courts to unprecedented intervention in the American political process. The Court is correct to refrain from directing this substantial intrusion into the Nation's political life. While agreeing with the plurality that the complaint the appellants filed in the District Court must be dismissed, and while understanding that great caution is necessary when approaching this subject, I would not foreclose all possibility of judicial relief if some limited and precise rationale were found to correct an established violation of the Constitution in some redistricting cases.

When presented with a claim of injury from partisan gerrymandering, courts confront two obstacles. First is the lack of comprehensive and neutral principles for drawing electoral boundaries. No substantive definition of fairness in districting seems to command general assent. Second is the absence of rules to limit and confine judicial intervention. With uncertain limits, intervening courts—even when proceeding with best intentions—would risk assuming political, not legal, responsibility for a process that often produces ill will and distrust.

That courts can grant relief in districting cases where race is involved does not answer our need for fairness principles here. Those controversies implicate a different inquiry. They involve sorting permissible classifications in the redistricting context from impermissible ones. Race is an impermissible classification. See *Shaw*. Politics is quite a different matter. See *Gaffney*.

A determination that a gerrymander violates the law must rest on something more than the conclusion that political classifications were applied. It must rest instead on a conclusion that the classifications, though generally permissible, were applied in an invidious manner or in a way unrelated to any legitimate legislative objective.

The object of districting is to establish "fair and effective representation for all citizens." *Reynolds*. At first it might seem that courts could determine, by the exercise of their own judgment, whether political classifications are related to this object or instead burden representational rights. The lack, however, of any agreed upon model of fair and effective representation makes this analysis difficult to pursue.

The second obstacle—the absence of rules to confine judicial intervention—is related to the first. Because there are yet no agreed upon substantive principles of fairness in districting, we have no basis on which to define clear, manageable, and politically neutral standards for measuring the particular burden a given partisan classification imposes on representational rights. Suitable standards for measuring this burden, however, are critical to our intervention. Absent sure guidance, the results from one gerrymandering case to the next would likely be disparate and inconsistent.

In this case, we have not overcome these obstacles to determining that the challenged districting violated appellants' rights. The fairness principle appellants propose is that a majority of voters in the Commonwealth should be able to elect a majority of the Commonwealth's congressional delegation. There is no authority for this precept. Even if the novelty of the proposed principle were accompanied by a convincing rationale for its adoption, there is no obvious way to draw a satisfactory standard from it for measuring an alleged burden on representational rights. The plurality demonstrates the shortcomings of the other standards that have been considered to date. I would add two comments to the plurality's analysis. The first is that the parties have not shown us, and I have not been able to discover, helpful discussions on the principles of fair districting discussed in the annals of parliamentary or legislative bodies. Our attention has not been drawn to statements of principled, well-accepted rules of fairness that should govern districting, or to helpful formulations of the legislator's duty in drawing district lines.

Second, even those criteria that might seem promising at the outset (*e.g.,* contiguity and compactness) are not altogether sound as independent judicial standards for measuring a burden on representational rights. They cannot promise political neutrality when used as the basis for relief. Instead, it seems, a decision under these standards would unavoidably have significant political effect, whether intended or not. For example, if we were to demand that congressional districts take a particular shape, we could not assure the parties that this criterion, neutral enough on its face, would not in fact benefit one political party over another.

The challenge in finding a manageable standard for assessing burdens on representational rights has long been recognized. See Lowenstein & Steinberg, The Quest for Legislative Districting in the Public Interest: Elusive or Illusory? 33 UCLA L.Rev. 1, 74 (1985) ("[W]hat matters to us, and what we think matters to almost all Americans when district lines are drawn, is how the fortunes of the parties and the policies the parties stand for are affected. When such things are at stake there is no neutrality. There is only political contest"). The dearth of helpful historical guidance must, in part, cause this uncertainty.

There are, then, weighty arguments for holding cases like these to be nonjusticiable; and those arguments may prevail in the long run. In my view, however, the arguments are not so compelling that they require us now to bar all future claims of injury from a partisan gerrymander. It is not in our tradition to foreclose the judicial process from the attempt to define standards and remedies where it is alleged that a constitutional right is burdened or denied. Nor is it alien to the Judiciary to draw or approve election district lines. Courts, after all, already do so in many instances. A determination by the Court to deny all hopes of intervention could erode confidence in the courts as much as would a premature decision to intervene.

Our willingness to enter the political thicket of the apportionment process with respect to one-person, one-vote claims makes it particularly difficult to justify a categorical refusal to entertain claims against this other type of gerrymandering. The plurality's conclusion that absent an "easily administrable standard," the appellants' claim must be nonjusticiable contrasts starkly with the more patient approach of *Baker v. Carr,* not to mention the controlling precedent on the question of justiciability of *Davis v. Bandemer,* the case the plurality would overrule.

In *Baker* the Court made clear that the more abstract standards that guide analysis of all Fourteenth Amendment claims sufficed to assure justiciability of a one-person, one-vote claim....

The Court said this before the more specific standard with which we are now familiar emerged to measure the burden nonequipopulous districting causes on representational rights.... Even putting *Baker* to the side—and so assuming that the existence of a workable standard for measuring a gerrymander's burden on representational rights distinguishes one-person, one-vote claims from partisan gerrymandering claims for justiciability purposes—I would still reject the plurality's conclusions as to nonjusticiability. Relying on the distinction between a claim having or not having a workable standard of that sort involves a difficult proof: proof of a categorical negative. That is, the different treatment of claims otherwise so alike hinges entirely on proof that no standard could exist. This is a difficult proposition to establish, for proving a negative is a challenge in any context.

That no such standard has emerged in this case should not be taken to prove that none will emerge in the future. Where important rights are involved, the impossibility of full analytical satisfaction is reason to err on the side of caution. Allegations of unconstitutional bias in apportionment are most serious claims, for we have long believed that "the right to vote" is one of "those political processes ordinarily to be relied upon to protect minorities." *United States v. Carolene Products Co.,* 304 U.S. 144, 153, n. 4 (1938). If a State passed an enactment that declared "All future apportionment shall be drawn so as most to burden Party X's rights to fair and effective representation, though still in accord with one-person, one-vote principles," we would surely conclude the Constitution had been violated. If that is so, we should admit the possibility remains that a legislature might attempt to reach the same result without that express directive. This possibility suggests that in another case a standard might emerge that suitably demonstrates how an apportionment's *de facto* incorporation of partisan classifications burdens rights of fair and effective representation (and so establishes the classification is unrelated to the aims of apportionment and thus is used in an impermissible fashion).

The plurality says that 18 years, in effect, prove the negative. As Justice SOUTER is correct to point out, however, during these past 18 years the lower courts could do no more than follow *Davis v. Bandemer,* which formulated a single, apparently insuperable standard. Moreover, by the timeline of the law 18 years is rather a short period. In addition, the rapid evolution of technologies in the apportionment field suggests yet unexplored possibilities. Computer assisted districting has become so routine and sophisticated that legislatures, experts, and courts can use databases to map electoral districts in a matter of hours, not months. See, *e.g., Larios v. Cox,* 305 F.Supp.2d 1335 (N.D.Ga.2004). Technology is both a threat and a promise. On the one hand, if courts refuse to entertain any claims of partisan gerrymandering, the temptation to use partisan favoritism in districting in an unconstitutional manner will grow. On the other hand, these new technologies may produce new methods of analysis that make more evident the precise nature of the burdens gerrymanders impose on the representational rights of voters and parties. That would facilitate court efforts to identify and remedy the burdens, with judicial intervention limited by the derived standards.

If suitable standards with which to measure the burden a gerrymander imposes on representational rights did emerge, hindsight would show that the Court prematurely abandoned the field. That is a risk the Court should not take. Instead, we should adjudicate only what is in the papers before us.

Because, in the case before us, we have no standard by which to measure the burden appellants claim has been imposed on their representational rights, appellants cannot establish that the alleged political classifications burden those same rights. Failing to show that the alleged classifications are unrelated to the aims of apportionment, appellants' evidence at best demonstrates only that the legislature adopted political classifications. That describes no constitutional flaw, at least under the governing Fourteenth Amendment standard. See *Gaffney.* As a consequence, appellants' complaint alleges no impermissible use of political classifications and so states no valid claim on which relief may be granted. . . .

The plurality thinks I resolve this case with reference to no standard, but that is wrong. The Fourteenth Amendment standard governs; and there is no doubt of that. My analysis only notes that if a subsidiary standard could show how an otherwise permissible classification, as applied, burdens representational rights, we could conclude that appellants' evidence states a provable claim under the Fourteenth Amendment standard.

Though in the briefs and at argument the appellants relied on the Equal Protection Clause as the source of their substantive right and as the basis for relief, I note that the complaint in this case also alleged a violation of First Amendment rights. The First Amendment may be the more relevant constitutional provision in future cases that allege unconstitutional partisan gerrymandering. After all, these allegations involve the First Amendment interest of not burdening or penalizing citizens because of their participation in the electoral process, their voting history, their association with a political party, or their expression of political views. See *Elrod v. Burns*. Under general First Amendment principles those burdens in other contexts are unconstitutional absent a compelling government interest.... First Amendment concerns arise where a State enacts a law that has the purpose and effect of subjecting a group of voters or their party to disfavored treatment by reason of their views. In the context of partisan gerrymandering, that means that First Amendment concerns arise where an apportionment has the purpose and effect of burdening a group of voters' representational rights.

The plurality suggests there is no place for the First Amendment in this area. The implication is that under the First Amendment any and all consideration of political interests in an apportionment would be invalid. ("Only an equal protection claim is before us in the present case — perhaps for the very good reason that a First Amendment claim, if it were sustained, would render unlawful *all* consideration of political affiliation in districting"). That misrepresents the First Amendment analysis. The inquiry is not whether political classifications were used. The inquiry instead is whether political classifications were used to burden a group's representational rights. If a court were to find that a State did impose burdens and restrictions on groups or persons by reason of their views, there would likely be a First Amendment violation, unless the State shows some compelling interest. Of course, all this depends first on courts' having available a manageable standard by which to measure the effect of the apportionment and so to conclude that the State did impose a burden or restriction on the rights of a party's voters.

Where it is alleged that a gerrymander had the purpose and effect of imposing burdens on a disfavored party and its voters, the First Amendment may offer a sounder and more prudential basis for intervention than does the Equal Protection Clause. The equal protection analysis puts its emphasis on the permissibility of an enactment's classifications. This works where race is involved since classifying by race is almost never permissible. It presents a more complicated question when the inquiry is whether a generally permissible classification has been used for an impermissible purpose. That question can only be answered in the affirmative by the subsidiary showing that the classification as applied imposes unlawful burdens. The First Amendment analysis concentrates on whether the legislation burdens the representational rights of the complaining party's voters for reasons of ideology, beliefs, or political association. The analysis allows a pragmatic or functional assessment that accords some latitude to the States.

Finally, I do not understand the plurality to conclude that partisan gerrymandering that disfavors one party is permissible. Indeed, the Court seems to acknowledge it is not. This is all the more reason to admit the possibility of later suits, while holding just that the parties have failed to prove, under our "well developed and familiar" standard, that these legislative classifications "reflec[t] *no* policy, but simply arbitrary and capricious action." *Baker*. That said, courts must be cautious about adopting a standard that turns on whether the partisan interests in the redistricting process were excessive. Excessiveness is not easily determined. Consider these apportionment schemes: In one State, Party X controls the apportionment process and draws the lines so it captures every congressional seat. In three other States, Party Y controls the apportionment process. It is not so blatant or egregious, but proceeds by a more subtle effort, capturing less than all the seats in each State. Still, the total effect of Party Y's effort is to capture more new seats than Party X captured. Party X's gerrymander was more egregious. Party Y's gerrymander was more subtle. In my view, however, each is culpable.

* * *

The ordered working of our Republic, and of the democratic process, depends on a sense of decorum and restraint in all branches of government, and in the citizenry itself. Here, one has the sense that legislative restraint was abandoned. That should not be thought to serve the interests of our political order. Nor should it be thought to serve our interest in demonstrating to the world how democracy works. Whether spoken with concern or pride, it is unfortunate that our legislators have reached the point of declaring that, when it comes to apportionment, "'We are in the business of rigging elections.'" J. Hoeffel, Six Incumbents Are a Week Away from Easy Election, Winston-Salem Journal, Jan. 27, 1998, p. B1 (quoting a North Carolina state senator).

Still, the Court's own responsibilities require that we refrain from intervention in this instance. The failings of the many proposed standards for measuring the burden a gerrymander imposes on representational rights make our intervention improper. If workable standards do emerge to measure these burdens, however, courts should be prepared to order relief. With these observations, I join the judgment of the plurality.

[Following is Justice Scalia's response to Justice Kennedy, taken from Part V of the plurality opinion:

… The first thing to be said about Justice KENNEDY's disposition is that it is not legally available. The District Court in this case considered the plaintiffs' claims *justiciable* but dismissed them because the standard for unconstitutionality had not been met. It is logically impossible to affirm that dismissal without either (1) finding that the unconstitutional-districting standard applied by the District Court, or some other standard that it *should* have applied, has not been met, or (2) finding (as we have) that the claim is nonjusticiable. Justice KENNEDY seeks to affirm "[b]ecause, in the case before us, we have no standard." But it is *our* job, not the plaintiffs', to explicate the standard that makes the facts alleged by the plaintiffs adequate or inadequate to state a claim. We cannot nonsuit *them* for our failure to do so.

Justice KENNEDY asserts that to declare nonjusticiability would be incautious. Our rush to such a holding after a mere 18 years of fruitless litigation "contrasts starkly" he says, "with the more patient approach" that this Court has taken in the past. We think not. When it has come to determining what areas fall beyond our Article III authority to adjudicate, this Court's practice, from the earliest days of the Republic to the present, has been more reminiscent of Hannibal than of Hamlet.[d] [Justice Scalia gives historical examples as early as 1793 and as late as 1993.]

The only cases Justice KENNEDY cites in defense of his never-say-never approach are *Baker v. Carr* and *Bandemer*. *Bandemer* provides no cover. There, all of the Justices who concluded that political gerrymandering claims are justiciable proceeded to describe what

---

d. Hannibal was a Carthaginian general, known for his bold and decisive campaigns against the Romans. Hamlet is the eponymous hero of Shakespeare's tragedy, regarded by many as fatally indecisive. Not everyone agrees. See John Dover Wilson, WHAT HAPPENS IN HAMLET (1935).—Eds.

they regarded as the discernible and manageable standard that rendered it so. The lower courts were set wandering in the wilderness for 18 years not because the *Bandemer* majority thought it a good idea, but because five Justices could not agree upon a single standard, and because the standard the plurality proposed turned out not to work.

As for *Baker v. Carr*: It is true enough that, having had no experience *whatever* in apportionment matters of any sort, the Court there refrained from spelling out the equal-protection standard. (It did so a mere two years later in *Reynolds v. Sims*.) But the judgment under review in *Baker,* unlike the one under review here, did not *demand* the determination of a standard. The lower court in *Baker* had held the apportionment claim of the plaintiffs *nonjusticiable,* and so it was logically possible to dispose of the appeal by simply disagreeing with the nonjusticiability determination. As we observed earlier, that is not possible here, where the lower court has held the claim *justiciable* but unsupported by the facts. We must either enunciate the standard that causes us to agree or disagree with that merits judgment, or else affirm that the claim is beyond our competence to adjudicate.

Justice KENNEDY worries that "[a] determination by the Court to deny all hopes of intervention could erode confidence in the courts as much as would a premature decision to intervene." But it is the function of the courts to provide relief, not hope. What we think would erode confidence is the Court's refusal to do its job—announcing that there may well be a valid claim here, but we are not yet prepared to figure it out. Moreover, that course does more than erode confidence; by placing the district courts back in the business of pretending to afford help when they in fact can give none, it deters the political process from affording genuine relief. . . .

But the conclusive refutation of Justice KENNEDY's position is the point we first made: it is not an available disposition. We can affirm because political districting presents a nonjusticiable question; or we can affirm because we believe the correct standard which identifies unconstitutional political districting has not been met; we cannot affirm because we do not know what the correct standard is. Reduced to its essence, Justice KENNEDY's opinion boils down to this: 'As presently advised, I know of no discernible and manageable standard that can render this claim justiciable. I am unhappy about that, and hope that I will be able to change my opinion in the future." What are the lower courts to make of this pronouncement? We suggest that they must treat it as a reluctant fifth vote against justiciability at district and statewide levels—a vote that may change in some future case but that holds, for the time being, that this matter is nonjusticiable.

Justice STEVENS, dissenting.

The central question presented by this case is whether political gerrymandering claims are justiciable. Although our reasons for coming to this conclusion differ, five Members of the Court are convinced that the plurality's answer to that question is erroneous. . . .

In my judgment, the *Bandemer* Court was correct to entertain that statewide challenge, because the plaintiffs in that case alleged a group harm that affected members of their party throughout the State. In the subsequent line of racial gerrymandering cases, however, the Court shifted its focus from statewide challenges and required, as a matter of standing, that plaintiffs stating race-based equal protection claims actually reside in the districts they are challenging. Because *Hays* has altered the standing rules for gerrymandering claims—and because, in my view, racial and political gerrymanders are species of the same constitutional concern—the *Hays* standing rule requires dismissal of the statewide claim. . . .

In a challenge to a statewide districting plan, the plaintiff-appellants complain that they have been injured because of their membership in a particular, identifiable group....

A challenge to a specific district or districts, on the other hand, alleges a different type of injury entirely—one that our recent racial gerrymandering cases have recognized as cognizable.... Undergirding the *Shaw* cases is the premise that racial gerrymanders effect a constitutional wrong when they disrupt the representational norms that ordinarily tether elected officials to their constituencies as a whole....

[I]n evaluating a challenge to a specific district, I would apply the standard set forth in the *Shaw* cases and ask whether the legislature allowed partisan considerations to dominate and control the lines drawn, forsaking all neutral principles. Under my analysis, if no neutral criterion can be identified to justify the lines drawn, and if the only possible explanation for a district's bizarre shape is a naked desire to increase partisan strength, then no rational basis exists to save the district from an equal protection challenge....

[Justice Scalia, writing for the plurality, said in response: "Justice STEVENS's confidence that what courts have done with racial gerrymandering can be done with political gerrymandering rests in part upon his belief that "the same standards should apply." But in fact the standards are quite different. A purpose to discriminate on the basis of race receives the strictest scrutiny under the Equal Protection Clause, while a similar purpose to discriminate on the basis of politics does not."]

Justice SOUTER, with whom Justice GINSBURG joins, dissenting....

.... For a claim based on a specific single-member district, I would require the plaintiff to make out a *prima facie* case with five elements. First, the resident plaintiff would identify a cohesive political group to which he belonged, which would normally be a major party, as in this case and in *Davis*. There is no reason in principle, however, to rule out a claimant from a minor political party (which might, if it showed strength, become the target of vigorous hostility from one or both major parties in a State) or from a different but politically coherent group whose members engaged in bloc voting, as a large labor union might do....

Second, a plaintiff would need to show that the district of his residence, see *Hays*, paid little or no heed to those traditional districting principles whose disregard can be shown straightforwardly: contiguity, compactness, respect for political subdivisions, and conformity with geographic features like rivers and mountains....

Third, the plaintiff would need to establish specific correlations between the district's deviations from traditional districting principles and the distribution of the population of his group.... Fourth, a plaintiff would need to present the court with a hypothetical district including his residence, one in which the proportion of the plaintiff's group was lower (in a packing claim) or higher (in a cracking one) and which at the same time deviated less from traditional districting principles than the actual district. This hypothetical district would allow the plaintiff to claim credibly that the deviations from traditional districting principles were not only correlated with, but also caused by, the packing or cracking of his group. Drawing the hypothetical district would, of course, necessarily involve redrawing at least one contiguous district, and a plaintiff would have to show that this could be done subject to traditional districting principles without packing or cracking his group (or another) worse than in the district being challenged.

Fifth, and finally, the plaintiff would have to show that the defendants acted intentionally to manipulate the shape of the district in order to pack or crack his group....

A plaintiff who got this far would have shown that his State intentionally acted to dilute his vote, having ignored reasonable alternatives consistent with traditional districting principles. I would then shift the burden to the defendants to justify their decision by reference to objectives other than naked partisan advantage. They might show by rebuttal evidence that districting objectives could not be served by the plaintiff's hypothetical district better than by the district as drawn, or they might affirmatively establish legitimate objectives better served by the lines drawn than by the plaintiff's hypothetical....

[Justice Scalia responded: "While this five-part test seems eminently scientific, upon analysis one finds that each of the last four steps requires a quantifying judgment that is unguided and ill suited to the development of judicial standards: *How much* disregard of traditional districting principles? *How many* correlations between deviations and distribution? *How much* remedying of packing or cracking by the hypothetical district? *How many legislators* must have had the intent to pack and crack — and *how efficacious* must that intent have been (must it have been, for example, a *sine qua non* cause of the districting, or a *predominant* cause)? ... Justice SOUTER's proposal is doomed to failure for a more basic reason: No test — yea, not even a five-part test — can possibly be successful unless one knows what he is testing *for*.... He vaguely describes the harm he is concerned with as vote dilution, a term which usually implies some actual effect on the weight of a vote. But no element of his test looks to the effect of the gerrymander on the electoral success, the electoral opportunity, or even the political influence, of the plaintiff group. We do not know the precise constitutional deprivation his test is designed to identify and prevent.]

Justice BREYER, dissenting.

[T]here is at least one circumstance where use of purely political boundary-drawing factors can amount to a serious, and remediable, abuse, namely the *unjustified* use of political factors to entrench a minority in power. By entrenchment I mean a situation in which a party that enjoys only minority support among the populace has nonetheless contrived to take, and hold, legislative power. By *unjustified* entrenchment I mean that the minority's hold on power is purely the result of partisan manipulation and not other factors. These "other" factors that could lead to "justified" (albeit temporary) minority entrenchment include sheer happenstance, the existence of more than two major parties, the unique constitutional requirements of certain representational bodies such as the Senate, or reliance on traditional (geographic, communities of interest, etc.) districting criteria.

[P]olitical gerrymandering that so entrenches a minority party in power violates basic democratic norms and lacks countervailing justification. For this reason, whether political gerrymandering does, or does not, violate the Constitution in other instances, gerrymandering that leads to entrenchment amounts to an abuse that violates the Constitution's Equal Protection Clause.

[Justice Scalia wrote in response: "The criterion Justice BREYER proposes is nothing more precise than "the *unjustified* use of political factors to entrench a minority in power" (emphasis in original). While he invokes in passing the Equal Protection Clause, it should be clear to any reader that what constitutes *unjustified* entrenchment depends on his own theory of "effective government." While one must agree with Justice BREYER's incredibly abstract starting point that our Constitution sought to create a "basically democratic" form of government, that is a long and impassable distance away from the conclusion that the judiciary may assess whether a group (somehow defined) has achieved a level of political power (somehow defined) commensurate with that to which they would be entitled absent *unjustified* political machinations (whatever that means).”]

Notes and Questions

1. Justice Scalia notes that with the exception of *Republican Party of Martin*, all the lower court decisions after *Bandemer* denied the plaintiffs' partisan gerrymandering claims. Does the conclusion follow that *Bandemer* failed to set a manageable standard?

2. Justice Kennedy's opinion appears to be pivotal. Under that opinion, is it harder for a major party plaintiff to win a partisan gerrymandering case than it was under *Bandemer*? Is it easier?

3. As Justice Scalia notes, the four dissenters came up with three different definitions of partisan gerrymandering that they regarded as unconstitutional. Is Justice Scalia correct that this panoply of proposed standards is itself evidence that the issue is nonjusticiable? For the suggestion that the dissenters were laying out a range of choices in the hope that Justice Kennedy would select one of them, see Richard L. Hasen, *Looking for Standards (in All the Wrong Places): Partisan Gerrymandering Claims after* Vieth, 3 ELECTION LAW JOURNAL 626 (2004).

4. Justice Scalia quotes a famous passage from *Baker v. Carr* setting forth the reasons why a federal claim may be nonjusticiable. The plurality in *Vieth* bases its conclusion on the second reason, “a lack of judicially discoverable and manageable standards for resolving” the controversy. The Constitution gives Congress the power to direct the states with respect to the “time, place, and manner” of conducting House elections. Congress has exercised that power on a number of occasions, specifically with reference to redistricting. Would the plurality have been on stronger grounds if it had found nonjusticiability under *Baker*'s first reason, “a textually demonstrable constitutional commitment of the issue to a coordinate political department”? Note that such a ruling would not have required overruling *Davis v. Bandemer*, a challenge to a state legislative plan. For discussion, see Daniel H. Lowenstein, Vieth's *Gap: Has the Supreme Court Gone from Bad to Worse on Partisan Gerrymandering?*, 14 CORNELL JOURNAL OF LAW AND PUBLIC POLICY 367, 370–73 (2005).

5. Justice Kennedy suggests in *Vieth* that partisan gerrymandering might violate the First Amendment. In an unpublished opinion, a three-judge District Court rejected a challenge on this ground to a mid-decade Republican plan adopted for the Georgia State Senate:

> Plaintiffs make no attempt to relate the burden imposed on their ability to elect the candidate of their choosing to any restriction or limitation on their freedom of political expression. Nor can they; Plaintiffs are every bit as free under the new plan to run for office, express their political views, endorse and campaign for their favorite candidates, vote, or otherwise influence the political process through their expression. Instead, Plaintiffs essentially contend that the First Amendment entitles them to success in those endeavors. We reject that suggestion.

Kidd v. Cox, 2006 WL 1341302 (N.D. Ga. 2006). The court rejected a claim that the plan infringed the Democrats' freedom of association on similar grounds. “Georgia's redistricting plan ... has no effect on Plaintiffs' ability to field candidates for office, participate in campaigns, vote for their preferred candidate, or otherwise associate with others for the advancement of common political beliefs." Is the court's analysis responsive to Justice Kennedy's comments on the First Amendment in *Vieth*?

6. How should litigants and lower courts proceed under *Vieth*? Various answers have been suggested. Michael A. Carvin & Louis K. Fisher, *"A Legislative Task": Why Four Types of Redistricting Challenges Are Not, or Should Not Be, Recognized by Courts*, 4 ELECTION LAW JOURNAL 2, 3–12 (2005), claim that "political gerrymandering claims are effectively dead." Hasen, *supra*, asserts that plaintiffs will not and should not win partisan gerrymandering claims until an "emerging social consensus" forms around the issue. James A. Gardner, *A Post-*Vieth *Strategy for Litigating Partisan Gerrymandering Claims*, 3 ELECTION LAW JOURNAL 643 (2004) suggests that plaintiffs can seek relief in state courts, which will therefore have an opportunity to develop standards that might eventually satisfy a majority on the Supreme Court. Lowenstein, *supra*, argues that something cannot be replaced by nothing. Justice Kennedy's pivotal opinion was "nothing" in the sense that it declined to approve either a negative rule such as that favored by the plurality or a positive rule such as those favored by the dissenters. Lowenstein concludes: "*Bandemer* was in effect when *Vieth* came to the Court. *Bandemer* was something and the outcome in *Vieth*, thanks to Justice Kennedy, was nothing. Not having been replaced, *Bandemer* is still binding precedent."

7. A federal appellate judge has identified *Vieth* as an example of what he describes as a strong tendency on the part of the Rehnquist Court in its later years to "split the difference" in constitutional litigation. Thus, although four justices would have declared partisan gerrymandering nonjusticiable and four others would have imposed standards that might have invalidated the Pennsylvania congressional plan, Justice Kennedy's pivotal opinion took an in-between position of neither setting forth a standard for judging districting plans nor exempting plans from review. J. Harvie Wilkinson III, *The Rehnquist Court at Twilight: The Lures and Perils of Split-the-Difference Jurisprudence*, 58 STANFORD LAW REVIEW 1969 (2006). Judge Wilkinson gives strong reasons both for and against split-the-difference adjudication, but on balance he is critical of the practice. One of his criticisms is based on the premise of *Erie R.R. Co. v. Tompkins*, 304 U.S. 64 (1938), that there is "no federal general common law." Judge Wilkinson writes:

> To the extent that constitutional interpretation adopts common law methods, and encourages judges to build case by case a corpus of constitutional law from the contours of their own experience, it would seem that Justice Brandeis himself [the author of *Erie*] might find something amiss. For the wisest, most reflective common law judge was always subject to being corrected by the most impulsive state legislature.... To see the common law method in the absence of this democratic check—i.e., to see it as a model for constitutional interpretation— is to grant the Justices a power that classic common law judges never possessed.

Wherever Justice Kennedy expects to find a standard for assessing partisan gerrymandering, he does not suggest he intends to look for it by reading the Constitution more carefully. He is looking for a policy that he and a majority of the Court will find workable. If he finds it, that policy will be binding on all of the states, without regard to the wishes or opinions of any other body, elected or otherwise. Is his position then vulnerable to Wilkinson's criticism? Some supporters of judicial intervention would claim that even if Wilkinson's criticism is sound as applied to substantive issues such as the death penalty or abortion rights, the judiciary is needed to police political processes such as redistricting. How would they support that claim? Would you agree?

8. Additional commentary on *Vieth* includes Mitchell N. Berman, *Managing Gerrymandering*, 83 TEXAS LAW REVIEW 781 (2005); Richard Briffault, *Defining the Constitu-*

tional Question in Partisan Gerrymandering, 14 CORNELL JOURNAL OF LAW AND PUBLIC POLICY 397 (2005); Adam B. Cox, *Partisan Gerrymandering and Disaggregated Redistricting*, 2004 SUPREME COURT REVIEW 409 (2004); Luis Fuentes-Rohwer, *Domesticating the Gerrymander: An Essay on Standards, Fair Representation, and the Necessary Question of Judicial Will*, 14 CORNELL JOURNAL OF LAW AND PUBLIC POLICY 423 (2005); Heather K. Gerken, *Lost in the Political Thicket: The Court, Election Law, and the Doctrinal Interregnum*, 153 UNIVERSITY OF PENNSYLVANIA LAW REVIEW 503 (2004); Samuel Issacharoff & Pamela S. Karlan, *Where to Draw the Line?: Judicial Review of Political Gerrymanders*, 153 UNIVERSITY OF PENNSYLVANIA LAW REVIEW 541 (2004); Michael S. Kang, *The Bright Side of Partisan Gerrymandering*, 14 CORNELL JOURNAL OF LAW AND PUBLIC POLICY 443 (2005).

9. A contentious legal and political issue in the 2000s was whether it is proper for a state legislature to change a districting plan after the first election held during a decade. In Colorado, the legislature changed a court-drawn congressional plan following a Republican victory in the 2002 election. The Colorado Supreme Court struck down the plan on state-law grounds, ruling that the Colorado Constitution prohibited a second redistricting plan during the decade. *People ex rel. Salazar v. Davidson*, 79 P.3d 1221 (Colo. 2003), *cert. denied*, *Colorado General Assembly v. Salazar*, 541 U.S. 1093 (2004). Chief Justice Rehnquist wrote an opinion, joined by Justices Scalia and Thomas, dissenting from the denial of certiorari.

The same issue arose in New Hampshire. The legislature was unable to update its own districts after the 2000 election, so a court-drawn plan was used in 2002. The New Hampshire Supreme Court upheld under state law a plan that the new legislature adopted in 2004. *In re Below*, 855 A.2d 459 (N.H. 2004). The court held that the legislature had authority under the state constitution to adopt only a single plan each decade, but that its authority was not obviated by the occurrence of an election under a court-drawn plan.

The fiercest controversy was in Texas. As in Colorado and New Hampshire, a divided legislature and governor had failed to produce a congressional plan after the 2000 census. Republicans claimed that a court-drawn plan simply carried forward a Democratic gerrymander enacted in 1991. The Republicans won control of the state government in the 2002 elections and decided to turn the tables. The nation was entertained by the spectacle of Democratic legislators fleeing to Oklahoma and New Mexico to prevent the Republicans from obtaining a quorum. Eventually the Republicans succeeded in passing their plan and the Democrats challenged it on a number of grounds. A federal three-judge court rejected the Democratic challenge in *Session v. Perry*, 298 F.Supp.2d 451 (E.D.Tex. 2004).

On appeal, the Supreme Court vacated the decision and asked the lower court to reconsider it in light of *Vieth*. *Henderson v. Perry*, 543 U.S. 941 (2004). Democrats argued that whatever the difficulty of finding constitutional standards in the case of ordinary redistricting that stumped the Court in *Vieth*, a mid-decade redistricting should be treated differently. Once a plan has been adopted that satisfies one person, one vote, no new plan is necessary. Therefore, a new plan adopted by a legislature controlled by one party should be treated as presumptively void. The three-judge court rejected this and other arguments, reaffirming the constitutionality of the Texas plan.

The Supreme Court affirmed in *League of United Latin American Citizens (LULAC) v. Perry*, 548 U.S. 399 (2006). As we have seen in Chapter 5, one Texas congressional district was found to have violated Section 2 of the Voting Rights Act. But the issue that received the most public attention was partisan gerrymandering. On that issue, the Court upheld the plan.

The Court was even more fractured than in *Vieth*.[e] Justice Kennedy again wrote the pivotal opinion. In one paragraph joined by the four *Vieth* dissenters and therefore speaking for the Court, he wrote that he would not revisit the holding of *Bandemer* and *Vieth* that partisan gerrymandering claims are justiciable.[f] Proceeding for himself only, Justice Kennedy emphasized that "a lawful, legislatively enacted plan should be preferable to one drawn by the courts," because "to prefer a court-drawn plan to a legislature's replacement would be contrary to the ordinary and proper operation of the political process."[g] In Part II-C of his opinion, Kennedy addressed the main arguments made by the Democrats against the Texas mid-decade redistricting:

> A rule, or perhaps a presumption, of invalidity when a mid-decade redistricting plan is adopted solely for partisan motivations is a salutary one, in appellants' view, for then courts need not inquire about, nor parties prove, the discriminatory effects of partisan gerrymandering—a matter that has proved elusive since *Bandemer*. Adding to the test's simplicity is that it does not quibble with the drawing of individual district lines but challenges the decision to redistrict at all.

> For a number of reasons, appellants' case for adopting their test is not convincing. To begin with, the state appellees dispute the assertion that partisan gain was the "sole" motivation for the decision to replace [the court-drawn plan that was in effect in 2002]. There is some merit to that criticism, for the pejorative label overlooks indications that partisan motives did not dictate the plan in its entirety. The legislature does seem to have decided to redistrict with the sole purpose of achieving a Republican congressional majority, but partisan aims did not guide every line it drew....

> Evaluating the legality of acts arising out of mixed motives can be complex, and affixing a single label to those acts can be hazardous.... We are skeptical, however, of a claim that seeks to invalidate a statute based on a legislature's unlawful motive but does so without reference to the content of the legislation enacted.

> Even setting this skepticism aside, a successful claim attempting to identify unconstitutional acts of partisan gerrymandering must do what appellants' sole-motivation theory explicitly disavows: show a burden, as measured by a reliable standard, on the complainants' representational rights. For this reason, a majority of the Court rejected a test proposed in *Vieth* that is markedly similar to the one appellants present today. [Kennedy's references to *Vieth* make it clear that the rejected test he is referring to is the one put forward by Justice Stevens.]

> The sole-intent standard offered here is no more compelling when it is linked to the circumstance that [the plan] is mid-decennial legislation. The text and structure of the Constitution and our case law indicate there is nothing inherently suspect about a legislature's decision to replace mid-decade a court-ordered plan with one of its own.[h] And even if there were, the fact of mid-decade redistricting alone is no sure indication of unlawful political

---

e. Even Part I of Justice Kennedy's lead opinion, which simply described the facts and background of the case, was joined only by Chief Justice Roberts and Justice Alito.

f. Part II-A of Kennedy's opinion.

g. Part II-B.

h. Suppose Party A controls the legislature after a census and adopts a partisan plan. Party B wins control in a later election that decade and adopts a new partisan plan benefiting itself. If Party A challenges the mid-decade plan, how does Kennedy's opinion in *LULAC* bear on the controversy? — Eds.

gerrymanders. Under appellants' theory, a highly effective partisan gerrymander that coincided with decennial redistricting would receive less scrutiny than a bumbling, yet solely partisan, mid-decade redistricting. More concretely, the test would leave untouched the 1991 Texas redistricting, which entrenched a party on the verge of minority status, while striking down the 2003 redistricting plan, which resulted in the majority Republican Party capturing a larger share of the seats. A test that treats these two similarly effective power plays in such different ways does not have the reliability appellants ascribe to it.

Furthermore, compared to the map challenged in *Vieth*, which led to a Republican majority in the congressional delegation despite a Democratic majority in the statewide vote, [the Texas plan] can be seen as making the party balance more congruent to statewide party power. To be sure, there is no constitutional requirement of proportional representation, and equating a party's statewide share of the vote with its portion of the congressional delegation is a rough measure at best. Nevertheless, a congressional plan that more closely reflects the distribution of state party power seems a less likely vehicle for partisan discrimination than one that entrenches an electoral minority. By this measure, [the Texas plan] can be seen as fairer than the plan that survived in *Vieth* and the two previous Texas plans—all three of which would pass the modified sole-intent test that [the Texas plan] would fail.

A brief for one of the *amici* proposes a symmetry standard that would measure partisan bias by "compar[ing] how both parties would fare hypothetically if they each (in turn) had received a given percentage of the vote."[i] Under that standard the measure of a map's bias is the extent to which a majority party would fare better than the minority party should their respective shares of the vote reverse. In our view *amici*'s proposed standard does not compensate for appellants' failure to provide a reliable standard of fairness. The existence or degree of asymmetry may in large part depend on conjecture about where possible vote-switchers will reside. Even assuming a court could choose reliably among different models of shifting voter preferences, we are wary of adopting a constitutional standard that invalidates a map based on unfair results that would occur in a hypothetical state of affairs. Presumably such a challenge could be litigated if and when the feared inequity arose. More fundamentally, the counterfactual plaintiff would face the same problem as the present, actual appellants: providing a standard for deciding how much partisan dominance is too much. Without altogether discounting its utility in redistricting planning and litigation, we conclude asymmetry alone is not a reliable measure of unconstitutional partisanship.

In the absence of any other workable test for judging partisan gerrymanders, one effect of appellants' focus on mid-decade redistricting could be to encourage partisan excess at the outset of the decade, when a legislature redistricts pursuant to its decennial constitutional duty and is then immune from the charge of sole-motivation. If mid-decade redistricting were barred or at least subject to close judicial oversight, opposition legislators would also have every incentive to prevent passage of a legislative plan and try their luck with a court that might give them a better deal than negotiation with their political rivals.[j]

---

i. For discussion of symmetry, see Note 3 in Part I of this chapter.—Eds.

j. Is this paragraph relevant to the question posed in footnote h, above?—Eds.

Finally, Kennedy, joined by Justices Souter and Ginsburg, rejected plaintiffs' argument that a mid-decade plan violates the one person, one vote rule, because it is based on the census taken at the beginning of the decade and fails to reflect population changes as the decade proceeds.

Justices Scalia and Thomas adhered to their position in *Vieth* that the partisan gerrymandering claim was nonjusticiable. Chief Justice Roberts, joined by Justice Alito, wrote this:

> I agree with the determination that appellants have not provided "a reliable standard for identifying unconstitutional political gerrymanders," [quoting from Kennedy's summation.] The question whether any such standard exists—that is, whether a challenge to a political gerrymander presents a justiciable case or controversy—has not been argued in these cases. I therefore take no position on that question, which has divided the Court, see *Vieth*, and I join the Court's disposition in Part II without specifying whether appellants have failed to state a claim on which relief can be granted, or have failed to present a justiciable controversy.

In *LULAC*, the Democrats and, more generally, those who favor judicial policing of gerrymandering, were hoping that a mid-decade plan was a sufficiently distinctive target that the Supreme Court could be induced to shoot at it without having to worry too much about the implications for the general run of redistrictings after each census. Plainly, that strategy failed. But the obvious question raised by *LULAC* is how, if at all, the general constitutional law of redistricting has been affected. Has anything changed from *Vieth*?

That question can be broken down into two distinct sub-questions, neither of which has an obvious answer:

1. Has the law, as it stands, changed? Suppose a districting plan is challenged as an unconstitutional partisan gerrymander before a panel of conscientious lower court judges whose only goal is to enforce the law. Is there anything that the conscientious judges should do after *LULAC* that is different from what they would have done after *Vieth*?

2. Some lower court judges and all litigants are more interested in what the courts (and particularly the Supreme Court) will do than in the state of the law at the moment a case is filed. Does *LULAC* change your prediction of whether and why the Supreme Court will find some districting plans to be unconstitutional partisan gerrymanders?

Chapter 7

Election Administration

Since the 2000 presidential election, public, legislative, and scholarly interest in the "nuts and bolts" of elections has surged. Among the subjects receiving prominent attention are voting technology, provisional ballots, voter registration, voter identification, challenges to voter eligibility, poll worker training and recruitment, and post-election dispute resolution processes. We collectively refer to this set of topics as election administration.

Two overarching themes appear in much of the post-2000 discourse over election administration. One is the pronounced *decentralization* of American election administration. For the most part, responsibility for the conduct of elections rests with local officials. While it is common to speak of the "election system," in reality there is not just one election system, or even fifty systems in the United States, but thousands of systems—comprised of the various county and municipal entities charged with running elections. Throughout American history, the federal government's role in administering elections has been very limited. See Daniel P. Tokaji, *The Birth and Rebirth of Election Administration*, 6 ELECTION LAW JOURNAL 118, 121–23 (2007). While Congress imposed some requirements on the states and provided some federal funding through the Help America Vote Act of 2002 ("HAVA") (discussed in detail in Part IV.B, below), election administration remains primarily a local matter.

The other prominent theme of American election administration is *partisanship*. In 33 states, the chief election official—typically the Secretary of State—is selected through a partisan electoral process, while in other states the chief election official is appointed by an official (such as a governor) elected as a representative of his or her party. Richard L. Hasen, *Beyond the Margin of Litigation: Reforming U.S. Election Administration to Avoid Electoral Meltdown*, 62 WASHINGTON & LEE LAW REVIEW 937, 976 (2005). At the local level, election officials are elected in roughly two-thirds of all jurisdictions, and party-affiliated officials run elections in almost half of all local jurisdictions. David C. Kimball, Martha Kropf & Lindsay Battles, *Helping America Vote? Election Administration, Partisanship, and Provisional Voting in the 2004 Election*, 5 ELECTION LAW JOURNAL 447, 453 (2006).

Concerns about partisanship emerged in the 2000 election. These concerns surrounded Florida's Secretary of State Katherine Harris—a Republican who supported then-Governor George W. Bush—as well as Democratic Attorney General Bob Butterworth who issued an opinion favorable to then-Vice-President Al Gore. In 2004, concerns of partisanship centered on Ohio's Republican Secretary of State Ken Blackwell, also a Bush supporter. The spectre of partisanship has also tainted Democratic chief election officials, including California's former Secretary of State Kevin Shelley, who was accused of using federal funds for partisan purposes. More recently, Ohio's Democratic Secretary of State Jennifer Brunner, who replaced Blackwell, has been accused by Republicans of exercising her authority in a partisan manner.

These features of American election administration raise important questions regarding the appropriate role of courts. The decentralization of elections introduces the possibility that different jurisdictions will adopt different practices, which may in turn deny equal treatment to some voters. Should courts intervene to ensure that voters in different parts of a state are treated equally, for example, when it comes to the equipment they use for voting or the manner in which their votes are counted? Partisanship in the administration of elections may also furnish an argument for judicial intervention—for example, where a Secretary of State adopts a rule for counting provisional ballots that tends to advantage his or her party. Should courts closely scrutinize such a rule? What about a voter identification law that is likely to benefit the party with a majority in the state legislature, while hurting voters who tend to support candidates of the other major party? Alternatively, should courts leave the regulation of elections to Congress, state legislatures, and election officials at the state and local level?

Part I of this Chapter discusses the Court's opinion in *Bush v. Gore*, the case that ended the 2000 election. That case and the controversy from which it arose gave rise to a new wave of legislative and judicial attention to the mechanics of elections. We next turn to two areas of election administration that have proven especially contentious since 2000: voting technology (Part II) and voter identification (Part III). Part IV considers the relationship between election law and voter participation, first surveying empirical research on turnout and then considering laws aimed at increasing or enhancing participation.

I. Equal Protection and the Counting of Votes

To what extent should courts insure that votes are counted using uniform standards? This issue attained national prominence following the 2000 presidential election. In the days before the 2000 election, everyone recognized that George W. Bush was locked in an extremely close race with Al Gore. In fact, the election turned out to be so close that the final outcome depended on the results in Florida, where the initial count showed Bush leading by 1,784 votes out of millions of votes cast in the state.

Florida law provided for an automatic machine recount of the votes in such a close election. While those recounts were being carried out, analysts examined more closely both the voting technology and ballot forms used in various Florida counties. Many previously ignored problems with election administration came to light as a result of the controversy. For example, Democrats focused on the "butterfly ballot" (see Figure 7.1) used in Palm Beach County, a ballot that listed candidates for president on two pages facing each other with a punch-card vote to be cast along the ballot's spine. Democrats claimed that ballot design made it unduly likely that voters would cast votes for someone other than their preferred candidate. Reform Party candidate Pat Buchanan received 3,704 votes in Palm Beach County, nearly 2,700 more than he received in any of Florida's other counties; in addition, approximately 19,000 ballots were thrown out as "overvotes" (ballots containing votes for more than one presidential candidate). Although legal challenges to the butterfly ballot eventually went nowhere, the issue energized many Democrats into supporting strong efforts by Gore to overturn the preliminary results.

As the automatic recounts continued, Gore filed an election "protest" asking for a manual recount of the vote in four counties, three of which used punch-card voting systems. When it seemed the recounts could not be finished in time to meet state deadlines, Gore sought an extension of time for the manual recounts. Republicans argued against the extension and also contended that the law did not allow for manual recounts absent a machine error in counting the votes. The Florida Supreme Court, however, allowed the

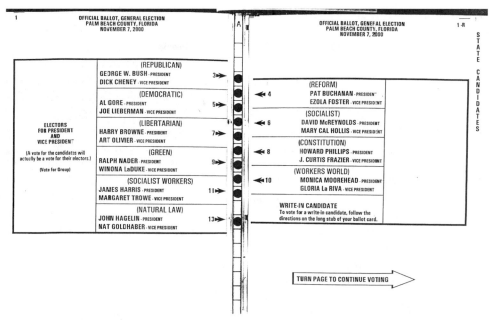

Figure 7.1 The Palm Beach County "Butterfly Ballot." Photo courtesy of Election Data Services.

recounts and extended the time to complete them, based upon its interpretation of Florida election statutes. Democrats and Republicans who could agree on little else agreed that the statutes were conflicting and unclear. In interpreting the statutes, the Florida court made background reference to provisions of the Florida Constitution that the Florida court characterized as calling for fair elections. *Palm Beach County Canvassing Board v. Harris*, 772 So.2d 1220 (Fla. 2000).

Bush appealed the decision to the United States Supreme Court. He argued that the Florida Supreme Court's opinion violated Article II of the Constitution, which provides that "[e]ach state shall appoint, in such manner as the legislature thereof may direct, a number of electors.... " Bush argued that the Florida opinion was in essence "new law" and therefore constituted the choosing of electors in a manner other than that directed by the Florida legislature. The Supreme Court issued a brief, unanimous, *per curiam* (unsigned) opinion remanding the case to the Florida Supreme Court for clarification as to whether the opinion was consistent with the Florida legislature's rules for choosing electors or was potentially in violation of Article II. *Bush v. Palm Beach County Canvassing Bd.*, 531 U.S. 70 (2000).

Despite Gore's victory in the first round of litigation, he still trailed Bush after the extended deadline the Florida Supreme Court had set. Gore then filed a separate election "contest," asking for a selective manual recount of nearly 10,000 undervotes from Miami-Dade County and approximately 4,000 votes set aside in Palm Beach County. (Undervotes are ballots that fail to record a valid vote for any candidate.) The trial court held that Gore failed to meet the statutory standard for a contest, and Gore appealed to the Florida Supreme Court.

The Florida Supreme Court, in a 4–3 vote, reversed the trial court. The court held that the trial court had applied the wrong legal standards in judging the merits of Gore's claim. *Gore v. Harris*, 772 So.2d 1243 (Fla. 2000). The court ordered that certain recounts, completed after the deadline it had set in the earlier case, be included in the totals and that a manual recount of undervotes in all the remaining counties in the state, not just the counties singled out by Gore, go forward. However, the recounts requested by Gore that had already been conducted would be grandfathered in. These recounts, unlike the new ones ordered by the court, had included all ballots, not just undervoted ballots.

The court further held that in examining the undervotes to determine whether the ballots indeed contained a valid vote for a presidential candidate, the counters should use a "clear intent of the voter" standard, as indicated in Florida statutes. The court failed to be more specific, perhaps out of fear that a more specific standard would violate the U.S. Supreme Court's understanding of Article II of the U.S. Constitution expressed in its earlier *per curiam* opinion.

While a state court judge was organizing the recount process, Bush filed a petition for a writ of certiorari and a stay in the U.S. Supreme Court. As the recounts began on Saturday, December 9, the Supreme Court, by a 5–4 vote, stayed the Florida Supreme Court's order, thereby suspending the recount. *Bush v. Gore*, 531 U.S. 1046 (2000). In an unusual move, Justice Scalia issued an opinion concurring in the granting of the stay. He wrote:

> Though it is not customary for the Court to issue an opinion in connection with its grant of a stay, I believe a brief response is necessary to Justice STEVENS' dissent. I will not address the merits of the case, since they will shortly be before us in the petition for certiorari that we have granted. It suffices to say that the issuance of the stay suggests that a majority of the Court, while not deciding the issues presented, believe that the petitioner has a substantial probability of success.
>
> On the question of irreparable harm, however, a few words are appropriate. The issue is not, as the dissent puts it, whether "[c]ounting every legally cast vote ca[n] constitute irreparable harm." One of the principal issues in the appeal we have accepted is precisely whether the votes that have been ordered to be counted are, under a reasonable interpretation of Florida law, "legally cast vote[s]." The counting of votes that are of questionable legality does in my view threaten irreparable harm to petitioner Bush, and to the country, by casting a cloud upon what he claims to be the legitimacy of his election. Count first, and rule upon legality afterwards, is not a recipe for producing election results that have the public acceptance democratic stability requires. Another issue in the case, moreover, is the propriety, indeed the constitutionality, of letting the standard for determination of voters' intent—dimpled chads, hanging chads, etc.—vary from county to county, as the Florida Supreme Court opinion, as interpreted by the Circuit Court, permits. If petitioner is correct that counting in this fashion is unlawful, permitting the count to proceed on that erroneous basis will prevent an accurate recount from being conducted on a proper basis later, since it is generally agreed that each manual recount produces a degradation of the ballots, which renders a subsequent recount inaccurate.
>
> For these reasons I have joined the Court's issuance of a stay, with a highly accelerated timetable for resolving this case on the merits.

Justice Stevens issued a strong dissent from the stay order for himself and Justices Breyer, Ginsburg and Souter:

> To stop the counting of legal votes, the majority today departs from three venerable rules of judicial restraint that have guided the Court throughout its history. On questions of state law, we have consistently respected the opinions of the highest courts of the States. On questions whose resolution is committed

at least in large measure to another branch of the Federal Government, we have construed our own jurisdiction narrowly and exercised it cautiously. On federal constitutional questions that were not fairly presented to the court whose judgment is being reviewed, we have prudently declined to express an opinion. The majority has acted unwisely.

Time does not permit a full discussion of the merits. It is clear, however, that a stay should not be granted unless an applicant makes a substantial showing of a likelihood of irreparable harm. In this case, petitioners have failed to carry that heavy burden. Counting every legally cast vote cannot constitute irreparable harm. On the other hand, there is a danger that a stay may cause irreparable harm to the respondents—and, more importantly, the public at large—because of the risk that "the entry of the stay would be tantamount to a decision on the merits in favor of the applicants." *National Socialist Party of America v. Skokie*, 434 U.S. 1327, 1328 (1977) (STEVENS, J., in chambers). Preventing the recount from being completed will inevitably cast a cloud on the legitimacy of the election.

It is certainly not clear that the Florida decision violated federal law. The Florida Code provides elaborate procedures for ensuring that every eligible voter has a full and fair opportunity to cast a ballot and that every ballot so cast is counted. See, *e.g.*, Fla. Stat. Ann. §§ 101.5614(5), 102.166 (Supp. 2001). In fact, the statutory provision relating to damaged and defective ballots states that "[n]o vote shall be declared invalid or void if there is a clear indication of the intent of the voter as determined by the canvassing board." § 101.5614(5). In its opinion, the Florida Supreme Court gave weight to that legislative command. Its ruling was consistent with earlier Florida cases that have repeatedly described the interest in correctly ascertaining the will of the voters as paramount.... Its ruling also appears to be consistent with the prevailing view in other States.... As a more fundamental matter, the Florida court's ruling reflects the basic principle, inherent in our Constitution and our democracy, that every legal vote should be counted. See *Reynolds v. Sims*; cf. *Hartke v. Roudebush*, 321 F.Supp. 1370, 1378–1379. (SD Ind. 1970) (STEVENS, J., dissenting); accord *Roudebush v. Hartke*, 405 U.S. 15 (1972).

Accordingly, I respectfully dissent.

On December 11, the Supreme Court heard oral argument on the merits. The same day, the Florida Supreme Court issued an opinion on remand in the first case. *Palm Beach County Canvassing Board v. Harris*, 772 So.2d 1273 (Fla. 2000). The Florida opinion was very similar to the initial opinion the court issued, but the court stated that its ruling was based upon Florida statutes, not the Florida constitution. Meanwhile, the Florida Legislature prepared to meet over the next two days in special session.

On the evening of December 12, the Supreme Court issued this opinion:

Bush v. Gore
531 U.S. 98 (2000)

PER CURIAM.

I

[The Court summarized the facts and procedural posture of the case. Bush's] petition presents the following questions: whether the Florida Supreme Court established new standards for resolving Presidential election contests, thereby violating Art. II, § 1, cl. 2, of the United States Constitution and failing to comply with 3 U.S.C. § 5, and whether the use of standardless manual recounts violates the Equal Protection and Due Process Clauses. With respect to the equal protection question, we find a violation of the Equal Protection Clause.

II

A

The closeness of this election, and the multitude of legal challenges which have followed in its wake, have brought into sharp focus a common, if heretofore unnoticed, phenomenon. Nationwide statistics reveal that an estimated 2% of ballots cast do not register a vote for President for whatever reason, including deliberately choosing no candidate at all or some voter error, such as voting for two candidates or insufficiently marking a ballot. In certifying election results, the votes eligible for inclusion in the certification are the votes meeting the properly established legal requirements.

This case has shown that punch card balloting machines can produce an unfortunate number of ballots which are not punched in a clean, complete way by the voter. After the current counting, it is likely legislative bodies nationwide will examine ways to improve the mechanisms and machinery for voting.

B

The individual citizen has no federal constitutional right to vote for electors for the President of the United States unless and until the state legislature chooses a statewide election as the means to implement its power to appoint members of the Electoral College. U.S. Const., Art. II, § 1. This is the source for the statement in *McPherson v. Blacker*, 146 U.S. 1, 35 (1892), that the State legislature's power to select the manner for appointing electors is plenary; it may, if it so chooses, select the electors itself, which indeed was the manner used by State legislatures in several States for many years after the Framing of our Constitution. History has now favored the voter, and in each of the several States the citizens themselves vote for Presidential electors. When the state legislature vests the right to vote for President in its people, the right to vote as the legislature has prescribed is fundamental; and one source of its fundamental nature lies in the equal weight accorded to each vote and the equal dignity owed to each voter. The State, of course, after granting the franchise in the special context of Article II, can take back the power to appoint electors. See *id.* ("[T]here is no doubt of the right of the legislature to resume the power at any time, for it can neither be taken away nor abdicated") (quoting S.Rep. No. 395, 43d Cong., 1st Sess.).

The right to vote is protected in more than the initial allocation of the franchise. Equal protection applies as well to the manner of its exercise. Having once granted the right to vote on equal terms, the State may not, by later arbitrary and disparate treatment, value one person's vote over that of another. See, *e.g., Harper v. Virginia Bd. of Elections*, 383 U.S. 663, 665 (1966) ("[O]nce the franchise is granted to the electorate, lines may not be drawn which are inconsistent with the Equal Protection Clause of the Fourteenth Amendment"). It must be remembered that "the right of suffrage can be denied by a debasement or dilution of the weight of a citizen's vote just as effectively as by wholly prohibiting the free exercise of the franchise." *Reynolds v. Sims.*

There is no difference between the two sides of the present controversy on these basic propositions. Respondents say that the very purpose of vindicating the right to vote justifies the recount procedures now at issue. The question before us, however, is whether the recount procedures the Florida Supreme Court has adopted are consistent with its obligation to avoid arbitrary and disparate treatment of the members of its electorate.

Much of the controversy seems to revolve around ballot cards designed to be perforated by a stylus but which, either through error or deliberate omission, have not been perforated with sufficient precision for a machine to count them. In some cases a piece of the card—a chad—is hanging, say by two corners. In other cases there is no separation at all, just an indentation.

The Florida Supreme Court has ordered that the intent of the voter be discerned from such ballots. For purposes of resolving the equal protection challenge, it is not necessary to decide whether the Florida Supreme Court had the authority under the legislative scheme for resolving election disputes to define what a legal vote is and to mandate a manual recount implementing that definition. The recount mechanisms implemented in response to the decisions of the Florida Supreme Court do not satisfy the minimum requirement for non-arbitrary treatment of voters necessary to secure the fundamental right. Florida's basic command for the count of legally cast votes is to consider the "intent of the voter." *Gore* v. *Harris*. This is unobjectionable as an abstract proposition and a starting principle. The problem inheres in the absence of specific standards to ensure its equal application. The formulation of uniform rules to determine intent based on these recurring circumstances is practicable and, we conclude, necessary.

The law does not refrain from searching for the intent of the actor in a multitude of circumstances; and in some cases the general command to ascertain intent is not susceptible to much further refinement. In this instance, however, the question is not whether to believe a witness but how to interpret the marks or holes or scratches on an inanimate object, a piece of cardboard or paper which, it is said, might not have registered as a vote during the machine count. The factfinder confronts a thing, not a person. The search for intent can be confined by specific rules designed to ensure uniform treatment.

The want of those rules here has led to unequal evaluation of ballots in various respects. See *Gore* v. *Harris* (Wells, J., dissenting) ("Should a county canvassing board count or not count a 'dimpled chad' where the voter is able to successfully dislodge the chad in every other contest on that ballot? Here, the county canvassing boards disagree"). As seems to have been acknowledged at oral argument, the standards for accepting or rejecting contested ballots might vary not only from county to county but indeed within a single county from one recount team to another.

The record provides some examples. A monitor in Miami-Dade County testified at trial that he observed that three members of the county canvassing board applied different standards in defining a legal vote. And testimony at trial also revealed that at least one county changed its evaluative standards during the counting process. Palm Beach County, for example, began the process with a 1990 guideline which precluded counting completely attached chads, switched to a rule that considered a vote to be legal if any light could be seen through a chad, changed back to the 1990 rule, and then abandoned any pretense of a *per se* rule, only to have a court order that the county consider dimpled chads legal. This is not a process with sufficient guarantees of equal treatment.

An early case in our one person, one vote jurisprudence arose when a State accorded arbitrary and disparate treatment to voters in its different counties. *Gray v. Sanders*, 372 U.S. 368 (1963). The Court found a constitutional violation. We relied on these principles in the context of the Presidential selection process in *Moore v. Ogilvie*, 394 U.S. 814 (1969), where we invalidated a county-based procedure that diluted the influence of citizens in larger counties in the nominating process. There we observed that "[t]he idea that one group can be granted greater voting strength than another is hostile to the one man, one vote basis of our representative government."

The State Supreme Court ratified this uneven treatment. It mandated that the recount totals from two counties, Miami-Dade and Palm Beach, be included in the certified total. The court also appeared to hold *sub silentio* that the recount totals from Broward County, which were not completed until after the original November 14 certification by the Secretary of State, were to be considered part of the new certified vote totals even though the county certification was not contested by Vice President Gore. Yet each of the counties used varying standards to determine what was a legal vote. Broward County used a more forgiving standard than Palm Beach County, and uncovered almost three times as many new votes, a result markedly disproportionate to the difference in population between the counties.

In addition, the recounts in these three counties were not limited to so-called undervotes but extended to all of the ballots. The distinction has real consequences. A manual recount of all ballots identifies not only those ballots which show no vote but also those which contain more than one, the so-called overvotes. Neither category will be counted by the machine. This is not a trivial concern. At oral argument, respondents estimated there are as many as 110,000 overvotes statewide. As a result, the citizen whose ballot was not read by a machine because he failed to vote for a candidate in a way readable by a machine may still have his vote counted in a manual recount; on the other hand, the citizen who marks two candidates in a way discernable by the machine will not have the same opportunity to have his vote count, even if a manual examination of the ballot would reveal the requisite indicia of intent. Furthermore, the citizen who marks two candidates, only one of which is discernable by the machine, will have his vote counted even though it should have been read as an invalid ballot. The State Supreme Court's inclusion of vote counts based on these variant standards exemplifies concerns with the remedial processes that were under way.

That brings the analysis to yet a further equal protection problem. The votes certified by the court included a partial total from one county, Miami-Dade. The Florida Supreme Court's decision thus gives no assurance that the recounts included in a final certification must be complete. Indeed, it is respondent's submission that it would be consistent with the rules of the recount procedures to include whatever partial counts are done by the time of final certification, and we interpret the Florida Supreme Court's decision to permit this. This accommodation no doubt results from the truncated contest period established by the Florida Supreme Court in *Bush I*, at respondents' own urging. The press of time does not diminish the constitutional concern. A desire for speed is not a general excuse for ignoring equal protection guarantees.

In addition to these difficulties the actual process by which the votes were to be counted under the Florida Supreme Court's decision raises further concerns. That order did not specify who would recount the ballots. The county canvassing boards were forced to pull together ad hoc teams comprised of judges from various Circuits who had no previous training in handling and interpreting ballots. Furthermore, while others were permitted to observe, they were prohibited from objecting during the recount.

The recount process, in its features here described, is inconsistent with the minimum procedures necessary to protect the fundamental right of each voter in the special instance of a statewide recount under the authority of a single state judicial officer. Our consideration is limited to the present circumstances, for the problem of equal protection in election processes generally presents many complexities.

The question before the Court is not whether local entities, in the exercise of their expertise, may develop different systems for implementing elections. Instead, we are presented with a situation where a state court with the power to assure uniformity has ordered a statewide recount with minimal procedural safeguards. When a court orders a statewide remedy, there must be at least some assurance that the rudimentary requirements of equal treatment and fundamental fairness are satisfied.

Given the Court's assessment that the recount process underway was probably being conducted in an unconstitutional manner, the Court stayed the order directing the recount so it could hear this case and render an expedited decision. The contest provision, as it was mandated by the State Supreme Court, is not well calculated to sustain the confidence that all citizens must have in the outcome of elections. The State has not shown that its procedures include the necessary safeguards. The problem, for instance, of the estimated 110,000 overvotes has not been addressed, although Chief Justice Wells called attention to the concern in his dissenting opinion.

Upon due consideration of the difficulties identified to this point, it is obvious that the recount cannot be conducted in compliance with the requirements of equal protection and due process without substantial additional work. It would require not only the adoption (after opportunity for argument) of adequate statewide standards for determining what is a legal vote, and practicable procedures to implement them, but also orderly judicial review of any disputed matters that might arise. In addition, the Secretary of State has advised that the recount of only a portion of the ballots requires that the vote tabulation equipment be used to screen out undervotes, a function for which the machines were not designed. If a recount of overvotes were also required, perhaps even a second screening would be necessary. Use of the equipment for this purpose, and any new software developed for it, would have to be evaluated for accuracy by the Secretary of State, as required by Fla. Stat. § 101.015 (2000).

The Supreme Court of Florida has said that the legislature intended the State's electors to "participat[e] fully in the federal electoral process," as provided in 3 U.S.C. § 5. That statute, in turn, requires that any controversy or contest that is designed to lead to a conclusive selection of electors be completed by December 12. That date is upon us, and there is no recount procedure in place under the State Supreme Court's order that comports with minimal constitutional standards. Because it is evident that any recount seeking to meet the December 12 date will be unconstitutional for the reasons we have discussed, we reverse the judgment of the Supreme Court of Florida ordering a recount to proceed.

Seven Justices of the Court agree that there are constitutional problems with the recount ordered by the Florida Supreme Court that demand a remedy.[a] See *post* (SOUTER, J., dissenting); *post* (BREYER, J., dissenting). The only disagreement is as to the remedy. Because the Florida Supreme Court has said that the Florida Legislature intended to obtain the safe-harbor benefits of 3 U.S.C. § 5, Justice BREYER's proposed remedy — remanding to the Florida Supreme Court for its ordering of a constitutionally proper contest until December 18 — contemplates action in violation of the Florida election code, and hence could not be part of an "appropriate" order authorized by Fla. Stat. § 102.168(8) (2000).

* * *

a. This statement in the opinion has been a source of some controversy. Dissenting opinions of Justices Breyer and Souter appear below. Is the Court correct that those justices agree that there is a constitutional problem? — Eds.

None are more conscious of the vital limits on judicial authority than are the members of this Court, and none stand more in admiration of the Constitution's design to leave the selection of the President to the people, through their legislatures, and to the political sphere. When contending parties invoke the process of the courts, however, it becomes our unsought responsibility to resolve the federal and constitutional issues the judicial system has been forced to confront.

The judgment of the Supreme Court of Florida is reversed, and the case is remanded for further proceedings not inconsistent with this opinion.[b] ...

It is so ordered.

CHIEF Justice REHNQUIST, with whom Justice SCALIA and Justice THOMAS join, concurring.

We join the *per curiam* opinion. We write separately because we believe there are additional grounds that require us to reverse the Florida Supreme Court's decision. [The concurring opinion began by setting forth the view that Article II gave the state *legislature* the sole power to set the rules for choosing presidential electors.]

II

Acting pursuant to its constitutional grant of authority, the Florida Legislature has created a detailed, if not perfectly crafted, statutory scheme that provides for appointment of Presidential electors by direct election....

The state legislature has also provided mechanisms both for protesting election returns and for contesting certified election results. Section 102.166 governs protests. Any protest must be filed prior to the certification of election results by the county canvassing board. Once a protest has been filed, "[t]he county canvassing board may authorize a manual recount." If a sample recount conducted pursuant to § 102.166(5) "indicates an error in the vote tabulation which could affect the outcome of the election," the county canvassing board is instructed to: "(a) Correct the error and recount the remaining precincts with the vote tabulation system; (b) Request the Department of State to verify the tabulation software; or (c) Manually recount all ballots." In the event a canvassing board chooses to conduct a manual recount of all ballots, § 102.166(7) prescribes procedures for such a recount.

Contests to the certification of an election, on the other hand, are controlled by § 102.168. The grounds for contesting an election include "[r]eceipt of a number of illegal votes or rejection of a number of legal votes sufficient to change or place in doubt the result of the election." Any contest must be filed in the appropriate Florida circuit court, and the canvassing board or election board is the proper party defendant. Section 102.168(8) provides that "[t]he circuit judge to whom the contest is presented may fashion such orders as he or she deems necessary to ensure that each allegation in the complaint is investigated, examined, or checked, to prevent or correct any alleged wrong, and to provide any relief appropriate under such circumstances." In Presidential elections, the contest

---

b. In the moments after the opinion was issued, legal commentators on television struggled to determine whether the Court's order of a reversal with remand would give the Florida Supreme Court another chance to order a recount under a uniform standard. The problem was complicated by the fact that the Court released the opinion without a summary of the decision, its usual practice. Within hours, it was clear to most observers that no further recounts would be possible. Gore's lawyers considered and then rejected the possibility of asking the Florida Supreme Court to order recounts under a uniform standard the next morning. Instead, Gore conceded the election. — EDS.

period necessarily terminates on the date set by 3 U.S.C. § 5 for concluding the State's "final determination" of election controversies.

In its first decision, *Palm Beach Canvassing Bd. v. Harris* (*Harris I*), the Florida Supreme Court extended the 7-day statutory certification deadline established by the legislature. This modification of the code, by lengthening the protest period, necessarily shortened the contest period for Presidential elections. Underlying the extension of the certification deadline and the shortchanging of the contest period was, presumably, the clear implication that certification was a matter of significance: The certified winner would enjoy presumptive validity, making a contest proceeding by the losing candidate an uphill battle. In its latest opinion, however, the court empties certification of virtually all legal consequence during the contest, and in doing so departs from the provisions enacted by the Florida Legislature.

The court determined that canvassing boards' decisions regarding whether to recount ballots past the certification deadline (even the certification deadline established by *Harris I*) are to be reviewed *de novo*, although the Election Code clearly vests discretion whether to recount in the boards, and sets strict deadlines subject to the Secretary's rejection of late tallies and monetary fines for tardiness. See Fla. Stat. Ann. § 102.112 (Supp. 2001). Moreover, the Florida court held that all late vote tallies arriving during the contest period should be automatically included in the certification regardless of the certification deadline (even the certification deadline established by *Harris I*), thus virtually eliminating both the deadline and the Secretary's discretion to disregard recounts that violate it.

Moreover, the court's interpretation of "legal vote," and hence its decision to order a contest-period recount, plainly departed from the legislative scheme. Florida statutory law cannot reasonably be thought to *require* the counting of improperly marked ballots. Each Florida precinct before election day provides instructions on how properly to cast a vote; each polling place on election day contains a working model of the voting machine it uses; and each voting booth contains a sample ballot. In precincts using punch-card ballots, voters are instructed to punch out the ballot cleanly:

> "AFTER VOTING, CHECK YOUR BALLOT CARD TO BE SURE YOUR VOT-ING SELECTIONS ARE CLEARLY AND CLEANLY PUNCHED AND THERE ARE NO CHIPS LEFT HANGING ON THE BACK OF THE CARD."

No reasonable person would call it "an error in the vote tabulation," Fla. Stat. Ann. § 102.166(5), or a "rejection of ... legal votes," Fla. Stat. Ann. § 102.168(3)(c), when electronic or electromechanical equipment performs precisely in the manner designed, and fails to count those ballots that are not marked in the manner that these voting instructions explicitly and prominently specify. The scheme that the Florida Supreme Court's opinion attributes to the legislature is one in which machines are *required* to be "capable of correctly counting votes," § 101.5606(4), but which nonetheless regularly produces elections in which legal votes are predictably *not* tabulated, so that in close elections manual recounts are regularly required. This is of course absurd. The Secretary, who is authorized by law to issue binding interpretations of the Election Code, rejected this peculiar reading of the statutes. The Florida Supreme Court, although it must defer to the Secretary's interpretations, rejected her reasonable interpretation and embraced the peculiar one. See *Palm Beach County Canvassing Board v. Harris* (*Harris II*).

But as we indicated in our remand of the earlier case, in a Presidential election the clearly expressed intent of the legislature must prevail. And there is no basis for reading the Florida statutes as requiring the counting of improperly marked ballots, as an examination of the Florida Supreme Court's textual analysis shows. We will not parse that analysis here, except to note that the principal provision of the election code on which it relied, § 101.5614(5), was, as Chief Justice Wells pointed out in his dissent in *Harris II*, entirely irrelevant. The State's Attorney General (who was supporting the Gore challenge) confirmed in oral argument here that never before the present election had a manual recount been conducted on the basis of the contention that "undervotes" should have been examined to determine voter intent. For the court to step away from this established practice, prescribed by the Secretary, the state official charged by the legislature with "responsibility to … [o]btain and maintain uniformity in the application, operation, and interpretation of the election laws," was to depart from the legislative scheme.

[The concurrence concluded in Part III that "[t]he scope and nature of the remedy ordered by the Florida Supreme Court jeopardizes the 'legislative wish' to take advantage of the safe harbor provided by 3 U.S.C. § 5."]

Justice STEVENS, with whom Justice GINSBURG and Justice BREYER join, dissenting.

The Constitution assigns to the States the primary responsibility for determining the manner of selecting the Presidential electors. See Art. II, § 1, cl. 2. When questions arise about the meaning of state laws, including election laws, it is our settled practice to accept the opinions of the highest courts of the States as providing the final answers. On rare occasions, however, either federal statutes or the Federal Constitution may require federal judicial intervention in state elections. This is not such an occasion.

The federal questions that ultimately emerged in this case are not substantial. [Justice Stevens rebutted the concurring opinion's interpretation of Article II and argued that Congress in enacting 3 U.S.C. § 5 "did not impose any affirmative duties upon the States that their governmental branches could 'violate.'"]

Nor are petitioners correct in asserting that the failure of the Florida Supreme Court to specify in detail the precise manner in which the "intent of the voter," Fla. Stat. § 101.5614(5) (Supp. 2001), is to be determined rises to the level of a constitutional violation.[2] We found such a violation when individual votes within the same State were weighted unequally, see, *e.g., Reynolds,* but we have never before called into question the substantive standard by which a State determines that a vote has been legally cast. And there is no reason to think that the guidance provided to the factfinders, specifically the various canvassing boards, by the "intent of the voter" standard is any less sufficient — or will lead to results any less uniform — than, for example, the "beyond a reasonable doubt" standard employed everyday by ordinary citizens in courtrooms across this country.

Admittedly, the use of differing substandards for determining voter intent in different counties employing similar voting systems may raise serious concerns. Those concerns are alleviated — if not eliminated — by the fact that a single impartial magistrate will ultimately adjudicate all objections arising from the recount process. Of course, as a general matter, "[t]he interpretation of constitutional principles must not be too literal. We must remember that the machinery of government would not work if it were not allowed a little play in its joints." *Bain Peanut Co. of Tex. v. Pinson,* 282 U.S. 499, 501 (1931) (Holmes, J.). If it were otherwise, Florida's decision to leave to each county the determination of

---

2. The Florida statutory standard is consistent with the practice of the majority of States, which apply either an "intent of the voter" standard or an "impossible to determine the elector's choice" standard in ballot recounts.…

what balloting system to employ—despite enormous differences in accuracy[4]—might run afoul of equal protection. So, too, might the similar decisions of the vast majority of state legislatures to delegate to local authorities certain decisions with respect to voting systems and ballot design.

Even assuming that aspects of the remedial scheme might ultimately be found to violate the Equal Protection Clause, I could not subscribe to the majority's disposition of the case. As the majority explicitly holds, once a state legislature determines to select electors through a popular vote, the right to have one's vote counted is of constitutional stature. As the majority further acknowledges, Florida law holds that all ballots that reveal the intent of the voter constitute valid votes. Recognizing these principles, the majority nonetheless orders the termination of the contest proceeding before all such votes have been tabulated. Under their own reasoning, the appropriate course of action would be to remand to allow more specific procedures for implementing the legislature's uniform general standard to be established.

In the interest of finality, however, the majority effectively orders the disenfranchisement of an unknown number of voters whose ballots reveal their intent—and are therefore legal votes under state law—but were for some reason rejected by ballot-counting machines. It does so on the basis of the deadlines set forth in Title 3 of the United States Code. But, as I have already noted, those provisions merely provide rules of decision for Congress to follow when selecting among conflicting slates of electors. They do not prohibit a State from counting what the majority concedes to be legal votes until a bona fide winner is determined. Indeed, in 1960, Hawaii appointed two slates of electors and Congress chose to count the one appointed on January 4, 1961, well after the Title 3 deadlines. See Josephson & Ross, Repairing the Electoral College, 22 J. Legis. 145, 166, n. 154 (1996). Thus, nothing prevents the majority, even if it properly found an equal protection violation, from ordering relief appropriate to remedy that violation without depriving Florida voters of their right to have their votes counted. As the majority notes, "[a] desire for speed is not a general excuse for ignoring equal protection guarantees." ...

What must underlie petitioners' entire federal assault on the Florida election procedures is an unstated lack of confidence in the impartiality and capacity of the state judges who would make the critical decisions if the vote count were to proceed. Otherwise, their position is wholly without merit. The endorsement of that position by the majority of this Court can only lend credence to the most cynical appraisal of the work of judges throughout the land. It is confidence in the men and women who administer the judicial system that is the true backbone of the rule of law. Time will one day heal the wound to that confidence that will be inflicted by today's decision. One thing, however, is certain. Although we may never know with complete certainty the identity of the winner of this year's Presidential election, the identity of the loser is perfectly clear. It is the Nation's confidence in the judge as an impartial guardian of the rule of law.

I respectfully dissent.

---

4. The percentage of nonvotes in this election in counties using a punch-card system was 3.92%; in contrast, the rate of error under the more modern optical-scan systems was only 1.43%. Put in other terms, for every 10,000 votes cast, punch-card systems result in 250 more nonvotes than optical-scan systems. A total of 3,718,305 votes were cast under punch-card systems, and 2,353,811 votes were cast under optical-scan systems.

Justice SOUTER, with whom Justice BREYER joins and with whom Justice STEVENS and Justice GINSBURG join with regard to all but Part C, dissenting.

The Court should not have reviewed either [*Bush I*], or this case, and should not have stopped Florida's attempt to recount all undervote ballots by issuing a stay of the Florida Supreme Court's orders during the period of this review. If this Court had allowed the State to follow the course indicated by the opinions of its own Supreme Court, it is entirely possible that there would ultimately have been no issue requiring our review, and political tension could have worked itself out in the Congress following the procedure provided in 3 U.S.C. § 15. The case being before us, however, its resolution by the majority is another erroneous decision. [Justice Souter expresses his disagreement with the concurrence's interpretations of Article II and 3 U.S.C. § 5.]

C

It is only on the third issue before us that there is a meritorious argument for relief, as this Court's *Per Curiam* opinion recognizes. It is an issue that might well have been dealt with adequately by the Florida courts if the state proceedings had not been interrupted, and if not disposed of at the state level it could have been considered by the Congress in any electoral vote dispute. But because the course of state proceedings has been interrupted, time is short, and the issue is before us, I think it sensible for the Court to address it.

Petitioners have raised an equal protection claim (or, alternatively, a due process claim, see generally *Logan v. Zimmerman Brush Co.*, 455 U.S. 422 (1982)), in the charge that unjustifiably disparate standards are applied in different electoral jurisdictions to otherwise identical facts. It is true that the Equal Protection Clause does not forbid the use of a variety of voting mechanisms within a jurisdiction, even though different mechanisms will have different levels of effectiveness in recording voters' intentions; local variety can be justified by concerns about cost, the potential value of innovation, and so on. But evidence in the record here suggests that a different order of disparity obtains under rules for determining a voter's intent that have been applied (and could continue to be applied) to identical types of ballots used in identical brands of machines and exhibiting identical physical characteristics (such as "hanging" or "dimpled" chads). I can conceive of no legitimate state interest served by these differing treatments of the expressions of voters' fundamental rights. The differences appear wholly arbitrary.

In deciding what to do about this, we should take account of the fact that electoral votes are due to be cast in six days. I would therefore remand the case to the courts of Florida with instructions to establish uniform standards for evaluating the several types of ballots that have prompted differing treatments, to be applied within and among counties when passing on such identical ballots in any further recounting (or successive recounting) that the courts might order.

Unlike the majority, I see no warrant for this Court to assume that Florida could not possibly comply with this requirement before the date set for the meeting of electors, December 18. Although one of the dissenting justices of the State Supreme Court estimated that disparate standards potentially affected 170,000 votes, the number at issue is significantly smaller. The 170,000 figure apparently represents all uncounted votes, both undervotes (those for which no Presidential choice was recorded by a machine) and overvotes (those rejected because of votes for more than one candidate). But as Justice BREYER has pointed out, no showing has been made of legal overvotes uncounted, and counsel for Gore made an uncontradicted representation to the Court that the statewide total of undervotes is about 60,000. To recount these manually would be a tall order, but before this Court stayed the effort to do that the courts of Florida were ready to do their best to get that job done. There is no justification for denying the State the opportunity to try to count all disputed ballots now.

I respectfully dissent.

Justice GINSBURG, with whom Justice STEVENS joins, and with whom Justice SOUTER and Justice BREYER join as to Part I, dissenting.

I

[In this part, Justice Ginsburg provides a lengthy explanation for her disagreement with Chief Justice Rehnquist's concurring opinion.]

II

I agree with Justice STEVENS that petitioners have not presented a substantial equal protection claim. Ideally, perfection would be the appropriate standard for judging the recount. But we live in an imperfect world, one in which thousands of votes have not been counted. I cannot agree that the recount adopted by the Florida court, flawed as it may be, would yield a result any less fair or precise than the certification that preceded that recount. See, *e.g.*, *McDonald v. Board of Election Comm'rs of Chicago*, 394 U.S. 802, 807 (1969) (even in the context of the right to vote, the state is permitted to reform "'one step at a time'").

Even if there were an equal protection violation, I would agree with Justice STEVENS, Justice SOUTER, and Justice BREYER that the Court's concern about "the December 12 deadline" is misplaced.... Equally important, as Justice BREYER explains, the December 12 "deadline" for bringing Florida's electoral votes into 3 U.S.C. §5's safe harbor lacks the significance the Court assigns it....

I dissent.

Justice BREYER, with whom Justice STEVENS and Justice GINSBURG join except as to Part I-A-1, and with whom Justice SOUTER joins as to Part I, dissenting.

The Court was wrong to take this case. It was wrong to grant a stay. It should now vacate that stay and permit the Florida Supreme Court to decide whether the recount should resume.

I

The political implications of this case for the country are momentous. But the federal legal questions presented, with one exception, are insubstantial.

A
1

The majority raises three Equal Protection problems with the Florida Supreme Court's recount order: first, the failure to include overvotes in the manual recount; second, the fact that *all* ballots, rather than simply the undervotes, were recounted in some, but not all, counties; and third, the absence of a uniform, specific standard to guide the recounts. As far as the first issue is concerned, petitioners presented no evidence, to this Court or to any Florida court, that a manual recount of overvotes would identify additional legal votes. The same is true of the second, and, in addition, the majority's reasoning would seem to invalidate any state provision for a manual recount of individual counties in a statewide election.

The majority's third concern does implicate principles of fundamental fairness. The majority concludes that the Equal Protection Clause requires that a manual recount be governed not only by the uniform general standard of the "clear intent of the voter," but also by uniform subsidiary standards (for example, a uniform determination whether indented, but not perforated, "undervotes" should count). The opinion points out that the Florida Supreme Court ordered the inclusion of Broward County's undercounted "legal votes" even though those votes included ballots that were not perforated but simply "dimpled," while newly recounted ballots from other counties will likely include only votes determined to be "legal" on the basis of a stricter standard. In light of our previous remand, the Florida Supreme Court may have been reluctant to adopt a more specific standard than that provided for by the legislature for fear of exceeding its authority under Article II. However, since the use of different standards could favor one or the other of the candidates, since time was, and is, too short to permit the lower courts to iron out significant differences through ordinary judicial review, and since the relevant distinction was embodied in the order of the State's highest court, I agree that, in these very special circumstances, basic principles of fairness may well have counseled the adoption of a uniform standard to address the problem. In light of the majority's disposition, I need not decide whether, or the extent to which, as a remedial matter, the Constitution would place limits upon the content of the uniform standard.

2

Nonetheless, there is no justification for the majority's remedy, which is simply to reverse the lower court and halt the recount entirely. An appropriate remedy would be, instead, to remand this case with instructions that, even at this late date, would permit the Florida Supreme Court to require recounting *all* undercounted votes in Florida, including those from Broward, Volusia, Palm Beach, and Miami-Dade Counties, whether or not previously recounted prior to the end of the protest period, and to do so in accordance with a single-uniform substandard.

The majority justifies stopping the recount entirely on the ground that there is no more time. In particular, the majority relies on the lack of time for the Secretary to review and approve equipment needed to separate undervotes. But the majority reaches this conclusion in the absence of *any* record evidence that the recount could not have been completed in the time allowed by the Florida Supreme Court. The majority finds facts outside of the record on matters that state courts are in a far better position to address. Of course, it is too late for any such recount to take place by December 12, the date by which election disputes must be decided if a State is to take advantage of the safe harbor provisions of 3 U.S.C. § 5. Whether there is time to conduct a recount prior to December 18, when the electors are scheduled to meet, is a matter for the state courts to determine. And whether, under Florida law, Florida could or could not take further action is obviously a matter for Florida courts, not this Court, to decide.

By halting the manual recount, and thus ensuring that the uncounted legal votes will not be counted under any standard, this Court crafts a remedy out of proportion to the asserted harm. And that remedy harms the very fairness interests the Court is attempting to protect. The manual recount would itself redress a problem of unequal treatment of ballots. As Justice STEVENS points out, the ballots of voters in counties that use punch-card systems are more likely to be disqualified than those in counties using optical-scanning systems. According to recent news reports, variations in the undervote rate are even more pronounced. Thus, in a system that allows counties to use different types of voting systems, voters already arrive at the polls with an unequal chance that their votes will be counted. I do not see how the fact that this results from counties' selection of different voting machines rather than a court order makes the outcome any more fair. Nor do I understand why the Florida Supreme Court's recount order, which helps to redress this inequity, must be entirely prohibited based on a deficiency that could easily be remedied.

B

The remainder of petitioners' claims, which are the focus of THE CHIEF JUSTICE's concurrence, raise no significant federal questions....

II

Despite the reminder that this case involves "an election for the President of the United States," no preeminent legal concern, or practical concern related to legal questions, required this Court to hear this case, let alone to issue a stay that stopped Florida's recount process in its tracks. With one exception, petitioners' claims do not ask us to vindicate a constitutional provision designed to protect a basic human right. See, e.g., *Brown v. Board of Education*, 347 U.S. 483 (1954). Petitioners invoke fundamental fairness, namely, the need for procedural fairness, including finality. But with the one "equal protection" exception, they rely upon law that focuses, not upon that basic need, but upon the constitutional allocation of power. Respondents invoke a competing fundamental consideration — the need to determine the voter's true intent. But they look to state law, not to federal constitutional law, to protect that interest. Neither side claims electoral fraud, dishonesty, or the like. And the more fundamental equal protection claim might have been left to the state court to resolve if and when it was discovered to have mattered. It could still be resolved through a remand conditioned upon issuance of a uniform standard; it does not require reversing the Florida Supreme Court.

Of course, the selection of the President is of fundamental national importance. But that importance is political, not legal. And this Court should resist the temptation unnecessarily to resolve tangential legal disputes, where doing so threatens to determine the outcome of the election.

The Constitution and federal statutes themselves make clear that restraint is appropriate. They set forth a road map of how to resolve disputes about electors, even after an election as close as this one. That road map foresees resolution of electoral disputes by *state* courts. See 3 U.S.C. § 5 (providing that, where a "State shall have provided, by laws enacted prior to [election day], for its final determination of any controversy or contest concerning the appointment of ... electors ... by judicial or other methods," the subsequently chosen electors enter a safe harbor free from congressional challenge). But it nowhere provides for involvement by the United States Supreme Court.

To the contrary, the Twelfth Amendment commits to Congress the authority and responsibility to count electoral votes. A federal statute, the Electoral Count Act, enacted after the close 1876 Hayes-Tilden Presidential election, specifies that, after States have tried to resolve disputes (through "judicial" or other means), Congress is the body primarily authorized to resolve remaining disputes. See Electoral Count Act of 1887, 3 U.S.C. §§ 5, 6, and 15.

The legislative history of the Act makes clear its intent to commit the power to resolve such disputes to Congress, rather than the courts. [Justice Breyer recounts the legislative history.]

Given this detailed, comprehensive scheme for counting electoral votes, there is no reason to believe that federal law either foresees or requires resolution of such a political issue by this Court. Nor, for that matter, is there any reason to that think the Constitution's Framers would have reached a different conclusion. Madison, at least, believed that allowing the judiciary to choose the presidential electors "was out of the question." Madison, July 25, 1787 (reprinted in 5 Elliot's Debates on the Federal Constitution 363 (2d ed. 1876)).

The decision by both the Constitution's Framers and the 1886 Congress to minimize this Court's role in resolving close federal presidential elections is as wise as it is clear. However awkward or difficult it may be for Congress to resolve difficult electoral disputes, Congress, being a political body, expresses the people's will far more accurately than does an unelected Court. And the people's will is what elections are about.

Moreover, Congress was fully aware of the danger that would arise should it ask judges, unarmed with appropriate legal standards, to resolve a hotly contested Presidential election contest. Just after the 1876 Presidential election, Florida, South Carolina, and Louisiana each sent two slates of electors to Washington. Without these States, Tilden, the Democrat, had 184 electoral votes, one short of the number required to win the Presidency. With those States, Hayes, his Republican opponent, would have had 185. In order to choose between the two slates of electors, Congress decided to appoint an electoral commission composed of five Senators, five Representatives, and five Supreme Court Justices. Initially the Commission was to be evenly divided between Republicans and Democrats, with Justice David Davis, an Independent, to possess the decisive vote. However, when at the last minute the Illinois Legislature elected Justice Davis to the United States Senate, the final position on the Commission was filled by Supreme Court Justice Joseph P. Bradley.

The Commission divided along partisan lines, and the responsibility to cast the deciding vote fell to Justice Bradley. He decided to accept the votes by the Republican electors, and thereby awarded the Presidency to Hayes.

Justice Bradley immediately became the subject of vociferous attacks. Bradley was accused of accepting bribes, of being captured by railroad interests, and of an eleventh-hour change in position after a night in which his house "was surrounded by the carriages" of Republican partisans and railroad officials. C. Woodward, Reunion and Reaction 159–160 (1966). Many years later, Professor Bickel concluded that Bradley was honest and impartial. He thought that "'the great question' for Bradley was, in fact, whether Congress was entitled to go behind election returns or had to accept them as certified by state authorities," an "issue of principle." The Least Dangerous Branch 185 (1962). Nonetheless, Bickel points out, the legal question upon which Justice Bradley's decision turned was not very important in the contemporaneous political context. He says that "in the circumstances the issue of principle was trivial, it was overwhelmed by all that hung in the balance, and it should not have been decisive."

For present purposes, the relevance of this history lies in the fact that the participation in the work of the electoral commission by five Justices, including Justice Bradley, did not lend that process legitimacy. Nor did it assure the public that the process had worked fairly, guided by the law. Rather, it simply embroiled Members of the Court in partisan conflict, thereby undermining respect for the judicial process. And the Congress that later enacted the Electoral Count Act knew it.

This history may help to explain why I think it not only legally wrong, but also most unfortunate, for the Court simply to have terminated the Florida recount. Those who caution judicial restraint in resolving political disputes have described the quintessential case for that restraint as a case marked, among other things, by the "strangeness of the issue," its "intractability to principled resolution," its "sheer momentousness, ... which tends to unbalance judicial judgment," and "the inner vulnerability, the self-doubt of an institution which is electorally irresponsible and has no earth to draw strength from." Bickel, *supra*. Those characteristics mark this case.

At the same time, as I have said, the Court is not acting to vindicate a fundamental constitutional principle, such as the need to protect a basic human liberty. No other strong reason to act is present. Congressional statutes tend to obviate the need. And, above all, in this highly politicized matter, the appearance of a split decision runs the risk of undermining the public's confidence in the Court itself. That confidence is a public treasure. It has been built slowly over many years, some of which were marked by a Civil War and the tragedy of segregation. It is a vitally necessary ingredient of any successful effort to protect basic liberty and, indeed, the rule of law itself. We run no risk of returning to the days when a President (responding to this Court's efforts to protect the Cherokee Indians) might have said, "John Marshall has made his decision; now let him enforce it." Loth, Chief Justice John Marshall and The Growth of the American Republic 365 (1948). But we do risk a self-inflicted wound—a wound that may harm not just the Court, but the Nation.

I fear that in order to bring this agonizingly long election process to a definitive conclusion, we have not adequately attended to that necessary "check upon our own exercise of power," "our own sense of self-restraint." *United States v. Butler*, 297 U.S. 1, 79 (1936) (Stone, J., dissenting). Justice Brandeis once said of the Court, "The most important thing we do is not doing." Bickel, *supra*. What it does today, the Court should have left undone. I would repair the damage done as best we now can, by permitting the Florida recount to continue under uniform standards.

I respectfully dissent.

Notes and Questions

1. *The Equal Protection Holding. Bush v. Gore* is the first Supreme Court case applying equal protection analysis to the "nuts and bolts" of elections. What is the holding? Why did the majority cite *Reynolds* and *Harper* (excerpted in Chapters 2 and 3) in support of its decision? Are the fact situations in those cases close enough to support the Court's result by force of analogy? Are there rules of doctrine in *Reynolds* and *Harper* that require the Court's result? If so, what rules?

According to one scholar, the Court's broad statements regarding the right to vote suggest that *Bush v. Gore*'s equal protection holding has implications far beyond Florida-like facts:

> [T]he Supreme Court may have given us an advancement in voting rights doctrine. It has asserted a new constitutional requirement: to avoid disparate and unfair treatment of voters. And this obligation obviously cannot be limited to the recount process alone.... The court's new standard may create a more robust constitutional examination of voting practices.

Samuel Issacharoff, *The Court's Legacy For Voting Rights*, N.Y. TIMES, Dec. 14, 2000, at A35.

A less expansive assessment appears in Richard L. Hasen, Bush v. Gore *and the Future of Equal Protection Law in Elections*, 29 FLORIDA STATE UNIVERSITY LAW REVIEW 377 (2001):

[A]lthough some have heralded the opinion as the (perhaps unintended) dawn of a new era in the jurisprudence of equal protection law in elections, there are good reasons for doubting that the Supreme Court majority intended anyone to take their equal protection holding seriously. Language in the *per curiam* opinion limits it to the facts of the case, or, at most, to cases where jurisdiction-wide recounts are ordered. Moreover, the Court's own analysis was superficial. It failed to explain or justify its large extension of precedent, and, most importantly, given the fact that a "fundamental right" was involved, the Court appeared to speak the language of strict scrutiny but apply something much less than strict scrutiny. Finally, the kind of equal protection claim favored by the conservative justices in the *Bush v. Gore* majority is a strong departure from the usual equal protection jurisprudence they favor. Time will tell whether the Court backs away from its ambitious new equal protection jurisprudence. To the extent that the Court does back away, it further undermines the already-questioned legitimacy of the opinion.

For yet another perspective, see Daniel H. Lowenstein, *The Meaning of* Bush v. Gore, 68 Ohio State Law Journal 1007, 1026–27 (2007):

The major premise [of *Bush v. Gore*] is that when a recount for a public election is conducted in a single judicial proceeding, then any avoidable disparate treatment of identical ballots is—presumptively, at least—a violation of the Equal Protection Clause. . . .

The broad principles regarding the right to vote stated ... in the opinion are not inconsistent with or in tension with the definition of the controversy as one arising in the setting of a judicially conducted recount. To the contrary, these elements are both essential to the holding, which is not that all disparate treatment of identical evidence in a single judicial proceeding violates the Equal Protection Clause and is not that all disparities in "election processes generally" violate the Equal Protection Clause, but that in a single judicial proceeding, disparate treatment of votes cast in a public election (presumptively) violates the Equal Protection Clause.

Which interpretation is most faithful to the majority opinion in *Bush v. Gore*? Consider this questions as you read the cases on voting technology and voter identification discussed in Parts II and III.

2. *The Level of Scrutiny.* In its discussion of the merits, the majority relies upon *Reynolds* and *Harper*, two cases in which the Court established that voting is a fundamental right. Violations of a fundamental right are generally thought to trigger strict scrutiny. Did the Court apply strict scrutiny? If so, why did the "safe harbor" provision of 3 U.S.C. § 5 get to trump the right of every voter to have each vote counted? Consider Hasen, *supra*:

Suppose evidence existed that Florida officials had failed to count the votes of African-American voters in Florida because of racial animus and the Florida Supreme Court ordered a recount of votes that would take time through December 12. It is not clear to me that the "safe harbor" provision should have trumped the right to have every vote count. Now perhaps one could argue even under those circumstances that Florida's interest in meeting the deadline was indeed compelling, and that there were no other means to achieve that goal. But the Supreme Court never even bothered to undertake the analysis in *Bush v. Gore*, suggesting that the fundamental right to vote was not so fundamental after all.

Consider also what the Court itself said earlier in *Bush v. Gore*: "The press of time does not diminish the constitutional concern. A desire for speed is not a general excuse for ignoring equal protection guarantees."

The level of scrutiny is significant. For example, a state might be able to defend the use of punch cards in only some counties as a resource allocation decision under a rational basis test but not under strict scrutiny. For an argument that rational basis is the test that courts *should* apply to local election decisionmaking to preserve the values of federalism, see Richard Briffault, Bush v. Gore *as an Equal Protection Case*, 29 FLORIDA STATE UNIVERSITY LAW REVIEW 325 (2001). For more on the level of scrutiny in election administration cases, see *Crawford v. Marion County Board of Elections* (2008) and the notes that follow, in Part III of this chapter.

3. *Other Constitutional Theories.* Was the essence of the problem in *Bush v. Gore* really one of due process rather than equal protection? See Roy A. Schotland, *In* Bush v. Gore: *Whatever Happened to the Due Process Ground?*, 34 LOYOLA UNIVERSITY OF CHICAGO LAW JOURNAL 211 (2002); Einer Elhauge, *The Lessons of Florida 2000*, POLICY REVIEW, Dec. 1 2001, at 15–36. Should the Court's decision be understood in light of First Amendment cases, which sharply limit the state's ability to rely on vague or ambiguous standards in regulating speech acts? *See* Abner S. Greene, *Is There a First Amendment Defense for* Bush v. Gore?, 80 NOTRE DAME LAW REVIEW 1643 (2005); Daniel P. Tokaji, *First Amendment Equal Protection*, 101 MICHIGAN LAW REVIEW 2409, 2487–95 (2003). Part of the justification for these First Amendment cases is that government officials cannot be trusted to implement such standards in an evenhanded fashion. Is the result in *Bush v. Gore* best explained by the Supreme Court's doubt of the neutrality of local election officials counting the ballots, or of the Florida Supreme Court? See Richard H. Pildes, *Foreword: The Constitutionalization of Democratic Politics*, 118 HARVARD LAW REVIEW 28, 49 (2004) (suggesting that *Bush v. Gore* may best be understood as concerned with the "unconstitutional risk of partisan manipulation in the recount and hence the election itself").

4. *The Remedy to End the Recount.* Perhaps the most controversial part of the Court's opinion was its decision to end the recount on December 12 rather than remand the case to the Florida Supreme Court to articulate a uniform standard for the counting of votes. The Court reached this decision after stating that the Florida supreme court indicated that the Florida legislature wished to take advantage of the safe harbor provision of 3 U.S.C. §5. According to the Court, the Florida court demonstrated this intention when it stated in *Palm Beach County Canvassing Board v. Harris* that Florida's Secretary of State could ignore late returns only if accepting them would "preclud[e] Florida voters from participating fully in the federal electoral process."

Should that be enough evidence of the Florida Supreme Court's interpretation of Florida law? The Supreme Court did not refer to other utterances of the Florida Supreme Court that might have supported its conclusion. In footnote 21 in the Florida Supreme Court's second opinion, *Gore v. Harris*, the court majority responded to the dissents' calls to end the count without questioning the dissents' statements that the safe harbor provisions mandated that the counting must end on December 12. See also *Palm Beach County Canvassing Board v. Harris*, 772 So.2d 1273, 1282 (Fla. 2000), in which the Florida Supreme Court, on remand from the first United States Supreme Court case, indicated that the Florida legislature enacted the Florida election code "[c]onsistent with" 3 U.S.C. §5. Is that enough?

5. *Federalism.* The five Justices in the Supreme Court majority were well known for their constitutional law opinions upholding the rights of the states over the federal gov-

ernment. Critics charge that the *Bush v. Gore* decision is inconsistent with strong federalism principles. See Briffault, *supra*. As we saw in Chapter 5, the Rehnquist Court's decisions establishing the constitutional claim of an "unconstitutional racial gerrymander" similarly has been criticized for deviating from federalism principles. Those cases may have something else in common with *Bush v. Gore*: "Whatever interest the Supreme Court's opinion [in *Bush v. Gore*] vindicated, it was not the interest of an identifiable individual voter. Rather[,] it was a perceived systemic interest in having recounts conducted according to a uniform standard or not at all. It was structural equal protection, just as the [racial gerrymandering] cases have been." Pamela S. Karlan, *Nothing Personal: The Evolution of the Newest Equal Protection from* Shaw v. Reno *to* Bush v. Gore, 79 NORTH CAROLINA LAW REVIEW 1345, 1364 (2001). For a further exploration of this idea, see Heather K. Gerken, *New Wine in Old Bottles: A Comment on Richard Hasen's and Richard Briffault's Essays on* Bush v. Gore, 29 FLORIDA STATE UNIVERSITY LAW REVIEW 407, 409–10 (2001) (under the structural view, *Bush* contains "a claim about how to order a well-functioning democracy, [but was] not a suit about individual rights.").

6. *A Results-Driven Decision?* The *Bush v. Gore* opinion was sharply criticized by liberals as result-oriented jurisprudence. See, for example, Bruce Ackerman, *The Court Packs Itself*, AMERICAN PROSPECT, Feb. 12, 2001. Conservative scholars seemed to agree that this was a result-oriented decision, and few appeared to defend its equal protection holding. Instead, one prominent conservative justified the result as "rough justice," if not "legal justice": "I cannot see the case for precipitating a political and constitutional crisis merely in order to fuss with a statistical tie that, given the inherent subjectivity involved in hand counting spoiled ballots, can never be untied." Richard A. Posner, *Florida 2000: A Legal and Statistical Analysis of the Election Deadlock and Ensuing Litigation*, 2000 SUPREME COURT REVIEW 1, 46. See also Richard A. Posner, BREAKING THE DEADLOCK: THE 2000 ELECTION, THE CONSTITUTION, AND THE COURTS (2001). How close was the United States to a crisis? If the Supreme Court had not intervened, the recounts would have gone forward. If Gore indeed won the recount (something that was far from assured), it was probable that the Florida Legislature would have sent a competing slate of electors to Congress. Congress then would have used one of a series of complicated rules to determine who was President. Under most of the scenarios, Bush would have been declared the President. Is that a crisis? How would you know a crisis if you saw one? What does Posner's analysis say about the line between law and politics? Posner's crisis rationale is criticized in Richard L. Hasen, *A "Tincture of Justice": Judge Posner's Failed Rehabilitation of* Bush v. Gore, 80 TEXAS LAW REVIEW 137 (2001) (book review); Ward Farnsworth, *"To Do a Great Right, Do a Little Wrong": A User's Guide to Judicial Lawlessness*, 86 MINNESOTA LAW REVIEW 227 (2001).

7. *The Article II Rationale*. Richard A. Epstein is probably the strongest academic supporter of the Article II rationale, set forth in Chief Justice Rehnquist's concurring opinion but not adopted by a majority of the Court. Calling the majority's equal protection rationale "a confused nonstarter at best, which deserves much of the scorn that has been heaped upon it," Epstein believes a constitutional violation occurs when "the state court's interpretation [of the legislative provisions governing the choosing of presidential electors] does not fall within the boundaries of acceptable interpretation, but rather represents what must be called, for want of a better term, a gross deviation from the scheme outlined in the statute." Richard A. Epstein, *"In Such Manner as the Legislature Thereof May Direct": The Outcome in* Bush v Gore *Defended*, in THE VOTE: BUSH, GORE AND THE SUPREME COURT 13, 20 (Cass R. Sunstein and Richard A. Epstein eds. 2001).

Criticisms of the Article II interpretation come in two varieties. Some argue that the scope of Article II has itself been misinterpreted, that at least historically it was not understood to favor state *legislatures* to the exclusion of state courts or state constitutions. Hayward H. Smith, *History of the Article II Independent State Legislature Doctrine*, 29 FLORIDA STATE UNIVERSITY LAW REVIEW 731 (2001). Others argue that the Florida Supreme Court's interpretation of Florida law did not violate Article II: "Although the principle underlying the Rehnquist concurrence is sound, the application is bewildering. The Florida Supreme Court's construction of Florida law, while in no way dictated by precedent or the plain language of the statutory scheme, was at a minimum, plausible." Harold J. Krent, *Judging Judging: The Problem of Second-Guessing State Judges' Interpretation of State Law in* Bush v. Gore, 29 FLORIDA STATE UNIVERSITY LAW REVIEW 493, 497 (2001).

8. *Who* Really *Won the Florida Vote?* The election results were final after *Bush v. Gore*, but that did not stop news organizations from attempting to recount the votes. Relying upon an extensive manual evaluation of Florida ballots by a research organization at the University of Chicago, news organizations drew their own conclusions. The *Wall Street Journal* reported that Bush would have won Florida by 493 votes if the counting ordered by the Florida Supreme Court had continued, and by 225 votes if hand recounts had been conducted in the four counties picked by Gore. Jackie Calmes & Edward P. Foldessy, *Florida Revisited: In Election Review, Bush Wins Without Supreme Court Help*, WALL STREET JOURNAL, Nov. 12, 2001, at p. A1. The *Washington Post* reported the same conclusion, and added that if Gore had found a way to trigger a statewide recount of all disputed ballots, or if the courts had required it, the election may have gone to Gore by "the narrowest of margins." Dan Keating & Dan Balz, *Florida Recounts Would Have Favored Bush; but Study Finds Gore Might Have Won Statewide Tally of All Uncounted Ballots*, WASHINGTON POST, Nov. 12, 2001, p. A01. The *New York Times* also reached similar conclusions, but noted that the review found statistical support for the claims of many voters, particularly elderly Democrats in Palm Beach County, that the confused ballot design there may have led them to spoil their ballots by voting for more than one candidate. Ford Fessenden and John M. Broder, *Study of Disputed Florida Ballots Finds Justices Did Not Cast the Deciding Vote*, NEW YORK TIMES, Nov. 12, 2001, at p. A1.

The *Times* also made reference to an earlier study the newspaper conducted showing that 680 of the late-arriving absentee ballots did not meet Florida's standards yet were still counted. A vast majority of those flawed ballots were accepted in counties that favored Bush. *See* David Barstow and Don Van Natta, Jr, *How Bush Took Florida: Mining the Overseas Absentee Vote*, NEW YORK TIMES, July 15, 2001, at p. A1.

To perform your own analysis of the data, visit the *Times'* interactive site at: http://www.nytimes.com/images/2001/11/12/politics/recount/index.html. If you want the raw data, go to the NORC website at: http://www.norc.uchicago.edu/fl/index.asp.

9. *The 2004 Election.* To what extent did *Bush v. Gore* fuel an explosion in election administration litigation? In the run-up to the 2004 presidential election, many observers worried that the election would again end up in the courts. Responding to Florida 2000, Democrats and Republicans dispatched "armies of lawyers" to litigate controversies over the rules of engagement. Controversy over everything from ballot access for Ralph Nader to the rules for counting provisional ballots under the new Help America Vote Act led to scores of court cases across the country.

The battle was most intense in the state of Ohio. There, Democrats and their allies were involved in litigation before Election Day over numerous issues, some stemming from discretionary decisions made by Ohio's Secretary of State, Kenneth Blackwell, a Republican. In his capacity as the state's Chief Elections Officer, he had decided, among other things, that provisional votes cast by a voter in the wrong precinct would not be counted and that voter registration forms printed on paper not of sufficient weight were to be rejected (a decision he later reversed). Though the presidential race was in fact closer in other states, such as Iowa (where Bush won by a little over 10,000 votes), the focus on Ohio turned out to be correct because the election results hinged on Ohio's 20 electoral votes. Preliminary results from Ohio that night showed incumbent President George W. Bush with an approximate 136,000-vote lead over Democratic candidate Senator John Kerry, out of approximately 5.5 million votes cast, with approximately 153,000 provisional ballots yet to be considered for inclusion in the totals.

Despite the potential for litigation, facing these numbers—a 136,000-vote lead with 153,000 votes to be counted—Kerry lawyers "did the math" and concluded that the election was beyond the "margin of litigation." Democrats had identified many problems with the way the Ohio election was conducted, but it was hard to come up with a legal theory that could capture enough votes to swing the results in Ohio, and therefore in the country, to Kerry. The morning after Election Day, Kerry conceded the race and agreed that Bush was victorious in his reelection quest. After the provisional ballots were counted, Ohio's final election results showed Bush finishing with 2,859,764 votes, compared to Kerry's 2,741,165, a difference of 118,599 votes. For more information on the Ohio litigation and related controversies, see Daniel P. Tokaji, *Early Returns on Election Reform: Discretion, Disenfranchisement, and the Help America Vote Act*, 73 George Washington Law Review 1206 (2005).

Despite the fears of some, the presidential election did not go into overtime, but some state and local elections did. Puerto Rico and Washington state saw extensive litigation over exceedingly close gubernatorial elections—following a statewide hand recount, the top two candidates in Washington's race were separated by 133 votes out of six million votes cast. The city of San Diego saw a very close mayor's race, where a write-in candidate might have won but for many of her supporters' failure to properly complete write-in ballots. In each race losing candidates tried to use *Bush v. Gore* to create an equal protection issue in the courts. The Washington and San Diego cases went to trial, and the Puerto Rico case made it all the way to the United States Court of Appeals for the First Circuit. None of the challenges succeeded. For background on the cases, see David Postman, *Rossi Loses in Court; Won't Appeal Ruling*, Seattle Times, Jun. 7, 2005; Istra Pacheco, *Anibal Acevedo Vila Officially Declared New Governor of Puerto Rico*, AP Newstream, Dec. 29, 2004; Greg Moran, *Court Case on Behalf of Frye Votes is Dropped*, San Diego Union-Tribune, May 13, 2005.

10. *Increased Election Litigation.* Nationwide, the number of election law cases has continued to grow. Consider Figure 7.2, reprinted with permission, from Richard L. Hasen, *The Untimely Death of Bush v. Gore*, 60 Stanford Law Review 1 (2007), showing that the average number of election-related cases in the 1996–99 period was 96 per year, compared to an average of 230 cases per year from 2001–06. This may be good news for election lawyers and bad news for everyone else. We discuss two of the most active areas of election-related litigation—voting technology and voter identification—in Parts II and III of this chapter. To what extent is the growth in election administration litigation attributable to the Florida controversy of 2000? Are there other reasons for the growth in litigation? See Charles Anthony Smith & Christopher Shortell, *The Suits That Counted: The Judicialization of Presidential Elections*, 6 Election Law Journal 251 (2007), finding an increase in pre-election litigation in 2000, which suggests more reliance on courts even before *Bush v. Gore*.

Figure 7.2

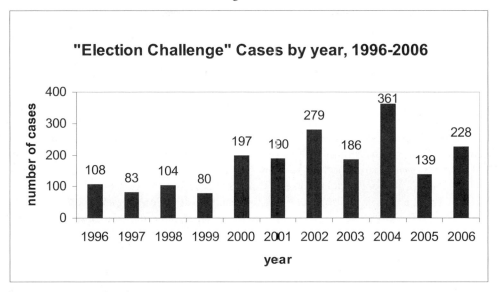

For a discussion of the types of problems that can and sometimes do wind up being litigated after an election, see Edward B. Foley, *The Analysis and Mitigation of Electoral Errors: Theory, Practice, Policy*, 18 STANFORD LAW & POLICY REVIEW 350, 362–74 (2007). For a comprehensive analysis of the remedies that courts have imposed in post-election litigation, see Steven F. Huefner, *Remedying Election Wrongs*, 44 HARVARD JOURNAL OF LEGISLATION 265 (2007). Huefner notes that provisional ballots and other recent electoral reforms may have the unintended consequences of increasing the likelihood of post-election disputes. *Id.* at 267.

11. *Bibliographical Note.* There is an enormous amount of academic and non-academic commentary on the Florida 2000 election and its resolution. One of the most valuable academic sources for varied perspectives on the case is THE VOTE: BUSH, GORE, AND THE SUPREME COURT (Cass R. Sunstein & Richard A. Epstein eds. 2001). The book features articles by Richard Epstein, Elizabeth Garrett, Samuel Issacharoff, Pamela S. Karlan, Michael W. McConnell, Frank I. Michelman, Richard H. Pildes, Richard A. Posner, David A. Strauss, Cass R. Sunstein, and John C. Yoo. Another valuable resource is the symposium in Volume 29, Number 2 of the FLORIDA STATE UNIVERSITY LAW REVIEW (2001), featuring articles by Steve Bickerstaff, Richard Briffault, Luis Fuentes-Rohwer & Guy-Uriel Charles, Richard D. Friedman, James A. Gardner, Elizabeth Garrett, Heather K. Gerken, Steven G. Gey, Richard L. Hasen, Pamela S. Karlan, Harold J. Krent, Sanford Levinson & Ernest A. Young, William P. Marshall, John O. McGinnis, Spencer Overton, Richard H. Pildes, Richard A. Posner, Robert J. Pushaw, Jr., Robert A. Schapiro, Peter M. Shane, and Hayward H. Smith. A readable survey of the legal issues may be found in Howard Gillman, THE VOTES THAT COUNTED: HOW THE SUPREME COURT DECIDED THE 2000 PRESIDENTIAL ELECTION (2001). Ronald Dworkin edited an anthology entitled: A BADLY FLAWED ELECTION: DEBATING BUSH V. GORE, THE SUPREME COURT AND AMERICAN DEMOCRACY (2003). For a review, see Bruce Cain, *Flaws Everywhere: A Review of a Badly Flawed Election*, 2 ELECTION LAW JOURNAL 525 (2003). Various other perspectives on the legal and political consequences of *Bush v. Gore* may be found in THE FINAL ARBITER: THE CONSEQUENCES OF *BUSH V. GORE* FOR LAW AND POLITICS (Christopher P. Banks et al., eds., 2005).

Other academic articles that readers may wish to consult include: Jack M. Balkin, Bush v. Gore *and the Boundary Between Law and Politics*, 110 YALE LAW JOURNAL 1407 (2001); Erwin Chemerinsky, Bush v. Gore *Was Not Justiciable*, 76 NOTRE DAME LAW REVIEW 1093 (2001); Michael C. Dorf & Samuel Issacharoff, *Can Process Theory Constrain the Courts?*, 72 UNIVERSITY OF COLORADO LAW REVIEW 923 (2001); Bradley W. Joondeph, Bush v. Gore, *Federalism, and the Distrust of Politics*, 62 OHIO STATE LAW JOURNAL 1781 (2001); Michael J. Klarman, Bush v. Gore *Through the Lens of Constitutional History*, 89 CALIFORNIA LAW REVIEW 1721 (2001); Nelson Lund, *The Unbearable Rightness of* Bush v. Gore, 23 CARDOZO LAW REVIEW 1219 (2002); Spencer Overton, *Rules, Standards, and* Bush v. Gore: *Form and the Law of Democracy*, 37 HARVARD CIVIL RIGHTS-CIVIL LIBERTIES LAW REVIEW 65 (2002); George Priest, *Reanalyzing* Bush v. Gore: *Democratic Accountability and Judicial Overreaching*, 72 UNIVERSITY OF COLORADO LAW REVIEW 953 (2001); Robert J. Pushaw, Jr., *Politics, Ideology, and the Academic Assault on Bush v. Gore*, 2 ELECTION LAW JOURNAL 97 (2003). Laurence H. Tribe, eroG v. hsuB *and Its Disguises: Freeing* Bush v. Gore *From Its Hall of Mirrors*, 115 HARVARD LAW REVIEW 170 (2001); and Mark Tushnet, *Renormalizing* Bush v. Gore: *An Anticipatory Intellectual History*, 90 GEORGETOWN LAW JOURNAL 113 (2001).

An overview of the legal issues in *Bush v. Gore* and other cases surrounding the 2000 election may be found in Abner Greene, UNDERSTANDING THE 2000 ELECTION: A GUIDE TO THE LEGAL BATTLES THAT DECIDED THE PRESIDENCY (2001). For a look at the Florida 2000 litigation surrounding the counting of military and other overseas ballots, see Diane H. Mazur, *The Bullying of America: A Cautionary Tale about Military Voting and Civil-Military Relations*, 4 ELECTION LAW JOURNAL 105 (2005). Julian M. Pleasants, HANGING CHADS: THE INSIDE STORY OF THE 2000 PRESIDENTIAL RECOUNT IN FLORIDA (2004) contains interviews with many of the major participants in the Florida controversy, including Florida Supreme Court Justice Major Harding, and Judges Nikki Ann Clark and Terry P. Lewis. See also Clifford A. Jones, *Out of Guatemala?: Election Law Reform in Florida and the Legacy of* Bush v. Gore *in the 2004 Presidential Election*, 5 ELECTION LAW JOURNAL 121 (2006).

Much of the academic commentary has been sharply critical of the Court's decision. Leading articles defending the Court's decision (though not necessarily its reasoning) include those by Richard Epstein and Michael McConnell (both in THE VOTE) and the Richard Posner book cited above. Nelson Lund takes a rare position defending both the opinion's reasoning and its remedy. Of course, most legal academics are Democrats. There appears to be a very strong correlation between partisan preferences and evaluations of *Bush v. Gore* among academics. For the view that the Florida controversy is best observed through the lens of the literary genre of comedy, see Daniel Lowenstein, *Lessons from the Florida Controversy*, in REALISING DEMOCRACY: ELECTORAL LAW IN AUSTRALIA 7 (Graeme Orr, Bryan Mercurio and George Williams, eds., 2003). For differing perspectives on *Bush v. Gore*'s legacy, see Richard L. Hasen, *The Untimely Death of* Bush v. Gore, 60 STANFORD LAW REVIEW 1 (2007); Edward Foley, *The Future of* Bush v. Gore, 68 OHIO STATE LAW JOURNAL 925 (2007); and Chad Flanders, Bush v. Gore *and the Uses of "Limiting,"* 116 YALE LAW JOURNAL 1159 (2007). For still more citations, see Richard L. Hasen, *A Critical Guide to* Bush v. Gore *Scholarship*, 7 ANNUAL REVIEW OF POLITICAL SCIENCE 297 (2004).

II. Voting Technology

Exercising the right to vote effectively requires that voters' intentions be recorded and counted accurately. Yet the issue of voting technology was not much on the public's radar screen before the 2000 presidential election. During and after that election, a great deal of evidence emerged regarding disparities in the accuracy of the various vote-counting technologies, resulting especially from deficiencies of the punch-card voting machines used in Florida and in many other parts of the country at the time.

A number of post-Florida commissions recommended changes to voting technology and ballot design. Perhaps the most influential study is the July 2001 Report of the Caltech-MIT Voting Technology Project, *Voting — What Is, What Could Be*, available at http://www.vote.caltech.edu/media/documents/july01/July01_VTP_Voting_Report_Entire.pdf. The study estimated that between 4 and 6 million votes for president were lost for a variety of reasons including faulty equipment and confusing ballots (1.5 to 2 million votes), registration mixups (1.5 to 3 million votes), polling place problems (up to 1 million votes), and absentee ballot problems (number of lost votes unknown). One of the report's main findings was that punch card technology was among the worst technologies. Other empirical studies found a "racial gap" in the number of lost votes resulting from punch card technologies, with more invalid votes cast in heavily African-American precincts. Michael Tomz & Robert P. Van Houweling, *How Does Voting Equipment Affect the Racial Gap in Voided Ballots?*, 47 AMERICAN JOURNAL OF POLITICAL SCIENCE 46 (2003). For a summary of the post-2000 empirical research concerning disparities in the number of lost votes resulting from different types of voting equipment, see Daniel P. Tokaji, *The Paperless Chase: Electronic Voting and Democratic Values*, 73 FORDHAM LAW REVIEW 1712, 1754–68 (2005) and Richard B. Saphire & Paul Moke, *Litigating* Bush v. Gore *in the States: Dual Voting Systems and the Fourteenth Amendment*, 51 VILLANOVA LAW REVIEW 229, 238–42 (2006).

The evidence of lost votes arising from certain types of voting equipment generated a new round of litigation after the 2000 election. Lawsuits challenging punch cards and other paper-based voting systems were filed in Florida, Georgia, Illinois, California, and Ohio. Congress also got into the act, passing the Help America Vote Act of 2002 ("HAVA"). HAVA did not require the replacement of existing voting equipment, but it did set standards and provide funds allowing states to purchase new voting technology.[c] As a result, punch cards were virtually extinct by the time of the 2006 elections.

With the demise of punch card voting machines, attention shifted to the security of new voting technology, most notably paperless direct record electronic (DRE) systems such as touchscreens. The switch to new voting systems has reduced the number of ballots that do not register a valid vote. Charles Stewart, *Residual Vote in the 2004 Election*, 5 ELECTION LAW JOURNAL 158 (2006), estimates that improvements in voting technology and procedures from 2000 to 2004 "saved" approximately one million votes. Others point out that DREs are easier to use and less error-prone than other voting systems, and that they are more accessible to voters with certain types of disabilities. For discussion of the advantages and disadvantages of new voting technology, see Paul S. Herrnson et al., VOTING TECHNOLOGY: THE NOT-SO-SIMPLE ACT OF CASTING A BALLOT (2008); R. Michael Alvarez & Thad E. Hall, ELECTRONIC ELECTIONS: THE PERILS AND PROMISES OF DIGITAL DEMOCRACY (2008); and Robert M. Stein, et al., *Voting Technology, Election Administration, and Voter Performance*, 7 ELECTION LAW JOURNAL 123 (2008).

DRE critics claim that the new technology raises security concerns, and some have filed lawsuits challenging paperless DRE systems. Relying in part on *Bush v. Gore*, critics have argued that the use of these systems deny voters equal protection due to the increased risk that their votes will not be counted. The following is one of those cases.

---

c. The requirements of HAVA are discussed in greater detail in Part IV.B.2 of this chapter.

Wexler v. Anderson

452 F.3d 1226 (11th Cir. 2006)

KRAVITCH, Circuit Judge:

The issue presented in this appeal is whether Florida's manual recount procedures in those counties employing paperless touchscreen voting machines violate the rights of voters in those counties to equal protection and due process under the Fifth and Fourteenth Amendments to the United States Constitution. For the reasons that follow, we hold that they do not.

I. Facts

Florida's Voting System

Florida's Electronic Voting Systems Act makes Florida's Department of State responsible for developing and adopting standards for electronic voting and for certifying electronic voting systems for use in the state. *See* Fla. Stat. §§ 101.5601–101.5614. Each county may then choose its own voting equipment from among those systems certified by the Department of State. In fifteen of Florida's sixty-seven counties, voters cast their votes using paperless touchscreen voting machines, which require that voters make their selections directly on computer screens by literally touching the screen as indicated. In the remaining fifty-two counties, voters cast optical scan ballots. To vote using an optical scan ballot, a voter uses a pencil to fill in a bubble or arrow by the name of the candidate he wishes to vote for; the ballot is then run through an automatic tabulation machine. Voters casting absentee or provisional ballots in touchscreen counties also submit optical scan ballots.

Manual Recount Procedures

Florida law provides for a two-stage recount procedure in certain close elections. First, if the margin of victory is one-half of a percent or less, election officials conduct a "machine recount," which entails re-tabulating ballots in precincts using optical scan ballots, and, in touchscreen voting precincts, examining "the counters on the precinct tabulators to ensure that the total of the returns on the precinct tabulators equals the overall election return." Second, if the results of the machine recount indicate a margin of victory of one-quarter of a percent or less, officials conduct a manual recount of all "overvotes" and "undervotes" (collectively, "residual votes"). An overvote results when "the elector marks or designates more names than there are persons to be elected to an office or designates more than one answer to a ballot question, and the tabulator records no vote for the office or question." An undervote results when "the elector does not properly designate any choice for an office or ballot question, and the tabulator records no vote for the office or question."

During the manual recount phase, auditors review residual votes to determine if there is a "clear indication on the ballot that the voter has made a definite choice." To that end, the Department of State is charged with: (1) adopting "specific rules for each certified voting system prescribing what constitutes a 'clear indication on the ballot that the voter has made a definite choice,'" and (2) issuing "detailed rules prescribing additional recount procedures for each certified voting system which shall be uniform to the extent practicable."

The manual recount is a fairly straightforward process in optical scan counties; auditors look for stray marks that may have misled the machines or other indicia that a voter has made a definite choice. For example, a voter might circle a candidate's name rather than making the prescribed mark to indicate his choice. In touchscreen counties, however, this process has proved more difficult. It is impossible to overvote in a touchscreen county; the touchscreen voting machines will not allow it. It is possible to undervote when using touchscreen voting machines, however, although the machines prompt a voter when he undervotes, providing him with an opportunity to choose a candidate for that race.

Emergency Rule

Because a touchscreen voter never records his vote onto paper, and there is no provision in these counties for contemporaneous print-outs of individual ballots, a "manual recount" in touchscreen counties does not allow for the same type of review of ballots for voter or machine error provided in optical scan counties. In light of these characteristics of touchscreen voting systems, the Florida Department of State originally did not require manual recounts in touchscreen counties. An administrative law judge struck down the original rule that failed to require manual recounts, however, and the Secretary of State [sought to comply by adopting Rule 1S-2.031].

Rule 1S-2.031 provides that if a manual recount becomes necessary, the canvassing board shall order the printing of one official copy of the ballot image report[4] from each touchscreen voting machine that has recorded undervotes for the affected race. If the certified voting system is capable of electronically sorting and identifying undervotes, then the canvassing board shall order the printing of a report indicating the undervotes. The ballot image report shall then be examined by the counting teams to identify and highlight ballot images containing undervotes for the affected race to determine if there is a clear indication on the ballot image that the voter made a definite choice to undervote. For those machines capable of electronically sorting, the undervotes shall be identified by the machine.

After identifying the undervotes, the counting teams shall maintain a running tally of the number of undervotes totaled per touchscreen voting machine in each precinct and then tabulate the total number of undervotes from all machines in that precinct. The counting teams shall then compare the total number of undervotes manually recounted for each precinct to the total number of undervotes reported by the voting system in the complete canvass report. If the comparison of the undervotes for each precinct matches the total number reported for such precinct, then the counting team shall certify the results of the machine recount to the canvassing board. If a discrepancy exists, however, the counting teams are to re-tabulate the number of undervotes for such precinct at least two additional times and, if necessary, the canvassing board must investigate and resolve the discrepancy.

The emergency rule instructs that "[t]he clear indication that the voter has made a definite choice to undervote shall be determined by the presence of the marking, or the absence of any marking, that the manufacturer of the certified voting system indicates shall be present or absent to signify an undervote." The rule goes on to specify how an undervote is designated for each of the three types of touchscreen voting machines currently certified for use in Florida....

On March 8, 2004, [U.S. Congressman Robert Wexler], Palm Beach County Commissioners Addie Greene and Burt Aaronson, and registered Florida voter Tony Fransetta

---

4. A "ballot image" is an electronic record of the content of a ballot cast by a voter and recorded by a voting device, and a "ballot image report" is a printout of ballot images for each machine or precinct.

brought the present action against Secretary of State Hood, LePore (Arthur Anderson's predecessor as the Supervisor of Elections for Palm Beach County) and Kay Clem, the Supervisor of Elections for Indian River County....

Following a bench trial, the district court ruled for defendants, holding that [the rule] established a manual recount procedure for touchscreen voting systems that both complies with Florida law and establishes a uniform, nondifferential standard for conducting manual recounts, satisfying the requirements of equal protection and due process. Plaintiffs now appeal....

III. Discussion

The basic theory of Plaintiffs' case is that by certifying touchscreen voting systems that are incapable of providing for the type of manual recounts contemplated by Florida law, the defendants have violated the equal protection and due process rights of voters in touchscreen counties. Although we agree with the district court that Florida's manual recount procedures for touchscreen counties comply with Florida law, the constitutional questions do not turn on that inquiry. Instead, we consider whether Florida's manual recount procedures, which vary by county according to voting system, accord arbitrary and disparate treatment to Florida voters, thereby depriving voters of their constitutional rights to due process and equal protection. *See Bush v. Gore.*

Equal Protection

Plaintiffs argue that the manual recount procedure for touchscreen counties fails to provide for meaningful review of undervotes. They contend that the ballot image summaries generated during recounts "do not permit the canvassing board to determine whether the voter made an intentional choice to undervote or that the machine failed to record the vote due to voter mistake, human error, or system error." Plaintiffs thus argue that Florida voters are not accorded equal treatment because those residing in optical scan counties will have an opportunity to have their residual votes reviewed in a meaningful way in certain very close elections whereas those residing in touchscreen counties will not.

Plaintiffs' fundamental error is one of perspective. By adopting the perspective of the residual voter, they have avoided the question that is of constitutional dimension: Are voters in touchscreen counties less likely to cast an effective vote than voters in optical scan counties? It is this question, and not the question of whether uniform procedures have been followed across a state regardless of differences in voting technology, that the Supreme Court consistently has emphasized in its voting jurisprudence. *See, e.g., Bush* ("Having once granted the right to vote on equal terms, the state may not, by later arbitrary treatment, value one person's vote over that of another."); *Dunn v. Blumstein* ("[A] citizen has a constitutionally protected right to participate in elections on an equal basis with other citizens in the jurisdiction."); *Reynolds v. Sims* ("Weighting the votes of citizens differently, by any method or means, merely because of where they happen to reside, hardly seems justifiable."); *Wesberry v. Sanders* ("[A]s nearly as is practicable[,] one man's vote in a congressional election is to be worth as much as another's.").

The right to vote is fundamental, forming the bedrock of our democracy. Nevertheless, states are entitled to burden that right to ensure that elections are fair, honest and efficient. *See Burdick v. Takushi; Anderson v. Celebrezze; Storer v. Brown.* Recognizing that "[e]lection laws will invariably impose some burden upon individual voters," the Supreme Court has explained that the level of scrutiny courts apply to state voting regulations should vary with the degree to which a regulation burdens the right to vote. Specifically, the Court has instructed that

> [a] court considering a challenge to a state election law must weigh "the character and magnitude of the asserted injury to the rights protected by the First and Fourteenth Amendments that the plaintiff seeks to vindicate" against "the precise interests put forward by the State as justifications for the burden imposed by its rule," taking into consideration "the extent to which those interests make it necessary to burden the plaintiff's rights."

Burdick. When a state election law imposes only "reasonable, nondiscriminatory restrictions" upon voters' rights, the "State's important regulatory interests are generally sufficient" to sustain the regulation. *Id.*

The plaintiffs argue that because voters in touchscreen counties have no opportunity to have their residual votes counted manually whereas voters in optical scan counties have such an opportunity, Florida's disparate treatment of these groups warrants strict scrutiny. The plaintiffs, however, did not plead that voters in touchscreen counties are less likely to cast effective votes due to the alleged lack of a meaningful manual recount procedure in those counties. Thus, if voters in touchscreen counties are burdened at all, that burden is the mere possibility that should they cast residual ballots, those ballots will receive a different, and allegedly inferior, type of review in the event of a manual recount. Such a burden, borne of a reasonable, nondiscriminatory regulation, is not so substantial that strict scrutiny is appropriate.... Thus, we review Florida's manual recount procedures to determine if they are justified by the State's "important regulatory interests." *See Burdick.*

Here, Florida has important reasons for employing different manual recount procedures according to the type of voting system a county uses. The differences between these procedures are necessary given the differences in the technologies themselves and the types of errors voters are likely to make in utilizing those technologies. Voters casting optical scan ballots can make a variety of mistakes that will cause their ballots not to be counted. For example, a voter casting an optical scan ballot might leave a stray pencil mark or circle a candidate's name rather than filling in the appropriate bubble. Thus, although an optical scan tabulation machine may register an undervote for a particular race on a particular ballot, there may be sufficient indicia on the ballot that the voter actually chose a candidate in that race such that the vote would be counted in a manual recount. In contrast, a voter in a touchscreen county either chooses a candidate for a particular race or does not; the touchscreen machines do not record ambiguous indicia of voter intent that can later be reviewed during a manual recount.

Plaintiffs do not contend that equal protection requires a state to employ a single kind of voting system throughout the state. Indeed, "local variety [in voting systems] can be justified by concerns about cost, the potential value of innovation, and so on." *Bush* (Souter, J., dissenting). Among other things, witnesses for the State testified that touchscreen machines have certain benefits for disabled voters and they prevent some of the voter errors that are characteristic of optical scan voting systems. Accordingly, we hold that Florida's manual recount procedures are justified by the State's important regulatory interests and, therefore, they do not violate equal protection.

Due Process

Plaintiffs argue that Florida's manual recount procedures are devoid of "fundamental fairness," thereby depriving voters of due process. However, as we noted above, whatever burden, if any, Florida's manual recount procedures place on voters, that burden is justified by the important regulatory interests outlined above. Therefore, we hold that Florida's manual recount procedures do not deprive voters of due process.

For the foregoing reasons, the judgment of the district court is AFFIRMED.

Notes and Questions

1. The *Wexler* court notes that plaintiffs "did not plead that voters in touchscreen counties are less likely to cast effective votes." If they had included such an allegation in their complaint, would this have been enough for their case to proceed? What sort of evidence should be required for plaintiffs to mount a successful equal protection challenge to new voting technology? Should courts be required to wait for an election meltdown before declaring that a particular voting system poses an unacceptable threat to voters' constitutional rights? Are courts better qualified to make such judgments than election officials?

Thus far, constitutional challenges to DRE systems have not fared well in the lower courts. See *Weber v. Shelley*, 347 F.3d 1101 (9th Cir. 2003); *Schade v. Maryland State Board of Elections*, 930 A.2d 304 (Md. 2007). For further discussion of the policy and legal issues in the debate over electronic voting, see Daniel P. Tokaji, *The Paperless Chase: Electronic Voting and Democratic Values*, 73 FORDHAM LAW REVIEW 1712 (2005). A bibliography of post-2000 scholarship on the issue may be found in Susan M. Boland & Therese Clarke Arado, *O Brave New World? Electronic Voting Machines and Internet Voting: An Annotated Bibliography*, 27 NORTHERN ILLINOIS UNIVERSITY LAW REVIEW 313 (2007).

2. *The Relevance of* Bush v. Gore. The *Wexler* opinion quotes *Bush v. Gore* for the proposition that "Having once granted the right to vote on equal terms, the state may not, by later arbitrary treatment, value one person's vote over that of another." If certain voters are less likely to have their votes counted due to untrustworthy voting technology, is the state "valu[ing] one's person vote over that of another"? Is the *Wexler* formulation a correct statement of *Bush v. Gore*'s holding? Consider, in this connection, the different interpretations summarized in Note 1 following *Bush v. Gore*, above.

3. *The Level of Scrutiny*. The *Wexler* court rejects plaintiffs' invitation to apply strict scrutiny, distinguishing other cases—like the "one person, one vote" cases—in which heightened scrutiny applied. At what point, if any, should strict scrutiny apply to disparities in voting technology? What if plaintiffs had introduced stronger statistical evidence, showing that certain voters are much less likely to have their votes counted? Suppose that a state uses two different types of voting equipment with 5% and 0.5 % error rates respectively? What if the difference were smaller, say 1% versus 0.5%? If relatively small statistical disparities in the likelihood of one's vote being counted violate the Equal Protection Clause, wouldn't a state effectively be required to use the same equipment in every precinct? Would that be a good result?

Consider also how courts should go about determining the applicable level of scrutiny when it comes to other disparities in running an election within a state, such as polling place operations. Suppose that in one county, the average voter must wait in a ten-minute line in order to vote while, in a neighboring county, the average voter need only wait in a two-minute line. Suppose one county provides free postage for voters to return absentee ballots, while another county requires voters to pay postage. Should such disparities trigger strict scrutiny?

4. *Punch Card Litigation*. Cases like *Wexler*, challenging electronic voting systems, may be thought of as the "second wave" of voting technology litigation since *Bush v.*

Gore. The first wave involved the challenges to punch card voting systems, mentioned earlier. Of the various cases challenging punch card voting equipment only the Ohio case went to trial. The district court rejected plaintiffs' equal protection claim, but a divided panel of the Sixth Circuit reversed in *Stewart v. Blackwell,* 444 F.3d 843 (6th Cir. 2006), a case that included a spirited exchange on the precedential value of *Bush v. Gore.* The majority opinion by Judge Boyce Martin cited statistical evidence that punch-card voting equipment results in more ballots that do not register a valid vote than newer voting technology providing voters with notice and the opportunity to correct mistakes. Judge Martin wrote:

> [V]oters in Ohio vote under two separate standards. Although voters approach the polls with the opportunity to vote in the same elections for the same candidates, once they step into the voting booth, they have an unequal chance of their vote being counted, *not* as a result of any action on the part of the voter, but because of the different technology utilized. Voters able to utilize notice technology [like touchscreen DREs] choose candidates and before their vote is turned in and counted, the technology notifies them of any errors that would result in the vote being disregarded. Those voters forced to use non-notice technology [like punch cards] are not notified of any errors in their ballot and, should errors exist, their votes are disregarded; moreover, voters using the two challenged technologies have an additional likelihood of disenfranchisement due to the inherent deficiencies of the punch-card and central-count optical scan.

In dissent, Judge Ronald Gilman argued that the majority had given too much weight to the Supreme Court's "murky" decision in *Bush v. Gore*:

> What actually provides the analytical basis for the majority opinion … is the Supreme Court's decision in *Bush v. Gore* and a series of lower-court cases that have purported to adopt the reasoning of that decision.… I believe that we should heed the Supreme Court's own warning and limit the reach of *Bush v. Gore* to the peculiar and extraordinary facts of that case. *See* Hasen, Bush v. Gore *and the Future of Equal Protection Law in Elections.* The majority has chosen a different path, one that unjustifiably expands *Bush v. Gore* into a landmark precedent designed to fundamentally transform federal election law.

This statement provoked a sharp reply from the *Stewart* majority, "reject[ing] the dissent's claim that Professor Hasen's article has overruled the Supreme Court's decision in *Bush v. Gore.*" In a footnote, the majority wrote:

> [T]he dissent begins by criticizing our "reliance on the Supreme Court's murky decision in *Bush v. Gore.*" Murky, transparent, illegitimate, right, wrong, big, tall, short or small; regardless of the adjective one might use to describe the decision, the proper noun that precedes it — 'Supreme Court" — carries more weight with us. Whatever else *Bush v. Gore* may be, it is first and foremost a decision of the Supreme Court of the United States and we are bound to adhere to it.

Who has the better of the argument over *Bush v. Gore*'s precedential value? Was there a stronger argument available to the dissenting judge in *Stewart v. Blackwell,* one that does not rest on the proposition that *Bush v. Gore* lacks precedential value? If you were representing a state using different voting systems in different counties with somewhat different residual vote rates, how would you defend against an argument predicated on *Bush v. Gore*?

After the panel opinion in *Stewart*, the Sixth Circuit granted the Ohio Secretary of State's petition for rehearing en banc and ultimately found the case moot because Ohio had by then replaced its punch card voting system. *Stewart v. Blackwell*, 473 F.3d 692 (6th Cir. 2007). The panel opinion holding Ohio's use of different voting equipment unconstitutional was therefore vacated.

Another state which saw litigation over its punch card voting equipment was California. After a settlement had been reached in that state providing for the replacement of punch cards, but before that equipment had actually been replaced, a dispute arose over the use of that equipment in the 2003 gubernatorial recall election. A three-judge panel of the United States Court of Appeals for the Ninth Circuit ordered the recall election to be delayed until punch cards were replaced. An eleven-judge *en banc* panel of the Ninth Circuit unanimously reversed the three-judge panel and allowed the election to go forward. See *Southwest Voter Registration Education Project v. Shelley*, 344 F.3d 882 (9th Cir.), *rev'd en banc* 344 F.3d 914 (9th. Cir. 2003). The *en banc* court's brief opinion focused not on the merits, but instead on the harm to the State of California from enjoining the recall election. The recall was therefore allowed to proceed, and Governor Gray Davis was recalled with actor Arnold Schwarzenegger elected as his successor. For divergent views on this litigation, see Richard L. Hasen, *Ninth Circuit Erred in Allowing Recall Election with Punch Card Votes*, 1 THE FORUM Issue 4 (2003), *available at* http://www.bepress.com/forum/vol1/iss4/art5; Daniel H. Lowenstein, *An Irresponsible Intrusion*, 1 THE FORUM Issue 4 (2003), *available at* http://www.bepress.com/vol1/iss4/art4.

As a doctrinal matter, the vacatur of the panel opinions in both the Ohio and California cases wipes the slate clean, meaning that there are no appellate precedents regarding the applicability of *Bush v. Gore* to punch card voting systems.

5. *Another Disputed Election in Florida.* In the November 2006 election for Florida's 13th Congressional District, Democrat Christine Jennings lost to Republican Vern Buchanan by 369 votes, according to the final tally, with over 18,000 "ballots" cast on electronic voting machines registering no vote in that contest. Most experts believe that poor ballot design was to blame for the high number of ballots registering no vote, but others think that there may have been flaws in the voting machine's software. Jennings was unsuccessful in her attempts to persuade courts to force the release of the software code and to obtain relief, either from the courts or the House of Representatives. See House Report 110–528, *Dismissing the Election Contest Relating to the Office of Representative from the Thirteenth Congressional District of Florida, Report of the Committee on House Administration to Accompany H. Res. 989* (2008). Court papers and other materials relating to this dispute may be found at http://moritzlaw.osu.edu/electionlaw/litigation/Jenningsv.ElectionsCanvassingCommission.php.

Would the result in *Wexler* have been different if it had been decided after the Buchanan-Jennings election? Should it have been? If the DRE system in use had been modified to provide a paper copy of each voter's ballot in order to allow for a manual recount, would that have had any effect in the Buchanan-Jennings contest?

III. Voter Identification

Since 2004, there has been a move in some states to enact voter identification laws. The Help America Vote Act ("HAVA") imposed a limited voter identification requirement, applicable to first-time voters who had registered by mail, but allowed either a photo ID or other documents (like a utility bill or bank statement).

A number of states have enacted requirements that go beyond HAVA. The most stringent of these state laws require voters to show government-issued *photo* identification in order to have their votes counted. Supporters, primarily Republicans, argue that stricter voter identification laws are needed to preserve the reality and appearance of election integrity, by ensuring that only eligible citizens may participate. Opponents, primarily Democrats, argue that the requirements impede participation by eligible voters, especially those who are poor, elderly, disabled, or minorities. Each side also disputes the other's claims, Democrats arguing that photo ID requirements prevent little or no voter fraud and Republicans arguing that the requirements prevent few if any eligible voters from voting. Why do Republicans support strict voter identification laws? Why do Democrats oppose them? See Richard L. Hasen, *Fraud Reform? How Efforts to ID Voting Problems Have Become a Partisan Mess*, SLATE, Feb. 22, 2006, *available at* http://www.slate.com/id/2136776/.

Several states' voter identification laws have been challenged as unconstitutional. In the following case, the Supreme Court upheld Indiana's voter identification law, probably the strictest law in the nation at the time the case was decided:

Crawford v. Marion County Election Board
128 S. Ct. 1610 (2008)

Justice STEVENS announced the judgment of the Court and delivered an opinion in which THE CHIEF JUSTICE and Justice KENNEDY join.

At issue in these cases is the constitutionality of an Indiana statute requiring citizens voting in person on election day, or casting a ballot in person at the office of the circuit court clerk prior to election day, to present photo identification issued by the government.

Referred to as either the "Voter ID Law" or "SEA 483," the statute applies to in-person voting at both primary and general elections. The requirement does not apply to absentee ballots submitted by mail, and the statute contains an exception for persons living and voting in a state-licensed facility such as a nursing home. A voter who is indigent or has a religious objection to being photographed may cast a provisional ballot that will be counted only if she executes an appropriate affidavit before the circuit court clerk within 10 days following the election. A voter who has photo identification but is unable to present that identification on election day may file a provisional ballot that will be counted if she brings her photo identification to the circuit county clerk's office within 10 days. No photo identification is required in order to register to vote, and the State offers free photo identification to qualified voters able to establish their residence and identity.

Promptly after the enactment of SEA 483 in 2005, the Indiana Democratic Party and the Marion County Democratic Central Committee (Democrats) filed suit in the Federal District Court for the Southern District of Indiana against the state officials responsible for its enforcement, seeking a judgment declaring the Voter ID Law invalid and enjoining its enforcement. A second suit seeking the same relief was brought on behalf of two elected officials and several nonprofit organizations representing groups of elderly, disabled, poor, and minority voters. The cases were consolidated, and the State of Indiana intervened to defend the validity of the statute.

The complaints in the consolidated cases allege that the new law substantially burdens the right to vote in violation of the Fourteenth Amendment; that it is neither a necessary nor appropriate method of avoiding election fraud; and that it will arbitrarily disfranchise qualified voters who do not possess the required identification and will place an unjustified burden on those who cannot readily obtain such identification.

[The district court granted defendants' motion for summary judgment, a divided panel of the Seventh Circuit affirmed, and the Seventh Circuit denied en banc review.]

I

In *Harper v. Virginia Bd. of Elections*, the Court held that Virginia could not condition the right to vote in a state election on the payment of a poll tax of $1.50. We rejected the dissenters' argument that the interest in promoting civic responsibility by weeding out those voters who did not care enough about public affairs to pay a small sum for the privilege of voting provided a rational basis for the tax. Applying a stricter standard, we concluded that a State "violates the Equal Protection Clause of the Fourteenth Amendment whenever it makes the affluence of the voter or payment of any fee an electoral standard." We used the term "invidiously discriminate" to describe conduct prohibited under that standard, noting that we had previously held that while a State may obviously impose "reasonable residence restrictions on the availability of the ballot," it "may not deny the opportunity to vote to a bona fide resident merely because he is a member of the armed services." Although the State's justification for the tax was rational, it was invidious because it was irrelevant to the voter's qualifications.

Thus, under the standard applied in *Harper,* even rational restrictions on the right to vote are invidious if they are unrelated to voter qualifications. In *Anderson v. Celebrezze,* however, we confirmed the general rule that "evenhanded restrictions that protect the integrity and reliability of the electoral process itself" are not invidious and satisfy the standard set forth in *Harper.* Rather than applying any "litmus test" that would neatly separate valid from invalid restrictions, we concluded that a court must identify and evaluate the interests put forward by the State as justifications for the burden imposed by its rule, and then make the "hard judgment" that our adversary system demands.

In later election cases we have followed *Anderson*'s balancing approach.... [I]n *Burdick v. Takushi,* we applied *Anderson* 's standard for "'reasonable, nondiscriminatory restrictions,'" and upheld Hawaii's prohibition on write-in voting despite the fact that it prevented a significant number of "voters from participating in Hawaii elections in a meaningful manner." (Kennedy, J., dissenting). We reaffirmed *Anderson* 's requirement that a court evaluating a constitutional challenge to an election regulation weigh the asserted injury to the right to vote against the "'precise interests put forward by the State as justifications for the burden imposed by its rule.'"[8]

In [none of the cases] did we identify any litmus test for measuring the severity of a burden that a state law imposes on a political party, an individual voter, or a discrete class of voters. However slight that burden may appear, as *Harper* demonstrates, it must be justified by relevant and legitimate state interests "sufficiently weighty to justify the limitation." *Norman v. Reed.* We therefore begin our analysis of the constitutionality of Indiana's statute by focusing on those interests.

---

8. Contrary to Justice SCALIA's suggestion, our approach remains faithful to *Anderson* and *Burdick.* The *Burdick* opinion was explicit in its endorsement and adherence to *Anderson,* and repeatedly cited *Anderson.* To be sure, *Burdick* rejected the argument that strict scrutiny applies to all laws imposing a burden on the right to vote; but in its place, the Court applied the "flexible standard" set forth in *Anderson. Burdick* surely did not create a novel "deferential 'important regulatory interests' standard."

II

The State has identified several state interests that arguably justify the burdens that SEA 483 imposes on voters and potential voters. While petitioners argue that the statute was actually motivated by partisan concerns and dispute both the significance of the State's interests and the magnitude of any real threat to those interests, they do not question the legitimacy of the interests the State has identified. Each is unquestionably relevant to the State's interest in protecting the integrity and reliability of the electoral process.

The first is the interest in deterring and detecting voter fraud. The State has a valid interest in participating in a nationwide effort to improve and modernize election procedures that have been criticized as antiquated and inefficient. The State also argues that it has a particular interest in preventing voter fraud in response to a problem that is in part the product of its own maladministration — namely, that Indiana's voter registration rolls include a large number of names of persons who are either deceased or no longer live in Indiana. Finally, the State relies on its interest in safeguarding voter confidence. Each of these interests merits separate comment.

Election Modernization

Two recently enacted federal statutes have made it necessary for States to reexamine their election procedures. Both contain provisions consistent with a State's choice to use government-issued photo identification as a relevant source of information concerning a citizen's eligibility to vote.

In the National Voter Registration Act of 1993 (NVRA), Congress established procedures that would both increase the number of registered voters and protect the integrity of the electoral process. The statute requires state motor vehicle driver's license applications to serve as voter registration applications. While that requirement has increased the number of registered voters, the statute also contains a provision restricting States' ability to remove names from the lists of registered voters. These protections have been partly responsible for inflated lists of registered voters. For example, evidence credited by [the district court] estimated that as of 2004 Indiana's voter rolls were inflated by as much as 41.4%, and data collected by the Election Assistance Committee in 2004 indicated that 19 of 92 Indiana counties had registration totals exceeding 100% of the 2004 voting-age population.

In HAVA, Congress required every State to create and maintain a computerized statewide list of all registered voters. HAVA also requires the States to verify voter information contained in a voter registration application and specifies either an "applicant's driver's license number" or "the last 4 digits of the applicant's social security number" as acceptable verifications. If an individual has neither number, the State is required to assign the applicant a voter identification number.

HAVA also imposes new identification requirements for individuals registering to vote for the first time who submit their applications by mail. If the voter is casting his ballot in person, he must present local election officials with written identification, which may be either "a current and valid photo identification" or another form of documentation such as a bank statement or paycheck. If the voter is voting by mail, he must include a copy of the identification with his ballot. A voter may also include a copy of the documentation with his application or provide his driver's license number or Social Security number for verification. Finally, in a provision entitled "Fail-safe voting," HAVA authorizes the casting of provisional ballots by challenged voters.

Of course, neither HAVA nor NVRA required Indiana to enact SEA 483, but they do indicate that Congress believes that photo identification is one effective method of establishing a voter's qualification to vote and that the integrity of elections is enhanced through improved technology. That conclusion is also supported by a report issued shortly after the enactment of SEA 483 by the Commission on Federal Election Reform chaired by former President Jimmy Carter and former Secretary of State James A. Baker III, which is a part of the record in these cases. In the introduction to their discussion of voter identification, they made these pertinent comments:

> A good registration list will ensure that citizens are only registered in one place, but election officials still need to make sure that the person arriving at a polling site is the same one that is named on the registration list. In the old days and in small towns where everyone knows each other, voters did not need to identify themselves. But in the United States, where 40 million people move each year, and in urban areas where some people do not even know the people living in their own apartment building let alone their precinct, some form of identification is needed.

> There is no evidence of extensive fraud in U.S. elections or of multiple voting, but both occur, and it could affect the outcome of a close election. The electoral system cannot inspire public confidence if no safeguards exist to deter or detect fraud or to confirm the identity of voters. Photo identification cards currently are needed to board a plane, enter federal buildings, and cash a check. Voting is equally important.

Voter Fraud

The only kind of voter fraud that SEA 483 addresses is in-person voter impersonation at polling places. The record contains no evidence of any such fraud actually occurring in Indiana at any time in its history. Moreover, petitioners argue that provisions of the Indiana Criminal Code punishing such conduct as a felony provide adequate protection against the risk that such conduct will occur in the future. It remains true, however, that flagrant examples of such fraud in other parts of the country have been documented throughout this Nation's history by respected historians and journalists,[11] that occasional examples have surfaced in recent years,[12] and that Indiana's own experience with fraudulent voting in the 2003 Democratic primary for East Chicago Mayor—though perpe-

---

11. One infamous example is the New York City elections of 1868. William (Boss) Tweed set about solidifying and consolidating his control of the city. One local tough who worked for Boss Tweed, "Big Tim" Sullivan, insisted that his "repeaters" (individuals paid to vote multiple times) have whiskers:

> When you've voted 'em with their whiskers on, you take 'em to a barber and scrape off the chin fringe. Then you vote 'em again with the side lilacs and a mustache. Then to a barber again, off comes the sides and you vote 'em a third time with the mustache. If that ain't enough and the box can stand a few more ballots, clean off the mustache and vote 'em plain face. That makes every one of 'em good for four votes.

A. Callow, THE TWEED RING 210 (1966) (quoting M. Werner, TAMMANY HALL 439 (1928)).

12. [The district court] cited record evidence containing examples from California, Washington, Maryland, Wisconsin, Georgia, Illinois, Pennsylvania, Missouri, Miami, and St. Louis. The Brief of *Amici Curiae* Brennan Center for Justice et al. in Support of Petitioners addresses each of these examples of fraud. While the brief indicates that the record evidence of in-person fraud was overstated because much of the fraud was actually absentee ballot fraud or voter registration fraud, there remain scattered instances of in-person voter fraud. For example, after a hotly contested gubernatorial election in 2004, Washington conducted an investigation of voter fraud and uncovered 19 "ghost voters." After a partial investigation of the ghost voting, one voter was confirmed to have committed in-person voting fraud. Le & Nicolosi, *Dead Voted in Governor's Race*, SEATTLE POST-INTELLIGENCER, Jan. 7, 2005, p. A1.

trated using absentee ballots and not in-person fraud—demonstrate that not only is the risk of voter fraud real but that it could affect the outcome of a close election.

There is no question about the legitimacy or importance of the State's interest in counting only the votes of eligible voters. Moreover, the interest in orderly administration and accurate recordkeeping provides a sufficient justification for carefully identifying all voters participating in the election process. While the most effective method of preventing election fraud may well be debatable, the propriety of doing so is perfectly clear.

In its brief, the State argues that the inflation of its voter rolls provides further support for its enactment of SEA 483. The record contains a November 5, 2000, newspaper article asserting that as a result of NVRA and "sloppy record keeping," Indiana's lists of registered voters included the names of thousands of persons who had either moved, died, or were not eligible to vote because they had been convicted of felonies. The conclusion that Indiana has an unusually inflated list of registered voters is supported by the entry of a consent decree in litigation brought by the Federal Government alleging violations of NVRA. Even though Indiana's own negligence may have contributed to the serious inflation of its registration lists when SEA 483 was enacted, the fact of inflated voter rolls does provide a neutral and nondiscriminatory reason supporting the State's decision to require photo identification.

Safeguarding Voter Confidence

Finally, the State contends that it has an interest in protecting public confidence "in the integrity and legitimacy of representative government." While that interest is closely related to the State's interest in preventing voter fraud, public confidence in the integrity of the electoral process has independent significance, because it encourages citizen participation in the democratic process. As the Carter-Baker Report observed, the "electoral system cannot inspire public confidence if no safeguards exist to deter or detect fraud or to confirm the identity of voters."

III

States employ different methods of identifying eligible voters at the polls. Some merely check off the names of registered voters who identify themselves; others require voters to present registration cards or other documentation before they can vote; some require voters to sign their names so their signatures can be compared with those on file; and in recent years an increasing number of States have relied primarily on photo identification. A photo identification requirement imposes some burdens on voters that other methods of identification do not share. For example, a voter may lose his photo identification, may have his wallet stolen on the way to the polls, or may not resemble the photo in the identification because he recently grew a beard. Burdens of that sort arising from life's vagaries, however, are neither so serious nor so frequent as to raise any question about the constitutionality of SEA 483; the availability of the right to cast a provisional ballot provides an adequate remedy for problems of that character.

The burdens that are relevant to the issue before us are those imposed on persons who are eligible to vote but do not possess a current photo identification that complies with the requirements of SEA 483. The fact that most voters already possess a valid driver's license, or some other form of acceptable identification, would not save the statute under our reasoning in *Harper,* if the State required voters to pay a tax or a fee to obtain a new photo identification. But just as other States provide free voter registration cards, the photo identification cards issued by Indiana's BMV are also free. For most voters who need them, the inconvenience of making a trip to the BMV, gathering the required documents, and posing for a photograph surely does not qualify as a substantial burden on the right to vote, or even represent a significant increase over the usual burdens of voting.[17]

Both evidence in the record and facts of which we may take judicial notice, however, indicate that a somewhat heavier burden may be placed on a limited number of persons. They include elderly persons born out-of-state, who may have difficulty obtaining a birth certificate; persons who because of economic or other personal limitations may find it difficult either to secure a copy of their birth certificate or to assemble the other required documentation to obtain a state-issued identification; homeless persons; and persons with a religious objection to being photographed. If we assume, as the evidence suggests, that some members of these classes were registered voters when SEA 483 was enacted, the new identification requirement may have imposed a special burden on their right to vote.

The severity of that burden is, of course, mitigated by the fact that, if eligible, voters without photo identification may cast provisional ballots that will ultimately be counted. To do so, however, they must travel to the circuit court clerk's office within 10 days to execute the required affidavit. It is unlikely that such a requirement would pose a constitutional problem unless it is wholly unjustified. And even assuming that the burden may not be justified as to a few voters,[19] that conclusion is by no means sufficient to establish petitioners' right to the relief they seek in this litigation.

IV

Given the fact that petitioners have advanced a broad attack on the constitutionality of SEA 483, seeking relief that would invalidate the statute in all its applications, they bear a heavy burden of persuasion. Only a few weeks ago we held that the Court of Appeals for the Ninth Circuit had failed to give appropriate weight to the magnitude of that burden when it sustained a preelection, facial attack on a Washington statute regulating that State's primary election procedures. *Washington State Grange v. Washington State Republican Party* [*infra*, Chapter 9—Eds]. Our reasoning in that case applies with added force to the arguments advanced by petitioners in these cases.

Petitioners ask this Court, in effect, to perform a unique balancing analysis that looks specifically at a small number of voters who may experience a special burden under the statute and weighs their burdens against the State's broad interests in protecting election integrity. Petitioners urge us to ask whether the State's interests justify the burden imposed on voters who cannot afford or obtain a birth certificate and who must make a second trip to the circuit court clerk's office after voting. But on the basis of the evidence in the record it is not possible to quantify either the magnitude of the burden on this narrow class of voters or the portion of the burden imposed on them that is fully justified.

First, the evidence in the record does not provide us with the number of registered voters without photo identification; Judge Barker found petitioners' expert's report to be

---

17. To obtain a photo identification card a person must present at least one "primary" document, which can be a birth certificate, certificate of naturalization, U.S. veterans photo identification, U.S. military photo identification, or a U.S. passport. Indiana, like most States, charges a fee for obtaining a copy of one's birth certificate. This fee varies by county and is currently between $3 and $12. Some States charge substantially more.

19. Presumably most voters casting provisional ballots will be able to obtain photo identifications before the next election. It is, however, difficult to understand why the State should require voters with a faith-based objection to being photographed to cast provisional ballots subject to later verification in every election when the BMV is able to issue these citizens special licenses that enable them to drive without any photo identification.

"utterly incredible and unreliable." Much of the argument about the numbers of such voters comes from extrarecord, postjudgment studies, the accuracy of which has not been tested in the trial court.

Further, the deposition evidence presented in the District Court does not provide any concrete evidence of the burden imposed on voters who currently lack photo identification. The record includes depositions of two case managers at a day shelter for homeless persons and the depositions of members of the plaintiff organizations, none of whom expressed a personal inability to vote under SEA 483. A deposition from a named plaintiff describes the difficulty the elderly woman had in obtaining an identification card, although her testimony indicated that she intended to return to the BMV since she had recently obtained her birth certificate and that she was able to pay the birth certificate fee.

Judge Barker's opinion makes reference to six other elderly named plaintiffs who do not have photo identifications, but several of these individuals have birth certificates or were born in Indiana and have not indicated how difficult it would be for them to obtain a birth certificate. One elderly named plaintiff stated that she had attempted to obtain a birth certificate from Tennessee, but had not been successful, and another testified that he did not know how to obtain a birth certificate from North Carolina. The elderly in Indiana, however, may have an easier time obtaining a photo identification card than the nonelderly, and although it may not be a completely acceptable alternative, the elderly in Indiana are able to vote absentee without presenting photo identification.

The record says virtually nothing about the difficulties faced by either indigent voters or voters with religious objections to being photographed. While one elderly man stated that he did not have the money to pay for a birth certificate, when asked if he did not have the money or did not wish to spend it, he replied, "both." From this limited evidence we do not know the magnitude of the impact SEA 483 will have on indigent voters in Indiana. The record does contain the affidavit of one homeless woman who has a copy of her birth certificate, but was denied a photo identification card because she did not have an address. But that single affidavit gives no indication of how common the problem is.

In sum, on the basis of the record that has been made in this litigation, we cannot conclude that the statute imposes "excessively burdensome requirements" on any class of voters. See *Storer v. Brown*.[20] A facial challenge must fail where the statute has a "plainly legitimate sweep." *Washington State Grange*. When we consider only the statute's broad ap-

---

20. Three comments on Justice SOUTER's speculation about the non-trivial burdens that SEA 483 may impose on "tens of thousands" of Indiana citizens are appropriate. First, the fact that the District Judge estimated that when the statute was passed in 2005, 43,000 citizens did not have photo identification tells us nothing about the number of free photo identification cards issued since then. Second, the fact that public transportation is not available in some Indiana counties tells us nothing about how often elderly and indigent citizens have an opportunity to obtain a photo identification at the BMV, either during a routine outing with family or friends or during a special visit to the BMV arranged by a civic or political group such as the League of Women Voters or a political party. Further, nothing in the record establishes the distribution of voters who lack photo identification. To the extent that the evidence sheds any light on that issue, it suggests that such voters reside primarily in metropolitan areas, which are served by public transportation in Indiana (the majority of the plaintiffs reside in Indianapolis and several of the organizational plaintiffs are Indianapolis organizations). Third, the indigent, elderly, or disabled need not "journey all the way to their county seat each time they wish to exercise the franchise," if they obtain a free photo identification card from the BMV. While it is true that obtaining a birth certificate carries with it a financial cost, the record does not provide even a rough estimate of how many indigent voters lack copies of their birth certificates. Supposition based on extensive Internet research is not an adequate substitute for admissible evidence subject to cross-examination in constitutional adjudication.

plication to all Indiana voters we conclude that it "imposes only a limited burden on voters' rights." *Burdick*. The "precise interests" advanced by the State are therefore sufficient to defeat petitioners' facial challenge to SEA 483.

Finally we note that petitioners have not demonstrated that the proper remedy—even assuming an unjustified burden on some voters—would be to invalidate the entire statute. When evaluating a neutral, nondiscriminatory regulation of voting procedure, "[w]e must keep in mind that [a] ruling of unconstitutionality frustrates the intent of the elected representatives of the people." *Washington State Grange*.

V

In their briefs, petitioners stress the fact that all of the Republicans in the General Assembly voted in favor of SEA 483 and the Democrats were unanimous in opposing it. In her opinion rejecting petitioners' facial challenge, Judge Barker noted that the litigation was the result of a partisan dispute that had "spilled out of the state house into the courts." It is fair to infer that partisan considerations may have played a significant role in the decision to enact SEA 483. If such considerations had provided the only justification for a photo identification requirement, we may also assume that SEA 483 would suffer the same fate as the poll tax at issue in *Harper*.

But if a nondiscriminatory law is supported by valid neutral justifications, those justifications should not be disregarded simply because partisan interests may have provided one motivation for the votes of individual legislators. The state interests identified as justifications for SEA 483 are both neutral and sufficiently strong to require us to reject petitioners' facial attack on the statute. The application of the statute to the vast majority of Indiana voters is amply justified by the valid interest in protecting "the integrity and reliability of the electoral process." *Anderson*.

The judgment of the Court of Appeals is affirmed.

Justice SCALIA, with whom Justice THOMAS and Justice ALITO join, concurring in the judgment.

The lead opinion assumes petitioners' premise that the voter-identification law "may have imposed a special burden on" some voters, but holds that petitioners have not assembled evidence to show that the special burden is severe enough to warrant strict scrutiny, That is true enough, but for the sake of clarity and finality (as well as adherence to precedent), I prefer to decide these cases on the grounds that petitioners' premise is irrelevant and that the burden at issue is minimal and justified.

To evaluate a law respecting the right to vote—whether it governs voter qualifications, candidate selection, or the voting process—we use the approach set out in *Burdick*. This calls for application of a deferential "important regulatory interests" standard for nonsevere, nondiscriminatory restrictions, reserving strict scrutiny for laws that severely restrict the right to vote. The lead opinion resists the import of *Burdick* by characterizing it as simply adopting "the balancing approach" of *Anderson v. Celebrezze*. Although *Burdick* liberally quoted *Anderson*, *Burdick* forged *Anderson*'s amorphous "flexible standard" into something resembling an administrable rule. Since *Burdick*, we have repeatedly reaffirmed the primacy of its two-track approach. See *Timmons v. Twin Cities Area New Party*; *Clingman v. Beaver*. "[S]trict scrutiny is appropriate only if the burden is severe." *Id*. Thus, the first step is to decide whether a challenged law severely burdens the right to vote. Ordinary and widespread burdens, such as those requiring "nominal effort" of everyone, are not severe. Burdens are severe if they go beyond the merely inconvenient.

Of course, we have to identify a burden before we can weigh it. The Indiana law affects different voters differently, but what petitioners view as the law's several light and heavy burdens are no more than the different *impacts* of the single burden that the law uniformly imposes on all voters. To vote in person in Indiana, *everyone* must have and present a photo identification that can be obtained for free. The State draws no classifications, let alone discriminatory ones, except to establish *optional* absentee and provisional balloting for certain poor, elderly, and institutionalized voters and for religious objectors. Nor are voters who already have photo identifications exempted from the burden, since those voters must maintain the accuracy of the information displayed on the identifications, renew them before they expire, and replace them if they are lost.

The Indiana photo-identification law is a generally applicable, nondiscriminatory voting regulation, and our precedents refute the view that individual impacts are relevant to determining the severity of the burden it imposes. In the course of concluding that the Hawaii laws at issue in *Burdick* "impose[d] only a limited burden on voters' rights to make free choices and to associate politically through the vote," we considered the laws and their reasonably foreseeable effect on *voters generally*. We did not discuss whether the laws had a severe effect on Mr. Burdick's own right to vote, given his particular circumstances.... Subsequent cases have followed *Burdick*'s generalized review of nondiscriminatory election laws. Indeed, *Clingman*'s holding that burdens are not severe if they are ordinary and widespread would be rendered meaningless if a single plaintiff could claim a severe burden.

Not all of our decisions predating *Burdick* addressed whether a challenged voting regulation severely burdened the right to vote, but when we began to grapple with the magnitude of burdens, we did so categorically and did not consider the peculiar circumstances of individual voters or candidates....

Insofar as our election-regulation cases rest upon the requirements of the Fourteenth Amendment, weighing the burden of a nondiscriminatory voting law upon each voter and concomitantly requiring exceptions for vulnerable voters would effectively turn back decades of equal-protection jurisprudence. A voter complaining about such a law's effect on him has no valid equal-protection claim because, without proof of discriminatory intent, a generally applicable law with disparate impact is not unconstitutional. The Fourteenth Amendment does not regard neutral laws as invidious ones, *even when their burdens purportedly fall disproportionately on a protected class*. A fortiori it does not do so when, as here, the classes complaining of disparate impact are not even protected.*

Even if I thought that *stare decisis* did not foreclose adopting an individual-focused approach, I would reject it as an original matter. This is an area where the dos and don'ts need to be known in advance of the election, and voter-by-voter examination of the burdens of voting regulations would prove especially disruptive. A case-by-case approach naturally encourages constant litigation. Very few new election regulations improve everyone's lot, so the potential allegations of severe burden are endless. A State reducing the number of polling places would be open to the complaint it has violated the rights of disabled voters who live near the closed stations. Indeed, it may even be the case that some laws

---

* A number of our early right-to-vote decisions, purporting to rely upon the Equal Protection Clause, strictly scrutinized nondiscriminatory voting laws requiring the payment of fees. See, *e.g., Harper v. Virginia Bd. of Elections* (1966) (poll tax); *Bullock v. Carter* (1972) (ballot-access fee); *Lubin v. Panish* (1974) (ballot-access fee). To the extent those decisions continue to stand for a principle that *Burdick* does not already encompass, it suffices to note that we have never held that legislatures must calibrate *all* election laws, even those totally unrelated to money, for their impacts on poor voters or must otherwise accommodate wealth disparities.

already on the books are especially burdensome for some voters, and one can predict lawsuits demanding that a State adopt voting over the Internet or expand absentee balloting.

That sort of detailed judicial supervision of the election process would flout the Constitution's express commitment of the task to the States. See Art. I, § 4. It is for state legislatures to weigh the costs and benefits of possible changes to their election codes, and their judgment must prevail unless it imposes a severe and unjustified overall burden upon the right to vote, or is intended to disadvantage a particular class. Judicial review of their handiwork must apply an objective, uniform standard that will enable them to determine, *ex ante*, whether the burden they impose is too severe.

The lead opinion's record-based resolution of these cases, which neither rejects nor embraces the rule of our precedents, provides no certainty, and will embolden litigants who surmise that our precedents have been abandoned. There is no good reason to prefer that course.

* * *

The universally applicable requirements of Indiana's voter-identification law are eminently reasonable. The burden of acquiring, possessing, and showing a free photo identification is simply not severe, because it does not "even represent a significant increase over the usual burdens of voting." And the State's interests are sufficient to sustain that minimal burden. That should end the matter. That the State accommodates some voters by permitting (not requiring) the casting of absentee or provisional ballots, is an indulgence—not a constitutional imperative that falls short of what is required.

Justice SOUTER, with whom Justice GINSBURG joins, dissenting.

Indiana's "Voter ID Law" threatens to impose nontrivial burdens on the voting right of tens of thousands of the State's citizens, and a significant percentage of those individuals are likely to be deterred from voting. The statute is unconstitutional under the balancing standard of *Burdick*: a State may not burden the right to vote merely by invoking abstract interests, be they legitimate, or even compelling, but must make a particular, factual showing that threats to its interests outweigh the particular impediments it has imposed. The State has made no such justification here, and as to some aspects of its law, it has hardly even tried. I therefore respectfully dissent from the Court's judgment sustaining the statute.

I

Voting-rights cases raise two competing interests, the one side being the fundamental right to vote. The Judiciary is obliged to train a skeptical eye on any qualification of that right. See *Reynolds*.

As against the unfettered right, however, lies the "[c]ommon sense, as well as constitutional law ... that government must play an active role in structuring elections; 'as a practical matter, there must be a substantial regulation of elections if they are to be fair and honest and if some sort of order, rather than chaos, is to accompany the democratic processes.'" *Burdick* (quoting *Storer v. Brown*).

Given the legitimacy of interests on both sides, we have avoided pre-set levels of scrutiny in favor of a sliding-scale balancing analysis: the scrutiny varies with the effect of the regulation at issue. And whatever the claim, the Court has long made a careful, ground-level appraisal both of the practical burdens on the right to vote and of the State's reasons for imposing those precise burdens. ...

The lead opinion does not disavow these basic principles. But I think it does not insist enough on the hard facts that our standard of review demands.

II

Under *Burdick*, "the rigorousness of our inquiry into the propriety of a state election law depends upon the extent to which a challenged regulation burdens First and Fourteenth Amendment rights," upon an assessment of the "character and magnitude of the asserted [threatened] injury," and an estimate of the number of voters likely to be affected.

A

The first set of burdens shown in these cases is the travel costs and fees necessary to get one of the limited variety of federal or state photo identifications needed to cast a regular ballot under the Voter ID Law. The travel is required for the personal visit to a license branch of the Indiana Bureau of Motor Vehicles (BMV), which is demanded of anyone applying for a driver's license or nondriver photo identification. The need to travel to a BMV branch will affect voters according to their circumstances, with the average person probably viewing it as nothing more than an inconvenience. Poor, old, and disabled voters who do not drive a car, however, may find the trip prohibitive,[4] witness the fact that the BMV has far fewer license branches in each county than there are voting precincts....

The burden of traveling to a more distant BMV office rather than a conveniently located polling place is probably serious for many of the individuals who lack photo identification. They almost certainly will not own cars, and public transportation in Indiana is fairly limited....

Although making voters travel farther than what is convenient for most and possible for some does not amount to a "severe" burden under *Burdick,* that is no reason to ignore the burden altogether. It translates into an obvious economic cost (whether in work time lost, or getting and paying for transportation) that an Indiana voter must bear to obtain an ID.

For those voters who can afford the roundtrip, a second financial hurdle appears: in order to get photo identification for the first time, they need to present " 'a birth certificate, a certificate of naturalization, U.S. veterans photo identification, U.S. military photo identification, or a U.S. passport.'" As the lead opinion says, the two most common of these documents come at a price: Indiana counties charge anywhere from $3 to $12 for a birth certificate (and in some other States the fee is significantly higher), and that same price must usually be paid for a first-time passport, since a birth certificate is required to prove U.S. citizenship by birth. The total fees for a passport, moreover, are up to about $100. So most voters must pay at least one fee to get the ID necessary to cast a regular ballot. As with the travel costs, these fees are far from shocking on their face, but in the *Burdick* analysis it matters that both the travel costs and the fees are dis-

---

4. The State asserts that the elderly and disabled are adequately accommodated through their option to cast absentee ballots, and so any burdens on them are irrelevant. But as petitioners' *amici* AARP and the National Senior Citizens Law Center point out, there are crucial differences between the absentee and regular ballot....

It is one thing (and a commendable thing) for the State to make absentee voting available to the elderly and disabled; but it is quite another to suggest that, because the more convenient but less reliable absentee ballot is available, the State may freely deprive the elderly and disabled of the option of voting in person.

proportionately heavy for, and thus disproportionately likely to deter, the poor, the old, and the immobile.

B

To be sure, Indiana has a provisional-ballot exception to the ID requirement for individuals the State considers "indigent" as well as those with religious objections to being photographed, and this sort of exception could in theory provide a way around the costs of procuring an ID. But Indiana's chosen exception does not amount to much relief.

The law allows these voters who lack the necessary ID to sign the poll book and cast a provisional ballot. As the lead opinion recognizes, though, that is only the first step; to have the provisional ballot counted, a voter must then appear in person before the circuit court clerk or county election board within 10 days of the election, to sign an affidavit attesting to indigency or religious objection to being photographed (or to present an ID at that point). Unlike the trip to the BMV (which, assuming things go smoothly, needs to be made only once every four years for renewal of nondriver photo identification), this one must be taken every time a poor person or religious objector wishes to vote, because the State does not allow an affidavit to count in successive elections. And unlike the trip to the BMV (which at least has a handful of license branches in the more populous counties), a county has only one county seat. Forcing these people to travel to the county seat every time they try to vote is particularly onerous for the reason noted already, that most counties in Indiana either lack public transportation or offer only limited coverage.

That the need to travel to the county seat each election amounts to a high hurdle is shown in the results of the 2007 municipal elections in Marion County, to which Indiana's Voter ID Law applied. Thirty-four provisional ballots were cast, but only two provisional voters made it to the County Clerk's Office within the 10 days. All 34 of these aspiring voters appeared at the appropriate precinct; 33 of them provided a signature, and every signature matched the one on file; and 26 of the 32 voters whose ballots were not counted had a history of voting in Marion County elections.

All of this suggests that provisional ballots do not obviate the burdens of getting photo identification. And even if that were not so, the provisional-ballot option would be inadequate for a further reason: the indigency exception by definition offers no relief to those voters who do not consider themselves (or would not be considered) indigent but as a practical matter would find it hard, for nonfinancial reasons, to get the required ID (most obviously the disabled).

C

Indiana's Voter ID Law thus threatens to impose serious burdens on the voting right, even if not "severe" ones, and the next question under *Burdick* is whether the number of individuals likely to be affected is significant as well. Record evidence and facts open to judicial notice answer yes.

Although the District Court found that petitioners failed to offer any reliable empirical study of numbers of voters affected, we may accept that court's rough calculation that 43,000 voting-age residents lack the kind of identification card required by Indiana's law. The District Court made that estimate by comparing BMV records reproduced in petitioners' statistician's report with U.S. Census Bureau figures for Indiana's voting-age population in 2004, and the State does not argue that these raw data are unreliable....

The upshot is this. Tens of thousands of voting-age residents lack the necessary photo identification. A large proportion of them are likely to be in bad shape economically.[25] The Voter ID Law places hurdles in the way of either getting an ID or of voting provisionally, and they translate into nontrivial economic costs. There is accordingly no reason to doubt that a significant number of state residents will be discouraged or disabled from voting.

Petitioners, to be sure, failed to nail down precisely how great the cohort of discouraged and totally deterred voters will be, but empirical precision beyond the foregoing numbers has never been demanded for raising a voting-rights claim. While of course it would greatly aid a plaintiff to establish his claims beyond mathematical doubt, he does enough to show that serious burdens are likely.

Thus, petitioners' case is clearly strong enough to prompt more than a cursory examination of the State's asserted interests. And the fact that Indiana's photo identification requirement is one of the most restrictive in the country makes a critical examination of the State's claims all the more in order.

III

Because the lead opinion finds only "limited" burdens on the right to vote, it avoids a hard look at the State's claimed interests. But having found the Voter ID Law burdens far from trivial, I have to make a rigorous assessment of "the precise interests put forward by the State as justifications for the burden imposed by its rule, [and] the extent to which those interests make it necessary to burden the plaintiff's rights." *Burdick*.

As this quotation from *Burdick* indicates, the interests claimed to justify the regulatory scheme are subject to discount in two distinct ways. First, the generalities raised by the State have to be shaved down to the precise "aspect[s of claimed interests] addressed by the law at issue." *California Democratic Party v. Jones*, 530 U.S. 567, 584 (2000) (emphasis omitted). And even if the State can show particularized interests addressed by the law, those interests are subject to further discount depending on "the extent to which [they] make it necessary to burden the plaintiff's rights." *Burdick*.

As the lead opinion sees it, the State has offered four related concerns that suffice to justify the Voter ID Law: modernizing election procedures, combating voter fraud, addressing the consequences of the State's bloated voter rolls, and protecting public confidence in the integrity of the electoral process. On closer look, however, it appears that the first two (which are really just one) can claim modest weight at best, and the latter two if anything weaken the State's case ...

[T]he State's interest in deterring a voter from showing up at the polls and claiming to be someone he is not must ... be discounted for the fact that the State has not come across a single instance of in-person voter impersonation fraud in all of Indiana's history. Neither the District Court nor the Indiana General Assembly that passed the Voter ID Law was given any evidence whatsoever of in-person voter impersonation fraud in the State....

The antifraud rationale is open to skepticism on one further ground, what *Burdick* spoke of as an assessment of the degree of necessity for the State's particular course of

---

25. Studies in other States suggest that the burdens of an ID requirement may also fall disproportionately upon racial minorities. See Overton, *Voter Identification*, 105 Mich. L.Rev. 631 (2007)....

action. Two points deserve attention, the first being that the State has not even tried to justify its decision to implement the photo identification requirement immediately on passage of the new law. A phase-in period would have given the State time to distribute its newly designed licenses, and to make a genuine effort to get them to individuals in need, and a period for transition is exactly what the Commission on Federal Election Reform, headed by former President Carter and former Secretary of State Baker, recommended in its report. See Building Confidence in U.S. Elections § 2.5 (Sept.2005).... Although Indiana claims to have adopted its ID requirement relying partly on the Carter-Baker Report, the State conspicuously rejected the Report's phase-in recommendation aimed at reducing the burdens on the right to vote, and just as conspicuously fails even to try to explain why.

What is left of the State's claim must be downgraded further for one final reason: regardless of the interest the State may have in adopting a photo identification requirement as a general matter, that interest in no way necessitates the particular burdens the Voter ID Law imposes on poor people and religious objectors. Individuals unable to get photo identification are forced to travel to the county seat every time they wish to exercise the franchise, and they have to get there within 10 days of the election. Nothing about the State's interest in fighting voter fraud justifies this requirement of a postelection trip to the county seat instead of some verification process at the polling places....

[I]f it is true that the State's fear of in-person voter impersonation fraud arises from its bloated voter checklist, the answer to the problem is in the State's own hands. The claim that the State has an interest in addressing a symptom of the problem (alleged impersonation) rather than the problem itself (the negligently maintained bloated rolls) is thus self-defeating; it shows that the State has no justifiable need to burden the right to vote as it does, and it suggests that the State is not as serious about combating fraud as it claims to be.

The State's final justification, its interest in safeguarding voter confidence, similarly collapses. The problem with claiming this interest lies in its connection to the bloated voter rolls; the State has come up with nothing to suggest that its citizens doubt the integrity of the State's electoral process, except its own failure to maintain its rolls. The answer to this problem is not to burden the right to vote, but to end the official negligence....

Without a shred of evidence that in-person voter impersonation is a problem in the State, much less a crisis, Indiana has adopted one of the most restrictive photo identification requirements in the country. The State recognizes that tens of thousands of qualified voters lack the necessary federally issued or state-issued identification, but it insists on implementing the requirement immediately, without allowing a transition period for targeted efforts to distribute the required identification to individuals who need it. The State hardly even tries to explain its decision to force indigents or religious objectors to travel all the way to their county seats every time they wish to vote, and if there is any waning of confidence in the administration of elections it probably owes more to the State's violation of federal election law than to any imposters at the polling places. It is impossible to say, on this record, that the State's interest in adopting its signally inhibiting photo identification requirement has been shown to outweigh the serious burdens it imposes on the right to vote.

If more were needed to condemn this law, our own precedent would provide it, for the calculation revealed in the Indiana statute crosses a line when it targets the poor and the weak. If the Court's decision in *Harper v. Virginia Bd. of Elections* stands for anything, it is that being poor has nothing to do with being qualified to vote. *Harper* made clear that "[t]o introduce wealth or payment of a fee as a measure of a voter's qualifications is to introduce a capricious or irrelevant factor." The State's requirements here, that people without cars travel to a motor vehicle registry and that the poor who fail to do that get to their county seats within 10 days of every election, likewise translate into unjustified economic burdens uncomfortably close to the outright $1.50 fee we struck down 42 years ago. Like that fee, the onus of the Indiana law is illegitimate just because it correlates with no state interest so well as it does with the object of deterring poorer residents from exercising the franchise.

* * *

The Indiana Voter ID Law is thus unconstitutional: the state interests fail to justify the practical limitations placed on the right to vote, and the law imposes an unreasonable and irrelevant burden on voters who are poor and old. I would vacate the judgment of the Seventh Circuit, and remand for further proceedings.

[A dissenting opinion from Justice Breyer is omitted.]

Notes and Questions

1. *What Is the Constitutional Standard After* Crawford? Six justices voted to uphold Indiana's voter ID law against a facial challenge under the Fourteenth Amendment, but no opinion commands a majority. Justice Stevens' opinion (for himself and two other justices) appears to embrace a balancing test for laws alleged to impede participation, under which the burden on voter participation is weighed against the state's asserted justifications. Rather than strict scrutiny being triggered by certain practices, with all others being subjected to rational basis review, the lead opinion suggests that courts should require a stronger justification from the state as the burdens on voters increase. As one commentator put it, the test is less like a "light switch" and "more like a dimmer." Justin Levitt, *Crawford — More Rhetorical Bark Than Legal Bite?*, May 2, 2008, *available at* http://www.brennancenter.org/blog/archives/crawford_more_rhetorical_bark_than_legal_bite /. Justice Scalia (also writing for himself and two other justices) criticizes the balancing approach of the lead opinion, and would instead apply a "two-track approach" that would function like a light switch rather than a dimmer. Under his test, a court should first determine whether the challenged practice imposes a "severe" burden, which he characterizes as one that "go[es] beyond the merely inconvenient." If it does, then he would apply strict scrutiny; if not, then he would apparently uphold them so long as they are reasonable, a standard he describes as imposing a "minimal burden." Is this a more appropriate (or at least more administrable) legal standard than the one embraced by Justice Stevens' lead opinion?

None of the opinions in *Crawford* cite *Bush v. Gore.* Should they have?

2. *The Poll Tax Comparison.* The plaintiffs and dissenters in *Crawford* sought to compare Indiana's photo identification requirement to the $1.50 poll tax struck down in *Harper v. Virginia Board of Elections*, based on its effect on poor voters. Even though Indiana provided photo ID cards free of charge, the argument goes, voters lacking identification are required to expend money to obtain the primary documents needed to obtain ID, such as a birth certificate or certificate of naturalization. Additionally, voters lacking ID would be put to the burden of either collecting these documents and going to the BMV to obtain photo ID, or of appearing at the county seat within 10 days after each election to sign an affidavit of indigency. Does the poll tax comparison hold? Should a "tax on the voter's time" be consid-

ered a severe burden, sufficient to trigger strict scrutiny? If so, what is the logical stopping point? Do all election practices that may incidentally burden poor people violate equal protection? For example, it is presumably more burdensome for voters lacking an automobile —who are likely to be less affluent than other voters—to get to their polling places. Does the poll tax analogy mean that the government might be required to provide additional polling places in poor neighborhoods, or even to subsidize transportation for poor voters?

For academic commentary comparing photo ID laws to poll taxes and other Jim Crow-era exclusionary practices, see David Schultz, *Less Than Fundamental: The Myth of Voter Fraud and the Coming of the Second Great Disenfranchisement*, 34 WILLIAM MITCHELL LAW REVIEW 483 (2008); E. Earl Parson & Monique McLaughlin, *The Persistence of Racial Bias in Voting: Voter ID, the New Battleground for Pretextual Race Neutrality*, 8 JOURNAL OF LAW IN SOCIETY 75 (2007). In contrast, Samuel P. Langholz, Note, *Fashioning a Constitutional Voter-Identification Requirement*, 93 IOWA LAW REVIEW 731 (2008), maintains that voter fraud is a significant problem and questions the poll tax analogy, so long as the required identification is provided free of charge.

3. *Facial vs. As-Applied Challenges.* Note that the lead opinion rejects plaintiffs' facial challenge to Indiana's law, but leaves the door open to a later as-applied challenge. For example, someone who objects to being photographed on religious grounds could argue that the law imposes an unconstitutional burden on his or her right to vote. Will this encourage case-by-case litigation, as Justice Scalia suggests? If the plaintiffs and dissenters are correct that the Indiana requirements will prevent significant numbers of eligible people from voting, will the availability of case-by-case relief be sufficient to prevent the requirements from operating as prerequisites for voting, in practice?

Consider the posture in which this type of issue might be litigated. After a close election, the losing candidate might argue that the votes of religious objectors who came to the polls without photo ID should be counted. Those voters would likely have cast provisional ballots, as the lead opinion explains. The losing candidate would then be in the position of arguing that Indiana's law is unconstitutional, as applied to those voters. This introduces the possibility of a post-election dispute over whether particular ballots should be counted. Is this the best posture in which to resolve election administration disputes? For an argument that pre-election litigation is preferable to post-election litigation, see Richard L. Hasen, *Beyond the Margin of Litigation: Reforming U.S. Election Administration to avoid Electoral Meltdown*, 62 WASHINGTON & LEE LAW REVIEW 937, 991 (2005). Note that the opinion does not preclude pre-election as-applied litigation by plaintiffs who can demonstrate a particularlized burden they would face under the identification requirement. In our hypothetical case, should the court decline to hear the issue posed after the election when the candidate or the voters could have raised the issue beforehand?

Suppose that a law imposes a large burden on a small segment of the voting population. Is such a law susceptible to a facial challenge after *Crawford*, or only an as-applied challenge? Take for example a law that required all newly registered voters without a fixed address to produce their birth certificates the first time they appear at the polls. Could a homeless voter affected by this law bring a facial challenge to it? Alternatively, could such a voter bring a claim alleging that the law is unconstitutional as applied to *all* homeless voters?

4. *The Empirical Void.* The legal and policy debates over voter identification depend in large measure on disputed factual questions, including the effect of identification laws on participation, the prevalence of voting fraud, and the likelihood that identification laws will curb fraud. In *Crawford*, the evidence of both the benefits and the burdens of

Indiana's law was quite weak. As the lead opinion notes, the only type of fraud that Indiana's law would prevent is in-person voter impersonation fraud, yet there was "no evidence of any such fraud actually occurring in Indiana at any time in its history." On the other hand, the lead opinion notes that plaintiffs' evidence of the Indiana law's burden on voters was also very weak. What is the appropriate course for a court to take under the circumstances?

The absence of evidence on both sides may indicate that the stakes in the debate over voter identification are really much smaller than they have appeared to some. See Bradley A. Smith, *Broken Windows and Voting Rights*, 156 UNIVERSITY OF PENNSYLVANIA LAW REVIEW PENNumbra 242, 243 (2008), *available at* http://www.pennumbra.com/debates/pdfs/voterid.pdf. Alternatively, it may be that the research on voter identification laws is not sufficiently well-developed to make an informed judgment about their effects, both positive and negative. See Spencer Overton, *Voter Identification*, 105 MICHIGAN LAW REVIEW 631 (2007). Was it a mistake for the Supreme Court to take the *Crawford* case, given the paucity of empirical evidence on both sides? See Daniel P. Tokaji, *Leave It to the Lower Courts: On Judicial Intervention in Election Administration*, 68 OHIO STATE LAW JOURNAL 1065, 1092 (2007).

5. *The "Danger Signs" Approach.* One way in which courts might deal with the lack of reliable empirical research when they consider challenges to election administration practices is to look out for "danger signs of a substantial threat to the democratic process." Christopher S. Elmendorf, *Structuring Judicial Review of Electoral Mechanics: Explanations and Opportunities*, 156 UNIVERSITY OF PENNSYLVANIA LAW REVIEW 313, 324 (2008). For comments, see Daniel P. Tokaji, *Judicial Review of Election Administration*, 156 UNIVERSITY OF PENNSYLVANIA LAW REVIEW PENNumbra 379, 387 (2008). Justice Souter's *Crawford* dissent relies on danger signs, citing Justice Breyer's plurality opinion in *Randall v. Sorrell*, from which the term derives. One of the danger signs that courts might consider is that a law was enacted along party lines, or threatens to have a "skewing effect" on the electorate. Does the danger-signs approach present a viable alternative to that taken by the lead opinion in *Crawford*?

6. *Advisory Commission Reports.* The lead opinion and both dissenting opinions give considerable weight to the report of the Commission on Federal Election Reform, a nongovernmental body jointly chaired by former President Jimmy Carter (a Democrat) and former Secretary of State James A. Baker III (a Republican). That report found no evidence of extensive fraud in American elections, but nevertheless recommended a photo ID requirement with a phase-in period. What weight should courts give to such advisory commission recommendations?

The opinions do not mention that the Carter-Baker Report was quite harshly criticized after its release for the absence of evidence supporting its recommendations. See, e.g., *Denying Access to the Ballot*, NEW YORK TIMES, Sept. 20, 2005. It triggered a sharp dissent—critical of both the substance and procedure followed by the commission—accompanied by an extensive counter-analysis of the voter ID issue. Spencer A. Overton, *Dissenting Statement, available at* http://www.carterbakerdissent.com/ ; Wendy R. Weiser, et al., *Response to the Report of the 2005 Commission on Federal Election Reform* (2005), *available at* http://brennan.3cdn.net/7aad4859cd1bf5f49e_4zm6i2f1i.pdf. Daniel P. Tokaji, *The Birth and Rebirth of Election Administration*, 6 ELECTION LAW JOURNAL 118, 131 (2007), criticizes Carter-Baker Report for "eschew[ing] careful research and rigorous analysis in favor of ex cathedra pronouncements of what ought to be done." On the other hand, some scholars argue that independent advisory commissions can play a constructive role in election reform in some circumstances. See Heather K. Gerken, *The Double-Edged Sword of Independence: Inoculating Electoral Reform Commissions Against Everyday Poli-*

tics, 6 ELECTION LAW JOURNAL 184 (2007); Christopher S. Elmendorf, *Representation Reinforcement Through Advisory Commissions: The Case of Election Law*, 80 N.Y.U. LAW REVIEW 1366 (2005).

Should the justices on both sides of *Crawford* have engaged in a more critical analysis of the Carter-Baker Report, rather than accepting its recommendations at face value? To what extent do you believe the Carter-Baker Report actually influenced the conclusions reached by either the majority or the dissenters?

6. *Arizona's ID Law.* Prior to *Crawford*, the Supreme Court had considered a challenge to an Arizona voter identification requirement in *Purcell v. Gonzalez*, 549 U.S. 1 (2006). Arizona's Proposition 200 required voters to show either one form of photo identification, or two forms of non-photo identification. Without deciding on Proposition 200's constitutionality, the Court's *per curiam* opinion vacated an injunction against the law that had been issued by the Ninth Circuit. The opinion in *Purcell* suggests that lower courts should be cautious in issuing injunctions against state election procedures shortly before an election:

> Faced with an application to enjoin operation of voter identification procedures just weeks before an election, the Court of Appeals was required to weigh, in addition to the harms attendant upon issuance or nonissuance of an injunction, considerations specific to election cases and its own institutional procedures. Court orders affecting elections, especially conflicting orders, can themselves result in voter confusion and consequent incentive to remain away from the polls. As an election draws closer, that risk will increase.

Is it prudent for courts to exercise particular restraint when deciding whether to issue an injunction shortly before an election? Is it better for courts to wait until after an election has been conducted, to see if the anticipated problems actually materialize? Are there advantages to resolving constitutional issues through pre-election litigation rather than post-election litigation? For criticism of *Purcell*, see Richard L. Hasen, *The Untimely Death of Bush v. Gore*, 60 STANFORD LAW REVIEW 1, 28–43 (2007).

7. *Racial Discrimination.* Plaintiffs' argument in *Crawford* was based upon the Fourteenth Amendment to the U.S. Constitution. Is there a plausible argument that strict voter identification laws violate Section 2 of the Voting Rights Act? As we saw in Chapter 5, Section 2 prohibits electoral practices that "result[] in a denial or abridgement of the right of any citizen of the United States to vote on account of race or color. . . ."? As noted in Part II of this chapter, Section 2 does not require discriminatory intent. What legal standard should courts apply to claims that a voter ID law "results in the denial or abridgement" of voting rights under Section 2? It might open the proverbial floodgates if any practice that has a disparate impact on racial minorities—including voting machines, felon disenfranchisement laws, or the location of polling places—were subject to a Section 2 claim. What sort of evidence should be required to prevail on a claim that an election administration practice violates Section 2? For a discussion of Section 2's applicability to voter ID and other election administration rules, see Daniel P. Tokaji, *The New Vote Denial: Where Election Reform Meets the Voting Rights Act*, 57 SOUTH CAROLINA LAW REVIEW 689 (2006).

IV. Law and Participation

To what extent can and should election administration laws be structured to increase and enhance voter participation? To answer this question, it is first helpful to examine what is known about American voter turnout and its effects on election results.

Voter Turnout, 1960–2000

Italy	92.15	Norway	79.89
Iceland	89.06	Germany	79.88
Belgium	87.13	Finland	78.81
Denmark	85.34	Ireland	75.46
Austria	84.79	United Kingdom	72.50
Sweden	84.64	Japan	67.75
Australia	83.74	Canada	66.74
Netherlands	83.00	France	64.86
New Zealand	82.73	United States	54.65
Israel	81.95	Switzerland	40.60

Source: David Hill, AMERICAN VOTER TURNOUT: AN INSTITUTIONAL PERSPECTIVE 8–9, 149 (2006) (relying on data from the Institute for Democracy and Electoral Assistance and the Federal Elections Commission).

A. Empirical Research on Voter Turnout

The proportion of Americans eligible to vote who actually *do* vote is low. You may ask, low compared to what? Low compared to other industrialized democracies, and low compared to our own experience earlier in our history. A comprehensive study of average turnout in national elections held in 140 countries holding at least two elections between 1945 and 1998 placed the United States 114th.[d] The table above shows the turnout between 1960 and 2000 in twenty stable, long-established democracies.

The United States ranks next to last among these twenty countries, ahead of only Switzerland, which has a long history of low voter turnout. Turnout has not always been so low in the United States. In the fifteen presidential elections from 1840 to 1896 (the peak period in American history), turnout averaged 78 percent.[e] Figure 7.3 on the next page shows that turnout declined precipitously during the period from around 1896 to 1920, that it gained some ground during the 1920s and 1930s, but that it has again declined significantly during the period since 1960.[f]

---

d. The only countries holding elections ranking lower in turnout than the United States were (in order of higher to lower turnout): Mexico, Peru, Brazil, Nigeria, Thailand, Sierra Leone, Botswana, Chile, Senegal, Ecuador, El Salvador, Haiti, Ghana, Pakistan, Zambia, Burkina Faso, Nauru, Yemen, Columbia, Niger, Sudan, Jordan, Guatemala, Djibouti, Egypt, and Mali. International Institute for Democracy and Electoral Assistance, *Turnout in the World—Country by Country Performance* (1945–98), *available at* http://www.idea.int/vt/survey/voter_turnout_pop2-2.cfm.

e. These figures were calculated using the table in Ruy A. Teixeira, THE DISAPPEARING AMERICAN VOTER 9 (1992) (Table 1-3).

f. Figure 7.3 shows turnout separately for the 11 former Confederate states and the rest of the country, because in the former, the drastic decline around the turn of the century was caused by the disfranchisement of African-Americans and the concomitant elimination of party competition, which discouraged many whites from voting. Turnout in the South remained low until after World War II, when blacks began to be reenfranchised and when competition between Democrats and Republicans reemerged. Separation of southern and northern turnout figures in this manner shows the extent of the recent turnout decline, which would be masked by the special developments in the South if only national figures were considered.

Figure 7.3 was prepared for this volume by J. Morgan Kousser, whose assistance is gratefully acknowledged.

Figure 7.3

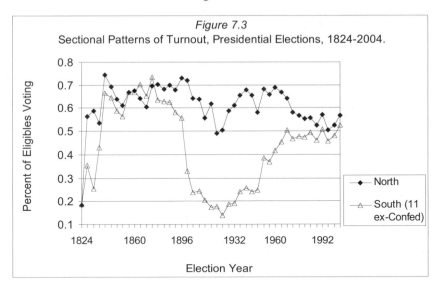

Figure 7.3
Sectional Patterns of Turnout, Presidential Elections, 1824-2004.

The above figures use percentages of *voting age population*, which can be somewhat misleading when it comes to American turnout. In some states, those convicted of a felony may not vote, and, as we know from Chapter 2, states impose a citizenship requirement for voting. Moreover, overseas voters are eligible to vote for president, but are not counted as part of the voting age population of a given state. Finally, population figures are based upon the United States census, which does not produce a perfectly accurate count. When considering voter turnout using percentages of *eligible voters* and adjusting for errors in the census, McDonald and Popkin found that there has been no significant change outside the South in *eligible* voter turnout rates since 1972. In the South, eligible voter turnout has *increased* since 1972. Michael P. McDonald & Samuel L. Popkin, *The Myth of the Vanishing Voter*, 95 AMERICAN POLITICAL SCIENCE REVIEW 963 (2001).

Even if the decline in voting rates is thus less dramatic than raw figures suggest, when one recalls the long struggle outlined in Chapter 2 to extend the suffrage to increased segments of the American population and the importance placed on the right to vote in the American civic culture, one may well be puzzled why so many citizens fail to take advantage of such a central part of their birthright. In a period when government's role in society is more far-reaching than ever before, why do not all citizens seek a voice in the decisions that affect their own lives? If people are dissatisfied with the performance of government, why do they abandon their best opportunity to enforce improvement? Given the elimination of poll taxes, how can so many people not find voting worth the minimal expenditure of time and effort required?

On the other hand, one can recognize the factors that may dissuade citizens in a democracy from political participation. In the 1830s, one of the most astute observers of American democracy, Alexis de Tocqueville, noted some of these factors:

> As the men who inhabit democratic countries have no superiors, no inferiors, and no habitual or necessary partners in their undertakings, they readily fall back upon themselves and consider themselves as beings apart.... Hence such men can never, without an effort, tear themselves from their private affairs

to engage in public business; their natural bias leads them to abandon the latter to the sole visible and permanent representative of the interests of the community; that is to say, to the state. Not only are they naturally wanting in a taste for public business, but they have frequently no time to attend to it. Private life in democratic times is so busy, so excited, so full of wishes and of work, that hardly any energy or leisure remains to each individual for public life. I am the last man to contend that these propensities are unconquerable, since my chief object in writing this book has been to combat them. I maintain only that at the present day a secret power is fostering them in the human heart, and that if they are not checked, they will wholly overgrow it.[g]

What conclusions can we draw from this brief discussion? The conventional perspective of the civic forum that expects people to welcome the opportunity to participate in public policymaking suggests that voter turnout will be higher to the extent citizens perceive that they have a civic obligation to vote and believe that the outcome of an election will matter to them and to the community generally. The public choice perspective predicts that individuals will not vote because the costs of doing so outweigh the expected benefit. If we accept this insight without applying it dogmatically, we may expect that the relative costliness of voting in time and effort will affect turnout.[h]

Even this assumption, that as costs go down voting goes up, appears unsupported by long-term evidence of the American experience. In the twentieth century, the period of turnout decline since 1960 coincided with substantial reductions in the barriers to voting. For example, during that period, poll taxes and literacy tests were eliminated, the typical year-long waiting requirement was reduced to thirty days in most places as a result of *Dunn v. Blumstein*, and at the state level, changes have almost invariably been in the direction of facilitating registration. How can the aggregate trend over time be reconciled with individual-level influences on voting? Even in the South, where because of the Voting Rights Act the lowering of the barriers was the most dramatic, turnout of eligible voters has at best shown a modest increase since 1960.

Perhaps it would not be a cause for public concern that only about half of the eligible registered voters vote in American presidential elections (and substantially less in other American elections) if those who voted mirrored those who did not vote. As we shall see, empirical studies show that voters tend not to be a random distribution of the population. It has long been believed that in twentieth-century America, persons of relatively high socioeconomic status (SES)—greater than average wealth and education, higher occupational status—were more likely to vote than persons of lower SES. Whites, who on average enjoy higher SES than blacks and Latinos, are more likely to vote than minority group members. Beginning in the early 1970s, data collected by the Census Bureau have made it possible to refine our understanding of demographic influences on voter turnout.

In a landmark study, Raymond E. Wolfinger and Steven J. Rosenstone discovered that of the socioeconomic factors, level of education has by far the greatest influence on propensity to vote.[i] Although published in 1980, it remains the best comprehensive source of data about who votes. Once education and other relevant factors are controlled, the effect of income is relatively small and almost entirely confined to those at the lowest income levels. That is, all else being equal, a person whose income is below the poverty

g. 2 Alexis de Tocqueville, Democracy in America 310 (Phillips Bradley ed., 1945).

h. For a qualified defense of the public choice model of voting see André Blais, To Vote or Not to Vote: The Merits and Limits of Rational Choice Theory (2000).

i. Raymond E. Wolfinger & Steven J. Rosenstone, Who Votes? 23–25 (1980).

level is somewhat less likely to vote than a person whose income is above the poverty level.[j] However, differences in income above the poverty level have almost no effect on the likelihood of voting. Wolfinger and Rosenstone did find some connection between voting and occupation, but it was not a straightforward correlation between voting and occupational status. Rather, persons in certain occupations — particularly farmers and people with lower status white-collar jobs such as clerical and sales positions — were especially likely to vote, all else being equal.[k] Aside from SES, two demographic factors that have a significant effect on voting include age (likelihood of voting increases with age, and a person between 18 and 24 is 28 percent less likely to vote than a 55-year-old)[l] and mobility (persons who have recently moved are less likely to vote).[m]

Turnout among white Anglos has been consistently higher than among racial and ethnic minorities. Between blacks and whites, the gap in 1988 was under eight percentage points, about five percentage points less than in 1964.[n] Though the turnout rate declined among blacks during this period, it declined even more among whites. Not surprisingly, these general trends mask differences between North and South during the period that the Voting Rights Act was enacted and took hold. In the South, the gap decreased from 15.5 percentage points in 1964 to 8.4 points in 1988, as black turnout increased by 4.0 points and white turnout declined by a modest (compared to the North) 3.1 points. In the rest of the country, the gap was less than three points in 1964. Both black and white turnout decreased substantially in subsequent elections, and in 1988 the gap was about five points. The gap had fluctuated considerably in the intervening period. Separate data for Latino citizens have been collected only since 1976. Nationwide, the turnout rate for Latino citizens of the United States has trailed that of blacks by about six points.[o]

Though racial minorities have voted at rates below that of the white Anglo majority, race does not appear to have been an *independent* cause of low turnout. To the contrary, Wolfinger and Rosenstone found that a black was slightly *more* likely to vote than a white with similar education and other demographic characteristics.[p] The same was true of

---

j.   *Id.* at 25–26.

k.   *Id.* at 28–33. Wolfinger & Rosenstone also found that after controlling for other factors, turnout among farm workers was 6 percentage points lower than what would be expected. *Id.* at 34.

l.   *Id.* at 50.

m.   *Id.* at 52–53. Wolfinger & Rosenstone had found this factor particularly strong in midterm elections. Moving is shown to have a substantial negative effect on the probability of voting in presidential elections in Peverill Squire, Raymond E. Wolfinger & David P. Glass, *Residential Mobility and Voter Turnout*, 81 AMERICAN POLITICAL SCIENCE REVIEW 45 (1987). Since there is no reason to expect a person's interest in a presidential election to be affected by moving, Squire et al. conclude that the effect is caused by the need to re-register.

n.   Data in this paragraph are taken from Teixeira, *supra*, 70–74. Not too much stock should be put in precise percentages, for the data are subject to a variety of technical problems and vary depending on which survey is used.

o.   For more detailed discussion of Latino voting rates, see Rodolfo O. de la Garza & Louis DeSipio, *Save the Baby, Change the Bathwater, and Scrub the Tub: Latino Electoral Participation After Seventeen Years of Voting Rights Act Coverage*, 71 TEXAS LAW REVIEW 1479 (1993). For further exploration which distinguishes the three largest Latino sub-groups (Cuban Americans, Mexican Americans, and Puerto Ricans), see Benjamin Highton & Arthur L. Burris, *New Perspectives on Latino Voter Turnout in the United States*, 30 AMERICAN POLITICS RESEARCH 285 (2002). Highton and Burris find that the gap in participation between Latinos and Anglos can largely be explained by socioeconomic status.

p.   Wolfinger & Rosenstone, *supra*, at 90. In more recent elections, the greater propensity of blacks to vote, demographic variables held constant, has become more pronounced. This was particularly true in 1984, which could have been the result of heightened mobilization activity among blacks in that election and of Walter Mondale being a particularly popular candidate among blacks, while Ronald Reagan was a particularly unpopular candidate. See Jan E. Leighley & Jonathan Nagler, *Indi-*

Mexican-Americans. Puerto Ricans, on the other hand, were seven percent less likely to vote than other citizens, after controlling for other variables.[q] In sum, they found that racial and ethnic minorities vote at lower rates than white Anglos, but the reason appears to be that racial minorities on average have received less education, are younger, and share other demographic attributes associated with nonvoting, and not that race or ethnicity is an independent factor lowering the probability of voting.

A more recent study by Hill and Leighley found that the more racially diverse a state's electorate, the lower the voter turnout. Kim Quaile Hill & Jan E. Leighley, *Racial Diversity, Voter Turnout, and Mobilizing Institutions in the United States*, 27 AMERICAN POLITICS QUARTERLY 275 (1999). The authors also found that "[s]tates with greater racial diversity have less-easy voter registration requirements, and they are less likely to have relatively liberal Republican party elites."

The overrepresentation among nonvoters of racial and ethnic minorities, people with less education, and people of low income, might suggest that if all nonvoters began voting, there would be a major electoral movement toward Democrats and liberal candidates. But most research shows that the political views of nonvoters are similar to those of voters. The percentages who favor the Democrats in each of the two groups tend to be almost identical. There are more independents among nonvoters, and therefore a smaller proportion of Republicans, but only by a few percentage points, not enough to have a major electoral impact. Opinions on policy issues of voters and nonvoters almost never diverge by more than a small amount, though there is a very slight tendency for voters to be more liberal than nonvoters on social issues and more conservative on economic issues.[r] Chronic nonvoters and irregular voters tend to be more politically independent and less interested and less informed about candidates, parties, and political issues than regular voters.

Recent research questions the "conventional wisdom," largely derived from Wolfinger and Rosenstone's work, that the policy preferences of voters are similar to those of nonvoters. Jan E. Leighley & Jonathan Nagler, *Who Votes Now? And Does It Matter?* (March 7, 2007), *available at* http://www.nyu.edu/gsas/dept/politics/faculty/nagler/leighley_nagler_midwest2007.pdf. Examining data from 1972 to 2004, Leighley and Nagler challenge the assumption that the policy preferences of voters and nonvoters are identical. Their study

---

vidual and Systemic Influences on Turnout: Who Votes? 1984, 54 JOURNAL OF POLITICS 718, 726 (1992). Studies of turnout in the 1950s and 1960s found that African Americans were especially likely to vote if they were both politically knowledgeable and relatively negative in their view of the political system. This contrasts with whites, whose propensity to vote is not associated with such political alienation. A study of more recent elections finds that this difference between blacks and whites has disappeared. However, the authors found that African Americans are more likely to vote in areas with black big-city mayors, and they suggest that whereas in earlier times blacks were motivated to vote by the need to protect themselves within a hostile system, currently they are most likely to vote when they feel empowered within the system. See Lawrence Bobo & Franklin D. Gilliam, Jr., *Race, Sociopolitical Participation, and Black Empowerment*, in CONTROVERSIES IN VOTING BEHAVIOR, at 39 (Richard G. Niemi & Herbert F. Weisberg eds., 3d ed. 1993).

q. See Wolfinger & Rosenstone, *supra*, at 92–93. Wolfinger and Rosenstone explained this difference between Mexican-Americans and Puerto Ricans on the ground that the former have to wait at least five years after arriving in the United States before they are eligible for citizenship, during which time they may acquire skills, information, and acculturation that make them more likely to vote, whereas Puerto Ricans are eligible to vote as soon as they arrive on the mainland. They go immediately into the denominator that forms the turnout rate, though some may regard themselves as merely temporary visitors to the mainland, and others may be less likely to vote until they have lived here at least a few years

r. See Wolfinger & Rosenstone, *supra*, at 109; Teixeira, *supra*, at 86–101.

finds that those who voted were "substantially more conservative than non-voters on class-based issues," such as union organizing, health insurance, and education.

Notes and Questions

1. Most public discussions of turnout assume that increasing the rate of voting is a desirable public goal. Why should this be so? Research indicates that the registration barriers that currently exist screen out people who are less well informed and have less education, without actually preventing many people from voting who are highly motivated to do so. Might this be regarded as a desirable state of affairs? Would the quality of public decisionmaking be improved by the participation of people who are less interested and less informed? If not, does it follow that higher turnout is a goal that ought to be abandoned? Does your answer depend upon whether you consider an election to be like an examination in which there is a "right" answer rather than as a means for dividing power among political equals? Does it depend on whether the policy preferences of non-voters are different from those of voters?

2. The American National Election Studies <www.electionstudies.org> is one of the most valuable sources for researchers interested in questions about trends in voting and turnout. One of the questions the NES asks survey participants is whether or not they voted in the last election. Occasionally NES verifies these responses by looking at local voting records. On average, about 25% of nonvoters in the validated NES voting surveys said they voted, compared to only 1% of confirmed voters who said they did not vote. See Brian D. Silver et al., *Who Overreports Voting?*, 80 AMERICAN POLITICAL SCIENCE REVIEW 613, 613–14 (1986). What explains this phenomenon? For recent empirical evidence supporting the view that people who are under the most social pressure to vote are the ones most likely to misrepresent their behavior when they fail to do so, see Robert Bernstein, Anita Chadha & Robert Montjoy, *Overreporting Voting: Why It Happens and Why It Matters*, 65 PUBLIC OPINION QUARTERLY 22 (2001).

3. Do negative political advertisements depress turnout? One study made such a claim based upon experimental data. Stephen Ansolabehere et al., *Does Attack Advertising Demobilize the Electorate?*, 88 AMERICAN POLITICAL SCIENCE REVIEW 829 (1994). Volume 93, No. 4 (December 1999) of the AMERICAN POLITICAL SCIENCE REVIEW presents a number of articles attacking and supporting the results of the study. If negative political advertisements do have such an effect, what can be done about them? Probably very little as a matter of constitutional law. See Chapter 11, Part II.

4. Democratic and Republican political operatives have less interest in increasing turnout overall than in increasing turnout of likely supporters. Suppose you wanted to increase the vote of a particular segment of the population. How would you do it? Perhaps you would like to pay people to vote. Of course, it is illegal in every state and in federal elections to pay people to vote for a particular candidate or for or against a particular ballot issue. See Richard L. Hasen, *Vote Buying*, 88 CALIFORNIA LAW REVIEW 1323, 1324 n.1 (2000), for a collection of statutes banning such vote buying. But what about payments to increase turnout? Federal law prohibits the practice, but at least three states— Alaska, California, and Mississippi—allow it when there are no federal candidates on the ballot. Should such a practice be illegal, legal but discouraged, or encouraged? For a discussion of these issues, see Hasen, *supra*, 88 CALIFORNIA LAW REVIEW at 1355–59.

Consider what happened in an Oakland, California, special election for a state assembly seat.

A candidate preferred by the state Democratic party, former Oakland Mayor Elihu Harris, was in electoral trouble. In response, the party offered $5 coupons for free chicken dinners exclusively in poor, African-American neighborhoods, where voters likely to support Harris lived. It is not clear how many voters cast their ballots because of the incentive. In any case, Harris did not get enough votes to avoid a runoff, and the chicken incident became part of racial politics in the runoff election, ultimately contributing to Harris' defeat and to the election of Audie Bock, the first Green Party candidate elected to state office, not to mention a barrage of chicken jokes.

Id. at 1355–56 (footnotes omitted); see also Benjamin Pimentel, *Chicken Dinners Don't Sit Well With Greens*, SAN FRANCISCO CHRONICLE, Feb. 11, 1999, at A19 ("The Green Party is crying foul over the Democratic Party's poultry politics.").

Who is most likely to vote when payments are given to increase turnout? Republicans in the Democratically-controlled California legislature have tried so far unsuccessfully to change California law on payments for turnout. In addition to vouchers for turnout, payments are sometimes made to get people to the polls. See *Dansereau v. Ulmer*, 903 P.2d 555, 561–66 (Alaska 1995) (holding that free gasoline vouchers to get voters to the polls do not violate federal law). Money is also sometimes given to "flushers" or "haulers" to get out the vote. No doubt some of that money ends up (illegally) in the hands of voters. Finally, how about a lottery with a valuable prize for anyone who turns in a voting stub? See *Naron v. Prestage*, 469 So.2d 83 (Miss. 1985) (upholding a lottery's legality under Mississippi law but condemning it for demeaning the electoral process). For an argument in favor of the lottery approach, see Pamela S. Karlan, *Not by Money but by Virtue Won? Vote Trafficking and the Voting Rights System*, 80 VIRGINIA LAW REVIEW 1455, 1472 (1994).

B. Laws Affecting Participation

Although election administration remains mostly a state and local matter, Congress has occasionally passed legislation aimed at increasing and enhancing voter participation. Three of the most important such laws are described below, along with other possibilities for additional federal or state legislation.

1. *The Language Assistance Provisions of the Voting Rights Act*

In 1975, Congress amended the Voting Rights Act to mandate that certain jurisdictions provide assistance to non-English proficient voters. The impetus for these amendments was Congress' finding of relatively low registration and participation rates among certain ethnic minority groups. For example, a congressional committee found that only 44.4% of Latino citizens, compared to 73.4% of other citizens, were registered to vote in 1972. S. Rep. No. 94-295, *reprinted in* 1975 U.S.C.C.A.N 774 (1975). Congress also found educational inequalities affecting Latino, Asian American, and American Indian groups that limited access to the electoral process:

> Through the use of various practices and procedures, citizens of language minorities have been effectively excluded from participation in the electoral process. Among other factors, the denial of the right to vote of such minority group citizens is ordinarily directly related to the unequal educational op-

portunities afforded them, resulting in high illiteracy and low voting participation.

42 U.S.C. § 1973aa-1a(a). The language assistance provisions of the VRA are temporary, but have been extended three times since their enactment, in 1982, 1992 and again
in 2006.

The key provisions of the VRA pertaining to language assistance are Sections 4(f)(4) and
Section 203. Section 4(f)(4) expanded the VRA's coverage formula, to include jurisdictions with low registration and participation rates, in which more than 5% are of a lan-
guage-minority group and in which English-only election materials had been provided in
the 1972 election. Covered jurisdictions are required to provide election materials in the
language of the relevant minority group, and to comply with the other VRA requirements
applicable to covered jurisdictions, including preclearance of electoral changes. Section
203 applies to jurisdictions with high concentrations of non-English proficient voters.
Under the current threshold, a jurisdiction is required to comply with the requirements
of Section 203 if more than 5% of the voting-age population or more than 10,000 citizens of voting age are members of a language minority group and are of limited English
proficiency.

Section 203 jurisdictions, like those covered by Section 4(f)(4), are required to provide all election materials in the languages of the relevant language minority groups.
That includes registration forms, instructions, oral assistance, and ballots. For more detailed descriptions of the requirements of Sections 4(f)(4) and 203, see James Thomas
Tucker, *Enfranchising Language Minority Citizens: The Bilingual Election Provisions of the
Voting Rights Act*, 10 N.Y.U. JOURNAL OF LEGISLATION & PUBLIC POLICY 195 (2006/2007)
and Jocelyn Friedrichs Benson, *Su Voto Es Su Voz: Incorporating Voters of Limited English Proficiency Into American Democracy*, 48 BOSTON COLLEGE LAW REVIEW 251 (2007).

The efficacy of the VRA's language assistance provisions remains the subject of considerable
debate. Supporters of the VRA's language assistance provisions argue that they have significantly increased registration and participation rates among Latino, Asian American,
and Native American voters. See Tucker, *supra*, at 233–34; Benson, *supra*, at 270–71; see
also Spencer Overton, STEALING DEMOCRACY: THE NEW POLITICS OF VOTER SUPPRESSION
121–47 (2006) (discussing benefits of VRA's language assistance provisions). A recent
GAO report found few quantitative data on the utility of the VRA's language assistance
requirements, though it noted that most election officials who were asked supported
bilingual voting assistance. Government Accountability Office, *Bilingual Voting Assistance:
Selected Jurisdictions' Strategies for Identifying Needs and Providing Assistance* (2008). Another study found that language assistance is widely used where it is available, but is frequently inadequate. James Thomas Tucker & Rodolfo Espino, *Government Effectiveness
and Efficiency? The Minority Language Assistance Provisions of the VRA*, 12 TEXAS JOUR-
NAL ON CIVIL LIBERTIES & CIVIL RIGHTS 163, 229–30, 231 (2007). This study also found
the costs of language assistance averaged 5% of total election expenses, an amount that
the authors characterize as modest. *Id.* at 230.

Are the language assistance provisions justified? With the significant exception of
Puerto Ricans, nearly all native-born American citizens grow up learning to speak and read
English. Immigrants are expected to learn some English as a condition of naturalization.
Putting aside Puerto Ricans, are voters unable to understand English entitled to foreign
language assistance in registering and voting?

A majority of Congress has consistently answered these questions in the affirmative,
most recently extending the language assistance provisions of the VRA in 2006. This

proved to be one of the more controversial aspects of the VRA reauthorization process, with some members of Congress disputing the need for bilingual language assistance. Questions were also raised about Congress' constitutional authority to require state and local governments to provide language assistance. In *Katzenbach v. Morgan*, 384 U.S. 641 (1966), the Supreme Court upheld a related provision of the original VRA, Section 4(e), which prohibited enforcement of state literacy requirements against those who had been educated in non-English speaking schools in Puerto Rico. The Court deferred to Congress' judgment that this requirement was needed to ensure that Puerto Ricans in the states would receive "nondiscriminatory treatment" with respect to voting and other public services. In later cases starting with *City of Boerne v. Flores*, 521 U.S. 507 (1997), however, the Court has adopted a much less deferential posture with respect to legislation enacted to enforce constitutional rights. It has required 'congruence and proportionality" between the means used and the ends that Congress seeks to achieve. But while striking down several laws as exceeding the proper scope of Congress' enforcement authority, the Court has distinguished its cases upholding various provisions of the VRA. (These cases are discussed in Chapter 5, Part II.)

Are the language assistance provisions of the VRA constitutional, under the test articulated in *Boerne* and later cases? What constitutional right do these provisions "enforce"? Are the provisions congruent and proportional to those rights? Should the Court adopt a more deferential posture when considering legislation aimed at protecting a fundamental right like voting? For discussion of these issues, see James Thomas Tucker, *The Battle over "Bilingual Ballots" Shifts to the Courts: A Post-*Boerne *Assessment of Section 203 of the Voting Rights Act*, 45 HARVARD JOURNAL ON LEGISLATION 507 (2008), and Daniel P. Tokaji, *Intent and Its Alternatives: Defending the New Voting Rights Act*, 58 ALABAMA LAW REVIEW 349 (2006).

2. *The National Voter Registration Act*

In 1993, Congress enacted the National Voter Registration Act (NVRA), 42 U.S.C. § 1973gg, better known as the "Motor Voter" law, because it ties voter registration to applying for or renewing one's driver's license. The law is much broader, however, providing that the state must designate as voter registration agencies all offices in the state that provide public assistance or state-funded programs for persons with disabilities. The law also requires each state to accept mail registration forms for voting and includes a number of other requirements.[s]

These provisions apply only to registration of voters in federal elections. However, in order to avoid dual systems of voter registration, almost all states use the procedures mandated by the Motor Voter law for registration to vote in state and local as well as federal elections. Illinois initially attempted to maintain a dual registration system, but as of 1997, Mississippi was the only state doing so. In that year, the Supreme Court ruled that Mississippi's dual registration system could not be kept in effect without preclearance under Section 5 of the Voting Rights Act. *Young v. Fordice*, 520 U.S. 273 (1997).

NVRA has been successful in raising voter registration. A report by the Federal Election Commission found that voter registration nationally rose 3.7% from 1994 to 1998.

---

s. For decisions upholding the constitutionality of the law against challenges based on principles of federalism, see *Association of Community Organizations for Reform Now v. Edgar*, 56 F.3d 791 (7th Cir. 1995) and *Voting Rights Coalition v. Wilson*, 60 F.3d 1411 (9th Cir. 1995), *cert. denied* 516 U.S. 1093 (1996).

Those figures so far have not translated into increased voter turnout in elections. See Robert D. Brown & Justin Wedeking, *People Who Have Their Tickets But Do Not Use Them: "Motor Voter," Registration, and Turnout Revisited*, 34 AMERICAN POLITICS RESEARCH 479 (2006); Stephen Knack, *Drivers Wanted: Motor Voter and the Election of 1996*, 32 PS: POLITICAL SCIENCE AND POLITICS 237 (1999); Michael D. Martinez & David Hill, *Did Motor Voter Work?*, 27 AMERICAN POLITICS QUARTERLY 296 (1999); see also Raymond E. Wolfinger & Jonathan Hoffman, *Registering and Voting with Motor Voter*, 34 PS: POLITICAL SCIENCE AND POLITICS 85 (2001). Knack argues, however, that the NVRA substantially slowed the decline in voter turnout. He also argues that the 1996 elections provide "absolutely no support" for the argument that new registrants under NVRA would be disproportionately Democratic. Knack, *supra*, 32 PS: POLITICAL SCIENCE AND POLITICS, at 241.

3. The Help America Vote Act

Two years after the Florida 2000 election, Congress passed the "Help America Vote Act of 2002," 42 U.S.C. § 15301 *et seq*. The Act, now commonly known as HAVA, represents the federal government's most significant intervention to date in the "nuts and bolts" of election administration.

In the deliberations leading up to HAVA's enactment, Congress attempted to balance the values of access and integrity. As Representative Steny Hoyer, one of HAVA's most prominent supporters, put it: "Everyone agrees that we should make it easier to vote ... and we should make it harder to cheat." David Nather, *Election Overhaul May Have to Wait in Line Behind Other 'Crisis' Issues*, CQ WEEKLY, July 27, 2002, at 2034. The difficulty was reaching agreement on how to promote these ends, with Democrats tending to emphasize access and Republican integrity.

HAVA contained both carrots and sticks to induce states to improve the administration of elections. Informed by the empirical research on voting technology that occurred in the wake of the 2000 election, Title I of HAVA authorized substantial federal funds for states to upgrade their voting technology and make other improvements in the administration of elections. 42 U.S.C. § 15302. Title II of HAVA set up a new agency, the Election Assistance Commission (EAC), to distribute these federal funds and to oversee implementation of the Act's requirements. 42 U.S.C. § 15321. Through Title III of HAVA, Congress imposed certain limited requirements upon states, including voting equipment standards, a statewide registration database, a limited identification requirement for first-time voters who registered by mail, and provisional voting. 42 U.S.C. §§ 15481–83.

From the beginning, the EAC encountered significant problems in performing its duties under HAVA. Congress delayed in approving sufficient funds and in confirming the EAC commissioners. More fundamentally, as one commentator put it: "The EAC was designed to have as little regulatory authority as possible." Leonard Shambon, *Implementing the Help America Vote Act*, 3 ELECTION LAW JOURNAL 424, 428 (2004). It is expressly denied the power to issue rules and regulations, except to implement certain provisions of the NVRA. 42 U.S.C. § 1973gg-7(a). The structure of the EAC—which is composed of four members, two from each major party, with a majority required for the Commission to act—also imposes a barrier to action. For more on the early problems encountered by the EAC, see Daniel P. Tokaji, *Early Returns on Election Reform: Discretion, Disenfranchisement, and the Help America Vote Act*, 73 GEORGE WASHINGTON LAW REVIEW 1206, 1218–20 (2005).

Among HAVA's key requirements is that provisional ballots be made available to certain voters—in particular, those who appear at the polls and find that their names are not on the registration list, and those who appear at the polls without required identification. 42 U.S.C. § 15482(a)(1), 15483(b)(2)(B). The idea behind this requirement is to provide a backstop, so that voters are not turned away without being able to cast a ballot due to an administrative error. One of the controversies that emerged during the 2004 election was whether voters should be allowed to cast a provisional ballot and have those ballots counted, if they mistakenly show up to vote at the wrong precinct. The operative language of HAVA provides that a voter

> shall be permitted to cast a provisional ballot at that polling place upon the execution of a written affirmation by the individual before an election official at the polling place stating that the individual is … a registered voter in the jurisdiction in which the individual desires to vote.. .

42 U.S.C. § 15482(a)(2). The dispute turned on whether "jurisdiction" meant the *precinct* at which the voter appeared (in which case voters at the wrong precinct need not be given a provisional ballot), or the *county or municipality* in which the voter resided (in which case voters were entitled to receive provisional ballots and, at least arguably, to have those ballots counted). Lower courts concluded that HAVA did not require states to count provisional ballots cast in the wrong precinct. See *Sandusky County Democratic Party v. Blackwell*, 387 F.3d 565 (6th Cir. 2004). For further discussion of HAVA's provisional voting requirements, see Leonard Shambon & Keith Abouchar, *Trapped by Precincts? The Help America Vote Act's Provisional Ballots and the Problem of Precincts*, 10 N.Y.U. JOURNAL OF LEGISLATION & PUBLIC POLICY 133 (2006–2007) and Edward B. Foley, *The Promise and Problems of Provisional Voting*, 73 GEORGE WASHINGTON LAW REVIEW 1193 (2005).

An unintended consequence of the provisional ballots mandated by HAVA is that they may provide fertile ground for post-election litigation, with opposing candidates disagreeing over which ones should be counted. According to Foley, such a scenario almost emerged in 2004, when "[t]housands of lawyers were at the ready, armed with numerous theories for disputing the standards and procedures for determining which provisional ballots should count and which should not." *Id.* at 1194. To minimize the likelihood of post-election disputes over provisional ballots, Foley recommends "development of clear rules for determining when provisional ballots are to be counted." *Id.* at 1203.

4. *Other Laws That Might Promote Participation*

What other legal changes to voting might be used in this country to increase or enhance voter participation?

Compulsory voting. If more participation in U.S. elections is desirable, then why not simply pass a law requiring that people vote or face a penalty? The idea is not as far-fetched as it might sound to American readers. Australia, Belgium, Italy and a number of other countries with high voter turnout have such laws.

Studies show that, controlling for other factors, turnout is about 10–15 percentage points higher in counties with compulsory voting. See Richard L. Hasen, *Voting Without Law?*, 144 UNIVERSITY OF PENNSYLVANIA LAW REVIEW 2135, 2171 n.144 (1996). The range of penalties for nonvoting range from Australia's $50 fine to Greece's penalty of imprisonment for up to one year, to Italy's posting of the names of nonvoters on the communal notice board. Despite this wide range of stated penalties, lack of enforcement is ubiquitous. See *id.* at 2169–70.

Should compulsory voting be adopted in the United States? For an argument in favor of its adoption by the former president of the American Political Science Association, see Arend Lijphart, *Unequal Participation: Democracy's Unresolved Dilemma*, 91 AMERICAN POLITICAL SCIENCE REVIEW 1 (1997). For a defense of compulsory voting drawn from Australia's experience, see Lisa Hill, *On the Reasonableness of Compelling Citizens to 'Vote': the Australian Case*, 50 POLITICAL STUDIES 80 (2002). Compulsory voting laws are rarely enforced in countries that have them. Why then do they appear to be so effective at raising turnout?

There do not appear to be any constitutional barriers against the adoption of compulsory voting in the United States. If the state can force you to serve on a jury, enlist in the army, and separate your trash for recycling purposes, the state can presumably make you show up and vote. A compulsory voting law allows you to cast a blank ballot, so it does not appear that you would be forced to choose from available candidates. Is the First Amendment a barrier? See Hasen, *supra*, 144 UNIVERSITY OF PENNSYLVANIA LAW REVIEW at 2175 n.163. Do you think compulsory voting is likely to be adopted in the United States in the near future? If not, why not? Note that jury duty, military service, and environmental compliance really *are* compulsory. It is not sufficient to show up but not perform. Might Americans regard it as bullying to require people to report to a polling place when they do not have to cast a vote?

Easing registration requirements. One way to increase turnout might be to reduce the cost of voting. The barrier most often discussed is the registration requirement. The United States is one of the few if not the only major democracy in the world that requires advance registration as a prerequisite to voting without the government assuming responsibility for seeing to it that all eligible people are registered. One scholar estimates that American registration requirements may account for fourteen percentage points of the turnout gap between the United States and most other democracies.[t] If this estimate is correct, then elimination of the registration requirement or the maintenance of universal registration by the government would not by itself put the United States near the top of the list in turnout, but could be predicted to close most of the gap between the United States and other low ranking countries such as Canada, France, and Japan. Furthermore, registration requirements have not always been imposed in the United States. Most were put in place around the turn of the century, possibly for the very purpose of discouraging voting by immigrants, workers, and others who were regarded by some as too ignorant to vote, though this is a point of contention among historians.[u]

Neither elimination of registration requirements nor universal registration is likely in the foreseeable future, but easing of barriers to registration is feasible. Though every state

---

t. G. Bingham Powell, Jr., *American Voter Turnout in Comparative Perspective*, in CONTROVERSIES IN VOTING BEHAVIOR, *supra*, at 56, 78. Note, however, that Powell's data do not reflect the results of NVRA.

u. See Dayna L. Cunningham, *Who Are to Be the Electors? A Reflection on the History of Voter Registration in the United States*, 9 YALE LAW & POLICY REVIEW 370, 380–85 (1991). Historians seeking to explain the drop in turnout in the North after 1896 disagree on how much was caused by registration laws and how much by lessened party mobilization. Party mobilization is believed to have decreased in part because after 1896, the South was safely controlled by Democrats and many areas in the North were almost as safely controlled by Republicans. Less competition might naturally lead to less mobilization. In addition, party mobilization may have been lessened because of the introduction, in approximately the same period, of the secret ballot, also referred to as the "Australian ballot." Previously, parties printed up their own ballots in a distinctive color and pre-marked, so that the fidelity of voters a party mobilized could be confirmed. Among historians who believe the introduction of registration requirements was a major cause of turnout decline, there is disagreement on the extent to which this consequence was intended.

but North Dakota requires voters to register, states vary considerably in their registration requirements. Several states allow election day registration (EDR), in which voters may appear at their polling place and vote on election day without having registered in advance. Social science research shows that EDR states enjoy significantly higher turnout than states requiring advance registration.[v] Presumably, this is because the desire to vote grows as the election nears and the campaign intensifies, to the point that some additional voters will have the incentive to take the effort to register[w].

Other differences in registration procedures that affect turnout, though not as much as the closing date, are whether the registration offices are open evenings or week-ends; whether the registration offices are open full-time during business hours; whether registration by mail is permitted for persons who are sick, disabled, or absent from home; and how quickly voters are "purged" from the registration lists for not voting in one or more elections. One recent study found that "registration portability"—the practice of allowing registrants who have moved within a state to change their registration and vote on election day at their new polling place—significantly increased turnout among people who had recently moved. Michael P. McDonald, *Portable Voter Registration*, 30 POLITICAL BEHAVIOR — (2008).

Perhaps surprisingly, the general availability of registration by mail and the availability of "deputy registrars" (private citizens who are deputized to register voters at homes, workplaces, shopping malls, etc.) do *not* appear to measurably increase turnout. But political scientists estimate that if all states had the most liberal registration procedures of the sort that have been shown to make a difference—i.e., voters can register up to election day; registration offices keep regular hours including being open evenings or weekends; people who are sick, disabled, or absent can register by mail; and voters are not purged without checks to confirm that they have either died or moved—then national turnout might increase by about seven to nine percentage points.[x]

Convenience Voting. Laws easing voter registration are only one way of lowering the costs of voting. Other possible methods include weekend voting, early voting (that is, giving voters the option of voting during a short period before the election), absentee voting, vote-by-mail, and (perhaps in the near future) internet voting. Each method makes it easier at least for some voters to cast ballots.

These other methods have costs as well as benefits, however. For example, weekend voting and early voting occur at polling places and require poll workers. Weekend voting might discourage some voters who are unwilling to sacrifice their recreational time.

The state of Oregon has moved to an all vote-by-mail voting system. Rather than having designated polling places, all registered voters are automatically sent a ballot that they may complete at home and mail back. Research on Oregon's experiment has revealed that

---

v. Craig L. Brians & Bernard Grofman, *Election Day Registration's Effect on U.S. Voter Turnout*, 82 SOCIAL SCIENCE QUARTERLY 170, 176–77 (2001), found a 7% increase with EDR on average. Benjamin Highton, *Easy Registration and Voter Turnout*, 59 JOURNAL OF POLITICS 565, 568 (1997) found turnout approximately 10% higher in states with EDR or no registration. Mark J. Fenster, *The Impact of Allowing Day of Registration Voting on Turnout in U.S. Elections from 1960 to 1992*, 22 AMERICAN POLITICS RESEARCH 74, 80, 84 (1994), found that three states adopting EDR in the mid-1970s saw increases in their turnout which were sustained over time.

w. Another advantage of EDR is that it tends to reduce reliance on provisional ballots. Eligible voters who do not appear on the registration list when they go to vote may, in EDR states, cast a regular ballot rather than voting provisionally. See Steven F. Huefner, et al., FROM REGISTRATION TO RECOUNTS: THE ELECTION ECOSYSTEMS OF FIVE MIDWESTERN STATES 177 (2007).

x. See Wolfinger & Rosenstone, *supra*, at 71–77; Teixeira, *supra*, at 107–12.

this system has increased turnout, particularly in local elections in which turnout is typically low. This research also suggests, however, that turnout has disproportionately increased among those already most likely to vote, specifically "those who are white, educated, older, and have higher incomes."[y] In sum, Oregon's vote-by-mail system seems to improve turnout, but may also increase the socioeconomic bias of the electorate. Is such a trade-off desirable? Are there intangible benefits from most people voting on the same day at designated places that are lost in vote-by-mail?

Absentee voting, vote-by-mail, and internet voting raise another problem—the methods eliminate the secret ballot. A rise in the use of these voting methods raises the specter of increased bribery of voters.[z] Consider *United States v. McCranie*, 169 F.3d 723 (11th Cir. 1999). Two competing candidates for county commissioner of Dodge County, Georgia, sent representatives to bid against each other for absentee ballots inside the county courthouse. "At trial, a Dodge County magistrate described the rowdy courthouse atmosphere during the absentee voting period as 'a successful flea market.'" As another example, massive absentee ballot fraud caused the voiding of all absentee ballots in the 1997 Miami mayoral election, leading to a change in the election results. See *Matter of Protest of Election Returns and Absentee Ballots in November 4, 1997 Election for City of Miami, Fla.*, 707 So.2d 1170 (Fla. App. 1998). For a readable discussion of the various issues surrounding absentee and early voting, see John C. Fortier, Absentee and Early Voting: Trends, Promises and Perils (2006).

Internet voting raises additional security concerns. For a comprehensive report on potential problems with a transition to internet voting, including the problem of hackers interfering with the counting of votes, see the Final Report of the California Internet Voting Task Force, *available at* www.ss.ca.gov/executive/ivote/. For suggestions on how these barriers might be overcome to make internet voting a reality, see R. Michael Alvarez & Thad E Hall, Point Click and Vote: The Future of Internet Voting (2004).

Besides concerns with fraud and security, there is a real question whether such efforts increase voter turnout rather than cause voters who used to vote at polling places on Election Day merely to shift to voting by an alternative method. In a recent survey of the literature, Michael W. Traugott wrote:

> Using a variety of data sources and analytical techniques, we conclude … that the effects of these reforms have been modest both in terms of increasing the size of the participating electorate and in altering its demographic and attitudinal characteristics....

> Analyses of alternative voting methods suggest … modest returns for turnout. These reforms seem to exert a small influence on the levels of participation, certainly not more than increases in the high single digits. It must be asked whether recent innovations will have any cumulative effects over a series of elections, or how durable some of these shifts might be, once the novelty of the changes and

---

y. Jeffrey A. Karp & Susan A. Banducci, *Going Postal: How All-Mail Elections Influence Turnout*, 22 Political Behavior 223, 233 (2000). Adam J. Berinsky et al., *Who Votes By Mail? A Dynamic Model of the Individual-Level Consequences of Voting-by-Mail Systems*, 65 Public Opinion Quarterly 178, 191 (2001) found that vote-by-mail "mobilizes older voters, those who are well educated, and those with substantial amounts of campaign interest."

z. Bribery of voters was far and away the greatest impediment to the integrity of elections before the introduction of the secret ballot, a fact well known not only to historians but to readers of great 19th century fiction. See, for example, Charles Dickens' *Bleak House*, George Eliot's *Felix Holt, Radical*, and Anthony Trollope's *Doctor Thorne*.

the associated high media coverage of the adoption wear off. In compositional terms, where most of the work has been among voters as opposed to registrants, these procedural changes do not seem to produce a less stratified electorate than we have now, or one that better reflects the underlying demographic or attitudinal characteristics of the population.

Michael W. Traugott, *Why Electoral Reform Has Failed: If You Build It, Will They Come?*, in RETHINKING THE VOTE: THE POLITICS AND PROSPECTS OF AMERICAN ELECTION REFORM 167, 181–82 (Ann N. Crigler, Marion R. Just and Edward J. McCaffery, eds., 2004). A study of absentee balloting similarly concluded that "[l]iberal absentee laws do appear to help stimulate turnout among certain groups, such as persons with disabilities and students. Yet, the extent to which overall turnout can be increased beyond these groups is doubtful. More likely, only those who are politically motivated (and thus likely to vote) will make plans in advance to vote absentee." Jeffrey A. Karp & Susan A. Banducci, *Absentee Voting, Mobilization, and Participation*, 29 AMERICAN POLITICS RESEARCH 183, 191 (2001).

Notes and Questions

1. *Federal involvement in election administration.* As noted at the beginning of this Chapter, the administration of American elections remains mostly a state and local matter. Though Congress has imposed some limited requirements through laws like the VRA, NVRA, and HAVA, most responsibility for running elections—including federal elections—still resides in officials in counties, cities, and towns throughout the United States. Is this a desirable state of affairs? Should we consider centralizing the administration of American elections? If so, what sort of structure might be implemented to promote fair and effective administration? The experience of the EAC in implementing HAVA's modest requirements might suggest that increasing federal responsibility over elections is not a panacea.

2. *Class bias?* Some proponents of registration reform have criticized the motor voter concept on the grounds that it is not only too limited but also biased.

> [M]otor voter programs ... expand the electorate without overcoming its upward class skew, a feature that may explain why both Republicans and Democrats sometimes support them. In 1983, only 47 percent of the 36 million adults in households with incomes under $10,000 held driver's licenses. But 93 percent of the 31 million adults in households with incomes over $40,000 had licenses.

Frances Fox Piven & Richard A. Cloward, WHY AMERICANS DON'T VOTE 222 (1988). See also Cunningham, *supra*, 9 YALE LAW & POLICY REVIEW at 389–90, asserting that the percentage of African Americans who have driver's licenses runs ten to eighteen points below the percentage for whites. Do these figures demonstrate that a motor voter registration law is likely to benefit whites and people who are affluent disproportionately? If so, do they provide a reason for opposing a motor voter system? Is the argument applicable to NVRA, the national Motor Voter law, which despite its nickname contains additional provisions intended to extend registration, including the availability of voter registration at welfare offices and offices providing services to people with disabilities?

3. *Absentee and early voting.* What effect would you expect absentee voting and early voting to have on the nature of political campaigns? Would those changes improve or detract from the nature of campaigns today? What effect would you expect voting at home to have on the nature of voting? Would voters feel less social pressure to vote if they knew no one could observe whether or not they showed up at the polling place?

4. *Internet voting and the digital divide.* The demographics of internet access are somewhat similar to the demographics of who votes. Those who are white, male, well-educated, and wealthy are most likely to have internet access. What is the relevance of this digital divide to the question whether internet voting should be adopted? For discussion of the digital divide, its impact on internet voting, and how these equality issues might be addressed, see Alvarez & Hall, POINT CLICK AND VOTE, *supra*, at 160–67 and Bryan Mercurio, *Democracy in Decline: Can Internet Voting Save the Electoral Process?*, 22 JOHN MARSHALL JOURNAL OF COMPUTER & INFORMATION LAW 409, 423–25 (2004).

Chapter 8

Ballot Propositions

Most of this book, like American political thought generally, centers around institutions of representative democracy, in which the people elect representatives who are empowered either directly or through their appointees to make governmental decisions. In most states, representative democracy has long been supplemented by direct votes on propositions. For example, every state but Delaware requires a vote of the people to amend the state constitution. However, near the end of the nineteenth century, the Populists and later the Progressives urged the extension of direct democracy to further supplement the ordinary legislative process. The three mechanisms most often advanced by the Progressives were the initiative, the referendum, and the recall.[a]

The *initiative* is a mechanism that permits a specified number of voters to propose a statute (and, in many states, a constitutional amendment) by signing petitions. Once the petitions qualify by receiving enough signatures the proposal is placed on the ballot, and it is enacted if the voters approve it. The initiative is the direct democracy device that usually receives by far the most public attention and debate.

The *referendum* permits voters to challenge a statute passed by the legislature. If a referendum petition qualifies, the challenged statute does not go into effect unless it is approved by the voters at the next election.[b] Some confusion is engendered by the fact that the word "referendum" sometimes is used as a generic term, referring to any type of ballot proposition.[c] In this chapter we use "referendum" in the more specific sense and use terms such as "ballot proposition" and "ballot measure" as generic terms for the direct democracy procedures.

The *recall* is a device whereby voters may attempt to unseat an elected official whose term has not expired. Logically, the recall might best be categorized as a part of the system of representative democracy, but it is customarily listed with the devices of direct democracy.

---

a. For a colorful account of the adoption of the initiative and referendum in Oregon, see David Schuman, *The Origin of State Constitutional Direct Democracy: William Simon U'Ren and "The Oregon System,"* 67 TEMPLE LAW REVIEW 947 (1994). More generally, see Nathaniel A. Persily, *The Peculiar Geography of Direct Democracy: Why the Initiative, Referendum and Recall Developed in the American West*, 2 MICHIGAN LAW & POLICY REVIEW 11 (1997).

b. Suppose a petition referring a legislatively-enacted redistricting statute to the voters qualifies for the ballot. According to the procedures governing the referendum process, the law is ineffective until and unless the voters approve it. If the first available election at which the referendum can be put to the voters occurs at the statewide primary, at which districts are needed for the nomination of candidates for Congress and the state legislature, what districts should be used? See *Assembly v. Deukmejian*, 30 Cal.3d 638, 639 P.2d 939, 180 Cal.Rptr. 297 (1982).

c. Although "referenda" is often used as the plural for "referendum," "referendums" is the more correct term, according to the OXFORD ENGLISH DICTIONARY. "Plebiscite" is another term sometimes used generically to refer to any type of ballot measure.

Another category of ballot propositions consists of measures submitted to the voters by the state legislature. Most often this is done because voter approval is required, as in the case of constitutional amendments and bond authorizations in most states. Occasionally, a state legislature will voluntarily pass a statute whose going into effect is conditional on voter approval.

Although ballot measure elections do not occur at the national level in the United States,[d] about half the states have adopted one or more of the above devices. All but five of these states did so before or during the first two decades of the twentieth century. Since 1978 only Mississippi, whose supreme court in 1922 had struck down an initiative law on procedural grounds,[e] has adopted (or, as in Mississippi's case, readopted) the initiative.

Despite the relative stability in availability of the initiative and referendum, a continuing controversy swirls around direct democracy. Even after nearly a century of experience, observers offer sharply differing assessments of the initiative, the most frequently used device. This chapter begins with background and an evaluation by Richard Ellis, a political scientist. Ensuing sections consider some limits on the content of initiative proposals and judicial oversight of the initiative process. Some of the most controversial issues surrounding the initiative relate to money, especially in connection with the qualification of initiative proposals for the ballot and the election campaigns that occur once those proposals have qualified. We shall consider the former in this chapter but the latter must be deferred to Chapters 15 and 16, after introduction to the Supreme Court's treatment of campaign finance regulation under the First Amendment.

I. Pros and Cons

Richard J. Ellis, Democratic Delusions:
The Initiative Process in America
26–43 (2002)[f]

THE INITIATIVE'S RADICAL PAST

Arguably the single most important event in the birth of the initiative and referendum in America was the publication, early in 1892, of a small book with the awkward title *Direct Legislation by the Citizenship through the Initiative and Referendum*. So electric was its impact that the title page of the 1893 edition boasted that it was "the book that started the Referendum Movement." Its author, James W. Sullivan, a member of the New York Typographers' Union, explicitly addressed the volume to the "radical world." In the mid-1880s Sullivan, who at the time was a devotee of Henry George and the single tax, had become interested in the Swiss model of direct legislation, and in 1888 he took a leave of absence from his job as editor of a reform weekly to visit Switzerland and investigate the impact direct legislation had had on the nation's economics and politics. Sullivan was not the first to describe the Swiss experience, but he was the first to make the Swiss model

---

d. The United States is one of five major democracies that have never had a nationwide referendum. The others are India, Israel, Japan, and the Netherlands. See David Butler & Austin Ranney, *Conclusion*, in Referendums around the World 258 (1994).

e. *Power v. Robinson*, 93 So. 769 (Miss. 1922). This ruling was reaffirmed in *Moore v. Molpus*, 578 So.2d 624 (Miss. 1991), a decision that prompted the readoption of the initiative in 1992.

f. Copyright 2002 by the University Press of Kansas. All Rights Reserved. Reprinted with permission.

seem relevant to the United States. Sullivan's message to American workers was simple and appealing: by empowering the wage-working majority, direct legislation would destroy "the American plutocracy." ... Introduce the initiative and the referendum, Sullivan preached, and the walls of the citadel would come crumbling down. The "straightforward politics of direct legislation" had peacefully and simply transformed Switzerland, and there was no reason it could not usher in a similarly bloodless social revolution in the United States.

Among the many American radicals to be captivated by Sullivan's message, none was more important than the founding father of Oregon's initiative and referendum, the blacksmith-turned-lawyer William Simon U'Ren.... Although U'Ren had come across the idea of the initiative and referendum a year or two earlier, Sullivan's study fired his imagination. U'Ren felt the veil lift from his eyes. "I forgot, for the time, all about Henry George and the single tax. All these I now saw to be details. The one important thing was to restore the law-making power where it belonged—into the hands of the people. Once give us that, we could get anything we wanted—single tax, anything."[g]

[U'Ren's efforts led to creation of a Joint Committee on Direct Legislation, consisting of five farm and labor organizations,] with U'Ren, the Farmers' Alliance representative, as secretary. The committee spearheaded a massive propaganda campaign designed to mobilize popular support for direct democracy. Its rhetoric was unabashedly radical and populist: the legislature was a bastion of "the monied and monopolistic classes," and only direct legislation would "make it impossible for corporations and boodlers to obtain unjust measures by which to profit at the expense of the people." More than just the rhetoric was radical, for the organization also demanded a mandatory referendum that would require all legislation passed at the state, county, or municipal level [to be] approved by voters before becoming law. U'Ren also pressed the direct democracy agenda from within the Populist party. After joining the party in 1893, he was soon selected secretary of the Populist state committee and then chair of the 1894 Populist state convention. In 1896 he carried the battle directly to the Oregon state legislature as a Populist state legislator.

FROM THE MARGINS TO THE MAINSTREAM

...

Since the mid-1880s radicals in the labor movement and agrarian protest movements had been attracted to direct legislation for its transformative promise. It would enable farmers and workers to turn the tables on corporate power and economic privilege, using numbers to defeat money. But so long as the vision was revolutionary or tied to a specific policy agenda—such as progressive taxation on land, income, and inheritances, or higher wages and shorter working days—it was difficult if not impossible to gain the support of the establishment: publishers and editors, bankers, lawyers, professionals, the comfortable middle class, and party politicians. The widespread economic distress and discontent of the early 1890s had created a window of opportunity for economic radicalism, but by 1896 the window was fast closing. If direct legislation were to be established across the country, it would need to appeal to more than just disaffected laborers and intellectuals; it would have to dance not just with those who brought it but with those who had initially spurned and spat upon it. After 1896 the initiative and referendum movement increasingly became a political movement divorced from any particular economic vision.

---

g. Ponder this statement in light of Irving Kristol's reflections on democracy in Chapter 1. Is it an example of what Kristol called "the absurdity of idolatry—of taking the symbolic for the real, the means for the end"?—EDS.

... U'Ren's rhetoric and position also shifted during this period. Through 1895 he had vigorously advocated a mandatory referendum on all or nearly all laws.... In 1896, however, U'Ren suddenly abandoned the mandatory referendum in favor of an optional referendum. Moreover, he began to downplay direct legislation's transformative powers. By the end of 1897, after the state legislature had again failed to act on the initiative and referendum, U'Ren stressed that direct legislation would be used infrequently. Far from citizens becoming political animals, the initiative would allow Oregonians to "give our time to our business and only touch politics occasionally as an incidental duty—and yet do vastly more effective work than was ever done by any amount of labor under the present system." The threat of the initiative and referendum would be sufficient to force the politicians to clean up their act and prevent them from passing wasteful, pernicious, or unjust laws. Direct legislation would be the "gun behind the door."

[I]n 1902, ... Oregon voters ... overwhelmingly approved [a] constitutional amendment establishing the initiative and referendum, making Oregon the third state to adopt direct legislation. (South Dakota was the first, and in Utah, the second, the initiative and referendum did not take effect until decades later because the legislature refused to pass enabling legislation.) In 1904 two initiatives qualified for the Oregon ballot, making it the first state to try out the new tools of direct democracy. Immediately thereafter the floodgates opened: over the next decade Oregonians voted on over one hundred statewide initiatives and popular referenda. Many longstanding friends of the initiative now worried that direct legislation was being abused. Even before the flood had begun, in January 1906, the *Oregon Journal* reminded Oregonians that "the real friends of the initiative law will be slow to invoke its aid, and when they do it will be to remedy a manifest evil that it is ordinarily difficult if not impossible to reach." ...

As states debated whether to adopt the initiative and referendum in the opening decades of the twentieth century, proponents continued to rely upon both millennial and minimalist justifications. The minimalist rationale appealed to those who feared that direct legislation made utopian demands upon the citizenry and subverted representative democracy, or who worried that the initiative process would be used to launch a class war against the rich and well-to-do or to wage a moral crusade against unpopular minorities. Direct legislation, Woodrow Wilson reassured the doubters, was not "a substitute for representative institutions, but only ... a means of stimulation and control ... a sobering means of obtaining genuine representative action on the part of legislative bodies." In this minimalist conception, which typically privileged the referendum over the initiative, direct legislation was just another "safeguard of politics," one which citizens would only need to deploy infrequently to keep politicians in check. The minimalist rationale effectively assuaged fears, but the millennial rationale spoke more directly to people's hopes and dreams. Although the Populist party had long since faded away, the Populist vision— which imagined that the initiative and referendum could usher in a radically transformed world "in which equal rights to all shall live on forever, and special privileges shall be known no more"—was still very much alive in the Progressive era. Direct legislation, in this view, would do more than just add another check on the behavior of legislators; it would, in the words of the *Boston Common*, transform politics by enabling "the rising tide of sentiment for social justice" to sweep away "the special interests which now play for delay." ...

A mixture of minimalist and millennial arguments helped to enact the initiative and referendum in nineteen states in the two decades between 1898 and 1918, but neither set of expectations proved a reliable guide to the subsequent history of the initiative. Certainly

Figure 8.1   Average Number of Initiatives per Two-Year Election Cycle

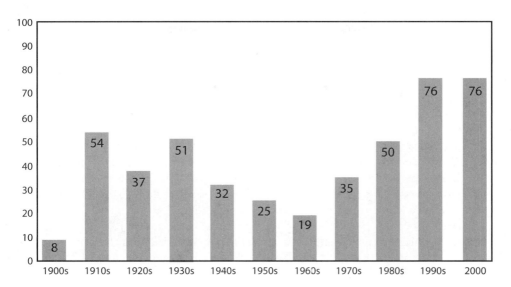

the initiative and referendum, despite notable and undeniable accomplishments, did little to justify the utopian, emancipatory hopes of radical transformation with which so many early advocates began. True, in some states Populist-backed governmental reforms, from direct election of senators to woman suffrage, were achieved through the initiative, but for the most part these reforms came about the old-fashioned way: through the legislative process. Useful reforms in working conditions (especially shorter hours) were sometimes enacted by initiative, but the more sweeping radical panaceas like the single tax were consistently defeated by voters. Moreover, far from disappearing, money, lobbyists, and powerful special interests continued to play a leading role in every state in the nation, whether the state possessed direct legislation or not. Indeed money and special interests usually played at least as prominent a part in initiative campaigns as they did in candidate campaigns.

The early years of direct legislation did little to vindicate the minimalists either. In Oregon in 1912 there were twenty-eight statewide initiatives on the November ballot, a national record that still stands to this day.... Activists in other states rushed to follow Oregon's lead. Coloradans voted on twenty initiatives in 1912, while in 1914 California's electorate faced seventeen initiatives and Arizona's fifteen. In 1920–21 North Dakota, which enacted the initiative in 1914, voted on sixteen initiatives, a record that the state eclipsed a decade later when citizens were asked to vote on eighteen in 1932. Outside of these hotbeds of initiative activity, the minimalist argument often fared much better. In states like Arkansas, Maine, Massachusetts, Michigan, Nebraska, and Nevada, for instance, the initiative was used sparingly in the first few decades of its existence....

The minimalist prediction was particularly relevant in the 1950s and 1960s as Figure 8.1 attests. [Even in] Oregon, the state that used the initiative more often than any other, citizens finally appeared to have learned to use direct democracy with discretion. Between 1956 and 1969 Oregonians voted on only nine initiatives and never faced more than two initiatives on the same ballot. Meanwhile, Oregonians took great pride in their government, turned out to vote in large numbers and had high levels of trust in their public officials. Elsewhere in the nation the story was much the same. In the thirty years between 1942 and 1971, nearly 350 statewide initiatives made it to the ballot, an average of about one initiative every two years for each of the initiative states. During these three decades, direct legislation did indeed seem to be the gun behind the door that the minimalists had promised, something more valuable for its potential than for its use.

THE SILENT REVOLUTION

Between 1990 and 2000 there were 458 initiatives nationwide. That is over three times the rate at which initiatives appeared on the ballot in the 1940s, 1950s, and 1960s. Today the initiative can no longer be plausibly portrayed as a gun behind the door, at least not in the states that have come to rely most heavily on the initiative process, particularly Oregon, California, Colorado, Washington, and Arizona. In these five states the gun is now madly brandished about and fired in almost every conceivable direction. Politicians scatter, running for cover, desperately trying to keep their heads down. Citizens appear bewildered, unsure what to think. The gunmen cry "power to the people," but few of the people seem to feel more empowered by the blaze of gunfire. To be sure, citizens take a certain delight at the occasional shot lodged in the politicians' posterior, but the gunslingers are not content to threaten only the political class. Vulnerable minorities are at least as likely to be the targets of the shootings as are the rich and powerful. To some it appears that beneath their populist masks, the gunslingers are the very same special interest groups and politicians from which the gun behind the door had promised to protect us.

When was the initiative transformed from a gun behind the door to a weapon of choice for interest groups and politicians? Many observers credit (or blame) California's Proposition 13, the 1978 property tax-cutting initiative that was spearheaded by Howard ("I'm mad as hell") Jarvis. Proposition 13, which passed by an overwhelming majority despite the opposition of virtually every major politician and newspaper in the state, dramatically illustrated direct legislation's enormous power to make public policy as well as to transform the political agenda. And yet Proposition 13 was as much symptom as it was cause. Increased reliance on the initiative, both in California and the nation, was already discernible even before Proposition 13 appeared on the June, 1978 ballot. In 1976–77 there were fifty-two initiatives across the nation, the highest number since the 1938–39 election cycle. Californians themselves had voted on ten initiatives in 1972–73; one has to go back a half century to 1922–23 to find more statewide initiatives on the California ballot. Even more telling evidence against the Proposition 13 explanation is that it was not until 1988 that initiative use shifted up into a higher gear nationwide (see Table 8.1). For almost a decade after Proposition 13, the average number of initiatives on the ballot nationally was actually less than the number of initiatives in the two-year election cycle immediately preceding Proposition 13.

Table 8.1   Number of Initiatives per Two-Year Election

	Mean	High	Low
1952–1971	20	31	10
1972–1975	32	39	25
1976–1987	48	58	42
1988–2001	75	103	61

Although no single event or year can be unambiguously identified as beginning the modern initiative revolution, there is little doubt about the magnitude of the change. [M]ore initiatives were approved by California in the last two decades of the twentieth century than were passed in the preceding sixty-eight years dating back to the initiative's adoption in 1912. Initiative-made law, once a minor feature of the California political landscape, has become its dominant and defining feature.

California and Oregon have been the clear leaders in initiative use, but there have been plenty of followers in the past two decades. Even states without a strong tradition of initiative use have increasingly gotten into the act. Idaho, Maine, Nevada, South Dakota, and Utah had more initiatives on the ballot in the 1980s and 1990s than in the previous eight decades of the century combined. Citizens in Maine, for instance, voted on twenty-six initiatives between 1980 and 2000, which is over double the number they had cast judgment on in the previous seventy years.... Across the nation, 35 percent of the approximately two thousand initiatives that have reached the ballot since 1904 qualified in the past two decades. More dramatically still, each of the past seven election cycles rank among the top ten election cycles in initiative use (see Table 8.2)....

Table 8.2   Ranking of the Top Ten Election Cycles in Initiative Use, 1904–2001

Rank	Election Cycle	No. of Initiatives
1	1996–1997	103
2	1914–1915	92
3	2000–2001	79
4	1932–1933	76
5	1994–1995	75
6	1990–1991	70
7	1992–1993	68
8	1912–1913	67
9	1998–1999	66
10	1988–1989	61

Initiative use indisputably became more widespread in the 1980s and 1990s than it had been in previous decades, but this national pattern is not reproduced in every state. In fact, Arkansas, North Dakota, and Oklahoma used the initiative less often in the 1980s and 1990s than they had in the preceding half century. For a few states it is the 1950s and 1960s that are exceptional, with the 1980s and 1990s representing something of a return to normalcy. In Missouri, for instance, there was only one initiative on the ballot in the 1950s and 1960s, but throughout the rest of the century, including the 1980s and 1990s, the state has consistently averaged about nine initiatives per decade. In other states the absolute number of initiatives remains small despite the increase in initiative use in recent decades. In Utah, for example, almost two-thirds of the state's initiatives appeared on the ballot between 1980 and 2000, but the total number of initiatives in those two decades was only eleven.... These statistics help to remind us that when we talk about an initiative revolution we are talking about a phenomenon that has transformed some states while leaving others relatively untouched.

Heavy initiative use remains concentrated in a relatively few states. Between 1980 and 2000 three states (California, Oregon, and Colorado) accounted for 40 percent of the total number of statewide initiatives in the nation. Indeed, Oregon and California alone accounted for 30 percent of statewide initiatives in the 1980s and 1990s and about the same percentage during the rest of the twentieth century. In 2000 these two pace-setting states accounted for close to 40 percent of the nation's initiatives. Six in ten initiatives between 1990 and 2000 came from six states (Arizona, California, Colorado, North Dakota, Oregon, and Washington), and those same six states account for better than 60 percent of the initiatives in the twentieth century. In short, although initiatives are more numerous today than ever before, a handful of high-use states continue to experience the effects of direct legislation in a way that is qualitatively different from other initiative states.

A POPULIST PARADOX

Among the most striking features of the contemporary period is that increased reliance on the initiative has not been accompanied by a rush to adopt direct legislation in other states. This stands in marked contrast to the first two decades of the twentieth century, when high rates of initiative use were accompanied by a rush of states enacting the initiative. In the sixteen years between 1902 and 1918, over two-fifths of the states then in the union adopted the initiative. Only five states have adopted the initiative since then, and four of those (Alaska [1959], Wyoming [1968], Florida [1968], and Illinois [1970]) adopted the initiative between 1959 and 1970, a period in which the initiative was little used across the country. Ironically, only one state has adopted the initiative during the decades of the initiative's greatest popularity. That state is Mississippi, which enacted the initiative in 1992.

More paradoxical still [are] the antipopulist constraints Mississippi placed upon the initiative power. The brand of direct democracy enacted in Mississippi bears little resemblance to the populist instrument used in California or in Oregon. To begin with, Mississippi established that no more than five initiatives could appear on any one ballot. The state also refused to permit statutory initiatives or popular referenda. Although voters can change the state constitution by means of an initiative petition, they cannot make laws through the initiative process, nor can they directly negate laws passed by the state legislature. Further constraining voters' ability to utilize the initiative process is a requirement that one-fifth of the petition signatures must come from each of the five congressional districts. The Mississippi initiative process also permits the legislature to place an alternative measure on the same ballot, thereby giving the voters a choice between two bills. To make things even more difficult, the legislature required that the majority in favor of an initiative must comprise at least 40 percent of the number of all voters who cast ballots in that election. Moreover, every initiative that has revenue implications must identify the amount and source of revenue required to implement it; if the initiative reduces revenues or reallocates funding it must specify which programs will be affected. Finally, Mississippi prohibits initiatives that would change the initiative process or alter either the state's bill of rights or its constitutional right-to-work guarantee.

Mississippi's emasculated initiative power resulted from intense opposition by an unlikely legislative alliance of rural conservatives and African-American liberals. Both saw themselves as minority groups who could be harmed by a purely majoritarian system. Blacks feared that whites would use the initiative power to discriminate against them, and legislators from rural districts feared that densely populated urban areas would be advantaged by the initiative. This coalition succeeded in defeating the initiative proposal no fewer than three times in the lower house, and with each defeat the proponents watered down the original proposal still further.

Not surprisingly, persuading legislatures to adopt the initiative process has proved a hard sell, but it is not only legislators who are responsible for the glacial pace of change. Legislators have been able to halt adoption of the initiative precisely because, unlike at the outset of the twentieth century, there has not been a deafening popular outcry in favor of adopting direct legislation....

The increased use of the initiative in the 1980s and 1990s is thus only half the story. If we are to understand the late-twentieth century initiative process, we must also understand the dog that didn't bark. In the last two decades of the twentieth century, bills to enact the initiative and referendum have been introduced in virtually every state in the nation, but with the exception of Mississippi no state has added the initiative to its democratic arsenal. The initiative's failure to spread to other states has come as a surprise to many political analysts [who predicted] that a substantial number of states would adopt the initiative and referendum before the end of the [twentieth] century.... Why have [their] predictions failed to come to pass even while direct legislation is used with increasing frequency in those states that possess the power?

Some initiative proponents might not see this development as paradoxical. In both cases the cause is the same: professional legislators looking out for their own interests or doing the bidding of powerful special interests. In states with the initiative power, this argument goes, the increase in initiative use is attributable to the legislature consistently ignoring popular demands and preferences. And in states without the initiative power, the failure to adopt direct legislation is also a result of the legislature ignoring the popular will. But there is an alternative explanation, namely that the explosion in initiative use in states like California has scared off many who were originally sympathetic to the idea. Certainly that is how many legislators explain their opposition to direct legislation....

In the late 1970s and early 1980s virtually every state that lacked the initiative was giving serious thought to adopting it. In 1977 the United States Senate held hearings on the possibility of adopting the initiative at the national level, which helped put the idea of a nationwide initiative and referendum on the national agenda for the next decade. But at the beginning of the twenty-first century, the idea of a national initiative has dropped almost completely off the national radar....

This is not to say that the initiative and referendum will not spread to other states in the coming years. Throughout the nation, particularly in the South, there are groups and politicians lobbying for the initiative and referendum. Republican governors in Louisiana and New York have come out in support of the initiative. And some antigovernment and antitax groups continue to push the initiative because they believe it is "a great tool for putting handcuffs on the government." But both the left and the right, Democrats and Republicans, are deeply divided over the desirability of the initiative. For every conservative who salivates at the thought of using direct legislation to cut taxes or end affirmative action, there are others who fear it may be used to further the liberal agenda. In Louisiana, for instance, business interests strongly opposed the Republican governor's direct legislation proposal, fearing it would be used to increase the minimum wage or enact environmental regulations that would increase the cost of doing business. And in Texas, the Christian Coalition resisted the initiative and referendum because they feared it would be used to legalize gambling. Among liberals, too, fears outnumber hopes. Apart from environmentalists, who have had some notable successes in initiative campaigns—particularly in the 1970s and 1980s (their record in recent years, however, has been decidedly poor)—much of the rest of the left fears that direct legislation will be used to cripple the government's capacity to provide much-needed social services. These kinds of fears were not absent in the early twentieth century, but for the most part they were limited to the business groups. As a result, the early-twentieth-century movement to pass direct legislation could plausibly be dramatized as a conflict between powerful special interests and the people. At the beginning of a new century, with groups from all sides of the political spectrum fearful of the initiative's enormous power to make sudden and drastic changes, that populist morality play no longer works as well.

If this analysis is correct, the initiative and referendum will at best be slow to spread across the country, particularly so long as high-use initiative states continue to dramatize the winner-take-all character of direct legislation politics. For most groups, so long as they have a reasonable chance of being heard in the legislature, the thought of what they might lose from direct legislation seems to far outweigh dreams of what they might gain. The Mississippi experience suggests that if another state does adopt the initiative process, intense pressure from interest groups will dilute and restrict the process in ways that make it unlikely that the state would have a large number of initiatives. In short, for the foreseeable future it is unlikely that direct legislation will become an important, let alone dominant force in the political life of those twenty-six states that do not currently have the initiative. Those critics who fear that direct legislation will spread across the country like a cancer are probably as misguided as the enthusiasts who anticipate national redemption through direct legislation's glorious march from sea to shining sea.

SUPPLY-SIDE POLITICS

If it is possible to speak about the future spread of direct legislation to non-initiative states with a modicum of certainty, it is more difficult to predict the future course of the initiative and referendum within those states that already possess the power. Is the current popularity of direct legislation just a fad or phase the nation is passing through, or is it here to stay as a permanent feature of a transformed political landscape? . . .

Our predictions of the future can only be as good as our explanations of the past. To forecast what will happen in the coming decades, we need to understand what has been driving initiative use over the past several decades. Probably the most common explanation of initiative use focuses on the mood of the voters. When the voters are angry and discontented, the number of initiatives increases. . . . Certainly trust in government has declined at roughly the same time that initiative use has increased. But although trust in government has an intuitive appeal as an explanation, the trust theory loses some its luster when it is inspected more closely. Trust in government after all has fluctuated substantially over the past several decades, but initiative use has remained relatively immune to those fluctuations. When trust has rebounded, as it did in the mid-1980s and again in the mid-1990s, initiative use has not declined. Nor has anyone provided any evidence that trust in government is lower in states that use the initiative more often. Although popular anger and distrust may have played an important role in triggering the renaissance of the initiative, it is much less clear that continued reliance on the initiative is closely related to levels of popular trust or discontent.

If initiative use seems to remain relatively constant in the face of wide swings in popular mood, we may be better off looking not at the demand side of the equation but rather at the supply side. A supply-side model of initiative use turns our attention away from the mood of the voters and toward those who produce the initiatives. According to this theory, the number of initiatives on the ballot is determined not by the demands of the people but by the suppliers of initiatives: the initiative activists and professionals who place initiatives on the ballot. The professionalization of signature gathering is particularly important in insulating initiative use from popular mood. If anyone with enough money can qualify an initiative for the ballot, then initiative use will vary independently of public demand. If we wish to predict the future of the initiative process in the United States, we must start by understanding the business of signature gathering.

Notes and Questions

1. Debate over the desirability of direct democracy has waxed and waned in the United States since the late nineteenth century. Thomas E. Cronin, DIRECT DEMOCRACY 224–32 (1989), evaluates empirically many of the pro and con arguments. Supportive arguments that he assesses include:

a. Direct democracy enhances government responsiveness and accountability.

b. It provides a safety valve "when legislators prove timid, corrupt, or dominated by special interests."

c. It protects against bossism.

d. It brings about rule by the common people.

e. It reduces the influence of special interests.

f. It permits less well-represented groups to bring their ideas before the public.

g. It stimulates educational debate on important policy issues.

h. It stimulates voter interest in public issues and stimulates turnout.

i. It promotes trust in government.

Cronin also evaluates arguments raised by opponents:

a. Direct democracy undermines representative democracy.

b. It produces unsound legislation.

c. It endangers minority rights.

d. It depends on voters who are not capable of competent policy judgments.

e. It amplifies special interest influence.

f. It lacks accountability because it is not subject to the usual checks and balances.

Cronin finds some merit in a couple of the supportive arguments, that direct democracy provides a safety valve and that it helps some less-represented groups find a forum. The opponents, he concludes, raise a serious objection with respect to the lack of checks and balances. Mostly, though, he finds that empirical support for the arguments on both sides ranges from none to mixed. "Both proponents and opponents have too often overstated their positions," he concludes. "The existing direct democracy processes have both virtues and liabilities."

Another study of the initiative process that reaches relatively balanced conclusions is Elisabeth R. Gerber, THE POPULIST PARADOX: INTEREST GROUP INFLUENCE AND THE PROMISE OF DIRECT LEGISLATION (1999). Gerber finds that in general, citizen groups are better able than economic groups to use the initiative successfully to pass new laws. However, she does not contend that her conclusion necessarily supports the process:

I do *not* say that citizen group dominance of the direct legislation process is necessarily good. The normative value one attributes to this finding depends very strongly on one's assessment of whether majoritarian interests already receive sufficient representation in modern American government. Certainly, the early

Populist and Progressive advocates of direct legislation took the position that minority interests, especially those of certain powerful industries, were overrepresented in state legislatures at the expense of broader middle-class interests. To the extent that one agrees that those same sorts of narrow economic interests are overrepresented in state legislatures today, the normative implication of citizen group dominance is favorable. In contrast, to those who believe that business or economic interests are limited in their ability to influence state legislatures or that they hold appropriate levels of power in the state legislative process, the shift of power toward majoritarian interests may be interpreted as bad. Most important, to those who believe the state legislative process facilitates compromise between competing interests, empowering the majority through the direct legislation process threatens to upset the delicate balance between majority and minority interests.

Id. at 142.

In contrast to Ellis, Cronin, and Gerber, all of whom take a relatively balanced view, most students of the initiative process approach the subject from a distinctly supportive or negative perspective. The last decade has seen a flurry of books hostile to the initiative, including David S. Broder, DEMOCRACY DERAILED (2000); Peter Schrag, PARADISE LOST (1998); Joseph F. Zimmerman, THE INITIATIVE: CITIZEN LAW-MAKING (1999). Supportive views are put forward in Shaun Bowler & Todd Donovan, DEMANDING CHOICES: OPINION, VOTING, AND DIRECT DEMOCRACY (1998).

2. Recall that in *Federalist No. 10*, contained in Chapter 1 of this book, James Madison distinguished between what he called republics and democracies. The former, which Madison preferred, embrace large populations and the representative system. The latter consist in small populations that meet and act directly. The initiative, at least at the state level, is a mixture of these forms. It is used by a large population—relative, that is, to a group that could meet together as a single assembly—but it operates directly rather than through representatives.

Although Madison's terminology distinguishing between republics and democracies is no longer widespread, serious debates still occur about the role of majorities in a democracy. Almost everyone agrees that majorities will and should be able to make public decisions. Within that broad agreement, however, there are many controversial issues. The two that are most relevant are the limits, if any, on the scope of majority rule and the process by which majority rule should be manifested.[h]

Limits on the scope of majority rule. Recall that in *Federalist No. 10*, Madison wrote that a faction, which by definition is a group working adversely to the rights of some citizens or to the permanent and aggregate interests of the community, can be either a minority or a majority of the population. Fear of "majority tyranny" or, less starkly, that majorities will treat minorities unfairly, has been a major theme of American political thought since Madison's time.[i] Some political philosophers have invoked various conceptions of natural rights in furtherance of the view that there are some things majorities are not en-

---

h. For a good overview of many of the theoretical issues surrounding majority rule, see Elaine Spitz, MAJORITY RULE (1984).

i. Two classics of American thought—though one was written by a Frenchman!—concerned themselves in significant part with this question. See Alexis de Tocquevelle, DEMOCRACY IN AMERICA (Harvey C. Mansfield and Delba Winthrop, trs., 2000) [1835, 1840]; John C. Calhoun, A DISQUISITION ON GOVERNMENT (1993) [1853].

titled to do. In American law and politics, the Bills of Rights in federal and state constitutions have been intended to limit the power of majorities.

Majoritarian processes. Aside from whatever limits on majority rule may exist, American political thought divides over how immediate the control of the majority over public policy should be. One view, sometimes referred to, especially by its detractors, as the plebiscitary view of democracy, holds that the most democratic procedures are those that facilitate the immediate conversion of a policy favored by a majority into law. Madison and many of his contemporaries opposed the majorities empowered by such procedures as "transient majorities" — as do many of our contemporaries. Their idea is that dramatic events or skillful propaganda may create a temporary public frenzy causing a majority to favor ill-considered measures that, given a chance for greater reflection, the majority would oppose. Aside from the problem of the transient majority, those opposed to plebiscitary democracy maintain that representation and other devices that mediate the transformation of majority preferences into law will result in better deliberation and wiser policies. Such mediation arises from what Americans refer to as the system of checks and balances.

Although, as was said above, nearly all Americans believe in some form of majority rule, there are considerable differences on the desirability of substantive and procedural limits or checks on majorities. Proposals and devices that will tend to reduce these limits are often referred to as majoritarian. Not surprisingly, the initiative is often thought of as the supremely majoritarian device. Debates on the desirability of the initiative are therefore often surrogates for debates on majoritarianism itself.

This is fair enough, but it is subject to two possible qualifications. The first, which is pointed to by some supporters of the initiative, is that even in the states identified by Ellis as using the initiative most widely, it remains the exception and not the rule. The overwhelming majority of laws in those states are enacted in the ordinary way by the state legislatures.[j] Thus, although the initiative is majoritarian with respect to whatever specific issue is being voted on at a particular time, it can also be thought of as part of the overall system of checks and balances. Groups that for one reason or another find it difficult to pursue their objectives in the ordinary legislative process have the opportunity to see if they can do better by taking their proposal to the electorate. For what may be the best defense of the initiative on this ground, see Maimon Schwarzschild, *Popular Initiatives and American Federalism, Or, Putting Direct Democracy In Its Place*, 13 Journal of Contemporary Legal Issues 531 (2004).

The second possible qualification attacks the premise that the initiative actually is a majoritarian institution. We consider that qualification in the following Note.

3. Although majoritarianism in its stronger forms has many critics among students of American government, its precepts often receive a favorable public reaction. Therefore, many supporters of the initiative eschew Schwarzschild's approach of emphasizing the compatibility of the initiative with checks and balances. Instead, they employ populist rhetoric declaring that the initiative embodies the true voice of the people, who can initiate and enact legislation free of the influence of interest groups.

In response to such rhetoric, some opponents of the initiative have sought to turn the tables by contending that the initiative is not majoritarian at all but is instead manipulated and controlled by special interests. The opponents point to the large amounts often

---

j. Of course, just counting laws can give a misleading picture, because the matters contained in initiatives are often of great importance.

spent by interest groups in initiative campaigns and, more generally, contend that the process has been captured by what is often referred to as the "initiative industry." That a high degree of professionalization has surrounded the initiative process in at least some of the high-use states is unquestionably true. See, for example, Jack Citrin, *Who's the Boss? Direct Democracy and Popular Control of Government*, in BROKEN CONTRACT? CHANGING RELATIONSHIPS BETWEEN AMERICANS AND THEIR GOVERNMENT (Stephen C. Craig, ed., 1996). Sometimes the professionalization is described in somewhat breathless terms:

> Increasingly, initiative proponents hire members of an "initiative industry," composed of professional campaign consultants who often specialize in direct democracy, to aid in this process. The proponents and their consultants are capable of conducting sophisticated research on the existing legal landscape in order to draft the measures to achieve their intended results with an eye toward future judicial review. Moreover, it is not unusual for them to use focus groups and conduct polls to determine how most effectively to promote or "spin" their measures to the voters.

Glen Staszewski, *Rejecting the Myth of Popular Sovereignty and Applying an Agency Model to Direct Democracy*, 56 VANDERBILT LAW REVIEW 395, 422 (2003).

Such language can perhaps serve as a corrective to excessive rhetoric extolling the initiative as a pure reflection of the public will. However, those who deny that the initiative works as a majoritarian device run into difficulties. The effects of campaign spending in initiative campaigns will be considered in Chapter 16. For present purposes we can mention that most studies have concluded that one-sided big spending can be quite effective when used in opposition to an initiative proposal but is remarkably ineffective when used to pass a measure. Because large economic resources can often stop the enactment of initiatives, the effectiveness of campaign spending can be said to limit the majoritarian effect of the initiative. But the more important point is that, by virtue of the usual ineffectiveness of spending to secure passage of proposals, spending does not bring into question the majoritarian nature of the initiative when it is used successfully.[k]

The suggestion that the rise of the initiative industry has permitted special interest groups to capture the initiative is subject to two objections. First, the initiative industry arose because the division of labor reduces costs, so that the services become more widely available, not less so. If it were generally true that the process is dominated by narrow interests, then a large percentage of initiatives would be supported by narrow interests and opposed by dispersed interests. There are such initiatives, but according to a recent study they amount to a small percentage—7.8 percent were of this type, and less than a third of these were approved by the voters.[l]

A second difficulty for those who deny the majoritarian nature of the initiative process is evidence suggesting that by and large, public policy is more in tune with majority pref-

---

k. A similar conclusion applies to another problem with the initiative that has been documented in recent years, namely that by reason of resistance from legislatures, executive agencies, or courts, many initiatives fail to be implemented, either entirely or in part. See Elisabeth R. Gerber, Arthur Lupia, Mathew D. McCubbins, and D. Roderick Kiewiet, STEALING THE INITIATIVE: HOW STATE GOVERNMENT RESPONDS TO DIRECT DEMOCRACY (2001). To the extent that enacted initiative measures are thus blocked, the majoritarian effect of the initiative is limited. But this does not detract from the majoritarian nature of initiatives to the extent they are implemented.

l. Howard R. Ernst, *The Historical Role of Narrow-Material Interests in Initiative Politics*, in Larry J. Sabato, Howard R. Ernst & Bruce A. Larson, DANGEROUS DEMOCRACY? THE BATTLE OVER BALLOT INITIATIVES IN AMERICA (2001).

erences in initiative states than in other states. Recently, researchers have assumed that in addition to the direct effects of successful initiative measures that go into effect, the availability of the process also has indirect effects. Legislators, interest groups, and others anticipate the possibility of an initiative being proposed and perhaps enacted, and adjust their actions accordingly. Therefore, instead of attempting to measure direct democracy's effects only by considering successful initiatives, these researchers compare policies in states that have the initiative with policies in states that do not.[m] Thus, John G. Matsusaka, in FOR THE MANY OR FOR THE FEW (2004), compares fiscal policy in states with and without the initiative and concludes that fiscal policy is closer to majority opinion in initiative states. A more recent study yielded similar findings on several social issues in initiative and non-initiative states.[n] Matsusaka summarizes his findings:

> The evidence turns out to tell a remarkably consistent story. For every policy I am able to examine, the initiative pushes policy in the direction a majority of people say they want to go. I am unable to find *any* evidence that the majority dislikes the policy changes caused by the initiative, as implied by the special interest subversive view.

FOR THE MANY OR FOR THE FEW at xi–xii (emphasis in original).

In sum, for better or for worse there are significant limits to the initiative's ability to convert majority opinion into public policy. Indeed, from one perspective the initiative plays a suitably modest role in an overall system marked by a complex array of checks and balances. But the evidence suggests that to the extent that the initiative does operate effectively, it does so in a majoritarian manner.

4. Ellis notes that the initiative originally won leftist support during the Populist era but achieved success when it won more moderate support in the Progressive period. Kenneth P. Miller, *Constraining Populism: The Real Challenge of Initiative Reform*, 41 SANTA CLARA LAW REVIEW 1037 (2001), argues that current supporters of the initiative are divided between progressivism and populism, two distinct and contradictory strains of thought. Populists, he asserts, are hostile to representative democracy and seek to displace it to the extent possible. Progressives seek to use the initiative to supplement and reinforce representative democracy. Miller argues that proposed reforms to the initiative process should be evaluated with this distinction in mind. In his view, only progressive-oriented reforms should be adopted. For further elaboration of these views, see Bruce E. Cain & Kenneth P. Miller, *The Populist Legacy: Initiatives and the Undermining of Representative Government*, in DANGEROUS DEMOCRACY? THE BATTLE OVER BALLOT INITIATIVES IN AMERICA 33 (Larry J. Sabato, Howard R. Ernst & Bruce A. Larson, eds., 2001).

If initiatives are supported, possibly for different reasons, by populists and progressives, what about pluralists? Is it clear that those inclined to pluralism should oppose direct democracy? For that matter, is it so clear that progressivists should support the initiative process? The author of one study summarized the values at stake in the controversy over direct democracy as follows:

> Not only do direct and indirect forms of democracy differ in the institutional arrangements they advocate but they pursue quite different ends and values as well. Direct democracy values participation, open access, and political equality.

---

m. For commentary on this research method, see Daniel H. Lowenstein, *Book Review: Competition and Competitiveness in American Elections*, 6 ELECTION LAW JOURNAL 278, ___ (2007).

n. John G. Matsusaka, "Direct Democracy and Social Issues," unpublished paper, May 2007, available at http://ssrn.com/abstract=989682.

It tends to deemphasize compromise, continuity, and consensus. In short, direct democracy encourages conflict and competition and attempts to expand the base of participants. Indirect democracy values stability, consensus, and compromise and seeks institutional arrangements that insulate fundamental principles from momentary passions or fluctuations in opinion.

David Magleby, DIRECT LEGISLATION 181 (1984). Although Magleby recognizes the legitimacy of both sets of values, he reaches conclusions generally critical of direct democracy, because he believes the benefits of the initiative and referendum are largely illusory, while some of their impairment of the values of representative democracy is real. For example, he writes:

Essential to the claim that more democratic government results from direct legislation is the assumption that the issues placed on ballots are representative of the issues people have on their minds and would like submitted to a public vote. Very few voters, however, can spontaneously name any particular issues on which they would like to see the public vote. Those issues that do appear on the ballot are typically not the same issues that voters list as the most important problems facing the state or the nation....

Because of voter disinterest and the signature threshold requirement, the agenda of issues to be decided is determined by proponents' capacity to hire professional signature-gathering firms or by the dedication of issue activists or single-issue groups who desire to place measures on the ballot.

Id. at 182.

Magleby's conclusions are criticized by Richard Briffault, *Distrust of Democracy*, 63 TEXAS LAW REVIEW 1347 (1985), who believes Magleby interprets the data in an unduly negative manner. For example, on the agenda-setting question, Briffault writes:

Although Magleby's analysis of the high hurdles tending to limit access to the initiative agenda to special interest organizations is difficult to refute, a significant number of ballot measures have been the product of forces outside the power elite who are not usually successful at the ordinary politics of working the lobbies of the State House. In the last decade, such outside groups have qualified proposals to control handguns, restrict indoor smoking, ban nonreturnable beverage containers, limit nuclear power plants, and legalize the possession and use of marijuana.[o]

Id. at 1357. More generally, Briffault contends that

although [Magleby's] discussion of direct democracy is well informed by an understanding of its defects in practice, his analysis of legislatures is at the abstract level of the textbook model. When direct legislation "in the field" is set against an idealized construct of the legislative process, it is bound to fall short.

Id. at 1350. Briffault points out that a high percentage of initiative proposals deal with areas such as governmental processes or taxation, in which legislatures may sometimes be prone to subordinate the public interest to their own interests or those of special interest supporters. Briffault gives a number of examples and concludes:

In these cases, the initiative served as a remedy for legislative failure — much as the Progressives had envisioned. Direct legislation did not serve as a substi-

---

o. The question of access to the ballot is closely related to the question of the increasingly common reliance by initiative proponents on professional circulators. That subject is considered in Part IV of this chapter.—EDS.

tute for the legislative process but as a complement when the legislature had displayed prolonged indifference to the wishes of a significant portion of the public. The initiative was an effective device for getting the legislature's attention and reminding representatives of the public outside the community of political insiders.

Id. at 1371.

5. In Chapter 1 we considered the view of some that the pluralist system reflects the intensity of voters' wishes in addition to the sheer number of voters who favor or oppose a particular policy. Some writers have criticized the initiative process for failing to take account of intensity. For example, Sherman J. Clark, *A Populist Critique of Direct Democracy*, 112 HARVARD LAW REVIEW 434, 465–66 (1998), writes:

> Representation lets each individual allocate that power where it matters most. Putting an issue to a direct vote by contrast, does two things. First, it prevents voters who care deeply about that particular issue from demonstrating the intensity of their concern. Second, it prevents voters who do *not* care deeply about that particular issue from using it as a vehicle for expressing the intensity of their concern about issues that matter more to them.

See also Sherman J. Clark, *The Character of Direct Democracy*, 13 JOURNAL OF CON-TEMPORARY LEGAL ISSUES 341 (2004). For the view that representative legislatures are not necessarily better than the initiative for recording the intensity of voter preferences, see Lynn A. Baker, *Preferences, Priorities, and Plebiscites*, 13 JOURNAL OF CON-TEMPORARY LEGAL ISSUES 313 (2004). One response to the exchange between Clark and Baker was that their debate "convinces me more than ever that the initiative process, like the legislative process involving legislators, should be judged by the outcome it produces rather than by the process by which it is passed." Richard L. Hasen, *Comments on Baker, Clark, and Direct Democracy*, 13 JOURNAL OF CONTEMPORARY LEGAL ISSUES 563 (2004).

6. Citrin, *supra*, makes an assertion that is widespread in the literature on initiatives, that "turnout rates generally are lower in American ballot proposition elections than in candidate elections." Such claims are based on data collected by David Magleby, DIRECT LEGISLATION 83–87 (1984), showing the dropoff rates in elections in California, Massachusetts, and Washington during the 1970s and early 1980s. "Dropoff" refers to the percentage of voters who cast a ballot but do not cast a vote for a particular office or on a particular proposition. Citrin's statement is accurate only because it is based on Magleby's data for *all* propositions and for *all* candidates. However, there is no controversy over the majority of ballot propositions, which are placed on the ballot by the state legislatures. The public officials who enact state laws and therefore provide an alternative to initiatives are the state legislators. Therefore, the relevant comparison is between the dropoff for initiatives and the dropoff in races for state legislators. Unfortunately, Magleby gives no data on dropoff in state legislative elections for Massachusetts and Washington. For California, he gives data for the Assembly, and the dropoff rate in California for the years he covers was an average of eight percent for both the Assembly and for initiatives. One could wish for data covering additional states and more recent elections, but at present the evidence available does not support a claim of superiority for either representative democracy or direct democracy with respect to participation rates.

A more important though less frequently discussed question relating to participation results from the fact that some states, including California, vote on statewide initiatives at primaries as well as at general elections. Turnout is substantially lower at primaries. Perhaps even more of a problem is that depending on whether there is a hot contest for president, governor, or senator in one party or the other, turnout at the primary may be skewed in favor of Democratic (and therefore liberal) or Republican (and therefore conservative) voters. The skewing is not likely to be decisive in an initiative election unless that election is very close, but clearly it would be preferable, all else being equal, for initiatives to be voted on at high-turnout general elections. The greatest resistance to eliminating initiative voting at primaries results from the fear that concentrating all the initiatives for an election year into the general election would compound the problem of burdening voters with too many matters to vote on. For discussion of that problem, see Philip L. Dubois & Floyd Feeney, LAWMAKING BY INITIATIVE 153–58 (1998).

7. As we have seen, one of the most prominent criticisms of direct democracy has been that it will facilitate tyranny of the majority over minorities. Derrick A. Bell, Jr., *The Referendum: Democracy's Barrier to Racial Equality*, 54 WASHINGTON LAW REVIEW 1, 16 (1978), contends that "the growing reliance on the referendum and initiative poses a threat to individual rights in general and in particular creates a crisis for the rights of racial and other discrete minorities." *Id.* at 2. He contends that the danger of majority tyranny in direct democracy exceeds the danger in representative democracy:

> Public officials, even those elected on more or less overtly racist campaigns, may prove responsive to minority pressures for civil rights measures once in office or, at least, be open to the negotiation and give-and-take that constitutes much of the political process. Thus, legislators may vote for, or executive officials may sign, a civil rights or social reform bill with full knowledge that a majority of their constituents oppose the measure. They are in the spotlight and do not wish publicly to advocate racism; they cannot openly attribute their opposition to "racist constituents." The more neutral reasons for opposition are often inadequate in the face of serious racial injustices, particularly those posing threats not confined to the minority community.
>
> When the legislative process is turned back to the citizenry either to enact laws by initiative or to review existing laws through the referendum, few of the concerns that can transform the "conservative" politician into a "moderate" public official are likely to affect the individual voter's decision. No political factors counsel restraint on racial passions emanating from long held and little considered beliefs and fears. Far from being the pure path to democracy . . . , direct democracy, carried out in the privacy of the voting booth, has diminished the ability of minority groups to participate in the democratic process. Ironically, because it enables the voters' racial beliefs and fears to be recorded and tabulated in their pure form, the referendum has been a most effective facilitator of that bias, discrimination, and prejudice which has marred American democracy from its earliest day.

Id. at 13–15.

Bell's criticism is probably on its strongest ground when directed against procedures that single out for referendum certain decisions, such as civil rights ordinances or land use regulations, that have particular effect on racial or other minorities. The Supreme Court has struck down procedures that require referendums before adoption of measures designed to benefit racial minorities, such as the adoption of fair housing ordinances or the imposition of school integration devices. See *Hunter v. Erickson*, 393 U.S. 385 (1969); *Washington v. Seattle School District No. 1*, 458 U.S. 457 (1982). However, it has permitted referendum requirements that apply only to measures benefiting poor people, such as approval of low-cost housing projects. See *James v. Valtierra*, 402 U.S. 137 (1971).

Defenders have contested the validity of Bell's charges as applied to initiatives, especially at the state level. Thus, Briffault, *supra*, 63 Texas Law Review at 1364–66, writes:

> [I]t is difficult to argue that historically minorities—in particular, blacks and other racial minorities did all that well in state legislatures. Racial discrimination was largely a product of state legislative action, not initiative votes. Nor are the great advances of minorities in recent decades attributable to state legislative action. The initial successes of the civil rights movement were won in the courts or on the streets. The legislatures resisted and delayed and became more responsive only under extraordinary political and legal pressures. Even today, in times of fiscal stringency, states may be more prone to cut programs that help minorities and the poor than those that serve more politically powerful groups.
>
> At another level, the challenge to the initiative for lack of sensitivity to minority interests is misguided; the initiative, like other devices of direct democracy, was designed as a *majoritarian* tool, to be used when the legislature failed to act on a program the majority desires. The appropriate question here is whether the initiative is more likely than the legislature to be a source of measures that discriminate against minorities or infringe upon the rights of the politically powerless. Without offering a firm answer, I suggest that there are two institutions that tend to mitigate the antiminority potential of direct legislation: the judiciary and the initiative process itself.
>
> The electorate-as-legislature can no more infringe upon constitutionally protected rights than can the representative legislature. Although the courts frequently bestow rhetorical plaudits on direct democracy, they have not hesitated to invalidate initiative measures as unconstitutional....
>
> The second constraint on majoritarian abuse lies in the nature of the initiative process. [I]t is difficult to get measures on the ballot and it is difficult to get them passed. Minority groups benefit from the "negative bias" in the system. A minority group that intensely opposes a measure can seek to block ballot qualification and it can mount a campaign that generates doubts and uncertainties about the proposition, exploiting the electorate's innate caution and reinforcing the tendency to reject initiatives even if the proposition appeals to antiminority prejudices. The "negative bias," although a barrier to "good" legislation, functions equally as a shield against "bad" legislation: a defect of direct democracy may also prevent its abuse.

In recent years, opponents of certain initiatives have revived the claim that the process may be abused by majorities against unpopular minorities. These initiatives include California's Proposition 187 in the 1994 general election, which sought to exclude illegal immigrants from various public benefits including education and non-emergency medical care, and initiatives in several states that have sought to prevent municipalities from prohibiting discrimination based on sexual orientation. For criticism of the "anti-gay" initiatives, see Hans A. Linde, *When Initiative Lawmaking Is Not "Republican Government": The Campaign Against Homosexuality*, 72 Oregon Law Review 19 (1993); *Symposium: The Bill of Rights vs. the Ballot Box: Constitutional Implications of Anti-Gay Ballot Initiatives*, 55 Ohio State Law Journal 491 (1994). As it happened, Briffault's claim that the judiciary constitutes an effective shield for minority groups against the initiative process was largely if not entirely vindicated in each of these instances. Most of Proposition 187 was struck down as either unconstitutional or preempted by federal law in *League of Latin American Citizens v. Wilson*, 997 F.Supp. 1244 (C.D.Cal. 1997). In *Romer v. Evans*, 517 U.S. 620 (1995), the Supreme Court struck down a Colorado initiative that would have barred state and local antidiscrimination protections based on sexual orientation.

In any event, the debate continues. Barbara Gamble, *Putting Civil Rights to a Popular Vote*, 41 AMERICAN JOURNAL OF POLITICAL SCIENCE 244 (1997), offers empirical evidence in favor of the view that initiatives jeopardize minority rights:

> By examining over three decades of civil rights laws that have appeared on state and local ballots across the nation, I find strong evidence that the majority has indeed used its direct legislative powers to deprive political minorities of their civil rights. In five issue areas — housing and public accommodations for racial minorities, school desegregation, gay rights, English language laws, and AIDS policies — the majority has been extraordinarily successful at using the ballot box to repeal existing legislative protections and to pass laws that block elected representatives from creating new laws. Furthermore, the judicial system, with its deference to the direct democratic process, provides only partial protection to the minorities whose rights have been taken away by popular vote.

Id. at 244–45. But Todd Donovan & Shaun Bowler, *Responsive or Responsible Government?* in CITIZENS AS LEGISLATORS: DIRECT DEMOCRACY IN THE UNITED STATES 249, 265 (Shaun Bowler, Todd Donovan & Caroline J. Tolbert, eds., 1998), argue that Gamble's and others' criticism may be valid at the local level, but "is overstated and not supported by data when examined at the state level." Donovan and Bowler claim that most of the initiatives in Gamble's study are local and that they are non-randomly selected. They also point out that in *The Federalist Papers*, Madison and Hamilton relied not only on representative democracy as a means of protecting minorities, but also on decision-making in large, diverse jurisdictions. By focusing on *statewide* initiatives hostile to minorities, Donovan and Bowler find that a much smaller percentage passed and that all the important ones that did pass were struck down by the courts. They cite another study finding that city councils are more likely to pass anti-discrimination ordinances for gays in large than in small jurisdictions, and conclude that the most important variable affecting how well minorities fare is not the existence of the initiative process but the size and diversity of the jurisdiction. *Id.* at 264–70.

8. Should the initiative be adopted as part of the federal government's legislative process? In the late 1970s, Senator James Abourezk, a liberal Democrat from South Dakota, proposed a constitutional amendment to do so. Senate Joint Resolution 67, 95th Cong., 1st Sess. (1977). For the text of Senator Abourezk's proposal see Bell, *supra*, at 21–22 n.79. The most extensive argument in favor of this proposal is Ronald J. Allen, *The National Initiative Proposal: A Preliminary Analysis*, 58 NEBRASKA LAW REVIEW 695 (1979). For additional views, see *Voter Initiative Constitutional Amendment: Hearings on S.J. Res. 67 Before the Subcommittee on the Constitution of the Senate Committee on the Judiciary*, 95th Cong., 1st Sess. (1977).

9. Another long-standing device of direct democracy that suddenly came into national prominence several years ago is the *recall*. In California, Governor Gray Davis was recalled from office in October 2003 and replaced by actor Arnold Schwarzenegger. This was the first time a governor had been recalled in any state since 1921. The run-up to the election featured a great deal of litigation over the meaning of California's seldom-used recall provisions; some of that litigation is described in Chapter 7.

Should those who favor the initiative process also favor the recall? What differences might there be between the two processes?

II. Content Restrictions

People's Advocate v. Superior Court
226 Cal. Rptr. 640 (Cal. App. 1986)

THE COURT:

At the June 5, 1984, election the people adopted a statutory initiative measure entitled the "Legislative Reform Act of 1983" (the Act). [The Act] makes sweeping changes in the organization and operation of the Assembly and Senate and limits the content of future legislation which appropriates money for their operations. Petitioners, [who were supporters of the initiative,] sought a declaration that the Act was valid and an order compelling compliance with its terms.

The real parties [in interest, i.e., the state legislature and others who opposed the initiative,] moved for judgment on the pleadings, challenging the provisions of the Act which regulate the internal rules, the selection of officers and employees, the selection and powers of committees of the houses of the Legislature and which limit prospectively the content of budget legislation as violative of the California Constitution; real parties challenged the remaining provisions as inseverable from the invalid provisions. The superior court granted the motion and entered judgment declaring the entire Act unconstitutional and of no force or effect....

We shall deny relief as to those provisions of the Act found by the trial court to be violative of the Constitution. However, the remaining provisions of the Act relating to secrecy in legislative proceedings are severable and as to those we shall issue a writ directing the trial court to vacate its judgment declaring their invalidity.

DISCUSSION

It is well to be clear at the outset what this case is and is not about. First, the issue before this court is one of law, not policy; it is whether the Act is constitutional, not whether it is necessary or wise. We address that issue and that issue alone. Second, this case is not about whether the will of the people shall be heeded. The Act is not the only relevant expression of popular sentiment in this case. The provisions of the California Constitution (art. IV, §7) which empower the houses of the Legislature to govern their own proceedings were first enacted almost 150 years ago and have twice been reenacted by the electorate. They are part of a constitutional structure of government by which the people have made statutes — even initiative statutes — subordinate to the Constitution, and have empowered the courts of this state in the exercise of the judicial power to interpret the state's fundamental charter. We are not presented with a conflict between the voice of the people expressed directly and through their elected representatives, but between two conflicting directives from the electorate: the Act and the California Constitution.[p]

The powers challenged by the Act are deeply rooted in constitutional soil. Since the inception of our state the power of a legislative body to govern its own internal workings has been viewed as essential to its functioning except as it may have been expressly constrained by the California Constitution. The fundamental charter of our state government was enacted by the people against a history of parliamentary common law. That law is implicit in the Constitution's structure and its separation of powers. As was said by

---

p. Why do you think the court saw fit to include this paragraph in its opinion? — EDS.

the California Supreme Court over one hundred years ago: "A legislative assembly, when established, becomes vested with all the powers and privileges which are necessary and incidental to a free and unobstructed exercise of its appropriate functions. These powers and privileges are derived not from the Constitution; on the contrary, they arise from the very creation of a legislative body, and are founded upon the principle of self preservation.[q] The Constitution is not a grant, but a restriction upon the power of the Legislature, and hence an express enumeration of legislative powers and privileges in the Constitution cannot be considered as the exclusion of others not named unless accompanied by negative terms. A legislative assembly has, therefore, all the powers and privileges which are necessary to enable it to exercise in all respects, in a free, intelligent, and impartial manner, its appropriate functions, except so far as it may be restrained by the express provisions of the Constitution, or by some express law made unto itself, regulating and limiting the same." (*Ex parte D.O. McCarthy* (1866) 29 Cal. 395, 403.)

McCarthy recognized as an integral part of this parliamentary common law the power of a house of the Legislature to "choose its own officers, and remove them at pleasure," to "establish its own rules of proceeding," and "[t]o be secret in its proceedings and debates." However, it is unnecessary for us to found our decision on that law for these powers have been made an express part of the California Constitution. They are to be found in article IV, sections 7 and 11 of the Constitution. The real parties claim that, with the exception of [certain] sections[,] each section of the Act facially violates these constitutional provisions. We agree with the claim.

I.

Article IV, section 7, subdivision (a), directs that "[e]ach house shall choose its officers and adopt rules for its proceedings." Article IV, section 11, provides that the "Legislature or either house may by resolution provide for the selection of committees necessary for the conduct of its business...."

The ... Act regulates the appointments of the Speaker of the Assembly and the President pro tempore of the Senate. It also seeks to regulate the appointment and powers of the standing, select, joint and interim committees of the houses. The Act would also regulate the method of adoption of rules for the conduct of the houses both generally and as applied to specific subject matters. It further provides that these statutory provisions may not be amended or modified except as permitted by the Act. The First part of the Act repeals the existing provisions of the Government Code which relate to these subjects These provisions of the Act manifestly invade one or more of the powers of the houses over their committees, staff and internal proceedings as expressly delegated to them by article IV, sections 7 and 11 of the Constitution.

A.

Petitioners respond that the Act is within a coordinate power of the people granted them by the Constitution, i.e. the initiative "power of the electors to propose statutes ... and to adopt or reject them." (Art. II, §8.) This power is shared with the Legislature and the Governor. See art. IV, §§8, 10; *Carlson v. Cory* 189 Cal.Rptr. 185 (Cal.App. 1983). A rule or resolution is solely the product of the house or houses which adopted it. The petitioners claim that a statute is superior to a rule or resolution and hence may supersede

---

q. Does this sentence suggest that the Legislative Reform initiative would have been void even if it had been a constitutional amendment? — Eds.

and control the subject matters of the rule making powers vested in the two houses by article IV, sections 7 and 11. Thus, so the petitioners' argument goes, there is no conflict between the Act and the Constitution. The claim presupposes that these *subject matters* are among those which may be regulated by statute. Therein lies the fallacy.

The subjects of statutes are categorically different from the subjects of the rule-making powers of article IV, sections 7 and 11. The subjects of statutes are laws. (Art. IV, §8: "The Legislature may make no law except by statute....") The kinds of rules and principles which are subsumed under the statutory "law" are addressed to the world outside the Legislature. Conversely, the internal rules of the Legislature do not have the force of law except as they may bind the house which adopted them. Since the subjects of statutory laws and rules of internal proceedings *categorically* differ, a statute may not control a rule of internal proceeding.

These subject matters are the prerogatives of different governmental entities. Laws, as expressed in statutes, are the prerogatives of the Legislature, together with the Governor, and of the electorate. Rules or resolutions which affect the selection of the officers of the houses or their rules of proceeding or rules for their committees or their employees are the exclusive prerogative of "[e]ach house" of the Legislature or the combined houses. (Art. IV, §7, subd. (a).) The people's initiative statutory power, being limited to the subject matter of statutes, does not extend to these matters.

There is one exception to this separation of powers, and it underscores this reading. Article IV, section 7, subdivision (c) (a part of the rule-making section at issue), provides that "[t]he proceedings of each house and the committees thereof shall be public except as provided by *statute or* by *concurrent resolution* ... adopted by a two-thirds vote ... of each house, provided, that if there is a conflict between such a statute and concurrent resolution, the last adopted shall prevail." (Emphasis added.) This is the only constitutional provision which authorizes the *statutory* control of a rule or resolution of internal proceeding and that authority is subject to revocation by resolution. The unmistakable implication is that none other was intended.

In sum, the people through the electorate have been given the power to make statutes, i.e. the power to make laws for all the people, but not the power to make rules for the selection of officers or rules of proceeding or rules which regulate the committees or employees of either or both houses of the Legislature. These powers (with the exception noted) are exclusively the province of the houses affected by them.

B.

Petitioners also defend the constitutionality of the Act by pointing to the apparent anomaly that the Legislature has in fact adopted statutes which purport to regulate the internal proceedings of its houses.

Petitioners offer no reasons why this practice is legally significant. There are none. The *form* (statute or rule or resolution) chosen by a house to exercise its rule-making power cannot preempt or estop a house from employing its *substantive* powers under Article IV, sections 7 and 11.[12] A rule of internal proceeding made in the guise of a statute is nonethe-

---

12. The houses have no doubt been encouraged to choose the statutory form for rule making because its parliamentary authority (Mason, Manual of Legis. Proc. (1979)) has told them that they may do so without precluding a subsequent change in the statute by *rule*. "The constitutional right of a state legislature to control its own procedure cannot be withdrawn or restricted by statute, but statutes may control procedure insofar as they do not conflict with the rules of the houses or with the rules contained in the constitution." (Mason, p. 35.) Pursuant to this advice, a statute adopted by the

less a *rule* "adopted" by the house and may be changed by an internal rule. "The enactment of statutes relating to internal proceedings was obviously accomplished by the voluntary participation of each of the two Houses. Thus each House was essentially engaged in its rule-making function." *Paisner v. Attorney General,* 458 N.E.2d 734, 739–740 (Mass. 1983). A rule of proceeding adopted by the Legislature by statute is, notwithstanding its means of adoption or label, a rule or resolution within the provisions of article IV, sections 7 and 11. It is not the form by which the rule is adopted but its substance which measures its place in the constitutional scheme. The people wholly lack this power whatever the form of its application.

Nor could a house estop itself or a future house by use of the statutory form from adopting any rule the substance of which is within the powers exclusively delegated to it by the Constitution. "The long indulgence in [a] custom cannot create a right in the legislature, or either house thereof, to do that which it has no power or authority to do." *Special Assembly Int. Com. v. Southard,* 90 P.2d 304 (Cal. 1939)....

Lastly, the petitioners seek to trade upon an assumption about the extent of the legislative power of the people. They assume that the initiative power includes the whole of the legislative power within which they locate the rule-making power. The assumption is incorrect. "The legislative power of this State is vested in the California Legislature which consists of the Senate and Assembly, but the people reserve to themselves the powers of initiative and referendum." (Art. IV, §1.) Such reserved powers are exclusively specified in article II, section 8, and are limited to that which has been specifically delegated. They do not include the power to regulate the internal workings of the houses....

To accomplish the purposes attempted by the Act, a constitutional amendment is required. Only by means of an initiative constitutional amendment may the people modify or impinge upon the freedom of the Legislature to exercise its constitutionally granted powers.

II.

Section 9934 is invalid for different reasons. It seeks to govern the content of future legislation by limiting the amount of monies appropriated for the support of the Legislature. It provides that "within 30 days following the enactment ... the total amount of monies appropriated for the support of the Legislature, ... shall be reduced by an amount equal to thirty percent of the total amount of monies appropriated for support of the Legislature for the 1983–84 fiscal year, and the amount so reduced shall revert to the General Fund. For each fiscal year thereafter, the total amount of monies appropriated ... shall not exceed an amount equal to that expended for support in the preceding fiscal year" adjusted up or down by the percentage increase or decrease in the general fund spending for the same year.

Real parties argue that section 9934 runs afoul of the "familiar principle of law that no legislative board, by normal legislative enactment, may divest itself or future boards of the power to enact legislation within its competence." *City and County of San Francisco v. Cooper* 120 Cal.Rptr. 707 (Cal. 1975). We agree.

Neither house of the Legislature may bind its own hands or those of future Legislatures by adopting rules not capable of change. "[T]he power of the electorate to enact legislation by use of the initiative process is circumscribed by the same limitations as the leg-

---

Legislature may govern an internal proceeding in the *absence* of a rule. It may not preclude a contrary rule.

islative powers resting in the legislative body concerned." *Mueller v. Brown*, 34 Cal.Rptr. 474 (Cal.App. 1963).

This principle has special application here. What is at issue is not the authority to amend a statute, however adopted, but the power to say what content a future statute may have. The authority to enact statutes which appropriate money for the support of the state government, including the Legislature, is set forth in article 4, section 12 of the California Constitution. It provides for the appropriation of such monies through the adoption of the budget bill. It also provides for special appropriations measures which may be adopted outside of the budget bill process. (Art. IV, §12, subd. (c).) Although either vehicle may be used to provide for the support of the Legislature, the budget bill is the vehicle historically used for the adoption of the Legislative budget.

The budget process takes special form. The Governor submits a budget bill accompanied by a budget document which supplies the budgetary detail for the budget bill. (Art. IV, §12, subds. (a) and (c). The Legislature is given the power inter alia to "control the ... enforcement of budgets...." (Art. IV, §12, subd. (e).)

Section 9934 limits the amount of monies that may be "appropriated" by statute for the support of the Legislature in each fiscal year beginning with the fiscal year 1984–1985. The limitation is based upon a formula tied to the budget bill enacted for the fiscal year 1982–1983. Section 9934 thus seeks to operate upon and condition the content of future statutes, appropriations statutes. In so doing it invades not only the *content* of the Governor's budget bill but displaces the process (budget and budget bill) by which article IV, section 12, commands the adoption and enforcement of the budget. It also affects any alternative means of appropriation by placing limits upon the content of any Legislative appropriations bill. By these means, section 9934 "divest[s] [the Legislature] of the power to enact legislation within its competence" and violates the specific injunctions of article IV, section 12 of the Constitution. (See *City and County of San Francisco v. Cooper, supra*.) Since the Legislature is denied such a statutory power, so are the people.[13] For these reasons section 9934 is invalid.

III.

This brings us to the question of severability. There remain a number of sections of the Act which have not been directly challenged by real parties as invalid for any of the reasons we have discussed. They relate inter alia to public meetings of the Legislature and the public reporting of legislative expenditures and by implication the repealed sections of the existing law. Real parties' claim is that these provisions are so intertwined with the invalid provisions of the Act that they may not be severed therefrom. On that point we disagree.

---

13. The limitation imposed by section 9934 upon the content of a budget measure must be distinguished from the constitutional authorization to appropriate money by statute by measures other than the budget bill. That power is specifically recognized in article IV, section 12. It authorizes the Legislature and hence the people to provide by statute for a continuing appropriation to pay for some specified program. However, the power so recognized does not authorize the placement of a *legal* limit upon the power of the Legislature to enact future appropriations legislation.

Although as a practical fiscal matter, a statute containing a continuous appropriation may limit the Legislature's *financial choices* in other appropriations measures, such a limitation is not one imposed by *law*. That is not the case here. The limitation mandated by section 9934 places legal limits upon the content of the legislation by which the Legislature is given the money to conduct its operations. That restriction exceeds the Legislature's own statutory power and hence exceeds the power of the people to do the same thing.

A.

As the California Supreme Court has said with respect to initiatives, "The rule on severability is set forth in *In re Blaney*, 184 P.2d 892 (Cal. 1947): '... if the statute is not severable, then the void part taints the remainder and the whole becomes a nullity.'" *Santa Barbara Sch. Dist. v. Superior Court*, 530 P.2d 605 (Cal. 1975). *Santa Barbara* also recognizes *Blaney's* presumption of constitutionality, "fortified" in its case, as here, by a severability clause. However, the presumption is subject to a number of tests.

Thus, *Santa Barbara*, following *Blaney*, posed the first test as grammatical. Severability "'*is possible and proper where the language of the statute is mechanically severable*, that is, where the valid and invalid parts can be separated by paragraph, sentence, clause, phrase, or even single words. [W]here there is no possibility of mechanical severance, as where the language is so broad as to cover subjects within and without the legislative power, and the defect cannot be cured by excising any word or group of words, the problem is quite different and more difficult of solution.'" (Emphasis in original.) Severance is akin to diamond cutting; a correct cut plumbs natural lines of cleavage if there are such; an incorrect one produces only diamond dust. If a grammatical cut is not possible, if the language "is incapable of mechanical severance [it] must survive, if at all, as a wholly integrated enactment." *Olson v. Cory*, 636 P.2d 532 (Cal. 1980).

The Act, like the enactment considered in the *Santa Barbara* case, contains a severability clause.[16] The courts have uniformly applied the grammatical test to enactments, however adopted, which contain severability clauses. We do so here.

The grammatical test is met by the sections at issue. As discrete sections of the Act they are grammatically complete and distinct. Thus, the only question of severance relates to the remaining sections as a whole.

B.

This tenders a second test of severance, the sections to be severed, though grammatically distinct, must be capable of independent application. Thus *Santa Barbara* says that "[s]uch a [severability] clause plus the ability to mechanically sever the invalid part while normally allowing severability, does not conclusively dictate it. The final determination [inter alia] depends on whether 'the remainder ... is complete in itself.... '" This might be called a functional test of severability. This too is contained in the severability clause. Section 9906 says that whatever language is left after severance must be capable of being "given effect". "[S]uch a clause does not require that we salvage provisions which even though valid are not intended to be independently operative." *Birkenfeld v. City of Berkeley*, 550 P.2d 1001 (Cal. 1976).

This means several things. The remainder must "'constitute[ ] a completely operative expression of the legislative intent....'" *Santa Barbara*. The part to be severed must not be part of a partially invalid but unitary whole. The remaining provisions must stand on their own, unaided by the invalid provisions nor rendered vague by their absence nor inextricably connected to them by policy considerations. They must be capable of separate enforcement.

---

16. Section 9906 provides: "If any provision of this chapter, or the application of any such provision to any person or circumstances, shall be held invalid, the remainder of this chapter to the extent it can be given effect; or the application of such provision to persons or circumstances other than those as to which it is held invalid, shall not be affected thereby, and to this end the provisions of this chapter are severable."

This test is also met here. The public meeting and public report sections are complete in themselves. They have an independent application wholly apart from and unaided by the provisions of the Act which invalidly regulate the internal proceedings of the houses of the Legislature. Moreover, the assumed justification of the severed sections rests upon an independent policy of our Constitution embodied in article IV, section 7, subdivision (c).

C.

There is a third test. As *Santa Barbara* said in applying the severability clause at issue here to an initiative, the "'remainder [must not only be] complete in itself [but] *would have been adopted by the legislative body had [it] foreseen the partial invalidation of the statute.*'" (Emphasis added.) This test logically requires that the remaining provisions must be viewed from the perspective of the enacting body.

Although the initiative process differs from the legislative process in that it does not permit amendments and a collective weighing of the relation of the parts of the enactment, it is nonetheless subject to the severability doctrine. However, the provisions to be severed must be so presented to the electorate in the initiative that their significance may be seen and independently evaluated in the light of the assigned purposes of the enactment. The test is whether it can be said with confidence that the electorate's attention was sufficiently focused upon the parts to be severed so that it would have separately considered and adopted them in the absence of the invalid portions.

This test is also met here.

The Act is preceded by policy sections which focus the attention of the electorate upon the issue of secrecy in government. Thus section 9902, in stating the purposes of the chapter, says "(e) No system of legislative voting which serves to deny or obscure the people's right to know how their representatives vote should be permitted in the Legislature." Similarly, subdivision (f) thereof says that "The people have the right to have notice of, see, and express their feelings on all proposed changes in the laws, including those changes proposed in reports of conference committees, and any knowing and willful violation of these rights should be a criminal offense...." We conclude that by this means, sufficient attention was drawn to the issue of secrecy to identify it as worthy of independent consideration. We conclude that had the electorate been separately given these provisions that they would have adopted them. There is no basis to suppose a differential popularity concerning these provisions of the Act.

It is argued, however, that 9936 and 9937 which provide for reports to the public concerning expenditures from the contingent funds of the Legislature and an independent public audit of them are inextricably linked to the provisions we have held invalid which control the use of contingent funds and limit the appropriations for support of the Legislature. This tenders a question whether these provisions were so presented to the electorate that they would have been identified as matters of governmental secrecy or as matters linked to the invalid limitations on legislative appropriations and expenditures. If solely the latter, they would be inseverable. The matter is equivocal as to choice. In this context we think the deciding factor is that there is a declared policy against the secrecy of legislative proceedings in the Act which provides a common linkage between these provisions. That fortifies our conclusion that had they been presented alone the electorate would have voted for them as a unit....

The validity of these provisions, apart from the issue of severability, has not been put in issue and nothing we say implicates such a conclusion. The provisions which we have severed may be repealed or replaced or rendered invalid by action of the Legislature pursuant to article IV, section 7, subdivision (c).…

PUGLIA, P.J., and EVANS and BLEASE, JJ., concur.

Notes and Questions

1. In footnote q, we asked whether the proposition would have been struck down if it had been circulated and enacted as a constitutional amendment. Assume the answer to that question is no. The only difference between enactment of an initiative statute and enactment of an initiative constitutional amendment in California, as well as in many other states, is that the constitutional amendment requires more signatures. Other than striking down the particular proposition, does *People's Advocate* have much significance if the same result can be reached by a group willing to spend the extra money needed to obtain enough signatures to qualify a constitutional amendment? Would you support a constitutional provision putting legislative rules beyond the reach of the initiative process altogether? Is it abusive to use the initiative to change legislative rules? To the contrary, might it be argued that changing legislative rules is an especially appropriate use of the initiative process? With respect to the last question, consider the Illinois constitutional provisions described in the following note.

2. In Illinois, the initiative is permitted *only* for the purpose of altering the legislative process.

> Amendments to Article IV [the legislative article] of this Constitution may be proposed by a petition signed by a [specified number of electors]. Amendments shall be limited to structural and procedural subjects contained in Article IV.…

Illinois Constitution, art. 14, §3. The rationale for this very limited scope of the initiative process has been explained as follows:

> Section 3 recognizes that the General Assembly is unlikely to propose any changes in its basic structure, but that some changes may appear to be necessary. Thus, a method of constitutional revision other than through the General Assembly is necessary.

Robert A. Helman & Wayne W. Whalen, *Constitutional Commentary*, in SMITH-HURD COMPILED STATUTES ANNOTATED, Const., art. 14, §3 (1993).

Paisner v. Attorney General, 458 N.E.2d 734 (Mass. 1983), was cited by the California court, because it interpreted the Massachusetts Constitution to place the legislature's power over its own rules and procedures beyond control by statutes, including initiative statutes. *Paisner* and *People's Advocate* could be crudely paraphrased as saying that the initiative can address most subjects but not the legislative process itself. Does the Illinois constitution take exactly the opposite approach? If so, which is better?

The Illinois provision for the initiative, narrow to begin with, has been interpreted strictly by the Illinois courts. In *Coalition for Political Honesty v. State Board of Elections*, 359 N.E.2d 138 (Ill. 1976), the Illinois Supreme Court ruled that an Illinois initiative must make both structural *and* procedural changes to the legislative process. On this basis it struck down three initiative proposals, including one that prohibited legislators from voting on bills in which they had conflicts of interest. Presumably, the court regarded that as a procedural but not as a structural change. In *Chicago Bar Association v. State Board of Elections*, 561 N.E.2d 50 (Ill. 1990), the court struck down a proposal that would have required a three-fifths vote in each house for any bill that would increase revenues and would have required a special revenue committee to be created in each house, with detailed specifications regarding number of members, method of appointment, and so on. The court explained:

> The [proponent] argues that the proposed Amendment does affect structural and procedural subjects of article IV, and thus complies with section 3 of article XIV. Even assuming that the [proponent] is correct in this regard, we find that the proposed Amendment is not *limited to* the structural and procedural subjects of article IV. Wrapped up in this structural and procedural package is a substantive issue not found in article IV — the subject of increasing State revenue or increasing taxes.

If an initiative like the one in *People's Advocate* were proposed in Illinois, would the Illinois courts permit it to go on the ballot?

3. The cases described above show that courts will often protect the legislature's autonomy from interference through the initiative process. Will they do so consistently and will they extend similar protection to the other two branches of government?

In *Citizens Coalition for Tort Reform v. McAlpine*, 810 P.2d 162 (Alaska 1991), the Supreme Court of Alaska struck from the ballot an initiative proposal to limit contingent attorney's fees in personal injury cases. The Alaska Constitution, art. XI, §7, barred initiative proposals to "create courts, define the jurisdiction of courts or prescribe their rules." The initiative in *Citizens Coalition* limited fees "regardless of whether the recovery is by settlement, arbitration, or judgment." The Alaska Supreme Court reasoned that since the regulation of the practice of law, including regulation of fees, was within its own power, the proposed initiative was an effort to prescribe a court rule.

In *Yute Air Alaska v. McAlpine*, 698 P.2d 1173 (1985), the Alaska court approved an initiative proposal that provided in part:

> The governor shall use best efforts and all appropriate means to persuade the United States Congress to repeal ... the Jones Act[, which required the use of United States vessels for shipping goods between United States ports]. Until that Act is repealed, the governor shall publish an annual report documenting the harmful effects of the Act on Alaska commerce, and progress made towards its repeal.

The court rejected a contention that this provision was not a "law" that could be enacted by the initiative process. What if this proposal were enacted and the governor did not favor repeal of the Jones Act? What if the Jones Act were still in effect and the governor or staff or consultants employed by the governor to prepare the required annual report concluded from the evidence that harm to Alaska commerce from the Jones Act either did not exist or could not be documented?

4. In some states the initiative may be used to "amend" the state constitution but not to "revise" it. See e.g., *McFadden v. Jordan*, 196 P.2d 787 (Cal. 1948), cert. denied 336 U.S. 918 (1949); *Holmes v. Appling*, 392 P.2d 636 (Or. 1964). This distinction is said to be "based on the principle that 'comprehensive changes' to the Constitution require more formality, discussion and deliberation than is available through the initiative process." See *Raven v. Deukmejian*, 276 Cal.Rptr. 326, 801 P.2d 1077 (1990).

Not surprisingly, California's famous Proposition 13 was challenged on the ground that it revised rather than amended the California Constitution. Proposition 13 has been described

> as a revolutionary measure for reducing the level and growth of state and local government expenditure as well as sharply restricting the use of the property tax as

a source of government revenue. [Proposition 13] 1) restricts the property tax rate to no more than 1 percent of assessed value; 2) sets assessed value for a property that has not been transferred since 1975–76 equal to its fair market value in that year plus 2 percent per year (compounded); in the event that the property has been transferred since 1975–76, the market value at the time of sale is used (plus the 2 percent growth factor); and 3) requires that new taxes or increases in existing taxes (except property taxes) receive a two-thirds approval of the legislature in the case of state taxes, or of the electorate, in the case of local taxes.

The potential fiscal impact of these provisions is enormous....

There are, among others, implications for financial markets; taxpayer equity; efficiency of the housing market; the structure of state and local government; and perhaps, most dramatically, for other governments, including the federal government.

William H. Oakland, *Proposition 13: Genesis and Consequences*, in THE PROPERTY TAX REVOLT: THE CASE OF PROPOSITION 13, 31, 31–32 (1981).ʳ In *Amador Valley Joint Union High School District v. State Board of Equalization*, 149 Cal.Rptr. 239, 583 P.2d 1281 (1978), the California Supreme Court ruled that Proposition 13 was valid as a constitutional "amendment." The court stated that

our analysis in determining whether a particular constitutional enactment is a revision or an amendment must be both quantitative and qualitative in nature. For example, an enactment which is so extensive in its provisions as to change directly the "substantial entirety" of the Constitution by the deletion or alteration of numerous existing provisions may well constitute a revision thereof. However, even a relatively simple enactment may accomplish such far reaching changes in the nature of our basic governmental plan as to amount to a revision also.

Proposition 13 was not a revision under this analysis, because its "changes operate functionally within a relatively narrow range to accomplish a new system of taxation which may provide substantial tax relief for our citizens."

However, in *Raven, supra,* the court ruled that a provision in an initiative known as Proposition 115 was void because it purported to revise the constitution. The provision in question required that various procedural rights of defendants in criminal cases

shall be construed by the courts of this state in a manner consistent with the Constitution of the United States. This Constitution shall not be construed by the courts to afford greater rights to criminal defendants than those afforded by the Constitution of the United States....

This provision admittedly was not a revision on quantitative grounds. Despite the fact that the California Supreme Court had a "general principle or policy" of being guided in its construction of state constitutional rights by the United States Supreme Court's interpretation of corresponding federal rights, the California court had departed from this pol-

---

r. The effects of Proposition 13 have been described less neutrally by Julian N. Eule, *Crocodiles in the Bathtub: State Courts, Voter Initiatives and the Threat of Electoral Reprisal*, 65 UNIVERSITY OF COLORADO LAW REVIEW 733 (1994):

Proposition 13 has left education, welfare, public safety, the economy, and the infrastructure in shambles. California, which once ranked as the nation's leader in primary and secondary education, now relishes a year in which it finishes forty-eighth rather than fiftieth. The University of California may still be a gem among public institutions of higher learning, but too often it is less a diamond than a zirconium.

icy on a number of occasions. Accordingly, from a qualitative standpoint, "the effect of Proposition 115 is devastating," because as to the rights in question, "California courts in criminal cases would no longer have authority to interpret the state Constitution in a manner more protective of defendants' rights than extended by the federal Constitution...."

Less than a year later the California court upheld Proposition 140 against a claim that it revised the state constitution. Proposition 140 imposed term limits on state legislators and other elected state officials; reduced the state legislature's budget by about 38 percent; and eliminated pensions for future state legislators. The court distinguished *Raven* as follows:

> As indicated in *Raven*, a qualitative revision includes one that involves a change in the basic plan of California government, i.e., a change in its fundamental structure or the foundational powers of its branches. *Raven* invalidated a portion of Proposition 115 because it deprived the state judiciary of its foundational power to decide cases by independently interpreting provisions of the state Constitution, and delegated that power to the United States Supreme Court.
>
> By contrast, Proposition 140 on its face does not affect either the structure or the foundational powers of the Legislature, which remains free to enact whatever laws it deems appropriate. The challenged measure alters neither the content of those laws nor the process by which they are adopted. No legislative power is diminished or delegated to other persons or agencies. The relationships between the three governmental branches, and their respective powers, remain untouched.

Legislature v. Eu, 286 Cal.Rptr. 283, 816 P.2d 1309 (1991), cert. denied 503 U.S. 919 (1992).

Amador Valley, *Raven*, and *Legislature* involved, respectively: Proposition 13, which dramatically lowered property taxes, greatly increased the difficulty of increasing taxes in the future, and predictably effected a major shift of power from local to state governments; Proposition 115, which converted a general principle of interpretation of certain rights into a mandatory principle; and Proposition 140, which adopted term limits and slashed the legislative budget. Which of these propositions brought about the most "comprehensive changes" in the California system of governance? Which brought about the least "comprehensive changes"?

Do the decisions summarized in this Note and in Note 3 suggest the possibility that courts are more sensitive to intrusions on their own powers than on those of the coordinate branches of government?

5. In Part II of *People's Advocate*, the court strikes down the portion of the initiative purporting to restrict future appropriations to cover the expenses of the legislature. The court's holding is a narrow one. It could be evaded if proponents qualified an initiative constitutional amendment rather than an initiative statute. Furthermore, as the court makes clear in its footnote 13, nothing prevents use of initiative statutes in California for appropriations, including appropriations extending permanently into the future. As the following makes clear, initiatives containing appropriations have become a common practice in California, though budgeting by initiative is restricted by the constitutions of some other states:

> Nine states place restrictions on the extent to which taxes can be levied or appropriations made through the initiative process. Even more states prohibit the use of the referendum to block or alter tax and appropriation measures....
>
> California is one of the states that does not impose restriction on the use of the initiative to raise revenue or spend money. One consequence is that a large proportion of the state's budget is now permanently subject to control by ini-

tiatives adopted in the past. Some believe that this not only creates annual budgeting problems but also encourages interest groups that lack the protected status conferred by the prior initiatives to seek protection for themselves....

California, like many other states, subjects its normal appropriations to a number of important processes. The budget must be balanced. Appropriations, except those for the public schools, must be passed by two-thirds of the membership of each house, and all appropriations are subject to an item veto by the governor. No bill except the budget bill may contain more than one item of appropriation, "and that for one certain, expressed purpose."[s] Appropriations contained in initiative measures are subject to none of these processes. This seems unduly lax, making it easier in some instances to secure appropriations through the initiative than through the legislative process. Because the appropriations process necessarily involves comparisons among programs, it also seems unwise and ultimately unworkable to allow a great proportion of a state's resources to be appropriated through the initiative process.

Philip L. Dubois & Floyd Feeney, LAWMAKING BY INITIATIVE 83 (1998).

6. Numerous additional subject-matter restrictions on the content of initiatives exist in one or more states. Following is a sampling:

In many jurisdictions, initiatives may not resolve "administrative" as opposed to "legislative" questions. This issue most commonly arises in connection with initiative proposals at the local level. For example, in *Foster v. Clark*, 790 P.2d 1 (Or. 1990), the Portland City Council had changed the name of a street from "Union Avenue" to "Martin Luther King, Jr. Boulevard." An initiative proposal to change the name of the street back to "Union Avenue" was struck off the ballot on the ground that it dealt with an administrative issue.

A few jurisdictions prohibit the reversal by initiative of a decision that already has been made by the legislative body. See, e.g., *Schaefer v. Village Board*, 501 N.W.2d 901 (Wis. 1993).

In at least some states, courts will remove from the ballot initiatives that declare an opinion on some question of public policy without legislating on the subject. The California Supreme Court adopted this view in *AFL-CIO v. Eu*, 206 Cal.Rptr. 89, 686 P.2d 609 (1984), while acknowledging that there may be value to permitting the people by direct vote not only to adopt statutes, but also to adopt resolutions, declare policy, and make known their views upon matters of statewide, national, or even international concern. Such initiatives, while not having the force of law, could nevertheless guide the lawmakers in future decisions. Indeed it may well be that the declaration of broad statements of policy is a more suitable use for the initiative than the enactment of detailed and technical statutes. Under the terms of the California Constitution, however, the initiative does not serve these hortatory objectives; it functions instead as a reserved legislative power, a method of enacting statutory law.

7. *Dueling initiatives.* The final issue in *People's Advocate* was whether the unchallenged portions of the proposition could survive after other provisions were declared unconstitutional. The answer to that question, which arises frequently with respect to initiatives as well as legislatively-enacted statutes in an era of active judicial review, depends on whether the unchallenged provisions, or those held to be constitutional, are "severable" from the provisions that are struck down.

A different issue of severability arises when two initiatives are adopted at the same election covering the same general subject matter. In the past one or two decades it has become increasingly common for interest groups threatened by an initiative to qualify one or more

---

s. Cal. Const. Art. IV, §12.

competing initiatives more to their liking. In general this has not been an effective technique, but it gives rise to the possibility of competing initiatives both being approved. This occurred in 1988 when the voters of California approved both Proposition 68 and Proposition 73, competing campaign finance initiatives. Although both propositions received a majority of affirmative votes, Proposition 73 received more votes than Proposition 68. Article II, section 10(b) of the California constitution provides: "If the provisions of 2 or more measures approved at the same election conflict, those of the measure receiving the highest affirmative vote shall prevail." In *Taxpayers to Limit Campaign Spending v. Fair Political Practices Commission*, 274 Cal.Rptr. 787, 799 P.2d 1220 (1990), the California Supreme Court stated the question and answered it as follows: "Does section 10(b) contemplate enforcement of any provisions of an initiative that receives a majority of the votes cast when another initiative on the same ballot, directed to the same subject and offered as a competing regulatory scheme, receives a greater majority? We conclude that it does not." The court relied in part on historical and textual analyses of section 10(b) and related provisions. The court also offered these more general observations:

> In order to further the fundamental right of the electorate to enact legislation through the initiative process, this court must on occasion indulge in a presumption that the voters thoroughly study and understand the content of complex initiative measures. Relying on this presumption we attempt to ascertain and implement the purposes of the measure. No case has been called to our attention, however, in which the court has assumed that voters not only recognized that they were approving initiatives with fundamentally conflicting provisions intended to regulate the same subject, but also analyzed the remaining provisions in order to predict which would be implemented if either measure received a lesser affirmative vote. A construction of section 10(b) that obligates the court to implement a fictitious electoral intent would be unreasonable and unjustified.

> In concluding that section 10(b) mandates an attempt to reconcile these competing initiatives, each of which offers a comprehensive but fundamentally different regulatory scheme, the dissent and the Court of Appeal apparently assume that a majority of the same voters cast their votes for both Proposition 73 and Proposition 68, and thus enforcement of parts of Proposition 68 will carry out the intent of the electorate. [H]owever, there is no sound basis for the predicate assumption. The parties concede that the court cannot determine whether a majority of the voters intended that both measures become effective if both passed. Absent some basis for such a determination, the court cannot logically conclude that it was the intent of a majority of the electorate that both propositions be implemented to the extent possible, or that the voters anticipated the amalgam created by the Court of Appeal.

> When competing initiatives are on the ballot, it is possible, if not probable, that many of the votes in favor of each measure were cast by the voters who cast votes against the alternative proposition. The arguments for and against the initiatives here asked the voters to do just that—to choose between the two measures. A construction of section 10(b) that invites judicial reconciliation of competing initiatives in these circumstances would lead as easily to thwarting the will of the electorate as to carrying it out.[t]

---

t. Suppose the arguments in support of two initiatives dealing with the same subject urged voters to vote in favor of both. Would the California Supreme Court uphold the non-conflicting provisions of the measure that received fewer votes?

[Supporters of Proposition 68] argue that a construction of section 10(b) that does not permit implementation of individual, non-conflicting provisions of initiative measures will "eviscerate" the initiative process, and will make it possible for opponents of an initiative to defeat it even when it has been adopted by an overwhelming majority of the voters. The opponents will be able to do so, they argue, by placing another, less complex, but conflicting, measure, on the same ballot in the hope that it will receive a greater vote.

The possibility of abuse of the initiative, however, does not offset the equally serious threat to the process that may occur when courts and regulatory agencies attempt to enforce provisions of conflicting initiatives in the absence of any assurance that the electorate anticipated the resulting regulatory scheme.

The process is better served by presentation at a subsequent election of a new initiative measure which the voters can consider in light of the scheme established by the measure that prevailed in the earlier election. We do not denigrate the conscientious efforts of the voters to familiarize themselves with ballot measures. The increasing number and complexity of statewide and local initiative measures, however, supports our conclusions that we should not read section 10(b) as mandating what constitutes judicial legislation in which portions of one regulatory scheme are excised and attached to another, quite different scheme. Nor should we assume … that the voters would have approved incorporation of these several Proposition 68 provisions into the regulatory scheme created by Proposition 73.

8. One content restriction that exists in most initiative states and that has been the subject of considerable litigation is the "single subject rule." For example, California Constitution, art. II, §8(d) provides: "An initiative measure embracing more than one subject may not be submitted to the electors or have any effect." Even in states whose constitutions contain no express single subject rule for initiatives, courts sometimes extend to initiatives the single subject rule that is explicitly applicable to the legislature. E.g., *Washington Federation of State Employees v. State*, 901 P.2d 1028 (Wash. 1995); *Montana Automobile Association v. Greely*, 632 P.2d 300, 311 (Mont. 1981).

The Single Subject Rule in Florida

For many years, challenges to initiatives on single-subject grounds had the greatest success in Florida, as the following case illustrates.

In re Advisory Opinion to the Attorney General
632 So.2d 1018 (Fla. 1994)

McDONALD, Justice.

[T]he Attorney General has petitioned this Court for an advisory opinion on the validity of an initiative petition.…

The petition seeks to amend article I, section 10 of the Florida Constitution, which provides:

No bill of attainder, ex post facto law or law impairing the obligation of contracts shall be passed.

The petition would amend the above provision in the following manner:

1) Article I, section 10 of the Constitution of the State of Florida is hereby amended by ... adding a new subsection "(b)" at the end thereof to read:

(b) The state, political subdivisions of the state, municipalities or any other governmental entity shall not enact or adopt any law regarding discrimination against persons which creates, establishes or recognizes any right, privilege or protection for any person based upon any characteristic, trait, status, or condition other than race, color, religion, sex, national origin, age, handicap, ethnic background, marital status, or familial status. As used herein the term 'sex' shall mean the biological state of either being a male person or a female person; 'marital status' shall mean the state of being lawfully married to a person of the opposite sex, separated, divorced, widowed or single; and 'familial status' shall mean the state of being a person domiciled with a minor, as defined by law, who is the parent or person with legal custody of such minor or who is a person with written permission from such parent or person with legal custody of such minor.

(2) All laws previously enacted which are inconsistent with this provision are hereby repealed to the extent of such inconsistency....

Our advisory opinion is limited to determining whether the proposed amendment complies with article XI, section 3 of the Florida Constitution and section 101.161, Florida Statutes (1993). Article XI, section 3 of the Florida Constitution requires that a proposed amendment "shall embrace but one subject and matter directly connected therewith." The Attorney General concluded that "on its face," the amendment appeared to satisfy the single-subject requirement. Looking beyond the surface, however, we find that the proposed amendment touches upon more than one subject and therefore violates the single-subject provision of the constitution.

Florida's state constitution reflects a consensus on the issues and values that the electorate has declared to be of fundamental importance. When voters are asked to consider a modification to the constitution, they should not be forced to "accept part of an initiative proposal which they oppose in order to obtain a change in the constitution which they support." *Fine v. Firestone*, 448 So.2d 984, 988 (Fla.1984). The single-subject rule is a constitutional restraint placed on proposed amendments to prevent voters from being trapped in such a predicament. Thus, to comply with the single-subject requirement, the proposed amendment must manifest a "logical and natural oneness of purpose." *Id.*

To ascertain whether the necessary "oneness of purpose" exists, we must consider whether the proposal affects separate functions of government and how the proposal affects other provisions of the constitution. *Id.* In support of the validity of the proposed amendment, the American Family Political Committee argues that discrimination is the sole subject of the proposed amendment. This Court has emphasized, however, that "enfolding disparate subjects within the cloak of a broad generality does not satisfy the single-subject requirement." *Evans v. Firestone*, 457 So.2d 1351, 1353 (Fla.1984). In *Fine*, we disapproved a proposed amendment that characterized the provisions as affecting the single subject of revenues because it actually affected the government's ability to tax, government user-fee operations, and funding of capital improvements through revenue bonds. Similarly we find that the subject of discrimination in the proposed amendment is an expansive generality that encompasses both civil rights and the power of all state and local governmental bodies. By including the language "any other governmental entity," the proposed amendment encroaches on municipal home rule powers and on the rulemaking authority of executive agencies and the judiciary. In addition, the amendment modifies article I, section 2 of the

Florida Constitution, dealing with the basic rights of all natural persons, and also affects article I, section 6 of the Florida Constitution, dealing with the right of employees to bargain collectively.

The proposed amendment also violates the single-subject requirement because it enumerates ten classifications of people that would be entitled to protection from discrimination if the amendment were passed. The voter is essentially being asked to give one "yes" or "no" answer to a proposal that actually asks ten questions. For example, a voter may want to support protection from discrimination for people based on race and religion, but oppose protection based on marital status and familial status. Requiring voters to choose which classifications they feel most strongly about, and then requiring them to cast an all or nothing vote on the classifications listed in the amendment, defies the purpose of the single-subject limitation. Therefore, the proposed amendment fails the single-subject requirement of article IV, section 3 of the Florida Constitution.

[The court also ruled that an additional reason for striking the measure from the ballot was that the proposed ballot title and summary were misleading. A concurring opinion by Justice Kogan is omitted.]

Notes and Questions

1. The initiative power was first inserted into the Florida Constitution in 1968, and is limited to constitutional amendments.[u] In 1970, the Florida Supreme Court ruled that an initiative proposal for a unicameral legislature was improper as a constitutional revision rather than a constitutional amendment. *Adams v. Gunter*, 238 So.2d 824 (1970). The legislature and the voters responded by amending the constitution to allow revisions as well as amendments by initiative, but also by inserting a single subject rule applicable to initiatives. Presumably, the purpose of the amendment was to assure greater leeway for changing the constitution through the initiative. Initially, the Florida Supreme Court interpreted the single subject rule in that spirit, applying the rule in the same deferential manner that it had long used in interpreting the single subject rule applicable to the legislature. See *Weber v. Smathers*, 338 So.2d 819 (Fla. 1976); *Floridians Against Casino Takeover v. Let's Help Florida*, 363 So.2d 337 (Fla. 1978).

In *Fine v. Firestone*, 448 So.2d 984 (Fla. 1984), cited in *In re Advisory Opinion*, the Florida Supreme Court "receded" from earlier decisions interpreting the two single-subject rules to establish the same standard. The court concluded that

> we should take a broader view of the legislative provision because any proposed law must proceed through legislative debate and public hearing. Such a process allows change in the content of any law before its adoption. This process is, in itself, a restriction on the drafting of a proposal which is not applicable to the scheme for constitutional revision or amendment by initiative.

Additional reasons, more specific to Florida, for applying the rule more strictly to initiatives than to legislative enactments, depended on the specific language used in the constitutional provisions and on the fact that the single-subject rule for the legislature applied

---

u. For a good account of the history of the initiative in Florida, see Joseph W. Little, *Does Direct Democracy Threaten Constitutional Governance in Florida?*, 24 STETSON LAW REVIEW 393 (1995). Thomas Rutherford, *The People Drunk or the People Sober? Direct Democracy Meets the Supreme Court of Florida*, 15 ST. THOMAS LAW REVIEW 61 (2002), provides an exhaustive analysis of the Florida court's activism in its treatment of initiatives.

only to statutes while the rule for initiatives applied only to constitutional amendments and revisions.

Most states that have considered the issue at least purport to apply the single-subject rule identically to the legislature and to the initiative process. Indeed, the Oregon Supreme Court canvassed decisions in a number of states on this point and concluded that "[i]t does appear ... that the Florida court stands alone." *Oregon Education Association v. Phillips*, 727 P.2d 602 (Or. 1986).[v]

The Florida Supreme Court continues to implement the single subject rule with a heavy hand. In 2005, redistricting reformers in Ohio and California placed proposals on the ballot to impose new redistricting criteria and to entrust the enactment of redistricting plans to commissions. Both proposals were decisively defeated, but the reformers had their day before the voters. In Florida, a similar effort was stifled by the Supreme Court, which ruled in *Advisory Opinion to the Attorney General*, 926 So.2d 1218 (Fla. 2006), that the redistricting initiative violated the single subject rule:

> Not only would the proposed amendment create a new redistricting commission, but it would also change the standards applicable to the districts that are created by the commission....
>
> The other provisions of the proposed amendment exhibit "a natural relation and connection as component parts or aspects of" the new method proposed for apportionment. These provisions explain the composition of the commission, specify the apportionment process, and provide for judicial apportionment if the commission fails to complete its duty. However, the creation of new standards to be used in apportioning the districts is not a component part of this apportionment plan and results in logrolling. A voter who advocates apportionment by a redistricting commission may not necessarily agree with the change in the standards for drawing legislative and congressional districts. Conversely, a voter who approves the change in district standards may not want to change from the legislative apportionment process currently in place. Thus, a voter would be forced to vote in the "all or nothing" fashion that the single subject requirement safeguards against.

2. What is the purpose of the single subject rule, as applied to initiatives? Two purposes are commonly articulated: to prevent voter confusion and, as the Florida court stated, to prevent logrolling. At least two types of logrolling are theoretically possible. The first type would combine two or more provisions, none of which alone would command majority support. Suppose, for example, a proposal contains provisions A and B, each of which is supported by one-third of the voters and opposed by two-thirds. The supporters of A are different voters from the supporters of B. The proponents hope that each group of voters will care more about the provision they support than the one they oppose, and vote for the proposal, which would then receive two-thirds of the total vote. The second type of logrolling occurs when a majority of voters supports A and opposes B. The proponents hope that they will care more about their support for A than their opposition to B and vote for the proposal. B in this example is known as a "rider," because if the proponents are successful, B, though opposed by a majority of voters, will ride to victory on the popularity of A.

Is the single subject rule well suited to accomplish its anti-confusion and anti-logrolling purposes? See Clayton P. Gillette, *Expropriation and Institutional Design in State and Local*

---

v. Footnote 4 of *Oregon Education Association* contains references to initiative single subject decisions from several states. A concurring opinion by Judge Hans Linde, a distinguished scholar on the initiative process, contains a thoughtful discussion of the single subject rule.

Government Law, 80 VIRGINIA LAW REVIEW 625, 664–70 (1994) (arguing that the single subject rule serves an anti-logrolling function); Daniel H. Lowenstein, *California Initiatives and the Single-Subject Rule*, 30 UCLA LAW REVIEW 936, 954–65 (1983) (arguing that the rule serves neither purpose, but proposing an alternative rationale for the rule).

3. Although Florida may be the only state that expressly applies the single-subject rule more rigorously to initiatives than to acts of the state legislature, for some time there have been other states that articulate relatively strict interpretations of the rule. For example, in Arizona, the rule is described as follows:

> If the different changes contained in the proposed amendment all cover matters necessary to be dealt with in some manner, in order that the Constitution, as amended, shall constitute a consistent and workable whole on the general topic embraced in that part which is amended, and if, logically speaking, they should stand or fall as a whole, then there is but one amendment submitted. But, if any one of the propositions, although not directly contradicting the others, does not refer to such matters, or if it is not such that the voter supporting it would reasonably be expected to support the principle of the others, then there are in reality two or more amendments to be submitted, and the proposed amendment falls within the constitutional prohibition.

Tilson v. Mofford, 737 P.2d 1367 (Ariz. 1987), quoting *Kerby v. Luhrs*, 36 P.2d 549 (Ariz. 1934). Nevertheless, at least until recently, no state other than Florida seems to have applied the rule strictly with any consistency.

Most states do not follow Arizona in requiring that all the provisions in an initiative be "necessary." For example, in Alaska, the "standard is that the 'act should embrace some one general subject; and by this is meant, merely, that all matters treated of should fall under some one general idea, be so connected with or related to each other, either logically or in popular understanding, as to be parts of, or germane to, one general subject.'" *Yute Air Alaska v. McAlpine*, 698 P.2d 1173 (Alaska 1985) (quoting from earlier decisions applying the single subject rule to legislatures). In California, likewise, the courts have applied the single subject rule liberally in order to sustain "statutes and initiatives which fairly disclose a reasonable and common sense relationship among their various components in furtherance of a common purpose." *Brosnahan v. Brown*, 186 Cal.Rptr. 30, 651 P.2d 274, 284 (1982).

One writer criticizes the liberal application of the rule in California on these grounds:

> The supreme court uses several artifices to avoid invalidating initiatives under the single-subject rule. Indeed, with these methods it can avoid altogether a meaningful application of the rule. These artifices include the broad manner of defining "subject," the loose relationship allowed between the measure's provisions and its "subject," the failure to distinguish between a measure's subject and objective, and the preference for delaying review until after an election. These artifices allow the court to sidestep serious review of complex initiative measures.

Marilyn E. Minger, Comment, *Putting the "Single" Back in the Single-Subject Rule: A Proposal for Initiative Reform in California*, 24 U.C. DAVIS LAW REVIEW 879, 899–900 (1991). For a defense of the liberal interpretation, see Lowenstein, *supra*.

4. Even in a state that interprets the rule liberally, anyone drafting an initiative—and anyone looking for a way to invalidate an initiative—should bear the single subject rule in mind. During the heyday of liberal interpretation of the rule by the California Supreme Court, lower courts nevertheless employed the rule to strike down two initiatives in 1988 and 1991.

California Trial Lawyers Association v. Eu, 200 Cal.App.3d 351, 245 Cal.Rptr. 916 (1988); *Chemical Specialties Manufacturers Assn., Inc. v. Deukmejian*, 227 Cal.App.3d 663, 278 Cal.Rptr. 128 (1991). More importantly, as the following materials will show, a sea change may be taking place in the interpretation of the initiative single subject rule.

The Single Subject Rule in California (and Elsewhere)

1. A good example of the liberal interpretation of the single subject rule that long prevailed in California is FAIR POLITICAL PRACTICES COMMISSION v. SUPERIOR COURT, 25 Cal.3d 33, 157 Cal.Rptr. 855, 599 P.2d 46 (1979). California's Political Reform Act, also known as Proposition 9, had been adopted by initiative in June, 1974. The court described Proposition 9 as follows:

> Chapters 1 and 2 contain general provisions and definitions, including a severability provision. Chapter 3 establishes the [Fair Political Practices Commission]. Chapter 4 establishes disclosure requirements for candidates' significant financial supporters. Chapter 5 places limitations on campaign spending. Chapter 6 regulates lobbyist activities. Chapter 7 establishes rules relating to conflict of interest. Chapter 8 establishes rules relating to voter pamphlet summaries of arguments on proposed ballot measures. Chapter 9 regulates ballot position of candidates. Chapter 10 establishes auditing procedures to aid enforcement of the law, and Chapter 11 imposes penalties for violations of the act.

The court applied its established test under the single subject rule and upheld Proposition 9 because its provisions were "reasonably germane" to the general subject of "elections and different methods for preventing corruption and undue influence in political campaigns and governmental activities." A membership group of California lobbyists urged the court to abandon the "reasonably germane" test, which the group contended was not sufficient to serve the rule's alleged purposes of allaying voter confusion and avoiding logrolling.

The court rejected this proposal: "Consistent with our duty to uphold the people's right to initiative process, we adhere to the reasonably germane test and, in doing so, find that the measure before us complies with the one subject requirement." The court responded to the lobbying group's contentions on the purposes of the rule:

> Although the initiative measure before us is wordy and complex, there is little reason to expect that claimed voter confusion could be eliminated or substantially reduced by dividing the measure into four or ten separate propositions.[w] Our society being complex, the rules governing it whether adopted by legislation or initiative will necessarily be complex. Unless we are to repudiate or cripple use of the initiative, risk of confusion must be borne.

> Nor does the possibility that some voters might vote for the measure—while objecting to some parts—warrant rejection of the reasonably germane test. Such risk is inherent in any initiative containing more than one sentence or even an "and" in a single sentence unless the provisions are redundant.

2. The *FPPC* court concludes that there is no single subject violation because the provisions of the Political Reform Act "are reasonably germane to the subject of political practices." It would be hard to argue that the measure was not confined to "political prac-

---

w. One of the editors of this volume wrote most of Proposition 9. He cheerfully concedes complexity but takes umbrage at wordiness.—EDS.

tices," and "political practices" presumably constitute a subject, albeit a broad one. The California constitution restricts initiatives to a single subject, but it does not say the subject has to be a narrow one. Does it follow that the court's conclusion is irrebuttably correct? Plainly not, because that argument proves too much. If *any* subject would do, then no measure could ever violate the single subject rule. Consider, for example, the initiative proposal that gave rise to the California single subject rule. Qualified for the ballot in 1948, it was the last of a series of initiatives sponsored in the 1930s and 1940s by the "ham and eggs" movement, so called because it favored public pensions that would put ham and eggs on the plates of senior citizens. The contents of the 1948 initiative were summarized as follow by the California Attorney General:

> Establishes 2 percent tax on gross receipts of all kinds. Legalizes, licenses and taxes bookmaking and other gambling. Abolishes all other State and local taxes and fees. Provides minimum monthly retirement pensions of $100 until July 1952, $130 thereafter, plus increases proportioned to cost-of-living increases since 1944, payable to aged persons, permanently disabled persons, widows, clergymen, teachers. Provides temporary disability and burial benefits. Regulates oleomargarine, certain healing arts, civic centers, public lands, water pollution, surface mining. Reapportions State Senate. Prohibits primary election cross-filing.

Relying on either common sense or on the legislative history of the single subject rule, we may take as a given that whatever else it may mean, the rule in California must at least rule out a repeat of the 1948 initiative. Yet, the above argument could be employed to vindicate the 1948 initiative just as easily as the 1974 Political Reform Act. All the provisions of the 1948 proposal, we might say, "are reasonably germane to the subject of public policy." True, public policy is an even broader subject than political practices, but it is still a subject. There has to be a limit on how broad the subject can be, if the rule is to have any meaning at all. The difficulty is that the rule gives no guidance as to what the limit should be.

The *FPPC* majority's approach, based on a case decided the year after the rule's adoption, allows broad subjects such as "political practices," but would prohibit measures approaching the 1948 ham and eggs measure in the disparateness of its provisions. Justice Wiley Manuel dissented, proposing that all the provisions in a measure should be functionally related to each other. Which interpretation is better as a matter of policy? Does the *Jones* case that follows employ the majority's interpretation of the single subject rule in *FPPC*, Justice Manuel's interpretation, or a different approach altogether?

3. SENATE OF THE STATE OF CALIFORNIA v. JONES, 21 Cal.4th 1142, 90 Cal.Rptr.2d 810, 988 P.2d 1089 (1999), was a 5–1 decision in which the California Supreme Court removed Proposition 24, an initiative, from the ballot because it violated the single subject rule. Proposition 24 contained four substantive provisions:

> a. It changed the method for setting salaries for state legislators. Instead of a state commission *setting* the salary changes, the commission would *recommend* changes, which had to be approved by both the legislature and the voters.

> b. It set restrictions on reimbursement of legislators for travel and living expenses.

> c. It imposed penalties on legislators if the budget was not approved each year by the deadline.

d. It took the power of redistricting away from the legislature. Districting plans were to be adopted by the California Supreme Court, subject to approval by the voters.

The court reaffirmed previous decisions holding that a measure is consistent with the single subject rule if, "despite its varied collateral effects, all of its parts are 'reasonably germane' to each other, and to the general purpose or object of the initiative."[x] The court said the rule does not require that an initiative's provisions "interlock in a functional relationship." The provisions merely had to be "reasonably related to a common theme or purpose." But the court claimed that the precedents "clearly recognize that the single-subject requirement serves an important role in preserving the integrity and efficacy of the initiative process."

The court acknowledged that the first three provisions described above were reasonably germane to one another, but found that the fourth, the redistricting provision, caused the violation. "[W]hen viewed from a realistic and commonsense perspective, the provisions of Proposition 24 appear to embrace at least two distinct subjects—state officers' compensation and reapportionment."

The initiative proponent claimed that because each of the four provisions called for voter approval of certain actions, "voter involvement" provided a single subject. The court rejected that proposed subject as too broad, observing that if it were accepted, it would validate a proposal calling for voter approval of matters as disparate as "fisheries, student class-size reduction, and securities fraud." The court then turned to a more serious defense of the measure, that all the provisions related to the problem of "legislative self-interest."

Without resolving the question whether remedying legislative self-interest would itself be too broad a "subject" for an initiative measure, the court rejected the argument because it found that the provision relating to legislative salaries was unrelated to that subject. The court emphasized that under the existing system, set up in 1990, the salaries were set entirely by the commission, which was appointed by the governor without legislative confirmation. Because it would turn that commission into a body that only recommended salaries rather than establishing them, and would "reinvest legislators with a direct role in the process," albeit subject to further approval by the voters, Proposition 24 could not "be defended as involving the single subject or theme of imposing a voter-approval requirement in areas in which legislators may act in their own self-interest." The court was unimpressed with arguments that by setting up the commission in 1990 the legislators had made salary increases politically feasible by removing themselves from political accountability for the increases and that as a result legislative salaries had more than doubled from $49,000 to $99,000 in eight years. That increase might "simply reflect that the current figure is a fairer and more accurate measure of the appropriate compensation for such officers." [y] The proponent of Proposition 24 might disagree, but the fact remains that the salary provision was not aimed at a legislative conflict of interest. Therefore, although the provision "can be viewed as reasonably related to the objective of minimizing legislators' salaries, this argument does not establish that the provision is reasonably germane to the subject or objective of providing a check upon legislator self-interest."

---

x. Emphasis is removed in this and other quotations in this paragraph.

y. Many readers of this book and, for that matter, its editors, may agree that a doubling of salary from $49,000 to $99,000 over the course of the relatively noninflationary 1990s made the legislative salaries "fairer and more accurate." Supporters of Proposition 24 presumably thought otherwise. Is the court improperly smuggling its disagreement with the premises and policies of Proposition 24 into the question of whether the measure contains more than a single subject?—Eds.

Not surprisingly, the proponent relied heavily on *FPPC*, among other precedents. The court responded:

> In *FPPC*, the initiative at issue embodied a broad and comprehensive reform of campaign contributions and other political practices and activities, among other things creating a new entity—the Fair Political Practices Commission—to regulate and oversee political campaign activity. In concluding that the measure did not violate the single-subject rule, the court in *FPPC* found that the provisions of the measure were "reasonably germane to the subject of political practices," explaining that "the voters may not be limited to brief general statements but may deal comprehensively and in detail with an area of the law." Unlike Proposition 24, the measure challenged in *FPPC* did not seek to combine one major structural change in the state constitutional framework (such as the transfer of the reapportionment power from the legislative to the judicial branch) with unrelated measures (such as those reducing and revising the pay of legislators and other state officers), but instead embodied a comprehensive package of provisions that were reasonably related to a common theme of reforming political campaign practices and related activities of candidates, lobbyists, and proponents of ballot measures.

The court concluded:

> In sum, we conclude that the initiative measure challenged in this case violates the single-subject rule. The portion of Proposition 24 that proposes to transfer the power of reapportionment from the Legislature, where it traditionally has resided, to the Supreme Court, itself involves a most fundamental and far-reaching change in the law. Assuming ... that the transfer of this traditional legislative power to this court does not rise to the level of a constitutional revision that never may be accomplished by initiative but only by a constitutional convention or legislative submission, the proposal to adopt such a significant change nonetheless clearly represents a separate "subject" within the meaning of the single-subject rule upon which a clear expression of the voters' intent is essential. To permit the drafters of an initiative petition to combine a provision transferring the power of reapportionment from the Legislature to this court with unrelated provisions relating to legislators' pay would inevitably create voter confusion and obscure the electorate's intent with regard to each of the separate subjects included within the initiative, undermining the basic objectives sought to be achieved by the single-subject rule.

4. To repeat the questions put at the end of Note 2, does *Jones* change the standard relied upon by the majority in *FPPC* for applying the single subject rule to initiatives? Does the majority in *Jones* adopt the standard favored by Justice Manuel in his *FPPC* dissent? And a new question: After *Jones*, is the single subject rule for initiatives applied in the same manner as the single subject rule applicable to statutes enacted by the legislature?

5. *Jones* distinguishes *FPPC* on the ground that the "comprehensive package of provisions" in the Political Reform Act of 1974 "were reasonably related to a common theme of reforming political campaign practices and related activities of candidates, lobbyists, and proponents of ballot measures." Is that an accurate characterization of the Political Reform Act or of the rationale given by the *FPPC* court? One major provision of the Political Reform Act limits personal gifts by lobbyists to a variety of elected and non-elected state officials. Other provisions require thousands of state and local officials and civil servants to disclose

their personal economic interests and to disqualify themselves from governmental decisions when the decisions conflict with their personal economic interests. How closely "related" are these regulated activities to "political campaign practices"? Are they more closely related to campaign practices than the provisions of Proposition 24 are to legislative self interest?

More generally, why did the California Supreme Court uphold the Political Reform Act of 1974 and strike down Proposition 24?

6. The *Jones* court's rejection of the "legislative self-interest" defense of Proposition 24 has been criticized by Daniel H. Lowenstein, *Initiatives and the New Single Subject Rule*, 1 ELECTION LAW JOURNAL 35, 40 (2002):

> The court's reasoning is either thick-headed politically, disingenuous, or both. As the proponent of Proposition 24 argued to the court, control over salaries was transferred from the legislature to a commission precisely to enable salary increases. Legislators were afraid of voter retaliation if they voted to increase their own salaries, so they passed the job to a commission that was electorally unaccountable. In fact, under the commission system, legislative salaries doubled during an eight-year period of low inflation, from $49,000 to $99,000....

> [The court displayed] its utter inability or unwillingness to acknowledge the political impulse behind a measure like Proposition 24. As is very well known and very well documented, distrust of government is widespread, as is the belief that public officials care more about themselves and about special interests than about ordinary people. The many people who hold such beliefs are not simply concerned with particular conflicts of interest, narrowly defined. Their concern is that the system as a whole is set up to favor insiders. For those who share that perception of politics, a system for increasing legislators' salaries without requiring legislators to put their fingerprints on the increases is worse than a system that requires legislators to pay a political price for increases, even if the Supreme Court might characterize that system as one of conflict of interest. A proposal that *in practice* reduces legislators' pecuniary benefits, reduces their control over their own districts, and punishes them for late enactment of a budget is a coherent and unified measure animated by a single purpose.

7. In a portion of the *Jones* opinion not reprinted above, the majority described how the proponents of Proposition 24 drafted several different versions of the proposal, each combining the redistricting provision with various additional provisions. The inference the majority drew was that the proponents were motivated exclusively to change redistricting procedures and that the additional provisions — the legislative compensation provisions in the version that was finally proposed — were intended as "sweeteners" to attract voter support. Assuming the truth of the court's inference regarding the proponents' motivation, what relevance does it have, if any, to the single subject determination? Gerald Uelmen, *Handling Hot Potatoes: Judicial Review of California Initiatives after* Senate v. Jones, 41 SANTA CLARA LAW REVIEW 999 (2001), finds the court's discussion of the proponents' purposes significant and predicts that in future single subject cases, "the court will look to the alternative drafts and other evidence of 'manipulation,' which support a claim that 'logrolling' is going on."

8. In *Manduley v. Superior Court*, 27 Cal.4th 537, 117 Cal.Rptr.2d 168, 41 P.3d 3 (Cal. 2002), the California Supreme Court upheld a lengthy initiative that addressed sentencing of repeat criminal offenders (by amending California's "three-strikes" law), gang-related crime, and the juvenile justice system. The common purpose was said to be addressing

the problem of juvenile and gang-related crime, but not "simply to reduce crime generally." The court then said that this was a subject or goal that "clearly is not so broad that an unlimited array of provisions could be considered relevant thereto. Indeed, ... in previous decisions we have upheld initiatives containing various provisions related to even broader goals in the criminal justice system." The court was willing to overlook the fact that the juvenile procedure provisions applied to juveniles who were not members of gangs, that the majority of gang members affected by the gang provisions were not juveniles, and that changes to the three-strikes law applied equally to adults and juveniles.

Does *Manduley* represent a retreat from *Jones*? Not overtly, but then *Jones* did not overtly represent a departure from *FPPC* and other California cases. It is undoubtedly too early to say, especially in light of the criticism offered by some that aggressive application of the single-subject rule inevitably entails inconsistent and even arbitrary results. One possible clue to the different results in *Jones* and *Manduley* is the court's statement that the provisions in the latter case do not "comprise 'a most fundamental and far-reaching change in the law' that clearly represents a single subject upon which a clear expression of the voters' intent is essential," quoting from *Jones*. If initiatives are more likely to violate the single-subject rule because one or more of their provisions are "fundamental and far-reaching," then the single-subject rule will come to resemble the constitutional revision doctrine, discussed above.

9. If *Manduley* notwithstanding, *Jones* was more than an aberration, then it marked a dramatic change from a half century of deferential application of the single subject rule by the California Supreme Court. In Florida also, as we have seen, aggressive application of the rule began only after early decisions construed the rule liberally. Indeed, the only state whose Supreme Court appears to have applied the rule aggressively from the start is Colorado. Colorado has permitted initiatives for both statutes and constitutional amendments since 1910, but the single subject rule for initiatives was not added to the state constitution until 1994. COLORADO CONSTITUTION art. V, §1(5.5). The most distinctive feature of the rule in Colorado is the procedure established for single subject review. A Ballot Title Setting Board, consisting of the Secretary of State and representatives of the Attorney General and Legislative Legal Services Office, rules on whether each initiative that is filed complies with the single subject rule, a determination that is reviewable by the state supreme court before the petition is circulated. The result is that an inordinate number of single subject cases come before the court. In the words of Anne Campbell, *In the Eye of the Beholder: The Single Subject Rule for Ballot Initiatives*, in THE BATTLE OVER CITIZEN LAWMAKING 131, 159 (M. Dane Waters, ed., 2001):

> Literally dozens of initiated measures have been challenged on single subject grounds since the restriction first went into effect in 1995. In the vast majority of the cases the Title Setting Board's title and judgment that an initiative encompasses a single subject are overturned. Either the Attorney General, the Secretary of State, and the Deputy for Legislative Legal Services are uncharacteristically inept when it comes to determining the validity of initiatives, or the Colorado Supreme Court is extremely strict in its scrutiny of initiatives.

10. In Oregon and Montana, the state supreme courts have strengthened their single subject review at least as dramatically as in California, but they have done so under a distinct rule, known as the "separate vote" requirement. Oregon, which in 1902 became the third state to adopt the initiative, added a single subject rule in 1968. OREGON CONSTITUTION art. IV, §1(2)(d). When the Oregon Supreme Court first had occasion to apply the rule to an initiative, it adopted the same deferential standard that was applicable to laws passed by the legislature. *Oregon Education Association v. Phillips*, 727 P.2d 602 (Or.

1986), and that standard was reiterated as recently as 1997. See *State ex rel. Caleb v. Beesley*, 949 P.2d 724 (Or. 1997). The following year, in *Armatta v. Kitzhaber*, 959 P.2d 49 (Or. 1998), the Oregon Supreme Court struck down a "victims' rights" constitutional amendment that had been approved by voters in 1996. The measure embraced a single subject under the standards set forth in the cases just mentioned. Therefore, instead of relying on Article IV, §1(2)(d), the Oregon court invoked the substantially overlapping separate vote requirement. OREGON CONSTITUTION art. XVII, §1. That section requires that when "two or more amendments shall be submitted … to the voters of this state at the same election, they shall be so submitted that each amendment shall be voted on separately." Such provisions are common in state constitutions, but no court before *Armatta* appears to have given them separate significance when there was also an applicable single subject rule. Nevertheless, the Oregon court stated that the separate vote requirement imposes a more restrictive requirement than the single subject rule.

According to *Armatta*, a proposed constitutional amendment violates the separate vote requirement if the proposal "would make two or more changes to the constitution that are substantive and that are not closely related." The court acknowledged that the purposes of the single subject rule and the separate vote requirement are similar. "Both serve to ensure that the voters will not be compelled to vote upon multiple 'subjects' or multiple constitutional changes in a single vote." Why should there be two rules serving the same purpose? Is the separate vote requirement easier to apply than the single subject rule? Consider the following:

> The only discernible "purpose" behind *Armatta*'s construal of the separate vote requirement as more restrictive than the single subject rule was that doing so enabled the Oregon Supreme Court to strike down an initiative constitutional amendment that its members did not like while pretending not to reverse its long string of precedents liberally interpreting both the legislative and initiative single subject rules. In addition, the court's conjuring up of the separate vote doctrine permitted it to throw out a constitutional amendment while avoiding rewriting the single subject rule as applied to initiative and legislatively-enacted statutes. But this advantage is paid for at the cost of greatly confusing the law as it applies to constitutional amendments. For what is the difference between saying that provisions belong to the same "subject" and that they are "closely related"? Provisions belong to the same subject *because* they are related. [The two formulations] use different words to describe the same concept. The establishment of two rules applicable to constitutional amendments, purporting to be distinct but delineated with words having the same meaning, can only muddy the waters considerably. And on top of this problem, the court's new rule requires it to decide the obscure questions whether provisions in a constitutional amendment make one change or several, and whether such changes as are made are "substantive."

Lowenstein, *Initiatives and the New Single Subject Rule, supra.*

The Oregon Supreme Court continues to apply the separate vote requirement with rigor. In *Lehman v. Bradbury*, 37 P.3d 989 (Or. 2002), it struck down an initiative that had been approved ten years earlier (!) purporting to impose term limits on executive and legislative elected officials in state government as well as on members of Congress elected from Oregon. Another Oregon initiative proposed to amend the state constitution by adding this paragraph:

> Notwithstanding any other provisions of this Constitution, the people through the initiative process, or the Legislative Assembly by a three-fourths vote of both

Houses, may enact and amend laws to prohibit or limit contributions and expenditures, of any type or description, to influence the outcome of any election.

This initiative was removed from the ballot on the ground that it made two changes to the Constitution: "by removing campaign contributions [and expenditures?] from the class of expression protected by [the constitution's free speech provision, and] carving out an exception to the rule ... that the legislature may pass and amend legislation by a simple majority." *Meyer v. Bradbury*, 134 P.3d 1005 (Or. App. 2006).

The Montana Supreme Court followed in the footsteps of its Oregon counterpart. As in Oregon, the single subject rule was applied to initiatives as deferentially as to statutes passed by the legislature. See *Martin v. State Highway Commission*, 88 P.2d 41 (Mont. 1939). In *Marshall v. Cooney*, 975 P.2d 325 (Mont. 1999), the Montana Supreme Court relied expressly on *Armatta* and invoked the separate vote requirement for constitutional amendments to strike down an initiative approved by the voters the previous year, requiring new taxes and tax increases to be subject to voter approval. However, the Montana court does not seem to have adopted the *Armatta* standard for applying the separate vote requirement. The reason it gave for striking down the tax initiative was that it would have changed or affected several different provisions of the Montana constitution. In Oregon, that would not have been sufficient. Assuming that the effect on each constitutional provision constituted a separate "change," in Oregon it would still have to be shown that the changes were substantive and that they were not "closely related." The Montana standard appears to be easier than the Oregon standard to apply, but it may encourage drafters of amendments to ignore loose ends that might be serious but that could only be tied up by referring to two or more existing constitutional articles or sections.

Finally, Washington probably can be added to the list of states whose courts have applied the single subject rule with a new stringency. See *Amalgamated Transit Union Local 587 v. State*, 11 P.3d 762 (Wash. 2000), and *City of Burien v. Kiga*, 31 P.3d 659 (Wash. 2001).

11. Numerous commentators have called for more aggressive single subject review of initiatives. E.g., Dubois & Feeney, *supra*, at 148–49. Until a few years ago, only the Florida Supreme Court had heeded that call with any consistency. The foregoing materials show that recently California, Colorado, Montana, Oregon, and Washington have joined the ranks, though Montana and Oregon have done so under the guise of the separate vote requirement. No one can say whether these recent developments will prove to be an aberration or an enduring trend. For the time being, those who draft initiatives would be well advised to pay close attention to the single subject requirements. Even in states that have not yet shown signs of aggressive review, a state Supreme Court that for any reason is unsympathetic with a measure may find that the recent developments in the states mentioned make it both easy and tempting to follow suit.

III. Procedural Requirements and Judicial Review

Laws passed by the initiative process are subject to judicial review under the state and federal constitutions, and state constitutional amendments passed by initiative are reviewed under the United States Constitution. One contention has been that the initiative process itself violates Article IV, §4 of the Constitution, which provides in part: "The United States shall guarantee to every state in this union a republican form of government, and shall protect each of them against invasion...." Those who believe the initiative process violates this "Guaranty Clause" maintain, relying in part on Madison's *Federalist*

No. 10, that the "republican form of government' that is guaranteed must consist of a representative government, in contrast with a "democratic" form relying on direct action by the voters. The constitutionality of a tax adopted by initiative in Oregon was challenged on this theory in *Pacific States Tel. & Tel. Co. v. Oregon*, 223 U.S. 118 (1912). The Supreme Court declined to reach the merits of this challenge, holding instead that questions raised under the Guaranty Clause are nonjusticiable.

State courts generally have followed *Pacific States* and declined to pass on whether the initiative process violates the Guaranty Clause. A former member of the Oregon Supreme Court has argued that state courts should not be bound by the federal nonjusticiability doctrine. He contends that if state courts are unwilling to strike down the initiative process as a whole, they should declare that the submission to the voters of certain types of measures, particularly those that stigmatize particular groups, may violate the requirement of a republican form of government. See Hans A. Linde, *When Initiative Lawmaking Is Not "Republican Government": The Campaign Against Homosexuality*, 72 OREGON LAW REVIEW 19 (1993); Hans A. Linde, *Who Is Responsible for Republican Government?*, 65 UNIVERSITY OF COLORADO LAW REVIEW 709 (1994). However, Linde's theory was rejected by an Oregon appellate court, which refused to remove from the ballot an "anti-gay" initiative:

> [P]laintiffs claim that Article IV, section 4 of the United States Constitution, which guarantees to the states a republican form of government, prohibits the use of the initiative for various purposes, including, among others, to enact a state constitutional amendment that "imposes unique disabilities on an identifiable group of citizens," and to propose a measure that asks voters to act on the basis of passion and interest. Plaintiffs assert that the Guaranty Clause forbids states from holding an election by popular vote on any "proposed laws aimed at restricting the substantive rights of unpopular minority groups." ...
>
> Plaintiffs ... do not cite *Pacific States* or make any argument about why we are not bound by the United States Supreme Court's interpretation of the federal constitution.... [W]e conclude that the United States Supreme Court's interpretation of the Guaranty Clause as presenting a purely political question that is exclusively for Congress and not the courts to decide, precludes the courts of this state from entering any declaration about compliance with the Guaranty Clause.

Lowe v. Keisling, 882 P.2d 91 (Or.App. 1994). For criticism of the Linde approach, see Jesse H. Choper, *Observations on the Guarantee Clause—As Thoughtfully Addressed by Justice Linde and Professor Eule*, 65 UNIVERSITY OF COLORADO LAW REVIEW 741, 744–46 (1994).

Although court challenges to the initiative process itself have been stymied to date, it is not surprising that specific measures enacted through a process designed to produce innovative and controversial laws should stimulate numerous judicial challenges. One type of challenge, considered in the preceding Part, contends that the measure is not one that may be adopted by the initiative process. The other most common types of challenges are those charging a failure to comply with procedural requirements and those claiming that the measure or some portion of it is substantively unconstitutional under either the federal or (in the case of an initiative statute) state constitution. Following a brief overview of the procedural requirements for initiatives, we discuss briefly the difficult question of how strictly procedural requirements should be enforced against initiative proponents—and in election law generally—and other questions distinctive to substantive judicial review of initiatives.

Recall that Richard Ellis, in the excerpt that opened this chapter, noted the strong differences in the frequency of use of the initiative among the states that allow for it. The differences may be influenced by the fact that the procedural requirements for qualification vary considerably from state to state. Some of the more common requirements are described by David B. Magleby, *Direct Legislation in the States*, in Referendums around the World 218, 225–29 (David Butler & Austin Ranney, eds., 1994):

> One of the most important legal requirements in all direct legislation processes is the signature threshold and related requirements.[z] All forms of the initiative and popular referendum require that petitioners gather sufficient signatures from registered voters to meet a signature threshold, typically set as a proportion of the vote for governor in the previous gubernatorial election. Signature requirements range from a low of 2 percent in North Dakota for statutory initiatives to a high of 15 percent in Wyoming for statutory initiatives and [referendums.]
>
> The stringency of a state's signature threshold is inversely related to the frequency of measures qualifying for the ballot. Thirteen states have a geographic distribution requirement for signatures on direct legislation petitions. The intent of this requirement is to force petitioners to demonstrate support for their measure outside a few highly populated counties. The presence of a geographic distribution requirement appears to hamper proponents in getting their measures on the ballot.[a] ...
>
> Other important procedural rules include the time period a measure can remain in circulation, the process whereby the measure is given its official title and summary, limitations on the subject matter that may be part of the measure, and whether the vote necessary for success is a simple majority of those voting on the measure, a majority of those voting in the election, or a supermajority of 60 percent or more of those voting in the election. Initiative petitions typically may circulate for up to 120 days, but the time limitation can be as short as 50 days or as long as 360 days. [R]eferendum petitions typically have a shorter time period for circulation, averaging about 90 to 120 days.
>
> Because initiatives are proposed laws or constitutional amendments, they can be very lengthy and technical in their wording. All states provide a short summary of the proposal, and most states give a short title as well. In some states, the proponents are permitted to title and summarize their own measures, but in most states this task is left to election officials. The process of summarizing and titling initiatives is often challenged in court....
>
> The vote needed for enactment of direct legislation also varies among the states. Some states require a majority of those voting on the measure, others a majority of those voting in the election, and still others an extraordinary majority of those voting in the election. At least one state requires a majority vote in two consecutive elections for a constitutional initiative to take effect. In 1988

---

z. Aside from the number of signatures required, the requirement that most affects the number of initiatives that qualify appears to be the time period allowed for circulation. These two requirements can be stated in combined form as the number of signatures required per day. According to Susan A. Banducci, *Direct Legislation: When Is It Used and When Does It Pass?* in Citizens as Legislators, *supra*, at 109, 116, each reduction of 2,000 required signatures per day results, on average, in an additional three initiatives that qualify in an election cycle. — Eds.

a. But will such provisions bear constitutional scrutiny? Not according to *Idaho Coalition United for Bears v. Cenarrussa*, 342 F.3d 1073 (9th Cir. 2003), which struck down as a violation of the one person, one vote principle an Idaho requirement that initiative proponents obtain signatures from at least six percent of voters in at least half Idaho's counties. — Eds.

and 1990, for instance, Nevada voters approved a constitutional initiative banning income taxes. When Minnesota voted on whether to adopt the initiative process in 1980, 53.2 percent of those voting on the question voted for the proposal, but a quarter of a million persons who voted in the election failed to vote on the question. Hence the affirmative vote was only 46.7 percent of all voters in the election. Since Minnesota law requires that a majority of those voting in the election vote affirmatively for changes in the state constitution, the proposal for a statewide initiative failed.

Only registered voters may sign petitions, except in North Dakota, which does not have voter registration. There is a wide variation in how states verify petition signatures, ranging from verifying each signature to verifying random samples of signatures. States routinely check for duplicate signatures and evidence of petition fraud.

For valuable commentary on a variety of issues relating to implementation of the initiative process, see Philip L. Dubois & Floyd Feeney, LAWMAKING BY INITIATIVE (1998). A good source for the procedural requirements in any given state, as well as for much other information about direct democracy in the United States, is the web site of the Initiative and Referendum Institute of the University of Southern California, <http://www.iandrinstitute.org>.

1. Strict Enforcement or Substantial Compliance?

Proponents of a redistricting initiative in California filed their petitions for what became known as Proposition 77 in early May, 2005. In mid-May, an attorney for the proponents discovered that there were differences between the text of the proposal filed with the Attorney General (and provided by the Attorney General to the legislature and to the public via the internet) and the version that was circulated. The attorney did not disclose the discrepancies to anyone except an attorney for Republican Governor Schwarzenegger, who was supporting the initiative. On June 10, a Friday, the Secretary of State certified that Proposition 77 had qualified for the ballot. The following Monday, the attorney for the proponents disclosed the discrepancies to the Secretary of State. The latter, also a Republican, waited until early July before reporting the problem to the Attorney General, a Democrat, who promptly made the problem known to the public and later joined in a challenge to the placement of Proposition 77 on the ballot. In the meantime, the governor called a special election for November to vote on Proposition 77 and several other initiatives.

Opponents of Proposition 77, joined by the Attorney General, sought removal of the proposal from the ballot. The trial judge ruled in their favor and a divided appellate court affirmed. In the appellate court, both the majority and the dissenter issued long and thoughtful opinions. Several days later, the California Supreme Court restored Proposition 77, saying in a two-paragraph decision that in "the absence of a showing that the discrepancies ... were likely to have misled the persons who signed the initiative petition, we conclude that it would not be appropriate to deny the electorate the opportunity to vote on Proposition 77 at the special election to be held on November 8, 2005, on the basis of such discrepancies." *Costa v. S. C. (Lockyer)*, 39 Cal.Rptr.3d 168, 128 P.3d 149 (2005).

In taking that action, did the Supreme Court overrule the appellate court on the merits, or simply rule that the merits should be decided after the election? Apparently the latter. As we shall see, the court issued an opinion on the merits long after Proposition 77 had been defeated. Is pre-election review appropriate in cases such as this one when there is a procedural question whether the measure is properly qualified for the ballot? One reason for denying pre-election review, which will be stronger in some cases and weaker in others, is that shortness of time may preclude a thorough review of the issues raised. To the extent that was true in the Proposition 77 case, were the delays caused by the proponents' failure to disclose the discrepancies relevant?

As mentioned, the Supreme Court resolved the merits after Proposition 77 had been defeated at the polls. The court reaffirmed the correctness of keeping the initiative on the ballot. COSTA v. SUPERIOR COURT, 39 Cal.Rptr.3d 470, 128 P.3d 675 (2006). Although there were a few opponents who thought otherwise, most observers agreed that the differences between the two versions of the proposal were unlikely to affect anyone's support or opposition. On the other hand, they were more than mere typographical errors or trivial changes. The version circulated accidentally failed to reflect a final edit that had been performed by the attorney for the proponents. In addition to a large number of wording changes, a paragraph of the statement of purposes was omitted, and a deadline was changed. Should changes of this order—neither insignificant nor politically salient—have resulted in removal of the proposition from the ballot? The court wrote:

> Although it has been suggested that the issue before us turns on whether the controlling decisions require "strict" or "substantial" compliance with the applicable election laws, in some respects such an approach presents a potentially misleading dichotomy....
>
> [T]he governing cases ... have recognized that an unreasonably literal or inflexible application of constitutional or statutory requirements that fails to take into account the purpose underlying the particular requirement at issue would be inconsistent with the fundamental nature of the people's constitutionally enshrined initiative power ...

Whether or not the terminology is potentially misleading, the question of substantial compliance comes up in a wide variety of settings in election law and poses a difficult jurisprudential question that is worth serious consideration. An orderly electoral system requires a wide variety of deadlines, thresholds, and specific rules of all types. Those rules make it possible for all actors in the system to know what they must do to accomplish their objectives. Because humans are fallible, failure to comply with the rules in various ways and to various degrees is inevitable. Most such failures will be inadvertent but some will be calculated, and it usually will be difficult for outsiders to tell the difference.

Should a candidate or a proposition lose a position on the ballot, or should some other valuable right be lost, because of failure to comply with rules? As the California Supreme Court said, an overly literal or inflexible application of rules can lead to a system that sets traps and barriers for the unwary. But bending the rules can be unfair to those who have complied and can lead to a state of affairs in which requirements are more impressionistic than defined. Furthermore, when a court decides important electoral questions on the basis of "substantial compliance" rather than the rules, the judges face the serious danger that their judgment will be affected by their political preferences. Judges are not likely to say to themselves that they will let this proposition or this candidate on the ballot because they support the proposition or because the candidate belongs to the judges' party. But judges who are favorably disposed to a candidate or proposition are likely to be more receptive to the idea that removal is unreasonable. It did not escape notice that the majority of justices who kept Governor Schwarzenegger's redistricting initiative on the ballot were Republicans.

The problem of substantial compliance is not limited to initiatives. Another difficult area in which it often comes up is in applying the qualifications for candidates. A celebrated example drew national attention in 2002 when the Democratic incumbent candidate for the United States Senate in New Jersey, Robert Torricelli, withdrew from the race in September because of a scandal. A straightforward reading of the New Jersey election statute suggested that it was too late for the Democrats to name a replacement candidate. That reading was strengthened by the relevant precedents. Nevertheless, the New Jersey Supreme Court gave the statute a surprising reading, in order to allow the replacement candidate, former Senator Frank Lautenberg, to be put on the ballot. *New Jersey Democratic Party v. Samson*, 814 A.2d 1028 (2002). The court was strongly and expressly motivated by the importance of providing voters with a choice between two major-party candidates in such an important election, and therefore adopted a standard permitting substitution of candidates so long as it was administratively feasible. The fact that absentee ballots had already been sent out and some had been received back did not make substitution of candidates infeasible, though the court required the Democratic Party to pay the significant additional costs of remailing. It proved to be a good investment, as Lautenberg was elected. For critical commentary on the *Samson* decision, see William E. Baroni, Jr., *Administrative Unfeasibility: The Torricelli Replacement Case and the Creation of a New Election Standard*, 27 SETON HALL LEGISLATIVE JOURNAL 53 (2003).

Probably everyone would agree with the New Jersey court that it is much better to permit candidates from each of the major parties to appear on the ballot in a Senate election. The difficult question is whether that desirable goal justifies a decision that seems to bend the rules that had been laid down in advance. Will courts uniformly interpret or even bend election laws liberally to remove procedural obstacles to major-party candidates appearing on the ballot? Apparently not. A more recent decision in another celebrated matter illustrates the point. After Tom DeLay, Republican minority leader in the House, resigned his seat amidst scandal in 2006, he sought to withdraw his candidacy for re-election, informing election officials that he had ceased to be an inhabitant of Texas. Under Texas law, DeLay could withdraw from the ballot only for certain reasons, including his ineligibility for the office. Although the Constitution makes residency within the state a qualification for being elected to the House of Representatives, the Fifth Circuit observed that the fact that DeLay was currently living in another state would not prevent him from moving back to Texas before the election. States are not permitted to add qualifications to those specified in the Constitution. According to the Fifth Circuit, by ruling DeLay ineligible because of his *current* residency outside the state, Texas was creating an additional qualification to the requirement that he be a Texas resident *at the time he was elected*. Accordingly, for Texas to allow DeLay to withdraw was to recognize a qualification not stated in the Constitution, which Texas was prohibited from doing. As a result, the Republicans were unable to put their replacement candidate on the ballot and had to resort to a write-in campaign. They were unsuccessful, and the Democrats won a House seat that the Republicans ordinarily could have been expected to win. *Texas Democratic Party v. Benkiser*, 459 F.3d 582 (5th Cir. 2006).

Benkiser was a questionable decision, in part because it turned on the Qualifications Clause of the Constitution despite the fact that Texas was not enforcing a qualification. That is, it was not preventing a candidate from running. Rather, it was permitting an unwilling candidate not to run. Although it was doing so on the basis of a conclusion that the candidate was ineligible, it still was not imposing a qualification, even if that conclusion was erroneous. In any event, it would be difficult to maintain that the Fifth Circuit in *Benkiser* and the New Jersey court in *Samson* approached the prospect of an election without both major parties being permitted on the ballot in a similar spirit. Although the Democrats happened to be the beneficiary in both these cases, there is no reason to suppose that in the long run, either party is more likely than the other to benefit either from strict enforcement of the rules or from liberal interpretation. Still, juxtaposition of the two cases shows that there is no assurance of even-handedness, especially in the short run. Do these considerations cast doubt on the wisdom of *Samson* and, by extension, a decision like *Costa*? Or should we commend the California and New Jersey courts for their flexibility and criticize the Fifth Circuit for failing to follow suit?

2. Pre-Election Judicial Review

Challenges to initiative measures may be brought on a variety of grounds, which are likely to fall into three categories: the proposal violates a substantive provision of the United States Constitution or, if it is a proposed statute, of the state constitution; the proposal is not one that can be enacted by initiative, for example, because it violates the single subject rule; the measure did not receive enough signatures or otherwise did not satisfy the procedural requirements to qualify for the ballot, as the respondents claimed in *Costa*. The challenge may be brought before the election, seeking to have the measure removed from the ballot, or after the election, seeking to have it declared void. The question arises whether a case brought before the election is premature.[b]

In *Wyoming National Abortion Rights League v. Karpan*, 881 P.2d 282 (Wyo. 1994), pro-choice groups challenged an initiative containing provisions apparently unconstitutional under abortion rulings of the United States Supreme Court. The Wyoming court cited cases from a number of states holding that review of such substantive constitutional issues would have to wait until after the election. For example, the Arizona Supreme Court had written:

> Just as under the separation of powers doctrine the courts are powerless to predetermine the constitutionality of legislation, so also they are powerless to predetermine the validity of the substance of an initiated measure....

> In the absence of any constitutional or statutory directive to the contrary, the proper place to argue about the potential impact of an initiative is in the political arena, in speeches, newspaper articles, advertisements and other forums. The constitutionality of the interpretation or application of the proposed amendment will be considered by this court only after the amendment is adopted and the issue is presented by litigants whose rights are affected.

---

b. The California Supreme Court recently sought to clarify its policy on pre-election review in terms of the three categories just set forth. Presumptively, substantive constitutional challenges are not to be heard until and unless the measure is approved by the voters. Challenges, such as *Costa*, to the procedures by which the measure qualified for the ballot should be heard before the election, if feasible. Challenges based not on substantive constitutionality but on the assertion that the proposal is not the type of measure that can be adopted as an initiative are in-between cases. Unlike a claim that the measure has not properly qualified, there is no likelihood that such a challenge will be moot after the election. Thus, such a claim is "susceptible to resolution either before or after the election." *Independent Energy Producers Association v. McPherson*, 38 Cal.4th 1020, 44 Cal.Rptr.3d 644, (2006).

Tilson v. Mofford, 737 P.2d 1367 (Ariz. 1987). The Wyoming court acknowledged that Arizona's position was that of the majority of states and was supported by the pragmatic consideration that the constitutional issue could be avoided if the initiative measure were defeated at the polls. Nevertheless, the Wyoming court declined to follow the majority rule:

> We hold that an initiative statute that contravenes direct constitutional language, or constitutional language as previously interpreted by the highest court of a state or of the United States, is subject to review under the declaratory judgment statutes.... [I]f such a measure were clearly unconstitutional, there would be no purpose in submitting it to the electorate under the initiative process. The initiative process was designed and intended for a different purpose than simply providing a formal straw vote.

On the other hand, the court said it would remove a measure from the ballot only if it were unconstitutional in its entirety. The anti-abortion initiative had some provisions that were constitutional and therefore remained on the ballot.

Proposition 187 was a controversial California initiative in 1994. One of its provisions was to prohibit children who are aliens illegally in the United States from attending public schools. Virtually everyone, including most knowledgeable supporters of Proposition 187, agreed that the public school provision violated the Equal Protection Clause as interpreted in *Plyler v. Doe*, 457 U.S. 202 (1982). Some supporters of Proposition 187 hoped that if the prohibition were enacted, a majority on the Supreme Court might be persuaded to reverse *Plyler*. Other provisions of Proposition 187, denying various public services to unlawful aliens, did not obviously violate existing constitutional doctrine. Would the Wyoming court that decided *Wyoming National Abortion Rights League* have ruled Proposition 187 off the ballot? Would it have done so if Proposition 187 had contained only the public school provision and had been proposed solely for the purpose of challenging *Plyler*? Does this hypothetical suggest that state courts should or should not provide pre-election constitutional review of initiatives?

Suppose you are consulted by a group in Wyoming that has drafted a law to bar unlawful aliens from public schools, in the belief that a majority on the Supreme Court would be willing to reverse *Plyler v. Doe*. The group proposes to circulate the proposed law as an initiative. How would you advise them to draft their law to assure that the Wyoming courts will permit it to go on the ballot?

In *Nasberg v. City of Augusta*, 662 A.2d 227 (Me. 1995), the Supreme Judicial Court of Maine upheld the refusal of a city to place an initiative proposal on the ballot. A statute provided that after a public hearing, municipal officers were to file with the city clerk

> a report containing the final draft of the proposed amendment and a written opinion by an attorney admitted to the bar of this State that the proposed amendment does not contain any provision prohibited by the general laws, the United States Constitution or the Constitution of Maine.

The city attorney believed the charter amendment in question violated a provision of the Maine Constitution and the City Council voted not to place the proposal on the ballot unless the proponents obtained a written opinion by an attorney upholding the proposal's constitutionality. The court stated that the intent of requiring an attorney's letter was "to prevent clearly unconstitutional provisions from being placed on municipal ballots." Suppose, under a requirement similar to Maine's, a group collected sufficient signatures to qualify an initiative whose sole purpose was to deny the ability of illegal aliens to enroll in public schools. Suppose it is your belief that the proposal is plainly unconstitutional under *Plyler v. Doe*, but that there is a substantial chance that the Supreme Court would overrule *Plyler v. Doe* and that therefore the proposal would be upheld. Under these circumstances, would you sign an opinion letter of the sort called for by the Maine statute? What if you did not think it likely that the Supreme Court would overrule *Plyler v. Doe* but you believed that the Court misinterpreted the Constitution in that decision?

Like the state courts, commentators are divided on the desirability of pre-election review of substantive constitutional questions. Opponents of pre-election review contend that it "involves issuing an advisory opinion, violates ripeness requirements, undermines the policy of avoiding unnecessary constitutional questions, and constitutes unwarranted judicial interference with a legislative process." James D. Gordon III & David B. Magleby, *Pre-Election Judicial Review of Initiatives and Referendums*, 64 NOTRE DAME LAW REVIEW 298 (1989). Gordon and Magleby elaborate on their ripeness point:

> Suits attacking the substantive validity of ballot measures involve a double contingency which renders any injury speculative and uncertain. First, the measure may not pass; only a minority do.... Second, even if the measure passes, there may be no threat of enforcement. Prosecutors and other government officials often exercise their discretion not to enforce a law because of their doubts about its constitutionality, their perception of its social disutility, or their allocation of resources to other tasks. Also, there is often the possibility that if enacted, the law may be applied in a constitutional manner. Therefore, the uncertainty about the measure's passage and the government's implementation of it creates a double contingency which makes suits attacking the substantive constitutionality of ballot measures unripe for review.

Id. at 310.

William E. Adams, Jr., *Pre-Election Anti-Gay Ballot Initiative Challenges: Issues of Electoral Fairness, Majoritarian Tyranny, and Direct Democracy*, 55 OHIO STATE LAW JOURNAL 583, 626 (1994), calls for pre-election substantive review, at least where necessary to protect groups such as the targets of "anti-gay" initiatives from oppression:

> In response to the argument that the judicial system would be subjected to criticism for removing a measure before an election, one should consider the alternatives. If a court strikes a measure passed by the electorate, the criticism of the judicial system certainly will not be less. Going through the charade of an election to pass a measure that cannot withstand legal scrutiny not only wastes time, energy, and other resources, it also mocks the electoral system it supposedly honors. Voters are given the option of either choosing what is constitutionally permissible or having their choice rejected for its illegality. Further, holding these elections has a harmful impact upon those whom the courts should be protecting. The controversy and animosity surrounding these measures has generated violent acts against the groups they target. This should not be surprising because the attempt to give discrimination an official sanction simply reinforces the bigoted notion that the persons being denied protection are worthy of the scorn and abuse they receive.

Most of the controversy involves judicial review of initiatives for substantive constitutionality. Courts typically will engage in pre-election review of procedural questions relating to the qualification of an initiative. See Douglas Michael, Comment, *Judicial Review of Initiative Constitutional Amendments*, 14 UC DAVIS LAW REVIEW 461, 468–74 (1980). "Indeed," according to one court, "the procedures leading up to an election cannot be questioned after the people have voted, but instead the procedures must be challenged before the election is held." *Tilson v. Mofford*, 737 P.2d 1367 (Ariz. 1987). It is questionable how many states follow the Arizona rule that approval of an initiative by the electorate obviates post-election challenges to procedural inadequacies. For example, a Nebraska term-limits initiative was voided because under an unexpected interpretation of the state constitution, the proponents had collected too few signatures to qualify the measure. See *Duggan v. Beermann*, 515 N.W.2d 738 (Neb. 1994).

3. Hard Looks?

Some critics of the initiative process, including Derrick Bell, whose writings were quoted in Section I of this chapter, have proposed that when initiatives are challenged for substantive unconstitutionality, they should be subjected to particularly rigorous review. In the words of another proponent of this view, challenged initiatives should receive a "hard look." Julian N. Eule, *Judicial Review of Direct Democracy*, 99 YALE LAW JOURNAL 1503 (1990). Eule bases his argument on the constitutional system of checks and balances, which he contends is largely circumvented by the initiative process:

> Where courts are but *one* of many checks on majority preferences, they serve predominantly as a safety net to catch those grains of tyrannical majoritarianism that slip through when the constitutional filtering system malfunctions. Most arguments for judicial restraint, I shall suggest, ought not to be perceived as pro-majoritarian. They are more on the order of "everything in its place." The claim is not that majorities do not need checking, but that courts are just one of several "solutions" to majority factions. The delicate balance put in place by the Framers is disturbed as much by judicial hyperactivity as by judicial dormancy. Where, however, the filtering system has been removed, courts must play a larger role—not because direct democracy is unconstitutional, nor because it frequently produces legislation that we may find substantively displeasing or short sighted, but because the judiciary stands *alone* in guarding against the evils incident to transient, impassioned majorities that the Constitution seeks to dissipate.

Id. at 1525. Eule does not propose that the "hard look" should be applied to all initiatives:

> Because the harder look is prompted by a concern for individual rights and equal application of laws, it is principally in these areas that the courts should treat [initiatives] with particular suspicion. Where, on the other hand, the electorate acts to improve the processes of legislative representation, the justification for judicial vigilance is absent. Measures to enforce ethics in government, regulate lobbyists, or reform campaign finance practices pose no distinctive threat of majoritarian tyranny. These measures install new filters rather than seeking to bypass the existing ones....
>
> I am unwilling, however, to group alterations of government structure and reapportionment efforts in the category of governmental reform. Too often these "reforms" are a facade for disenfranchising minorities; courts should be watchful of such chicanery. Neither do I ignore the threat of majority tyranny in fiscal measures like taxation and spending limitations. The beneficiaries of these so-called taxpayer revolts are principally upper and upper-middle class white citizens. The brunt of the burdens, in contrast, is borne by the underrepresented poor and by racial minorities.

Id. at 1559–60. Even where the "hard look" is applicable, Eule would apply it in a flexible manner:

I do not perceive the concept of a hard judicial look to be a rigid one. Unlike "strict scrutiny" — a standard which on paper at least can be reduced to precise formulation — it is not intended to take on a unitary form. What I have in mind is more a general notion that courts should be willing to examine the realities of [initiatives] — that the unspoken assumptions about the legislative process that so often induce judicial restraint deserve less play in a setting where they are more fanciful. Sometimes a hard judicial look will take the form ... of a candid "We know what's going on here and we won't allow any of it." In other situations[,] recognition that the burden of plebiscitary action falls on political actors able to defend their interests in the popular arena, combined with a need to conserve limited judicial capital, will appropriately lead to a more modest form of review.

Id. at 1572–73.

Eule concedes that, to date at least, courts addressing the question almost invariably have said that for purposes of substantive constitutional review, it makes no difference whether a law was passed by the legislature or by initiative. *Id.* at 1505–06. Furthermore, his call for a "hard judicial look" has been criticized by some scholars. Lynn Baker, *Direct Democracy and Discrimination: A Public Choice Perspective*, 67 CHICAGO-KENT LAW REVIEW 707, 756 (1991), argues that the "hard look" is unnecessary:

[From Eule's discussion,] one might expect the United States Reports to be littered with instances in which the Court has upheld arguably racially discriminatory legislation enacted by plebiscites. In fact, the Court has heard only four cases in which plebiscitary legislation was challenged as racially discriminatory in violation of the Fourteenth Amendment. Applying the same equal protection standards that it applies to the enactments of representative bodies, the Court found that three of the four plebiscitary enactments violated the Equal Protection Clause.

Eule responds that although the Court *purported* to use the same equal protection standards it applies to laws produced by legislatures, in fact it may silently have been giving the initiatives in question a hard look. See Julian N. Eule, *Representative Government: The People's Choice*, 67 CHICAGO-KENT LAW REVIEW 777, 780–82 (1991).

The "hard look" approach is also criticized by Robin Charlow, *Judicial Review, Equal Protection and the Problem with Plebiscites*, 79 CORNELL LAW REVIEW 527 (1994), who contends that heightened judicial review is a misplaced remedy for the defects that critics find in the initiative process:

[T]he real problem that proponents of special judicial review have with plebiscites lies with the plebiscitary process, not with plebiscitary results. But, having concluded that the process, although undesirable, is constitutional, they are left with no constitutional recourse but to attack the results.

Either state and local plebiscitary processes are constitutional forms of lawmaking or they are not. If they are constitutional, dissatisfaction with the perceived efficacy of these processes for particular groups should not, in and of itself, warrant different constitutional treatment of the products of such processes. In other words, if plebiscitary lawmaking does not violate the Guarantee Clause, it should not matter whether state and local plebiscitary schemes fulfill the structural goals of the system prescribed for federal decisionmaking. That federal structure, and its tripartite, minority-protective safeguards, could have been, but was not, imposed on the states. In terms of the structure of state governments, the federal constitution imposes no limits beyond those contained in the Guarantee Clause. If that clause condemns only the extremes of state government excess (pure democracy and monarchy), then that is all the structural protection against state and local majoritarianism that minorities were intended to receive under the Constitution.

Id. at 556–57. Furthermore, Charlow contends that heightened judicial review of initiatives may hinder rather than further the constitutional system of checks and balances:

It could be said that the implementation of plebiscites was motivated by a desire to have the populace perform in a new power-checking capacity. Plebiscites grew out of the populist Progressive reform movement of the late 19th and early 20th centuries. According to conventional historical analyses, public lawmaking was approved in an effort to break the perceived stranglehold that certain minority, monied interests — in particular, wealthy corporations — had managed to secure over elected state and local legislatures. The plebiscitary institution, therefore, like conventional branches of government, has a tradition of serving a distinct part in assuring against the overconcentration of power in one governmental body.

... One purpose of separating power among the three branches of government was to diminish the influence of majoritarian faction expressed in the politically responsive legislative branch. The special review thesis seems to conclude that the populace must be checked by the judiciary precisely because it presents a similar and even more exceptional threat of majoritarian tyranny. Thus, with regard to the peril of majoritarian tyranny, plebiscites are supposedly worse than legislatures, and therefore more in need of judicial oversight or, conversely, less deserving of judicial deference.

However, it could also be said that separation of powers was adopted to prevent minoritarian tyranny, for example, in the unelected judicial branch. This would support the separation of powers explanation for the judiciary's deference to the will of the majoritarian legislative branch. Plebiscites were likewise instituted to allay minority faction, albeit in the usually majoritarian legislative body rather than in the judiciary. Therefore, if courts are supposed to defer to legislatures in order to guard against an excessive concentration of their own minoritarian power, perhaps they ought likewise defer to the electorate in the case of plebiscites in order to ensure against the overconcentration of minoritarian power within the usually majoritarian legislature. Indeed, in theory plebiscites embody the will of the ultimate politically responsive body — the electorate itself — so courts should defer to them even more readily than they do to legislative action in order to avoid minority tyranny.

Id. at 580–82. In her conclusion, Charlow says that she agrees with Bell, Eule, and other critics, that the initiative process creates dangers for some groups, but she contends that heightened substantive constitutional review of initiatives is neither called for nor an adequate solution. She proposes instead that the initiative process be improved or, if it is perceived to be sufficiently dangerous, that it be scrapped. Alternatively, she suggests that remedies may be found within the political process, by defeating oppressive initiative proposals, or repealing those that are enacted. Finally, she suggests that if discriminatory laws still survive, the solution is in improvement of equal protection doctrine generally, rather than heightened application of the Equal Protection Clause only to laws that were enacted by initiative. *Id.* at 625–30.

IV. Financing Qualification Drives

Meyer v. Grant

486 U.S. 414 (1988)

Justice STEVENS delivered the opinion of the Court.

In Colorado [o]ne section of the state law regulating the initiative process makes it a felony to pay petition circulators. The question in this case is whether that provision is unconstitutional....

I ...

Under Colorado law, ... the proponents of [a measure] have six months to obtain the necessary signatures, which must be in an amount equal to at least five percent of the total number of voters who cast votes for all candidates for the Office of Secretary of State at the last preceding general election. If the signature requirements are met, the petitions may be filed with the Secretary of State, and the measure will appear on the ballot at the next general election.

State law requires that the persons who circulate the approved drafts of the petitions for signature be registered voters. Before the signed petitions are filed with the Secretary of State, the circulators must sign affidavits attesting that each signature is the signature of the person whose name it purports to be and that, to the best of their knowledge and belief, each person signing the petition is a registered voter. The payment of petition circulators is punished as a felony.

Appellees are proponents of an amendment to the Colorado Constitution that would remove motor carriers from the jurisdiction of the Colorado Public Utilities Commission. In early 1984 they obtained approval of a title, submission clause, and summary for a measure proposing the amendment and began the process of obtaining the 46,737 signatures necessary to have the proposal appear on the November 1984 ballot. Based on their own experience as petition circulators, as well as that of other unpaid circulators, appellees concluded that they would need the assistance of paid personnel to obtain the required number of signatures within the allotted time. They then brought this action ... against the Secretary of State and the Attorney General of Colorado seeking a declaration that the statutory prohibition against the use of paid circulators violates their rights under the First Amendment.

[The trial court upheld the law, but was reversed by the Tenth Circuit Court of Appeals.][3]

II

We fully agree with the Court of Appeals' conclusion that this case involves a limitation on political expression subject to exacting scrutiny. *Buckley*....

---

3. In support of its conclusion that the prohibition against the use of paid circulators did not inhibit the placement of initiative measures on the general ballot, the District Court compared Colorado's experience with that of 20 States which have an initiative process but do not prohibit paid circulators. It noted that since 1910, Colorado has ranked fourth in the total number of initiatives placed on the ballot. This statistic, however, does not reject the possibility that even more petitions would have been successful if paid circulators had been available, or, more narrowly, that these appellees would have had greater success if they had been able to hire extra help. As the District Court itself noted, "the evidence indicates [appellees'] purposes would be enhanced if the corps of volunteers could be augmented by a cadre of paid workers."

The circulation of an initiative petition of necessity involves both the expression of a desire for political change and a discussion of the merits of the proposed change. Although a petition circulator may not have to persuade potential signatories that a particular proposal should prevail to capture their signatures, he or she will at least have to persuade them that the matter is one deserving of the public scrutiny and debate that would attend its consideration by the whole electorate. This will in almost every case involve an explanation of the nature of the proposal and why its advocates support it.[4] Thus, the circulation of a petition involves the type of interactive communication concerning political change that is appropriately described as "core political speech."

The refusal to permit appellees to pay petition circulators restricts political expression in two ways: First, it limits the number of voices who will convey appellees' message and the hours they can speak and, therefore, limits the size of the audience they can reach. Second, it makes it less likely that appellees will garner the number of signatures necessary to place the matter on the ballot, thus limiting their ability to make the matter the focus of statewide discussion....

Appellants argue that even if the statute imposes some limitation on First Amendment expression, the burden is permissible because other avenues of expression remain open to appellees and because the State has the authority to impose limitations on the scope of the state-created right to legislate by initiative. Neither of these arguments persuades us that the burden imposed on appellees' First Amendment rights is acceptable.

That appellees remain free to employ other means to disseminate their ideas does not take their speech through petition circulators outside the bounds of First Amendment protection. Colorado's prohibition of paid petition circulators restricts access to the most effective, fundamental, and perhaps economical avenue of political discourse, direct one-on-one communication. That it leaves open "more burdensome" avenues of communication, does not relieve its burden on First Amendment expression. The First Amendment protects appellees' right not only to advocate their cause but also to select what they believe to be the most effective means for so doing.

---

4. The record in this case demonstrates that the circulation of appellees' petition involved political speech. Paul Grant, one of the appellees, testified about the nature of his conversations with voters in an effort to get them to sign the petition:

"[T]he way we go about soliciting signatures is that you ask the person—first of all, you interrupt the person in their walk or whatever they are doing. You intrude upon them and ask them, 'Are you a registered voter? ...' If you get a yes, then you tell the person your purpose, that you are circulating a petition to qualify the issue on the ballot in November. and tell them what about, and they say, 'Please let me know a little bit more.' Typically, that takes maybe a minute or two, the process of explaining to the persons that you are trying to put the initiative on the ballot to exempt Colorado transportation from [State Public Utilities Commission] regulations.

"Then you ask the person if they will sign your petition. If they hesitate, you try to come up with additional arguments to get them to sign.... [We try] to explain the not just deregulation in this industry, that it would free up to industry from being cartelized, allowing freedom from moral choices, price competition for the first time, lowering price costs, which we estimate prices in Colorado to be $150 million a year in monopoly benefits. We have tried to convey the unfairness and injustice of the existing system, where some businesses are denied to go into business simply to protect the profits of existing companies.

"We tried to convey the unfairness of the existing system, which has denied individuals the right to start their own businesses. In many cases, individuals have asked for an authority and been turned down because huge corporate organizations have opposed them."

This testimony provides an example of advocacy of political reform that falls squarely within the protections of the First Amendment.

Relying on *Posadas de Puerto Rico Associates v. Tourism Co. of Puerto Rico*, 478 U.S. 328 (1986), Colorado contends that because the power of the initiative is a state-created right, it is free to impose limitations on the exercise of that right. That reliance is misplaced. In *Posadas* the Court concluded that "the greater power to completely ban casino gambling necessarily includes the lesser power to ban advertising of casino gambling." The Court of Appeals quite properly pointed out the logical flaw in Colorado's attempt to draw an analogy between the present case and *Posadas*. The decision in *Posadas* does not suggest that "the power to ban casino gambling entirely would include the power to ban public discussion of legislative proposals regarding the legalization and advertising of casino gambling." Thus it does not support the position that the power to ban initiatives entirely includes the power to limit discussion of political issues raised in initiative petitions. And, as the Court of Appeals further observed:

> *Posadas* is inapplicable to the present case for a more fundamental reason — the speech restricted in *Posadas* was merely "commercial speech which does 'no more than propose a commercial transaction....'" Here, by contrast, the speech at issue is "at the core of our electoral process and of the First Amendment freedoms," *Buckley* — an area of public policy where protection of robust discussion is at its zenith.

We agree with the Court of Appeals' conclusion that the statute trenches upon an area in which the importance of First Amendment protections is "at its zenith." For that reason the burden that Colorado must overcome to justify this criminal law is well-nigh insurmountable.

III

We are not persuaded by the State's arguments that the prohibition is justified by its interest in making sure that an initiative has sufficient grass roots support to be placed on the ballot, or by its interest in protecting the integrity of the initiative process. As the Court of Appeals correctly held, the former interest is adequately protected by the requirement that no initiative proposal may be placed on the ballot unless the required number of signatures has been obtained.

The State's interest in protecting the integrity of the initiative process does not justify the prohibition because the State has failed to demonstrate that it is necessary to burden appellees' ability to communicate their message in order to meet its concerns. The Attorney General has argued that the petition circulator has the duty to verify the authenticity of signatures on the petition and that compensation might provide the circulator with a temptation to disregard that duty. No evidence has been offered to support that speculation, however, and we are not prepared to assume that a professional circulator — whose qualifications for similar future assignments may well depend on a reputation for competence and integrity — is any more likely to accept false signatures than a volunteer who is motivated entirely by an interest in having the proposition placed on the ballot.

Other provisions of the Colorado statute deal expressly with the potential danger that circulators might be tempted to pad their petitions with false signatures. It is a crime to forge a signature on a petition, to make false or misleading statements relating to a petition, or to pay someone to sign a petition. Further, the top of each page of the petition must bear a statement printed in red ink warning potential signatories that it is a felony to forge a signature on a petition or to sign the petition when not qualified to vote and admonishing signatories not to sign the petition unless they have read and understand the proposed initiative. These provisions seem adequate to the task of minimizing the risk of improper conduct in the circulation of a petition, especially since the risk of fraud or corruption, or the appearance thereof, is more remote at the petition stage of an initiative than at the time of balloting.

"[L]egislative restrictions on advocacy of the election or defeat of political candidates are wholly at odds with the guarantees of the First Amendment." *Buckley*. That principle applies equally to "the discussion of political policy generally or advocacy of the passage or defeat of legislation." *Id*. The Colorado statute prohibiting the payment of petition circulators imposes a burden on political expression that the State has failed to justify. The Court of Appeals correctly held that the statute violates the First and Fourteenth Amendments. Its judgment is therefore affirmed.

Notes and Questions

1. Is the Colorado ban on paid petition circulators properly viewed as a restriction on speech or as a method of self-regulation by the state to determine which measures will be placed on the ballot? Consider a hypothetical statute that permits proponents of initiatives to employ paid circulators but requires the circulators to indicate on the face of the petitions that they have been paid. When the petitions are filed, the signatures acquired by paid circulators are ignored for purposes of determining whether the measure has qualified for the ballot. Paid circulators are required to disclose this fact to signers, who remain free to sign a petition circulated by a volunteer.

Would the hypothetical statute violate the First Amendment? Does it prohibit anyone from engaging in any speech activity or from paying others to engage in speech activity? As a practical matter, are its effects any different from the statute struck down in *Meyer v. Grant*? See Daniel Hays Lowenstein & Robert M. Stern, *The First Amendment and Paid Initiative Petition Circulators: A Dissenting View and a Proposal*, 17 HASTINGS CONSTITUTIONAL LAW QUARTERLY 175, 184–87 (1989).

2. In recent years, Congress has inserted a provision known as the Barr Amendment into the District of Columbia appropriation law. The Barr Amendment prohibits the District from spending money "to enact or carry out" any law legalizing or reducing penalties associated with certain controlled substances, including marijuana. In *Marijuana Policy Project v. District of Columbia Board of Elections and Ethics*, 191 F.Supp.2d 196 (D.D.C. 2002), plaintiffs sought to circulate an initiative petition that would legalize marijuana under some circumstances. The D.C. Board of Elections and Ethics refused to certify the petition for circulation because the attendant expenses would violate the Barr Amendment. The court acknowledged that Congress had power to prevent the implementation of the proposed initiative, but relied on *Meyer v. Grant* to require the Board to permit plaintiffs to seek to qualify their measure for the ballot. Were plaintiffs' speech rights infringed? The District Court thought so: "Circulation of a Board-approved petition necessarily involves expressive interaction with the public." But the D.C. Circuit disagreed in *Marijuana Policy Project v. United States*, 304 F.3d 82 (D.C. Cir. 2002): The Barr Amendment "restricts no speech; to the contrary, medical marijuana advocates remain free to lobby, petition, or engage in other First Amendment-protected activities to reduce marijuana penalties. The Barr Amendment merely requires that, in order to have legal effect, their efforts must be directed to Congress rather than to the D.C. legislative process." Is the Court of Appeals' reasoning consistent with *Meyer*?

3. In footnote 4, Justice Stevens presents one version of the typical signature solicitation process. Here is another, given by the late Ed Koupal, who was head of an organi-

zation that had considerable success using volunteer circulators to qualify measures for the ballot in California in the early 1970's, quoted in Carla Lazzareschi Duscha, *The Koupals' Petition Factory*, 6 CALIFORNIA JOURNAL 83, 83 (1975):

> "Generally the people who are out getting signatures are too god-damned interested in their ideology to get the required number in the required time," Koupal said. "We use the hoopla process. First, you set up a table with six petitions taped to it and a sign in front that says, SIGN HERE. One person sits at the table. Another person stands in front. That's all you need—two people.
>
> "While one person sits at the table, the other walks up to people and asks two questions. (We operate on the old selling maxim that two yesses make a sale.) First, we ask if they are a registered voter. If they say yes, we ask them if they are registered in that county. If they say yes to that, we immediately push them up to the table where the person sitting points to a petition and says, 'Sign this.' By this time the person feels, 'Oh, goodie, I get to play,' and signs it. If a table doesn't get 80 signatures an hour using this method, it's moved the next day."
>
> Koupal said that about 75 percent of the people sign when they're told to. "Hell no, people don't ask to read the petition and we certainly don't offer," he added. "Why try to educate the world when you're trying to get signatures?"

From the standpoint of the First Amendment, does it matter whether this process described by Ed Koupal, or the process described by Paul Grant in footnote 4 of the Stevens opinion is more typical? See *Buckley v. American Constitutional Law Foundation*, 525 U.S. 182, 211 n.3 (1999) (Thomas, J., concurring) (noting anecdotal evidence that petition circulators do not discuss merits of initiatives in any great depth, but commenting that "[i]n my view, the level of scrutiny cannot turn on the content or sophistication of a political message.").

4. After reviewing social science studies and a variety of anecdotal information regarding the petition circulation process, Lowenstein & Stern, *supra*, 17 HASTINGS CONSTITUTIONAL LAW QUARTERLY at 199–200, drew the following conclusions:

> The degree to which potential signers agree with the merits of a petition is a significant but not crucial factor in their willingness to sign. Many other considerations go into the decision. These considerations undoubtedly are more important for some people, such as those particularly susceptible to casual social pressure, than for others. Petition circulators, whether professional or volunteer, can succeed, if they are willing to put in the effort, by relying on two general principles. First, they can use their experience and training to attempt to create a situation in which the social pressure to sign is relatively high. Second, they can adapt to the need for large numbers of signatures by ignoring potential signers for whom persuasion requires more than a few seconds....
>
> As to the signers, if the question is whether as a group they are more likely to support the substance of the petition than a comparable group of nonsigners, the answer is yes. If the question is whether the ability to obtain signatures is a reasonably accurate measure of public support for the substance of the petition, the answer is no. The latter point is vividly demonstrated by this statistic: One petition management firm was retained in a total of fifty-three petition drives through 1988, and fifty-two of these qualified for the ballot. The statement that

under present conditions, anyone willing to put up the funds can buy a place on the ballot, is no hyperbole.

If these conclusions are valid empirically, what affect do they have, if any, on the constitutional analysis in *Meyer v. Grant*? See *id.* at 200–205.

5. Is Justice Stevens correct in arguing that because the Colorado statute "makes it less likely that appellees will garner the number of signatures necessary to place the matter on the ballot, thus limiting their ability to make the matter the focus of statewide discussion," it follows that the statute restricts political expression? Does it restrict political expression if a state does not have an initiative process at all? If Colorado wished to raise the number of required signatures to qualify an initiative for the ballot, would it have to justify its action under the First Amendment?

6. In California (and increasingly in some other states that use the initiative process) the reliance on professional circulators to qualify initiatives has become immense. Consider the following from a report issued by a non-profit research organization:

> Professional signature-gathering firms now boast that they can qualify *any* measure for the ballot (one "guarantees" qualification) if paid enough money for cadres of individual signature gatherers, and their statement is probably true. Any individual, corporation or organization with approximately $1 million to spend can now place any issue on the ballot and at least have a chance of enacting a state law. Qualifying an initiative for the statewide ballot is thus no longer so much a measure of general citizen interest as it is a test of fundraising ability. Instead of waging volunteer petition campaigns for broad-based grassroots support, initiative proponents now engage in intense searches for large contributors willing to fund increasingly expensive paid circulation drives....
>
> In recent elections, *one* business organization or individual has single-handedly qualified an initiative for the ballot. In 1984, for example, Scientific Games of Atlanta, a manufacturer of lottery tickets, contributed 99.6% ($1.1 million) of the total qualification funding raised ($1.11 million) to qualify Proposition 37 (the successful lottery initiative) for the ballot. In 1988, San Francisco Bay Area attorney Jim Rogers, with approximately $300,000 (93% of the total $324,000 raised) qualified his advertising disclosure Proposition 105 for the ballot. In 1990, Harold Arbit contributed nearly $1 million to qualify Proposition 130 ("Forests Forever") for the ballot and in 1991 Frank Wells contributed over $500,000 to re-qualify the forest protection initiative.

California Commission on Campaign Financing, Democracy By Initiative 265 (1992).

Elizabeth Garrett, *Money, Agenda Setting, and Direct Democracy*, 77 Texas Law Review 1845 (1999), argues that the widespread reliance on professional circulators for the qualification of initiatives in many states turns the initiative into a preserve for well-funded groups. But Daniel H. Lowenstein, *Election Law Miscellany: Enforcement, Access to Debates, Qualification of Initiatives*, 77 Texas Law Review 2001, 2002–08 (1999), criticizes the system's reliance on professional circulation firms for the opposite reason, that the efficiency of the firms and the consequent low cost of qualifying a measure result in qualification of proposals that have not demonstrated widespread support.

7. Asserting that "it can be both too hard and too easy to qualify an initiative," Lowenstein & Stern, *supra*, propose a two-tier system, in which signatures obtained by volunteer circulators would weigh more heavily toward qualification than signatures obtained

by professionals.[c] 17 Hastings Constitutional Law Quarterly at 220–23. A state could then lower the required number of signatures, making it easier for all-volunteer groups to qualify their measures, while making it substantially more difficult for groups relying solely on professionals. What values would be served and disserved by this proposal? Is the proposal constitutional?

The Lowenstein-Stern proposal is criticized by Philip L. Dubois & Floyd F. Feeney, Improving the California Initiative Process: Options for Change 84 (1992):

> It could be cumbersome to administer in practice, susceptible to fraud and deception by those seeking the bonus, difficult to enforce, and possibly unconstitutional on equal-protection grounds by valuing some signatures more than others....
>
> Even assuming that the Lowenstein/Stern proposal could be administered, enforced, survive constitutional challenge, and be effective, it suffers from a more fundamental flaw: it fails to come to grips with the fact that signatures, whether gathered by volunteers or paid solicitors, are simply not meaningful gauges of public discontent or even interest.

Dubois and Feeney suggest a different means of assuring that signatures are a "meaningful gauge," which they believe requires separating the solicitation of signatures from the collection of signatures:

> Solicitors could be limited to discussing ballot measures with prospective signators and to distributing the official ballot title and summary along with appropriate campaign literature urging voters to support placing the matter on the ballot. Petitions for signatures could then be made available for voters to sign in a number of prominent public locations, such as state and local government offices, public libraries, and fire stations. Alternatively, solicitors might provide voters with a stamped or unstamped postcard bearing the official title and summary with a space for voters to provide their names and addresses as required by law, preaddressed to the county registrar of voters where it would be sent for verification.

Id. at 86. Is the Dubois-Feeney proposal an improvement on the Lowenstein-Stern proposal? Is the Dubois-Feeney proposal more enforceable? Can the Dubois-Feeney proposal be improved?

8. Another method of circulating initiative petitions is by direct mail. Of course, this method is very expensive, but if the proposal has sufficiently intense support, it sometimes is possible to raise sufficient funds through the mailings to pay for the circulation drive as it goes along. Some measures were qualified in this manner in California in the period around 1980, and many thought this would be the wave of the future. However, it has proved difficult to raise adequate funds for most proposals, so that in most cases direct mail has been at best a supplemental means of obtaining signatures. From a public interest standpoint, is the use of direct mail better or worse than the use of volunteer circulators? Professional circulators? See Thomas E. Cronin, Direct Democracy 216–17 (1989); Lowenstein & Stern, *supra*, 17 Hastings Constitutional Law Quarterly at 205–9.

9. If it is unconstitutional to ban paid circulators, is it constitutional to regulate the *manner* in which they are paid? The North Dakota legislature passed a statute in 1987 allow-

---

c. Under this proposal, a person who signed a professionally circulated petition would be permitted later to sign a petition circulated by a volunteer, in order to receive the benefit of the higher weighting.

ing petition circulators to be paid, but prohibiting payment on a per signature basis. The United States Court of Appeals for the Eighth Circuit upheld the law on grounds that the state legislature could have concluded that payments per signature (rather than payments by the hour) increased the risk of fraud. *Initiative and Referendum Institute v. Jaeger*, 241 F.3d 614 (8th Cir. 2001); see also *Prete v. Bradbury*, 438 F.3d 949 (9th Cir. 2006) (upholding similar measure passed by Oregon voters); *Person v. New York State Board of Elections*, 467 F.3d 141 (2d Cir. 2006) (upholding similar New York measure). The Sixth Circuit, however, recently struck down an Ohio law barring the payment of initiative circulators on any basis other than time-worked. *Citizens for Tax Reform v. Deters*, 518 F.3d 375 (6th Cir. 2008). The court held the Ohio law was more onerous than the other laws and therefore deserving of stricter scrutiny:

> [Under the Ohio law petition circulating companies] could not give a bonus to a circulator based on productivity or longevity. [A company] could not set a minimum signature requirement because, in order to earn a day's wages, for example, a circulator would both have to work a certain number of hours and have to collect a certain number of signatures, thereby partially tying earnings to the number of signatures. Arguably, [a company] could not terminate a circulator who consistently did not collect enough signatures because, again, to earn a wage (and keep the job) the circulator would, among other things, have to collect a minimum number of signatures. Furthermore, [a company] could not base a circulator's earnings on the geographic area covered (pay per city block, for example). It is even unclear whether [the company] could pay a salary to a circulator unless it strictly limited the hours worked. If, instead, a salaried circulator were responsible for completing a number of duties each day or week regardless of the number of hours worked (i.e., the typical plight of the salaried worker), then in a sense the circulator would be compensated on a basis other than strictly time worked.

The court declined to reach the question whether a law similar to North Dakota's or Oregon's would be constitutional.

Though these laws were passed in the name of fraud prevention, no doubt some supporters believe the law will decrease the amount of initiative activity, because it will be more expensive to collect signatures (why?). Should this intent be relevant to the constitutional inquiry?

10. States place other restrictions on the circulation of initiatives besides restricting payment to circulators. One common requirement is that the circulator reside in the county in which he or she circulates the petition. Is such a requirement unconstitutional under *Meyer v. Grant*? In *Buckley v. American Constitutional Law Foundation*, 525 U.S. 182, 197 (1999) [*ACLF*], the Supreme Court struck down a Colorado law requiring that circulators be registered voters. In a majority opinion by Justice Ginsburg, the Court stated that the registration requirement limited speech because "the choice not to register implicates political thought and expression." *Id.* at 183–84.[d] The Court held that this limit on speech was not justified by the state's interest in insuring that lawbreaking circulators were amenable to a subpoena in the state. According to the Court, that interest was met by a requirement that circulators sign an affidavit listing their addresses and by a resi-

---

d. Is this statement inconsistent with *Burdick v. Takushi*, 504 U.S. 428 (1992)? In *Burdick*, the Court rejected the idea that voting has an expressive value holding that ballots are for choosing candidates, not fora for political expression. See Adam Winkler, Note, *Expressive Voting*, 68 NYU LAW REVIEW 330 (1993).

dence requirement, not challenged in the case. *Id.* at 197. After *ACLF*, courts have upheld residency requirements on grounds that they prevent campaign fraud. *Initiative and Referendum Institute v. Jaeger, supra; Kean v. Clark*, 56 F.Supp.2d 719, 733 (S.D. Miss. 1999).

The *ACLF* Court did not consistently apply "exacting" or strict scrutiny to its constitutional analysis, as *Meyer* appears to require. Justice Thomas, concurring in the judgment in *ACLF*, argued that strict scrutiny should be applied to all the issues in the case. 525 U.S. at 206 (Thomas, J., concurring in the judgment). The *ACLF* court also declined to reach the question whether paid circulators could be compelled to wear a badge disclosing whether the circulator is paid or a volunteer. Garrett, *supra*, 77 TEXAS LAW REVIEW at 1888, believes disclosure of such information might help voters identify whether signature gatherers are part of a "grassroots movement" rather than representatives of "special interests." She argues:

> The effect of disclosure on public behavior could be enhanced if social norms developed that stigmatized campaigns using paid workers. Through advertisements and other methods, private reform groups could convince the public that paid workers are the tools of monied special interest groups. Thus, PAID would signify more than a professional worker; it would also identify someone working for groups with interests that conflict with the public good. Reformers could work to associate volunteer circulators with the values of dedication to a cause and civic-mindedness. In this way, the identification tags could play into a social norm that would impede groups relying on paid workers.

Given the empirical evidence that even "grassroots" organizations like Common Cause rely upon paid circulators, what effect would stigmatization of paid workers (assuming it could be developed) have on the initiative process as a whole? Is there any reason to believe that ordinary people (in contrast to law professors) will think there is anything wrong with a worker being paid?

11. For a survey of the qualification requirements in states that use the initiative and referendum processes, see David B. Magleby, *Ballot Access for Initiatives and Popular Referendums: The Importance of Petition Circulation and Signature Validation Procedures*, 2 JOURNAL OF LAW & POLITICS 287 (1985).

12. Section 203 of the Voting Rights Act requires a jurisdiction with significant numbers or percentages of members of a "single language minority [who] are limited-English proficient" to make available translations into that language when it "provides any registration or voting notices, forms, instructions, assistance, or other materials or information relating to the electoral process, including ballots." In *Padilla v. Lever*, 429 F.3d 910 (9th Cir. 2005), a federal appellate panel ruled that petitions to recall a school board member in Santa Ana, California, were invalid because neither the petitions nor required accompanying material—a statement of the reasons for the recall, and a rebuttal provided by the board member—had been translated into Spanish.

This was, to say the least, an innovative ruling. Two other circuits had held that initiative petitions were not subject to the translation requirement. *Montero v. Meyer*, 861 F.2d 603 (10th Cir. 1988); *Delgado v. Smith*, 861 F.2d 1489 (11th Cir. 1988). The majority in *Padilla* regarded the plain language of the statute as covering recall petitions, especially when reinforced by the general practice of broad interpretation of the Voting Rights Act as a remedial statute. The dissenting judge maintained that the petitions and accompanying documents are "provided" by the proponents, not by the jurisdiction. The majority contended that the requirement that election officials approve the format of the petitions was sufficient to support the conclusion that the jurisdiction "provided" the document. The majority did not think the burden on proponents could override the command of the Voting Rights Act. As the dissent pointed out, the burden can be substantial. If it had been an Orange County official rather than a school board member who was being recalled, the proponents would have had to provide translations of their documents into Spanish, Vietnamese, Korean, and Chinese. Perhaps the dissent's most interesting argument amounted to the contention that the translation requirement would serve little purpose:

> Those who circulate recall petitions ... have no incentive to exclude anyone from signing their petitions. There is no way, and no need, to vote "no" on a recall petition itself; those eligible voters who do not sign, for any reason, are effectively counted as "no" votes on the question of whether to have an election [because the required number of signatures is calculated as a percentage of total registered voters]. The purpose, therefore, of those who circulate recall petitions is to obtain as many signatures as possible in order to precipitate an election that otherwise would not occur. To the extent that they fail to provide translations of their petitions, they take the risk of failure of their enterprise.

> It might be argued, however, that minority language voters ought to be able to have the opportunity to sign a petition in their language in order to help precipitate a recall election. It is difficult to see how such an argument can lead to an enforceable right, however. Certainly the circulators have no obligation to present a petition to any particular voter. Again, the incentive operating on the circulator is to reach as many potential voters as possible but if, for any number of reasons, the circulator does not reach an eligible voter and provide an opportunity for that voter to sign the petition, it is hard to see how there has been a violation of voting rights remediable by the Voting Rights Act and the courts.

The decision in *Padilla* prompted opponents of initiatives and recalls in several California jurisdictions to file challenges based on the failure to provide translations, sometimes with success. See, for example, *In re County of Monterey Initiative Matter*, 427 F.Supp.2d 958 (N.D.Cal. 2006); *Imperial v. Castruita*, 418 F.Supp.2d 1174 (C.D.Cal. 2006). The flurry of such cases ended when the Ninth Circuit granted en banc review of *Padilla* and overruled the panel's decision. *Padilla v. Lever*, 463 F.3d 1046 (9th Cir. 2006). According to the en banc majority,

> It is true that California regulates recall petitions in some detail. The petitions must follow a format provided by the Secretary of State, and must use a minimum type size. The petition also must include a copy of the Notice of Intention, the statement of grounds for recall, and the answer of the targeted officer if the officer submitted one. But these regulations do not mean that the petitions are *provided* by the State or subdivision. The form is regulated by the State, but the proponents fill out the petition, supply the grounds of recall, and have the petitions printed at their own expense. The fact that ... the Secretary of State "provides" the format does not mean that the State "provides" the petitions themselves within the meaning of the Voting Rights Act.

Chapter 9

Major Political Parties

Political parties play a central role in the working of electoral systems in every national democracy (and, for that matter, in most dictatorships). Some countries, such as Italy and Israel, rely on a multi-party, coalition-building system. Japan was an example, from 1955 until the ruling Liberal Democratic Party finally fell from power in 1993, of a system characterized by a single party that dominated the government, more or less indefinitely, with a fractured opposition. In the United States, at least since the 1830s, politics has centered around two major political parties.

For most of our history, the national parties in the United States were essentially federations of state organizations. In the past half century, the national parties have grown in importance as independent organizations, though this development came about by different means in the two major parties. Growth of the Republican National Committee began after the Republican disaster in the 1964 presidential election, as the national party organization became increasingly important as a provider of administrative and fundraising support for Republican candidates and state organizations. In the Democratic Party, beginning in 1968, the national organization successfully began to assert power over state organizations on various matters, especially the procedures for selecting delegates to national nominating conventions. Later, the national Democratic organizations increased their fundraising and administrative support activities, though the Democrats have continued to lag behind the Republicans in these respects. See generally John F. Bibby, *Party Renewal in the National Republican Party*, in PARTY RENEWAL IN AMERICA: THEORY AND PRACTICE (Gerald M. Pomper ed. 1980); James A. Reichley, *The Rise of National Parties*, in THE NEW DIRECTION IN AMERICAN POLITICS (J. Chubb & P. Peterson eds. 1985).

At the national level, law has played comparatively little role in creating or shaping the parties, which have been thought of as autonomous, private organizations to be kept free from legal regulation. Yet the activities of political parties—nominating candidates for office, building and reflecting support for legislation—are central to the actual working of government. A tension reflected in a variety of legal issues thus arises between the private nature of party organizations and the essential political functions they perform. To what extent should the parties be subject to the same constitutional constraints as the government? To what extent should party activities be regulated in the public interest? To the extent regulation is necessary or desirable, should it be a matter of federal law or should it be left to the states? To what extent do parties have constitutional protection from regulation? More generally, how does the party system, particularly in presidential elections, relate to the federal system? How active or restrained should the courts be in party affairs?

At the state level, parties went similarly unregulated through most of the nineteenth century. During the twentieth century there was a strong tendency toward regulation of the parties by state law. The centerpiece in this movement was the state-mandated direct primary election for choosing party candidates, but party activities have been regulated in many other significant respects as well. To some extent, regulation of parties is self-regulation, as party members in state legislatures codify by statute the governing arrangements the parties choose. Alternatively, regulation may put into effect the interests or opinions of some elements of a party over other elements. When the legislature governs the major parties, it is never entirely external to the entities it regulates, as it is when it regulates, say, businesses or labor unions. Sometimes the parties are regulated by initiatives, over which they have less control. Even then, however, the major parties are rarely helpless, and sometimes they use initiatives as a means of pursuing their objectives.[a]

Like federal non-regulation, state law regulation gives rise to many questions: Do the particular regulations serve the interests of the parties? Of the public? Would a different system of regulation be preferable? Would it be better to deregulate the parties and let them decide on their own structure? Do parties have a constitutional right to deregulation? If parties are to be deregulated, who should be able to set the rules for the parties? Party members (i.e., voters)? Party activists? Party officials? Partisan elected officials? Should the allocation of power within the party be determined by law?

This chapter considers these and other questions relating to the major political parties. Issues more important to minor parties and independent candidates are addressed in Chapter 10.

I. The Party and the Political System

The role parties do and should play in American politics has long been a subject of controversy among political scientists, party activists, government officials, lawyers and, at times, the general public. In reading the following materials, consider whether law has much to do with the controversy or should have much to do with it.

The Constitution does not mention political parties. The framers of the Constitution, of course, recognized the power of organized groups and public opinion and took steps to curb them through the indirect election of the Senate, the electoral college, and the system of checks and balances described by Madison in *Federalist* Nos. 10 and 51. None of these measures, however, seems directed expressly against political parties as opposed to other types of associations formed for political purposes. The majority of the framers, if asked, probably would have included political parties in the "factions" the constitutional system should guard against. See Richard Hofstadter, THE IDEA OF A PARTY SYSTEM 40–73 (1969).

Despite their relegation to a constitutional no-man's land, political parties arose quickly in America for reasons described by Justice Reed in *Ray v. Blair*, 343 U.S. 214, 220–21 (1952):

> As is well known, political parties in the modern sense were not born with the Republic. They were created by necessity, by the need to organize the rapidly increasing population, scattered over our Land, so as to coordinate efforts to secure needed legislation and oppose that deemed undesirable.

---

a. See Richard L. Hasen, *Parties Take the Initiative (and Vice Versa)*, 100 COLUMBIA LAW REVIEW 731 (2000).

Political parties are, to some extent, an anomaly engrafted onto a constitutional system that did not plan for them.[b]

One controversy over the role political parties should play in our political system generally has crystallized around the issue of how ideologically-oriented or "disciplined" the parties should be. One's position on the proper scope of legal regulation of political parties may well turn on one's view of the propriety or impropriety of "party discipline" and of means to achieve party ideological unity and coherence.

The most disciplined political party is one whose leaders pick the candidates for office on the basis of fealty to the party's positions and have the capacity to discipline non-adherents. It is probably also the party whose members — the voters — have the least to say about who the candidates should be. A disciplined party is thus arguably less democratic in organization and structure and more "boss" dominated than a looser ideological coalition. It is also the party whose structure arguably can produce the clearest ideological choice for voters at the general election.[c] A leading school of thought among students of political parties holds that parties serve the public best when they are firmly controlled by leaders, not voters. Joseph Schlesinger, *On the Theory of Party Organizations*, 46 JOURNAL OF POLITICS 369, 377 (1984), a proponent of this view, remarked that definitions of parties "must exclude the voters. Voters are choosers among parties, not components of them." See also Gerald M. Pomper, *The Alleged Decline of American Parties*, in John G. Geer, ed., POLITICIANS AND PARTY POLITICS 14, 18 (1998).[d]

Nevertheless, the history of American political parties has been to give voters more, not less direct control over party candidates and positions. No doubt this trend is strongly related to the ascendancy of progressivist ideas in American politics. To quote Justice Reed again:

> The party conventions of locally chosen delegates, from the county to the national level, succeeded the caucuses of self-appointed legislators or other interested individuals. Dissatisfaction with the manipulation of conventions caused that system to be largely superseded by the direct primary.

Ray v. Blair, 343 U.S. at 221. Direct primaries, which have become by far the most common method of selecting party nominees, allow candidates to appeal over the heads of party leaders directly to the voters. They have become a prime device for weakening party discipline.

Our major parties usually have been ideologically loose confederations of people of varying political persuasions, seeking to moderate their position on issues so as to attract the maximum number of voters. But in recent years the parties have become increasingly

---

b. For an important analysis by a social scientist of the process by which parties arose and evolved, see John H. Aldrich, WHY PARTIES? THE ORIGIN AND TRANSFORMATION OF PARTY POLITICS IN AMERICA (1995). For a lively historical summary of the rise of the American parties and their fortunes down through the 1950s, see James MacGregor Burns, THE DEADLOCK OF DEMOCRACY 8–203 (1963).

c. For a careful analysis of leading American theories of party government, see Austin Ranney, THE DOCTRINE OF RESPONSIBLE PARTY GOVERNMENT (1954). For a useful account that is more concise and more up-to-date, see Leon Epstein, POLITICAL PARTIES IN THE AMERICAN MOLD 9–39 (1986).

d. An important forerunner of these views was Part IV of the celebrated book by Joseph Schumpeter, CAPITALISM, SOCIALISM AND DEMOCRACY (1942). Schumpeter rejected as unrealistic the "classical doctrine" of democracy, in which the public set policies that were then carried out by elected officials. Rather, he saw elections as opportunities for parties and leaders to compete with each other for public support.

cohesive. For example, in Congress, a very large majority of Democrats oppose a very large majority of Republicans on a growing number of issues.[e] Still, American parties are relatively undisciplined ideologically, compared with their counterparts in many other countries.

In 1950, a time when the parties were much less cohesive than they are now, the Committee on Political Parties of the American Political Science Association submitted a still cited, seminal report called TOWARD A MORE RESPONSIBLE TWO PARTY SYSTEM (reprinted as a supplement to 44 AMERICAN POLITICAL SCIENCE REVIEW No. 3, Part 2 (1950)), criticizing the undisciplined type of party organization. The thesis of the report was:

> Historical and other factors have caused the American two-party system to operate as two loose associations of state and local organizations, with very little national machinery and very little national cohesion. As a result, either major party, when in power, is ill-equipped to organize its members in the legislative and the executive branches into a government held together and guided by the party program. Party responsibility at the polls thus tends to vanish. This is a very serious matter, for it affects the very heartbeat of American democracy. It also poses grave problems of domestic and foreign policy in an era when it is no longer safe for the nation to deal piecemeal with issues that can be disposed of only on the basis of coherent programs.

The Committee argued that "an effective party system requires, first, that the parties are able to bring forth programs to which they commit themselves and, second, that the parties possess sufficient internal cohesion to carry out these programs." *Id.* at 17–18. The Committee made a number of recommendations to bring about centralized, ideologically coherent parties. One typical recommendation would have given the national party the right to exclude ideologically disloyal state organizations from party deliberations (such as refusing to seat them at the national convention).

The Association's report and recommendations caused substantial controversy when published. See, e.g., J. Roland Pennock, *Responsiveness, Responsibility and Majority Rule*, 46 AMERICAN POLITICAL SCIENCE REVIEW 790 (1952) (arguing disciplined parties could be created only by polarizing the country along class lines and are inadequate for the task of "political brokerage" in America); Murray S. Stedman & Herbert Sonthoff, *Party Responsibility—A Critical Inquiry*, 4 WESTERN POLITICAL QUARTERLY 454 (1951) (arguing disciplined parties are incompatible with principles of federalism and with a non-partisan approach to local government, and that they would lead to the evils of bossism on a national scale).

For better or for worse, the kind of political party envisioned in the Committee's report did not exist in 1950, and as the following excerpts from an article by Morris Fiorina show, some observers have believed that the problems that existed then grew worse over the next three decades. Fiorina wrote at a time when many scholars and journalists believed American parties were in a state of serious decline. In the intervening years, there has been a resurgence of parties on many fronts and scholars have begun to doubt that parties ever were

---

e. There is now a large body of research on the increasing polarization of the parties in both the electorate and among elected officials, especially in Congress. A good place to start is Gary C. Jacobson, *Party Polarization in National Politics: The Electoral Connection*, in Jon R. Bond & Richard Fleisher, eds., POLARIZED POLITICS: CONGRESS AND THE PRESIDENT IN A PARTISAN ERA (2000). For an explanation of the consequences and dynamics of polarization in Congress, see John H. Aldrich & David W. Rohde, *The Logic of Conditional Party Government: Revisiting the Electoral Connection*, in Lawrence C. Dodd & Bruce I. Oppenheimer, eds., CONGRESS RECONSIDERED (7th ed. 2001).

in as bad a state as was previously believed. The examples in Fiorina's article are now dated and Fiorina himself has let it be known he no longer holds some of the views he expressed. We include his article here, however, because it remains an unusually cogent description of the role of the parties in the system of government accountability.

Morris P. Fiorina, *The Decline of Collective Responsibility in American Politics*
109 Daedalus 25 (1980)

Though the founding fathers believed in the necessity of establishing a genuinely national government, they took great pains to design one that could not lightly do things *to* its citizens; what government might do *for* its citizens was to be limited to the functions of what we know now as the "watchman state." Thus the Founders composed the constitutional litany familiar to every schoolchild: they created a federal system, they distributed and blended powers within and across the federal levels, and they encouraged the occupants of the various positions to check and balance each other by structuring incentives so that one officeholder's ambitions would be likely to conflict with others'. The resulting system of institutional arrangements predictably hampers efforts to undertake major initiatives and favors maintenance of the status quo.

Given the historical record faced by the Founders, their emphasis on constraining government is understandable. But we face a later historical record, one that shows two hundred years of increasing demands for government to act positively. Moreover, developments unforeseen by the Founders increasingly raise the likelihood that the uncoordinated actions of individuals and groups will inflict serious damage on the nation as a whole. The by-products of the industrial and technological revolutions impose physical risks not only on us, but on future generations as well. Resource shortages and international cartels raise the spectre of economic ruin. And the simple proliferation of special interests with their intense, particularistic demands threatens to render us politically incapable of taking actions that might either advance the state of society or prevent foreseeable deteriorations in that state. None of this is to suggest that we should forget about what government can do *to* us—the contemporary concern with the proper scope and methods of government intervention in the social and economic orders is long overdue. But the modern age demands as well that we worry about our ability to make government work *for* us. The problem is that we are gradually losing that ability, and a principal reason for this loss is the steady erosion of *responsibility* in American politics.

What do I mean by this important quality, responsibility? To say that some person or group is responsible for a state of affairs is to assert that he or they have the ability to take legitimate actions that have a major impact on that state of affairs. More colloquially, when someone is responsible, we know whom to blame. Human beings have asymmetric attitudes toward responsibility, as captured by the saying "Success has a thousand fathers, but failure is an orphan." This general observation applies very much to politicians, not surprisingly, and this creates a problem for democratic theory, because clear location of responsibility is vitally important to the operation of democratic governments. Without responsibility, citizens can only guess at who deserves their support; the act of voting loses much of its meaning. Moreover, the expectation of being held responsible provides representatives with a personal incentive to govern in their constituents' interest. As ordinary citizens we do not know the proper rate of growth of the money supply, the appropriate level of the federal deficit, the advantages of the MX over alternative missile systems, and so forth. We elect people to make those decisions. But only if those elected know they will be held accountable for the results of their decisions (or nondecisions, as the case may be), do they have a personal incentive to govern in our interest.[1]

Unfortunately, the importance of responsibility in a democracy is matched by the difficulty of attaining it. In an autocracy, individual responsibility suffices; the location of power in a single individual locates responsibility in that individual as well. But individual responsibility is insufficient whenever more than one person shares governmental authority. We can hold a particular congressman individually responsible for a personal transgression such as bribe-taking. We can even hold a president individually responsible for military moves where he presents Congress and the citizenry with a *fait accompli*. But on most national issues individual responsibility is difficult to assess. If one were to go to Washington, randomly accost a Democratic congressman, and berate him about a 20-percent rate of inflation, imagine the response. More than likely it would run, "Don't blame me. If 'they' had done what I've advocated for *x* years, things would be fine today." And if one were to walk over to the White House and similarly confront President Carter, he would respond as he already has, by blaming Arabs, free-spending congressmen, special interests, and, of course, us.

American institutional structure makes this kind of game-playing all too easy. In order to overcome it we must lay the credit or blame for national conditions on all those who had any hand in bringing them about: some form of collective responsibility is essential.

The only way collective responsibility has ever existed, and can exist given our institutions, is through the agency of the political party; in American politics, responsibility requires cohesive parties. This is an old claim to be sure, but its age does not detract from its present relevance. In fact, the continuing decline in public esteem for the parties and continuing efforts to "reform" them out of the political process suggest that old arguments for party responsibility have not been made often enough or, at least, convincingly enough, so I will make these arguments once again in this essay.

A strong political party can generate collective responsibility by creating incentive for leaders, followers, and popular supporters to think and act in collective terms. First, by providing party leaders with the capability (e.g., control of institutional patronage, nominations, and so on) to discipline party members, genuine leadership becomes possible. Legislative output is less likely to be a least common denominator—a residue of myriad conflicting proposals—and more likely to consist of a program actually intended to solve a problem or move the nation in a particular direction. Second, the subordination of individual officeholders to the party lessens their ability to separate themselves from party actions. Like it or not, their performance becomes identified with the performance of the collectivity to which they belong. Third, with individual candidate variation greatly reduced, voters have less incentive to support individuals and more incentive to support or oppose the party as a whole. And fourth, the circle closes as party-line voting in the electorate provides party leaders with the incentive to propose policies that will earn the support of a national majority, and party back-benchers with the personal incentive to cooperate with leaders in the attempt to compile a good record for the party as a whole.

In the American context, strong parties have traditionally clarified politics in two ways. First, they allow citizens to assess responsibility easily, at least when the government is

---

1. This may sound cynical, but it is a standard assumption in American democratic theory. Certainly the Founders believed that the government should not depend on the nobility of heart of officialdom in order to operate properly.

unified, which it more often was in earlier eras when party meant more than it does today.[3] Citizens need only evaluate the social, economic, and international conditions they observe and make a simple decision for or against change. They do not need to decide whether the energy, inflation, urban, and defense policies advocated by their congressman would be superior to those advocated by Carter—were any of them to be enacted![f]

The second way in which strong parties clarify American politics follows from the first. When citizens assess responsibility on the party as a whole, party members have personal incentives to see the party evaluated favorably. They have little to gain from gutting their president's program one day and attacking him for lack of leadership the next, since they share in the president's fate when voters do not differentiate within the party. Put simply, party responsibility provides party members with a personal stake in their collective performance.

Admittedly, party responsibility is a blunt instrument. The objection immediately arises that party responsibility condemns junior Democratic representatives to suffer electorally for an inflation they could do little to affect. An unhappy situation, true, but unless we accept it, Congress as a whole escapes electoral retribution for an inflation they *could* have done something to affect. Responsibility requires acceptance of both conditions. The choice is between a blunt instrument or none at all.

Of course, the United States is not Great Britain. We have neither the institutions nor the traditions to support a British brand of responsible party government, and I do not see either the possibility or the necessity for such a system in America. In the past the United States has enjoyed eras in which party was a much stronger force than today. And until recently—a generation, roughly—parties have provided an "adequate" degree of collective responsibility. They have done so by connecting the electoral fates of party members, via presidential coattails, for example, and by transforming elections into referenda on party performance, as with congressional off-year elections.

In earlier times, when citizens voted for the party, not the person, parties had incentives to nominate good candidates, because poor ones could have harmful fallout on the ticket as a whole.[4] In particular, the existence of presidential coattails (positive and negative) provided an inducement to avoid the nomination of narrowly based candidates, no matter how committed their supporters. And, once in office, the existence of party voting in the electorate provided party members with the incentive to compile a good *party* record. In particular, the tendency of national midterm elections to serve as ref-

---

3. During the postwar period the national government has experienced divided party control about half the time. In the preceding half century there were only six years of divided control. [Since the publication of Fiorina's article, divided control prevailed continuously through 2000, except for the period 1993–94. Unified government was in place by the barest of margins during the first five months of 2001 and from 2003–06.—Eds.]

f. Most theories of party accountability—and probably most popular thought on the subject— have emphasized the party platforms, which consist of promises to adopt or follow specified policies. Fiorina espouses an alternate view: that rather than choosing among the parties on the basis of beliefs about policies, it is easier and more feasible for voters to evaluate the results of recent governmental policies. In effect, they decide how to vote by answering the famous question Ronald Reagan posed in one of his 1980 debates against President Carter, when Reagan asked voters whether they felt better off than four years previously. For an elaboration of this approach, see Morris P. Fiorina, RETROSPECTIVE VOTING IN AMERICAN NATIONAL ELECTIONS (1981).—Eds.

4. At this point skeptics invariably ask, "What about Warren G. Harding?" The statement in the text is meant to express a tendency. Certainly, in the first sixty years of this century we did not see a string of candidates comparable to the products of the amateur politics of the past fourteen years (Goldwater, McGovern, Carter, Reagan).

erenda on the performance of the president provided a clear inducement for congressmen to do what they could to see that their president was perceived as a solid performer. By stimulating electoral phenomena such as coattail effects and midterm referenda, party transformed some degree of personal ambition into concern with collective performance.

In the contemporary period, however, even the preceding tendencies toward collective responsibility have largely dissipated. As background for a discussion of this contemporary weakening of collective responsibility and its deleterious consequences, let us briefly review the evidence for the decline of party in America.

The Continuing Decline of Party in the United States

Party is a simple term that covers a multitude of complicated organizations and processes. It manifests itself most concretely as the set of party organizations that exist principally at the state and local levels. It manifests itself most elusively as a psychological presence in the mind of the citizen. Somewhere in between, and partly a function of the first two, is the manifestation of party as a force in government. The discussion in this section will hold to this traditional schema, though it is clear that the three aspects of party have important interconnections.

Party Organizations

In the United States, party organization has traditionally meant state and local party organization. The national party generally has been a loose confederacy of subnational units that swings into action for a brief period every four years. This characterization remains true today, despite the somewhat greater influence and augmented functions of the national organizations. Though such things are difficult to measure precisely, there is general agreement that the formal party organizations have undergone a secular decline since their peak at the end of the nineteenth century. The prototype of the old-style organization was the urban machine, a form approximated today only in Chicago.

Several long-term trends have served to undercut old-style party organizations. The patronage system has been steadily chopped back since passage of the Civil Service Act of 1883. The social welfare functions of the parties have passed to the government as the modern welfare state developed. And, less concretely, the entire ethos of the old-style party organization is increasingly at odds with modern ideas of government based on rational expertise. These longterm trends spawned specific attacks on the old party organizations. In the late nineteenth and early twentieth centuries the Populists, Progressives, and assorted other reformers fought electoral corruption with the Australian Ballot and personal registration systems. They attempted to break the hold of the party bosses over nominations by mandating the direct primary. They attacked the urban machines with drives for nonpartisan at-large elections and nonpartisan city managers. None of these reforms destroyed the parties; they managed to live with the reforms better than most reformers had hoped. But the reforms reflected changing popular attitudes toward the parties and accelerated the secular decline in the influence of the party organizations.

The New Deal period temporarily arrested the deterioration of the party organizations, at least on the Democratic side. Unified party control under a "political" president provided favorable conditions for the state and local organizations. But following the heyday of the New Deal (and ironically, in part, because of government assumption of subnational parties' functions) the decline continued.

In the 1970s two series of reforms further weakened the influence of organized parties in American national politics. The first was a series of legal changes deliberately intended to lessen organized party influence in the presidential nominating process. In the Democratic party, "New Politics" activists captured the national party apparatus and imposed a series of rules changes designed to "open up" the politics of presidential nominations. The Republican party—long more amateur and open than the Democratic party—adopted weaker versions of the Democratic rules changes. In addition, modifications of state electoral laws to conform to the Democratic rules changes (enforced by the federal courts) stimulated Republican rules changes as well. [T]he presidential nominating process has indeed been opened up. In little more than a decade after the disastrous 1968 Democratic conclave, the number of primary states has more than doubled, and the number of delegates chosen in primaries has increased from little more than a third to three-quarters. Moreover, the remaining delegates emerge from caucuses far more open to mass citizen participation, and the delegates themselves are more likely to be amateurs, than previously....

A second series of 1970s reforms lessened the role of formal party organizations in the conduct of political campaigns. These are financing regulations growing out of the Federal Election Campaign Act of 1971 as amended in 1974 and 1976. In this case the reforms were aimed at cleaning up corruption in the financing of campaigns; their effects on the parties were a by-product, though many individuals accurately predicted its nature....

The ultimate results of such reforms are easy to predict. A lesser party role in the nominating and financing of candidates encourages candidates to organize and conduct independent campaigns, which further weakens the role of parties.[g] Of course, party is not the entire story in this regard. Other modern day changes contribute to the diminished party role in campaign politics. For one thing, party foot soldiers are no longer so important, given the existence of a large leisured middle class that participates out of duty or enjoyment, but that participates on behalf of particular candidates and issues rather than parties. Similarly, contemporary campaigns rely heavily on survey research, the mass media, and modern advertising methods—all provided by independent consultants outside the formal party apparatus. Although these developments are not directly related to the contemporary reforms, their effect is the same: the diminution of the role of parties in conducting political campaigns. And if parties do not grant nominations, fund their choices, and work for them, why should those choices feel any commitment to their party?

---

g. Many political scientists have agreed with this conclusion. A prominent example is Nelson W. Polsby, CONSEQUENCES OF PARTY REFORM (1983). However, others have contested the assertion that campaign finance reforms have harmed parties. See David Adamany, *Political Finance and the American Political Parties*, 10 HASTINGS CONSTITUTIONAL LAW QUARTERLY 497 (1983). For an excellent discussion, see Frank J. Sorauf, MONEY IN AMERICAN ELECTIONS 120–53 (1988). There has been more widespread agreement with Fiorina and Polsby that party leaders have lost control of presidential nominations by virtue of the post-1968 reforms. Until recently, that is, when scholars began to notice that since 1980, presidential candidates favored by party leaders and insiders have had excellent success in the nomination process. See Pomper, *The Alleged Decline, supra*, at 19–22; Marty Cohen, David Karol, Hans Noel & John Zaller, "Beating Reform: The Resurgence of Parties in Presidential Nominations," forthcoming as a book and meanwhile available online as a conference paper (2001) (http://www.sscnet.ucla.edu/polisci/faculty/zaller/APSA_Parties%20Are%20Back.pdf).—EDS.

Party in the Electorate

In the citizenry at large, party takes the form of a psychological attachment. The typical American traditionally has been likely to identify with one or the other of the two major parties. Such identifications are transmitted across generations to some degree, and within the individual they tend to be fairly stable. But there is mounting evidence that the basis of identification lies in the individual's experiences (direct and vicarious, through family and social groups) with the parties in the past. Our current party system, of course, is based on the dislocations of the Depression period and the New Deal attempts to alleviate them. Though only a small proportion of those who experienced the Depression directly are active voters today, the general outlines of citizen party identifications much resemble those established at that time.

Again, there is reason to believe that the extent of citizen attachments to parties has undergone a long-term decline from a late nineteenth century high.[12] [More recently, scholars have found a rebound of partisan voting after a low in the 1970s. See Larry M. Bartels, *Partisanship and Voting Behavior, 1952–1996*, 44 AMERICAN JOURNAL OF POLITICAL SCIENCE 35 (2000); Bruce E. Keith et al., THE MYTH OF THE INDEPENDENT VOTER (1992).—EDS.]

Party in Government

If the organizational capabilities of the parties have weakened, and their psychological ties to the voters have loosened, one would expect predictable consequences for the party in government. In particular, one would expect to see an increasing degree of split party control within and across the levels of American government. The evidence on this point is overwhelming.

At the state level, twenty-seven of the fifty governments were under divided party control after the 1978 election. In seventeen states a governor of one party opposed a legislature controlled by the other, and in ten others a bicameral legislature was split between the parties.[h] By way of contrast, twenty years ago the number of states with divided party control was sixteen.

At the federal level the trend is similar. In 1953 only twelve states sent a senator of each party to Washington. The number increased to sixteen by 1961, to twenty-one by 1972, and stands at twenty-seven today.[i] Of course, the senators in each state are elected at different times. But the same patterns emerge when we examine simultaneous elections. There is an increasing tendency for congressional districts to support a congressman of one party and the presidential candidate of the other.... At the turn of the century it was

---

12. For a discussion, see Walter Dean Burnham, CRITICAL ELECTIONS AND THE MAINSPRINGS OF AMERICAN POLITICS (1970).

h. After the 2006 (or 2007 in a few states) elections, there were 25 states with unified government and 24 with divided government. One of the divided government states was Tennessee, which after the 2006 election had a Democratic governor and House, but a Senate that was Republican by 17–16. In 2007, one of the Republican senators became an independent, leaving the Senate evenly divided between the major parties. One state, Nebraska, has a nonpartisan one-house legislature.—EDS.

i. This number stood at 21 after the 1992 election. Although this is a decline from the post-1978 figure that Fiorina reports, both figures are consistent with what one would expect if party choices for the Senate were random. However, after the 2006 election, the number had declined to 15. The senators from two states, Connecticut and Vermont, consist of a Democrat and an independent.—EDS.

extremely rare for a congressional district to report a split result. But since that time the trend has been steadily upward....[j]

Seemingly unsatisfied with the increasing tendencies of the voters to engage in ticket-splitting, we have added to the split of party in government by changing electoral rules in a manner that lessens the impact of national forces. For example, in 1920 thirty-five states elected their legislators, governors, and other state officials in presidential election years. In 1944 thirty-two states still did so. But in the past generation the trend has been toward isolation of state elections from national currents: as of 1970 only twenty states still held their elections concurrently with the national ones. This legal separation of the state and national electoral arenas helps to separate the electoral fates of party office-holders at different levels of government, and thereby lessens their common interest in a good party record.

The increased fragmentation of the party in government makes it more difficult for government officeholders to work together than in times past (not that it has ever been terribly easy). Voters meanwhile have a more difficult time attributing responsibility for government performance, and this only further fragments party control. The result is lessened collective responsibility in the system....

By now it is widely understood that senatorial races are in a class by themselves. The visibility of the office attracts the attention of the media as well as that of organized interest groups. Celebrities and plutocrats find the office attractive. Thus massive media campaigns and the politics of personality increasingly affect these races. Senate elections now are most notable for their idiosyncrasy, and consequentially for their growing volatility; correspondingly, such general forces as the president and the party are less influential in senatorial voting today than previously.

What is less often recognized is that House elections have grown increasingly idiosyncratic as well. I have already discussed the declining importance of party identification in House voting and the increasing number of split results at the district level. These trends are both cause and consequence of incumbent efforts to insulate themselves from the electoral effects of national conditions.

[Fiorina presents data showing that between the late 1940s and the early 1970s, House incumbents as a group were able to increase the margins by which they were typically re-elected. Fiorina argues that not only partisan but also programmatic and ideological influences have diminished as factors in House elections. These have been replaced, to a significant extent, by "personal and local influences." In particular, the growth of the federal government has greatly increased the opportunity for House incumbents to provide ombudsman and other individualized services to individuals and organizations in their districts. This activity enables the incumbents to build personal followings that may insulate them from national tides detrimental to their party. For elaboration of this argu-

---

j. The trend Fiorina refers to leveled off and now appears to have reversed. In the two elections preceding his article, the figures were 192 (1972) and 124 (1976). In the next three elections the figures were 143 (1980), 196 (1984), and 148 (1988). It is not surprising that the two largest figures were in 1972 and 1984, when Democratic presidential candidates suffered disastrous losses, but many Democratic House members were able to hold onto districts lost by McGovern and Mondale. In 1992, when the results may have been influenced by the Perot independent candidacy, the figure was 100. That was the lowest figure since 1952, when the figure was 86. All earlier figures in the twentieth century were below 100. In 1996, the figure remained at what seemed a low level at 111. But then a new drop occurred. In 2000 the number was 86, and in 2004 it was 59. See Harold W. Stanley & Richard G. Niemi, eds., VITAL STATISTICS ON AMERICAN POLITICS 46 (2005–06).—EDS.

ment, see Morris P. Fiorina, Congress: Keystone of the Washington Establishment (2d ed. 1989).

In the present context, Fiorina argues that the greater insulation of incumbents from national partisan tides means a severe diminution in electoral phenomena such as presidential coattails and the midterm election as a referendum on presidential performance.[k]

.... The withering away of the party organizations and the weakening of party in the electorate have begun to show up as disarray in the party in government. As the electoral fates of congressmen and the president have diverged, their incentives to cooperate have diverged as well. Congressmen have little personal incentive to bear any risk in their president's behalf, since they no longer expect to gain much from his successes or suffer much from his failures. Only those who personally agree with the president's program and/or those who find that program well suited for their particular district support the president. And there are not enough of these to construct the coalitions necessary for action on the major issues now facing the country. By holding only the president responsible for national conditions, the electorate enables officialdom as a whole to escape responsibility. This situation lies at the root of many of the problems that now plague American public life.

Some Consequences of the Decline of Collective Responsibility

The weakening of party has contributed directly to the severity of several of the important problems the nation faces....

Immobilism

As the electoral interdependence of the party in government declines, its ability to act also declines. If responsibility can be shifted to another level or to another officeholder, there is less incentive to stick one's own neck out in an attempt to solve a given problem. Leadership becomes more difficult, the ever-present bias toward the short-term solution becomes more pronounced, and the possibility of solving any given problem lessens.

[Often] the problem lies in the future, while the solutions impose costs in the present. So politicians dismiss the solutions as unfeasible and act as though the problem will go away. When it doesn't, popular concern increases. The president, in particular, feels compelled to act—he will be held responsible, both at election time and in the judgment of history. But congressmen expect to bear much less responsibility; moreover, the representatives face an election in less than two years, whereas the president can wait at least four (longer for the lame duck) for the results of his policy to become evident. Congressmen, logically enough, rebel. They denounce every proposed initiative as unfair, which simply means that it imposes costs on their constituents, whereas they prefer the costs to fall on everyone else's constituents. At first, no policy will be adopted; later, as pressure builds, Congress adopts a weak and ineffectual policy for symbolic purposes. Then, as the problem continues to worsen, congressmen join with the press and the public and attack the president for failures of leadership.

---

k. More detailed and up-to-date information on the "incumbency advantage" is contained in Chapter 12 of this book. — Eds.

The preceding scenario is simplified, to be sure, but largely accurate, and in my opinion, rather disgusting. What makes it possible is the electoral fragmentation produced by the decline of party. Members of Congress are aware that national problems arising from inaction will have little political impact on them, and that the president's failures in dealing with those problems will have similarly little impact. Responsibility for inflation and energy problems? Don't look at congressmen....

Single-Issue Politics

In recent years both political analysts and politicians have decried the increased importance of single-issue groups in American politics. Some in fact would claim that the present immobilism in our politics owes more to the rise of single-issue groups than to the decline of party. A little thought, however, should reveal that the two trends are connected. Is single-issue politics a recent phenomenon? The contention is doubtful; such groups have always been active participants in American politics. The gun lobby already was a classic example at the time of President Kennedy's assassination. And however impressive the antiabortionists appear today, remember the temperance movement, which succeeded in getting its constitutional amendment. American history contains numerous forerunners of today's groups, from anti-Masons to abolitionists to the Klan—singularity of purpose is by no means a modern phenomenon. Why, then, do we hear all the contemporary hoopla about single-issue groups? Probably because politicians fear them now more than before and thus allow them to play a larger role in our politics. Why should this be so? Simply because the parties are too weak to protect their members and thus to contain single-issue politics.

In earlier times single-issue groups were under greater pressures to reach accommodations with the parties. After all, the parties nominated candidates, financed candidates, worked for candidates, and, perhaps most important, party voting protected candidates. When a contemporary single-issue group threatens to "get" an officeholder, the threat must be taken seriously. The group can go into his district, recruit a primary or general election challenger, or both, and bankroll that candidate. Even if the sentiment espoused by the group is not the majority sentiment of the district, few officeholders relish the thought of a strong, well-financed opponent. Things were different when strong parties existed. Party leaders controlled the nomination process and would fight to maintain that control. An outside challenge would merely serve to galvanize the party into action to protect its prerogatives. Only if a single-issue group represented the dominant sentiment in a given area could it count on controlling the party organization itself, and thereby electoral politics in that area.

Not only did the party organization have greater ability to resist single-issue pressures at the electoral level, but the party in government had greater ability to control the agenda, and thereby contain single-issue pressures at the policymaking level....

In sum, a strong party that is held accountable for the government of a nation-state has both the ability and the incentive to contain particularistic pressures. It controls nominations, elections, and the agenda, and it collectively realizes that small minorities are small minorities no matter how intense they are. But as the parties decline they lose control over nominations and campaigns, they lose the loyalty of the voters, and they lose control of the agenda. Party officeholders cease to be held collectively accountable for party performance, but they become individually exposed to the political pressure of myriad interest groups. The decline of party permits interest groups to weld greater influence, their success encourages the formation of still more interest groups, politics becomes increasingly fragmented, and collective responsibility becomes still more elusive.

Popular Alienation from Government

For at least a decade political analysts have pondered the significance of survey data indicative of a steady increase in the alienation of the American public from the political process. [According to the 1978 National Election Studies survey,] two-thirds of the American public feel the government is run for the benefit of big interests rather than for the people as a whole, three-quarters believe that government officials waste a lot of tax money, and half flatly agree with the statement that government officials are basically incompetent. The American public is in a nasty mood, a cynical, distrusting, and resentful mood. The question is, Why?

Specific events and personalities clearly have some effect: we see pronounced "Watergate effects" between 1972 and 1976. But the trends clearly began much earlier. Indeed, the first political science studies analyzing the trends were based on data no later than 1972. At the other extreme it also appears that the American data are only the strongest manifestation of a pattern evident in many democracies, perhaps for reasons common to all countries in the present era, perhaps not. I do think it probable, however, that the trends thus far discussed bear some relation to the popular mood in the United States.

If the same national problems not only persist but worsen while ever-greater amounts of revenue are directed at them, why shouldn't the typical citizen conclude that most of the money must be wasted by incompetent officials? If narrowly based interest groups increasingly affect our politics, why shouldn't citizens increasingly conclude that the interests run the government? For fifteen years the citizenry has listened to a steady stream of promises but has seen very little in the way of follow-through. An increasing proportion of the electorate does not believe that elections make a difference, a fact that largely explains the much-discussed post-1960 decline in voting turnout.

Continued public disillusionment with the political process poses several real dangers. For one thing, disillusionment begets further disillusionment. Leadership becomes more difficult if citizens do not trust their leaders and will not give them the benefit of a doubt. Policy failure becomes more likely if citizens expect the policy to fail. Waste increases and government competence decreases as citizen disrespect for politics encourages a lesser breed of person to make careers in government. And "government by a few big interests" becomes more than a cliché if citizens increasingly decide the cliché is true and cease participating for that reason.

Finally, there is the real danger that continued disappointment with particular government officials ultimately metamorphoses into disillusionment with government per se. Increasing numbers of citizens believe that government is not simply overextended but perhaps incapable of any further bettering of the world. Yes, government is overextended, inefficiency is pervasive, and ineffectiveness is all too common. But government is one of the few instruments of collective action we have, and even those committed to selective pruning of government programs cannot blithely allow the concept of an activist government to fall into disrepute.

* * *

The concept of democracy does not submit to precise definition, a claim supported by the existence of numerous nonidentical definitions. To most people democracy embodies a number of valued qualities. Unfortunately, there is no reason to believe that all such valued qualities are mutually compatible. At the least, maximizing the attainment of one quality may require accepting middling levels of another.

Recent American political thought has emphasized government *of* the people and *by* the people. Attempts have been made to insure that all preferences receive a hearing, especially through direct expression of those preferences, but if not, at least through faithful representation. Citizen *participation* is the reigning value, and arrangements that foster widespread participation are much in favor.

Of late, however, some political commentators have begun to wonder whether contemporary thought places sufficient emphasis on government *for* the people. In stressing participation have we lost sight of *accountability*? Surely, we should be as concerned with what government produces as with how many participate. What good is participation if the citizenry is unable to determine who merits their support?[27]

Participation and responsibility are not logically incompatible, but there is a degree of tension between the two, and the quest for either may be carried to extremes. Participation maximizers find themselves involved with quotas and virtual representation schemes, while responsibility maximizers can find themselves with a closed shop under boss rule. Moreover, both qualities can weaken the democracy they supposedly underpin. Unfettered participation produces Hyde Amendments and immobilism. Responsible parties can use agenda power to thwart democratic decision—for more than a century the Democratic party used what control it had to suppress the racial issue. Neither participation nor responsibility should be pursued at the expense of all other values, but that is what has happened with participation over the course of the past two decades, and we now reap the consequences in our politics....

The depressing thing is that no rays of light shine through the dark clouds. The trends that underlie the decline of parties continue unabated, and the kinds of structural reforms that might override those trends are too sweeping and/or outlandish to stand any chance of adoption.[30] Through a complex mixture of accident and intention we have constructed for ourselves a system that articulates interests superbly but aggregates them poorly. We hold our politicians individually accountable for the proposals they advocate, but less so for the adoption of those proposals, and not at all for overseeing the implementation of those proposals and the evaluation of their results. In contemporary America officials do not govern, they merely posture.

Notes and Questions

1. For an expression of similar views, see Gerald Pomper, *The Decline of the Party in American Elections*, 92 POLITICAL SCIENCE QUARTERLY 21 (1977). Notice that Fiorina and Pomper wrote after the 1976 election but before the 1980 election. Would subsequent elections have compelled Fiorina and Pomper to change their views? Recall that in 1980, Ronald Reagan's presidential victory was accompanied by a Republican takeover of the Senate (though not of the House), and the Republicans maintained their control until the 1986 election. From 1986 through 1992 we reverted to the situation in which the Re-

27. There is, of course, a school of thought, dating back at least to John Stuart Mill, that holds that participation is a good in itself. While I am prepared to concede that self-expression is nice, I strongly object to making it the *raison d'être* of democratic politics.

30. For example, party cohesion would no doubt be strengthened by revising existing statutes to prevent split-ticket voting and to permit campaign contributions only to parties. At the constitutional level, giving the president the power of dissolution and replacing the single-member district system with proportional representation would probably unify the party in government much more than at present. Obviously, changes such as these are not only highly improbable but also exceedingly risky, since we cannot accurately predict the unintended consequences that surely would accompany them.

publicans control the White House while the Democrats control both houses of Congress. After two years of united government under President Clinton and the Democrats, the Republicans won control of Congress for the first time in 40 years. Was the 1994 election good news for one holding Fiorina's view of the need for greater political accountability?

Divided government with a Democratic president and a Republican Congress persisted through 2000. As a result of the 2000 election, the Republicans won back the presidency. They also maintained their majority in the House, albeit by a small margin. The Senate divided 50–50, with the Republicans maintaining control solely because the Vice-President—in this case Republican Dick Cheney—casts tie-breaking votes in the Senate. However, the situation changed when, as is described below, Republican Senator Jim Jeffords left the Republican Party, throwing majority control of the Senate to the Democrats, and thus restoring divided government. Unified government returned more firmly when the Republicans won control of both houses in 2002. The Republicans remained in control until 2006, when the Democrats won a resounding victory and took control of both houses of Congress. As with the Republican victory in 1994, the Democratic victory in 2006 was widely perceived as prompted by discontent with the incumbent party's performance.

In many respects, parties are unquestionably stronger than they were at the time Fiorina wrote his essay. Is American government more accountable as a consequence? Do the 1994 and 2006 elections suggest an affirmative answer to that question? What about some of Fiorina's other concerns, such as the power of single interest groups and popular alienation from government? Have stronger parties caused other problems? Many complain that partisan polarization, at least in conditions in which the two parties are very closely balanced, has reduced civility in public discourse and brought about an immobilism at least equal to that which worried Fiorina. Caution is advisable in seeking answers to the questions in this paragraph, because although by some of Fiorina's measures the parties are unquestionably stronger than in 1980, other conditions that he describes have endured or even become stronger. Still, one benefit of reading Fiorina's article may be as a reminder that the grass tends to look greener on the other side of the fence. When the parties were weak, we longed for stronger parties. Now that we have them, we look nostalgically back at the days when polarization sounded like a method of photography.

2. A number of observers have agreed with Fiorina that divided government—the situation in which neither party controls both the presidency and both houses of Congress—creates severe structural problems for the working of government. See, e.g., James Sundquist, *Needed: A Political Theory for the New Era of Coalition Government in the United States*, 103 POLITICAL SCIENCE QUARTERLY 613 (1988). Some have regarded the problem as so serious that they have recommended major constitutional changes, comparable to those dismissed by Fiorina in footnote 30 of his article, as remedies. E.g., Lloyd N. Cutler, *Party Government Under the American Constitution*, 125 UNIVERSITY OF PENNSYLVANIA LAW REVIEW 134 (1985). During the Reagan and George H.W. Bush administrations, political scientists devoted considerable effort to trying to identify causes for the frequent occurrence of divided government since World War II. See Morris P. Fiorina, *An Era of Divided Government*, in DEVELOPMENTS IN AMERICAN POLITICS 324 (Gillian Peele et al., eds., 1992); Gary C. Jacobson, THE ELECTORAL ORIGINS OF DIVIDED GOVERNMENT: COMPETITION IN U.S. HOUSE ELECTIONS, 1946–1988 (1990); John R. Petrocik, *Divided Government: Is It All in the Campaigns?*, in THE POLITICS OF DIVIDED GOVERNMENT 13 (Gary W. Cox & Samuel Kernell, eds., 1991).

Probably the most common concern about divided government is that with the president and at least one house of Congress controlled by different parties, the two branches will be unable to work together to formulate legislation or coordinated government policy in order to solve important problems facing the country. This concern seems logical, but an important study poses a serious challenge to it on empirical grounds. See David R. Mayhew, DIVIDED WE GOVERN: PARTY CONTROL, LAWMAKING AND INVESTIGATIONS, 1946–1990 (1990). Mayhew made a list of laws that were regarded as major by contemporaries and that were passed by Congress during the 45 years covered by his study. He found that the enactment of major legislation was no more frequent during periods of unified government than during periods of divided government.

It is difficult to imagine that divided partisan control of the government has *no* systematic consequences, but as Fiorina himself has acknowledged in a book that provides a useful overview of the subject, Mayhew's study makes it difficult to blame divided government for "gridlock." See Morris P. Fiorina, DIVIDED GOVERNMENT 86–92 (1992). If Mayhew's findings are accepted, does it follow that Fiorina's concerns about divided government expressed in his 1980 article are misplaced? See *id.* at 109–111.

3. Divided government is only one of the causes and one of the symptoms of the distress of the American party system perceived by Fiorina, Pomper, and many other observers. Although these writers suggested that American parties had declined since World War II, concern about the weakness of American parties long predates that period. For example, a prominent political scientist writing in 1901 found very little incidence of strong party-line voting in Congress or in state legislatures, and he gave this explanation, which sounds as if it could have been excerpted from Fiorina's article:

> If in England a member of the majority in the House of Commons refuses to support an important measure upon which the cabinet insists, and if enough of his colleagues share his opinion to turn the scale, the consequence must be a change of ministry or a dissolution; but under similar circumstances in America no such dire results will follow. The measure will simply be lost, but the member can retain his seat undisturbed till the end of his term, and the administration will go on as before. Hence the difficulty in carrying out party platforms, and the discredit into which they have fallen in consequence.

A. Lawrence Lowell, *The Influence of Party upon Legislation in England and America*, 1 ANNUAL REPORT OF THE AMERICAN HISTORICAL ASSOCIATION FOR THE YEAR 1901 321, 346.

4. Assessments of the American party system often overlook two of the bedrock strengths of the major parties. Each came under modest pressure in the period following the 2000 election, but each is likely to endure for the foreseeable future.

The first is the strength of the parties when it comes to organizing legislatures. By custom, American legislators may be put under some pressure to vote in accordance with the party position on legislation, but they remain free to defect. Indeed, party leaders are usually reluctant to place great pressure on members to vote the party line, because it is more important to the leaders to have party members reelected than to receive their votes on particular issues. A different custom prevails on votes to organize the chamber of the legislature, i.e., to vote for leaders, to organize committees and install committee chairs, and the like. Here, there has been a virtually absolute rule that party members vote with the party. That is one reason there was a great furor in 2001, when a Republican senator from Vermont, Jim Jeffords, announced that he would become an independent and decline to vote with the Republicans on organizational issues. The Senate was divided 50–50 at the time. Jeffords' move meant the Democrats gained a majority. Although Jeffords became an independent, the Democrats rewarded him with a committee chair.

Many in the press and most Democrats and liberals applauded Jeffords for his independence. Many Republicans and conservatives reviled him as a traitor who betrayed Republican voters who elected him. Jeffords supporters responded that people who voted for Jeffords were independent-minded and often liberal, so that in making the switch he was representing them well. In point of fact, many who voted for him met this description, but many were traditional Republicans. Jeffords supporters pointed out that numerous members of Congress had switched parties in the past, without much controversy. Republicans responded that there was harm and therefore a wrong only when the switch would affect control of the chamber. Before the start of the 83rd Congress (1953–54), Wayne Morse, a Republican senator from Oregon, switched to being an independent. In the 1952 election, the Republicans won 48 seats in the 96-member Senate, not counting Morse. Because Richard Nixon, the new vice president, was a Republican, the Republicans were assured control of the Senate regardless of how Morse voted. However, Republican Senator Robert A. Taft died on July 31, 1953 and was replaced by a Democrat. Morse at this point could have switched control of the Senate to the Democrats. However, Morse took the position that because he had been elected as a Republican, he should not vote with the Democrats on organizational issues for the remainder of that Congress, and the Republicans maintained their control.

Which side was right in this argument? A situation similar to the Jeffords incident arose in California after the 1994 election, when the Republicans gained control of the state Assembly by a margin of one vote. A Republican member, Paul Horcher, switched parties and voted to retain the speakership for Democrat Willie Brown. Republicans successfully circulated a recall petition against Horcher in his district. At the ensuing election a few months later, his constituents removed him from office. Was that a proper or abusive use of the recall process?

The Australian Democrats, a minor party in that country, have a provision in their constitution requiring that if a party nominee is elected to Parliament and then resigns from the party, he or she must also resign from Parliament. Should such a provision be enforced if the member resigns from the party but seeks to retain the parliamentary seat? If so, by whom? By a court? By the parliamentary chamber? For discussion, see Graeme Orr, *A Politician's Word: The Legal (Un)enforceability of Political Deals*, 5 CONSTITUTIONAL LAW & POLICY REVIEW 1 (2002).

The other arena in which party discipline is relatively ironclad is the electoral college. Occasionally electors will vote for someone other than the candidate they were elected to support, but such incidents are rare and have never been meaningful. See Jack W. Peltason, *Constitutional Law for Political Parties*, in Nelson W. Polsby & Raymond F. Wolfinger, eds., ON PARTIES: ESSAYS HONORING AUSTIN RANNEY 9, 11–13 (1999). Because the 2000 presidential election was so close, there were rumors that the Democrats might attempt to swing enough Republican electors to win the election for Al Gore. Such efforts quickly dwindled.

5. Is there really any evidence that old-fashioned "strong" party organizations have better satisfied the functions required for a working democratic government than the currently predominant system in which a candidate forms his or her own organization to appeal directly to the voters through the mass media to compete for a party nomination in a primary election? Which system of nomination is likely to foster greater public trust in candidates? More coherent and far-seeing public policy? Greater responsiveness to voter concerns?

Many states in the west and upper midwest have used the direct primary since around the turn of the century, whereas many eastern and southern states have had stronger party organizations until more recently. Which regions have been characterized by more efficient, honest, and innovative state and local governments? Does the party structure significantly affect the quality of the government? If so, does the historical record support Fiorina's position? Might Fiorina argue that so far as the issues he is dealing with are concerned, the state and federal governments are not comparable?

6. Suppose you wanted to strengthen the Republican and Democratic parties. What steps would you take to do it? Consider the pros and cons of the following proposals and, to the extent you believe they are desirable, consider whether they should be adopted by state or national party organizations or by state or national law:

A. Allocating a fixed number of seats for elected officials and other party leaders as delegates to the national convention.

B. Requiring all candidates in a party's primary for national, state, and local office to sign a pledge under oath that if elected they will faithfully adhere to and attempt to enact the party's platform as adopted at its convention. (If you agree with this proposal, would there be some system of discipline and punishment if the promise were broken?)

C. Requiring all candidates in a party's primary for national, state, and local office to sign a pledge that they will support the candidate of the party chosen in the primary even if they are defeated.

D. Providing public funding for any or all of a party's internal operations.

E. Requiring a candidate for statewide office who is not the designee of a party convention to obtain the signatures of 5 or 10 percent of registered party members in order to qualify for the ballot in the upcoming primary.

F. Requiring voters who want to switch parties to wait out one primary election before they could reregister. See *Kusper v. Pontikes*, 414 U.S. 51 (1973). Cf. *Rosario v. Rockefeller*, 410 U.S. 752 (1973).

Some of the foregoing proposals might raise substantial constitutional and legal questions, especially if they were implemented by state or federal statute. The materials that follow should help you identify some of these questions.

II. Obligations of Parties under the Constitution

For a long time, courts treated political parties as private associations, subject only to the comparatively minimal legal restraints imposed on purely private groups. See *Developments in the Law—Judicial Control of Actions of Private Associations*, 76 HARVARD LAW REVIEW 983, 1020–37 (1963). The courts' reluctance to intervene in the internal operations of political parties was influenced by the view that their functions of compromise, negotiation and conciliation between competing political factions would be hampered by deciding disputes through litigation. See Comment, *Judicial Intervention in Political Party Disputes: The Political Thicket Reconsidered*, 22 UCLA LAW REVIEW 622, 625 (1975).

The scope of state regulation of political party operations increased dramatically, however, beginning in 1903 when Wisconsin mandated that parties choose candidates through the direct primary and established procedures for conducting the primary. The primary quickly became a critical locus of party activity and a battlefront in the courts. Once state government began to direct the way political parties were to operate, legal questions inevitably arose as to the extent parties thus became subject to a higher standard of constitutional constraint than a purely private association. More recently, courts have considered the extent to which the Constitution may immunize political parties from state regulation.[1]

In the remainder of this section, we shall consider the extent to which the courts have imposed or should impose constraints on the parties in the name of protecting constitutional rights. In the following section, we shall consider the extent to which parties are immune under the First Amendment from regulation by state legislatures. In the final section of this chapter we shall consider the constitutional limits on patronage, a practice that for much of this country's history was an important means for the parties to maintain power and influence.

A. The Federal Interest in Regulating Party Primaries

Before the constitutional constraints on parties could be explored, the initial question whether the federal constitution had any impact on the party primary had to be answered. As previously mentioned, the Constitution makes no mention of parties or primaries. Article I, §4 of the Constitution gives state legislatures the power to prescribe the "times, places and manner of holding *elections* for Senators and Representatives," subject to Congress' power to "make or alter such regulations" (emphasis added). The Fifteenth and Nineteenth Amendments prohibit discrimination on grounds of race or sex in extension of the right to vote. Was a state party primary an "election" under article I, §4 subject to federal regulation? Were the antidiscrimination guarantees of the Fifteenth and Nineteenth Amendments applicable to the right to vote in primaries of political parties, which many viewed as purely private associations?

By a 5–4 decision in *Newberry v. United States*, 256 U.S. 232 (1921), the Supreme Court temporarily delayed the application of federal statutory and constitutional constraints to state party primaries. The defendants in *Newberry*—a candidate for Michigan's Republican nomination for Senate and his supporters—were charged with violating federal statutes that limited campaign expenditures. Newberry's lawyer, former Justice and future Chief Justice Charles Evans Hughes, argued that Congress' power under article I, §4 extended only to general elections, not primaries, and thus the statute did not apply to his clients. The Court held that the statute was inapplicable, but only four justices agreed with Hughes' position. They concluded that primaries "are in no sense elections for office, but merely methods by which party adherents agree upon candidates." 256 U.S. at 740. The virtual necessity of party nomination for election did not impress these four justices. "Birth must precede, but it is no part of either funeral or apotheosis," reasoned the plurality. 256 U.S. at 757. The fifth vote was supplied by Justice McKenna, who reasoned that Congress might have the power to regulate senatorial primaries in the future because of the passage of the Seventeenth Amendment, which provided for the direct election of senators. Four justices dissented.

---

1. For an overview of the history of legal regulation of political parties, see John W. Epperson, The Changing Legal Status of Political Parties in the United States (1986). For a more detailed account of a crucial period including the initial adoption of direct primaries, see Adam Winkler, *Voters' Rights and Parties' Wrongs: Early Political Party Regulation in the State Courts, 1886–1915* 100 Columbia Law Review 873 (2000).

B. The White Primary Cases and the State Action Doctrine

The *Newberry* plurality's philosophy could not forever withstand the increasing use of the primary as the main method of selecting candidates, or the necessity of a federal role in protecting the voting rights of African-Americans, particularly in the then one-party southern states where victory in the Democratic primary was tantamount to election. The Texas Democratic primary became the main constitutional battleground over a quarter of a century as the state party tried a variety of increasingly sophisticated devices to exclude African-American participation and as African-Americans responded with court challenges.

In *Nixon v. Herndon*, 273 U.S. 536 (1927), the Court unanimously held that Texas' state law expressly disqualifying African-Americans from voting in the Democratic primary denied African-American voters equal protection under the *Fourteenth* Amendment. The Court did not discuss whether the *Fifteenth* Amendment right to vote extended to a primary election. Texas then repealed the statute, but gave the party's executive committee the right to determine who was qualified to vote in the primary. The executive committee promptly obliged by passing a resolution prohibiting African-Americans from participating.

In *Nixon v. Condon*, 286 U.S. 73 (1932), the Court invalidated the executive committee's resolution on the ground that the state had, by statute, given the executive committee a power it never had previously held. The executive committee thereby acted as an agent of the state and the result was the same as in *Nixon v. Herndon*. Again, the Fourteenth Amendment's equal protection clause was the ground for decision.

Undaunted, the Texas Democratic Party in convention then adopted a resolution restricting party membership to whites. No legislation authorized this resolution. The issue of the constitutional power of the party to do something the state could not do itself was squarely presented. In *Grovey v. Townsend*, 295 U.S. 45 (1935), the Court temporarily stepped back from the principle that racial discrimination in party affairs central to the electoral process was constitutionally unacceptable. It held unanimously that the Texas party's resolution did not violate federally guaranteed constitutional rights. The philosophy of *Newberry*, that the party was a private association and its primary not a subject of federal constitutional interest, was temporarily reaffirmed.

The landmark decision in *United States v. Classic*, 313 U.S. 299 (1941), though not involving issues of racial discrimination, resumed the course of placing party primaries under the restraint of federal constitutional law. The indictment in *Classic* charged several Louisiana election officials with dishonest practices in a primary election for Congress. The district court dismissed the indictment on the ground that no federal statutory right was violated by a dishonest count in a state-administered congressional primary. The Supreme Court reversed, and overruled *Newberry* explicitly. The Court held Congress had the power to regulate primary elections under article I, §4. The new thinking of the Court on Congress' expansive powers in the elections area was analogous to its new thinking regarding the power of the federal government in economic regulation, inspired by Franklin Roosevelt's abortive Court packing plan and his recent appointees.

Grovey v. Townsend also succumbed to this new trend, in *Smith v. Allwright*, 321 U.S. 649 (1944), decided three years after *Classic*. In *Allwright* the Court emphasized the *Fifteenth* Amendment as the source of the voter's right to be free from racial discrimination in casting a ballot in a party primary. The Court stated that *Classic* "fused the primary and general elections into a single instrumentality." Texas' detailed regulation and involvement in the primary process turned that process into a state function, even though it was conducted by the ostensibly private Democratic Party.

The Court's new activism in protecting African-American voting rights in party primaries took its final step in *Terry v. Adams*, 345 U.S. 461 (1953). The Jaybird Democratic Association of Fort Bend County, Texas, a group founded in 1889, held a straw vote every year several months before the official Democratic primary. The Jaybird vote was open to any white voter. The Jaybird election victor had no special official status under state law and had to compete on an equal basis with every other candidate in the primary.[m] In practice, however, the Jaybird victor always won the primary and general elections. In a result reached by a majority that was split between three separate opinions, the Court held that the Jaybird action excluding African-Americans from the straw vote violated the Fifteenth Amendment.

Justice Black, writing for three justices, noted that the Fifteenth Amendment clearly includes "any election in which public issues are decided or public officials selected," but just as clearly excludes social or business clubs. He also noted that the qualifications for voting in the Jaybird straw vote were identical to those for voting in the Democratic primary, with the one additional proviso of race. He concluded:

> For a state to permit such a duplication of its election processes is to permit a flagrant abuse of those processes to defeat the purposes of the Fifteenth Amendment. The use of the county-operated primary to ratify the result of the prohibited election merely compounds the offense. It violates the Fifteenth Amendment for a state, by such circumvention, to permit within its borders the use of any device that produces an equivalent of the prohibited election.

Justice Frankfurter said he found the case "by no means free of difficulty. Whenever the law draws a line between permissive and forbidden conduct cases are bound to arise which are not obviously on one side or the other." Crucial to his decision was his view that "[a]s the action of the entire white voting community, the Jaybird primary is as a practical matter the instrument of those few in this small county who are politically active— the officials of the local Democratic party and, we may assume, the elected officials of the county." In particular, those officials "participate by voting in the Jaybird primary," and they "join the white voting community in proceeding with elaborate formality, in almost all respects parallel to the procedures dictated by Texas law for the primary itself, to express their preferences in a wholly successful effort to withdraw significance from the State-prescribed primary, to subvert the operation of what is formally the law of the State for primaries in this county." He then concluded that the state had "entered into a comprehensive scheme of regulation of political primaries, including procedures by which election officials shall be chosen.... If the Jaybird Association, although not a political party, is a device to defeat the law of Texas regulating primaries, and if the electoral officials, clothed with State power in the county, share in that subversion, they cannot divest themselves of the State authority and help as participants in the scheme."

Justice Clark, writing for four justices, found that the Jaybird Association was a political party for purposes of the Fifteenth Amendment, and therefore covered by *Smith v. Allwright*:

---

m. The Jaybird Association had a rule barring candidates who had already served more than two consecutive terms, though no such term limit appeared in state law.

Not every private club, association or league organized to influence public candidacies or political action must conform to the Constitution's restrictions on political parties. Certainly a large area of freedom permits peaceable assembly and concerted private action for political purposes to be exercised separately by white and colored citizens alike. More, however, is involved here....

Quite evidently the Jaybird Democratic Association operates as an auxiliary of the local Democratic Party organization, selecting its nominees and using its machinery for carrying out an admitted design of destroying the weight and effect of Negro ballots in Fort Bend County. To be sure, the Democratic primary and the general election are nominally open to the colored elector. But his must be an empty vote cast after the real decisions are made. And because the Jaybird-indorsed nominee meets no opposition in the Democratic primary, the Negro minority's vote is nullified at the sole stage of the local political process where the bargaining and interplay of rival political forces could make it count.

Justice Minton dissented.

Terry held that Texas "violated the Fifteenth Amendment by permitting within its borders a private device that would have been forbidden in a public election," according to Ronald D. Rotunda, *Constitutional and Statutory Restrictions on Political Parties in the Wake of Cousins v. Wigoda*, 53 TEXAS LAW REVIEW 935, 954 (1975). Rotunda adds that the "logic of the *White Primary Cases* supports the conclusion that an election for public office is a public function and that any integral part of that function must be constitutional." *Id.* at 955.

Another commentator has suggested that *Terry* "went too far." John G. Kester, *Constitutional Restrictions on Political Parties*, 60 VIRGINIA LAW REVIEW 735, 738 (1974). In Kester's view: "For the judiciary now to place constitutional limitations on endorsements by a private group simply because the electorate respects and normally follows the group's endorsements is nothing less than a judicial subversion of the American political process." *Id.* Further, as Kester interprets the *White Primary Cases*, the "right of a political party to determine its own membership by any standard it pleases is unimpaired so long as it does not abridge the *right to vote* free from racial, and probably sexual discrimination. The arguments in favor of granting a party such freedom are even more forceful today ... in light of the intervening recognition of constitutionally protected rights of association which parties and its members may claim." *Id.* at 759–60.

Do you agree with Kester that *Terry* goes too far? Suppose a hypothetical Jaybird Association never conducts straw votes, but consists of a handful of local leaders who publicize their recommendations to the voters before each primary election. If this small group's recommended candidates always or nearly always win in the primaries, and if the group's members are all whites, would their activities violate the Fifteenth Amendment? If the group includes members of all races and all ethnic groups but are all males, would their activities violate the Nineteenth Amendment? What if the members are all white males, but the candidates they endorse come from all racial and ethnic groups and both sexes? What if their recommendations appear to be influential but fall way short of being decisive? What if they do not publicize their recommendations at all, but contribute substantial campaign funds to the candidates they support?

Do you share Kester's concern that the *White Primary Cases*, by treating parties and even non-party groups such as the Jaybird Association as subject to constitutional constraints, may impair legitimate associational freedoms of parties? Consider the following.

Daniel Hays Lowenstein, *Associational Rights of Major Political Parties: A Skeptical Inquiry*
71 Texas Law Review 1741, 1747–54 (1993)

Nearly everyone who has written about the constitutional rights or obligations of parties seems to have assumed that whether parties or their activities are to be classified as "private" or "public" is a crucial issue....

To the uninitiated, this must seem odd. Parties are not government agencies. In ordinary conversation, to suggest that they are would be bizarre. However, the Supreme Court's continued adherence to the state action doctrine has forced the Justices to depart from ordinary conceptions of what entities are "public." Under the doctrine, unless an entity's actions affecting others are regarded as "public," the entity need not conform to the requirements of due process of law, equal protection, freedom of speech, or other provisions of the Bill of Rights. Accordingly, when the Supreme Court was confronted in the *White Primary Cases* with the question of whether the Texas Democratic Party could exclude African-Americans from voting in its primaries, the only way it could find to prohibit such an exclusion was to declare that parties, at least when they nominate candidates in primary elections, are acting as public agencies.

The difficulty created by the *White Primary Cases* for proponents of freedom of association for political parties is that the public/private distinction is generally perceived as governing not only whether an entity must conform to constitutional requirements in its treatment of others, but also whether the entity itself enjoys constitutional rights against the government. Thus, by declaring parties to be "public," the *White Primary Cases* not only prohibited them from depriving racial minorities of their right to vote but also seemed to deprive the parties of the protections of the Bill of Rights. If instead parties were declared to be "private," they would enjoy constitutional rights, but the foundation for the *White Primary Cases* would be undercut.

One response to this dilemma would be to disavow the *White Primary Cases* and treat parties as purely private in nature. The proposal is not monstrous, because the *White Primary Cases* had only modest success in extending the franchise to African-Americans in the southern states and, more importantly, because federal voting rights legislation and greatly changed mores make it extremely unlikely that the parties would seek to exclude primary voters on grounds of race in the foreseeable future. Renunciation now of the *White Primary Cases* would have no tangible cost in racial discrimination, would bring constitutional doctrine into accord with the common sense notion that parties are not government agencies, and would clear the way for a full extension of constitutional freedoms to parties. However, the *White Primary Cases*, despite their limited effectiveness, are rightly remembered as one of the bright spots in the history of the Supreme Court and the struggle for racial equality. For the Supreme Court now to declare that the cases were wrong would be unpleasant, even disillusioning. Most of us would never believe the Court anyway. Furthermore, it is always possible that at some time in the future the parties will act in a manner perceived to deny fundamental rights to some group of Americans. The possibility of constitutional relief, won so painstakingly from the 1920s to the 1950s, should not be tossed away lightly. In any event, few commentators and no courts have suggested the disavowal of the *White Primary Cases*.

At the opposite extreme is the position that the parties are public, pure and simple. [But this position is not viable after the cases considered in Part III of the present chapter. Therefore,] as the Justices like to say, it is "too late in the day" for the argument to succeed. Nor should it. The idea of parties as "public" is in tension not only with the everyday recognition that parties are not government agencies, but also with the need to assure that the party system maintains a basic autonomy from the state so that the parties may serve as vehicles for expressing the public's needs and sentiments. Such autonomy distinguishes democracies from authoritarian systems, and our constitutional law may as well recognize this fact. It is one thing to argue about the nature of the protection accorded to parties by the First Amendment, but to argue that the parties are entitled to *no* such protection has an incongruous ring to it.

A third approach is the middle ground that parties are a mixture of public and private elements or that some of their activities are public and others private. Leon Epstein captures this idea by analogizing parties to public utilities.[45] Of course, the key question for any middle-ground approach is: When is the party private, and when is it public? The most common answer has been that it is the election process that is a governmental activity; therefore, when parties nominate candidates or engage in other activities directly connected with the conduct of elections, their activities are public. Other activities, such as internal governance and the adoption of platforms, are private.

This distinction between electoral and internal activities is another casualty of *Tashjian* [*infra*]. The activity in question in *Tashjian*, determination of who could vote in a primary election, was the same as in the *White Primary Cases*, but in *Tashjian* the party was treated as a bearer of First Amendment rights, and therefore presumably private rather than public.

Aside from its fate at the hands of the *Tashjian* Court, the middle-ground approach might mitigate but cannot solve the public/private dilemma that exists for anyone who believes that there are at least some situations in which parties should be required to honor constitutional rights and other situations in which parties should bear constitutional rights. A middle ground allows for both possibilities by dividing party activities into two categories. But within the "public" category it must still be the case that the parties bear no constitutional rights, and within the "private" category the party will be free to deny equal protection, freedom of speech, and other constitutional protections to others.

The final approach is to ignore the problem. Thus, the *White Primary Cases* are limited to their "unusual context: a state-mandated racially discriminatory primary scheme in a one-party state where nomination is tantamount to election."[48] If we take the public/private distinction seriously, this will not do. To suggest that political parties act as agents of the government when and only when they violate the fundamental rights of citizens is to do violence to the English language, if the terms "public" and "private" are taken to have any descriptive meaning whatever.

But should we take the public/private distinction seriously? If we set the distinction aside momentarily, we are free simply to conclude, as the Ninth Circuit did in *Eu*, [*infra*], that parties bear constitutional rights *and* that they act unconstitutionally when they deprive any group of citizens of the opportunity for political participation. Surely this is the result most of us want. We can obtain this result by recognizing that the question of whether a party action is public or private is not a tool of analysis used in deciding a constitutional controversy, but is instead the attachment, after the fact, of a more or less superfluous label to a result reached for other reasons. For example, the reason parties are prohibited from excluding African-Americans from primaries is not that they act in a public capacity when they exclude. Rather, the action of excluding African-Americans is labeled a state

---

45. Leon D. Epstein, POLITICAL PARTIES IN THE AMERICAN MOLD 155–59 (1986).
48. San Francisco County Democratic Cent. Comm. v. Eu, 826 F.2d 814, 826 n.21 (9th Cir. 1987), *aff'd*, [*infra*].

action because we have chosen to interpret the Constitution as prohibiting it. Similarly, the party has a First Amendment right to permit independents to vote in its primaries, but not because analysis has shown the party to be a private association. Rather, it is because the Court decided *Tashjian* as it did that we label the decision whether independents should be able to vote in the party's primary as a private associational decision.

Thus the terms "public" and "private" (like many similar terms in the law) actually function as *post hoc* labels, rather than as the *a priori* analytical devices that conventional doctrine supposes them to be. They do so because the world is too diverse for all its phenomena to fit comfortably within a small set of categories that can suffice for an acceptable normative ordering. A dichotomy such as the public/private distinction is devised because it is found to be a useful way of ordering some range of activities, but it is an artificial categorization.... As such, it is susceptible to manipulation, and it is virtually certain to be manipulated for at least two reasons. First, different people (such as different Justices) who apply the categories will be guided by different values and life experiences. Second, although the categories may be straightforward and acceptable within a range of problems, outside of that range their application will be obscure or even perverse.

So it is with the public/private distinction as applied to political parties. We have seen that the distinction leads to perverse results, for it permits parties either to be subject to constitutional rights or to bear them, but not both (at least with respect to any given party activity). However, the greatest harm caused by fixation on the public/private distinction is not that it requires an embarrassing and illogical confinement of the *White Primary Cases* "to their facts," but that it tends to preclude consideration of the actual relationship between the government and major political parties. That relationship does not justify denying First Amendment Rights to parties, but it significantly affects the way in which those rights should be applied.

Notes and Questions

1. As this excerpt reflects, considerable attention has been given to the tension that may exist between the constitutional *rights* of parties and the constitutional *obligations* of parties. Similar tension may exist between parties' *constitutional* rights and their *statutory* obligations. Consider, for example, the requirement of Section 5 of the Voting Rights Act that a covered "State or political subdivision" must seek preclearance before implementing changed voting procedures. If eligibility for voting in primaries in a covered jurisdiction is set by parties and a party wishes to change the requirements, must it seek preclearance? By the logic of *Smith v. Allwright*, if the primary and general elections are "fused," then preclearance must be required to prevent the state from evading Section 5 by handing control of the primaries to the parties. See, e.g., *MacGuire v. Amos*, 343 F.Supp. 119 (M.D.Ala. 1972). However, suppose candidates are nominated at party conventions rather than at primaries. Must a change in the method of selecting delegates to the convention be precleared?

This question was answered affirmatively in a 5–4 decision in *Morse v. Republican Party*, 517 U.S. 186 (1996). The facts of the case were unusual. Virginia law assures the candidates of the two major parties a position on the ballot and leaves it to the parties to determine how to nominate their candidates. The Republicans had used various nomination methods, but for 1994 they adopted a "convention" method under which any Republican could be a delegate and have a vote upon payment of a fee up to $45.

There was no opinion for the Court. In a lengthy opinion Justice Stevens, joined by Justice Ginsburg, gave numerous reasons for believing the party's adoption of the fee was subject to preclearance, particularly Congress' intent when it passed the Voting Rights Act to assure effective enforcement of the Fifteenth Amendment. The *White Primary Cases*, and the persistent efforts in southern states to set up nomination processes that would evade the Fifteenth Amendment, were well known to the Congress that passed the Voting Rights Act. Justice Breyer, joined by Justices O'Connor and Souter, relied even more heavily on this point. But he recognized the burden on parties' associational rights that could result from overly broad application of the preclearance requirement to parties. Given *Smith v. Allwright* and *Terry v. Adams*, Congress surely intended that changes in eligibility to vote in primaries were subject to preclearance. Breyer went on:

> We need not go further in determining when party activities are, in effect, substitutes for state nominating primaries because the case before us involves a nominating convention that resembles a primary about as closely as one could imagine. The convention (but for the $45 fee) was open to any voter declaring loyalty to the Party, just like a primary....
>
> Nor need we go further to decide just which party nominating convention practices fall within the scope of the Act. There are already substantial limits as to which voting related "practices and procedures" must be precleared. See *Presley v. Etowah County Commission*, 502 U.S. 491 (1992).... I would note, moreover, that the lower courts have applied §5 only to a small category of party rules.
>
> While these limitations exclude much party activity—including much that takes place at an assembly of its members—I recognize that some of the First Amendment concerns raised by the dissents may render these limits yet more restrictive in the case of party conventions. But the practice challenged here—the fee—lies within the Act, and well outside the area of greatest "associational" concern. Like the more obviously evasive "all-white" devices, it is of a kind that is the subject of a specific constitutional Amendment. U.S. Const., Amdt. 24, §1 (banning poll tax).
>
> We go no further in this case because, as the dissents indicate, First Amendment questions about the extent to which the Federal Government, through preclearance procedures, can regulate the workings of a political party convention, are difficult ones, as are those about the limits imposed by the state action cases. Those questions, however, are properly left for a case that squarely presents them.

2. The Texas Log Cabin Republicans are a group of Republicans seeking to influence their party to be more supportive of positions favorable to gays and lesbians. In 1996, the Texas Republican Party refused to permit the Log Cabin Republicans to lease a booth at the state party convention and to purchase an advertisement in the convention program. Is this refusal state action for purposes of a free speech challenge by the Log Cabin Republicans? Applying the state action doctrine under the *state* constitution, the Supreme Court of Texas ruled it was not state action in *Republican Party of Texas v. Dietz*, 940 S.W.2d 86 (Tex. 1997), and gave the following reasons:

> We agree that a political party is a state actor in some instances, such as when it is conducting elections, but a private organization in other instances, such as when it is conducting certain of its internal affairs. We must determine where, along this spectrum, the Republican Party's conduct falls. We hold that the actions of the Republican Party in denying LCR the booth and advertisement were mere internal party affairs. The stated purpose of LCR in attempting to obtain a booth and advertising space was to work toward changing the Party's internal platform. However, a Party's platform is not an element of the electoral process.

Party candidates are free to accept in part and reject in part the platform, and there is no requirement that a party member adhere to all portions of the platform. While there are many provisions of the Texas Election Code regulating the conduct of political parties, these provisions do not regulate or even require that a political party have a platform.

If the Texas Republican Party adopted a policy of not renting booths or selling advertising space to members of a particular racial group, would an Equal Protection challenge be denied on the ground that the refusal is not state action?

C. The Constitution and the Party in the Legislature

Ammond v. McGahn

390 F.Supp. 655 (D.N.J. 1975)

COHEN, Senior District Judge:

Perhaps, for the first time in the history of the New Jersey State Legislature, a federal court is asked to decide whether a political caucus may exclude one of its members for her critical public statements without violating the First and Fourteenth Amendments to the Federal Constitution....

Plaintiff, Alene S. Ammond, in November, 1973, was elected [as a Democrat] to the New Jersey State Senate by the voters of the Sixth Senatorial District. [Additional plaintiffs were residents of Senator Ammond's district.]

The defendants are 28 Democratic Senators who comprise the New Jersey State Democratic Caucus; the Sergeant-at-Arms of the State Senate; the Executive Director of the Senate Majority; and both counsel for the Senate Majority Caucus.

It is contended by the plaintiff, Senator Ammond, that the decision by her fellow-Democratic Senators to exclude her from the Caucus was in retaliation for public statements she made regarding the Caucus and its members; that the Senate Democratic Caucus is a vital and integral part of the New Jersey State Legislative process; and that her right to free speech guaranteed under the First Amendment has been violated.

Plaintiffs, Karp, Paull and Powers contend that the exclusion of their duly elected representative from the Caucus denies them the Equal Protection of the Law guaranteed by the Fourteenth Amendment....

Defendants while not conceding that the conduct of the Caucus is "state action," ... seem to rest primarily on the defense of immunity. Plaintiffs, on the other hand, maintain that the Caucus is inextricably bound up with the affairs of the Senate, and, therefore, a symbiotic relationship exists between the Caucus and the Senate.... [I]f, as plaintiff alleges, the Caucus is a vital and integral part of the legislative process, then there can be no question as to state action. For, as the Supreme Court indicated in *Jackson v. Metropolitan Edison Co.*, 419 U.S. 345, 352 (1974), "We have of course found state action present in the exercise by private entity of powers traditionally exclusively reserved to the State. If we were dealing with the exercise by Metropolitan of some power delegated to it by the State which is traditionally associated with sovereignty, such as eminent domain, our case would be quite a different one." Thus, the question presented here resolves itself to whether the Caucus is, in fact, an integral part of the legislative process in New Jersey.

In deciding this issue, the testimony of Senator Ammond, supported by that of Bolton Schwartz, who has been characterized as the "Dean of the Press Corps," must be considered. At the hearing, it was revealed that on or about January 20, 1975, in her absence, the Democratic Caucus voted unanimously to exclude Senator Ammond from the Caucus. She received no official communication informing her that she had been so barred, nor was she accorded any hearing whatsoever in connection with her exclusion. On January 27, 1975, she attempted to attend the regularly scheduled meeting of the Caucus. The sergeant-at-arms barred her entry, and informed her that the President of the Senate, Frank J. Dodd, had authorized him to convey to her that she could not enter the Caucus as a result of the exclusion vote adopted the previous week. Senator Ammond maintains that the decision to exclude her was in retaliation for public statements she made regarding the caucus and its members.

The Caucus is a body composed of all Democratic members of the State Senate who receive compensation from the State of New Jersey. Its sessions are conducted in the State House on State property and attended by elected and appointed State officials; it is serviced by State paid employees, who include, among others, the sergeant-at-arms for the Senate, the Executive Director of the Senate Majority and its counsel; and notice of the Caucus meetings, by telegrams listing proposed legislative bills and other matters on the agenda, are paid by the State.

Bills pending before the Senate are discussed by their sponsors followed by general discussion and debate among the members of the Caucus. The views of members of the Executive Branch of the State Government are presented. Often, "Straw" votes are taken to determine the likelihood of passage of a bill. Since the Democratic members of the Senate are a large majority, the result of a "Straw" vote will often determine the outcome of a bill on the floor of the Senate. Bills which do not command a majority are often withdrawn. Majority counsel participate in the Caucus and render advisory opinions on the legislative proposals.

Additionally, a "consent list" is prepared in Caucus, consisting of those bills which will pass on the floor without debate. The purpose of this list is to free legislative time by obviating the necessity for debate on routine matters.

It is the determination of the Court that the Caucus functions as an arm of the State Legislature and is an essential part of the legislative process in New Jersey. We hold that the Caucus exercises legislative power which is normally associated with sovereignty and, therefore, action by the Caucus is "state action" ... *Jackson*; *Terry v. Adams*.

The Caucus is not, as the defendants attempted to elicit on cross-examination, an informal social gathering—a luncheon club consisting of members of the same political party. It conducts the business of the State. [Telegrams were introduced into evidence,] paid for by the State, signed by Frank J. Dodd, Senate President, addressed to Senator Ammond at her residence, notifying her that the Senate will convene on a specified date; requesting her to be prepared to vote on certain enumerated Senate Bills; advising her that certain Senate Committees will meet at specified times; and that party conferences will be held at specified times. Obviously, all of the aforementioned State business was to be discussed at the Conference or party Caucus.

The exclusion of Senator Ammond from the Caucus in retaliation for her critical public statements is violative of her right of free speech under the First Amendment. Given the fact that the Caucus often decides the course of legislation before it ever reaches the floor of the Senate, exclusion from the Caucus is tantamount to exclusion from the Senate....

It is further determined that the exclusion of Senator Ammond from the Caucus without a prior hearing violates the Due Process Clause of the Fourteenth Amendment. No elected representative of the people may be barred from participation in the forum to which he or she was elected for misconduct, no matter how egregious, without some type of hearing. *Bond v. Floyd*, 385 U.S. 116 (1966); see *Goss v. Lopez*, 419 U.S. 565 (1975). The action by the Caucus in denying Senator Ammond the opportunity to attend its deliberations deprived her constituents of the Equal Protection of the law. In effect, the action by the Caucus created two classes of voters. One class consists of those citizens whose Senators could effectively participate fully in the legislative process and another class whose Senator could participate only to a limited degree. As the Supreme Court has indicated:

> ... The right of suffrage can be denied by a debasement or dilution of the weight of a citizen's vote as effectively as by wholly prohibiting the free exercise of the franchise. *Reynolds.*

While it is true that Senator Ammond was not barred from voting on the floor of the New Jersey Senate, her exclusion from the Caucus could vastly diminish her efficacy as an elected representative.

This court need not consider the merits of the controversy between Senator Ammond and her colleagues and while we are not confronted with the question of whether her public statements are defamatory, we note that the alleged "injury to official reputation affords no more warrant for repressing speech that would otherwise be free than does factual error." *New York Times Co. v. Sullivan*, 376 U.S. 254, 272 (1964).

We also note, in passing, that if these defendants were to seek redress in the courts for the alleged injury to their reputations caused by Senator Ammond's remarks, they would be met by "the constitutional guarantees ... that prohibit[] a public official from recovering damages for a defamatory falsehood relating to his official conduct unless he proves that the statement was made with 'actual malice'—that is, with knowledge that it was false or with reckless disregard of whether it was false or not." *Id.* at 279–80; see *Gertz v. Welch, Inc.*, 418 U.S. 323 (1974). While we intimate no view as to the defamatory nature of Senator Ammond's statements, it is significant that defendants concede that Senator Ammond's exclusion was a result of her public statements.

It was rather well established from the testimony that Senator Ammond is an outspoken critic of the Legislature and its members. She has been characterized as "The Terror of Trenton." As was legendarily and so forcefully proclaimed by Voltaire:[3]

I disapprove of what you say, but I will defend to the death your right to say it.

[Earlier in the proceedings, the court had issued a temporary restraining order against the defendants, ordering them not to deny Senator Ammond access to the Caucus meetings during the pendency of the law suit. The Caucus then voted to readmit Senator Ammond. The court nevertheless concluded that the case was not moot.]

This court believes a preliminary injunction is appropriate. We are convinced that plaintiffs have a reasonable chance of ultimate success in this suit, and that unless injunctive relief is provided, freedom of speech may suffer a chilling effect....

---

3. Although this quote is commonly attributed to Voltaire, it is actually a paraphrase of his attitude by S. G. Tallentyre in *Friends of Voltaire* 199 (London, 1907).

Notes and Questions

1. On appeal, the District Court's granting of a preliminary injunction in favor of Senator Ammond was reversed on the ground that the Democratic Caucus had voted to readmit her, so that there was "no clear showing of immediate irreparable injury. Under such circumstances, a court should not exercise the delicate power of injunctive relief." *Ammond v. McGahn*, 532 F.2d 325, 329 (3d Cir. 1976). The appellate court thus found it unnecessary to discuss "the possible conflict between the associational and political rights of the members of the Caucus, ... and the constitutional rights of the plaintiffs...."

2. The majority faction on a city council, angry at an opposing council member for his votes and statements, fires the legislative aide and close associate of the opposing member from his position on the legislative payroll. Does the aide have a First Amendment claim against the city? See *Camacho v. Brandon*, 317 F.3d 153 (2d Cir. 2003).

3. Republicans win 55% of the seats in a state legislative chamber and Democrats win the remaining 45%. The Republican speaker appoints disproportionately large numbers of Republicans to committees, with Democrats receiving as few as 10% of the seats in several of the key committees. The Democratic representatives, joined by Democratic voters in their districts, seek injunctive relief ordering the speaker to reappoint the committees so that the membership of each will be approximately proportionate to the partisan breakdown in the chamber as a whole. How should the court rule? See *Davids v. Akers*, 549 F.2d 120 (9th Cir. 1977).

4. The Democrats in the New Jersey legislature got back into federal court a few years after the *Ammond* litigation in *Gewertz v. Jackman*, 467 F.Supp. 1047 (D.N.J. 1979). Gewertz, a Democratic member of the General Assembly, had "a reputation for being outspoken and [had] expressed frequent opposition to the leadership of his party," as well as to the governor, also a Democrat. The Speaker removed him from the Appropriations Committee, an action ratified by the Democratic Caucus. Gewertz claimed his removal violated his rights to free speech, equal protection of the laws, and due process. The District Court denied a preliminary injunction on the grounds that under the evidence, Gewertz was unlikely to prevail on any of those claims. But the court explicitly took the view that it was proper for it to consider these claims on the merits:

> Without directly attacking this court's jurisdiction or the justiciability of this action, defendants assert it is improper for this court to become involved in the operations of a state legislative body or to conduct an inquiry into the motivations of its leaders. While the court recognizes the delicacy of the task, we are convinced that the law requires us to do so when an individual legislator alleges that his constitutional rights have been violated by the legislature or its leaders.

Compare *Vander Jagt v. O'Neill*, 699 F.2d 1166 (D.C.Cir. 1983), in which Republican members of the House of Representatives objected to their party's disproportionately small representation on key House committees. The claim was thus similar to the claim by state legislators in Note 3 above, except that this case arose in Congress and the disproportion was much smaller than in Note 3. The D.C. Circuit majority recognized that it had jurisdiction and found no other procedural impediment to its hearing the case on the merits. However, it exercised its "remedial discretion" not to do so because of its "respect for a coequal branch of government." Judge Bork concurred in the judgment on the ground that the plaintiffs lacked standing

III. Associational Rights of Parties

A. Presidential Nominations

For most of our history party organization was centered at the state and local levels. National parties were confederations of these state organizations, and for the most part were inactive except during the quadrennial periods of presidential nomination and campaigning. Since the 1830s, presidential candidates have been nominated at national party conventions, which, until the 1970s, were dominated by the state organizations.

Each state could decide for itself by what means its delegation to the convention would be selected. When disputes arose over who could properly represent a state party at the National Convention, these disputes were referred to the Credentials Committee, whose decisions were subject to appeal to the Convention as a whole. Often these disputes were treated more as ploys in the competition for the nomination than as matters to be resolved on the basis of principle or legal propriety.

Since there were few restrictions on the manner in which states could select delegates, state legislatures could regulate the process without much danger of coming into conflict with national party rules or requirements. Dating from the Progressive period in the early twentieth century, a number of states used presidential primaries, but these states did not constitute close to a majority at the conventions. Although the presidential primaries provided a test of the popularity of competing candidates, they were by no means the predominant factor in the awarding of a presidential nomination. The great majority of delegates at the conventions were more or less selected and controlled by the state party leaders and organizations, and it was the state leaders who ultimately had the greatest say in who would be the presidential candidates.

Because of the controversies attending their troubled 1968 convention, the Democrats created a commission to propose reformed delegate selection procedures. The commission was originally chaired by Senator George McGovern, who later became a candidate for President and was succeeded by Representative Donald Fraser. The reforms proposed by the McGovern-Fraser commission and later adopted almost intact by the Democratic National Committee had three major thrusts.

First, whether the state used a primary or a caucus system,[n] the procedure had to be open to all registered Democrats and held at a time and in a manner that would permit each participant to vote for a specific presidential candidate. Previously, in many states, delegates or those empowered to name the delegates were selected long before the presidential campaign began, or otherwise in a manner calculated to discourage participation by anyone but supporters of the dominant party organization.

Second, the tallying of voter preferences had to be roughly though not necessarily precisely proportional. In other words, "winner-take-all" primaries or caucus procedures would be prohibited. However, in a compromise, states were permitted to retain winner-

---

n. "Caucuses," in this context, are meetings held simultaneously across the state in each neighborhood. Participants in each caucus select representatives, usually chosen according to the presidential candidates they support, to a higher level caucus or convention. A pyramidal process eventuates in a statewide convention of representatives whose selection is ultimately traceable to the preferences expressed at the original caucuses. The statewide convention selects the actual presidential nominating delegation.

take-all primaries through the 1972 election. As we shall see shortly, this compromise helped trigger the first round of litigation under the new rules.

Third, the demographic makeup of the delegation, especially with respect to race and sex, but also with respect to characteristics such as age and income, must not depart excessively from the population of the states. By 1980 the Democratic Convention required that each delegation include equal numbers of men and women.[o]

One important consequence of the adoption of the reforms, commented upon by Fiorina, *supra*, was that there was a dramatic increase in the number of states that selected their delegates by holding a presidential primary. This was not required by the new rules, and it probably was not even desired by many of the reformers, who consisted primarily of liberal activists who undoubtedly expected to be overrepresented among voters turning out at caucuses held in accordance with the new requirements. However, the caucus requirements were complex, and many states found it easier to assure compliance with the new rules by opting for a primary election. Furthermore, those state parties that were still dominated by old-line organizations may have preferred a presidential primary to a caucus proceeding that could spread the new "democratization" to state party governance. See Shafer, *supra*; Nelson W. Polsby, CONSEQUENCES OF PARTY REFORM (1983).

Although the Republican Party did not adopt all the reforms that the Democrats adopted, the Republicans were influenced significantly by them. They did adopt some of the reforms, though usually in a more moderate version. In addition, when the reforms were adopted via state legislation, the new laws often applied to the Republicans as well. This was especially true in the case of the adoption of presidential primaries, which with very few exceptions was done either for both parties or for neither.

By inducing greatly increased use of presidential primaries, the new rules helped bring about a basic change in the method of selecting the president. As we have seen, success in primaries was only a part of a campaign for the nomination prior to 1972. Its major significance was to demonstrate to party leaders that an aspirant would make a strong candidate. For example, John Kennedy's victory over Hubert Humphrey in the West Virginia primary in 1960 went a long way toward overcoming doubts of some party leaders as to whether a Roman Catholic could win votes in heavily Protestant parts of the country. But the final decision was determined not by primaries, but by negotiations between state delegation leaders at the convention. In contrast, since 1972, the nominee of each party has been the candidate who could win a majority of delegate votes in the primaries and state caucuses.

The parties, especially the Democrats, continued to tinker with the delegate selection rules in advance of each convention after 1972, at least through 1984. Of greater consequence to us in this section is that the rules changes have stimulated litigation presenting complex new constitutional problems.

State parties on occasion have resisted one or another aspect of the delegate selection rules. Since the state party is likely to have influence over the state legislature on such matters, the state party's resistance sometimes is buttressed by state law. When such conflicts arise, they raise the question whether the national party rules, state party rules, or state legislation should be supreme with respect to the selection of the state party dele-

---

o. For a detailed history of the McGovern-Fraser proposals, see Byron E. Shafer, QUIET REVOLUTION: THE STRUGGLE FOR THE DEMOCRATIC PARTY AND THE SHAPING OF POST-REFORM POLITICS (1983).

gation to a national convention.[p] When such conflicts are brought to court, they present an additional question: Should the conflicts be resolved by the judiciary at all, or should they be left to the political process for resolution.

Brown v. O'Brien, 409 U.S. 1 (1972), went to the Supreme Court on the eve of the 1972 Democratic National Convention. The Credentials Committee, whose rulings would be subject to review by the convention delegates, had upheld challenges to the California and Illinois delegations. The California challenge was based on the fact that California had conducted a winner-take-all primary. George McGovern, who had won the primary, virtually was assured the nomination if he received all the California delegates, whereas the nomination might be up for grabs if the California delegation were divided among the candidates in proportion to their vote percentages. The Illinois delegation, which was controlled by Chicago Mayor Richard Daley, was challenged for underrepresenting women, minorities, and young people.

The D.C. Circuit, while rejecting the Illinois claim, held the credentials committee ruling unseating the California McGovern delegates violated due process, since those delegates were selected in accordance with then existing state law. The losing sides both applied to the Supreme Court for stays of the D.C. Circuit's orders. Three days before the Convention opened, the Court granted those requests, in part because of the "grave doubts" it had about the action of the D.C. Circuit. In the *per curiam* opinion in *O'Brien*, 409 U.S. at 4, the Court said:

> It has been understood since our national political parties first came into being as voluntary associations of individuals that the convention itself is the proper forum for determining intra-party disputes as to which delegates shall be seated. Thus, these cases involve claims of the federal judiciary to review actions heretofore thought to lie in the control of political parties. Highly important questions are presented concerning justiciability, whether the action of the Credentials Committee is state action, and if so, the reach of the Due Process Clause in this unique context. Vital rights of association guaranteed by the Constitution are also involved.

The Court did not, however, definitively resolve the issues it identified, because of the lack of time for adequate briefing of them and "the availability of the Convention as a forum to review the recommendations of the Credentials Committee." The Convention did ultimately uphold the Credentials Committee on the Illinois challenge but reversed its decision on the California challenge, thus assuring the nomination for Senator McGovern.

Meanwhile, the Daley delegation (also called the Wigoda delegation) had obtained an injunction from an Illinois state judge prohibiting the challengers (the Cousins delegation) from acting as delegates. The Cousins delegation ignored the injunction and participated in the Convention as the delegates from Illinois. The Illinois state judge who had issued the injunction then held the Cousins delegation in contempt of court for violating it. The issue was thus clearly joined over the power of state election law to govern the con-

---

p. One constitutional question that has not been tested is the degree to which Congress has the power to regulate the national conventions or other national or state party processes. To date, Congress has withheld its legislative hand. For discussion of constitutional issues that would be raised by congressional efforts to regulate, see William Mayer & Andrew E. Busch, THE FRONT-LOADING PROBLEM IN PRESIDENTIAL ELECTIONS 131–40 (2004); Daniel Lowenstein, *Presidential Nomination Reform: Legal Restraints and Procedural Possibilities*, in REFORMING THE PRESIDENTIAL NOMINATION PROCESS (Steven S. Smith & Melanie J. Springer, eds., forthcoming).

Congress has regulated party finances, and the constitutional issues raised by that regulation are considered in Chapter 15.

duct of a national party's Convention. The Supreme Court ultimately held that the Illinois judge had no power to control the actions of the Convention. *Cousins v. Wigoda*, 419 U.S. 477 (1975).

The Democratic National Committee's call for the 1980 Democratic National Convention required that participation in the delegate selection process must be limited to Democrats only. Wisconsin had employed an "open" primary since 1903, when it became one of the first states to adopt the direct primary system for nominating candidates. An open primary is one in which each voter may request to vote in the primary of whichever party he or she chooses on election day, without regard to party membership or affiliation. Wisconsin Democrats defied the national Democratic Party by conducting an open primary in 1980. A Wisconsin court ordered the national party to seat Wisconsin's delegates at the convention, despite the violation of the national party rules. In *Democratic Party of the United States v. Wisconsin ex rel. La Follette*, 450 U.S. 107 (1981), the Supreme Court reversed the state court's order.

Justice Stewart's opinion for the majority emphasized that the Court was not ruling that the national Democrats could prevent Wisconsin from conducting an open primary. He wrote that Wisconsin had an interest in conducting its elections as it chose and that the national Democrats had an interest in how the delegates to their convention were selected. He went on:

> But these interests are not incompatible, and to the limited extent they clash in this case, both interests can be preserved. The National Party rules do not forbid Wisconsin to conduct an open primary. But if Wisconsin does open its primary, it cannot require that Wisconsin delegates to the National Party Convention vote there in accordance with the primary results, if to do so would violate Party rules.

Justice Powell, joined by Justices Blackmun and Rehnquist, dissented.

Notes and Questions

1. Justice Stewart emphasized the National Democratic Party's constitutional right to freedom of association as an important reason for the result he reached in *La Follette*. Yet, the Wisconsin Democratic Party strongly supported the open primary and attempted to defend it in the litigation. Is the majority's ruling an infringement on the state party's freedom of association? Why is the state party's right to select delegates to the National Convention by the process it chooses of less constitutional weight than the National Party's right to decide which delegates to seat?

2. At first glance, the passage from *La Follette* quoted above seems silly. The purpose of holding a primary is to determine how much support the competing presidential candidates will receive from the state's delegation to the national convention. What good does it do to tell the state that it is perfectly free to run its primary any way it chooses, but that the primary will count only if it is run the way the national party orders? Justice Powell made this seemingly telling point in dissent.

But first glances can be deceiving, and subsequent events showed that Justice Stewart was right and Justice Powell was wrong. *La Follette* left Wisconsin with more leverage than at first appeared. In 1980, the Democratic National Convention seated the Wisconsin delegation despite the fact that the state's open primary violated the national rules and despite the fact that the Supreme Court had stayed the lower court order requiring that the delegates be seated. In 1984, the Wisconsin Democrats yielded by selecting delegates at caucuses open only to Democrats, but by 1988 the national Democrats had given in, revising the national rules to permit Wisconsin to use an open primary.

The law of *Cousins* and *La Follette* is that although the states may select delegates pretty much as they choose within their own borders, the national party at its convention is free to accept or reject the delegates sent by the state and may choose to replace these delegates with substitutes selected using any method it cares to honor. This *seems* to be a victory for the national party because it has the last word. But the last word that the national party actually will utter will be determined politically, and in the political process the states carry considerable weight.

Despite increasing disenchantment with the national conventions, they still draw considerable attention and are regarded as significant events in the presidential election campaign. Let us imagine what would happen if the national Democratic rulemakers and the State of Wisconsin each decided to press their respective positions on the open primary to the hilt. Wisconsin would send its delegation, and the credentials committee, if it adhered to the rules, would recommend that the delegation not be seated. The matter would then be decided in an open vote on the floor of the convention. In the typical modern convention, this would be one of the few newsworthy events in a week of intensive news coverage. Would the delegates vote to exclude a state's democratically elected delegation because of an obscure technicality, poorly understood by most of the delegates themselves, not to mention millions of television viewers? The person being nominated for president at the convention would be unlikely to permit the matter to go to a floor vote, and the nominee would be even less likely to permit the exclusion of a state's elected delegation, an action that could only mystify the public.

The national party's ultimate weapon in rules conflicts with state parties and state governments was protected in *La Follette*, but the states can make that weapon very costly to use by sending to the convention a delegation clothed with the aura of having been selected democratically and legitimately. The result is that each side has a strong incentive to accommodate the other. The give-and-take that occurred between the national Democrats and the Wisconsin Democrats over the open primary suggests that consigning such controversies to the political process is unlikely to lead to one-sided results.

The foregoing discussion assumes that by the time of the convention, the presidential candidate has been determined by the primaries and the caucuses, as was the case in both parties in every election after 1972 through 2004. But what if the contest is still undecided and a controversy like the ones described above in Wisconsin were to arise? That possibility almost came to pass in 2008. The nomination battle in the Democratic Party between Hillary Clinton and Barack Obama was close through the last primaries, and some of Clinton's supporters hoped she would bring the contest to the convention. Two states, Michigan and Florida, held presidential primaries on January 29, 2008, in violation of Democratic party rules prohibiting those states from holding primaries before February 5. According to the party rules, no delegates selected in such primaries would be seated at the convention. The precise details varied in the two states, but roughly speaking Clinton campaigned much more actively than Obama in the two states, in primaries that, at the time, seemed only symbolic. Clinton won significant majorities of the "delegates" in both Florida and Michigan, though if the rules were followed, no actual delegates would be seated.

As the possibility arose that the primaries and caucuses might fail to produce a clear winner between Clinton and Obama, it was not surprising that Clinton proposed that the Florida and Michigan delegates should be seated, the party rules to the contrary notwithstanding. State party leaders from both states joined in. Frantic efforts were made, unsuccessfully, to arrange some sort of "do-over" primary on short notice. Had the nomination been uncertain at the convention, the Florida and Michigan issues would have been resolved by a political battle between the Clinton and Obama forces. The incident was a reminder that the national party's power to determine which state delegations will be seated is profoundly subject to political influence.

3. Would the result in *La Follette* have been different if Congress had passed a statute allowing state legislatures to choose between an open and closed primary and Wisconsin had opted for an open primary in opposition to national party rules? See Note, *Freedom of Association and Selection of Delegates to National Political Conventions*, 56 CORNELL LAW REVIEW 148, 152–60 (1970). Would it be relevant that the great majority of Democrats in the House and Senate voted for the bill and that it was signed by a Democratic president?

Could Congress require the political parties to hold their primaries in every state on a single day? Should it? In the absence of any such action by Congress, New Hampshire has a statute that sets its primary date one week earlier than the next earliest state. What would happen if Vermont passed the same statute?

If one of the national parties stated it would not seat delegates selected in primaries unless the primary were held on a date specified, would its refusal to seat the delegates be constitutionally protected under *La Follette*? Would such a rule be materially different for constitutional purposes than a rule that states not hold their primaries before a specified date? What if the state required by the national party to vote on a particular date proved (1) that it had traditionally held its primary on a different date; (2) that change in the date was strongly resisted by the other major party; and (3) that holding the two parties' primaries on separate dates would entail considerable public expense and would be likely to reduce turnout, not only in the presidential primaries but in other elections held concurrently, such as state and local primaries and ballot measure elections?

4. *La Follette* does not really answer the question of the extent to which the decision of a national political party in allocation and selection of delegates is "state action" subject to constitutional restraint. See generally the numerous cases and secondary sources cited in *Cousins v. Wigoda*, 419 U.S. at 483, n.4. Consider the following:

A. Can the party require all candidates for president to swear in advance of the nomination to support and abide by its platform with the sanction of withdrawal of the nomination if the candidate deviates? If so, is the victorious candidate who allegedly deviates entitled to a trial where he or she can challenge the allegations and evidence? Before whom? Under what procedures?

B. Is allocation of delegates to states at national party conventions subject to the principles of the redistricting decisions? Suppose, for example, the Republicans decide to award substantial numbers of extra delegates at their next convention to states carried by Republican candidates for President or Senator or that elected a majority of Republicans to the seats in the House allocated to their state. The Republicans' theory is that the bonus allocation will encourage state organizations to work harder to get out the Republican vote. See Ronald D. Rotunda, *Constitutional and Statutory Restrictions on Political Parties in the Wake of Cousins v. Wigoda*, 53 TEXAS LAW REVIEW 935, 938–43 (1975), and cases and sources discussed therein. What are the practical consequences of such a system, compared to apportionment of delegates strictly by population?

C. Is it constitutional for a party to require that a state's delegation to a nominating convention must contain women, identified racial minorities, and young people in the exact percentage that those groups are present in the population of the state? See *Bachur v. Democratic National Party*, 836 F.2d 837 (4th Cir. 1987), holding that Maryland rules to implement policies of the national Democratic Party, requiring individuals to vote for equal numbers of men and women for delegate to the convention, did not infringe on the right to vote. See generally John G. Kester, *Constitutional Restrictions on Political Parties*, 60 VIRGINIA LAW REVIEW 735, 770–72 (1974).

D. Is your answer to any of the above questions affected by the fact that the major parties receive public funds to finance their conventions? Would your answer be influenced if Congress appropriated funds to pay for the parties' internal operations? Their public relations activities?

E. Is your view of when a political party's action is state action different for the national, state, and local parties? Suppose, for example, that in a given state, trial court judges are not nominated in primaries but by the party county committees. A party committee in a given county is taken over by a reform faction. Assume further that the party's nomination for trial court judge in that county is tantamount to election. Wholly on its own volition, the party committee establishes a screening committee of distinguished lawyers and non-lawyers to recommend nominees for judge to it, and the party committee agrees to be bound by the screening committee's choice. A candidate for judge rejected by the screening committee sues the county party, alleging that the screening committee considered hearsay statements of unidentified lawyers and former clients in rejecting the candidate and did not give the rejected candidate the opportunity to confront accusers and be heard on the charges. The candidate alleges the screening committee is in effect an arm of the county party, whose nomination of the candidate endorsed by the screening committee is state action subject to the due process clause of the fourteenth amendment. What result, and why?

5. As we have seen the controversies that raised questions of parties' associational freedoms in the 1970s centered on presidential nominations. In the ensuing decades, the legal battles more often have pitted competing viewpoints within particular states. Before we move to those developments, it is worth pausing to note two additional areas of controversy around presidential elections. In this Note we mention the timing of presidential primaries. In the next one we will discuss the electoral college.

As we have seen, the 1968 reforms in the Democratic Party's nominating process had the unanticipated consequence of altering the process in both parties to one dominated by primaries. Even the states that declined to adopt presidential primaries have used caucuses that are closer in nature to primaries than to the old processes dominated by state party leaders. Caucuses, like primaries, are open to voters who choose among the contenders for the party's nominations.

It has become a modern tradition that the first decisive event in the nomination process is the Iowa caucus in each party, followed by the New Hampshire primary. After these events, states have been free to schedule their primaries and caucuses whenever they wished. At first the nominating events were fairly evenly spread out between February and June. However, a pattern began to emerge. Going into Iowa and New Hampshire, there were typically anywhere up to ten or so reasonably serious candidates in each party—with the exception of a party in which an incumbent president was seeking reelection. Of these, two or three would be regarded as front-runners and the rest as "dark horses." Iowa and New Hampshire would winnow the field down, usually to two or at the most three candidates. One or two of these might be dark horses who had done unexpectedly well in Iowa or, especially, New Hampshire. The surviving candidates would then fight it out in the ensuing primaries and caucuses. Often, for one reason or another, attention would be focused on one or a small number of primaries that were regarded as crucial. Eventually—often before many states had conducted their primaries or caucuses—it would become clear that a particular candidate was going to win. Usually the other candidates withdrew from the race, so that the later contests were purely pro forma.

Whatever the merits of this system as a method of choosing a pair of finalists in the competition to be President of the United States, it began to draw the ire of partisan activists in states that were holding their primaries and caucuses late in the process. Many of these people thought that their states were being frozen out, as the contests were over for all practical purposes by the time their citizens had a chance to vote. Gradually, states began to move their primary and caucus dates earlier. And then not so gradually.

All this came to a head as the 2008 election approached. States sought to hold their contests earlier and earlier. It began to appear that Iowa and New Hampshire, determined to retain their positions at the head of the line, might have to hold their contests before Christmas. The parties responded to complaints about the non-representative quality of Iowa and New Hampshire by extending to two additional states—Nevada and South Carolina—the privilege of an early place in line. All other states were prohibited by both parties from acting before February 5. The Republicans would penalize a state that breached the February 5 limit by seating only half the state's delegates. The Democrats would not seat any delegates from a state in violation. As we have already seen in Note 2, above, two large states—Florida and Michigan—defied the national parties by holding their primaries on January 29.

Other states all complied, but twenty states, including such large ones as California, New York, and Illinois, set their primaries on the first legal date, February 5, which became known as "Super-Tuesday." As the schedule took shape and the year 2008 approached, many observers looked ahead with trepidation. In the past, after the field was winnowed, there had been time for the remaining candidates to collect resources and for voters, in the succeeding primaries, to closely evaluate them. In 2008, soon after the early contests, the remaining candidates would be thrown into a massive Super-Tuesday contest with little time for preparation and little time for voters to get to know them.

In the contemporary era of presidential nomination contests, which may be said to have begun in 1972, there have been plenty of surprising turns. But never so many as occurred in 2008. To be sure, the compressed schedule of front-loaded primaries was not the only cause. Perhaps most important were the intense divisions in the country over foreign policy and social issues, together with increasing concern about a declining economy. These divisions made the stakes seem unusually high. Another factor was what may have been the most remarkable group of presidential candidates in any election in history—candidates with remarkable strengths, striking weaknesses, and collectively, great diversity in their backgrounds, their temperaments and, of course, their political viewpoints. But these factors interacted with the difficult schedule of contests to heighten the unpredictability of events.

On the Republican side, despite the surprising turns, events were reasonably close to the pattern established since 1972. In mid to late 2007, Rudy Giuliani and Mitt Romney appeared to be the frontrunners, with John McCain and Fred Thompson also waging serious candidacies, and a number of darker horses trailing behind. Mike Huckabee's surprising victory in the Iowa caucuses thrust him into the field of frontrunners, while Giuliani and Thompson faded. McCain's victory in New Hampshire made him the new frontrunner, with Romney his main challenger and Huckabee still in the running. McCain strengthened his lead as the other early primaries progressed and delivered the knockout blow on Super-Tuesday. Romney quickly withdrew and although Huckabee waited to do so until McCain had the nomination mathematically clinched, the race was all but over.

Things went differently on the Democratic side. Through most of 2007, Hillary Clinton was viewed as a strong frontrunner in a large field. As 2007 neared its end, Barack Obama surged to a position competitive with Clinton, while John Edwards led the rest of the pack, though without ever getting very close to Clinton and Obama. A big Iowa victory for Obama made it appear that he might win the nomination early, but Clinton came back with an upset victory in New Hampshire. Edwards and the others faded, but even after Super-Tuesday, no clear winner had emerged between Clinton and Obama. Obama again seemed on the brink of victory with a string of twelve straight victories after Super-Tuesday, but Clinton stayed alive with primary wins in Ohio, Texas, and Pennsylvania. Though Obama still maintained a lead, the contest was not over, and there even seemed a possibility that the contest would still be open at the time of the Democratic convention — an eventuality that many observers thought would be seriously harmful for the party's chances in the election. In the end, though Clinton did surprisingly well in the late primaries, she was unable to overcome Obama's lead and she conceded in June, after the last primaries.

Not surprisingly, these developments have caught the attention of Congress. The Senate Committee on Rules and Administration conducted hearings on the subject in September, 2007.[q] Legislation has been introduced in both houses.[r] The national parties are also studying the problem. As this book goes to press, it is impossible to say what remedies are likely or even how the problem will be perceived when observers can look back on the 2008 contests with some distance. But there seems very little doubt that the presidential nominating system will be high on the national agenda for the next few years. Stay tuned to the annual supplements to this volume!

6. Under article II, section 1 of the Constitution, "Each state shall appoint, in such manner as the Legislature thereof may direct, a number of electors, equal to the whole number of Senators and Representatives to which the State may be entitled in the Congress...." In the first two elections, George Washington was the consensus candidate and the only serious question was who would be chosen as vice-president. Under the original Constitution, each elector voted for two people, with no differentiation between president and vice-president. If one candidate received votes equal to a majority of the electors that candidate was elected president and the candidate with the next highest number of votes was vice-president. If no candidate received votes from a majority of the electors, the president was selected by the House of Representatives, with each state having one vote.

---

q. A witness list and a link to the transcript may be found at < http://rules.senate.gov/hearings/2007/091907hrg.htm>.

r. At least as this book goes to press, descriptions of the bills that have been introduced may be found at < http://www.federalelectionreform.com/bill_tables/110_primary_elections.html>.

Beginning with the election of 1796, the electors began to divide between two national parties, a development not anticipated by the authors of the Constitution. This created no particular problem in 1796, but in 1800, when the Republican Thomas Jefferson defeated the Federalist John Adams, each Republican elector cast one vote for Jefferson and one for his running mate Aaron Burr, with the result that they each received the same number of electoral votes and the election was thrown into the House. The Federalists, hostile to Jefferson, sought to elect Burr as president. A deadlock arose that was finally broken when the sole Representative from Delaware, a Federalist, withheld his state's vote from Burr, enabling Jefferson to win. In the aftermath of this constitutional crisis, the Twelfth Amendment was passed. In effect it adapted the electoral college to the party system by requiring electors to specify the presidential and vice-presidential candidates they were voting for, so that votes for the two offices could be counted separately.

Article II, section 1 permits the state legislature to decide the manner in which the state will appoint its electors. In early elections two methods were used predominantly, selection by the legislature and popular election. Popular election took place in districts in some states and on a statewide, winner-take-all basis in others. Over time, nearly all the states settled on the statewide popular vote. As of 2008, all but two states use that method. Maine and Nebraska pick two electors, corresponding to their two senators, by statewide election, and their remaining electors in their congressional districts.

The electoral college has long been criticized, usually by people who favor a national popular election. There is an extensive literature on the subject. A useful introduction is John C. Fortier, ed., AFTER THE PEOPLE VOTE: A GUIDE TO THE ELECTORAL COLLEGE (3d ed. 2004). Works critical of the electoral college include Robert W. Bennett, TAMING THE ELECTORAL COLLEGE (2006); George C. Edwards III, WHY THE ELECTORAL COLLEGE IS BAD FOR AMERICA (2004). The electoral college is defended in Gary L. Gregg II, ed., SECURING DEMOCRACY: WHY WE HAVE AN ELECTORAL COLLEGE (2001); Tara Ross, ENLIGHTENED DEMOCRACY: THE CASE FOR THE ELECTORAL COLLEGE (2004). A good source for information on the Twelfth Amendment is Tadahisa Kuroda, THE ORIGINS OF THE TWELFTH AMENDMENT: THE ELECTORAL COLLEGE IN THE EARLY REPUBLIC, 1787–1804 (1994). For a short but lively debate, see Sanford Levinson, John McGinnis & Daniel H. Lowenstein, *Should We Dispense with the Electoral College?*, 156 UNIVERSITY OF PENNSYLVANIA LAW REVIEW PENNumbra 10 (2007), *available at* http://www.pennumbra.com/debates/pdfs/electoral_college.pdf.

Seemingly, changing the method for selecting a president prescribed by the Constitution requires a constitutional amendment. At least, that is what has been generally assumed. Recently a group of reformers began espousing a plan, known as the National Popular Vote Plan, intended to get around the electoral college without amending the Constitution. The idea is that state legislatures should adopt a procedure that would select electors pledged not to the presidential candidate winning the most votes within the states, but to the candidate winning the national popular vote. The plan does not go into effect until and unless states representing a majority of the electoral college sign on. At that point, the popular vote in non-cooperating states would be taken into account but the electoral votes from non-cooperating states would become irrelevant. Supporters have produced a volume that opponents of the plan as well as supporters will find a useful reference work, John R. Koza et al., EVERY VOTE EQUAL: A STATE-BASED PLAN FOR ELECTING THE PRESIDENT BY NATIONAL POPULAR VOTE (2006). As of early 2008, three states, Maryland, New Jersey, and Illinois, had adopted the plan.

If they succeed in obtaining states with a majority of the electoral votes to sign up for the plan, they can anticipate two constitutional challenges. The first will be that the plan is an interstate compact of the sort that requires congressional approval. For divergent views on this question, see Jennings "Jay" Wilson, *Bloc Voting in the Electoral College: How the Ignored States Can Become Relevant and Implement Popular Election Along the Way*, 5 ELECTION LAW JOURNAL 384 (2006); Derek T. Muller, *The Compact Clause and the National Popular Vote Interstate Compact*, 6 ELECTION LAW JOURNAL 372 (2007); Jennifer Hendricks, *Popular Election of the President: Using or Abusing the Electoral College?*, 7 ELECTION LAW JOURNAL ___ (2008); Derek T. Muller, *More Thoughts on the Compact Clause and the National Popular Vote: A Response to Professor Hendricks*, 7 ELECTION LAW JOURNAL ___ (2008). The second will be that although under article II, section 1, the legislature is authorized to determine the manner of appointing the electors, it is the state that must do the appointing. The contention will be that determining the identity of the electors by the national popular vote is not appointment by the state.

B. State Parties

1. *Establishing the Right*

In the *White Primary Cases*, constitutional rights of voters were asserted successfully against political parties. In *Cousins* and *La Follette*, parties were able to assert their own associational rights to defend national party control of the national conventions against state judicial interference. We now turn to cases in which state parties, or individuals claiming to act on a party's behalf, assert associational rights under the First Amendment as a means of striking down state regulation.

Tashjian v. Republican Party of Connecticut
479 U.S. 208 (1986)

Justice MARSHALL delivered the opinion of the Court.

Appellee Republican Party of the State of Connecticut (Party) in 1984 adopted a Party rule which permits independent voters — registered voters not affiliated with any political party — to vote in Republican primaries for federal and state-wide offices. Appellant Julia Tashjian, the Secretary of the State of Connecticut, is charged with the administration of the State's election statutes, which include a provision requiring voters in any party primary to be registered members of that party. Conn. Gen. Stat. §9-431 (1985). Appellees, who in addition to the Party include the Party's federal officeholders and the Party's state chairman, challenged this eligibility provision on the ground that it deprives the Party of its First Amendment right to enter into political association with individuals of its own choosing. The District Court granted summary judgment in favor of appellees. The Court of Appeals affirmed. We ... now affirm.

I

In 1955, Connecticut adopted its present primary election system. For major parties, the process of candidate selection for federal and statewide offices requires a statewide convention of party delegates; district conventions are held to select candidates for seats in the state legislature. The party convention may certify as the party-endorsed candidate any person receiving more than 20% of the votes cast in a roll-call vote at the convention. Any candidate not endorsed by the party who received 20% of the vote may challenge the party-endorsed candidate in a primary election, in which the candidate receiving the plurality of votes becomes the party's nominee. Candidates selected by the major parties, whether through convention or primary, are automatically accorded a place on the ballot at the general election....

Motivated in part by the demographic importance of independent voters in Connecticut politics,[3] in September 1983 the Party's Central Committee recommended calling a state convention to consider altering the Party's rules to allow independents to vote in Party primaries. In January 1984 the state convention adopted the Party rule now at issue, which provides:

> Any elector enrolled as a member of the Republican Party and any elector not enrolled as a member of a party shall be eligible to vote in primaries for nomination of candidates for the offices of United States Senator, United States Representative, Governor, Lieutenant Governor, Secretary of the State, Attorney General, Comptroller and Treasurer.

During the 1984 session, the Republican leadership in the state legislature, in response to the conflict between the newly enacted Party rule and §9-431, proposed to amend the statute to allow independents to vote in primaries when permitted by Party rules. The proposed legislation was defeated, substantially along party lines, in both houses of the legislature, which at that time were controlled by the Democratic Party....[4]

II

... The nature of appellees' First Amendment interest is evident. "It is beyond debate that freedom to engage in association for the advancement of beliefs and ideas is an inseparable aspect of the 'liberty' assured by the Due Process Clause of the Fourteenth Amendment, which embraces freedom of speech." *NAACP v. Alabama ex rel. Patterson*, 357 U.S. 449 (1958). The freedom of association protected by the First and Fourteenth Amendments includes partisan political organization. "The right to associate with the political party of one's choice is an integral part of this basic constitutional freedom." *Kusper.*

The Party here contends that §9-431 impermissibly burdens the right of its members to determine for themselves with whom they will associate, and whose support they will seek, in their quest for political success. The Party's attempt to broaden the base of public participation in and support for its activities is conduct undeniably central to the exercise of the right of association. As we have said, the freedom to join together in furtherance of common political beliefs "necessarily presupposes the freedom to identify the people who constitute the association." *La Follette.*

A major state political party necessarily includes individuals playing a broad spectrum of roles in the organization's activities. Some of the Party's members devote substantial portions of their lives to furthering its political and organizational goals, others provide substantial financial support, while still others limit their participation to casting their votes for some or all of the Party's candidates. Considered from the standpoint of the Party itself, the act of formal enrollment or public affiliation with the Party is merely one

---

3. The record shows that in October 1983 there were 659,268 registered Democrats, 425,695 registered Republicans, and 532,723 registered and unaffiliated voters in Connecticut.

4. In the November 1984 elections, the Republicans acquired a majority of seats in both houses of the state legislature, and an amendment to §9-431 was passed, but was vetoed by the Democratic Governor.

element in the continuum of participation in Party affairs, and need not be in any sense the most important.

Were the State to restrict by statute financial support of the Party's candidates to Party members, or to provide that only Party members might be selected as the Party's chosen nominees for public office, such a prohibition of potential association with nonmembers would clearly infringe upon the rights of the Party's members under the First Amendment to organize with like-minded citizens in support of common political goals. As we have said, "'[a]ny interference with the freedom of a party is simultaneously an interference with the freedom of its adherents.'" *La Follette* (quoting *Sweezy v. New Hampshire*, 354 U.S. 234 (1957).[6] The statute here places limits upon the group of registered voters whom the Party may invite to participate in the "basic function" of selecting the Party's candidates. *Kusper*. The State thus limits the Party's associational opportunities at the crucial juncture at which the appeal to common principles may be translated into concerted action, and hence to political power in the community.[7]

It is, of course, fundamental to appellant's defense of the State's statute that this impingement upon the associational rights of the Party and its members occurs at the ballot box, for the Constitution grants to the States a broad power to prescribe the "Times, Places and Manner of holding Elections for Senators and Representatives," Art. I, §4, cl. 1, which power is matched by state control over the election process for state offices. But this authority does not extinguish the State's responsibility to observe the limits established by the First Amendment rights of the State's citizens. The power to regulate the time, place, and manner of elections does not justify, without more, the abridgment of fundamental rights, such as the right to vote, see *Wesberry*, or, as here, the freedom of political association. We turn then to an examination of the interests which appellant asserts to justify the burden cast by the statute upon the associational rights of the Party and its members.

------

6. It is this element of potential interference with the rights of the Party's members which distinguishes the present case from others in which we have considered claims by nonmembers of a party seeking to vote in that party's primary despite the party's opposition. In this latter class of cases, the nonmember's desire to participate in the party's affairs is overborne by the countervailing and legitimate right of the party to determine its own membership qualifications. See *Rosario*. Similarly, the Court has upheld the right of national political parties to refuse to seat at their conventions delegates chosen in state selection processes which did not conform to party rules. See *La Follette*; *Cousins*. These situations are analytically distinct from the present case, in which the Party and its members seek to provide enhanced opportunities for participation by willing nonmembers. Under these circumstances, there is no conflict between the associational interests of members and nonmembers.

7. Appellant contends that any infringement of the associational right of the Party or its members is de minimis, because Connecticut law, as amended during the pendency of this litigation, provides that any previously unaffiliated voter may become eligible to vote in the Party's primary by enrolling as a Party member as late as noon on the last business day preceding the primary. Thus, appellant contends, any independent voter wishing to participate in any Party primary may do so.

This is not a satisfactory response to the Party's contentions for two reasons. First, as the Court of Appeals noted, the formal affiliation process is one which individual voters may employ in order to associate with the Party, but it provides no means by which the members of the Party may choose to broaden opportunities for joining the association by their own act, without any intervening action by potential voters. Second, and more importantly, the requirement of public affiliation with the Party in order to vote in the primary conditions the exercise of the associational right upon the making of a public statement of adherence to the Party which the State requires regardless of the actual beliefs of the individual voter. As counsel for appellees conceded at oral argument, a requirement that independent voters merely notify state authorities of their intention to vote in the Party primary would be acceptable as an administrative measure, but "[t]he problem is that the State is insisting on a public act of affiliation ... joining the Republican Party as a condition of this association."

III

Appellant contends that §9-431 is a narrowly tailored regulation which advances the State's compelling interests by ensuring the administrability of the primary system, preventing raiding, avoiding voter confusion, and protecting the responsibility of party government.

A

[Appellant argues] that the administrative burden imposed by the Party rule is a sufficient ground on which to uphold the constitutionality of §9-431. Appellant contends that the Party's rule would require the purchase of additional voting machines, the training of additional poll workers, and potentially the printing of additional ballot materials specifically intended for independents voting in the Republican primary. In essence, appellant claims that the administration of the system contemplated by the Party rule would simply cost the State too much.

Even assuming the factual accuracy of these contentions…, the possibility of future increases in the cost of administering the election system is not a sufficient basis here for infringing appellees' First Amendment rights. Costs of administration would likewise increase if a third major party should come into existence in Connecticut, thus requiring the State to fund a third major-party primary. Additional voting machines, poll workers, and ballot materials would all be necessary under these circumstances as well. But the State could not forever protect the two existing major parties from competition solely on the ground that two major parties are all the public can afford. While the State is of course entitled to take administrative and financial considerations into account in choosing whether or not to have a primary system at all, it can no more restrain the Republican Party's freedom of association for reasons of its own administrative convenience than it could on the same ground limit the ballot access of a new major party.

B

Appellant argues that §9-431 is justified as a measure to prevent raiding, a practice "whereby voters in sympathy with one party designate themselves as voters of another party so as to influence or determine the results of the other party's primary." *Rosario*. While we have recognized that "a State may have a legitimate interest in seeking to curtail 'raiding,' since that practice may affect the integrity of the electoral process," *Kusper*; *Rosario*, that interest is not implicated here. The statute as applied to the Party's rule prevents independents, who otherwise cannot vote in any primary, from participating in the Republican primary. Yet a raid on the Republican Party primary by independent voters, a curious concept only distantly related to the type of raiding discussed in *Kusper* and *Rosario*, is not impeded by §9-431; the independent raiders need only register as Republicans and vote in the primary. Indeed, under Conn.Gen.Stat. §9-56 (1985), which permits an independent to affiliate with the Party as late as noon on the business day preceding the primary, the State's election statutes actually *assist* a "raid" by independents, which could be organized and implemented at the 11th hour. The State's asserted interest in the prevention of raiding provides no justification for the statute challenged here.

C

Appellant's next argument in support of §9-431 is that the closed primary system avoids voter confusion. Appellant contends that "[t]he legislature could properly find that it would be difficult for the general public to understand what a candidate stood for who was nominated in part by an unknown amorphous body outside the party, while never-theless using the party name." Appellees respond that the State is attempting to act as the ideological guarantor of the Republican Party's candidates, ensuring that voters are not misled by a "Republican" candidate who professes something other than what the State regards as true Republican principles.

As we have said, "[t]here can be no question about the legitimacy of the State's in-terest in fostering informed and educated expressions of the popular will in a general election." *Anderson v. Celebrezze*, 460 U.S. 780 (1983). To the extent that party labels provide a shorthand designation of the views of party candidates on matters of public concern, the identification of candidates with particular parties plays a role in the process by which voters inform themselves for the exercise of the franchise. Appellant's argument depends upon the belief that voters can be "misled" by party labels. But "[o]ur cases re-flect a greater faith in the ability of individual voters to inform themselves about cam-paign issues." *Id.* Moreover, appellant's concern that candidates selected under the Party rule will be the nominees of an "amorphous" group using the Party's name is inconsis-tent with the facts. The Party is not proposing that independents be allowed to choose the Party's nominee without Party participation; on the contrary, to be listed on the Party's primary ballot continues to require, under a statute not challenged here, that the primary candidate have obtained at least 20% of the vote at a Party convention, which only Party members may attend. Conn. Gen. Stat. §9-400 (1985). If no such can-didate seeks to challenge the convention's nominee in a primary, then no primary is held, and the convention nominee becomes the Party's nominee in the general election without any intervention by independent voters. Even assuming, however, that puta-tive candidates defeated at the Party convention will have an increased incentive under the Party's rule to make primary challenges, hoping to attract more substantial support from independents than from Party delegates, the requirement that such challengers garner substantial minority support at the convention greatly attenuates the State's con-cern that the ultimate nominee will be wedded to the Party in nothing more than a mar-riage of convenience.

In arguing that the Party rule interferes with educated decisions by voters, appellant also disregards the substantial benefit which the Party rule provides to the Party and its members in seeking to choose successful candidates. Given the numerical strength of in-dependent voters in the State, one of the questions most likely to occur to Connecticut Republicans in selecting candidates for public office is how can the Party most effectively appeal to the independent voter? By inviting independents to assist in the choice at the polls between primary candidates selected at the Party convention, the Party rule is in-tended to produce the candidate and platform most likely to achieve that goal. The state statute is said to decrease voter confusion, yet it deprives the Party and its members of the opportunity to inform themselves as to the level of support for the Party's candidates among a critical group of electors. "A State's claim that it is enhancing the ability of its citizenry to make wise decisions by restricting the flow of information to them must be viewed with some skepticism." *Anderson*. The State's legitimate interests in preventing voter confusion and providing for educated and responsible voter decisions in no respect "make it necessary to burden the [Party's] rights." *Id.*[s]

---

s. Connecticut is unusual both in its requirement that candidates surpass a percentage thresh-old at a party convention as a prerequisite to appearing on the ballot in a primary and in its high per-centage of independent voters. If a controversy like *Tashjian* arose in a state that was unlike Connecticut in both these respects, what should the result be? — EDS.

D

Finally, appellant contends that §9-431 furthers the State's compelling interest in protecting the integrity of the two-party system and the responsibility of party government. Appellant argues vigorously and at length that the closed primary system chosen by the state legislature promotes responsiveness by elected officials and strengthens the effectiveness of the political parties.

The relative merits of closed and open primaries have been the subject of substantial debate since the beginning of this century, and no consensus has as yet emerged.[11] Appellant invokes a long and distinguished line of political scientists and public officials who have been supporters of the closed primary. But our role is not to decide whether the state legislature was acting wisely in enacting the closed primary system in 1955, or whether the Republican Party makes a mistake in seeking to depart from the practice of the past 30 years.[12]

We have previously recognized the danger that "splintered parties and unrestrained factionalism may do significant damage to the fabric of government." *Storer v. Brown*, 415 U.S. 724 (1974). We upheld a California statute which denied access to the ballot to any independent candidate who had voted in a party primary or been registered as a member of a political party within one year prior to the immediately preceding primary election. We said:

> [T]he one-year disaffiliation provision furthers the State's interest in the stability of its political system. We also consider that interest as not only permissible, but compelling and as outweighing the interest the candidate and his supporters may have in making a late rather than an early decision to seek independent ballot status.

The statute in *Storer* was designed to protect the parties and the party system against the disorganizing effect of independent candidacies launched by unsuccessful putative party nominees. This protection, like that accorded to parties threatened by raiding in *Rosario*, is undertaken to prevent the disruption of the political parties from without, and not, as in this case, to prevent the parties from taking internal steps affecting their own process for the selection of candidates. The forms of regulation upheld in *Storer* and *Rosario* imposed certain burdens upon the protected First and Fourteenth Amendment interests of some individuals, both voters and potential candidates, in order to protect the interests of others. In the present case, the state statute is defended on the ground that it protects the integrity of the Party against the Party itself.

Under these circumstances, the views of the State, which to some extent represent the views of the one political party transiently enjoying majority power, as to the optimum methods for preserving party integrity lose much of their force. The State argues that its statute is well designed to save the Republican Party from undertaking a course of conduct de-

---

11. At the present time, 21 States provide for "closed" primaries of the classic sort, in which the primary voter must be registered as a member of the party for some period of time prior to the holding of the primary election. Sixteen States allow a voter previously unaffiliated with any party to vote in a party primary if he affiliates with the party at the time of, or for the purpose of, voting in the primary. Four States provide for nonpartisan primaries in which all registered voters may participate, while nine States have adopted classical "open" primaries, in which all registered voters may choose in which party primary to vote.

12. We note that appellant's direst predictions about destruction of the integrity of the election process and decay of responsible party government are not borne out by the experience of the 29 States which have chosen to permit more substantial openness in their primary systems than Connecticut has permitted heretofore.

structive of its own interests. But on this point "even if the State were correct, a State, or a court, may not constitutionally substitute its own judgment for that of the Party." *La Follette.* The Party's determination of the boundaries of its own association, and of the structure which best allows it to pursue its political goals, is protected by the Constitution. "And as is true of all expressions of First Amendment freedoms, the courts may not interfere on the ground that they view a particular expression as unwise or irrational." *Id.*[13]

We conclude that the State's enforcement, under these circumstances, of its closed primary system burdens the First Amendment rights of the Party. The interests which the appellant adduces in support of the statute are insubstantial, and accordingly the statute, as applied to the Party in this case, is unconstitutional.

IV

[In Part IV, the Court considers and rejects a different defense of the statute, based on provisions in the Constitution requiring that the qualifications for voters be the same in elections for Congress as they are for voters in elections for the more numerous branch of the state legislature. Art. 1, §2; Seventeenth Amendment. The state argued that since the Republican Party rule allowed independents to vote in congressional but not state legislative primaries, different qualifications for voting in the two types of election were being imposed, contrary to the dictate of the Constitution. The Court agreed with the state that the constitutional provisions apply to voter qualifications in primaries as well as in general elections, but concluded that the Constitution was intended to prevent congressional voter qualifications from being *more* restrictive than the qualifications for state legislative voting but not to prevent *less* restrictive qualifications. Justice Stevens, in an opinion joined by Justice Scalia, dissented from this latter conclusion.]

V

We conclude that §9-431 impermissibly burdens the rights of the Party and its members protected by the First and Fourteenth Amendments. The interests asserted by appellant in defense of the statute are insubstantial. The judgment of the Court of Appeals is

Affirmed.

Justice SCALIA, with whom THE CHIEF JUSTICE and Justice O'CONNOR join, dissenting....

In my view, the Court's opinion exaggerates the importance of the associational interest at issue, if indeed it does not see one where none exists. There is no question here of restricting the Republican Party's ability to recruit and enroll Party members by offering them the ability to select Party candidates; Conn. Gen. Stat. §9-56 (1985) permits an independent voter to join the Party as late as the day before the primary. Nor is there any question of restricting the ability of the Party's members to select whatever candidate

---

13. Our holding today does not establish that state regulation of primary voting qualifications may never withstand challenge by a political party or its membership. A party seeking, for example, to open its primary to all voters, including members of other parties, would raise a different combination of considerations. Under such circumstances, the effect of one party's broadening of participation would threaten other parties with the disorganization effects which the statutes in *Storer* and *Rosario* were designed to prevent. We have observed on several occasions that a State may adopt a "policy of confining each voter to a single nominating act," a policy decision which is not involved in the present case. See *Anderson*; *Storer*. The analysis of these situations derives much from the particular facts involved....

they desire. Appellees' only complaint is that the Party cannot leave the selection of its candidate to persons who are not members of the Party, and are unwilling to become members. It seems to me fanciful to refer to this as an interest in freedom of association between the members of the Republican Party and the putative independent voters. The Connecticut voter who, while steadfastly refusing to register as a Republican, casts a vote in the Republican primary, forms no more meaningful an "association" with the Party than does the independent or the registered Democrat who responds to questions by a Republican Party pollster. If the concept of freedom of association is extended to such casual contacts, it ceases to be of any analytic use....

The ability of the members of the Republican Party to select their own candidate, on the other hand, unquestionably implicates an associational freedom—but it can hardly be thought that that freedom is unconstitutionally impaired here. The Party is entirely free to put forward, if it wishes, that candidate who has the highest degree of support among Party members and independents combined. The State is under no obligation, however, to let its party primary be used, instead of a party-funded opinion poll, as the means by which the party identifies the relative popularity of its potential candidates among independents. Nor is there any reason apparent to me why the State cannot insist that this decision to support what might be called the independents' choice be taken *by the party membership in a democratic fashion*, rather than through a process that permits the members' votes to be diluted—and perhaps even absolutely outnumbered—by the votes of outsiders.

The Court's opinion characterizes this, disparagingly, as an attempt to "protec[t] the integrity of the Party against the Party itself." There are two problems with this characterization. The first, and less important, is that it is not true. We have no way of knowing that a majority of the Party's members is in favor of allowing ultimate selection of its candidates for federal and statewide office to be determined by persons outside the Party. That decision was not made by democratic ballot, but by the Party's state convention—which, for all we know, may have been dominated by officeholders and office seekers whose evaluation of the merits of assuring election of the Party's candidates, vis-à-vis the merits of proposing candidates faithful to the Party's political philosophy, diverged significantly from the views of the Party's rank and file. I had always thought it was a major purpose of state-imposed party primary requirements to protect the general party membership against this sort of minority control. Second and more important, however, *even if* it were the fact that the majority of the Party's members wanted its candidates to be determined by outsiders, there is no reason why the State is bound to honor that desire—any more than it would be bound to honor a party's democratically expressed desire that its candidates henceforth be selected by convention rather than by primary, or by the party's executive committee in a smoke-filled room. In other words, the validity of the state-imposed primary requirement itself, which we have hitherto considered "too plain for argument," *American Party of Texas v. White*, 415 U.S. 767 (1974), presupposes that the State *has* the right "to protect the Party against the Party itself." Connecticut may lawfully require that significant elements of the democratic election process be democratic—whether the Party wants that or not. It is beyond my understanding why the Republican Party's delegation of its democratic choice to a Republican Convention can be proscribed, but its delegation of that choice to nonmembers of the Party cannot.

In the case before us, Connecticut has said no more than this: Just as the Republican Party may, if it wishes, nominate the candidate recommended by the Party's executive committee, so long as its members select that candidate by name in a democratic vote;

so also it may nominate the independents' choice, so long as its members select him by name in a democratic vote. That seems to me plainly and entirely constitutional.

I respectfully dissent.

Notes and Questions

1. Connecticut law was changed to allow the parties to open their primaries to non-members, but the rules of both major parties now allow only registered members to vote. See Elizabeth Garrett, *Is the Party Over? Courts and the Political Process*, 2002 SUPREME COURT REVIEW 95, 120.

2. Suppose state law requires the selection of nominees for state office by party primary, but the leaders of one of the major parties decide they would prefer to select the party's nominees by means of a state convention. The party therefore brings an action challenging the statutory requirement that the party choose its nominees in primary elections. What result? See generally Stephen E. Gottlieb, *Rebuilding the Right of Association: The Right to Hold a Convention as a Test Case*, 11 HOFSTRA LAW REVIEW 191 (1982).

In 1969, Arkansas revised its election code and required parties to select their candidates by holding primaries. However, Arkansas also required the parties to pay the costs of their primaries, except to the extent counties were willing to pay for them. Many counties declined to pay. The combination of the state's requiring a primary and requiring the party to pay for it was declared unconstitutional in *Republican Party of Arkansas v. Faulkner County*, 49 F.3d 1289 (8th Cir. 1995).

3. Article I, §4, cl. 1 of the United States Constitution, referred to in *Tashjian*, provides in part as follows:

> The times, places and manner of holding elections for Senators and Representatives, shall be prescribed in each state by the legislature thereof; but the Congress may at any time by law make or alter such regulations....

If Congress passed a law requiring that party nominations in congressional elections be determined by nominating conventions, could the law be enforced over the objection of a state party that preferred to select its nominees in primaries? Would it matter in this dispute whether the state statutes provided for primaries, provided for conventions, or were silent? Would the result be different in the opposite case: Congress requires primaries, and a state party prefers nominating conventions? If a federal statute required that only persons registered in the party be permitted to vote in congressional primaries, would this requirement be enforceable against the Republican Party of Connecticut?

4. Suppose the Democratic Party of Connecticut decided to adopt the same rule as the Republicans. In that event, registered Democrats would vote only in the Democratic primary, registered Republicans would vote only in the Republican primary, and independent voters would be permitted to vote in whichever party's primary they chose at any given election. This type of primary is described "semi-closed," as we shall see shortly in connection with *Clingman v. Beaver*. What incentive would a voter have to register as a party member under this system? Does the state have a legitimate interest in encouraging voters to affiliate with parties? Is the political system better off if voters are so encouraged?

One who took the perspective of Morris Fiorina in Section I above would be likely to answer the last question in the affirmative. If the open primary validated in *Tashjian* had the effect of weakening the party system by reducing incentives for voters to affiliate with parties, should a supporter of strong parties accept this setback as the price of the increased associational freedom *Tashjian* recognizes in parties? On the whole, how are parties likely to use such associational freedom? Will the choices they make be more or less likely than choices made by state legislatures to promote a stronger party system?

5. The Court relied on *Tashjian* in *Eu v. San Francisco County Democratic Central Committee*, 489 U.S. 214 (1989), to strike down numerous California statutes regulating parties. One of the statutes prohibited the parties from nominating candidates in primaries.

Recall the view of political scientists, summarized in Fiorina's article, that parties consist of at least three parts: the party in the electorate, the party in elective office, and the party organization. Why should the latter of these be able to speak for the party in endorsing candidates in the primary? If the party organization really does speak for the party, what is the point in holding the primary at all? Would a statute be constitutional that permitted state and county central committees to endorse candidates and to publicize those endorsements, but required that such publicity refer to the endorsement as that of the committee, not of the party? Consider footnote 19 of the Justice Marshall's opinion for the Court in *Eu*:

> The State suggested at oral argument that the endorsement ban prevents fraud by barring party officials from misrepresenting that they speak for the party. To the extent that the State suggests that only the primary election results can constitute a party endorsement, it confuses an endorsement from the official governing bodies that may influence election results with the results themselves. . . .

Does a ban on party endorsements in *non*partisan primaries violate the First Amendment? In *Geary v. Renne*, 911 F.2d 280 (9th Cir. 1990), an 8–3 majority struck down a 1986 amendment to the California Constitution that prohibited such endorsements. In *Renne v. Geary*, 501 U.S. 312 (1991), the Supreme Court reversed on procedural grounds without reaching the merits. If the chairs of the San Francisco County Republican and Democratic Central Committees asked you whether the committees could legally endorse candidates in the next nonpartisan mayoral election, what advice would you give?

The other statutes struck down in *Eu* were detailed provisions for internal governance of the parties, dealing with such matters as the term of office for party chairs. In the California Elections Code, there were separate chapters setting governance rules and procedures for each of the two major parties, as well as for certain of the minor parties. The practice in California was that Democrats would go along with any changes the Republican members of the legislature wanted to make in the Republican chapter, and vice versa. The plaintiffs in *Eu* were a handful of county central committees, candidates, and party activists. At their behest, the Court struck down the statutes that had been enacted by the parties' elected representatives in the legislature. The Court did so to protect the parties' freedom of association. As between the plaintiffs in *Eu* and the elected legislators from either the Democratic or Republican Party, which had a better claim to speak for the party?

For criticism of *Tashjian* and *Eu*, see Daniel Hays Lowenstein, *Associational Rights of Major Political Parties: A Skeptical Inquiry*, 71 Texas Law Review 1741 (1993).

6. Suppose a state statute provides that all members of the state Senate who are affiliated with a political party are members of the Senate Caucus of that party. Under factual circumstances similar to those of *Ammond v. McGahn, supra*, the Senate Democratic Caucus votes to expel Senator Ammond. She goes to court seeking reinstatement as a

member of the Caucus, relying on the statute. The Caucus asserts that the statute is unconstitutional as an infringement of the party's freedom of association. What result?

7. *Rosario v. Rockefeller*, 410 U.S. 752 (1973), and *Kusper v. Pontikes*, 414 U.S. 51 (1973), both involved waiting periods before voters who switched parties could vote in the primary of their new party. In *Rosario*, voters challenged a New York requirement that in order to vote in a party's primary, they must affiliate with the party 30 days before the previous general election. For example, a Republican voter who wanted to switch to the Democratic Party would have to have enrolled as a Democrat by early October of an election year in order to vote in the next Democratic primary held in the state. The Court upheld this long waiting period, in part because it protected parties against "raiding" by supporters of an opposing party. Raiding would occur if there were an uncontested primary in Party *A* and supporters of Party *A* therefore decided to vote in the primary of Party *B*, where their votes might prove decisive. Because few voters could anticipate this situation prior to the preceding general election, the waiting period was expected to make raiding impossible. However, this anti-raiding purpose was insufficient to justify Illinois' longer waiting period of 23 months in *Kusper*. Illinois conducted primaries each year, so that the 23-month waiting period meant that voters who wished to switch parties would have to go through at least one primary election without being able to vote within either party. The Court regarded this denial of the right to vote as unnecessary and as outweighing the state's anti-raiding purpose.

No political party participated as a litigant in either *Rosario* or *Kusper*. Yet the Court was willing to assume that the statutes being challenged were intended to protect the associational integrity of the political parties. Why shouldn't the same assumption be made in *Eu*? The obvious answer would seem to be that in disputes like *Rosario* and *Kusper* between individual voters and the state it can be assumed that the state is in accord with the wishes of the parties, but that this assumption would obviously be inappropriate in a dispute such as *Eu* between one or more parties and the state. But on what basis can we characterize *Eu* as a dispute between the major parties and the state? Recall that neither the Democratic nor the Republican State Central Committee was a plaintiff. Even if the state committees had been plaintiffs, why should the "party organization" be regarded as speaking for "the Democratic Party" or "the Republican Party" more than the Democratic and Republican elected officials who enacted the statutes under attack? See generally Lowenstein, *supra*.

8. The firm establishment in *Tashjian* and *Eu* of parties' associational freedom cannot eliminate the likelihood of conflicts between the exercise of that freedom and alleged rights of those aggrieved by the parties' actions. Consider the case of David Duke, a former Ku Klux Klan officer who received nationwide notoriety when he was elected to the Louisiana state legislature and then made it to a run-off election as a gubernatorial candidate. Duke announced that he was a candidate for the 1992 Republican presidential nomination. Under Georgia law, it was the Secretary of State's responsibility to create a preliminary list of candidates "who are generally advocated or recognized in news media throughout the United States" as candidates for president. However, the statutes provided that a candidate could be removed from the ballot if a committee consisting of the Republican leaders of both houses of the state legislature and the Republican state chairperson unanimously agreed. Duke appeared on the preliminary list of Republican candidates, but the three-member committee unanimously removed his name from the ballot. Duke and some of his Georgia supporters brought an action in federal court seeking to restore his name to the ballot. How should the court rule? Compare *Duke v. Cleland*, 954 F.2d 1526 (11th Cir. 1992) (*Duke I*), with *Duke v.*

Cleland, 5 F.3d 1399 (11th Cir. 1993) (*Duke II*), and with *Duke v. Massey*, 87 F.3d 1226 (11th Cir.1996) (*Duke III*). See also *Duke v. Smith*, 13 F.3d 388 (11th Cir. 1994), involving a similar dispute in Florida, though under a somewhat different statutory scheme.

2. The Extent of the Right—Recent Cases

In 1996, California voters approved an initiative measure, Proposition 198, over the opposition of Democratic and Republican party leaders as well as several minor parties. Proposition 198 changed California's historic closed primary to a form of open primary known as a "blanket primary." In the usual open primary, voters may select a ballot of whichever party they choose, but must vote in that party's primary for each office. In a blanket primary, the voter may vote in one party's primary for one office and a different party's primary for another office. For example, in the 1998 California primary, many voters voted for a Democrat for governor and a Republican for U.S. senator, because the Republican nomination for governor and the Democratic nomination for senator were essentially uncontested.

The Democratic and Republican parties and two minor parties filed an action contending that under *Tashjian*, they could not be forced by state law to nominate their candidates through a blanket primary. The United States District Court and the Ninth Circuit upheld the imposition of the blanket primary on the parties, but the Supreme Court struck it down in CALIFORNIA DEMOCRATIC PARTY v. JONES, 530 U.S. 567 (2000).

Justice Scalia, whom you will recall dissented in *Tashjian*, wrote for the Court: "[We have not held] that the processes by which political parties select their nominees are, as respondents would have it, wholly public affairs that States may regulate freely. To the contrary, we have continually stressed that when States regulate parties' internal processes they must act within limits imposed by the Constitution. See, *e.g., Eu; La Follette.* In this regard, respondents' reliance on *Smith* v. *Allwright* and *Terry* v. *Adams* is misplaced. In *Allwright,* we invalidated the Texas Democratic Party's rule limiting participation in its primary to whites; in *Terry,* we invalidated the same rule promulgated by the Jaybird Democratic Association, a 'self-governing voluntary club.' These cases held only that, when a State prescribes an election process that gives a special role to political parties, it 'endorses, adopts and enforces the discrimination against Negroes,' that the parties (or, in the case of the Jaybird Democratic Association, organizations that are 'part and parcel' of the parties, (Clark, J., concurring)) bring into the process—so that the parties' discriminatory action becomes state action under the Fifteenth Amendment. They do not stand for the proposition that party affairs are public affairs, free of First Amendment protections—and our later holdings make that entirely clear. See, *e.g., Tashjian.*...

"In no area is the political association's right to exclude more important than in the process of selecting its nominee. That process often determines the party's positions on the most significant public policy issues of the day, and even when those positions are predetermined it is the nominee who becomes the party's ambassador to the general electorate in winning it over to the party's views....

"Proposition 198 forces political parties to associate with—to have their nominees, and hence their positions, determined by—those who, at best, have refused to affiliate with the party, and, at worst, have expressly affiliated with a rival. In this respect, it is qualitatively different from a closed primary. Under that system, even when it is made

470 · MAJOR POLITICAL PARTIES

quite easy for a voter to change his party affiliation the day of the primary, and thus, in some sense, to 'cross over,' at least he must formally *become a member of the party*; and once he does so, he is limited to voting for candidates of that party.[8]

"[The Court cited statistics seeming to show that the votes of non-party members in major-party primaries could often be decisive.] The impact of voting by nonparty members is much greater upon minor parties, such as the Libertarian Party and the Peace and Freedom Party. In the first primaries these parties conducted following California's implementation of Proposition 198, the total votes cast for party candidates in some races was more than *double* the total number of *registered party members*....

"[T]he deleterious effects of Proposition 198 are not limited to altering the identity of the nominee. Even when the person favored by a majority of the party members prevails, he will have prevailed by taking somewhat different positions—and, should he be elected, will continue to take somewhat different positions in order to be renominated. As respondents' own expert concluded, '[t]he policy positions of Members of Congress elected from blanket primary states are ... more moderate, both in an absolute sense and relative to the other party, and so are more reflective of the preferences of the mass of voters at the center of the ideological spectrum' (expert report of Elisabeth R. Gerber). It is unnecessary to cumulate evidence of this phenomenon, since, after all, the whole purpose of Proposition 198 was to favor nominees with 'moderate' positions. It encourages candidates—and officeholders who hope to be renominated—to curry favor with persons whose views are more 'centrist' than those of the party base. In effect, Proposition 198 has simply moved the general election one step earlier in the process, at the expense of the parties' ability to perform the 'basic function' of choosing their own leaders. *Kusper*....

"In sum, Proposition 198 forces petitioners to adulterate their candidate-selection process—the 'basic function of a political party'—by opening it up to persons wholly unaffiliated with the party. Such forced association has the likely outcome—indeed, in this case the intended outcome—of changing the parties' message. We can think of no heavier burden on a political party's associational freedom. Proposition 198 is therefore unconstitutional unless it is narrowly tailored to serve a compelling state interest....

"[The Court considered and rejected seven suggested state interests. One of these was] that the blanket primary is the only way to ensure that disenfranchised persons enjoy the right to an effective vote. By 'disenfranchised,' respondents do not mean those who cannot vote; they mean simply independents and members of the minority party in 'safe' districts. These persons are disenfranchised, according to respondents, because under a closed primary they are unable to participate in what amounts to the determinative election—the majority party's primary; the only way to ensure they have an 'effective' vote is to force the party to open its primary to them. This also appears to be nothing more than reformulation of an asserted state interest we have already rejected—recharacterizing nonparty members' keen desire to participate in selection of the party's nominee as 'disenfranchisement' if that desire is not fulfilled. We have said, however, that a 'nonmember's desire to participate in the party's affairs is overborne by the countervailing and legitimate right of the party to determine its own membership qualifications.' *Tashjian*. The voter's desire to participate does not become more weighty simply because the State supports it. Moreover, even if it were accurate to describe the plight of the non-party-member in a safe district as 'disenfranchisement,' Proposition 198 is not needed to solve the problem. The voter who feels him-

---

8. In this sense, the blanket primary also may be constitutionally distinct from the open primary, in which the voter is limited to one party's ballot. This case does not require us to determine the constitutionality of open primaries.

self disenfranchised should simply join the party. That may put him to a hard choice, but it is not a state-imposed restriction upon his freedom of association, whereas compelling party members to accept his selection of their nominee is a state-imposed restriction upon theirs....

"Finally, we may observe that even if all these state interests were compelling ones, Proposition 198 is not a narrowly tailored means of furthering them. Respondents could protect them all by resorting to a nonpartisan blanket primary. Generally speaking, under such a system, the State determines what qualifications it requires for a candidate to have a place on the primary ballot—which may include nomination by established parties and voter-petition requirements for independent candidates. Each voter, regardless of party affiliation, may then vote for any candidate, and the top two vote getters (or however many the State prescribes) then move on to the general election. This system has all the characteristics of the partisan blanket primary, save the constitutionally crucial one: Primary voters are not choosing a party's nominee.[t] Under a nonpartisan blanket primary, a State may ensure more choice, greater participation, increased 'privacy,' and a sense of 'fairness'—all without severely burdening a political party's First Amendment right of association...."

Justice Kennedy wrote a concurring opinion and Justices Stevens and Ginsburg dissented.

Notes and Questions

1. Was the result in *Jones* dictated by *Tashjian*?

2. Much of the reporting of the *Jones* decision in the popular press and, indeed, some of the language in Justice Scalia's opinion, may give the impression that the Court's decision had the effect of striking down blanket primaries in the two additional states (Alaska and Washington) that then used them and of jeopardizing open primaries in the much larger number of states that use them. That impression is just as misleading as it would be to say that *Tashjian* jeopardizes closed primaries. What both decisions do is give the parties rather than the state legislatures the last word. However, the state legislature usually will provide for the type of primary favored by the major parties. *Tashjian* arose because the Democratic-controlled legislature refused to permit the Republicans to modify their primary. *Jones* arose because of an initiative. The likelihood that many states will change their primary systems because of *Jones* is probably low. Nor is there evidence to date of widespread change in the states.

3. Under *Jones*, what are the constitutional limits on the ability of a state to permit nonparty members to affect the nomination processes of a party, other than by voting in its primary? Is it unconstitutional to permit nonparty members to initiate a challenge to a candidate's nominating petitions for the primary? See *Queens County Republican Committee v. New York State Board of Elections*, 222 F.Supp.2d 341 (E.D.N.Y. 2002).

---

t. Justice Scalia's statement that a nonpartisan primary has all the characteristics of a partisan blanket primary save that voters are not selecting a party's nominee may be misleading. The difference is by no means a conceptual one alone. In a nonpartisan primary, which is the electoral procedure followed in Louisiana, all candidates are running against each other in the primary. In a partisan blanket primary such as the one struck down in this case, Republican candidates run against Republicans, Democratic candidates against Democrats, and so on. Thus, in the partisan blanket primary, there will always be a general election with one candidate from each party. In a nonpartisan primary, as conducted in Louisiana and at the local level in many states, there will not be a general election if one candidate gets a majority of the votes in the primary. Even if there is a general (or run-off) election, the candidates might both be members of the same party.—EDs.

4. Even in a blanket primary, Republicans run against Republicans and Democrats run against Democrats for their parties' nominations. As is discussed in *Jones*, Louisiana goes one step further, by eliminating even this feature from primary elections. In Louisiana, all candidates from all parties run against each other, and if one gets a majority of the vote, he or she is elected. If no candidate gets a majority, there is a run-off between the two top vote-getters, even if they are both from the same party.

The Louisiana system has run into a snag as applied to congressional elections. Its "primary," or first-round election, is held in October. The run-off is held on the Tuesday following the first Monday in November, which is required to be the date for federal elections by 2 U.S.C. §§1 and 7. However, the Supreme Court ruled that the possibility of a candidate being elected in the primary violates the statutory requirement of a uniform nationwide date for electing the members of Congress. See *Foster v. Love*, 522 U.S. 67 (1997).

5. *Jones* is criticized by Richard L. Hasen, *Do the Parties or the People Own the Electoral Process?*, 149 UNIVERSITY OF PENNSYLVANIA LAW REVIEW 815 (2001). Hasen maintains that parties' right to control their internal affairs is protected by the First Amendment, but that nominating candidates is not an internal matter. "Rather, primaries are a means for voters to structure the electoral process by winnowing down candidates to a list of finalists to run in the general election. Voters through the initiative process or the state legislature should be allowed to dictate the form of that winnowing process...." He argues that if members of party organizations object to losing control of the nomination process to voters, their real complaint is with the direct primary itself, not with the particular form of the blanket primary. "Yet," he points out, "the Supreme Court in *Jones* rejected the idea that the direct primary is unconstitutional...." Finally, he questions the empirical premises put forth by opponents of the blanket primary:

> The evidence we have on the effect of the form in which primary elections are held on the strength of parties does not demonstrate that parties are in great danger from more open primaries. Despite the existence of the blanket primary in the State of Washington for many years, the Republican Party there is among the strongest party organizations in the nation. More generally, during the same period that almost half of the states had open or blanket primaries, party cohesion in Congress reached high levels unprecedented in American history. It appears that the openness of the primaries has not caused candidates to become so moderate that they cannot engage in party-line voting most of the time.

An even broader attack on the Court's application of the First Amendment to political parties is contained in Gregory P. Magarian, *Regulating Political Parties Under a "Public Rights" First Amendment*, 44 WILLIAM & MARY LAW REVIEW 1939 (2003). But the Court's decision is defended by Bruce E. Cain, *Party Autonomy and Two Party Electoral Competition*, 149 UNIVERSITY OF PENNSYLVANIA LAW REVIEW 793 (2001):

> As decades of political science research amply demonstrates, the party label has enormous informational value—indeed since a majority of the electorate tends to vote predictably along the lines of party label, it is the most important resource that the party possesses. Giving up control of that label is a significant blow to the party's capacity to determine its nominees....

Cain believes that the threat to the party's control of its nominations is real:

> Studies of the 1998 California primary revealed two main types of strategic voters: hedgers who had no competitive race in their own primary and therefore voted for the most preferred candidate in another party's primary (thereby ensuring that they at least get their second favorite candidate in November), and

raiders/saboteurs who voted for the weakest candidate in order to help their own party's candidate in the fall. While the number of raiders/saboteurs is small and the total number of strategic voters will normally be less than the total number of sincere crossover voters, it is clear that a party's nomination in the spring may be determined by a significant number of voters who will not support the nominee in November. This raises serious questions about the authenticity and legitimacy of party nominees made under a blanket system and about the system's vulnerability to strategic manipulation.

For additional commentary on *Jones*, see Samuel Issacharoff, *Political Parties with Public Purposes: Political Parties, Associational Freedoms, and Partisan Competition*, 101 COLUMBIA LAW REVIEW 274 (2001); Nathaniel Persily, *Toward a Functional Defense of Political Party Autonomy*, 76 NEW YORK UNIVERSITY LAW REVIEW 750 (2001). For empirical studies of the blanket primary, see VOTING AT THE POLITICAL FAULT LINE: CALIFORNIA'S EXPERIMENT WITH THE BLANKET PRIMARY (Bruce E. Cain & Elisabeth R. Gerber, eds., 2002).

6. The Democratic primary in Georgia's Fourth Congressional District in 2002 featured a spirited contest between incumbent Cynthia McKinney and challenger Denise Majette, both African Americans. Majette won the primary by a 58–42 margin and went on to win the general election easily. Georgia has an open primary, and McKinney's supporters claimed that Majette's margin of victory in the primary was provided by Republican crossover voters.[u]

* * *

Oklahoma uses a "semiclosed" primary. Only members of a party may vote in primaries, unless the party permits independent voters to participate. In CLINGMAN v. BEAVER, 544 U.S. 581 (2005), the Court rejected a challenge to these rules brought by the Libertarian Party, which wanted to allow any voters, including those who were members of other parties, to vote in its primaries.[v]

Writing for a plurality that included Chief Justice Rehnquist and Justices Kennedy and Scalia, Justice Thomas wrote that there was no real "association" being denied by the Oklahoma rules, because any of the voters who wanted to significantly associate with the Libertarians were free to do so by disaffiliating from their other party. Alternatively, if there was a burden on association, it was a minimal one.

In the rest of Justice Thomas' opinion he spoke for the Court, as he was joined by Justices O'Connor and Breyer.[w] He rejected the plaintiffs' reliance on *Tashjian*, writing that:

> As our cases since *Tashjian* have clarified, strict scrutiny is appropriate only if the burden is severe. In *Tashjian* itself, independent voters could join the Connecticut Republican Party as late as the day before the primary. As explained above, requiring voters to register with a party prior to participating in the party's primary minimally burdens voters' associational rights.

Justice Thomas also said *Tashjian* was distinguishable, primarily on the obvious ground that in *Clingman*, unlike *Tashjian*, the state was not requiring voters to register as Liber-

---

u. Empirically, that claim is doubtful, but it does appear that McKinney received a large majority of the votes cast by African Americans. See Michael Barone with Richard E. Cohen and Grant Ujifusa, THE ALMANAC OF AMERICAN POLITICS 2004 471 (2003).

v. The plaintiffs also included Republican and Democratic voters who wanted to vote in the Libertarian primary.

w. There was a procedural issue in the case, not discussed here, on which Justice Breyer declined to join the majority.

tarians in order to vote in the Libertarian primary. Is *Tashjian* a viable precedent after *Clingman*?

The foregoing reasoning led Justice Thomas to the conclusion that because of the lack of a severe burden on associational rights, strict scrutiny was not compelled. Several government interests justified the restrictions under less severe scrutiny. First was the state's interest in preserving the parties as "visible and identifiable interest groups." Allowing members of other parties to vote could result in the nomination of candidates out of accord with the preference of Libertarian members. Although the party might be willing to take this risk in exchange for possible electoral benefit, the state had an interest in avoiding confusion. The state could believe democracy would be facilitated when voters classify themselves by party affiliations. Removing the connection between affiliation and voting in primaries could disrupt that system.

Second, the state could seek to facilitate efficient campaigning and party-building, which would be difficult without advance identification of which voters were likely to vote in the party's primary. Third, the state could seek to prevent party switching, or what political scientists call "strategic voting" (i.e., a vote cast for a candidate in order to give another candidate or party a tactical advantage). For example, if there were no competitive race in the Democratic Party, some Democrats might vote in the Libertarian Primary to try to nominate a candidate they thought would draw Republican votes in the general election.

In a concurring opinion, joined in part by Justice Breyer, Justice O'Connor wrote that when the state prohibits a party from allowing voters to participate in its primaries it implicates important associational interests. But she agreed with the Court that these interests were not seriously burdened in the Oklahoma case. Justice Stevens, joined by Justices Ginsburg and Souter, dissented.

The most recent case in the line beginning with *Tashjian* is WASHINGTON STATE GRANGE v. WASHINGTON STATE REPUBLICAN PARTY, 128 S.Ct. 1184 (2008). Since 1935, Washington had been using blanket primaries similar to the one struck down in *California Democratic Party v. Jones, supra.* That case gave parties the right to opt out of a mandatory blanket primary, and the parties in Washington rapidly exercised that option.[x] You will recall that in *Jones*, the Court suggested a "less restrictive alternative" that states could use, a nonpartisan blanket primary. This device, which has been used in Louisiana, consists of primary elections that avoid party nominations altogether. As it works in Louisiana, all candidates for an office appear on the ballot in the primary. Any candidate who receives a majority of votes is elected. If no candidate gets a majority, the two top candidates oppose each other in the general election, which is a run-off election. Typically, these two candidates would be a Democrat and a Republican, but they might be two Democrats or two Republicans, and occasionally they might include an independent or a member of a third party. Because the candidates are not categorized by party, the primary does not result in any official party nominees, even if it does result in a run-off between one candidate who is a Republican and one who is a Democrat.

If Washington had adopted the Louisiana system, apparently it would have had clear sailing. Instead, an initiative approved by Washington's voters, called I-872, adopted what the state called a nonpartisan blanket primary system, but with a partisan wrinkle. Candidates can list a "party preference" on the ballot.[y] The parties objected to the system on

---

x. See *Democratic Party of Washington State v. Reed*, 343 F.3d 1198 (2003).

y. Another difference between the Louisiana and Washington systems is that in Washington, the two top candidates run against each other in the general election, even if one of them won a majority in the primary. This difference is not material to the constitutional question.

the ground that if the name of a party appeared next to each candidate's name on the ballot, the primaries would for all practical purposes result in a party nomination so far as most voters would be concerned. The party would thus end up with a *de facto* nominee selected in part by voters with no affiliation with the party, which under *Jones* is what the parties are entitled to object to.[z] The Ninth Circuit accepted this argument and ruled that the parties were entitled to opt out of the system.

The Supreme Court, in an opinion by Justice Thomas, upheld the Washington system against what it pointed out was a "facial challenge." "The State has had no opportunity to implement I-872, and its courts have had no occasion to construe the law in the context of actual disputes arising from the electoral context, or to accord the law a limiting construction to avoid constitutional questions." Facial challenges are disfavored, in part because they "often rest on speculation."

The Court did not accept the parties' and the Ninth Circuit's contention that candidates in the general election would be *de facto* party nominees.

> The flaw in this argument is that, unlike the California primary [in *Jones*], the I-872 primary does not, by its terms, choose parties' nominees. The essence of nomination—the choice of a party representative—does not occur under I-872. The law never refers to the candidates as nominees of any party, nor does it treat them as such.... The top two candidates from the primary election proceed to the general election regardless of their party preferences.

The Court added in a footnote:

> It is true that parties may no longer indicate their nominees on the ballot, but that is unexceptionable: The First Amendment does not give political parties a right to have their nominees designated as such on the ballot. Parties do not gain such a right simply because the State affords candidates the opportunity to indicate their party preferences on the ballot.

The Court continued:

> Respondents counter that, even if the I-872 primary does not actually choose parties' nominees, it nevertheless burdens their associational rights because voters will assume that candidates on the general election ballot are the nominees of their preferred parties. This brings us to the heart of respondents' case—and to the fatal flaw in their argument. At bottom, respondents' objection to I-872 is that voters will be confused by candidates' party-preference designations. Respondents' arguments are largely variations on this theme. Thus, they argue that even if voters do not assume that candidates on the general election ballot are the nominees of their parties, they will at least assume that the parties associate with, and approve of, them. This, they say, compels them to associate with candidates they do not endorse, alters the messages they wish to convey, and forces them to engage in counterspeech to disassociate themselves from the candidates and their positions on the issues.
>
> We reject each of these contentions for the same reason: They all depend, not on any facial requirement of I-872, but on the possibility that voters will be confused as to the meaning of the party-preference designation. But respondents' assertion that voters will misinterpret the party-preference designation is sheer

---

z. Indeed, there was not even a requirement that candidates be members of the party they listed as their "party preference."

speculation. It "depends upon the belief that voters can be 'misled' by party labels...."

Of course, it is *possible* that voters will misinterpret the candidates' party-preference designations as reflecting endorsement by the parties. But these cases involve a facial challenge, and we cannot strike down I-872 on its face based on the mere possibility of voter confusion. Because respondents brought their suit as a facial challenge, we have no evidentiary record against which to assess their assertions that voters will be confused. Indeed, because I-872 has never been implemented, we do not even have ballots indicating how party preference will be displayed. It stands to reason that whether voters will be confused by the party-preference designations will depend in significant part on the form of the ballot....

As long as we are speculating about the form of the ballot—and we can do no more than speculate in this facial challenge—we must, in fairness to the voters of the State of Washington who enacted I-872 and in deference to the executive and judicial officials who are charged with implementing it, ask whether the ballot could conceivably be printed in such a way as to eliminate the possibility of widespread voter confusion and with it the perceived threat to the First Amendment.

It is not difficult to conceive of such a ballot. For example, petitioners propose that the actual I-872 ballot could include prominent disclaimers explaining that party preference reflects only the self-designation of the candidate and not an official endorsement by the party. They also suggest that the ballots might note preference in the form of a candidate statement that emphasizes the candidate's personal determination rather than the party's acceptance of the candidate, such as "my party preference is the Republican Party." Additionally, the State could decide to educate the public about the new primary ballots through advertising or explanatory materials mailed to voters along with their ballots. We are satisfied that there are a variety of ways in which the State could implement I-872 that would eliminate any real threat of voter confusion. And without the specter of widespread voter confusion, respondents' arguments about forced association and compelled speech fall flat....

Because we have concluded that I-872 does not severely burden respondents, the State need not assert a compelling interest. The State's asserted interest in providing voters with relevant information about the candidates on the ballot is easily sufficient to sustain I-872.

Chief Justice Roberts, joined by Justice Alito, added a concurring opinion. Justice Scalia, joined by Justice Kennedy, dissented.

Notes and Questions

1. If you were an attorney advising the Washington officials charged with implementing I-872, how would you advise them to proceed? Suppose what may or may not be true, that the groups supporting I-872 want the Washington primaries to be as close as possible to the former partisan blanket primaries that Washington conducted since 1935, before *Jones*. In other words, suppose these groups *do* want the surviving Democratic and Republican candidates in the general election to be *de facto* nominees of their parties. If you were counsel to those groups and you were consulted about what their lobbying efforts on the implementation of I-872 should be directed toward, how would you advise them?

2. One aspect of *Washington State Grange* that is worth considering is its formalism. At least for purposes of a facial challenge, the Court is unreceptive to claims of the *de facto* effect of I-872. Rather, the law is taken on its own terms, which do not include the concept of party nomination, whatever the actual political effect of the system created by the law may be. Formalism also seemed conspicuous in another election law case the Supreme Court decided in the same term, *New York State Board of Elections v. López Torres*, 128 S.Ct. 791 (2008). In *López Torres*, plaintiffs objected to the system for party nominations of candidates for the New York Supreme Court, which despite its name is a trial court of general jurisdiction. The judicial candidates are nominated through a complex system of election of delegates to nominating conventions. The Second Circuit struck down the system on the ground that, as a practical matter, it assured party insiders almost complete control of the nominating process. As in *Washington State Grange*, the *López Torres* Court overruled the lower court and upheld the nominating system, offering a formalist reliance on the system "on paper" rather than on the system's practical effects. Here, Justice Scalia, who dissented in *Washington State Grange*, wrote for a unanimous Court:[a]

> Our cases invalidating ballot-access requirements have focused on the requirements themselves, and not on the manner in which political actors function under those requirements. Here respondents complain not of the state law, but of the voters' (and their elected delegates') preference for the choices of the party leadership.
>
> To be sure, we have ... permitted States to set their faces against "party bosses" by requiring party-candidate selection through processes more favorable to insurgents, such as primaries. But to say that the State can require this is a far cry from saying that the Constitution demands it. None of our cases establishes that an individual's constitutional right is to have a "fair shot" at winning the party's nomination. And with good reason. What constitutes a "fair shot" is a reasonable enough question for legislative judgment, which we will accept so long as it does not too much infringe upon the party's associational rights. But it is hardly a manageable constitutional question for judges—especially for judges in our legal system, where traditional electoral practice gives no hint of even the existence, much less the content, of a constitutional requirement of a "fair shot" at party nomination.[b]

Do *Washington State Grange* and *López Torres* signify a trend toward increased formalism in election law jurisprudence or is their issuance within a couple of months of each other a coincidence? It will be a question worth watching over the next several years.

* * *

You may at this point wish to think in general terms about the pros and cons of judicial oversight of political parties and the laws regulating them. One scholar, at least, has expressed considerable skepticism:

> Not only do political parties adapt to new circumstances, but most other aspects of the political environment also change over time. These changes then further affect political parties. The interactions and feedback effects increase the dynamic complexity facing courts and virtually guarantee that judicial decisions in this arena will have unforeseen consequences for all facets of government. Ad-

---

a. Justice Kennedy, joined in part by Justice Breyer, concurred in the result only.

b. We shall revisit *López Torres* in Chapter 12, to consider the Court's statements on the significance of competitiveness in election law. There is also perhaps some connection between the question of formalism that we raise here and the question of strict enforcement of election law requirements and "substantial compliance," considered in Chapter 8.

judication is a blunt and often counterproductive tool. Courts do not have the resources to gather reliable information about the political environment or to make accurate predictions about the likely effects of their rulings on parties and other institutions. Courts are presented only with a partial picture and often cannot grasp the entirety of a problem. Moreover, if the system adapts to a particular ruling in unexpected ways, courts do not have the ability to modify the law unless someone brings a case that allows adjustment. In an area of rapidly changing institutions and complex relationships among entities, the ability to revise policy over time, engage in new and expanded fact-finding, and make decisions incrementally can be crucial to success. None of these features plays to the strengths of the courts …

Elizabeth Garrett, *Is the Party Over? Courts and the Political Process*, 2002 SUPREME COURT REVIEW 95, 114–15. Garrett therefore takes the view that judicial review "in political party cases should be limited to only the most extreme cases in which one segment of a party works successfully, perhaps with other party entities, to impose anticompetitive structures." Do you agree? Or might Garrett's observations support the sort of enhanced formalism we just noticed in the two 2008 cases? Such formalism would often but not always lead to greater judicial restraint of the sort Garrett recommends. Garrett bases part of her argument on cases involving minor parties, so you may wish to revisit this question after studying Chapter 10.

IV. Parties and Patronage

"Patronage" refers to the practice of awarding governmental benefits to allies of the party or the individuals in power. Broadly speaking the term can refer to a variety of governmental benefits, such as the awarding of profitable contracts or of government franchises, loans or grants. Commonly, the term is used more narrowly to refer to the providing of government jobs to allies and party loyalists. These jobs can run the spectrum from very high level positions, such as ambassadorships and judgeships, to the lowest level manual or clerical positions. They can be full-time jobs or particular assignments, such as, in many states, inheritance tax appraisers.

Patronage, and the controversy it arouses, has played a conspicuous part in American history and even in American culture. Mention of a few highlights will illustrate the point. After Republican Thomas Jefferson defeated Federalist incumbent John Adams in the 1800 presidential election, Adams appointed as many Federalists as possible to a variety of offices, including the notorious "midnight judges," one of whom was the great Chief Justice John Marshall. Jefferson later wrote:

> I can say with truth that one act of Mr. Adams's life, and one only, ever gave me a moment's personal displeasure. I did consider his last appointments to office as personally unkind. They were from among my most ardent political enemies, from whom no faithful cooperation could ever be expected, and laid me under the embarrassment of acting thro' men whose views were to defeat mine; or to encounter the odium of putting others in their places. It seemed but common justice to leave a successor free to act by instruments of his own choice.[c]

---

c. Letter from Thomas Jefferson to Abigail Adams, June 13, 1804, in Thomas Jefferson, *Writings* 1144, 1145–46 (Library of America, 1984).

Upon taking office, Jefferson seemed to promise a new policy, when he declared,

> every difference of opinion is not a difference of principle. We have called by different names brethren of the same principle. We are all Republicans, we are all Federalists.[d]

Nevertheless, within a few months, Jefferson was forced to explain his replacement of Federalist officeholders with Republicans:

> Declarations of myself in favor of *political tolerance*, exhortations to *harmony* and affection in social intercourse, and to respect for the *equal rights* of the minority, have, on certain occasions, been quoted & misconstrued into assurances that the tenure of offices was to be undisturbed. But could candor apply such a construction? ... When it is considered, that during the late administration, those who were not of a particular sect of politics were excluded from all office; when, by a steady pursuit of this measure, nearly the whole offices of the U S were monopolized by that sect; when the public sentiment at length declared itself, and burst open the doors of honor and confidence to those whose opinions they more approved, was it to be imagined that this monopoly of office was still to be continued in the hands of the minority? Does it violate their *equal rights*, to assert some rights in the majority also? Is it *political intolerance* to claim a proportionate share in the direction of the public affairs? Can they not *harmonize* in society unless they have everything in their own hands?[e]

During the so-called "era of good feelings" that followed, partisan patronage was not an issue at the national level, since national politics was dominated by a single party. During the 1820s, the Democratic-Republican Party split between the supporters, respectively, of John Quincy Adams and Andrew Jackson. The Jacksonians, finally victorious in the 1828 election, openly declared their policy of filling offices by partisan criteria. In the ensuing decades, there was alternation in the presidency between the Democrats and the Whigs and, after 1860, between the Democrats and the Republicans. Each time the presidency was transferred from one party to the other, federal officeholders were swept out of office to be replaced by adherents of the newly victorious party.

Even during its heyday, the practice of federal patronage did not go without criticism. The otherwise routine firing of the manager of the Salem, Massachusetts, custom-house in 1848, by the Whigs after the victory of their candidate, Zachary Taylor, became immortalized because its victim, Nathaniel Hawthorne, recorded the incident in his introductory essay to one of America's greatest novels.

"[I]t is a strange experience," Hawthorne wrote.

> to a man of pride and sensibility, to know that his interests are within the control of individuals who neither love nor understand him, and by whom, since one or the other must needs happen, he would rather be injured than obliged. Strange, too, for one who has kept his calmness throughout the contest, to observe the bloodthirstiness that is developed in the hour of triumph, and to be conscious that he is himself among its objects! There are few uglier traits of human nature than this tendency—which I now witnessed in men no worse than their neighbours—to grow cruel, merely because they possessed the power of inflicting harm. If the guillotine, as applied to office-hold-

d. Thomas Jefferson, First Inaugural Address, March 4, 1801, in *ibid.*, 492, 493.
e. Thomas Jefferson, Letter to Elias Shipman and Others, a Committee of the Merchants of New Haven, July 12, 1801, in *ibid.*, 497, 498 (emphasis in original).

ers, were a literal fact, instead of one of the most apt of metaphors, it is my sincere belief, that the active members of the victorious party were sufficiently excited to have chopped off all our heads, and have thanked Heaven for the opportunity![f]

Opposition to patronage at the federal level grew, especially after the Civil War, and came to a head when a disappointed office seeker assassinated President James Garfield in 1881. The Pendleton Act, introducing the federal civil service system and sharply reducing the number of federal positions subject to patronage appointments, was enacted in 1883.

Patronage played a more important role and lasted longer in state and local politics. Patronage, in both the narrow and the broad senses, was the mainstay of party "machines" in state and, most notoriously, in big city politics around the country. Patronage and the corruption many people associated with it were a prime target of the "muckraking" journalists of the turn of the century and of the early twentieth century Progressive movement. The result was a gradual displacement of a great deal of patronage in state and local governments with civil service systems over the course of most of the twentieth century.

The best known strong patronage systems to survive into the 1970s were those of the state of Illinois and the city of Chicago, the latter controlled by then Mayor Richard Daley.[g] By 1976, when the Supreme Court decided *Elrod v. Burns*, patronage in the narrow sense had declined considerably in most of the country, so that the significance of the Court's patronage cases may not be as great as the justices in both the majority and the minority in *Elrod* and subsequent cases seem to have believed. However, patronage in the narrow sense has by no means entirely disappeared, and patronage in the broader sense is likely to endure in one form or another so long as democracy as we know it exists.[h] One question you might bear in mind, as you read the patronage cases that follow, is to what extent their conclusions ought to be applicable to other types of government benefits, such as the awarding of franchises or contracts, or even broader policy matters such as the adoption of legislation. Does it violate the First Amendment for government officials to base such decisions in whole or in part on the party affiliation of interested persons? On whether or not interested persons have made campaign contributions to the right party or the right candidates? The Supreme Court discussed some of these issues in two 1996 cases, discussed at the end of this chapter.

Elrod v. Burns

427 U.S. 347 (1976)

Mr. Justice BRENNAN announced the judgment of the Court and delivered an opinion in which Mr. Justice WHITE and Mr. Justice MARSHALL joined.

This case presents the question whether public employees who allege that they were discharged or threatened with discharge solely because of their partisan political affiliation or nonaffiliation state a claim for deprivation of constitutional rights secured by the First and Fourteenth Amendments....

---

f. Nathaniel Hawthorne, *The Custom-House*, in THE SCARLET LETTER 4, 31 (3d Norton Critical Edition, 1988).

g. See generally Cynthia Grant Bowman, *"We Don't Want Anybody Anybody Sent": The Death of Patronage Hiring in Chicago*, 86 NORTHWESTERN UNIVERSITY LAW REVIEW 57 (1991).

h. See generally Raymond E. Wolfinger, *Why Political Machines Have Not Withered Away and Other Revisionist Thoughts*, 34 JOURNAL OF POLITICS 365 (1972).

In December 1970, the Sheriff of Cook County, a Republican, was replaced by Richard Elrod, a Democrat. At that time, respondents, all Republicans, were employees of the Cook County Sheriff's Office. They were non-civil-service employees and, therefore, not covered by any statute, ordinance, or regulation protecting them from arbitrary discharge....

It has been the practice of the Sheriff of Cook County, when he assumes office from a Sheriff of a different political party, to replace non-civil-service employees of the Sheriff's Office with members of his own party when the existing employees lack or fail to obtain requisite support from, or fail to affiliate with, that party. Consequently, subsequent to Sheriff Elrod's assumption of office, respondents, with the exception of Buckley, were discharged from their employment solely because they did not support and were not members of the Democratic Party and had failed to obtain the sponsorship of one of its leaders. Buckley is in imminent danger of being discharged solely for the same reasons....

The Cook County Sheriff's practice of dismissing employees on a partisan basis is but one form of the general practice of political patronage. The practice also includes placing loyal supporters in government jobs that may or may not have been made available by political discharges. Nonofficeholders may be the beneficiaries of lucrative government contracts for highway construction, buildings, and supplies. Favored wards may receive improved public services. Members of the judiciary may even engage in the practice through the appointment of receiverships, trusteeships, and refereeships. Although political patronage comprises a broad range of activities, we are here concerned only with the constitutionality of dismissing public employees for partisan reasons.

Patronage practice is not new to American politics. It has existed at the federal level at least since the Presidency of Thomas Jefferson, although its popularization and legitimation primarily occurred later, in the Presidency of Andrew Jackson. The practice is not unique to American politics. It has been used in many European countries, and in darker times, it played a significant role in the Nazi rise to power in Germany and other totalitarian states. More recent times have witnessed a strong decline in its use, particularly with respect to public employment. Indeed, only a few decades after Andrew Jackson's administration, strong discontent with the corruption and inefficiency of the patronage system of public employment eventuated in the Pendleton Act, the foundation of modern civil service. And on the state and local levels, merit systems have increasingly displaced the practice.[8] ...

The decline of patronage employment is not, of course relevant to the question of its constitutionality. It is the practice itself, not the magnitude of its occurrence, the constitutionality of which must be determined. Nor for that matter does any unacceptability of the practice signified by its decline indicate its unconstitutionality. Our inquiry does not begin with the judgment of history, though the actual operation of a practice viewed in retrospect may help to assess its workings with respect to constitutional limitations....

The cost of the practice of patronage is the restraint it places on freedoms of belief and association. In order to maintain their jobs, respondents were required to pledge their political allegiance to the Democratic Party, work for the election of other candidates

---

8. See *Broadrick v. Oklahoma*, 413 U.S. 601, 604–605 n.2 (1973). Factors contributing to the declining use of patronage have not been limited to the proliferation of merit systems. New methods of political financing, the greater necessity of job expertise in public employment, growing issue orientation in the elective process, and new incentives for political campaigners have also contributed.

of the Democratic Party, contribute a portion of their wages to the Party, or obtain the sponsorship of a member of the Party, usually at the price of one of the first three alternatives. Regardless of the incumbent party's identity, Democratic or otherwise, the consequences for association and belief are the same. An individual who is a member of the out-party maintains affiliation with his own party at the risk of losing his job. He works for the election of his party's candidates and espouses its policies at the same risk. The financial and campaign assistance that he is induced to provide to another party furthers the advancement of that party's policies to the detriment of his party's views and ultimately his own beliefs, and any assessment of his salary is tantamount to coerced belief....

It is not only belief and association which are restricted where political patronage is the practice. The free functioning of the electoral process also suffers. Conditioning public employment on partisan support prevents support of competing political interests. Existing employees are deterred from such support, as well as the multitude seeking jobs. As government employment, state or federal, becomes more pervasive, the greater the dependence on it becomes, and therefore the greater becomes the power to starve political opposition by commanding partisan support, financial and otherwise. Patronage thus tips the electoral process in favor of the incumbent party, and where the practice's scope is substantial relative to the size of the electorate, the impact on the process can be significant.

[The practice of patronage firings] unavoidably confronts decisions by this Court either invalidating or recognizing as invalid government action that inhibits belief and association through the conditioning of public employment on political faith....

Particularly pertinent to the constitutionality of the practice of patronage dismissals are *Keyishian v. Board of Regents*, 385 U.S. 589 (1967), and *Perry v. Sindermann*, 408 U.S. 593 (1972). In *Keyishian*, the Court invalidated New York statutes barring employment merely on the basis of membership in "subversive" organizations. *Keyishian* squarely held that political association alone could not, consistently with the First Amendment, constitute an adequate ground for denying public employment. In *Perry*, the Court broadly rejected the validity of limitations on First Amendment rights as a condition to the receipt of a governmental benefit....

Patronage practice falls squarely within the prohibitions of *Keyishian* and *Perry*. Under that practice, public employees hold their jobs on the condition that they provide, in some acceptable manner, support for the favored political party. The threat of dismissal for failure to provide that support unquestionably inhibits protected belief and association, and dismissal for failure to provide support only penalizes its exercise. The belief and association which government may not ordain directly are achieved by indirection....

Although the practice of patronage dismissals clearly infringes First Amendment interests, our inquiry is not at an end, for the prohibition on encroachment of First Amendment protections is not an absolute. Restraints are permitted for appropriate reasons....

It is firmly established that a significant impairment of First Amendment rights must survive exacting scrutiny....

One interest which has been offered in justification of patronage is the need to insure effective government and the efficiency of public employees. It is argued that employees of political persuasions not the same as that of the party in control of public office will not have the incentive to work effectively and may even be motivated to subvert the incumbent administration's efforts to govern effectively. We are not persuaded. The inefficiency resulting from the wholesale replacement of large numbers of public employees every time political office changes hands belies this justification. And the prospect of dismissal after an election in which the incumbent party has lost is only a disincentive to good work. Further, it is not clear that dismissal in order to make room for a patronage appointment will result in replacement by a person more qualified to do the job since appointment often occurs in exchange for the delivery of votes, or other party service, not job capability. More fundamentally, however, the argument does not succeed because it is doubtful that the mere difference of political persuasion motivates poor performance; nor do we think it legitimately may be used as a basis for imputing such behavior. The Court has consistently recognized that mere political association is an inadequate basis for imputing disposition to ill-willed conduct.... At all events, less drastic means for insuring government effectiveness and employee efficiency are available to the State. Specifically, employees may always be discharged for good cause, such as insubordination or poor job performance, when those bases in fact exist.

Even if the first argument that patronage serves effectiveness and efficiency be rejected, it still may be argued that patronage serves those interests by giving the employees of an incumbent party the incentive to perform well in order to insure their party's incumbency and thereby their jobs. Patronage, according to the argument, thus makes employees highly accountable to the public. But the ability of officials more directly accountable to the electorate to discharge employees for cause and the availability of merit systems, growth in the use of which has been quite significant, convince us that means less intrusive than patronage still exist for achieving accountability in the public work force and, thereby, effective and efficient government. The greater effectiveness of patronage over these less drastic means, if any, is at best marginal, a gain outweighed by the absence of intrusion on protected interests under the alternatives.

The lack of any justification for patronage dismissals as a means of furthering government effectiveness and efficiency distinguishes this case from *CSC v. Letter Carriers*, 413 U.S. 548 (1973), and *United Public Workers v. Mitchell*, 330 U.S. 75 (1949). In both of those cases, legislative restraints on political management and campaigning by public employees were upheld despite their encroachment on First Amendment rights because, *inter alia*, they did serve in a necessary manner to foster and protect efficient and effective government. Interestingly, the activities that were restrained by the legislation involved in those cases are characteristic of patronage practices. As the Court observed in *Mitchell*, "The conviction that an actively partisan governmental personnel threatens good administration has deepened since [1882]. Congress recognizes danger to the service in that political rather than official effort may earn advancement and to the public in that governmental favor may be channeled through political connections."

A second interest advanced in support of patronage is the need for political loyalty of employees, not to the end that effectiveness and efficiency be insured, but to the end that representative government not be undercut by tactics obstructing the implementation of policies of the new administration, policies presumably sanctioned by the electorate. The justification is not without force, but is nevertheless inadequate to validate patronage wholesale. Limiting patronage dismissals to policymaking positions is sufficient to achieve this governmental end. Nonpolicymaking individuals usually have only limited responsibility and are therefore not in a position to thwart the goals of the in-party.

No clear line can be drawn between policymaking and nonpolicymaking positions. While nonpolicymaking individuals usually have limited responsibility, that is not to say that one with a number of responsibilities is necessarily in a policymaking position. The nature of the responsibilities is critical. Employee supervisors, for example, may have many responsibilities, but those responsibilities may have only limited and well-defined objectives. An employee with responsibilities that are not well defined or are of broad scope more likely functions in a policymaking position. In determining whether an employee occupies a policymaking position, consideration should also be given to whether the employee acts as an adviser or formulates plans for the implementation of broad goals. Thus, the political loyalty "justification is a matter of proof, or at least argument, directed at particular kinds of jobs." *Illinois State Employees Union v. Lewis*, 473 F.2d 561 (7th Cir. 1972). Since, as we have noted, it is the government's burden to demonstrate an overriding interest in order to validate an encroachment on protected interests, the burden of establishing this justification as to any particular respondent will rest on the petitioners on remand, cases of doubt being resolved in favor of the particular respondent.

It is argued that a third interest supporting patronage dismissals is the preservation of the democratic process. According to petitioners, "we have contrived no system for the support of party that does not place considerable reliance on patronage. The party organization makes a democratic government work and charges a price for its services."[21] The argument is thus premised on the centrality of partisan politics to the democratic process.

Preservation of the democratic process is certainly an interest protection of which may in some instances justify limitations on First Amendment freedoms. But however important preservation of the two-party system or any system involving a fixed number of parties may or may not be, we are not persuaded that the elimination of patronage practice or, as is specifically involved here, the interdiction of patronage dismissals, will bring about the demise of party politics. Political parties existed in the absence of active patronage practice prior to the administration of Andrew Jackson, and they have survived substantial reduction in their patronage power through the establishment of merit systems.

Patronage dismissals thus are not the least restrictive alternative to achieving the contribution they may make to the democratic process. The process functions as well without the practice, perhaps even better, for patronage dismissals clearly also retard that process. Patronage can result in the entrenchment of one or a few parties to the exclusion of others. And most indisputably, as we recognized at the outset, patronage is a very effective impediment to the associational and speech freedoms which are essential to a meaningful system of democratic government. Thus, if patronage contributes at all to the elective process, that contribution is diminished by the practice's impairment of the same. Indeed, unlike the gain to representative government provided by the Hatch Act in *CSC v. Letter Carriers*, supra, and *United Public Workers v. Mitchell*, supra, the gain to representative government provided by the practice of patronage, if any, would be insufficient to justify its sacrifice of First Amendment rights.

To be sure, *Letter Carriers* and *Mitchell* upheld Hatch Act restraints sacrificing political campaigning and management, activities themselves protected by the First Amendment. But in those cases it was the Court's judgment that congressional subordination of those activities was permissible to safeguard the core interests of individual belief and associa-

---

21. Brief for Petitioners, quoting V.O. Key, Politics, Parties and Pressure Groups 369 (5th ed. 1964).

tion. Subordination of some First Amendment activity was permissible to protect other such activity. Today, we hold that subordination of other First Amendment activity, that is, patronage dismissals, not only is permissible, but also is mandated by the First Amendment. And since patronage dismissals fall within the category of political campaigning and management, this conclusion irresistibly flows from *Mitchell* and *Letter Carriers*. For if the First Amendment did not place individual belief and association above political campaigning and management, at least in the setting of public employment, the restraints on those latter activities could not have been judged permissible in *Mitchell* and *Letter Carriers*.

It is apparent that at bottom we are required to engage in the resolution of conflicting interests under the First Amendment. The constitutional adjudication called for by this task is well within our province. The illuminating source to which we turn in performing the task is the system of government the First Amendment was intended to protect, a democratic system whose proper functioning is indispensably dependent on the unfettered judgment of each citizen on matters of political concern. Our decision in obedience to the guidance of that source does not outlaw political parties or political campaigning and management. Parties are free to exist and their concomitant activities are free to continue. We require only that the rights of every citizen to believe as he will and to act and associate according to his beliefs be free to continue as well.

In summary, patronage dismissals severely restrict political belief and association. Though there is a vital need for government efficiency and effectiveness, such dismissals are on balance not the least restrictive means for fostering that end. There is also a need to insure that policies which the electorate has sanctioned are effectively implemented. That interest can be fully satisfied by limiting patronage dismissals to policymaking positions. Finally, patronage dismissals cannot be justified by their contribution to the proper functioning of our democratic process through their assistance to partisan politics since political parties are nurtured by other, less intrusive and equally effective methods. More fundamentally, however, any contribution of patronage dismissals to the democratic process does not suffice to override their severe encroachment on First Amendment freedoms. We hold, therefore, that the practice of patronage dismissals is unconstitutional under the First and Fourteenth Amendments, and that respondents thus stated a valid claim for relief....

The judgment of the Court of Appeals is

Affirmed.

Mr. Justice STEVENS did not participate in the consideration or decision of this case.

Mr. Justice STEWART, with whom Mr. Justice BLACKMUN joins, concurring in the judgment.

Although I cannot join the plurality's wide-ranging opinion, I can and do concur in its judgment.

This case does not require us to consider the broad contours of the so-called patronage system, with all its variations and permutations. In particular, it does not require us to consider the constitutional validity of a system that confines the hiring of some governmental employees to those of a particular political party, and I would intimate no views whatever on that question.

The single substantive question involved in this case is whether a nonpolicymaking, nonconfidential government employee can be discharged or threatened with discharge from a job that he is satisfactorily performing upon the sole ground of his political beliefs. I agree with the plurality that he cannot. See *Perry v. Sindermann.*

[A short dissenting opinion by Chief Justice BURGER is omitted.]

Mr. Justice POWELL, with whom THE CHIEF JUSTICE and Mr. Justice REHNQUIST join, dissenting.

The Court holds unconstitutional a practice as old as the Republic, a practice which has contributed significantly to the democratization of American politics. This decision is urged on us in the name of First Amendment rights, but in my view the judgment neither is constitutionally required nor serves the interest of a representative democracy. It also may well disserve rather than promote core values of the First Amendment. I therefore dissent.

The Cook County Sheriff's Office employs approximately 3,000 people. Roughly half of these employees are "merit" employees given various protections from discharge. The other half of the employees have no such protection. Customary Illinois political practice has allowed such "non-merit" positions to be awarded on "patronage" grounds. This tradition has entitled newly elected officeholders to replace incumbent nonmerit employees with patronage appointments.

[Patronage] in employment played a significant role in democratizing American politics. Before patronage practices developed fully, an "aristocratic" class dominated political affairs, a tendency that persisted in areas where patronage did not become prevalent. Patronage practices broadened the base of political participation by providing incentives to take part in the process, thereby increasing the volume of political discourse in society. Patronage also strengthened parties, and hence encouraged the development of institutional responsibility to the electorate on a permanent basis. Parties became "instrument(s) through which discipline and responsibility may be achieved within the Leviathan." Sorauf, "Patronage and Party," 3 *Midwest J. Pol. Sci.* 115 (1959).

In many situations patronage employment practices also entailed costs to government efficiency. These costs led eventually to reforms placing most federal and state civil service employment on a nonpatronage basis. But the course of such reform is of limited relevance to the task of constitutional adjudication in this case. It is pertinent to note, however, that a perceived impingement on employees' political beliefs by the patronage system was not a significant impetus to such reform. Most advocates of reform were concerned primarily with the corruption and inefficiency that patronage was thought to induce in civil service and the power that patronage practices were thought to give the "professional" politicians who relied on them. Moreover, it generally was thought that elimination of these evils required the imposition both of a merit system and of restrictions on First Amendment activities by government employees.

[In this case we] have complaining employees who apparently accepted patronage jobs knowingly and willingly, while fully familiar with the "tenure" practices long prevailing in the Sheriff's Office. Such employees have *benefited* from their political beliefs and activities; they have not been penalized for them. In these circumstances, I [believe] that beneficiaries of a patronage system may not be heard to challenge it when it comes their turn to be replaced....

It is difficult to disagree with the view, as an abstract proposition, that government employment ordinarily should not be conditioned upon one's political beliefs or activities. But we deal here with a highly practical and rather fundamental element of our political system, not the theoretical abstractions of a political science seminar. In concluding that patronage hiring practices are unconstitutional, the plurality seriously underestimates the strength of the government interest—especially at the local level—in allowing some patronage hiring practices, and it exaggerates the perceived burden on First Amendment rights.

As indicated above, patronage hiring practices have contributed to American democracy by stimulating political activity and by strengthening parties, thereby helping to make government accountable. It cannot be questioned seriously that these contributions promote important state interests....

The complaining parties are or were employees of the Sheriff. In many communities, the sheriff's duties are as routine as process serving, and his election attracts little or no general public interest. In the States, and especially in the thousands of local communities, there are large numbers of elective offices, and many are as relatively obscure as that of the local sheriff or constable. Despite the importance of elective offices to the ongoing work of local governments, election campaigns for lesser offices in particular usually attract little attention from the media, with consequent disinterest and absence of intelligent participation on the part of the public. Unless the candidates for these offices are able to dispense the traditional patronage that has accrued to the offices, they also are unlikely to attract donations of time or money from voluntary groups. In short, the resource pools that fuel the intensity of political interest and debate in "important" elections frequently "could care less" about who fills the offices deemed to be relatively unimportant. Long experience teaches that at this local level traditional patronage practices contribute significantly to the democratic process. The candidates for these offices derive their support at the precinct level, and their modest funding for publicity, from cadres of friends and political associates who hope to benefit if their "man" is elected. The activities of the latter are often the principal source of political information for the voting public. The "robust" political discourse that the plurality opinion properly emphasizes is furthered—not restricted—by the time-honored system.

Patronage hiring practices also enable party organizations to persist and function at the local level. Such organizations become visible to the electorate at large only at election time, but the dull periods between elections require ongoing activities: precinct organizations must be maintained; new voters registered; and minor political "chores" performed for citizens who otherwise may have no practical means of access to officeholders. In some communities, party organizations and clubs also render helpful social services.

It is naive to think that these types of political activities are motivated at these levels by some academic interest in "democracy" or other public service impulse. For the most part, as every politician knows, the hope of some reward generates a major portion of the local political activity supporting parties. It is difficult to overestimate the contributions to our system by the major political parties, fortunately limited in number compared to the fractionalization that has made the continued existence of democratic government doubtful in some other countries. Parties generally are stable, high-profile, and permanent institutions. When the names on a long ballot are meaningless to the average voter, party affiliation affords a guidepost by which voters may rationalize a myriad of political choices. Voters can and do hold parties to long-term accountability, and it is not too much to say that, in their absence, responsive and responsible performance in low-profile offices, particularly, is difficult to maintain.

It is against decades of experience to the contrary, then, that the plurality opinion concludes that patronage hiring practices interfere with the "free functioning of the electoral process."... One would think that elected representatives of the people are better equipped than we to weigh the need for some continuation of patronage practices in light of the interests above identified, and particularly in view of local conditions....

Notes and Questions

1. In *CSC v. Letter Carriers*, 413 U.S. 548 (1973), and *United Public Workers v. Mitchell*, 330 U.S. 75 (1949), the Court upheld the constitutionality of the Hatch Act. The Hatch Act prohibited most partisan political activity by the great majority of federal employees. In *Elrod*, Justice Brennan distinguishes the Hatch Act cases in part by saying, "in those cases it was the Court's judgment that congressional subordination of those activities was permissible to safeguard the core interests of individual belief and association." The belief that the individual is the fundamental unit in democratic politics is central to the school of thought known as progressivism. In Chapter 1 of this book we were introduced to a competing school of thought, pluralism, which views the group as the fundamental unit. In this chapter, we have seen that some scholars believe that a particular form of group, the political party, must stand at the center of the political process if democracy is to succeed.

In the Hatch Act cases, as Justice Brennan wrote, severe restriction of public employees' political freedom was permitted in order to promote the value of political individualism. In *Elrod*, the state's desire to promote the value of collective activity through political parties is held insufficient to justify an equally severe restriction on public employees' political freedom. Read together, do the Hatch Act cases and *Elrod* suggest that progressivism is preferred by the Constitution over competing beliefs such as pluralism and party government? Should progressivism be a constitutionally preferred value? Are there special characteristics of patronage and public employment that might distinguish these cases from others in which competing progressivist and pluralist or party government values might be in conflict?

2. In *Branti v. Finkel*, 445 U.S. 507 (1980), a public defender appointed by a newly-elected county legislature quickly proceeded to fire several attorneys in the public defender's office, allegedly because they were Democrats. The public defender sought to defend the firings, in part, on the ground that attorneys were "policymakers," and therefore not protected by *Elrod*. Justice Stevens, writing for the Court, disagreed:

> As Mr. Justice Brennan noted in *Elrod*, it is not always easy to determine whether a position is one in which political affiliation is a legitimate factor to be considered.... Under some circumstances, a position may be appropriately considered political even though it is neither confidential nor policymaking in character. As one obvious example, if a State's election laws require that precincts be supervised by two election judges of different parties, a Republican judge could be legitimately discharged solely for changing his party registration. That conclusion would not depend on any finding that the job involved participation in policy decisions or access to confidential information. Rather, it would simply rest on the fact that party membership was essential to the discharge of the employee's governmental responsibilities.
>
> It is equally clear that party affiliation is not necessarily relevant to every policymaking or confidential position. The coach of a state university's football team formulates policy, but no one would seriously claim that Republicans make better coaches than Democrats, or vice versa, no matter which party is in control of the state government. On the other hand, it is equally clear that the governor of a state may appropriately believe that the official duties of various assistants who help him write speeches, explain his views to the press, or communicate with the legislature cannot be performed effectively unless those persons share his political beliefs and party commitments. In sum, the ultimate inquiry is not whether the label "policymaker" or "confidential" fits a particular

position; rather the question is whether the hiring authority can demonstrate that party affiliation is an appropriate requirement for the effective performance of the public office involved.

Since "whatever policymaking occurs in the public defender's office must relate to the needs of individual clients and not to any partisan political interests," Justice Stevens concluded that the attorneys in the public defender's office were protected by the *Elrod* doctrine. He added, in footnote 13, that "an official such as a prosecutor" has broader public responsibilities, and that the Court was expressing no opinion on whether "the deputy of such an official could be dismissed on grounds of political party affiliation or loyalty." Justices Powell, Rehnquist, and Stewart dissented in *Branti*.

If you were an incumbent running for reelection to the county legislature, how would you respond if your opponent attacked you on grounds of incompetence in the public defender's office?

If a new public defender is unconcerned about partisanship but simply wants to employ attorneys in whom he or she has a high degree of confidence and with whom he or she feels compatible, does the Constitution permit firing the old attorneys and hiring new ones?

Considering footnote 13 in *Branti*, how would you advise a newly-elected district attorney who wishes to fire all deputies who are not members of his or her party? May a party membership test be a condition of employment in the civil division of a state attorney general's office?

Could Branti, the public defender, fire Finkel if Finkel made a speech criticizing Branti's management of the public defender's office? If he made a speech criticizing the county legislature for providing too low a budget to the public defender's office? If he made a speech criticizing the county legislature for actions unrelated to the public defender's office? Cf. *Pickering v. Board of Education*, 391 U.S. 563 (1968). Reconsider this question after reading the *Umbehr* and *O'Hare* cases below.

3. *Branti* seems to have modified *Elrod*'s exception for "policymaking" employees, by stating that the question is whether party affiliation is "an appropriate requirement" for the position. Justice Stevens' examples of a football coach (inappropriate) and an assistant to the governor (appropriate) may seem intuitively obvious, but what is the standard of "appropriateness"? Would it be appropriate to fire a prison warden on grounds of partisan affiliation? The head of a city construction project? The director of an agency that enforces the state's campaign finance laws? The personal secretary to the mayor? With respect to the last of these questions, see *Faughender v. City of North Olmsted*, 927 F.2d 909 (6th Cir. 1991), holding the mayor's personal secretary could be fired on political grounds. What about the personal secretary to the head of a city department? What about a receptionist in the mayor's office?

Despite more than a generation of cases arising under the *Branti* exception, litigation over the policymaking exception continues unabated. See, e.g., *Biggs v. Best, Best & Krieger*, 189 F.3d 989 (9th Cir. 1999) (attorney who worked at private law firm with contract to provide services of city attorney occupied policy position and could be fired because of her political activities and those of her family). Professor Bowman argues that the lower courts have shown hostility to the Supreme Court's patronage decisions, and therefore they use doctrines such as the "policymaking exception" to prevent application of the Court's patronage rules. Cynthia Grant Bowman, *The Law of Patronage at a Crossroads*, 12 JOURNAL OF LAW & POLITICS 341 (1996).

* * *

Elrod bars firing non-policymaking employees on grounds of their partisan affiliation. In RUTAN V. REPUBLICAN PARTY OF ILLINOIS, 497 U.S. 62 (1990), the Supreme Court extended the *Elrod* rule to patronage hiring and transfer decisions. Justice Brennan, writing for the Court, saw no constitutional difference between hiring and firing:

"The same First Amendment concerns that underlay our decisions in *Elrod* and *Branti* are implicated here. Employees who do not compromise their beliefs stand to lose the considerable increases in pay and job satisfaction attendant to promotions, the hours and maintenance expenses that are consumed by long daily commutes, and even their jobs if they are not rehired after a 'temporary' layoff. These are significant penalties and are imposed for the exercise of rights guaranteed by the First Amendment. Unless these patronage practices are narrowly tailored to further vital government interests, we must conclude that they impermissibly encroach on First Amendment freedoms.

"We find, however, that our conclusions in *Elrod* and *Branti* are equally applicable to the patronage practices at issue here. A government's interest in securing effective employees can be met by discharging, demoting, or transferring staff members whose work is deficient. A government's interest in securing employees who will loyally implement its policies can be adequately served by choosing or dismissing certain high-level employees on the basis of their political views. Likewise, the 'preservation of the democratic process' is no more furthered by the patronage promotions, transfers, and rehires at issue here than it is by patronage dismissals. First, 'political parties are nurtured by other, less intrusive and equally effective methods.' *Elrod*. Political parties have already survived the substantial decline in patronage employment practices in this century. Second, patronage decidedly impairs the elective process by discouraging free political expression by public employees. Respondents, who include the Governor of Illinois and other state officials, do not suggest any other overriding government interest in favoring Republican Party supporters for promotion, transfer, and rehire.

"We therefore determine that promotions, transfers, and recalls after layoffs based on political affiliation or support are an impermissible infringement on the First Amendment rights of public employees....

"Petitioner James W. Moore presents the closely related question whether patronage hiring violates the First Amendment. Patronage hiring places burdens on free speech and association similar to those imposed by the patronage practices discussed above. A state job is valuable. Like most employment, it provides regular paychecks, health insurance, and other benefits. In addition, there may be openings with the State when business in the private sector is slow. There are also occupations for which the government is a major (or the only) source of employment, such as social workers, elementary school teachers, and prison guards. Thus, denial of a state job is a serious privation...."

Justice Scalia wrote a dissenting opinion. He talked about the demise of patronage in American politics and what this meant for the party system:

> It may well be that the Good Government Leagues of America were right, and that Plunkitt, James Michael Curley, and their ilk were wrong; but that is not entirely certain. As the merit principle has been extended and its effects increasingly felt; as the Boss Tweeds, the Tammany Halls, the Pendergast Machines, the Byrd Machines, and the Daley Machines have faded into history; we find that political leaders at all levels increasingly complain of the helplessness of elected government, unprotected by 'party discipline,' before the demands of small and cohesive interest groups.

The choice between patronage and the merit principle—or, to be more realistic about it, the choice between the desirable mix of merit and patronage
principles in widely varying federal, state, and local political contexts—is not so
clear that I would be prepared, as an original matter, to chisel a single, inflexible prescription into the Constitution. Fourteen years ago, in *Elrod*, the Court
did that. *Elrod* was limited however, as was the later decision of *Branti*, to patronage
firings, leaving it to state and federal legislatures to determine when and where
political affiliation could be taken into account in hirings and promotions. Today
the Court makes its constitutional civil service reform absolute, extending to all
decisions regarding government employment. Because the First Amendment has
never been thought to require this disposition, which may well have disastrous
consequences for our political system, I dissent....

The whole point of my dissent is that the desirability of patronage is a policy
question to be decided by the people's representatives; I do not mean, therefore,
to endorse that system. But in order to demonstrate that a legislature could reasonably determine that its benefits outweigh its "coercive" effects, I must describe those benefits as the proponents of patronage see them: As Justice Powell
discussed at length in his *Elrod* dissent, patronage stabilizes political parties and
prevents excessive political fragmentation—both of which are results in which
States have a strong governmental interest....

The Court simply refuses to acknowledge the link between patronage and
party discipline, and between that and party success.... It is unpersuasive to
claim, as the Court does, that party workers are obsolete because campaigns are
now conducted through media and other money-intensive means. Those techniques have supplemented but not supplanted personal contacts. Certainly they
have not made personal contacts unnecessary in campaigns for the lower level
offices that are the foundations of party strength, nor have they replaced the
myriad functions performed by party regulars not directly related to campaigning. And to the extent such techniques have replaced older methods of campaigning (partly in response to the limitations the Court has placed on patronage),
the political system is not clearly better off. Increased reliance on money-intensive campaign techniques tends to entrench those in power much more effectively than patronage—but without the attendant benefit of strengthening the
party system. A challenger can more easily obtain the support of party workers
(who can expect to be rewarded even if the candidate loses—if not this year,
then the next) than the financial support of political action committees (which
will generally support incumbents, who are likely to prevail).

It is self-evident that eliminating patronage will significantly undermine party
discipline; and that as party discipline wanes, so will the strength of the two-
party system. But, says the Court, "[p]olitical parties have already survived the
substantial decline in patronage employment practices in this century." This is almost verbatim what was said in *Elrod*. Fourteen years later it seems much less convincing. Indeed, now that we have witnessed, in 18 of the last 22 years, an
Executive Branch of the Federal Government under the control of one party
while the Congress is entirely or (for two years) partially within the control of
the other party; now that we have undergone the most recent federal election,
in which 98% of the incumbents, of whatever party, were returned to office; and
now that we have seen elected officials changing their political affiliation with
unprecedented readiness, the statement that "political parties have already sur-

vived' has a positively whistling-in-the-graveyard character to it. Parties have assuredly survived—but as what? As the forges upon which many of the essential compromises of American political life are hammered out? Or merely as convenient vehicles for the conducting of national Presidential elections?

The patronage system does not, of course, merely foster political parties in general; it fosters the two-party system in particular. When getting a job, as opposed to effectuating a particular substantive policy, is an available incentive for party workers, those attracted by that incentive are likely to work for the party that has the best chance of displacing the "ins," rather than for some splinter group that has a more attractive political philosophy but little hope of success. Not only is a two-party system more likely to emerge, but the differences between those parties are more likely to be moderated, as each has a relatively greater interest in appealing to a majority of the electorate and a relatively lesser interest in furthering philosophies or programs that are far from the mainstream. The stabilizing effects of such a system are obvious....

Equally apparent is the relatively destabilizing nature of a system in which candidates cannot rely upon patronage-based party loyalty for their campaign support, but must attract workers and raise funds by appealing to various interest groups. There is little doubt that our decisions in *Elrod* and *Branti*, by contributing to the decline of party strength, have also contributed to the growth of interest-group politics in the last decade. See, e.g., Fitts, *The Vice of Virtue*, 136 U.Pa.L.Rev. 1567, 1603–1607 (1988). Our decision today will greatly accelerate the trend. It is not only campaigns that are affected, of course, but the subsequent behavior of politicians once they are in power. The replacement of a system firmly based in party discipline with one in which each office-holder comes to his own accommodation with competing interest groups produces "a dispersion of political influence that may inhibit a political party from enacting its programs into law." *Branti* (Powell, J., dissenting).

Patronage, moreover, has been a powerful means of achieving the social and political integration of excluded groups. By supporting and ultimately dominating a particular party 'machine,' racial and ethnic minorities have—on the basis of their politics rather than their race or ethnicity—acquired the patronage awards the machine had power to confer. No one disputes the historical accuracy of this observation, and there is no reason to think that patronage can no longer serve that function. The abolition of patronage, however, prevents groups that have only recently obtained political power, especially blacks, from following this path to economic and social advancement....

While the patronage system has the benefits argued for above, it also has undoubted disadvantages. It facilitates financial corruption, such as salary kickbacks and partisan political activity on government-paid time. It reduces the efficiency of government, because it creates incentives to hire more and less-qualified workers and because highly qualified workers are reluctant to accept jobs that may only last until the next election. And, of course, it applies some greater or lesser inducement for individuals to join and work for the party in power.

To hear the Court tell it, this last is the greatest evil. That is not my view, and it has not historically been the view of the American people. Corruption and inefficiency, rather than abridgement of liberty, have been the major criticisms leading to enactment of the civil service laws—for the very good reason that the patronage system does not have as harsh an effect upon conscience, expression, and association as the Court suggests. As described above, it is the nature of the pragmatic, patronage-based, two-party system to build alliances and to suppress rather than foster ideological tests for participation in the division of political "spoils." What the patronage system ordinarily demands of the party worker is loyalty to, and activity on behalf of, the organization itself rather than a set of political beliefs. He is generally free to urge *within the organization* the adoption of any political position; but if that position is rejected he must vote and work for the party nonetheless. The diversity of political expression (other than expression of party loyalty) is channeled, in other words, to a different stage — to the contests for party endorsement rather than the partisan elections. It is undeniable, of course, that the patronage system entails some constraint upon the expression of views, particularly at the partisan-election stage, and considerable constraint upon the employee's right to associate with the other party. It greatly exaggerates these, however, to describe them as a general 'coercion of belief.' Indeed, it greatly exaggerates them to call them 'coercion' at all, since we generally make a distinction between inducement and compulsion.... In sum, I do not deny that the patronage system influences or redirects, perhaps to a substantial degree, individual political expression and political association. But like the many generations of Americans that have preceded us, I do not consider that a significant impairment of free speech or free association.

In emphasizing the advantages and minimizing the disadvantages (or at least minimizing one of the disadvantages) of the patronage system, I do not mean to suggest that that system is best. It may not always be; it may never be. To oppose our *Elrod-Branti* jurisprudence, one need not believe that the patronage system is *necessarily* desirable; nor even that it is always and everywhere *arguably* desirable; but merely that it is a political arrangement that may sometimes be a reasonable choice, and should therefore be left to the judgment of the people's elected representatives. The choice in question, I emphasize, is not just between patronage and a merit-based civil service, but rather among various combinations of the two that may suit different political units and different eras: permitting patronage hiring, for example, but prohibiting patronage dismissal; permitting patronage in most municipal agencies but prohibiting it in the police department; or permitting it in the mayor's office but prohibiting it everywhere else. I find it impossible to say that, always and everywhere, all of these choices fail our 'balancing' test.

Notes and Questions

1. The most famous patronage-based machine to survive into the 1970s was the Chicago Democratic organization headed by Mayor Richard Daley. Based primarily on historical and social science accounts of the Chicago machine and its consequences, Cynthia Grant Bowman, "*We Don't Want Anybody Anybody Sent*": *The Death of Patronage Hiring in Chicago*, 86 NORTHWESTERN UNIVERSITY LAW REVIEW 57 (1991), contends that in practice patronage has not brought about the benefits attributed to it by Justices Powell and Scalia in their dissents in *Elrod* and *Rutan*. For example, addressing the contention that patronage helps disadvantaged groups to begin their climb up the societal ladder, Professor Bowman writes:

Machines clearly did function to bring in *some* new groups during *some* historical periods. The early Chicago machine is an example of a patronage party which did in fact incorporate a series of ethnic groups into political life, but it did so only because it faced substantial competition both from the Republican Party and from factions within the Democratic Party. Thus, as Republican Thompson reached out to newer ethnic groups, including Blacks, and [Democrat] Cermak struggled with the Irish for control of the Democratic party, the machine competed for Polish, Czech, Jewish, and Italian votes in addition to those of the older Irish immigrants.

In other cities, however, the classic urban machine did not perform a democratizing function on any consistent basis. Recent studies show that the typical Irish machine was slow to incorporate the Southern and Eastern European immigrants who arrived after the Irish. In cities other than Chicago, where Irish machines succeeded in putting together a 'minimal winning electoral coalition' without appealing to newer immigrants who might compete with the Irish for jobs and political power, urban machines had no incentive to mobilize the more recently arrived ethnic groups, and did not do so. In Boston, for example, where the Irish comprised a majority of the population and could thus control city government without relying upon the votes of any of the newer groups, the machine played virtually no role in integrating those other ethnic groups into political life. Thus, the more a machine was able to consolidate its power by use of patronage, the less likely it was to fulfill the function of broadening the number of groups involved in the political process.

It is not difficult to understand why mature urban political machines did not consistently perform the democratizing functions Scalia and Powell have alleged that they did. A patronage party depends on the allocation of a scarce resource — public jobs. After the initial spurts in the growth of public employment in the late nineteenth and early twentieth centuries, it was simply not possible to increase the supply of municipal jobs without limit. Hence, the only workable strategy for a patronage party was to 'deflate' the demand for this scarce resource so that it would not exceed the supply of employment opportunities. If new groups continually entered the process, this delicate economy would be destroyed. Thus, patronage parties which have consolidated power generally have not sought to maximize participation of new groups in the political process. Instead, they are highly selective mobilizers and have emphasized the deliverability and controllability of votes over vote-maximization.

If such criticism is sound empirically, to what extent does it undermine the Powell-Scalia position? How would you expect Justice Scalia to respond to Professor Bowman?

2. Justice Scalia attributes a decline in the power of political parties to the Supreme Court's prohibition on patronage in employment. An alternative hypothesis is that the Court has followed, rather than created, a trend. Consider the following: "In part, the debate over the virtues of patronage comes too late. The replacement of party-centered, labor intensive political campaigns with candidate-centered, capital-intensive ones has lessened politicians' demand for patronage employment. Politicians want money for media campaigns, not precinct workers. This increased demand for campaign contributions puts pressure on politicians to exchange government favors, including contracts, for such contributions." Richard L. Hasen, *Patronage*, in 4 ENCYCLOPEDIA OF THE AMERICAN CONSTITUTION 1885 (Leonard W. Levy & Kenneth L. Karst eds., 2d ed. 2000).

3. Professor Bowman observes that "Contract patronage was the route taken when other forms of patronage were foreclosed by the Court; this trend was exacerbated by the decrease in government employment after 1980 and the privatization of many functions

previously performed by government workers. From 1982 to 1992, for example, the rate of increase in Illinois state employment declined, while spending on government contracts doubled." Cynthia Grant Bowman, *The Supreme Court's Patronage Decisions and the Theory and Practice of Politics*, in THE U.S. SUPREME COURT AND THE ELECTORAL PROCESS 124, 138 (David K. Ryden ed., 2000).

4. The Court addressed the question of patronage contracting in two companion cases, extending the First Amendment rights of public employees that had been protected in the *Elrod* and *Pickering* lines of cases (see note 2 following *Elrod*) to independent contractors that do business with government agencies. In *Board of County Commissioners, Wabaunsee County v. Umbehr*, 518 U.S. 668 (1996), Umbehr had a contract with the county for hauling trash. The contract had been renewed on an annual basis, until Umbehr sharply criticized the County Board of Commissioners on various matters. Allegedly in retaliation for the criticism, the Board voted to terminate the contract. The Supreme Court held that Umbehr was entitled to relief for violation of his speech rights under the First Amendment if he proved that the termination was indeed retaliatory and that under a balancing analysis, his free speech interests outweigh the County's "legitimate interests as contractor, deferentially viewed...."

In *O'Hare Truck Service v. City of Northlake*, 518 U.S. 712 (1996), the city had a list of towing services that it called upon by a rotation system. O'Hare allegedly was dropped from the list when its owner declined to make a campaign contribution in response to a request from the mayor, who was running for reelection. The Court ruled that the *Elrod-Branti-Rutan* line of cases was applicable, notwithstanding that O'Hare provided services to the city as an independent contractor, whereas the plaintiffs in the earlier cases were individuals who were or desired to be government employees. As we have seen, the Court had stated in *Branti* that retaliation for a disfavored party affiliation was unconstitutional unless party affiliation was an "appropriate requirement" for the position in question. There was no "balancing," except to determine the appropriateness of conditioning the job on the basis of partisan affiliation. In the *Pickering* line of cases, including *Umbehr*, the Court balanced the interests in free speech against the government's interests. Thus, the Court in *O'Hare* attempted to define the circumstances under which one approach or the other would be employed. After describing the *Branti* test, the Court went on:

> Our cases call for a different, though related, inquiry where a government employer takes adverse action on account of an employee or service provider's right of free speech. There, we apply the balancing test from *Pickering*. *Elrod* and *Branti* involved instances where the raw test of political affiliation sufficed to show a constitutional violation, without the necessity of an inquiry more detailed than asking whether the requirement was appropriate for the employment in question. There is an advantage in so confining the inquiry where political affiliation alone is concerned, for one's beliefs and allegiances ought not to be subject to probing or testing by the government. It is true, on the other hand..., that the inquiry is whether the affiliation requirement is a reasonable one, so it is inevitable that some case-by-case adjudication will be required even where political affiliation is the test the government has imposed. A reasonableness analysis will also accommodate those many cases, perhaps including the one before us, where specific instances of the employee's speech or expression, which require balancing in the *Pickering* context, are intermixed with a political affiliation requirement. In those cases, the balancing *Pickering* mandates will be inevitable. This case-by-case process will allow the courts to consider the necessity of according to the government the discretion it requires in the administration

and awarding of contracts over the whole range of public works and the delivery of governmental service.

Do you find these distinctions clear and persuasive?

You will not be surprised to learn that Justice Scalia wrote a lengthy and heated dissent. He was joined by Justice Thomas, but three of the justices who joined Scalia in dissent in *Rutan*—Kennedy, O'Connor, and Rehnquist—joined the majority in both cases. Indeed, O'Connor and Kennedy, respectively, wrote the majority opinions in *Umbehr* and *O'Hare*. If Kennedy, O'Connor, and Rehnquist had held to their positions in *Rutan*, *Umbehr* and *O'Hare* would have been decided differently and, perhaps, the Court might have cut back on the patronage line of cases.

Scalia criticizes the majority on many grounds, including what he perceives as deficiencies in the distinction drawn in the *O'Hare* passage quoted above:

> If ... the Court is newly to announce that it has discovered that the granting or withholding of a contract is a First Amendment issue, a coherent statement of the new law is the least that those who labor in the area are entitled to expect. They do not get it from today's decisions, which contradict each other on a number of fundamental points.
>
> The decision in *Umbehr* appears to be an improvement on our *Elrod-Branti-Rutan* trilogy in one sense. *Rutan*, the most recent of these decisions, provided that the government could justify patronage employment practices only if it proved that such patronage was "narrowly tailored to further vital governmental interests." The four of us in dissent explained "[t]hat strict-scrutiny standard finds no support in our cases"' and we argued that, if the new constitutional right was to be invented, the criterion for violation should be "the test announced in *Pickering*." It thus appears a happy development that the Court in *Umbehr* explicitly rejects the suggestion ... that "on proof of viewpoint-based retaliation for contractors' political speech, the government should be required to justify its actions as narrowly tailored to serve a compelling state interest," and instead holds "that the *Pickering* balancing test, adjusted to weigh the government's interests as contractor rather than as employer, determines the extent of [independent contractors'] protection" under the First Amendment. *Pickering* balancing, of course, requires a case-by-case assessment of the government's and the contractor's interests.... It is clear that this is what the Court's opinion in *Umbehr* anticipates: "a *fact-sensitive* and deferential weighing of the government's legitimate interests," which accords "[d]eference ... to the government's reasonable assessments of its interests as contractor." "[S]uch a nuanced approach," *Umbehr* says, "which recognizes the variety of interests that may arise in independent contractor cases, is superior to a brightline rule."
>
> What the Court sets down in *Umbehr*, however, it rips up in *O'Hare*.... Indeed, what is quite astonishing, the Court concludes that it "need not inquire" into any government interests that patronage contracting may serve—even generally, much less in the particular case at hand—"for *Elrod* and *Branti* establish that patronage does not justify the coercion of a person's political beliefs and associations." Leaving aside that there is no coercion here, the assertion obviously contradicts the need for "balancing" announced in the companion *Umbehr* decision. This rejection of "balancing" is evident elsewhere in *O'Hare*—as when the Court rejects as irrelevant the Seventh Circuit's observation in *LaFalce v. Houston*, 712 F.2d 292 (1983), that some contractors elect to "curr[y] favor with di-

verse political parties," on the ground that the fact "[t]hat some citizens [thus] find a way to mitigate governmental overreaching, or refrain from complaining, does not excuse wrongs done to those who exercise their rights." But whether the government action at issue here is a "wrong" is precisely the issue in this case, which we thought (per *Umbehr*) was to be determined by "balancing."

One would have thought these two opinions the products of the courts of last resort of two different legal systems, presenting fertile material for a comparative-law course on freedom of speech were it not for a single paragraph in *O'Hare*, a veritable *deus ex machina* of legal analysis, which reconciles the irreconcilable. [The paragraph quoted above] advises that henceforth "the freedom of speech" alluded to in the Bill of Rights will be divided into two categories: (1) the "right of free speech," where "we apply the balancing test from *Pickering*," and (since this "right of free speech" presumably does not exhaust the Free Speech Clause), (2) "political affiliation," where we apply the rigid rule of *Elrod* and *Branti*. The Court (or at least the *O'Hare* Court) says that "[t]here is an advantage in so confining the inquiry where political affiliation alone is concerned, for one's beliefs and allegiances ought not to be subject to probing or testing by the government."

Frankly, the only "advantage" I can discern in this novel distinction is that it provides some explanation (no matter how difficult to grasp) of how these two opinions can issue from the same Court on the same day. It raises many questions. Does the "right of free speech" (category (1), that is) come into play if the contractor not only *is* a Republican, but *says* "I am a Republican"? (At that point of course, the fatal need for "probing or testing" his allegiance disappears.) Or is the "right of free speech" at issue only if he goes still further, and says, "I believe in the principles set forth in the Republican platform"? Or perhaps one must decide whether the Rubicon between the "right of free speech" and the more protected "political affiliation" has been crossed on the basis of the contracting authority's *motivation,* so that it does not matter whether the contractor *says* he is a Republican, or even *says* that he believes in the Republican platform, so long as the reason he is disfavored is simply that (whatever he says or believes) he is a Republican. But the analysis would change, perhaps, if the contracting authority really has nothing against Republicans as such, but can't stand people who believe what the Republican platform stands for. Except perhaps it would *not* change if the contractor never actually *said* he was a Republican—or perhaps only if he never actually *said* that he believed in the Republican platform. The many variations will provide endless diversion for the courts of appeals.

If one is so sanguine as to believe that facts involving the "right of free speech" and facts involving "political affiliation" can actually be segregated into separate categories, there arises, of course, the problem of what to do when both are involved. One would expect the more rigid test (*Elrod* nonbalancing) to prevail. That is certainly what happens elsewhere in the law. If one is categorically liable for a *defamatory* statement, but liable for a *threatening* statement only if it places the subject in immediate fear of physical harm, an utterance that combines both ("Sir, I shall punch you in your lying mouth!") would be (at least as to the defamatory portion) categorically actionable. Not so, however, with our new First Amendment law. Where, we are told, "specific instances of the employee's speech or expression, which require balancing in the *Pickering* context, are intermixed with a political affiliation requirement," *balancing* rather than categorical liability will be the result.

Were all this confusion not enough, the explanatory paragraph makes doubly sure it is not setting forth any comprehensible rule by adding, immediately after its description of how *Elrod*, rather than the *Pickering* balancing test, applies in "political affiliation" cases, the following: "It is true, on the other hand, ... that the inquiry is whether the affiliation requirement is a reasonable one, so it is inevitable that some case-by-case adjudication will be required even where political affiliation is the test the government has imposed." As I said in *Rutan*, "[w]hat that means is anybody's guess." Worse still, we learn that *O'Hare* itself, where the Court does *not* conduct balancing, may "perhaps [be] includ[ed]" among "those many cases ... which require balancing" because it is one of the "intermixed" cases I discussed in the paragraph immediately above. Why, then, one is inclined to ask, did not the Court *conduct* balancing?

Justice Scalia appears correct that lower courts have had trouble distinguishing when to apply the *Elrod* test rather than the *Pickering* test. The Ninth Circuit, for example, has held that "a public employee's claim that he or she was fired for exercising his or her First Amendment speech rights would generally be analyzed using the *Pickering* balancing test. If, however, a public employee is a policymaker, then the claim would fall under the rubric of *Elrod* and *Branti*." *Fazio v. City and County of San Francisco*, 125 F.3d 1328, 1332 (9th Cir. 1997), cert. denied 523 U.S. 1074 (1998). The Seventh Circuit, by contrast, has held that "[a]lthough an employee's status as a policymaker bears considerable attention when weighing the interests of the government, the policymaking employee exception [of *Elrod* and *Branti*] does not apply and courts must apply *Pickering* balancing when the speech at issue does not implicate the employee's politics or substantive policy viewpoints." *Bonds v. Milwaukee County*, 207 F.3d 969, 979 (7th Cir. 2000), cert. denied 531 U.S. 944 (2000). Do either of these tests find support in *Umbehr* or *O'Hare*?

One reason for taking seriously the question of what standard the Court is erecting for different situations is that *Umbehr* and *O'Hare* significantly extend the potential applicability of the *Pickering* and *Elrod* doctrines, especially the latter. Even before *Elrod*, the old-fashioned type of patronage involving public jobs was in decline. Government officials in many parts of the country probably had little practical reason to be concerned by *Elrod*, even as it was extended in *Rutan*. However, it is probably far more widespread for state and local governments to reward party and political loyalists in ways other than providing employment. *Umbehr* and *O'Hare* leave open the question of just how far the First Amendment will interfere with such practices. Consider these comments from Scalia's dissent:

I believe the Court accepts (any sane person *must* accept) the premise that it is utterly impossible to erect, and enforce through litigation, a system in which *no* citizen is intentionally disadvantaged by the government because of his political beliefs. I say the Court accepts that, because the *O'Hare* opinion, in a rare brush with the real world, points out that "O'Hare was not part of a constituency that must take its chance of being favored or ignored in the larger political process—for example by residing or doing business in a region the government rewards or spurns in the construction of public works." Of course. Government favors those who agree with its political views, and disfavors those who disagree, every day—in where it builds its public works, in the kinds of taxes it imposes and collects, in its regulatory prescriptions, in the design of its grant and benefit programs—in a *million* ways, including the letting of contracts for government business. What good reason has the Court given for separating out this last way, and declaring it to be (as all the others for some reason are not) an "abridgment of the freedom of speech"?

Professor Bowman observes that "[n]otably missing from Justice Scalia's dissent ... are the earlier arguments about the dangers presented by special interests. Indeed, who are these contributors in exchange for contracts except special interests? Instead, the defendants' arguments focused solely on the effect that prohibiting patronage would have on the administration's ability to ensure the efficient provision of services and thus to remain faithful to its electoral mandate." Bowman, *supra*, at 138–39.

Do you believe the *Elrod* and *Pickering* doctrines should be limited to public employment and the letting of government contracts? If not, to which additional government activities would you extend the doctrines and to which, if any, would you not extend them? Do you agree with Scalia that there is no rational ground for limiting the doctrines to those two activities? The Court in *Umbehr* tried to put a limit on the reach of the decision along a different dimension:

> [W]e emphasize the limited nature of our decision today. Because Umbehr's suit concerns the termination of a pre-existing commercial relationship with the government, we need not address the possibility of suits by bidders or applicants for new government contracts who cannot rely on such a relationship.

Scalia criticized this passage, particularly the vagueness of the term "pre-existing commercial relationship." He pointed out that Umbehr had a more specific, contractual relationship, but suggested that the majority used the more general term in order to include O'Hare, which according to Scalia "had not paid or promised anything to be placed on a list of tow-truck operators who would be offered individual contracts as they came up. The company had no right to sue if the city failed to call it, nor the city any right to sue if the company turned down an offered tow. It had, in short, only what might be called (as an infinity of things might be called) 'a pre-existing commercial relationship' with the city: it was one of the tow-truck operators they regularly called. [The majority's statement, quoted above,] invites the bar to believe, therefore, that the Court which declined to draw the line of First Amendment liability short of firing from government employment (*Elrod* and *Branti*); short of nonhiring for government employment (*Rutan*); short of termination of a government contract (*Umbehr*); and short of *denial* of a government contract to someone who had a 'pre-existing commercial relationship'(*O'Hare*); may take a firm stand against extending the Constitution into every little thing when it comes to denying a government contract to someone who had *no* 'pre-existing commercial relationship.' Not likely; in fact, not even believable."

Suppose you are legal adviser to a local government that is undertaking a new public works project. A businessperson who has never before contracted with the city enters a bid. The businessperson has been a major contributor to and supporter of a political faction that has at various times controlled the city government but whose opponents are now in power. The bidding and other rules governing the contract give the city discretion to accept this businessperson or a competitor, and neither of these two bidders is markedly superior to the other in qualifications to do the job or other, similar criteria. The mayor and city council would like to reject the businessperson because of his or her political support for the opposition. Would you accept Scalia's assertions and advise that *O'Hare* prohibits rejecting the bid for that reason? Do you think the Constitution ought to prohibit rejecting the bid for that reason?

Chapter 10

Third Parties and Independent Candidates

In Chapter 9 we gave extended attention to legal questions affecting the major political parties because, for most of its history, the national politics of the United States have been dominated by two parties—since 1856, the Democrats and the Republicans. Somewhat less uniformly, politics at the state and local levels also have been dominated by the two major parties. Questions about the rights and obligations of the major parties therefore have the most direct and obvious influence on the functioning of democratic government.

Despite the two-party dominance, third parties and independent candidates sometimes have played a significant role in American politics. For example, in seven presidential elections since 1856, more than ten percent of the votes cast have gone to a candidate who was not a Democrat or Republican. The most recent example is the 1992 election, in which 18.9% of the votes were cast for independent candidate H. Ross Perot.[a] Below the level of the presidency, third-party and independent candidates are occasionally elected. Socialist Bernard Sanders represented Vermont in the House of Representatives starting in 1991 and was elected to the Senate in 2006. Joe Lieberman was reelected to the Senate as an independent from Connecticut in 2006, after having lost the Democratic primary to a more liberal opponent. A handful of state governors, most famously in recent years Governor Jesse Ventura of Minnesota, have also been independents or third-party candidates.

Despite their limited role in American politics, third parties and independent candidates account for more litigation than the major parties. This is hardly surprising, because the major parties are far more likely to be able to resolve their problems through legislation or other political means.[b] In addition, major parties control the legislature and at best have little reason to ease burdens facing third parties and independent candidates. The most persistent form of litigation brought by third parties and independent candidates in recent decades has consisted of challenges to denial of listing on the ballot. The first principal case in this chapter, *Munro v. Socialist Workers Party*, is an example. In the remaining principal cases, third parties challenge their exclusion from publicly provided campaign benefits or other laws that the third parties claim discriminate against them.

A natural question to consider at the beginning of this chapter is to what extent election laws have been responsible for the generally peripheral role played by third parties

---

a. When Perot ran for President in 1996, he received about 8 percent of the vote.

b. For a comparison and analysis of the use of litigation by major and minor parties in cases that reach the Supreme Court, see Lee Epstein & Charles D. Hadley, *On the Treatment of Political Parties in the U.S. Supreme Court, 1900–1986*, 52 JOURNAL OF POLITICS 413 (1990).

and independent candidates in American politics. The probable answer is that election laws have been of overriding importance, but not the laws at issue in cases such as the ones considered in this chapter. It is the single-member district system in accordance with which most American elections are conducted that makes it extremely difficult for third parties to succeed or to endure. Unless a third party's support is very concentrated regionally, it can win a substantial percentage of votes but win few or no legislative seats because it cannot ordinarily win a plurality in any given district. In presidential elections, the electoral college works to the same effect, as the example of H. Ross Perot indicates. In 1992, Perot won 18.9% of the popular vote, but because he did not win a plurality in any state, he did not win any electoral votes.

In electoral systems with a higher degree of proportional representation than the American system, parties can win legislative representation with vote proportions much lower than the 18.9% won by Perot in 1992. Since that usually does not occur in the single-member district system, it is difficult for third parties to attract strong candidates, who will recognize the small likelihood of winning office under a third-party banner. The lack of strong candidates makes it even more difficult to attract support from voters, who may already be predisposed not to "waste" their votes on candidates and parties with no realistic chance of winning. Again, recent presidential elections illustrate the problem facing third parties. In 2000, consumer group activist Ralph Nader ran as a candidate for the Green Party. Nader's support in public opinion polls slipped in the days before the election, amid the charges of some Democrats that Nader's candidacy would "spoil" Democratic candidate Al Gore's chances and lead to the election of Republican George W. Bush. A third party candidate often faces charges of being a "spoiler" from backers of the major party candidate who appears likely to lose support to the third party candidate.

The strong tendency of the single-member district system to bring about a two-party system was first demonstrated in an early classic of American political science:

> The system does not operate to destroy the defeated major party because the defeated major party is able to retain a *monopoly of the opposition*. The cutting edge of the two-party system is precisely at the point of contact of the second major party and the third party (or the first minor party aspiring to become [the] third major party). What it amounts to is this: the advantage of the second party over the third is overwhelming. It usually wins all seats or very nearly all seats not won by the first party. Among all the opposition parties in the field it has by a very wide margin the best chance of displacing the party in power. Because this is true it is extremely likely that it can assemble about its banner nearly all of the elements in the country seriously opposed to the party in power and seriously interested in an early party overturn. *The monopoly of the opposition* is the most important asset of the second major party. As long as it can monopolize the movement to overthrow the party in power, the second party is important; any party able to monopolize the opposition is certain to come into power sooner or later. The second major party is able to argue, therefore, that people who vote for minor opposition parties dissipate the opposition, that the supporters of the minor parties *waste their votes*. All who oppose the party in power are made to feel a certain need for concentrating their support behind the party most likely to lead a successful opposition. As a consequence the tendency to support minor parties is checked. The tendency of the single-member district system to give the second major party a great advantage over all minor parties is extremely important. In this way it is possible to explain the *longevity* of the major parties and the instability of

the minor parties. Thus, while the major parties seem to go on forever, what has become of, and who remembers a long series of Labor, Farmer-Labor, Workers', United Labor, Socialist-Labor, Peoples', Union, and American parties launched since the Civil War?

Why are third parties with highly sectional support unable to survive? In this case, the single-member district system operates in favor of the third party and against one or the other of the major parties within the section. A third party ought therefore to be able to entrench itself in a region and maintain itself permanently. Obviously, the system of representation cannot account for the tendency of sectional third parties to fade away; the explanation must be found elsewhere. As a matter of fact, it is not necessary to go far afield for an explanation. Even more important than congressional elections are presidential elections, which might properly be described as the focus of American politics.... Now it is clear that a purely sectional party can never win a presidential election. Presidents can be elected only by combinations of sections, by parties that cross sectional lines. An exclusively sectional party is doomed to permanent futility, therefore, in the pursuit of the most important single objective of party strategy. Sooner or later exclusively sectional parties are likely to lose even their sectional support in favor of a major party which has a real chance of winning the supreme prize. For this reason narrowly sectional parties cannot displace the traditional type of major party, even though the single-member district system of electing representatives might sometimes give them an advantage.

E.E. Schattschneider, Party Government 81–83 (1942). That single-member district systems lead to two-party systems while more proportional systems lead to multi-party systems was shown to be true across a great number of democracies and over an extended period by Maurice Duverger, Political Parties 216–28 (2d English ed., 1959), and has therefore come to be known as Duverger's Law.[c]

Another election law that makes it difficult for third parties to prosper is the nomination of major party candidates by direct primary elections. Primaries are intended to increase the ability of voters to control the ideological direction of the major parties. If primaries in fact accomplish this purpose then they are likely to harm third parties, whose chances of winning votes depend primarily on voter dissatisfaction with the major parties. In the words of the leading empirical study of third party voting:

> The story of why people vote for third parties is a story of major party deterioration. To be sure, third parties can help their own causes by selecting high caliber candidates or by building a loyal following over the years. But, overwhelmingly, it is the failure of the major parties to do what the electorate expects of them — reflect the issue preferences of voters, manage the economy, select attractive and acceptable candidates, and build voter loyalty to the parties and the political system — that most increases the likelihood of voters backing a minor party. Citi-

---

c. For more recent commentary, see, e.g., Douglas W. Rae, The Political Consequences of Electoral Laws 87–103 (1967); William H. Riker, *The Number of Political Parties: A Reexamination of Duverger's Law*, 9 Comparative Politics 93 (1976). Duverger's Law has greater empirical validity if it is modified, in the way suggested by Schattschneider, by recognizing that regionally concentrated third parties can survive in a single-member district system when there is no presidential election creating pressure for a two-party system. Canada and India are examples of countries in which regional third parties have had some success. See Jae-On Kim & Mahn-Geum Ohn, *A Theory of Minor-Party Persistence: Election Rules, Social Cleavage, and the Number of Political Parties*, 70 Social Forces 575 (1992).

zens by and large cast third party ballots because they are dissatisfied with the major parties, not because they are attracted to the alternatives.

Steven J. Rosenstone, Roy L. Behr & Edward H. Lazarus, THIRD PARTIES IN AMERICA 162 (2d ed. 1996).

Compared to single-member districts, the Electoral College, and the major parties' primary system, ballot access requirements and the exclusion of minor parties and candidates from publicly provided benefits probably have a slight impact on third parties' chances of electoral success. Nevertheless, ballot access is unquestionably of crucial importance to any independent candidate or third party, as well as for those who believe that the presence of third parties makes an important contribution to American democracy. In the words of Rosenstone, Behr and Lazarus, *supra*, at 8:

> [T]he power of third parties lies in their capacity to affect the content and range of political discourse, and ultimately public policy, by raising issues and options that the two major parties have ignored. In so doing, they not only promote their cause but affect the very character of the two-party system.

I. Ballot Access

The issue of ballot access for parties and candidates did not arise in the 19th century, because before the introduction of the secret (or "Australian") ballot around the end of that century, the state did not typically provide a ballot at all. It was the responsibility of the voter to supply a ballot. In practice, this usually meant that the parties provided printed ballots, each containing the names of their own candidates, and each distinctively colored so that observers could easily tell which party's ballot an individual was casting. This system made it relatively difficult for voters to "split their tickets," and it also made it difficult to support a party that was not sufficiently well organized to print and distribute its own ballots.

To permit secret voting, states had to print their own ballots with the names of competing candidates, so that voters could choose in private. This meant that the state had to set rules for the eligibility of parties and candidates to be listed on the state-supplied ballots. For parties and candidates who qualified, the Australian ballot was a considerable boon, because the obstacles that hindered voters wishing to depart from the major parties were removed. But for parties and candidates who did not qualify, the Australian ballot made a bad situation worse. Although most states permit write-in votes,[d] it is easier to vote for a listed candidate, and unlisted candidates typically are not considered serious ones. For a wealth of information on past and current ballot access requirements, see Richard Winger, *How Ballot Access Laws Affect the U.S. Party System*, 16 AMERICAN REVIEW OF POLITICS 321 (1996).

Until 1968, the states were free to set whatever ballot qualifications they chose. In that year, a strong challenge to the Democrats and Republicans was mounted by George Wallace, running under the banner of the American Independent Party. Wallace was able to satisfy the petition requirements for listing on the ballot for every state but one, Ohio. Even in Ohio, Wallace was able to satisfy the relatively stiff 15% signature requirement, but he was not able to do so by the early deadline of February 7 of the election year. Such an

---

d. In *Burdick v. Takushi*, 504 U.S. 428 (1992), the Supreme Court ruled that the Constitution does not necessarily require a state to permit write-in votes. Nevertheless, most states do permit such votes.

early deadline can be particularly difficult for third party and independent challenges, which often develop in response to the candidates chosen by the major parties.

In *Williams v. Rhodes*, 393 U.S. 23 (1968), the Supreme Court ordered Wallace to be placed on the Ohio ballot. Ohio's laws, according to the Court, made it "virtually impossible for any party to qualify on the ballot except the Republican and Democratic Parties," which retained automatic ballot status by receiving at least ten percent of the votes in gubernatorial elections. The Court has not relied on a constitutional right to be a candidate for public office, in *Williams* or in subsequent cases. Rather, the Court said that Ohio's restrictions placed burdens on "two different, although overlapping, kinds of rights — the right of individuals to associate for the advancement of political beliefs, and the right of qualified voters, regardless of their political persuasion, to cast their votes effectively."

The Court rejected Ohio's claim that its strict requirements could be justified under the Equal Protection Clause by its interest in promoting a two-party system.

> The fact is ... that the Ohio system does not favor a "two-party system"; it favors two particular parties — the Republicans and the Democrats — and in effect tends to give them a complete monopoly.... New parties struggling for their place must have the time and opportunity to organize in order to meet reasonable requirements for ballot position, just as the old parties have had in the past.
>
> ... Concededly, the State does have an interest in attempting to see that the election winner be the choice of a majority of its voters. But to grant the State power to keep all political parties off the ballot until they have enough members to win would stifle the growth of all new parties working to increase their strength from year to year.

This language in *Williams* indicated that the Court was willing to concede a state interest in requiring some demonstration of support for a candidate or party as a prerequisite to ballot access. In *Jenness v. Fortson*, 403 U.S. 431 (1971), the Court made it clear that more than token support could be required. *Jenness* upheld Georgia's requirement that independent candidates obtain signatures from electors equal in number to five percent of the number of registered voters in the jurisdiction. The deadline was the same as that for candidates who wished to be listed on the ballot as candidates in party primaries. The Court regarded the Georgia requirements as significantly less onerous than the ones struck down in *Williams*.

> Unlike Ohio, Georgia does not require every candidate to be the nominee of a political party, but fully recognizes independent candidacies. Unlike Ohio, Georgia does not fix an unreasonably early filing deadline for candidates not endorsed by established parties. Unlike Ohio, Georgia does not impose upon a small party or a new party the Procrustean requirement of establishing elaborate primary election machinery. Finally, and in sum, Georgia's election laws, unlike Ohio's do not operate to freeze the political status quo....
>
> There is surely an important state interest in requiring some preliminary showing of a significant modicum of support before printing the name of a political organization's candidate on the ballot — the interest, if no other, in avoiding confusion, deception, and even frustration of the democratic process at the general election. The 5% figure is, to be sure, apparently somewhat higher than the percentage of support required to be shown in many States as a condition for ballot position, but this is balanced by the fact that Georgia has imposed no ar-

bitrary restrictions whatever upon the eligibility of any registered voter to sign as many nominating petitions as he wishes.

Although the Court viewed the Georgia requirements in *Jenness* as less onerous than the Ohio requirements in *Williams*, in fact the Georgia requirements—by keying to the number of *registered*, rather than *actual* voters—may have been much more onerous. *See* Richard Winger, *The Supreme Court and the Burial of Ballot Access: A Critical Review of* Jenness v. Fortson, 1 ELECTION LAW JOURNAL 235, 242 (2002).

Numerous ballot access cases have found their way to the Supreme Court, but the Court has generally adhered to the pattern set in *Williams* and *Jenness*: it will uphold ballot access requirements that are difficult for many minor parties and independent candidates to satisfy, but will intervene when it believes the requirements are so severe that they pose obstacles even to parties and candidates that can demonstrate significant electoral support.

Munro v. Socialist Workers Party
479 U.S. 189 (1986)

Justice WHITE delivered the opinion of the Court.

The State of Washington requires that a minor-party candidate for partisan office receive at least 1% of all votes cast for that office in the State's primary election before the candidate's name will be placed on the general election ballot. The question for decision is whether this statutory requirement, as applied to candidates for statewide offices, violates the First and Fourteenth Amendments to the United States Constitution. The Court of Appeals for the Ninth Circuit declared the provision unconstitutional. We reverse.

In 1977, the State of Washington enacted amendments to its election laws, changing the manner in which candidates from minor political parties qualify for placement on the general election ballot. Before the amendments, a minor-party candidate did not participate in the State's primary elections, but rather sought his or her party's nomination at a party convention held on the same day as the primary election for "major" parties. The convention-nominated, minor-party candidate secured a position on the general election ballot upon the filing of a certificate signed by at least 100 registered voters who had participated in the convention and who had not voted in the primary election. The 1977 amendments retained the requirement that a minor-party candidate be nominated by convention, but imposed the additional requirement that, as a precondition to general ballot access, the nominee for an office appear on the primary election ballot and receive at least 1% of all votes cast for that particular office at the primary election.

Washington conducts a "blanket primary" at which registered voters may vote for any candidate of their choice, irrespective of the candidates' political party affiliation....

The events giving rise to this action occurred in 1983, after the state legislature authorized a special primary election to be held on October 11, 1983, to fill a vacancy in the office of United States Senator. Appellee Dean Peoples qualified to be placed on the primary election ballot as the nominee of appellee Socialist Workers Party. Also appearing on that ballot were 32 other candidates. At the primary, Mr. Peoples received approximately nine one-hundredths of one percent of the total votes cast for the office,[9] and, accordingly, the State did not place his name on the general election ballot....

---

9. Mr. Peoples received 596 of the 681,690 votes cast in the primary.

Restrictions upon the access of political parties to the ballot impinge upon the rights of individuals to associate for political purposes, as well as the rights of qualified voters to cast their votes effectively, *Williams*, and may not survive scrutiny under the First and Fourteenth Amendments.... These associational rights, however, are not absolute and are necessarily subject to qualification if elections are to be run fairly and effectively. *Storer v. Brown*, 415 U.S. 724, 730 (1974).

While there is no "litmus-paper test" for deciding a case like this, *ibid.*, it is now clear that States may condition access to the general election ballot by a minor-party or independent candidate upon a showing of a modicum of support among the potential voters for the office. In *Jenness*, the Court unanimously rejected a challenge to Georgia's election statutes that required independent candidates and minor-party candidates, in order to be listed on the general election ballot, to submit petitions signed by at least 5% of the voters eligible to vote in the last election for the office in question. Primary elections were held only for those political organizations whose candidate received 20% or more of the vote at the last gubernatorial or Presidential election. The Court's opinion observed that "[t]here is surely an important state interest in requiring some preliminary showing of a significant modicum of support before printing the name of a political organization's candidate on the ballot—the interest, if no other, in avoiding confusion, deception, and even frustration of the democratic process at the general election." And, in *American Party of Texas v. White*, 415 U.S. 767 (1974), candidates of minor political parties in Texas were required to demonstrate support by persons numbering at least 1% of the total vote cast for Governor at the last preceding general election. Candidates could secure the requisite number of petition signatures at precinct nominating conventions and by supplemental petitions following the conventions. Voters signing these supplemental petitions had to swear under oath that they had not participated in another party's primary election or nominating process. In rejecting a First Amendment challenge to the 1% requirement, we asserted that the State's interest in preserving the integrity of the electoral process and in regulating the number of candidates on the ballot was compelling and reiterated the holding in *Jenness* that a State may require a preliminary showing of significant support before placing a candidate on the general election ballot.

Jenness and *American Party* establish with unmistakable clarity that States have an "undoubted right to require candidates to make a preliminary showing of substantial support in order to qualify for a place on the ballot...." *Anderson v. Celebrezze*, 460 U.S. 780, 788–789, n. 9 (1983). We reaffirm that principle today.

The Court of Appeals determined that Washington's interest in insuring that candidates had sufficient community support did not justify the enactment of [the 1% requirement] because "Washington's political history evidences no voter confusion from ballot overcrowding." We accept this historical fact, but it does not require invalidation....

We have never required a State to make a particularized showing of the existence of voter confusion, ballot overcrowding, or the presence of frivolous candidacies prior to the imposition of reasonable restrictions on ballot access....

To require States to prove actual voter confusion, ballot overcrowding, or the presence of frivolous candidacies as a predicate to the imposition of reasonable ballot access restrictions would invariably lead to endless court battles over the sufficiency of the "evidence" marshaled by a State to prove the predicate. Such a requirement would necessitate that a State's political system sustain some level of damage before the legislature could take corrective action. Legislatures, we think, should be permitted to respond to potential deficiencies in the electoral process with foresight rather than reactively, provided that the response is reasonable and does not significantly impinge on constitutionally protected rights.

In any event, the record here suggests that [imposition of the 1% requirement] was, in fact, linked to the state legislature's perception that the general election ballot was becoming cluttered with candidates from minor parties who did not command significant voter support. In 1976..., the largest number of minor political parties in Washington's history—12—appeared on the general election ballot. The record demonstrates that at least part of the legislative impetus for [the 1% requirement] was concern about minor parties having such easy access to Washington's general election ballot.

The primary election in Washington ... is "an integral part of the entire election process ... [that] functions to winnow out and finally reject all but the chosen candidates." *Storer v. Brown*, 415 U.S. 724, 735 (1974). We think that the State can properly reserve the general election ballot "for major struggles," *ibid.*, by conditioning access to that ballot on a showing of a modicum of voter support. In this respect, the fact that the State is willing to have a long and complicated ballot at the primary provides no measure of what it may require for access to the general election ballot. The State of Washington was clearly entitled to raise the ante for ballot access, to simplify the general election ballot, and to avoid the possibility of unrestrained factionalism at the general election.

Neither do we agree with the Court of Appeals and appellees that the burdens imposed on appellees' First Amendment rights by the 1977 amendments are far too severe to be justified by the State's interest in restricting access to the general ballot. Much is made of the fact that prior to 1977, virtually every minor-party candidate who sought general election ballot position so qualified, while since 1977 only 1 out of 12 minor-party candidates has appeared on that ballot. Such historical facts are relevant, but they prove very little in this case, other than the fact that [the 1% requirement] does not provide an insuperable barrier to minor-party ballot access.[11] It is hardly a surprise that minor parties appeared on the general election ballot before [the requirement was imposed]; for, until then, there were virtually no restrictions on access. Under our cases, however, Washington was not required to afford such automatic access and would have been entitled to insist on a more substantial showing of voter support. Comparing the actual experience before and after 1977 tells us nothing about how minor parties would have fared in those earlier years had Washington conditioned ballot access to the maximum extent permitted by the Constitution.

Appellees urge that this case differs substantially from our previous cases because requiring primary votes to qualify for a position on the general election ballot is qualitatively more restrictive than requiring signatures on a nominating petition. In effect, their submission would foreclose any use of the primary election to determine a minor party's qualification for the general ballot. We are unpersuaded, however, that the differences between the two mechanisms are of constitutional dimension. Because Washington provides a "blanket primary," minor party candidates can campaign among the entire pool of registered voters. Effort and resources that would otherwise be directed at securing petition signatures can instead be channeled into campaigns to "get the vote out," foster candidate name recognition, and educate the electorate. To be sure, candidates must demonstrate, through their ability to secure votes at the primary election, that they enjoy a modicum of community support in order to advance to the general election. But requiring

11. [The requirement] apparently poses an insubstantial obstacle to minor-party candidates for nonstatewide offices and independent candidates for statewide offices. Since 1977, 36 out of 40 such minor-party candidates have qualified for the general election ballot and 4 out of 5 independent candidates for statewide office have so qualified.

candidates to demonstrate such support is precisely what we have held States are permitted to do.

Appellees argue that voter turnout at primary elections is generally lower than the turnout at general elections, and therefore … the pool of potential supporters from which Party candidates can secure 1% of the vote [is reduced]. We perceive no more force to this argument than we would with an argument by a losing candidate that his supporters' constitutional rights were infringed by their failure to participate in the election. Washington has created no impediment to voting at the primary elections; every supporter of the Party in the State is free to cast his or her ballot for the Party's candidates.... States are not burdened with a constitutional imperative to reduce voter apathy or to "handicap" an unpopular candidate to increase the likelihood that the candidate will gain access to the general election ballot. As we see it, Washington has done no more than to visit on a candidate a requirement to show a "significant modicum" of voter support, and it was entitled to require that showing in its primary elections.

We also observe that [Washington's statute] is more accommodating of First Amendment rights and values than were the statutes we upheld in *Jenness, American Party*, and *Storer*. Under each scheme analyzed in those cases, if a candidate failed to satisfy the qualifying criteria, the State's voters had no opportunity to cast a ballot for that candidate and the candidate had no ballot-connected campaign platform from which to espouse his or her views; the unsatisfied qualifying criteria served as an absolute bar to ballot access. Undeniably, such restrictions raise concerns of constitutional dimension, for the "exclusion of candidates … burdens voters' freedom of association, because an election campaign is an effective platform for the expression of views on the issues of the day...." *Anderson*. Here, however, Washington virtually guarantees what the parties challenging the Georgia, Texas, and California election laws so vigorously sought—candidate access to a statewide ballot. This is a significant difference. Washington has chosen a vehicle by which minor-party candidates must demonstrate voter support that serves to promote the very First Amendment values that are threatened by overly burdensome ballot access restrictions. It can hardly be said that Washington's voters are denied freedom of association because they must channel their expressive activity into a campaign at the primary as opposed to the general election. It is true that voters must make choices as they vote at the primary, but there are no state-imposed obstacles impairing voters in the exercise of their choices....

The judgment of the Court of Appeals for the Ninth Circuit is therefore reversed.

It is so ordered.

Justice MARSHALL, with whom Justice BRENNAN joins, dissenting.

… The minor party's often unconventional positions broaden political debate, expand the range of issues with which the electorate is concerned, and influence the positions of the majority, in some instances ultimately becoming majority positions. And its very existence provides an outlet for voters to express dissatisfaction with the candidates or platforms of the major parties. Notwithstanding the crucial role minor parties play in the American political arena, the Court holds today that the associational rights of minor parties and their supporters are not unduly burdened by a ballot access statute that, in practice, completely excludes minor parties from participating in statewide general elections.

I

The Court fails to articulate the level of scrutiny it applies in holding that the Washington 1% primary vote requirement is not an unconstitutional ballot access restriction....

By contrast, the standard of review set forth in our prior decisions is clear: Whether viewed as a burden on the right to associate or as discrimination against minor parties, a provision that burdens minor-party access to the ballot must be necessary to further a compelling state interest, and must be narrowly tailored to achieve that goal. The necessity for this approach becomes evident when we consider that major parties, which by definition are ordinarily in control of legislative institutions, may seek to perpetuate themselves at the expense of developing minor parties. The application of strict scrutiny to ballot access restrictions ensures that measures taken to further a State's interest in keeping frivolous candidates off the ballot do not incidentally impose an impermissible bar to minor-party access.

Appellant argues that there is no ballot access limitation here at all, and thus no need for the application of heightened scrutiny, because minor parties can appear on a primary ballot simply by meeting reasonable petition requirements. I cannot accept, however, as a general proposition, that access to any ballot is always constitutionally adequate. The Court, in concluding here that the State may reserve the general election ballot for "major struggles," appears to acknowledge that, because of its finality, the general election is the arena where issues are sharpened, policies are hotly debated, and the candidates' positions are clarified. Nonetheless, the Court deems access to the primary adequate to satisfy minor-party rights to ballot access, even though we have characterized the primary election principally as a "forum for continuing intraparty feuds," *Storer v. Brown*, 415 U.S. 724, 735 (1974), rather than an arena for debate on the issues. Access to a primary election ballot is not, in my view, all the access that is due when minor parties are excluded entirely from the general election.

The Court's conclusion stems from a fundamental misconception of the role minor parties play in our constitutional scheme. To conclude that access to a primary ballot is adequate ballot access presumes that minor-party candidates seek only to get elected. But, as discussed earlier, minor-party participation in electoral politics serves to expand and affect political debate.... That contribution cannot be realized if they are unable to participate meaningfully in the phase of the electoral process in which policy choices are most seriously considered. A statutory scheme that excludes minor parties entirely from this phase places an excessive burden on the constitutionally protected associational rights of those parties and their adherents....

I am unconvinced that the Washington statute serves the asserted justification for the law: avoiding ballot overcrowding and voter confusion. The statute streamlines the general election, where overcrowding and confusion appear never to have been much of a problem before the 1977 amendments, at the expense of an already cumbersome primary ballot. Between 1907 and 1977, no more than six minor party candidates ever appeared on the general election ballot for any statewide office, and no more than four ever ran for any statewide office other than Governor, suggesting that the ballot was never very crowded. But in the 1983 special election that prompted this lawsuit, appellee Peoples, instead of being placed on the general election ballot with 2 other candidates, was placed on the primary ballot along with *32* other candidates: 18 Democrats and 14 Republicans.

The Court notes that we have not previously required a State seeking to impose reasonable ballot access restrictions to make a particularized showing that voter confusion in fact existed before those restrictions were imposed. But where the State's solution exacerbates the very problem it claims to solve, the State's means cannot be even rationally related to its asserted ends....

Additionally, while a State may have an interest in eliminating frivolous candidates by requiring candidates to demonstrate "a significant modicum of support" to qualify for a place on the ballot, Washington already had a mechanism that required minor-party candidates to show such support, which it retained after its imposition of the 1% primary vote requirement in 1977. Appellees did not challenge the legitimacy of the convention and petition requirements in this case, but the fact that a mechanism for requiring some showing of support previously existed casts doubt on the need for the imposition of still another requirement on minor-party candidates. Moreover, the application of the 1% requirement suggests it is overbroad, avoiding frivolous candidacies only by excluding virtually all minor-party candidates from general elections for statewide office.

The only purpose this statute seems narrowly tailored to advance is the impermissible one of protecting the major political parties from competition precisely when that competition would be most meaningful. Because the statute burdens appellees' First Amendment interests, it must be subjected to strict scrutiny; because it fails to pass such scrutiny, it is unconstitutional.

II

Even if I were prepared to adopt the nebulous logic the Court employs in preference to the mandatory strict standard of review in this case, I could not reach the majority's result. While this Court has in the past acknowledged that limits on minor-party access to the ballot may in some circumstances be appropriate, we have made equally clear that States may not employ ballot access limitations which result in the exclusion of minor parties from the ballot....

Under this reasoning, the validity of ballot access limitations is a function of empirical evidence: A minor party is not impermissibly burdened by ballot access restrictions when "a reasonably diligent independent candidate" could be expected to satisfy the ballot access requirement. *Storer*....

Washington's primary law acts as an almost total bar to minor-party access to statewide general election ballots.... The Court of Appeals found that by 1984, only one minor-party candidate had been able to surmount the 1% barrier and earn the right to participate in the general election. The legislation leading to this substantial elimination of minor parties from the political arena in Washington's general elections should not be sustained as a legitimate requirement of a demonstration of significant support.

Notes and Questions

1. In his dissenting opinion, Justice Marshall asserts:

> The minor party's often unconventional positions broaden political debate, expand the range of issues with which the electorate is concerned, and influence the positions of the majority, in some instances ultimately becoming majority positions. And its very existence provides an outlet for voters to express dissatisfaction with the candidates or platforms of the major parties.

It is undoubtedly the case that many third party and independent candidates recognize that they have no chance of being elected and therefore are running for other reasons. For the government, however, the function served by elections—determining who shall hold public office—is a crucial one. In designing election procedures, should the government be permitted to exalt its own purpose over other uses to which parties and candidates may wish to put elections?

Some scholars have contended that the right to vote has expressive elements—one can send a message by the vote one casts. See Adam Winkler, Note, *Expressive Voting*, 68 New York University Law Review 330 (1993). In *Burdick v. Takushi*, 504 U.S. 428, 438 (1992), the Supreme Court rejected such a role for voting, holding that "[a]ttributing to elections a more generalized expressive function would undermine the ability of States to operate elections fairly and efficiently." Was the Court right to reject the idea that voting serves an expressive function?

2. To what extent should judicial review of ballot access rules consider their impact upon political competition? Consider the 2004 cases involving presidential candidate Ralph Nader, who unsuccessfully sought injunctive relief to get his name on the ballot in six states. The issues included the constitutionality of state rules regarding the deadline for petitions, the number of signatures required to get on the ballot, and the use of out-of-state petition circulators. See Richard Winger, *An Analysis of the 2004 Nader Ballot Access Federal Court Cases*, 32 Fordham Urban Law Journal 567 (2005).

In one of those cases, *Nader v. Keith*, 385 F.3d 729, 732–34 (7th Cir. 2004), Judge Posner wrote the following in regard to Nader's attempt to get on the Illinois ballot, despite having gathered insufficient signatures by the filing deadline:

> Nader argues that [Illinois's] rules that in combination ruled him off the ballot impose an unreasonable burden on third-party and independent (nonparty) candidacy (though the Libertarian Party's candidate was able to qualify), and if this is so the rules are unconstitutional. Nader emphasizes the role that third parties have played in American democracy. The Republican Party started as a third party; and such third parties as the Progressive Party of Theodore Roosevelt, LaFollette's Progressive Party, and the Reform Party have made significant contributions to political competition, whether by injecting new ideas or, in the case of the Republican Party, by actually displacing one of the major parties.

> So the barriers to the entry of third parties must not be set too high; yet the two major parties, who between them exert virtually complete control over American government, are apt to collude to do just that. For like other duopolists they would prefer not to be challenged by some upstart—although if a major party believes that a third party will take more votes from the other party than from itself, it will support that third party (surreptitiously, because it's supporting an ideological opponent), and the other party will oppose it (also surreptitiously, because it's opposing an ideological ally)....

> It doesn't follow from what we said about the importance of preserving opportunities for the entry of new parties into the political arena that it would be a good thing if there were no barriers at all to third-party candidacies. A multiplication of parties would make our politics more ideological by reducing the influence of the median voter (who in a two-party system determines the outcome of most elections), and this could be a very bad thing. More mundanely, terminal voter confusion might ensue from having a multiplicity of Presidential candidates on the ballot—for think of the confusion caused by the "butterfly" ballot used in Palm Beach County, Florida in the 2000 Presidential election. That fiasco was a consequence of the fact that the ballot listed ten Presidential candidates. The butterfly ballot was a folded punchcard ballot in which the ten candidates for President were listed on facing pages.

> This unusual design was innocently adopted in order to enable the candidates' names to be printed in large type, in consideration of the number of el-

derly voters in the county, while at the same time placing all the candidates for each office in sight of the voter at one time so that he would be less likely to over-vote. Another ballot design might have effectively disfranchised voters who had poor eyesight, or who cast their vote before realizing there were additional candidates for the same office on the next page of the ballot, or who cast two votes for candidates for the same office because they didn't realize that candidates for the same office appeared on different pages. But with names on each side and the chads (the places in the ballot that the voter punches out in order to vote) in the middle, it was easy to punch the chad of the candidate on one of the facing pages meaning to vote for the candidate on the opposite page. Apparently a significant number of voters did just that: intending to vote for Al Gore, they voted for Patrick Buchanan. With fewer candidates, the "butterfly" design and resulting confusion would have been avoided.

Less obviously, third-party candidates would themselves be harmed if there were no barriers to including such candidates on the ballot. It is to the Libertarian Party's advantage that if Nader's challenge fails, its candidate will be the only independent candidate for President on the ballot. If there were 98 independent candidates, none could hope for a nontrivial vote.

So there have to be hurdles to getting on the ballot and the requirement of submitting a minimum number of nominating petitions is a standard one. In a state the size of Illinois—the population exceeds 12 million, of whom more than 7 million are registered voters—requiring a third-party candidate to obtain 25,000 signed nominating petitions cannot be thought excessive. *Jenness* upheld a Georgia law that required petitions from 5 percent of the registered voters—in Illinois that would mean 350,000 petitions! Equally stringent requirements have been upheld in other cases. And especially in a state as notorious for election fraud as Illinois, the fact that the nominating petitions that a candidate submits have actually been signed by registered voters has to be verified. If the petition were not required to contain any identifying information (such as date of birth, mother's maiden name, or, the identifier that Illinois has chosen, the address at which the petitioner is registered to vote), there would be no practical impediment to a person's signing the name of anyone he knew to be a registered voter.

Consider as well these comments of Justice O'Connor (joined by Justice Breyer) concurring in *Clingman v. Beaver*, 544 U.S. 581 (2005) which rejected the Libertarian Party of Oklahoma's challenge to that state's semiclosed primary system:[e]

We have sought to balance the associational interests of parties and voters against the States' regulatory interests through the flexible standard of review reaffirmed by the Court today. Under that standard, "the rigorousness of our inquiry into the propriety of a state election law depends upon the extent to which a challenged regulation burdens First and Fourteenth Amendment rights." *Burdick*. Regulations imposing severe burdens on associational rights must be narrowly tailored to advance a compelling government interest. *Timmons*. Regulations imposing lesser burdens are subject to less intensive scrutiny, and rea-

---

e. *Clingman* is discussed more fully in Chapter 9.

sonable, nondiscriminatory restrictions ordinarily will be sustained if they serve important regulatory interests.

This regime reflects the limited but important role of courts in reviewing electoral regulation. Although the State has a legitimate — and indeed critical — role to play in regulating elections, it must be recognized that it is not a wholly independent or neutral arbiter. Rather, the State is itself controlled by the political party or parties in power, which presumably have an incentive to shape the rules of the electoral game to their own benefit. Recognition of that basic reality need not render suspect most electoral regulations. Where the State imposes only reasonable and genuinely neutral restrictions on associational rights, there is no threat to the integrity of the electoral process and no apparent reason for judicial intervention. As such restrictions become more severe, however, and particularly where they have discriminatory effects, there is increasing cause for concern that those in power may be using electoral rules to erect barriers to electoral competition. In such cases, applying heightened scrutiny helps to ensure that such limitations are truly justified and that the State's asserted interests are not merely a pretext for exclusionary or anticompetitive restrictions.

Should a similar analysis apply where state ballot access rules make it difficult for third-party or independent candidates to get on the ballot? See also *id.* at 2045 ("The semi-closed primary law, standing alone, does not impose a significant obstacle to participation in the [Libertarian party's] primary, nor does it indicate partisan self dealing or a lockup of the political process that would warrant heightened judicial scrutiny.")

For a criticism of Judge Posner's analysis of the third party issues in *Nader v. Keith*, see Richard Winger, *How Many Parties Ought to Be on the Ballot?: An Analysis of Nader v. Keith*, 5 ELECTION LAW JOURNAL 170 (2006). See also Dmitri Evseev, *A Second Look at Third Parties: Correcting the Supreme Court's Understanding of Elections*, 85 BOSTON UNIVERSITY LAW REVIEW 1277 (2005). For further discussion of the scholarly debate regarding competition, see *infra* Chapter 12, Part III.

3. *Bad Legislative Intent?* Why did the Washington legislature adopt the system challenged in *Munro*? Apparently, to avoid becoming a "laughing stock" and to save money. In the 1976 elections, a Jazz musician named Red Kelly formed the OWL Party, which stood for "Out With Logic; On With Lunacy," which ran a series of joke candidates to mock the political system. For example, "Fast" Lucie Griswold ran for secretary of state as an OWL candidate. She advocated that the next secretary be able to "take shorthand or do typing." She also took "unequivocal stands" against "(1) The heartbreak of psoriasis; (2) Bed wetting; (3) The big 'O'; [and] (4) Post nasal drip." The legislature may have been motivated, at least in part, to save the expense of having the OWL Party's statements appear in ballot materials printed at public expense. If that more benign explanation of the legislature's intent is correct, should it have any bearing on the constitutionality of its ballot access law? For an argument in the negative, see Richard L. Hasen, *Bad Legislative Intent*, 2006 WISCONSIN LAW REVIEW 843.

4. Consider the State of Washington's present system, which the Supreme Court upheld against a facial challenge in *Washington State Grange v. Washington State Republican Party*, 128 S. Ct. 1184 (2008) (discussed at greater length in Chapter 9). In Washington, all voters may now vote for candidates of any party in the primary election, but only the top two votegetters (regardless of party) proceed to the general election. This makes it very unlikely that any third-party candidates will make it to the general election ballot.

Does this present a serious problem, to the extent one believes that elections should provide a forum for citizens to express dissatisfaction with the major parties? Should Washington's system be struck down as applied to third-party candidates repeatedly frustrated in their efforts to obtain access to the general election ballot?

5. Critics argue that although the Court continues to pay lip service to *Williams*, in practice it has been willing to tolerate overly restrictive ballot access requirements. Thus, Bradley A. Smith, Note, *Judicial Protection of Ballot-Access Rights: Third Parties Need Not Apply*, 28 HARVARD JOURNAL ON LEGISLATION 167, 184 (1991), claims that in *Jenness*:

> [The Court] overstated the historical ability of third parties to gain access to the Georgia ballot. The Court emphasized that, while the Ohio law [in *Williams*] had foreclosed any third-party competition, "[t]he open quality of the Georgia system is far from merely theoretical." In support of this characterization, the Court noted that the petition procedure had been used in 1966 and again in 1968. Prior to 1966, however, no candidate had ever successfully used the petition procedure to appear on Georgia's statewide ballot. The candidate who qualified in 1966 was not a minor party or independent candidate, but the Republican nominee for Governor. Thus, the differences between the Ohio and Georgia systems, in "totality," were not nearly so great as the Court's opinion in *Jenness* would make it seem.

Smith is also critical of *Munro*, whose "most devastating part" in Smith's opinion is its ruling that the state does not need to defend the validity of the interests it asserts against empirical challenge. *Id.* at 191. Smith concludes:

> The *Munro* holding that no particularized showing of state interest is required, combined with the *Jenness* test that virtually any past success by third parties in obtaining ballot status establishes the legitimacy of a ballot-access statute, undermines most constitutional challenges to ballot-access restrictions. In *Munro*, the Court recognized compelling state interests in imposing restrictions, which future plaintiffs are unable to challenge empirically. At the same time, plaintiffs will rarely be able to show an impermissible burden, for so long as even one third-party candidate has previously met a state's requirement, the law would meet the *Jenness* test. If the Court adheres to these rulings, ballot-access laws will be unassailable.

Id. at 192.

6. Many commentators have found the Court's ballot access doctrine nebulous and inconsistent. See, e.g., Laurence H. Tribe, AMERICAN CONSTITUTIONAL LAW 1102 (2d ed. 1988) ("the border between permissible and impermissible ballot access requirements remains ill-defined"). Probably the reason is that the 'standard of review" employed by the Court has been shifting and unclear. In *Williams*, the Court required a compelling state interest to justify the burden on voting and associational rights. In a subsequent case, *Anderson v. Celebrezze*, 460 U.S. 780, 788–90 (1983), the Court set forth a more flexible standard that is important because it also has been referred to in a number of election law cases not involving ballot access:

> Although [the] rights of voters are fundamental, not all restrictions imposed by the States on candidates' eligibility for the ballot impose constitutionally suspect burdens on voters' rights to associate or to choose among candidates. We have recognized that, "as a practical matter, there must be a substantial regulation of elections if they are to be fair and honest and if some sort of order, rather than chaos, is to accompany the democratic processes." *Storer v. Brown*, 415 U.S.

724, 730 (1974). To achieve these necessary objectives, States have enacted comprehensive and sometimes complex election codes. Each provision of these schemes, whether it governs the registration and qualifications of voters, the selection and eligibility of candidates, or the voting process itself, inevitably affects—at least to some degree—the individual's right to vote and his right to associate with others for political ends. Nevertheless, the State's important regulatory interests are generally sufficient to justify reasonable, nondiscriminatory restrictions.

Constitutional challenges to specific provisions of a State's election laws therefore cannot be resolved by any "litmus-paper test" that will separate valid from invalid restrictions. *Storer.* Instead, a court must resolve such a challenge by an analytical process that parallels its work in ordinary litigation. It must first consider the character and magnitude of the asserted injury to the rights protected by the First and Fourteenth Amendments that the plaintiff seeks to vindicate. It then must identify and evaluate the precise interests put forward by the State as justifications for the burden imposed by its rule. In passing judgment, the Court must not only determine the legitimacy and strength of each of those interests, it also must consider the extent to which those interests make it necessary to burden the plaintiff's rights. Only after weighing all these factors is the reviewing court in a position to decide whether the challenged provision is unconstitutional. The results of this evaluation will not be automatic; as we have recognized, there is "no substitute for the hard judgments that must be made." *Storer.*

For detailed analysis of the standard of review in the ballot access cases, see Martin E. Latz, *The Constitutionality of State-Passed Congressional Term Limits*, 25 AKRON LAW REVIEW 155, 189–97 (1991).

Despite the uncertainty that may exist regarding standard of review, if we look at the results in the ballot access cases that have reached the Supreme Court, the pattern does not seem particularly unclear. With the assistance of the Court in *Williams*, George Wallace was able to appear on every state's ballot in the 1968 presidential election. John Anderson, an independent candidate in 1980, also appeared on the ballot in all states, again with the help of the Court, which in *Anderson v. Celebrezze* repeated its 1968 performance by striking down overly restrictive Ohio requirements.[f] In 1992 and 1996, Ross Perot appeared on the ballot of every state, without the necessity for Supreme Court intervention.[g] It thus appears that under the Court's present doctrine, states cannot enforce requirements whose effect is to bar from the ballot candidates or parties with enough support to make a substantial showing in the election. As Smith argues (Note 3, *supra*), the Court permits exclusion of third party and independent candidacies that cannot demonstrate the likelihood of such a substantial showing.

7. *Filing fees.* One type of case may be an exception to the foregoing generalization. The Court has been intolerant of state laws conditioning ballot appearance on the payment of filing fees. In *Bullock v. Carter*, 405 U.S. 134 (1972), the Court struck down filing fees for local offices in Texas as violative of equal protection. The decision was based in part of the excessive size of the filing fees:

---

f. More precisely, a United States District Judge ordered that Anderson's name be placed on the ballot in Ohio, and this ruling was vindicated by the Supreme Court in 1983. Anderson also required judicial assistance to reach the ballot in Maine and Maryland.

g. Green Party candidate Ralph Nader appeared on the ballot in all but seven states in 2000.

Unlike a filing-fee requirement that most candidates could be expected to fulfill from their own resources or at least through modest contributions, the very size of the fees imposed under the Texas system gives it a patently exclusionary character. Many potential office seekers lacking both personal wealth and affluent backers are in every practical sense precluded from seeking the nomination of their chosen party, no matter how broad or enthusiastic their popular support. The effect of this exclusionary mechanism on voters is neither incidental nor remote. Not only are voters substantially limited in their choice of candidates, but also there is the obvious likelihood that this limitation would fall more heavily on the less affluent segment of the community, whose favorites may be unable to pay the large costs required by the Texas system.... [W]e would ignore reality were we not to recognize that this system falls with unequal weight on voters, as well as candidates, according to their economic status.

Two years later, the Court considered a challenge to a filing fee of $701.60 for candidates for the Los Angeles County Board of Supervisors. Considering that the supervisorial districts had populations close to two million people, the filing fee surely qualified as nominal. Nevertheless, the Court struck it down in *Lubin v. Panish*, 415 U.S. 709 (1974), finding that because there was no alternative way of qualifying for the ballot, the filing fee "inevitably renders the California system exclusionary as to some aspirants." The Court added that the state could require a candidate unable to pay the filing fee to "demonstrate the 'seriousness' of his candidacy by persuading a substantial number of voters to sign a petition in his behalf." Is *Lubin* consistent with cases like *Jenness v. Fortson*? Is it of much benefit to third parties and independent candidates?

While filing fees tend to impede both major-party and third-party candidates from running for office, there is empirical evidence that they have a greater impact on the latter. See Thomas Stratmann, *Ballot Access Restrictions and Candidate Entry in Elections*, 21 EUROPEAN JOURNAL OF POLITICAL ECONOMY 59 (2005). For an argument that filing fees for federal elected office violate the Qualification Clauses of the U.S. Constitution, see Mark R. Brown, *Ballot Fees as Impermissible Qualifications for Federal Office*, 54 AMERICAN UNIVERSITY LAW REVIEW 1283 (2005).

8. *Ballot access in major party primaries.* Ballot access laws occasionally pose difficulties for major party candidates, as well as third party and independent candidates. The New York Republican State Committee, for example, has enacted into law a series of ballot access rules (such as onerous signature requirements) intended to benefit candidates preferred by the party organization and to disadvantage those who are not preferred. The rules have been challenged repeatedly in court with some success, most recently by John McCain and others in the 2000 presidential primary. See *Molinari v. Powers*, 82 F.Supp.2d 57 (E.D.N.Y. 2000). In *Molinari*, the district court, in striking down the most recent provisions, noted that while the discriminatory ballot access requirements "may further the interest of the Republican State Committee, as distinguished from the 3.1 million New York voters affiliated with the Republican Party, it undermines the very purpose of a primary, which is 'to protect the general party membership against this sort of minority control [by the party leadership]' *Tashjian....*" Should courts apply a different standard to ballot access claims involving intraparty disputes? What interest does the party or the state have in keeping certain major party candidates off the primary ballot? For an exploration of these issues, see Nathaniel Persily, *Candidates v. Parties: The Constitutional Constraints on Primary Ballot Access Laws*, 89 GEORGETOWN LAW JOURNAL 2181 (2001).

9. *"Sore loser" laws.* To what extent should state election laws be upheld on the ground that they prevent candidates who lose major-party primaries from running in the general election as independent or third-party candidates? A recent example of such a candidacy is that of U.S. Senator Joe Lieberman. After having served in the Senate since 1988, Senator Lieberman ran for reelection in 2006 but lost the Democratic Party's primary to Ned Lamont. Targeting the Democratic Party's base, Lamont campaigned in vigorous opposition to the War in Iraq, which Lieberman had strongly supported. Because Connecticut does not have a "sore-loser" law, Lieberman was able to run as an independent candidate in the general election and retained his seat, defeating both Lamont and a Republican challenger, Alan Schlesinger. Does this example strengthen the argument for upholding laws that limit the ability of primary-election losers to run in the general election? Alternatively, does it furnish an argument *against* "sore loser" laws, given that Senator Lieberman won reelection in the general election by appealing to moderate voters of both major parties? Is it possible that allowing "sore loser" candidacies may improve the electoral process by facilitating the election of more centrist candidates?

In *Storer v. Brown*, 415 U.S. 724 (1974), the Court indicated it would uphold statutes designed to prevent "sore loser" candidacies. One of the statutes at issue in *Storer*, California Elections Code §6830(d), broadly prohibited a candidate from running in the general election as an independent if he or she had been affiliated with a party that was qualified to appear on the ballot within a year prior to that party's primary. The Court explained:

> The direct party primary in California is not merely an exercise or warm-up for the general election but an integral part of the entire election process, the initial stage in a two-stage process by which the people choose their public officers. It functions to winnow out and finally reject all but the chosen candidates. The State's general policy is to have contending forces within the party employ the primary campaign and primary election to finally settle their differences. The general election ballot is reserved for major struggles; it is not a forum for continuing intraparty feuds. The provision against defeated primary candidates running as independents effectuates this aim, the visible result being to prevent the losers from continuing the struggle and to limit the names on the ballot to those who have won the primaries and those independents who have properly qualified. The people, it is hoped, are presented with understandable choices and the winner in the general election with sufficient support to govern effectively.

> Section 6830(d) ... carries very similar credentials. It protects the direct primary process by refusing to recognize independent candidates who do not make early plans to leave a party and take the alternative course to the ballot. It works against independent candidacies prompted by short-range political goals, pique, or personal quarrel. It is also a substantial barrier to a party fielding an "independent" candidate to capture and bleed off votes in the general election that might well go to another party.

In *Wood v. Meadows*, 207 F.3d 708 (4th Cir. 2000), the court rejected a challenge to a Virginia requirement that nominating petitions for independent candidates be filed by the date of the primary election, which occurred on the second Tuesday in June, approximately 150 days before the general election. Applying the balancing test of *Anderson v. Celebrezze*, the appellate court held that Virginia "has articulated legitimate interests justifying its reasonable, nondiscriminatory ballot access requirements." The reasons Virginia put forward included "administrative convenience," as well as "limiting the number of candidates on the general election ballot, requiring those candidates who will be included to demonstrate a preliminary showing of sufficient voter support, and designating the primary election date as the date for determining the full field of candidates."

The Virginia deadline requires that independent candidacies be mounted before the party nominees are determined. Suppose Candidate *A* in a contested party primary supports the views of a particular social movement. If *A* is defeated in the primary, the movement would like to mount an independent candidacy. However, if *A* becomes the party nominee, the last thing the movement would want would be for an independent candidate to split the pro-movement vote with *A*. *Storer v. Brown* upholds a rule intended to prevent "sore losers" within the party from challenging the party's nominee in the general election. Should this result be extended to genuinely independent candidates?

In *Council of Alternative Political Parties v. Hooks*, 179 F.3d 64 (3d Cir. 1999), the Third Circuit upheld a New Jersey deadline for independent and minor party candidates on the date of the primary election similar to the Virginia deadline. The court rejected the plaintiffs' argument that potential independent and minor party candidates should be able to make decisions based on knowledge of the outcome of major party primary contests. The court said that permitting independent and minor party candidacy decisions to be made after the major parties chose their candidates in primaries would be to give the independent and minor party candidates preferential treatment.

10. *Qualifications and ballot access.* The *Williams* line of cases that has been described in this section assumes that the candidate is eligible to be elected to and serve in the office in question. States typically have leeway to set actual qualifications for state and local office, though not without limit. Thus, in *Turner v. Fouche*, 396 U.S. 346 (1970), the Court ruled that a requirement that appointed school board members be freeholders had no rational basis and therefore violated the Equal Protection Clause.

A plurality of the Supreme Court may have obscured the distinction between qualifications for office and requirements for access to the ballot in *Clements v. Fashing*, 457 U.S. 957 (1982). The issues in this case included an equal protection challenge to a Texas constitutional provision that disqualified judges from serving in the state legislature during the judicial term for which they had been elected, even if they were willing to resign their judicial offices. Justice Rehnquist, writing for a four-member plurality, summarized the holdings of the ballot access cases and observed that "[n]ot all ballot access restrictions require 'heightened' equal protection scrutiny.' Because the disqualification in question did not impose "special burdens" based on political affiliation or viewpoint, and because the plurality regarded it as imposing merely a reasonable "waiting period" on judges who wanted to run for the legislature, the provision needed only a rational basis to be upheld. That rational basis was found in Texas' interest in discouraging judges from vacating their terms of office.

Was the plurality correct to regard this issue as controlled by the ballot access decisions? (Justice Stevens provided a fifth vote to uphold the Texas provision, but without referring to any of the *Williams* line of cases.) If Texas permitted judges to run for and serve in the state legislature before their judicial terms expired, but required that they run as write-in candidates, would the exclusion from the ballot be upheld on the authority of *Clements*?

11. Ballot access aficionados have their very own newsletter. *Ballot Access News*, available at nominal cost, is a useful source of information on legislative and judicial developments relating not only to ballot access, but also to a range of election law issues. For more information, visit <http://www.ballot-access.org>.

II. Minor Parties, Public Benefits, and Laws Favoring the Two-Party System

Ballot access has probably been the issue most frequently litigated by third parties and independent candidates in recent decades, but it has by no means been the only issue litigated. In this section, we shall consider the extent to which such parties and candidates may be entitled to a share of other benefits sometimes provided by the government and the extent to which the government can enact laws favoring the two-party system.

In 1974, Congress passed comprehensive amendments to the previously enacted Federal Election Campaign Act (FECA). The amended FECA provided for campaign disclosure, a variety of limits on campaign contributions and expenditures, and public financing of presidential campaigns. Nearly every significant provision of the Act was quickly challenged in *Buckley v. Valeo*. In later chapters we shall consider in some detail both the amended FECA and the *Buckley* decision. In this chapter, we consider only the portion of *Buckley* responding to the claim that the presidential public financing provisions unconstitutionally discriminated against third parties and independent candidates.

Buckley v. Valeo
424 U.S. 1, 85–109 (1976)

PER CURIAM ...

III. PUBLIC FINANCING OF PRESIDENTIAL ELECTION CAMPAIGNS

A series of statutes for the public financing of Presidential election campaigns produced the scheme now found in 26 U.S.C. §6096 and Subtitle H of the Internal Revenue Code of 1954....

A. Summary of Subtitle H

Section 9006 establishes a Presidential Election Campaign Fund (Fund), financed from general revenues in the aggregate amount designated by individual taxpayers, under §6096, who on their income tax returns may authorize payment to the Fund of one dollar of their tax liability in the case of an individual return or two dollars in the case of a joint return.[h] The Fund consists of three separate accounts to finance (1) party nominating conventions, (2) general election campaigns, and (3) primary campaigns.

Chapter 95 of Title 26, which concerns financing of party nominating conventions and general election campaigns, distinguishes among "major," "minor," and "new" parties. A major party is defined as a party whose candidate for President in the most recent election received 25% or more of the popular vote. A minor party is defined as a party whose candidate received at least 5% but less than 25% of the vote at the most recent election. All other parties are new parties, including both newly created parties and those receiving less than 5% of the vote in the last election.

Major parties are entitled to $2,000,000 to defray their national committee Presidential nominating convention expenses, must limit total expenditures to that amount, and may not use any of this money to benefit a particular candidate or delegate. A minor

---

h. Since the 1994 tax year, taxpayers have been able to designate three dollars on an individual return and six dollars on a joint return. — EDS.

party receives a portion of the major-party entitlement determined by the ratio of the votes received by the party's candidate in the last election to the average of the votes received by the major parties' candidates. The amounts given to the parties and the expenditure limit are adjusted for inflation, using 1974 as the base year. No financing is provided for new parties, nor is there any express provision for financing independent candidates or parties not holding a convention.

For expenses in the general election campaign, §9004(a)(1) entitles each major-party candidate to $20,000,000. This amount is also adjusted for inflation. To be eligible for funds the candidate must pledge not to incur expenses in excess of the entitlement under §9004(a)(1) and not to accept private contributions.... Minor-party candidates are also entitled to funding, again based on the ratio of the vote received by the party's candidate in the preceding election to the average of the major-party candidates. Minor-party candidates must certify that they will not incur campaign expenses in excess of the major-party entitlement and that they will accept private contributions only to the extent needed to make up the difference between that amount and the public funding grant. New-party candidates receive no money prior to the general election, but any candidate receiving 5% or more of the popular vote in the election is entitled to post-election payments according to the formula applicable to minor-party candidates. Similarly, minor-party candidates are entitled to post-election funds if they receive a greater percentage of the average major-party vote than their party's candidate did in the preceding election; the amount of such payments is the difference between the entitlement based on the preceding election and that based on the actual vote in the current election. A further eligibility requirement for minor- and new-party candidates is that the candidate's name must appear on the ballot, or electors pledged to the candidate must be on the ballot, in at least 10 States.

Chapter 96 establishes a third account in the Fund, the Presidential Primary Matching Payment Account. This funding is intended to aid campaigns by candidates seeking Presidential nomination "by a political party" in "primary elections." The threshold eligibility requirement is that the candidate raise at least $5,000 in each of 20 States, counting only the first $250 from each person contributing to the candidate. In addition, the candidate must agree to abide by [overall campaign spending limits]. Funding is provided according to a matching formula: each qualified candidate is entitled to a sum equal to the total private contributions received, disregarding contributions from any person to the extent that total contributions to the candidate by that person exceed $250. Payments to any candidate under Chapter 96 may not exceed 50% of the overall expenditure ceiling accepted by the candidate.

B. Constitutionality of Subtitle H

Appellants argue that Subtitle H is invalid [among other reasons] because Subtitle H invidiously discriminates against certain interests in violation of the Due Process Clause of the Fifth Amendment. We find no merit in these contentions....

Equal protection analysis in the Fifth Amendment area is the same as that under the Fourteenth Amendment. In several situations concerning the electoral process, the principle has been developed that restrictions on access to the electoral process must survive exacting scrutiny. The restriction can be sustained only if it furthers a "vital" governmental interest, *American Party of Texas v. White*, that is "achieved by a means that does not unfairly or unnecessarily burden either a minority party's or an individual candidate's equally important interest in the continued availability of political opportunity." *Lubin v. Panish*. These cases, however, dealt primarily with state laws requiring a candidate to satisfy certain requirements in order to have his name appear on the ballot. These were, of course, direct burdens not only on the candidate's ability to run for office but also on the voter's ability to voice preferences regarding representative government and contemporary issues. In contrast, the denial of public financing to some Presidential candidates is not restrictive of voters' rights and less restrictive of candidates'.[128] Subtitle H does not prevent any candidate from getting on the ballot or any voter from casting a vote for the candidate of his choice; the inability, if any, of minor-party candidates to wage effective campaigns will derive not from lack of public funding but from their inability to raise private contributions. Any disadvantage suffered by operation of the eligibility formulae under Subtitle H is thus limited to the claimed denial of the enhancement of opportunity to communicate with the electorate that the formulae afford eligible candidates. But eligible candidates suffer a countervailing denial. As we more fully develop later, acceptance of public financing entails voluntary acceptance of an expenditure ceiling. Noneligible candidates are not subject to that limitation.[129] Accordingly, we conclude that public financing is generally less restrictive of access to the electoral process than the ballot-access regulations dealt with in prior cases. In any event, Congress enacted Subtitle H in furtherance of sufficiently important governmental interests and has not unfairly or unnecessarily burdened the political opportunity of any party or candidate.

It cannot be gainsaid that public financing as a means of eliminating the improper influence of large private contributions furthers a significant governmental interest. In addition, the limits on contributions necessarily increase the burden of fundraising, and Congress properly regarded public financing as an appropriate means of relieving major-party Presidential candidates from the rigors of soliciting private contributions. The States have also been held to have important interests in limiting places on the ballot to those candidates who demonstrate substantial popular support. Congress' interest in not funding hopeless candidacies with large sums of public money necessarily justifies the withholding of public assistance from candidates without significant public support. Thus, Congress may legitimately require "some preliminary showing of a significant modicum of support," *Jenness*, as an eligibility requirement for public funds. This requirement also serves the important public interest against providing artificial incentives to "splintered parties and unrestrained factionalism." *Storer*.

At the same time Congress recognized the constitutional restraints against inhibition of the present opportunity of minor parties to become major political entities if they obtain widespread support. As the Court of Appeals said, "provisions for public funding of Presidential campaigns ... could operate to give an unfair advantage to established parties, thus reducing, to the nation's detriment, ... the 'potential fluidity of American political life.'"

---

128. Appellants maintain that denial of funding is a more severe restriction than denial of access to the ballot, because write-in candidates can win elections, but candidates without funds cannot. New parties will be unfinanced, however, only if they are unable to get private financial support, which presumably reflects a general lack of public support for the party. Public financing of some candidates does not make private fundraising for others any more difficult; indeed, the elimination of private contributions to major-party Presidential candidates might make more private money available to minority candidates.

129. Appellants dispute the relevance of this answer to their argument on the ground that they will not be able to raise money to equal major-party spending. As a practical matter, however, Subtitle H does not enhance the major parties' ability to campaign; it substitutes public funding for what the parties would raise privately and additionally imposes an expenditure limit. If a party cannot raise funds privately, there are legitimate reasons not to provide public funding, which would effectively facilitate hopeless candidacies.

1. General Election Campaign Financing

Appellants insist that Chapter 95 falls short of the constitutional requirement in that its provisions supply larger, and equal, sums to candidates of major parties, use prior vote levels as the sole criterion for pre-election funding, limit new-party candidates to post-election funds, and deny any funds to candidates of parties receiving less than 5% of the vote. These provisions, it is argued, are fatal to the validity of the scheme, because they work invidious discrimination against minor and new parties in violation of the Fifth Amendment. We disagree.[131]

As conceded by appellants, the Constitution does not require Congress to treat all declared candidates the same for public financing purposes. As we said in *Jenness*, "there are obvious differences in kind between the needs and potentials of a political party with historically established broad support, on the one hand, and a new or small political organization on the other.... Sometimes the grossest discrimination can lie in treating things that are different as though they were exactly alike, a truism well illustrated in *Williams*." Since the Presidential elections of 1856 and 1860, when the Whigs were replaced as a major party by the Republicans, no third party has posed a credible threat to the two major parties in Presidential elections. Third parties have been completely incapable of matching the major parties' ability to raise money and win elections. Congress was, of course, aware of this fact of American life, and thus was justified in providing both major parties full funding and all other parties only a percentage of the major-party entitlement.[133] Identical treatment of all parties, on the other hand, "would not only make it easy to raid the United States Treasury, it would also artificially foster the proliferation of splinter parties." The Constitution does not require the Government to "finance the efforts of every nascent political group," *American Party of Texas*, merely because Congress chose to finance the efforts of the major parties.

Furthermore, appellants have made no showing that the election funding plan disadvantages nonmajor parties by operating to reduce their strength below that attained without any public financing. First, such parties are free to raise money from private sources, and by our holding today new parties are freed from any expenditure limits, although admittedly those limits may be a largely academic matter to them. But since any major-party candidate accepting public financing of a campaign voluntarily assents to a spending ceiling, other candidates will be able to spend more in relation to the major-party candidates. The relative position of minor parties that do qualify to receive some public funds because they received 5% of the vote in the previous Presidential election is also enhanced. Public funding for candidates of major parties is intended as a substitute for private contributions; but for minor-party candidates such assistance may be viewed as a supplement to private contributions since these candidates may continue to solicit private funds up to the applicable spending limit. Thus, we conclude that the general election funding system does not work an invidious discrimination against candidates of nonmajor parties.

---

131. The allegations of invidious discrimination are based on the claim that Subtitle H is facially invalid; since the public financing provisions have never been in operation, appellants are unable to offer factual proof that the scheme is discriminatory in its effect. In rejecting appellants' arguments, we of course do not rule out the possibility of concluding in some future case, upon an appropriate factual demonstration, that the public financing system invidiously discriminates against nonmajor parties.

133. Appellants suggest that a less discriminatory formula would be to grant full funding to the candidate of the party getting the most votes in the last election and then give money to candidates of other parties based on their showing in the last election relative to the "leading" party. That formula, however, might unfairly favor incumbents, since their major-party challengers would receive less financial assistance.

Appellants challenge reliance on the vote in past elections as the basis for determining eligibility. That challenge is foreclosed, however, by our holding in *Jenness*, that popular vote totals in the last election are a proper measure of public support. And Congress was not obliged to select instead from among appellants' suggested alternatives. Congress could properly regard the means chosen as preferable, since the alternative of petition drives presents cost and administrative problems in validating signatures, and the alternative of opinion polls might be thought inappropriate since it would involve a Government agency in the business of certifying polls or conducting its own investigation of support for various candidates, in addition to serious problems with reliability.

Appellants next argue, relying on the ballot-access decisions of this Court, that the absence of any alternative means of obtaining pre-election funding renders the scheme unjustifiably restrictive of minority political interests. Appellants' reliance on the ballot-access decisions is misplaced. To be sure, the regulation sustained in *Jenness*, for example, incorporated alternative means of qualifying for the ballot, and the lack of an alternative was a defect in the scheme struck down in *Lubin*. To suggest, however, that the constitutionality of Subtitle H therefore hinges solely on whether some alternative is afforded overlooks the rationale of the operative constitutional principles. Our decisions finding a need for an alternative means turn on the nature and extent of the burden imposed in the absence of available alternatives. We have earlier stated our view that Chapter 95 is far less burdensome upon and restrictive of constitutional rights than the regulations involved in the ballot-access cases. Moreover, expenditure limits for major parties and candidates may well improve the chances of nonmajor parties and their candidates to receive funds and increase their spending. Any risk of harm to minority interests is speculative due to our present lack of knowledge of the practical effects of public financing and cannot overcome the force of the governmental interests against use of public money to foster frivolous candidacies, create a system of splintered parties, and encourage unrestrained factionalism.

Appellants' reliance on the alternative-means analyses of the ballot-access cases generally fails to recognize a significant distinction from the instant case. The primary goal of all candidates is to carry on a successful campaign by communicating to the voters' persuasive reasons for electing them. In some of the ballot-access cases the States afforded candidates alternative means for qualifying for the ballot, a step in any campaign that, with rare exceptions, is essential to successful effort. Chapter 95 concededly provides only one method of obtaining pre-election financing; such funding is, however, not as necessary as being on the ballot. Plainly, campaigns can be successfully carried out by means other than public financing; they have been up to this date, and this avenue is still open to all candidates. And, after all, the important achievements of minority political groups in furthering the development of American democracy were accomplished without the help of public funds. Thus, the limited participation or nonparticipation of nonmajor parties or candidates in public funding does not unconstitutionally disadvantage them.

Of course, nonmajor parties and their candidates may qualify for post-election participation in public funding and in that sense the claimed discrimination is not total. Appellants contend, however, that the benefit of any such participation is illusory due to §9004(c), which bars the use of the money for any purpose other than paying campaign expenses or repaying loans that had been used to defray such expenses. The only meaningful use for post-election funds is thus to repay loans; but loans, except from national banks, are "contributions" subject to the general limitations on contributions. Further, they argue, loans are not readily available to nonmajor parties or candidates before elections to finance their campaigns. Availability of post-election funds therefore assertedly gives them nothing. But in the nature of things the willingness of lenders to make loans will depend upon the pre-election probability that the candidate and his party will attract 5% or more of the voters. When a reasonable prospect of such support appears, the party and candidate may be an acceptable loan risk since the prospect of post-election participation in public funding will be good.

Finally, appellants challenge the validity of the 5% threshold requirement for general election funding. They argue that, since most state regulations governing ballot access have threshold requirements well below 5%, and because in their view the 5% requirement here is actually stricter than that upheld in *Jenness*, the requirement is unreasonable. We have already concluded that the restriction under Chapter 95 is generally less burdensome than ballot-access regulations. Further, the Georgia provision sustained in *Jenness* required the candidate to obtain the signatures of 5% of all eligible voters, without regard to party. To be sure, the public funding formula does not permit anyone who voted for another party in the last election to be part of a candidate's 5%. But under Chapter 95 a Presidential candidate needs only 5% or more of the actual vote, not the larger universe of eligible voters. As a result, we cannot say that Chapter 95 is numerically more, or less, restrictive than the regulation in *Jenness*. In any event, the choice of the percentage requirement that best accommodates the competing interests involved was for Congress to make. Without any doubt a range of formulations would sufficiently protect the public fisc and not foster factionalism, and would also recognize the public interest in the fluidity of our political affairs. We cannot say that Congress' choice falls without the permissible range.

2. Nominating Convention Financing

The foregoing analysis and reasoning sustaining general election funding apply in large part to convention funding under Chapter 95 and suffice to support our rejection of appellants' challenge to these provisions. Funding of party conventions has increasingly been derived from large private contributions, and the governmental interest in eliminating this reliance is as vital as in the case of private contributions to individual candidates.... We therefore conclude that appellants' constitutional challenge to the provisions for funding nominating conventions must also be rejected.

3. Primary Election Campaign Financing

Appellants' final challenge is to the constitutionality of Chapter 96, which provides funding of primary campaigns. They contend that these provisions are constitutionally invalid (1) because they do not provide funds for candidates not running in party primaries and (2) because the eligibility formula actually increases the influence of money on the electoral process. In not providing assistance to candidates who do not enter party primaries, Congress has merely chosen to limit at this time the reach of the reforms encompassed in Chapter 96.... The choice to limit matching funds to candidates running in primaries may reflect that concern about large private contributions to candidates centered on primary races and that there is no historical evidence of similar abuses involving contributions to candidates who engage in petition drives to qualify for state ballots. Moreover, assistance to candidates and nonmajor parties forced to resort to petition drives to gain ballot access implicates the policies against fostering frivolous candidacies, creating a system of splintered parties, and encouraging unrestrained factionalism.

The eligibility requirements in Chapter 96 are surely not an unreasonable way to measure popular support for a candidate, accomplishing the objective of limiting subsidization to those candidates with a substantial chance of being nominated....

For the reasons stated, we reject appellants' claims that Subtitle H is facially uncon-stitutional.

Notes and Questions

1. Should the Court have struck down the public financing system on the ground that it was unfair to new parties? See Marlene Arnold Nicholson, *Buckley v. Valeo: The Constitutionality of the Federal Election Campaign Act Amendments of 1974*, 1977 WISCONSIN LAW REVIEW 323, 363:

> One of the most persuasive arguments against the allocation formula is its discrimination against new political parties. A new party could have the support of 5 percent of the electorate, or even much more, but would receive no funding from the government because of the lack of a showing of support at the previous general presidential election. Although the new party may be entitled to a grant after the election, funds will only be dispersed to such a party in the amount of outstanding debts. Therefore, the new party must gamble that it will obtain 5 percent of the vote and find creditors also willing to gamble. The new party is thus caught in what has been described as a "Catch-22" situation: it cannot obtain public funding without a showing of electoral support, but it may not be able to get electoral support without public funding.

The appellants, who were challenging the statute, argued that this problem could have been solved by permitting eligibility for receipt of public funding to be established by petition. Nicholson criticizes the Court for rejecting this argument:

> When considering whether a means other than prior electoral support would have been a less restrictive alternative, the opinion did refer to the various possible alternatives and the major objections to them. However, the Court did not take upon itself the task of second-guessing Congress as to whether the objections to the alternative means were substantial enough to outweigh the burdens upon the first amendment interests of third parties created by the use of prior electoral support as the funding criterion. One might question whether such deference to Congress was appropriate given the first amendment rights at stake....
>
> The alternative of petition signatures as a means of addressing the problem of new parties was largely ignored in Appellees' briefs, other than a conclusory statement that it was not feasible. If Appellees had the burden of demonstrating "the absence of less burdensome means," it does not appear that the burden was met, at least not with respect to the use of petitions. The Court itself referred to petitions as presenting "cost and administrative problems in validating signatures." However, the benefits of such a system seem so great that such problems could perhaps be tolerated. The procedure could be used both in the general election and in the primary. Formulas which discriminate against third parties would not be necessary. The problem of lack of funding for new parties could be dealt with.

Id. at 367–70.

2. Addressing what is perhaps a more fundamental question, Nicholson challenges what the Court described as "the important public interest against providing artificial incentives to 'splintered parties and unrestrained factionalism.'" Nicholson writes:

> Evidently it was thought that the availability of funds on a more liberal basis to third parties would encourage persons to split from the major parties and

form their own parties in situations where, but for the availability of funds, such factionalization would not take place. However, it seems more likely that the present statute is an artificial influence which actually discourages factionalization, because of burdens upon parties not qualifying for public subsidies. A more liberal funding formula might merely compensate for the disincentives to factionalization created by contribution limitations and disclosure laws. It seems clear from the legislative history of the Act that at least some members of Congress purposely sought to protect the two-party system not just from artificial incentives to factionalism, but also from the old fashioned natural factionalism, which has disturbed the major parties at infrequent intervals in the past....

The only concern voiced by the majority opinion with respect to third parties was that the subsidies must not inhibit "the present opportunity of minority parties to become major political entities if they obtain widespread support." Apparently the Court concluded that it had not been proven that the subsidy provisions would function in such a manner. It should be noted, however, that the Court showed no solicitude for parties and candidates who have no realistic chance of gaining widespread support. The Court ignored the fact that even "hopeless candidacies" serve important first amendment functions and are also subject to other restraints under the 1974 legislation which inhibit the performance of such functions.

Id. at 364–66.

3. Should the Court have struck down the matching requirement for eligibility to receive public funding in presidential primaries? Writing before the *Buckley* decision, Joel L. Fleishman, *The 1974 Federal Election Campaign Act Amendments: The Shortcomings of Good Intentions*, 1975 DUKE LAW JOURNAL 851, 886–89, argued that the matching requirement was unconstitutional in the absence of an alternative method of qualification, such as petition signatures:

Despite its simplicity and reliability..., a monetary eligibility criterion has a serious constitutional flaw. Instead of manifesting general public support for a contender, it reflects a candidate's support among those who can afford to spend discretionary income or capital on politics—a sizable, but nonetheless minority, proportion of the population. In view of the Court's holdings and language in the filing fee cases[,] it is difficult to see how an exclusively monetary eligibility criterion could be sustained against an equal protection attack....

The Court's heavy reliance [in the filing fee cases] on the interests of a candidate's prospective supporters and on their socio-economic background is even more appropriate with respect to the subsidy-qualifying mechanism than it is to filing fees. To qualify for the subsidy, a candidate must raise the necessary funds from his supporters. If his supporters are without means sufficient to contribute, it is *their* indigency which is being discriminated against in the political arena, not *his*.

Nicholson, *supra*, at 351, adds:

Certainly matching grants are an effective means of screening frivolous candidates from public funding, but they are grossly overinclusive. Also screened out in the process are candidates supported by the poor.

4. One independent candidate, John Anderson, was paid $4.2 million after the 1980 election because his 6.6 percent of the popular vote exceeded the five percent threshold

for general election funding. Because he exceeded that threshold, Anderson would also have been eligible to receive pre-election public funding in 1984, but he chose not to be a candidate that year. Reform party candidate Ross Perot received over $29 million in public funds in 1996. In 2000, the FEC awarded $12.6 million to Reform Party candidate Pat Buchanan, after an initial question over whether Buchanan or another candidate was the true Reform Party standard-bearer. See News Release, FEC, FEC Certifies General Election Public Funds for Buchanan-Foster Ticket (Sept. 14, 2000).

5. When state statutes have authorized provision of voter registration lists to the major parties for use in campaigning and get-out-the-vote drives, federal courts have ruled that election officials are constitutionally required to provide the lists to minor parties on the same terms. See *Libertarian Party of Indiana v. Marion County Board of Voter Registration*, 778 F.Supp. 1458 (S.D. Ind. 1991); *Socialist Workers Party v. Rockefeller*, 314 F.Supp. 984 (S.D.N.Y. 1970), aff'd., 400 U.S. 806 (1970).

A statute passed by Congress in 1978 permitted national and state committees of political parties to send mail at subsidized postage rates. In 1980, Congress amended the statute so that only parties whose presidential candidate in the most recent election had received at least five percent of the vote were eligible for the subsidy. In *Greenberg v. Bolger*, 497 F.Supp. 756 (E.D.N.Y. 1980), this exclusion of small parties from the postal subsidy was found to violate both the First Amendment and the Equal Protection Clause.

Is *Greenberg* consistent with *Buckley*? The *Greenberg* opinion pointed out some salient differences between the two cases:

> The definitions [establishing eligibility for the postal subsidy] are derived from the Campaign Fund Act.... But, unlike the Campaign Fund Act, the 1978 Act [as amended in 1980] does not require major or minor parties to accept expenditure or contribution limitations as a condition of the receipt of public funds in the form of a postal subsidy. Moreover, the 1978 Act unlike the Campaign Fund Act makes no provision for the possible reimbursement of a political party unable to qualify for advance funds given past results (or the lack of results in the case of a newly created party), but making the requisite showing in a current election. In addition, the 5 percent requirement reflects a concern for nationwide impact neglecting the local or statewide success that some third parties enjoy.

6. Campaign finance laws are not the only laws that may (intentionally or not) benefit or hinder third parties. In New York, the Liberal Party since the 1940s and the Conservative Party since the 1960s have played a more prominent role than third parties in other states. An important reason is that in New York, individuals may appear on the ballot as the candidate of more than one party. Thus, in New York, the Liberal Party often nominates the same candidate as the Democrats and the Conservative Party often nominates the same candidate as the Republicans. These minor parties typically receive enough votes so that major party politicians have some incentive to prove themselves sufficiently "pure" ideologically to retain the support of the relevant minor party. Most states have "anti-fusion" laws that either prevent candidates from appearing on the ballot under the label of more than one party or otherwise prevent minor parties from following the New York strategy. See generally Daniel A. Mazmanian, THIRD PARTIES IN PRESIDENTIAL ELECTIONS 115–135 (1974); Howard A. Scarrow, *Duverger's Law, Fusion, and the Decline of American "Third" Parties*, 39 WESTERN POLITICAL QUARTERLY 634 (1986). In 1997, the Supreme Court considered a constitutional attack on Minnesota's anti-fusion law, and in the process may have made some broad pronouncements about the acceptability of laws favoring the two-party system.

Timmons v. Twin Cities Area New Party
520 U.S. 351 (1997)

CHIEF JUSTICE REHNQUIST delivered the opinion of the Court.

Most States prohibit multiple-party, or "fusion," candidacies for elected office.[1] The Minnesota laws challenged in this case prohibit a candidate from appearing on the ballot as the candidate of more than one party. Minn. Stat. §§204B.06, subd. 1(b) and 204B.04, subd. 2 (1994). We hold that such a prohibition does not violate the First and Fourteenth Amendments to the United States Constitution.

Respondent is a chartered chapter of the national New Party. Petitioners are Minnesota election officials. In April 1994, Minnesota State Representative Andy Dawkins was running unopposed in the Minnesota Democratic-Farmer-Labor Party's (DFL) primary.[2] That same month, New Party members chose Dawkins as their candidate for the same office in the November 1994 general election. Neither Dawkins nor the DFL objected,[i] and Dawkins signed the required affidavit of candidacy for the New Party. Minnesota, however, prohibits fusion candidacies. Because Dawkins had already filed as a candidate for the DFL's nomination, local election officials refused to accept the New Party's nominating petition....

Fusion was a regular feature of Gilded Age of American politics. Particularly in the West and Midwest, candidates of issue-oriented parties like the Grangers, Independents, Greenbackers, and Populists often succeeded through fusion with the Democrats, and vice versa. Republicans, for their part, sometimes arranged fusion candidacies in the South, as part of a general strategy of encouraging and exploiting divisions within the dominant Democratic Party.

Fusion was common in part because political parties, rather than local or state governments, printed and distributed their own ballots. These ballots contained only the names of a particular party's candidates, and so a voter could drop his party's ticket in the ballot box without even knowing that his party's candidates were supported by other parties as well. But after the 1888 presidential election, which was widely regarded as having been plagued by fraud, many States moved to the "Australian ballot system." Under that system, an official ballot, containing the names of all the candidates legally nominated by all the parties, was printed at public expense and distributed by public officials at polling places. By 1896, use of the Australian ballot was widespread. During the same period, many States enacted other election-related reforms, including bans on fusion candidacies. Minnesota banned fusion in 1901. This trend has continued and, in this century, fusion has become the exception, not the rule. Today, multiple-party candidacies are permitted in just a few States, and fusion plays a significant role only in New York....

When deciding whether a state election law violates First and Fourteenth Amendment associational rights, we weigh the "character and magnitude" of the burden the State's rule

---

1. "Fusion," also called "cross-filing" or "multiple-party nomination," is "the electoral support of a single set of candidates by two or more parties." Argersinger, "A Place on the Ballot": Fusion Politics and Antifusion Laws, 85 American History Review 287, 288 (1980).

2. The DFL is the product of a 1944 merger between Minnesota's Farmer-Labor Party and the Democratic Party, and is a "major party" under Minnesota law.

i. Is the constitutional attack on the antifusion law stronger if the DFL consents to Dawkins being both its own candidate and that of the New Party? If so, should the fact that the DFL, as Chief Justice Rehnquist says, did not object, be regarded as the equivalent of consent? Since the statute prohibited the fusion candidacy in any event, there was neither a reason for nor a mechanism for the DFL to register a formal objection. —Eds.

imposes on those rights against the interests the State contends justify that burden, and consider the extent to which the State's concerns make the burden necessary. *Burdick*. Regulations imposing severe burdens on plaintiffs' rights must be narrowly tailored and advance a compelling state interest. Lesser burdens, however, trigger less exacting review, and a State's "important regulatory interests" will usually be enough to justify "reasonable, nondiscriminatory restrictions." *Burdick*. No bright line separates permissible election-related regulation from unconstitutional infringements on First Amendment freedoms. *Storer*.

The New Party's claim that it has a right to select its own candidate is uncontroversial, so far as it goes. See, *e.g.*, *Cousins*. That is, the New Party, and not someone else, has the right to select the New Party's "standard bearer." It does not follow, though, that a party is absolutely entitled to have its nominee appear on the ballot as that party's candidate. A particular candidate might be ineligible for office, unwilling to serve, or, as here, another party's candidate. That a particular individual may not appear on the ballot as a particular party's candidate does not severely burden that party's association rights.

The New Party relies on *Eu* and *Tashjian*.... But while *Tashjian* and *Eu* involved regulation of political parties' internal affairs and core associational activities, Minnesota's fusion ban does not. The ban, which applies to major and minor parties alike, simply precludes one party's candidate from appearing on the ballot, as that party's candidate, if already nominated by another party. Respondent is free to try to convince Representative Dawkins to be the New Party's, not the DFL's, candidate. Whether the party still wants to endorse a candidate who, because of the fusion ban, will not appear on the ballot as the party's candidate, is up to the party.

The Court of Appeals also held that Minnesota's laws "keep the New Party from developing consensual political alliances and thus broadening the base of public participation in and support for its activities." The burden on the party was, the court held, severe because "[h]istory shows that minor parties have played a significant role in the electoral system where multiple party nomination is legal, but have no meaningful influence where multiple party nomination is banned." In the view of the Court of Appeals, Minnesota's fusion ban forces members of the New Party to make a "no-win choice" between voting for "candidates with no realistic chance of winning, defect[ing] from their party and vot[ing] for a major party candidate who does, or declin[ing] to vote at all."

But Minnesota has not directly precluded minor political parties from developing and organizing. Nor has Minnesota excluded a particular group of citizens, or a political party, from participation in the election process. The New Party remains free to endorse whom it likes, to ally itself with others, to nominate candidates for office, and to spread its message to all who will listen.

The Court of Appeals emphasized its belief that, without fusion-based alliances, minor parties cannot thrive. This is a predictive judgment which is by no means self-evident.[9]

---

9. Between the First and Second World Wars, for example, various radical, agrarian, and labor-oriented parties thrived, without fusion, in the Midwest. See generally R. Vallely, Radicalism in the States (1989). One of these parties, Minnesota's Farmer-Labor Party, displaced the Democratic Party as the Republicans' primary opponent in Minnesota during the 1930's. As one historian has noted: "The Minnesota Farmer-Labor Party elected its candidates to the governorship on four occasions, to the U.S. Senate in five elections, and to the U.S. House in twenty-five campaigns.... Never less than Minnesota's second strongest party, in 1936 Farmer-Laborites dominated state politics.... The Farmer-Labor Party was a success despite its independence of America's two dominant national parties and despite the sometimes bold anticapitalist rhetoric of its platforms." J. Haynes, Dubious Alliance 9 (1984). It appears that factionalism within the Farmer-Labor Party, the popular successes of New Deal programs and ideology, and the gradual movement of political power from the States to the Na-

But, more importantly, the supposed benefits of fusion to minor parties does not require that Minnesota permit it. Many features of our political system — *e.g.*, single-member districts, "first past the post" elections, and the high costs of campaigning — make it difficult for third parties to succeed in American politics. But the Constitution does not require States to permit fusion any more than it requires them to move to proportional-representation elections or public financing of campaigns.

The New Party contends that the fusion ban burdens its "right ... to communicate its choice of nominees on the ballot on terms equal to those offered other parties, and the right of the party's supporters and other voters to receive that information," and insists that communication on the ballot of a party's candidate choice is a "critical source of information for the great majority of voters ... who ... rely upon party 'labels' as a voting guide."

It is true that Minnesota's fusion ban prevents the New Party from using the ballot to communicate to the public that it supports a particular candidate who is already another party's candidate. In addition, the ban shuts off one possible avenue a party might use to send a message to its preferred *candidate* because, with fusion, a candidate who wins an election on the basis of two parties' votes will likely know more — if the parties' votes are counted separately — about the particular wishes and ideals of his constituency. We are unpersuaded, however, by the party's contention that it has a right to use the ballot itself to send a particularized message, to its candidate and to the voters, about the nature of its support for the candidate. Ballots serve primarily to elect candidates, not as forums for political expression. See *Burdick*. Like all parties in Minnesota, the New Party is able to use the ballot to communicate information about itself and its candidate to the voters, so long as that candidate is not already someone else's candidate. The party retains great latitude in its ability to communicate ideas to voters and candidates through its participation in the campaign, and party members may campaign for, endorse, and vote for their preferred candidate even if he is listed on the ballot as another party's candidate.

In sum, Minnesota's laws do not restrict the ability of the New Party and its members to endorse, support, or vote for anyone they like. The laws do not directly limit the party's access to the ballot. They are silent on parties' internal structure, governance, and policymaking. Instead, these provisions reduce the universe of potential candidates who may appear on the ballot as the party's nominee only by ruling out those few individuals who both have already agreed to be another party's candidate and also, if forced to choose, themselves prefer that other party. They also limit, slightly, the party's ability to send a message to the voters and to its preferred candidates. We conclude that the burdens Minnesota imposes on the party's First and Fourteenth Amendment associational rights — though not trivial — are not severe.

The Court of Appeals determined that Minnesota's fusion ban imposed "severe" burdens on the New Party's associational rights, and so it required the State to show that the ban was narrowly tailored to serve compelling state interests. We disagree; given the burdens imposed, the bar is not so high. Instead, the State's asserted regulatory interests need only be "sufficiently weighty to justify the limitation" imposed on the party's rights. *Norman v. Reed*, 502 U.S. 279, 288–289 (1992). Nor do we require elaborate, empirical verification of the weightiness of the State's asserted justifications. See *Munro*.

---

tional Government contributed to the party's decline. Eventually, a much-weakened Farmer-Labor Party merged with the Democrats, forming what is now Minnesota's Democratic-Farmer-Labor Party, in 1944.

... Minnesota argues here that its fusion ban is justified by its interests in avoiding voter confusion, promoting candidate competition (by reserving limited ballot space for opposing candidates), preventing electoral distortions and ballot manipulations, and discouraging party splintering and "unrestrained factionalism."

States certainly have an interest in protecting the integrity, fairness, and efficiency of their ballots and election processes as means for electing public officials. Petitioners contend that a candidate or party could easily exploit fusion as a way of associating his or its name with popular slogans and catchphrases. For example, members of a major party could decide that a powerful way of "sending a message" via the ballot would be for various factions of that party to nominate the major party's candidate as the candidate for the newly-formed "No New Taxes," "Conserve Our Environment," and "Stop Crime Now" parties. In response, an opposing major party would likely instruct its factions to nominate that party's candidate as the "Fiscal Responsibility," "Healthy Planet," and "Safe Streets" parties' candidate.

Whether or not the putative "fusion" candidates' names appeared on one or four ballot lines, such maneuvering would undermine the ballot's purpose by transforming it from a means of choosing candidates to a billboard for political advertising. The New Party responds to this concern, ironically enough, by insisting that the State could avoid such manipulation by adopting more demanding ballot-access standards rather than prohibiting multiple-party nomination. However, as we stated above, because the burdens the fusion ban imposes on the party's associational rights are not severe, the State need not narrowly tailor the means it chooses to promote ballot integrity. The Constitution does not require that Minnesota compromise the policy choices embodied in its ballot-access requirements to accommodate the New Party's fusion strategy.

Relatedly, petitioners urge that permitting fusion would undercut Minnesota's ballot-access regime by allowing minor parties to capitalize on the popularity of another party's candidate, rather than on their own appeal to the voters, in order to secure access to the ballot. That is, voters who might not sign a minor party's nominating petition based on the party's own views and candidates might do so if they viewed the minor party as just another way of nominating the same person nominated by one of the major parties. Thus, Minnesota fears that fusion would enable minor parties, by nominating a major party's candidate, to bootstrap their way to major-party status in the next election and circumvent the State's nominating-petition requirement for minor parties. The State surely has a valid interest in making sure that minor and third parties who are granted access to the ballot are bona fide and actually supported, on their own merits, by those who have provided the statutorily required petition or ballot support.

States also have a strong interest in the stability of their political systems. This interest does not permit a State to completely insulate the two-party system from minor parties' or independent candidates' competition and influence, nor is it a paternalistic license for States to protect political parties from the consequences of their own internal disagreements. That said, the States' interest permits them to enact reasonable election regulations that may, in practice, favor the traditional two-party system, and that temper the destabilizing effects of party-splintering and excessive factionalism. The Constitution permits the Minnesota Legislature to decide that political stability is best served through a healthy two-party system. And while an interest in securing the perceived benefits of a stable two-party system will not justify unreasonably exclusionary restrictions, States need not remove all of the many hurdles third parties face in the American political arena today.

In *Storer,* we upheld a California statute that denied ballot positions to independent candidates who had voted in the immediately preceding primary elections or had a registered party affiliation at any time during the year before the same primary elections. After surveying the relevant caselaw, we "ha[d] no hesitation in sustaining" the party-disaffiliation provisions. We recognized that the provisions were part of a "general state policy aimed at maintaining the integrity of ... the ballot,' and noted that the provision did not discriminate against independent candidates. We concluded that while a "State need not take the course California has, ... California apparently believes with the Founding Fathers that splintered parties and unrestrained factionalism may do significant damage to the fabric of government. See The Federalist No. 10 (Madison). It appears obvious to us that the one-year disaffiliation provision furthers the State's interest in the stability of its political system."[12]

Our decision in *Burdick v. Takushi* is also relevant. There, we upheld Hawaii's ban on write-in voting against a claim that the ban unreasonably infringed on citizens' First and Fourteenth Amendment rights. In so holding, we rejected the petitioner's argument that the ban "deprive[d] him of the opportunity to cast a meaningful ballot," emphasizing that the function of elections is to elect candidates and that "we have repeatedly upheld reasonable, politically neutral regulations that have the effect of channeling expressive activit[ies] at the polls."

Minnesota's fusion ban is far less burdensome than the disaffiliation rule upheld in *Storer*, and is justified by similarly weighty state interests.... Under the California disaffiliation statute at issue in *Storer*, *any* person affiliated with a party at any time during the year leading up to the primary election was absolutely precluded from appearing on the ballot as an independent or as the candidate of another party. Minnesota's fusion ban is not nearly so restrictive; the challenged provisions say nothing about the previous party affiliation of would-be candidates but only require that, in order to appear on the ballot, a candidate not be the nominee of more than one party. California's disaffiliation rule limited the field of candidates by thousands; Minnesota's precludes only a handful who freely choose to be so limited. It is also worth noting that while California's disaffiliation statute absolutely banned many candidacies, Minnesota's fusion ban only prohibits a candidate from being named twice.

We conclude that the burdens Minnesota's fusion ban imposes on the New Party's associational rights are justified by "correspondingly weighty" valid state interests in ballot integrity and political stability. In deciding that Minnesota's fusion ban does not unconstitutionally burden the New Party's First and Fourteenth Amendment rights, we express no views on the New Party's policy-based arguments concerning the wisdom of fusion. It may well be that, as support for new political parties increases, these arguments will carry the day in some States' legislatures. But the Constitution does not require Minnesota, and the approximately 40 other States that do not permit fusion, to allow it. The judgment of the Court of Appeals is reversed.

It is so ordered.

JUSTICE STEVENS, with whom JUSTICE GINSBURG joins, and with whom JUSTICE SOUTER joins as to Parts I and II, dissenting.

... The Court's conclusion that the Minnesota statute prohibiting multiple-party candidacies is constitutional rests on three dubious premises: (1) that the statute imposes

---

12. [The dissent] insists that New York's experience with fusion politics undermines Minnesota's contention that its fusion ban promotes political stability. California's experiment with cross-filing, on the other hand, provides some justification for Minnesota's concerns. In 1946, for example, Earl Warren was the nominee of both major parties, and was therefore able to run unopposed in California's general election. It appears to be widely accepted that California's cross-filing system stifled electoral competition and undermined the role of distinctive political parties.

only a minor burden on the Party's right to choose and to support the candidate of its choice; (2) that the statute significantly serves the State's asserted interests in avoiding ballot manipulation and factionalism; and (3) that, in any event, the interest in preserving the two-party system justifies the imposition of the burden at issue in this case. I disagree with each of these premises.

I

The members of a recognized political party unquestionably have a constitutional right to select their nominees for public office and to communicate the identity of their nominees to the voting public. Both the right to choose and the right to advise voters of that choice are entitled to the highest respect.

The Minnesota statutes place a significant burden on both of those rights. The Court's recital of burdens that the statute does not inflict on the Party does nothing to minimize the severity of the burdens that it does impose. The fact that the Party may nominate its second choice surely does not diminish the significance of a restriction that denies it the right to have the name of its first choice appear on the ballot. Nor does the point that it may use some of its limited resources to publicize the fact that its first choice is the nominee of some other party provide an adequate substitute for the message that is conveyed to every person who actually votes when a party's nominees appear on the ballot. . . .

II

. . . [E]ven accepting the majority's view that the burdens imposed by the law are not weighty, the State's asserted interests must at least bear some plausible relationship to the burdens it places on political parties. Although the Court today suggests that the State does not have to support its asserted justifications for the fusion ban with evidence that they have any empirical validity, we have previously required more than a bare assertion that some particular state interest is served by a burdensome election requirement.[3]

While the State describes some imaginative theoretical sources of voter confusion that could result from fusion candidacies, in my judgment the argument that the burden on First Amendment interests is justified by this concern is meritless and severely underestimates the intelligence of the typical voter. . . .

The State's concern about ballot manipulation, readily accepted by the majority, is similarly farfetched. The possibility that members of the major parties will begin to create dozens of minor parties with detailed, issue-oriented titles for the sole purpose of nominating candidates under those titles is entirely hypothetical. The majority dismisses out-of-hand the Party's argument that the risk of this type of ballot manipulation and crowding is more easily averted by maintaining reasonably stringent requirements for the creation of minor parties. In fact, though, the Party's point merely illustrates the idea that a State can place some kinds — but not every kind — of limitation on the abilities of small parties to thrive. If the State wants to make it more difficult for any group to achieve

---

3. In any event, the parade of horribles that the majority appears to believe might visit Minnesota should fusion candidacies be allowed is fantastical, given the evidence from New York's experience with fusion. Thus, the evidence that actually is available diminishes, rather than strengthens, Minnesota's claims. The majority asserts [in n.12] that California's cross-filing system, in place during the first half of this century, provides a compelling counterexample. But cross-filing, which "allowed candidates to file in the primary of any or all parties without specifying party affiliation," D. Mazmanian, Third Parties in Presidential Elections 132–133 (1974), is simply not the same as fusion politics, and the problems suffered in California do not provide empirical support for Minnesota's position.

the legal status of being a political party, it can do so within reason and still not run up against the First Amendment. *Anderson*; *Jenness*. But once the State has established a standard for achieving party status, forbidding an acknowledged party from putting on the ballot its chosen candidate clearly frustrates core associational rights.[5]

The State argues that the fusion ban promotes political stability by preventing intraparty factionalism and party raiding. States do certainly have an interest in maintaining a stable political system. *Eu*. But the State has not convincingly articulated how the fusion ban will prevent the factionalism it fears. Unlike the law at issue in *Storer*, for example, this law would not prevent sore-loser candidates from defecting with a disaffected segment of a major party and running as an opposition candidate for a newly formed minor party. Nor does this law, like those aimed at requiring parties to show a modicum of support in order to secure a place on the election ballot, prevent the formation of numerous small parties. Indeed, the activity banned by Minnesota's law is the formation of coalitions, not the division and dissension of "splintered parties and unrestrained factionalism."

As for the State's argument that the fusion ban encourages candidate competition, this claim treats "candidates" as fungible goods, ignoring entirely each party's interest in nominating not just any candidate, but the candidate who best represents the party's views. Minnesota's fusion ban simply cannot be justified with reference to this or any of the above-mentioned rationales. I turn, therefore, to what appears to be the true basis for the Court's holding—the interest in preserving the two-party system.

III

… In most States, perhaps in all, there are two and only two major political parties. It is not surprising, therefore, that most States have enacted election laws that impose burdens on the development and growth of third parties. The law at issue in this case is undeniably such a law. The fact that the law was both intended to disadvantage minor parties and has had that effect is a matter that should weigh against, rather than in favor of, its constitutionality.

Our jurisprudence in this area reflects a certain tension: On the one hand, we have been clear that political stability is an important state interest and that incidental burdens on the formation of minor parties are reasonable to protect that interest, see *Storer*; on the other, we have struck down state elections laws specifically because they give "the two old, established parties a decided advantage over any new parties struggling for existence," *Williams*. Between these boundaries, we have acknowledged that there is "no litmus-paper test for separating those restrictions that are valid from those that are invidious … The rule is not self-executing and is no substitute for the hard judgments that must be made." *Storer*.

Nothing in the Constitution prohibits the States from maintaining single-member districts with winner-take-all voting arrangements. And these elements of an election sys-

---

5. A second "ballot manipulation" argument accepted by the majority is that minor parties will attempt to "capitalize on the popularity of another party's candidate, rather than on their own appeal to the voters, in order to secure access to the ballot." What the majority appears unwilling to accept is that *Andy Dawkins was the New Party's chosen candidate.* The Party was not trying to capitalize on his status as someone else's candidate, but to identify him as their own choice.

[Is Justice Stevens correct that the New Party was not trying to capitalize on Dawkins' status as the DFL nominee? Doesn't the fusion strategy for minor parties crucially depend on nominating the candidates of major parties, at least in many cases?—Eds]

tem do make it significantly more difficult for third parties to thrive. But these laws are different in two respects from the fusion bans at issue here. First, the method by which they hamper third-party development is not one that impinges on the associational rights of those third parties; minor parties remain free to nominate candidates of their choice, and to rally support for those candidates. The small parties' relatively limited likelihood of ultimate success on election day does not deprive them of the right to try. Second, the establishment of single-member districts correlates directly with the States' interests in political stability. Systems of proportional representation, for example, may tend toward factionalism and fragile coalitions that diminish legislative effectiveness. In the context of fusion candidacies, the risks to political stability are extremely attenuated. Of course, the reason minor parties so ardently support fusion politics is because it allows the parties to build up a greater base of support, as potential minor party members realize that a vote for the smaller party candidate is not necessarily a "wasted" vote. Eventually, a minor party might gather sufficient strength that—were its members so inclined—it could successfully run a candidate not endorsed by any major party, and legislative coalition-building will be made more difficult by the presence of third-party legislators. But the risks to political stability in that scenario are speculative at best.

In some respects, the fusion candidacy is the best marriage of the virtues of the minor party challenge to entrenched viewpoints and the political stability that the two-party system provides. The fusion candidacy does not threaten to divide the legislature and create significant risks of factionalism, which is the principal risk proponents of the two-party system point to. But it does provide a means by which voters with viewpoints not adequately represented by the platforms of the two major parties can indicate to a particular candidate that—in addition to his support for the major party views—he should be responsive to the views of the minor party whose support for him was demonstrated where political parties demonstrate support—on the ballot.

The strength of the two-party system—and of each of its major components—is the product of the power of the ideas, the traditions, the candidates, and the voters that constitute the parties. It demeans the strength of the two-party system to assume that the major parties need to rely on laws that discriminate against independent voters and minor parties in order to preserve their positions of power....

In my opinion legislation that would otherwise be unconstitutional because it burdens First Amendment interests and discriminates against minor political parties cannot survive simply because it benefits the two major parties. Accordingly, I respectfully dissent.

JUSTICE SOUTER, dissenting.

[Justice Souter did not believe that the defense that an anti-fusion law helped strengthen the two-party system was properly before the Court, a question addressed by Chief Justice Rehnquist and Justice Stevens in portions of their opinions that have been omitted above. Justice Souter added these paragraphs:]

I am, however, unwilling to go the further distance of considering and rejecting the majority's "preservation of the two-party system" rationale. For while Minnesota has made no such argument before us, I cannot discount the possibility of a forceful one. There is considerable consensus that party loyalty among American voters has declined significantly in the past four decades. In the wake of such studies, it may not be unreasonable to infer that the two-party system is in some jeopardy.

Surely the majority is right that States "have a strong interest in the stability of their political systems," that is, in preserving a political system capable of governing effectively. If it could be shown that the disappearance of the two-party system would undermine that interest, and that permitting fusion candidacies poses a substantial threat to the two-party scheme, there might well be a sufficient predicate for recognizing the constitutionality of the state action presented by this case. Right now, however, no State has attempted even to make this argument, and I would therefore leave its consideration for another day.

Notes and Questions

1. The Democratic-Farmer-Labor Party enjoyed a comfortable majority in both houses of the Minnesota legislature. If it is true that the DFL did not object to its candidates being endorsed by other parties, then why didn't the legislature repeal the sections that the New Party is challenging?

2. Suppose the Supreme Court had struck down the Minnesota anti-fusion laws and the DFL passed a rule prohibiting its candidates from appearing on the ballot additionally as the candidate of other parties. Would the DFL have the right to enforce this rule under *Tashjian*, *Eu*, and *California Democratic Party v. Jones*?

3. If Justice Stevens' dissenting view had prevailed, would the role of third parties have been enhanced? Some third party activists have suggested that a constitutional right to engage in fusion would help third parties grow. See. e.g., John B. Anderson & Jeffrey L. Freeman, *Taking the First Steps Towards a Multiparty System in the United States*, 21 Fletcher Forum of World Affairs 73, 81 (1997). Other commentators take the opposite view, arguing that New York's experience demonstrates that fusion relegates third parties to a permanent secondary pressure group role. James Gray Pope, *Fusion*, Timmons v. Twin Cities Area New Party, *and the Future of Third Parties in the United States*, 50 Rutgers Law Review 473 (1998). A third view holds that the fusion ban should have little marginal effect on the power of third parties in the United States, given Duverger's Law. See Richard L. Hasen, *Entrenching the Duopoly: Why the Supreme Court Should Not Allow the States to Protect the Democrats and Republicans from Political Competition*, 1997 Supreme Court Review 331, 367–71.

4. According to Hasen, *supra*, the real significance of *Timmons* is that it marks the first time the Supreme Court has recognized preservation of the two-party system as a legitimate state interest that may justify a state regulation against constitutional attack. Compare *Timmons* ("the States' interest permits them to enact reasonable election regulations that may, in practice, favor the traditional two-party system") with *Williams v. Rhodes*, *supra* ("The fact is, however, that the Ohio system does not merely favor a "two-party system"; it favors two particular parties—the Republicans and the Democrats—and in effect tends to give them a complete monopoly.... New parties struggling for their place must have the time and opportunity to organize in order to meet reasonable requirements for ballot position, just as the old parties have had in the past."). Hasen argues that this newly-recognized interest might allow states to further limit the ability of third parties to serve as pressure groups as well as limiting information available to voters through the third party labels. This first assertion is borne out by post-*Timmons* cases such as *Wood v. Meadows*, *supra*, 207 F.3d at 712, in which the Fourth Circuit cited *Timmons*' statements regarding state promotion of the two-party system as a justification for a 150-day filing deadline for independent candidates.

But consider this:

> The scholarly opposition to *Timmons* was led by Richard Hasen, who read the case as permitting infringement of First Amendment rights in furtherance of the state's interest in preserving the two-party system. He based his interpreta-

tion primarily on the Court's statement that "the Constitution permits the Minnesota Legislature to decide that political stability is best served through a healthy two-party system.".…

> Hasen's reading is a possible one, but it is not the most plausible reading and certainly not the friendliest. He emphasizes the term "two-party" in the final phrase of the quoted passage. The phrase takes on a different meaning if instead we emphasize "healthy." So read, the Court's statement does not suggest that *preservation* of the two-party system is a state interest that can justify constitutional infringements, but rather that *given* the existence of a two-party system, the state has an interest in keeping it healthy.

Daniel H. Lowenstein, *Legal Regulation and Protection of American Parties*, in HANDBOOK OF PARTY POLITICS 456, 464 (Richard S. Katz & William Crotty, eds., 2006). Lowenstein adds that in the quotation following the reference to Hasen's article in the previous paragraph, the Court says that the state may pursue valid interests in a manner that will benefit the two-party system, not that the preservation of the two-party system is itself an interest that would justify infringement of first amendment rights.

5. Pennsylvania generally banned cross-party candidacies, but it made an exception for certain local elections. Presumably in order to encourage but not require non-partisan politics in those local elections, cross-party candidacies were permitted, but only among the major parties. Thus, a candidate could appear on the general election ballot as the candidate of the Democratic and Republican parties. However, the minor parties were not permitted to participate in the cross-party candidacies. A federal court had struck down this disparity before the Supreme Court decided *Timmons*. After *Timmons*, that ruling was reaffirmed in *Reform Party of Allegheny County v. Department of Elections*, 174 F.3d 305 (3d Cir. 1999):

> Nothing in the *Timmons* opinion itself weakens the equal protection analysis of [the former ruling], because no equal protection claim was asserted or considered by the Court in *Timmons*. The statutory scheme in *Timmons* differs from the Pennsylvania scheme in a manner crucial for the equal protection analysis. *Timmons* involved an across-the-board ban on fusion by both major and minor parties. In contrast, the Pennsylvania statutes involve a ban on cross-nomination that facially discriminates against minor parties by allowing major parties, but not minor parties, to cross-nominate in certain circumstances. The Supreme Court in *Timmons* did not hold that states can treat minor parties in a discriminatory way.

Id. at 312.

6. Major party candidates receive a number of additional benefits, including more press coverage and invitations to speak or debate. When the state is involved in organizing debates, may it exclude third party candidates? The Supreme Court considered that question in the next case.

Arkansas Educational Television Commission v. Forbes
523 U.S. 666 (1998)

Justice KENNEDY delivered the opinion of the Court.

[The Arkansas Educational Television Commission (AETC) is a state agency that owns and operates a network of five noncommercial television stations. In 1992, AETC decided to sponsor and televise a series of five debates, one for the Senate candidates and one for candidates in each of the four Arkansas congressional districts. Having decided to limit participation in the debates to candidates of the major parties or other candidates "who had strong popular support," the AETC staff declined to invite Forbes, an independent House candidate qualified to appear on the ballot in the Third Congressional District.

Forbes challenged his exclusion from the debate on First Amendment grounds. The District Court dismissed for failure to state a cause of action, but was overruled by the Court of Appeals. The case was remanded for trial, at which "AETC professional staff testified Forbes was excluded because he lacked any campaign organization, had not generated appreciable voter support, and was not regarded as a serious candidate by the press covering the election. The jury made express findings that AETC's decision to exclude Forbes had not been influenced by political pressure or disagreement with his views."

The District Court entered judgment for AETC but was again overruled by the Court of Appeals.]

II

[The "public forum doctrine" is a complex and controversial doctrine established by the Supreme Court for adjudicating claims of a right to use government-owned facilities for speech purposes.[j] Justice Kennedy turned to a consideration of the doctrine in the context of this case.] Having first arisen in the context of streets and parks, the public forum doctrine should not be extended in a mechanical way to the very different context of public television broadcasting. In the case of streets and parks, the open access and viewpoint neutrality commanded by the doctrine is "compatible with the intended purpose of the property." *Perry Ed. Assn. v. Perry Local Educators' Assn.*, 460 U.S. 37 (1983). So too was the requirement of viewpoint neutrality compatible with the university's funding of student publications in *Rosenberger v. Rector and Visitors of Univ. of Va.*, 515 U.S. 819 (1995). In the case of television broadcasting, however, broad rights of access for outside speakers would be antithetical, as a general rule, to the discretion that stations and their editorial staff must exercise to fulfill their journalistic purpose and statutory obligations.

Congress has rejected the argument that "broadcast facilities should be open on a nonselective basis to all persons wishing to talk about public issues." *Columbia Broadcasting System, Inc. v. Democratic National Committee*, 412 U.S. 94 (1973). Instead, television broadcasters enjoy the "widest journalistic freedom" consistent with their public responsibilities. *Id.* Among the broadcaster's responsibilities is the duty to schedule programming that serves the "public interest, convenience, and necessity." 47 U.S.C. §309(a). Public and private broadcasters alike are not only permitted, but indeed required, to exercise substantial editorial discretion in the selection and presentation of their programming.

As a general rule, the nature of editorial discretion counsels against subjecting broadcasters to claims of viewpoint discrimination. Programming decisions would be particularly vulnerable to claims of this type because even principled exclusions rooted in sound journalistic judgment can often be characterized as viewpoint based. To comply

---

j. For overviews, see William B. Lockhart et al., Constitutional Law 799–817 (8th ed. 1996); Laurence H. Tribe, American Constitutional Law 986–97 (2d ed. 1988). The many excellent commentaries include Robert C. Post, *The History and Theory of the Public Forum*, 34 UCLA Law Review 1713 (1987); Daniel A. Farber & John E. Nowak, *The Misleading Nature of Public Forum Analysis: Content and Context in First Amendment Adjudication*, 70 Virginia Law Review 1219 (1984).

with their obligation to air programming that serves the public interest, broadcasters must often choose among speakers expressing different viewpoints. "That editors — newspaper or broadcast — can and do abuse this power is beyond doubt," *CBS*; but "[c]alculated risks of abuse are taken in order to preserve higher values." *Id.* Much like a university selecting a commencement speaker, a public institution selecting speakers for a lecture series, or a public school prescribing its curriculum, a broadcaster by its nature will facilitate the expression of some viewpoints instead of others. Were the judiciary to require, and so to define and approve, pre-established criteria for access, it would risk implicating the courts in judgments that should be left to the exercise of journalistic discretion.

When a public broadcaster exercises editorial discretion in the selection and presentation of its programming, it engages in speech activity. Cf. *Turner Broadcasting System, Inc. v. FCC*, 512 U.S. 622, 636 (1994). Although programming decisions often involve the compilation of the speech of third parties, the decisions nonetheless constitute communicative acts.

Claims of access under our public forum precedents could obstruct the legitimate purposes of television broadcasters. Were the doctrine given sweeping application in this context, courts "would be required to oversee far more of the day-to-day operations of broadcasters' conduct, deciding such questions as whether a particular individual or group has had sufficient opportunity to present its viewpoint and whether a particular viewpoint has already been sufficiently aired." *CBS.* "The result would be a further erosion of the journalistic discretion of broadcasters," transferring "control over the treatment of public issues from the licensees who are accountable for broadcast performance to private individuals" who bring suit under our forum precedents. *Id.* In effect, we would "exchange 'public trustee' broadcasting, with all its limitations, for a system of self-appointed editorial commentators." *Id.*

In the absence of any congressional command to "[r]egimen[t] broadcasters" in this manner, *id.*, we are disinclined to do so through doctrines of our own design. This is not to say the First Amendment would bar the legislative imposition of neutral rules for access to public broadcasting. Instead, we say that, in most cases, the First Amendment of its own force does not compel public broadcasters to allow third parties access to their programming.

Although public broadcasting as a general matter does not lend itself to scrutiny under the forum doctrine, candidate debates present the narrow exception to the rule. For two reasons, a candidate debate like the one at issue here is different from other programming. First, unlike AETC's other broadcasts, the debate was by design a forum for political speech by the candidates. Consistent with the long tradition of candidate debates, the implicit representation of the broadcaster was that the views expressed were those of the candidates, not its own. The very purpose of the debate was to allow the candidates to express their views with minimal intrusion by the broadcaster. In this respect the debate differed even from a political talk show, whose host can express partisan views and then limit the discussion to those ideas.

Second, in our tradition, candidate debates are of exceptional significance in the electoral process.... Deliberation on the positions and qualifications of candidates is integral to our system of government, and electoral speech may have its most profound and widespread impact when it is disseminated through televised debates. A majority of the population cites television as its primary source of election information, and debates are regarded as the "only occasion during a campaign when the attention of a large portion of the American public is focused on the election, as well as the only campaign information format which potentially offers sufficient time to explore issues and policies in depth in a neutral forum." Congressional Research Service, Campaign Debates in Presidential General Elections, summ. (June 15, 1993).

As we later discuss, in many cases it is not feasible for the broadcaster to allow unlimited access to a candidate debate. Yet the requirement of neutrality remains; a broadcaster cannot grant or deny access to a candidate debate on the basis of whether it agrees with a candidate's views.[k] Viewpoint discrimination in this context would present not a "[c]alculated ris[k]," *CBS*, but an inevitability of skewing the electoral dialogue.

The special characteristics of candidate debates support the conclusion that the AETC debate was a forum of some type. The question of what type must be answered by reference to our public forum precedents, to which we now turn.

III

Forbes argues, and the Court of Appeals held, that the debate was a public forum to which he had a First Amendment right of access. Under our precedents, however, the debate was a nonpublic forum, from which AETC could exclude Forbes in the reasonable, viewpoint-neutral exercise of its journalistic discretion.

A

For our purposes, it will suffice to employ the categories of speech fora already established and discussed in our cases. "[T]he Court [has] identified three types of fora: the traditional public forum, the public forum created by government designation, and the nonpublic forum." *Cornelius v. NAACP Legal Defense & Ed. Fund, Inc.*, 473 U.S. 788 (1985). Traditional public fora are defined by the objective characteristics of the property, such as whether, "by long tradition or by government fiat," the property has been "devoted to assembly and debate." *Perry Ed. Assn.* The government can exclude a speaker from a traditional public forum "only when the exclusion is necessary to serve a compelling state interest and the exclusion is narrowly drawn to achieve that interest." *Cornelius.*

Designated public fora, in contrast, are created by purposeful governmental action. "The government does not create a [designated] public forum by inaction or by permitting limited discourse, but only by intentionally opening a nontraditional public forum for public discourse." *Id.* Hence "the Court has looked to the policy and practice of the government to ascertain whether it intended to designate a place not traditionally open to assembly and debate as a public forum." *Id.* If the government excludes a speaker who falls within the class to which a designated public forum is made generally available, its action is subject to strict scrutiny.

Other government properties are either nonpublic fora or not fora at all. The government can restrict access to a nonpublic forum "as long as the restrictions are reasonable and [are] not an effort to suppress expression merely because public officials oppose the speaker's view." *Id.*...

B

The parties agree the AETC debate was not a traditional public forum.... The issue, then, is whether the debate was a designated public forum or a nonpublic forum.

---

k. Justice Kennedy here refers without qualification to "a broadcaster," though he does so in the context of a case dealing with a public broadcaster. Would it be unconstitutional for a privately owned television station to broadcast a debate limited to candidates who took a particular position on a given issue? — EDS.

Under our precedents, the AETC debate was not a designated public forum. To create a forum of this type, the government must intend to make the property "generally available," *Widmar v. Vincent*, 454 U.S. 263 (1981), to a class of speakers.... A designated public forum is not created when the government allows selective access for individual speakers rather than general access for a class of speakers....

[The] distinction between general and selective access furthers First Amendment interests. By recognizing the distinction, we encourage the government to open its property to some expressive activity in cases where, if faced with an all-or-nothing choice, it might not open the property at all. That this distinction turns on governmental intent does not render it unprotective of speech. Rather, it reflects the reality that, with the exception of traditional public fora, the government retains the choice of whether to designate its property as a forum for specified classes of speakers.

Here, the debate did not have an open-microphone format. Contrary to the assertion of the Court of Appeals, AETC did not make its debate generally available to candidates for Arkansas' Third Congressional District seat. Instead..., AETC reserved eligibility for participation in the debate to candidates for the Third Congressional District seat (as opposed to some other seat). At that point..., AETC made candidate-by-candidate determinations as to which of the eligible candidates would participate in the debate. "Such selective access, unsupported by evidence of a purposeful designation for public use, does not create a public forum." *Cornelius*. Thus the debate was a non-public forum.

In addition to being a misapplication of our precedents, the Court of Appeals' holding would result in less speech, not more. In ruling that the debate was a public forum open to all ballot-qualified candidates, the Court of Appeals would place a severe burden upon public broadcasters who air candidates' views. In each of the 1988, 1992, and 1996 Presidential elections, for example, no fewer than 19 candidates appeared on the ballot in at least one State. In the 1996 congressional elections, it was common for 6 to 11 candidates to qualify for the ballot for a particular seat. In the 1993 New Jersey gubernatorial election, to illustrate further, sample ballot mailings included the written statements of 19 candidates. On logistical grounds alone, a public television editor might, with reason, decide that the inclusion of all ballot-qualified candidates would "actually undermine the educational value and quality of debates."

Were it faced with the prospect of cacophony, on the one hand, and First Amendment liability, on the other, a public television broadcaster might choose not to air candidates' views at all. A broadcaster might decide "'the safe course is to avoid controversy'.... and by so doing diminish the free flow of information and ideas." *Turner Broadcasting System*. In this circumstance, a "[g]overnment-enforced right of access inescapably 'dampens the vigor and limits the variety of public debate.'"

These concerns are more than speculative. As a direct result of the Court of Appeals' decision in this case, the Nebraska Educational Television Network canceled a scheduled debate between candidates in Nebraska's 1996 United States Senate race. A First Amendment jurisprudence yielding these results does not promote speech but represses it.

C

The debate's status as a nonpublic forum, however, did not give AETC unfettered power to exclude any candidate it wished.... To be consistent with the First Amendment, the exclusion of a speaker from a nonpublic forum must not be based on the speaker's viewpoint and must otherwise be reasonable in light of the purpose of the property. *Cornelius*.

In this case, the jury found Forbes' exclusion was not based on "objections or opposition to his views." The record provides ample support for this finding, demonstrating as well that AETC's decision to exclude him was reasonable. AETC Executive Director Susan Howarth testified Forbes' views had "absolutely" no role in the decision to exclude him from the debate. She further testified Forbes was excluded because (1) "the Arkansas voters did not consider him a serious candidate"; (2) "the news organizations also did not consider him a serious candidate"; (3) "the Associated Press and a national election result reporting service did not plan to run his name in results on election night"; (4) Forbes "apparently had little, if any, financial support, failing to report campaign finances to the Secretary of State's office or to the Federal Election Commission"; and (5) "there [was] no 'Forbes for Congress' campaign headquarters other than his house." Forbes himself described his campaign organization as "bedlam" and the media coverage of his campaign as "zilch." It is, in short, beyond dispute that Forbes was excluded not because of his viewpoint but because he had generated no appreciable public interest.

There is no substance to Forbes' suggestion that he was excluded because his views were unpopular or out of the mainstream. His own objective lack of support, not his platform, was the criterion. Indeed, the very premise of Forbes' contention is mistaken. A candidate with unconventional views might well enjoy broad support by virtue of a compelling personality or an exemplary campaign organization. By the same token, a candidate with a traditional platform might enjoy little support due to an inept campaign or any number of other reasons.

Nor did AETC exclude Forbes in an attempted manipulation of the political process. The evidence provided powerful support for the jury's express finding that AETC's exclusion of Forbes was not the result of "political pressure from anyone inside or outside [AETC]." There is no serious argument that AETC did not act in good faith in this case. AETC excluded Forbes because the voters lacked interest in his candidacy, not because AETC itself did.

The broadcaster's decision to exclude Forbes was a reasonable, viewpoint-neutral exercise of journalistic discretion consistent with the First Amendment. The judgment of the Court of Appeals is

Reversed.

JUSTICE STEVENS, with whom JUSTICE SOUTER and JUSTICE GINSBURG join, dissenting.

The Court has decided that a state-owned television network has no "constitutional obligation to allow every candidate access to" political debates that it sponsors. I do not challenge that decision. The judgment of the Court of Appeals should nevertheless be affirmed....

I

Two months before Forbes was officially certified as an independent candidate qualified to appear on the ballot under Arkansas law, the AETC staff had already concluded that he "should not be invited" to participate in the televised debates because he was "not a serious candidate as determined by the voters of Arkansas." He had, however, been a serious contender for the Republican nomination for Lieutenant Governor in 1986 and again in 1990. Although he was defeated in a runoff election, in the three-way primary race conducted in 1990—just two years before the AETC staff decision—he had received 46.88% of the statewide vote and had carried 15 of the 16 counties within the Third Congressional District by absolute majorities. Nevertheless, the staff concluded that Forbes did not have "strong popular support."

Given the fact that the Republican winner in the Third Congressional District race in 1992 received only 50.22% of the vote and the Democrat received 47.20%, it would have been necessary for Forbes, who had made a strong showing in recent Republican primaries, to divert only a handful of votes from the Republican candidate to cause his defeat. Thus, even though the AETC staff may have correctly concluded that Forbes was "not a serious candidate," their decision to exclude him from the debate may have determined the outcome of the election in the Third District.[1]

If a comparable decision were made today by a privately owned network, it would be subject to scrutiny under the Federal Election Campaign Act[5] unless the network used "pre-established objective criteria to determine which candidates may participate in [the] debate." 11 CFR §110.13(c) (1997). No such criteria governed AETC's refusal to permit Forbes to participate in the debate. Indeed, whether that refusal was based on a judgment about "newsworthiness"—as AETC has argued in this Court—or a judgment about "political viability"—as it argued in the Court of Appeals—the facts in the record presumably would have provided an adequate basis either for a decision to include Forbes in the Third District debate or a decision to exclude him, and might even have required a cancellation of two of the other debates.[6]

The apparent flexibility of AETC's purported standard suggests the extent to which the staff had nearly limitless discretion to exclude Forbes from the debate based on ad hoc justifications. Thus, the Court of Appeals correctly concluded that the staff's appraisal of "political viability" was "so subjective, so arguable, so susceptible of variation in individual opinion, as to provide no secure basis for the exercise of governmental power consistent with the First Amendment."

II

AETC is a state agency whose actions "are fairly attributable to the State and subject to the Fourteenth Amendment, unlike the actions of privately owned broadcast licensees." The AETC staff members therefore "were not ordinary journalists: they were employees of government." The Court implicitly acknowledges these facts by subjecting

---

1. In the situation hypothesized by Justice Stevens, the independent candidate has no serious popular support (however "serious" may be defined), but the race is expected to be so close that even a slight increase or decrease in the vote share of the independent candidate—such as might result from inclusion in a candidates' debate—might affect the outcome between the leading candidates. Would the presence of such circumstances provide a reason for including the independent candidate in the debate, or a reason for excluding that candidate?—EDS.

5. See 2 U.S.C. §441b(a); see also *Perot v. FEC*, 97 F.3d 553, 556 (CADC 1996), cert. denied *sub nom. Hagelin v. FEC*, 520 U.S. 1210 (1997).

6. Although the contest between the major-party candidates in the Third District was a relatively close one, in two of the other three districts in which both major-party candidates had been invited to debate, it was clear that one of them had virtually no chance of winning the election. Democrat Blanche Lambert's resounding victory over Republican Terry Hayes in the First Congressional District illustrates this point: Lambert received 69.8% of the vote compared with Hays' 30.2%. [The inconsistent spelling of the Republican candidate's name appears in the U.S. Reports.—EDS.] Similarly, in the Second District, Democrat Ray Thornton, the incumbent, defeated Republican Dennis Scott and won with 74.2% of the vote. Note that Scott raised only $6,000, which was less than Forbes raised; nevertheless, Scott was invited to participate in a debate while Forbes was not.

[Recall that according to the testimony, AETC's policy was to include Republican and Democratic candidates regardless of their support and other candidates "who had strong popular support." Should it be unconstitutional for a publicly owned station to apply the test of popular support to third party and independent candidates when the test is not applied to Republicans and Democrats?—EDS.]

the decision to exclude Forbes to constitutional analysis. Yet the Court seriously underestimates the importance of the difference between private and public ownership of broadcast facilities, despite the fact that Congress and this Court have repeatedly recognized that difference.

In *CBS*, the Court held that a licensee is neither a common carrier nor a public forum that must accommodate "'the right of every individual to speak, write, or publish.'" Speaking for a plurality, Chief Justice Burger expressed the opinion that the First Amendment imposes no constraint on the private network's journalistic freedom....

The case before us today involves only the right of a state-owned network to regulate speech that plays a central role in democratic government. Because AETC is owned by the State, deference to its interest in making ad hoc decisions about the political content of its programs necessarily increases the risk of government censorship and propaganda in a way that protection of privately owned broadcasters does not.

III

The Court recognizes that the debates sponsored by AETC were "by design a forum for political speech by the candidates." The Court also acknowledges the central importance of candidate debates in the electoral process. Thus, there is no need to review our cases expounding on the public forum doctrine to conclude that the First Amendment will not tolerate a state agency's arbitrary exclusion from a debate forum based, for example, on an expectation that the speaker might be critical of the Governor, or might hold unpopular views about abortion or the death penalty. Indeed, the Court so holds today.

It seems equally clear, however, that the First Amendment will not tolerate arbitrary definitions of the scope of the forum. We have recognized that "[o]nce it has opened a limited forum, ... the State must respect the lawful boundaries it has itself set." *Rosenberger*. It follows, of course, that a State's failure to set any meaningful boundaries at all cannot insulate the State's action from First Amendment challenge. The dispositive issue in this case, then, is not whether AETC created a designated public forum or a nonpublic forum, as the Court concludes, but whether AETC defined the contours of the debate forum with sufficient specificity to justify the exclusion of a ballot-qualified candidate.

AETC asks that we reject Forbes' constitutional claim on the basis of entirely subjective, ad hoc judgments about the dimensions of its forum. The First Amendment demands more, however, when a state government effectively wields the power to eliminate a political candidate from all consideration by the voters. All stations must act as editors, and when state-owned stations participate in the broadcasting arena, their editorial decisions may impact the constitutional interests of individual speakers. A state-owned broadcaster need not plan, sponsor, and conduct political debates, however. When it chooses to do so, the First Amendment imposes important limitations on its control over access to the debate forum....

No written criteria cabined the discretion of the AETC staff. Their subjective judgment about a candidate's "viability" or "newsworthiness" allowed them wide latitude either to permit or to exclude a third participant in any debate. Moreover, in exercising that judgment they were free to rely on factors that arguably should favor inclusion as justifications for exclusion. Thus, the fact that Forbes had little financial support was considered as evidence of his lack of viability when that factor might have provided an independent reason for allowing him to share a free forum with wealthier candidates.

The televised debate forum at issue in this case may not squarely fit within our public forum analysis, but its importance cannot be denied. Given the special character of political speech, particularly during campaigns for elected office, the debate forum implicates constitutional concerns of the highest order, as the majority acknowledges. Indeed, the planning and management of political debates by state-owned broadcasters raise serious constitutional concerns that are seldom replicated when state-owned television networks engage in other types of programming....

The reasons that support the need for narrow, objective, and definite standards to guide licensing decisions apply directly to the wholly subjective access decisions made by the staff of AETC. The importance of avoiding arbitrary or viewpoint-based exclusions from political debates militates strongly in favor of requiring the controlling state agency to use (and adhere to) preestablished, objective criteria to determine who among qualified candidates may participate. When the demand for speaking facilities exceeds supply, the State must "ration or allocate the scarce resources on some acceptable neutral principle." *Rosenberger.* A constitutional duty to use objective standards — i.e., "neutral principles" — for determining whether and when to adjust a debate format would impose only a modest requirement that would fall far short of a duty to grant every multiple-party request.[19] Such standards would also have the benefit of providing the public with some assurance that state-owned broadcasters cannot select debate participants on arbitrary grounds.

Like the Court, I do not endorse the view of the Court of Appeals that all candidates who qualify for a position on the ballot are necessarily entitled to access to any state-sponsored debate. I am convinced, however, that [constitutional imperatives] command that access to political debates planned and managed by state-owned entities be governed by pre-established, objective criteria. Requiring government employees to set out objective criteria by which they choose which candidates will benefit from the significant media exposure that results from state-sponsored political debates would alleviate some of the risk inherent in allowing government agencies — rather than private entities — to stage candidate debates.

Accordingly, I would affirm the judgment of the Court of Appeals.

Notes and Questions

1. Assume Justice Kennedy is right that Forbes was excluded in the exercise of reasonable journalistic discretion. Is it inherently wrong for public broadcasters to pick and choose among parties and candidates to participate in debates? If so, can public broadcasters be good journalists? For an examination of these issues, see Daniel H. Lowenstein, *Election Law Miscellany: Enforcement, Access to Debates, Qualification of Initiatives*, 77 TEXAS LAW REVIEW 2001, 2012–13 (1999).

2. Perhaps Forbes was excluded because the public journalists determined that Forbes' views on the issues were too far out of the mainstream. Would that be an exercise of "journalistic discretion" or government viewpoint discrimination (or both)? Consider Jamin B. Raskin, *The Debate Gerrymander*, 77 TEXAS LAW REVIEW 1943, 1956 (1999): "[E]ven (charitably) granting that there was no bureaucratic animus against Forbes as a person,

---

19. The Court expresses concern that as a direct result of the Court of Appeals' holding that all ballot-qualified candidates have a right to participate in every debate, a state-owned network canceled a 1996 Nebraska debate. If the Nebraska station had realized that it could have satisfied its First Amendment obligations simply by setting out standards before the debate, however, it seems quite unlikely that it would have chosen instead to cancel the debate.

the whole purpose and effect of excluding his appearance as a candidate was to block out presentation in the debate of a political viewpoint deemed unpopular by a candidate deemed unpopular. This is the very definition of viewpoint discrimination and, by definition, it radically changed the nature and dynamics of AETN's televised debate."

Raskin goes on to question whether the government is "clairvoyant" in its ability do determine the "viability" of candidates, pointing to the gubernatorial victory of Minnesota Reform party gubernatorial candidate Jesse Ventura. "Governor Ventura's victory over his Democratic and Republican rivals stunned even close observers of the race. Significantly, one apparently indispensable component of his success was that he was invited to face his rivals on an equal basis in at least eight statewide televised debates. This fact suggests not only that the normal exclusion of third-party candidates on grounds of viability is a self-fulfilling prophecy, but also that debate inclusion can become a wedge for opening up democracy to new voices and new choices." *Id.* at 1964.

3. Perhaps Forbes was excluded not because he was out of the mainstream, but because he threatened mainstream candidates. Raskin, *supra*, gives this history:

> Ralph Forbes was a thorn in the side of the Arkansas political establishment for years—not a pest or a gadfly, but a serious rival to better-financed politicians. His maverick campaigns in the Republican party struck a deep chord in conservative white precincts. In 1990, Forbes ran for lieutenant governor and won forty-six percent of the vote in a three-way primary race for the Republican party nomination, defeating his two rivals. He had become a force to be reckoned with in conservative politics.
>
> In that 1990 race for lieutenant governor, Forbes captured a majority of the vote in fifteen of the sixteen counties that make up the Third Congressional District of Arkansas. So Forbes set his sights on Washington, and when the House seat in the district fortuitously opened in 1992, Forbes announced his candidacy, this time stepping outside of the Republican party and declaring as an independent. He knocked on doors throughout the summer, sweating his way across the district to collect more than six thousand signatures from registered voters, earning a place on the general election ballot next to Republican Tim Hutchison and Democrat John Van Winkle.

Id. at 1949–50 (footnotes omitted). Does this background change your view of the propriety of Forbes' exclusion from the race? Suppose he was excluded because the journalists thought he might be a "spoiler" who would take votes away from the Republican candidate, leading to the election of a Democrat. Would that be proper? If not, can *Storer's* recognition of the state's interest in preventing spoiler candidates be justified?

4. Does Justice Stevens provide a workable alternative to the majority's holding? In his view, when can public broadcasters exclude candidates from debates?

5. *Forbes* and similar cases raise two distinct issues: first, whether broadcasters ought to be required by law to open candidate debates to at least some third party and independent candidates; and second, whether such a requirement should be imposed by courts or, alternatively, by legislation. Keith Darren Eisner, Comment, *Non-Major-Party Candidates and Televised Presidential Debates: The Merits of Legislative Inclusion*, 141 UNIVERSITY OF PENNSYLVANIA LAW REVIEW 973 (1993), argues strenuously for a *legislative* requirement of inclusion, but he is skeptical about judicial imposition:

> Even if the judicial treatment of minor-party candidates seeking inclusion in nationally televised presidential debates were more solicitous than it has been ...

the judiciary is not the appropriate body to grant relief to such candidates. Judicially mandated inclusion would likely be a simplistic, narrow, fact-specific determination that would not concern itself with the necessarily complex, fine-tuned political judgments that need to be made. Such inclusion would likely encourage a spate of lawsuits by third-party or independent candidates of varying national stature, each claiming to be similarly situated to a candidate who has already been granted judicial relief.

Which third-party or independent candidates should be included in the debates? Certainly, practical considerations dictate that allowing dozens of fringe candidates to participate in a nationally televised debate with the two major candidates is neither wise nor predictable. What realistic criteria can be formulated to determine which third-party or independent candidates to include and which to exclude? How can one be certain that the major parties will agree to participate in such debate? The task of answering these and similar questions, of ironing out solutions to political problems, is a job for which the legislature is uniquely qualified. Only Congress has the time, the resources, and the knowledge to restructure, in programmatic fashion, nationally televised debates.

Id. at 1009–10.

6. Justice Stevens in dissent alludes to FEC rules that require private broadcasters and corporations sponsoring debates to use "pre-established objective criteria to determine which candidates may participate in [the] debate." 11 C.F.R. §110.13(c). Ross Perot in 1996 and Ralph Nader in 2000 challenged their exclusion from presidential debates by the Commission for Presidential Debates, which is dominated by Democrats and Republicans, for failure to use such criteria. They did not succeed. See *Perot '96 v. FEC*, 97 F.3d 553 (D.C. Cir. 1996), cert denied sub. nom *Hagelin v. FEC*, 520 U.S. 1210 (1997) *Becker v. FEC*, 230 F.3d 381 (1st Cir. 2000). See also Raskin, *supra*, 1976–94 (arguing against the commission and its criteria).

7. If major party candidates have the right to organize a debate for themselves only, public or private broadcasters might well broadcast it as a newsworthy event. If that is not prohibited, how successful is litigation challenging broadcaster-organized debates likely to be, even if the plaintiffs prevail? See Lowenstein, *supra*, at 2014.

8. In this chapter, we have considered cases in which third parties and independent candidates have sought entitlement to benefits — ballot access, public funding, and participation in broadcast debates — that were being provided to major party candidates. In these cases, the third parties and independent candidates claim a constitutional right to be treated the same as major parties. In other cases, third parties or independent candidates seek to be relieved of burdens that are imposed on major party candidates. In such cases, third parties and independent candidates claim a right to differential treatment.

An important example is the claim of some third parties to exemption from campaign financial disclosure requirements. In *Buckley v. Valeo*, *supra*, the Supreme Court upheld generally the constitutionality of disclosure requirements. However, the Court stated that where a third party could show that disclosure might subject it, its contributors, or its vendors to public or private harassment, the third party could be entitled to a constitutional exemption from the requirement of itemizing contributions and expenditures. In *Brown v. Socialist Workers '74 Campaign Committee*, 459 U.S. 87 (1982), the Court ruled that the Socialist Workers Party had made a sufficient showing and must be granted an exemption.

Chapter 11

Campaigns

In almost any theory of democracy, the election plays a central role in assuring that government policy will bear some relationship to popular sentiment. For elections to play this role, voters must have information regarding the choices that appear on the ballot. The election campaign is the concentrated and purposive communication of information with the specific objective of influencing voter choice. While campaigns are neither the only nor necessarily the most important source of information for voters, few would deny their importance in the American political system.

This chapter considers some of the laws related to campaigning. We necessarily focus on just a few questions, but candidates considering a run for office must negotiate a maze of laws regulating their campaigns. For example, a local statute requires that candidates for city council must reside in the district in which they run.[a] Candidate A has a large home outside the district, but lists as his residence a guest house of his campaign consultant that is within the district Candidate B challenges Candidate A's qualifications. Should Candidate A — in this case liberal activist turned politician Tom Hayden — be disqualified? See Patrick McGreevy, *Hayden Feeling Heat Over Addresses; Council race: Rivals raise residency requirement concerns, citing candidate's use of homes in Sherman Oaks and Westwood*, Los Angeles Times, Feb. 22, 2001, Valley Edition, at B1.

Nuts-and-bolts legal issues become very important even as potential candidates explore whether to run for election; the first thing a prudent potential candidate should do is hire a lawyer and an accountant. In many states, the law will require filing regular reports on campaign finances with appropriate administrative agencies. Those who fail to file proper reports may face fines, or at least face embarrassment when the matter comes to light. Chapter 18 considers campaign finance disclosure rules in some detail.

This chapter considers other legal issues related to the law of campaigns. To inform the legal debate, we begin in Part I with a brief review of the political science of campaigns. How, if at all, does negative speech affect campaigns? How does media coverage influence voter choice? Do party conventions and presidential debates affect how voters choose a presidential candidate?

---

a. Under the Constitution's Qualifications Clauses, members of the United States Senate and the House of Representatives must be residents of the state they represent. See U.S. Const., Art. I, §2, cl. 2; §3, cl. 1. Numerous courts have struck down state statutes attempting to impose additional requirements such as that a candidate for the House be a resident of the Congressional district. See Daniel H. Lowenstein, *Are Congressional Term Limits Constitutional?*, 18 Harvard Journal of Law and Public Policy 1, 43–44 (1994) (collecting cases); see also *Schaefer v. Townsend*, 215 F.3d 1031 (9th Cir. 2000), cert denied sub nom. *Jones v. Schaefer*, 532 U.S. 904 (2001), in which the Ninth Circuit held that "California's requirement that candidates to the House of Representatives reside within the state *before* election violates the Constitution by handicapping the class of nonresident candidates who otherwise satisfy the Qualifications Clause."

We then turn to two legal questions. First, many people are concerned about the content of campaigns. Some view campaigns as full of negative, misleading, and false speech. Part II considers whether campaign speech may be regulated. Part III explores the intersection of election law and communications law, specifically, rules regulating how broadcasters must treat candidates and campaign advertisements.

I. What We Know about American Political Campaigns

A common theme of the political science literature is that not all campaigns are created equal. The dynamics differ depending upon the office sought, whether or not the election is a party primary, a partisan general election (in which candidates run under a party label) or a nonpartisan general election, and whether or not the candidates are running for an open seat or in an election in which an incumbent seeks reelection.

Given their importance in American political life, presidential elections have received a great deal of political scientists' attention. More money and national media attention are spent on presidential races than on any other race for public office. Political scientists have noted an apparent paradox in presidential elections: they have been able to accurately "forecast" the Democratic and Republican candidate's share of the presidential vote based upon a statistical model that considers only a few factors, most importantly the state of the economy in the months before the election. Models that ignore issues related to the campaign, including major campaign "events" such as conventions or debates,[b] remain highly accurate in predicting the outcome of most presidential races. The accuracy of forecasting suggests that presidential election campaigns do not matter. The paradox is that polls of voters' preferences for president are volatile, and fluctuate in response to events as they occur during the campaign, suggesting that campaigns do matter to election outcomes.

Two political scientists have sought to resolve this paradox by hypothesizing that voters typically pay little attention to a presidential campaign until shortly before the election. In the period when voters are ignorant, there may be a considerable gap (or disequilibrium) between their presidential candidate preferences expressed to pollsters in the months before the election and how these voters ultimately vote on election day. During the campaign period, voters receive information through the media that helps them to make decisions consistent with their enlightened self-interest, eventually lining up voter preferences with those predicted by the forecasting models. Andrew Gelman & Gary King, *Why Are American Election Campaign Polls So Variable When Votes are So Predictable?*, 23 BRITISH JOURNAL OF POLITICAL SCIENCE 409 (1993).

In this understanding, presidential campaigns matter in a peculiar way. Both presidential campaigns are likely to be well-funded and well-run, leading to a situation where neither major-party candidate can gain a political advantage by campaigning. But a can-

---

b. Wlezien and Erikson find that more than half the reported post-convention "bounce"—whereby a presidential candidate receives additional support in polls after the candidate's party convention—is due not to increase in a candidate's support but to sampling error in the polls. Christopher Wlezien & Robert S. Erikson, *Campaign Effects in Theory and Practice*, 29 AMERICAN POLITICS RESEARCH 419, 426 (2001). Nonetheless, the authors believe that "events that happen during the campaign cause voters preferences to change.... The problem is empirically identifying those effects." *Id.* at 419.

didate could not abandon campaigning because doing so would allow the other campaign to gain an advantage with voters. Thomas M. Holbrook, Do CAMPAIGNS MATTER? 147 (1996).

How do campaigns impart information to voters? Some campaign messages come directly from candidates or campaigns, such as through campaign appearances, debates, and campaign advertising (whether on television or radio, or by mail, phone, or Internet). These messages often contain appeals to emotions, either to impart positive feelings about the candidate or fear about the candidates' opponent. Though some have derided such emotional appeals as distracting voters from making good decisions about whom to vote for, others defend such emotional appeals as providing a sound basis for voter choice. Ted Brader, CAMPAIGNING FOR HEARTS AND MINDS (2006). Somewhat surprisingly, Brader found "the most knowledgeable or 'sophisticated' citizens are also the most responsive to emotional appeals." *Id.* at 183. Brader believes voters can make sound decisions about which candidates to vote for by relying on their emotional responses.

If campaign advertising appeals to emotions, is it manipulative, causing voters to vote against their true preferences? Ansolabehere and Iyengar do not think so: "In the end, political advertising does not produce wholesale manipulation and deception of the electorate. Rather, it leads partisans to cast 'informed' votes. Exposure to advertising induces less-informed Democrats and Republicans to vote like their fellow partisans, who are more knowledgeable about the candidates and public affairs." Stephen Ansolabehere & Shanto Iyengar, GOING NEGATIVE: HOW POLITICAL ADVERTISEMENTS SHRINK AND POLARIZE THE ELECTORATE 66 (1995). Indeed, "Democrats and Republicans tend to reject messages from the opposing party, and liberals and conservatives reject persuasive communications that are inconsistent with their ideologies." John R. Zaller, THE NATURE AND ORIGIN OF MASS PUBLIC OPINION 267 (1992).

Other information on campaigns comes through media coverage of the candidates. There seems little question that much of the news media coverage aims to make politics entertaining to viewers—after all, newspaper publishers want to sell newspapers and television executives want to sell advertising. Media coverage typically focuses on the "horserace" aspect of the campaign (who's ahead in the polls) as well as "gaffe" coverage, such as when a candidate makes a mistake in a debate or elsewhere. There is much less coverage of the candidates' various positions on issues and policies, a fact often lamented by some civic minded activists.

Political scientists are divided, however, on whether this media coverage has a negative influence on voter choices. Thomas Patterson, for example, believes that media coverage deprives voters of valuable information on the candidates, and leads to the choosing of candidates who are telegenic and can speak in sound bites. Thomas E. Patterson, OUT OF ORDER (1994). Samuel Popkin, in contrast, believes that media coverage can give voters the information they need to make choices consistent with their interests. Samuel L. Popkin, THE REASONING VOTER: COMMUNICATION AND PERSUASION IN PRESIDENTIAL CAMPAIGNS (1991). For example, Popkin defends "gaffe" coverage. He points to President Ford's 1976 campaign gaffe when he tried to take a bite of the inedible husk of a Mexican tamale. Popkin explains that Ford's unfamiliarity with the tamale told Latino voters that he was unfamiliar with their culture and unlikely to be sympathetic to their interests. *Id.* at 111. Because the gaffe coverage was entertaining, voters had a rational incentive to obtain the information.

Gelman and King, *supra* at 449, find horserace coverage largely irrelevant: "[J]ournalists should realize that they can report the polls all they want, and continue to make incorrect causal inferences about them, but they are not helping to predict or even influence the election."

Campaigns for other offices differ in significant ways from presidential campaigns. Some campaigns for lower office will be lopsided (for example, because one campaign will have more resources than the other, or a more competent campaign staff), and a superior campaign organization could be a decisive factor in some elections. Other elections may be swayed by national events (such as 9/11 or corruption scandals) beyond the message control of ordinary campaigns.

Unlike presidential and U.S. Senate campaigns, which rely heavily on television advertising, about one-third of U.S. House campaigns (and fewer campaigns in expensive media markets) rely on means other than television to get their messages out. Gary C. Jacobson, THE POLITICS OF CONGRESSIONAL ELECTIONS 88 (6th ed. 2004.) In state elections, statewide campaigns in large states such as California may depend heavily on television advertisements and direct mail; in smaller states, and in district races even in larger states, in-person contact, radio, phone and mail are likely to be much more important than television.

Increasingly, voters are turning to the Internet for campaign information. With many campaigns sending opposition researchers to video record the opposing candidate, a controversial remark or gaffe made on the campaign trail can mushroom into a major campaign issue when the video is posted on the internet. Consider Virginia U.S. Senator George Allen, who was considered a shoo-in for reelection to the Senate in 2006 until his "macaca moment." Allen was being videotaped by an opposition researcher from the campaign of his opponent, James Webb. On video quickly posted on the Internet's YouTube website, "[h]e called a Webb volunteer of Indian descent 'macaca' and welcomed him to 'America and the real world of Virginia.'" Michael D. Shear & Tim Craig, *After 2 Decades in Ascent, A Stunning Breakdown*, WASHINGTON POST, Nov. 10, 2006, at A01. His campaign tumbled after that moment. What, if anything, did Virginia voters learn about Allen from the extensive gaffe coverage of the so-called "macaca moment?"

In low salience races, such as races for superior court judge or local dog catcher, voters may have seen no advertising and know nothing about the candidate before entering the voting booth, and will rely upon various voting cues in deciding how to vote.[c] A party label is a useful cue for voters—knowing the candidate is a Republican or Democrat may be all the voter needs to know. In the absence of a party label (be it in a party primary or nonpartisan election), voters may rely upon the candidate's listed occupation, whether or not the candidate is the incumbent, and even the likely ethnic background of the candidate based upon the candidate's surname to choose how to vote. See Richard L. Hasen, *"High Court Wrongly Elected:" A Public Choice Model of Judging and Its Implications for the Voting Rights Act*, 75 NORTH CAROLINA LAW REVIEW 1305, 1316 (1997) (collecting citations to the political science literature). There is also evidence, though it is disputed across different types of races, that being listed first on a ballot can benefit a candidate, particularly in a low salience race. See J.A. Krosnick, J.M. Miller, & M.P. Tichy, *An Unrecognized Need For Ballot Reform: Effects of Candidate Name Order, in* RETHINKING THE VOTE: THE

---

c. That is, if they do vote. Voters are more likely to vote for more prominent races (the "top of the ticket") than in less salient local races, even though the chances of affecting the outcome of larger races are much smaller. For roll-off figures in judicial retention elections, see PHILIP L. DUBOIS, FROM BALLOT TO BENCH 48 tbl. 2 (1980).

Politics and Prospects of American Election Reform 51 (A.N. Crigler, M.R. Just, & E.J. McCaffery eds., 2004); Jonathan GS Koppell & Jennifer A. Steen, *The Effects of Ballot Position on Election Outcomes*, 66 Journal of Politics 267 (2004); R. Michael Alvarez, Betsy Sinclair, and Richard L. Hasen, *How Much is Enough? The "Ballot Order Effect" and the Use of Social Science Research in Election Law Disputes*, 5 Election Law Journal 40 (2006).

Though voters typically express disapproval of the job done by many state legislatures and Congress, being an incumbent is a decided advantage for both state and federal officeholders. The extent of this advantage and possible reasons for it are explored in Chapter 12.

Political scientists have also studied a number of popular perceptions about campaigns. Many in the public believe that campaigns, especially presidential campaigns, are too long. Some believe that there is too much negative campaigning, which increases voter cynicism about the political process. Some political scientists defend negative campaigning as imparting valuable information to voters. John G. Geer, In Defense of Negativity: Attack Ads in Presidential Campaigns (2006). Others counter that negative campaigning can demobilize voters, especially independent voters, leading to a decline in voter turnout. Ansolabehere & Iyengar, *supra*, ch. 5. The effect of negative campaigning on turnout continues to be debated. For a summary and critique, see Deborah Jordan Brooks, *The Resilient Voter: Moving Toward Closure in the Debate over Negative Campaigning and Turnout*, 68 Journal of Politics 684 (2006).

In sum, political scientists appear to have moved beyond the question of "Do campaigns matter" to the question of "When and how do campaigns matter? Campaign effects are themselves quite variable, and therefore we must identify which conditions narrow or broaden the scope for manipulation." Henry Brady, Richard Johnston, & John Sides, *The Study of Political Campaigns*, in Capturing Campaign Effects 1, 12 (Henry Brady & Richard Johnston, eds. 2006).

Notes and Questions

1. Depending upon how one diagnoses the problems, if any, of American political campaigns, it is possible to imagine a whole series of laws that might be passed to regulate campaigns, some of which have been adopted in other democracies. For example, laws might seek to shorten the campaign period, require candidates to participate in a number of debates, bar candidate television advertising except for free air time provided by the government, prevent false or negative campaign speech, require newscasts to broadcast campaign conventions and cover issues, not "horserace" coverage or campaign gaffes, require candidates to run in elections with party labels, limit fundraising by independent groups that are more likely to run negative advertisements, and require candidates to abide by an oath of civility. Many, if not most, of these proposed laws would run afoul of the First Amendment of the U.S. Constitution, as we will see in Parts II and III of this Chapter. Putting aside the constitutional issue for a moment, would you favor adopting any of these laws? Why or why not?

Considering existing law, James A. Gardner, *Deliberation or Tabulation? The Self Undermining Constitutional Architecture of Election Campaigns*, 54 Buffalo Law Review 1413 (2007), argues that American law purports to understand campaigns to be about reasoned deliberation, but that campaign finance laws, ballot access laws, and other current election laws discourage such deliberation:

Sometimes the law delivers what it promises, sometimes not. In the case of election campaigns, the law publicly proclaims a strong commitment to a widely held social conception of what election campaigns ought to be. In that understanding, campaigns ought to be deliberative in that their characteristic activity should be the practice of thoughtful and reasoned persuasion. Instead, the laws and jurisprudential doctrines structuring American election campaigns are built around a very different assumption: that the purpose of campaigns is primarily to tabulate exogenous voter preferences, and that political actors cannot reasonably expect, and therefore need not by law enjoy, meaningful opportunities during the campaign period to persuade voters to their points of view. Reasoned persuasion, in this environment, can thus be expected to play at most a minor, supporting role in most campaigns. Nothing in the law affirmatively prevents persuasion from occurring, but certainly the architecture of campaign law does nothing to facilitate it, and in some cases throws up obstacles to persuasion that may well be significant.

Id. at 1481. What changes to election law might facilitate more deliberation? Should election law be changed to facilitate more deliberation?

2. Dirty tricks have always been a part of campaigns. Recent examples include New Hampshire Republican Party officials jamming the phone lines of an election day assistance program of the Democratic Party and Democrats in Milwaukee slashing tires of vans taking Republican voters to the polls. *See* Thomas B. Edsall, *GOP Official Faces Sentence in Phone Jamming Case*, WASHINGTON POST, May 17, 2006, at A10; Meg Jones, *4 Get Jail in Election Day Tire Slashing*, MILWAUKEE JOURNAL-SENTINEL, April 26, 2006.

Many of these practices are already illegal under state and local law, and some under federal law as well. Should a new federal law be passed to deal specifically with campaign dirty tricks? Bills have been proposed to expand coverage or increase penalties, but none have yet passed. For a recent example, see Deceptive Practices and Voter Intimidation Act of 2007, S. 453, 110th Cong., 1st session. Among other provisions, the bill would prohibit any person, whether acting under color of law or otherwise, from knowingly deceiving any other person regarding: (1) the time, place, or manner of conducting any federal election; or (2) the qualifications for or restrictions on voter eligibility in such an election.

3. *Campaign Hang-ups.* In recent years, many campaigns have turned to automated, prerecorded telephone calls (or "robocalls") to voters to get out the vote, even though it is not clear that robocalls are effective as a voter mobilization tool. See Donald P. Green & Alan S. Gerber, GET OUT THE VOTE! HOW TO INCREASE VOTER TURNOUT (2004). Indeed, voters have complained about the frequency of these calls and a number of states have considered legislation to ban the practice. See Susan Saulny, *Limits Sought on "Robocalls" in Campaigns*, NEW YORK TIMES, April 25, 2007.

A less reputable practice is "push polling:" "Push polls are not really polls at all; their object is not to measure public opinion, but to manipulate it by providing as many 'respondents' as possible, with hypothetical, sometimes blatantly false information about candidates, political parties, or initiatives." Evan Gerstmann & Matthew J. Streb, *Putting an End to Push Polling: Why It Should Be Banned and Why the First Amendment Lets Congress Ban It*, 3 ELECTION LAW JOURNAL 37 (2004). Do you agree with Gerstmann and Streb that banning push polling is a good idea? Consider the constitutional question of banning the practice after you have reviewed the material in Part II.

II. Regulating Campaign Speech

State of Washington v. 119 Vote No! Committee

957 P.2d 691 (Wash. 1998)

SANDERS, Justice.

[The State of Washington through its Public Disclosure Commission (PDC) alleged that the 119 Vote No! Committee violated Revised Code of Washington (RCW) section 42.17.530(1)(a) by publishing false political advertising during the course of its campaign in opposition to Initiative 119, the so-called "Death with Dignity Act." Ultimately the initiative went down to defeat at the polls on November 5, 1991. The one-page printed advertisement began with the words "Vote No!" superimposed over the words "Initiative 119," and generally suggested that the initiative invited assisted suicide without sufficient safeguards.[d]

At the time, RCW § 42.17.530(1)(a) prohibited any person from sponsoring, with actual malice, a political advertisement containing a false statement of material fact.[e] The PDC's referral arose from a complaint filed by proponents of the initiative. The PDC's complaint asked that the Committee and individual defendants be fined up to $10,000 plus costs, attorney fees, and treble damages.

The trial court concluded the advertisement did not contain materially false statements and dismissed, but the intervenor, the American Civil Liberties Union (ACLU), pursued its claim for a declaratory judgment of invalidity. The trial court then held the statute valid on its face.]

---

d. The leaflet stated in pertinent part:
　　* * *

Initiative 119: Vote No
IT WOULD LET DOCTORS END PATIENTS' LIVES WITHOUT BENEFIT OF SAFE-GUARDS ...
　　* * *

　　No special qualifications—
　　your eye doctor could kill you.
　　No rules against coercion—
　　Nothing to prevent "selling" the idea to the aged, the poor, the homeless.
　　No reporting requirements—
　　No records kept.
　　No notification requirements—
　　Nobody need tell family members beforehand.
　　No protection for the depressed—
　　No waiting period; no chance to change your mind.
INITIATIVE 119 ... IS A DANGEROUS LAW
VOTE NO ON INITIATIVE 119

e. RCW §42.17.530 provided:
　　(1) It is a violation of this chapter for a person to sponsor with actual malice:
　　　　(a) Political advertising that contains a false statement of material fact;
　　　　(b) Political advertising that falsely represents that a candidate is the incumbent for the office sought when in fact the candidate is not the incumbent;
　　　　(c) Political advertising that makes either directly or indirectly, a false claim stating or implying the support or endorsement of any person or organization when in fact the candidate does not have such support or endorsement.
　　(2) Any violation of this section shall be proven by clear and convincing evidence.

III. Legal Analysis

… The Committee and the ACLU argue the statute is a facially unconstitutional abridgment of free speech. The State asserts its interest in an informed electorate justifies this burden upon political debate.

The constitutional guarantee of free speech has its "fullest and most urgent application" in political campaigns. *Brown v. Hartlage*, 456 U.S. 45,53 (1982). Therefore, the State bears a "well-nigh insurmountable" burden to justify RCW 42.17.530's restriction on political speech. *Meyer v. Grant*, 486 U.S. 414 (1988). This burden requires the court to apply "exacting scrutiny" to RCW 42.17.530(1)(a). *Meyer*. *See also Buckley*. Exacting scrutiny will invalidate the statute unless the State demonstrates a compelling interest that is both narrowly tailored and necessary. *McIntyre v. Ohio Elections Commission*, 514 U.S. 334 (1995); *Burson v. Freeman*, 504 U.S. 191, 198 (1992). Such burdens are rarely met. *Burson*.

A. RCW 42.17.530(1)(a) infringes on speech protected by the First Amendment

… The State asserts it may prohibit false statements of fact contained in political advertisements. This claim presupposes the State possesses an independent right to determine truth and falsity in political debate. However, the courts have "consistently refused to recognize an exception for any test of truth — whether administered by judges, juries, or administrative officials — and especially one that puts the burden of proving truth on the speaker." *New York Times Co. v. Sullivan*, 376 U.S. 254, 271 (1964).

Rather, the First Amendment operates to insure the public decides what is true and false with respect to governance. *Meyer*; *Riley v. National Fed. of the Blind of North Carolina, Inc.*, 487 U.S. 781 (1988)….

Particularly in the religious and political realms, "the tenets of one man … seem the rankest error to his neighbor." *Cantwell v. Connecticut*, 310 U.S. 296, 310 (1940). Therefore, the Supreme Court has recognized that to sustain our constitutional commitment to uninhibited political discourse, the State may not prevent others from "resort[ing] to exaggeration, to vilification of men who have been, or are, prominent in church and state, and *even to false statement*." *Id.* (emphasis added). At times such speech seems unpalatable, but the value of free debate overcomes the danger of misuse. *McIntyre*. For even false statements make valuable contributions to debate by bringing about "the clearer perception and livelier impression of truth, produced by its collision with error." *New York Times* (quoting John S. Mill, *On Liberty* 15 (Oxford, Blackwell 1947)).

Specifically, the First Amendment prohibits the State from silencing speech it disapproves, particularly silencing criticism of government itself. Threats of coerced silence chill uninhibited political debate and undermine the very purpose of the First Amendment. See *Riley*; *Brown*; *Meyer*….

Instead of relying on the State to silence false political speech, the First Amendment requires our dependence on even more speech to bring forth truth. *Brown*. See also *Gertz v. Robert Welch, Inc.*, 418 U.S. 323, 339–40 (1974). In the political context, a campaign's factual blunder is most likely noticed and corrected by the campaign's political opponent rather than the State. *Id.* Contrary to claims made by Justice Talmadge in his concurrence, the Supreme Court has refused to recognize the possibility of "'an eleventh-hour anonymous smear campaign'" as enough to justify a restriction on speech. *McIntyre*. Moreover, a well-publicized, yet bogus, complaint to the PDC on election eve raises the same concern. Therefore, "[t]he preferred First Amendment remedy of 'more speech, not enforced silence' thus has special force." *Brown*. Underlying our dependence upon more speech is the presupposition "that right conclusions are more likely to be gathered out of a multitude of tongues, than through any kind of authoritative selection. To many this is, and always will be, folly; but we have staked upon it our all.'" *New York Times*. . . .

Even assuming, as per Justice Talmadge's concurrence, that malicious falsehoods against candidates are beyond constitutional protection, this statute has broader reach and brings within its sweep every maliciously false statement of "material fact" whether it is defamatory to an individual or not. Justice Talmadge's concurrence cites no authority to support its broad claim that all false statements in a political advertisement, including statements relating to issues campaigns, may be prohibited as unprotected speech. Moreover, the statutory requirement that malice be proved by a high standard of proof does not cure the infirmity as the chilling effect of possible governmental sanction will not be lost on the faint of heart.

B. RCW 42.17.530(1)(a) does not serve a compelling state interest

. . . The State claims its interest to foster an informed electorate outweighs the imposition upon political expression by RCW 42.17.530(1)(a). The State relies heavily on defamation cases to prove a compelling interest to justify intrusion into public debate citing *Gertz*, which states: "[T]here is no constitutional value in false statements of fact. Neither the intentional lie nor the careless error materially advances society's interest in 'uninhibited, robust, and wide-open' debate on public issues." . . . The State argues the language in these defamation cases applies with equal force to all political speech, even if no one is defamed.

However the State's reliance on the law of defamation is misplaced. By its nature defamation concerns statements made by one person against another and is designed to protect the property of an individual in his or her good name.

> The legitimate state interest underlying the law of libel is the compensation of individuals for the harm inflicted on them by a defamatory falsehood. . . . [T]he individual's right to the protection of his own good name "reflects no more than our basic concept of the essential dignity and worth of every human being—a concept at the root of any decent system of ordered liberty."

Gertz. Clearly, a competing interest exists in defamation cases which is absent here. . . .

However RCW 42.17.530(1)(a) restricts political speech absent the competing interest present in defamation cases, and, unlike a defamation suit, creates a cause of action for the government to pursue against a private person. "The legitimate state interest underlying the law of libel is the compensation of individuals for the harm inflicted on them for defamatory falsehood." *Gertz*. . . .

Additionally, the State relies upon the United States Supreme Court's decision in *McIntyre* . . . to support its contention that it has a compelling interest to regulate maliciously false speech. But neither case supports its claim.

In *McIntyre* the Supreme Court held a statute prohibiting anonymous leaflets violated the First Amendment. The Court noted Ohio's Elections Code contained detailed prohibitions against making false statements. Therefore the State asserts *McIntyre* impliedly suggested laws prohibiting false political statements are constitutional.

However the inference to be drawn from *McIntyre* is just the opposite. *McIntyre* explained that speech made in the heat of a political contest receives more protection than any other form of political speech. The state in *McIntyre* argued the speech restrictions were necessary because false advertising might be distributed as "an eleventh-hour anonymous smear campaign." The Court explained the statute could not be upheld on that ground because it swept within it speech unrelated to the state's concern. Describing the statute's unconstitutional breadth, the Court distinguished between literature supporting or opposing candidates from referenda as "[a] public question clearly cannot be the victim of character assassination." *McIntyre* indicates the State does not possess an independent right to determine truth and falsity in public issues.

Additionally, even if the State possessed a compelling interest here, it must also prove the statute at issue is necessary to serve that interest. *Burson*. However, the record here demonstrates RCW 42.17.530(1)(a) may be manipulated by candidates to impugn the electoral process rather than promote truthfulness.

Ultimately, the State's claimed compelling interest to shield the public from falsehoods during a political campaign is patronizing and paternalistic. *See Eu; Brown*. It assumes the people of this state are too ignorant or disinterested to investigate, learn, and determine for themselves the truth or falsity in political debate, and it is the proper role of the government itself to fill the void. This assumption is especially flawed in cases like this where the truth of the assertion may be readily tested against the text of the initiative. At its worst the statute is pure censorship, allowing government to undertake prosecution of citizens who, in their view, have abused the right of political debate....

IV. Conclusion

The First Amendment to the United States Constitution renders [the statute] facially unconstitutional. The ACLU [and 119 Vote No! Committee are awarded their] reasonable attorney fees....

[Justice Guy concurred, stating that the statute was constitutional but the advertisement did not violate the statute. Justice Madsen concurred with the majority that the statute was unconstitutional as it applied to ballot elections, but she stated that Washington could constitutionally penalize a deliberate falsehood about candidates for public office.]

TALMADGE, Justice, concurring.

Today the Washington State Supreme Court becomes the first court in the history of the Republic to declare First Amendment protection for calculated lies. In so doing, the majority opinion flouts numerous United States Supreme Court pronouncements to the contrary. The majority determines RCW 42.17.530, a statute providing penalties for dissemination of false political advertising, is facially violative of the First Amendment because the State has no compelling interest in preventing lies in the course of an initiative or referendum campaign, no matter how egregious the lies may be.

The sweep of the majority's rhetoric is so encompassing that no statute designed to ensure statements of fact in political campaigns are truthful would survive a First Amendment challenge. Moreover, the breadth of the majority's rhetoric has untold impacts on existing law regarding political campaigns for candidates and ballot measures.

The majority is also shockingly oblivious to the increasing nastiness of modern American political campaigns. This trend is highlighted by a "win at any cost" attitude involving vilification of opponents and their ideas. This new type of campaign neither illuminates nor exemplifies the best of our democratic tradition, and has caused too many of our fellow citizens to turn away from participation in the political process.

While I believe the First Amendment properly presents extraordinarily difficult hurdles for statutes addressing political speech and conduct, I cannot agree RCW 42.17.530 violates the First Amendment. However, because I believe the 119 Vote No! Committee (Committee) did not violate RCW 42.17.530(1)(a), I concur in the majority's disposition of the case....

B. Constitutionality of RCW 42.17.530

The majority cites only a small portion of the challenged statute, and undertakes no analysis of the wording of the statute. Thus, one must guess as to the constitutional infirmities the majority claims exist. The majority tells us the State may not prohibit "unpalatable" speech. But the statute addresses only lies, not vitriol. The majority tells us the State may not silence criticism of the government. But the statute addresses only calculated falsehoods, not censure. The majority tells us the State may not chill uninhibited political debate. But the statute addresses only malicious prevarication, not honest, robust, political debate. The majority tells us factual blunders are best corrected by the opponent. But the statute addresses deliberate falsehoods, not innocent errors of fact.

The key to the majority's analysis of the statute is found in the following two sentences: "The State asserts it may prohibit false statements of fact contained in political advertisements. The claim presupposes the State possesses an independent right to determine truth or falsity in political debate." The majority thus presumes the people of Washington have no authority to require persons to tell the truth. This presumption is, of course, wrong. Perjury has been a part of Washington's criminal code since territorial days. Prohibitions against lying and bearing false witness may be found in cultures worldwide from time immemorial.

Although perjury itself concerns lying under oath or in official proceedings, there is no reason the State may not prohibit lying in other contexts pursuant to the exercise of its police power. That is precisely what the State has done by enacting the challenged statute in this case.

The challenged statute is plainly a valid exercise of the police power. *Lawton v. Steele*, 152 U.S. 133 (1894). If the elected representatives of the people of Washington, who are accountable to their constituents every two and four years, in their considered judgment believe calculated lying does not belong in electoral politics, it is not for us to question the wisdom of or necessity for such legislation.

Turning to the First Amendment, the threshold question is whether the statute affects speech over which the First Amendment affords protection. Without examining the wording or effect of the statute, the majority simply assumes protected speech is involved. Subsuming the answer in the question falls a good way short of the penetrating rigor a legitimate constitutional analysis requires. We start with the wording of the statute....

[The statute was amended in 1988 to include an "actual malice" requirement. In] RCW 42.17.505(1), the Legislature defined actual malice to mean "to act with knowledge of falsity or with reckless disregard as to truth or falsity." By requiring the intermediate standard of proof, clear and convincing evidence, the new statute made violations more difficult to prove. Thus, a person violates the statute if and only if he or she sponsors political advertising that is (1) a false statement of material fact (2) with actual malice, as defined, and (3) is found to have done so by clear and convincing evidence. One example of a violation of this statute might be a political flyer from a candidate who declares herself to be the incumbent when in fact she is not. She has acted with "knowledge of falsity." Another example could be one candidate's accusing an opponent of having been convicted of desertion during the Vietnam War. In a case such as this, the accuser may have no actual knowledge one way or the other, but has violated the statute by acting with "reckless disregard as to the truth or falsity" of the accusation. These examples are what men and women of common understanding would describe as deliberate lies. Do deliberate lies come under the protective umbrella of the First Amendment? The majority opinion says "yes." The Supreme Court of the United States has said "no" on numerous occasions, as have all other courts addressing the same question.

The Supreme Court has unequivocally and repeatedly refused to extend First Amendment protection to *deliberate lies*. [Justice Talmadge discussed United States Supreme Court cases, Washington Supreme Court cases, and cases from other jurisdictions on this point.]

Despite the mountain of United States Supreme Court and state court authority to the contrary, the majority decides the First Amendment condones deliberate falsehoods in campaigns. As support for its position, the majority cites to *New York Times* on four separate occasions. Yet *nowhere* does the majority opinion reveal the *holding* of *New York Times*, which is "a public official cannot recover for defamation unless he or she establishes the defendant made the defamatory statement with actual malice, that is, knowledge of its falsity or with reckless disregard for whether it was false or not." *Richmond v. Thompson*, 922 P.2d 1343 (Wash.1996). The new RCW 42.17.530(1)(a), having added actual malice as a required element of the violation and having adopted from *New York Times* the exact language defining "actual malice," plainly passes muster under that case. Similarly, the new statute's requirement of clear and convincing evidence mirrors the requirement for the higher standard of proof set forth in *Gertz*. How, then, can a statute on all fours with controlling United States Supreme Court authority be unconstitutional in Washington? As long as *New York Times* remains the supreme law of the land, we are not free to ignore it, or to interpret it to our liking, short of articulating independent state grounds for doing so under the Washington constitution. Nobody has made such an argument in this case. The United States Supreme Court would not find RCW 42.17.530(1)(a) unconstitutional under its First Amendment jurisprudence. Nor may we.

The Court's holding in *New York Times* and its repeated refusals to grant First Amendment protection to lies are completely dispositive of the issues in this case. The majority is undeterred by authority, however, and finding no case extending First Amendment protection to deliberate lies in political campaigns, asserts a novel proposition to support its conclusion: the majority decides that everything the Supreme Court said in *New York Times, Garrison,* and *Gertz* concerning deliberate lies is applicable only to defamation cases, and not to ballot issues that, because they do not involve individuals, are not susceptible to defamation actions. The Supreme Court itself has never indicated such a dichotomy exists, nor has any other court in any other jurisdiction....

The chilling effect of the statute on free speech is infinitesimal, if it exists at all. The scope of RCW 42.17.530(1)(a) is severely proscribed. It does not reach hyperbole or rhetoric, polemic or beguiling commentary, satire or mockery, zealotry or insanity, insincerity or low cunning, true beliefs or mere mistakes. It does not concern itself with opinion or political position. The communists, the fascists, the socialists, the New Democrats, the Old Democrats, the moderate Republicans, the radical right Republicans, the liberals, the Luddites, the conservatives, the Christian Coalition, the Reform Party, the Socialist Workers Party, the Wobblies, the Webeloes, the cranks, the crackpots, the naive, the foolish, the property rights advocates, the environmentalists, the Tsarists, the monarchists, the anarchists, the disgruntled, the Sandanistas, the survivalists, the Ku Klux Klan, the America Firsters—all have nothing to fear from the law.

The statute speaks to only one person: the calculating liar, who with clear mind and steadfast, deliberate purpose, coldly composes and diligently distributes knowing lies to effect a desired political result. The statute chills only this devious liar, not free speech.... Accordingly, I do not find RCW 42.17.530(1)(a) facially unconstitutional.[5]

---

5. The majority's disapproval of RCW 42.17.530(1)(a) goes further than its analysis warrants. The majority's analysis recognizes two different situations—the first, where candidates are involved, implicating defamation concerns, and the second, where only ballot issues are involved, and defamation

C. Compelling State Interest

Because I conclude calculated lies are not protected speech under the First Amendment, it is not necessary to address the second question, which is, does the state have a compelling interest in prohibiting calculated lies in political campaigns. Nevertheless, I address it because the majority implies the State does not have a compelling interest in preserving the sanctity of the electoral process....

Do the people of Washington have a compelling interest in penalizing deliberate lies in political campaigns? The answer is obvious.... The State has a compelling interest in ensuring the integrity of the electoral process, for ballot measures as well as for election of candidates. That compelling interest includes punishing calculated deceit and knowing lies.

A distressing feature of the majority's analysis is its fundamental lack of any connection with the real world of political campaigns. Its entire answer to any concerns about an electoral process flowing from deliberate lies is that more speech will cure such falsehoods. I wish this were true, and, in the best of all possible worlds, it could be. But, in modern American politics, it isn't reality. It is indeed all too common for candidates, political committees and individuals in political campaigns to make last minute charges, usually distributed the weekend before election day or in a fashion calculated to forestall a reply through whatever means at their disposal. There is simply no time to use any of the traditional means of political communication—leaflets, direct mail, newspaper, radio or television advertising—to combat late hour, outrageously false statements. Further speech, in the classic formulation, will not cure such a situation....

Ironically, in the case of defamation in a campaign involving candidates, the remedies for such conduct may actually be greater than those available to address outright lies in a ballot measure campaign. A defamed candidate has a cause of action in court. That candidate may also suggest to the legislative body that the offending candidate should not be seated. That candidate could even challenge the offender in the next election. By contrast, the ballot measure enacted on the basis of a campaign of lies may be amended only by a two-thirds vote of the Legislature for the period of two years after its enactment. Few legislators would choose to risk proposing the repeal of a popularly enacted measure, let alone two-thirds of all legislators necessary for such repeal, to express antagonism to a campaign flawed by deliberate lies.

American political campaigns in general and campaigns in the State of Washington have become all too often campaigns of vilification and mudslinging, rather than campaigns of communication. While this has been true throughout the course of American history, the sophistication of recent political campaigns coupled with the ability of the media to reach so many so quickly have only enhanced the power of last minute campaign smears. Moreover, money talks in elections. If the victim is without significant campaign resources, the "Big Lie" technique can, unfortunately prevail over the truth. All too many of our fellow citizens, turned off by these kinds of political maneuvers, have turned away from the political system, expressing indifference to the extreme tactics taken by partisans of candidates or issues.[7]

---

is not an issue. It is not clear at all from the majority's analysis that the statute should be unconstitutional under the first circumstance. Indeed, insofar as the statute tracks the *New York Times* test, it plainly cannot be unconstitutional. At most, then, the majority's reasoning supports a holding of unconstitutionality only when ballot issues are involved, yet the majority strikes down the statute in its entirety.

7. In a 1988 campaign for the State House of Representatives, for example, the successful candidate sent out a mailing over the last weekend of the campaign against his opponent, a former Super-

Because of the foregoing realities of modern electoral politics, the State Legislature was justified in declaring a compelling interest in ensuring that at least a modicum of propriety be observed in political campaigns, that modicum being honesty. In particular, the State has a compelling interest to ensure no deliberately false statements of fact are disseminated in the course of a campaign involving candidates or ballot measures. The majority would destroy any statutory effort to prohibit deliberate falsehoods in campaigns or, for that matter, disclosure of information to the public regarding adherence to campaign ethics standards. With this, the majority sends out the wrong message to a public troubled by rampant problems in the campaign process while it condones lies in ballot measure campaigns as constitutionally protected, leaving our society powerless to take the most minimal steps to stop them. Unlike the majority, I am unwilling to find, as a matter of First Amendment principles, that any and all lies, no matter how egregious, are constitutionally protected in ballot measure campaigns.

The majority considers invocation of society's interest in campaign integrity "patronizing and paternalistic." This is a novel approach to constitutional analysis. We have no authority to strike down legislation because we consider it to be patronizing and paternalistic. No constitutional standard of review with which I am familiar encompasses those terms. I consider it remarkably patronizing to claim the people of Washington have no compelling interest in preventing political campaigns from being corrupted by deliberate liars....

D. Application of RCW 42.17.530

Having found the statute constitutional, I next address whether it was violated. The trial court correctly determined the 119 Vote No! Committee did not violate RCW 42.17.530 because the Committee engaged in traditional political campaign hyperbole in the campaign against Initiative 119. The Committee distributed a leaflet with statements of opinion regarding the contents of the proposed law; those opinions did not constitute facts within the meaning of the statute....

In construing a similar statute, Oregon courts have consistently held that a statement that can in any way be inferred to be either factually correct or a mere opinion is not prohibited by Oregon's statute, even though it could also be interpreted as a false factual statement. *See, e.g., Committee of One Thousand to Re-Elect State Senator Walt Brown v. Eivers*, 674 P.2d 1159, 1164 (Or. 1983). The Oregon standard is a very difficult one to establish, but still provides that factually false statements may be actionable....

The leaflet here stated Initiative 119 would permit doctors to end patients' lives "without safeguards," arguing the Initiative did not specify special qualifications for physicians under the Initiative, rules against coercion of patients, reporting requirements for when the authority under the Initiative was exercised, notification requirements for family members, or special protections for vulnerable individuals. These concerns relate particularly to the operation or effect of the law. As the PDC indicates in its brief, these statements are often far beyond the actual text of the Initiative.

However, these statements are debatable assertions of opinion regarding the impact of the Initiative from the perspective of the Initiative's opponents, who believed the Initia-

---

intendent of Public Instruction, implying that his opponent had "something to hide" in his refusal to remove licenses of teachers investigated for illicit relations with students. [The statute at issue in this case was in effect during this race; before 1988 one could violate the statute even without "actual malice." What does that say about the effectiveness of the statute in deterring false political speech? — Eds.]

tive went too far in allowing physician-assisted suicide and did too little to protect individuals subject to its authority.

Political campaigns are communications exercises and often involve heated debate rife with hyperbole that pushes the truth to its edge. The Committee's statements in its leaflet were statements of opinion about the effect of the proposed law. They were sufficiently debatable to fall within the wide latitude this Court has traditionally given to political speech.[11] ...

Notes and Questions

1. On the level of constitutional doctrine, the majority opinion and Justice Talmadge's concurrence agree that a person may not be fined for making a false statement in a political campaign unless the statement was made with *actual malice*, that is, knowingly false or made with reckless disregard as to truth or falsity. In addition to the actual malice requirement, the majority also requires that the statement be *defamatory*, that is, injuring the reputation of an individual. Justice Talmadge argues that actual malice is sufficient to meet constitutional concerns. The Sixth Circuit upheld portions of an Ohio law regulating false political statements because it contained an actual malice requirement. *Pestrak v. Ohio Elections Commission*, 926 F.2d 573, 577 (6th Cir. 1991). Should something more than actual malice be required? For an argument that the Supreme Court's cases allowing regulation of corporate and labor union campaign expenditures provide support for regulating false campaign speech made with actual malice, see William P. Marshall, *False Campaign Speech and the First Amendment*, 152 UNIVERSITY OF PENNSYLVANIA LAW REVIEW 285 (2004).

For a case confirming that actual malice is required to sanction candidate speech, see *Ancheta v. Watada*, 135 F.Supp.2d 1114, 1122 (D. Hawaii 2001). The court rejected the argument that Hawaii's regulation of candidate speech could be justified on grounds of preventing candidates from being discouraged from running for public office.

2. In *McKimm v. Ohio Elections Commission*, 729 N.E.2d 364 (Ohio 2000), cert. denied, 531 U.S. 1078 (2001), the Ohio Supreme Court upheld the reprimand of a candidate who published a cartoon depicting his opposing candidate holding a bundle of cash underneath a table along with accompanying words that the court held connoted to the reasonable reader that the candidate had taken a bribe or kickback. The cartoon appears in Figure 11.1.

The court upheld the reprimand after examining the commission's finding of actual malice: the court stated that the candidate "had no basis to believe that [the opposing candidate] had participated in ... any illegal acts ... during his tenure as trustee.... After our independent review of the record, we agree with the commission and the trial court that [the candidate] disseminated his cartoon well aware of its false implication." *Id.* at 374–75. Should a "false implication" be enough for constitutional purposes? Do such "implications" meet the actual malice standard? What chilling effect will a law reprimanding candidates for statements (or pictures!) with false implications have on candidates?

---

11. Notwithstanding the wide latitude given to political speech in the campaign context, I do confess some concern at the timing of the distribution of the leaflet at issue in this case. One million copies of the leaflet were distributed by the Committee over the weekend before the election. In the real world of political campaigns, there was no possibility whatsoever that the opponents of the Committee could prepare a responsive leaflet, prepare a direct mail response, or purchase newspaper, radio, or TV time sufficient to respond to any statements contained in the leaflet, even if they were outright falsehoods as contemplated by RCW 42.17.530.

Figure 11.1

7.   Which of the following is true?
A. Trustees have a policy of bidding **all**
   contracts greater than $10,000.
B. Randy Gonzalez **ignored** bidding policy.
   He voted to contract an architect for
   $51,000 to design the Social Hall
   (pavilion) *without taking bids.*
C. This one
   is tricky.
   Both A....
   and B.
   are true.

3. Statements made during ballot measure campaigns usually concern issues, not individuals; thus, in the ballot context, few malicious false statements would be defamatory and therefore subject to state regulation under the majority opinion in *119 Vote No! Committee*. Given that defamatory statements may be made with greater frequency in candidate campaigns, why did the majority not limit its holding to ballot measure campaigns? Note that with or without the statute, candidates can still sue for defamation under state law. Of the 17 states with laws in 2001 prohibiting false speech regarding political candidates, at least ten of them also prohibited false speech regarding ballot propositions. See Becky Kruse, Comment, *The Truth in Masquerade: Regulating False Ballot Proposition Ads Through State Anti-False Speech Statutes*, 89 CALIFORNIA LAW REVIEW 129, 132 (2001). Are all of these laws unconstitutional as applied to ballot propositions? Kruse argues against *119 Vote No! Committee* and for the constitutionality of laws regulating false speech in ballot proposition campaigns "[t]o protect the public debate, encourage more representative voting, and support the integrity of the electoral process...." *Id.* at 162. Assuming these goals are good ones, does that answer the constitutional objection? Another commentator has acknowledged the greater reputational interest at stake in candidate campaigns, but argues that the Washington law should be constitutional in ballot measure elections based upon a compelling state interest in ensuring the accuracy of information that is transmitted to voters participating in the initiative process. Carlton F.W. Larson, Note, *Bearing False Witness*, 108 YALE LAW JOURNAL 1155 (1999).

4. The majority opinion in *119 Vote No! Committee* and Justice Talmadge's concurrence disagree over whether the government can be trusted to police false statements in campaigns. The majority's distrust may be the reason it struck down the statute in its entirety. Washington's governor appoints the five members of the Public Disclosure Commission with the consent of the state senate; no more than three PDC members can be

from the same political party. RCW §42.17.350. Can such a commission avoid partisan politics?

5. In response to this case, the Washington Legislature amended the statute so that it applies only to political advertising made with actual malice that contains a false statement of material fact "about a candidate for public office. However, this subsection (1)(a) does not apply to statements made by a candidate or the candidate's agent about the candidate himself or herself." See RCW §42.17.530(1)(a) (1999).

In *Rickert v. State*, 168 P.3d 826 (Wash. 2007), a divided Washington Supreme Court struck down the revised statute even though it applied only to candidates. The Chief Justice issued a concurring opinion for himself only that controlled the outcome of the case. The opinion in its entirety reads:

> In my view, the majority goes too far in concluding that any government censorship of political speech would run afoul of the First Amendment to the United States Constitution. The United States Supreme Court has ruled that defamation is not protected by the First Amendment. *Bose Corp. v. Consumers Union of U.S., Inc.*, 466 U.S. 485, 504 (1984); *Beauharnais v. Illinois*, 343 U.S. 250, 266, (1952). The government, thus, may penalize defamatory political speech. The statute at issue here, however, prohibits nondefamatory speech in addition to defamatory speech. Thus, I concur in the majority's conclusion that RCW 42.17.530(1)(a) is unconstitutionally overbroad.

6. If false campaign statement laws (with or without a defamation requirement) are constitutional, must a court, rather than a commission, decide the question of a violation? In *Pestrak, supra*, 926 F.2d at 578, the Sixth Circuit held that the Ohio Elections Commission could not issue fines for false political statements because, as a non-judicial body, the Commission was not subject to the *Gertz* rule that punishment in this area must be based upon "clear and convincing evidence." The *Pestrak* court upheld the commission's ability to (1) recommend prosecution for violating the Ohio law to the appropriate county prosecutor, and (2) make a public declaration as to the truth of various campaign allegations.

7. The Washington statute at issue in *119 Vote No! Committee* applied only to false statements of *material* fact. Certainly the statute should not apply to immaterial or irrelevant false statements. But how does one determine materiality? Would it have been a *material* false statement if the 119 Vote No! Committee falsely claimed that Initiative 119 would allow chiropractors to assist a patient with suicide, if chiropractors were not considered "doctors" under the initiative?

8. Even if some false campaign statement laws are constitutional, how effective are they? According to a press report, the PDC had received fewer than 200 complaints since 1990, and in only 16 of those cases had a violation been found. The largest fine the PDC had levied was $2,500. Terry McDermott, *Law to Curb Political Lies Runs Afoul of Higher Truth: The 1st Amendment*, LOS ANGELES TIMES, June 18, 1998, at A5. The low fines and the inability of the PDC to respond quickly to last-minute smear campaigns make the law seem largely ineffective at controlling lying. Nor could a commission constitutionally issue "cease and desist orders" against someone accused of making false statements to prevent future false statements. Such orders violate the constitutional prohibition on prior restraint of speech. See *Pestrak, supra*, 926 F.2d at 578. The Ohio statute reviewed in *Pestrak* made intentionally disseminating a falsehood concerning a candidate for election a misdemeanor of the first degree. The *Pestrak* court did not discuss the constitutionality of this provision, which certainly would be a greater deterrent than a $2,500 fine. Is jail time for malicious false campaign statements a constitutional punishment?

9. Should it be easier to reprimand or otherwise punish a *judge* running for office for false campaign statements than to reprimand or punish a candidate for other offices? Are judges expected to be more honest than other public officials? The trend appears to be for states to impose penalties for false judicial election speech. See William Glaberson, *States Rein In Truth-Bending In Court Races*, NEW YORK TIMES, Aug. 23, 2000, at A1.

The Supreme Court took up the issue of judicial campaign speech in *Republican Party of Minnesota v. White*, 536 U.S. 765 (2002). In *White*, the Court by a 5–4 vote struck down a Minnesota judicial rule that prohibited candidates for judicial election from "announcing" their views on political or legal issues. The state had asserted the ban was necessary to promote judicial impartiality and the appearance of impartiality in the judiciary. Applying strict scrutiny, the Court held the rule violated the First Amendment because it was not narrowly tailored to promote a compelling state interest.

The Court considered three different meanings of "impartiality." It first held that the rule did not serve to further impartiality in the sense of lack of bias for or against particular *parties* likely to come before the judge because the rule targeted *issues*, not parties. As for impartiality as a "lack of preconception in favor or against a particular *legal view*," the Court held the interest was not compelling.

> A judge's lack of predisposition regarding the relevant legal issues in a case has never been thought a necessary component of equal justice, and with good reason. For one thing, it is virtually impossible to find a judge who does not have preconceptions about the law.... Indeed, even if it were possible to select judges who did not have preconceived views on legal issues, it would hardly be desirable to do so.... And since avoiding judicial preconceptions on legal issues is neither possible nor desirable, pretending otherwise by attempting to preserve the 'appearance' of that type of impartiality can hardly be a compelling state interest either.

Finally, the Court rejected the idea that the rule was justified to preserve judicial openmindedness:

> The short of the matter is this: In Minnesota, a candidate for judicial office may not say "I think it is constitutional for the legislature to prohibit same-sex marriages." He may say the very same thing, however, up until the very day before he declares himself a candidate, and may say it repeatedly (until litigation is pending) after he is elected. As a means of pursuing the objective of openmindedness that respondents now articulate, the announce clause is so woefully underinclusive as to render belief in that purpose a challenge to the credulous.

Justice O'Connor concurred, but expressed her belief that judicial elections are undesirable. Justice Kennedy filed a concurring opinion as well, in which he, among other things, distanced himself from Justice O'Connor's remarks.

Justice Stevens and Justice Ginsburg filed dissenting opinions, both joined by Justices Breyer and Souter. Justice Stevens wrote: "By obscuring the fundamental distinction between campaigns for the judiciary and the political branches, and by failing to recognize the difference between statements made in articles or opinions and those made on the campaign trail, the Court defies any sensible notion of the judicial office and the importance of impartiality in that context." Justice Ginsburg wrote: "I would differentiate elections for political offices, in which the First Amendment holds full sway, from elections designed to select those whose office it is to administer justice without respect to persons. Minnesota's choice to elect its judges, I am persuaded, does not preclude the State from installing an election process geared to the judicial office."

The Court majority was careful to note that it was not striking down rules preventing judges from making *explicit promises* in campaigns. Given the logic of *White*, are such rules constitutional under the First Amendment? If the state can no longer forbid a candidate from saying "I think it is constitutional for the legislature to prohibit same-sex marriages," what interest is served by a state law that prevents the candidate from saying, "If elected, I promise to rule that it is constitutional for the legislature to prohibit same-sex marriages"? In discussing campaign promises, Justice Scalia remarked: "one would be naive not to recognize that campaign promises are — by long democratic tradition — the least binding form of human commitment." If so, by what logic may they be banned?

On remand, the Eighth Circuit, sitting en banc, went further than the Supreme Court in *White*, striking down both a clause limiting judges' partisan political activities and their personal solicitation of campaign contributions. *Republican Party of Minnesota v. White*, 416 F.3d 738 (8th Cir. 2005) (en banc), cert. denied sub. nom. *Dimick v. Republican Party of Minnesota*, 546 U.S. 1157 (2006). A flurry of suits challenging judicial conduct rules are working their way through the courts, and it is unclear whether the new Roberts Court will tackle the constitutional questions any time soon. For an overview of the legal issues, see Richard L. Hasen, *First Amendment Limits on Regulating Judicial Campaigns*, in Running for Judge 15 (Matthew Streb, ed. 2007).

New York's judicial conduct rules have been subject to conflicting judicial analysis after *White*. Compare *Spargo v. New York State Commission of Judicial Conduct*, 244 F.Supp.2d 72 (N.D.N.Y 2003) (striking down certain provisions of New York's judicial code prohibiting partisan political activity by judges) with *In re Raab*, 793 N.E.2d 1287 (N.Y. 2003) (upholding other provisions of New York's judicial code prohibiting partisan political activity by judges) and *In re Watson*, 794 N.E.2d 1 (N.Y. 2003) (upholding provisions of New York's judicial code prohibiting judicial candidates from making campaign promises). The Second Circuit vacated the district court ruling in *Spargo* without reaching the merits, holding that the federal courts should abstain from deciding the case. *Spargo v New York State Commission of Judicial Conduct*, 351 F.3d 65 (2d Cir. 2003).

For a careful examination of the issues surrounding regulation of judicial campaigns, see Richard Briffault, *Judicial Campaign Codes after* Republican Party of Minnesota v. White, 152 University of Pennsylvania Law Review 181 (2004).

10. Some people complain that negative campaigning and a lack of civility between opponents, rather than false statements, are the greatest problems with campaigns. Even under *Pestrak*, laws purporting to regulate truthful (or non-malicious) negative or uncivil statements violate the First Amendment. One commentator has proposed that candidates targeted in negative television or radio advertisements be given the right to a contemporaneous equal time response, which would air immediately after the negative ad. "Unless the candidate himself speaks about an opponent in a negative ad, the sponsor of the negative ad would be required to share the media cost of a response ad." Michael Kimmel, *A Proposal To Strengthen the Right of Response to Negative Campaign Commercials*, 49 Catholic University Law Review 89, 91 (1999). What should be considered a "negative" ad to trigger the statute? Is it constitutional to require candidates to pay for their opposing candidates' advertisements? To require television and radio stations to run such advertisements? We consider this last question more generally in Part III.

III. The Intersection of Communications Law and Election Law

Radio-Television News Directors Association v. FCC

184 F.3d 872 (D.C. Cir. 1999)

ROGERS, Circuit Judge:

These consolidated appeals challenge the Federal Communications Commission's ("FCC") decision to not repeal the personal attack and political editorial rules. Petitioners[1] maintain that the rules are "two vestiges of a bygone area of broadcasting regulation" that should have disappeared when the FCC abrogated the fairness doctrine that the two rules were allegedly intended to "effectuate." Preserving the rules when their rationale has evaporated, petitioners contend, is arbitrary and capricious, and violates the First Amendment. The FCC has deadlocked on its proposal to repeal the rules, so we review the joint statement of Commissioners Ness and Tristani supporting retention of the rules as the opinion of the agency.

Although the FCC issued a notice of proposed rulemaking ("NPRM") proposing to repeal or modify the two challenged rules because it had concluded that the rules might no longer be in the public interest, and that "especially searching" reexamination was necessary, the FCC now defends the rules primarily by negative implication, rejecting attacks on the rules while assuming their underlying validity. Absent affirmative justification of the two rules as being in the public interest, or explanation of why the rules should survive in light of FCC precedent rejecting the fairness doctrine, the court is left in large part to guess the rationale that shields the rules from critiques the FCC found persuasive when reviewing the fairness doctrine, and which the FCC itself proffered in the NPRM. Such an approach to defending an existing rule against a suggestion that it be repealed might in other circumstances be sufficient to withstand judicial review under the Administrative Procedure Act, 5 U.S.C. §706 (1994) ("APA"), but not where the NPRM and subsequent FCC precedent frame the proceeding to require a persuasive rationale for rules that seem unnecessary. Without a clear explanation for the rules, the court is not in a position to review whether they continue to serve the public interest, and whether they burden First Amendment interests too severely. The court, therefore, cannot affirm the FCC's order, but neither can it conclude that the FCC could not on remand justify the rules consistently with principles of administrative law. Accordingly, rather than enjoining enforcement of existing rules that the FCC might be able to justify, we must remand the case for the FCC to further explain its decision not to repeal or modify them. Should a further challenge be made to the FCC's decision on remand, the court will be in a position to test the FCC's rationale against the factual and legal attacks that petitioners raise against it.

I.

From the early days of spectrum regulation in the 1930s and 1940s, the FCC imposed upon broadcasters a duty that came to be known as the "fairness doctrine." To merit a broadcast license, applicants were obliged, first, "to cover vitally important controversial issues of interest in their communities," and second, "to provide a reasonable opportunity for the presentation of contrasting viewpoints." *Syracuse Peace Council*, 2 F.C.C.R.

---

1. Petitioners are the Radio-Television News Directors Association ("RTNDA"), the National Association of Broadcasters ("NAB"), and the Freedom of Expression Foundation, Inc ("FEF").

5043, 5058 n.2 (1987), *recon. denied,* 3 F.C.C.R. 2035 (1988). The fairness doctrine persisted until 1987, although its death knell sounded in 1985, when the FCC released an exhaustive "Fairness Report" declaring the doctrine obsolete and "no longer [in] ... the public interest." *Fairness Report,* 102 F.C.C.2d 142, 246 (1985). The report concluded that new media technologies and outlets ensured dissemination of diverse viewpoints without need for federal regulation, that the fairness doctrine chilled speech on controversial subjects, and that the doctrine interfered too greatly with journalistic freedom. The FCC did not immediately abrogate the doctrine, however, electing instead to await resolution of proposals percolating in Congress. At the time, the FCC was concerned that the 1959 amendments to the Communications Act rendered the fairness doctrine a statutory necessity, subject to repeal only by Congress. Less than a year later, the court held that the fairness doctrine derived from the FCC's mandate to serve the public interest, subject to changing agency interpretation, and was not compelled by statute. *See Telecommunications Research & Action Ctr. v. FCC,* 801 F.2d 501, 517–18 (D.C. Cir. 1986). The doctrine's demise swiftly followed.

In 1987, the FCC announced during an adjudication that it would no longer enforce the fairness doctrine. Relying heavily on its 1985 Fairness Report, the FCC reasoned that the doctrine imposed substantial burdens on broadcasters without countervailing benefits. As a result, the FCC concluded that the doctrine was inconsistent with both the public interest and the First Amendment principles it was intended to promote. The court affirmed the conclusion that the fairness doctrine no longer served the public interest, but did not reach the constitutional question. *See Syracuse Peace Council v. FCC,* 867 F.2d 654, 656 (D.C. Cir.1989).

The *Syracuse* order covered the fairness doctrine only as applied generally, and did not review each of its evolving permutations. In particular, the FCC noted that the order created precedent for, but did not directly resolve, reconsideration of the political editorial and personal attack rules, much less what effect general abrogation of the fairness doctrine would have on the doctrine's "every conceivable application." *Syracuse Peace Council.*

The FCC promulgated the political editorial and personal attack rules in 1967, although it had previously enforced them as corollaries to the fairness doctrine. *See Amendment of Part 73 of the Rules to Provide Procedures in the Event of a Personal Attack or Where a Station Editorializes as to Political Candidates,* 8 F.C.C.2d 721 (1967) ("Personal Attacks & Political Editorials"). The two rules are distinct, although petitioners attack them for essentially the same reasons.

The personal attack rule provides that:

> When, during the presentation of views on a controversial issue of public importance, an attack is made upon the honesty, character, integrity, or like personal qualities of an identified person or group, the licensee shall ... transmit to the persons or group attacked ... [the substance of the attack] and an offer of a reasonable opportunity to respond over the licensee's facilities.

47 C.F.R. § 73.1920(a) (1998). Several exceptions limit the rule, including exclusion of attacks in "bona fide newscasts." 47 C.F.R. § 73.1920(b)(4). The political editorial rule has a similar structure, affording political candidates notice of and an opportunity to respond to editorials opposing them or endorsing another candidate.[2] *See* 47 C.F.R. § 73.1930 (1998).

---

2. Specifically, the political editorial rule provides, in part, that:
[w]here a licensee, in an editorial ... [e]ndorses or ... [o]pposes a legally qualified can-

The Supreme Court has rejected facial First Amendment challenges to both rules. *See Red Lion Broad. Co. v. FCC,* 395 U.S. 367 (1969).[3] The Court started from the premise that "[t]here is no sanctuary in the First Amendment for unlimited private censorship operating in a medium not open to all." Given the scarcity of broadcast spectrum relative to interested users, the Court concluded that victims of personal attacks and candidates opposed by editorials might be "unable without governmental assistance to gain access to ... [broadcast media] for expression of their views." Because dissemination of these views would serve the public's right "to receive suitable access to social, political, esthetic, moral, and other ideas and experiences," the First Amendment benefits of the personal attack and political editorial rules justified the imposition on licensees' asserted right "continuously to broadcast whatever they choose." The Court cautioned, however, that "if experience with the administration of [these] doctrines indicates that they have the net effect of reducing rather than enhancing the volume and quality of coverage [of public issues], there will be time enough to reconsider the constitutional implications."

The instant case arises from a petition for rulemaking filed by the NAB to repeal the political editorial and personal attack rules. The petition asserted that the rules entailed unnecessarily severe administrative burdens and were counter-productive because they chilled controversial speech rather than encouraging balanced debate. In light of the FCC's experience administering the rules and *Red Lion's* cautionary limitation to then-prevailing facts, the petition invited the FCC to conclude that the rules were obsolete and had undermined, rather than furthered, First Amendment goals. In 1983, the FCC issued an NPRM proposing to repeal or modify the political editorial and personal attack rules. *See Repeal or Modification of the Personal Attack and Political Editorial Rules,* 48 Fed. Reg. 28,295 (1983). The NPRM outlined the development of First Amendment law after *Red Lion,* noting a need to test the challenged rules under the "more exacting framework of current law." The FCC went so far as to state that "[w]e believe the petitioner [NAB] and other commenters have presented a compelling case that the personal attack and political editorial rules do not serve the public interest." Consequently, the FCC concluded, "our reexamination of the public interest justification for the ... rules must be especially searching."

And then nothing happened for a long time. [The court further recounts the FCC's failure to act.]

II.

[The court rejected the contention that the *Syracuse* order "of its own force drags the political editorial and personal attack rules down with the fairness doctrine to which they were moored...."]

III.

The question remains whether the rules can survive petitioners' challenge in light of the NPRM, the Fairness Report, the *Syracuse* order, and petitioners' contention that

---

didate[,] ... the licensee shall, with[in] 24 hours after the editorial, transmit to [the endorsed or opposed candidate] ... (A) [n]otification of the date and the time of the editorial, (B) [a] script or tape of the editorial and (C) [a]n offer of reasonable opportunity for the candidate or a spokesman of the candidate to respond over the licensee's facilities.
47 C.F.R. §73.1930(a).

3. Although *Red Lion* has been "the subject of intense criticism," it is still binding precedent. *Time Warner Entertainment Co. v. FCC,* 105 F.3d 723, 724 n. 2 (D.C. Cir.1997).

changes in the industry since 1967, including an expansion of communications outlets, undermine support for the rules. *See* 5 U.S.C. § 706....

B.

The FCC appears to acknowledge its duty to explain the reasons for its action, noting in the Joint Statement that:

> In the end, our task in this proceeding, just as it was in our review of the fairness doctrine, is to "make predictive and normative judgments" about the benefits and the burdens resulting from the two rules, and ultimately to determine whether the benefits outweigh the burdens. In our judgment this calculus leads us to a different result than the one reached by the prior Commission with respect to the fairness doctrine given the different considerations raised by the political editorial and personal attack rules.

Joint Statement. Yet, to the extent the FCC employed some sort of "calculus," its analysis in the Joint Statement is opaque, relying on broad policy statements to justify much narrower rules despite having recently rejected similar policies in a related context. With only minor modifications, the rationales discussed in the Joint Statement could have been used, verbatim, to defend the fairness doctrine. In short, the FCC's analysis in the Joint Statement bears little relation to the FCC's present and past actions.

For the sake of argument, we will assume that the Joint Statement correctly negates the charge that the rules chill protected expression, impose undue administrative burdens on broadcasters, and have been rendered obsolete by the proliferation of new media technologies and outlets. Even so, the rules to some degree interfere with the editorial judgment of professional journalists and entangle the government in day-to-day operations of the media. The Supreme Court and the FCC have noted that both effects are cause for concern, though not fatal in moderation. *See Arkansas Educ. Television Comm'n v. Forbes*; *FCC v. League of Women Voters*, 468 U.S. 364, 378 (1984); *CBS v. Democratic Nat'l Comm.*, 412 U.S. 94, 110 (1973); *see also Syracuse Peace Council*; NPRM; *Fairness Report*.[8] Because the FCC is bound to regulate in the public interest, it must explain why the public would benefit from rules that raise these policy and constitutional doubts; yet the Joint Statement fails to present an adequate basis upon which to affirm retention of the rules and dispel concerns previously raised by the FCC itself. Although the Joint Statement recites that the rules "serve as important components of a broadcaster's public interest obligations," it does not persuasively explain, in light of FCC precedent, why this is so or why less intrusive alternatives would be less desirable.

The first theory offered in the Joint Statement is that the "rules serve the public interest by helping to ensure that the same audience that heard the broadcast of an endorsement or personal attack be accessible to the individual concerned." The theory relies on an unstated premise that the public has a clear interest in hearing both sides of each issue on which a broadcaster elects to focus. The premise is no doubt sound. But, in abrogating the fairness doctrine, the FCC rejected the notion that this interest automatically justifies government intervention in the editorial processes of broadcasters. *See Syracuse Peace Council.* The rules therefore make sense only if there is a special interest, greater than the general interest addressed by the now-discarded fairness doctrine, in hearing re-

---

8. Outside the broadcast context, a regulation requiring a media outlet to provide a right of reply to victims of personal or political attacks would face more severe First Amendment constraints. *See Miami Herald Publ'g Co. v. Tornillo*, 418 U.S. 241, 256–58 (1974).

sponses to political editorials or personal attacks. The Joint Statement offers no such explanation. Although repeal of the fairness doctrine could in theory have left the challenged rules intact, the Joint Statement never presents a plausible explanation why political editorials and personal attacks are sufficiently meaningful to warrant regulation when other kinds of topics, editorials, and attacks do not. The FCC generally need not explain why it has declined to regulate something in order to justify a particular rule, but having expressly decided to repeal broad rules, it must explain why retaining similar (albeit narrower) rules is appropriate.

Second, the Joint Statement justifies retention of the rules for "precisely the same reasons" as the Supreme Court noted in *Red Lion*. According to the Joint Statement, these reasons were that, absent the rules, "station owners and a few networks would have unfettered power to make time available only to the highest bidders, to communicate only their own views on public issues, people and candidates, and to permit on the air only those with whom they agreed." *Id.* (quoting *Red Lion*).

The quoted language from *Red Lion* appears in the Court's consideration of whether the political editorial and personal attack rules were "inconsistent with the First Amendment goal of producing an informed public capable of conducting its own affairs." The Court concluded that there was no inconsistency. It did not purport, however, to hold that the rules would always be in the public interest. The mere fact that a rule is not unconstitutional does not therefore mean that its perpetuation is not arbitrary and capricious. Accordingly, the Joint Statement is flawed to the extent that it relies on a thirty-year-old conclusion that the challenged rules survive First Amendment scrutiny to justify the decision not to repeal them in the face of modern challenges to the rules' consistency with the FCC's regulatory mandate.

Moreover, the Joint Statement's quotation from *Red Lion* rings hollow in view of the FCC's repeal of the fairness doctrine. Licensees now have greater opportunities to "make time available only to the highest bidders, … communicate only their own views on public issues, people and candidates, and … permit on the air only those with whom they agree[ ]." *Red Lion*. The caveat is that they must be careful not to editorialize about candidates and not to allow personal attacks. Such artful evasion of a duty to provide balanced programming would have been far less possible when the fairness doctrine supplemented the rules challenged here, but is easier to accomplish today. It is therefore difficult to conceive how retention of the rules can be for "precisely" the reasons noted in *Red Lion* when those reasons were offered for a different purpose and in the context of a now defunct regulatory regime.

Third, the Joint Statement notes that the "scarcity of broadcast frequencies provides a rationale for imposing public interest obligations on broadcasters." Even accepting the factual premise of this statement, it provides no support for the specific rules under review. The mere fact that the FCC has the power to regulate broadcasters more intensely than other media does not also mean that it may impose any obligation it sees fit. Each regulation must be in the "public interest," and none can be "arbitrary" or "capricious." The scarcity rationale does not address either limit on the FCC's discretion.

Fourth, the Joint Statement attempts to justify the challenged rules by reference to its authority under the equal time doctrine, which provides that "[i]f any licensee shall permit any person who is a legally qualified candidate for any public office to use a broadcasting station, he [or she] shall afford equal opportunities to all other such candidates for that office in the use of such broadcasting station." 47 U.S.C. §315(a) (1994); *see also* 47 U.S.C. §312(a)(7) (1994). According to the Joint Statement, the challenged rules "complement" the "policies" underlying § 315(a).[10] Yet the equal time doctrine does not compel either the political editorial or personal attack rules. Both rules apply when the licensee itself distributes proscribed content, while the statute contemplates situations where the licensee allows a candidate use of the station's facilities. Moreover, the personal attack rule applies to all attacks, not just attacks on candidates. Thus, the challenged rules are substantially broader than the equal time doctrine. This breadth does not invalidate the rules, but it lessens the persuasive force of the Joint Statement's reliance on the statute to justify its decision. This is particularly so because the Joint Statement ignores the fact that the fairness doctrine also complemented § 315(a), illustrating the point that mere consistency with a statute does not justify a regulation; a statutory policy can be implemented in numerous ways, but the agency is limited to solutions that are not arbitrary and capricious.

Fifth, the Joint Statement explains that the political editorial rule:

> is intended to provide citizens with the information necessary to enable them to exercise their vote in a more responsible and informed manner. In such respects, we believe that this particular rule goes to the very heart of our democratic electoral process.

Few would disagree with the idea that vibrant debate is good for democracy, but that alone cannot explain why editorials about candidates justify federal intervention when other types of editorials or non-editorial programming does [*sic*] not. The Joint Statement's rationale would justify numerous salutary regulations—including the fairness doctrine— but it offers no explanation for the FCC's choice to impose the ones at issue here. Moreover, the Joint Statement's reasoning fails to address the concern raised in the NPRM that nothing inherent in the nature of an editorial necessitates countervailing speech to ensure balanced debate. Many programming decisions add to and detract from the balance within the marketplace of ideas without regulatory consequence, but the Joint Statement never explains why editorials warrant special treatment.

There may be good reasons to focus on political editorials. If broadcasters want to use public resources overtly to push a private agenda by advocating a result in an election, a right of reply might be a minimally intrusive means of countering a licensee's government-granted monopoly on access to the resource. The same could be said, however, to defend rights of reply on many issues of public concern.[13] Yet the FCC has emphatically rejected such a broad regulatory regime. It therefore falls on the FCC to explain why editorials about candidates are particularly appropriate subjects for regulation.

Finally, the Joint Statement justifies the personal attack rule by noting that the airwaves should not be a "platform for attacks on personal character," that the rule is targeted to provide a limited right of reply to the same audience that heard the attack, and that the FCC only enforces the rule when a licensee acts in "bad faith." This defense of the rule may be appealing—personal attacks can be distasteful and detract from reasoned discourse— but it fails to make a sustainable case for the rule. Most troubling is the fact that the Joint

---

10. The FCC has developed a related rule that governs cases in which a candidate's supporters, rather than the candidate herself, appear on a station. *See Nicholas Zapple,* 23 F.C.C.2d 707 (1970).

13. For example, the FCC would permit a network to editorialize about tax policy, but would constrain a network's discretion to endorse a particular candidate based on her views about tax policy. Likewise, a network has more freedom to endorse a ballot initiative than to endorse a candidate championing such an initiative. The FCC has not articulated a basis for the distinction.

Statement ignores the concerns that the FCC raised in the NPRM about the rule's utility. The NPRM notes that newspapers are not bound by a similar right of reply and yet no serious consequences seem to have ensued, that at least some victims (those who are public figures) of personal attacks have sufficient access to broadcast media that a right-of-reply requirement is unnecessary, that the rule does not apply to newscasts and yet its inapplicability does not seem to have led to the problems that the rule is designed to address, that the rationale for applying the rule to non-news programming was even less sound than applying it to newscasts, and that the FCC lacked any "evidence that personal attacks are inherently more persuasive than other [types of] arguments." *NPRM*. There may be valid responses to each of these concerns, but the Joint Statement's conclusory assertion that the rule is a necessary prerequisite for balanced debate on public issues is insufficient to allay the doubts that the FCC itself previously raised. Indeed, having in the past conceded that it lacked "evidence" that the rule was necessary, the FCC at a minimum should point to evidence to support the rule or explain why none is needed.

As with the political editorial rule, there may be sound reasons to regulate personal attacks. The problem here, however, is that whether viewed individually or as a whole, the explanations in the Joint Statement do not articulate them.

C.

The foregoing deficiencies in the FCC's analysis render its present explanation of its decision to retain the rules insufficient to permit judicial review....

Consequently, as a matter of administrative law, the court cannot affirm the FCC's order. Neither, however, is the court in a position to hold on this record that the challenged rules are inconsistent with the public interest or the First Amendment. The FCC's failure to address relevant factors, distinguish applicable precedents, and explain the scope of its rules despite acknowledging that the rules might be too broad renders meaningful judicial review impossible because the court lacks a coherent rationale against which to weigh petitioners' factual, policy, and constitutional claims. Petitioners' claims each require the court to balance the rationale for the rules against their consequences.[19] In theory, balancing could be avoided if the rules so obviously entailed no ill effects that they would survive even if only marginally useful. That, however, is not the case, as illustrated in the NPRM and the Fairness Report. Even were the court to assume that some of petitioners' arguments are overstated, the challenged rules by their nature interfere with at least some journalistic judgment, chill at least some speech, and impose at least some burdens on activities at the heart of the First Amendment. Because the court must weigh the rules' benefits against their burdens, the inadequacy of the explanation in the Joint Statement is apparent. Wooden application of principles underlying rhetoric about the FCC's vast power, its broad discretion, and the importance of vibrant debate in democracy to a specific set of rules would force the court to adopt an impressionistic approach that would

---

19. The First Amendment "requires a critical examination of the interests of the public and broadcasters in light of the particular circumstances of each case." *League of Women Voters*. Although *Red Lion* affirmed the rules challenged here, the Court recognized that changed circumstances might be salient in future cases. *See Red Lion*. Also, the Court since *Red Lion* has increasingly focused on the editorial discretion of broadcasters, *see, e.g., Forbes*, indicating that while the *Red Lion* framework may still be good law, its application to the instant rules may require updating. *See also Fairness Report* (critiquing the scarcity rationale).

disserve the parties and muddle the First Amendment analysis. The FCC must therefore explain its rationale for these rules in more detail, thereby permitting the court to test that rationale against petitioners' factual assertions and, if necessary, the demands of the First Amendment.

IV ...

Accordingly, we grant the petitions for review and remand the case to afford the FCC an opportunity to provide an adequate justification for retaining the personal attack and political editorial rules, and for such proceedings as the FCC may determine are appropriate to implement this mandate. Given its prior delay in this proceeding, the FCC need act expeditiously.

Notes and Questions

1. As you might expect given the past deadlock, the FCC did not act expeditiously even after the Court of Appeals decided this case. After petitioners returned to the court seeking an order overturning the rules, the FCC, over two dissents, issued an order temporarily suspending the rules for 60 days. The Court of Appeals held that the suspension did not render the matter moot. It then struck down the rules:

> The court has afforded repeated opportunities for the Commission to take final action. Despite its filings suggesting to the court that something would happen, the Commission, once again, has done nothing to cure the deficiencies of which it as been long aware. Of course, the Commission may institute a new rule-making proceeding to determine whether, consistent with constitutional constraints, the public interest requires the personal attack and political editorial rules. These are issues that the court has yet to decide. Nevertheless, extraordinary action by the court is warranted in this case, particularly in view of the fact that the six reasons proffered in support of the rules were all wanting. The Commission has delayed final action for two decades, to the detriment of petitioners.

Radio-Television News Directors Association v. FCC, 229 F.3d 269, 272 (D.C. Cir. 2000). Why was the FCC deadlocked for so long? Is it relevant that the five FCC commissioners are appointed by the President, with no more than three from any single political party? The two commissioners who supported retention of the rules were appointed by Democratic President Clinton and the chair of the commission declined to vote because of a potential conflict of interest. It is not surprising that Republican appointees should be more supportive of deregulation than Democrats. If, when they control the FCC, the Republicans bring about a partial deregulation, should Democrats be legally required to justify their refusal to finish the job?

2. The demise of the rule allowing political candidates attacked on radio or television a right to reply is not too surprising. As the opinion above explains, such rules (and similar rules promoting "fairness" by broadcasters) emerged as broadcast media gained widely in popularity even as the number of broadcasters remained small. In the *Red Lion* case discussed in the *Radio-Television News Directors Association* opinion, the Supreme Court upheld the FCC's Fairness Doctrine and the related rules discussed above on grounds of scarcity in the broadcast spectrum: competitors could not begin rival stations because there were no available frequencies with which to broadcast them.

Given the lack of a scarcity problem with print media, the Court struck down a right-of-reply statute (similar to the FCC's personal attack rules) applied to newspapers. See *Miami Herald Publishing Co. v. Tornillo*, 418 U.S. 241, 256–58 (1974). The scarcity rationale for broadcast media has been considerably weakened with the emergence of cable and satellite television, along with the Internet. Are there grounds other than scarcity for mandating a candidate's right-of-reply on broadcast stations? On broadcast stations but not in newspapers? See Charles W. Logan, Jr. *Getting Beyond Scarcity: A New Paradigm for Assessing the Constitutionality of Broadcast Regulation*, 85 CALIFORNIA LAW REVIEW 1687, 1722 (1997) ("Political broadcasting requirements promote political dialogue, which goes to the heart of deliberative democracy."); Lee C. Bollinger, IMAGES OF A FREE PRESS (1991) (arguing that it is valuable to have one type of media subject to regulation and the other unregulated); Lucas A. Powe, Jr., AMERICAN BROADCASTING AND THE FIRST AMENDMENT 31 (1987) (attacking the Supreme Court's broadcast media cases). Note that the Supreme Court declined to extend its rules for broadcasters to cable television. *Turner Broadcasting System v. FCC*, 512 U.S. 622, 638 (1994) ("Although courts and commentators have criticized the scarcity rationale since its inception, we have declined to question its continuing validity as support for our broadcast jurisprudence, and see no reason to do so here. The broadcast cases are inapposite in the present context because cable television does not suffer from the inherent limitations that characterize the broadcast medium.") Nonetheless, the Court held that cable operators could be subject to greater regulation than newspapers. Thus, there are at least three constitutional standards in assessing rules regulating candidate access and coverage.

3. One possible consequence of treating broadcasters and print media differently is that unlike the print media, few broadcasters endorse political candidates for office. See Richard L. Hasen, *Campaign Finance Laws and the Rupert Murdoch Problem*, 77 TEXAS LAW REVIEW 1627, 1644 (1999) (citing 1983 report by the National Association of Broadcasters reporting that only 3.1% of broadcasters endorse candidates). Do you expect broadcasters to endorse more candidates now that a court has struck down the personal attack rule?

4. Despite the demise of the Fairness Doctrine and the personal attack rule, three important statutory provisions still regulate campaigns over the broadcast media. First, the equal time doctrine, 47 U.S.C. § 315(a), provides that if a broadcast licensee "shall permit any person who is a legally qualified candidate for any public office to use a broadcasting station, he shall afford equal opportunities to all other such candidates for that office in the use of such broadcasting station." The statute creates an exception for an appearance by a candidate on bona fide news programs. Is a press conference by a President running for reelection a bona fide news event subject to an exception to the equal time rules? See *Kennedy for President Committee v. FCC*, 636 F.2d 417 (D.C. Cir. 1980). Is the equal time rule constitutional given the demise of the scarcity rationale? Would broadcasters on major television networks, for example, fail to provide balanced coverage in the absence of the rule? Do they provide balanced coverage now?

It is important to note that the equal time doctrine does *not* require a station to assure that all candidates actually receive equal time. Because of the exception for news broadcasts, the doctrine mainly affects paid advertisements. If the station sells advertising to one candidate, it must offer advertising on the same terms to all other candidates for the same office. But if the opponent is unwilling or unable to pay the offered price, the station is not required to provide free time.

5. The second statutory provision relevant to campaigns (this time, only federal campaigns) is 47 U.S.C. §312(a)(7), sometimes known as the "reasonable access" statute. It provides that the FCC may revoke a license for a broadcaster's "willful or repeated failure to allow reasonable access to or to permit purchase of reasonable amounts of time for the use of a broadcasting station by a legally qualified candidate for Federal elective office on behalf of his candidacy." The Supreme Court upheld the regulation against constitutional challenge in *CBS v. FCC*, 453 U.S. 367, 397 (1981) ("Section 312(a)(7) represents an effort by Congress to assure that an important resource—the airwaves—will be used in the public interest. We hold that the statutory right of access ... properly balances the First Amendment rights of federal candidates, the public, and broadcasters."). What First Amendment rights do federal candidates have to be on a private television station against the station owner's wishes? If federal candidates have such First Amendment rights, what about candidates for state or local offices? Should *CBS* be reconsidered given the demise of the scarcity rationale? If not, could such a reasonable access requirement be applied to newspapers in light of *Tornillo*?

6. The final statutory provision relevant to campaigns is 47 U.S.C. §315(b). This section provides that candidates for public office who wish to run campaign advertisements must be charged "during the forty-five days preceding the date of a primary or primary runoff election and during the sixty days preceding the date of a general or special election in which such person is a candidate, the lowest unit charge of the station for the same class and amount of time for the same period." This is a significant benefit for candidates, because demand for broadcast advertising rises heavily during some election periods, and rates rise as well. The rate charged to candidates must be the same as the rate broadcasters charge to their largest high-volume advertisers. The low rate does not apply to non-candidates, even to the candidate's political party. Note that because the "reasonable access" rules apply only to federal candidates, no provision of federal law requires that broadcasters sell *any* advertising to non-federal candidates or others wishing to run political advertisements. If it is sold, however, it must be at the low rate. And under the equal time doctrine if it is sold to one candidate it must be offered to the candidate's opponents.

Would it be constitutional for Congress to require broadcast media to provide *free* advertising to candidates for political office? Proposals for campaign finance reform sometimes include such provisions. Broadcast stations have threatened to sue if such provisions are enacted into law. If you represented the broadcasters challenging such a law, what arguments would you advance? Which would be more persuasive: a First Amendment challenge or a challenge that such a provision is an unconstitutional government "taking" of property without compensation in violation of the Fifth Amendment of the Constitution? Proponents of such laws argue that there is no taking because broadcast licensees receive very valuable licenses (including to the new digital broadcast spectrum) without providing any other payment. Consider Logan, *supra*, 85 CALIFORNIA LAW REVIEW at 1726 ("Existing broadcasters have received a very valuable resource—a license to use the spectrum—without being required to pay a fee. Rather, their licenses are conditioned on their serving the public interest, including in the programming they air. This *quid pro quo* provides another rationale for upholding broadcast regulation under the First Amendment.").

Chapter 12

Incumbency

In the last few decades, the difficulty of defeating incumbents, especially in legislative elections, has been an issue of growing interest to students of politics, in part because it has been central to numerous policy debates, especially campaign finance, legislative term limits, and redistricting. As the following materials will demonstrate, concern has revolved not only around the high success rate for incumbents but also the various laws and practices that may benefit incumbent officeholders in their quests for reelection or for election to higher office. We shall consider some of these institutional issues and the legal questions that surround them. We shall also consider whether the "entrenchment" of incumbents is or should be an element in election law jurisprudence. As you read this chapter, keep the following questions in mind:

1. What are the pros and cons of an electoral system in which incumbents usually can count on reelection as opposed to one in which they usually face a difficult struggle each election year?

2. Most of the "perquisites" considered in this chapter involve at least some gain to the public as well as some political benefit to the incumbent officeholder. Would a change or curtailment of the practice be desirable on balance? If you believe political benefit should be minimized, are there alternative arrangements that would preserve the public benefit while reducing or eliminating the political effect?

3. Can the practices be justified as assurances to officeholders that their accomplishments in behalf of the public will become known and be rewarded politically, thus creating an incentive and a just reward for high quality public service? To what extent does a given practice encourage substantive accomplishments? To what extent does it encourage creating a false or exaggerated appearance of accomplishment?

4. To what extent are the practices the inevitable result of the demands we make on our public officials? Officials are generally expected to act as ombudsmen able to perform a variety of individual services for constituents, and as party leaders with informed opinions on a broad range of issues, even those which are unrelated to the official's specific responsibilities. Would it be fair for society to demand that officials play these roles and then require that they pay for the necessary resources with private funds?

5. Many officials pay for some activities which have mixed governmental, constituent service, and political purposes with private funds, which may be either campaign contributions or contributions to separate accounts usually known as "office accounts" or, less reverently, "slush funds." In the past the contributions to and expenditures from the accounts were often secret, but most modern campaign disclosure laws require that they be disclosed. Is private financing of these activities preferable to public financing? To what extent, if at all, are the arguments for public financing of election campaigns (described more fully in Chapter 17) applicable here?

6. Granted the high success rate of incumbent candidates, how significant a cause are the perquisites considered in this chapter? How significant are patterns of campaign financing? Could the success rate be explained by the existence of gerrymandered election districts, or a tendency by some voters to vote for an incumbent who is doing an adequate job?

7. The two most likely determinants of a vote are the voter's party preference and the voter's evaluation of the individual candidates. The latter is likely to benefit the incumbent, who is usually better known, more experienced and, by virtue of having been elected previously, has demonstrated appeal in the district or jurisdiction. In the 19th century, straight party voting was often regarded as desirable. Increasingly in the 20th and 21st centuries, voters are much more likely to say they vote for the candidate rather than for the party (though their behavior often suggests otherwise). What are the advantages and disadvantages of party-oriented elections compared with candidate, and therefore incumbent-oriented elections?

8. Perhaps most importantly, what is the relationship between performance in office and electoral practices that benefit incumbents? How does the desire of incumbents for reelection affect the ability of parties to function effectively in legislatures and elsewhere in government? In what ways is the accountability of elected officials for the performance of government either reinforced or obscured? Ask the same questions with respect to any proposed reform intended to minimize or eliminate the incumbency advantage.

I. The Incumbency Advantage

A. The Permanent Campaign

"The campaign is never over." After quoting that comment by Robert Squier, a campaign media consultant, Hedrick Smith twenty years ago provided a lengthy and colorful account of a Senate committee hearing that exemplified what he called "permanent campaigning." Hedrick Smith, THE POWER GAME (1988). The hearings were to investigate the effects of "porn rock," described by Smith as "an escalating trend of violent, brutal erotica in rock music (*heavy metal* in the argot of its fans."[a] Leading the charge against porn rock were Susan Baker, wife of the then Republican Treasury Secretary, and Tipper Gore, wife of a then Democratic Senator from Tennessee. According to Mrs. Baker, porn rock was "glorifying rape, sadomasochism, incest, the occult, and suicide." The hearings featured celebrated performers of porn rock as well as more tame genres, and were presided over by Senator John Danforth, chair of the Commerce Committee. But, according to Smith,

> On the network news that night, the star was none of the above. It was Senator Paula Hawkins of Florida, a petite, politically canny and assertive grandmother, who made drug abuse, child abuse, missing children, and pornography her cornerstone issues in the Senate. Hawkins was not a member of the Senate Commerce Committee, but she has a nose for media events and a knack for attracting publicity that enabled her to upstage the committee. Through senatorial courtesy, Senator Hawkins arranged to be invited and appeared, eye-catching and camera-catching, in a fire-engine-red suit.

---

a. The editors of this volume disclaim any knowledge of these matters. The portion of Smith's book summarized here appears at pages 119–126.

Several other senators made predictable statements of moral outrage, but Hawkins had a shrewder gambit. She had her statement, too, but knowing that words were no match for pictures, she came armed with some near-irresistible visuals crafted by the graphic-arts staff of the Senate Republican Conference. On her own television set, plopped on her dais, she played a couple of sizzling porn-rock videocassettes … to demonstrate for one and all that the new raunchiness of rock made Elvis Presley seem as innocent as a choirboy.[b]

Smith goes on to observe that elective officeholders had been publicizing themselves through such activities from the early days of television, in events such as the Kefauver investigations of organized crime in 1951 and the Watergate hearings in 1973–74. "The new wrinkle is that politics has become a prime time vehicle for virtually every incumbent, even a relatively unnoticed freshman" like Hawkins. It should be observed that the exploitation of television news in this manner is much more suited to the presidency, the Senate, and governorships than to other offices. It is usually impossible for House members or state legislators to benefit much from television news. Incumbents in these less visible offices use different techniques, but they also are usually focused on reelection throughout their terms of office. A campaign, Hedrick concludes, "has become a perpetual-motion machine.… The techniques, mentality, and mercenary consultants of the campaign follow the winners right into office."

Smith contends that Congress provides its incumbents with important advantages, which he refers to as "the five pillars of incumbency." These are "1. video feeds; 2. high-tech computerized mail; 3. elaborately staffed casework, involving myriad little favors for constituents; 4. personal presence back home, often ingeniously publicized; and 5. political money."

Notes and Questions

1. What, if anything, does the Paula Hawkins incident tell us about the American political process? Did she do anything wrong? Does her ability to garner publicity in the way she did suggest anything dysfunctional about the way that either the press or the Congress operates?

2. Paula Hawkins was defeated by Democrat Bob Graham in her quest for reelection in 1986.

3. Smith asserted that House members "have become especially skilled at modern survival techniques" and pointed out that since the mid-1960s, House incumbents seeking reelection had been successful ninety-one percent of the time, compared to Senators prevailing 78 percent of the time. Such figures leave out of account the fact that House members have to run for reelection every two years, while Senators have six-year terms. If a House incumbent has a ninety-one percent chance of winning reelection, then that member's chance of being reelected for the three terms that make up a Senate term are .91 x .91 x .91, or a fraction over seventy-five percent. This is a slightly *lower* figure than the Senate reelection rate Smith reports. See Amihai Glazer & Bernard Grofman, *Two Plus Two Plus Two Equals Six: Tenure in Office of Senators and Representatives, 1953–1983*, 12 Legislative Studies Quarterly 555 (1987), finding that the reelection chances of House members over three elections are about equal to those of Senators in one election.

Does this suggest that the "incumbency advantage," however great it may be, is equal in the Senate and the House, or is the percentage of successful incumbents in any given

---

b. We omit Smith's description of Hawkins' visual props in this family-oriented volume.

election the more relevant comparison? In any event, what could explain the higher House reelection rate in a given election?

4. Much theorizing and investigation have been devoted to the ways in which the desire for reelection affects official performance. In the simplest conception of democracy, reelection provides the incentive to make officials accountable to the public. Concerns about incumbents' electoral advantages suggest that neither the general public nor students of government accept this simple conception as entirely adequate. Although the point cannot be explored in depth in this book, the following brief discussion may suggest some lines of thought and starting places for research.

A particularly influential work has been David R. Mayhew, CONGRESS: THE ELECTORAL CONNECTION (1974). Mayhew hypothesizes that members of Congress are motivated *solely* by the desire for reelection. Of course, Mayhew recognizes that this is at least an oversimplification and an exaggeration. Nevertheless, he concludes that a great deal of the behavior of individual legislators and of the structure and performance of the Congress as a whole are consistent with this simplified assumption. In particular, Mayhew argues that the reelection goal prompts legislators to engage primarily in three activities:

> One activity is *advertising*, defined here as any effort to disseminate one's name among constituents in such a fashion as to create a favorable image but in messages having little or no issue content. A successful congressman builds what amounts to a brand name.... The personal qualities to emphasize are experience, knowledge, responsiveness, concern, sincerity, independence, and the like. Just getting one's name across is difficult enough; only about half the electorate, if asked, can supply their House members' names. It helps a congressman to be known....

> A second activity may be called *credit claiming*, defined here as acting so as to generate a belief in a relevant political actor (or actors) that one is personally responsible for causing the government, or some unit thereof, to do something that the actor (or actors) considers desirable. The political logic of this, from the congressman's point of view, is that an actor who believes that a member can make pleasing things happen will no doubt wish to keep him in office so that he can make pleasing things happen in the future. The emphasis here is on individual accomplishment (rather than, say, party or governmental accomplishment) and on the congressman as doer (rather than as, say, expounder of constituency views). Credit claiming is highly important to congressmen, with the consequence that much of congressional life is a relentless search for opportunities to engage in it.

> [I]t becomes necessary for each congressman to try to peel off pieces of governmental accomplishment for which he can believably generate a sense of responsibility. For the average congressman the staple way of doing this is to traffic in what may be called "particularized benefits." Particularized governmental benefits ... have two properties: (1) Each benefit is given out to a specific individual, group, or geographical constituency, the recipient unit being of a scale that allows a single congressman to be recognized (by relevant political actors and other congressmen) as the claimant for the benefit (other congressmen being perceived as indifferent or hostile). (2) Each benefit is given out in apparently ad hoc fashion (unlike, say, social security checks) with a congressman apparently having a hand in the allocation. A particularized benefit can normally be regarded as a member of a class. That is, a benefit given out to an individual, group, or constituency can normally be looked upon by congressmen as one of a class of similar benefits given out to sizable numbers

of individuals, groups, or constituencies. Hence, the impression can arise that a congressman is getting "his share" of whatever it is the government is offering. . . .

In sheer volume the bulk of particularized benefits come under the heading of "casework"—the thousands of favors congressional offices perform for supplicants in ways that normally do not require legislative action. . . . But many benefits require new legislation, or at least they require important allocative decisions on matters covered by existent legislation. Here the congressman fills the traditional role of supplier of goods to the home district. It is a believable role; when a member claims credit for a benefit on the order of a dam, he may well receive it. ["Sometimes without justification," Mayhew adds in a footnote.] . . .

The third activity congressmen engage in may be called *position taking*, defined here as the public enunciation of a judgmental statement on anything likely to be of interest to political actors. The statement may take the form of a roll call vote. The most important classes of judgmental statements are those prescribing American governmental ends (a vote cast against the war; a statement that "the war should be ended immediately") or governmental means (a statement that "the way to end the war is to take it to the United Nations"). . . . The congressman as position taker is a speaker rather than a doer. The electoral requirement is not that he make pleasing things happen but that he make pleasing judgmental statements. The position itself is the political commodity. Especially on matters where governmental responsibility is widely diffused it is not surprising that political actors should fall back on positions as tests of incumbent virtue.

Id. at 49–62.

Although Mayhew contends that a great deal of congressional activity is consistent with the hypothesis of reelection as the only goal, he acknowledges that the hypothesis cannot explain everything.

Quite the contrary. It is not too much to say that if all members did nothing but pursue their electoral goals, Congress would decay or collapse. Some of the institutional maintenance problems are implicit in the earlier discussion, including a serious one arising from the difficulty of getting members to do grueling and unrewarding legislative work. (Sometimes in the Senate it is even hard to get them to appear and vote.)

Id. at 141. Thus, although many analysts have attempted to refine and elaborate Mayhew's single-motivation explanation of Congress, others have attempted to build on the presumably more realistic premise that most legislators have multiple goals—though concededly these almost always will prominently include reelection, which is a prerequisite to being able to continue to pursue other goals. Following the lead of Richard Fenno, many scholars assume that three motivations tend to be paramount, though in different balances for different legislators: "re-election, influence within the House, and good public policy." Richard F. Fenno, Jr., CONGRESSMEN IN COMMITTEES 1 (1973).

Some social scientists are uncomfortable with a multiple-goal assumption, on the ground that the assumption does not predict which goals will be paramount on which occasions, and thus cannot predict congressional performance. Furthermore, critics argue, the multiple-goal assumption is not "falsifiable," because after the fact, whatever Congress does can be explained by an assumption that is so protean that it could have as easily explained the opposite outcome. Nevertheless, the multiple-goal assumption can provide the foundation for rich and insightful accounts of congressional action on important matters, as in Daniel Shaviro's analysis of major tax changes in the 1980s. In 1981, Congress seemed to adhere closely to Mayhew's model, passing legislation that contained numerous particularized benefits for a variety of interest groups. But in 1986, it passed new legislation that was strongly opposed by many of the same groups. See Daniel Shaviro, *Beyond Public Choice and Public Interest: A Study of the Legislative Process as Illustrated by Tax Legislation in the 1980s*, 139 UNIVERSITY OF PENNSYLVANIA LAW REVIEW 1 (1990).

Another important study proposes an in-between position, assuming that reelection is always the paramount goal, but that often legislators can choose between different courses of action without risk to the goal of reelection, in which case they will pursue other goals such as influence within Congress and public policy. See R. Douglas Arnold, THE LOGIC OF CONGRESSIONAL ACTION 5 (1990). Arnold also adds certain elements to Mayhew's analysis. Arnold concedes that at the time legislators act on many issues, most constituents are unaware of their actions and may be unaware of the issue or of what is the best way for the government to deal with it. But Arnold argues that the legislators must nevertheless take into account how the issue will affect constituents, because the issue may become more salient by election time and the press, interest groups, and especially an incumbent's challenger will take steps to inform voters of unpopular actions taken by the incumbent. (A striking example is the savings and loan debacle. In the 1980s, very few Americans were aware of the policies the government was following affecting the savings and loan industry. When that issue exploded, imposing enormous costs on an already troubled national fisc, many members of Congress suffered electoral costs because of past connections with savings and loans. The 2002 vote on authorization of the invasion of Iraq illustrates how tricky these choices can be. Depending on the fortunes of war, a vote that was a benefit in one subsequent election became a detriment in another.) Within this framework, Arnold attempts to show that numerous factors, including the way an issue is framed in debate, influence whether legislators work for particularized interests or behave in a more "public-regarding" way.

5. Hedrick Smith describes and David Mayhew theorizes about a Congress composed of professional politicians, sophisticated in the use of modern communications devices and other resources to maintain themselves in office. This environment is by no means unique to Congress. Indeed, one of the most striking phenomena in American politics in recent decades is the spread of such "professional" politics beyond Congress and the largest state and local governments to state legislatures in most states and to localities of only modest size. For an insightful account of this phenomenon (despite its rather lurid title), see Alan Ehrenhalt, THE UNITED STATES OF AMBITION (1991). As Ehrenhalt has noted, the ascendency of career, professional politicians has been as complete in Britain as in the United States.

> [I]n the late twentieth century, both political systems have generated a similar cast of characters, people whose dedication to a political career is overwhelming and, in many cases, all but lifelong.

Alan Ehrenhalt, *Political pros*, THE PUBLIC INTEREST, Fall, 1994, at 131, 132.

B. Incumbency and Electoral Competition[c]

The first two elections after the 1990 census temporarily diminished but did not eliminate concern over the "incumbency advantage" and its effects on electoral competition. The 325 incumbents reelected to the House of Representatives in 1992 were the lowest number since 1948. This occurred in large part because 52 incumbents declined to run for reelection, a post-World War II record. But the 19 incumbents defeated in primaries also set a post-World War II record, and the percentage of incumbents seeking reelection and winning dipped below 90 percent for the first time since the Watergate election of 1974 and only the second time since 1964. Although a relatively high total of 49 House seats changed parties, the parties' gains partially canceled each other out, with the result that the Republicans gained a modest net of 10 seats.[d]

In 1994, voters showed that they could use a sharper partisan focus in defeating incumbents. The Republican Party won control of both houses of Congress and not a single Republican incumbent governor, senator, or House member was defeated. 1994 marked the first time since 1952 that the Republicans won control of the House, and only the third time since 1928.

Although the 1992 and 1994 elections made the "incumbency advantage" a less salient political concern, the issue began to revive as incumbent success in the House returned to high levels in the following five elections. 2002 was especially noteworthy, considering it was a post-redistricting election.[e] The 2006 election, which was something of a mirror image of 1994 and restored the Democrats to control of the House, again may have muted the issue to some degree. The decades of the 1990s and 2000s taken as a whole suggest that very high reelection rates are not inexorable features of contemporary elections, but that they will occur in the absence of strong partisan tides or other events that disturb the electoral *status quo*.

Incumbency in legislative elections has received an enormous amount of study, nearly all of it in the last four decades. Much is known, but much remains obscure. Little of what has been learned—and even less of the researchers' awareness of the limits of their knowledge—has found its way into popular debates about incumbency. This section will review research on the nature and extent of the incumbency advantage and on its causes and consequences. As we have seen, in any given election, the incumbency advantage is stronger in House races than in Senate contests, at least in any given year. The incumbency advantage is a major factor in state legislative elections, sometimes as much as or more than in U.S. House races. However, most of the published research has focused on the U.S. House. Perforce, this section will do the same.

---

c. The following is adapted and partially updated from a paper presented by Daniel Lowenstein at the annual meetings of the American Political Science Association, Chicago, September 4, 1992.

d. All figures in this paragraph are derived from VITAL STATISTICS ON AMERICAN POLITICS 125, 206, 208 (4th ed. 1994). The figure of 49 seats changing parties is complicated by the fact that House districts were reapportioned (between states) and redistricted (within states) between the 1990 and 1992 elections.

e. For sharp commentary on competitiveness in the 2002 House elections, see Sam Hirsch, *The United States of Unrepresentatives: What Went Wrong in the Latest Round of Congressional Redistricting*, 2 ELECTION LAW JOURNAL 179 (2003).

1. *Extent of the Incumbency Advantage*

It might seem that the extent of the incumbency advantage could be measured easily, by calculating the average vote percentage obtained by incumbents. Unfortunately, the simple approach is insufficient. Consider, for example, a Democratic incumbent who runs for reelection in an inner-city Chicago district, and a Republican incumbent running in a rock-ribbed Republican district in downstate Illinois. Suppose each wins by a margin of 70 percent or higher. Are their victory margins attributable to incumbency? Perhaps any Chicago Democrat or downstate Republican could have done equally well. Or consider a district with no strong partisan bias, in which there is no incumbent, and the Republican candidate, Roy, receives 60 percent of the vote. Perhaps this victory suggests that Roy was a stronger candidate than the Democrat, Doris. Suppose the same two candidates run two years later, and again Roy receives 60 percent of the vote. Is this victory the result of an incumbency advantage or of the same superior candidacy that was determinative in the first election?

Despite these and similar problems, political scientists trying to measure the incumbency advantage have sought answers to three distinct questions: First, how much is incumbency worth to the average legislator in terms of expected enhancement of his or her percentage of the two-party vote? Second, how does incumbency affect the number of "marginal" districts? Third, how much does incumbency improve a legislator's chance of being reelected?

Vote percentage. The first systematic estimate of the incumbency advantage was performed by Robert Erikson.[f] Erikson attempted to exclude the effects of district partisanship and candidate superiority by estimating the "sophomore surge" and the "retirement slump." In the above example, the sophomore surge would be the increase in Roy's vote percentage from his *initial* election to his first *reelection*, i.e., zero. If Roy had received 65 percent in the second election, his sophomore surge would have been 5 percentage points. Suppose that before Roy's election, the district was represented by another Republican, Ruby, who received 70 percent of the vote in her last reelection effort. The retirement slump would be the decrease from her 70 percent margin to Roy's initial victory margin of 60 percent, i.e., 10 percentage points.

Applying this procedure to the 1954–1960 period, Erikson estimated the incumbency advantage at two percentage points. He concluded that such a small benefit could have been decisive in only a small number of districts and that therefore the fact that a high percentage of incumbents won reelection should be attributed primarily to the fact that most districts were safe for their parties and not to the advantage deriving specifically from the fact of incumbency. However, when he applied the same procedures to later elections, Erikson found that although the two percent estimate remained accurate through 1964, in the 1966–70 elections the incumbency advantage jumped to about five percent.

Subsequent studies using the sophomore surge or retirement slump or both tended to confirm Erikson's finding of a sharp jump in the incumbency advantage in the mid-1960s. Different studies have generated somewhat different results (as well as some methodological controversies) but there is a near-consensus that the incumbency advantage, measured by vote percentage, jumped in the mid-1960s to the 5–10 percent range.[g] A similar jump appears to have occurred in state legislatures, but one to two decades later. But in

---

f. See Robert S. Erikson, *The Advantage of Incumbency in Congressional Elections*, 3 POLITY 395 (1971).

g. Bear in mind that these are averages. They do not necessary apply to any given incumbent and may vary considerably from one election year to another.

the meantime, the incumbency advantage in House races seems to have dropped to the 4–5 percent range.[h]

Vanishing marginals. The research of Erikson and those who followed him showed a surge in the incumbency advantage in the 1960s, but because their research dealt with averages across districts, it could do no more than suggest a possible adverse effect on electoral competition. The case for such an adverse effect was strengthened in an influential article by David Mayhew.[i]

Political scientists and political practitioners alike have long regarded a representative's margin of victory in one election as a useful indicator of his or her prospects in the next election. There is no single threshold of vulnerability, but political scientists have usually used either 55 or 60 percent as a convenient point for identification of "marginal" districts. Mayhew showed that in the early and mid-1960s, the number of House elections falling within the marginal range declined sharply. By 1972 there were only about half as many marginal elections as in 1956. The decline appeared to be connected to incumbency, because there was no decline when only "open seat" races (those in which no incumbent was running) were considered. Furthermore, when the presidential vote was broken down by House districts, there was no decline in the number of districts that were marginal.

Another drop in marginal districts occurred in the early 1980s. Using more elaborate statistical methods than Mayhew had used, Gary Jacobson estimated the proportion of incumbent races that were marginal (defined as less than a 60% vote total for the winner) as 39 percent for 1946–64, 27 percent for 1966–82, and 17 percent for 1984–88.[j]

Reelection Rates. The vanishing marginals seemed to indicate that incumbents' average advantage in winning votes was indeed paying off in terms of electoral security, with a resultant decline in competition. At least a portion of the extra votes incumbents were getting were boosting many of them from close victories indicating vulnerability to comfortable victories indicating safety. Indeed, the combination of enhanced average vote percentage and vanishing marginals seemed for over a decade to have completed the case for increased electoral safety. However, when scholars in the late 1980s began to look at the incumbency advantage from the seemingly simple perspective of actual rates of reelection, the picture became surprisingly murky.

Table 12-1 (on the next page) shows that from 1950–1990, incumbents who sought reelection enjoyed a high success rate. In only three years were more than 10 percent of incumbents running in general elections defeated, and the figure never reached as high as 12 percent. If incumbents defeated in primaries are included, there were four years in which over 10 percent of the incumbents seeking reelection lost, but the figure never reached 14 percent. The percentage of incumbents defeated in 1992 and 1994 was at the high end of the range that prevailed in the previous four decades, but 1992 and 1994 did not break out of that range.

---

h. See Bruce J. Oppenheimer, *Deep Red and Blue Congressional Districts*, in Lawrence C. Dodd & Bruce I. Oppenheimer, eds., CONGRESS RECONSIDERED (8th ed., 2005); Alan I. Abramowitz, Brad Alexander & Matthew Gunning, *Incumbency, Redistricting, and the Decline of Competition in U.S. House Elections*, 68 JOURNAL OF POLITICS 75 (2006).

i. See David R. Mayhew, *Congressional Elections: The Case of the Vanishing Marginals*, 6 POLITY 295 (1974).

j. See Gary C. Jacobson, THE ELECTORAL ORIGINS OF DIVIDED GOVERNMENT: COMPETITION IN U.S. HOUSE ELECTIONS, 1946–1988, at 26–29 (1990).

Table 12.1   Electoral Fortunes of U.S. House Incumbents, 1946–2002

Year(s)	Total Running	Lost Primary	Lost General	Total Lost	Total Won	% Won General	% Won Total
1946	398	18	52	70	328	86.3%	82.4%
1948	400	15	68	83	317	82.3%	79.3%
1950	400	6	32	38	362	91.9%	90.5%
1952	389	9	26	35	354	93.2%	91.0%
1954	407	6	22	28	379	94.5%	93.1%
1956	411	6	16	22	389	96.0%	94.6%
1958	396	3	37	40	356	90.6%	89.9%
1960	405	5	25	30	375	93.8%	92.6%
1962	402	12	22	34	368	94.4%	91.5%
1964	397	8	45	53	344	88.4%	86.6%
1966	411	8	41	49	362	89.8%	88.1%
1968	409	4	9	13	396	97.8%	96.8%
1970	401	10	12	22	379	96.9%	94.5%
1972	390	12	13	25	365	96.6%	93.6%
1974	391	8	40	48	343	89.6%	87.7%
1976	384	3	13	16	368	96.6%	95.8%
1978	382	5	19	24	358	95.0%	93.7%
1980	398	6	31	37	361	92.1%	90.7%
1982	393	10	29	39	354	92.4%	90.1%
1984	409	3	16	19	390	96.1%	95.4%
1986	393	2	6	8	385	98.5%	98.0%
1988	409	1	6	7	402	98.5%	98.3%
1990	407	1	15	16	391	96.3%	96.1%
1992	368	19	24	43	325	93.1%	88.3%
1994	386	4	35	39	347	90.8%	89.9%
1996	384	2	21	23	361	94.5%	94.0%
1998	404	3	6	9	395	98.5%	97.8%
2000	403	3	6	9	394	98.5%	97.8%
2002	398	8	8	16	382	98.0%	96.0%
2004	404	2	7	9	395	98.3%	97.8%
2006	405	2	22	24	381	94.5%	94.1%
1952–60	2008	29	126	155	1853	93.6%	92.3%
1962–70	2020	42	129	171	1849	93.5%	91.5%
1972–80	1945	34	116	150	1795	93.9%	92.3%
1982–90	2011	17	72	89	1922	96.4%	95.6%
1992–2000	1945	31	92	123	1822	95.1%	93.7%
2002–06	1207	12	37	49	1158	96.9%	95.9%
1952–66	3218	57	234	291	2927	92.6%	91.0%
1968–2006	7916	108	338	446	7470	95.7%	94.4%

Source: Vital Statistics on American Politics 2005–2006 (2005), Table 1-17.
For 2006, compiled from The Almanac of American Politics 2008.

Column 7 shows the percentage of incumbents in the general election who were reelected. The denominator is the total seeking reelection (column 2) minus the number defeated in primaries (column 3).

Column 8 shows the percentage of incumbents seeking reelection who were reelected. The denominator is the total seeking reelection (column 2).

As we have noted, incumbents may be reelected because of party dominance in their districts or because they are superior candidates, without any need for an electoral advantage inherent in incumbency. However, given the boost in incumbents' vote percentage and the sharp drop in marginal districts that occurred in the mid-1960s, an increase in the reelection rate for incumbents at the same time might have been expected and could have been attributed to a heightened incumbency advantage.

Gary Jacobson challenged conventional wisdom regarding the benefits of incumbency by pointing out that for the period 1952–1980, on a decade-by-decade basis, there had been no increase in incumbents' reelection rate.[k] In the 1950s and the 1970s they were reelected at identical rates, with a slight dip in the 1960s. General election reelection rates were nearly the same in all three decades.

How was it possible for incumbents' vote percentages to surge and for the marginals to vanish without a dramatic increase in the incumbency reelection rate? Jacobson's answer lay in another development: At the same time that the average incumbent's vote percentage was increasing, the variation about the mean was also surging.[l] What this meant was that the threshold of marginality needed to be raised. For example, an "incumbent elected in the 1970s with between 60 and 65 percent of the vote was just as likely to lose in the next election as was an incumbent in the 1950s who had been elected with 55 to 60 percent of the vote."[m] The reduced correlation between an incumbent's vote percentage in one election and the next made it possible for incumbents to increase their average vote percentages and to move out of the ranges that had been thought of as marginal while still losing elections as often as they had before.

Jacobson's studies created a new conventional wisdom that incumbents were *not* safer than they had been before the mid-1960s, but not one that lasted long. There was strong scholarly criticism,[n] but the biggest blows to Jacobson's assertions were leveled by the elections of the 1980s. Reelection rates went up noticeably, and more than 96 percent of incumbents running in general elections from 1982 to 1990 were reelected.

Jacobson was not cowed by a mere decade. He argued that the low number of incumbent defeats in the 1980s was a short-term phenomenon, occurring because "national conditions and issues [were not] conducive to change."[o] The 1992 and 1994 elections supported Jacobson's position, but 1996 and especially 1998 through 2004 suggest that "national conditions not conducive to change" are more the norm than the exception. 2006

k. See Gary C. Jacobson, The Politics of Congressional Elections (1987); Gary C. Jacobson, *The Marginals Never Vanished: Incumbency and Competition in Elections to the U.S. House of Representatives, 1952–1982*, 31 American Journal of Political Science 126 (1987).

l. Much the same point had been documented earlier by Thomas E. Mann, Unsafe at any Margin: Interpreting Congressional Elections (1978).

m. Jacobson, *The Marginals Never Vanished*, at 130.

n. See Monica Bauer & John R. Hibbing, *Which Incumbents Lose in House Elections: A Response to Jacobson's "The Marginals Never Vanished,"* 33 American Journal of Political Science 262 (1989).

o. Gary C. Jacobson, The Electoral Origins of Divided Government: Competition in U.S. House Elections, 1946–1988 133 (1990).

shows that exceptions still occur. If instead of dividing the postwar period by decades, as Jacobson does, one instead separates 1952–1966 from 1968–2006, the picture is one of a noticeable decline in competition. But if 1968–2006 has constituted an "era" of low competition, years like 1992, 1994, and 2006 show that the era is also punctuated with some highly competitive election years.

Before turning to possible causes of the incumbency advantage, we should note another implication of the increased variance in incumbents' vote percentages noted above. Even if the actual number of incumbents who will be defeated or face a close call in a given year is low, increased variance means that the number of incumbents who face *potential* jeopardy increases. Incumbents who contemplate a lengthy career in Congress need to be concerned not only with their jeopardy in the next election, but over a series of elections. Often it takes only one defeat to derail a congressional and perhaps a political career. Mayhew's finding that the marginal elections were declining in races with incumbents but remained high in open seat races might create an expectation that most representatives elected initially in close races will win thereafter by safe margins. However, even after the mid-1960s, only a third of the House members elected initially by close margins were able to follow with three consecutive "safe" victories.[p] Even representatives initially elected with a "safe" margin were found to have a one-out-of-four chance of going down to electoral defeat at some time in the future.[q]

It thus appears that fewer incumbents enjoy long-term security than would appear from looking at one of Mayhew's charts of vanishing marginals. This fact helps to explain the seeming paradox that despite widespread belief that incumbents are "entrenched," observers of congressional behavior universally report that members usually "run scared" and engage in what Hedrick Smith called "the perpetual campaign."

2. Causes

The previous discussion shows that although the incumbency advantage is a more complex question than is sometimes supposed, it is no myth or popular delusion. Not surprisingly, very soon after it was detected, scholars began to search for causes and to speculate over consequences. Explanations fall into two categories: district-based explanations, which posit that voters prone to support the party of the incumbents are concentrated within districts, and candidate-based explanations, which posit that incumbents possess personal qualities or other advantages that enable them to do better than challengers.

Gerrymandering. An early suspect was gerrymandering, a district-based explanation. This was a natural surmise, since the mid-1960s jump in the incumbency advantage coincided with *Wesberry*, which required that congressional districts within a state contain equal populations and thereby triggered a round of mid-decade congressional redistricting.

Despite its initial plausibility, several reasons exist for rejecting gerrymandering as a major explanation of the incumbency advantage. If the marginals were vanishing because of redistricting and not because of the dynamics of House elections, then the

---

p. See Melissa P. Collie, *Incumbency, Electoral Safety, and Turnover in the House of Representatives, 1952–76*, 75 AMERICAN POLITICAL SCIENCE REVIEW 119, 138 (1981).

q. See Robert S. Erikson, *Is There Such a Thing as a Safe Seat?*, 8 POLITY 623 (1976).

results of national and statewide elections should have become more polarized when broken down by congressional districts. Yet, as Mayhew pointed out, there was no decline of marginal results in presidential elections broken down by congressional districts during the period that the marginals were declining in House races with incumbents. Similar results have been found more recently, in statewide as well as presidential elections.[r]

Furthermore, the temporal correlation between the incumbency surge and court-coerced redistricting turned out upon closer inspection to be illusory. For example, the percentage of marginal districts declined at least as much in the 1960s in states that did not redistrict as in states that did.[s]

Bipartisan redistricting plans are universally understood to emphasize incumbent protection, and even partisan gerrymanders are likely to target a few opposition districts while keeping most districts safe for incumbents of both parties. Therefore, intuition strongly suspects that redistricting should have a pro-incumbent, anti-competitive effect. Many scholars have looked for such effects using many research methods, but mostly they have come up empty.[t] One study found some anticompetitive effects of bipartisan redistricting for the House,[u] and a more recent study found modest but significant pro-incumbent effects in partisan and racial redistrictings for state legislatures.[v] But another recent study compared the vote for president in the old and new congressional districts at the time of redistricting, and found little or no change in the competitiveness of the districts caused by the redistricting.[w] The same study found ample evidence that House districts became less competitive *between* redistricting, suggesting a different district-based explanation. We turn to that next.

The Fall and Rise of Partisanship. The decline and rise of partisanship in voting provides a better, though only a partial explanation of the incumbency advantage. In the late 19th century there was no popular cultural support for the "independent" voter as the citizen who evaluated candidates and issues on the merits and arrived at an informed decision. On the contrary, such people tended to be scorned as "traitors," "turncoats," or corrupt sellers of their votes.[x] Times have changed. In a 1986 survey, 92 percent agreed that "I always vote for the person I think is best, regardless of what party they [*sic*] belong to," while only 14 percent agreed that "I always support the candidates of just one party."[y]

In fact, people vote more consistently along party lines than the 1986 survey suggests, but decreased party loyalty from the 1960s through the 1980s was nevertheless an im-

r. See Jacobson, ELECTORAL ORIGINS, at 96.

s. See John A. Ferejohn, *On the Decline of Competition in Congressional Elections*, 71 AMERICAN POLITICAL SCIENCE REVIEW 166 (1977).

t. See Albert D. Cover, *One Good Term Deserves Another: The Advantage of Incumbency in Congressional Elections*, 21 AMERICAN JOURNAL OF POLITICAL SCIENCE 523 (1977); Albert D. Cover & David R. Mayhew, *Congressional Dynamics and the Decline of Competitive Congressional Elections*, in Lawrence C. Dodd & Bruce I. Oppenheimer, eds., CONGRESS RECONSIDERED (1st ed. 1977).

u. Michael Lyons & Peter F. Galderisi, *Incumbency, Reapportionment, and U.S. House Redistricting*, 48 POLITICAL RESEARCH QUARTERLY 857 (1995).

v. David Lublin & Michael P. McDonald, *Is It Time to Draw the Line?: The Impact of Redistricting on Competition in State House Elections*, 5 ELECTION LAW JOURNAL 144 (2006).

w. Abramowitz et al., *Incumbency, Redistricting, and the Decline of Competition in U.S. House Elections*, at 79.

x. Walter Dean Burnham, CRITICAL ELECTIONS AND THE MAINSPRINGS OF AMERICAN POLITICS 73 (1970).

y. Larry J. Sabato, THE PARTY'S JUST BEGUN: SHAPING POLITICAL PARTIES FOR AMERICA'S FUTURE 133 (1988) (Table 4.5).

portant cause of the incumbency advantage.[z] By its nature, however, it was an incomplete explanation. Strong party voting helps incumbents who represent safe partisan districts or whose party is benefiting from shifts in voter sentiments in a given year. But by the same token, strong party voting prevents incumbents from protecting themselves against adverse partisan tides. Increased voter willingness to cross party lines and to split tickets creates the *opportunity* for incumbents to increase their vote shares and electoral security by winning votes from adherents of the opposing party. However, there is no logical necessity for votes that become less determined by party identification to favor incumbents. The decline in party voting made the enhanced incumbency advantage possible, but cannot by itself explain why that possibility came to fruition.

The same mechanism has worked in reverse since the 1980s, when voters began voting more consistently as Democrats or Republicans. As voting in Congress became more polarized between the two parties, voters responded by voting more consistently according to their ideologies as liberals or conservatives. This created even stronger reasons for representatives to act in a polarized manner, and so on.[a]

The result was a decline, starting in the 1990s, in the incumbency advantage per se, as even a popular incumbent of the other party was less likely to sway a voter to cross party lines. Why, then, did incumbents' margins of victory and ability to get reelected remain strong and perhaps grow stronger? Research suggests that for various reasons there has been a trend toward Democrats living near Democrats and Republicans living near Republicans.[b] As a recent study concluded:

> The most significant changes in the competitiveness of House districts occurred between redistricting cycles. This pattern is consistent with the partisan polarization hypothesis. As a result of population movement, immigration, and ideological realignment within the electorate, Republicans are increasingly surrounded by other Republicans and Democrats by other Democrats. This trend has been evident since the 1970s, but it appears to have accelerated in recent years. Between 1992 and 2004, the number of marginal districts fell from 157 to 112 while the number of safe districts rose from 156 to 208.[c]

Though recent research shows the electoral value of incumbency to be reduced, it does not show it to have disappeared, so it is still worth looking for its causes.

Incumbents' activities. Some popular rhetoric seems to treat the incumbency advantage as if it were an axiomatic phenomenon, without any particular cause and somehow immune to voter preferences. Although it is possible that some voters use incumbency as a positive voting cue, there is little evidence for this and it may be offset, especially in recent elections, by hostility toward incumbency. Incumbency is probably best thought of not as an intrinsic electoral advantage but as a resource that a candidate can use to enhance his or her chances.

As Hedrick Smith described, incumbents do many things, aside from their actual reelection campaigns, to try to assure their reelection. Their legislative activities such as

---

z. See, e.g., Keith Krehbiel & John R. Wright, *The Incumbency Effect in Congressional Elections: A Test of Two Explanations*, 27 AMERICAN POLITICAL SCIENCE REVIEW 140 (1983).

a. See Gary C. Jacobson, *Party Polarization in National Politics: The Electoral Connection*, in Jon R. Bond & Richard Fleisher, eds., POLARIZED POLITICS: CONGRESS AND THE PRESIDENT IN A PARTISAN ERA (2000).

b. E.g., Oppenheimer, *Deep Red and Blue Congressional Districts.*

c. Abramowitz et al., *Incumbency, Redistricting, and the Decline of Competition in U.S. House Elections*, at 79.

votes on bills are calculated to avoid grounds for attack and to build support from the interests they regard as important to their electoral coalitions. They seek favorable publicity in the news media, and they further publicize themselves through mail sent to constituents at public expense. They deploy their staffs to act in their names as ombudsmen, helping constituents in matters ranging from simple provision of information to assistance in winning grants or other government funding for a variety of projects in their districts. They spend time attending meetings, functions, and other events to bring them into contact with constituents.[d]

Incumbents engage in these activities to assist in their reelection, and it seems reasonable to assume that the activities have this effect. Nevertheless, it has been very difficult to find solid empirical evidence of a correlation between the activities and the incumbent's vote share. To the contrary, almost all studies have found a lack of correlation.[e] In addition, researchers have been unable to find evidence that incumbent activities discourage strong challenges.[f]

Despite these studies several scholars have attempted to demonstrate that incumbent activities are effective, but none with as great perseverance and creativity as Morris Fiorina. Fiorina and his colleagues have focused on one incumbent activity, "casework," the assistance that House members provide to constituents in their dealings with agencies of the federal government. In what may be the most comprehensive study of casework, they were still unable to show a direct connection between casework and votes for incumbents, but they did show in various ways that casework is associated with favorable attitudes, and that persons who hold these favorable attitudes are more likely to vote for the incumbent.[g]

If such indirect evidence is less than compelling, it is not difficult to find reasons for difficulty in proving the electoral effectiveness of casework and other incumbent activities. First, "casework" is a somewhat vague term that includes a range of activities, and there is no very accurate way to measure it. Second, no members of the House have volunteered to suspend casework or other reelection-oriented activity in order to provide a controlled experiment from which political scientists can determine the electoral effectiveness of each activity, in isolation or in combination with one another. Once it is borne in mind that in *all* the districts measured in political scientists' models, the incumbents are engaging in casework and other activities to the extent they think necessary to assure their reelection, the inability to find correlations between varying levels of activities and the electoral results becomes less surprising.

These considerations help explain the studies that find no correlation between casework and votes, but they also point beyond a narrow focus on casework. None of the more general evidence that is available about representatives and their constituents suggests that members seek to impress constituents or that constituents evaluate their representatives on the basis of a single activity. Rather, incumbents try to win the trust of their constituents, and they do this by trying to establish that they are qualified to hold the

---

d. See generally Richard F. Fenno, Jr., HOME STYLE: HOUSE MEMBERS IN THEIR DISTRICTS (1978).

e. See, e.g., John R. Johannes & John C. McAdams, *The Congressional Incumbency Effect: Is It Casework, Policy Compatibility, or Something Else? An Examination of the 1978 Election*, 25 AMERICAN JOURNAL OF POLITICAL SCIENCE 512 (1981). For additional references, see John C. McAdams & John R. Johannes, *Congressmen, Perquisites, and Elections*, 50 JOURNAL OF POLITICS 412, 419–20 (1988).

f. See, e.g., Lyn Ragsdale & Timothy E. Cook, *Representatives' Actions and Challengers' Reactions: Limits to Candidate Connections in the House*, 31 AMERICAN JOURNAL OF POLITICAL SCIENCE 45 (1987).

g. See Bruce Cain, John Ferejohn & Morris Fiorina, THE PERSONAL VOTE: CONSTITUENCY SERVICE AND ELECTORAL INDEPENDENCE (1987).

position and that they both identify and empathize with the people in their districts.[h] The "home style" by which each incumbent relates to his or her district varies with the nature of the district and its expectations, as well as with the personality and priorities of the representative.

Campaign finance. The advantage that incumbents have in fund-raising in congressional elections is well-known and well-documented. We shall look more closely at the connection between campaign finance and the incumbency advantage in Chapter 14. For now, we should note that comparing the amounts spent by incumbents and challengers is not the most helpful way to understand the effects of campaign money on electoral competition. There is considerable evidence that the absolute amount spent by the challenger has more of an effect on vote percentages than the ratio of incumbent to challenger spending. For present purposes, then, the causal significance of campaign finance can be subsumed under the broader question of the quality of candidates who challenge incumbents. We turn to that question next.

Strategic politicians. There is some irony in the theory of strategic politicians. The theory was put forth by its originators, Gary Jacobson and Samuel Kernell,[i] as a solution to a puzzling disparity between aggregate national election data and data from voter surveys. As it turned out, the theory would not have provided much of a solution and the puzzle it was designed to solve was shown to be illusory. Nevertheless, by focusing attention on the importance of the challenge that is leveled against the incumbent and by providing a framework within which the interplay of national and local conditions in House campaigns could be studied, the theory has helped generate some of the most important insights into congressional elections during the last three decades.

Aggregate data had shown that votes cast in midterm congressional elections reflected national conditions. The better the state of the economy and the more popular the president, the smaller were the vote losses of the House candidates of the president's party in the midterm election. However, national surveys at best could find only weak and inconsistent evidence at the level of the individual voter that opinions on national conditions affected House votes. How could national conditions be reflected in aggregate vote totals if individual voters were not influenced by them?

Jacobson and Kernell's answer was that even if voters were not influenced by national conditions, political elites were. Potentially strong challengers to an incumbent would be more likely to run when national partisan trends appeared favorable. When the partisan winds were blowing in the opposite direction, they were more likely to wait. Similarly, potential campaign contributors and other supporters would be attracted to likely winners, and therefore would be more forthcoming in years when the partisan trends were favorable. When conditions were adverse, they would be more likely to channel their efforts and their funds to support endangered incumbents. These inclinations of candidates and supporters would mutually reinforce each other. Strong challengers would be more likely to run when the prospects of picking up support seemed good, and contributors would be attracted to strong challengers.

The result would be that for a voter in a district with an incumbent whose party was benefiting from national trends, the challenger would probably be a weak candidate with little money or support. On the other hand, a voter in a district with an incumbent from

---

h. See e.g., Fenno, HOME STYLE, at 56–67.
i. See Gary C. Jacobson & Samuel Kernell, STRATEGY AND CHOICE IN CONGRESSIONAL ELECTIONS (1981).

the party that was disadvantaged by national trends had a better chance of having the opportunity to vote for a strong, experienced, well-financed challenger. The voter, then, as the survey evidence seemed to suggest, could make a choice based on evaluation of the candidates. It would be the correlation of strong challenges with national trends that would produce the aggregate vote in accordance with national phenomena such as presidential approval, without the necessity for voters to be directly influenced by the national trends at all.

This explanation, clever though it was, contained a central flaw, which Jacobson and Kernell themselves acknowledged would prevent the system they described from being very stable. If voters really were not influenced by national trends in deciding between House candidates, why should potential challengers be influenced by those trends in deciding to run, and why should supporters and contributors be influenced by national trends in their allocations? Citing V.O. Key's dictum that "voters are not fools," Jacobson and Kernell (p. 19) had declared: "Neither ... are politicians." The trouble was that their system depended precisely on politicians being fools.

Furthermore, their explanation turned out to be unnecessary. Improved analyses of the survey data showed that direct influence on votes could be found from perceptions of national conditions.[j] Ironically, the discovery that undermined the theory's initial premise gave new plausibility and significance to a modified version. Strategic politicians, if they really were strategic, would not base their actions in House campaigns on national conditions unless voter behavior provided a reason for doing so. Once it became apparent that national conditions had a discernible influence on votes, it became possible for the actions of strategic politicians to *amplify* the effects of national conditions.

This amplification can occur only if voters are influenced by both candidate evaluations and by national conditions. If voters responded solely to national conditions, strong challengers would run only when partisan conditions were favorable, but there could be no amplification because voters would already be voting on a referendum basis and the strength of the challengers would have no effect on outcomes. If, as Jacobson and Kernell initially assumed, voters were moved solely by their evaluations of the candidates, strategic politicians would form their strategies without regard to national conditions. But if both candidate evaluations and national conditions influence votes, strategic politicians will have reason to make their challenges in favorable partisan years, and the presence of strong challengers will amplify the already beneficial effects of favorable national conditions for that party.

Strong incumbents. A great deal of research has been conducted on the difference a strong challenger can make in a House race. The most popular test of quality is a simple one, whether the challenger has previously held elective office. It should not be forgotten that all incumbents, by definition, have held elective office. Furthermore, the incumbents have already won the very office for which they are seeking reelection. Occasional incumbents may be weak candidates who won office originally because they faced even weaker opponents or were lucky in other ways. On average, however, a can-

---

j. See, e.g., Eric M. Uslaner & M. Margaret Conway, *The Responsible Congressional Electorate: Watergate, the Economy, and Vote Choice in 1974*, 79 AMERICAN POLITICAL SCIENCE REVIEW 788 (1985). Jacobson and Kernell later conceded the point. See Gary C. Jacobson, *Strategic Politicians and the Dynamics of U.S. House Elections, 1946–86*, 83 AMERICAN POLITICAL SCIENCE REVIEW 773, 774 (1989); Gary C. Jacobson & Samuel Kernell, *National Forces in the 1986 U.S. House Elections*, 15 LEGISLATIVE STUDIES QUARTERLY 65, 74 (1990).

didate who can win a highly coveted congressional seat is likely to have a high measure of the skills and qualities it takes to win in that district. Furthermore, the few weak candidates who get elected to Congress are likely either to acquire skills or be defeated. Some challengers may also be highly skilled, but as a group challengers do not have the track record of success that incumbents have and therefore are likely to be less skilled on average. Therefore, incumbents who run for reelection in any given year are likely to be more skillful than their opponents, and for that reason alone are likely to win most elections.

That, at any rate, is the theory recently proposed by John Zaller:

> The reason that [House incumbents] win reelection at very high rates is the same reason that world heavyweight boxing champions win most of their title defenses: owing to their manner of selection, incumbent champions in both professions are simply better competitors than most of the opponents they face.[k]

Divided government and partisan bias. Our discussion to this point has treated all incumbents alike, without distinguishing between Democrats and Republicans. However, a phenomenon that makes change more difficult would seem on its face likely to benefit the party that is favored by the status quo. Republicans, in particular, often contended, prior to the 1994 election, that the incumbency advantage trapped them in a minority position in the House during a period when they dominated presidential elections and temporarily (from 1980–1986) were able to win control of the Senate.[l] Other commentators, less concerned with the partisan welfare of Republicans, have expressed concern over the frequent occurrence since 1954 of divided government[m] or over possible deleterious effects on legislators that can result from being either in a permanent majority or a permanent minority.[n]

The assumption that divided government is harmful to the country has long been a mainstay of party government theory. As we saw in Chapter 9, that assumption has received a major challenge from David Mayhew, who surveyed the postwar era and was unable to find any pattern that periods of united government were superior to periods of divided government when measured by the passage of significant legislation.[o] Mayhew does not address the argument that united government is important for government accountability to the public,[p] even if it is true that it has no true superiority in government performance. One possible interpretation of the 1994 election is that the two-year period of united government following President Clinton's election made it possible for the electorate to hold the Democratic Party accountable for the performance of government. The perhaps ironical result was the quick reintroduction of divided government. The same in reverse can be said of 2006.

---

k. John Zaller, *Politicians as Prize Fighters: Electoral Selection and Incumbency Advantage*, in John G. Geer, ed., POLITICIANS AND PARTY POLITICS 131, 131 (1998).

l. See, e.g., Lee Atwater, *Altered States: Redistricting Law and Politics in the 1990s*, 6 JOURNAL OF LAW & POLITICS 661 (1990).

m. See, e.g., James L. Sundquist, *Needed: A Political Theory for the New Era of Coalition Government in the United States*, 103 POLITICAL SCIENCE QUARTERLY 613 (1988).

n. See, e.g., Thomas E. Mann, *Is the House of Representatives Unresponsive to Political Change?*, in ELECTIONS AMERICAN STYLE 261, 268 (A. James Reichley, ed., 1987).

o. See David R. Mayhew, DIVIDED WE GOVERN: PARTY CONTROL, LAWMAKING AND INVESTIGATIONS, 1946–1990 (1990).

p. See Morris P. Fiorina, *An Era of Divided Government*, in DEVELOPMENTS IN AMERICAN POLITICS 324 (Gillian Peele et al., eds., 1992).

Even if it is assumed that divided government is a bad thing, it is not clear how much the incumbency advantage has been a major contributor to its existence. The incumbency advantage may have reduced the rate at which shifts in the vote from one party to the other are translated into seat shifts in the House.[q] However, for some time scholars generally doubted that this effect had a major long-term partisan effect. They pointed to the fact that during the long period of Democratic dominance following the mid-1960s growth in the incumbency advantage, Republicans were unable to make consistent gains in open seat races. From 1968 to 1990, the Democrats won 80 previously Republican open seats while the Republicans won 71 previously Democratic open seats. Even during the Reagan and Bush years, the Republicans had only a 31–29 lead in capturing open seats from the opposing party, more than offset by a net Democratic gain of five seats in newly created districts.[r] And these results must be read against the fact that the Democrats had more seats to defend.

But there, according to more recent research, is the rub. Membership in the House of Representatives is a good job, but being a member of the majority party makes it even better. When a shift in partisan control of the House seems remote, members of the minority are more likely to step down. Because of the incumbency advantage, each time a member retires, the other party has an enhanced chance to gain that seat. Though the majority has more seats to defend, the minority is more likely to find itself defending open seats, and thus will have to run hard to avoid losing further ground. The increase in the incumbency advantage starting in the mid-1960s may therefore have contributed to the Democrats' remarkable 40-year control of the House.[s]

One other study should be mentioned as we wind up this survey. The study considered the incumbency advantage in state executive and legislative elections as well as congressional elections from 1942–2000. The authors concluded that changes in the incumbency advantage tended to come at about the same times in all the types of elections they studied. This is potentially an important finding, because it casts considerable doubt on all assertions that the increases in the incumbency advantage in elections for the House of Representatives are caused by factors specific to the House or to Congress or to national elections generally.[t]

3. Conclusion

This survey of research on the incumbency advantage has yielded these conclusions:

1. House incumbents have enjoyed considerable success since 1950, though over the long term a House member's electoral security is comparable to that of a Senator.

2. There was a lasting surge in the incumbency advantage, as measured by vote percentage, in the mid-1960s. A second celebrated surge in reelection rates occurred in the 1980s, but was interrupted in 1992 and 1994. The high reelection rate of incumbents resumed in subsequent elections until 2006, but their success appears to be the result of

---

q. See Stephen Ansolabehere, David W. Brady & Morris Fiorina, *The Vanishing Marginals and Electoral Responsiveness*, 22 British Journal of Political Science 21, 31–32 (1992).

r. See Gary C. Jacobson, *The Persistence of Democratic House Majorities*, in The Politics of Divided Government 57, 62–63 (Gary W. Cox & Samuel Kernell, eds., 1991).

s. See Stephen Ansolabehere & Alan Gerber, *Incumbency Advantage and the Persistence of Legislative Majorities*, 22 Legislative Studies Quarterly 161 (1997).

t. See Stephen Ansolabehere & James M. Snyder, Jr., *The Incumbency Advantage in U.S. House Elections: An Analysis of State and Federal Offices, 1942–2000*, 1 Election Law Journal 315 (2002).

higher partisan loyalty and cohesion among voters in districts than advantages accruing particularly to incumbency. The incumbency advantage itself appears to have receded to about the level reached in the mid-1960s.

3. Electoral success is not something that comes automatically to incumbents. Rather, they work hard to accomplish it, by a variety of activities. The effectiveness of these activities in winning votes has been surprisingly difficult to document by rigorous statistical methods. Nevertheless, until the contrary is demonstrated, it seems reasonable to assume that incumbents' activities have been effective in boosting their vote percentages.

4. Although the assumption that incumbents' activities increase their vote percentages seems reasonable, how resistant this advantage will be to a strenuous challenge is harder to say. Experienced, well-funded challengers can cut substantially into incumbents' margins and are successful in a surprisingly high percentage of attempts. The high reelection rate from 1984 to 1990 and again from 1996 to 2004 has not occurred because incumbents regularly defeated strong challengers but because they were rarely confronted with strong challengers.

6. It does not necessarily follow, however, that many more incumbents would have been defeated if there had been more strong challengers. Strong challenges are much more likely to occur when there is a good chance of success. Furthermore, incumbents by definition are successful, experienced candidates whose track record alone should make us expect high reelection rates.

7. As the 1992, 1994, and 2006 elections demonstrated, all of the above are subject to change.

This complex and in some respects unclear picture does not suggest firm answers to the legal and policy questions that will be considered in the remainder of this chapter and in the chapters on campaign finance. Perhaps it will help us to avoid facile responses based on unfounded or oversimplified assumptions.

II. Perquisites

People v. Ohrenstein
77 N.Y.2d 38, 565 N.E.2d 493 (1990)

WACHTLER, Chief Judge.

The primary question on this appeal is whether the Minority Leader of the State Senate may be prosecuted criminally for having assigned employees of his Senate staff, largely during the year 1986, to work on political campaigns for members of his party seeking election or reelection to the Senate. The case also presents the question whether defendants may be prosecuted criminally for having placed on the Senate payroll, during that same period, "no-show" employees—persons who did no work and were not expected to do anything to earn their salaries.

The trial court dismissed hundreds of counts relating to the use of Senate staff employees in political campaigns, and the Appellate Division precluded the prosecutor from proceeding on the remaining counts in that category. However, both courts sustained the counts relating to the "no-show" employees. The prosecutor and the defendants have cross-appealed. We now affirm, emphasizing that we are not dealing here with a civil action to enjoin the expenditure of funds or to recover funds already expended. Nor do we condone the challenged expenditures. Our focus is solely on whether defendants' acts subjected them to criminal prosecution under the circumstances of this case.

I. The Facts....

The defendant Manfred Ohrenstein is a Democratic Senator and the Minority Leader of the State Senate. The indictment alleges that in 1986 he conspired with his chief of staff, defendant Francis Sanzillo, and Senator Howard Babbush to use Senate employees from their staffs in seven campaigns for the Senate in which the incumbents were considered vulnerable. In two of the campaigns Democratic Senators were seeking reelection; in the others Democratic candidates challenged Republican incumbents.

[T]hese employees fell into three categories. Some were regular legislative aides who were temporarily assigned to work on the campaigns (Category 1). Others were hired for the campaigns and retained afterwards (Category 2) or let go when the campaigns were over (Category 3). These employees received regular salaries biweekly from the Senate payroll. In each instance the Senator or his designee certified that the employee was on the Senate staff and had performed "proper duties" during the relevant period. If the campaign efforts had been wholly successful, it is likely that the Democrats would have obtained a majority in the Senate and that Senator Ohrenstein would have become the Majority Leader. But the efforts did not succeed entirely; in all seven of the targeted campaigns the incumbents, including the two Democratic incumbents, were reelected.

In 1988, the defendants and others were indicted by a Manhattan Grand Jury. The indictment contains 665 counts charging the defendants, individually or in various combinations, with felonies and misdemeanors generally related to theft allegedly committed between 1981 and 1986. The bulk of the charges concern the use of Senate staff in political campaigns and most of these charges relate to the 1986 election. The defendants were also charged with placing four persons on the payroll who performed no services of any kind. It is alleged that the defendants knew that these employees did nothing and, in fact, had no duties but that the Senators or their designees nevertheless certified that the employees had performed "proper duties."

[The trial court dismissed the counts relating to employees in Categories 1 and 2, but denied defendants' motion to dismiss the counts relating to Category 3 and "no-show" employees. The Appellate Division ruled that the Category 3 counts should have been dismissed, and otherwise affirmed the rulings of the trial court. In this opinion, the Court of Appeals— the highest court in the New York system—affirms the decision of the Appellate Division.]

II. The Campaign Worker Counts

[The court found it unnecessary to reach constitutional questions, because it concluded the acts alleged were not subject to prosecution.]

The indictment charges the defendants with violating various generic sections of the Penal Law dealing with theft, but all of the charges relating to the campaign workers rest on a single prosecutorial premise: political campaign activities were not a "proper duty" of a legislative staff member. Based on this premise the defendants are charged with filing false instruments for certifying that members of the staff active in political campaigns performed "proper duties," and are further charged with committing larceny by false pretenses for inducing the State to pay the salaries in reliance on the allegedly false statements. The defendants are also charged with theft of services on the theory that legislative employees assigned to campaign work have been diverted from their "proper duties". Counts charging the defendants with engaging in a conspiracy and a scheme to defraud the government rest on the same premise.

It is important to emphasize that we are not dealing here with broad policy and ethics questions concerning the propriety of permitting State employees generally to participate in political campaign activities. This case focuses narrowly on alleged criminal activities of legislative employees who are unique in several respects because of the nature of the Legislature's function.... The Legislative Law delegates to the Minority Leader the power to "appoint such employees to assist him in the performance of his duties as may be authorized and provided for in the legislative appropriation bill" (§6[2]) and to determine their tenure (§8) and salaries (§10). Similar powers are delegated with respect to committees (§9). However, there is no statute fixing the hours of work for such employees or defining the duties of legislative aides or the duties of the Minority Leader they are hired to assist. And at the times relevant here, there was no rule or regulation concerning these matters. The Legislature is not always in session, and when it is in session, legislators and their staffs often work late into the night and through holidays and weekends until the Legislature's work is done. They were not required to account for their time and received no additional compensation or formal compensatory time allowances for overtime. Legislative staff members worked when they were needed and were often given free time when they were not needed, at the discretion of the particular legislator.

The appropriation bill that authorized the salaries in this case limited the amount of money available but did not otherwise limit the legislator's powers with respect to the allocation of staff time or function. It provided simply that the funds were to be used for "personal service of employees and for temporary and expert services of legislative and program operations ... [and] of standing committees."

Thus the statutes permitted the individual legislator to appoint staff members, to determine the terms and conditions of their employment and to assign duties and the hours of work as the legislator deemed necessary to fulfill the broad range of legislative duties. Despite this extensive grant of authority, the prosecutor urges that a Senator's power to assign duties to legislative assistants should be limited to governmental activities and should not include purely political ones. Although this distinction may be relevant to other State employees, the line between political and governmental activities is not so easily drawn in cases dealing with legislators and their assistants.

The Legislature is the "political" branch of government. All of its members are elected every two years and all legislation is the product of political activity both inside and outside the Legislature. Indeed, by statute the State Legislature itself is structured along party lines with the majority and minority parties in both houses organized behind elected party leaders. As noted, the Minority Leader is expressly authorized to appoint persons to assist him with his duties, and annual appropriations specifically authorize the expenditure of State funds to compensate these employees and enable the party leaders to carry out that party's "program operations." In addition to political activities formally recognized at law, there are additional functions which a legislator performs to gain support in the community, such as distributing newsletters and meeting constituents. Although these activities may be fairly characterized as political, as opposed to governmental, they are considered an inherent part of the job of an elected representative and thus perfectly legitimate acts for a legislator or legislative assistant to perform (*Hutchinson v. Proxmire*, 443 U.S. 111 (1979)). Indeed, the prosecutor does not suggest that every legislator who uses State facilities or personnel for any type of political activity should be indicted for misuse of government funds. As the People make clear in their reply brief, for example: "The People recognize that some 'political' activities of legislators and their aides do fall into an uncertain or 'gray' area." Conduct is not illegal "merely because legislative employees worked on election campaigns." It has "never been [the People's] position that legislative employees are prohibited from engaging in political campaign activity." Thus the prosecutor's objection to the defendants' use of Senate staff for the campaigns is not based on the fact that it is a political activity but on the belief that it is too political.... Although prior to 1987 some felt that the use of staff employees in political campaigns should be prohibited or subject to limitations, it is apparent that for many years that was not the prevailing view.

In 1945, a Joint Legislative Committee recommended that legislative staff employees not be included with other State employees in the Civil Service system. The study notes that: "Under our theory of government where party programs have been the basis for legislation, it might hamstring a legislator to surround him with employees unsympathetic to his point of view or to whom party strategy cannot be confided ... [furthermore] civil service employees would not be free to participate in the political activity generally required of a legislator." In subsequent years..., critics and concerned legislators recommended curtailing the practice or suggested imposing restrictions or "guidelines" regulating the use of legislative staff members in political campaigns. But it was not until 1987 that the Legislature placed any restrictions on the practice.

In that year the Legislature created a commission to study the subject and adopted interim guidelines reaffirming the right of legislative employees to participate in political campaigns, provided that did not interfere with legislative duties, which for the first time was defined to include specified activities excluding political campaigns. Later in the year Governor Cuomo signed the Ethics in Government Act, establishing a Legislative Ethics Committee to review such matters (L.1987, ch. 813) and adopted the New York State Governmental Accountability, Audit and Internal Control Act of 1987 (L.1987, ch. 814), which required the Senate to adopt procedures regulating its personnel and their salaries.

Thus prior to 1987, when the activities at issue here occurred, the Legislature was aware of the fact that its members were using staff employees in political campaigns perhaps excessively, and nevertheless chose to place no restrictions on the practice. Although it is arguable that the defendants' conduct might have exceeded the custom in some respects, the controlling factor for the purposes of a criminal prosecution is that there was no law which, either expressly or as interpreted by the courts, declared the acts to be criminal. Moreover, it cannot fairly be said that the Legislature otherwise forbade the conduct so that it could serve as a predicate for a conviction under general Penal Law provisions.

The prosecutor urges that the matter does not end here. He contends that the defendants' conduct is prohibited by article VII, §8 of the State Constitution, which prohibits the use of State moneys for "private undertaking[s]." ... In other words, the prosecutor's position is that if prior to 1987 the Legislature did not actually prohibit the defendants' use of Senate staff in political campaigns, it nevertheless must be deemed to have done so because the Constitution would not permit the Legislature to expend State moneys in this manner or authorize others to do so.... The prosecutor recognizes the need for a legislator or someone in the legislator's office to respond to constituent inquiries, as well as the need to have staff members take some part in a legislator's reelection campaign which may incidentally involve some use of State facilities. He argues, however, that exclusive or extensive use of legislative personnel for election campaigns is prohibited by the Constitution, although he concedes that this provision would not preclude the Legislature from authorizing public funding for political campaigns but urges that it would have to be done impartially to avoid being treated as a "private undertaking."

These arguments are far removed from the type of analysis appropriate to a criminal prosecution and need not be resolved here. Notably although this provision has been a part of the State Constitution for well over a century, and the courts have frequently been called upon to construe it, this is the first time that it has been suggested that a violation, if it be that, should serve as a predicate for criminal prosecution. A review of the section and its history shows that it was never intended to be used in this manner.

[The court's review of the history of article VII, §8, which is omitted here, leads it to this conclusion:] The constitutional prohibition limits the power of the Legislature to appropriate, but it does not create a hidden limitation in every appropriation so that any expenditure which is facially valid, but constitutionally prohibited, can be deemed an unauthorized expenditure and therefore a predicate for a criminal prosecution. That would elevate and convert an ordinary fiscal responsibility measure into an extraordinary penal one and distort the purposes of the constitutional prohibition.

The dissent agrees that all the charges relating to the use of Senate staff in political campaigns should be dismissed, except those dealing with employees hired for the campaigns and released afterward (Category 3). Dismissal of those charges, the dissenter contends, will permit the Legislature to determine how State funds should be spent without any oversight by the courts. However, it should be emphasized that in this case we have not been called upon to decide whether what occurred here should be civilly enjoined in the future or whether the money spent in the past may be recovered as an unauthorized expenditure of State funds. All we have before us is a criminal indictment and we hold only that the defendants cannot be held criminally liable for their use of Senate staff in these campaigns under the practice that existed prior to 1987.

Nor are we saying, as the dissent suggests, that such conduct would be permitted today or that it can continue in the future with impunity unless the Legislature adopts a statute specifically prohibiting it. The statutes dealing generically with theft provide a basis for prosecution in cases where government employers use State employees for activities which are prohibited or are not within the employees' duties as defined by statute, rule or regulation. The point we are making in this case is that at the time the defendants acted, their conduct was not prohibited in any manner; nor could they have known that they were subject to criminal prosecution for their acts; there was no statute, nor was there any rule or regulation defining the duties of legislative assistants or limiting the nature or extent of their permissible political activities. In a criminal prosecution where these defendants are charged with engaging in activities prohibited by law, the absence of any such legal prohibition is fatal to the prosecution.

Our holding is a narrow one based on circumstances which no longer exist. As indicated, the Legislature, acting as employer, has now adopted a joint resolution which defines some of the duties of legislative assistants and imposes limitations on a legislator's use of such assistants. Additionally, the Legislature has adopted statutes requiring such staff members and their employers to make a more extensive account of their activities and has also created a panel to further study the matter and make additional recommendations. The joint resolution specifically addresses the dissenter's concerns and prohibits legislators in the future from hiring staff assistants solely to work in political campaigns. We cannot decide future cases not before us; but in response to the dissent it is only fair to note that those who engage in such conduct in the future will not be able to make the arguments that we find determinative here in the event they are criminally prosecuted.

III. The "No-Show" Counts

On the defendants' appeal they urge that the Appellate Division erred in holding that prosecution of the counts relating to the "no-show" employees is not prohibited by … the separation of powers doctrine. We agree with the Appellate Division.

The theory underlying these counts is that the defendants filed false instruments when they certified on the payroll records that these employees performed "proper duties," and committed larceny when they induced the State to rely on the false statements. Here there is no question as to what "proper duties" include, because no matter how they are defined, they must at least include the performance of some services, of some type, at some time. Here it is alleged that these employees did nothing, that the defendants knew this and that the defendants also knew that they had no duties. These allegations are sufficient to sustain these criminal counts.

This should also dispose of the defendants' argument that the indictment and prosecution constitutes an unwarranted intrusion into the affairs of the Legislature in violation of the separation of powers concept because it will permit the executive and the courts to determine what are proper duties for legislative staff. No such inquiry is necessary in this case if, as alleged, these staff members did nothing and were not expected to perform any duties.

Accordingly, the order of the Appellate Division should be affirmed and the judgment of the Appellate Division should be affirmed, without costs.

SIMONS, Judge (dissenting in part).

I agree with the majority that the counts of the indictment founded on defendants' use of their regular employees for political activities in addition to legislative duties must be dismissed (Categories 1 and 2). I also agree that the counts of the indictment charging defendants with certifying the salary of four "no-shows," persons placed on the legislative payroll who performed no duties, should stand (Category 4). I disagree, however, with the dismissal of the charges alleging that defendants unlawfully authorized payment from State funds to persons whose only duties consisted of working for Democratic senatorial candidates during the election campaign (Category 3). Certifying their payment from State funds was criminal and the counts alleging defendants did so should be reinstated.

I would have thought the use of public funds to finance the election campaigns of the candidates of one party and defeat candidates of the opposition was so clearly unlawful that it was not worth discussion. Any other view devalues the democratic process by leaving incumbent legislators free to perpetuate themselves in office at government expense. The majority concludes otherwise, however, reasoning that partisan political activities are "proper duties" of a legislative employee. Once this premise is accepted, it follows easily that employees may be hired to engage in a broad range of purely political activities and be paid for it by the State because they are doing no more than fulfilling their public duties. The Legislature may restrict such political activities, the majority holds, but since it had not done so in 1986, defendants' conduct was not criminal and the charges involving employees in Categories 1, 2 and 3 must be dismissed.

I know of no authority, and the majority cites none, which would support such reasoning. Political activities are private, not public, matters and the use of public funds to pay employees hired for private purposes is unlawful. Thus, the question is not whether the Legislature has ever restricted the power of its members to hire campaign workers at State expense or criminalized such conduct. It has never had the power to authorize such employment....

I

[The work performed by the Category 3 employees] served no public purpose. On the contrary, everything they did was political. Thus, a determination that defendants were guilty of criminal conduct for certifying their payment from State funds does not involve intrusion by the Court into matters of legislative discretion. It involves no more than a determination of whether political activities are a part of a legislator's public duties which may be paid for from public funds.... The employees performed a wide range of political duties. For example, one was assigned as an employee of the Commission for Water Resources and Needs for Long Island at a salary of $500 per week but acted as the campaign manager for one of the candidates. She was not even aware that she was assigned to a commission until terminated after the election. Another worked as a "gofer" for one of the candidates and was paid $1,400 from funds allocated to the Commission on Rural Resources. One appointee, listed on defendant Ohrenstein's payroll as a Senate "research analyst", received a total of $10,000 from the State for checking the biographical backgrounds of two Republican incumbents. Others were hired as publicists, campaign coordinators, poll takers or in similar jobs at comparable salaries....

II

... The statutes in question, like penal laws generally, do not proscribe specific practices or methods but rather focus on whether the conduct causing the injury was blameworthy. The essence of the larceny charges against defendants is that they used State funds knowing the use was unauthorized, i.e., that the funds could not be used for the private purpose of campaign activity. The defendants' claim, accepted by the Appellate Division and the majority in this Court, is that the charges cannot stand because no provision in the Penal Law defines this conduct as criminal. There is no statute proscribing payments of State funds to "no shows" either, but doing so is a crime. The myriad ways in which the improper use of governmental funds may be accomplished precludes such specificity and the majority, by sustaining the counts in the indictment involving "no shows", recognize as much.

The majority asserts a specific statute is required in this case, however, because political activities are an inherent part of a legislator's public duties. They hold that unless the Legislature proscribes the use of legislative aides for political purposes the practice is proper. The presence or absence of a statute prohibiting the specific conduct is irrelevant. As New York and every other jurisdiction which has addressed the issue has found, partisan political activities are private, not public functions, and the use of public funds for such purposes is improper....

Some of these authorities relate to the use of public funds by State agencies to support propositions rather than candidates but the logic of applying them to legislative election campaigns is inescapable. Campaigning, whether for a cause or a candidate, is a private activity. The government has no interest in paying for partisan activity to obtain a particular election result. Political parties, by definition, represent only a portion of the public and their purpose is to advance the views of the group they represent. It is not possible, therefore, to render a service to the public or perform "proper duties" of the Legislature by working solely to elect the candidates of a particular party or to increase the power and influence of a particular political leader. Such work has no reasonable connection with serving the public....

The necessity for the rule is apparent when viewed from a broader perspective also. Elections are the central event in any democratic society. If they are to fulfill their function, two aspects must be preserved: (1) voters must have an effective voice in choosing their representatives and (2) candidates, whether incumbents or challengers, must have a reasonably equal chance at success. Permitting the Legislature, which has access to the biggest campaign war chest of all, the public treasury, to use public funds solely for campaign purposes in an attempt to dominate elections, threatens the basic integrity of the democratic process and implicates important constitutional concepts of government neutrality and fair dealing....[u]

The majority, in holding that political activities are part of a legislator's public duties, has failed to distinguish between the many legitimate representational activities performed by legislative staff, e.g., distributing newsletters and answering constituent inquiries, and those purely political activities directed at securing reelection. There is a world of difference between paying a staffer performing proper and legitimate duties to handle constituent concerns, however, and paying an employee from funds appropriated for the Commission on Water Resources to be the campaign manager for a Democratic candidate seeking to oust a Senate incumbent. The former is perfectly proper; the latter most certainly is not....

The majority in support of its position that staffing Democratic headquarters and campaign organizations at public expense is in the "gray area" between legitimate representational activity and purely political activity, cites the prosecutor's acknowledgment that sometimes differentiation between the two is difficult. The prosecutor did not concede that the work performed by the campaign-only employees was proper in this case, however. He contended that the activities of employees in all three categories covered by the indictment were not "even near" the gray area.... It is difficult to disagree with that assessment when workers in Category 3 did only political work, many were on commission, not Senate payrolls, and most worked to elect five private citizens seeking office and could not be performing public duties of a representational nature for legislators.

If the State had given conflicting interpretations of the propriety of hiring campaign workers at public expense, defendants could reasonably contend that they acted in good faith and that the authorities cited should not serve as a predicate for conviction under the general Penal Law provisions. But neither the New York courts nor the State's agencies have ever authorized this conduct....

Moreover, defendants knew the law on the subject for they had researched the issue themselves. [In] 1984, two years before the events covered in this indictment, defendant Ohrenstein retained a law professor to thoroughly research the question. The professor issued a 26-page opinion which discussed the Penal Law provisions at issue and analyzed most of the same judicial authorities relied on in this dissent. He concluded that the use of legislative employees for campaign purposes could be illegal. More importantly, he carefully distinguished between staffers who performed legislative functions but devoted part of their time to political activities and employees hired solely for campaign purposes, noting that while permanent staffers might justifiably use free time for political activities, the employment of persons at public expense solely for campaign work would present grave questions under the Penal Law sections relating to larceny, offering false instruments for filing and theft of services. Instead of heeding their lawyer's warnings or inquiring of State agencies about the propriety of their intended conduct, however, defendants chose to hire people at public expense to staff these Senate campaigns.... Had defendants genuinely believed that campaigning was a proper public duty, they would have identified the employees listed on the payroll certifications as "campaign workers", not as "research assistants", "legislative aides", etc. Moreover, had they believed their conduct proper, there would have been no need for the efforts revealed in the Grand Jury testimony to conceal the payments from the public. There was evidence, for example, that one candidate had

---

u. These principles do not render legislation for the public financing of political campaigns unlawful. It is only the partisan use of the public treasury which is prohibited....

two "campaign managers", one figurehead whose name was disclosed to the press and a counterpart not publicly acknowledged but paid by the State; that several "farmed out" staffers were instructed to avoid the media or to use pseudonyms when dealing with reporters so that they would not be recognized; that campaign workers paid from public funds left campaign headquarters at the first sign of a reporter to avoid disclosure and that message boards at campaign headquarters were altered to avoid reporters recognizing names. These actions bespeak guilty knowledge, not a good-faith belief by defendants that their conduct was permissible under the law....

V ....

The majority's assertion that defendants' conduct cannot be repeated, notwithstanding its concession that the Legislature possesses the authority to finance purely political campaign activities at State expense and its broad view of the Legislature's power over its employees, virtually assures that similar conduct will occur in the future. Only the bounds of human ingenuity will limit it. Accordingly, I dissent and would reinstate the counts relating to the 18 employees who worked only on campaigns.

Notes and Questions

1. If some plaintiffs had brought a civil action in 1986 seeking to enjoin Ohrenstein and the other defendants from assigning public employees to pure campaign activities, would the New York Court of Appeals have upheld an injunction? Should the fact that the actual *Ohrenstein* case was a criminal prosecution make a decisive difference?

2. Given the majority's decision to throw out all the counts related to public employees engaging in campaign work, was it correct to uphold the counts related to public employees who were not required to work at all? If it is a crime to appropriate state funds to pay "employees" not to do any work at all, why is it less of a crime to use those funds to pay "employees" to work, but not to work for the state? If a state legislator is accused in New York of theft for using state funds to hire an individual to tutor the legislator's children, would the charge be upheld under *Ohrenstein*?

3. Is the dissenter right to agree with the dismissal of the counts based on Category 1 and 2 employees while voting to uphold the counts based on Category 3 employees? If the dissenter's view had prevailed, what incentives would be created for legislative party leaders who want to have state-paid employees available to perform important campaign functions?

4. Charles Chvala, Democratic leader in the Wisconsin Senate, was charged with the felony of "misconduct in office." The offense applied to an officer who "exercises a discretionary power in a manner inconsistent with the duties of the officer's ... office ... or the rights of others and with intent to obtain a dishonest advantage for the officer ... or another...." Chvala allegedly hired and oversaw employees of the Senate Democratic Caucus to work on campaigns. His motion to dismiss the charges on several grounds, including that the prohibition was vague as applied to his alleged conduct, was rejected in *State v. Chvala*, 678 N.W.2d 880 (Wis. App. 2004). The Wisconsin Supreme Court unanimously affirmed the Court of Appeals' rejection of some of Chvala's objections, but was evenly divided on others, including the vagueness claim. That had the effect of affirming the lower court's decision, thereby allowing Chvala to be tried. *State v. Chvala*, 693 N.W.2d 747 (Wis. 2005).

Wisconsin enjoyed equal opportunity prosecutions. A couple of Republican legislators were charged under the same statute with hiring legislative employees for political purposes. The results in the Court of Appeals and the Wisconsin Supreme Court were similar to those in *Chvala*. See *State v. Jensen*, 681 N.W.2d 230 (Wis. App. 2004), *affirmed*, 694 N.W.2d 56 (Wis. 2005).

5. The *Ohrenstein* majority emphasizes that it is holding only that abuse of legislative perquisites cannot be regulated by means of criminal charges based on general criminal offenses such as theft. Nevertheless, other courts often have been equally inhospitable to efforts to employ civil remedies against abuse of legislative perquisites.

One such case was UNITED STATES ex rel. JOSEPH v. CANNON, 642 F.2d 1373 (D.C.Cir. 1981), cert. denied, 455 U.S. 999 (1982). *Cannon* was an action brought under the False Claims Act, a Civil War statute permitting citizens who have discovered fraudulent claims against the government to bring an action requiring reimbursement and, if successful, recover a portion of the repayment. The claim in this case was that a United States Senator, Howard Cannon, had defrauded the government by assigning one of his staff aides, Chester B. Sobsey, to do full-time campaign work while Sobsey was drawing a federal salary. The only specific regulation of the subject was Senate Rule 43, prohibiting Senate aides from soliciting or receiving campaign contributions unless the aide had been designated by the Senator to perform such services. The court denied the claim, basing its conclusion on an interpretation of the False Claims Act. However, this interpretation was based in large part on the possibility that the form of review that would be required if such claims were permissible would require the resolution of a nonjusticiable question, namely, which "political" activities are permissible for legislative staff. Excerpts from the *Cannon* opinion follow:

> [T]he construction of the Act for which appellant contends — the only construction through which appellant could hope to achieve victory — would require us to venture far beyond the limits of acceptable judicial action....

> [S]o-called political questions are denied judicial scrutiny, not only because they invite courts to intrude into the province of coordinate branches of government, but also because courts are fundamentally underequipped to formulate national policies or develop standards of conduct for matters not legal in nature. A challenge to the interworkings of a Senator and his staff member raises at the outset the specter that such a question lurks....

> Even assuming, as fairly we may, that the funds appropriated were intended solely to compensate staffers for performance of their "official" duties, we are left with the perplexing question whether campaign work is official activity. Not even the Senate itself has been able to reach a consensus on the propriety of using staff members in reelection campaigns; rather, the history of its attempts to develop a suitable rule reveals the lack of a firm standard during the period relevant to this case, and vividly portrays the keen difficulties with which courts would be faced were they to attempt to design guidelines on their own.

> [As of 1976, when the alleged fraudulent claim occurred, the only regulation of staff campaign activity was Rule 43. Even after 1976, although serious efforts were made in the Senate to adopt regulations, it proved difficult to do so. For example, one proposal] met a very early demise..., a fate reflective of the still-continuing inability of the Senate to prescribe binding standards of behavior in that regard, as well as of the perceived need for further study of the problem....

> [T]he interpretation of the False Claims Act suggested by appellant would license the courts to monitor every action taken by a Senator and his aide in an effort to determine whether it is sufficiently "official" or too "political."

The dilemma thus posed is just as unsurmountable here as we found it to be in another recent case — one involving a presidential reelection campaign. *Winpisinger v. Watson*, 628 F.2d 133 (D.C.Cir. 1980). There we cited both lack of standing and general prudential considerations in declining to exercise jurisdiction to deal with claims of misuse of federal power and funds by a candidate who allegedly had followed

> a concerted course of conduct designed to use the public treasury for salaries, travel expenses, costs of meetings and other political outlays; to grant and withhold public employment based upon political support by the employee; and to promise and award federal programs and funds to communities as political inducements and rewards, all in order to obtain support for President Carter's renomination.

These accusations, we noted, "relate[d], quite literally, to virtually every discretionary decision made by the Administration acting through ... high government officials;" "[c]onsequently," we said, "any relief, to be effective, would have to be as broad as the authority of the high offices held by the federal defendants." So,

> [w]hether shaped as declaratory relief, or injunctive relief, or both, the court's judgment would have to interject itself into practically every facet of the Executive Branch of the federal government, on a continuing basis, for the purpose of appraising whether considerations other than pure public service motivated a particular defendant in the performance of his or her official duties.

But this, we concluded, was beyond the ability of the judiciary, for the courts simply are "not suited to undertake neutral consideration of every Executive action." And we pointed out that resolving the issue drawn would compel us to make fundamental policy decisions:

> For this court to undertake the inquiry which would be required in this case would be to invade the far corners of the Executive Branch by subjecting countless Administration decisions to judicial scrutiny for any vestige of political motivation.... [I]n addition to being unmanageable[,] [n]either would that inquiry proceed on the basis of a discrete judicial standard.... Rather the court would be assessing the correctness of an action assigned to the Executive Branch and often requiring substantial supporting personnel and expertise, as well as a significant time investment.

In the absence of any discernible legal standard or even of a congressional policy determination that would aid consideration and decision of the question..., we are loathe to give the False Claims Act an interpretation that would require the judiciary to develop rules of behavior for the Legislative Branch. We are unwilling to conclude that Congress gave the courts a free hand to deal with so sensitive and controversial a problem, or invited them to assume the role of political overseer of the other branches of Government.... We do not, of course, say that Members of Congress or their aides may defraud the Government without subjecting themselves to statutory liabilities. We simply hold that under the facts alleged in count one of appellant's complaint, no cause of action has been made out under the Act.

In both *Cannon* and *Ohrenstein*, the fact that the legislative bodies themselves had not developed standards of conduct was given as a reason for the judiciary to decline to intervene. Is this the equivalent of saying the gate to the chicken coop should be left open because the foxes are unable to agree on how it should be closed?

6. Erwin Chemerinsky, *Protecting the Democratic Process: Voter Standing to Challenge Abuses of Incumbency*, 49 OHIO STATE LAW JOURNAL 773 (1988), calls for a more active judicial policing of what he calls "abuse of incumbency." He catalogues the abusive practices as follows:

> The phrase "abuse of incumbency" refers to the use of government resources, not available to any other candidates, to aid an incumbent running for reelection. There are many ways in which officeholders have used their positions to further their election campaigns. For example, some candidates have tried to use government funds to pay campaign expenses, including the costs of travel, publications, and salaries. Many officials have been accused of abusing the "franking privilege," sending campaign literature to constituents at government expense.
>
> Another form of abuse of incumbency is using government workers to perform campaign tasks while they are on the government payroll. In fact, some incumbents purportedly threatened to fire workers who refused to support the officeholders' campaigns for reelection. Incumbents also allegedly have manipulated the award of government grants and contracts to reward supporters and thereby encourage potential receipts to support the reelection effort.
>
> Other forms of abuse of incumbency are more subtle and virtually impossible to control. For example, some presidents have been accused of manipulating government statistics around the time of an election to make their administration look better. Officials at all levels have manipulated news events to coincide with the election. The common theme in all of these examples is that the incumbent is taking advantage of government powers and resources which are not available to challengers. The government is aiding one candidate and no others.

Id. at 774–76. Despite his belief that incumbents' abusive practices "are inconsistent with the very definition of a democratic government," id. at 776, Chemerinsky reports that the federal judiciary, as in *Cannon*, has been reluctant to intervene:

> No other institution but the judiciary has the authority to restrain unconstitutional behavior by government officials. Unfortunately, most courts have held that it is not the role of the federal judiciary to resolve challenges to improper actions by incumbents. Although occasionally courts have allowed candidates to bring suit, most courts have held that such litigation is not justiciable. Relying on restrictive interpretations of the standing doctrine, courts have declared that challengers and their supporters lack standing to sue. As a result, voters in many areas of the country have no way of restraining unconstitutional actions by an incumbent during an election campaign.

Id. at 774.

7. An indirect effort to regulate the use of legislative staff for campaign purposes succeeded in FAIR POLITICAL PRACTICES COMMISSION (FPPC) v. SUITT, 90 Cal. App.3d 125, 153 Cal.Rptr. 311 (1979). The FPPC alleged that a legislative staff member worked for the reelection of Assemblyman Tom Suitt and contended that because the staffer's salary was paid by the state legislature, Suitt's campaign committee should have disclosed receipt of an in-kind contribution from the legislature. The court agreed that campaign services from legislative employees constituted reportable in-kind contribu-

tions. The California campaign disclosure law required listing the name of each "person" who made a contribution over a specified amount. "Person" was defined as "an individual, proprietorship, firm, partnership, joint venture, syndicate, business trust, company, corporation, association, committee, and any other organization or group of persons acting in concert." Does the catch-all phrase at the end of the definition include the state legislature or other governmental entities? The *Suitt* court thought so, and gave the following responses to counterarguments:

> Respondents assert first that "much of what is done by the Legislature, and consequently by legislative aides, is done for a political purpose;" therefore application of the Act to the Legislature would result in "... an interference with the normal functioning of the sovereign powers of the Legislature." Just how this comes about is not clear to us; presumably the claim is that the effort of legislators would be hampered by their inability to distinguish work on a political campaign from work on legislation in deciding what is or is not a contribution under [Government Code] section 82015. As the FPPC points out in response, this argument is not convincing; for even if the definition of "contribution" might be unclear as applied to certain legislative activities not here involved, the Act obviously does not infringe on the performance of Suitt's official duties insofar as the activities alleged in this case are concerned. The use of state employees by a legislator's campaign committee to solicit contributions, plan campaign strategy, coordinate volunteers, and prepare the campaign budget, all at state expense, is in no way a proper part of a legislator's official functions; that is not to be questioned. If it is to be done at all, the public has a serious interest in its disclosure.

> The Legislature's asserted difficulty here, if indeed it exists, is no different from that faced by government officials in distinguishing between the improper expenditure of public funds for "campaign" purposes and the proper expenditure thereof for "informational" activities. In *Stanson v. Mott*, 17 Cal.3d 206, 223, 130 Cal.Rptr. 697, (1976), the Supreme Court resolved that problem by holding governmental officials liable only if they fail to use due care in authorizing the expenditure. Analogously the Legislature need not be absolutely perfect in distinguishing between the performance by its employees of proper legislative functions as distinguished from election campaigning; it should nonetheless exercise due care in separating the two activities.... [T]he alleged activities in the present case were unambiguously political. Of course, there may be certain marginal activities which are neither specifically included by the Act's campaign disclosure provisions nor excluded from them. Thus, there may be some ambiguity as to whether certain activities by legislators are "contributions." However, any ambiguity can be cured through regulations or judicial constructions which draw clear lines for the marginal cases. The FPPC points out that analogous line-drawing is required and has taken place in other types of campaign activity....

> With respect to campaign activities by publicly paid staff, the FPPC acknowledges that a situation may arise in which lines are difficult to draw, although no such difficulty is presented by the instant case. Therefore, the FPPC advises us in its reply brief that pursuant to its rule making authority it is now preparing to take public testimony and to develop guidelines which will eliminate any possible ambiguity with respect to campaign activities involving public employees, office facilities and supplies. The solution to any ambiguity that may exist in the statute is to develop clear, enforceable standards for the marginal cases, not, as respondents suggest, to eliminate the reporting requirement entirely.

Respondents' next argument is that the stated policy of the Political Reform Act, along with the arguments in the Voter's Handbook accompanying the initiative measure, show that the Act was intended to apply only to private entities. Indeed the Act and the handbook demonstrate a preoccupation with the influence of private campaign contributions on elections. But a very obvious reason for the absence of discussion of *public* campaign contributions is not that the Act intended such to remain secret and undisclosed, but that contributions by governmental entities to political campaigns are per se illegal. Gifts of public money to private persons, associations, or corporations are prohibited by article XVI, section 6 of the California Constitution. It was thus inconceivable in 1974 to the draftsmen of the initiative measure, and to the electorate, that public funds would be expended by or for the benefit of certain legislators to reelect themselves rather than their adversaries. Hence the need to specify such a proscription in the Act would have been deemed unnecessary, and even demeaning to lawmakers and public employees generally. It does not follow however that such expenditures were meant to be unreportable, for the electorate would then be saying in effect: "We recognize that such a use of public money is illegal and unconstitutional, but where it nonetheless occurs, it may be kept secret." This is absurd. The Act's silence bespeaks incredulity that such practices would occur rather than an intent to exempt them from disclosure.

The Act undeniably was intended to deal comprehensively with the influence of money, *all money,* on electoral and governmental processes. Its paramount purpose, as expressed in section 81002, subdivision (a), is that "(r)eceipts and expenditures in election campaigns should be fully and truthfully disclosed in order that the voters may be fully informed and *improper practices may be inhibited.*" (Emphasis added.) It would be anomalous in the extreme to hold that such a blatantly improper practice as a gift of public money to a candidate was nevertheless intended to remain undisclosed under the Act.... Section 82047's definition of "person" broadly includes "... any other organization or group of persons acting in concert." The Legislature and the Assembly Democratic Caucus are unmistakably "other organization[s] or group[s] of persons acting in concert," and thus literally within the definition....

8. As the *Suitt* court notes, the California Supreme Court held in *Stanson v. Mott* that it is illegal to use public resources to advocate a position in a political campaign in the absence of express statutory authorization. The same conclusion has been reached in the courts of several states, though most of the cases involve use of public funds to support or oppose a ballot measure. See generally Note, *Governmental Referendum Advocacy: An Emerging Free Speech Problem,* 29 CASE WESTERN RESERVE LAW REVIEW 886, 895–900 (1979), containing citation of cases from several jurisdictions and discussion. However, most such decisions permit agencies to disseminate information on public subjects, including those that are the subject of a pending ballot measure. How would you distinguish between "information" regarding the issues in a campaign and advocacy?

A Colorado statute permits a policymaking official to spend up to $50 in public funds to express his or her opinion on a ballot proposition. In *Regents of the University of Colorado v. Meyer,* 899 P.2d 316 (Colo.App. 1995), a university official wrote a paragraph taking a position on a statewide proposition and included it in a newsletter that was regularly inserted into the pay envelopes of the university's 19,000 employees. The Colorado appellate court ruled that the paragraph came within the statutory exemption, because its inclusion did not increase the cost of printing or distributing the newsletter. Without discussion, the court assumed that the $50 limit should be applied to the marginal cost attributable to the paragraph rather than the pro rata share of the cost of the entire newsletter. Do you agree? Is the $50 exemption justifiable in the first place?

If an elected official engages in campaign activities during "working hours" (or even full-time during part of his or her term of office) without refunding all or part of the salary, is the official acting unlawfully under *Stanson*? Must the official disclose all or a portion of the salary as a campaign contribution from the government under *Suitt*? If the official uses his or her government office for a campaign-related meeting, is there a violation of law? Should the official's campaign committee disclose an in-kind contribution of the office space from the government? Cf. *Colorado Taxpayers Union v. Romer*, 750 F.Supp. 1041 (D.Colo. 1990), dismissed on other grounds, 963 F.2d 1394 (10th Cir. 1992).

18 U.S.C. §607 prohibits soliciting and receiving federal campaign contributions in federal offices. This previously obscure statute suddenly became better known following disclosure that Vice President Al Gore had used telephones in White House offices to solicit 46 contributions for the 1996 Clinton-Gore reelection campaign, which paid for the calls. Gore initially stated the solicitations were for "soft money" donations (see Chapter 15), which would not have been "contributions" within the meaning of Section 607. It later turned out that at least some of the donations had gone into "hard money" accounts, and therefore were contributions under the statute, though Gore continued to maintain that he had believed he was raising soft money. Setting aside the question of whether Gore actually violated Section 607, is the prohibition good public policy? If it is, should it be extended to other campaign activity besides soliciting and receiving contributions?

9. Suppose Sam Staffer is a state-paid administrative assistant to Barbara Boss, a member of the California legislature who is actively seeking reelection. Which, if any, of the following activities are unlawful under *Stanson* or reportable under *Suitt*?

A. He writes a speech on tax policy for Boss to deliver to the Chamber of Commerce in her district. Boss is chairman of the Tax Committee.

B. He writes a speech on immigration for Boss to deliver to the PTA in her district. There are no bills pending in the legislature relating to immigration, but immigration is a very controversial subject in the district.

C. He writes a speech covering a variety of legislative subjects for Boss to deliver to the state convention of her party.

D. He prepares a press release defending Boss' tax policies against attacks by her opponent in the election.

E. He engages in numerous lengthy discussions with Boss over her votes and other actions on bills. These discussions cover both the substantive merits of the bills and the likely effect of various actions on Boss' reelection prospects.

F. At the request of Boss' campaign manager, Staffer reviews all campaign literature, advertisements and speeches to assure that they are consistent with Boss' legislative record.

G. Throughout the year, he coordinates Boss' schedule. During the campaign he continues to do this, in consultation with Boss' campaign manager.

10. To what extent are the questions in note 9 answered by the following regulation, adopted by the FPPC a few months after the *Suitt* decision?

18420. (a) Any candidate or committee that receives contributions from a state or local government agency shall report receipt of those contributions.

(b) The payment by a state or local government agency of the salary or expenses of its employees or agents is an expenditure or contribution only if the salary or expenses are for campaign activities and meet the requirements of 2 Cal. Adm. Code Section 18423.ᵛ For purposes of this subsection, "campaign activities" shall include, but are not limited to, the following:

(1) Arranging or coordinating a campaign-related event;

(2) Acting in the capacity of the campaign manager or coordinator;

(3) Soliciting, receiving or acknowledging campaign contributions or arranging for the raising of contributions;

(4) Developing, writing or distributing campaign literature or making arrangements for campaign literature;

(5) Arranging for the development, production or distribution of campaign literature;

(6) Preparing television, radio or newspaper campaign advertisements;

(7) Arranging for the development, production, publishing or broadcast of campaign advertisements;

(8) Establishing liaison with or coordinating activities of campaign volunteers;

(9) Preparing campaign budgets;

(10) Preparing campaign statements; and

(11) Participating in partisan get out the vote drives.

Nothing in this subsection shall require the reporting of employee's campaign activities if such activities are performed on vacation time or other than during publicly paid working hours.

(c) Notwithstanding subsection (b), the payment of salary or expenses by a state or local government agency to an elected official shall not be an expenditure or contribution. . . .ʷ

Does the FPPC regulation prevent abusive use of staff by incumbents? Note that under subsection (b) the employee's campaign activities are exempt from disclosure if they are performed "on vacation time or other than during publicly paid working hours." May an employee who has worked overtime during a nonelection year use "compensatory time off" during the election year to work on the campaign? A common practice is for legislative staff members to take unpaid leaves of absence for the two or three months prior to an election and work on the campaign during that period. Does this practice satisfy the legal requirements? If you were a challenger to a legislative incumbent, would you regard the system of regulation as providing much benefit to you if this practice is permitted?

---

v. Section 18423 deals generally with the question of the contribution of an employee's services to a political campaign. It does not deal specifically with government employees. It requires that an employee must spend more than 10% of his or her compensated time working for the campaign before the donation of services will be regarded as a reportable contribution by the employer. What is the purpose of this threshold requirement? Do you agree with it?—Eds.

w. A "comment" is appended to the regulation, stating that "[n]othing in this regulation should be read as condoning or authorizing campaign-related activities by a state or local government agency," pointing out that such activities may be illegal, and containing references to the California Penal Code and to *Stanson* and two additional California cases.—Eds.

11. The houses of Congress have taken some steps to control campaign work by congressional staff. For example, the HOUSE ETHICS MANUAL 283 (1992), states that "House employees are compensated from funds of the Treasury for regular performance of official duties. They are not paid to do campaign work." The Manual notes, however, that congressional employees are free to do campaign work during their free time, so long as they are not required to do so as a condition of keeping their jobs. The manual acknowledges, quoting *Bolger*, *infra*, that "it is simply impossible to draw and enforce a perfect line between the official and political business of Members of Congress," *id.*, but gives several examples intended to illustrate the distinction. See *id.* at 284–85.

12. One of the perquisites most commonly cited as giving incumbents an electoral advantage is the ability to send mass mail to constituents at government expense. In state legislatures, postage and printing may be paid out of the legislative budget, though reformers have had success in some states in controlling political use of state-paid mail. See, e.g., California Government Code §89001 for a simple prohibition, and 2 California Code of Regulations §18901 for complex implementing regulations.

It is around Congress that the greatest controversy over government-paid political mail has centered. By reason of the franking privilege, members of Congress can send mail that may or may not be politically motivated at the expense not of their own legislative budgets, but at the expense of the Postal Service. The congressional franking privilege is governed by 39 U.S.C. §3210, which permits Senators and Representatives to frank their mail for a variety of purposes, the most controversial of which are:

(B) The usual and customary congressional newsletter or press release which may deal with such matters as the impact of laws and decisions on State and local governments and individual citizens; reports on public and official actions taken by Members of Congress; and discussions of proposed or pending legislation or governmental actions and the positions of the Members of Congress on, and arguments for or against, such matters;

(C) the usual and customary congressional questionnaire seeking public opinion on any law, pending or proposed legislation, public issue, or subject.

39 U.S.C. §3210(a)(3)(B) and (C). The statute does contain some restrictions, including one against "mail matter which specifically solicits political support," Section 3210(a)(5)(C), and one against sending mass franked mail less than 60 days prior to a primary or general election in which the sender is a candidate. Section 3210(a)(6)(A).

In COMMON CAUSE v. BOLGER, 574 F.Supp. 672 (D.D.C. 1982), *aff'd without hearing* 461 U.S. 911 (1983), plaintiffs challenged the use of the frank for political purposes as unconstitutional on a number of grounds. After receiving extensive evidence, the court found that Senators and Representatives systematically used the frank for electoral purposes, and that indeed they were trained in how to do so by their respective parties. Many franked mailings were used "in ways that frequently have no relationship to official business and which are closely connected to reelection plans and strategy." Other findings included:

The volume and timing of franked mass mailings … indicate widespread use to promote incumbents' reelection efforts. The volume of franked mass mailings is significantly higher in the year preceding House or Senate elections than in the year following elections. The volume builds to a peak just before the preelection cutoff and drops sharply. The volume of non-mass franked mailings stays relatively constant from year to year in both the House and the Senate. It is an undeniable conclusion that the fluctuations in the volume of franked mass mailings are caused by the electoral cycle, rather than by fluctuations in legislative activity.

> Measured in financial terms, the franking privilege confers a substantial advantage to incumbent Congressional candidates over their challengers....

However, consistent with the social science research reported earlier in this chapter, the court added:

> We make no specific finding concerning the extent to which use of the franking privilege has contributed to the electoral victories of any incumbent Members of Congress. We are inclined by the lack of evidence on this point to conclude only that there is no statistical relationship between the use of the frank and the outcome of an election and that proof of the decisive impact of the privilege in any particular election is elusive, whatever the potential financial benefit of the frank.

Despite its findings that the frank was being used extensively for electoral benefit, the court upheld the constitutionality of Section 3210. Following are excerpts from the court's opinion:

> Were the frank shown to be available and widely used for reelection purposes and had plaintiffs demonstrated that such use has a substantial detrimental impact on opposing candidates or members of the voting public seeking to educate themselves on the candidates and the issues, plaintiffs' claims, particularly those based on the First Amendment, would have considerable merit. But such level of interference with the electoral process has not been shown in this case. We are hesitant to apply a standard under the guise of strict judicial scrutiny to a situation where there has been no demonstration of significant harm to the plaintiffs' constitutional rights. The conceded and undisputed legitimate interests promoted by the franking statute are sufficient to justify the limited impacts on the rights of the plaintiff class and to satisfy the invocation of the rational basis test, which we apply in this case. We cannot hold the franking statute unconstitutional simply because it sets forth a standard to determine "official" uses of the frank different from that proposed by plaintiffs.
>
> It is important to view the franking activities of Members of Congress from an overall perspective. It seems undeniable that all mailings, franked and unfranked, from any particular Member of Congress may be grouped into three types. The first type is composed of "official" mailings, those related directly to the legislative and representative functions of Congress. This is the type of communication which Members of Congress arguably are under a duty to provide and to which the frank has been extended over the past 200 years. At the other extreme are mailings which are on their face political or private and therefore "unofficial" in nature. Congress itself has recognized the dangers, constitutional as well as practical, of extending the franking privilege to these types of mailings and has excluded them or expressly prohibited them under the statute and rules in both Houses. Between these two extremes lies a class of mailings whose purposes are less easily discernible. For example, it is undeniable that Senator X, acting in his elected capacity, should have a right to make mailings within this middle area related to his official duties. It is equally obvious that this same individual acting as candidate for the Senate has an interest in mailing the same material to prospective voters to promote his campaign efforts. Thus the motivations, even behind a particular mailing, may be mixed. Plaintiffs' complaints here can only be about the actions and purposes of the candidate, however, and not the senator.

Congress drafted the franking statute expressly to include many of the types of mailings which unquestionably fall within this middle area. This of itself does not require that we invalidate the scheme as unconstitutional. The question before us is not whether the particular line which Congress has drawn between "official" and "unofficial" uses of the frank necessarily has the least possible potential, in comparison with other methods of drawing the line, for adversely affecting challengers' effective access to the mails. The question is only whether the line is a reasonable one....

To state the obvious, it simply is impossible to draw and enforce a perfect line between the official and political business of Members of Congress. The franking privilege is only one of many perquisites afforded to them which may be turned one way or another into a campaign advantage over any challenger. [A]n incumbent is, by virtue of his incumbency alone, much more visible to the voting public than is a would-be challenger. He has greater access to the media, both local and national; he usually has one or more offices in his home district, in addition to his Washington office; he has a staff paid out of public funds; he has a WATS line for telephone calls which he may use to communicate with his constituents.

Plaintiffs do not suggest that the incumbents' use of these tools of office be strictly limited to purposes which cannot possibly contribute to efforts at reelection. This would be a most difficult standard to administer in any case, for each and every act of an elected representative may, in a political context, be seen as an effort to demonstrate that the voters' choice was a good one. It is impossible, without probing into the deepest thoughts and motives of an individual Member of Congress, to determine exactly why he votes as he does on a particular issue, why he casts a letter to a constituent in the terms in which it is cast, why he communicates with other Members of Congress as he does, why he assigns particular staff functions as he does, or why he does any of the myriad of things that a Member does in his day-to-day routine. It is no less difficult to apply and administer a subjective standard in the use of the frank. Moreover, we cannot require that such a standard be substituted for what we accept as an already reasonable objective standard adopted under section 3210.

In 1992, a federal judge relied on *Bolger* to reject a narrower challenge to congressional franking practices. In particular, plaintiffs challenged the sending by a House member of franked mass mailings to persons who were not residents of the district from which he or she had been elected, but who lived in the newly reapportioned district from which the Representative intended to seek reelection. See *Coalition to End the Permanent Congress v. Runyon*, 796 F.Supp. 549 (D.D.C. 1992). On July 30, 1992, the Court of Appeals reversed, thus ruling that the practice was unconstitutional. The court announced its ruling and indicated it would issue an opinion later. See 971 F.2d 765. However, Congress quickly responded to the publicity that the court's ruling attracted, by amending Section 3210 to prohibit franked mass mailings by House members into the new portions of their districts. The Court of Appeals decided that in light of this development, it would refrain from issuing an opinion explaining its ruling that the now-prohibited practice was unconstitutional. See *Coalition to End the Permanent Congress v. Runyon*, 979 F.2d 219 (D.C.Cir. 1992). If state legislative incumbents are permitted to send publicly-paid mail to new areas they seek to represent after a redistricting, would *Runyon* be a precedent that the practice is unconstitutional?(The editors of this book do not know the answer, but we encourage students to ask their civil procedure instructors.)

13. *Term Limits.* The simplest and most drastic way of eliminating the incumbency advantage is to prohibit incumbents from running for reelection. The principle of "rotation in office" was popular at the time of the American Revolution, and many state constitutions that were adopted in the mid-1770s restricted the ability of incumbents to run for reelection. The popularity of rotation diminished over the next decade. Although mandatory rotation for members of Congress was proposed at the constitutional convention in 1787, it was rejected.

Term limits for executive officials—governor and mayor, primarily—became fairly common in the United States in the twentieth century, and an executive term limit was added to the federal government system in 1951, with the approval of the 22nd Amendment, which limits presidents to two terms. Legislative term limits were rare, however, until 1990, when initiatives were passed in Colorado, limiting terms of congressional representatives and state legislators, and in California and Oklahoma, limiting state legislative terms. By the end of 1994, 22 states had adopted congressional term limits (all but one, Utah, had done so by the initiative process), and a similar number had adopted state legislative term limits. A number of local governments, including the cities of New York and Los Angeles, also adopted term limits in the 1990s.[x]

The election returns suggest that the movement for term limits strongly resonated with popular sentiment in the early 1990s. Probably an equally strong majority of students of government have been opposed to term limits. The debate has been vigorous. In part it has been a partisan debate, but history has a way of confounding those who seek or oppose structural changes for short term partisan reasons. The 22nd Amendment, for example, was advocated by Republicans who reacted to Franklin Roosevelt having been elected four times as a Democrat. Yet, three of the four presidents to date who have been affected by the 22nd Amendment, Dwight Eisenhower, Ronald Reagan, and George W. Bush, were Republicans. Similarly, part of the drive for congressional term limits was supplied by Republicans hoping to break the long-term Democratic control of the House of Representatives. In 1994 the Republicans won control of Congress without the help of term limits, and many of them faced the prospect of their own careers being cut short. However, as we shall see in Note 14, the Supreme Court gave them a reprieve by declaring congressional term limits unconstitutional.

14. Are term limits constitutional? Challenges to state and local term limits based on the First and Fourteenth Amendments have generally been rejected by both state courts, see, e.g., *Legislature v. Eu,* 816 P.2d 1309 (Cal. 1991), cert. denied 503 U.S. 919 (1992); *U.S. Term Limits v. Hill,* 872 S.W.2d 349 (Ark. 1994), affirmed on other grounds 514 U.S. 779 (1995), and federal courts, see, e.g., *Citizens for Legislative Choice v. Miller,* 144 F.3d 916 (6th Cir. 1998); *Bates v. Jones,* 131 F.3d 843 (9th Cir. 1997) (en banc), cert. denied 523 U.S. 1021.

The constitutionality of *congressional* term limits was vigorously debated. The debate centered on the fact that the Constitution itself sets forth qualifications for Congress, primarily minimum age, citizenship and residency requirements. Opponents of term limits claimed that these qualifications are exclusive, and that states cannot prohibit anyone who satisfies them, including a person who has already served in Congress for a specified period, from running for Congress. Supporters said that the qualifications set forth in the Constitution are minimum qualifications, not a bar to adding additional qualifications.

---

x. For a description and evaluation of the New York City term limits, see Eric Lane, *The Impact of Term Limits on Lawmaking in the City of New York,* 3 ELECTION LAW JOURNAL 670 (2004).

Three lower courts declared congressional term limits unconstitutional. *Stumpf v. Lau*, 839 P.2d 120 (Nev. 1992); *Thorsted v. Gregoire*, 841 F.Supp. 1068 (W.D.Wash. 1994); *U.S. Term Limits v. Hill*, 872 S.W.2d 349 (Ark. 1994). In 1995, the Supreme Court affirmed the Arkansas decision, ruling that the "Qualifications Clauses" prohibit the states from imposing term limits or any other qualifications on candidates for Congress. *U.S. Term Limits v. Thornton*, 514 U.S. 779 (1995). Justice Thomas wrote a dissenting opinion joined by Chief Justice Rehnquist and Justices O'Connor and Scalia.

III. Competitiveness in Election Law Jurisprudence

In the past decade a number of election law scholars have called for heightened judicial oversight of rules and procedures that they believe "entrench" incumbents or parties or, using language from antitrust, "lock up" the "marketplace" of the electoral system. Two early statements of this view were Michael J. Klarman, *Majoritarian Judicial Review: The Entrenchment Problem*, 85 Georgetown Law Journal 491 (1997), and Samuel Issacharoff & Richard H. Pildes, *Politics as Markets: Partisan Lockups of the Democratic Process*, 50 Stanford Law Review 643 (1998). Issacharoff and Pildes went so far as to suggest that in judicial review of election law, nurturing of competitiveness should displace the principles of rights and equality based on the text of the Constitution:

> In cases involving the regulation of politics, we argue that courts should shift from the conventional first-order focus on rights and equality to a second-order focus on the background markets in partisan control. Rather than seeking to control politics directly through the centralized enforcement of individual rights, we suggest courts would do better to examine the background structure of partisan competition. Where there is an appropriately robust market in partisan competition, there is less justification for judicial intervention. Where courts can discern that existing partisan forces have manipulated these background rules, courts should strike down those manipulations to ensure an appropriately competitive political environment.

Id. at 648. How does one know when a political market is "appropriately" robust or competitive? Richard L. Hasen, *The "Political Market" Metaphor and Election Law: A Comment on Issacharoff and Pildes*, 50 Stanford Law Review 719, 725–28 (1998) argues that Issacharoff and Pildes do not adequately define the meaning of these terms.

Issacharoff and Pildes criticize a number of Supreme Court cases including *Timmons v. Twin Cities Area New Party*, 520 U.S. 351 (1997), upholding a ban on fusion candidacies, and *Burdick v. Takushi*, 504 U.S. 428 (1992), upholding Hawaii's ban on write-in votes.[y] After declaring that a "political process case more wrongly decided than *Burdick* is difficult to imagine," Issacharoff and Pildes, *supra*, 50 Stanford Law Review, at 670, the authors argue that the ban on write-in votes worked with other election laws to insure Democratic party dominance over Hawaii politics:

> The critical issue for the Court should not have been Burdick's individual interest in using the ballot for mere "expressive purposes," nor should it have been the purported abstract state interests. Instead, when interpreting the various constitutional provisions that protect self-government, such as the First

---

y. Both these cases are described in Chapter 10.

Amendment, the Court should construe those provisions against a background conception of democracy that recognizes the importance of competitive political markets to ensuring appropriately responsive representation. As part of that inquiry, the Court ought to focus on whether the process remains sufficiently open to challenge and reform, or whether the costs of mobilizing effective challenge have been raised so high as to leave the system insufficiently responsive. In the one-party state of Hawaii ... the state-enacted barriers to competition were ingeniously effective at stifling potential competition.[z] The state's ability to recite abstract state interests in political stability, avoidance of factionalism, or prevention of party raiding, should hardly obstruct more penetrating judicial analysis of the actual anti-competitiveness effects. Indeed, given the context [of the case], the very interests that could be asserted in the names of the states are no more than thinly veiled formulas for disguising self-serving arguments of incumbent powers. Far from justifying these state practices, such interests should be the very reason the Court strikes those practices down.

Id. at 673–74.

The anti-entrenchment rationale is criticized in Daniel H. Lowenstein, *The Supreme Court Has No Theory of Politics—And Be Thankful for Small Favors*, in THE U.S. SUPREME COURT AND THE ELECTORAL PROCESS 245 (David K. Ryden ed., 2000). Lowenstein faults Issacharoff and Pildes for focusing on election laws like Hawaii's ban on write-in votes rather than on the more significant legal structures favoring the two-party system like single-member districts and the direct primary:

Issacharoff and Pildes do not expect the Supreme Court to eliminate single-member districts, presidential elections, or direct primaries. It is not clear, therefore, what difference it would make if the Court were to subscribe to their theory of partisan lockups as the key to election law adjudication. If the Court accepted the theory and were truly sophisticated regarding the causes of Democratic and Republican predominance in American politics, they would simply deconstitutionalize election law and have done with it.

Id. at 263.

Pildes and Issacharoff have separately responded to criticisms of their "political markets" approach in ways that suggest the two authors have diverged on how far their approach goes. In Richard H. Pildes, *The Theory of Political Competition*, 85 VIRGINIA LAW REVIEW 1605 (1999), Pildes responds to an argument by Bruce Cain, *Garrett's Temptation*, 85 VIRGINIA LAW REVIEW 1589, 1600 (1999), to the effect that the logical implication of the approach is court-mandated proportional representation. Pildes lists a number of "countervailing values [that] could be marshaled against judicial imposition of proportional representation," including original intent, history, and the importance of public acceptability of judicial decisions.

In Samuel Issacharoff, *Gerrymandering and Political Cartels*, 116 HARVARD LAW REVIEW 593 (2002), Issacharoff calls upon the courts to strike down virtually all legislative districting conducted by partisan officials as unconstitutional, leading to districting conducted solely by nonpartisan commissions or by computer. To Issacharoff, the risk of gerrymandering is that it "constrict[s] the competitive processes by which voters can express choice."

---

z. Linda Lingle, the governor of the "one-party" Democratic state of Hawaii, first elected in 2002 and reelected in 2006, is a Republican.—EDS.

Nathaniel Persily disagrees with Issacharoff on the question whether gerrymandering stifles political competition. Nathaniel Persily, Reply, *In Defense of Foxes Guarding Henhouses: The Case for Judicial Acquiescence to Incumbent-Protecting Gerrymanders*, 116 HARVARD LAW REVIEW 649 (2002). Launching a broader attack on the political markets approach is Richard L. Hasen, THE SUPREME COURT AND ELECTION LAW: JUDGING EQUALITY FROM BAKER V. CARR TO BUSH V. GORE 138–56 (2003). Hasen sees connections between the Supreme Court's "structural equal protection" jurisprudence in *Shaw v. Reno* and *Bush v. Gore* and the "political markets approach," finding both "symptomatic of a belief in unlimited judicial wisdom."

Some political scientists also have become increasingly concerned by lack of competitiveness in some elections. A vigorous statement of this viewpoint is contained in Michael McDonald & John Samples, *The Marketplace of Democracy: Normative and Empirical Issues*, which is the introduction to their edited volume, THE MARKETPLACE OF DEMOCRACY: ELECTORAL COMPETITION AND AMERICAN POLITICS (2006). McDonald & Samples begin with the idea that the best chance for a political system to avoid tyranny is the accountability imposed on public officials by competitive elections. They survey a number of respects in which they believe American elections are deficient in competitiveness. "Competition in the United States," they say, "bears a troubling resemblance to that in nations where candidates run unopposed or with token opposition, nations that American leaders condemn as lacking truly democratic or legitimate elections."

The contributors to *The Marketplace of Democracy*, including some of the best contemporary political science writers on American politics, provide a wealth of ideas and analysis on aspects of competitiveness in elections, though they vary widely in their agreement with the editors on the degree of the problem. Lowenstein concluded a review of the volume by observing:

> I, for one, marvel at those who find this the moment to bewail a supposed lack of competitiveness. We are living through a period featuring the most intense partisan competitiveness between the most evenly divided parties in my now lengthy lifetime (and a considerable period before that). Incumbent legislators may show lack of vision or lack of wisdom or lack of courage, but the one thing they do not show is a lack of concern for their districts, which presumably is what is meant by lack of accountability.

Daniel H. Lowenstein, *Competition and Competitiveness in American Elections*, 6 ELECTION LAW JOURNAL 278 (2007).

Supporters of the idea that the courts should police entrenchment took heart from the lead opinion in a campaign finance decision, *Randall v. Sorrell*, 548 U.S. 230 (2006), in which Justice Breyer spoke for himself, Chief Justice Roberts, and Justice Alito. *Randall*, which appears in Chapter 15, struck down a limit on campaign contributions that the Court regarded as too low. One reason for the decision, according to Justice Breyer, was that "contribution limits that are too low can ... harm the electoral process by preventing challengers from mounting effective campaigns against incumbent officeholders, thereby reducing democratic accountability."

Following is an excerpt from an opinion by federal appellate judge J. Harvie Wilkinson III, dissenting from denial of an en banc hearing to review a panel decision striking down an unusual nominating procedure in Virginia. The general statutory rule in Virginia was that party organizations could select from a number of different nominating procedures, including an open primary. An exception allowed an incumbent state legislator who was seeking reelection to choose a procedure, even if it was not the procedure favored by the party organization. Stephen Miller, an incumbent legislator, opted for an open primary. The party preferred a semi-closed primary, which was not a form recognized by Virginia law. Two constitutional issues were raised in the case. First, did the party have the right to a semi-closed primary in the face of Virginia law providing for an open primary? Second, was it constitutional to allow incumbents individually to select the procedure under which they would seek reelection?

Judge Wilkinson objected to the narrow grounds on which the panel ruled in favor of the party. The panel declared the Virginia statute unconstitutional, "but only 'as applied' to the situation in which an incumbent elects to hold an open primary against his party's wishes." In other words, the panel did not decide whether the party had the general right to opt for a semi-closed primary, nor did it decide whether it was generally unconstitutional to allow the incumbent to select the nomination method. Judge Wilkinson dissented from the denial of en banc review because he believed each of these questions ought to have been decided. In the course of his opinion he made these comments on the significance of incumbency in election law jurisprudence:

Miller v. Cunningham
512 F.3d 98 (4th Cir. 2007)

...

WILKINSON, Circuit Judge, dissenting from the denial of the petition for rehearing en banc:

... The first important issue not addressed by the panel opinion is the constitutionality of Virginia's incumbent selection provision, Va. Code Ann. § 24.2-509(B) (2006). To me, the unconstitutionality of this provision is clear. I fully recognize that governance is an immensely complicated business and that the ability of parties to re-nominate and electorates to re-elect incumbent officeholders is essential to the fund of experience and expertise that enables a large Commonwealth such as Virginia to be well-run. Notwithstanding the benefits that length of service confers upon the public welfare, the incumbent selection provision at issue here facially discriminates in favor of incumbents, shutting down the political process and violating the most essential requirements of equal protection....

I believe that the constitutionality of § 24.2-509(B) is properly presented in this case: the parties are treating it as such, and the panel necessarily considered the provision in reaching its holding. However, failure to address the constitutionality of this provision can only mean more litigation down the road. I see no reason to refrain from striking down a provision that plainly runs afoul of our most fundamental constitutional rights.

A.

I start my analysis of Virginia's incumbent selection provision with a very simple proposition: if there is going to be election law, it will be written and enacted by incumbents. Both the United States and Virginia Constitutions explicitly grant the legislative branch the authority to regulate elections....

Given this, there is certainly nothing unconstitutional *per se* about incumbents shaping the electoral process to their advantage. This is merely a feature of American politics. The Framers were surely aware of the desire of those who hold elective office to retain elective office, yet they were clearly comfortable giving incumbents the authority to write election law. Judicial intervention into the electoral process, merely for the purpose of rooting out self-interested political behavior, would therefore be a "substantial" incursion into textually and traditionally legislative prerogatives. *See Vieth* (Kennedy, J., concurring in the judgment). Furthermore, elections are "pervasively regulated," Richard H. Pildes, *The Supreme Court, 2003 Term-Foreword: The Constitutionalization of Democratic Politics,* 118 Harv. L.Rev. 28, 51 (2004), and aggressive review of legislative motivation in this area would leave the federal judiciary time to do little else but analyze election laws. The Supreme Court has therefore been appropriately reluctant to police enactments in the election law context, even while explicitly recognizing that self-interest may be a partial driver of legislative action in this area. *See Vieth* (plurality opinion) (holding political gerrymandering to be non-justiciable for lack of a judicially manageable standard despite the fact that redistricting is always conducted with an intent to gain "political advantage").

Nonetheless, there are limits to this deference. As the Supreme Court suggested in the famous fourth footnote of *United States v. Carolene Products Co.,* 304 U.S. 144 (1938), the judiciary has a basic obligation to keep the political process open and well-functioning. "The first instinct of power is the retention of power," and those who hold public office can be expected to attempt to insulate themselves from meaningful electoral review. *McConnell v. FEC,* 540 U.S. 93, 263 (2003) (Scalia, J., concurring in part and dissenting in part). It is therefore necessary for an independent and co-equal branch of government—the judiciary—to ensure that incumbents are unable to create a system where the "ins ... will stay in and the outs will stay out." John Hart Ely, *Democracy and Distrust* 103 (1980); *see also* Klarman, *supra.*

This is because any political system that lacks accountability, "democracy's essential minimal condition," Pildes, *supra,* at 44, does not conform with even the barest requirements of equal protection, which demand, at a minimum, that the majority is not systematically frustrated in enacting its policies into law.

At the very least, therefore, the need to "clear the channels of political change," *see* Ely, *supra,* at 105–34, requires the judiciary to presume that election laws that *facially* discriminate in *favor* of incumbents are unconstitutional.[3] Two reasons support this conclusion. First, election laws that facially discriminate in favor of existing officeholders simply go "too far": if incumbents are allowed to pass laws explicitly and exclusively for their own benefit, there would be no end to the advantages they could provide themselves. Incumbents could therefore diminish the possibility for change and competition in American politics to a degree never envisioned by the Constitution. Second, the problems presented by judicial intervention into the political process are not nearly as pronounced when the courts are faced with laws that facially favor incumbents. Facially neutral laws, like legislative redistricting schemes, may produce a *de facto* advantage for incumbents, but uncovering whether that advantage reaches unconstitutional limits requires an intrusive—and potentially error-prone—inquiry into legislative motive. The biases of facially discriminatory laws, on the other hand, are readily apparent.

Given the foregoing, Virginia's incumbent selection statute is plainly unconstitutional, at least when state legislators are passing laws dealing with their own re-election prospects. The statute facially discriminates in favor of existing officeholders, by compelling polit-

---

3. Laws may, of course, facially benefit incumbents without posing constitutional problems. For example, laws that enable state legislators to provide constituent services—e.g., hire staff or pay office expenses—are clearly constitutional, despite the fact that these statutes may provide resources that produce a *de facto* advantage for legislators in campaigning for reelection. But these laws are clearly passed for a legitimate purpose, unlike election laws passed solely to entrench incumbents in office.

ical parties to "nominate [their] candidate[s] for election ... by the method[s] designated" by incumbents. In doing so, the law leaves no doubt as to who its purported beneficiaries are—the incumbents in Virginia's General Assembly. These incumbent legislators already possess numerous structural advantages over their electoral competition: money, name-recognition, staff, etc. To this pre-existing array of *de facto* advantages, Virginia's incumbent selection provision now adds the *de jure* advantage that the incumbent can dictate his or her recommended preference as to renomination procedures over a party's express wishes. Such an explicit advantage given to existing officeholders surely threatens to entrench Virginia's incumbents to an unconstitutional extent....

Notes and Questions

1. If the state permits the word "incumbent" to appear on the ballot to identify incumbents seeking reelection, does the state "facially favor" incumbents so as to make the practice presumptively unconstitutional, under Judge Wilkinson's opinion?

2. In the book review referred to previously, Lowenstein distinguishes two distinct concepts signified by the word "competition," and designates one of them by the word "competition" and the other by "competitiveness":

> There are two senses in which the word "competitiveness" is used. For example, we say that baseball is a competitive sport. But suppose you go to a game in which the score is 12–1 in the second inning. Nothing much happens after that and the final score is 16–3. You might say that the game was not competitive. Yet, you would not mean by that to deny that baseball is a competitive sport or that the 16–3 game was a fair competition.
>
> A few weeks later you go to another game. In the bottom of the ninth with the score 3–2, two out and runners on second and third, the batter hits a sinking line drive. The outfielder charges and reaches down to attempt a shoestring catch. A matter of an inch separates his making the catch and the ball skipping off the web of his mitt. On that inch the outcome of the game depends. This, you will say, was a highly competitive game. As spectator entertainment, it was also no doubt a much better game than the previous one. But there is a sense in which the purpose of the competition is that the team that plays the best should win. If the question is which game was better from this standpoint, surely the answer is the 16–3 game, even though the 3–2 game (or 4–3, depending on whether the ball stayed in the mitt) was by far the more "competitive."
>
> ... If the only purpose of holding elections were to provide entertainment for political junkies, [then it would be justifiable to assume that closeness of elections is the measure of electoral competition], for the relevant sense of competitiveness would be the same as the one that makes us prefer the close baseball game to the blowout. But we might bear in mind that even in baseball, there are children young and old who would prefer the 16–3 game if their favorite team won over the close game if their team lost. Thus, we now have three criteria by which to assess competitiveness: the better team wins, the outcome is in suspense to the end, my favored team wins. All of these criteria are valid. Which we prefer depends on the goals we are pursuing....
>
> One of the most important insights to emerge in American political science in the last few decades is the recognition that influence often can be exercised because of the potential to take action without the need for actually taking ac-

tion. So, for example, Congress can oversee executive agencies without continually monitoring their activities. Rather, it can wait until it receives complaints and then swing into action. The knowledge of this potential on the part of the agencies provides them with an incentive to anticipate and act in accordance with congressional goals, with the result that actual congressional action may be infrequent. Similarly, members of Congress who wish to get reelected will seek to avoid actions that will be distressing to voters, even if the voters are inattentive, because of the possibility that interest groups, the press, or an opposing candidate will bring the member's offensive action to the attention of the voters before the next election. For the same reason, close elections or a lot if incumbents being defeated are not necessary for representatives to be held accountable. So long as opposing parties and candidates are free to run, they and others are free to speak, and voters are free to vote as they choose, the incumbents know that if they fail to maintain the trust of their constituents, they will be vulnerable to defeat....

Unfortunately, the two conceptions of electoral competition—a system whose features make it freely open to contestation as opposed to closely contested races in particular elections—are easy to confuse. The conceptions are related to each other and our language uses the same terms—"competition" and "competitive"—to apply to each. To help keep the conceptions distinct, I shall use the noun "competition" (sometimes "free competition" for emphasis) to refer to the electoral system that freely allows for contestation, and "competitiveness" to refer to races that are actually closely contested. As there is only one adjective, I shall say "freely competitive" to describe the free system or elections within the free system, and simply "competitive" to describe the elections that are actually closely contested.

Using this terminology, when Judge Wilkinson makes it presumptively unconstitutional to "facially favor" incumbents in a statute, is he protecting competition or competitiveness?

3. The anti-entrenchment scholars who were encouraged by the passage in *Randall v. Sorrell* that we have quoted, were probably less pleased with this decision of the Supreme Court:

New York State Board of Elections v. López Torres
128 S.Ct. 791 (2008)

Justice SCALIA delivered the opinion of the Court.

The State of New York requires that political parties select their nominees for Supreme Court Justice at a convention of delegates chosen by party members in a primary election. We consider whether this electoral system violates the First Amendment rights of prospective party candidates.

I
A

The Supreme Court of New York is the State's trial court of general jurisdiction, with an Appellate Division that hears appeals from certain lower courts. Under New York's current Constitution, the State is divided into 12 judicial districts and Supreme Court Justices are elected to 14-year terms in each such district....

In 1911, the New York Legislature enacted a law requiring political parties to select Supreme Court nominees (and most other nominees who did not run statewide) through direct primary elections. The primary system came to be criticized as a "device capable of astute and successful manipulation by professionals," Editorial, The State Convention, N.Y. Times, May 1, 1917, p. 12, and the Republican candidate for Governor in 1920 campaigned against it as "a fraud" that "offered the opportunity for two things, for the demagogue and the man with money." A law enacted in 1921 required parties to select their candidates for the Supreme Court by a convention composed of delegates elected by party members.

New York retains this system of choosing party nominees for Supreme Court Justice to this day. Section 6-106 of New York's election law sets forth its basic operation: "Party nominations for the office of justice of the supreme court shall be made by the judicial district convention." ... In a September "delegate primary," party members elect delegates from each of New York's 150 assembly districts to attend the party's judicial convention for the judicial district in which the assembly district is located. An individual may run for delegate by submitting to the Board of Elections a designating petition signed by 500 enrolled party members residing in the assembly district, or by five percent of such enrolled members, whichever is less. These signatures must be gathered within a 37-day period preceding the filing deadline, which is approximately two months before the delegate primary. The delegates elected in these primaries are uncommitted; the primary ballot does not specify the judicial nominee whom they will support.

The nominating conventions take place one to two weeks after the delegate primary. Each of the 12 judicial districts has its own convention to nominate the party's Supreme Court candidate or candidates who will run at large in that district in the general election. The general election takes place in November. The nominees from the party conventions appear automatically on the general-election ballot. They may be joined on the general-election ballot by independent candidates and candidates of political organizations that fail to meet the 50,000 vote threshold for "party" status; these candidates gain access to the ballot by submitting timely nominating petitions with (depending on the judicial district) 3,500 or 4,000 signatures from voters in that district or signatures from five percent of the number of votes cast for Governor in that district in the prior election, whichever is less.

B

Respondent López Torres was elected in 1992 to the civil court for Kings County—a court with more limited jurisdiction than the Supreme Court—having gained the nomination of the Democratic Party through a primary election. She claims that soon after her election, party leaders began to demand that she make patronage hires, and that her consistent refusal to do so caused the local party to oppose her unsuccessful candidacy at the Supreme Court nominating conventions in 1997, 2002, and 2003. The following year, López Torres—together with other candidates who had failed to secure the nominations of their parties, voters who claimed to have supported those candidates, and the New York branch of a public-interest organization called Common Cause—brought suit in federal court against the New York Board of Elections, which is responsible for administering and enforcing the New York election law. They contended that New York's election law burdened the rights of challengers seeking to run against candidates favored by the party leadership, and deprived voters and candidates of their rights to gain access to the ballot and to associate in choosing their party's candidates. As relevant here, they sought a declaration that New York's convention system for selecting Supreme Court Justices violates their First Amendment rights, and an injunction mandating the establishment of a direct primary election to select party nominees for Supreme Court Justice.

The District Court issued a preliminary injunction granting the relief requested, pending the New York Legislature's enactment of a new statutory scheme. A unanimous panel of the United States Court of Appeals for the Second Circuit affirmed....

II
A

A political party has a First Amendment right to limit its membership as it wishes, and to choose a candidate-selection process that will in its view produce the nominee who best represents its political platform. *La Follette*; *Jones*. These rights are circumscribed, however, when the State gives the party a role in the election process—as New York has done here by giving certain parties the right to have their candidates appear with party endorsement on the general-election ballot. Then, for example, the party's racially discriminatory action may become state action that violates the Fifteenth Amendment. And then also the State acquires a legitimate governmental interest in assuring the fairness of the party's nominating process, enabling it to prescribe what that process must be. We have, for example, considered it to be "too plain for argument" that a State may prescribe party use of primaries or conventions to select nominees who appear on the general-election ballot. *American Party of Tex. v. White*, 415 U.S. 767, 781 (1974). That prescriptive power is not without limits. In *Jones*, for example, we invalidated on First Amendment grounds California's blanket primary, reasoning that it permitted non-party members to determine the candidate bearing the party's standard in the general election.

In the present case, however, the party's associational rights are at issue (if at all) only as a shield and not as a sword. Respondents are in no position to rely on the right that the First Amendment confers on political parties to structure their internal party processes and to select the candidate of the party's choosing. Indeed, both the Republican and Democratic state parties have intervened from the very early stages of this litigation to defend New York's electoral law.[a] The weapon wielded by these plaintiffs is their *own* claimed associational right not only to join, but to have a certain degree of influence in, the party. They contend that New York's electoral system does not go far enough—does not go as far as the Constitution demands—in assuring that they will have a fair chance of prevailing in their parties' candidate-selection process.

This contention finds no support in our precedents. We have indeed acknowledged an individual's associational right to vote in a party primary without undue state-imposed impediment. In *Kusper v. Pontikes*, we invalidated an Illinois law that required a voter wishing to change his party registration so as to vote in the primary of a different party to do so almost two full years before the primary date. But *Kusper* does not cast doubt on all state-imposed limitations upon primary voting. In *Rosario v. Rockefeller*, we upheld a New York State requirement that a voter have enrolled in the party of his choice at least 30 days before the previous general election in order to vote in the next party primary. In any event, respondents do not claim that they have been excluded from voting in the primary. Moreover, even if we extended *Kusper* to cover not only the right to vote in the party primary but also the right to run, the requirements of the New York law (a 500-signature petition collected during a 37-day window in advance of the primary) are entirely reasonable. Just as States may require persons to demonstrate "a significant modicum

---

a. Would the result have been different if the political parties had not participated in the litigation at all? If they had intervened or filed *amicus* briefs supporting the plaintiffs rather than defending the law? If one of the major parties had intervened to defend the law but the other had intervened on the side of the plaintiffs?—Eds.

of support" before allowing them access to the general-election ballot, lest it become unmanageable, *Jenness v. Fortson*, they may similarly demand a minimum degree of support for candidate access to a primary ballot. The signature requirement here is far from excessive.

Respondents' real complaint is not that they cannot vote in the election for delegates, nor even that they cannot run in that election, but that the convention process that follows the delegate election does not give them a realistic chance to secure the party's nomination. The party leadership, they say, inevitably garners more votes for its slate of delegates (delegates uncommitted to any judicial nominee) than the unsupported candidate can amass for himself. And thus the leadership effectively determines the nominees. But this says nothing more than that the party leadership has more widespread support than a candidate not supported by the leadership. No New York law compels election of the leadership's slate—or, for that matter, compels the delegates elected on the leadership's slate to vote the way the leadership desires. And no state law prohibits an unsupported candidate from attending the convention and seeking to persuade the delegates to support her. Our cases invalidating ballot-access requirements have focused on the requirements themselves, and not on the manner in which political actors function under those requirements. Here respondents complain not of the state law, but of the voters' (and their elected delegates') preference for the choices of the party leadership.

To be sure, we have, as described above, permitted States to set their faces against "party bosses" by requiring party-candidate selection through processes more favorable to insurgents, such as primaries. But to say that the State can require this is a far cry from saying that the Constitution demands it. None of our cases establishes an individual's constitutional right to have a "fair shot" at winning the party's nomination. And with good reason. What constitutes a "fair shot" is a reasonable enough question for legislative judgment, which we will accept so long as it does not too much infringe upon the party's associational rights. But it is hardly a manageable constitutional question for judges—especially for judges in our legal system, where traditional electoral practice gives no hint of even the existence, much less the content, of a constitutional requirement for a "fair shot" at party nomination. Party conventions, with their attendant "smoke-filled rooms" and domination by party leaders, have long been an accepted manner of selecting party candidates. "National party conventions prior to 1972 were generally under the control of state party leaders" who determined the votes of state delegates. American Presidential Elections: Process, Policy, and Political Change 14 (H. Schantz ed.1996). Selection by convention has never been thought unconstitutional, even when the delegates were not selected by primary but by party caucuses.

The Second Circuit's judgment finesses the difficulty of saying how much of a shot is a "fair shot" by simply mandating a primary until the New York Legislature acts. This was, according to the Second Circuit, the New York election law's default manner of party-candidate selection for offices whose manner of selection is not otherwise prescribed. Petitioners question the propriety of this mandate, but we need not pass upon that here. Even conceding its propriety, there is good reason to believe that the elected members of the New York Legislature remain opposed to the primary, for the same reasons their predecessors abolished it 86 years ago: because it leaves judicial selection to voters uninformed about judicial qualifications, and places a high premium upon the ability to raise money. Should the New York Legislature persist in that view, and adopt something different from a primary and closer to the system that the Second Circuit invalidated, the question whether *that* provides enough of a "fair shot" would be presented. We are not inclined to open up this new and excitingly unpredictable theater of election jurisprudence. Selection by convention has been a traditional means of choosing party nominees. While a State may determine it is not desirable and replace it, it is not unconstitutional.

B

Respondents put forward, as a special factor which gives them a First Amendment right to revision of party processes in the present case, the assertion that party loyalty in New York's judicial districts renders the general-election ballot "uncompetitive." They argue that the existence of entrenched "one-party rule" demands that the First Amendment be used to impose additional competition in the nominee-selection process of the parties. (The asserted "one-party rule," we may observe, is that of the Democrats in some judicial districts, and of the Republicans in others.) This is a novel and implausible reading of the First Amendment.

To begin with, it is hard to understand how the competitiveness of the general election has anything to do with respondents' associational rights in the party's selection process. It makes no difference to the person who associates with a party and seeks its nomination whether the party is a contender in the general election, an underdog, or the favorite. Competitiveness may be of interest to the voters in the general election, and to the candidates who choose to run *against* the dominant party. But we have held that those interests are well enough protected so long as all candidates have an adequate opportunity to appear on the general-election ballot.... New York's general-election balloting procedures for Supreme Court Justice easily pass muster under this standard. Candidates who fail to obtain a major party's nomination via convention can still get on the general-election ballot for the judicial district by providing the requisite number of signatures of voters resident in the district. To our knowledge, outside of the Fourteenth and Fifteenth Amendment contexts, see *Jones,* no court has ever made "one-party entrenchment" a basis for interfering with the candidate-selection processes of a party. (Of course, the *lack* of one-party entrenchment will not cause free access to the general-election ballot to validate an otherwise unconstitutional restriction upon participation in a party's nominating process. See *Bullock v. Carter.*)

The reason one-party rule is entrenched may be (and usually is) that voters approve of the positions and candidates that the party regularly puts forward. It is no function of the First Amendment to require revision of those positions or candidates. The States can, within limits (that is, short of violating the parties' freedom of association), discourage party monopoly—for example, by refusing to show party endorsement on the election ballot. But the Constitution provides no authority for federal courts to prescribe such a course. The First Amendment creates an open marketplace where ideas, most especially political ideas, may compete without government interference. See *Abrams v. United States,* 250 U.S. 616, 630 (1919) (Holmes, J., dissenting). It does not call on the federal courts to manage the market by preventing too many buyers from settling upon a single product.

Limiting respondents' court-mandated "fair shot at party endorsement" to situations of one-party entrenchment merely multiplies the impracticable lines courts would be called upon to draw. It would add to those alluded to earlier the line at which mere party popularity turns into "one-party dominance." In the case of New York's election system for Supreme Court Justices, that line would have to be drawn separately for each of the 12 judicial districts—and in those districts that are "competitive" the current system would presumably remain valid. But why limit the remedy to *one*-party dominance? Does not the dominance of two parties similarly stifle competing opinions? Once again, we decline to enter the morass.

* * *

New York State has thrice (in 1846, 1911, and 1921) displayed a willingness to reconsider its method of selecting Supreme Court Justices. If it wishes to return to the primary system that it discarded in 1921, it is free to do so; but the First Amendment does not compel that. We reverse the Second Circuit's contrary judgment.

It is so ordered.

Justice STEVENS, with whom Justice SOUTER joins, concurring.

While I join Justice SCALIA's cogent resolution of the constitutional issues raised by this case, I think it appropriate to emphasize the distinction between constitutionality and wise policy. Our holding with respect to the former should not be misread as endorsement of the electoral system under review, or disagreement with the findings of the District Court that describe glaring deficiencies in that system and even lend support to the broader proposition that the very practice of electing judges is unwise. But as I recall my esteemed former colleague, Thurgood Marshall, remarking on numerous occasions: "The Constitution does not prohibit legislatures from enacting stupid laws."

Justice KENNEDY, with whom Justice BREYER joins as to Part II, concurring in the judgment.

The Court's analysis, in my view, is correct in important respects; but my own understanding of the controlling principles counsels concurrence in the judgment and the expression of these additional observations.

I

When a state-mandated primary is used to select delegates to conventions or nominees for office, the State is bound not to design its ballot or election processes in ways that impose severe burdens on First Amendment rights of expression and political participation. Respondents' objection to New York's scheme of nomination by convention is that it is difficult for those who lack party connections or party backing to be chosen as a delegate or to become a nominee for office. Were the state-mandated-and-designed nominating convention the sole means to attain access to the general election ballot there would be considerable force, in my view, to respondents' contention that the First Amendment prohibits the State from requiring a delegate selection mechanism with the rigidities and difficulties attendant upon this one. The system then would be subject to scrutiny from the standpoint of a "reasonably diligent independent candidate," *Storer v. Brown.* The Second Circuit took this approach.

As the Court is careful to note, however, New York has a second mechanism for placement on the final election ballot. One who seeks to be a Justice of the New York Supreme Court may qualify by a petition process.... This requirement has not been shown to be an unreasonable one, a point respondents appear to concede. True, the candidate who gains ballot access by petition does not have a party designation; but the candidate is still considered by the voters.

The petition alternative changes the analysis.

This is not to say an alternative route to the general election exempts the delegate primary/nominating convention from all scrutiny. For instance, the Court in *Bullock,* after determining that Texas' primary election filing fees were so "patently exclusionary" on the basis of wealth as to invoke strict scrutiny under the Equal Protection Clause, rejected the argument that candidate access to the general election without a fee saved the statute. But there is a dynamic relationship between, in this case, the convention system and the petition process; higher burdens at one stage are mitigated by lower burdens at the other. And, though the point does not apply here, there are certain injuries (as in *Bullock*) that are so severe they are unconstitutional no matter how minor the burdens at the other stage. As the Court recognized in *Kusper,* moreover, there is an individual right to associate with the political party of one's choice and to have a voice in the selection of that party's candidate for public office. On the particular facts and circumstances of this case, then, I reach the same conclusion the Court does.

II

[Part II comments on elections as a means of judicial selection.]

III

With these observations, I concur in the judgment of the Court.

Notes and Questions

1. Part II-B gives little credence to the idea that entrenchment is a prime target for judicial review. Does the Court's analysis suggest that this skepticism is limited to challenges to a party's means of selecting candidates, or does Part II-B have broader implications?

2. Is *López Torres* at odds with the views expressed by Judge Wilkinson in *Miller?* Suppose a state statute calls for selection of nominees by majority vote at a party convention, but provides that a losing candidate who receives at least twenty percent of the votes can challenge the convention winner in a primary. Now suppose there is an additional provision that if the convention winner is the incumbent for the office, then the nomination is final. Would this system be unconstitutional under Judge Wilkinson's principles? Under *López Torres?*

Chapter 13

Bribery

Our primary concern in the remainder of this book will be the campaign finance system and problems related to that system. One of the main reasons campaign finance has become a prominent issue in American politics is the belief of many that the raising of campaign funds provides the occasion for conduct that is corrupt or improper. As we shall see in later chapters, whether and under what circumstances campaign contributions are corrupt is a point of practical and theoretical controversy. The law of bribery, which attempts to deal with the most obviously corrupt forms of political activity, thus provides an appropriate preface to our consideration of campaign finance. In addition, developments in recent decades have made the law of bribery of increasing practical importance to people in and around politics.

Bribery was a common law offense, applicable originally only to official actions of a judicial nature, but extended gradually during the eighteenth and nineteenth centuries to all official actions. See generally *State v. Ellis*, 33 N.J.L. 102 (1868). Today, bribery is generally a statutory offense. It is not only one of the oldest legal concepts developed to protect the integrity of government and politics, but it is one of the most basic.[a] Most people probably would agree with the Supreme Court's characterization of bribery laws as dealing "with only the most blatant and specific attempts of those with money to influence governmental action." *Buckley v. Valeo*, 424 U.S. 1, 28 (1976). The bribe is at the heart of our concept of corruption, whatever other conduct may be included within that concept.

While bribery prosecutions are not rare and the appellate reports contain numerous bribery cases, the bribery laws have received surprisingly little attention, except by participants in specific bribery prosecutions. In this chapter we will be particularly concerned with bribery of policy-making officials, and with the question of what counts as a bribe in situations that may arise commonly in politics. As you read the chapter, think about these questions:

1. What are the elements of the crime of bribery? Which elements seem to depend on the specific language of the statutes and which elements, if any, seem to be intrinsic to the crime of bribery?

2. How accurate is the Supreme Court's characterization, quoted above, of the coverage of bribery laws as they are written and as they have been interpreted by the courts? Is bribery limited to the most "blatant and specific" conduct?

---

a. For a comprehensive history of the evolution of the concept of bribery throughout the course of western civilization, see John T. Noonan, Jr., BRIBES (1984). For a cross-section of social scientific research on bribery and corruption, see the anthology, POLITICAL CORRUPTION: CONCEPTS AND CONTEXTS (Arnold J. Heidenheimer and Michael Johnston, eds., 2002). For an economic analysis of corruption, see Susan Rose-Ackerman, CORRUPTION: A STUDY IN POLITICAL ECONOMY (1978). A variety of approaches to corruption, including the historical and the literary as well as the legal, may be found in the essays collected in PUBLIC AND PRIVATE CORRUPTION (William C. Heffernan & John Kleinig, eds., 2004).

3. Are the bribery statutes too vague, either as a matter of constitutional law or as a matter of fairness and effectiveness? Can you think of ways to make them clearer? At what cost, if any?

4. What should be the precise role of the bribery laws, especially in relation to other laws seeking to promote the integrity of the political system, such as those regulating campaign finances, lobbying practices, and conflicts of interest? Should the bribery laws be used solely against individuals who obviously have violated widely accepted norms, or should prosecutors and judges employ them aggressively as instruments of reform, to eliminate practices that are questionable or worse but may be widespread?

5. In particular, should *federal* prosecutors and judges use federal bribery and related statutes as an instrument for the reform of *state* and *local* political practices? As we shall see, in recent decades federal prosecutors have vigorously pursued state and local officials in some states, but the United States Supreme Court has partially curtailed their ability to do so. Should federal prosecutorial oversight of state and local government be expanded? Or should the Supreme Court go even further to limit such prosecutions?

6. Do the bribery statutes prohibit those acts and only those acts that are most plainly corrupt from a common sense standpoint? Should they? Are you sure you have a non-vague sense of what is a plainly corrupt act? Are you confident that you know a corrupt act when you see one?

It is difficult to think of the meaning of corruption without relying on one's conception of how the democratic process ought to function. Indeed, perhaps the best reason for studying the law of bribery is that the subject provides a concrete setting for evaluating and applying democratic norms. As an illustration, Section I of this chapter deals with unusual and relatively simple cases in which bribery of a candidate is alleged. Competing conceptions of political competition can have a major influence on how one believes such cases should be resolved. In Section II we consider the far more common and far more complex case of bribery of a public official.[b]

I. Bribery of Candidates

People v. Hochberg

62 App.Div.2d 239, 404 N.Y.S.2d 161 (1978)

MIKOLL, Justice.

The People charged that the defendant, Assemblyman Alan Hochberg, met with one, Charles Rosen, in January and February, 1976, to secure Rosen's promise not to run against him in the 1976 Primary for the Assembly in exchange for Hochberg's promise to give Rosen a $20,000 a year job in the Legislature, a session job for Rosen's brother-in-law paying approximately $3,000, and a $5,000 political campaign contribution. The defense contended that Hochberg's discussions with Rosen were for the purpose of establishing a working political coalition between Rosen, the political group in Co-op City which

---

b. Anyone doing research on bribery and related subjects can benefit from consulting Elaine R. Johansen, POLITICAL CORRUPTION: SCOPE AND RESOURCES: AN ANNOTATED BIBLIOGRAPHY (1990).

evolved during the rent strike and defendant's group in Pelham Park, as well as filling positions on his legislative staff with qualified persons.

The defendant was convicted of violating section 421 (subd. 5) of the Election Law (Penal Law, §110.00) which prohibits the fraudulent or wrongful doing of any act tending to affect the result of a primary election;[c] section 448 of the Election Law which prohibits any person, while holding public office, from corruptly using or promising to use his official authority to secure public employment upon consideration that the person so to be benefited or any other person will give or use their political influence or action in behalf of any candidate, or upon any other corrupt condition or consideration; and section 77 of the Public Officers Law which makes it a felony for any member of the Legislature to ask, receive, consent or agree to receive "any money, property or thing of value or of personal advantage" for performing any discretionary act which he may exercise by virtue of his office....

The People's evidence established that defendant was the State Assemblyman from the heavily Democratic 81st Assembly District (A.D.) located in the Bronx, New York. He was to be a candidate for re-election in the 1976 elections for the term of office commencing January 1, 1977. The district was divided into two sections, 81st A.D. West, which consisted of an area known as Pelham Parkway where defendant resided and which area he controlled and 81st A.D. East, known as Co-op City, a large housing development community of about 60,000 people, where Charles Rosen, Chairman of Steering Committee III, was the very popular leader of a rent strike supported by 86% of the residents. Co-op City was 99% Democratic in party affiliation and comprised about 40% of the Democratic primary vote in the district. Pelham Parkway supplied about 60% of that vote. Success in the Democratic primary was tantamount to election in the 81st A.D.

[In 1975–76, the Democratic Party in the 81st A.D. was split between regular and reform factions. Defendant Hochberg attempted to form an alliance with a Democratic leader, Larry Dolnick, who also was associated with Rosen as a leader of the rent strike. He informed Dolnick that he, Hochberg, wanted to be reelected to the Assembly in 1976 and then run for Civil Court Judge in 1977. He offered to support Dolnick to fill the Assembly vacancy that would result. When Dolnick said he was not interested in public office, Hochberg offered Dolnick either a legislative staff job at a salary of $19–20,000 or a job for less where "he wouldn't have to appear." Finally, Hochberg offered to contribute $750 to the New Democratic Club, of which Dolnick was a leader.]

Defendant told Dolnick that he did not want a primary in 1976 because it would be expensive. On different occasions he inquired of Dolnick whether Charles Rosen intended to run against him. Dolnick said Rosen did not. However, defendant said he wanted to hear it from "the horse's mouth" and wanted Dolnick to set up a meeting. He stated that Rosen would be a viable candidate, that a primary campaign for the Assembly would cost upwards of $25,000 and that he wanted to run for Civil Judge in 1977 and that that was the reason he wanted to be sure Rosen would not run. Dolnick thereafter advised Rosen that the defendant wanted to talk to him and told Rosen of the offers the defendant had made to him.

Charles Rosen testified that he visited the office of the Special Prosecutor for Nursing Homes in December, 1975, to discuss defendant's connection with the Nursing Home Industry. He mentioned what he characterized as defendant's "third party bribe" offer and the Special Prosecutor subsequently suggested that Rosen meet with the defendant to allow him to repeat the "bribe."

---

c. Does such a generally worded statute cover the defendant's conduct in this case? See *People v. Lang*, 36 N.Y.2d 366, 368 N.Y.S.2d 492, 329 N.E.2d 176 (1975). — EDS.

On January 27, 1976, Dolnick and Rosen went to the Special Prosecutor's office and arrangements were made to record the meeting defendant requested. The first tape recording played at trial revealed that Dolnick, Rosen and defendant met at Dolnick's apartment on January 30, 1976, where defendant stated he did not want a primary in 1976, that he wanted to run for the bench in 1977 and that he wanted their support for that office. The discussion included references to defendant's job offer to Dolnick and his proposed $750 contribution for the New Democratic Club campaign. At this meeting defendant stated that he was willing to help Rosen achieve his dreams because the $25,000 he would probably have to spend in a tough primary against Rosen would kill his judgeship race. Defendant stated that he would not have the resources for two campaigns. Defendant offered the $20,000 job on his staff to Rosen but said they would have to work it out with Dolnick first because he had offered the same job to him. Defendant also said he would raise $5,000 for Rosen's 1978 Special Election campaign for the Assembly by recommending that other people contribute to Rosen's campaign fund.

On February 5, 1976, Rosen and the defendant met alone at the Larchmont Diner. The tape recording of this meeting disclosed that defendant offered to place Rosen in a $3,000 job on his committee at the current session. It was agreed Rosen could not take it, but that any name would be acceptable to defendant as a "stand-in" for Rosen. That conversation went like this:

> ROSEN: Now, you talked about this job on your committee. I can't take that job.
>
> HOCHBERG: Who can? Is that a thought?
>
> ROSEN: That somebody would be a stand-in.
>
> HOCHBERG: Right. Does it look bad if your wife?
>
> ROSEN: What about my sister-in-law … or my brother-in-law[?]
>
> HOCHBERG: Matter of fact … as I told you, as of Monday, at least for the figure I had quoted you they can … come up and sign on. Immediately.…
>
> ROSEN: So who will know.
>
> HOCHBERG: That's right. All right. That's. That's that.

Defendant further stated in the taped conversation that he could guarantee Rosen $5,000 for his Special Election campaign and that the $3,000 session job was evidence of his good faith in that it would be completely paid before the primary. Rosen testified that in addition defendant said, "I will give you ___" and then proceeded to write on a napkin the figure $5,000, asking him to nod if it was acceptable.

He also said that if the rent strike was not over, Rosen's stand-in could be placed in the $20,000 job. When Rosen asked defendant not to put the stand-in's name on the payroll until Wednesday instead of the Monday, as planned, the defendant made reference to the stand-in losing. Rosen replied, "Schmuck, he's losing nothing, I'm getting the money." Defendant agreed, "But that's it, you're losing, why … ?" Rosen explained he had to talk the matter over with his wife.

At a subsequent recorded meeting on February 8, 1976, Rosen advised the defendant that the "stand-in" would be in Albany the following day. Rosen asked him when the arrangement regarding the $5,000 contribution which he had written on the napkin would be consummated. Defendant said that he had an "excellent mechanism to protect both of us." Rosen could set up a bank account in the name of a campaign committee and contributions could be made to that entity by defendant. "No problems, it's perfectly legal." he assured Rosen.

The stand-in for Rosen, his brother-in-law, Chris Johnson, who was equipped with a recording device, arrived in Albany the next day and defendant accompanied him to the necessary offices so that he could be put on the payroll. Defendant told Johnson that he would not have to come to Albany again but he would like Johnson to answer some mail at home.

The defense, through cross-examination of Rosen, and the testimony of defense witness, Philip Luce, sought to establish that Rosen was biased against defendant in that Rosen was a militant communist, out to destroy the government of the United States and in the process to destroy Assemblyman Hochberg as a political force in the community.[d] At the same time, through cross-examination of Dolnick and Rosen, the defense attempted to show that the discussions with Rosen were merely political in nature, made to establish a political coalition in the 81st Assembly District. The defendant also attempted to develop a basis for the defense of entrapment through cross-examination and the establishment of bias on the part of Rosen towards defendant. In addition, the defense offered the testimony of several character witnesses.

Defendant on this appeal first contends that there was a failure to prove beyond a reasonable doubt that the offers made by defendant were contingent on Rosen not running in the primary since they were made as part of a larger political accommodation involving the 81st Assembly District. We disagree. While certainly on this record a question of fact was created for the jury, there was sufficient evidence for the jury to find that the job offers were made on the condition that Rosen not run in the primary. Defendant said he did not want a primary against Rosen, that it would cost him $25,000 and would "kill his judgeship race," because he would not then have the financial resources for such a race. Defendant's knowledge that the offers were made contingent upon Rosen's not running in the primary appears from his statement in reference to the offer of the $3,000 session job, that: "That's my good faith ... it is completely paid ... before the petitions are filed." Further, the fact that the $20,000 and the $3,000 staff jobs were offered by defendant without regard to the duties to be performed or the skills required indicated the presence of an ulterior motive. Defendant's reference to their "agreement," their "deal" and "personal *quid pro quo*" during both meetings with Rosen, in connection with their discussions, along with his caution to Rosen to "deny everything" is sufficient to establish that defendant attempted to condition the job offers on Rosen's promise not to run in the primary.

It is also urged by defendant that the People failed to prove that he accepted "or thing of value or of personal advantage." This is without merit. Unlawful fees and payments (Public Officers Law, §77) are obviously a form of bribery. The benefit accruing to the public official need not be tangible or monetary to constitute a bribe (*People v. Hyde*, 156 App.Div. 618, 141 N.Y.S. 1089; *People ex rel. Dickinson v. Van De Carr*, *infra*). Here, Rosen's agreement not to run in the 1976 Primary was a sufficiently direct benefit to the defendant to be included within the term "thing of personal advantage."

---

d. Aside from the obvious drawbacks of this defense tactic, consider its effect on the more substantial defense described in the following sentence. — Eds.

Defendant next claims that there was a failure to prove that he acted with a wrongful intent because the People failed to prove that he knew he was violating sections 421 (subd. 5) and 448 (subd. 1) of the Election Law. We find this contention is without merit. There are sufficient facts in the record from which the jury could find that defendant acted with a corrupt intent (*People v. Lang*, 36 N.Y.2d 366, 370–371, 368 N.Y.S.2d 492, 495–497, 329 N.E.2d 176, 179–180). The trial court charged that a corrupt intent involved "an intentional and knowing disregard of the law." "Intentional" requires a conscious objective to engage in the prohibited conduct while "knowing" requires an awareness that one's conduct is of such nature or that such circumstances exist (Penal Law, §15.05, subds. 1 and 2). Here, evidence existed that defendant used or promised to use his authority as a legislator to secure staff jobs for Rosen and Johnson with the intent and purpose of obtaining Rosen's promise to refrain from entering the primary in violation of section 448 (subd. 1) of the Election Law. Likewise, evidence existed that defendant deliberately attempted to cause Rosen to refrain from entering the primary in exchange for the said jobs and offers of campaign contributions in violation of section 421 (subd. 5) of the Election Law.

Defendant urges that, at best, the evidence only supports attempted unlawful fees and payments and attempted corrupt use of position or authority, in that, Rosen testified that he never intended to run in the primary. The argument must be rejected since both crimes encompass an attempt. Unlawful fees and payments requires only the mere asking, consenting or agreeing to receive anything of value or personal advantage in exchange for performing a discretionary act. Corrupt use of position or authority includes only corruptly *promising* to use official authority in exchange for a promise not to enter the primary.

Further, defendant argues that because Rosen said he never had the intention to run in the primary, there could be no actual *effect* on the primary, as required by section 448 (subd. 1) of the Election Law, and that likewise, Rosen's promise not to run in the primary was not a thing of value as required under section 77 of the Public Officers Law. This argument is defeated by the fact that Rosen's state of mind was a present but transient state of mind at the time, subject to change and unbound by the obligations inherent in a promise not to run. Such a promise would take away his unfettered freedom to be a candidate and change the transitory nature of his state of mind to permanency. Thus, the promise not to run affected the primary by removing Rosen as a viable potential primary candidate and, also, consequently, was a thing of value or personal advantage to defendant.

Defendant contends that the statutes under which he was convicted are (1) unconstitutional in that they are overbroad and inhibit First Amendment activities relative to free political discussion; and (2) unconstitutionally vague in prohibiting the use of official position or authority in exchange for the benefit of another's "political influence or action" or "upon any other corrupt condition or consideration." We find the first contention is without merit. The statutes place reasonable restrictions on the use of official position and authority which is corruptive of a free elective process. No one has a constitutional right to corruptly use official position or authority to obtain political gain. Secondly, the statutes here under attack are sufficiently definite to give a reasonable person notice of the nature of the acts prohibited. They are generally aimed at corrupt bargaining to obtain public office and specifically at the use of the public payroll in such bargains. In view of the myriad ways in which the objects sought to be prohibited may be accomplished, laws framed with narrow particularity would afford easy circumvention of their purpose and be ineffectual. Thus, the statutes are neither impermissibly vague nor overbroad. A person of ordinary intelligence would realize that it is illegal to offer Assembly staff positions to another as a payoff not to run against him in an election for public office....

Judgment affirmed.

Notes and Questions

1. Hochberg's first contention is that there was insufficient proof "that the offers made by defendant were contingent on Rosen not running in the primary since they were made as part of a larger political accommodation involving the 81st Assembly District." Is the defendant arguing that Rosen's not running was no part of the "larger accommodation," or that a deal that includes Rosen's agreement not to run is permissible so long as the agreement is part of a "larger political accommodation"? How does the court interpret this contention? Why is the contention unsuccessful? If the second meaning is intended, is the contention persuasive?

2. The court states in response to one of Hochberg's claims that under the evidence the jury could have found "that defendant acted with a corrupt intent." In this passage, the court is referring to the convictions under both Sections 421 and 448 of the Election Law. The latter section states that a violator must act "corruptly," but Section 421(5) contains no such requirement. Was the court mistaken in assuming that the prosecutor had to prove that Hochberg acted "corruptly" in order to violate Section 421(5)?

3. You are consulted by Assemblyman Alex Alvarez, the favored candidate in next year's Democratic primary for an open State Senate seat. Barbara Bell has been mentioned as a possible opponent who might give Alvarez a strong race. Yesterday Bell had a meeting with Alvarez, during which she offered to run in the primary for the Assembly seat Alvarez will be vacating instead of challenging Alvarez for the Senate, if Alvarez will agree to support Bell in the Assembly primary and help her to raise money. Alvarez anticipates a tough general election contest against the likely Republican candidate and therefore would like to avoid strong opposition in the primary. He has no strong feelings one way or the other about Bell as a candidate for the Assembly. All things considered, he would like to accept Bell's offer if he may do so legally. How would you advise him, in New York? What would your advice be in California, where Elections Code §18205 provides:

> A person shall not ... advance, pay, solicit, or receive ... any money or other valuable consideration ... in order to induce a person not to become or to withdraw as a candidate for public office....

Aside from whatever legal advice you would give, do you regard Bell's offer as improper? Would your legal or ethical judgment be different if the proposal was first made by the Democratic state chair, who thought that the proposed arrangement would improve the Democrats' chances of winning both the Senate and the Assembly seats?

If one purpose of the New York and California statutes is to encourage and promote electoral competition, which solution to the problem would best promote competition in primary elections? Which solution would best promote competition in general elections? See generally Daniel H. Lowenstein, *Political Bribery and the Intermediate Theory of Politics*, 32 UCLA LAW REVIEW 784, 791–95 (1985).

4. *A personal postscript from Professor Lowenstein.* The article just cited was theoretically oriented and stated that "many of the transactions identified in this Article as definite or likely bribes are engaged in by public officials and those who deal with them on virtually a daily basis, with only the remotest chance of triggering a bribery prosecution."

Id. at 789. It was therefore a surprise to read in the *Los Angeles Times* only a few months after the article was published that Representative Bobbi Fiedler was being indicted on the basis of alleged facts resembling those of the Alvarez-Bell problem.

Fiedler was a California member of the House of Representatives who was planning to run in the 1986 Republican primary for the right to run against then Democratic Senator Alan Cranston. She and her aide, Paul Clarke, were accused of attempting to induce another potential candidate, Ed Davis, to withdraw from the Republican primary by offering Davis assistance in raising funds to pay off a considerable deficit that he had incurred. According to the indictment, this offer violated California Elections Code §18205, quoted above.[e] So far as is known, it was the first time anyone had ever been prosecuted under the section, which had originally been enacted in 1893.

About a week after the indictment I was retained to serve on the defense team, in part because my article supported the position that the allegations against Fiedler and Clarke did not violate California law even if they were true. As it turned out, there was so little evidence against Fiedler that the Los Angeles District Attorney agreed to the charge against her being dismissed. Although we believed the evidence against Clarke was equally weak, the District Attorney disagreed and pursued the case against him. We moved to have the case dismissed on a variety of legal grounds, including our contention that an offer of *political* benefits such as assistance in raising funds to pay off a campaign deficit did not constitute "valuable consideration" under Section 18205.

The good news from my perspective was that the Superior Court granted the motion to dismiss, and the District Attorney decided not to appeal. The bad news was that instead of deciding whether the statute covered political benefits in exchange for a withdrawal of candidacy, the court ruled on the very narrow ground that the list of verbs in Section 18205 does not include "offer." Thus, although a candidate who *solicits* a benefit in exchange for withdrawing is covered, a person who *offers* a benefit to a candidate in exchange for a withdrawal is not.

The Fiedler-Clarke case was very widely publicized. Furthermore, the events just described took place shortly before the California deadline for candidates to file for public office. Consequently, I received inquiries from several politicians who asked whether they could engage in variations on the Alvarez-Bell problem. What advice would you have given? Would your advice have been influenced by the pendency of the Fiedler-Clarke case? By the result, once the Fiedler-Clarke case had been dismissed?

Prior to my joining the Fiedler-Clarke defense team, I was interviewed by a large number of reporters, because I was virtually the only person who had done any research on the issue who was not connected to either the prosecution or (at that time) the defense. One of the reporters was from the *New York Times*, and in that interview I pointed out that *Hochberg*, a New York decision, was the closest judicial precedent to the Fiedler-Clarke case. The next morning, among my phone messages was one from Alan Hochberg!

After trying to remember exactly what I had said to the *New York Times* and briefly wondering whether I ought to consult a specialist in the law of defamation, I returned Hochberg's call. Far from being offended, Hochberg expressed considerable interest in the Fiedler-Clarke case and offered his services if there were any way he could assist them. Hochberg told me that as a result of losing his appeal he had served a prison term and had also been disbarred. He found occupation as a taxi driver, but one day, while he was sitting in his parked cab, another vehicle ran into it and disabled him. A judicial decision

---

e. The section had a different number in 1986, but its language has not been changed.

that to me had previously been an abstract treatment of an interesting intellectual problem suddenly took on a very human face.[f]

5. In *Kaisner v. State*, 772 S.W.2d 528 (Tex.App. 1989), the defendant was an incumbent sheriff running in a Republican primary for reelection. Because his 41% share of the vote was less than a majority, Texas law called for a runoff against the second-place candidate, one Robinson. Defendant was convicted of bribery for offering Robinson the job of Chief Deputy Sheriff if Robinson withdrew from the runoff election. The bribery statute applied to a "public servant," which was defined in the Texas Penal Code as including "a candidate for nomination or election to public office." The Texas Court of Appeals affirmed the conviction, stating that the decision to withdraw as a candidate "would have been the exercise of discretion as a public servant." The court went on:

> Appellant's argument is that the offer of a job to a political opponent falls within the traditional notion of political patronage and is therefore outside the statutory prohibition. We disagree. No such exception, justification or defense was authorized by the legislature. While it may have been acceptable or traditional behavior in Texas or other jurisdictions to "buy off" opponents, it is certainly within the province of the legislature to criminalize such acts.

Perhaps a more remarkable example of a court reaching to find a legal basis for a conviction for bribery of candidates to withdraw is *State v. Woodward*, 689 A.2d 801 (N.J.Super.A.D. 1997), which appears to hold that paying a potential candidate not to run comes under a statute banning bribery of voters.

6. In *Grunseth v. Boschwitz*, Hennepin County, Minnesota, District Court, 4th Judicial District, File No. 93-15958 (Feb. 1, 1994), Rudy Boschwitz and Jon Grunseth were Republican candidates, respectively, for senator and governor. Grunseth received some unfavorable publicity, to the point that Boschwitz regarded Grunseth's presence on the ticket as a liability in his own race. Boschwitz encouraged Grunseth to withdraw his candidacy and allegedly offered to pay $100,000 of Grunseth's campaign deficit. Grunseth withdrew but Boschwitz did not pay. Grunseth sued Boschwitz for damages in breach of contract. The court, in an unreported opinion, granted summary judgment for Boschwitz. Contracts are not enforceable if they violate public policy, and the alleged contract in this case was believed by the judge to violate Minn. Stat. Chapter 211B:

> A person may not reward or promise to reward another in any manner to induce the person to be or refrain from or cease being a candidate. A person may not solicit or receive a payment, promise, or reward from another for this purpose.

7. Hochberg was convicted of bribery both in his capacity as a public official *and* in his capacity as a candidate. The remainder of this chapter will concern itself with bribery of public officials. Most such bribery cases involve relatively lower level or even ministerial officials. We shall concentrate on bribery in connection with higher level public policymaking. At higher levels, most decisionmaking is inherently discretionary and officials are subject to various pressures. To the extent that it is unclear what counts as a bribe, does

---

f. In 1995, I spoke with Hochberg again. He reported that in all respects his life had gotten back on track in the past decade and was offering him considerable satisfaction. Alas, one of the other principals in the *Hochberg* case, Charles Rosen, has run into legal difficulties of his own. See Sewell Chan, "Bronx Odyssey: From Rebel to Executive to Felon," New York Times, October 10, 2006 (available at http://www.nytimes.com/2006/10/10/nyregion/10rosen.html). Those who are familiar with the medieval concept of the wheel of fortune will find these events unsurprising.

this reflect lack of an underlying consensus on what pressures on officials are desirable, or at least acceptable, in a democratic society?

II. The Elements of Bribery

The wording of bribery statutes in the United States varies considerably, and in some instances the variations are or may be significant. Nevertheless, for the most part the elements of the crime are similar. The federal statute, 18 U.S.C. §201, is representative. Subsection (a), which contains definitions, is followed by subsections (b)(1) and (2), defining, respectively, bribery and acceptance of a bribe:

(b) Whoever—

(1) directly or indirectly, corruptly gives, offers or promises anything of value to any public official ... or offers or promises any public official ... to give anything to any other person or entity, with intent—

(A) to influence any official act; or

(B) to influence such public official ... to commit ... or allow, any fraud ... on the United States; or

(C) to induce such public official ... to do or omit to do any act in violation of the lawful duty of such official or person ... ;

(2) being a public official ... directly or indirectly, corruptly demands, seeks, receives, accepts, or agrees to receive or accept anything of value personally or for any other person or entity, in return for:

(A) being influenced in the performance of any official act;

(B) being influenced to commit ... or allow, any fraud ... on the United States; or

(C) being induced to do or omit to do any act in violation of the official duty of such official ... ;

...

shall be fined ... or imprisoned ... or both....

There are five elements to the crime defined in this and most other American bribery statutes:

1. There must be a *public official.*

2. The defendant must have a *corrupt intent.*

3. A benefit, *anything of value*, must redound to the public official.

4. There must be an *intent to influence* the public official (or to be influenced if the recipient of the bribe is the defendant).

5. That which is intended to be influenced must be an *official act.*

Of these elements, are all present in *Hochberg*? Which, if any, might be doubtful?

Of the five elements only the first, that the bribee must be a public official, is relatively straightforward. It is true that the boundary between the public and private sectors is often unclear, and there can be difficult questions as to whether officials in entities that straddle both sectors are "public officials" within the meaning of a bribery statute. In addition, some state bribery statutes apply to persons who are not public officials, such as party officials or, as in *Hochberg*, candidates for public office. But this element of the crime ordinarily is not in issue. The materials that follow in this chapter will consider the remaining four elements.

First, however, the elements of bribery should be contrasted with those of the lesser offense of giving or receiving an unlawful gratuity a federal offense and an offense in many states. The federal statute, 18 U.S.C. §201(c), is again representative:

(c) Whoever—

(1) otherwise than as provided by law for the proper discharge of official duty—

(A) directly or indirectly gives, offers, or promises anything of value to any public official ... for or because of any official act performed or to be performed by such public official ... ; or

(B) being a public official ... otherwise than as provided by law for the proper discharge of official duty, directly or indirectly demands, seeks, receives, accepts, or agrees to receive or accept anything of value personally for or because of any official act performed or to be performed by such official ... ;

...

shall be fined ... or imprisoned ... or both.

A comparison of the elements of the unlawful gratuity offense with bribery yields the following:

1. The requirement that there be a public official is substantially the same, except that a transaction involving a former official can be an unlawful gratuity but not a bribe. This is because a bribe must look forward to an official act, whereas an unlawful gratuity may look forward or backward.

2. The actions proscribed by the bribery subsection must be done "corruptly." There is no such requirement for an unlawful gratuity.

3. The requirement that a benefit, "anything of value," must redound to the benefit of the official is identical to the bribery requirement, except that under the bribery provision the benefit may be received by the official or any other person, while under the unlawful gratuity provision the benefit must be received by the official "personally."

4. While there must be an intent that the benefit pass to the official "for or because of" the official act, there need be no intent, as in bribery, that the official be influenced by the benefit.

5. The requirement of an official act is seemingly identical for bribes and unlawful gratuities.

If, during an election year, Victoria strongly favors a particular bill and therefore mails $25 campaign contributions to each of the three members of the House of Representatives from her state who voted in favor of the bill, is she guilty of making an unlawful gratuity?

A. Corrupt Intent

What does the word "corruptly" in 18 U.S.C. §201(b) mean? Is a gift or benefit to a public official made with the expectation that the gift or benefit will influence the official's conduct in a manner beneficial to the donor always a bribe under the federal statute? Is it the presence of such an expectation that is meant by "corrupt"? If so, is the word "cor-ruptly" surplusage? Courts will read the requirement of a corrupt intent into a bribery statute where it is not stated expressly. E.g., *State v. O'Neill*, 700 P.2d 711 (Wash. 1985). Indeed, one court did so even when the bribery statute had been amended to omit the word "cor-ruptly." *State v. Alfonsi*, 147 N.W.2d 550 (Wisc. 1967). What is the significance, if any, of these holdings?

Could there be a bribe without an expectation that the gift or benefit will influence the public official's conduct? Is such an expectation necessary for a violation of the un-lawful gratuity offense, 18 U.S.C. §201(c)?

Compare with the federal statute these definitions from the California Penal Code:

> *Section 7(6)*: The word "bribe" signifies anything of value or advantage, pre-sent or prospective, or any promise or undertaking to give any, asked, given, or accepted, with a corrupt intent to influence, unlawfully, the person to whom it is given, in his or her action, vote, or opinion, in any public or official capacity.

> *Section 7(3)*: The word "corruptly" imports a wrongful design to acquire or cause some pecuniary or other advantage to the person guilty of the act or omis-sion referred to, or to some other person.

Does the definition of "corruptly" in Section 7(3) help you answer any of the questions above? What does the word "unlawfully" in Section 7(6) mean? What does the word "wrongful" in Section 7(3) mean?

Problem

Linda Lewis, a newly-elected president of the state labor federation, issues a public statement that is reported in the press to the effect that the most important item on labor's legislative agenda is to defeat bill number 100. Accordingly, the federation will support and contribute to those legislators and only those legislators who vote against the bill. Senator Sam Scott, who has been publicly uncommitted on bill number 100 and who is in a difficult struggle for reelection, has decided, after taking into account his need for a contribution from the labor federation as well as many other considerations, including the merits of the bill, that he would like to vote against the bill. He also would like to ac-cept the contribution. How would you advise him?

Senator Susan Smith, who was publicly and firmly opposed to the bill prior to Lewis' statement, also would like to vote against the bill and accept a contribution. How would you advise her?

If both senators vote against the bill and accept a contribution, is Lewis guilty of brib-ing either or both state senators under the language of the federal bribery statute? Under the California statute? Is she guilty of making one or more unlawful gratuities under the language of the federal statute? Should her conduct be prohibited?

Whether or not they have violated the law, is Lewis acting unethically? Senator Scott? Senator Smith?

B. Anything of Value

The standard bribe, as it usually is thought of, consists of a payment of money to an official for the official's personal use. On the official's part, it is motivated by venality.

However, it is clear from the language of the statutes ("anything of value") and numerous judicial decisions that bribery is not limited to the "standard" case. Still within the category of venality, loans to an official, business transactions resulting in a sales commission for the official, and numbers for the official in an illegal lottery are among the diverse personal benefits that have been held to be bribes. Some statutes, including 18 U.S.C. §201(b), expressly include benefits provided to third persons.

The most interesting questions that arise regarding the benefit to the official under bribery laws involve benefits that are political rather than personal. Of central importance are campaign contributions. Without apparent exception, American courts have held that a campaign contribution is a "thing of value" for purposes of typical bribery statutes. See Daniel H. Lowenstein, *Political Bribery and the Intermediate Theory of Politics*, 32 UCLA LAW REVIEW 784, 808–09 (1985). The difficult question is not *whether* a campaign contribution may be a bribe but *when* it is a bribe. We shall consider that question in the following section.

What about political benefits, other than campaign contributions, that are provided to influence an official act? Could an endorsement of a public official running for re-election be a bribe if it is given with intent to influence or in exchange for some official action? If the endorsing organization is very influential in the official's district, might not the endorsement have considerable value? Would you regard such an occurrence as improper? Would it depend on the surrounding circumstances? What if the endorsement were a prerequisite to a campaign contribution by the organization? See Lowenstein, *supra*, at 809–11.

Another type of political benefit can come in the form of official actions performed by other government officials. "Logrolling" is the term commonly used when legislators trade votes. For example, suppose Carol represents a corn-growing district and William represents a wheat-growing district. If Carol is sponsoring a corn bill and William a wheat bill and each agrees reciprocally to vote for the other's bill in committee, have they bribed each other? Which, if any, of the elements of bribery are not present? In the following case, the "logroll" is not between two legislators but between a legislator and an executive branch official.

People ex rel. Dickinson v. Van de Carr
87 App.Div. 386, 84 N.Y.S. 461 (1903)

LAUGHLIN, J.:

[Dickinson, the relator, was an alderman of New York City charged with violating Penal Code §72, a bribery statute. Rather than plead guilty or innocent, he filed a "traverse," an old-fashioned means of seeking dismissal of the case without trial.] The testimony showed that John McGaw Woodbury, the commissioner of street cleaning of the city of New York, wrote a letter to the relator on the 23d day of September, 1902, saying: "In reply to your letter of September 20th, I would say that the department is so short of horses, particularly in the borough of Brooklyn, that we have been very strict with the drivers during the warm weather to prevent any possibility of overheating or damaging the stock. We are many behind our complement. Should, however, the Honorable Board grant me the moneys for new stock and plant, this would give employment to more drivers, and as the heavy season comes on, having made a note of your favorable recommendation, the case of Covino will be reconsidered;" that on the thirtieth day of the same month the relator wrote and mailed a letter to Commissioner Woodbury in reply saying:

"If you will reinstate Antonio Covino, who I think was too severely punished by being dismissed from your department, I will vote and otherwise help you to obtain the money needed for a new plant in Brooklyn;" and at this time there was pending in the board of aldermen a bill to authorize an issue of corporate stock "for new stock or plant for Department of Street Cleaning, Borough of Brooklyn."

... Section 72 of the Penal Code provides as follows:

> Officer accepting bribe—A [public official] who asks, receives, or agrees to receive a bribe, or any money, property, or value of any kind, or any promise or agreement therefor, upon any agreement or understanding that his vote, opinion, judgment, action, decision, or other official proceeding, shall be influenced thereby, or that he will do or omit any act or proceeding, or in any way neglect or violate any official duty, is punishable by imprisonment ... or fine ... or both....

It will be observed that the clause "asks, receives or agrees to receive a bribe, or any money, property, or value of any kind, or any promise or agreement therefor," is disjunctive. It first specifically includes certain officers who ask, receive or agree to receive a *bribe*. In the absence of any statute defining a bribe, we must have recourse to the decisions and text writers to determine what was embraced in that term at common law. Bribery was an indictable offense at common law, and although in the early days it was limited to judicial officers and those engaged in the administration of justice, it was later extended to all public officers. It was variously defined as taking or offering an "*undue reward*" or a "*reward*" to influence official action. Bribery is defined in the American and English Encyclopaedia of Law to be "the giving, offering or receiving of anything of value, or any valuable service, intended to influence one in the discharge of a legal duty." The cases of bribery that have been before the courts of this State, so far as brought to our attention, have related to the offering or giving of property or something of intrinsic value. The relator claims that, inasmuch as no money or property was asked or agreed to be received by him to influence his official action, he has not violated this statute. In view of the circumstances disclosed his letter is open to the inference that he desired to obtain a political or other personal advantage from or by securing Covino's reinstatement in the public service, and that he took advantage of the known desire on the part of the street commissioner to obtain this appropriation of public moneys, to improperly influence the action of the street commissioner on the application of Covino for reinstatement, by offering, in case that were done, to vote for and further the desired ... appropriation, and impliedly threatening in case of refusal to withhold his support therefrom. The interests of the public service require that public officers shall act honestly and fairly upon propositions laid before them for consideration, and shall neither be influenced by nor receive pecuniary benefit from their official acts or enter into bargains with their fellow-legislators or officers or with others for the giving or withholding of their votes conditioned upon their receiving any valuable favor, political or otherwise, for themselves or others. It was the duty of the relator to act fairly and honestly and according to his judgment upon the proposition of the street commissioner. It does not appear to have been the mandatory duty of the board of aldermen to favor the recommendation of Commissioner Woodbury. In these circumstances it was the duty of relator to favor or oppose the recommendation according to its merits or demerits. If in his judgment it should have been disapproved, he should have opposed it, and he should not bargain to vote for it upon obtaining an agreement from the street commissioner to reinstate Covino. It is quite as demoralizing to the public service and as much against the spirit and intent of the statute for a legislator or other public official to bargain to sell his vote or official action for a political or other favor or reward as for money. Either is a bribe, and they only differ in degree. Nor should he, by holding out this inducement, have tempted the commissioner to act favorably upon Covino's application for reinstatement. This was undue influence and would be detrimental to the public service. In addition to the word "bribe" in section 72 of the Penal Code other words are employed sufficiently broad to reach this case. It is a violation of the statute for a public officer to ask, receive or agree to receive "property or value of any kind or any promise or agreement therefor" upon any agreement or understanding that his vote or official action shall be influenced thereby. It is clear that the words "value of any kind," as here used, are more comprehensive than "property." The benefit which the relator expected to receive from the reinstatement of his constituent would, we think, be embraced in the meaning of this clause and would also constitute a bribe. We are, therefore, of the opinion that the facts tend to show that the relator has offended against the provisions of section 72 of the Penal Code and that he was properly held to answer upon the charge....

Order affirmed.

Notes and Questions

1. American legislators at all levels see it as one of their primary functions to intercede in behalf of their constituents in dealings with executive agencies of the government. Whether or not they are usually as direct in their negotiations as was the defendant in *Van de Carr*, there is never any doubt that the basis of the legislator's influence with the agencies is the legislature's control over each agency's budget, programs, salaries, governing statutes and the like. Is such intercession by legislators wrong? What harm results? See generally Morris P. Fiorina, CONGRESS: KEYSTONE OF THE WASHINGTON ESTABLISHMENT (2d ed. 1989). Can it be argued that the practice is beneficial? In any event, is such intercession by a legislator a bribe?

2. Can a campaign contribution by one legislator to another be a bribe if given in exchange for or to influence a vote on a bill? What if the donor is a candidate for Speaker or Majority Leader and the contribution is in exchange for or to influence the recipient's vote on the donor's candidacy? What if the "donor" legislator does not actually make a contribution, but agrees to help the recipient raise money? Can it be a bribe for one legislator to vote for a bill favored by a second legislator in exchange for or to influence the second legislator's vote in a contest for a leadership position? Consider *People v. Montgomery*, 61 Cal.App.3d 718, 132 Cal.Rptr. 558 (1976), in which the bribery conviction of a city council member was upheld. The offense consisted of agreeing to give favorable consideration to another council member's favored projects in return for the other member's vote for the defendant for mayor, an office that was filled by vote of the city council. Defendant did not raise on appeal the question whether such an agreement could constitute a bribe. If he had, how should the court have ruled? Is *Van de Carr* relevant?

3. Consider again the problem of Carol and William, set forth above immediately before *Van de Carr*. Does *Van de Carr* suggest that "logrolling" in its most traditional form constitutes bribery? If so, would a current-day court be likely to reach the same conclusion?

Some states have constitutional or statutory provisions making logrolling unlawful. See, e.g., California Penal Code §86: "Every member of either of the houses composing the Legislature of this state who ... gives ... any official vote in consideration that another Member of the Legislature shall give any such vote either upon the same or another question, is punishable by imprisonment...."

Such prohibitions are old and, to say the least, rarely enforced.

4. Elizabeth, a well-known businesswoman who would be a strong challenger for a city council seat, tells Frank, the incumbent council member, that she will agree not to run against him if he helps her obtain a zoning variance for a commercial development that she wants to build. Has Elizabeth offered Frank a bribe? Is this problem identical to *Hochberg* and *Kaisner*? See Lowenstein, *supra*, 32 UCLA LAW REVIEW at 812–13.

C. Intent to Influence

Bribery often is assumed to require a *quid pro quo*, an agreement that in exchange for such and such a benefit, the official will perform such and such an official act in the desired manner. It is often easy to accomplish a corrupt purpose while avoiding an express agreement and it is usually difficult to prove the existence of such an agreement even if it has occurred. As a result, bribery has a reputation as a crime of narrow scope.

However, the supposed *quid pro quo* requirement is equivocal. On its face, the typical bribery statute does not require an agreement. There are some statutes that require the benefit to be given as "consideration" for the desired official act. *E.g.*, Texas Penal Code Ann. §36.02. This language could support an interpretation that an agreement is required. Most of the statutes, however, including the federal bribery statute, require only that the benefit be given (or received) with an intent to influence (or to be influenced on) the official action.

In this section we shall consider the "intent to influence" element of bribery, with particular focus on cases in which the "thing of value" is a campaign contribution. Many contributions are made in the hope that they will influence the recipient to act favorably to the donor. Explicit exchanges of contributions for particular official actions (such as favorable votes on legislation) are less common. We saw in the preceding section that courts generally hold that campaign contributions *may* be bribes. In this section we shall consider *when* they are bribes.

To help keep your bearings as you work through the complex material that follows, it may be helpful to consider the following hypothetical cases. In the first four cases, campaign contributions are made to incumbent legislators, each of whom is regarded as relatively safe in his or her district and none of whom knows of any likely strong challengers in the foreseeable future.

Case 1: The ABC Corporation contributes $10,000 to Larry.[g] ABC has a large, permanent lobbying staff, because it has numerous, ongoing legislative interests on matters such as taxation and regulation. At the time of the contribution, no particular issue dominates ABC's agenda. In none of the discussions between ABC and Larry relative to the contribution is there any allusion to legislative issues. ABC makes the contribution because it hopes and believes that it will influence Larry to support ABC's positions more often than he would do if ABC made no contribution. Larry accepts the contribution with a similar expectation that when it is more or less costless for him to do so, he will support ABC in the future.

Case 2: The XYZ Corporation has no ongoing interest in legislation and has not previously engaged in either lobbying or contributing to campaigns. However, for the last

---

g. We assume in each of these hypotheticals that the contribution is legal under any applicable campaign finance regulations and is properly disclosed.

year, XYZ has been intensively lobbying in support of a large public works project that, if approved by the legislature, is likely to result in large contracts for XYZ. Analysts inside and outside the company believe the continued solvency of XYZ depends on approval of the project, which is the only issue on which XYZ is lobbying. XYZ contributes $10,000 to Laura. In none of the discussions between XYZ and Laura relating to the contribution is there any allusion made to the project or any other legislative issue. XYZ makes the contribution because it hopes and believes it will increase the chances that Laura will vote for the project. Laura has been undecided on the project and continues to be undecided after receiving the contribution. However, she appreciates the contribution and she mentions to her legislative assistant that because of the contribution she has switched from a position of leaning against the project to leaning in favor, pending further debate and possible reactions to the proposal in her district or among other interest groups.

Case 3: ABC Corporation, situated as in Case 1 above, contributes $10,000 to Lenny. During the meeting in which the head of ABC's political action committee hands over the contribution, the following dialogue occurs:

> *Lenny*: You know, I can't promise to support you on every issue. Sometimes we're just on opposite sides. But I realize that $10,000 is a big contribution, and if you give it to me I guarantee you that I'll give you my support whenever I can, consistent with other commitments and with the situation in my district.
>
> *PAC Director*: That's all we can ask. Here's your check.

Case 4: XYZ Corporation, situated as in Case 2 above, contributes $10,000 to Lucy. During the meeting in which the head of XYZ's political action committee makes the contribution, the following dialogue occurs:

> *Lucy*: There is some vocal opposition to your project in my district, and up to now I have been planning to vote against it. But I'll support it if you contribute $10,000 to my campaign.
>
> *PAC Director*: It's a deal. Here's your check.

Case 5: An issue-oriented group makes campaign contributions out of funds it raises from individuals who support the group's ideology. The group does no lobbying. Rather, it seeks to influence policy by helping to elect candidates with compatible views and defeat candidates with opposing views. In a given legislative district, a candidate who avidly supports the group's ideology is challenging an incumbent who, from the group's point of view, has one of the worst voting records in the legislature. The group contributes $10,000 to the challenger's campaign but otherwise has no contact with the candidate.

In Case 5, the group follows an "electoral strategy," seeking to influence policy by enhancing the chances of candidates who are likely, if elected, to pursue the policies the contributor favors. Some would object to a campaign finance system in which electoral strategies are broadly effective, because of an equity objection that those with resources to devote to large contributions attain a disproportionate influence on public policy. Even if such an objection is accepted, most would agree that the problem is with the system, not with the conduct of the contributor or the recipient of the contribution. No one has contended that contributions made pursuant to an electoral strategy are corrupt or that they are bribes.

The contributors in Cases 1 through 4 pursue a "legislative strategy," consisting of contributing to a person presently in office or a candidate who is likely to be elected, in the hopes of influencing the recipient to pursue the favored policies by reason of gratitude, a desire to encourage future donations from the same or additional sources, or similar mo-tivations. Interest group contributions in the United States are often, though by no means always, made partly or entirely in pursuit of a legislative strategy. They are often received by candidates who know why the contribution is made.

It may help you to organize Cases 1 through 4 in your mind to see that they differ along two dimensions. In Cases 1 and 3, ABC Corporation contributes to promote its legislative agenda generally but not to influence any particular vote or other legislative action. In the other two cases, XYZ Corporation's contributions are targeted to a partic-ular bill. Thus, one difference relates to the specificity of the influence sought by the con-tributor. In Cases 1 and 2, the contributor hopes for influence but receives no assurances. In Cases 3 and 4, there is an explicit agreement that the contributor will receive favorable official action in exchange for the contribution. Thus, the second difference relates to the explicitness (and therefore certainty) of the influence.

As you read the statutes and cases in the following materials, consider which, if any, of Cases 1 through 4 would constitute a bribe or other offense under the legal doctrines being put forth. What if in each instance, the transfer were a personal gift of money to the legislator rather than a campaign contribution. Would the result be affected under the given statute or case?

State v. Agan

384 S.E.2d 863 (Georgia 1989), cert. denied 494 U.S. 1057 (1990)

HUNT, Justice.

We granted certiorari to the Court of Appeals in *Agan v. State*, 191 Ga.App. 92, 380 S.E.2d 757 (1989) to review that opinion, with emphasis upon "[t]he correct interpreta-tion of the offering of a bribe, as prohibited by OCGA §16-10-2(a)(1), and the accep-tance of a 'campaign contribution,' as defined in OCGA §21-5-3(6)."

The facts, more fully set forth in the Court of Appeals' opinion, are summarized as follows. Agan, the Honorary Turkish Consul in Atlanta, sought a building height variance for the construction of a hotel on his property. Agan and Sarper, an Emory University pro-fessor, had discussed with officials of the Emory Medical Clinic a plan to bring Turkish patients to the Clinic who would stay at the hotel. The Dekalb County Commission had twice rejected Agan's application for a variance. Agan submitted a third application, and spoke with two Dekalb County commissioners, Lanier and Fletcher, inquiring what Agan could do to insure the approval of his application. Agan told Fletcher he had a number of friends in the local Turkish-American Association who wished to contribute to Fletcher's campaign. At a meeting between Agan and Fletcher, Agan urged Fletcher to support the variance application, then left Fletcher with four checks totaling $3,700.00, made to Fletcher personally, and marked "for campaign contribution," despite Fletcher's protests that he did not even have a campaign bank account. The checks were drawn on the ac-counts of Sarper and three others who testified they were reimbursed for the checks by Agan and believed Agan wanted contributions to come from different people in order to give the impression he enjoyed broad support in the Turkish community. After another meeting between Agan and Fletcher in which Agan reiterated his need for the variance, Agan presented Fletcher with a fifth check for $800.00 marked as a campaign contribu-tion, from a third party. Agan, accompanied by Sarper, also met with Lanier to discuss the variance. As they left Lanier's office, Sarper gave Agan an envelope at Agan's request and, back in Lanier's office, without Sarper, Agan presented Lanier with the envelope containing Sarper's check to Lanier for $3,000.00 marked "campaign contribution," despite Lanier's statement to him that he was not up for re-election for three years....

Sufficiency of the Evidence

1(a). The Court of Appeals correctly determined ... that a rational trier of fact could have found the essential elements of the crime of bribery to have been established beyond a reasonable doubt in regard to Agan. There was ample evidence at trial that Agan gave payments to Lanier and Fletcher for the specific purpose of influencing their votes on his application for a building height variance, thus committing the crime of bribery....

The Charge

[Bribery is defined] in OCGA §16-10-2(a)(1), which provides that:

> [a] person commits the offense of bribery when ... [h]e gives or offers to give to any person acting for or on behalf of the state or any political subdivision thereof ... any benefit, reward, or consideration to which he is not entitled with the purpose of influencing him in the performance of any act related to the functions of his office.

....

2(b). The Court of Appeals found the trial court's charge faulty for failing to read the bribery statute, OCGA §16-10-2, in conjunction with the Ethics in Government Act, OCGA §21-5-1 et seq., which defines political contributions and sets forth the manner in which they may be received and reported. In particular, the Court of Appeals held the language of the bribery statute prohibiting the giving or offering to a public officer of a benefit to which that officer "is not entitled," is to be read very narrowly to proscribe the giving or offering to a public official of a benefit to which that officer "*is not qualified or privileged to receive or has no grounds or right to seek, request, or receive.*" [Emphasis supplied]. The Court of Appeals further held

> a campaign contribution, whether made to a candidate in the heat of a campaign or to encourage or influence the official after he is elected, is something which a candidate or elected official is qualified or privileged to request or receive and thus something to which he is "entitled" within the meaning of OCGA §16-10-2.

We interpret this holding as meaning, in effect, that if money given to an office holder qualifies as a campaign contribution, requiring reporting under the Ethics in Government Act, OCGA §21-5-1 et seq., then it cannot be a bribe. With this conclusion we respectfully disagree.

The Ethics in Government Act has in no manner altered the bribery statute. The Act simply defines a campaign contribution and, having defined, requires disclosure. Specifically, nothing in the Act permits a public officeholder to request or receive anything of value "to which he is not entitled with the purpose of influencing him in the performance of any act related to the functions of his office or employment...." (OCGA §16-10-2(a)). Nor is the term "entitled," as contained in the bribery statute, modified in any way by the Ethics in Government Act. Other than those emoluments of public office that are expressly authorized and established by law, no holder of public office is entitled to request or receive—from any source, directly or indirectly—anything of value in exchange for the performance of any act related to the functions of that office.[2] ....

---

2. Our holding means that a transfer that is a bribe as defined by OCGA §16-10-2 also may come within the definition of "contribution" as contained in the third sentence of OCGA §21-5-3(6). The fact that such a transfer must be reported does not change its character as a bribe.

Constitutionality of the Bribery Statute

Vagueness Challenge

3. We find no merit to Agan's contention that OCGA §16-10-2(a) is unconstitutionally vague, hence void....

First Amendment Challenge

4. Agan contends the bribery statute must be interpreted as condemning only a payment to a public officer who agrees to a clearly delineated *quid quo pro*, i.e., an explicit purchase of an explicit official act. Were that not so, he insists, the bribery statute would be an impermissible restraint upon free speech under the First Amendment to the Constitution of the United States. He relies principally upon *Buckley v. Valeo*, 424 U.S. 1 (1976).

In *Buckley*, the Supreme Court examined the application of the First Amendment to limitations upon campaign expenditures by a candidate for public office, and limitations upon amounts that might be contributed to a campaign, finding a violation of the right of free speech for the former, and none for the latter. The holdings in *Buckley* do not apply to the bribery statute, which places no limitation upon amounts of contributions or expenditures, but, rather, restricts the purposes for which any "benefit, reward or consideration" may be offered or given to, or solicited or accepted by, a public officer. Even assuming the First Amendment might relate to the purposes of political transfers, it cannot be understood to shield the bribing of a public officer.[3]

Citizens of Georgia have every right to try to influence their public officers — through petition and protest, promises of political support and threats of political reprisal. They do *not* have, nor have they ever had, the "right" to buy the official act of a public officer. OCGA §16-10-2(a). Public officers are not prohibited from receiving legitimate financial aid in support of nomination or election to public office. They do *not* have, nor have they ever had, the "right" to sell the powers of their offices.[4] OCGA §16-10-2(b). The bribery statute does not serve to weaken free speech. It serves to strengthen free government....

---

3. "Where the letter of the statute results in absurdity or injustice or would lead to contradictions, the meaning of general language may be restrained by the spirit or reason of the statute." *Sirmans v. Sirmans*, 149 S.E.2d 101 (Ga. 1966). That logic should apply alike to all legal authorities, including the Constitution.

We decline to follow the "rule," as urged by Agan, of *People v. Brandstetter*, 430 N.E.2d 731 (Ill.App. 1982), that: "[P]ublic officials are 'authorized by law' to receive campaign contributions from those who might seek to influence the candidate's performance as long as no promise for or performance of a specific official act is given in exchange." In that case, a political activist was convicted of bribery for handing to a state legislator a note that read: "Mr. _____, the offer for help in your election & $1000 for your campaign for Pro ERA vote."

While Brandstetter's conviction was affirmed on appeal, we are concerned that its "rule" would proliferate corrupt practices. As example, note this story in *The Atlanta Journal and Constitution* of July 8, 1989: "A millionaire who handed out $10,000 checks on the [Texas] Senate floor while legislation that interested him was pending said the checks were political contributions, not an attempt to bribe lawmakers. 'It would be difficult to make it into a bribery case,' said [the district attorney], who believes it's time to change Texas's loose campaign finance laws. 'In Texas, it's almost impossible to bribe a public official as long as you report it....'"

4. The acceptance of a bribe is an egregious conflict of interest, and will vitiate official acts that otherwise appear to be lawful. [The footnote goes on to refer to several Georgia decisions in which zoning and other decisions were set aside at the behest of private citizens because they were infected by corruption or conflict of interest.] — Eds.

Notes and Questions

1. In a portion of the *Agan* opinion that is not reprinted here, the court ruled that Agan was entitled to a hearing to determine whether he had been a victim of selective prosecution. To succeed, Agan would have to show that others similarly situated had not been prosecuted and that he had been singled out for an improper reason, such as his Turkish ethnicity. At the hearing that ensued, the trial court ruled against Agan. This ruling was affirmed in *Agan v. State*, 417 S.E.2d 156 (Ga.App. 1992), affirmed 426 S.E.2d 552 (Ga.), cert. denied 510 U.S. 819 (1993). The Georgia Court of Appeals decision included the following:

> [A]ppellant has not shown that others in a similar situation were not prosecuted. While appellant did show that other developers made contributions while they had zoning matters pending, he failed to show that the contributions of those developers were accompanied by the following factors attendant to the contributions made by appellant: the contributions were made at a time when the commissioners did not have an active campaign structure; appellant propounded his zoning request at the same meeting that he gave the contributions, in envelopes, directly to the commissioners; at the same meetings, appellant promised future contributions; the checks were make out to the commissioners personally rather than to their campaigns; appellant was very persistent in talking to the commissioners and giving them contributions; a videotape of the contact with the commissioners was made and was available as evidence; the votes of either of the two commissioners involved were necessary for appellant's zoning to be passed; and the two commissioners approached the district attorney with the evidence of the bribe. When all these factors coalesce, appellant's situation becomes of a different category than the situations attempted to be shown at the hearing. We find no evidence that anyone else crossed the line of illegality as did appellant. While the district attorney indicated that other situations may appear improper, appellant failed to show that the district attorney knew or should have known of other situations in which the line of illegality was crossed.

Suppose any or all of the factors mentioned in this passage had not been present in Agan's case, but that Agan was convicted on the same jury instructions that occurred in the actual case. Would the Georgia Supreme Court have reversed the conviction?

2. It is commonly said that one of the elements of bribery is "consideration," or what is often referred to as a *quid pro quo*.[h] Does *Agan* require a *quid pro quo*? Does 18 U.S.C. §201(b)? Should a *quid pro quo* be required? If not, what more than a gift to the official and an official act favorable to the donor should be required for a bribe? Following are excerpts from three *federal* decisions of the 1970s and early 1980s interpreting *state* bribery statutes. Do they provide answers to these questions?

In *United States v. Isaacs*, 493 F.2d 1124, 1145 (7th Cir.), cert. denied, *sub nom. Kerner v. United States*, 417 U.S. 976 (1974), the court said (construing the Illinois bribery statute):

> [B]ribery occurs when property is accepted by a public official with knowledge that it is offered with intent to influence the performance of any act related to his public position. No particular act need be contemplated by the offeror or offeree. There is bribery if the offer is made with intent that the offeree act favorably to the offeror when necessary.

---

h. This is a Latin phrase whose literal translation is "something for something." See David Mellinkoff, MELLINKOFF'S DICTIONARY OF AMERICAN LEGAL USAGE 116 (1992).

Under *Isaacs*, is our Case 1 a bribe? Should it be? Suppose it is shown that an interest group makes sizeable campaign contributions to all the members of a legislative committee that hears bills affecting the group. Contributions are made to members of the committee without regard to party or ideology. This would not be an unusual occurrence. See, e.g., Fred Wertheimer, *The PAC Phenomenon in American Politics*, 22 Arizona Law Review 603, 607–11 (1980). Under *Isaacs*, does such a showing constitute a prima facie case of bribery?

In *United States v. Arthur*, 544 F.2d 730 (4th Cir. 1976), defendant was an officer of a national bank in West Virginia, charged with misapplying bank funds in violation of federal law. In particular, he was charged with using bank funds for bribery, "to entertain, do favors and buy gifts for state and local officials who might be influential in securing government deposits for the bank." The Court of Appeals found improper a jury instruction that

> The payment of money to government officials for the purpose of obtaining deposits of government funds in the bank and to influence the judgment of such officials in connection with such deposits is, in itself, illegal in that such activity constitutes the bribery or attempted bribery of public officials.

The appellate court wrote:

> It is universally recognized that bribery occurs only if the gift is coupled with a particular criminal intent.... That intent is not supplied merely by the fact that the gift was motivated by some generalized hope or expectation of ultimate benefit on the part of the donor, *see United States v. Brewster, infra*.... "Bribery" imports the notion of some more or less specific *quid pro quo* for which the gift or contribution is offered or accepted....
>
> This requirement of criminal intent would, of course, be satisfied if the jury were to find a "course of conduct of favors and gifts flowing" to a public official *in exchange for* a pattern of official actions favorable to the donor even though no particular gift or favor is directly connected to any particular official act.... Moreover, as the Seventh Circuit has held, it is sufficient that the gift is made on the condition "that the offeree act favorably to the offeror when necessary." *United States v. Isaacs.*[i] ... It does not follow, however, that the traditional business practice of promoting a favorable business climate by entertaining and doing favors for potential customers becomes bribery merely because the potential customer is the government. Such expenditures, although inspired by the hope of greater government business, are not intended as a *quid pro quo* for that business: they are in no way conditioned upon the performance of an official act or pattern of acts or upon the recipient's express or implied agreement to act favorably to the donor when necessary.

The *Arthur* court also pointed to the West Virginia bribery statute, which referred to "[a]ny pecuniary benefit *as consideration for* the recipient's official action as a public servant or party official...." West Virginia Code Ann. §61-5A-3 (Supp. 1975) (emphasis added). The use of the word "consideration" helped indicate that the statute "was not intended to depart from the general rule as to the requisite criminal intent discussed above." Because the jury instruction did not set forth with sufficient clarity the "crucial distinction between 'goodwill' expenditures" and bribes, which require criminal intent based on a *quid pro quo*, the case was remanded.

In *United States v. L'Hoste*, 609 F.2d 796 (5th Cir), cert. denied 449 U.S. 833 (1980), defendants were convicted of federal conspiracy and racketeering offenses based on charges

---

i. Is this an accurate paraphrase of *Isaacs*? — Eds.

that they obtained numerous no-bid, cost-plus sewer contracts in violation of the Louisiana bribery statute. There was evidence that the defendants' company received the preponderance of such contracts during the period in question and that inadequate supervision of performance under the contracts had permitted various types of fraud. There was also evidence that during this period the defendants gave various gifts to the public officials responsible for the contracts, including construction and landscaping work at their residences, trips to places such as Mexico, Las Vegas, and Hawaii, and campaign contributions. The conviction was affirmed on appeal. In upholding the trial court's refusal to give a jury instruction requested by the defendants, the appellate court wrote:

> In the instructions formally requested by the defendants, the final sentence states: "If you find that the gifts were made, but that the gifts were motivated by no more than customary business reasons ... then you should find that bribery did not take place." ... The jury would have been bound to treat as innocent any gifts made for customary business reasons. This, in our view, would be a rank misapplication of the Louisiana bribery law. Customary business practice could embrace all sorts of extravagant favors intended to influence important business decisions. The type of favor, the manner in which it is given, and its timing are things a businessman no doubt considers in courting his client; he has an economic incentive to employ his resources in a manner that will produce the greatest return. It is obvious that the same incentive motivates [businessmen] in their commercial dealings with governmental bodies; by the size and timing of their favors, however, they may transgress the bribery laws. In our view, the instruction proposed by the defense would have foreclosed such a finding of such transgression.

> ... As we have observed, certain practices designed to promote business in the private sector may very well be intended as a *quid pro quo* for that business. Yet, in the public sector, the same practices may run counter to a bribery statute. Even if appellants' theory is correct — that some *quid pro quo* must be found to satisfy the requisite criminal intent for bribery — the [rejected instruction] misstated the law.... In summary, defendants wanted the jury to be bound to find that any favor falling within the amorphous categories of "customary" or "traditional" business practice was not bribery, when it easily could have been.

The *L'Hoste* court distinguished *Arthur*, in part, on the ground that the Louisiana bribery statute requires only "intent to influence" official action, whereas the West Virginia statute required consideration.

3. The cases discussed in Note 2 involved enforcement of federal statutes that incorporated *state* bribery laws. Some of the more significant interpretations of the *federal* bribery laws during the 1970s arose out of some transactions between Senator Daniel Brewster of Maryland and lobbyist Cyrus Anderson. Brewster was a member of the Senate Post Office and Civil Service Committee, and Anderson's client, mail-order catalogue merchant Spiegel, Inc., had a strong interest in keeping postal rates as low as possible. Anderson made several payments to Brewster during a period when potential postal rate increases were either pending or foreseeable. In 1967, when these payments were made, campaign reporting and accounting requirements were minimal. The payments could reasonably have been characterized as either campaign contributions or personal payments to Brewster. Brewster and Anderson were accused of both bribes and unlawful gratuities.

Preliminarily, Brewster objected that for a member of Congress to be charged with bribery or an unlawful gratuity in connection with legislative business would violate the Speech or Debate Clause in Art. I, §6 of the Constitution, which reads in part:

> The Senators and Representatives ... shall in all cases, except treason, felony and breach of the peace, be privileged from arrest during their attendance at the session of their respective houses, and in going to and returning from the same; and for any speech or debate in either house, they shall not be questioned in any other place.

In *United States v. Brewster*, 408 U.S. 501 (1972), the Supreme Court ruled that the Speech or Debate Clause does not preclude charging members of Congress with bribery, but that the prosecution's case may not depend on either legislative acts or on the motivation for legislative acts. The Court's theory was that the offense of bribery is completed when the benefit is sought or accepted with the proscribed intent, regardless of the actual official behavior that ensues. Although, as you might imagine, the Court's ruling in *Brewster* poses challenging practical problems for prosecutors and judges in bribery cases in which members of Congress are charged, the Court reaffirmed its position in *United States v. Helstoski*, 442 U.S. 477 (1979). However, the Court has not extended the privilege to officials other than members of Congress. In *United States v. Gillock*, 445 U.S. 360 (1980), it declined to protect state legislators who are defendants in federal prosecutions from having their legislative acts introduced as evidence against them.

After the Supreme Court had ruled that Brewster could be prosecuted, he and Anderson stood trial. Anderson was convicted of bribery.[j] Brewster was convicted of accepting unlawful gratuities but was acquitted of the bribery charges. Brewster appealed on the grounds, among others, that the unlawful gratuity statute is unconstitutionally vague and overbroad, and that the trial judge's instructions to the jury were inadequate to distinguish conduct falling within three categories: 1) guilt of bribery, 2) guilt of unlawful gratuity, and 3) innocence. In a long and difficult opinion, the Court of Appeals upheld the constitutionality of the unlawful gratuity statute but reversed Brewster's conviction because of the jury instructions. *United States v. Brewster*, 506 F.2d 62 (D.C.Cir. 1974). The court summarized its view of the two offenses as follows:

> To accept a thing of value "*in return for*: (1) *being influenced* in [the] performance of any official act," [as required by the bribery offense,] appears to us to imply a higher degree of criminal intent than to accept the same thing of value "for or because of any official act performed or to be performed." Perhaps the difference in meaning is slight, but Congress chose different language in which to express comparable ideas. The bribery section makes necessary an explicit *quid pro quo* which need not exist if only an illegal gratuity is involved; the briber is the mover or producer of the official act, but the official act for which the gratuity is given might have been done without the gratuity, although the gratuity was produced because of the official act.

As we shall see later in this chapter, in the *Sun-Diamond* case, the Supreme Court ruled on the connection between a gift to an official and an official act that is necessary for a violation of Section 201(c), the gratuity offense. With respect to Section 201(b), the bribery offense, is the *Brewster* court correct that an "explicit *quid pro quo*" is required for a violation? If so, is there an "explicit *quid pro quo*" in Case 1, presented above, in which there was a mutual expectation of generalized influence? Is there an "explicit *quid pro quo*" in Case 2, in which there is an expectation of influence on a particular matter, but no explicit agreement to that effect nor even an assurance that the influence will be

---

j. For Anderson's appeal, see *United States v. Anderson*, 509 F.2d 312 (D.C.Cir. 1974), cert. denied 420 U.S. 991 (1975).

decisive? If there is an "explicit *quid pro quo*" in those cases, does the phrase "explicit *quid pro quo*" mean anything like what it appears to mean? But if there is no "explicit *quid pro quo*" in Cases 1 and 2, is the requirement of an "explicit *quid pro quo*" consistent with the statutory language? If there is a requirement of an "explicit *quid pro quo*" and if that requirement excludes Cases 1 and 2 from being bribes under Section 201(b), does the requirement apply to all cases, or only to cases of campaign contributions? In other words, if there is an "explicit *quid pro quo*" requirement and if that requirement excludes Cases 1 and 2, would the courts be likely to reach the same result if the payment in Case 1 or Case 2 were a personal payoff rather than a campaign contribution? If not, is there a justification for applying the statute differently to campaign contributions and other types of benefits?

There are no firm answers to these questions, though the following materials surely bear on them. As to the last of the questions, the *Brewster* court seemed to rule out the possibility of campaign contributions violating the federal *gratuity* offense, at least as long as the contribution is made to a campaign committee rather than to the candidate directly, as is now invariably the case. This aspect of *Brewster* has been criticized by Joseph R. Weeks, *Bribes, Gratuities and the Congress: The Institutionalized Corruption of the Political Process, the Impotence of Criminal Law to Reach It, and a Proposal for Change*, 13 JOURNAL OF LEGISLATION 123, 130–31 (1986):

> The *Brewster* "perfectly legitimate, honest campaign contribution" exception to [the unlawful gratuity offense] is not based on the statutory language. Although Congress is certainly free to create an exception in the statute for campaign contributions or, indeed, to exempt its members entirely from the reach of section 201, it has consistently rejected suggestions that it do so. The rationale for a campaign contribution exception to section 201, as suggested by the *Brewster* discussion, instead appears to be a kind of "rule of necessity." Since it is known that members of Congress regularly accept campaign contributions and it is thought that such a practice is required as a practical matter to become or remain an elected federal officeholder, campaign contributions are deemed innocent and thus not capable of restriction by section 201....
>
> [But such arguments] are both amoral and, at their core, a repudiation of the concept of democratic government. They accept as not only not improper but, indeed, an expected and perhaps creditable example of democracy in action for elected officials to seek and accept campaign contributions in exchange for being influenced in their legislative conduct. The arguments thus endorse not simply the receipt of gratuities but outright bribes as appropriate conduct by federal officeholders. Such arguments simply ignore the familiar concept of universal and equal suffrage as well as the historic American abhorrence for legislative decision-making based on the profit motive.

Earlier in this chapter we posed the question whether Victoria, a voter who sends $25 campaign contributions to each of the members of the House of Representatives from her state who voted for a bill she favors is guilty of making an unlawful gratuity. Does that question suggest a possible objection to Weeks' position?

4. The foregoing cases indicate that coming into the 1980s, the federal courts had no clear and uniform understanding of what was required by way of an "intent to influence" under federal or state bribery laws or when a campaign contribution could be a bribe or an unlawful gratuity. In the meantime, federal prosecutors became increasingly aggressive in attempting to enforce anti-corruption laws against state and local elected officials

and, in some cases, against members of Congress. For example, several officials and lobbyists in California and South Carolina were imprisoned in the early 1990s because of federal "sting" investigations of corruption in and around the state legislatures. Three cases decided by the Supreme Court—*McNally v. United States* (1987), *McCormick v. United States* (1991), and *Evans v. United States* (1992)—reflect an apparent desire upon the part of the Supreme Court to control the extent of federal engagement in anti-corruption activity in states and localities. Together with a fourth decision, *United States v. Sun-Diamond Growers* (1999), they may also reflect concern by the Court with possibly excessively broad interpretation of anti-corruption laws.

In order to understand the significance as well as the limits of these decisions, it will be helpful to bear in mind four possible situations in which bribes may be prosecuted.

(1) Federal prosecutors may bring charges against federal officials and those who attempt to influence them under federal bribery statutes, such as 18 U.S.C. §201. *Brewster*, *supra*, and *Sun-Diamond* are examples of this type of case.

(2) Federal prosecutors may bring charges under federal statutes that establish federal standards that may be imposed, under specified circumstances, on state and local officials. *McNally*, *McCormick*, and *Evans* all fall into this category. The most commonly used statutes of this type have been the Hobbs Act, 18 U.S.C. §1951, and the Mail Fraud law, 18 U.S.C. §1341.[k]

(3) Federal prosecutors may bring charges against state or local officials under federal statutes that, in effect, incorporate the standards of "predicate" statutes, including state bribery statutes. *Isaacs*, *Arthur*, and *L'Hoste* were in this category. Under statutes of this type, violation of one or more predicate statutes, combined with certain additional circumstances, becomes a federal violation. The most important statutes under this heading are the Travel Act, 18 U.S.C. §1952, and the Racketeer Influenced and Corrupt Organizations Act (RICO), 18 U.S.C. §§1961–68. Statutes of the second and third types require that the corrupt activity impinge on some federal interest, such as by affecting interstate commerce or involving use of the mail, but these requirements are often satisfied and therefore have little effect in restraining federal enforcement of corrupt activity.

(4) State prosecutors may prosecute state or local officials under state bribery laws. *Agan* is an example of this type of case.

Because *McNally*, *McCormick*, and *Evans* each were examples of the second situation, they did not entail interpretation of the federal or state bribery statutes. Nevertheless, the decisions are of considerable interest, both theoretical and practical. From a practical standpoint, various factors can inhibit anti-corruption investigations and prosecutions by state and local prosecutors. Federal prosecutions under the Hobbs Act (construed in *McCormick* and *Evans*) and other federal statutes are the most visible and possibly the most numerous anti-corruption actions affecting state and local government.[l] Furthermore, it

---

k. An additional statute, passed in 1984 and used increasingly by federal prosecutors against state and local officials after 1990, is referred to as the "federal program bribery" provision, 18 U.S.C. §666. It prohibits bribery, and also embezzlement and other forms of theft, by employees of governmental entities that receive federal grants. The prohibition is applicable to bribes without regard to whether federal funds are demonstrably affected. See *Salinas v. United States*, 522 U.S. 52 (1997). For commentary on federal program bribery, see George D. Brown, *Stealth Statute—Corruption, The Spending Power, and the Rise of 18 U.S.C. §666*, 73 Notre Dame Law Review 247 (1998).

l. By one count, nearly six thousand state and local officials were convicted of federal corruption charges between 1977 and 1987. See Kenneth J. Meier & Thomas M. Holbrook, *"I Seen My Opportunities and I Took 'Em:" Political Corruption in the American States*, 54 Journal of Politics 135, 136 (1992).

is at least possible that these decisions will affect bribery statutes themselves. The Supreme Court may bring similar views to bear when it comes to interpreting the federal bribery statute, and state courts may find the views of the Supreme Court persuasive when construing their own statutes.

McCormick is the most significant of the cases for our purposes, but each is worth noting. In the first case, *McNally v. United States*, 483 U.S. 350 (1987), Kentucky public officials and others who participated in a scheme to steer state insurance business to benefit either themselves or their political allies were convicted of violating the federal Mail Fraud statute, 18 U.S.C. §1341, which read:

> Whoever, having devised or intending to devise any scheme or artifice to defraud, or for obtaining money or property by means of false or fraudulent pretenses, representations, or promises, ... for the purpose of executing such scheme or artifice [uses the mails or causes them to be used], shall be fined ... or imprisoned ... or both.

Although the diversion of insurance business for defendants' benefit did not actually cost the state any money, they were convicted on an interpretation of the Mail Fraud law that had been accepted by several lower courts, holding that the statute's prohibition extends to "schemes to defraud citizens of their intangible rights to honest and impartial government."

In *McNally*, the Supreme Court rejected this view, holding that the Mail Fraud law "clearly protects property rights, but does not refer to the intangible right of the citizenry to good government." Among several other reasons for this conclusion, the Court stated a preference to avoid an interpretation that "involves the Federal Government in setting standards of disclosure and good government for local and state officials."

The practical effect of *McNally* was short-lived, as Congress in 1988 adopted a new section stating that for purposes of the Mail Fraud law, "the term 'scheme or artifice to defraud' includes a scheme or artifice to deprive another of the intangible right of honest services." 18 U.S.C. §1346. For commentary on *McNally* and the Mail Fraud law, see John C. Coffee, *Modern Mail Fraud: The Restoration of the Public/Private Distinction*, 35 AMERICAN CRIMINAL LAW REVIEW 427 (1998). In your opinion, is the setting of standards of good government for states and localities an appropriate function for the federal government? For a careful and thoughtful consideration of this question, see George D. Brown, *New Federalism's Unanswered Question: Who Should Prosecute State and Local Officials for Political Corruption?*, 60 WASHINGTON AND LEE LAW REVIEW 417 (2003).

McCormick v. United States
500 U.S. 257 (1991)

Justice WHITE delivered the opinion of the Court.

This case requires us to consider whether the Court of Appeals properly affirmed the conviction of petitioner, an elected public official, for extorting property under color of official right in violation of the Hobbs Act, 18 U.S.C. §1951.

I

[McCormick was a member of the West Virginia state legislature who represented a district that had suffered from a shortage of doctors. In 1984, he supported legislation to permit foreign medical school graduates to practice under temporary permits while they were studying for the state licensing examinations. During his reelection campaign, Mc-Cormick told the lobbyist for an organization of the foreign medical graduates "that his campaign was expensive, that he had paid considerable sums out of his own pocket, and that he had not heard anything from the foreign doctors." The lobbyist raised some money from the members of his group and gave McCormick an envelope containing $900 in cash. West Virginia law prohibited cash contributions over $50, and neither McCormick nor the organization reported the gift as a campaign contribution.

McCormick was convicted of extortion under the Hobbs Act, which provides:

(a) Whoever in any way or degree obstructs, delays, or affects commerce ... by way of robbery or extortion ... in violation of this section shall be fined ... or imprisoned ... or both.

(b) as used in this section —

...

(2) The term "extortion" means the obtaining of property from another with his consent, induced by wrongful use of actual or threatened force, violence, or fear, or under color of official right.]

II

McCormick's challenge to the judgment below affirming his conviction is limited to ... his claim that the payments made to him by or on behalf of the doctors were campaign contributions, the receipt of which did not violate the Hobbs Act.... McCormick does not challenge any rulings of the courts below with respect to the application of the Hobbs Act to payments made to nonelected officials or to payments made to elected officials that are properly determined not to be campaign contributions. Hence, we do not consider how the "under color of official right" phrase is to be interpreted and applied in those contexts....

B

We agree with the Court of Appeals that in a case like this it is proper to inquire whether payments made to an elected official are in fact campaign contributions, and we agree that the intention of the parties is a relevant consideration in pursuing this inquiry. But we cannot accept the Court of Appeals' approach to distinguishing between legal and illegal campaign contributions. The Court of Appeals stated that payments to elected officials could violate the Hobbs Act without proof of an explicit *quid pro quo* by proving that the payments "were never intended to be *legitimate* campaign contributions." ...

Serving constituents and supporting legislation that will benefit the district and individuals and groups therein is the everyday business of a legislator. It is also true that campaigns must be run and financed. Money is constantly being solicited on behalf of candidates, who run on platforms and who claim support on the basis of their views and what they intend to do or have done. Whatever ethical considerations and appearances may indicate, to hold that legislators commit the federal crime of extortion when they act for the benefit of constituents or support legislation furthering the interests of some of their constituents, shortly before or after campaign contributions are solicited and received from those beneficiaries, is an unrealistic assessment of what Congress could have meant by making it a crime to obtain property from another, with his consent, "under color of official right." To hold otherwise would open to prosecution not only conduct that has long been thought to be well within the law but also conduct that in a very real sense is unavoidable so long as election campaigns are financed by private contributions or expenditures, as they have been from the beginning of the Nation. It would require statutory language more explicit than the Hobbs Act contains to justify a contrary conclusion.

This is not to say that it is impossible for an elected official to commit extortion in the course of financing an election campaign. Political contributions are of course vulnerable if induced by the use of force, violence, or fear. The receipt of such contributions is also vulnerable under the Act as having been taken under color of official right, but only if the payments are made in return for an explicit promise or undertaking by the official to perform or not to perform an official act. In such situations the official asserts that his official conduct will be controlled by the terms of the promise or undertaking. This is the receipt of money by an elected official under color of official right within the meaning of the Hobbs Act.

This formulation defines the forbidden zone of conduct with sufficient clarity. As the Court of Appeals for the Fifth Circuit observed in *United States v. Dozier*, 672 F.2d 531, 537 (1982):

> A moment's reflection should enable one to distinguish, at least in the abstract, a legitimate solicitation from the exaction of a fee for a benefit conferred or an injury withheld. Whether described familiarly as a payoff or with the Latinate precision of *quid pro quo*, the prohibited exchange is the same: a public official may not demand payment as inducement for the promise to perform (or not to perform) an official act.

The United States agrees that if the payments to McCormick were campaign contributions, proof of a *quid pro quo* would be essential for an extortion conviction and quotes the instruction given on this subject in 9 Department of Justice Manual §9-85A.306, p. 9-1938.134 (Supp.1988-2): "[C]ampaign contributions will not be authorized as the subject of a Hobbs Act prosecution unless they can be proven to have been given in return for the performance of or abstaining from an official act; otherwise any campaign contribution might constitute a violation."

We thus disagree with the Court of Appeals' holding in this case that a *quid pro quo* is not necessary for conviction under the Hobbs Act when an official receives a campaign contribution.[10] By the same token, we hold, as McCormick urges, that the District Court's instruction to the same effect was error.

III

[I]t is true that the trial court instructed that the receipt of voluntary campaign contributions did not violate the Hobbs Act. But under the instructions a contribution was not "voluntary" if given with any expectation of benefit; and as we read the instructions, taken as a whole, the jury was told that it could find McCormick guilty of extortion if any of the payments, even though a campaign contribution, was made by the doctors with the expectation that McCormick's official action would be influenced for their benefit and if McCormick knew that the payment was made with that expectation. It may be that the jury found that none of the payments was a campaign contribution, but it is mere speculation that the jury convicted on this basis rather than on the impermissible

---

10. As noted previously, McCormick's sole contention in this case is that the payments made to him were campaign contributions. Therefore, we do not decide whether a *quid pro quo* requirement exists in other contexts, such as when an elected official receives gifts, meals, travel expenses, or other items of value.

basis that even though the first payment was such a contribution, McCormick's receipt of it was a violation of the Hobbs Act....

V

Accordingly we reverse the judgment of the Court of Appeals and remand for further proceedings consistent with this opinion.

Justice STEVENS, with whom Justice BLACKMUN and Justice O'CONNOR join, dissenting....

In my opinion there is no statutory requirement that illegal agreements, threats, or promises be in writing, or in any particular form. Subtle extortion is just as wrongful—and probably much more common—than the kind of express understanding that the Court's opinion seems to require.

Nevertheless, to prove a violation of the Hobbs Act, I agree with the Court that it is essential that the payment in question be contingent on a mutual understanding that the motivation for the payment is the payer's desire to avoid a specific threatened harm or to obtain a promised benefit that the defendant has the apparent power to deliver, either through the use of force or the use of public office. In this sense, the crime does require a "*quid pro quo.*" ...

This Court's criticism of the District Court's instructions focuses on this single sentence:

Voluntary is that which is freely given without expectation of benefit.

The Court treats this sentence as though it authorized the jury to find that a legitimate campaign contribution is involuntary and constitutes extortion whenever the contributor expects to benefit from the candidate's election. In my opinion this is a gross misreading of that sentence in the context of the entire set of instructions.

In context, the sentence in question advised the jury that a payment is voluntary if it is made without the expectation of a benefit that is specifically contingent upon the payment. An expectation that the donor will benefit from the election of a candidate who, once in office, would support particular legislation regardless of whether or not the contribution is made, would not make the payment contingent or involuntary in that sense; such a payment would be "voluntary" under a fair reading of the instructions, and the candidate's solicitation of such contributions from donors who would benefit from his or her election is perfectly legitimate. If, however, the donor and candidate know that the candidate's support of the proposed legislation is contingent upon the payment, the contribution may be found by a jury to have been involuntary or extorted.

In my judgment, the instructions, read as a whole, properly focused the jury's attention on the critical issue of the candidate's and contributor's intent at the time the specific payment was made....

I respectfully dissent.

[A concurring opinion by Justice Scalia is omitted.]

Notes and Questions

1. Is Justice Stevens' conception of a *quid pro quo* the same as the majority's?

2. From a practical standpoint, the important question about *McCormick* is where it leads. Does the same *quid pro quo* requirement apply to benefits that are not campaign contributions? When campaign contributions are at issue, will the same *quid pro quo* re-

quirement be read into other federal anti-bribery statutes, especially 18 U.S.C. §201? Will state and federal courts read the same requirement into *state* bribery laws? Will the Supreme Court and other courts adhere to *McCormick*'s strict definition of the *quid pro quo* requirement wherever it is applicable? Although there have been many decisions since then, a few of which are mentioned in these notes, there are few definitive answers.

3. Should the *McCormick* requirement of an "explicit promise or undertaking" be applied to a Hobbs Act prosecution when the benefit provided to the official is not a campaign contribution? In *United States v. Montoya*, 945 F.2d 1068, 1074 n.2 (9th Cir. 1991), the court wrote:

> In his defense to several of the extortion charges, Montoya has argued that the cash payments he received were legitimate honoraria. Although *McCormick* involved claimed campaign contributions, we see no rational distinction between cash payments claimed by the official to be lawful campaign contributions or those alleged to be legitimate honoraria. The critical question is whether the payments were induced and whether a *quid pro quo* exists, not how an official labels the payments in his defense to a charge that the payments were extorted.

Do you agree? In *United States v. Torcasio*, 959 F.2d 503, 506 (4th Cir. 1992), cert. denied 507 U.S. 909 (1993), a different court rejected the claim that *McCormick* required the government to prove a specific *quid pro quo* in a case not involving campaign contributions.

4. Is the question addressed in Note 3 affected by EVANS v. UNITED STATES, 504 U.S. 255 (1992), the third and last Supreme Court decision in our series? The central issue in *Evans* was whether the word "induced" in paragraph (b)(2) of the Hobbs Act means that the official must ask for or in some other way initiate or actively bring about the forbidden transaction.[m] The majority opinion in *Evans* is introduced by the statement:

> We granted certiorari to resolve a conflict in the Circuits over the question whether an affirmative act of inducement by a public official, such as a demand, is an element of the offense of extortion "under color of official right" prohibited by the Hobbs Act. We agree with the Court of Appeals for the Eleventh Circuit that it is not, and therefore affirm the judgment of the court below.

Evans, a member of the Board of Commissioners of DeKalb County, Georgia, had numerous conversations over a period of a year-and-a-half with an undercover FBI agent posing as a real estate developer seeking to rezone a tract of land. All or nearly all of the conversations were initiated by the agent. Near the end of the period, the agent gave Evans $7,000 in cash and a campaign contribution of $1,000. The jury could have found that Evans

> accepted the cash knowing that it was intended to ensure that he would vote in favor of the rezoning application and that he would try to persuade his fellow commissioners to do likewise. Thus, although petitioner did not initiate the transaction, his acceptance of the bribe constituted an implicit promise to use his official position to serve the interests of the bribe-giver.

The jury instructions correctly anticipated *McCormick*, advising that a campaign contribution by a person with business pending before an official was not sufficient for a vi-

---

m. Paragraph (b)(2), it will be recalled, reads:
The term "extortion" means the obtaining of property from another, with his consent, induced by wrongful use of actual or threatened force, violence, or fear, or under color of official right.

olation of the Hobbs Act. But if the official "demands or accepts money in exchange for [a] specific requested exercise of his or her official power, such a demand or acceptance does constitute a violation of the Hobbs Act regardless of whether the payment is made in the form of a campaign contribution." Evans' objection to the jury instruction was that it permitted a conviction based on a mere "acceptance" of money in exchange for favorable official action, without requiring a demand or any affirmative act of inducement.

Relying in large part on historical research and analysis by James Lindgren, *The Elusive Distinction Between Bribery and Extortion: From the Common Law to the Hobbs Act*, 35 UCLA LAW REVIEW 815 (1988), the Court concluded inducement by the official was not an element of the offense.

> At common law, extortion was an offense committed by a public official who took "by colour of his office" money that was not due to him for the performance of his official duties. Extortion by the public official was the rough equivalent of what we would now describe as "taking a bribe." It is clear that petitioner committed that offense.

Since a portion of the payment to Evans was a campaign contribution, the Court briefly addressed *McCormick*.

> We reject petitioner's criticism of the instruction and conclude that it satisfies the *quid pro quo* requirement of *McCormick*, because the offense is completed at the time when the public official receives a payment in return for his agreement to perform specific official acts;[n] fulfillment of the *quid pro quo* is not an element of the offense.... We hold today that the Government need only show that a public official has obtained a payment to which he was not entitled, knowing that the payment was made in return for official acts.[o]

Referring to the last sentence of this quotation, Justice Kennedy, concurring in *Evans*, said that "this language requires a *quid pro quo* as an element of the Government's case in a prosecution" under the "color of official right" portion of the Hobbs Act. In other words, Kennedy interpreted the majority opinion as extending *McCormick* to all "color of official right" cases, whether or not the payment to the official is a campaign contribution. Do you agree?

5. Both *McCormick* and *Evans* arose under the Hobbs Act, whose definition of extortion is stated in general terms. Is the requirement of a *quid pro quo* applicable to cases in which campaign contributions are prosecuted under bribery statutes whose elements are specified in greater detail, such as 18 U.S.C. §201? In *United States v. McDade*, 827 F.Supp. 1153, 1171 (E.D. Pa. 1993), the court expressed the view that *McCormick* is probably inapplicable to Section 201(c), the unlawful gratuities prohibition:

> Any comparison of *McCormick* to the case at bar must, of course, start with the obvious observation that *McCormick* was a Hobbs Act case, while the current argument is about the gratuities statute. It is thus doubtful whether *McCormick* controls at all.

Do you agree? If so, would you also regard *McCormick* as inapplicable to a bribery prosecution under Section 201(b)?

---

n. Note that in its description of what the jury presumably found, quoted above, the Court referred to an *implicit* promise. Compare this to *McCormick*'s requirement of an *explicit* promise or undertaking.— EDS.

o. The majority opinion in *Evans* was written by Justice Stevens, who had dissented in *McCormick*. Justice Thomas dissented, joined by Justice Scalia and Chief Justice Rehnquist.

A similar question arises when state and local officials are prosecuted under federal statutes that incorporate state bribery laws. Violations of the state laws can constitute "predicate" offenses that, when added to other elements, result in a federal crime. For example, RICO, 18 U.S.C. §§1961–1968, defines a "pattern of racketeering activity" as at least two acts of racketeering activity, which can include violations of state bribery laws. Section 1962(c) defines the circumstances in which a "pattern of racketeering activity" violates RICO. If the transaction that allegedly violates a state bribery law in a RICO prosecution is a campaign contribution, must the *quid pro quo* requirement of *McCormick* be satisfied? See *United States v. Mokol*, 957 F.2d 1410 (7th Cir.), cert. denied 506 U.S. 899 (1992); *United States v. Allen*, 10 F.3d 405, 410–11 (7th Cir. 1993).

6. In Notes 3 through 5 we considered whether the *quid pro quo* required by *McCormick* is applicable in various situations. Now we must consider the nature of that requirement. *McCormick* says there is a violation "only if the payments are made in return for an explicit promise or undertaking by the official to perform or not to perform an official act. In such situations the official asserts that his official conduct will be controlled by the terms of the promise or undertaking." This formulation has the virtue at least of being relatively clear. But does it serve to distinguish corrupt from innocent conduct? Not according to Dennis F. Thompson, *Mediated Corruption: The Case of the Keating Five*, 87 AMERICAN POLITICAL SCIENCE REVIEW 369, 374–75 (1993):

> There is ... no good reason to believe that connections between contributions and benefits that are proximate and explicit are any more corrupt than connections that are indirect and implicit. The former may be only the more detectable — not necessarily the more deliberate or damaging — form of corruption.

The *McCormick* formulation is criticized as both unnecessary and too restrictive by James Lindgren, *The Theory, History, and Practice of the Bribery-Extortion Distinction*, 141 UNIVERSITY OF PENNSYLVANIA LAW REVIEW 1695, 1710–11 (1993):

> It appears that Justice White was concerned about either the unjust conviction of public officials for innocent campaign contributions or the chilling effect on campaign financing. He doesn't give any examples of the pre-existing law being too vigorously applied. Indeed, I can't think of a single case in which a conviction for extortion has withstood challenge when the official acted properly and the court applied the usual common law rule requiring that the official taking be wrongful or corrupt. Certainly, even Congress can't claim that the pre-existing law chilled too many large contributions. If we ask whether we have too little influence peddling in the context of campaign finances, too much influence peddling, or an optimal amount, I think everyone thinks that we have too much. So over-deterrence isn't a problem....

> Let's look at two situations, both involving corrupt takings without an explicit quid pro quo:

>> (1) An elected judge approaches a lawyer in a major case pending before the judge and says, "I haven't heard from you yet. Would you donate $100,000 to my re-election fund?" Result: not official extortion under Justice White's test.

>> (2) An elected legislator approaches a businessman and says, "If you pay me $100,000 for my campaign, I can't promise you how I'll vote on the many pieces of legislation affecting your company — that would be illegal. But if you contribute, I *predict* that I will vote your way." Result: not official extortion under Justice White's test.

Although both of these situations would have been Hobbs Act extortion under color of official right before *McCormick*, were one to judge only from Justice White's odd opinion in *McCormick*, they wouldn't be now. Quid pro quos may or not be implied in these situations, but they certainly aren't explicit. Neither explicitly promises any specific action.

Must the *McCormick* test be applied as strictly as Professor Lindgren suggests? See *United States v. Carpenter*, 961 F.2d 824, 827 (9th Cir.), cert. denied 506 U.S. 919 (1992). Whether or not it must be, is the test as stated in *McCormick* still in effect? We have seen that in *Evans*, Justice Stevens' summary of the majority's holding was "that the Government need only show that a public official has obtained a payment to which he was not entitled, knowing that the payment was made in return for official acts." Was the phrase "in return for" intended to set forth a standard, as opposed to being simply a general reference to some connection, whatever it might be, that must exist between the payment and the official acts? If it was intended to set forth a standard, is it different from the *McCormick quid pro quo* requirement?

Justice Kennedy, concurring in *Evans*, set forth his conception of *quid pro quo*:

> The requirement of a *quid pro quo* means that without pretense of any entitlement to the payment, a public official violates [the Hobbs Act] if he intends the payor to believe that absent payment the official is likely to abuse his office and his trust to the detriment and injury of the prospective payor or to give the prospective payor less favorable treatment if the *quid pro quo* is not satisfied. The official and the payor need not state the *quid pro quo* in express terms, for otherwise the law's effect could be frustrated by knowing winks and nods. The inducement from the official is criminal if it is express or if it is implied from his words and actions, so long as he intends it to be so and the payor so interprets it.

Is Kennedy's conception of *quid pro quo* different from *McCormick*'s? From Stevens' phrase, "in return for"? See *United States v. Coyne*, 4 F.3d 100, 111 (2d Cir. 1993), cert. denied 510 U.S. 1095 (1994) ("Proof of an explicit promise at the time of payment to perform certain acts is not necessary....); *United States v. Hairston*, 46 F.3d 361, 365 (4th Cir. 1995) (describing the *quid pro quo* requirement as "not onerous."). Neither *Coyne* nor *Hairston* involved campaign contributions. Should that have mattered?

7. *McCormick* and the other cases we have been considering are based on the premise that a requirement of a *quid pro quo* will prevent extortion and bribery laws from overly broad coverage that may criminalize innocent or at least tolerable conduct. This premise is challenged by Lindgren, *supra*, 141 University of Pennsylvania Law Review at 1736–38, who nonetheless finds Justice Stevens' "in return for" formulation in *Evans* an acceptable standard:

> The problem that the Court is trying to solve is that elected officials often receive contributions from people with pending government business. Such contributions aren't necessarily corrupt. The old way to separate corrupt takings from noncorrupt contributions was to ask the ultimate question: Are they corrupt or wrongful? It appears that the Court thinks that a quid pro quo requirement does the same job separating wrongful takings from legitimate contributions. But does it?

Consider these explicit quid pro quos that aren't corrupt (or at least aren't corrupt enough to count as official extortion):

(1) A legislator says to a trucking company owner, "If you make this large contribution to my campaign, I promise you three things. First, I won't vote on any trucking legislation without calling you first. Second, when you call me, I will drop whatever official business I am doing to take your call personally. Third, when you or your clients come to town, I will rearrange my schedule whenever possible to entertain you in the legislative dining room. I can't promise you how I'll vote, but you can buy what any large contributor buys: direct access to me."

(2) A legislator says to a large contributor, "If you give me a large contribution, I'll consult you on my choice of my next chief of staff. Understand me, he'll be working for me, not you. But I promise you that I'll pick someone you can work with."

The contributor gets an explicit quid pro quo — access to the legislator or consultation on a staff appointment. Someone with very high ethical standards may view these last two examples as corrupt, but the Supreme Court probably wouldn't. Indeed, the legislators' willingness to state the deals clearly suggests that they wouldn't think they are corrupt. Yet both situations might meet Justices White's, Stevens's, and Kennedy's reciprocity tests, at least without a specific filter that the agreements be corrupt. Only by bringing in the corrupt intent element ... can a jury make sense of these examples. Thus, if these examples don't involve obtaining property corruptly or wrongfully, even an explicit quid pro quo isn't enough for extortion.

But then, what does the explicit quid pro quo requirement add other than noise? If one must test extortion by whether it's corrupt in any event, a reciprocity requirement only adds another layer that may exculpate those otherwise guilty of wrongful extortion. The nature of the exchange must be examined in any event.

The obvious objection to relying on the corruption requirement alone is its vagueness. A quid pro quo requirement will give better notice than a simple corruption requirement. Anytime you're dealing with behavior as complex as promises and threats, you can't nail down every possible permutation in advance. The best approach is to use judicial decisionmaking to clarify ambiguities and give guidance to triers of fact. *Evans* does this by requiring reciprocity.

8. At this point, it is perhaps appropriate to say that if you are not confused, you have not been following the argument![p] If anything emerges from the case law we have reviewed, it is that courts are torn between the desire to set forth clear standards for applying bribery-type offenses and the recognition that the only clear standard that suggests itself — requirement of a more or less explicit agreement between the parties that the gift or campaign contribution is made in exchange for favorable official action — fails to match normative intuitions about what is and is not corrupt conduct. To borrow Justice Kennedy's phrase, if winks and nods suffice for an "intent to influence" or *quid pro quo* requirement, then the standard of conduct imposed by the law can never be clear. But if something

---

p. But if you regret we have not provided more detail, you can satisfy your odd tastes with Daniel Lowenstein, *When Is a Campaign Contribution a Bribe?*, in PUBLIC AND PRIVATE CORRUPTION (William C. Heffernan & John Kleinig, eds., 2004).

more explicit than winks and nods is required for a violation, then the law will punish the most inept, not the most corrupt. When considered in light of the intractability of the underlying problem, no wonder the case law is confused. Perhaps as a measure of that confusion, consider again Cases 1 through 4 in the hypotheticals at the beginning of this section. Are the contributors and legislators guilty of bribery or related offenses? And consider again whether the result would be different if the payments in each case were a personal gift rather than a campaign contribution.

United States v. Sun-Diamond Growers of California
526 U.S. 398 (1999)

Justice SCALIA delivered the opinion of the Court.

Talmudic sages believed that judges who accepted bribes would be punished by eventually losing all knowledge of the divine law. The Federal Government, dealing with many public officials who are not judges, and with at least some judges for whom this sanction holds no terror, has constructed a framework of human laws and regulations defining various sorts of impermissible gifts, and punishing those who give or receive them with administrative sanctions, fines, and incarceration. One element of that framework is 18 U.S.C. §201(c)(1)(A), the "illegal gratuity statute," which prohibits giving "anything of value" to a present, past, or future public official "for or because of any official act performed or to be performed by such public official." In this case, we consider whether conviction under the illegal gratuity statute requires any showing beyond the fact that a gratuity was given because of the recipient's official position.

I

Respondent is a trade association that engaged in marketing and lobbying activities on behalf of its member cooperatives, which were owned by approximately 5,000 individual growers of raisins, figs, walnuts, prunes, and hazelnuts. Petitioner United States is represented by Independent Counsel Donald Smaltz, who, as a consequence of his investigation of former Secretary of Agriculture Michael Espy, charged respondent with, *inter alia*, making illegal gifts to Espy in violation of §201(c)(1)(A). That statute provides, in relevant part, that anyone who

> otherwise than as provided by law for the proper discharge of official duty ... directly or indirectly gives, offers, or promises anything of value to any public official, former public official, or person selected to be a public official, for or because of any official act performed or to be performed by such public official, former public official, or person selected to be a public official ... shall be fined under this title or imprisoned for not more than two years, or both.

Count One of the indictment charged Sun-Diamond with giving Espy approximately $5,900 in illegal gratuities: tickets to the 1993 U.S. Open Tennis Tournament (worth $2,295), luggage ($2,427), meals ($665), and a framed print and crystal bowl ($524). The indictment alluded to two matters in which respondent had an interest in favorable treatment from the Secretary at the time it bestowed the gratuities. [First, Sun-Diamond hoped for favorable regulations from the Secretary of Agriculture defining which agricultural entities would be eligible for export subsidies. Second, Sun-Diamond sought the Secretary's assistance in persuading the Environmental Protection Agency to abandon or soften a proposed rule regulating a certain pesticide, methyl bromide.]

Although describing these two matters before the Secretary in which respondent had an interest, the indictment did not allege a specific connection between either of them — or between any other action of the Secretary — and the gratuities conferred....

II

[Justice Scalia described the textual juxtaposition of the bribery offense in Section 201(b) and the gratuity offense in Section 201(c), as at the beginning of Part II of this chapter.]

The distinguishing feature of each crime is its intent element. Bribery requires intent "to influence" an official act or "to be influenced" in an official act, while illegal gratuity requires only that the gratuity be given or accepted "for or because of" an official act. In other words, for bribery there must be a *quid pro quo* — a specific intent to give or receive something of value *in exchange* for an official act. An illegal gratuity, on the other hand, may constitute merely a reward for some future act that the public official will take (and may already have determined to take), or for a past act that he has already taken....

The District Court's instructions in this case, in differentiating between a bribe and an illegal gratuity, correctly noted that only a bribe requires proof of a *quid pro quo*. The point in controversy here is that the instructions went on to suggest that §201(c)(1)(A), unlike the bribery statute, did not require any connection between respondent's intent and a specific official act. It would be satisfied, according to the instructions, merely by a showing that respondent gave Secretary Espy a gratuity because of his official position — perhaps, for example, to build a reservoir of goodwill that might ultimately affect one or more of a multitude of unspecified acts, now and in the future....

In our view, this interpretation does not fit comfortably with the statutory text, which prohibits only gratuities given or received "for or because of *any official act* performed or to be performed" (emphasis added). It seems to us that this means "for or because of some particular official act of whatever identity" — just as the question "Do you like any composer?" normally means "Do you like some particular composer?" It is linguistically possible, of course, for the phrase to mean "for or because of official acts in general, without specification as to which one" — just as the question "Do you like any composer?" could mean "Do you like all composers, no matter what their names or music?" But the former seems to us the more natural meaning, especially given the complex structure of the provision before us here. Why go through the trouble of requiring that the gift be made "for or because of any official act performed or to be performed by such public official," and then defining "official act" (in §201(a)(3)) to mean "any decision or action on any question, matter, cause, suit, proceeding or controversy, which may at any time be pending, or which may by law be brought before any public official, in such official's official capacity," when, if the Government's interpretation were correct, it would have sufficed to say "for or because of such official's ability to favor the donor in executing the functions of his office"? The insistence upon an "official act," carefully defined, seems pregnant with the requirement that some particular official act be identified and proved.

Besides thinking that this is the more natural meaning of §201(c)(1)(A), we are inclined to believe it correct because of the peculiar results that the Government's alternative reading would produce. It would criminalize, for example, token gifts to the President based on his official position and not linked to any identifiable act — such as the replica jerseys given by championship sports teams each year during ceremonial White House visits. Similarly, it would criminalize a high school principal's gift of a school baseball cap to the Secretary of Education, by reason of his office, on the occasion of the latter's visit to the school. That these examples are not fanciful is demonstrated by the fact that counsel for the United States maintained at oral argument that a group of farmers would violate §201(c)(1)(A) by providing a complimentary lunch for the Secretary of Agriculture in conjunction with his speech to the farmers concerning various matters of USDA policy— so long as the Secretary had before him, or had in prospect, matters affecting the farmers. Of course the Secretary of Agriculture *always* has before him or in prospect matters that affect farmers, just as the President always has before him or in prospect matters that affect college and professional sports, and the Secretary of Education matters that affect high schools.

It might be said in reply to this that the more narrow interpretation of the statute can also produce some peculiar results. In fact, in the above-given examples, the gifts could easily be regarded as having been conferred, not only because of the official's position as President or Secretary, but also (and perhaps principally) "for or because of" the official acts of receiving the sports teams at the White House, visiting the high school, and speaking to the farmers about USDA policy, respectively. The answer to this objection is that those actions—while they are assuredly "official acts" in some sense—are not "official acts" within the meaning of the statute, which, as we have noted, defines "official act" to mean "any decision or action on any question, matter, cause, suit, proceeding or controversy, which may at any time be pending, or which may by law be brought before any public official, in such official's official capacity, or in such official's place of trust or profit." 18 U.S.C. §201(a)(3). Thus, when the violation is linked to a particular "official act," it is possible to eliminate the absurdities *through the definition of that term.* When, however, no particular "official act" need be identified, and the giving of gifts by reason of the recipient's mere tenure in office constitutes a violation, nothing but the Government's discretion prevents the foregoing examples from being prosecuted.

[We omit Justice Scalia's responses to additional statutory arguments tendered by the government. In Part III, Justice Scalia rejected the government's argument that the erroneous jury instruction was harmless error.]

We hold that, in order to establish a violation of 18 U.S.C. §201(c)(1)(A), the Government must prove a link between a thing of value conferred upon a public official and a specific "official act" for or because of which it was given. . . .

Notes and Questions

1. The Court's interpretation of Section 201(c)(1)(A) in *Sun-Diamond* is narrower than the interpretation urged by the government and adopted by the lower courts. But is it narrow enough for the gratuities statute to be applied comfortably to campaign contributions? Consider again the hypothetical case of Victoria, presented earlier in this chapter. Victoria strongly favored a particular bill and mailed $25 campaign contributions to each of the three members of the House of Representatives from her state who voted in favor of the bill. Has she violated 18 U.S.C. §201(c)? Does *Sun-Diamond* have any bearing on her case?

2. Consider Justice Scalia's statement relating to Section 201(b), the bribery offense:

Bribery requires intent "to influence" an official act or "to be influenced" in an official act, while illegal gratuity requires only that the gratuity be given or accepted "for or because of" an official act. In other words, for bribery there must be a *quid pro quo*—a specific intent to give or receive something of value *in exchange* for an official act.

Is this statement dictum, or part of the *Sun-Diamond* holding? Does the second sentence simply paraphrase the quoted statutory phrases in the first sentence or does it change the meaning of those phrases? In this passage, does the Court apply the standard set up in *McCormick* for Hobbs Act campaign contribution cases to *all* cases arising under the main federal bribery statute? Recall that in *McCormick*, Justice White said the agreement had to be explicit. Under Justice Scalia's reading of the bribery statute, must the exchange be explicit? Would Justice Scalia find a violation if the exchange occurred through winks and nods?

3. The gratuity statute refers to a benefit conferred or received for or because of an official act "performed or to be performed." Charles B. Klein, *What Exactly Is an Unlawful Gratuity After* United States v. Sun-Diamond Growers?, 68 George Washington Law Review 117, 119 (1999), explains:

> A lobbyist commits a traditional "backward-looking gratuity" violation when giving a gift to a U.S. senator to reward (or thank) the senator for previously voting to pass a particular bill. A lobbyist commits a traditional forward-looking gratuity when giving a gift to a U.S. senator to reward (or thank) the senator for a vote the senator already has committed to make, but has not yet made.

Some courts, especially the D.C. Circuit in *Brewster, supra,* and other cases, have extended the forward-looking gratuity violation to situations in which the official has not decided or has not made his or her intention clear, so that the gift cannot be regarded as a reward. If the gift is a violation at all, it must be on the theory that it is intended to influence the official decision, albeit to a lesser degree than is required for violation of the bribery statute. Thus, *Brewster* held that unlawful gratuity is a lesser included offense within bribery. Klein argues strenuously against the D.C. Circuit's interpretation of the gratuity statute. He maintains that only a "reward" should constitute an unlawful gratuity, so that there could be no forward-looking violation except when the official has made his or her intention known. Klein contends that *Sun-Diamond* is at least compatible with the "reward" interpretation of Section 201(c). But Klein concedes that the reward interpretation implies a broad interpretation of the "intent to influence" component of the bribery offense. Otherwise, under his interpretation, a person making a gift as a reward under circumstances showing that influence is out of the question would be guilty of an unlawful gratuity, while a person making a gift intending it to influence the official would not commit either a bribe or an unlawful gratuity, so long as the intent to influence falls short of whatever *quid pro quo* is required for a bribe. Whether *Sun-Diamond* is compatible with a broad reading of Section 201(b)'s "intent to influence" is questionable, to say the least.

4. Since the 1960s, scandal and corruption have played a more prominent role in American politics than had been true in the decades before. The press and activist groups such as Common Cause have played a major part in this development, but one can find periods of similar activity earlier in American history. What is perhaps unprecedented in the past few decades is the extent to which numerous federal, state, and local regulations have been enacted to combat corruption and other forms of impropriety, real or imagined, and the amount of civil and criminal litigation to enforce such regulations. There has been a considerable backlash against these developments. See, e.g., Frank Anechiaricho & James B. Jacobs, The Pursuit of Absolute Integrity: How Corruption Control Makes Government Ineffective (1996); Steven G. Calabresi, *Some Structural*

Consequences of the Increased Use of Ethics Probes as Political Weapons, 11 JOURNAL OF
LAW & POLITICS 521 (1995); Suzanne Garment, SCANDAL: THE CULTURE OF MISTRUST IN
AMERICAN POLITICS (1992); Benjamin Ginsberg & Martin Shefter, POLITICS BY OTHER
MEANS: POLITICIANS, PROSECUTORS, AND THE PRESS FROM WATERGATE TO WHITEWATER
(1999); Peter W. Morgan & Glenn H. Reynolds, THE APPEARANCE OF IMPROPRIETY: HOW
THE ETHICS WARS HAVE UNDERMINED AMERICAN GOVERNMENT, BUSINESS, AND SOCI-
ETY (1997). In decisions like *McNally, McCormick*, and *Sun-Diamond*, has the Supreme
Court brought its considerable weight to bear on the side of those reacting against what
they see as the excesses of the post-Watergate era? A qualifiedly affirmative answer to this
question is given by George D. Brown, *Putting Watergate Behind Us*—Salinas, Sun-Dia-
mond, *and Two Views of the Anticorruption Model*, 74 TULANE LAW REVIEW 747 (2000).
For more particular focus on the gratuity offense, see George D. Brown, *The Gratuities
Debate and Campaign Reform: How Strong Is the Link?*, 52 WAYNE LAW REVIEW 1371
(2006).

5. Meanwhile, back in the states, *Agan* is one of very few cases defining the circumstances under which bribery statutes apply to campaign contributions. In *People
v. Deegan*, 509 N.E.2d 345 (N.Y. 1987), the New York Court of Appeals said without
supporting analysis that evidence was sufficient to support a bribery charge when it
supported an inference that an elected official "changed his vote on a proposed rate
increase ... in exchange for a promise of future campaign contributions." Was such an
exchange necessary for a conviction? In *People v. Bac Tran*, 603 N.E.2d 950 (N.Y. 1992),
which did not involve campaign contributions, the Court of Appeals considered the effects of changes in the New York bribery statute in 1965 that substituted the requirement of an "agreement or understanding" for the previous requirement of an "intent
to influence." The court regarded this change in language as signaling "a new and different notion. The key element was changed on its face to something qualitatively and
quantitatively higher than the long-standing, simple 'intent to influence.'" In particular, a benefit conferred with only "the hope that the public servant would be influenced thereby" did not constitute a bribe. "Ironically," the court added, "the crime of
attempted bribery ... may be proved when a prosecutor satisfies its burden of proof by
a showing of only intent."

In a few states, bribery statutes avoid the problem by specifically exempting many contributions. Thus, Texas Penal Code §36.02(a)(4) and (d) exempt campaign contributions
from the bribery statute if they are made and reported in accord with Texas campaign finance regulations, unless the contribution is offered or accepted "pursuant to an express
agreement to take or withhold a specific exercise of official discretion if such exercise of official discretion would not have been taken or withheld but for" the contribution. In *People v. Brandstetter*, 430 N.E.2d 731 (Ill.App.), cert. denied 459 U.S. 988 (1982), several
Illinois statutes were read together to reach a result similar to that set forth in the Texas statute.
In *Brandstetter*, the defendant was a volunteer active in the effort to persuade the Illinois
legislature to ratify the Equal Rights Amendment. She handed a legislator a hand-written
note reading: "Mr. Swanstrom the offer for help in your election & $1000 for your cam-
paign for Pro ERA vote." On the basis of this note, her bribery conviction was affirmed.q

A statutory exemption in Oregon goes further than those in Texas and Illinois. Oregon Revised Statutes §162.015(1) requires a "pecuniary benefit" for a bribe, but "pecuniary
benefit" is defined by Section 162.005(1) to exclude "a political campaign contribution reported in accordance with" Oregon campaign finance regulations. The exclusion appears

---

q. Review, in light of this paragraph, footnote 3 of the *Agan* decision.

to apply even if the contribution is made expressly in exchange for a particular official action.[r]

D. Official Act

Officials have private lives within the bounds of which they presumably are free to be influenced by whatever considerations they choose. Between those actions that clearly are performed in an official capacity and those that are clearly private, there are actions that have mixed public and private elements, particularly in the case of higher level officials whose influence is likely to extend beyond their legally defined powers.

State v. Bowling
427 P.2d 928 (Ariz. App. 1967)

MOLLOY, Judge.

The defendants in this action appeal from convictions ... of receiving a bribe, while a member of the Arizona State Legislature, "... upon an understanding that their official opinions, judgments and actions should be influenced thereby ...".

The facts giving rise to these charges are substantially without dispute. A resident of Pima county by the name of Jerry Hanson, the co-proprietor of a tavern, was desirous of obtaining a new liquor license for his business, which would permit the sale of additional types of liquor. He had a conversation with Bowling, one of the defendants, who was at the time a member of the House of Representatives of the Arizona State Legislature, about assistance in obtaining such license. Bowling informed Hanson that he might be able to assist him, and arranged a meeting between Hanson, himself, and the other defendant, Cook, who was also a member of the Arizona House of Representatives. Hanson testified that Cook was introduced to him only as a legislator, while Bowling testified that Cook was introduced as a real estate broker. At this meeting, Hanson was informed that it would cost approximately $5,000 for the license over and above regular license fees and at a subsequent meeting, it was agreed that Hanson would pay $4,200, over and above the normal license fees, if the liquor license was obtained for him.

An application for such a license was duly submitted and a personal conference with Mr. John Duncan, Superintendent of Liquor Licenses and Control for the State of Arizona, followed, with Hanson, Bowling and Cook all speaking in behalf of the issuance of the license. The statements made in support of issuing the license were in the nature of character references for Hanson and his father, who was a partner in the tavern, and included the argument that such a license was needed because two families were to be supported from this one business. There was no showing in the evidence of any inducements being offered to Mr. Duncan to issue the license nor of any improper persuasions advanced. The testimony is undisputed that Hanson was fully qualified under applicable law for the issuance of the license and that the location as to which the license application pertained fulfilled all of the legal requirements for such a license.

---

r. In *State v. Gyenes*, 855 P.2d 642 (Or.App. 1993), the exclusion was extended to certain cases in which the contribution is not reported.

About a month after the conversation with Duncan, Cook contacted Hanson to inform him that the license had been issued, and Cook together with Bowling, brought the license to Hanson's home, where Hanson gave them $4,200 in cash. Bowling testified that all of this money was received and retained by Cook; Cook did not take the stand during the trial....

Applicable law gives to the Superintendent of Liquor Licenses and Control carte blanche discretion in selecting the recipients of the "quota" of new licenses available each year.... The statutes do not provide for a hearing at which various applicants may be given the opportunity to establish better entitlement. [T]here were approximately thirty-five applicants for [the Pima County quota of] eleven licenses....

[Appellants were convicted of] the acceptance of a bribe by a legislator as proscribed in A.R.S. §13-286, reading as follows:

> A member of the legislature who asks, receives or agrees to receive a bribe upon an understanding that his *official* vote, opinion, judgment or action shall be influenced thereby, or shall be given in any particular manner, or upon any particular side of a question or matter upon which he may be required to act in his *official capacity*, or casts, or offers or promises to cast, an *official* vote in consideration that another member of the legislature will cast such vote, either upon the same or another question, shall be punished by imprisonment.... (Emphasis added)

The appellants contend that there is a complete absence of any proof that there was any understanding, that the "official vote, opinion, judgment or action" of these defendants would be influenced by the monies received as established in this record. A leading case in Arizona in this area of our law, *State v. Hendricks*, 66 Ariz. 235, 186 P.2d 943 (1947), quotes with approval from 1 Burdick, Law of Crime §291, as follows:

> The act intended to be influenced must be connected with one's official or public duty, although the duty may possibly arise only in the future, but if the act is associated with official duty, it is immaterial whether the bribed person has, or has not, authority to do that specific thing, since the essence of the crime is the fact that he agreed to do it under color of office.

The court in *Hendricks* proceeded to expound on this requirement as follows:

> The rule requiring that the matter in which the bribe is attempted be related to the officer's duty before it can be a crime, is a wise one. The possible perversion of justice is the touchstone and guide. And though it might be morally improper and may well involve some other crime to give or offer money to an officer to do an act totally unrelated to his job, it would not be bribery.

... No statute has been called to our attention which in any way suggests that a legislator has a duty to solicit liquor licenses before the Superintendent of Liquor Licenses and Control. Under our statutes, there is little connection between a member of the lower house of our legislature and this licensing agency. The Superintendent is appointed by the Governor of this State with the advice and consent of the State Senate and it is only the Governor who may remove him, subject to review in the court. That there is an inherent impropriety in the defendants' solicitation, however, is apparent when it is remembered that they made no disclosure to the Superintendent that they were appearing before him for remuneration and that as legislators they had some control over his salary and over all monies expended by his department.

We accept the proposition, urged by the State, that the official duties of a public officer need not be prescribed by statute but may be imposed by regulation or by usage and custom. Cited decisions, such as *United States v. Birdsall*, 233 U.S. 223 (1913), *Daniels v. United States*, 17 F.2d 339 (9th Cir. 1927), and *Cohen v. United States*, 144 F.2d 984 (9th Cir. 1944), so hold.

... In these cases we see proof that is lacking here. In order to satisfy the requirements of these cases, we believe there would have to be substantial proof that there was a custom or usage for legislators to make fair and impartial—and hence "official"—recommendations to the Superintendent of Liquor Licenses and Control as to which applicants should receive an available license.

Apparently realizing a deficiency in this regard, the prosecuting attorney elicited from the witness Hanson the following testimony:

> Q I believe you testified before the jury went out that you were familiar around 1963 of the habit, custom and tradition here in Pima County for applicants obtaining licenses out of Mr. Duncan's office; is that correct?
>
> A Yes.
>
> Q What is that habit, custom and usage, sir? What was it at that time?
>
> A Going through a legislator to obtain one.
>
> Q In what capacity did you have to go through a legislator?
>
> A Money.

The foundation for this testimony was that Mr. Hanson was acquainted with 90 per cent of the bar owners in Tucson; that he had been on a board of directors and a member of the Retail Liquor Dealers Association; and that he knew from "hearsay" that it was customary to go through a legislator to get a liquor license. There was no other evidence of similar import. The proof presented leaves one with the innuendo that it is customary for legislators to accept money to do exactly what the defendants did in this case. However, Hanson was unable to give the name of any other legislator who had ever acted similarly and professed to know, without giving any names, only four other instances when a license had ever been secured through a legislator.

This proof, we hold, fails to close the gap in the establishment of criminality in two respects. First, the proof submitted in no way tends to prove that there was an obligation under any custom or usage for the legislator to make a good faith recommendation on the merits of the issuance of liquor licenses. Absent this, it is our belief that the purported custom only tended to show conduct of other legislators equally unsavory, but equally outside of the "official" duties of legislators.

Secondly, we do not believe that the testimonial qualifications of Hanson were such as to establish in sufficient probative force a custom and usage so as to predicate a conviction in a criminal court thereon. Generally, proof of custom is said to require "clear and satisfactory" evidence. The testimony of Hanson as to this "custom and usage" fails to rise above common gossip. We hold this unsupported testimony to be insufficient to meet the standard above expressed.

In attempting to show the inapplicability of the bribery statute to the subject conduct, the appellants ask in their brief:

> Would they violate the statute by accepting remuneration for a speaking engagement on behalf of a local candidate for office? How about a legislator-attorney who represents a property holder on a variance before a local zoning board? Or a legislator-physician who accepted a free dinner to speak for or against medicare?

While we can see a distinction in degree of impropriety between these postulated activities of a legislator and that presented here, we are of the opinion that the subject statute draws no discernible line separating this type of concededly noncriminal conduct from that sought to be punished as a felony in this action. That the legislature has the power to delineate for punishment the type of conduct under consideration is not the question before us,[8] but rather whether it had done so at the time of the commission of these acts. We hold that it had not.

The decision reached here we believe to be in accord with all case law called to our attention. The State has cited no decision holding similar "influence peddling" by a legislator to be a violation of a bribery statute. *State v. Nadeau*, 105 A.2d 194 (R.I. 1954), held that a city councilman could not be bribed to favor a particular candidate for appointment to the city police force, because appointments to the city police force under pertinent law were within the authority of a board of police commissioners, of which the city councilman was not a member and over which he had no control. *State v. Hibicke*, 56 N.W.2d 818 (Wis. 1953), holds that a police constable could not be bribed to recommend to a town council the issuance of a trailer-camp license to a particular applicant because the making of such recommendation was not a part of the constable's "duty in law enforcement." *People v. Leve*, 16 N.W.2d 72 (Mich. 1944), held, under a similar statute, that it was reversible error to instruct a jury that a conviction might lie if the defendant had agreed that "his vote, opinion or judgment or 'influence'" (emphasis added) be given in any particular manner. The court said:

> In the instant case the statute provides for vote, opinion or judgment. It does not make it a crime to use influence.

For the reasons expressed herein the judgment is reversed and judgment of acquittal ... is ordered to be entered as to both defendants.

HATHAWAY, C.J., and KRUCKER, J., concur.

Notes and Questions

1. Do you think Bowling and Cook acted improperly? Did the court think they acted improperly? Would your opinion be affected if Bowling and Cook had let their services for Hanson and the compensation they received be known publicly? Would your opinion be affected if Bowling and Cook were lawyers and it was customary for applicants to be represented by counsel at interviews with the Superintendent?

2. Did the prosecution lose on appeal in *Bowling* because as a matter of law the legislators were not acting in their official capacity or because of a failure of proof? If the latter, what factual showing was necessary?

3. A notorious incident of influence-peddling in the 1980s was the affair of the "Keating Five," who consisted of four Democratic senators—Alan Cranston (California), Dennis De Concini (Arizona), John Glenn (Ohio), and Donald Riegle (Michigan)—and one Republican—John McCain (Arizona). A brief account of the affair is given by Dennis F. Thompson, *Mediated Corruption: The Case of the Keating Five*, 87 AMERICAN POLITICAL SCIENCE REVIEW 369, 369–70 (1993):

---

8. We note in passing that the [Arizona legislature has adopted a new statute] dealing with the subject of "ethics" of members of the legislature. [A subsection of the new statute,] pertaining to the acceptance of compensation for services rendered in relation to any matter or proceeding pending before a state agency, would appear to [criminalize] conduct similar to that charged herein....

They were brought together by Charles Keating, Jr., now in prison in California, convicted on charges of fraud and racketeering. As chairman of a home construction company in Phoenix, he bought Lincoln Savings and Loan in California in 1984 and began to shift its assets from home loans to high-risk projects, violating a wide variety of state and federal regulations in the process. In 1989, Lincoln collapsed, wiping out the savings of twenty-three thousand (mostly elderly) uninsured customers and costing taxpayers over two billion dollars. It was the biggest failure in what came to be the most costly financial scandal in American history. Lincoln came to symbolize the savings-and-loan crisis.

[Keating's] most visible political lobbying was directed against the new rule prohibiting direct investment by savings-and-loans, which many legitimate financial institutions and many members of Congress also opposed. His most prominent and persistent target was Edwin Gray, the head of the three-member bank board that regulated the industry, himself a controversial figure.

The five senators met jointly with Gray, asking him why the investigation of Lincoln and Keating, whom they described as their "friend," was taking so long. Gray said later that he felt intimidated by the show of force. Some of the senators made additional efforts on Keating's behalf. Later, all of them were rebuked, though to differing degrees, by the Senate Ethics Committee.[s]

Thompson recognizes that "constituency service" is a common function performed by legislators, though he questions whether it should be accorded the legitimacy it often receives. Implicitly, therefore, Thompson rejects the approach of *Bowling* of attempting to classify a transaction as a bribe by determining whether the legislator's behavior is or is not "official."

Among the details of the Keating Five affair that Thompson believes permit moral condemnation of the senators are: that although the senators would regularly intervene in behalf of constituents whether or not they were contributors, the nature of the intervention — "[f]ive senators meeting in private with regulators on a specific case" — was extraordinary; that the intervention went well beyond a status inquiry, which Thompson regards as "perfectly proper," to the point of appearing to the regulators more like a threat; and that the contributions were extraordinarily large and, in some cases, involved "ideological incongruence," as when the conservative Republican Keating gave to the liberal Democrat Alan Cranston.

In commenting on the Senate Ethics Committee's report, Thompson writes:

The committee found the contributions and services [in Cranston's case] to be "substantially linked" through an "impermissible pattern of conduct," but they stopped short of finding "corrupt intent." Why did the committee decline to find corruption here? The connection, it would seem, could hardly be closer.... Part of the answer probably is that "corrupt intent" is the language of the bribery statutes, and the committee did not dare suggest that campaign contributions could be bribes. The line between contributions and bribes must be kept bright.

But *is* the line so bright? ... Courts have not been able to provide a principled way of distinguishing the two.

Id. at 374. On this note, we may end this chapter about where it began.

---

s. An account of the Keating Five affair in the context of the savings and loan scandal is contained in Peter DeLeon, THINKING ABOUT POLITICAL CORRUPTION 130–163 (1993). Both Thompson and DeLeon provide references to more detailed accounts.

Chapter 14

The *Buckley* Framework

I. Introduction: Basic Facts and Figures about Campaign Financing in the U.S.

The remainder of this casebook considers efforts to regulate and reform the system of campaign finance in American politics, as well as the constitutional constraints on such efforts. We will focus in this chapter on the Supreme Court's opinion in *Buckley v. Valeo*, the fountainhead of modern American campaign finance jurisprudence, as well as on arguments for and against regulation of money in politics.

Before turning to these readings, it is worth considering a few of the basic facts and figures relating to campaign finance in the United States. More information will be presented in later in this chapter and in subsequent chapters. But we need not present a comprehensive description of the campaign finance system here, because nowadays there is a steady stream of books that do this very well. Among the worthy volumes published in recent years are THE ELECTION AFTER REFORM: MONEY, POLITICS, AND THE BIPARTISAN CAMPAIGN REFORM ACT (Michael J. Malbin, ed. 2006); FINANCING THE 2004 ELECTION (David B. Magleby, Anthony Corrado, and Kelly D. Patterson, eds. 2006); FINANCING THE 2000 ELECTION (David B. Magleby, ed. 2002); FINANCING THE 1996 ELECTION (John C. Green, ed., 1999); Herbert E. Alexander & Anthony Corrado, FINANCING THE 1992 ELECTION (1995); Herbert E. Alexander, FINANCING POLITICS: MONEY, ELECTIONS & POLITICAL REFORM (4th ed., 1992); Frank J. Sorauf, INSIDE CAMPAIGN FINANCE: MYTHS AND REALITIES (1992); Frank J. Sorauf, MONEY IN AMERICAN ELECTIONS (1988).[a]

Campaign finance spending in the U.S. consistently grew each election period from the 1970s through the 1990s. One estimate placed total spending for the 1976 elections at $540 million (about $1.98 billion in 2007 dollars), compared to $4.2 billion for the 1996 elections (about $5.6 billion in 2007 dollars).[b] These numbers are rough estimates; it is very difficult to get accurate figures on total spending in all elections across the country.

Compiling statistics on *federal* election activity (presidential and congressional) is easier, thanks to the uniform reporting requirements of the Federal Election Commission (FEC). These figures reveal that total spending may be leveling off, or at least not growing as

---

a. Perhaps the classic work on American campaign finance is Alexander Heard, THE COSTS OF DEMOCRACY (1960). Of course, it is now hopelessly obsolete, but it remains a source of wisdom.

b. The nominal dollar figures are from Herbert E. Alexander, *Spending in the 1996 Elections*, 11, 15, in FINANCING THE 1996 ELECTION, *supra*. The editors of this book converted the figures in this chapter to 2007 dollars using the inflation calculator available at the Bureau of Labor Statistics website, <www.bls.gov>. Using somewhat different methodology, Candice Nelson concluded that total spending on 1999–2000 election-related activity was just under $4 billion. Candice J. Nelson, *Spending in the 2000 Election*, 22–24, in FINANCING THE 2000 ELECTION, *supra*.

rapidly. Total spending on federal election activity related to the 2004 election reached about $4.3 billion ($4.74 billion in 2007 dollars), up from $3.8 billion in 2000 ($4.6 billion in 2007 dollars). Kelly D. Patterson, *Spending in the 2004 Election,* 68, 69 in FINANCING THE 2004 ELECTION, *supra.* Presidential candidates spent $1.2 billion in the 2004 cycle, and $1.3 billion was spent on congressional races. Parties spent over $1 billion on federal election activity during the period. *Id.*

Why are campaigns so expensive? Television time and postage, which dominate many federal campaigns, have gone up more rapidly than the consumer price index. Some things purchased by campaigns have become cheaper, especially computer technology. But this has not lowered campaign costs; it has simply made it possible — and therefore necessary, because campaigning is a competitive enterprise — for campaigns to function at a level of sophistication that was not previously possible. For example, campaigns now routinely engage in polling and targeted mail activities that would not have been imaginable one or two or three decades ago. Internet campaigning is the latest target for campaign consultants. Whether costs will decrease as the Internet becomes a more important campaign tool remains to be seen.

Many people regard high campaign spending as a problem in itself. Most politicians, journalists, academics, and other close observers of electoral politics do not share this view. They point out that the total amount spent on political campaigns is miniscule compared, say, to what is spent to advertise commercial goods and services, or to government budgets generally. They maintain that communication is central to a democratic system and there is no reason to assume that such communication will be costless.

Part of the public sentiment against the growth of campaign spending probably reflects disapproval of the content of political advertising, which is often negative, misleading, superficial, strident, or all of the above. Many close observers of politics share this disapproval, though no one seems to have come up with a very good idea for what can be done about it and, as Chapter 11 shows, the Constitution would permit very little regulation in this area.

Aside from the content of campaigning, close observers tend to be less concerned about the growth in spending in itself than about some of the stresses and strains accompanying that growth. As the following pages will show, there are many such concerns, and different observers have very different ideas about how important they are. Debate has centered primarily around the distribution of campaign resources and the implications that the distribution has for electoral competition; and on the pressures that are generated by the need to raise increasing amounts of campaign contributions.

This chapter and the ones that follow explore whether, why, and how campaign financing should be regulated. "Regulation" could be anything from disclosure of the source and use of campaign funds, to limits on amounts contributed or spent, to public financing of campaigns. Before you begin reading these materials, ask yourself whether you believe campaign financing should be regulated. Why or why not? Does your answer depend upon whether you are a pluralist, civic republican, or progressivist?

Consider the following non-exhaustive list of reasons some have suggested for regulating campaign finances:

1. Prevent corruption of elected officials

2. Promote political equality

3. Enhance the competitiveness of elections

4. Instill public confidence in the democratic process

5. Free candidates from excessive time spent on fundraising

Note that these reasons may be at odds with one another. For example, imposing a low dollar limit on the amount individuals may contribute to candidate campaigns might serve the goals of preventing corruption or promoting equality, but such a limit almost surely will increase the time that candidates must spend raising funds. Note also that these reasons may not be as distinct from one another as they may first appear. For example, sometimes people speak of "corruption" when they really have a concern about equality.[c] In addition, campaign finance regulation would not instill "public confidence" in the democratic process unless the public was concerned about some other underlying problem, such as corruption or inequality. Finally, these reasons must be considered in light of concerns about the free speech and associational rights guaranteed by the First Amendment of the Constitution, an issue to which we now turn.

II. *Buckley v. Valeo:* The Foundation of American Campaign Finance Jurisprudence

The modern era of campaign finance regulation began, at the federal level, with the Federal Election Campaign Act Amendments of 1974 (FECA), codified at 2 U.S.C. §431 *et seq.*[d] There were four basic forms of regulation contained in the FECA, and with some variations, these have remained the basic elements of most debate on campaign finance regulation ever since: disclosure; limits on the size of campaign contributions; limits on campaign expenditures; and public financing of campaigns. In addition, the FECA retained older forms of federal election regulation, most prominently a ban on contributions by corporations and labor unions.

The FECA applies to congressional and presidential elections, only a small fraction of the elections held in the United States. However, around the same period, most of the states adopted roughly comparable laws that included some or all of the same forms of regulation.

Congress was aware when it enacted the FECA that there would be serious challenges to the law's constitutionality. The FECA includes a provision, 2 U.S.C. §437h, allowing such challenges to receive expedited consideration in the federal courts. Almost before the ink of the statute had dried, a comprehensive challenge to most of its provisions was filed by an ideologically diverse group of plaintiffs.[e] The Court of Appeals upheld the law in its entirety with one very minor exception, 519 F.2d 821 (D.C. Cir. 1975), and the case went to the Supreme Court under the name *Buckley v. Valeo.*

---

c. As we shall see, the Supreme Court has encouraged this practice — perhaps inadvertently — by recognizing corruption but not equality as a rationale to justify campaign finance laws.

d. The public financing provisions of FECA are codified separately, in the Internal Revenue Code. The entire text of the statute as it stood following the 1974 amendments is set forth as an appendix to *Buckley v. Valeo*, 424 U.S. 1, 144–235 (1976).

The Federal Election Campaign Act was originally enacted in 1971, but before most of its provisions were scheduled to go into effect, the 1971 system of regulation was replaced by the 1974 amendments.

e. The disclosure requirements were alleged to be overbroad. All the other major provisions were alleged to be unconstitutional in their entirety.

On three previous occasions, the Court had taken pains to avoid deciding constitutional controversies over congressional attempts to regulate campaign finances.[f] In *Buckley*, the Court showed no such restraint. The Court adjudicated the validity of a large number of different provisions, and attempted to write a virtual treatise setting forth both general principles and considerable doctrinal detail, delineating the limits of regulation in this contentious field. The result was a *per curiam* decision (a decision "by the Court," i.e., not signed by any one justice) extending over 138 pages of the United States Reports, almost certainly the longest *per curiam* opinion in the history of the Supreme Court. The opinion was drafted by a committee of Justices, with the portion reprinted in this chapter drafted primarily by Justice Potter Stewart. See Richard L. Hasen, *The Untold Drafting History of* Buckley v. Valeo, 2 ELECTION LAW JOURNAL 241 (2003). In addition to the *per curiam* opinion, five of the eight justices who participated in the case added separate views, disagreeing with one aspect or another of the majority decision. These separate statements fill an additional 83 pages of the official reports.

Buckley's major rulings were as follows:

1. The campaign disclosure requirements, the least controversial portion of FECA, were upheld. However, the Court stated that it would be unconstitutional to impose the disclosure requirements on parties or candidates who could show that disclosure might subject themselves, their contributors, or their vendors to governmental or private harassment. In *Brown v. Socialist Workers '74 Campaign Committee*, 459 U.S. 87 (1982), the Court ruled that a party was entitled to an exemption from disclosure requirements on this ground. We return to disclosure issues in Chapter 18.

2. In the portion of the opinion that is reprinted in this chapter, the Court upheld the limits on the size of contributions but struck down the expenditure limits. There were three different expenditure limits in the FECA: limits on independent spending in behalf of a candidate; limits on how much of his or her own money the candidate could spend; and limits on the total spending of a candidate's campaign. Prior to *Buckley*, most supporters of the legislation probably would have characterized the first two as corollaries of the FECA's contribution limits. The limit on independent expenditures prevented evasion of the contribution limits and the limits on use of the candidate's own money prevented unfairness to a wealthy candidate's less wealthy opponents, for whom raising money might be made more difficult as a result of the contribution limits. As will be seen, the *Buckley* Court regarded all the expenditure limits as comprising a separate category, sharply distinct from the contribution limits. This chapter and the two that follow explore issues growing out of the constitutional structure set up in *Buckley*.

3. The FECA enacted public financing in presidential but not congressional campaigns. In presidential primaries, candidates can receive public funds on a matching basis for private contributions up to $250. In general elections, the presidential campaigns of candidates who opt for public financing are entirely publicly financed, and the major party candidates receive no private contributions. These public financing provisions were upheld in *Buckley*. Footnote 65, appended to the section on expenditure limits and reprinted below, stated that despite the unconstitutionality of such limits if they are mandatory, it is permissible to attach spending limits as a condition of acceptance of public financing, on the theory that the limits then become voluntary. Chapter 17 explores public financ-

---

f. See United States v. CIO, 335 U.S. 106 (1948); United States v. UAW-CIO, 352 U.S. 567 (1957); Pipefitters Local Union No. 562 v. United States, 407 U.S. 385 (1972).

ing issues. In Chapter 10 we considered the question whether the public financing plan unconstitutionally infringed the rights of third party and independent candidates.

4. The FECA created a new agency, the Federal Election Commission, for the purpose of administering and enforcing the new legislation. In *Buckley*, the Court ruled that the manner in which the FEC was constituted—two members each were appointed by the President, the Senate, and the House—violated the system of separation of powers established by the Constitution. The last point required that the Act be amended in 1976, to reconstitute the FEC with all members appointed by the President. The Act was amended again in 1979 and 2002, and we will consider those amendments in Chapter 17. Even with those amendments, the basic framework of the FECA that emerged from *Buckley* continues to govern federal elections. That FECA is considerably different from the one passed by Congress, since it does not include expenditure limits in congressional elections. Indeed, Chief Justice Burger, in a separate opinion in *Buckley*, declared that he would have struck down the entire law rather than leave standing such a modified version of what Congress wrote:

> [T]he Court's result does violence to the intent of Congress in this comprehensive scheme of campaign finance. By dissecting the Act bit by bit, and casting off vital parts, the Court fails to recognize that the whole of this Act is greater than the sum of its parts. Congress intended to regulate all aspects of federal campaign finances, but what remains after today's holding leaves no more than a shadow of what Congress contemplated. I question whether the residue leaves a workable program.

424 U.S. at 235–36 (Burger, C.J., concurring in part and dissenting in part).

Buckley is therefore a crucially important case for its direct effect on federal campaign law. There are several additional reasons why the decision, and especially the portion that is reprinted in this chapter, must be mastered by the student of election law. First, as mentioned above, the Court's opinion attempts to define in general outline and in considerable detail the constitutional limits on campaign finance reform in the United States. To be sure, critics have questioned *Buckley*'s internal consistency and its consistency with subsequent campaign finance decisions. Nevertheless, *Buckley* is still the most basic text against which any existing or proposed federal, state, or local campaign finance regulation must be tested. Second, because the case covers so much conceptual, doctrinal, polemical and even empirical ground, it provides a useful starting point for discussion of legal and policy aspects of the campaign finance problem. Finally, because of its breadth, and the contrast between its interventionism and the Court's earlier restraint in campaign finance cases, *Buckley* is an important case study for consideration of the judiciary's role in coping with the campaign finance problem and, more broadly, the Court's exercise of its function of judicial review in general.

Buckley v. Valeo
424 U.S. 1, 12–59 (1976)

I. CONTRIBUTION AND EXPENDITURE LIMITATIONS

The intricate statutory scheme adopted by Congress to regulate federal election campaigns includes restrictions on political contributions and expenditures that apply broadly to all phases of and all participants in the election process. The major contribution and expenditure limitations in the Act prohibit individuals from contributing more than

$25,000 in a single year or more than $1,000 to any single candidate for an election campaign[12] and from spending more than $1,000 a year "relative to a clearly identified candidate." Other provisions restrict a candidate's use of personal and family resources in his campaign and limit the overall amount that can be spent by a candidate in campaigning for federal office.

The constitutional power of Congress to regulate federal elections is well established and is not questioned by any of the parties in this case.[16] Thus, the critical constitutional questions presented here go not to the basic power of Congress to legislate in this area, but to whether the specific legislation that Congress has enacted interferes with First Amendment freedoms or invidiously discriminates against nonincumbent candidates and minor parties in contravention of the Fifth Amendment.[g]

A. General Principles

The Act's contribution and expenditure limitations operate in an area of the most fundamental First Amendment activities. Discussion of public issues and debate on the qualifications of candidates are integral to the operation of the system of government established by our Constitution. The First Amendment affords the broadest protection to such political expression in order "to assure [the] unfettered interchange of ideas for the bringing about of political and social changes desired by the people." *Roth v. United States*, 354 U.S. 476, 484 (1957). Although First Amendment protections are not confined to "the exposition of ideas," *Winters v. New York*, 333 U.S. 507, 510 (1948), "there is practically universal agreement that a major purpose of that Amendment was to protect the free discussion of governmental affairs, ... of course includ[ing] discussions of candidates...." *Mills v. Alabama*, 384 U.S. 214, 218 (1966). This no more than reflects our "profound national commitment to the principle that debate on public issues should be uninhibited, robust, and wide-open," *New York Times Co. v. Sullivan*, 376 U.S. 254, 270 (1964). In a republic where the people are sovereign, the ability of the citizenry to make informed choices among candidates for office is essential, for the identities of those who are elected will inevitably shape the course that we follow as a nation. As the Court observed in *Monitor Patriot Co. v. Roy*, 401 U.S. 265, 272 (1971), "it can hardly be doubted that the constitutional guarantee has its fullest and most urgent application precisely to the conduct of campaigns for political office."

The First Amendment protects political association as well as political expression. The constitutional right of association explicated in *NAACP v. Alabama*, 357 U.S. 449, 460

---

12. An organization registered as a political committee for not less than six months which has received contributions from at least 50 persons and made contributions to at least five candidates may give up to $5,000 to any candidate for any election.... [These are the organizations generally known as "political action committees," or "PACs."—Eds.]

16. Article I, §4, of the Constitution grants Congress the power to regulate elections of members of the Senate and House of Representatives. See *Smiley v. Holm*, 285 U.S. 355 (1932); *Ex parte Yarbrough*, 110 U.S. 651 (1884). Although the Court at one time indicated that party primary contests were not "elections" within the meaning of Art. I, §4, *Newberry v. United States*, 256 U.S. 232 (1921), it later held that primary elections were within the Constitution's grant of authority to Congress. *United States v. Classic*, 313 U.S. 299 (1941). The Court has also recognized broad congressional power to legislate in connection with the elections of the President and Vice President. *Burroughs v. United States*, 290 U.S. 534 (1934).

g. References to the Fifth Amendment in this opinion are to what is sometimes referred to as the "equal protection component" of the Fifth Amendment. The Equal Protection Clause itself, in the 14th Amendment, restricts only the states. The Court has found, in the due process provisions of the Fifth Amendment, restrictions on the federal government that are virtually identical to those of the Equal Protection Clause.—Eds.

(1958), stemmed from the Court's recognition that "(e)ffective advocacy of both public and private points of view, particularly controversial ones, is undeniably enhanced by group association." Subsequent decisions have made clear that the First and Fourteenth Amendments guarantee "freedom to associate with others for the common advancement of political beliefs and ideas," a freedom that encompasses "[t]he right to associate with the political party of one's choice." *Kusper v. Pontikes*, 414 U.S. 51, 56, 57 (1973), quoted in *Cousins v. Wigoda*, 419 U.S. 477, 487 (1975).

It is with these principles in mind that we consider the primary contentions of the parties with respect to the Act's limitations upon the giving and spending of money in political campaigns. Those conflicting contentions could not more sharply define the basic issues before us. Appellees contend that what the Act regulates is conduct, and that its effect on speech and association is incidental at most. Appellants respond that contributions and expenditures are at the very core of political speech, and that the Act's limitations thus constitute restraints on First Amendment liberty that are both gross and direct.

In upholding the constitutional validity of the Act's contribution and expenditure provisions on the ground that those provisions should be viewed as regulating conduct, not speech, the Court of Appeals relied upon *United States v. O'Brien*, 391 U.S. 367 (1968). The *O'Brien* case involved a defendant's claim that the First Amendment prohibited his prosecution for burning his draft card because his act was "symbolic speech" engaged in as a "demonstration against the war and against the draft." On the assumption that "the alleged communicative element in O'Brien's conduct [was] sufficient to bring into play the First Amendment," the Court sustained the conviction because it found "a sufficiently important governmental interest in regulating the nonspeech element" that was "unrelated to the suppression of free expression" and that had an "incidental restriction on alleged First Amendment freedoms ... no greater than [was] essential to the furtherance of that interest." The Court expressly emphasized that *O'Brien* was not a case "where the alleged governmental interest in regulating conduct arises in some measure because the communication allegedly integral to the conduct is itself thought to be harmful."

We cannot share the view that the present Act's contribution and expenditure limitations are comparable to the restrictions on conduct upheld in *O'Brien*. The expenditure of money simply cannot be equated with such conduct as destruction of a draft card. Some forms of communication made possible by the giving and spending of money involve speech alone, some involve conduct primarily, and some involve a combination of the two. Yet this Court has never suggested that the dependence of a communication on the expenditure of money operates itself to introduce a nonspeech element or to reduce the exacting scrutiny required by the First Amendment[h] ....

Even if the categorization of the expenditure of money as conduct was accepted, the limitations challenged here would not meet the *O'Brien* test because the governmental

---

h. This passage is criticized by J. Skelly Wright, *Politics and the Constitution: Is Money Speech?*, 85 YALE LAW JOURNAL 1001, 1007–08 (1976): "I am bound to say that this passage performs a judicial sleight of hand. The real question in the case was: Can the use of money be regulated, by analogy to conduct such as draft-card burning, where there is an undoubted incidental effect on speech? However, what the Court asked was whether pure speech can be regulated where there is some incidental effect on money. Naturally the answer to the Court's question was 'No.' But this left untouched the real question in the case. The Court riveted its attention on what the money could buy—be it communication, or communication mixed with conduct. Yet the campaign reform law did not dictate what could be bought. It focused exclusively on the giving and spending itself. In short, the Court turned the congressional telescope around and looked through the wrong end." — EDS.

interests advanced in support of the Act involve "suppressing communication." The interests served by the Act include restricting the voices of people and interest groups who have money to spend and reducing the overall scope of federal election campaigns. Although the Act does not focus on the ideas expressed by persons or groups subject to its regulations, it is aimed in part at equalizing the relative ability of all voters to affect electoral outcomes by placing a ceiling on expenditures for political expression by citizens and groups. Unlike *O'Brien*, where the Selective Service System's administrative interest in the preservation of draft cards was wholly unrelated to their use as a means of communication, it is beyond dispute that the interest in regulating the alleged "conduct" of giving or spending money "arises in some measure because the communication allegedly integral to the conduct is itself thought to be harmful."

Nor can the Act's contribution and expenditure limitations be sustained, as some of the parties suggest, by reference to the constitutional principles reflected in [decisions such as *Kovacs v. Cooper*, 336 U.S. 77 (1949), standing] for the proposition that the government may adopt reasonable time, place, and manner regulations, which do not discriminate among speakers or ideas, in order to further an important governmental interest unrelated to the restriction of communication. In contrast to *O'Brien*, where the method of expression was held to be subject to prohibition, [*Kovacs*, etc.] involved place or manner restrictions on legitimate modes of expression — picketing, parading, demonstrating, and using a soundtruck. The critical difference between this case and those time, place, and manner cases is that the present Act's contribution and expenditure limitations impose direct quantity restrictions on political communication and association by persons, groups, candidates, and political parties in addition to any reasonable time, place, and manner regulations otherwise imposed.[17]

A restriction on the amount of money a person or group can spend on political communication during a campaign necessarily reduces the quantity of expression by restricting the number of issues discussed, the depth of their exploration, and the size of the audience reached.[18] This is because virtually every means of communicating ideas in today's mass society requires the expenditure of money. The distribution of the humblest handbill or leaflet entails printing, paper, and circulation costs. Speeches and rallies generally necessitate hiring a hall and publicizing the event. The electorate's increasing dependence

---

17. The nongovernmental appellees argue that just as the decibels emitted by a sound truck can be regulated consistently with the First Amendment, *Kovacs*, the Act may restrict the volume of dollars in political campaigns without impermissibly restricting freedom of speech. This comparison underscores a fundamental misconception. The decibel restriction upheld in *Kovacs* limited the manner of operating a soundtruck but not the extent of its proper use. By contrast, the Act's dollar ceilings restrict the extent of the reasonable use of virtually every means of communicating information. As the *Kovacs* Court emphasized, the nuisance ordinance only barred sound trucks from broadcasting "in a loud and raucous manner on the streets," and imposed "no restriction upon the communication of ideas or discussion of issues by the human voice, by newspapers, by pamphlets, by dodgers," or by soundtrucks operating at a reasonable volume.

[The Court's argument has been criticized by a number of commentators who analogize controlling the volume of a soundtruck to controlling the "volume" of monetary expenditures. Lillian R. BeVier, *Money and Politics: A Perspective on the First Amendment and Campaign Finance Reform*, 73 CALIFORNIA LAW REVIEW 1045, 1060 n.72 (1985), argues that this analogy "is flawed because the evil created by too much sound is noise in a strictly physical sense, whereas that thought to be created by too many dollars is noise only in a normative sense — namely that, in the view of the person drawing the analogy, too many dollars permit certain messages to be heard too much." — EDS.]

18. Being free to engage in unlimited political expression subject to a ceiling on expenditures is like being free to drive an automobile as far and as often as one desires on a single tank of gasoline.

on television, radio, and other mass media for news and information has made these expensive modes of communication indispensable instruments of effective political speech.

The expenditure limitations contained in the Act represent substantial rather than merely theoretical restraints on the quantity and diversity of political speech. The $1,000 ceiling on spending "relative to a clearly identified candidate," 18 U.S.C. §608(e)(1), would appear to exclude all citizens and groups except candidates, political parties, and the institutional press from any significant use of the most effective modes of communication.[20] Although the Act's limitations on expenditures by campaign organizations and political parties provide substantially greater room for discussion and debate, they would have required restrictions in the scope of a number of past congressional and Presidential campaigns[21] and would operate to constrain campaigning by candidates who raise sums in excess of the spending ceiling.

By contrast with a limitation upon expenditures for political expression, a limitation upon the amount that any one person or group may contribute to a candidate or political committee entails only a marginal restriction upon the contributor's ability to engage in free communication. A contribution serves as a general expression of support for the candidate and his views, but does not communicate the underlying basis for the support. The quantity of communication by the contributor does not increase perceptibly with the size of his contribution, since the expression rests solely on the undifferentiated, symbolic act of contributing.[i] At most, the size of the contribution provides a very rough index of the intensity of the contributor's support for the candidate. A limitation on the amount of money a person may give to a candidate or campaign organization thus involves little direct restraint on his political communication, for it permits the symbolic expression of support evidenced by a contribution but does not in any way infringe the contributor's freedom to discuss candidates and issues. While contributions may result in political expression if spent by a candidate or an association to present views to the voters, the transformation of contributions into political debate involves speech by someone other than the contributor.

Given the important role of contributions in financing political campaigns, contribution restrictions could have a severe impact on political dialogue if the limitations prevented candidates and political committees from amassing the resources necessary for effective advocacy. There is no indication, however, that the contribution limitations im-

---

20. The record indicates that, as of January 1, 1975, one full-page advertisement in a daily edition of a certain metropolitan newspaper cost $6,971.04 — almost seven times the annual limit on expenditures "relative to" a particular candidate imposed on the vast majority of individual citizens and associations by §608(e)(1).

21. The statistical findings of fact agreed to by the parties in the District Court indicate that 17 of 65 major-party senatorial candidates in 1974 spent more than the combined primary-election, general-election, and fundraising limitations imposed by the Act. The 1972 senatorial figures showed that 18 of 66 major-party candidates exceeded the Act's limitations. This figure may substantially underestimate the number of candidates who exceeded the limits provided in the Act, since the Act imposes separate ceilings for the primary election, the general election, and fundraising, and does not permit the limits to be aggregated. The data for House of Representatives elections are also skewed, since statistics reflect a combined $168,000 limit instead of separate $70,000 ceilings for primary and general elections with up to an additional 20% permitted for fundraising. Only 22 of the 810 major-party House candidates in 1974 and 20 of the 816 major-party candidates in 1972 exceeded the $168,000 figure. Both Presidential candidates in 1972 spent in excess of the combined Presidential expenditure ceilings.

i. One critic argues that the Court omitted "any discussion of the contributor who wished to delegate his speech to a more effective communicator, as he freely could under the Court's invalidation of spending limitations if he picked an ad agency rather than a candidate." L.A. Powe, Jr., *Mass Speech and the Newer First Amendment*, 1982 SUPREME COURT REVIEW 243, 253. — EDS.

posed by the Act would have any dramatic adverse effect on the funding of campaigns and political associations.[23] The overall effect of the Act's contribution ceilings is merely to require candidates and political committees to raise funds from a greater number of persons and to compel people who would otherwise contribute amounts greater than the statutory limits to expend such funds on direct political expression, rather than to reduce the total amount of money potentially available to promote political expression.

The Act's contribution and expenditure limitations also impinge on protected associational freedoms. Making a contribution, like joining a political party, serves to affiliate a person with a candidate. In addition, it enables like-minded persons to pool their resources in furtherance of common political goals. The Act's contribution ceilings thus limit one important means of associating with a candidate or committee, but leave the contributor free to become a member of any political association and to assist personally in the association's efforts on behalf of candidates. And the Act's contribution limitations permit associations and candidates to aggregate large sums of money to promote effective advocacy. By contrast, the Act's $1,000 limitation on independent expenditures "relative to a clearly identified candidate" precludes most associations from effectively amplifying the voice of their adherents, the original basis for the recognition of First Amendment protection of the freedom of association. See *NAACP v. Alabama*. The Act's constraints on the ability of independent associations and candidate campaign organizations to expend resources on political expression "is simultaneously an interference with the freedom of (their) adherents," *Sweezy v. New Hampshire*, 354 U.S. 234, 250 (1957) (plurality opinion).

In sum, although the Act's contribution and expenditure limitations both implicate fundamental First Amendment interests, its expenditure ceilings impose significantly more severe restrictions on protected freedoms of political expression and association than do its limitations on financial contributions.

B. Contribution Limitations

1. The $1,000 Limitation on Contributions by Individuals and Groups to Candidates and Authorized Campaign Committees

Section 608(b) provides, with certain limited exceptions, that "no person shall make contributions to any candidate with respect to any election for Federal office which, in the aggregate, exceed $1,000." The statute defines "person" broadly to include "an individual,

---

23. Statistical findings agreed to by the parties reveal that approximately 5.1% of the $73,483,613 raised by the 1,161 candidates for Congress in 1974 was obtained in amounts in excess of $1,000. In 1974, two major-party senatorial candidates, Ramsey Clark and Senator Charles Mathias, Jr., operated large-scale campaigns on contributions raised under a voluntarily imposed $100 contribution limitation.

[Compare this footnote with footnote 21, *supra*, in which the Court documents the proposition that campaign spending limits would have a substantial repressive effect on campaign speech. In footnote 21 the Court considers the ratio of campaigns that would have exceeded the limits to those that spent within the limits. In footnote 23, the Court considers the ratio of money contributed in excess of the limits to that of money contributed within the limits. Why consider apples (the number of campaigns over the limit) in one case and oranges (the amount of money contributed over the limit) in the other?

Whatever the ratio that may be selected, how large must the ratio be for the Court to regard it as indicating that the limits in question will have a "dramatic adverse effect on the funding of campaigns and political associations"? According to the figures the Court gives in footnote 21, a total of 4.3% of House and Senate campaigns in 1972 and 1974 spent amounts that would have exceeded the campaign spending limits. Why does this indicate a "dramatic adverse effect" while the 5.1% figure the Court gives in footnote 23 shows the absence of such an effect? — EDS.]

partnership, committee, association, corporation, or any other organization or group of persons." §591(g). The limitation reaches a gift, subscription, loan, advance, deposit of anything of value, or promise to give a contribution, made for the purpose of influencing a primary election, a Presidential preference primary, or a general election for any federal office.[24] §§591(e)(1), (2).... The restriction applies to aggregate amounts contributed to the candidate for each election with primaries, run-off elections, and general elections counted separately, and all Presidential primaries held in any calendar year treated together as a single election campaign. §608(b)(5).

Appellants contend that the $1,000 contribution ceiling unjustifiably burdens First Amendment freedoms, employs overbroad dollar limits, and discriminates against candidates opposing incumbent officeholders and against minor-party candidates in violation of the Fifth Amendment. We address each of these claims of invalidity in turn.

(a)

As the general discussion in Part I-A, *supra*, indicated, the primary First Amendment problem raised by the Act's contribution limitations is their restriction of one aspect of the contributor's freedom of political association. The Court's decisions involving associational freedoms establish that the right of association is a "basic constitutional freedom," *Kusper*, that is "closely allied to freedom of speech and a right which, like free speech, lies at the foundation of a free society." *Shelton v. Tucker*, 364 U.S. 479, 486 (1960). In view of the fundamental nature of the right to associate, governmental "action which may have the effect of curtailing the freedom to associate is subject to the closest scrutiny." *NAACP v. Alabama*. Yet, it is clear that "(n)either the right to associate nor the right to participate in political activities is absolute." *CSC v Letter Carriers*, 413 U.S. 548, 567 (1973). Even a "'significant interference' with protected rights of political association" may be sustained if the State demonstrates a sufficiently important interest and employs means closely drawn to avoid unnecessary abridgment of associational freedoms. *Cousins*.

Appellees argue that the Act's restrictions on large campaign contributions are justified by three governmental interests. According to the parties and *amici*, the primary interest served by the limitations and, indeed, by the Act as a whole, is the prevention of corruption and the appearance of corruption spawned by the real or imagined coercive influence of large financial contributions on candidates' positions and on their actions if elected to office. Two "ancillary" interests underlying the Act are also allegedly furthered by the $1,000 limits on contributions. First, the limits serve to mute the voices of affluent persons and groups in the election process and thereby to equalize the relative ability of all citizens to affect the outcome of elections. Second, it is argued, the ceilings may to some extent act as a brake on the skyrocketing cost of political campaigns and thereby serve to open the political system more widely to candidates without access to sources of large amounts of money.

It is unnecessary to look beyond the Act's primary purpose to limit the actuality and appearance of corruption resulting from large individual financial contributions in order to find a constitutionally sufficient justification for the $1,000 contribution limitation. Under a system of private financing of elections, a candidate lacking immense personal or family wealth must depend on financial contributions from others to provide the resources necessary to conduct a successful campaign. The increasing importance of the

---

24. The Act exempts from the contribution ceiling the value of all volunteer services provided by individuals to a candidate or a political committee and excludes the first $500 spent by volunteers on certain categories of campaign-related activities. §§591(e)(5)(A)–(D)....

communications media and sophisticated mass-mailing and polling operations to effective campaigning make the raising of large sums of money an ever more essential ingredient of an effective candidacy. To the extent that large contributions are given to secure a political *quid pro quo* from current and potential office holders, the integrity of our system of representative democracy is undermined. Although the scope of such pernicious practices can never be reliably ascertained, the deeply disturbing examples surfacing after the 1972 election demonstrate that the problem is not an illusory one.

Of almost equal concern as the danger of actual *quid pro quo* arrangements is the impact of the appearance of corruption stemming from public awareness of the opportunities for abuse inherent in a regime of large individual financial contributions. In *CSC v. Letter Carriers, supra,* the Court found that the danger to "fair and effective government" posed by partisan political conduct on the part of federal employees charged with administering the law was a sufficiently important concern to justify broad restrictions on the employees' right of partisan political association. Here, as there, Congress could legitimately conclude that the avoidance of the appearance of improper influence "is also critical … if confidence in the system of representative Government is not to be eroded to a disastrous extent."

Appellants contend that the contribution limitations must be invalidated because bribery laws and narrowly drawn disclosure requirements constitute a less restrictive means of dealing with "proven and suspected *quid pro quo* arrangements." But laws making criminal the giving and taking of bribes deal with only the most blatant and specific attempts of those with money to influence governmental action.[j] And while disclosure requirements serve the many salutary purposes discussed elsewhere in this opinion, Congress was surely entitled to conclude that disclosure was only a partial measure, and that contribution ceilings were a necessary legislative concomitant to deal with the reality or appearance of corruption inherent in a system permitting unlimited financial contributions, even when the identities of the contributors and the amounts of their contributions are fully disclosed.

The Act's $1,000 contribution limitation focuses precisely on the problem of large campaign contributions—the narrow aspect of political association where the actuality and potential for corruption have been identified—while leaving persons free to engage in independent political expression, to associate actively through volunteering their services, and to assist to a limited but nonetheless substantial extent in supporting candidates and committees with financial resources.[31] Significantly, the Act's contribution limitations in themselves do not undermine to any material degree the potential for robust and effec-

---

j. Is this an accurate statement of the scope of the law of bribery under federal and state laws? See Chapter 13, *supra.*—EDS.

31. While providing significant limitations on the ability of all individuals and groups to contribute large amounts of money to candidates, the Act's contribution ceilings do not foreclose the making of substantial contributions to candidates by some major special-interest groups through the combined effect of individual contributions from adherents or the proliferation of political funds each authorized under the Act to contribute to candidates. As a prime example, §610 permits corporations and labor unions to establish segregated funds to solicit voluntary contributions to be utilized for political purposes. Corporate and union resources without limitation may be employed to administer these funds and to solicit contributions from employees, stockholders, and union members. Each separate fund may contribute up to $5,000 per candidate per election so long as the fund qualifies as a political committee under §608(b)(2).

The Act places no limit on the number of funds that may be formed through the use of subsidiaries or divisions of corporations, or of local and regional units of a national labor union….

The Act allows the maximum contribution to be made by each unit's fund provided the decision or judgment to contribute to particular candidates is made by the fund independently of control or direction by the parent corporation or the national or regional union.

tive discussion of candidates and campaign issues by individual citizens, associations, the institutional press, candidates, and political parties.

We find that, under the rigorous standard of review established by our prior decisions, the weighty interests served by restricting the size of financial contributions to political candidates are sufficient to justify the limited effect upon First Amendment freedoms caused by the $1,000 contribution ceiling.

(b)

Appellants' first overbreadth challenge to the contribution ceilings rests on the proposition that most large contributors do not seek improper influence over a candidate's position or an officeholder's action. Although the truth of that proposition may be assumed, it does not undercut the validity of the $1,000 contribution limitation. Not only is it difficult to isolate suspect contributions, but, more importantly, Congress was justified in concluding that the interest in safeguarding against the appearance of impropriety requires that the opportunity for abuse inherent in the process of raising large monetary contributions be eliminated.

A second, related overbreadth claim is that the $1,000 restriction is unrealistically low because much more than that amount would still not be enough to enable an unscrupulous contributor to exercise improper influence over a candidate or officeholder, especially in campaigns for statewide or national office. While the contribution limitation provisions might well have been structured to take account of the graduated expenditure limitations for congressional and Presidential campaigns, Congress' failure to engage in such fine tuning does not invalidate the legislation. As the Court of Appeals observed, "(i)f it is satisfied that some limit on contributions is necessary, a court has no scalpel to probe, whether, say, a $2,000 ceiling might not serve as well as $1,000." Such distinctions in degree become significant only when they can be said to amount to differences in kind.

(c)

Apart from these First Amendment concerns, appellants argue that the contribution limitations work such an invidious discrimination between incumbents and challengers that the statutory provisions must be declared unconstitutional on their face. In considering this contention, it is important at the outset to note that the Act applies the same limitations on contributions to all candidates regardless of their present occupations, ideological views, or party affiliations. Absent record evidence of invidious discrimination against challengers as a class, a court should generally be hesitant to invalidate legislation which on its face imposes evenhanded restrictions.

There is no such evidence to support the claim that the contribution limitations in themselves discriminate against major-party challengers to incumbents. Challengers can and often do defeat incumbents in federal elections. Major-party challengers in federal elections are usually men and women who are well known and influential in their community or State. Often such challengers are themselves incumbents in important local, state, or federal offices. Statistics in the record indicate that major-party challengers as well as incumbents are capable of raising large sums for campaigning. Indeed, a small but nonetheless significant number of challengers have in recent elections outspent their incumbent rivals. And, to the extent that incumbents generally are more likely than challengers to attract very large contributions, the Act's $1,000 ceiling has the practical effect of benefiting challengers as a class. Contrary to the broad generalization drawn by the appellants, the practical impact of the contribution ceilings in any given election will clearly depend upon the amounts in excess of the ceilings that, for various reasons, the candidates in that election would otherwise have received and the utility of these additional amounts to the candidates. To be sure, the limitations may have a significant effect on particular challengers or incumbents, but the record provides no basis for predicting that such adventitious factors will invariably and invidiously benefit incumbents as a class. Since the danger of corruption and the appearance of corruption apply with equal force to challengers and to incumbents, Congress had ample justification for imposing the same fundraising constraints upon both.

The charge of discrimination against minor-party and independent candidates is more troubling, but the record provides no basis for concluding that the Act invidiously disadvantages such candidates. As noted above, the Act on its face treats all candidates equally with regard to contribution limitations. And the restriction would appear to benefit minor-party and independent candidates relative to their major-party opponents because major-party candidates receive far more money in large contributions. Although there is some force to appellants' response that minor-party candidates are primarily concerned with their ability to amass the resources necessary to reach the electorate rather than with their funding position relative to their major-party opponents, the record is virtually devoid of support for the claim that the $1,000 contribution limitation will have a serious effect on the initiation and scope of minor-party and independent candidacies. Moreover, any attempt to exclude minor parties and independents en masse from the Act's contribution limitations overlooks the fact that minor-party candidates may win elective office or have a substantial impact on the outcome of an election.

In view of these considerations, we conclude that the impact of the Act's $1,000 contribution limitation on major-party challengers and on minor-party candidates does not render the provision unconstitutional on its face.

2. The $5,000 Limitation on Contributions by Political Committees

Section 608(b)(2) permits certain committees, designated as "political committees" [and popularly known as political action committees, or PACs—EDS.], to contribute up to $5,000 to any candidate with respect to any election for federal office. In order to qualify for the higher contribution ceiling, a group must have been registered with the Commission as a political committee under 2 U.S.C. §433 for not less than six months, have received contributions from more than 50 persons, and, except for state political party organizations, have contributed to five or more candidates for federal office. Appellants argue that these qualifications unconstitutionally discriminate against *ad hoc* organizations in favor of established interest groups and impermissibly burden free association. The argument is without merit. Rather than undermining freedom of association, the basic provision enhances the opportunity of bona fide groups to participate in the election process, and the registration, contribution, and candidate conditions serve the permissible purpose of preventing individuals from evading the applicable contribution limitations by labeling themselves committees....

4. The $25,000 Limitation on Total Contributions During any Calendar Year

In addition to the $1,000 limitation on the nonexempt contributions that an individual may make to a particular candidate for any single election, the Act contains an overall $25,000 limitation on total contributions by an individual during any calendar year. §608(b)(3). A contribution made in connection with an election is considered, for purposes of this subsection, to be made in the year the election is held. Although the constitutionality of this provision was drawn into question by appellants, it has not been separately addressed at length by the parties. The overall $25,000 ceiling does impose an ultimate restriction upon the number of candidates and committees with which an individual may associate himself by means of financial support. But this quite modest restraint upon protected political activity serves to prevent evasion of the $1,000 contribution limitation by a person who might otherwise contribute massive amounts of money to a particular candidate through the use of unearmarked contributions to political committees likely to contribute to that candidate, or huge contributions to the candidate's political party. The limited, additional restriction on associational freedom imposed by the overall ceiling is thus no more than a corollary of the basic individual contribution limitation that we have found to be constitutionally valid.

C. Expenditure Limitations

The Act's expenditure ceilings impose direct and substantial restraints on the quantity of political speech. The most drastic of the limitations restricts individuals and groups, including political parties that fail to place a candidate on the ballot, to an expenditure of $1,000 "relative to a clearly identified candidate during a calendar year." Other expenditure ceilings limit spending by candidates, their campaigns, and political parties in connection with election campaigns. It is clear that a primary effect of these expenditure limitations is to restrict the quantity of campaign speech by individuals, groups, and candidates. The restrictions, while neutral as to the ideas expressed, limit political expression "at the core of our electoral process and of the First Amendment freedoms." *Williams v. Rhodes.*

1. The $1,000 Limitation on Expenditures "Relative to a Clearly Identified Candidate"

Section 608(e)(1) provides that "[no] person may make any expenditure ... relative to a clearly identified candidate during a calendar year which, when added to all other expenditures made by such person during the year advocating the election or defeat of such candidate, exceeds $1,000." The plain effect of §608(e)(1) is to prohibit all individuals, who are neither candidates nor owners of institutional press facilities, and all groups, except political parties and campaign organizations, from voicing their views "relative to a clearly identified candidate" through means that entail aggregate expenditures of more than $1,000 during a calendar year. The provision, for example, would make it a federal criminal offense for a person or association to place a single one-quarter page advertisement "relative to a clearly identified candidate" in a major metropolitan newspaper.[k]

Before examining the interests advanced in support of §608(e)(1)'s expenditure ceiling, consideration must be given to appellants' contention that the provision is unconstitutionally vague. Close examination of the specificity of the statutory limitation is required where, as here, the legislation imposes criminal penalties in an area permeated by First Amendment interests....

---

k. Consider Daniel D. Polsby, *Buckley v. Valeo: The Special Nature of Political Speech*, 1976 SUPREME COURT REVIEW 1, 6: "Under the FECA amendments, a person who, independently and on his own initiative, placed a full-page advertisement in the Washington Post urging the defeat of an incumbent president ... could be fined and sent to prison. Even granting the seriousness of the problem, solutions so rigorous give off a whiff of brimstone." — EDS.

But a different concern is expressed by John S. Shockley, *Money in Politics: Judicial Roadblocks to Campaign Finance Reform*, 10 HASTINGS CONSTITUTIONAL LAW QUARTERLY 679, 695–96 (1983): "In thus striking down limits on expenditures the Court freed the wealthy to engage in significant use of the most effective modes of communication. But what are the Justices saying about the great majority of the American people who cannot spend more than $1,000 on candidates they support? By the Court's own words, a majority of the American people are excluded from effective communication." — EDS.

The key operative language of the provision limits "any expenditure ... relative to a clearly identified candidate." Although "expenditure," "clearly identified," and "candidate" are defined in the Act, there is no definition clarifying what expenditures are "relative to" a candidate. The use of so indefinite a phrase as "relative to" a candidate fails to clearly mark the boundary between permissible and impermissible speech, unless other portions of §608(e)(1) make sufficiently explicit the range of expenditures covered by the limitation. The section prohibits "any expenditure ... relative to a clearly identified candidate during a calendar year which, *when added to all other expenditures ... advocating the election or defeat of such candidate*, exceeds, $1,000." (Emphasis added.) This context clearly permits, if indeed it does not require, the phrase "relative to" a candidate to be read to mean "advocating the election or defeat of" a candidate.

But while such a construction of §608(e)(1) refocuses the vagueness question, the Court of Appeals was mistaken in thinking that this construction eliminates the problem of unconstitutional vagueness altogether. For the distinction between discussion of issues and candidates and advocacy of election or defeat of candidates may often dissolve in practical application. Candidates, especially incumbents, are intimately tied to public issues involving legislative proposals and governmental actions. Not only do candidates campaign on the basis of their positions on various public issues, but campaigns themselves generate issues of public interest....

[These] constitutional deficiencies ... can be avoided only by reading §608(e)(1) as limited to communications that include explicit words of advocacy of election or defeat of a candidate, much as the definition of "clearly identified" in §608(e)(2) requires that an explicit and unambiguous reference to the candidate appear as part of the communication.[51] This is the reading of the provision suggested by the non-governmental appellees in arguing that "[f]unds spent to propagate one's views on issues without expressly calling for a candidate's election or defeat are thus not covered." We agree that in order to preserve the provision against invalidation on vagueness grounds, §608(e)(1) must be construed to apply only to expenditures for communications that in express terms advocate the election or defeat of a clearly identified candidate for federal office.[52]

We turn then to the basic First Amendment question whether §608(e)(1), even as thus narrowly and explicitly construed, impermissibly burdens the constitutional right of free expression. The Court of Appeals summarily held the provision constitutionally valid on the ground that "section 608(e) is a loophole-closing provision only" that is necessary to prevent circumvention of the contribution limitations. We cannot agree.

The discussion in Part I-A, *supra*, explains why the Act's expenditure limitations impose far greater restraints on the freedom of speech and association than do its contribution limitations. The markedly greater burden on basic freedoms caused by §608(e)(1) thus cannot be sustained simply by invoking the interest in maximizing the effectiveness

---

51. Section 608(e)(2) defines "clearly identified" to require that the candidate's name, photograph or drawing, or other unambiguous reference to his identity appear as part of the communication. Such other unambiguous reference would include use of the candidate's initials (e.g., FDR), the candidate's nickname (e.g., Ike), his office (e.g., the President or the Governor of Iowa), or his status as a candidate (e.g., the Democratic Presidential nominee, the senatorial candidate of the Republican Party of Georgia).

52. This construction would restrict the application of §608(e)(1) to communications containing express words of advocacy of election or defeat, such as "vote for," "elect," "support," "cast your ballot for," "Smith for Congress," "vote against," "defeat," "reject." [Pay close attention to this footnote. The entire controversy regarding "issue advocacy" in federal elections, discussed in detail in Chapter 16, begins with an understanding of the footnote and the accompanying text. — EDS.]

of the less intrusive contribution limitations. Rather, the constitutionality of §608(e)(1) turns on whether the governmental interests advanced in its support satisfy the exacting scrutiny applicable to limitations on core First Amendment rights of political expression.

We find that the governmental interest in preventing corruption and the appearance of corruption is inadequate to justify §608(e)(1)'s ceiling on independent expenditures. First, assuming, *arguendo*, that large independent expenditures pose the same dangers of actual or apparent *quid pro quo* arrangements as do large contributions, §608(e)(1) does not provide an answer that sufficiently relates to the elimination of those dangers. Unlike the contribution limitations' total ban on the giving of large amounts of money to candidates, §608(e)(1) prevents only some large expenditures. So long as persons and groups eschew expenditures that in express terms advocate the election or defeat of a clearly identified candidate, they are free to spend as much as they want to promote the candidate and his views. The exacting interpretation of the statutory language necessary to avoid unconstitutional vagueness thus undermines the limitation's effectiveness as a loophole-closing provision by facilitating circumvention by those seeking to exert improper influence upon a candidate or office-holder. It would naively underestimate the ingenuity and resourcefulness of persons and groups desiring to buy influence to believe that they would have much difficulty devising expenditures that skirted the restriction on express advocacy of election or defeat but nevertheless benefited the candidate's campaign. Yet no substantial societal interest would be served by a loophole-closing provision designed to check corruption that permitted unscrupulous persons and organizations to expend unlimited sums of money in order to obtain improper influence over candidates for elective office.[1]

Second, quite apart from the shortcomings of §608(e)(1) in preventing any abuses generated by large independent expenditures, the independent advocacy restricted by the provision does not presently appear to pose dangers of real or apparent corruption comparable to those identified with large campaign contributions. The parties defending §608(e)(1) contend that it is necessary to prevent would-be contributors from avoiding the contribution limitations by the simple expedient of paying directly for media advertisements or for other portions of the candidate's campaign activities. They argue that expenditures controlled by or coordinated with the candidate and his campaign might well have virtually the same value to the candidate as a contribution and would pose similar dangers of abuse. Yet such controlled or coordinated expenditures are treated as contributions rather than expenditures under the Act.[53] Section 608(b)'s contribution ceilings

---

1. Is the Court playing fast and loose in this paragraph? Very little contemporary election advertising is known for its subtlety, presumably because campaign advertisers believe most voters are paying little attention. Assuming this "loophole" would undermine the statute's effectiveness, should not the Court have considered whether a different interpretation of §608(e)(1) existed that would both alleviate vagueness concerns and better prevent evasion? For an argument that the Court should have and could have done so, see Marlene Arnold Nicholson, *Buckley v. Valeo: The Constitutionality of the Federal Election Campaign Act Amendments of 1974*, 1977 WISCONSIN LAW REVIEW 323, 342–44. Finally, consider the Court's footnote 31, in which it acknowledged that the anti-corruption effect of the contribution limits could be evaded by major special interests. Why does the possibility of evasion undermine the constitutionality of expenditure limits but not of contribution limits? — EDS.

53. Section 608(e)(1) does not apply to expenditures "on behalf of a candidate" within the meaning of §608(c)(2)(B). The latter subsection provides that expenditures "authorized or requested by the candidate, an authorized committee of the candidate, or an agent of the candidate" are to be treated as expenditures of the candidate and contributions by the person or group making the expenditure. The House and Senate Reports provide guidance in differentiating individual expenditures that are contributions and candidate expenditures under §608(c)(2)(B) from those treated as independent expenditures subject to the §608(e)(1) ceiling. The House Report speaks of independent expenditures as costs "incurred without the request or consent of a candidate or his agent." The Senate

rather than §608(e)(1)'s independent expenditure limitation prevent attempts to circumvent the Act through prearranged or coordinated expenditures amounting to disguised contributions. By contrast, §608(e)(1) limits expenditures for express advocacy of candidates made totally independently of the candidate and his campaign. Unlike contributions, such independent expenditures may well provide little assistance to the candidate's campaign and indeed may prove counterproductive. The absence of prearrangement and coordination of an expenditure with the candidate or his agent not only undermines the value of the expenditure to the candidate, but also alleviates the danger that expenditures will be given as a *quid pro quo* for improper commitments from the candidate. Rather than preventing circumvention of the contribution limitations, §608(e)(1) severely restricts all independent advocacy despite its substantially diminished potential for abuse.[m]

While the independent expenditure ceiling thus fails to serve any substantial governmental interest in stemming the reality or appearance of corruption in the electoral process, it heavily burdens core First Amendment expression. For the First Amendment right to "speak one's mind ... on all public institutions" includes the right to engage in "'vigorous advocacy' no less than 'abstract discussion.'" *New York Times Co. v. Sullivan*, 376 U.S., at 269. Advocacy of the election or defeat of candidates for federal office is no less entitled to protection under the First Amendment than the discussion of political policy generally or advocacy of the passage or defeat of legislation.

It is argued, however, that the ancillary governmental interest in equalizing the relative ability of individuals and groups to influence the outcome of elections serves to justify the limitation on express advocacy of the election or defeat of candidates imposed by §608(e)(1)'s expenditure ceiling. But the concept that government may restrict the speech of some elements of our society in order to enhance the relative voice of others is wholly foreign to the First Amendment, which was designed "to secure 'the widest possible dissemination of information from diverse and antagonistic sources,'" and "to assure unfettered interchange of ideas for the bringing about of political and social changes de-

---

report addresses the issue in greater detail. It provides an example illustrating the distinction between "authorized or requested" expenditures excluded from §608(e)(1) and independent expenditures governed by §608(e)(1):

> "[A] person might purchase billboard advertisements endorsing a candidate. If he does so completely on his own, and not at the request or suggestion of the candidate or his agent's [sic] that would constitute an 'independent expenditure on behalf of a candidate' under section 614(c) of the bill. The person making the expenditure would have to report it as such.
>
> "However, if the advertisement was placed in cooperation with the candidate's campaign organization, then the amount would constitute a gift by the supporter and an expenditure by the candidate just as if there had been a direct contribution enabling the candidate to place the advertisement himself. It would be so reported by both."

The Conference substitute adopted the provision of the Senate bill dealing with expenditures by any person "authorized or requested" to make an expenditure by the candidate or his agents. In view of this legislative history and the purposes of the Act, we find that the "authorized or requested" standard of the Act operates to treat all expenditures placed in cooperation with or with the consent of a candidate, his agents, or an authorized committee of the candidate as contributions subject to the limitations set forth in §608(b).

m. In Part I.B.4 of its opinion, the Court upheld the $25,000 limitation on total contributions by an individual on the ground that the individual could evade the $1,000 limit on contributions to candidates by making "massive" contributions to PACs likely to support such candidates or "huge" contributions to the candidates' political parties. Was the "potential for abuse" addressed by the $25,000 limit more of a danger than the potential addressed by the limit on independent expenditures? — EDS.

sired by the people." *New York Times Co.* The First Amendment's protection against governmental abridgment of free expression cannot properly be made to depend on a person's financial ability to engage in public discussion. *Cf. Eastern R. Conf. v. Noerr Motors*, 365 U.S. 127, 139 (1961).[55] ....

For the reasons stated, we conclude that §608(e)(1)'s independent expenditure limitation is unconstitutional under the First Amendment.

2. Limitation on Expenditures by Candidates from Personal or Family Resources

The Act also sets limits on expenditures by a candidate "from his personal funds, or the personal funds of his immediate family, in connection with his campaigns during any calendar year." §608(a)(1). These ceilings vary from $50,000 for Presidential or Vice Presidential candidates to $35,000 for senatorial candidates, and $25,000 for most candidates for the House of Representatives.

The ceiling on personal expenditures by candidates on their own behalf, like the limitations on independent expenditures contained in §608(e)(1), imposes a substantial restraint on the ability of persons to engage in protected First Amendment expression.[n] The candidate, no less than any other person, has a First Amendment right to engage in the discussion of public issues and vigorously and tirelessly to advocate his own election and the election of other candidates. Indeed, it is of particular importance that candidates have the unfettered opportunity to make their views known so that the electorate may intelligently evaluate the candidates' personal qualities and their positions on vital public issues before choosing among them on election day. Mr. Justice Brandeis' observation that in our country "public discussion is a political duty," *Whitney v. California*, 274 U.S. 357, 375 (1927) (concurring opinion), applies with special force to candidates for public office. Section 608(a)'s ceiling on personal expenditures by a candidate in furtherance of his own candidacy thus clearly and directly interferes with constitutionally protected freedoms.

The primary governmental interest served by the Act—the prevention of actual and apparent corruption of the political process—does not support the limitation on the candidate's expenditure of his own personal funds. As the Court of Appeals concluded: "Manifestly, the core problem of avoiding undisclosed and undue influence on candidates from outside interests has lesser application when the monies involved come from the candidate himself or from his immediate family." Indeed, the use of personal funds

---

55. Neither the voting rights cases nor the Court's decision upholding the Federal Communications Commission's fairness doctrine lends support to appellees' position that the First Amendment permits Congress to abridge the rights of some persons to engage in political expression in order to enhance the relative voice of other segments of our society. Cases invalidating governmentally imposed wealth restrictions on the right to vote or file as a candidate for public office rest on the conclusion that wealth "is not germane to one's ability to participate intelligently in the electoral process" and is therefore an insufficient basis on which to restrict a citizen's fundamental right to vote. *Harper*. These voting cases and the reapportionment decisions serve to assure that citizens are accorded an equal right to vote for their representatives regardless of factors of wealth or geography. But the principles that underlie invalidation of governmentally imposed restrictions on the franchise do not justify governmentally imposed restrictions on political expression. Democracy depends on a well-informed electorate, not a citizenry legislatively limited in its ability to discuss and debate candidates and issues....

n. Shockley, *supra*, 10 HASTINGS CONSTITUTIONAL LAW QUARTERLY at 694–95, asks: "If one agrees with the Court that being able to spend only $25,000 to $50,000 annually on campaigning is in fact a substantial restraint upon constitutional expression, what does this say about the rights of the ninety-nine percent of the American electorate who cannot expend even this 'substantially restrained' amount? Since their ability to speak is presumably restrained even more, where are they to look for the protection of their First Amendment rights?"—EDS.

reduces the candidate's dependence on outside contributions and thereby counteracts the coercive pressures and attendant risks of abuse to which the Act's contribution limitations are directed.

The ancillary interest in equalizing the relative financial resources of candidates competing for elective office, therefore, provides the sole relevant rationale for §608(a)'s expenditure ceiling. That interest is clearly not sufficient to justify the provision's infringement of fundamental First Amendment rights. First, the limitation may fail to promote financial equality among candidates. A candidate who spends less of his personal resources on his campaign may nonetheless outspend his rival as a result of more successful fundraising efforts. Indeed, a candidate's personal wealth may impede his efforts to persuade others that he needs their financial contributions or volunteer efforts to conduct an effective campaign. Second, and more fundamentally, the First Amendment simply cannot tolerate §608(a)'s restriction upon the freedom of a candidate to speak without legislative limit on behalf of his own candidacy. We therefore hold that §608(a)'s restriction on a candidate's personal expenditures is unconstitutional.

3. Limitations on Campaign Expenditures

Section 608(c) places limitations on overall campaign expenditures by candidates seeking nomination for election and election to federal office. Presidential candidates may spend $10,000,000 in seeking nomination for office and an additional $20,000,000 in the general election campaign. §§608(c)(1)(A), (B). The ceiling on senatorial campaigns is pegged to the size of the voting-age population of the State with minimum dollar amounts applicable to campaigns in States with small populations. In senatorial primary elections, the limit is the greater of eight cents multiplied by the voting-age population or $100,000, and in the general election the limit is increased to 12 cents multiplied by the voting-age population or $150,000. §§608(c)(1)(C), (D). The Act imposes blanket $70,000 limitations on both primary campaigns and general election campaigns for the House of Representatives with the exception that the senatorial ceiling applies to campaigns in States entitled to only one Representative. §§608(c)(1)(C)–(E). These ceilings are to be adjusted upwards at the beginning of each calendar year by the average percentage rise in the consumer price index for the 12 preceding months. §608(d).

No governmental interest that has been suggested is sufficient to justify the restriction on the quantity of political expression imposed by §608(c)'s campaign expenditure limitations. The major evil associated with rapidly increasing campaign expenditures is the danger of candidate dependence on large contributions. The interest in alleviating the corrupting influence of large contributions is served by the Act's contribution limitations and disclosure provisions rather than by §608(c)'s campaign expenditure ceilings. The Court of Appeals' assertion that the expenditure restrictions are necessary to reduce the incentive to circumvent direct contribution limits is not persuasive. There is no indication that the substantial criminal penalties for violating the contribution ceilings combined with the political repercussion of such violations will be insufficient to police the contribution provisions. Extensive reporting, auditing, and disclosure requirements applicable to both contributions and expenditures by political campaigns are designed to facilitate the detection of illegal contributions. Moreover, as the Court of Appeals noted, the Act permits an officeholder or successful candidate to retain contributions in excess of the expenditure ceiling and to use these funds for "any other lawful purpose." This provision undercuts whatever marginal role the expenditure limitations might otherwise play in enforcing the contribution ceilings.

The interest in equalizing the financial resources of candidates competing for federal office is no more convincing a justification for restricting the scope of federal election campaigns. Given the limitation on the size of outside contributions, the financial resources available to a candidate's campaign, like the number of volunteers recruited, will normally vary with the size and intensity of the candidate's support.[63] There is nothing invidious, improper, or unhealthy in permitting such funds to be spent to carry the candidate's message to the electorate.[64] Moreover, the equalization of permissible campaign expenditures might serve not to equalize the opportunities of all candidates, but to handicap a candidate who lacked substantial name recognition or exposure of his views before the start of the campaign.

The campaign expenditure ceilings appear to be designed primarily to serve the governmental interests in reducing the allegedly skyrocketing costs of political campaigns. Appellees and the Court of Appeals stressed statistics indicating that spending for federal election campaigns increased almost 300% between 1952 and 1972 in comparison with a 57.6% rise in the consumer price index during the same period. Appellants respond that during these years the rise in campaign spending lagged behind the percentage increase in total expenditures for commercial advertising and the size of the gross national product. In any event, the mere growth in the cost of federal election campaigns in and of itself provides no basis for governmental restrictions on the quantity of campaign spending and the resulting limitation on the scope of federal campaigns. The First Amendment denies government the power to determine that spending to promote one's political views is wasteful, excessive, or unwise. In the free society ordained by our Constitution it is not the government, but the people individually as citizens and candidates and collectively as associations and political committees who must retain control over the quantity and range of debate on public issues in a political campaign.[65]

For these reasons we hold that §608(c) is constitutionally invalid.

In sum, the provisions of the Act that impose a $1,000 limitation on contributions to a single candidate, §608(b)(1), a $5,000 limitation on contributions by a political committee to a single candidate, §608(b)(2), and a $25,000 limitation on total contributions

---

63. This normal relationship may not apply where the candidate devotes a large amount of his personal resources to his campaign.

64. As [Judge Tamm's] opinion dissenting in part from the decision below noted: "If a senatorial candidate can raise $1 voter from each voter, what evil is exacerbated by allowing that candidate to use all that money for political communication? I know of none."

65. For the reasons discussed in Part III, *infra*, Congress may engage in public financing of election campaigns and may condition acceptance of public funds on an agreement by the candidate to abide by specified expenditure limitations. Just as a candidate may voluntarily limit the size of the contributions he chooses to accept, he may decide to forgo private fundraising and accept public funding.

[This footnote, number 65, is cryptic but extremely important, as the tying of permissible campaign spending limits to public funding has profoundly shaped the politics of campaign finance regulation. In Part III of its opinion the Court does give reasons for the permissibility of public financing, but contrary to the statement in footnote 65, there is no explanation in Part III or elsewhere in Buckley why Congress may "condition acceptance of public funds on an agreement by the candidate to abide by ... expenditure limitations."

The text in the opinion immediately prior to footnote 65 should not be overshadowed by the footnote itself. If, collectively, the people favor a lower level of campaign expenditures, is it realistic for the Court to suggest that they may control the "quantity and range of debate" by reducing the contributions they make (as individuals or through associations) or receive (as candidates or political committees)? Consider Harold Leventhal, *Courts and Political Thickets*, 77 COLUMBIA LAW REVIEW 345, 368 (1977): "This answer ignores the possibility that the dynamics of some campaign problems are such that they cannot be solved by individual decisions; the race for campaign funds—like an arms race—requires global regulation."—EDS.]

by an individual during any calendar year, §608(b)(3), are constitutionally valid. These limitations, along with the disclosure provisions, constitute the Act's primary weapons against the reality or appearance of improper influence stemming from the dependence of candidates on large campaign contributions. The contribution ceilings thus serve the basic governmental interest in safeguarding the integrity of the electoral process without directly impinging upon the rights of individual citizens and candidates to engage in political debate and discussion. By contrast, the First Amendment requires the invalidation of the Act's independent expenditure ceiling, §608(e)(1), its limitation on a candidate's expenditures from his own personal funds, §608(a), and its ceilings on overall campaign expenditures, §608(c). These provisions place substantial and direct restrictions on the ability of candidates, citizens, and associations to engage in protected political expression, restrictions that the First Amendment cannot tolerate.

Notes and Questions on Buckley *and the First Amendment*

1. *Campaign Finance and the First Amendment.* Few are likely to quarrel with the majority's opening assertion that the contribution and spending limits "operate in an area of the most fundamental First Amendment activities." Yet most commentators agree that *Buckley* is characterized by "fluctuating deference to congressional determinations." Marlene Arnold Nicholson, *Buckley v. Valeo: The Constitutionality of the Federal Election Campaign Act Amendments of 1974*, 1977 WISCONSIN LAW REVIEW 323, 325. One reason, no doubt, is that if the restrictions operate within the core of the First Amendment, the governmental interests at stake lie within the core of the democratic process. Supporters of campaign finance regulation often claim that the governmental interests furthered are not only important, but are themselves intended to further First Amendment values, by making the opportunity to participate effectively in political debate more widespread. Whether this is the case and the implications for constitutional doctrine if it is have been questions of continuing controversy.

Those who believe there were First Amendment values on both sides accuse the *Buckley* majority of excessive formalism or mechanical jurisprudence. Such views were expressed by a member of the Court of Appeals panel whose ruling in *Buckley* upholding virtually all of the FECA Amendments was partially overruled by the Supreme Court:

> By ritual incantation of the notion of absolute protection, by applying it to the quantity as well as the content of political expression, and by making the unexamined and unprecedented assertion that money is speech, the Court elevated dry formalism over substantive constitutional reasoning. Political discussion is indeed at the core of the first amendment's guarantees, but the very centrality of political speech calls for a thorough rather than a conclusory analysis.

J. Skelly Wright, *Money and the Pollution of Politics: Is the First Amendment an Obstacle to Political Equality?*, 82 COLUMBIA LAW REVIEW 611, 633 (1982). Another member of the Court of Appeals panel in *Buckley* argued that the presence of First Amendment considerations on both sides required a more pragmatic approach than the Supreme Court had displayed:

> The first amendment works to promote an open market in ideas. But we restrict the freedom of monopolists controlling a market to enhance the freedom of others in the market. At a time when the liberty of contract had the constitutional preeminence today assigned to freedom of expression, Justice Holmes declared that principles of freedom cannot preclude government limits on the power

of wealth in order to create a fair competition.... These examples ... are suggestive of a pragmatic mode of thinking, which avoids focusing on the initial impact of a law, as a restriction, and looks at its overall effect.

Harold Leventhal, *Courts and Political Thickets*, 77 COLUMBIA LAW REVIEW 345, 373 (1977).

These critics have themselves drawn criticism from those who believe it is dangerous to give greater weight to "First Amendment values" than to what they regard as the First Amendment's direct command that the government not regulate political speech:

> The most important aspect of *Buckley v. Valeo* is what it did not do—specifically, the Supreme Court's refusal to follow the lead of the Court of Appeals and announce a radical new departure in the meaning of constitutional free speech. Although the revelations that accompanied Watergate undoubtedly pose hazards to the idea of self-government fully as great as the Court of Appeals apparently assumed, speech is not "free" in any very important sense if it is protected only when and to the extent that such protection is consistent with a congressionally defined notion of political equality....
>
> If we set any store by what Mr. Justice White in his dissenting opinion called "the word of those who know," the strong consensus is that, considering the state of American politics, very substantial sacrifices of the individual speech interest are warranted, indeed are necessary for the preservation of democratic values in government. The Court of Appeals capped its opinion with a disturbing metaphor—that of the dog in Aesop's fable who, lunging for the illusive bone reflected in the water, loses the real one that he had in his mouth. That real bone is the speech interest that is compatible with what [Alexander] Meiklejohn called "the common cause in which we all share." The bone in the water, the idea of free speech as an individual liberty—something that belongs to a person by inherent right regardless of what Congress may desire—may have, as the Court of Appeals suggests, a tincture of unreality. But the other bone is all too familiar. It is, at present, lodged in the throat of almost everyone in the world. Almost every country in the world, including those behind the iron curtain, can display a constitution that guarantees freedom of expression to the people—to the extent, of course, that the people's representatives may deem proper. With *Buckley v. Valeo* in hand, we can boast that our Constitution protects something far scarcer in history than that sort of freedom. And with the knowledge of the caliber of people who sometimes get their hands on our government, it is well that this is so.

Daniel D. Polsby, Buckley v. Valeo: *The Special Nature of Political Speech*, 1976 SUPREME COURT REVIEW 1, 42–43.

Following are two more extended statements of the competing sides of this debate. The first is from L.A. Powe, Jr., *Mass Speech and the Newer First Amendment*, 1982 SUPREME COURT REVIEW 243, 245–46, 268–69, 280–84:

> [T]he possibility [exists] that even if differing viewpoints are present there may be so overwhelming a predominance of communication in support of some of them that other viewpoints simply do not have a chance to be considered on the merits. For those who believe this occurs there is the not unnatural conclusion that the prevailing viewpoint has done so in an unfair way. Had the issue been joined between equals, a differing viewpoint would (or might) have prevailed. Most typically such concerns are expressed in the context of elections, and over

the past decade there have been a variety of attempts to even up the potential clash of ideas through either contribution or expenditure limitations on candidates and their supporters.... The structure of argument in the campaign finance cases is fairly simple. Because any contribution or expenditure will be translated into media advertising, a legislative restriction will necessarily limit speech. This is valid only if the government offers very important reasons. Typically, the government has two reasons, both going to the perceived purity of the electoral process. The first is that citizens may view large contributions to candidates as akin to bribery. But this rationale has not been sufficient to sustain all of the legislation. Thus the second justification: an election ought to have the elements of a fair fight, and when one side grossly outspends the other for advertising, a fair fight is impossible. Accordingly the marketplace of ideas is better served, and freedom of speech is enhanced, when one side of an issue is prevented from being repeated so often that it overwhelms rational thought about the merits of the election. This second justification for limiting contributions and expenditures is what I call the enhancement theory of freedom of speech. The theory has developed over the years on foundations that are foreign to the First Amendment; the theory has no place in any sensible treatment of the First Amendment and should, in the future, be summarily rejected....

To surrender the interests of individual autonomy and to attempt to tone down a debate (or one side of it) in the interests of enhancing the marketplace is to give up something that is directly traceable to the First Amendment in order to achieve a speculative gain. It is attempted on the speculative basis that a legislature knows at what points the problem of market failure is likely to surface and that enhancement is an effective means of avoiding them.... Furthermore, it rests on an assumption that less speech may well be better than more, an assumption that appears wildly at odds with the normal First Amendment belief that more speech is better....

The fundamental tenet of enhancement theory that less speech is better at some points seems to rest on two assumptions: first, additional speech on the other side either will not be forthcoming or is not worth the effort, and second, the "reach" of modern mass communications is of such a new order that it needs a different theory to make it function "consistently with the ends and purposes of the First Amendment." Yet just as there is a problem with determining how much is too much, there is also a gap in the explanation of why there will be no further speech on the other side to counter the speech that is being repeated too often. And how "new" is the problem? But for the "mass" communications of newspapers, specifically Pulitzer's and Hearst's, there would not have been a Spanish American War in 1898 to make Theodore Roosevelt next in line to the Presidency in 1900.

Enhancement has been articulated as a rationale only for dealing with the mass media. The soapbox orator, that classic and heroic lone dissenter of so much of the First Amendment case law, seems exempt. He does not fit within enhancement, because he cannot, from his soapbox, create the necessary imbalance. In his case we cannot shut him off because we dislike him, dislike his message, are sick and tired of being bothered, are angry that someone could be so wrong-headed, or feel that he creates such an imbalance in the marketplace that it would be unfair to let him continue. We are stuck with walking away from him or maybe even countering what he says with our own position.

The traditional solution, more rather than less speech, is both possible and desirable in the mass speech area as well. [A]s Brandeis recognized over fifty years ago, speech is a part of political liberty. Public discussion is a citizen's duty. As a society we have more to fear from an inert than an active citizenry. Fear and repression menace stable government; speech does not.... It is not so much that we retain a naive belief that truth is knowable or that the electorate will rationally choose it, as that the simple recognition that no theory requiring people to stop speaking (or stop listening) better fits with our traditions than the one we have adopted. The theory that a speaker has the right to choose his message and the intensity and frequency of its delivery reflects the recognition that a free-for-all on public issues serves both the ideals [of] self-government and those of maximizing individual choices.... It is hard to dispute that the wealthy seem to enjoy tremendous influence — and not only in this country. But if this is the concern, I would suspect that the best way of dealing with the power of wealth would be to attack its source rather than its consequences. In other words, if the wealthy are too powerful, change the tax and inheritance laws to prevent accumulations of wealth. If that is too extreme, then significant additional public funding can be made available for electoral campaigns, so that the advantages of wealth can either be eliminated or minimized. These are neither easy nor cost-free choices, but by not seeking to operate directly on speech in one case and by adding more speech without limiting anyone in the other, both are consistent with the traditions of the First Amendment.

I think it not unlikely that at least part of the impetus to do something toward limiting mass speech flows from a disdain for those that would use this type of speech and the message that they offer as well as the not inconceivable fear that people might listen. The nice thing about Abrams dropping pamphlets out of an upper floor window to the street below, or Gitlow distributing that horribly turgid and dull "Left Wing Manifesto," or Dennis and his handful of colleagues reading Marx and Lenin and plotting to find the proletariat for a revolution, or Brandenburg spouting his racism and anti-Semitism to the cattle of Hamilton County, was that we know that even if someone listens, nothing happens.[o] The speech reaches few people and affects even fewer. But the mass speech cases involve speech that everyone has seen, and the New Right mass mailing distortion squads appear to have done what the lone dissenter never managed to do, convince people to vote the wrong way. It is easy to defend speech we hate so long as it is ineffective, but it is much harder to do so when people actually respond positively.... The sloganeering of mass speech does not require thought or invite dialogue. It preys on the basest instincts and, unfortunately, may well convince the masses to make our society a less enjoyable place to live.

This is, of course, true of a lot of speech.... But [freedom of speech has come down] to us with but a single tradition: that the "State's fear that voters might make an ill-advised choice does not provide the State with a compelling justification for limiting speech" and if there is concern, more, not less, speech is the best remedy. Thus far the Court's results in the mass speech cases have been reasonably consistent with this tradition. What remains is to strengthen them by recognizing that the mass speech cases present but the modern version of a much older problem to which we have long since known the appropriate remedy.

---

o. In this sentence, Powe refers to a series of classic twentieth-century First Amendment decisions of the Supreme Court. — EDS.

For other recent similar defenses to Powe's, see Kathleen M. Sullivan, *Political Money and Freedom of Speech*, 30 U.C. DAVIS LAW REVIEW 663 (1997) and Robert Post, *Regulating Election Speech Under the First Amendment*, 77 TEXAS LAW REVIEW 1837 (1999).

The second excerpt is from Owen M. Fiss, *Free Speech and Social Structure*, 71 IOWA LAW REVIEW 1405, 1407–16 (1986).

> Democracy promises collective self-determination—a freedom to the people to decide their own fate—and presupposes a debate on public issues that is (to use Justice Brennan's now classic formula) "uninhibited, robust, and wide-open." [*Buckley* and other] free speech decisions of the seventies, however, seemed to impoverish, rather than enrich public debate and thus threatened one of the essential preconditions for an effective democracy. And they seemed to do so in a rather systematic way.
>
> [A]t issue was not simply a conflict between equality and liberty, but also and more importantly, a conflict between two conceptions of liberty. The battle being fought was not just Liberty v. Equality, but Liberty v. Liberty, or to put the point another way, not just between the first amendment and the equal protection clause, but a battle *within* the first amendment itself. [T]he Court was not advancing an idiosyncratic or perverted conception of liberty, but was in fact working well within the Free Speech Tradition. The Court was not crudely substituting entrepreneurial liberty (or property) for political liberty; the rich or owners of capital in fact won, but only because they had advanced claims of political liberty that easily fit within the received Tradition. Money is speech—just as much as picketing is.
>
> [T]he difficulties the Court encountered in the free speech cases of the seventies could ultimately be traced to inadequacies in the Free Speech Tradition itself. The problem was the Tradition not the Court. [O]n balance, it seemed that the Tradition oriented the Justices in the wrong direction and provided ample basis for those who formed the majority to claim, quite genuinely, that they were protecting free speech when, in fact, they were doing something of a different, far more ambiguous, character. This meant that criticism would have to be directed not simply at the Burger Court but at something larger: at a powerfully entrenched, but finally inadequate body of doctrine.
>
> [T]he key to fulfilling the ultimate purposes of the first amendment is not autonomy, which has a most uncertain or double-edged relationship to public debate, but rather the actual effect of a broadcast: On the whole does it enrich public debate? Speech is protected when (and only when) it does, and precisely because it does, not because it is an exercise of autonomy. In fact, autonomy adds nothing and if need be, might have to be sacrificed, to make certain that public debate is sufficiently rich to permit true collective self-determination. What the phrase 'the freedom of speech' in the first amendment refers to is a social state of affairs, not the action of an individual or institution.
>
> The risk posed to freedom of speech by autonomy ... occurs whenever speech takes place under conditions of scarcity, that is, whenever the opportunity for communication is limited. In such situations one utterance will necessarily displace another. With the street corner, the element of scarcity tends to be masked; when we think of the street corner we ordinarily assume that every speaker will have his or her turn, and that the attention of the audience is virtually unlimited. Indeed, that is why it is such an appealing story. But in politics, scarcity is the rule

rather than the exception. The opportunities for speech tend to be limited, either by the time or space available for communicating or by our capacity to digest or process information. This is clear and obvious in the case of the mass media, which play a decisive role in determining which issues are debated, and how, but it is true in other contexts as well. In a referendum or election, for example, there is every reason to be concerned with the advertising campaign mounted by the rich and powerful, because the resources at their disposal enable them to fill all the available space for public discourse with their message....

Classical liberalism presupposes a sharp dichotomy between state and citizen. It teaches us to be wary of the state and equates liberty with limited government. The Free Speech Tradition builds on this view of the world when it reduces free speech to autonomy and defines autonomy to mean the absence of government interference. Liberalism's distrust of the state is represented by the antagonism between the policeman and soapbox orator and by the assumption that the policeman is the enemy of speech.

[W]e can no longer assume that the state is all censorship. [I]n the modern world the state can enrich as much as it constricts public debate: The state can do this, in part, through the provision of subsidies and other benefits....

We can also look beyond the provision of subsidies, and consider whether the state might enrich public debate by regulating in a manner similar to the policeman.... The power of the media to decide what it broadcasts must be regulated because, as we saw through an understanding of the dynamic of displacement, this power always has a double edge: It subtracts from public debate at the very moment that it adds to it. Similarly expenditures of political actors might have to be curbed to make certain all views are heard. To date we have ambivalently recognized the value of state regulation of this character on behalf of speech—we have a fairness doctrine for the broadcast media and limited campaign financing laws. But these regulatory measures are today embattled, and in any event, more, not less, is needed.... A commitment to rich public debate will allow, and sometimes even require the state to act in these ways, however elemental and repressive they might at first seem. Autonomy will be sacrificed, and content regulation sometimes allowed, but only on the assumption that public debate might be enriched and our capacity for collective self-determination enhanced. The risks of this approach cannot be ignored, and at moments they seem alarming, but we can only begin to evaluate them when we weigh in the balance the hidden costs of an unrestricted regime of autonomy.

At the core of my approach is a belief that contemporary social structure is as much an enemy of free speech as is the policeman.... We should learn to recognize the state not only as an enemy, but also as a friend of speech; like any social actor, it has the potential to act in both capacities, and, using the enrichment of public debate as the touchstone, we must begin to discriminate between them. When the state acts to enhance the quality of public debate, we should recognize its actions as consistent with the first amendment.

On what points, if any, are Polsby, Powe, and Fiss in agreement? What is the fundamental disagreement between Fiss on the one hand, and Polsby and Powe on the other? Does the pragmatic approach recommended by Judges Wright and Leventhal necessarily entail Fiss's outlook?

Consider also Cass R. Sunstein, *Political Equality and Unintended Consequences*, 94 COLUMBIA LAW REVIEW 1390, 1397 (1994). Sunstein argues that *Buckley* is the "modern-day analogue of the infamous and discredited case of *Lochner v. New York* [198 U.S. 45 (1905)], in which the Court invalidated maximum hour laws." Sunstein explains:

> Just as the due process clause once forbade government "interference" with the outcomes of the economic marketplace [the holding of *Lochner* — EDS.], so too the First Amendment now bans government "interference" with the political marketplace, with the term "marketplace" understood quite literally. In this way *Buckley* replicates *Lochner....*

> Because it involves speech, *Buckley* is in one sense even more striking than *Lochner*. As I have noted, the goal of political equality is time-honored in the American constitutional tradition, as the goal of economic equality is not. Efforts to redress economic inequalities, or to ensure that they are not turned to political inequalities, should not be seen as impermissible redistribution, or as the introduction of government regulation into a place where it did not exist before. A system of unlimited campaign expenditures should be seen as a regulatory decision to allow disparities in resources to be turned into disparities in political influence. That may be the best decision, all things considered; but why is it unconstitutional for government to attempt to replace this system with an alternative? The Court offered no answer. Its analysis was startlingly cavalier. Campaign finance laws should be evaluated not through axioms, but pragmatically in terms of their consequences for free expression.

Id. at 1398–99; see also John Rawls, POLITICAL LIBERALISM 362 (1993) (making a similar argument); Frank Michelman, *Political Truth and the Rule of Law*, 8 TEL AVIV UNIVERSITY STUDIES IN LAW 281 (1988) (putting forth a civic republican defense of campaign finance regulation). How does one engage in such a pragmatic evaluation? Would Polsby and Powe reach the same conclusions in conducting such an evaluation as Fiss and Sunstein?

2. *Neutrality*. In the past quarter-century, "content neutrality" has emerged as a major component of the Supreme Court's doctrine in applying the First Amendment. "The Court applies 'the most exacting scrutiny' to regulations that discriminate among instances of speech based on its content." LAURENCE H. TRIBE, AMERICAN CONSTITUTIONAL LAW 798 (2d ed., 1988) (quoting *Widmar v. Vincent*, 454 U.S. 263, 276 (1981)).

In *Buckley*, the majority conceded that the FECA did not "focus on the ideas expressed by persons or groups subject to its regulations," while noting that the Act was "aimed in part at equalizing the relative ability of all voters to affect electoral outcomes." Defenders of regulation assert that "the equal money limits are concededly neutral as to the content of ideas expressed—a crucial point." Leventhal, *supra*, 77 COLUMBIA LAW REVIEW at 359. However, critics of regulation do not invariably concede this point.

> In no case will the effects upon individuals, interest groups, and other political actors be precisely evenhanded. Indeed, it is ironic that the most forceful argument supporting campaign finance legislation praises the FECA for depriving the wealthy of the advantage of their position. The argument implies that the chief *virtue* of reform measures is their lack of neutrality of impact. Statutes that are supported precisely because they deprive a particular group of its ability to engage relatively effectively in politics, therefore, may not be as "entirely content neutral" as they seem.

Lillian R. BeVier, *Money and Politics: A Perspective on the First Amendment and Campaign Finance Reform*, 73 CALIFORNIA LAW REVIEW 1045, 1062 (1985); see also Bradley A. Smith, *Money Talks: Speech, Corruption, Equality, and Campaign Finance*, 86 GEORGETOWN LAW JOURNAL 45, 54 (1997) ("To suggest that any [campaign finance] scheme could be content neutral is to misunderstand the purpose of the enterprise: People who favor campaign finance reform do so because they believe that the present system of finance gives some individuals too much influence, thus leading to disfavored electoral and legislative results."); Sanford Levinson, *Book Review: Regulating Campaign Activity: The New Road to Contradiction?*, 83 MICHIGAN LAW REVIEW 939, 945 (1985) ("[I]t is worth considering to what extent we in fact support such restrictions because of tacit assumptions about the contents of the views held by the rich, who would obviously feel most of the burden of the restrictions."). Indeed, according to two of the attorneys who litigated *Buckley*, plaintiffs considered but rejected the idea of arguing that the regulations were not neutral:

> An argument plaintiffs decided against making in *Buckley*, in part on the ground that it sounded too political, is that restrictions on campaign financing generally favor Democrats over Republicans because the latter needed to exploit their generally greater access to substantial contributors or larger total contributions to overcome the Democrats' much larger registered membership. Moreover, it can be argued persuasively that so long as our social system is based on the premise that inequalities of wealth serve valid and useful purposes, the wealthy need means to exercise their financial power to defend themselves politically against the greater numbers who may believe that their economic interests militate toward leveling.

Brice M. Clagett & John R. Bolton, Buckley v. Valeo, *Its Aftermath, and Its Prospects: The Constitutionality of Government Restraints on Political Campaign Financing*, 29 VANDERBILT LAW REVIEW 1327, 1335 (1976).

As a matter of tactics, do you believe the plaintiffs were correct to withhold this argument in the *Buckley* case? Do you believe contribution and expenditure limits are neutral?

3. *Is money speech?* The *Buckley* majority said that limiting campaign expenditures was tantamount to limiting speech, because such a limit "necessarily reduces the quantity of expression by restricting the number of issues discussed, the depth of their exploration, and the size of the audience reached." As a practical matter, a limit on spending by a major campaign may limit the *repetition* of the same message to the same audience. Is a reduction of repetition the same as a reduction of the size of the audience? What if the reason for the repetition is that many or most people are inclined to "tune out" the message (if it is broadcast) or throw it away unopened (if it is mailed)?

Though the question was hotly debated in the period leading up to *Buckley*, most defenders of reform until recently have accepted the Court's conclusion that spending limits need to be treated as speech limitations though, as we have seen, they often contend that the limits also serve First Amendment goals. One writer who refused to concede the point was J. Skelly Wright, *Politics and the Constitution: Is Money Speech?*, 85 YALE LAW JOURNAL 1001, 1012 (1976):

> [T]he effectiveness of political speakers is not necessarily diminished by reasonable contribution and expenditure ceilings. The giving and spending restrictions may cause candidates and other individuals to rely more on less expensive means of communication. But there is no reason to believe that such a shift in means reduces the number of issues discussed in a campaign. And, by forcing candidates to put more emphasis on local organizing or leafletting or door-to-door canvassing and less on full-page ads and television spot commercials, the restrictions may well generate deeper exploration of the issues raised. Finally, even to the extent that smaller audiences result from diminished use of the most expensive and pervasive media—and the campaigning so far gives no substan-

tial indication that this happens—the effectiveness of a given speaker does not decline in relation to that of his opponents. All similarly situated competitors face the same constraints. Within those limits effectiveness still depends on the creativity of the speaker—and on the soundness of his ideas.

How persuasive is Judge Wright's argument? When candidates are limited in the amount they can spend in their campaigns—either because of the limits in their fund-raising capabilities or because of legally imposed spending limits—they are likely to use their scarce economic resources in the manner they regard as most cost-effective. If mass media—especially television and direct mail—are perceived as the most cost-effective media, then the imposition of spending limits may cause campaigns to cut back on "grass roots" expenditures and thereby increase their overall dependence on mass media. Spending in the 1976 presidential campaign was limited, because the major candidates accepted public financing. The perception that the campaigns sharply cut back on grass roots expenditures, such as bumper stickers and campaign buttons, led to the adoption of amendments in 1979 that made it possible for parties to spend sums outside the regular spending limits for grass roots activities.

Even if spending limits did have the effect of diverting campaigns from reliance on mass media to reliance on volunteers, as Wright supposes, would this necessarily be desirable? Political spot advertising on television is widely reviled, but the message is one that is controlled by the candidate. Volunteers might engage in more extended dialogue with voters, but anyone who has ever "walked precincts" in campaigns is likely to have mastered a brief, "canned" statement and been acutely aware of the need not to spend more than a few moments at any one residence. In any event, the volunteer may not be accurately reflecting the views of the candidate, especially in presidential or statewide elections in which few volunteers are likely to have any significant acquaintance with the candidate.

Justice Stevens revived the question, if cryptically, in a short concurrence in *Nixon v. Shrink Missouri Government PAC*, 528 U.S. 377 (2000). There, Stevens said that money was property, not speech. We therefore return to this question in Chapter 15, which reprints and discusses *Shrink Missouri*.

4. *Balancing the First Amendment with Concerns over Corruption or Equality*. In *Buckley*, the Court applied a *balancing test* to determine if the government's interest in preventing corruption, the appearance of corruption, or equality could trump First Amendment concerns. In your view, how should the proper balance be struck? You may wish to consider your answer in light of the readings in Part III of this chapter.

5. *The standard of review*. As students of constitutional law are well aware, since the 1960s the Supreme Court has devoted considerable time to elaborating the "standard of review" that will be employed to test the constitutionality of various government measures. To simplify, it is ordinarily assumed that regulation that impinges on First Amendment rights—especially when it is political speech and association that are at stake—will be reviewed under the most rigorous standard, often described as "strict scrutiny." The *Buckley* majority having concluded that both contribution limits and spending limits impinge on the freedom of political speech or association, it would seem to follow that they should be subjected to strict scrutiny. But did the *Buckley* majority test all the limits against the strictest standard? This question has seemed to some to have at least some tactical significance, because if strict scrutiny was applied, future limits are likely to be struck down, even though certain limits (those on the size of contributions) were upheld in *Buckley*. On the other hand, if a more lenient standard of review was applied, then it may be easier to de-

fend various campaign regulations. The doctrinal debate is summarized by Marlene Arnold Nicholson, *Political Campaign Expenditure Limitations and the Unconstitutional Condition Doctrine*, 10 HASTINGS CONSTITUTIONAL LAW QUARTERLY 601, 607–08 (1983):

> It is difficult to determine the standard of review employed by the Court to evaluate the various restrictions in *Buckley*. Although the per curiam opinion relied upon cases in which strict scrutiny was explicitly applied, it was less than explicit in describing the standard it was actually employing. The decision in *Buckley* may be viewed as a case in which the strictest First Amendment review was applied to all of the limitations. The fact that contribution limitations were upheld may simply mean that those restrictions alone were found to be necessary to further a compelling government interest. The Court's initial rejection of the argument that a lesser standard of review than strict scrutiny should apply because the limitations applied to "speech plus" rather than "pure speech," supports this view. On the other hand, the Court seemed to scrutinize some of the limitations more closely than others, giving credence to the interpretation that the level of scrutiny was subject to a sliding scale, depending upon the Court's view of the burden upon First Amendment interests. [L]imitations upon overall campaign expenditures seemed to fall somewhere in the middle. Unlike its treatment of independent expenditures and the use of a candidate's personal wealth, the Court did not greatly stress the seriousness of the burden, and did not speak in absolutist terms. Rather, the primary emphasis was upon the inadequacy of the proffered rationales.

In *Shrink Missouri*, the Supreme Court clarified that something less than strict scrutiny applies to review of challenged contribution limits. How much less than strict scrutiny remains to be seen, especially given more recent cases by the Court that have pulled back from the deference the Court showed in *Shrink Missouri*.

Notes and Questions on the Court's Differing Treatment of Contribution Limits and Spending Limits

1. The *Buckley* majority distinguished sharply between contribution limits and expenditure limits, treating the latter as more offensive to the First Amendment than the former. Chief Justice Burger, in his separate opinion concurring in part and dissenting in part, criticized this distinction, asserting that "contributions and expenditures are two sides of the same First Amendment coin." He explained:

> The Court's attempt to distinguish the communication inherent in political *contributions* from the speech aspects of political *expenditures* simply "will not wash." We do little but engage in word games unless we recognize that people— candidates and contributors—spend money on political activity because they wish to communicate ideas, and their constitutional interest in doing so is precisely the same whether they or someone else utters the words.

> The Court attempts to make the Act seem less restrictive by casting the problem as one that goes to freedom of association rather than freedom of speech. I have long thought freedom of association and freedom of expression were two peas from the same pod. The contribution limitations of the Act impose a restriction on certain forms of associational activity that are for the most part, as the Court recognizes, harmless in fact. And the restrictions are hardly incidental in their effect upon particular campaigns. Judges are ill-equipped to gauge the precise

impact of legislation, but a law that impinges upon First Amendment rights requires us to make the attempt. It is not simply speculation to think that the limitations on contributions will foreclose some candidacies. The limitations will also alter the nature of some electoral contests drastically.

Justice Blackmun, concurring in part and dissenting in part, also said he was "not persuaded that the Court makes, or indeed is able to make, a principled constitutional distinction between the contribution limitations, on the one hand, and the expenditure limitations, on the other, that are involved here." In later cases, individual justices have occasionally rejected *Buckley*'s decisive distinction between contribution and expenditure limits, see *Federal Election Commission v. National Conservative Political Action Committee*, 470 U.S. 480, 518, 519 (1985) (Marshall, J., dissenting) ("Although I joined the portion of the *Buckley per curiam* that distinguished contributions from independent expenditures for First Amendment purposes, I now believe that the distinction has no constitutional significance."), or sought to limit the scope of the distinction. See *Austin v. Michigan Chamber of Commerce*, 494 U.S. 652, 678 (1990) (Stevens, J., concurring) ("In my opinion the distinction between individual expenditures and individual contributions that the Court identified in *Buckley* should have little, if any, weight in reviewing corporate participation in candidate elections.") Most recently, Justice Thomas has rejected the distinction between contributions and expenditures in *Colorado I* and *Shrink Missouri* (both discussed in Chapter 15).

The distinction has also come in for heavy criticism from commentators outside the Supreme Court. The viability of the distinction has been doubted both by those who favor more stringent review of campaign finance regulations, e.g., BeVier, *supra*, 73 CALIFORNIA LAW REVIEW at 1063; Clagett & Bolton, *supra*, 29 VANDERBILT LAW REVIEW at 1332, and by those who favor greater constitutional tolerance for such regulations. For example, Judge Leventhal, *supra*, 77 COLUMBIA LAW REVIEW at 358–59, wrote:

> With a limitation of contributions, political freedom is rendered less than absolute. The conclusion that the limitations on these freedoms were supported by an overriding public interest was sound, in my view, but certainly debatable. What strikes a careful reader of the opinion, however, is the Court's acceptance for the present of the legislative judgment that the public interest in reform is overriding, while reserving for the future the possibility of reconsidering whether the provision operates in the real world not merely as a limitation but as an effective exclusion from the political process.

> Strikingly different from the pragmatic tone, experimental outlook, and fact-and-record oriented discussion of the passages upholding the foregoing provisions, are the virtually adjoining passages that invalidate ceilings on overall campaign expenditures in a campaign for federal office, on a candidate's expenditures from his own funds, and on amounts that can be expended by a supporter directly on behalf of a candidate rather than by contribution.

> A close look at these passages discloses that the Court rested its conclusions on undemonstrated, and possibly undemonstrable, assertions about the way the statute would affect political life.

One commentator, Nicholson, *supra*, 1977 WISCONSIN LAW REVIEW at 327, suggested that to explain the distinction, one must view *Buckley* in the "context of its time." The Watergate scandals

> produced a political climate in which wholesale invalidation of the 1974 reforms could have brought about widespread distrust of the Court as an institution. In-

deed, the scandals probably convinced the Court that stringent measures were necessary to prevent illegal campaign activities from weakening our political system. However, the Court was clearly not convinced that the political power balance between the rich and the nonrich need be upset. Indeed, it was in dealing with the policy goal of equalizing the relative political influence of various economic classes that the Court accorded the least deference to Congress. The Court rejected the equalization of political influence as a rationale for restrictions upon the use of money for political expression. Although the rationale of preventing the appearance and reality of corruption was accepted as a compelling interest to restrict contributions, it refused to defer to Congress' determination that restrictions upon expenditures were necessary to prevent corruption.

Despite the distinction's possible origin in the political climate of its time, and despite the criticism it has received on and off the Court, the Court has continued to treat the distinction between contributions and expenditures as the cornerstone of First Amendment doctrine affecting campaign finance regulation.[p] Attempting to benefit from hindsight, one of the editors of this volume reviewed experience since 1976 and concluded:

> [T]here is *some* basis for the Court's preference of contribution limits over expenditure limits. Contribution limits address the conflict of interest problem more directly, though not necessarily more effectively, than campaign spending limits, whereas spending limits restrict speech more directly than contribution limits. Indirect effects can be equally or more serious than direct effects, but in a world of great empirical uncertainty, one may have a higher degree of confidence in judgments of causation when the causal chain is direct.... Although the jury of social scientists is still out, there is reason to believe that to the extent spending limits reduce spending more than contribution limits, this will tend to make spending limits more detrimental to electoral competition....
>
> These advantages of contribution limits over spending limits are modest, at best, and very much subject to changing circumstances. They do not support a general principle that expenditure limits are nearly always unconstitutional while contribution limits are nearly always valid.

Daniel Hays Lowenstein, *A Patternless Mosaic: Campaign Finance and the First Amendment After* Austin, 21 CAPITAL UNIVERSITY LAW REVIEW 381, 401–02 (1992). For a stronger defense of *Buckley*'s distinction between contributions and expenditures, see Eugene Volokh, *Freedom of Speech and Speech about Political Candidates: The Unintended Consequences of Three Proposals*, 24 HARVARD JOURNAL OF LAW AND PUBLIC POLICY 47, 65 (2000) ("Especially given the ability of many people to pool their independent expenditures — the expenditures would only have to be independent of the candidate, not of each other — a regime that allowed unlimited expenditures but only modest contributions would still leave people with considerable opportunities to speak.").

2. *The validity of contribution limits.* The Court upheld the FECA contribution limits as an effort "to limit the actuality and appearance of corruption resulting from large individual financial contributions." Although the Court was willing to assume "that most large contributors do not seek improper influence over a candidate's position or an officeholder's action," the Court quoted approvingly the Court of Appeals' statement that "a court has no scalpel to probe, whether, say, a $2,000 ceiling might not serve as well as

---

p. However, as we shall see in later chapters, the distinction has had less force in cases involving ballot measure elections or the regulation of corporate and labor union political activity.

$1,000." Does this approach provide adequate protection to First Amendment rights? BeVier, *supra*, 73 CALIFORNIA LAW REVIEW at 1086–88, believes it does not:

> Campaign contributions are valuable first amendment activities which, in *most* instances, involve little genuine risk of corrupting public decision-making. Contribution limitations thus systematically restrict protected, *non*dangerous activities....
>
> In contrast to its customary strategy of overprotecting speech in order to protect speech that matters, the Court's willingness to defer to corruption-prevention measures represents an apparent strategy of underprotecting speech in order to protect a governmental interest that matters. The Court, in effect, has permitted Congress to outlaw entirely political activity that presents no genuine danger of corruption—the substantive evil that Congress has the right to prevent....
>
> The question that must be faced, then, is whether "where corruption is the evil feared," the Court should underprotect speech. Genuine corruption, of course, undermines the integrity of any government. Moreover, it is difficult to detect and difficult to define precisely in a statute. Therefore it arguably is impossible to prevent with narrowly drawn prohibitions. Thus, the argument would go, the Court can reasonably permit the legislature to treat the problem with broad prophylactic rules and need not impose any requirement that the government demonstrate either the rules' necessity or their efficacy.
>
> This argument is troublesome because it treats the nature of the government interest as the only variable that determines how the Court should deal with plainly overbroad legislative rules. There is, of course, another variable to be considered, namely the fact that rules deter and punish legitimate political behavior. Strict scrutiny of legislative means is the first amendment norm, and overprotection of speech rights is a substantively and procedurally defensible judicial practice. The fact that corruption is the evil to be feared does not render political activity itself intrinsically less valuable. Moreover, no one has ever tried to explain why legislatures should in principle have more leeway to infringe upon first amendment rights to prevent corruption than they have, for example, to prevent subversion.

Despite such criticism, the Court has continued to regard restrictions on contributions permissively. A strong reaffirmation of this permissiveness occurred in *California Medical Association (CMA) v. Federal Election Commission*, 453 U.S. 182 (1981), a case that arose because of the intricate provisions in FECA regulating the financial activities of political action committees. When a corporation or union organizes a PAC, the corporation or union is permitted to pay the PAC's administrative expenses without limit. These can be quite high, often exceeding the amounts of campaign funds that the PAC raises and distributes. On the other hand, corporations and unions are not permitted to contribute campaign funds to their PACs or directly to federal candidates. Individuals and unincorporated associations are permitted to contribute campaign funds, but these are subject to the general limits. In particular, they can give a PAC no more than $5,000. CMA, an unincorporated association, gave more than $5,000 to CALPAC, a PAC established as the vehicle for campaign money raised from California doctors. CMA argued that for First Amendment purposes, its payments to CALPAC should be treated as similar to expenditures rather than contributions, because such payments constituted the only way CMA could engage in political activity through a political committee. Furthermore, since

CMA's payments went only to CALPAC, not directly to candidates, and since CALPAC's contributions to candidates were subject to the normal limits, the CMA payments posed no danger of corruption. Finally, CMA argued that it was denied equal protection as compared to corporations and unions that were permitted to pay the administrative expenses of their PACs without limit.

Speaking for a plurality of four, Justice Marshall wrote this often-quoted passage:

> We would naturally be hesitant to conclude that CMA's determination to fund CALPAC rather than to engage directly in political advocacy is entirely unprotected by the First Amendment. Nonetheless, the "speech by proxy" that CMA seeks to achieve through its contributions to CALPAC is not the sort of political advocacy that this Court in *Buckley* found entitled to full First Amendment protection.

There were four justices who dissented on jurisdictional grounds without reaching the merits. Therefore, the fifth vote required for the decision against CMA was cast by Justice Blackmun, who repeated his opinion, stated in *Buckley*, that restrictions on contributions and expenditures were subject to the same "rigorous standard of review." Nonetheless, Justice Blackmun suggested that under *Buckley*, limits on contributions to political committees making only independent expenditures would be unconstitutional. Perhaps more significant than Marshall's and Blackmun's contrasting rhetoric was the fact that a majority was willing to uphold a contribution restriction whose efficacy as an instrument against corruption or conflict of interest seems tenuous at best. Blackmun joined with the other four justices to make a majority in rejecting CMA's equal protection argument on the ground that when the whole pattern of restrictions on corporations and unions was considered, there was no discrimination against an unincorporated association such as CMA.

3. *The invalidity of expenditure limits.* If the purpose of preventing contributors from gaining improper influence over elected officials justifies contribution limits, why is the same purpose not also a justification of overall limits on how much a candidate's campaign may spend? One reason in *Buckley* was that spending limits are subject to more stringent review under the First Amendment. In addition, the *Buckley* majority regarded contribution limits as the primary weapon against undue influence, and spending limits as a redundancy. "The interest in alleviating the corrupting influence of large contributions is served by the Act's contribution limitations and disclosure provisions rather than by ... campaign expenditure restrictions."

This conclusion, like so many others in *Buckley*, has come in for criticism:

> Sixteen years after *Buckley*, few would argue that the FECA contribution limits have prevented conflicts of interest arising from campaign contributions. The Court seems to have assumed that the contribution limits set by Congress were fixed solely for the purpose of preventing contributions that could exert improper pressure. If so, the Court's assumption was erroneous. Although limits could prevent the most flagrant and dangerous contributions, to set the limits low enough to remove the likelihood of pressure would have been to preclude the possibility of raising funds for an adequate campaign. Congress recognized that in the absence of public financing, realistic contribution limits without expenditure limits could not effectively prevent the campaign finance system from being a system of institutionalized conflict of interest.

Lowenstein, *supra*, 21 CAPITAL UNIVERSITY LAW REVIEW at 398–99. Even if this argument that campaign spending limits are not redundant as an anti-corruption device is accepted, a spending limit itself would not prevent receipt of a contribution large enough for potential improper influence to exist. On what theory could a campaign spending limit prevent "a system of institutionalized conflict of interest"?

The other major argument in favor of expenditure limits that was rejected by the *Buckley* majority is that such limits would equalize the opportunity to participate in electoral politics and to influence outcomes. In earlier notes in this chapter and in the last chapter we considered some contrasting views on equality as a general goal of campaign finance regulation. Was this equalization rationale rejected in *Buckley* because it was insufficient or because it was not even a permissible objective under the Constitution? Probably the most frequently quoted statement in *Buckley* is that "the concept that government may restrict the speech of some elements of our society in order to enhance the relative voice of others is wholly foreign to the First Amendment." This strong statement, written in the context of rejecting the FECA limits on independent expenditures, prompted Professor Nicholson, writing shortly after the *Buckley* decision was issued, to find "that the Court viewed the purpose to equalize as the impropriety." 1977 WISCONSIN LAW REVIEW at 330.

> As will be seen, later campaign finance decisions have seemed to show fluctuating attitudes on the Court toward equalizing regulations. Even in *Buckley* itself, the Court's hostility was not uniform in intensity. The strong language quoted above occurred in the context of a drastically restrictive provision, the $1,000 limit on individual expenditures in a federal election campaign. In the context of limits on a candidate's overall campaign spending, which, as the Court noted, provided "substantially greater room for discussion and debate," the Court appeared to treat the equalization rationale with less animosity, rejecting it because there was nothing invidious about permitting the candidate who could raise more to spend more, *so long as only modest contributions were permitted.*

4. Even if expenditure limits are impermissible in public elections, might they be permissible in university student association elections, in light of a university's educational mission? *See Flint v. Dennison*, 361 F.Supp.2d 1215, 1221 (D. Mont. 2005) ("When the cynicism of wealth invades the academy, students learn not the lessons of ordinary governance but instead are imbued with the anti-egalitarian notion that wealth is power."), *aff'd*, 488 F.3d 816 (9th Cir. 2007), cert.denied, 128 S. Ct. 882 (2008).

5. *Footnote 65.* Footnote 65 of the *Buckley* majority opinion stated that "Congress may engage in public financing of election campaigns and may condition acceptance of public funds on an agreement by the candidate to abide by specified expenditure limitations." Footnote 65 is an important and controversial qualification of the otherwise comprehensive condemnation of spending limits. Critics of public financing conditioned on the acceptance of spending limits point out that the simultaneous enactment of contribution limits may put considerable pressure on candidates to accept the public financing/spending limits package. We return to this issue of voluntariness versus coercion in Chapter 17.

6. These notes have considered "substantive" constitutional questions raised by *Buckley*. A related but distinct question is the extent to which the judiciary should be resolving such issues, rather than leaving them to be resolved through political institutions. For an excellent theoretical discussion of this issue, see Frederick Schauer, *Judicial Review of the Devices of Democracy*, 94 COLUMBIA LAW REVIEW 1326 (1994). For a less theoretical (and less excellent) discussion, see Lowenstein, *supra*, 21 CAPITAL UNIVERSITY LAW REVIEW at 424–27.

7. The Court's treatment of contribution and expenditure limits has become more complex since *Buckley*. Chapter 15 looks at post-*Buckley* developments on contribution

limits. Chapter 16 considers post-*Buckley* developments on spending limits. The remainder of this chapter considers in greater depth both political science questions related to campaign financing and the corruption and equality rationales for campaign finance regulation.

III. Empirical Observations about, and Theoretical Justifications for, Campaign Finance Regulation

A. Empirical Observations

The Court in *Buckley* permitted Congress to impose individual contribution limits on the grounds that such limits can prevent corruption or the appearance of corruption. As we shall see, many opponents of campaign finance regulation believe that legislative bodies often pass campaign finance regulations not to prevent corruption, but to protect their members from political competition.

These kinds of arguments raise empirical questions. Do large campaign contributions buy votes or otherwise "corrupt" legislators? Do campaign finance regulations promote public confidence in the electoral process by diminishing the "appearance of corruption?" Do such regulations harm political competition? Political scientists have been examining these questions for many years, and here we briefly summarize some of their findings.

What Do Campaign Contributions Buy? One of the enduring questions considered by political scientists and others is the extent to which campaign contributions and spending affect the decisions made by lawmakers. Although popular sentiment leans toward viewing contributions as "buying votes," finding empirical support for this claim is more difficult than one might think. As Frank Sorauf summarizes the literature:

> First, and most important, there simply are no data in the systematic studies that would support the popular assertions about the "buying" of the Congress or about any other massive influence of money on the legislative process. Second, even taking the evidence selectively, there is at best a case for a modest influence of money, a degree of influence that puts it well behind the other major influences on congressional behavior. Third, in some of the studies with a time dimension, there is evidence that vote support for the PAC's legislative position leads to greater campaign contributions. They do not, however, answer the question whether the legislative votes changed in order to "earn" the reward of increased contributions.

Frank J. Sorauf, MONEY IN AMERICAN ELECTIONS (1988). Sorauf acknowledges that large campaign contributions might buy access to elected officials but he found "no systematic evidence" supporting even the access hypothesis.

Most of the studies Sorauf relied on attempt to find systematic causal relationships between campaign contributions and congressional *floor votes*. As Sorauf reports, the results are mixed. Some commentators have suggested that influence derived from campaign contributions, to the extent that it exists, would be more likely to manifest itself in committees and in other legislative activities with less visibility than floor votes. Unfortunately, most other activities are much more difficult to measure than floor votes. One study, published after Sorauf's book, found some evidence of influence from contributions over committee activity. See Richard L. Hall & Frank W. Wayman, *Buying Time:*

Moneyed Interests and the Mobilization of Bias in Congressional Committees, 84 AMERICAN POLITICAL SCIENCE REVIEW 797 (1990). Following Hall and Wayman, another study found that the American Medical Association's PAC gives contributions to congressional candidates in a manner consistent with the PAC's presumed desire to secure access to Members of Congress. See John D. Wilkerson & David Carrell, *Money, Politics, and Medicine: The American Medical PAC's Strategy of Giving in U.S. House Races*, 24 JOURNAL OF HEALTH POLITICS, POLICY AND LAW 335 (1999).

For a more skeptical view of the idea the contributors give to influence legislation or secure access, see Stephen Ansolabehere, John M. de Figueiredo, and James M. Snyder, Jr., *Why Is There So Little Money in U.S. Politics?*, 17 JOURNAL OF ECONOMIC PERSPECTIVES 105 (2003):

> Much of the academic research and public discussion of campaign contributions appears to be starting from some misguided assumptions. Campaign spending, measured as a share of GDP, does not appear to be increasing. Most of the campaign money does not come from interest group PACs, but rather from individual donors. Most donors give substantially less than the current hard money limits. It doesn't seem accurate to view campaign contributions as a way of investing in political outcomes. Instead, aggregate campaign spending in the United States, we conjecture, mainly reflects the consumption value that individuals receive from giving to campaigns. In addition, individual contributors provide the average and marginal dollar to political campaigns. Because politicians can readily raise campaign funds from individuals, rent-seeking donors lack the leverage to extract large private benefits from legislation.

For a further exploration, see Stephen Ansolabehere, James M. Snyder, Jr., and Michiko Ueda, *Did Firms Profit From Soft Money?*, 3 ELECTION LAW JOURNAL 193 (2004).

As the foregoing suggests, the goals of different contributors may vary. Contributors who seek to attain their goals by helping candidates who support the same goals are sometimes said to follow an "electoral strategy." Those who contribute to candidates they believe are likely to win anyway in an attempt to influence their policies follow a "legislative strategy." See generally Kay Lehman Schlozman & John T. Tierney, ORGANIZED INTERESTS AND AMERICAN DEMOCRACY 206–08 (1986). Of course, a single contribution could be intended to serve both purposes. But a contributor following a predominantly electoral strategy would be likely to contribute primarily to candidates in competitive races, while a legislative strategy would point toward contributions to secure incumbents, particularly those in leadership positions or serving on committees of importance to the contributor.

That many interest group contributions are made in pursuit of a legislative strategy seems beyond doubt. Consider, for example, the 1982 Texas gubernatorial election. A Democrat unexpectedly defeated the Republican incumbent. Shortly after the election, the newly-elected Democrat received ninety contributions in amounts from $10,000 to $50,000 from sources that had contributed to his Republican opponent before the election.

Nevertheless, there are many contributions, including many interest group contributions, that are made in pursuit of an electoral strategy. Even when contributors follow a legislative strategy, Sorauf raises the question whether they succeed. As he reports, the empirical research on this question has produced mixed results. Furthermore, Sorauf appears to regard the question as crucial from a normative or policy perspective.

Do you agree? Suppose that instead of votes in Congress following campaign money, campaign money follows the votes. If it is assumed that campaign spending has a significant influence on who wins an election—an assumption that will be examined below—the result would be that well-funded interests would be able to influence public policy by electing sympathetic candidates but not by using their money to induce unsympathetic candidates to change their positions. This might still give well-funded interests a big advantage over poorly-funded adversaries. Is this a problem? If so, can you articulate what the problem is?

Do Campaign Finance Laws Instill Public Confidence in the Democratic Process? In *Buckley*, the Court wrote that "Congress could legitimately conclude that the avoidance of the appearance of improper influence is also critical … if confidence in the system of representative Government is not to be eroded to a disastrous extent" (internal quotations omitted). The Court wrote those words in upholding FECA's contribution limits. But do campaign contribution limits instill public confidence in the democratic process?

Nathaniel Persily and Kelli Lammie, *Perceptions of Corruption and Campaign Finance: When Public Opinion Determines Constitutional Law*, 153 UNIVERSITY OF PENNSYLVANIA LAW REVIEW 119, 121 (2004), argue that "the Court's invocation of this novel state interest has less to do with the importance of removing unsavory appearances and more to do with the difficulty of proving actual corruption. Reliance on combating the appearance or perception of impropriety serves as a fallback state interest in the likely event that one cannot make the difficult showing that campaign contributions have actually influenced a representative's vote or official conduct."

Looking empirically at public opinion polling on corruption over time, the authors conclude that "trends in general attitudes of corruption seem unrelated to anything happening in the campaign finance system (e.g., a rise in contributions or the introduction of a particular reform)." *Id.* at 122. Indeed, public perceptions of corruption *went up* after Congress passed the most important campaign finance law in decades, the Bipartisan Campaign Reform Act of 2002.

The authors conclude:

> While believing that campaign contributions corrupt parties and candidates and that campaign finance reform is desirable, a majority of Americans also agree that special interests will continue to have undue influence even once such reforms are passed. Moreover, available survey data suggest that Americans' perceptions of corruption are related to their views about their position in society, the incumbents in office, or their attitudes about how government ought to tax and spend.

Id. at 173. Does this evidence mean that the Court should no longer rely on the "appearance of corruption" to justify campaign finance regulation?

Campaign Finance Regulation and Political Competition. Whether or not legislators pass campaign finance laws in order to stifle political competition, political scientists have considered whether limiting how much a candidate can spend to run for election (or limiting the contributions a candidate may raise, which in turn affects spending) can affect competition.

Gary Jacobson's influential work in this area, beginning with Gary C. Jacobson, *The Effects of Campaign Spending on Congressional Elections*, 72 AMERICAN POLITICAL SCIENCE REVIEW 469 (1978) has argued that, at least as to races for the U.S. House of Representatives, any campaign finance law restricting campaign spending will help incumbents and diminish electoral competition. *See also* Gary C. Jacobson, *Enough is Too Much: Money and Competition in House Elections*, in ELECTIONS IN AMERICA 173 (Kay Lehman Schlozman, ed., 1987).

As Jacobson later explained it:

> Campaign spending is subject to diminishing returns; the more dollars spent, the less gained by each additional dollar. Congressional incumbents usually exploit their official resources reaching constituents so thoroughly that the additional increment of information about their virtues put forth during the campaign adds comparatively little to what is already known and felt about them....
>
> In general, then, spending should matter more to nonincumbent candidates than to incumbents because they have yet to get their message out, and getting a message out costs money. Spending may also matter to incumbents if they have to get out a *new* message. That is, when an incumbent is in trouble for some reason.... Regardless of their potential, if challengers cannot raise lots of money, they can forget about winning. If incumbents are strongly challenged, raising and spending lots of money may not help them much, although there is no reason to think it hurts....
>
> Plainly, though, spending huge sums of money does not ensure reelection.... This means that *the incumbent's most effective electoral strategy is to discourage serious opposition.*

Gary C. Jacobson, *The Politics of Congressional Elections* 46–47 (6th ed. 2004).

Some research has found that the benefits incumbents gain from increased spending are greater than Jacobson suggests. See, e.g., Donald P. Green & Jonathan S. Krasno, *Salvation for the Spendthrift Incumbent: Reestimating the Effects of Campaign Spending in House Elections*, 32 AMERICAN JOURNAL OF POLITICAL SCIENCE 884 (1988); Scott J. Thomas, *Do Incumbent Campaign Expenditures Matter?*, 51 JOURNAL OF POLITICS 965 (1989); Kevin B. Grier, *Campaign Spending and Senate Elections, 1974–84*, 63 PUBLIC CHOICE 201 (1989); Donald P. Green & Jonathan S. Krasno, *Rebuttal to Jacobson's "New Evidence for Old Arguments*," 34 AMERICAN JOURNAL OF POLITICAL SCIENCE 363 (1990). Jacobson and others continue to find that the effects of increased incumbent spending are slight (albeit potentially decisive in close elections). See, e.g., Gary C. Jacobson, *The Effects of Campaign Spending in House Elections: New Evidence for Old Arguments*, 34 AMERICAN JOURNAL OF POLITICAL SCIENCE 334 (1990); Alan I. Abramowitz, *Incumbency, Campaign Spending, and the Decline of Competition in U.S. House Elections*, 53 JOURNAL OF POLITICS 35 (1991).

Alan Gerber contests Jacobson's findings in *Estimating the Effect of Campaign Spending on Senate Election Outcomes Using Instrumental Variables*, 92 AMERICAN POLITICAL SCIENCE REVIEW 401 (1998). Gerber finds that in Senate elections, incumbent spending is as effective as challenger spending. One possible explanation for the discrepant findings is that Senate challengers tend to be better known than House challengers, so that the dynamics of the two types of races may be different. Gerber explains the significance of the empirical debate in terms that both sides would agree on:

> The finding that incumbent spending wins elections has important implications for recent American politics. Campaign finance, and specifically the level of incumbent spending, is a potentially critical factor in the competitiveness of congressional elections. The finding that incumbent spending effects are important also requires reconsideration of the consequences of campaign finance reform. The debate typically turns on what happens to challengers and neglects incumbents. Spending limits that apply to both are seen as severely biased in favor of incumbents. As Jacobson argues, "campaign spending does have an important effect on who wins [congressional elections] and it is the amount spent by challengers (and other disadvantaged candidates) that actually makes the difference.

Spending limits, if they have any effect at all on competition, can only work to the detriment of the challenger." In a companion paper, I conduct simulations of policy alternatives and show that, when the new estimates of incumbent spending effects are used, the conclusions inspired by the traditional view of campaign spending need major revision.... For example, spending caps, even if set lower than some challengers' campaign spending levels, can significantly increase the chances of challenger victory.

Id. at 410.

B. Preventing Corruption

Daniel Hays Lowenstein, *On Campaign Finance Reform: The Root of All Evil Is Deeply Rooted*
18 HOFSTRA LAW REVIEW 301, 322–29 (1989)

What Is Meant By Influence?

Ironically, the inability of the econometric studies to answer whether campaign contributions have measurable effects on legislators' actions may result, in part, from the single-mindedness with which they have asked the question. Apparently believing that the extent of such measurable effects is of overriding importance, econometric analysts have attempted to tease out answers from data and mathematical tools ill-suited for the task. These analysts might make greater progress if they conducted a more open-ended inquiry into the dynamics of how campaign contributions enter into the legislative process and how they interact with other influences, rules and institutional factors to guide the conduct of individual legislators and the legislature as a whole. They would be well-advised to do so, not only to produce better social science, but because the degree of measurable aggregate influence of campaign contributions over legislative activity does not have the crucial normative significance that they have assumed.

It is commonly observed that any influence over legislative behavior generated by campaign contributions is intertwined with other influences. Michael Malbin, for example, points out that it is "difficult to separate the importance of PAC contributions from the lobbying efforts they are supposedly meant to enhance."[97] Some writers conclude that because it is impossible to be confident that legislative actions favorable to contributors have been caused by contributions, concern over contributions may be minimized. Their premise of intertwining is correct and important, but the conclusion they draw from it is wrong by 180 degrees.

---

97. See Michael Malbin, *Looking Back at the Future of Campaign Finance Reform*, in MONEY AND POLITICS IN THE UNITED STATES 232, 249 (Malbin ed., 1984); see also Sorauf, *supra* (stating that "[i]t is ... very hard to separate the effects of lobbying and of constituency pressures from the effects of a campaign contribution.").

John Kingdon quoted a House member who stated: "A close friend of mine, who's been associated with me for years and is an important campaign contributor, is in the oil business. I had no idea how this bill would affect the oil people until I heard from him." John Kingdon, CONGRESSMEN'S VOTING DECISIONS 34 (3d ed. 1989). Would the friendship have been sufficient to make this legislator pay such heed without the contributions? If so, why did the member mention the fact that the friend is a contributor? Would the friendship be as close without the contributions? Could the legislator answer these questions with certainty?

The conclusion is wrong because the question of campaign finance is a question of conflict of interest. [For present purposes, a] conflict of interest exists when the consequences of a decision made in the course of a relationship of trust are likely to have an effect, not implicit in the trust relationship, on … the decisionmaker's self-interest.…

Often, and in various contexts, we take institutional steps to minimize the occurrence of conflicts of interest, or we disqualify a person from acting when a conflict of interest arises. Why do we do so? Part of the reason, and not necessarily the most important part, is our concern that the individual may deliberately set aside his or her obligations of trust in favor of self-interest. Even if we were sure we could identify all such cases of overt dishonesty, we would continue to regulate conflicts of interest because of the probability that even an honest person's judgment will be impaired when in a position of conflict. Centuries before terms such as "selective perception" were current, it was understood that an individual whose own self-interest is at stake finds it difficult to view a situation dispassionately and objectively. That is why we refer to a person without conflict as "disinterested."

Some people in a conflict situation may be able to act in the position of trust without being the slightest bit moved by the potential effects on self-interest. Others may find that considerations of self-interest are present in their minds but may be able, nonetheless, to struggle through to a conclusion based only on proper considerations. Still other people may be biased in their judgments in situations not conventionally regarded as conflicts of interest. The reason these situations can, and commonly do exist, is that conflict of interest is a concept based on the average person. Sometimes individuals are unusually resistant to being moved by self-interest, sometimes they are unusually susceptible, and sometimes their goals and preferences are sufficiently idiosyncratic that what constitutes self-interest is unusual. Therefore, conflict of interest regulation sometimes disqualifies an individual who is *not* biased, while at other times it fails to disqualify an individual who *is* biased. This does not mean that the regulation is faulty. It happens because there is no alternative to regulating on the basis of what we believe are typical human reactions.

What is the significance of the fact that the campaign finance question is a question of conflict of interest? First consider this statement from one of the econometric studies: "It is useful to imagine that the exogenous variables [such as party, ideology and constituency] determine an 'initial position' on the issue for a candidate, and that contributions cause shifts away from that position."[104] As a heuristic device, this is often a useful procedure. As a description of reality it is woefully inadequate because of the intertwining of campaign contributions with other influencing factors. From the beginning of an issue's life, legislators know of past contributions and the possibility of future ones from the interest groups that are affected, just as the legislators know of relevant constituency effects, party positions, various aspects of the merits of the issue and so on. All of these combine in a manner no one fully understands to form an initial predisposition in the legislator. Thereafter, the legislator may receive new information on any or all of these factors. The new information may modify the legislator's initial position, but the information that is received and the manner in which it is processed will themselves be influenced by the initial position.

In reality, then, the influence of campaign contributions is present from the start, and it interacts in the human mind with other influences in an unfathomable but complex dynamic. It affects the "chemistry" or the "mix" of the legislator's deliberations. It may or

---

104. Chappell, *Campaign Contributions and Congressional Voting: A Simultaneous Probit-Tobit Model*, 64 Review of Economics & Statistics 77, 78 (1982).

may not affect the legislator's ultimate actions, but setting aside the most flagrant cases, no one can be sure, perhaps not even the legislator in question. For this reason, to say that campaign contributions "taint" the legislative process is to use the language with precision. It is not that the entire legislative process or even a great deal of it is corrupt; rather, it is that the corrupt element is intermingled with the entire process, in a way that cannot be isolated.

The conflicts of interest caused by campaign contributions are illustrated routinely in nearly every daily newspaper. For instance, the following example appeared in the *Los Angeles Times* while these paragraphs were being written. It is from an article about six Democrats, mostly from the south, on the House Ways and Means Committee.[109] At the time of the article, it was believed that these six members of Congress might swing the committee to report out a reduction in the tax on capital gains, supported by President Bush and the Republicans but opposed by a majority of the Democrats:

> Whatever the outcome, Bush has laid bare a deep split between Democrats' traditional ideology of opposing special treatment for the wealthy and the party's growing dependence on contributions from a host of business special interest groups, particularly real estate developers, that would benefit from the tax cut.

> "We've got wealthy Democrats in this country too," said a longtime supporter of a capital gains cut, Beryl Anthony Jr. (D-Ark.), who is a key party fund-raiser as head of the Democratic Congressional Campaign Committee.

A common way of describing this type of situation is to say that there is an "appearance of impropriety." While not exactly wrong, discussion of the campaign finance question in terms of appearances is misleading. It suggests that there is an underlying reality that is either proper or not proper, and if we could only look behind the locked door or, perhaps, into the legislator's head, we would know. Used as a rationale for reform measures, the argument is that the appearance of impropriety is a sufficient justification for reform, because it undermines popular confidence in government. Depending on who is speaking and who is listening, there may be an implied wink to the effect that impropriety is really very unlikely but that some sop must be thrown to the ignorantly suspicious public. Alternatively, the implied wink may suggest that of course there is impropriety, but it would be impolitic to say so directly.

Rather than saying there is an *appearance of impropriety* in the Democrats' dependence on contributions from interests demanding a capital gains reduction or in similar situations, it is more precise to say that there is a *reality of conflict of interest*. There was no meeting, behind closed doors or otherwise, not even a moment in a single legislator's mind, in which a decision was made either to succumb to the contributors or not to succumb. The pressure from the contributors is simply part of the mix of considerations out of which a position evolves. At best, one can exercise a judgment as to whether the outcome would have been different if there had been no contributions and no possibility of contributions. Even if the hypothetical outcome would have been the same, however, it does not change the fact that the real outcome results from an actual, tainted process. That is why the question of how much contributions affect legislative outcomes, while surely important, is not normatively crucial.

It may be objected that the conflict of interest argument applies equally to many of the major influences on the legislative process other than campaign contributions. Leg-

---

109. Redburn, "Six Democrats Backing Capital Gains Tax Cut," L.A. Times, July 25, 1989, pt. 1, at 1.

islators who are highly responsive to their constituents, for example, most likely act in that manner because they believe it will help them get reelected a self-interested reason. Legislators who adhere to the party position or the wishes of influential colleagues may do so because they hope for reciprocity in the future, or for advancement within the legislative chamber. They also act out of self-interest.

The fallacy in this objection is its assumption that all considerations of self-interest are equal. No one ever claimed that systems are corrupt simply because they contain incentives. If this were the case, there would be a conflict of interest any time an employer paid an employee a salary, since the employee who did a good job in hopes of keeping the job or being promoted would be acting corruptly. Such incentives are not conflicts of interest because they are implicit in the relationship of trust, in this case between the employer and employee.

A variety of pressures characterize political life in America. Sorting out which pressures are proper and which are not is difficult. There are, however, some easy cases. Constituency influence is an example. One side of the Burkean debate maintains that while legislators should regard constituent opinions as relevant data for public policy, they should be guided only by their own best judgments. There is no consensus in favor of that position. Accordingly, some degree of responsiveness to constituents' views is at least permissible in legislative positions of trust in this country.

The paradigm case of improper influence is the payment of money to the official for the official's benefit. That is what a campaign contribution is. Indeed, the distinction between a campaign contribution and a payment for the recipient's personal use can be blurred or nonexistent. Nevertheless, there are some differences. Campaign contributions, under current conditions, are more likely to be indispensable to an elected official than personal payments. This makes campaign contributions the more dangerous, though not the more unethical practice. A second difference is that the contributor may be motivated not to influence the recipient but to promote a cause that the recipient represents. In other words, contributors may follow an electoral rather than a legislative strategy.... [T]he fact that many contributions are ideological may affect the way people think about all contributions.

Despite differences, it is clear that our culture regards it as inappropriate for public officials to be influenced by campaign contributions. We need not look to Common Cause, Elizabeth Drew, and Brooks Jackson to establish this point. Stronger evidence comes from the scholars with whom I have joined issue in this part. Frank Sorauf, Michael Malbin, and others with similar views would not be at such great pains to characterize the influence of campaign contributions as minimal if they did not believe that it would be wrong if the contributions were influential, or at least that the overwhelming majority of their fellow citizens believe that it would be wrong.

Further confirmation can be found in the fact that a campaign contribution made with the intent to influence official conduct constitutes bribery, as that crime is defined in most American jurisdictions. It is true that the typical special interest bribe in the form of a campaign contribution is very rarely prosecuted. I doubt that this reflects approval of the practice as much as recognition of its pervasiveness, which in turn results from the fact that the receipt of special interest contributions is more or less a practical necessity for most legislators. This necessity may constitute an excellent reason for not prosecuting such routine transactions as bribes, but it does not justify preservation of the system that creates the necessity.

It is a fact of our political culture that although a great variety of the pressures brought to bear on politicians embody forces that are regarded as more or less democratic and therefore legitimate, this is not true of pressure imposed by payments of money to politicians, either for their personal benefit or for campaign use. At best, the existence of such pressures is tolerated as a necessary evil. The evil is necessary within the existing campaign finance system, but the existence of the evil provides a compelling reason for reforming that system.

Notes and Questions

1. The symposium in which this article appeared included several commentaries, pertinent excerpts of which will be set forth in these notes. First, Gary C. Jacobson, *Campaign Finance and Democratic Control: Comments on Gottlieb and Lowenstein's Papers*, 18 HOFSTRA LAW REVIEW 369, 377–78 (1989):

> Reelection depends on many other things besides money, and actions that promote reelection do not always serve constituents or conscience. Elected officials routinely confront choices between doing what helps them stay in office and doing what they think is best for their constituents, their party or their country. To give some familiar examples, the prevalence in Congress [of] wasteful pork barrel politics, of vacuous position taking, and of endless self-promotion, suggests that money is by no means the only electoral necessity that promotes shirking. Lowenstein falls short of demonstrating that the current campaign finance system, which, after all, limits the amount of money supplied by any particular individual or political action committee (PAC), is an especially egregious source of shirking and, therefore, requires the sweeping reforms he proposes.

2. Martin Shapiro, *Corruption, Freedom and Equality in Campaign Financing*, 18 HOFSTRA LAW REVIEW 385, 387 (1989):

> Lowenstein ... operates as a cultural anthropologist and discovers that there is an anti-corruption norm in American society and that campaign financing legislation is an expression of that norm. The norm is legitimated by its existence and the statutes are legitimated by the norm. This approach is not entirely satisfactory from the standpoint of constitutional law. There is a cultural norm of racism in our society. Does the existence of such a norm give constitutional legitimacy to racist statutes? Such an argument would not appear terribly attractive or constitutional. Moreover, there is that old bromide of cultural anthropology. Is the best evidence of a norm profession or behavior? If there is an anti-corruption norm in American society, surely there is also a pro-corruption norm in the widespread proclivity of Americans to seek to influence the behavior of legislators by any means short of assassination.

3. Sanford Levinson, *Electoral Regulation: Some Comments*, 18 HOFSTRA LAW REVIEW 411, 412–13 (1989):

> I remain unpersuaded by any analysis that expresses justified worry about the impact of money on the behavior of public officials and, at the same time, wholly ignores the power of the media to influence these same public officials in part through the media's ability to structure public consciousness. Almost a decade ago my colleague, L.A. Powe, queried why Congress should be able to limit the ability to influence the outcomes of elections of everyone, except those fortunate enough to be owners of mass media.... The potential for conflicts of interests at the heart of Lowenstein's analysis is also present when a candidate confronts the

owners and editors of major newspapers on issues and when such a candidate beseeches the same owners and editors to support ... his or her campaign.[q]

4. Does it help to reconsider the corruption problem using the metaphor of pollution? See John Copeland Nagle, *Corruption, Pollution, and Politics*, 110 YALE LAW JOURNAL 293, 322 (2000):

> To say that the political system is polluted avoids the implication that particular representatives are polluted. It also avoids the connotation of corruption that suggests that no corruption can be tolerated. By contrast, the law tolerates some environmental pollution. The law intervenes to regulate or prohibit pollution only when the amount of a particular type of pollutant has harmful effects. Under this view, campaign contributions and spending would be permissible up to the point where they begin to produce harmful effects, including but not limited to corruption.

5. Some scholars have argued that Lowenstein is concerned less with corruption than with equality. See Bruce E. Cain, *Moralism and Realism in Campaign Finance Reform*, 1995 UNIVERSITY OF CHICAGO LEGAL FORUM 111 and David A. Strauss, *What is the Goal of Campaign Finance Reform?*, 1995 UNIVERSITY OF CHICAGO LEGAL FORUM 141. Consider the following argument from Strauss:

> One way to set aside any concern with inequality is to assume, as a thought experiment, that everyone has an equal opportunity to "bribe" the official or candidate of his or her choice by making campaign contributions. This will isolate the problem of corruption. For example, one might assume that the law requires campaign contributions to be made in vouchers that are distributed according to some conception of equality. Or one might assume a scheme that equalizes people's ability to make contributions by multiplying contributions by a factor inversely related to the contributor's income.
>
> One could argue that even in such an "equal" world, the corrupting effects of campaign contributions will be a problem because officials will be unduly responsive to contributors. But the question, once inequality is removed from the picture, is why this is troubling. Elected officials also respond to the wishes of past and potential future voters. While that may sometimes be a problem, no one thinks it is the same kind of problem as bribery. If everyone had the same capacity to contribute to campaigns—that is, if equality were somehow secured (or if we decided it was not an issue)—the difference between contributions and votes would diminish sharply.

Id. at 143–44; see also Kathleen M. Sullivan, *Political Money and Freedom of Speech*, 30 U.C. DAVIS LAW REVIEW 663, 680 (1997). Is Strauss right that at bottom Lowenstein is concerned not with corruption, but inequality?

In response to Cain's and Strauss's criticism, Lowenstein offered a hypothetical of his own in which four legislators agree to vote for a bill for different reasons. The first legislator made her decision along Burkean lines. The second followed the public opinion in his district. The third followed the wishes of her party leadership. The fourth, however, gave the following answer to why he voted for the bill:

> It's true that my judgment of good public policy, the views of most of my constituents, and the demands of party loyalty all pointed toward voting against the

---

q. We return to the question of media influence in the notes following the *Austin* case in Chapter 16.

bill. But these considerations, even in combination, were outweighed by my desire to raise funds to help me get reelected. Therefore, I agreed to vote for this bill in exchange for a large contribution from Barbara Bigbucks.

Daniel Hays Lowenstein, *Campaign Contributions and Corruption: Comments on Strauss and Cain*, 1995 UNIVERSITY OF CHICAGO LEGAL FORUM 163, 171–72. Why, if at all, should we be concerned with this answer? Lowenstein remarks that "the unequivocal disapproval of this transaction in the American political culture cannot be explained by concerns about equality or structural problems of collective action. Americans disapprove of this transaction because they recognize it as corrupt." *Id.* at 172. If Barbara Bigbucks could give no more than anyone else to Demetrios, would Demetrios's answer still be a problem? Is the answer that under those conditions Bigbucks could no longer give a (relatively) "large" contribution?

C. Promoting Equality

As noted above, Lowenstein vigorously contends that corruption and equality concerns in campaign finance are analytically distinct. We turn now to consider equality on its own merits. Does a concern for political equality justify campaign finance regulation? If so, what kinds of regulation?

Edward B. Foley, *Equal-Dollars-Per-Voter: A Constitutional Principle of Campaign Finance*
94 COLUMBIA LAW REVIEW 1204 (1994)

The Constitution of the United States should contain a principle, which I shall call "equal-dollars-per-voter," that would guarantee to each eligible voter equal financial resources for purposes of supporting or opposing any candidate or initiative on the ballot in any election held within the United States. The argument for adopting this principle is that wealthy citizens should not be permitted to have a greater ability to participate in the electoral process simply on account of their greater wealth. This argument, in turn, depends upon a belief that the electoral process must be wealth-neutral in order to be fair to rich and poor alike.

An important function of electoral politics is to determine how wealth should be distributed among society's members. The existing distribution of wealth at the time of any particular election should not affect the electorate's determination of what the distribution should be henceforth. Money, however, is an indispensable element of any electoral campaign because money pays for the publicity and advertising that attempt to convince the undecided voters to support the campaign on election day. Consequently, if rich citizens are free to spend their own money to support or oppose candidates or ballot initiatives, they will have a greater opportunity than poor citizens to attempt to persuade undecided voters to agree with their positions. In this way, then, permitting wealthy citizens to use their wealth in electoral politics biases the electoral process in favor of their political objectives and against the political objectives of the poor. This bias contradicts the premise, stated above, that the electoral process should not be affected by whatever distribution of wealth exists in society at election time. In order to eliminate this bias, the Constitution should guarantee that all voters receive equal financial resources for the purpose of participating in electoral politics....

I. An Explanation of Equal-Dollars-Per-Voter

A. What Equal-Dollars-Per-Voter Requires

The principle of equal-dollars-per-voter means that each eligible voter should receive the same amount of financial resources for the purpose of participating in electoral politics. In other words, pursuant to this principle, the government would provide all eligible voters with the same sum of money—the principle does not specify any particular amount—and the voters could then donate this money to the electoral organizations of their choice. Electoral organizations consist of three types: (1) a candidate's campaign organization; (2) a broad-based interest group, otherwise known as a political party; or (3) a more narrowly-focused "special interest" group.

The only money that voters would be permitted to donate to an electoral organization would be the money they receive from the government pursuant to the equal-dollars-per-voter principle. Voters would not be permitted to supplement the electoral funds they receive from the government with their own personal funds, no matter how extensive their wealth and no matter how strong their desire. In this way, the principle of equal-dollars-per-voter would prohibit affluent citizens from spending any more on electoral politics than impoverished citizens.

The same principle applies to candidates as well as voters. Candidates would be permitted to spend only the money they had received either directly from voters or indirectly through an interest group (either broad-based or narrowly-focused). The only money candidates would be permitted to contribute to their own campaigns would be the money they had received from the government pursuant to the equal-dollars-per-voter principle. Thus, the principle would prohibit affluent candidates from using their personal wealth to advance their own candidacies.

Likewise, the only money that interest groups (either broad-based or narrowly-focused) would be permitted to spend to support or oppose a candidate would be the money they had received from voters pursuant to the equal-dollars-per-voter principle. Interest groups could spend this money in either of two ways. First, as already indicated, they could hand it over to a candidate's campaign, thus acting as a conduit between voters and candidates. Voters might prefer to donate their electoral funds to an interest group, rather than to a candidate directly, because they trust the interest group's judgment about which candidate most deserves their support. Alternatively, the interest group might decide to keep some or all of the money it had received from voters to spend on its own independent activities in support of or opposition to a candidate (e.g., newspaper advertisements endorsing a candidate).

Either way, interest groups would spend only the money they receive from voters. They would not be permitted to receive electoral funds from any other source—neither from a corporation, nor from a labor union, nor from any other club or voluntary association that engages in nonelectoral activities. If individuals associated with corporations, labor unions, or other nonelectoral organizations wished to spend money in connection with a campaign, they would be required to set up separate electoral organizations with separate accounts. The only money that these individuals could give to these electoral organizations would be the money they had received as voters pursuant to the equal-dollars-per-voter principle.

Individual voters would also be free to make their own independent expenditures to support or oppose a candidate or ballot initiative. For example, a voter might photocopy several hundred leaflets to distribute among her neighbors, urging them to vote for or against a particular candidate. Or, if sufficient funds were available, a voter might purchase advertising space in a local newspaper to endorse a candidate. But the principle of equal-dollars-per-voter would still apply to these independent expenditures. The principle requires all voters to receive the same amount of funds for all their expenditures in support of, or in opposition to, an electoral campaign. For this reason, voters would not be permitted to use their own personal funds to make independent expenditures.

In sum, the principle of equal-dollars-per-voter calls for a closed system of electoral funds. Within the system, the money may flow freely—from voter to interest group to candidate or from voter to candidate directly. The money could even pass from one interest group to another, and to yet another, before it is given to a candidate's campaign or spent independently to support or oppose a candidate—just so long as all the money originates with the individual voters pursuant to the basic principle. The principle requires simply that all individuals start with the same amount and that no outside funds be introduced into the system....

II. Distributive Justice and the Anti-Plutocracy Principle

The argument for equal-dollars-per-voter consists of two parts. First, I shall argue that a citizen's wealth should have no bearing upon her opportunity to participate in the electoral process. This proposition I call the "anti-plutocracy principle," as a plutocracy is a system of government in which a citizen's ability to participate as an elector depends upon the amount of wealth belonging to the citizen. Second, I shall argue that this anti-plutocracy principle encompasses the more specific principle that a citizen's wealth should have no bearing on her opportunity to attempt to persuade fellow citizens of the merits of her views. This more specific principle, which I call "equal-opportunity-for-persuasion," necessarily entails equal-dollars-per-voter.[33]

My argument for the anti-plutocracy principle is based upon the premise that political philosophy cannot yield a definitive answer to the question of distributive justice (i.e., how should society's wealth be distributed among its various members?). Because philosophy cannot answer this question, the members of society must adopt a decision-making process in which they collectively choose whatever principles of distributive justice they wish to govern their society. No particular pattern of distribution carries a presumption of validity from the perspective of political philosophy—not even the pattern that happens to exist at the time the members of society gather together to choose the principles of distributive justice. Accordingly, the decision-making process should be structured in such a way that it is not affected by the existing distribution of wealth in society.

In section B of this Part, I shall elaborate upon this argument. But first, in section A, I shall explain the premise that the question of distributive justice has no philosophically definitive answer.

A. *The Indeterminacy of Distributive Justice*

The problem of distributive justice, simply put, is the problem of who should get what—which members of society should obtain property rights to which of society's resources. The problem of distributive justice is by no means the only problem that confronts the polity. On the contrary, the state must address many other sorts of problems,

---

33. In calling this principle "equal opportunity for persuasion," I do not mean to imply that it guarantees citizens an equal *ability* to persuade. On the contrary, as I shall repeatedly emphasize, it guarantees only an equal opportunity for *attempting* to persuade.

including those caused by the failure of a market economy to allocate goods and services efficiently. In this Article, however, I focus solely on the problem of distributive justice. Even if the other problems confronting the polity miraculously disappeared, there would still be the fundamental problem of who is entitled to what. Moreover, the conclusions that I reach about distributive justice have profound implications for the specific issue of campaign finance

In thinking about distributive justice, I start with the basic premise that all persons have equal intrinsic worth, which I call the principle of intrinsic equality. This idea of equal intrinsic worth is widely recognized by contemporary political philosophers to be the first principle of a just society. Ronald Dworkin, for example, invokes this basic principle when he says that the most fundamental requirement of a constitutional democracy is that it treat its citizens *as equals*, with equal concern and respect.

Different religious and metaphysical traditions provide different justifications for this principle of intrinsic equality....

Perhaps at some future stage of human history, some philosopher will succeed in demonstrating that one of the ... competing principles of justice ... is the only one consistent with intrinsic equality, or else is the only reasonable one in light of other compelling considerations. But that day has not yet arrived. Until then, it is legitimate and reasonable for individual citizens to adopt whichever of these principles they prefer. Alternatively, individuals legitimately and reasonably might decide to adopt some sort of compromise among these principles. In any event, for the foreseeable future, philosophers will remain unable to identify a definitive principle of distributive justice that all reasonable individuals must accept as the only valid principle—and which they must acknowledge to be binding upon society as a fundamental postulate from which the polity must not deviate. Instead, because different citizens legitimately and reasonably may adopt different principles of distributive justice, society must adopt some sort of collective decision-making procedure in which each individual expresses her preferences concerning distributive justice. This decision-making procedure must then tally these conflicting preferences into a coherent social result.

B. *The Anti-Plutocracy Principle*

Whatever the particulars of the decision-making procedure society adopts to resolve the disputes concerning distributive justice, this decision-making procedure should comply with the anti-plutocracy principle. Society might decide to restrict participation in the decision-making process on a variety of reasonable grounds. For example, society might set a minimum age requirement or perhaps even some minimum competency requirement (e.g., no mental impairment so severe as to prevent a person from understanding what it means to cast a vote in an election). But all members of society should have an equal opportunity to participate in this decision-making process *without regard to the amount of wealth they have at the time the decision-making process occurs.*

In Part III, I explain why the equal opportunity to participate must mean more than just an equal vote at the end of the decision-making process. Instead, it must include an equal opportunity to attempt to persuade one's fellow citizens to agree with one's own views about distributive justice. In the meantime, however, there is no doubt that the anti-plutocracy principle encompasses the proposition that all citizens should have equal voting rights without regard to wealth. Thus, I will state the case for the anti-plutocracy principle by focusing on the specific subject of wealth qualifications for voting.

1. *Wealth Qualifications for Voting.*—Suppose the decision-making process for choosing society's principles of distributive justice provided each citizen with one vote for each dollar of income the citizen had received in the previous year. Most of us instinctively recoil at the idea, but why exactly is it wrong?

To give the rich more votes than the poor just because they are rich would be a form of elitism in violation of the principle of intrinsic equality. The interests of poor citizens must count the same as the interests of rich citizens. Thus, there must be a justification for unequal voting rights other than the elitist assertion that the interests of the rich are inherently more deserving of satisfaction because the rich are inherently better than the poor.

But no such justification is available. The rich cannot claim that they are more likely to espouse better views of distributive justice than the poor. As we have seen, there is no way to determine in advance of the collective decision-making process which views of distributive justice are better or worse for society. A poor person's views about distributive justice deserve to have just as much input into the decision-making process as a rich person's views because there is no independent standard for evaluating the relative merit of the different views.

Moreover, human nature being what it is (i.e., substantially self-interested), there is a significant chance that rich citizens will simply cast their votes to support policies that will permit them to retain their wealth and to pass it on to their own offspring. Giving the rich more votes per capita than the poor will build into the decision-making process a bias in favor of the interests of rich citizens and against the interests of poor citizens. But because the interests of the poor must count as much as the interests of the rich, and because their views about distributive justice are equally legitimate, this risk of built-in bias is unacceptable.

To be sure, poor citizens may vote for distributive policies that maximize the amount of wealth to be redistributed from the rich to the poor (and to their offspring). There is no reason to believe, however, that the vote of poor citizens will be more self-interested than the vote of rich citizens. Whatever else they may possess, the rich have no monopoly on moral virtue.

Thus, if rich and poor alike are likely to use their votes to advance their own self-interests, the decision-making process should be structured to give each citizen, regardless of wealth, an equal opportunity to do so. The consequence may be an unseemly contest of self-interest against self-interest, but at least it will be a contest in which no one has an inherent advantage just because she happens to be wealthier at the outset of the decision-making process. In short, the likelihood of self-interested voting, combined with the inability of philosophy to identify an independent standard of distributive justice, requires adherence to the anti-plutocracy principle.

The following question inevitably arises: how can I insist upon adherence to the anti-plutocracy principle when I say that philosophy cannot provide society with an unassailable principle of distributive justice? The answer is that the anti-plutocracy principle follows necessarily from the foundational principle of intrinsic equality, whereas none of the competing principles of distributive justice follows inevitably from intrinsic equality. Moreover, the anti-plutocracy principle follows necessarily from intrinsic equality *precisely because* none of the competing principles of distributive justice follows inevitably from intrinsic equality. It is the very indeterminacy of distributive justice (together with the fact that citizens largely vote their own self-interests) which yields the conclusion that all citizens should have equal voting rights regardless of their respective wealth. The premise of indeterminacy compels this conclusion once one has already accepted the elementary proposition that the interests of all citizens must count equally.

Now, the rich may argue that they need extra voting rights to protect their greater wealth from the self-interested designs of the poor but that the poor need less protection because they have so much less to lose. This argument, however, must fail because it presumes that the rich are entitled to protect their wealth against redistributivist efforts by the poor (and the middle class). Whether the rich have a valid claim to the wealth they possess is precisely the issue to be decided by the decision-making process. Given the philosophical indeterminacy of distributive justice, one cannot presume in advance of the decision-making process that the rich have any valid claim at all to the wealth in their possession.

To be sure, the legitimate property rights of rich and poor alike may be protected by constitutional devices, like the Takings Clause, that prohibit the government from demanding specific individual citizens to sacrifice their property for public benefit without just compensation. But such constitutional provisions should not be construed to prevent the electorate, by majority vote, from enacting tax laws that redistribute wealth from the rich, as a class, to the poor, as a class. What is more, the existence of such constitutional devices cannot justify giving rich citizens more voting rights than poor citizens, thereby granting to rich citizens a built-in check against the pursuit of redistributivist tax laws by poor citizens. On the contrary, when society votes on whether to pursue redistributivist tax legislation, rich citizens and poor citizens must be equal participants in the process, each with an equal vote regardless of wealth. The only legitimate presumption in favor of the existing distribution of wealth at the time of voting is contained within the principle of majority rule itself: a tie vote favors the status quo. Otherwise, the electorate must be free to adopt whatever distributive policies it wishes, as none has any intrinsic philosophical advantage.

The argument is also sometimes made that the poor outnumber the rich and, therefore, if everyone has an equal vote, the masses of poor will overwhelm the relatively few affluent citizens. But no matter what the distribution of income happens to be, each citizen should have an equal say in what the distribution ought to be. Under majority rule, both those above and those below the median must convince the median voter to side with them on issues of distributive justice. Consequently, if there is a small percentage of super-rich citizens, to obtain a majority they must form a coalition with enough of those less affluent than they. Likewise, if there is a small percentage of super-poor citizens, they must build a coalition with those more affluent. Requiring both the rich and poor to build these coalitions is surely preferable to an electoral system that gives either the rich or the poor extra votes to protect themselves from majority rule. Majority rule may be an imperfect procedure, but it remains the best available device to decide issues of distributive justice, given a commitment to the fundamental proposition that the interests of each citizen count equally.

2. No Buying or Selling of Votes.—Adherence to the anti-plutocracy principle requires that no one be permitted to buy or sell votes. If citizens were permitted to trade votes for dollars, rich citizens would buy votes from poor citizens, thereby disenfranchising the poor who had sold their votes. This result is inevitable because of the declining marginal utility of income. Even if a poor person has a greater desire to vote in an election than does a rich person, the poor person may sell his vote to the rich person because of a pressing need to feed his family. Thus, to permit the exchange of votes for dollars would make a person's ability to participate in electoral politics dependent upon the person's wealth, precisely the result that the anti-plutocracy principle condemns as invalid.

Libertarians may argue that the prohibition on vote-selling is an illegitimate restraint of liberty. After all, the transaction is voluntary: the poor person wants to sell, and the rich person wants to buy. The poor person, however, should not be put in a position of having to choose between the right to vote and other, more pressing goods. Even though a transaction is voluntary, the transaction may not be fair if conditions at the time the agreement is made are themselves unfair. A person who is starving to death may be willing to sell one of his kidneys in exchange for food, but should the person be forced to make this choice? This question is one of distributive justice and has no definitive answer. Suppose, for example, the person is starving because he squandered all of his inheritance, refuses to work for a living, and thinks society owes him a decent standard of living even if he refuses to work.

The very indeterminacy of distributive justice is, again, precisely the relevant point for our purposes. No one can say *in advance of the electoral process* that the existing distribution of wealth is fair, thereby making it legitimate to permit a poor person to sell her vote if she wishes. Rather, the only way to determine the fairness of the existing distribution of wealth is to ask for its ratification in an electoral process in which each poor citizen has the same amount of input as does each rich person. And the only way to ensure that poor citizens have equal input is to prohibit the poor from selling their votes....

III. THE ANTI-PLUTOCRACY PRINCIPLE AND CAMPAIGN FINANCE

The case for the equal-dollars-per-voter principle depends upon the following crucial proposition: the equal opportunity to participate in electoral politics, which is guaranteed to all regardless of wealth, must be understood to encompass not only an equal vote, but also the equal opportunity to attempt to persuade one's fellow voters to share one's own views about distributive justice. Once this crucial proposition is established, the argument for equal-dollars-per-voter becomes relatively straightforward: the argument is essentially a repetition of the argument for the anti-plutocracy principle in general, of which equal-dollars-per-voter is now recognized to be an integral component. Thus, society must accept that equal-dollars-per-voter, like the anti-plutocracy principle, is an essential precondition of democratic government.

A. *An Equal Vote Is Not Enough*

Voting is only the final stage of the electoral process. It is preceded not only by the agenda-formation stage (in which matters to be voted upon are identified) but also by what might be called the "argumentative stage," in which competing factions of the electorate attempt to persuade the mass of undecided voters to agree with their positions. Even if we put aside the problem of agenda formation and thus define the electoral process as commencing once the items on the ballot have been determined, we must acknowledge that a citizen does not have equal input in the electoral process if she is denied an equal opportunity to participate in the argumentative stage of the process.

The importance of the argumentative stage must not be underestimated. Many voters do not enter the electoral process with fixed and intransigent views about distributive justice. On the contrary, they are open to persuasion. Consequently, other citizens, who do enter the electoral process with strong and firm opinions about distributive justice, must have an opportunity to attempt to persuade the undecided voters.[82] Some citizens

---

82. Recall here that I am limiting my discussion of the electoral process to its decisions on issues of distributive justice. My argument does not apply to other kinds of issues that might be put before the electorate. But as long as voters make decisions about issues of distributive justice—as they must do in a democracy committed to the anti-plutocracy principle—then my argument pertains.

Voters in a democracy need not vote directly for or against propositions of distributive justice (although they may do so in referenda, as in the case of California's famous Proposition 13). Instead, voters may vote on candidates who act as proxies for propositions about distributive justice (as was true

will be committed egalitarians, attempting to convince the undecided to support higher taxes, which would be spent on redistributivist social policies. Other citizens will be equally committed libertarians, attempting to convince the undecided to oppose such taxes. If both groups of citizens are to have truly equal opportunities to participate in the electoral process, they both must have equal opportunities to attempt to persuade the undecided voters. They need more than just an equal vote on election day.

If one of these groups has a greater opportunity to attempt to persuade the undecided voters, the members of this group will have an inherent structural advantage in the electoral process. To be sure, this advantage may not result in victory on election day. Attempts to persuade often fail. Nonetheless, having a greater opportunity to attempt to persuade is still an inherent advantage because, by definition, it is denied to one's opponents. Thus, if the electoral process is to avoid this kind of structural bias, the electoral process must guarantee all citizens an equal opportunity for persuading one another on issues of distributive justice.

Guaranteeing this equal opportunity for persuasion requires adherence to the principle of equal-dollars-per-voter. This point, although perhaps obvious, is worth making explicit. The attempt to persuade voters of the merits of one's views requires considerable financial resources. To attempt to persuade, one must advertise and publicize one's views. This advertising and publicity require resources, whether in the form of television time, billboard space, or door-to-door distribution of campaign literature.

Consequently, if all citizens are to have a truly equal opportunity to attempt to persuade their fellow citizens, then all citizens must have equal financial resources for this purpose.

And thus the argument for equal-dollars-per-voter is complete. The anti-plutocracy principle requires an equal opportunity for persuasion regardless of wealth, which in turn entails equal-dollars-per-voter....

Notes and Questions

1. Foley argues that equality requires each voter to have "the equal opportunity to attempt to persuade one's fellow voters to share one's own views about distributive justice." Thus, Foley attempts to regulate equality for those pursuing an "electoral strategy," as described in the notes following the Sorauf excerpt above. Can one make an equality argument for those pursuing a "legislative strategy?" Consider Richard L. Hasen, *Campaign Finance Laws and the Rupert Murdoch Problem*, 77 TEXAS LAW REVIEW 1627, 1645–46 (1999):

> Many critics of equality-based campaign finance reform miss the crucial role of access, and assume that the *only* equality argument against unequal contributions to or expenditures in favor of political candidates is that such contributions or expenditures increase the chances of a politician gaining election—what Lowenstein terms an "electoral strategy." Because money alone usually cannot buy an election contest, the anti-reform argument goes, this concern over use of money to buy elections is overblown.

in the 1992 presidential election, Clinton being the candidate who favored higher taxes for the purpose of higher spending on redistributive policies, and Bush being the candidate who opposed these tax-and-spend measures). When the office to be voted upon has the authority to make policy decisions in additional areas besides distributive justice, then voters will be concerned about the candidates' views on these matters as well. Nonetheless, regardless of whatever other types of issues might come before the elective office, as long as this office addresses issues of distributive justice, then voters will be concerned about the candidates' views about distributive justice, and thus the election must be governed by the principle of equal-dollars-per-voter.

However, the retort that money does not buy elections ignores the access argument. If corporate PACs truly were solely interested in influencing the outcome of elections, they would not give so evenhandedly to parties, or to candidates running against each other in the same electoral contest. The money buys access, giving the contributor (assuming the most benign purposes) a greater chance of gaining the ear of the politician to make an argument in favor of the contributor's position on legislation. This is an advantage that non-contributors are much less likely to have. Those buying access are using their campaign expenditures as part of a *legislative strategy* to influence the outcome of the legislative process.

Equality demands that every individual be given, so far as practical, the same political capital, so that each individual has a roughly equal ability to pursue both an electoral strategy and a legislative strategy. The most important step to ensure such equality is preventing vastly unequal expenditures of money in campaigns.

2. Critics of the equality rationale for campaign finance regulation make a number of counterarguments. As we saw in *Buckley* and in the notes following the case, perhaps the most important argument (at least to the courts) has been that regulating campaign finances to achieve equality conflicts with First Amendment's rights of freedom of speech and association.

In addition to the argument that regulating finances to achieve equality is unconstitutional under the First Amendment, anti-equality arguments fall into two broad categories.

(a) *It is unfair to single out money to be regulated when other inequalities would remain.* Consider Bradley A. Smith, *Money Talks: Speech, Corruption, Equality, and Campaign Finance*, 86 GEORGETOWN LAW JOURNAL 45, 91–92 (1997): "[A] ban on private monetary contributions tends to favor those with volunteer time, such as students and retirees, over working people, who have less time but may have money. It favors persons skilled in producing political advertising over persons skilled in growing corn or building homes." Consider in response Burt Neuborne, *Is Money Different?*, 77 TEXAS LAW REVIEW 1609, 1613 (1999): "The power of ... money would be less troubling if there existed substitutes that allowed persons without great wealth to exercise equivalent power. Talent can occasionally play that role, enabling extraordinary persons without great wealth to play significant roles in the political process. But the link between money and effective speech is so strong that, over time, I believe it overwhelms talent." See also Ronald Dworkin, SOVEREIGN VIRTUE: THE THEORY AND PRACTICE OF EQUALITY 366–67 (2000) ("Experience has shown—and never more dramatically than in recent elections—that any group's political success is so directly related to the sheer magnitude of its expenditures, particularly on television and radio, that this factor dwarfs others in accounting for political success. That is the heart of the democratic argument for expenditure limits in political campaigns."). If Dworkin is correct, how is it that during the second half of the twentieth century, when campaign costs were growing rapidly, Congress enacted the Clean Air Act of 1970, the Tax Reform Act of 1986, and any number of additional major laws that were strenuously opposed by well-financed interests? Is Dworkin's assertion about what experience shows consistent with the empirical research described in Section III.A above?

(b) *It is unnecessary to regulate wealth in campaign financing to achieve equality.* This argument has three separate components: (i) Some critics argue that money spent on elections does not correlate with legislative votes. We considered this argument in connection with the Sorauf excerpt above. Even if wealth does not correlate with legislative votes, it may correlate with other legislative action, such as a committee's decision to amend or table a bill. Is that reason enough to regulate campaign finances?; (ii) Some critics argue that the views of the wealthy are distributed randomly: "[T]he views of the 'rich' are, it appears, much less homogeneous than many other groups with a large amount of political influence." Smith, *supra*, 86 Georgetown Law Journal at 94; but see Neuborne, *supra*, 77 Texas Law Review at 1613 ("While there are wealthy left-wing radicals, and impoverished right-wing conservatives, by and large, the wealthy are likely to cluster at given points on the political spectrum that do not overlap with the places where the poor cluster."); (iii) Others object to the idea that "the poor" and "the rich" are immutable categories. In this regard, consider Lillian R. BeVier, *Campaign Finance Reform: Specious Arguments, Intractable Dilemmas*, 94 Columbia Law Review 1258, 1263–64 (1994):

> Wealth is always unequally distributed in a market economy because not only are initial material endowments unequal but so are intangible ones such as intellectual skills, energy, personality, judgment, and luck. However, where free exchange and the opportunity to exploit or to squander one's initial endowment exists, no distribution is permanent. The familiar saying "three generations from shirtsleeves to shirtsleeves" is but a homely way of capturing this universal flux.... A static conception [of wealth distribution] provides at best an incomplete, and at worst an inaccurate and irrelevant, account of reality because it fails to credit the continual redistribution of rights and entitlements that takes place in an inherently dynamic world where private property rights are protected and free markets prevail.

BeVier provides no empirical support for her claim about redistribution of wealth across generations, and long-term longitudinal empirical studies (studying the same people or families over time) may not exist. In the shorter term, the empirical picture does not support BeVier. One study found that in 1983 non-Hispanic African-Americans had mean net worth only 19% of whites ($43,700, compared to $232,300 in 1995 dollars), and in 1995 their mean net worth was a similar 17% of whites ($40,800, compared to $242,400 in 1995 dollars). Edward N. Wolff, *Recent Trends in the Size Distribution of Household Wealth*, Journal of Economic Perspectives Summer 1998, at 131, 141. The study concluded that:

> The only households that saw their mean net worth and financial wealth rise in absolute terms between 1983 and 1995 were those in the top 20 percent of their respective distributions and the gains were particularly strong for the top 1 percent. All other groups suffered real wealth or income losses, and the declines were particularly precipitous at the bottom. Slicing the numbers by black and white, or by young and old, only confirms the growth in inequality of wealth.

Id. at 150. See also Javier Diaz-Giménez, Vincenzo Quadrini, and José-Víctor Ríos-Rull, *Dimensions of Inequality: Facts on the U.S. Distributions of Earnings, Income, and Wealth*, Federal Reserve Bank of Minneapolis Quarterly Review, Spring 1997, at 3, 14 (table 7) (finding that over 90% of those in the bottom fifth of net worth in 1984 were in the bottom two-fifths in 1989, and over 92% of those in the top fifth of net worth in 1984 were in the top two-fifths in 1989).

In considering these competing viewpoints, bear in mind that many of the resources that flow into campaigns come from organizations, not individuals. Thus, few teachers are especially wealthy, but teachers' unions are one of the major sources of campaign resources—financial and otherwise—in contemporary America.

Spencer Overton takes issue with BeVier's arguments as well. After noting that "Professor BeVier's focus on the *income* of taxpayers also overlooks the important role of *wealth* in measuring class mobility," Overton offers statistics showing that when measured by wealth, economic mobility is "dismal." He continues by noting some racial disparities:

> In a study of men who turned twenty-one after 1980, 47% of whites reached middle class earnings by age thirty, whereas only 19% of blacks had done so. African Americans are nearly five times more likely than whites to fall from the top income quartile to the bottom quartile, while African Americans born to the bottom quartile attain the top quartile at less than one-half the rate of whites. In a study of American wealth mobility over 15 years, 0% of African American males in the study rose from the lowest wealth decile to the highest.

Spencer Overton, *The Donor Class: Campaign Finance, Democracy, and Participation*, 153 UNIVERSITY OF PENNSYLVANIA LAW REVIEW 73, 94–96 (2004).

3. Smith and BeVier are two of a number of prominent writers who have written in favor of deregulating campaign finance. Readers interested in this debate might wish to start with Bradley A. Smith, *Faulty Assumptions and Undemocratic Consequences of Campaign Finance Reform*, 105 YALE LAW JOURNAL 1049 (1996) and a response by a supporter of regulation, E. Joshua Rosenkranz, *Faulty Assumptions in "Faulty Assumptions": A Response to Professor Smith's Critiques of Campaign Finance Reform*, 30 CONNECTICUT LAW REVIEW 867 (1998). For another debate, see Kathleen M. Sullivan, *Political Money and Freedom of Speech*, 30 U.C. DAVIS LAW REVIEW 663, 668–69 (1997) and Frank Askin, *Political Money and Freedom of Speech: Kathleen Sullivan's Seven Deadly Sins—An Antitoxin*, 31 U.C. DAVIS LAW REVIEW 1065 (1998). Other notable deregulationist works include: Bradley A. Smith, UNFREE SPEECH: THE FOLLY OF CAMPAIGN FINANCE REFORM (2001); Joel M. Gora, *Campaign Finance Reform: Still Searching Today for a Better Way*, 6 JOURNAL OF LAW AND POLICY 137 (1997); and Stephen E. Gottlieb, *The Dilemma of Election Campaign Finance Reform*, 18 HOFSTRA LAW REVIEW 213 (1989). For a skeptical, though not necessarily deregulationist, view, see Roy A. Schotland, *Proposals for Campaign Finance Reform: An Article Dedicated to Being Less Dull Than Its Title*, 21 CAPITAL UNIVERSITY LAW REVIEW 429 (1992). Professors Issacharoff and Karlan argue that effective campaign finance regulation is simply impossible because the money will have to "flow" somewhere. See Samuel Issacharoff and Pamela S. Karlan, *The Hydraulics of Campaign Finance Reform*, 77 TEXAS LAW REVIEW 1705 (1999).

4. Claiming that "[l]egal academics who call for campaign finance reform ... have overlooked the significance of race," Spencer Overton argues that a focus on race significantly bolsters the equality argument for such regulation. Spencer Overton, *But Some Are More Equal: Race, Exclusion, and Campaign Finance*, 80 TEXAS LAW REVIEW 987 (2002). According to Overton, "[e]xisting frameworks fail to acknowledge that past state-mandated discrimination against racial minorities has shaped the current distribution of property, which in turn hinders the ability of many people of color to participate fully in a privately financed political system.... By using the First Amendment to undermine legislative restrictions on the use of political money, courts effectively enshrine the existing distribution of property as a baseline for political advantage." *Id*. See also Terry Smith, *Race and Money in Politics*, 79 NORTH CAROLINA LAW REVIEW 1469 (2001). The Smith article is part of a symposium, *Democracy in a New America*, and includes commentaries on the article by Samuel Issacharoff, Daniel H. Lowenstein, and Spencer Overton.

5. Note that Foley does not argue that the Constitution requires equality in campaign finance. For an argument that it does, see Jamin Raskin and John Bonifaz, *The Constitutional Imperative and Practical Superiority of Democratically Financed Elections*, 94 COLUMBIA LAW REVIEW 1160 (1994). For a criticism of Raskin and Bonifaz, see Smith, *supra*,

86 Georgetown Law Journal at 79–88. See also Sullivan, *supra*, 30 U.C. Davis Law Review at 672–73 (arguing that campaign finance is more analogous to political speech than voting, for which formal equality is the constitutional standard).

6. Is there a connection between equality arguments for campaign finance regulation and civic republicanism? Consider Cass R. Sunstein, *Political Equality and Unintended Consequences*, 94 Columbia Law Review 1390, 1392 (1994):

> [Political equality] is a time-honored goal in American constitutional thought. People who are able to organize themselves in such a way as to spend large amounts of cash should not be able to influence politics more than people who are not similarly able. Certainly, economic equality is not required in a democracy; but it is most troublesome if people with a good deal of money are allowed to translate their wealth into political influence. It is equally troublesome if the electoral process translates poverty into an absence of political influence. Of course economic inequalities cannot be made altogether irrelevant for politics. But the link can be diminished between wealth or poverty on the one hand and political influence on the other. The "one person-one vote" rule exemplifies the commitment to political equality. Limits on campaign expenditures are continuous with that rule.
>
> The third interest is in some ways a generalization of the [interests in preventing corruption and in political equality]. Campaign finance laws might promote the goal of ensuring political deliberation and reason-giving. Politics should not simply register existing preferences and their intensities, especially as these are measured by private willingness to pay. In the American constitutional tradition, politics has an important deliberative function. The constitutional system aspires to a form of "government by discussion." Grants of cash to candidates might compromise that goal by, for example, encouraging legislatures to vote in accordance with private interest rather than reasons.
>
> The goals of political equality and political deliberation are related to the project of distinguishing between the appropriate spheres of economic markets and politics. In democratic politics, a norm of equality is important: disparities in wealth ought not lead to disparities in power over government. Similarly, democracy requires adherence to the norm of reason-giving. Political outcomes should not be based only on intensities of preferences as these are reflected in the criterion of private willingness to pay. Taken together, the notions of equality and reason-giving embody a distinctive conception of political respect. Markets are operated on the basis of quite different understandings. People can purchase things because they want them, and they need not offer or even have reasons for their wants. Markets embody their own conception of equality insofar as they entail a principle of "one dollar-one 'vote'"; but this is not the conception of equality appropriate to the political sphere.

See also Dworkin, Sovereign Virtue, *supra*, at 351–85; C. Edwin Baker, *Campaign Expenditures and Free Speech*, 33 Harvard Civil Rights-Civil Liberties Law Review 1, 3 (1998); Issacharoff & Karlan, *supra*, 77 Texas Law Review 1705. Sullivan, *supra*, 30 U.C. Davis Law Review at 681–82, contends that "[c]ampaign finance reformers necessarily reject pluralist assumptions about the operation of democracy and would restrict speech in the form of political money to foster either" a Burkean/civic republican view or a populist view "in which the representative ought be as close as possible to a transparent vehicle for plebiscitary democracy...."

Compare Sunstein's argument with Daniel Ortiz's comments on Issacharoff and Karlan:

Several times in passing Issacharoff and Karlan tar [campaign finance] reform with the brush of civic republicanism. Because campaign finance reform elevates thoughtfulness in individual political decision-making, they believe reform rests on "republican-communitarian" assumptions. Although they correctly identify reform's central premise—that thoughtful voters are better ones—their conclusion does not follow. Some reformers follow the "republican-communitarian" flag; some do not. Again, I am largely agnostic. Thoughtfulness in individual decision-making improves both civic republican and pluralist decision-making. In a pluralistic system, it aims to ensure that people thoughtfully vote their *real* self-interests rather than passively follow the affective comforts of political advertising.

Daniel R. Ortiz, *Water, Water Everywhere*, 77 TEXAS LAW REVIEW 1739, 1749 (1999); see also Richard L. Hasen, *Clipping Coupons for Democracy: An Egalitarian/Public Choice Defense of Campaign Finance Vouchers*, 84 CALIFORNIA LAW REVIEW 1, 6 (1996), which proposes an equality-based voucher plan that "does not depend upon utopian hopes that politics can become less self-regarding." Ortiz's comments follow upon his exploration of the question whether equality-based arguments for campaign reform are based upon doubts about voters' abilities to exercise informed, independent judgments. See Daniel R. Ortiz, *The Democratic Paradox of Campaign Finance Reform*, 50 STANFORD LAW REVIEW 893 (1998). Does your view of the equality rationale depend upon whether you are a pluralist, progressivist, civic republican, or something else?

7. A final note relevant not only to equality-based arguments for campaign finance regulation, but for campaign finance regulation as a whole: Beware of unintended consequences. Sunstein, *supra*, 94 COLUMBIA LAW REVIEW at 1400–1411, argues that campaign finance legislation may prove unhelpful or counterproductive. He notes a number of possible unintended consequences:

(a) Campaign finance limits may entrench incumbents

(b) Limits on individual contributions will produce more (and more influential) PACs

(c) Limits on hard money encourage a shift to soft money

(d) Limits on PACs lead to an increase in individual expenditures

(e) Limits on PACs may increase secret gifts

(f) Limits on both PACs and contributions could hinder campaign activity

See also Issacharoff & Karlan, *supra*, 77 TEXAS LAW REVIEW at 1714: "We are particularly worried that reforms would exacerbate the already disturbing trend toward politics being divorced from the mediating influence of candidates and political parties."

Sunstein concludes that because of congressional self-dealing in campaign finance regulation, "considerable judicial suspicion ... is justified." He states that "we might try to avoid rigid, command-and-control regulation, which poses special dangers, and move instead toward more flexible, incentive-based strategies." Sunstein, *supra*, 94 COLUMBIA LAW REVIEW at 1400. Sunstein tentatively endorses campaign finance vouchers, *id.* at 1412–13, discussed in more detail in Chapter 17.

Chapter 15

Contribution Limits after *Buckley*

In *Buckley v. Valeo*, the Supreme Court upheld a number of laws limiting campaign contributions to candidates for federal office. The Court held such limits only "marginally" restricted free speech rights and were justified by the government's interest in preventing corruption and the appearance of corruption.

Though *Buckley* answered some fundamental questions about the constitutionality of campaign contribution limits, it left open a number of others, including the following important questions:

- May a state or local government limit campaign contributions in ballot measure campaigns?
- Can campaign contribution limits be so low as to become unconstitutional?
- Is it constitutional to limit contributions to political committees that make *independent expenditures* favoring or opposing candidates, but do not make any contributions to candidates or coordinate spending with candidates?[a] This issue gained increased salience after Congress passed a new campaign finance law, the Bipartisan Campaign Reform Act of 2003 (BCRA), which led to a dramatic increase in spending by "527 organizations" in the 2004 elections, including "Americans Coming Together," a Democratic-leaning organization supported by a few very wealthy donors, and the "Swift Boat Veterans for Truth," which ran advertisements attacking Democrat John Kerry.

We consider each of these questions in turn.

I. Campaign Contribution Limits in Ballot Measure Elections

Buckley concerned *federal* campaign finance law, which means it concerned exclusively *candidate* elections; there is no initiative process on the federal level. In *First National Bank of Boston v. Bellotti*, set forth in Chapter 16, the Supreme Court held that the First Amendment bars any limit on spending by corporations in ballot measure campaigns. *Bellotti* is important for our purposes now because the *Bellotti* Court's premise was that

---

a. As was pointed out in *Buckley,* federal law counts coordinated spending as a contribution rather than as an independent expenditure. *See* FEC v. Wisconsin Right to Life, 127 S.Ct. 2652, 2678 (2007) (Scalia, J., concurring in part and concurring in the judgment).

"Referenda are held on issues, not candidates for public office. The risk of corruption perceived in cases involving candidate elections simply is not present in a popular vote on a public issue."

Building upon *Bellotti*, the Court in CITIZENS AGAINST RENT CONTROL V. CITY OF BERKELEY, 454 U.S. 290 (1981) (*CARC*), struck down a $250 limit on contributions to committees formed to support or oppose municipal ballot measures. The Court relied heavily on the First Amendment right of association:

> We begin by recalling that the practice of persons sharing common views banding together to achieve a common end is deeply embedded in the American political process. The 18th-century Committees of Correspondence and the pamphleteers were early examples of this phenomena [*sic*] and the Federalist Papers were perhaps the most significant and lasting example. The tradition of volunteer committees for collective action has manifested itself in myriad community and public activities; in the political process it can focus on a candidate or on a ballot measure. Its value is that by collective effort individuals can make their views known, when, individually, their voices would be faint or lost.

> The Court has long viewed the First Amendment as protecting a marketplace for the clash of different views and conflicting ideas. That concept has been stated and restated almost since the Constitution was drafted. The voters of the city of Berkeley adopted the challenged ordinance which places restrictions on that marketplace.

The *CARC* Court then found the contribution limit unconstitutional under *Buckley*:

> [*Buckley* noted] that the freedom of association "is diluted if it does not include the right to pool money through contributions, for funds are often essential if 'advocacy' is to be truly or optimally 'effective.'" Under the Berkeley ordinance an affluent person can, acting alone, spend without limit to advocate individual views on a ballot measure. It is only when contributions are made in concert with one or more others in the exercise of the right of association that they are restricted by [the ordinance].

> *Buckley* identified a single narrow exception to the rule that limits on political activity were contrary to the First Amendment. The exception relates to the perception of undue influence of large contributors to a *candidate* ...

> *Buckley* thus sustained limits on contributions to candidates and their committees.

> In *Bellotti*, we held that a state could not prohibit corporations any more than it could preclude individuals from making contributions or expenditures advocating views on ballot measures. The *Bellotti* Court relied on *Buckley* to strike down state legislative limits on advocacy relating to ballot measures ...

> Notwithstanding *Buckley* and *Bellotti*, the city of Berkeley argues that [the ordinance] is necessary as a prophylactic measure to make known the identity of supporters and opponents of ballot measures. It is true that when individuals or corporations speak through committees, they often adopt seductive names that may tend to conceal the true identity of the source. Here, there is no risk that the Berkeley voters will be in doubt as to the identity of those whose money supports or opposes a given ballot measure since contributors must make their identities known under [another provision] of the ordinance, which requires publication of lists of contributors in advance of the voting.

Contributions by individuals to support concerted action by a committee advocating a position on a ballot measure is beyond question a very significant form of political expression. As we have noted, regulation of First Amendment rights is always subject to exacting judicial scrutiny. The public interest allegedly advanced by [the ordinance] — identifying the sources of support for and opposition to ballot measures — is insubstantial because voters may identify those sources under the [other] provisions. In addition, the record in this case does not support the California Supreme Court's conclusion that [the ordinance] is needed to preserve voters' confidence in the ballot measure process. Cf. *Bellotti*. It is clear, therefore, that [the ordinance] does not advance a legitimate governmental interest significant enough to justify its infringement of First Amendment rights.

Apart from the impermissible restraint on freedom of association, but virtually inseparable from it in this context, [the ordinance] imposes a significant restraint on the freedom of expression of groups and those individuals who wish to express their views through committees. As we have noted, an individual may make expenditures without limit under [the ordinance] on a ballot measure but may not contribute beyond the $250 limit when joining with others to advocate common views. The contribution limit thus automatically affects expenditures,[b] and limits on expenditures operate as a direct restraint on freedom of expression of a group or committee desiring to engage in political dialogue concerning a ballot measure.

Whatever may be the state interest or degree of that interest in regulating and limiting contributions to or expenditures of a candidate or a candidate's committees there is no significant state or public interest in curtailing debate and discussion of a ballot measure. Placing limits on contributions which in turn limit expenditures plainly impairs freedom of expression. The integrity of the political system will be adequately protected if contributors are identified in a public filing revealing the amounts contributed; if it is thought wise, legislation can outlaw anonymous contributions. Id at 297–300.

Justices Blackmun and O'Connor issued a brief opinion concurring in the judgment. On the question of the state's interest in preserving voter confidence in government, they wrote:

We would not deny the legitimacy of that interest.... We did not find those interests threatened in *Bellotti*, however, in part because the State failed to show "by record or legislative findings that corporate advocacy threatened imminently to undermine democratic processes" or "the confidence of the citizenry in government." The city's evidentiary support in this case is equally sparse. Id at 302, 303.

Justice Marshall agreed in his separate opinion that the state failed to present adequate evidence the ordinance was needed to preserve voter confidence, but Justice White disagreed:

It is bad enough that the Court overstates the extent to which First Amendment interests are implicated. But the Court goes on to assert that the ordinance furthers no legitimate public interest and cannot survive "any degree of scrutiny." Apparently the Court assumes this to be so because the ordinance is not directed at *quid pro quos* between large contributors and candidates for office, "the single narrow exception" for regulation that it viewed *Buckley* as endorsing. The

---

b. Is this statement consistent with the analysis in *Buckley* supporting the constitutionality of the FECA contribution limits? If not, which analysis is more sound, the *per curiam* opinion's in *Buckley* or Chief Justice Burger's here? — EDS.

Buckley Court, however, found it "unnecessary to look beyond the Act's primary purpose," the prevention of corruption, to uphold the contribution limits, and thus did not consider other possible interests for upholding the restriction. Indeed, at least since *United States v. Automobile Workers*, 352 U.S. 567 (1957), the Court has recognized that "sustaining the active alert responsibility of the individual citizen in a democracy for the wise conduct of government" is a valid state interest. The *Bellotti* Court took care to note that this objective, along with "[p]reserving the integrity of the electoral process [and] the individual citizen's confidence in government" "are interests of the highest importance."

In *Bellotti*, the Court found inadequate evidence in the record to support these interests, but it suggested that some regulation of corporate spending might be justified if "corporate advocacy threatened imminently to undermine democratic processes, thereby denigrating rather than serving First Amendment interests." The Court suggested that such a situation would arise if it could be shown that "the relative voice of corporations ha[d] been overwhelming [and] ... significant in influencing referenda." It is quite possible that such a test is fairly met in this case. Large contributions, mainly from corporate sources, have skyrocketed as the role of individuals has declined. Staggering disparities have developed between spending for and against various ballot measures. While it is not possible to prove that heavy spending "bought" a victory on any particular ballot proposition, there is increasing evidence that large contributors are at least able to block the adoption of measures through the initiative process. Recognition that enormous contributions from a few institutional sources can overshadow the efforts of individuals may have discouraged participation in ballot measure campaigns and undermined public confidence in the referendum process.

By restricting the size of contributions, the Berkeley ordinance requires major contributors to communicate directly with the voters. If the ordinance has an ultimate impact on speech, it will be to assure that a diversity of views will be presented to the voters.... Of course, entities remain free to make major direct expenditures. But because political communications must state the source of funds, voters will be able to identify the source of such messages and recognize that the communication reflects, for example, the opinion of a single powerful corporate interest rather than the views of a large number of individuals. As the existence of disclosure laws in many States suggests, information concerning who supports or opposes a ballot measure significantly affects voter evaluation of the proposal. The Court asserts, without elaboration, that existing disclosure requirements suffice to inform voters of the identity of contributors. Yet, the inadequacy of disclosure laws was a major reason for the adoption of the Berkeley ordinance. Section 101(d) of the ordinance constitutes a finding by the people of Berkeley that "the influence of large campaign contributors is increased because existing laws for disclosure of campaign receipts and expenditures have proved to be inadequate."

Admittedly, Berkeley cannot present conclusive evidence of a causal relationship between major undisclosed expenditures and the demise of the referendum as a tool of direct democracy. But the information available suffices to demonstrate that the voters had valid reasons for adopting contribution ceilings. It was on a similar foundation that the Court upheld contribution limits in *Buckley* and *California Medical Assn*. In my view, the ordinance survives scrutiny under the *Buckley* and *Bellotti* cases.

Notes and Questions

1. For commentary on *Citizens Against Rent Control (CARC)* and the issue it addresses, see Marlene Nicholson, *The Constitutionality of Contribution Limitations in Ballot Measure Elections*, 9 ECOLOGY LAW QUARTERLY 683 (1981); Daniel H. Lowenstein, *Campaign Spending and Ballot Propositions: Recent Experience, Public Choice Theory and the First Amendment*, 29 UCLA LAW REVIEW 505, 583–602 (1982).

2. The Court in *Bellotti* and *CARC* proceeded on the assumption that there is a clear line separating candidate elections and ballot measure elections. That is not always true. In California, for example, governors and others have used ballot measure elections as a means to boost their own chances for reelection or to further other political goals. "There were at least thirty-seven committees controlled by candidates or elected officials and organized to affect the outcome of ballot measure elections from 1990 to 2004, and together they have raised at least $84 million." See Richard L. Hasen, *Rethinking the Unconstitutionality of Contribution and Expenditure Limits in Ballot Measure Campaigns*, 78 SOUTHERN CALIFORNIA LAW REVIEW 885, 898 (2005). On the strength of this evidence, may contributions to candidate-controlled ballot measure committees be limited consistent with the First Amendment? It should be added that while we are unaware of any systematic studies, our impression is that more often than not these efforts to exploit initiatives for electoral gain are distinct failures.

3. The Court rejected the California Supreme Court's view that a contribution limit could be justified as "needed to preserve voters' confidence in the ballot measure process," because it was not supported by the record. What evidence would be sufficient to sustain this argument? Consider the following evidence, which had not been published prior to the trial in *CARC* and therefore could not have been made part of the record.

Some scholars have asserted that even when one side greatly outspends its adversaries its chances for success do not increase materially. *E.g.*, Ronald J. Allen, *The National Initiative Proposal: A Preliminary Analysis*, 58 NEBRASKA LAW REVIEW 965, 1028–38 (1979). Others have found one-sided spending to have a dominant effect. *E.g.*, John S. Shockley, THE INITIATIVE PROCESS IN COLORADO POLITICS: AN ASSESSMENT (1980). Research relative to California ballot propositions held between 1968 and 1980 suggests that one-sided spending has generally been very effective, to the point of "dominance," when it has been on the negative side, but surprisingly ineffective when it has been on the affirmative side. See Lowenstein, *supra*. Lowenstein's study is deservedly criticized for its statistical crudeness by John R. Owens & Larry L. Wade, *Campaign Spending on California Ballot Propositions, 1924–1984: Trends and Voting Effects*, 39 WESTERN POLITICAL QUARTERLY 675, 682–87 (1986). Owens and Wade considered vote percentages rather than passage or defeat of ballot propositions, and the effects of campaign spending that they found were relatively weak. Nevertheless, a study of California initiative campaigns for the period 1976–88 generally found the same effects on outcomes as had appeared in Lowenstein's study, i.e., dominance of big negative spending and ineffectiveness of big affirmative spending. See California Commission on Campaign Financing, DEMOCRACY BY INITIATIVE 290–91 (1992).

If another jurisdiction adopted a contribution limit, would introduction of that research be sufficient to sustain the limit? If you were persuaded that this conclusion (that one-sided spending usually prevails if it is on the negative side but not on the affirmative side) holds generally in ballot proposition campaigns, would it lead you to regard some control as desirable or as unnecessary? Would your answer be affected by whether you regard the institutions of direct democracy as desirable?

4. Elisabeth R. Gerber, THE POPULIST PARADOX: INTEREST GROUP INFLUENCE AND THE PROMISE OF DIRECT LEGISLATION (1999), argues that "it is a mistake to equate money with influence in the context of direct legislation." Gerber studied how both "economic" interest groups (such as trade associations) and "citizen" interest groups (such as the National Rifle Association or the Sierra Club) used the political process in states with initiatives. Gerber noted that economic groups are generally rich in capital and citizen groups are rich in labor, leading to different strategies:

> If citizen and economic interest groups have the comparative advantages described above, then I expect to observe the following patterns between group resources and strategies. Because citizen groups tend to have the personnel resources required to mobilize broad-based electoral support, they are better able to amass an electoral majority. When they have sufficient capital to participate at all, I therefore expect citizen groups to employ strategies aimed at proposing and passing new initiatives. Economic interest groups, by contrast, should anticipate a more difficult time using their resources to achieve victory at the ballot box and should instead pursue largely defensive or indirect strategies. Analyzing surveys of interest group activities and motivations, as well as campaign finance data from 161 initiative and referendum campaigns in eight states, I find strong empirical evidence in support of these theoretical conclusions. Citizen groups report using the direct legislation process to pass new laws and contribute to campaigns to support new initiative legislation. Economic groups report using the direct legislation process to pressure the legislature and direct a large share of their financial resources to opposition campaigns ...
>
> I expect these patterns of interest group behavior to translate into patterns of policy outcomes. Specifically, I expect the laws that pass by initiative to reflect the interests of citizen groups that use the process to achieve direct modifying influence. I expect the laws that fail to reflect economic group interests. I also expect legislatures in initiative states to respond to interest group pressures by passing different laws than do legislatures in noninitiative states. Further analyses of the campaign finance data, plus comparisons of policies in the fifty states, provide strong empirical evidence that is consistent with these expectations.
>
> Together, these theoretical and empirical results show that citizen and economic interest groups use direct legislation for different purposes and to different ends. The largely conservative and indirect influence by economic interest groups is a form of influence much different from—although perhaps no less important than—the one portrayed by modern critics of direct legislation.[c]

Id. at 8–9. Assume Gerber's empirical evidence supports her case. Would that fact lead you to support different (or no) controls over initiative campaign finance?

5. Suppose that in a ballot proposition campaign side A can raise $1,000,000 in relatively small contributions, and side B can raise only $100,000 in such contributions. Suppose further that XYZ Corporation would like to contribute $900,000 to side B. Is it fair to permit the large contribution under these circumstances? Is it fair to prohibit it? From whose point of view are you applying a standard of fairness? Consider Lowenstein, *supra,* 29 UCLA LAW REVIEW at 515–17:

---

c. On the specific question of blocking initiatives, Gerber found that economic groups have an easier time than citizen groups blocking initiatives they oppose. *Id.* at 119.

There are two conceptions of fairness that may inform our evaluation. First, the campaign may be regarded as fair when both sides have a roughly equal opportunity to present their arguments to the voters. We shall call this the *equality* standard of fairness. Second, the campaign may be regarded as fair when the ability of either side to present its arguments more or less reflects the number of people who actively support that side and the strength of their feelings. We shall call this the *intensity* standard of fairness.

The equality standard is based on the voter's interest in receiving a balanced presentation of the arguments. If the equality standard is met, the voter is least likely to be deceived and most likely to be apprised of considerations relevant to his assessment of the proposition. The intensity standard is based on the interest of activists on each side who wish to translate their own strong feelings into an advantage for their side. The intensity standard minimizes the likelihood that an apathetic majority will impose severe harm on an intense minority. In addition, it incorporates the idea that widespread political participation is desirable and therefore should be encouraged by assuring that participation will be effective.

While both the equality and intensity standards have intuitive appeal, they can be incompatible. If large numbers of people feel strongly and are prepared to contribute money, speak out and otherwise assist one side of the issue while most of their opponents remain apathetic, under the intensity standard the result is regarded as fair although voters are exposed to a relatively one-sided debate. On the other hand, if measures are taken to assure a relatively even-handed debate, the intense feelings on one side will not significantly enhance that side's chances of success.

In the above problem, is permitting the contribution by the XYZ Corporation to Side B fair under the equality standard of fairness? Under the intensity standard? Suppose the XYZ Corporation instead wants to contribute $900,000 to side A. Is permitting this contribution fair under either or both standards of fairness?

Now consider a variation that is often more realistic in ballot measure campaigns. Side A has sufficiently widespread and intense support that it can raise $500,000 in small contributions, and it receives no large contributions. Side B receives virtually no small contributions, but four corporations contribute $5 million each. Because of the large size of the state and the high prices for advertising in media of all types, political experts agree that a $500,000 campaign will have almost no success in communicating its message to voters, whereas $20 million is just about what is needed to get a message heard often enough to make an impression. Furthermore, because of other, more newsworthy matters that will be on the ballot at the same time, newspapers and broadcasters are giving little attention to the proposition in question. The proposition is sufficiently complex and its likely consequences sufficiently debatable that the electorate would unquestionably benefit from debate and information. Under these circumstances, if the choice is between a one-sided campaign favoring side B and virtually no campaign at all, which is more in the public interest?

6. The effects of large contributions can be dramatic. Consider the case of Proposition 5 in the California 1978 general election, an initiative proposal to require separate smoking and no-smoking sections in public places. In contributions *under* $1,000, the supporters raised $541,621 compared with the opponents' $48,236. In contributions *over* $1,000, the supporters raised $111,960, while the opponents raised $6,302,252. Almost

all of this last figure came from five major tobacco companies and the Tobacco Institute. One company alone, R.J. Reynolds Tobacco Company, put up $2,403,600. See Fair Political Practices Commission, Campaign Contributions and Spending Report, November 7, 1978 General Election. These large contributions were not made in vain. Although early polls showed Proposition 5 leading by 20 percentage points, the proposition was defeated. See Lowenstein, *supra*, 29 UCLA Law Review at 537–40.

The absence of any limit on the size of contributions to ballot measure campaigns, combined with the high cost of advertising media in large states, can render small contributions by ordinary citizens insignificant. To a large extent, this has occurred in California.

> With large contributions coming from all sides, ballot measure campaigns become battles between fewer and fewer major interests. A majority of the funding for some 1990 initiative contests came from fewer than 10 contributors. In the campaign for forest protection Proposition 130, for example, the proponents were funded almost entirely by two contributors—Harold Arbit and Frank Wells—who gave contributions of $1 million or more. The opposition campaign was almost entirely supported by 16 lumber companies giving in amounts of $100,000 or more.... In 1990, two-thirds (67%) of the total dollars raised by all campaigns were received in amounts of $100,000 or more.... Over one-third (37%) of all 1990 contributions came in amounts of $1 million or more....
>
> Contributions from small donors were least significant. Though contributors of less than $1,000 accounted for 78% of the total *number* of contributions to 1990 campaigns, they totaled just 6% of the total dollars contributed.

California Commission on Campaign Financing, Democracy By Initiative 279–80 (1992) (some emphasis deleted).

7. Would public financing of ballot measure campaigns be desirable? What would be the objective of public financing? Would money be provided in all ballot proposition campaigns? Bear in mind that many ballot propositions involve relatively obscure amendments to state constitutions that generate little interest. If money is not to be provided in all campaigns, how would it be decided which propositions would be eligible? Would funds go to both sides of the campaign or to one side only? If it were decided that a given side in a given campaign were entitled to funds, what would happen if more than one committee on that side applied for the funds? Would public financing be joined with a limit on the size of contributions or would it be an alternative to such limits? For discussion of these issues, see Elizabeth Garrett, *Money, Agenda Setting, and Direct Democracy*, 77 Texas Law Review 1845, 1876–79 (1999); Richard Briffault, *Ballot Propositions and Campaign Finance Reform*, 1 New York University Journal of Legislation & Public Policy 41 (1997); Lowenstein, *supra*, 29 UCLA Law Review at 578–83.

II. When Are Contribution Limits Too Low?

You may recall from *Buckley* that the Court rejected a challenge to the *amount* of the FECA's contribution limits as unconstitutionally low. The Court quoted approvingly from the lower court opinion that it lacked "a scalpel to probe, whether, say, a $2,000 ceiling might not serve as well as $1,000." The Court continued that "[s]uch distinctions in degree become significant only when they can be said to amount to differences in kind." 424 U.S. 1, 30 (1976).

In 1994, voters in Missouri and Montana approved initiatives imposing general contribution limits of $100 in many elections. Other jurisdictions also adopted very low contribution limits, usually through the initiative process. As these laws passed, opponents challenged them, arguing that the contribution limits were unconstitutionally low under *Buckley*. For example, in *Carver v. Nixon*, 72 F.3d 633 (8th Cir. 1995), cert. denied 518 U.S. 1033 (1996), the Eighth Circuit held that Missouri's campaign contribution limits enacted by initiative were unconstitutional because they were not narrowly tailored to meet the state's interest in limiting the potential corruption associated with large campaign contributions.

In *Shrink Missouri Government PAC v. Adams*, 161 F.3d 519 (8th Cir. 1998), the Eighth Circuit struck down Missouri's legislatively-enacted $250–$1,000 campaign contribution limits that went into effect after the court had struck down the lower initiative-enacted limits in *Carver*. *Shrink Missouri* started off as a typical low contribution limits case. The court's reasoning, however, was surprising. Only one judge on the three-judge panel believed that the $1,075 limit was unconstitutionally low. That judge was joined by a second judge in holding the contribution law unconstitutional because the state failed to provide "some demonstrable evidence that there were genuine problems that resulted from contributions in amounts greater than the limits in place." The ruling called into question all contribution limits, including the FECA's $1,000 individual contribution limit originally upheld in *Buckley*.[d]

The Supreme Court granted certiorari in *Shrink Missouri* and reversed the Eighth Circuit in the following opinion. The opinion is important not only for its holding, but also for the concurring opinion of Justice Breyer, which stakes out an egalitarian "participatory self-government" theory of how courts should review campaign finance laws, and the dissenting opinion of Justice Thomas, which defends a deregulationist approach to such laws under the First Amendment.

Nixon v. Shrink Missouri Government PAC
528 U.S. 377 (2000)

Justice SOUTER delivered the opinion of the Court.

The principal issues in this case are whether *Buckley v. Valeo* is authority for state limits on contributions to state political candidates and whether the federal limits approved in *Buckley*, with or without adjustment for inflation, define the scope of permissible state limitations today. We hold *Buckley* to be authority for comparable state regulation, which need not be pegged to *Buckley*'s dollars.

I

In 1994, the Legislature of Missouri enacted Senate Bill 650 (SB650) to restrict the permissible amounts of contributions to candidates for state office. Before the statute became effective, however, Missouri voters approved a ballot initiative with even stricter contribution limits, effective immediately. The United States Court of Appeals for the

---

d. As we will see in Part III of this chapter, the federal individual contribution limit was raised to $2,000 in 2003 and indexed to inflation.

Eighth Circuit then held the initiative's contribution limits unconstitutional under the First Amendment, *Carver v. Nixon*, with the upshot that the previously dormant 1994 statute took effect.

As amended in 1997, that statute imposes contribution limits ranging from $250 to a $1,000, depending on specified state office or size of constituency. The particular provision challenged here reads that

> "[t]o elect an individual to the office of governor, lieutenant governor, secretary of state, state treasurer, state auditor or attorney general, [[t]he amount of contributions made by or accepted from any person other than the candidate in any one election shall not exceed] one thousand dollars."

The statutory dollar amounts are baselines for an adjustment each even-numbered year, to be made "by multiplying the base year amount by the cumulative consumer price index … and rounded to the nearest twenty-five-dollar amount, for all years since January 1, 1995." When this suit was filed, the limits ranged from a high of $1,075 for contributions to candidates for statewide office (including state auditor) and for any office where the population exceeded 250,000, down to $275 for contributions to candidates for state representative or for any office for which there were fewer than 100,000 people represented.

Respondents Shrink Missouri Government PAC, a political action committee, and Zev David Fredman, a candidate for the 1998 Republican nomination for state auditor, sought to enjoin enforcement of the contribution statute as violating their First and Fourteenth Amendment rights (presumably those of free speech, association, and equal protection, although the complaint did not so state). Shrink Missouri gave $1,025 to Fredman's candidate committee in 1997, and another $50 in 1998. Shrink Missouri represented that, without the limitation, it would contribute more to the Fredman campaign. Fredman alleged he could campaign effectively only with more generous contributions than [the statute] allowed.

On cross-motions for summary judgment, the District Court sustained the statute. Applying *Buckley v. Valeo*, *supra*, the court found adequate support for the law in the proposition that large contributions raise suspicions of influence peddling tending to undermine citizens' confidence "in the integrity of … government." The District Court rejected respondents' contention that inflation since *Buckley*'s approval of a federal $1,000 restriction meant that the state limit of $1,075 for a statewide office could not be constitutional today.

The Court of Appeals for the Eighth Circuit nonetheless enjoined enforcement of the law pending appeal, and ultimately reversed the District Court. Finding that *Buckley* had "'articulated and applied a strict scrutiny standard of review,'" the Court of Appeals held that Missouri was bound to demonstrate "that it has a compelling interest and that the contribution limits at issue are narrowly drawn to serve that interest." The appeals court treated Missouri's claim of a compelling interest "in avoiding the corruption or the perception of corruption brought about when candidates for elective office accept large campaign contributions" as insufficient by itself to satisfy strict scrutiny. Relying on Circuit precedent, see *Russell, Carver*, the Court of Appeals required

> "some demonstrable evidence that there were genuine problems that resulted from contributions in amounts greater than the limits in place.…"

> "[T]he Buckley Court noted the perfidy that had been uncovered in federal campaign financing in 1972.… But we are unwilling to extrapolate from those ex-

amples that in Missouri at this time there is corruption or a perception of corruption from 'large' campaign contributions, without some evidence that such problems really exist."

The court thought that the only evidence presented by the State, an affidavit from the co-chairman of the state legislature's Interim Joint Committee on Campaign Finance Reform when the statute was passed, was inadequate to raise a genuine issue of material fact about the State's alleged interest in limiting campaign contributions. *Ibid.*[2]

Given the large number of States that limit political contributions, we granted certiorari to review the congruence of the Eighth Circuit's decision with *Buckley*. We reverse.

II

The matters raised in *Buckley* included claims that federal campaign finance legislation infringed speech and association guarantees of the First Amendment and the Equal Protection Clause of the Fourteenth. The Federal Election Campaign Act of 1971, as amended by the Federal Election Campaign Act Amendments of 1974, limited (and still limits) contributions by individuals to any single candidate for federal office to $1,000 per election. Until *Buckley* struck it down, the law also placed a $1,000 annual ceiling on independent expenditures linked to specific candidates. We found violations of the First Amendment in the expenditure regulations, but held the contribution restrictions constitutional. *Buckley*.

A

Precision about the relative rigor of the standard to review contribution limits was not a pretense of the *Buckley per curiam* opinion. To be sure, in addressing the speech claim, we explicitly rejected both *O'Brien* intermediate scrutiny for communicative action, see *United States v. O'Brien*, 391 U.S. 367 (1968), and the similar standard applicable to merely time, place, and manner restrictions, see *Adderley v. Florida*, 385 U.S. 39 (1966); *Cox v. Louisiana*, 379 U.S. 536 (1965); *Kovacs v. Cooper*, 336 U.S. 77 (1949). In distinguishing these tests, the discussion referred generally to "the exacting scrutiny required by the First Amendment," *Buckley*, and added that "'the constitutional guarantee has its fullest and most urgent application precisely to the conduct of campaigns for political office,'" *id.* (quoting *Monitor Patriot Co. v. Roy*, 401 U.S. 265, 272 (1971)).

We then, however, drew a line between expenditures and contributions, treating expenditure restrictions as direct restraints on speech, which nonetheless suffered little direct effect from contribution limits:

> "[A] limitation upon the amount that any one person or group may contribute to a candidate or political committee entails only a marginal restriction upon the contributor's ability to engage in free communication. A contribution serves as a general expression of support for the candidate and his views, but does not communicate the underlying basis for the support The quantity of communication by the contributor does not increase perceptibly with the size of his contribution, since the expression rests solely on the undifferentiated symbolic act of con-

2. Chief Judge Bowman also would have found the law invalid because the contribution limits were severely tailored beyond any need to serve the State's interest. Comparing the Missouri limits with those considered in *Buckley*, the Chief Judge said that "[a]fter inflation, limits of $1,075, $525, and $275 cannot compare with the $1,000 limit approved in *Buckley* twenty-two years ago," and "can only be regarded as 'too low to allow meaningful participation in protected political speech and association.'" ...

tributing. At most, the size of the contribution provides a very rough index of the intensity of the contributor's support for the candidate. A limitation on the amount of money a person may give to a candidate or campaign organization thus involves little direct restraint on his political communication, for it permits the symbolic expression of support evidenced by a contribution but does not in any way infringe the contributor's freedom to discuss candidates and issues." [*Buckley*] (footnote omitted).

We thus said, in effect, that limiting contributions left communication significantly unimpaired.

We flagged a similar difference between expenditure and contribution limitations in their impacts on the association right. While an expenditure limit "precludes most associations from effectively amplifying the voice of their adherents," *id.* (thus interfering with the freedom of the adherents as well as the association, *ibid.*), the contribution limits "leave the contributor free to become a member of any political association and to assist personally in the association's efforts on behalf of candidates," *ibid.*; see also *id.*, at 28. While we did not then say in so many words that different standards might govern expenditure and contribution limits affecting associational rights, we have since then said so explicitly in *MCFL*: "We have consistently held that restrictions on contributions require less compelling justification than restrictions on independent spending." It has, in any event, been plain ever since *Buckley* that contribution limits would more readily clear the hurdles before them. Cf. *Colorado I* [described *infra* this chapter—EDS.] (opinion of BREYER, J.) (noting that in campaign finance case law, "[t]he provisions that the Court found constitutional mostly imposed *contribution* limits" (emphasis in original)). Thus, under *Buckley*'s standard of scrutiny, a contribution limit involving "significant interference" with associational rights, could survive if the Government demonstrated that contribution regulation was "closely drawn" to match a "sufficiently important interest," though the dollar amount of the limit need not be "fine tun[ed]." [*Buckley.*]

While we did not attempt to parse distinctions between the speech and association standards of scrutiny for contribution limits, we did make it clear that those restrictions bore more heavily on the associational right than on freedom to speak. *Id.* We consequently proceeded on the understanding that a contribution limitation surviving a claim of associational abridgment would survive a speech challenge as well, and we held the standard satisfied by the contribution limits under review.

"[T]he prevention of corruption and the appearance of corruption," was found to be a "constitutionally sufficient justification," *id.*:

> "To the extent that large contributions are given to secure a political *quid pro quo* from current and potential office holders, the integrity of our system of representative democracy is undermined...." "Of almost equal concern as the danger of actual *quid pro quo* arrangements is the impact of the appearance of corruption stemming from public awareness of the opportunities for abuse inherent in a regime of large individual financial contributions.... Congress could legitimately conclude that the avoidance of the appearance of improper influence 'is also critical ... if confidence in the system of representative Government is not to be eroded to a disastrous extent.'" *Id.* (quoting *Civil Service Comm'n v. Letter Carriers*, 413 U.S. 548, 565 (1973)).

See also *NCPAC* [discussed in the next chapter—EDS.] ("Corruption is a subversion of the political process. Elected officials are influenced to act contrary to their obligations of office by the prospect of financial gain to themselves or infusions of money into their campaigns"); *Federal Election Comm'n v. National Right to Work Comm.* (noting that Government interests in preventing corruption or the appearance of corruption "directly implicate 'the integrity of our electoral process, and, not less, the responsibility of the individual citizen for the successful functioning of that process'"); *Bellotti* ("The importance of the governmental interest in preventing [corruption] has never been doubted").

In speaking of "improper influence" and "opportunities for abuse" in addition to "*quid pro quo* arrangements," we recognized a concern not confined to bribery of public officials, but extending to the broader threat from politicians too compliant with the wishes of large contributors. These were the obvious points behind our recognition that the Congress could constitutionally address the power of money "to influence governmental action" in ways less "blatant and specific" than bribery. *Buckley*.[4]

B

In defending its own statute, Missouri espouses those same interests of preventing corruption and the appearance of it that flows from munificent campaign contributions. Even without the authority of *Buckley*, there would be no serious question about the legitimacy of the interests claimed, which, after all, underlie bribery and anti-gratuity statutes. While neither law nor morals equate all political contributions, without more, with bribes, we spoke in *Buckley* of the perception of corruption "inherent in a regime of large individual financial contributions" to candidates for public office, as a source of concern "almost equal" to *quid pro quo* improbity, *ibid.* The public interest in countering that perception was, indeed, the entire answer to the overbreadth claim raised in the *Buckley* case. This made perfect sense. Leave the perception of impropriety unanswered, and the cynical assumption that large donors call the tune could jeopardize the willingness of voters to take part in democratic governance. Democracy works "only if the people have faith in those who govern, and that faith is bound to be shattered when high officials and their appointees engage in activities which arouse suspicions of malfeasance and corruption." *United States v. Mississippi Valley Generating Co.*, 364 U.S. 520, 562 (1961).

Although respondents neither challenge the legitimacy of these objectives nor call for any reconsideration of *Buckley*, they take the State to task, as the Court of Appeals did, for failing to justify the invocation of those interests with empirical evidence of actually corrupt practices or of a perception among Missouri voters that unrestricted contributions must have been exerting a covertly corrosive influence. The state statute is not void, however, for want of evidence.

The quantum of empirical evidence needed to satisfy heightened judicial scrutiny of legislative judgments will vary up or down with the novelty and plausibility of the justification raised. *Buckley* demonstrates that the dangers of large, corrupt contributions and the suspicion that large contributions are corrupt are neither novel nor implausible. The opinion noted that "the deeply disturbing examples surfacing after the 1972 election demonstrate that the problem [of corruption] is not an illusory one." Although we did not ourselves

---

4. In arguing that the *Buckley* standard should not be relaxed, respondents Shrink Missouri and Fredman suggest that a candidate like Fredman suffers because contribution limits favor incumbents over challengers. This is essentially an equal protection claim, which *Buckley* squarely faced. We found no support for the proposition that an incumbent's advantages were leveraged into something significantly more powerful by contribution limitations applicable to all candidates, whether veterans or upstarts. Since we do not relax *Buckley*'s standard, no more need be said about respondents' argument, though we note that nothing in the record here gives respondents a stronger argument than the *Buckley* petitioners made.

marshal the evidence in support of the congressional concern, we referred to "a number of the abuses" detailed in the Court of Appeals's decision, which described how corporations, well-financed interest groups, and rich individuals had made large contributions, some of which were illegal under existing law, others of which reached at least the verge of bribery. See *Buckley v. Valeo*, 519 F.2d 821, 839–840, and nn. 36–38 (C.A.D.C. 1975). The evidence before the Court of Appeals described public revelations by the parties in question more than sufficient to show why voters would tend to identify a big donation with a corrupt purpose.

While *Buckley*'s evidentiary showing exemplifies a sufficient justification for contribution limits, it does not speak to what may be necessary as a minimum.[5] As to that, respondents are wrong in arguing that in the years since *Buckley* came down we have "supplemented" its holding with a new requirement that governments enacting contribution limits must "'demonstrate that the recited harms are real, not merely conjectural,'" Brief for Respondents (quoting *United States v. Treasury Employees*, 513 U.S. 454, 475 (1995) (in turn quoting *Turner Broadcasting System, Inc. v. FCC*, 512 U.S. 622, 664, (1994))), a contention for which respondents rely principally on *Colorado I*. We have never accepted mere conjecture as adequate to carry a First Amendment burden, and *Colorado I* did not deal with a government's burden to justify limits on contributions. Although the principal opinion in that case charged the Government with failure to show a real risk of corruption, the issue in question was limits on independent expenditures by political parties, which the principal opinion expressly distinguished from contribution limits: "limitations on independent expenditures are less directly related to preventing corruption" than contributions are. In that case, the "constitutionally significant fact" that there was no "coordination between the candidate and the source of the expenditure" kept the principal opinion "from assuming, absent convincing evidence to the contrary, that [a limitation on expenditures] is necessary to combat a substantial danger of corruption of the electoral system." *Colorado I* thus goes hand in hand with *Buckley*, not toe to toe.

In any event, this case does not present a close call requiring further definition of whatever the State's evidentiary obligation may be. While the record does not show that the Missouri Legislature relied on the evidence and findings accepted in *Buckley*, the evidence introduced into the record by respondents or cited by the lower courts in this action and the action regarding Proposition A is enough to show that the substantiation of the congressional concerns reflected in *Buckley* has its counterpart supporting the Missouri law. Although Missouri does not preserve legislative history, the State presented an affidavit from State Senator Wayne Goode, the co-chair of the state legislature's Interim Joint Committee on Campaign Finance Reform at the time the State enacted the contribution limits, who stated that large contributions have "'the real potential to buy votes.'" The District Court cited newspaper accounts of large contributions supporting inferences of impropriety. One report questioned the state treasurer's

---

5. Cf. *NRWC* ("Nor will we second-guess a legislative determination as to the need for prophylactic measures where corruption is the evil feared"); *Bellotti*; *CMA v. FEC* (noting that *Buckley* held that contribution limits "served the important governmental interests in preventing the corruption or appearance of corruption of the political process that might result if such contributions were not restrained"); *CARC* ("*Buckley* identified a single narrow exception to the rule that limits on political activity were contrary to the First Amendment. The exception relates to the perception of undue influence of large contributors to a *candidate*"); see also *NCPAC*(observing that *Buckley* upheld contribution limits as constitutional, and noting the Court's "deference to a congressional determination of the need for a prophylactic rule where the evil of potential corruption had long been recognized").

decision to use a certain bank for most of Missouri's banking business after that institution contributed $20,000 to the treasurer's campaign. Editorial, *The Central Issue is Trust*, St. Louis Post-Dispatch, Dec. 31, 1993, p. 6C. Another made much of the receipt by a candidate for state auditor of a $40,000 contribution from a brewery and one for $20,000 from a bank. J. Mannies, *Auditor Race May Get Too Noisy to be Ignored*, St. Louis Post-Dispatch, Sept. 11, 1994, at 4B. In *Carver*, the Eighth Circuit itself, while invalidating the limits Proposition A imposed, identified a $420,000 contribution to candidates in northern Missouri from a political action committee linked to an investment bank, and three scandals, including one in which a state representative was "accused of sponsoring legislation in exchange for kickbacks," and another in which Missouri's former attorney general pleaded guilty to charges of conspiracy to misuse state property after being indicted for using a state workers' compensation fund to benefit campaign contributors. And although majority votes do not, as such, defeat First Amendment protections, the statewide vote on Proposition A certainly attested to the perception relied upon here: "[A]n overwhelming 74 percent of the voters of Missouri determined that contribution limits are necessary to combat corruption and the appearance thereof." *Carver*.

There might, of course, be need for a more extensive evidentiary documentation if petitioners had made any showing of their own to cast doubt on the apparent implications of *Buckley*'s evidence and the record here, but the closest respondents come to challenging these conclusions is their invocation of academic studies said to indicate that large contributions to public officials or candidates do not actually result in changes in candidates' positions. Smith, *Money Talks: Speech, Corruption, Equality, and Campaign Finance*, 86 Georgetown Law Journal 45, 58 (1997); Smith, *Faulty Assumptions and Undemocratic Consequences of Campaign Finance Reform*, 105 Yale Law Journal 1049, 1067–1068 (1995). Other studies, however, point the other way. F. Sorauf, Inside Campaign Finance 169 (1992); Hall & Wayman, *Buying Time: Moneyed Interests and the Mobilization of Bias in Congressional Committees*, 84 American Political Science Review 797 (1990); D. Magleby & C. Nelson, The Money Chase 78 (1990). Given the conflict among these publications, and the absence of any reason to think that public perception has been influenced by the studies cited by respondents, there is little reason to doubt that sometimes large contributions will work actual corruption of our political system, and no reason to question the existence of a corresponding suspicion among voters.

C

Nor do we see any support for respondents' various arguments that in spite of their striking resemblance to the limitations sustained in *Buckley*, those in Missouri are so different in kind as to raise essentially a new issue about the adequacy of the Missouri statute's tailoring to serve its purposes. Here, as in *Buckley*, "[t]here is no indication ... that the contribution limitations imposed by the [law] would have any dramatic[ally] adverse effect on the funding of campaigns and political associations," and thus no showing that "the limitations prevented the candidates and political committees from amassing the resources necessary for effective advocacy." [*Buckley*.] The District Court found here that in the period since the Missouri limits became effective, "candidates for state elected office [have been] quite able to raise funds sufficient to run effective campaigns," and that "candidates for political office in the state are still able to amass impressive campaign war chests." The plausibility of these conclusions is buttressed by petitioners' evidence that in the 1994 Missouri elections (before any relevant state limitations went into effect), 97.62 percent of all contributors to candidates for state auditor made contributions of $2,000 or less.[9] Even if we were to assume that the contribution limits affected respondent Fredman's ability to wage a competitive campaign (no small assumption given that Fredman only identified one contributor, Shrink Missouri, that would have given him more than $1,075 per election), a showing of one affected individual does not point up a system of suppressed political advocacy that would be unconstitutional under *Buckley.*

These conclusions of the District Court and the supporting evidence also suffice to answer respondents' variant claim that the Missouri limits today differ in kind from *Buckley*'s owing to inflation since 1976. Respondents seem to assume that *Buckley* set a minimum constitutional threshold for contribution limits, which in dollars adjusted for loss of purchasing power are now well above the lines drawn by Missouri. But this assumption is a fundamental misunderstanding of what we held.

In *Buckley*, we specifically rejected the contention that $1,000, or any other amount, was a constitutional minimum below which legislatures could not regulate. As indicated above, we referred instead to the outer limits of contribution regulation by asking whether there was any showing that the limits were so low as to impede the ability of candidates to "amas[s] the resources necessary for effective advocacy." [*Buckley*.] We asked, in other words, whether the contribution limitation was so radical in effect as to render political association ineffective, drive the sound of a candidate's voice below the level of notice, and render contributions pointless. Such being the test, the issue in later cases cannot be truncated to a narrow question about the power of the dollar, but must go to the power to mount a campaign with all the dollars likely to be forthcoming. As Judge Gibson [the Eighth Circuit dissenting judge] put it, the dictates of the First Amendment are not mere functions of the Consumer Price Index.

D

The dissenters in this case think our reasoning evades the real issue. Justice Thomas chides us for "hiding behind" *Buckley*, and Justice Kennedy faults us for seeing this case as "a routine application of our analysis" in *Buckley* instead of facing up to what he describes as the consequences of *Buckley.* Each dissenter would overrule *Buckley* and thinks we should do the same.

The answer is that we are supposed to decide this case. Shrink and Fredman did not request that *Buckley* be overruled; the furthest reach of their arguments about the law was that subsequent decisions already on the books had enhanced the State's burden of justification beyond what *Buckley* required, a proposition we have rejected as mistaken.

III

There is no reason in logic or evidence to doubt the sufficiency of *Buckley* to govern this case in support of the Missouri statute. The judgment of the Court of Appeals is, accordingly, reversed, and the case is remanded for proceedings consistent with this opinion.

JUSTICE STEVENS, concurring.

JUSTICE KENNEDY suggests that the misuse of soft money tolerated by this Court's misguided decision in *Colorado I* demonstrates the need for a fresh examination of the con-

---

9. Similarly, data showed that less than 1.5 percent of the contributors to candidates in the 1992 election for Missouri secretary of state made aggregate contributions in excess of $2,000.

stitutional issues raised by Congress' enactment of the Federal Election Campaign Acts of 1971 and 1974 and this Court's resolution of those issues in *Buckley*. In response to his call for a new beginning, therefore, I make one simple point. Money is property; it is not speech.

Speech has the power to inspire volunteers to perform a multitude of tasks on a campaign trail, on a battleground, or even on a football field. Money, meanwhile, has the power to pay hired laborers to perform the same tasks. It does not follow, however, that the First Amendment provides the same measure of protection to the use of money to accomplish such goals as it provides to the use of ideas to achieve the same results.*

Our Constitution and our heritage properly protect the individual's interest in making decisions about the use of his or her own property. Governmental regulation of such decisions can sometimes be viewed either as "deprivations of liberty" or as "deprivations of property," see, *e.g., Moore v. East Cleveland*, 431 U.S. 494, 513 (1977) (STEVENS, J., concurring in judgment). Telling a grandmother that she may not use her own property to provide shelter to a grandchild—or to hire mercenaries to work in that grandchild's campaign for public office—raises important constitutional concerns that are unrelated to the First Amendment. Because I did not participate in the Court's decision in *Buckley*, I did not have the opportunity to suggest then that those property and liberty concerns adequately explain the Court's decision to invalidate the expenditure limitations in the 1974 Act.

Reliance on the First Amendment to justify the invalidation of campaign finance regulations is the functional equivalent of the Court's candid reliance on the doctrine of substantive due process as articulated in the two prevailing opinions in *Moore v. East Cleveland*. The right to use one's own money to hire gladiators, or to fund "speech by proxy," certainly merits significant constitutional protection. These property rights, however, are not entitled to the same protection as the right to say what one pleases.

JUSTICE BREYER, with whom JUSTICE GINSBURG joins, concurring.

The dissenters accuse the Court of weakening the First Amendment. They believe that failing to adopt a "strict scrutiny" standard "balance[s] away First Amendment freedoms." (opinion of THOMAS, J.). But the principal dissent oversimplifies the problem faced in the campaign finance context. It takes a difficult constitutional problem and turns it into a lopsided dispute between political expression and government censorship. Under the cover of this fiction and its accompanying formula, the dissent would make the Court absolute arbiter of a difficult question best left, in the main, to the political branches. I write separately to address the critical question of how the Court ought to review this kind of problem, and to explain why I believe the Court's choice here is correct.

If the dissent believes that the Court diminishes the importance of the First Amendment interests before us, it is wrong. The Court's opinion does not question the constitutional importance of political speech or that its protection lies at the heart of the First Amendment. Nor does it question the need for particularly careful, precise, and independent judicial review where, as here, that protection is at issue. But this is a case where constitutionally protected interests lie on both sides of the legal equation. For that rea-

---

* Unless, of course, the prohibition entirely forecloses a channel of communication, such as the use of paid petition circulators. See, *e.g., Meyer v. Grant* ("Colorado's prohibition of paid petition circulators restricts access to the most effective, fundamental, and perhaps economical avenue of political discourse, direct one-on-one communication.... The First Amendment protects appellees' right not only to advocate their cause but also to select what they believe to be the most effective means for so doing").

son there is no place for a strong presumption against constitutionality, of the sort often thought to accompany the words "strict scrutiny." Nor can we expect that mechanical application of the tests associated with "strict scrutiny"—the tests of "compelling interests" and "least restrictive means"—will properly resolve the difficult constitutional problem that campaign finance statutes pose....

On the one hand, a decision to contribute money to a campaign is a matter of First Amendment concern—not because money *is* speech (it is not); but because it *enables* speech. Through contributions the contributor associates himself with the candidate's cause, helps the candidate communicate a political message with which the contributor agrees, and helps the candidate win by attracting the votes of similarly minded voters. *Buckley*. Both political association and political communication are at stake.

On the other hand, restrictions upon the amount any one individual can contribute to a particular candidate seek to protect the integrity of the electoral process—the means through which a free society democratically translates political speech into concrete governmental action. *See id., Burroughs v. United States*, 290 U.S. 534, 545 (1934) (upholding 1925 Federal Corrupt Practices Act by emphasizing constitutional importance of safeguarding the electoral process); see also *Burson v. Freeman*, 504 U.S. 191, 199 (1992) (plurality opinion) (recognizing compelling interest in preserving integrity of electoral process). Moreover, by limiting the size of the largest contributions, such restrictions aim to democratize the influence that money itself may bring to bear upon the electoral process. Cf. *Reynolds v. Sims* (in the context of apportionment, the Constitution "demands" that each citizen have "an equally effective voice"). In doing so, they seek to build public confidence in that process and broaden the base of a candidate's meaningful financial support, encouraging the public participation and open discussion that the First Amendment itself presupposes. See *Mills v. Alabama*, 384 U.S. 214, 218–219 (1966); *Whitney v. California*, 274 U.S. 357, 375–376 (1927) (Brandeis, J., concurring); A. Meiklejohn, FREE SPEECH AND ITS RELATION TO SELF-GOVERNMENT 24–27 (1948).

In service of these objectives, the statute imposes restrictions of degree. It does not deny the contributor the opportunity to associate with the candidate through a contribution, though it limits a contribution's size. Nor does it prevent the contributor from using money (alone or with others) to pay for the expression of the same views in other ways. Instead, it permits all supporters to contribute the same amount of money, in an attempt to make the process fairer and more democratic.

Under these circumstances, a presumption against constitutionality is out of place. I recognize that *Buckley* used language that could be interpreted to the contrary. It said, for example, that it rejected "the concept that government may restrict the speech of some elements of our society in order to enhance the relative voice of others." But those words cannot be taken literally. The Constitution often permits restrictions on the speech of some in order to prevent a few from drowning out the many—in Congress, for example, where constitutionally protected debate, Art. I, §6, is limited to provide every Member an equal opportunity to express his or her views. Or in elections, where the Constitution tolerates numerous restrictions on ballot access, limiting the political rights of some so as to make effective the political rights of the entire electorate. See, *e.g., Storer v. Brown*, 415 U.S. 724, 736 (1974). Regardless, as the result in *Buckley* made clear, the statement does not automatically invalidate a statute that seeks a fairer electoral debate through contribution limits, nor should it forbid the Court to take account of the competing constitutional interests just mentioned.

In such circumstances—where a law significantly implicates competing constitutionally protected interests in complex ways—the Court has closely scrutinized the statute's impact on those interests, but refrained from employing a simple test that effectively presumes unconstitutionality. Rather, it has balanced interests. And in practice that has meant asking whether the statute burdens any one such interest in a manner out of proportion to the statute's salutary effects upon the others (perhaps, but not necessarily, because of the existence of a clearly superior, less restrictive alternative). Where a legislature has significantly greater institutional expertise, as, for example, in the field of election regulation, the Court in practice defers to empirical legislative judgments—at least where that deference does not risk such constitutional evils as, say, permitting incumbents to insulate themselves from effective electoral challenge. This approach is that taken in fact by *Buckley* for contributions, and is found generally where competing constitutional interests are implicated.... For the dissenters to call the approach "*sui generis*" overstates their case.

Applying this approach to the present case, I would uphold the statute essentially for the reasons stated by the Court. I agree that the legislature understands the problem— the threat to electoral integrity, the need for democratization—better than do we. We should defer to its political judgment that unlimited spending threatens the integrity of the electoral process. But we should not defer in respect to whether its solution, by imposing too low a contribution limit, significantly increases the reputation-related or media-related advantages of incumbency and thereby insulates legislators from effective electoral challenge. The statutory limit here, $1,075 (or 378, 1976 dollars), is low enough to raise such a question. But given the empirical information presented—the type of election at issue; the record of adequate candidate financing post-reform; and the fact that the statute indexes the amount for inflation—I agree with the Court that the statute does not work disproportionate harm. The limit may have prevented the plaintiff, Zev David Fredman, from financing his own campaign for office, for Fredman's support among potential contributors was not sufficiently widespread. But any contribution statute (like any statute setting ballot eligibility requirements, see, *e.g., Jenness v. Fortson*, 403 U.S. 431, 442 (1971)) will narrow the field of conceivable challengers to some degree. Undue insulation is a practical matter, and it cannot be inferred automatically from the fact that the limit makes ballot access more difficult for one previously unsuccessful candidate.

The approach I have outlined here is consistent with the approach this Court has taken in many complex First Amendment cases. The *Buckley* decision, as well, might be interpreted as embodying sufficient flexibility for the problem at hand. After all, *Buckley*'s holding seems to leave the political branches broad authority to enact laws regulating contributions that take the form of "soft money." It held public financing laws constitutional. It says nothing one way or the other about such important proposed reforms as reduced-price media time. And later cases presuppose that the Federal Election Commission has the delegated authority to interpret broad statutory provisions in light of the campaign finance law's basic purposes, despite disagreements over whether the Commission has exercised that authority in a particular case. See *Colorado I* (whether claimed "independent expenditure" is a "coordinated expenditure"); accord, *id.* at 648–650 (STEVENS, J., dissenting). Alternatively, it might prove possible to reinterpret aspects of *Buckley* in light of the post-*Buckley* experience stressed by JUSTICE KENNEDY (dissenting opinion), making less absolute the contribution/expenditure line, particularly in respect to independently wealthy candidates, whose expenditures might be considered contributions to their own campaigns.

But what if I am wrong about *Buckley*? Suppose *Buckley* denies the political branches sufficient leeway to enact comprehensive solutions to the problems posed by campaign finance. If so, like JUSTICE KENNEDY, I believe the Constitution would require us to reconsider *Buckley*. With that understanding I join the Court's opinion.

JUSTICE KENNEDY, dissenting.

The Court's decision has lasting consequences for political speech in the course of elections, the speech upon which democracy depends. Yet in defining the controlling standard of review and applying it to the urgent claim presented, the Court seems almost indifferent. Its analysis would not be acceptable for the routine case of a single protester with a hand-scrawled sign, see *City of Ladue v. Gilleo*, 512 U.S. 43 (1994), a few demonstrators on a public sidewalk, see *United States v. Grace*, 461 U.S. 171 (1983), or a driver who taped over the motto on his license plate because he disagreed with its message, see *Wooley v. Maynard*, 430 U.S. 705 (1977). Surely the Court's approach is unacceptable for a case announcing a rule that suppresses one of our most essential and prevalent forms of political speech.

It would be no answer to say that this is a routine application of our analysis in *Buckley* to a similar set of facts, so that a cavalier dismissal of the petitioners' claim is appropriate. The justifications for the case system and *stare decisis* must rest upon the Court's capacity, and responsibility, to acknowledge its missteps. It is our duty to face up to adverse, unintended consequences flowing from our own prior decisions. With all respect, I submit the Court does not accept this obligation in the case before us. Instead, it perpetuates and compounds a serious distortion of the First Amendment resulting from our own intervention in *Buckley*. The Court is concerned about voter suspicion of the role of money in politics. Amidst an atmosphere of skepticism, however, it hardly inspires confidence for the Court to abandon the rigors of our traditional First Amendment structure.

I

Zev David Fredman asks us to evaluate his speech claim in the context of a system which favors candidates and officeholders whose campaigns are supported by soft money, usually funneled through political parties. The Court pays him no heed. The plain fact is that the compromise the Court invented in *Buckley* set the stage for a new kind of speech to enter the political system. It is covert speech. The Court has forced a substantial amount of political speech underground, as contributors and candidates devise ever more elaborate methods of avoiding contribution limits, limits which take no account of rising campaign costs. The preferred method has been to conceal the real purpose of the speech. Soft money may be contributed to political parties in unlimited amounts, see *Colorado I*, and is used often to fund so-called issue advocacy, advertisements that promote or attack a candidate's positions without specifically urging his or her election or defeat. Briffault, *Issue Advocacy: Redrawing the Elections/Politics Line*, 77 TEXAS LAW REVIEW 1751, 1752–1753 (1999). Issue advocacy, like soft money, is unrestricted, see *Buckley*, while straightforward speech in the form of financial contributions paid to a candidate, speech subject to full disclosure and prompt evaluation by the public, is not. Thus has the Court's decision given us covert speech. This mocks the First Amendment. The current system would be unfortunate, and suspect under the First Amendment, had it evolved from a deliberate legislative choice; but its unhappy origins are in our earlier decree in *Buckley*, which by accepting half of what Congress did (limiting contributions) but rejecting the other (limiting expenditures) created a misshapen system, one which distorts the meaning of speech.

The irony that we would impose this regime in the name of free speech ought to be sufficient ground to reject *Buckley*'s wooden formula in the present case. The wrong goes deeper, however. By operation of the *Buckley* rule, a candidate cannot oppose this system in an effective way without selling out to it first. Soft money must be raised to attack the problem of soft money. In effect, the Court immunizes its own erroneous ruling from change. Rulings of this Court must never be viewed with more caution than when they provide immunity from their own correction in the political process and in the forum of unrestrained speech. The melancholy history of campaign finance in *Buckley*'s wake shows what can happen when we intervene in the dynamics of speech and expression by inventing an artificial scheme of our own.

The case in one sense might seem unimportant. It appears that Mr. Fredman was an outsider candidate who may not have had much of a chance. Yet, by binding him to the outdated limit of $1075 per contribution in a system where parties can raise soft money without limitation and a powerful press faces no restrictions on use of its own resources to back its preferred candidates, the Court tells Mr. Fredman he cannot challenge the status quo unless he first gives into it. This is not the First Amendment with which I am familiar.

To defend its extension of *Buckley* to present times, the Court, of course, recites the dangers of corruption, or the appearance of corruption, when an interested person contributes money to a candidate. What the Court does not do is examine and defend the substitute it has encouraged, covert speech funded by unlimited soft money. In my view that system creates dangers greater than the one it has replaced. The first danger is the one already mentioned: that we require contributors of soft money and its beneficiaries to mask their real purpose. Second, we have an indirect system of accountability that is confusing, if not dispiriting, to the voter. The very disaffection or distrust that the Court cites as the justification for limits on direct contributions has now spread to the entire political discourse. *Buckley* has not worked.

My colleagues in the majority, in my respectful submission, do much disservice to our First Amendment jurisprudence by failing to acknowledge or evaluate the whole operation of the system that we ourselves created in *Buckley*. Our First Amendment principles surely tell us that an interest thought to be the compelling reason for enacting a law is cast into grave doubt when a worse evil surfaces in the law's actual operation. And our obligation to examine the operation of the law is all the more urgent when the new evil is itself a distortion of speech. By these measures the law before us cannot pass any serious standard of First Amendment review.

Among the facts the Court declines to take into account is the emergence of cyberspace communication by which political contributions can be reported almost simultaneously with payment. The public can then judge for itself whether the candidate or the officeholder has so overstepped that we no longer trust him or her to make a detached and neutral judgment. This is a far more immediate way to assess the integrity and the performance of our leaders than through the hidden world of soft money and covert speech.

Officeholders face a dilemma inherent in the democratic process and one that has never been easy to resolve: how to exercise their best judgment while soliciting the continued support and loyalty of constituents whose interests may not always coincide with that judgment. Edmund Burke captured the tension in his *Speeches at Bristol*. "Your representative owes you, not his industry only, but his judgment; and he betrays instead of serving you, if he sacrifices it to your opinion." Whether our officeholders can discharge their duties in a proper way when they are beholden to certain interests both for reelection and for campaign support is, I should think, of constant concern not alone to citizens but to conscientious officeholders themselves. There are no easy answers, but the Constitution relies on one: open, robust, honest, unfettered speech that the voters can examine and assess in an ever-changing and more complex environment.

II

To this point my view may seem to be but a reflection of what JUSTICE THOMAS has written, and to a large extent I agree with his insightful and careful discussion of our precedents. If an ensuing chapter must be written, I may well come out as he does, for his reasoning and my own seem to point to the conclusion that the legislature can do little by way of imposing limits on political speech of this sort. For now, however, I would leave open the possibility that Congress, or a state legislature, might devise a system in which there are some limits on both expenditures and contributions, thus permitting officeholders to concentrate their time and efforts on official duties rather than on fundraising. For the reasons I have sought to express, there are serious constitutional questions to be confronted in enacting any such scheme, but I would not foreclose it at the outset. I would overrule *Buckley* and then free Congress or state legislatures to attempt some new reform, if, based upon their own considered view of the First Amendment, it is possible to do so. Until any reexamination takes place, however, the existing distortion of speech caused by the half-way house we created in *Buckley* ought to be eliminated. The First Amendment ought to be allowed to take its own course without further obstruction from the artificial system we have imposed. It suffices here to say that the law in question does not come even close to passing any serious scrutiny.

For these reasons, though I am in substantial agreement with what JUSTICE Thomas says in his opinion, I have thought it necessary to file a separate dissent.

JUSTICE THOMAS, with whom JUSTICE SCALIA joins, dissenting.

In the process of ratifying Missouri's sweeping repression of political speech, the Court today adopts the analytic fallacies of our flawed decision in *Buckley*. Unfortunately, the Court is not content to merely adhere to erroneous precedent. Under the guise of applying *Buckley*, the Court proceeds to weaken the already enfeebled constitutional protection that *Buckley* afforded campaign contributions. In the end, the Court employs a *sui generis* test to balance away First Amendment freedoms. Because the Court errs with each step it takes, I dissent. As I indicated in *Colorado I* (opinion concurring in judgment and dissenting in part), our decision in *Buckley* was in error, and I would overrule it. I would subject campaign contribution limitations to strict scrutiny, under which Missouri's contribution limits are patently unconstitutional.

I

I begin with a proposition that ought to be unassailable: Political speech is the primary object of First Amendment protection. The Founders sought to protect the rights of individuals to engage in political speech because a self-governing people depends upon the free exchange of political information. And that free exchange should receive the most protection when it matters the most — during campaigns for elective office. "The value and efficacy of [the right to elect the members of government] depends on the knowledge of the comparative merits and demerits of the candidates for public trust, and on the equal freedom, consequently, of examining and discussing these merits and demerits of the candidates respectively." Madison, *Report on the Resolutions* (1799), in 6 WRITINGS OF JAMES MADISON 397 (G. Hunt ed. 1906).

I do not start with these foundational principles because the Court openly disagrees with them — it could not, for they are solidly embedded in our precedents. Instead, I start with them because the Court today abandons them. For nearly half a century, this Court has extended First Amendment protection to a multitude of forms of "speech," such as making false defamatory statements, filing lawsuits, dancing nude, exhibiting drive-in movies with nudity, burning flags, and wearing military uniforms. Not surprisingly, the Courts of Appeals have followed our lead and concluded that the First Amendment protects, for example, begging, shouting obscenities, erecting tables on a sidewalk, and refusing to wear a necktie. In light of the many cases of this sort, today's decision is a most curious anomaly. Whatever the proper status of such activities under the First Amendment, I am confident that they are less integral to the functioning of our Republic than campaign contributions. Yet the majority today, rather than going out of its way to *protect* political speech, goes out of its way to *avoid* protecting it. As I explain below, contributions to political campaigns generate essential political speech. And contribution caps, which place a direct and substantial limit on core speech, should be met with the utmost skepticism and should receive the strictest scrutiny.

II

At bottom, the majority's refusal to apply strict scrutiny to contribution limits rests upon *Buckley*'s discounting of the First Amendment interests at stake. The analytic foundation of *Buckley*, however, was tenuous from the very beginning and has only continued to erode in the intervening years. What remains of *Buckley* fails to provide an adequate justification for limiting individual contributions to political candidates.

A

To justify its decision upholding contribution limitations while striking down expenditure limitations, the Court in *Buckley* explained that expenditure limits "represent substantial rather than merely theoretical restraints on the quantity and diversity of political speech," *Buckley*, while contribution limits "entai[l] only a marginal restriction upon the contributor's ability to engage in free communication," *id*. In drawing this distinction, the Court in *Buckley* relied on the premise that contributing to a candidate differs qualitatively from directly spending money. It noted that "[w]hile contributions may result in political expression if spent by a candidate or an association to present views to the voters, the transformation of contributions into political debate involves speech by someone other than the contributor." *Id*. See also *CMA v. FEC*(plurality opinion) ("[T]he 'speech by proxy' that [a contributor] seeks to achieve through its contributions ... is not the sort of political advocacy that this Court in *Buckley* found entitled to full First Amendment protection").

But this was a faulty distinction *ab initio* because it ignored the reality of how speech of all kinds is disseminated:

> "Even in the case of a direct expenditure, there is usually some go-between that facilitates the dissemination of the spender's message — for instance, an advertising agency or a television station. To call a contribution 'speech by proxy' thus does little to differentiate it from an expenditure. The only possible difference is that contributions involve an extra step in the proxy chain. But again, that is a difference in form, not substance." *Colorado I* (THOMAS, J., concurring in judgment and dissenting in part) (citations omitted).

And, inasmuch as the speech-by-proxy argument was disconnected from the realities of political speech to begin with, it is not surprising that we have firmly rejected it since *Buckley*. In *NCPAC*, we cast aside the argument that a contribution does not represent the constitutionally protected speech of a contributor, recognizing "that the contributors obviously like the message they are hearing from these organizations and want to add their voices to that message; otherwise they would not part with their money." Though in that case we considered limitations on expenditures made by associations, our holding that the speech-by-proxy argument fails to diminish contributors' First Amendment rights is directly applicable to this case. In both cases, donors seek to disseminate information by giving to an organization controlled by others. Through contributing, citizens see to it that their views on policy and politics are articulated. In short, "they are aware that however great the confidence they may justly feel in their own good sense, their interests can be more effectually promoted by [another] than by themselves." The Federalist No. 35, p. 214 (C. Rossiter ed. 1961) (A. Hamilton).

Without the assistance of the speech-by-proxy argument, the remainder of *Buckley*'s rationales founder. Those rationales — that the "quantity of communication by the contributor does not increase perceptibly with the size of his contribution," that "the size of the contribution provides a very rough index of the intensity of the contributor's support for the candidate," and that "[a] contribution serves as a general expression of support for the candidate and his views, but does not communicate the underlying basis for the support" — still rest on the proposition that speech by proxy is not fully protected. These contentions simply ignore that a contribution, by amplifying the voice of the candidate, helps to ensure the dissemination of the messages that the contributor wishes to convey. Absent the ability to rest on the denigration of contributions as mere "proxy speech," the arguments fall apart.[3]

The decision of individuals to speak through contributions rather than through independent expenditures is entirely reasonable.[4] Political campaigns are largely candidate fo-

---

3. If one were to accept the speech-by-proxy point and consider a contribution a mere symbolic gesture, *Buckley*'s auxiliary arguments still falter. The claim that a large contribution receives less protection because it only expresses the "intensity of the contributor's support for the candidate" fails under our jurisprudence because we have accorded full First Amendment protection to expressions of intensity. See *Cohen v. California*, 403 U.S. 15, 25–26 (1971) (protecting the use of an obscenity to stress a point). Equally unavailing is the claim that a contribution warrants less protection because it "does not communicate the underlying basis for the support." *Buckley*. We regularly hold that speech is protected when the underlying basis for a position is not given. See, e.g., *City of Ladue v. Gilleo* (sign reading "For Peace in the Gulf"); *Tinker v. Des Moines Independent Community School Dist.*, 393 U.S. 503, 510–511 (1969) (black armband signifying opposition to Vietnam war). See also *Colorado Republican I* (THOMAS, J., concurring in judgment and dissenting in part) ("Even a pure message of support, unadorned with reasons, is valuable to the democratic process"). Cf. *Hurley v. Irish-American Gay, Lesbian and Bisexual Group of Boston*, 515 U.S. 557, 569 (1995) (opinion of the Court by SOUTER, J.) ("[A] narrow, succinctly articulable message is not a condition of constitutional protection").

4. JUSTICE STEVENS asserts that "[m]oney is property; it is not speech," (concurring opinion), and contends that there is no First Amendment right "to hire mercenaries" and "to hire gladiators." These propositions are directly contradicted by many of our precedents. For example, in *Meyer v. Grant*, (opinion of the Court by STEVENS, J.), this Court confronted a state ban on payments to petition circulators. The District Court upheld the law, finding that the ban on monetary payments did not restrain expression and that the would-be payors remained free to use their money in other ways. We disagreed and held that "[t]he refusal to permit appellees to pay petition circulators restricts political expression" by "limit[ing] the number of voices who will convey appellees' message and the hours they can speak and, therefore, limits the size of the audience they can reach." In short, the Court held that the First Amendment protects the right to pay others to help get a message out. In other cases, this Court extended such protection, holding that the First Amendment prohibits laws that do not ban, but instead only regulate, the terms upon which so-called mercenaries and gladiators are retained. See *Riley* (holding that the First Amendment prohibits state restriction on the amount a charity may pay a professional fundraiser); *Secretary of State of Md. v. Joseph H. Munson Co.*, 467 U.S. 947 (1984) (same). Cf. also, *e.g., Teachers v. Hudson*, 475 U.S. 292 (1986) (opinion of the Court by STEVENS, J.) (holding that the First Amendment restrains government-compelled exactions of money); *Abood v. Detroit Bd. of Ed.*, 431 U.S. 209 (1977) (same). In these cases, the Court did not resort to JUSTICE STEVENS' assertion that money "is not speech" to dismiss challenges to monetary regulations. Instead, the Court properly examined the impact of the regulations on free expression. See also, *e.g., NCPAC* (First Amendment protects political com-

cused and candidate driven. Citizens recognize that the best advocate for a candidate (and the policy positions he supports) tends to be the candidate himself. And candidate organizations also offer other advantages to citizens wishing to partake in political expression. Campaign organizations offer a ready-built, convenient means of communicating for donors wishing to support and amplify political messages. Furthermore, the leader of the organization—the candidate—has a strong self-interest in efficiently expending funds in a manner that maximizes the power of the messages the contributor seeks to disseminate. Individual citizens understandably realize that they "may add more to political discourse by giving rather than spending, if the donee is able to put the funds to more productive use than can the individual." *Colorado I* (THOMAS, J., concurring in judgment and dissenting in part). See also *MCFL*("[I]ndividuals contribute to a political organization in part because they regard such a contribution as a more effective means of advocacy than spending the money under their own personal direction").[5]

In the end, *Buckley*'s claim that contribution limits "d[o] not in any way infringe the contributor's freedom to discuss candidates and issues" ignores the distinct role of candidate organizations as a means of individual participation in the Nation's civic dialogue.[6] The result is simply the suppression of political speech. By depriving donors of their right to speak through the candidate, contribution limits relegate donors' points of view to less effective modes of communication. Additionally, limiting contributions curtails individual participation. "Even for the affluent, the added costs in money or time of taking out a newspaper advertisement, handing out leaflets on the street, or standing in front of one's house with a hand-held sign may make the difference between participating and not participating in some public debate." *City of Ladue v. Gilleo*. *Buckley* completely failed in its attempt to provide a basis for permitting government to second-guess the individual choices of citizens partaking in quintessentially democratic activities. "The First Amendment mandates that we presume that speakers, not the government, know best both what they want to say and how to say it." *Riley.*

B

The Court in *Buckley* denigrated the speech interests not only of contributors, but also of candidates. Although the Court purported to be concerned about the plight of candidates, it nevertheless proceeded to disregard their interests without justification. The Court did not even attempt to claim that contribution limits do not suppress the speech of political candidates. See [*Buckley*] ("[C]ontribution ... limitations impose direct quantity restrictions on political communication and association by ... candidates"); *id.* ("[T]he [contribution] limitations may have a significant effect on particular challengers or incumbents"). It could not have, given the reality that donations "mak[e] a significant contribution to freedom of expression by enhancing the ability of candidates to present, and

---

mittee's expenditures of money); *CARC*(First Amendment protects monetary contributions to political committee); *Bellotti*(First Amendment protects "spend[ing] money to publicize [political] views").

5. Even if contributions to a candidate were not the most effective means of speaking—and contribution caps left political speech "significantly unimpaired"—an individual's choice of that mode of expression would still be protected. "The First Amendment protects [individuals'] right not only to advocate their cause but also to select what they believe to be the most effective means for so doing." *Meyer.*

6. *Buckley*'s approach to associational freedom is also unsound. In defense of its decision, the Court in *Buckley* explained that contribution limits "leave the contributor free to become a member of any political association and to assist personally in the association's efforts on behalf of candidates." In essence, the Court accepted contribution limits because alternative channels of association remained open. This justification, however, is peculiar because we have rejected the notion that a law will pass First Amendment muster simply because it leaves open other opportunities.

the public to receive, information necessary for the effective operation of the democratic process." *CBS, Inc. v. FCC.* See also *CARC* ("Placing limits on contributions which in turn limit expenditures plainly impairs freedom of expression"). Instead, the Court abstracted from a candidate's individual right to speak and focused exclusively on aggregate campaign funding. See *Buckley* ("There is no indication … that the contribution limitations imposed by the Act would have any dramatic adverse effect on the funding of campaigns"); (There is "no showing that 'the limitations prevented the candidates and political committees from amassing the resources necessary for effective advocacy'" [majority opinion above, quoting *Buckley*].)

The Court's flawed and unsupported aggregate approach ignores both the rights and value of individual candidates. The First Amendment "is designed and intended to remove governmental restraints from the arena of public discussion, putting the decision as to what views shall be voiced largely into the hands of *each of us*, in the hope that use of such freedom will ultimately produce a more capable citizenry and more perfect polity and in the belief that no other approach would comport with the premise of *individual* dignity and choice upon which our political system rests." *Cohen v. California* (emphases added). See also *Sweezy v. New Hampshire*, 354 U.S. 234, 250 (1957) (plurality opinion) ("Our form of government is built on the premise that every citizen shall have the right to engage in political expression and association"); *Richmond v. J.A. Croson Co.*, 488 U.S. 469, 493 (1989) (plurality opinion) ("As this Court has noted in the past, the 'rights created by the first section of the Fourteenth Amendment are, by its terms, guaranteed to the individual. The rights established are personal rights.'". In short, the right to free speech is a right held by each American, not by Americans en masse. The Court in *Buckley* provided no basis for suppressing the speech of an individual candidate simply because other candidates (or candidates in the aggregate) may succeed in reaching the voting public. And any such reasoning would fly in the face of the premise of our political system—liberty vested in individual hands safeguards the functioning of our democracy. In the case at hand, the Missouri scheme has a clear and detrimental effect on a candidate such as petitioner Fredman, who lacks the advantages of incumbency, name recognition, or substantial personal wealth, but who has managed to attract the support of a relatively small number of dedicated supporters: It forbids his message from reaching the voters. And the silencing of a candidate has consequences for political debate and competition overall. See *Arkansas Ed. Television Comm'n v. Forbes* (STEVENS, J., dissenting) (noting that the suppression of a minor candidate's speech may directly affect the outcome of an election); cf. *NAACP v. Button*, 371 U.S. 415, 431 (1963) ("'All political ideas cannot and should not be channeled into the programs of our two major parties. History has amply proved the virtue of political activity by minority, dissident groups …'").

In my view, the Constitution leaves it entirely up to citizens and candidates to determine who shall speak, the means they will use, and the amount of speech sufficient to inform and persuade. *Buckley*'s ratification of the government's attempt to wrest this fundamental right from citizens was error.

III

Today, the majority blindly adopts *Buckley*'s flawed reasoning without so much as pausing to consider the collapse of the speech-by-proxy argument or the reality that *Buckley*'s remaining premises fall when deprived of that support.[7]

---

7. Implicitly, however, the majority downplays its reliance upon the speech-by-proxy argument. In fact, the majority reprints nearly all of *Buckley*'s analysis of contributors' speech interests, block quoting almost an entire paragraph from that decision. Tellingly, the only complete sentence from that

After ignoring these shortcomings, the Court proceeds to apply something less—much less—than strict scrutiny. Just how much less the majority never says. The Court in *Buckley* at least purported to employ a test of "'closest scrutiny.'" (The Court's words were belied by its actions, however, and it never deployed the test in the fashion that the superlative instructs. See *Colorado I* (THOMAS, J., concurring in judgment and dissenting in part) (noting that *Buckley* purported to apply strict scrutiny but failed to do so in fact).) The Court today abandons even that pretense and reviews contributions under the *sui generis* "*Buckley*'s standard of scrutiny," which fails to obscure the Court's ad hoc balancing away of First Amendment rights. Apart from its endorsement of *Buckley*'s rejection of the intermediate standards of review used to evaluate expressive conduct and time, place, and manner restrictions, the Court makes no effort to justify its deviation from the tests we traditionally employ in free speech cases. See *Denver Area Educational Telecommunications Consortium, Inc. v. FCC*, 518 U.S. 727, 774, (1996) (SOUTER, J., concurring) ("Reviewing speech regulations under fairly strict categorical rules keeps the starch in the standards for those moments when the daily politics cries loudest for limiting what may be said").

Unfortunately, the majority does not stop with a revision of *Buckley*'s labels. After hiding behind *Buckley*'s discredited reasoning and invoking "*Buckley*'s standard of scrutiny," the Court proceeds to significantly extend the holding in that case. The Court's substantive departure from *Buckley* begins with a revision of our compelling-interest jurisprudence. In *Buckley*, the Court indicated that the only interest that could qualify as "compelling" in this area was the government's interest in reducing actual and apparent corruption. And the Court repeatedly used the word "corruption" in the narrow *quid pro quo* sense, meaning "[p]erversion or destruction of integrity in the discharge of public duties by bribery or favour." 3 OXFORD ENGLISH DICTIONARY 974 (2d ed. 1989). See also WEBSTER'S THIRD NEW INTERNATIONAL DICTIONARY 512 (1976) ("inducement (as of a political official) by means of improper considerations (as bribery) to commit a violation of duty"). When the Court set forth the interest in preventing actual corruption, it spoke about "large contributions ... given to secure a political *quid pro quo* from current and potential office holders." *Buckley*. The Court used similar language when it set forth the interest in protecting against the appearance of corruption: "Of almost equal concern as the danger of actual *quid pro quo* arrangements is the impact of the appearance of corruption stemming from public awareness of the opportunities for abuse inherent in a regime of large individual financial contributions." *Id.* Later, in discussing limits on independent expenditures, the Court yet again referred to the interest in protecting against the "dangers of actual or apparent *quid pro quo* arrangements." *Id.* See also *id.*, (referring to "the danger that expenditures will be given as a *quid pro quo* for improper commitments"); *id.*(corruption relates to "post-election special favors that may be given in return" for contributions). To be sure, after mentioning *quid pro quo* transactions, the Court went on to use more general terms such as "opportunities for abuse," "potential for abuse," "improper influence," "attempts ... to influence," and "buy[ing] influence." But this general language acquires concrete meaning only in light of the preceding specific references to *quid pro quo* arrangements.

Almost a decade after *Buckley*, we reiterated that "corruption" has a narrow meaning with respect to contribution limitations on individuals:

---

paragraph that the majority fails to quote is the final sentence—which happens to be the one directly setting forth the speech-by-proxy rationale. ("While contributions may result in political expression if spent by a candidate or an association to present views to the voters, the transformation of contributions into political debate involves speech by someone other than the contributor").

"Corruption is a subversion of the political process. Elected officials are influenced to act contrary to their obligations of office by the prospect of financial gain to themselves or infusions of money in their campaigns. The hallmark of corruption is the financial *quid pro quo*: dollars for political favors." *NCPAC.*

In that same opinion, we also used "giving official favors" as a synonym for corruption. *Id.*

The majority today, by contrast, separates "corruption" from its *quid pro quo* roots and gives it a new, far-reaching (and speech-suppressing) definition, something like "[t]he perversion of anything from an original state of purity." 3 Oxford English Dictionary at 974. See also Webster's Third New International Dictionary at 512 ("a departure from what is pure or correct"). And the Court proceeds to define that state of purity, casting aspersions on "politicians too compliant with the wishes of large contributors." "But precisely what the 'corruption' may consist of we are never told with assurance." *NCPAC.* Presumably, the majority does not mean that politicians should be free of attachments to constituent groups.[9] And the majority does not explicitly rely upon the "harm" that the Court in *Buckley* rejected out of hand, namely, that speech could be regulated to equalize the voices of citizens. *Buckley.* Instead, without bothering to offer any elaboration, much less justification, the majority permits vague and unenumerated harms to suffice as a compelling reason for the government to smother political speech.

In refashioning *Buckley*, the Court then goes on to weaken the requisite precision in tailoring, while at the same time representing that its fiat "do[es] not relax *Buckley*'s standard." The fact is that the majority ratifies a law with a much broader sweep than that approved in *Buckley*. In *Buckley*, the Court upheld contribution limits of $1,000 on individuals and $5,000 on political committees (in 1976 dollars). Here, by contrast, the Court approves much more restrictive contribution limitations, ranging from $250 to $1,000 (in 1995 dollars) for both individuals and political committees. The disparity between Missouri's caps and those upheld in *Buckley* is more pronounced when one takes into account some measure of inflation. See *Shrink Missouri Government PAC v. Adams*, 161 F.3d 519, 523, and n. 4 (C.A.8 1998) (noting that, according to the Consumer Price Index, a dollar today purchases about a third of what it did in 1976 when *Buckley* was decided). Yet the Court's opinion gives not a single indication that the two laws may differ in their tailoring. See [majority opinion] (Missouri's caps are "striking [in their] resemblance to the limitations sustained in *Buckley*"). The Court fails to pay any regard to the drastically lower level of the limits here, fails to explain why political committees should be subjected to the same limits as individuals, and fails to explain

---

9. The Framers of course thought such attachments inevitable in a free society and that faction would infest the political process. As to controlling faction, James Madison explained, "There are again two methods of removing the causes of faction: the one, by destroying the liberty which is essential to its existence; the other, by giving to every citizen the same opinions, the same passions, and the same interests." The Federalist No. 10. Contribution caps are an example of the first method, which Madison contemptuously dismissed:

"It could never be more truly said than of the first remedy that it was worse than the disease. Liberty is to faction what air is to fire, an aliment without which it instantly expires. But it could not be a less folly to abolish liberty, which is essential to political life, because it nourishes faction than it would be to wish the annihilation of air, which is essential to animal life, because it imparts to fire its destructive agency." *Ibid.*

The Framers preferred a political system that harnessed such faction for good, preserving liberty while also ensuring good government. Rather than adopting the repressive "cure" for faction that the majority today endorses, the Framers armed individual citizens with a remedy. "If a faction consists of less than a majority, relief is supplied by the republican principle, which enables the majority to defeat its sinister views by regular vote." *Id.*

why caps that vary with the size of political districts are tailored to corruption. I cannot fathom how a $251 contribution could pose a substantial risk of "secur[ing] a political *quid pro quo.*" *Buckley.* Thus, contribution caps set at such levels could never be "closely drawn" to preventing *quid pro quo* corruption. The majority itself undertakes no such defense.

The Court also reworks *Buckley*'s aggregate approach to the free speech rights of candidates. It begins on the same track as *Buckley*, noting that "a showing of one affected individual does not point up a system of suppressed political advocacy that would be unconstitutional under *Buckley.*" See also, *e.g.,* [majority opinion] (claiming that candidates "'are still able to amass impressive campaign war chests'".) But the Court quickly deviates from *Buckley*, persuading itself that Missouri's limits do not suppress political speech because, prior to the enactment of contribution limits, "97.62 percent of all contributors to candidates for state auditor made contributions of $2,000 or less." But this statistical anecdote offers the Court no refuge and the citizenry no comfort. As an initial matter, the statistic provides no assurance that Missouri's law has not reduced the resources supporting political speech, since the largest contributors provide a disproportionate amount of funds. The majority conspicuously offers no data revealing the percentage of funds provided by large contributors. (At least the Court in *Buckley* relied on the percentage of funds raised by contributions in excess of the limits.) But whatever the data would reveal, the Court's position would remain indefensible. If the majority's assumption is incorrect—*i.e.,* if Missouri's contribution limits actually do significantly reduce campaign speech—then the majority's calm assurance that political speech remains unaffected collapses. If the majority's assumption is correct—*i.e.,* if large contributions provide very little assistance to a candidate seeking to get out his message (and thus will not be missed when capped)—then the majority's reasoning still falters. For if large contributions offer as little help to a candidate as the Court maintains, then the Court fails to explain why a candidate would engage in "corruption" for such a meager benefit. The majority's statistical claim directly undercuts its constitutional defense that large contributions pose a substantial risk of corruption.[10]

Given the majority's ill-advised and illiberal aggregate rights approach, it is unsurprising that the Court's *pro forma* hunt for suppressed speech proves futile. Such will always be the case, for courts have no yardstick by which to judge the proper amount and effectiveness of campaign speech. See, *e.g.,* Smith, *Faulty Assumptions and Undemocratic Consequences of Campaign Finance Reform.* I, however, would not fret about such matters. The First Amendment vests choices about the proper amount and effectiveness of political advocacy not in the government—whether in the legislatures or the courts—but in the people.

---

10. The majority's statistical analysis also overlooks the quantitative data in the record that directly undercut its position that Missouri's law does not create "a system of suppressed political advocacy." For example, the Court does not bother to note that following the imposition of contribution limits, total combined spending during primary and general elections for five statewide offices was cut by over half, falling from $21,599,000 to $9,337,000. Significantly, total primary election expenditures in each of the races decreased. In fact, after contribution limits were imposed, overall spending in statewide primary elections plummeted 89 percent, falling from $14,249,000 to $1,625,000. Most importantly, the majority does not bother to mention that before spending caps were enacted each of the 10 statewide primary elections was contested, with two to four candidates vying for every nomination in 1992. After caps were enacted, however, only 1 of the 10 primary elections was contested. Overall, the total number of candidates participating in statewide primaries fell from 32 to 11. Even if these data do not conclusively show that Missouri's contribution limits diminish political speech (although it is undeniable that the data strongly suggest such a result), they at least cast great doubt on the majority's assumption that the picture is rosy.

IV

In light of the importance of political speech to republican government, Missouri's substantial restriction of speech warrants strict scrutiny, which requires that contribution limits be narrowly tailored to a compelling governmental interest. See *Buckley v. American Constitutional Law Foundation, Inc.,* (THOMAS, J., concurring in judgment); *Colorado I* (THOMAS, J., concurring in judgment and dissenting in part).

Missouri does assert that its contribution caps are aimed at preventing actual and apparent corruption. As we have noted, "preventing corruption or the appearance of corruption are the only legitimate and compelling government interests thus far identified for restricting campaign finances." *NCPAC.* But the State's contribution limits are not narrowly tailored to that harm. The limits directly suppress the political speech of both contributors and candidates, and only clumsily further the governmental interests that they allegedly serve. They are crudely tailored because they are massively overinclusive, prohibiting all donors who wish to contribute in excess of the cap from doing so and restricting donations without regard to whether the donors pose any real corruption risk. See *Colorado I* (THOMAS, J., concurring in judgment and dissenting in part) ("'Where First Amendment rights are involved, a blunderbuss approach which prohibits mostly innocent speech cannot be held a means narrowly and precisely directed to the governmental interest in the small minority of contributions that are not innocent.'"). See also *Martin v. City of Struthers,* 319 U.S. 141, 145 (1943) (Though a method of speaking may be "a blind for criminal activities, [it] may also be useful [to] members of society engaged in the dissemination of ideas in accordance with the best tradition of free discussion"). Moreover, the government has less restrictive means of addressing its interest in curtailing corruption. Bribery laws bar precisely the *quid pro quo* arrangements that are targeted here. And disclosure laws "'deter actual corruption and avoid the appearance of corruption by exposing large contributions and expenditures to the light of publicity.'" *ACLF.* In fact, Missouri has enacted strict disclosure laws.

In the end, contribution limitations find support only in the proposition that other means will not be as effective at rooting out corruption. But when it comes to a significant infringement on our fundamental liberties, that some undesirable conduct may not be deterred is an insufficient justification to sweep in vast amounts of protected political speech. Our First Amendment precedents have repeatedly stressed this point. For example, in *Martin v. City of Struthers, supra,* we struck down an ordinance prohibiting door-to-door distribution of handbills. Although we recognized that "burglars frequently pose as canvassers," we also noted that door-to-door distribution was "useful [to] members of society engaged in the dissemination of ideas in accordance with the best tradition of free discussion." We then struck down the ordinance, observing that the "dangers of distribution can so easily be controlled by traditional legal methods." Similarly, in *Riley,* we struck down a law regulating the fees charged by professional fundraisers. In response to the assertion that citizens would be defrauded in the absence of such a law, we explained that the State had an antifraud law which "we presume[d] that law enforcement officers [we]re ready and able to enforce," and that the State could constitutionally require fundraisers to disclose certain financial information. We concluded by acknowledging the obvious consequences of the narrow tailoring requirement: "If this is not the most efficient means of preventing fraud, we reaffirm simply and emphatically that the First Amendment does not permit the State to sacrifice speech for efficiency." *Ibid.* See also, *e.g., Schneider v. State (Town of Irvington),* 308 U.S. 147, 162 (1939) ("There are obvious methods of preventing littering. Amongst these is the punishment of those who actually throw papers on the streets").

The same principles apply here, and dictate a result contrary to the one the majority reaches. States are free to enact laws that directly punish those engaged in corruption and require the disclosure of large contributions, but they are not free to enact generalized laws that suppress a tremendous amount of protected speech along with the targeted corruption.

V

Because the Court unjustifiably discounts the First Amendment interests of citizens and candidates, and consequently fails to strictly scrutinize the inhibition of political speech and competition, I respectfully dissent.

Notes and Questions

1. Is the majority opinion a "routine application" of *Buckley*? Just about all of the majority's arguments find some support in the *Buckley* opinion. Nevertheless, in the course of the opinion, the majority appears to weaken *Buckley's* protection of contributions in four ways:

a. *The majority opinion lowers the level of scrutiny.* The *Shrink Missouri* majority is surely right that "[p]recision about the relative rigor of the standard to review contribution limits was not a pretense of the *Buckley per curiam* opinion." Isn't Justice Thomas correct as well in his dissent that the *Shrink Missouri* majority applies "something less— much less—than strict scrutiny"?

b. *The majority opinion expands the definition of corruption and the appearance of corruption.* What does it mean for politicians to be "too compliant" with the wishes of contributors or for the public to believe that large contributors "call the tune?" The majority states that *quid pro quo* corruption is not necessary to sustain campaign contribution limits. What is necessary?

c. *The majority opinion lessens the evidentiary standard to support the government's interest in contribution limits.* Was the Court actually persuaded by the affidavit of a state legislator that large contributions have the "real potential to buy votes"? Should such a *potential* be enough to survive constitutional scrutiny? Are citations to newspaper articles now enough evidence to support a contribution limit law? For a case following *Shrink Missouri* suggesting the answer is "yes," see *Daggett v. Commission on Governmental Ethics and Election Practices*, 205 F.3d 445, 456–57 (1st Cir. 2000). And what of public support for campaign finance reform as proof of corruption? Perhaps Missouri voters supported campaign finance reform to equalize the electoral playing field, and not (merely) to prevent corruption. Should more evidence be required? If so, what evidence?

d. *The majority opinion seemingly makes it very difficult to challenge the amount of contribution limits as too low.* If you were attorney for a candidate or group challenging a contribution limit as too low, how would you challenge it following *Shrink Missouri*? In particular, how would you prove that a "contribution limitation was so radical in effect as to render political association ineffective, drive the sound of a candidate's voice below the level of notice, and render contributions pointless?" How low would a contribution limit have to be before contributions are pointless? Note that the cost of e-mails and faxing is quite low. What kind of "campaign" must a candidate "lack the power to mount" in order for a court to void contribution limits? Might your best bet be to challenge contribution limits through a "showing of [your] own to cast doubt on the apparent implications of *Buckley's* evidence"? Think about these questions as you read *Randall v. Sorrell*, which follows.

2. Justice Breyer in his concurring opinion explicitly endorses an equality rationale for campaign finance regulation. Justice Ginsburg concurred in this opinion. Justice Stevens made a similar argument in his dissenting opinion in the *Colorado I* case discussed below. That makes three Justices ready to reconsider *Buckley* in a way to allow for greater campaign finance regulation. Justices Kennedy, Thomas, and Scalia have indicated in *Shrink Missouri* and other cases that they would overrule those portions of *Buckley* upholding most contribution limits. If there are at least six Justices wishing to overrule *Buckley*, why does it still stand?

3. Justice Stevens in his brief concurring opinion reopens the question whether money is speech. For a more detailed argument that money should be considered property, not speech, see Spencer A. Overton, *Mistaken Identity: Unveiling the Property Characteristics of Political Money*, 53 VANDERBILT LAW REVIEW 1235, 1269 (2000). According to Overton, "Courts should recognize that, as in the property context, issues of scarcity and distribution of political money may result in situations in which those with abundant political money unfairly interfere with the interests of those with less political money, and legislatures should be able to enact laws to prevent these harms. Just as some landlords and large companies may have unfair bargaining power over tenants, employees, and small competitors, those with abundant political money often have unfair bargaining power over those without political money." Compare Eugene Volokh, *Freedom of Speech and Speech About Political Candidates: The Unintended Consequences of Three Proposals*, 24 HARVARD JOURNAL OF LAW & PUBLIC POLICY 47, 57–58 (2000): "Now Justice Stevens's 'simple point' is literally true — money is not speech — but it doesn't show much by itself. After all, expenditure limits don't just bar the use of money; they single out the use of money *to speak*. A law restricting people from flying places to give speeches would be a speech restriction, not because 'flying is speech' but because giving a speech is speech and burdening such speech (you may not fly in order to do it) is a speech restriction. Likewise for restrictions on spending money for speech."

4. Consider the empirical evidence cited by the majority opinion and Justice Thomas in dissent on the effects of the contribution limits in Missouri. Do the figures tell you anything about the quality of campaigns in Missouri? About any infringement on First Amendment rights? Which set of figures, if either, are more relevant to that inquiry? On these questions, see Roy A. Schotland, *Act I: BCRA Wins in Congress. Act II: BCRA Wins Big at the Court. Act III: BCRA Loses to Reality*, 3 ELECTION LAW JOURNAL 335, 342 (2004) (listing the numerous ways that Missouri's low contribution limit is easily evaded and noting that Missouri had the tenth highest incumbent reelection rates for its legislators in the 1980–2001 period).

5. Under *Shrink Missouri*, may the government prevent candidates from carrying over campaign contributions from one election to another? For a pre-*Shrink Missouri* case (with some of the same parties) striking down a ban on such transfers, see *Shrink Missouri Government PAC v. Maupin*, 71 F.3d 1422 (8th Cir. 1995), cert. denied 518 U.S. 1033 (1996). For a case reaching a contrary conclusion but not citing *Maupin*, see *Citizens for Responsible Government State Political Action Committee v. Buckley*, 60 F. Supp. 2d 1066, 1093 (D. Colo. 1999). The court held a Colorado provision limiting carry-over funds was justified because "the State has a legitimate governmental interest in preventing candidates from using contributions obtained in one campaign to avoid contribution limits in the next campaign." The court also concluded that the law "is justified as preventing incumbents from stockpiling large amounts of money and eluding other provisions of [Colorado's campaign finance law]. There is evidence in the record of substantial carry-overs retained as 'war chests' or contributed to other candidates or to political parties." The

Tenth Circuit vacated this part of the decision as moot because Colorado amended its law to eliminate this provision. *Citizens for Responsible Government State Political Action Committee v. Davidson*, 236 F.3d 1177, 1181 (10th Cir. 2000). Can these spend-down provisions be justified as furthering a governmental interest in increasing the competitiveness of elections?

6. *Treating judicial elections differently.* Canon 7(C)(8) of the Ohio Code of Judicial Conduct prohibits a judicial candidate from spending funds on a campaign for judicial office if those funds were raised while campaigning for a non-judicial office. In upholding the constitutionality of Canon 7(C)(8), the court distinguished *Maupin* and another case holding that bans on intra-candidate transfers generally are unconstitutional: "in neither case did the parties argue, nor did the courts consider, the more particular compelling state interest of avoiding corruption or the appearance of corruption *of elected judges.*" *Suster v. Marshall*, 951 F. Supp. 693, 703 (N.D. Ohio 1996), *aff'd*, 149 F.3d 523, cert. denied 525 U.S. 1114 (1999). As noted in Chapter 5, courts also treat judicial elections differently for purposes of Section 2 of the Voting Rights Act.

The issue of campaign finance in judicial campaigns has received increased attention as judicial races have become nastier and more expensive. For a summary of the recent issues, see Roy A. Schotland, *Financing Judicial Elections, 2000: Change and Challenge*, 2001 LAW REVIEW OF MICHIGAN STATE UNIVERSITY DETROIT COLLEGE OF LAW 849. Schotland also edited a symposium that will interest readers interested in judicial campaign finance in particular or judicial elections generally. See *Symposium, National Summit on Improving Judicial Selection: Call to Action*, 34 LOYOLA OF LOS ANGELES LAW REVIEW 1353 (2001).

7. *Limits on accepting campaign contributions during legislative sessions.* According to a Georgia statute, "No member of the General Assembly [i.e., state legislature] or that member's campaign committee … shall accept a contribution during a legislative session." Teper, a member of the General Assembly contemplating a run for Congress, challenged the statute as preempted by the Federal Election Campaign Act, as applied to a person raising money for a federal campaign. By a 2–1 majority, the Eleventh Circuit agreed. *Teper v. Miller*, 82 F.3d 989 (11th Cir. 1996).

Of course, this ruling leaves the Georgia prohibition in effect for legislators running for reelection or other state or local office. Judge Kravitch, in the lead opinion, wrote that the purpose of the prohibition is "to prevent the appearance of impropriety—bribery, to be precise—that may arise when state legislators accept campaign contributions during the period of time when they are actually legislating.… [T]he Georgia Ethics in Government Act is an admirable example of self-regulation by incumbent state legislators.…" Admirable or not, is it consistent with the First Amendment? For a case holding that such a ban is unconstitutional, see *State v. Dodd*, 561 So. 2d 263, 265 (Fla. 1990). The *Dodd* court held that although such a ban may be justified by a compelling interest in preventing corruption and the appearance of corruption, it is not narrowly tailored to prevent corruption. The law "applies to all office-seekers without exception. As a result, it places restrictions on some public officials and candidates who could not possibly be subject to a corrupting quid pro quo arrangement." What about a ban applying only to incumbents? See *Arkansas Right to Life State Political Action Committee v. Butler*, 29 F. Supp. 2d 540, 553 (W.D.Ark. 1998). A ban on contributions by lobbyists during legislative sessions? See *North Carolina Right to Life v. Bartlett*, 168 F.3d 705 (4th Cir. 1999).

8. *Residency requirements for campaign contributions.* Oregon voters amended their constitution to penalize state and local candidates who accepted more than ten percent of their funds from out-of-district contributors. The Ninth Circuit struck down the ban as un-

constitutional. *VanNatta v. Keisling*, 151 F.3d 1215 (9th Cir. 1998), cert. denied *sub nom. Miller v. VanNatta*, 525 U.S. 1104 (1999). It held that the ban was not narrowly tailored to prevent corruption because the measure "bans all out-of-district donations, regardless of size or any other factor that would tend to indicate corruption." In *State v. Alaska Civil Liberties Union*, 978 P.2d at S97, 616 (Alaska 1999), the Alaska Supreme Court distinguished *VanNatta* in upholding Alaska's ban on campaign contributions by non-residents. "Oregon's out-of-district restrictions applied to both nonresidents and residents of Oregon. But Alaska's challenged provisions apply only to nonresidents of Alaska, and do not limit speech of those most likely to be directly affected by the outcome of a campaign for state office — Alaska residents regardless of what district they live in." Does one need to be affected by an issue to have a first amendment right to speak on it? The Alaska court further rejected the relevance of what it termed the "largeness" of the outside contributions. The restrictions "are aimed not at very large individual contributions, by which a single contributor can influence a candidate, but at cumulatively vast out-of-state contributions." Does this reasoning mean that people lose their constitutional right to make a campaign contribution because others who are similarly situated also try to exercise those rights?

9. Other novel constitutional issues related to contributions and expenditures remain open. For example, is it constitutional to limit the aggregate amount of contributions a candidate may take from all political committees? See *Gard v. Wisconsin State Elections Board*, 456 N.W.2d 809 (Wis. 1990), cert. denied 498 U.S. 982 (1990). Are aggregate limits contribution limits or expenditure limits? For a diversity of opinion, see California Commission on Campaign Financing, THE NEW GOLD RUSH: FINANCING CALIFORNIA'S LEGISLATIVE CAMPAIGNS 242–43 (1985) (aggregate limits are contribution limits); Fred Wertheimer, *The PAC Phenomenon in American Politics*, 22 ARIZONA LAW REVIEW 603, 625 (1980) (same conclusion); Eric S. Anderson, Comment, *Campaign Finance in Wisconsin After Buckley*, 1976 WISCONSIN LAW REVIEW 816, 856 (aggregate limit "has aspects of expenditure limits"); Daniel Hays Lowenstein, *A Patternless Mosaic: Campaign Finance and the First Amendment After Austin*, 21 CAPITAL UNIVERSITY LAW REVIEW 381, 417 (1992) ("the contribution limit/expenditure limit contrast is not a dichotomy after all, but a spectrum," and most proposed aggregate limits are in the middle of that spectrum); Lawton Chiles, *PAC's: Congress on the Auction Block*, 11 JOURNAL OF LEGISLATION 193, 213 (1984) ("the limitation might be viewed as … limiting campaign expenditures"); Don M. Millis, *The Best Laid Schemes of Mice and Men: Campaign Finance Reform Gone Awry*, 1989 WISCONSIN LAW REVIEW 1465, 1475 (aggregate limits are "de facto expenditure limits").

Citizens for Responsible Government State Political Action Committee v. Buckley, 60 F. Supp. 2d 1066, 1092 (D. Colo. 1999), followed *Gard* in upholding an aggregate contribution limit on contributions from political committees to candidate committees. See also *Kentucky Right to Life, Inc. v. Terry*, 108 F.3d 637, 649–51 (6th Cir. 1997), cert. denied 522 U.S. 860 (1997) (upholding $150,000 aggregate limit on permanent committee contributions to gubernatorial candidates).

10. Many of the Justices writing opinions in *Shrink Missouri* cited to a 1996 Supreme Court case, *Colorado Republican Federal Campaign Committee v. Federal Election Commission*, 518 U.S. 604 (1996) ("*Colorado I*"). The case arose out of spending by the Colorado Republican Party attacking Timothy Wirth, the likely Democratic Senate nominee in the 1986 Senate election. The FECA contained a special provision allowing political parties to make a certain amount of coordinated expenditures (set through a formula contained in the statute) supporting that party's Senate candidates. But the Act did not allow for independent spending by parties, on the assumption that in the nature of things, the activities of parties and candidates are coordinated. The Colorado Republican Party had assigned its $103,000 in

permissible coordinated expenditures to the National Republican Senatorial Committee, and when the Colorado Republican Party paid for a radio advertisement attacking Wirth, the Democrats claimed that the Republicans violated the FECA. The Colorado Republican Party claimed, first, that the spending was independent of any candidate—a plausible claim, because the anti-Wirth ads ran before the Republican candidate was known—and second, that it was unconstitutional to deny parties the right to engage in independent spending. The Republicans also contended that even if the expenditures in question were coordinated, parties had the constitutional right to unlimited coordinated spending.

The Supreme Court issued no majority opinion. Justice Breyer, joined by Justices O'-Connor and Souter, declined to reach the question whether parties' *coordinated* expenditures could be limited. These Justices concluded that the FECA provision was unconstitutional insofar as it prohibited the party from making *independent* expenditures. Following *Buckley*, the three Justices held that the government could not demonstrate an adequate danger of corruption to justify limiting such expenditure:

> We are not aware of any special dangers of corruption associated with political parties that tip the constitutional balance in a different direction. When this Court considered, and held unconstitutional, limits that FECA had set on certain independent expenditures by PAC's, it reiterated *Buckley*'s observation that "the absence of prearrangement and coordination" does not eliminate, but it does help to "alleviate," any "danger" that a candidate will understand the expenditure as an effort to obtain a "*quid pro quo.*" See *NCPAC*. The same is true of independent party expenditures.

> We recognize that FECA permits individuals to contribute more money ($20,000) to a party than to a candidate ($1,000) or to other political committees ($5,000). 2 U.S.C. §441a(a). We also recognize that FECA permits unregulated "soft money" contributions to a party for certain activities, such as electing candidates for state office, see §431(8)(A)(i), or for voter registration and "get out the vote" drives, see §431(8)(B)(xii). But the opportunity for corruption posed by these greater opportunities for contributions is, at best, attenuated. Unregulated "soft money" contributions may not be used to influence a federal campaign, except when used in the limited, party-building activities specifically designated in the statute. See §431(8)(B). Any contribution to a party that is earmarked for a particular campaign is considered a contribution to the candidate and is subject to the contribution limitations. §441a(a)(8). A party may not simply channel unlimited amounts of even undesignated contributions to a candidate, since such direct transfers are also considered contributions and are subject to the contribution limits on a "multicandidate political committee." §441a(a)(2). The greatest danger of corruption, therefore, appears to be from the ability of donors to give sums up to $20,000 to a party which may be used for independent party expenditures for the benefit of a particular candidate. We could understand how Congress, were it to conclude that the potential for evasion of the individual contribution limits was a serious matter, might decide to change the statute's limitations on contributions to political parties. Cf. *California Medical Assn.*, (plurality opinion) (danger of evasion of limits on contribution to candidates justified prophylactic limitation on *contributions* to PAC's). But we do not believe that the risk of corruption present here could justify the "markedly greater burden on basic freedoms caused by" the statute's limitations on *expenditures*. *Buckley*. Contributors seeking to avoid the effect of the $1,000 contribution limit indirectly by donations to the national party could spend that

same amount of money (or more) themselves more directly by making their own independent expenditures promoting the candidate.... If anything, an independent expenditure made possible by a $20,000 donation, but controlled and directed by a party rather than the donor, would seem less likely to corrupt than the same (or a much larger) independent expenditure made directly by that donor. In any case, the constitutionally significant fact, present equally in both instances, is the lack of coordination between the candidate and the source of the expenditure. See *Buckley*; *NCPAC*. This fact prevents us from assuming, absent convincing evidence to the contrary, that a limitation on political parties' independent expenditures is necessary to combat a substantial danger of corruption of the electoral system.

Justices Kennedy, Scalia and Chief Justice Rehnquist agreed that the provision was unconstitutional as applied to party independent expenditures, but they would have struck down the limit as applied to party *coordinated* expenditures as well: "We have a constitutional tradition of political parties and their candidates engaging in joint First Amendment activity; we also have a practical identity of interests between the two entities during an election. Party spending 'in cooperation, consultation, or concert with' a candidate therefore is indistinguishable in substance from expenditures by the candidate or his campaign committee. We held in *Buckley* that the First Amendment does not permit regulation of the latter, and it should not permit this regulation of the former." Justice Thomas issued a separate opinion in which he agreed with Justice Kennedy's analysis under *Buckley*, but also argued that the *Buckley* framework should be abandoned in favor of a strict scrutiny approach to all regulation. Justice Stevens, joined by Justice Ginburg dissented, identifying three reasons to limit even independent spending by political parties:

First, such limits serve the interest in avoiding both the appearance and the reality of a corrupt political process. A party shares a unique relationship with the candidate it sponsors because their political fates are inextricably linked. That interdependency creates a special danger that the party—or the persons who control the party—will abuse the influence it has over the candidate by virtue of its power to spend. The provisions at issue are appropriately aimed at reducing that threat....

Second, these restrictions supplement other spending limitations embodied in the Act, which are likewise designed to prevent corruption. Individuals and certain organizations are permitted to contribute up to $1,000 to a candidate. Since the same donors can give up to $5,000 to party committees, if there were no limits on party spending, their contributions could be spent to benefit the candidate and thereby circumvent the $1,000 cap. We have recognized the legitimate interest in blocking similar attempts to undermine the policies of the Act. See *CMA*; *Buckley*.

Finally, I believe the Government has an important interest in leveling the electoral playing field by constraining the cost of federal campaigns.

On remand, the district court addressed the Colorado Republican Federal Campaign Committee's counterclaim that the ban on party spending coordinated with candidates was unconstitutional. Such coordinated spending is treated as a contribution under the FECA; see 2 U.S.C. §441a(a)(7)(B)(i). The court struck down the party expenditure provision because the FEC "failed to offer relevant, admissible evidence which suggests that coordinated party expenditures must be limited to prevent corruption or the appearance thereof...." *Federal Election Commission v. Colorado Republican Federal Campaign Committee*, 41 F.

Supp. 2d 1197, 1213 (D. Colo. 1999). The Tenth Circuit affirmed. 213 F.3d 1221 (10th Cir. 2000).

In *Federal Election Commission v. Colorado Republican Federal Campaign Committee*, 533 U.S. 431 (2001) (*Colorado II*), the Supreme Court, by a 5–4 vote, reversed the Tenth Circuit. Following its opinion in *Shrink Missouri*, the Court treated the coordinated expenditure rules as a "functional[]" contribution limit. It then held that Congress could impose such a limit to prevent corruption and its appearance:

> When we look directly at a party's function in getting and spending money, it would ignore reality to think that the party role is adequately described by speaking generally of electing particular candidates. The money parties spend comes from contributors with their own personal interests. PACs, for example, are frequent party contributors who (according to one of the Party's own experts) "do not pursue the same objectives in electoral politics," that parties do (statement of Professor Anthony Corrado). PACs "are most concerned with advancing their narrow interest[s]" and therefore "provide support to candidates who share their views, regardless of party affiliation." *Ibid.* In fact, many PACs naturally express their narrow interests by contributing to both parties during the same electoral cycle, and sometimes even directly to two competing candidates in the same election. Parties are thus necessarily the instruments of some contributors whose object is not to support the party's message or to elect party candidates across the board, but rather to support a specific candidate for the sake of a position on one, narrow issue, or even to support any candidate who will be obliged to the contributors.

> Parties thus perform functions more complex than simply electing candidates; whether they like it or not, they act as agents for spending on behalf of those who seek to produce obligated officeholders. It is this party role, which functionally unites parties with other self-interested political actors, that the [challenged provision] targets. This party role, accordingly, provides good reason to view limits on coordinated spending by parties through the same lens applied to such spending by donors, like PACs, that can use parties as conduits for contributions meant to place candidates under obligation.

Justice Thomas, joined by Justices Scalia and Kennedy, dissented, calling for *Buckley* to be overruled. Then, joined by those Justices and Chief Justice Rehnquist, Justice Thomas argued that even under *Buckley* the law failed to pass constitutional muster. On the point raised by the majority about parties acting as agents for donors, Justice Thomas responded:

> The Court contends that parties are not organized simply to "elec[t] particular candidates" as evidenced by the fact that many political action committees donate money to both parties and sometimes even opposing candidates. According to the Court, "[p]arties are thus necessarily the instruments of some contributors whose object is not to support the party's message or to elect party candidates across the board." There are two flaws in the Court's analysis. First, no one argues that a party's role is merely to get particular candidates elected. Surely, among other reasons, parties also exist to develop and promote a platform. The point is simply that parties and candidates have shared interests, that it is natural for them to work together, and that breaking the connection between parties and their candidates inhibits the promotion of the party's message. Second, the mere fact that some donors contribute to both parties and their candidates does not necessarily imply that the donors control the parties or their candidates. It certainly does not mean that the parties are mere "instruments" or "agents" of the donors. Indeed, if a party receives

money from donors on both sides of an issue, how can it be a tool of both donors? If the Green Party were to receive a donation from an industry that pollutes, would the Green Party necessarily become, through no choice of its own, an instrument of the polluters? The Court proffers no evidence that parties have become pawns of wealthy contributors. Parties might be the target of the speech of donors, but that does not suggest that parties are influenced (let alone improperly influenced) by the speech. Thus, the Court offers no explanation for why political parties should be treated the same as individuals and political committees.

11. Political parties and the candidates they nominate normally work closely together in campaigns. *Colorado I* and *Colorado II* taken together allow parties to spend independently without limit but permit controls on their spending that is coordinated with candidates. The cases therefore create a strong incentive for parties to separate their activities from their candidates. Is any public purpose served?

12. In the summer of 2005, Justice O'Connor announced her retirement from the Supreme Court (effective upon the confirmation of her successor). Soon after the announcement, Chief Justice Rehnquist died. John G. Roberts, Jr., was confirmed as the new Chief Justice and Samuel Alito was confirmed to replace Justice O'Connor. As noted earlier, the Court's deferential campaign finance rulings such as *Shrink Missouri* had become dependent on the crucial fifth vote of Justice O'Connor. Will the replacement of Justice O'Connor with Justice Alito change the Court's campaign finance jurisprudence away from deference? It appears so based upon the first few campaign finance cases decided by the Roberts Court. We consider one case here, and the second, the *Wisconsin Right to Life* case, at the end of the next chapter.

Randall v. Sorrell

548 U.S. 230 (2006)

Justice BREYER announced the judgment of the Court, and delivered an opinion in which THE CHIEF JUSTICE joins, and in which Justice ALITO joins except as to Parts II-B-1 and II-B-2.

We here consider the constitutionality of a Vermont campaign finance statute that limits both (1) the amounts that candidates for state office may spend on their campaigns (expenditure limitations) and (2) the amounts that individuals, organizations, and political parties may contribute to those campaigns (contribution limitations). Vt. Stat. Ann., Tit. 17, § 2801 *et seq.* (2002). We hold that both sets of limitations are inconsistent with the First Amendment. Well-established precedent makes clear that the expenditure limits violate the First Amendment. *Buckley.* The contribution limits are unconstitutional because in their specific details (involving low maximum levels and other restrictions) they fail to satisfy the First Amendment's requirement of careful tailoring. That is to say, they impose burdens upon First Amendment interests that (when viewed in light of the statute's legitimate objectives) are disproportionately severe.

I
A

Prior to 1997, Vermont's campaign finance law imposed no limit upon the amount a candidate for state office could spend. It did, however, impose limits upon the amounts that individuals, corporations, and political committees could contribute to the campaign of such a candidate. Individuals and corporations could contribute no more than

$1,000 to any candidate for state office. Political committees, excluding political parties, could contribute no more than $3,000. The statute imposed no limit on the amount that political parties could contribute to candidates.

In 1997, Vermont enacted a more stringent campaign finance law, Pub. Act No. 64 (hereinafter Act or Act 64), the statute at issue here. Act 64, which took effect immediately after the 1998 elections, imposes mandatory expenditure limits on the total amount a candidate for state office can spend during a "two-year general election cycle," *i.e.*, the primary plus the general election, in approximately the following amounts: governor, $300,000; lieutenant governor, $100,000; other statewide offices, $45,000; state senator, $4,000 (plus an additional $2,500 for each additional seat in the district); state representative (two-member district), $3,000; and state representative (single member district), $2,000. These limits are adjusted for inflation in odd-numbered years based on the Consumer Price Index. Incumbents seeking reelection to statewide office may spend no more than 85% of the above amounts, and incumbents seeking reelection to the State Senate or House may spend no more than 90% of the above amounts. The Act defines "[e]xpenditure" broadly to mean the:

> payment, disbursement, distribution, advance, deposit, loan or gift of money or anything of value, paid or promised to be paid, for the purpose of influencing an election, advocating a position on a public question, or supporting or opposing one or more candidates.

With certain minor exceptions, expenditures over $50 made on a candidate's behalf by others count against the candidate's expenditure limit if those expenditures are "intentionally facilitated by, solicited by or approved by" the candidate's campaign. These provisions apply so as to count against a campaign's expenditure limit any spending by political parties or committees that is coordinated with the campaign and benefits the candidate. And any party expenditure that "primarily benefits six or fewer candidates who are associated with the political party" is "presumed" to be coordinated with the campaign and therefore to count against the campaign's expenditure limit.

Act 64 also imposes strict contribution limits. The amount any single individual can contribute to the campaign of a candidate for state office during a "two-year general election cycle" is limited as follows: governor, lieutenant governor, and other statewide offices, $400; state senator, $300; and state representative, $200. Unlike its expenditure limits, Act 64's contribution limits are not indexed for inflation.

A political committee is subject to these same limits. So is a political party, defined broadly to include "any subsidiary, branch or local unit" of a party, as well as any "national or regional affiliates" of a party (taken separately or together). Thus, for example, the statute treats the local, state, and national affiliates of the Democratic Party as if they were a single entity and limits their total contribution to a single candidate's campaign for governor (during the primary and the general election together) to $400.

The Act also imposes a limit of $2,000 upon the amount any individual can give to a political party during a 2-year general election cycle.

The Act defines "contribution" broadly in approximately the same way it defines "expenditure." Any expenditure made on a candidate's behalf counts as a contribution to the candidate if it is "intentionally facilitated by, solicited by or approved by" the candidate. And a party expenditure that "primarily benefits six or fewer candidates who are associated with the" party is "presumed" to count against the party's contribution limits.

There are a few exceptions. A candidate's own contributions to the campaign and those of the candidate's family fall outside the contribution limits. Volunteer services do not count as contributions. Nor does the cost of a meet-the-candidate function, provided that the total cost for the function amounts to $100 or less.

In addition to these expenditure and contribution limits, the Act sets forth disclosure and reporting requirements and creates a voluntary public financing system for gubernatorial elections. None of these is at issue here. The Act also limits the amount of contributions a candidate, political committee, or political party can receive from out-of-state sources. The lower courts held these out-of-state contribution limits unconstitutional, and the parties do not challenge that holding.

B

The petitioners are individuals who have run for state office in Vermont, citizens who vote in Vermont elections and contribute to Vermont campaigns, and political parties and committees that participate in Vermont politics. Soon after Act 64 became law, they brought this lawsuit in Federal District Court against the respondents, state officials charged with enforcement of the Act. Several other private groups and individual citizens intervened in the District Court proceedings in support of the Act and are joined here as respondents as well.

The District Court agreed with the petitioners that the Act's expenditure limits violate the First Amendment. See *Buckley*. The court also held unconstitutional the Act's limits on the contributions of political parties to candidates. At the same time, the court found the Act's other contribution limits constitutional. *Landell v. Sorrell*, 118 F. Supp. 2d 459 (Vt. 2000).

Both sides appealed. A divided panel of the Court of Appeals for the Second Circuit held that *all* of the Act's contribution limits are constitutional. It also held that the Act's expenditure limits may be constitutional. *Landell v. Sorrell*, 382 F.3d 91 (2004). It found those limits supported by two compelling interests, namely, an interest in preventing corruption or the appearance of corruption and an interest in limiting the amount of time state officials must spend raising campaign funds. The Circuit then remanded the case to the District Court with instructions to determine whether the Act's expenditure limits were narrowly tailored to those interests.

The petitioners and respondents all sought certiorari. They asked us to consider the constitutionality of Act 64's expenditure limits, its contribution limits, and a related definitional provision. We agreed to do so.

II

We turn first to the Act's expenditure limits. Do those limits violate the First Amendment's free speech guarantees?

A

In *Buckley* the Court considered the constitutionality of the Federal Election Campaign Act of 1971 (FECA), a statute that, much like the Act before us, imposed both expenditure and contribution limitations on campaigns for public office. The Court, while upholding FECA's contribution limitations as constitutional, held that the statute's expenditure limitations violated the First Amendment.

[The Court summarized *Buckley*'s differing treatment of contribution and expenditure limits.] Over the last 30 years, in considering the constitutionality of a host of different campaign finance statutes, this Court has repeatedly adhered to *Buckley*'s constraints, including those on expenditure limits. See *McConnell* [discussed after this case—EDs]; *Colorado II*; *Shrink Missouri*; *Colorado I*; *MCFL*; *NCPAC*; *CMA*.

B[e]

1

The respondents recognize that, in respect to expenditure limits, *Buckley* appears to be a controlling-and unfavorable-precedent. They seek to overcome that precedent in two ways. First, they ask us in effect to overrule *Buckley* Post-*Buckley* experience, they believe, has shown that contribution limits (and disclosure requirements) alone cannot effectively deter corruption or its appearance; hence experience has undermined an assumption underlying that case. Indeed, the respondents have devoted several pages of their briefs to attacking *Buckley*'s holding on expenditure limits.

Second, in the alternative, they ask us to limit the scope of *Buckley* significantly by distinguishing *Buckley* from the present case. They advance as a ground for distinction a justification for expenditure limitations that, they say, *Buckley* did not consider, namely that such limits help to protect candidates from spending too much time raising money rather than devoting that time to campaigning among ordinary voters. We find neither argument persuasive.

2

The Court has often recognized the "fundamental importance" of *stare decisis,* the basic legal principle that commands judicial respect for a court's earlier decisions and the rules of law they embody. The Court has pointed out that *stare decisis* "'promotes the evenhanded, predictable, and consistent development of legal principles, fosters reliance on judicial decisions, and contributes to the actual and perceived integrity of the judicial process.'" *Stare decisis* thereby avoids the instability and unfairness that accompany disruption of settled legal expectations. For this reason, the rule of law demands that adhering to our prior case law be the norm. Departure from precedent is exceptional, and requires "special justification." This is especially true where, as here, the principle has become settled through iteration and reiteration over a long period of time.

We can find here no such special justification that would require us to overrule *Buckley*. Subsequent case law has not made *Buckley* a legal anomaly or otherwise undermined its basic legal principles. We cannot find in the respondents' claims any demonstration that circumstances have changed so radically as to undermine *Buckley*'s critical factual assumptions. The respondents have not shown, for example, any dramatic increase in corruption or its appearance in Vermont; nor have they shown that expenditure limits are the only way to attack that problem. Cf. *McConnell*. At the same time, *Buckley* has promoted considerable reliance. Congress and state legislatures have used *Buckley* when drafting campaign finance laws. And, as we have said, this Court has followed *Buckley*, upholding and applying its reasoning in later cases. Overruling *Buckley* now would dramatically undermine this reliance on our settled precedent.

For all these reasons, we find this a case that fits the *stare decisis* norm. And we do not perceive the strong justification that would be necessary to warrant overruling so well es-

---

e. Recall that in Parts II-B-1 and II-B-2 Justice Breyer writes for himself and Chief Justice Roberts, but not Justice Alito.

tablished a precedent. We consequently decline the respondents' invitation to reconsider *Buckley*.

3

The respondents also ask us to distinguish these cases from *Buckley*. But we can find no significant basis for that distinction. Act 64's expenditure limits are not substantially different from those at issue in *Buckley*. In both instances the limits consist of a dollar cap imposed upon a candidate's expenditures. Nor is Vermont's primary justification for imposing its expenditure limits significantly different from Congress' rationale for the *Buckley* limits: preventing corruption and its appearance.

The sole basis on which the respondents seek to distinguish *Buckley* concerns a further supporting justification. They argue that expenditure limits are necessary in order to reduce the amount of time candidates must spend raising money. Increased campaign costs, together with the fear of a better-funded opponent, mean that, without expenditure limits, a candidate must spend too much time raising money instead of meeting the voters and engaging in public debate. *Buckley*, the respondents add, did not fully consider this justification. Had it done so, they say, the Court would have upheld, not struck down, FECA's expenditure limits.

In our view, it is highly unlikely that fuller consideration of this time protection rationale would have changed *Buckley*'s result. The *Buckley* Court was aware of the connection between expenditure limits and a reduction in fundraising time. In a section of the opinion dealing with FECA's public financing provisions, it wrote that Congress was trying to "free candidates from the rigors of fundraising." The Court of Appeals' opinion and the briefs filed in this Court pointed out that a natural consequence of higher campaign expenditures was that "candidates were compelled to allow to fund raising increasing and extreme amounts of money and energy." And, in any event, the connection between high campaign expenditures and increased fundraising demands seems perfectly obvious.

Under these circumstances, the respondents' argument amounts to no more than an invitation so to limit *Buckley*'s holding as effectively to overrule it. For the reasons set forth above, we decline that invitation as well. And, given *Buckley*'s continued authority, we must conclude that Act 64's expenditure limits violate the First Amendment.

III

We turn now to a more complex question, namely the constitutionality of Act 64's contribution limits. The parties, while accepting *Buckley*'s approach, dispute whether, despite *Buckley*'s general approval of statutes that limit campaign contributions, Act 64's contribution limits are so severe that in the circumstances its particular limits violate the First Amendment.

A

As with the Act's expenditure limits, we begin with *Buckley*. In that case, the Court upheld the $1,000 contribution limit before it. *Buckley* recognized that contribution limits, like expenditure limits, "implicate fundamental First Amendment interests," namely, the freedoms of "political expression" and "political association." But, unlike expenditure limits (which "necessarily reduc[e] the quantity of expression by restricting the number of issues discussed, the depth of their exploration, and the size of the audience reached"), contribution limits "involv[e] little direct restraint on" the contributor's speech. They do restrict "one aspect of the contributor's freedom of political association," namely, the contributor's ability to support a favored candidate, but they nonetheless "permi[t] the symbolic expression of support evidenced by a contribution," and they do "not in any way infringe the contributor's freedom to discuss candidates and issues."

Consequently, the Court wrote, contribution limitations are permissible as long as the Government demonstrates that the limits are "closely drawn" to match a "sufficiently important interest." It found that the interest advanced in the case, "prevent[ing] corruption" and its "appearance," was "sufficiently important" to justify the statute's contribution limits.

The Court also found that the contribution limits before it were "closely drawn." It recognized that, in determining whether a particular contribution limit was "closely drawn," the amount, or level, of that limit could make a difference. Indeed, it wrote that "contribution restrictions could have a severe impact on political dialogue if the limitations prevented candidates and political committees from amassing the resources necessary for effective advocacy." But the Court added that such "distinctions in degree become significant only when they can be said to amount to differences in kind." Pointing out that it had "no scalpel to probe, whether, say, a $2,000 ceiling might not serve as well as $1,000," the Court found "no indication" that the $1,000 contribution limitations imposed by the Act would have "any dramatic adverse effect on the funding of campaigns." It therefore found the limitations constitutional.

Since *Buckley*, the Court has consistently upheld contribution limits in other statutes. *Shrink* ($1075 limit on contributions to candidates for Missouri state auditor); *CMA* ($5,000 limit on contributions to multicandidate political committees). The Court has recognized, however, that contribution limits might *sometimes* work more harm to protected First Amendment interests than their anticorruption objectives could justify. See *Shrink*; *Buckley*. And individual Members of the Court have expressed concern lest too low a limit magnify the "reputation-related or media-related advantages of incumbency and thereby insulat[e] legislators from effective electoral challenge." *Shrink* (BREYER, J., joined by GINSBURG, J., concurring). In the cases before us, the petitioners challenge Act 64's contribution limits on that basis.

B

Following *Buckley*, we must determine whether Act 64's contribution limits prevent candidates from "amassing the resources necessary for effective [campaign] advocacy," whether they magnify the advantages of incumbency to the point where they put challengers to a significant disadvantage; in a word, whether they are too low and too strict to survive First Amendment scrutiny. In answering these questions, we recognize, as *Buckley* stated, that we have "no scalpel to probe" each possible contribution level. We cannot determine with any degree of exactitude the precise restriction necessary to carry out the statute's legitimate objectives. In practice, the legislature is better equipped to make such empirical judgments, as legislators have "particular expertise" in matters related to the costs and nature of running for office. *McConnell*. Thus ordinarily we have deferred to the legislature's determination of such matters.

Nonetheless, as *Buckley* acknowledged, we must recognize the existence of some lower bound. At some point the constitutional risks to the democratic electoral process become too great. After all, the interests underlying contribution limits, preventing corruption and the appearance of corruption, "directly implicate the integrity of our electoral process." *McConnell*. Yet that rationale does not simply mean "the lower the limit, the better." That is because contribution limits that are too low can also harm the electoral process by preventing challengers from mounting effective campaigns against incumbent officeholders, thereby reducing democratic accountability. Were we to ignore that fact, a statute that seeks to regulate campaign contributions could itself prove an obstacle to the very electoral fairness it seeks to promote. Thus, we see no alternative to the exercise of independent judicial judgment as a statute reaches those outer limits. And, where there is strong indication in a particular case, *i.e.,* danger signs, that such risks exist (both present in kind and likely serious in degree), courts, including appellate courts, must review the record independently and carefully with an eye toward assessing the statute's "tailoring," that is, toward assessing the proportionality of the restrictions. See *Bose Corp. v. Consumers Union of United States, Inc.,* 466 U.S. 485, 499 (1984) ("[A]n appellate court has an obligation to 'make an independent examination of the whole record' in order to make sure that 'the judgment does not constitute a forbidden intrusion on the field of free expression' ").

We find those danger signs present here. As compared with the contribution limits upheld by the Court in the past, and with those in force in other States, Act 64's limits are sufficiently low as to generate suspicion that they are not closely drawn. The Act sets its limits per election cycle, which includes both a primary and a general election. Thus, in a gubernatorial race with both primary and final election contests, the Act's contribution limit amounts to $200 per election per candidate (with significantly lower limits for contributions to candidates for State Senate and House of Representatives). These limits apply both to contributions from individuals and to contributions from political parties, whether made in cash or in expenditures coordinated (or presumed to be coordinated) with the candidate.

These limits are well below the limits this Court upheld in *Buckley*. Indeed, in terms of real dollars *(i.e.,* adjusting for inflation), the Act's $200 per election limit on individual contributions to a campaign for governor is slightly more than one-twentieth of the limit on contributions to campaigns for federal office before the Court in *Buckley*. Adjusted to reflect its value in 1976 (the year *Buckley* was decided), Vermont's contribution limit on campaigns for statewide office (including governor) amounts to $113.91 per 2-year election cycle, or roughly $57 per election, as compared to the $1,000 per election limit on individual contributions at issue in *Buckley*. (The adjusted value of Act 64's limit on contributions from political parties to candidates for statewide office, again $200 per candidate per election, is just over one one-hundredth of the comparable limit before the Court in *Buckley*, $5,000 per election.) Yet Vermont's gubernatorial district-the entire State-is no smaller than the House districts to which *Buckley*'s limits applied. In 1976, the average congressional district contained a population of about 465,000. Indeed, Vermont's population is 621,000-about one-third *larger*.

Moreover, considered as a whole, Vermont's contribution limits are the lowest in the Nation. Act 64 limits contributions to candidates for statewide office (including governor) to $200 per candidate per election. We have found no State that imposes a lower per election limit. Indeed, we have found only seven States that impose limits on contributions to candidates for statewide office at or below $500 per election, more than twice Act 64's limit. Cf. Ariz.Rev.Stat. Ann. § 16-905 ($760 per election cycle, or $380 per election, adjusted for inflation); Colo. Const., Art. XXVIII, § 3 ($500 per election, adjusted for inflation); Fla. Stat. § 106.08(1)(a) (2003) ($500 per election); Me.Rev.Stat. Ann., Tit. 21A, § 1015(1) (1993) ($500 for governor, $250 for other statewide office, per election); Mass. Gen. Laws, ch. 55, §7A (West Supp.2006) ($500 per year, or $250 per election); Mont.Code

Ann. § 13-37-216(1)(a) (2005) ($500 for governor, $250 for other statewide office, per election); S.D. Codified Laws § 12-25-1.1 (2004) ($1,000 per year, or $500 per election). We are aware of no State that imposes a limit on contributions from political parties to candidates for statewide office lower than Act 64's $200 per candidate per election limit. Cf. Me.Rev.Stat. Ann., Tit. 21A, § 1015(1) (1993) (next lowest: $500 for contribution from party to candidate for governor, $250 for contribution from party to candidate for other statewide office, both per election). Similarly, we have found only three States that have limits on contributions to candidates for state legislature below Act 64's $150 and $100 per election limits. Ariz.Rev.Stat. Ann. § 16-905 (West Cum.Supp.2005) ($296 per election cycle, or $148 per election); Mont.Code Ann. § 13-37-216(1)(a) (2005) ($130 per election); S.D. Codified Laws § 12-25-1.1 (2004) ($250 per year, or $125 per election). And we are aware of no State that has a lower limit on contributions from political parties to state legislative candidates. Cf. Me.Rev.Stat. Ann., Tit. 21A, § 1015(1) (1993) (next lowest: $250 per election).

Finally, Vermont's limit is well below the lowest limit this Court has previously upheld, the limit of $1,075 per election (adjusted for inflation every two years) for candidates for Missouri state auditor. *Shrink*. The comparable Vermont limit of roughly $200 per election, not adjusted for inflation, is less than one-sixth of Missouri's current inflation-adjusted limit ($1,275).

We recognize that Vermont's population is much smaller than Missouri's. Indeed, Vermont is about one-ninth of the size of Missouri. Thus, *per citizen,* Vermont's limit is slightly more generous. As of 2006, the ratio of the contribution limit to the size of the constituency in Vermont is .00064, while Missouri's ratio is .00044, 31% lower.

But this does not necessarily mean that Vermont's limits are less objectionable than the limit upheld in *Shrink*. A campaign for state auditor is likely to be less costly than a campaign for governor; campaign costs do not automatically increase or decrease in precise proportion to the size of an electoral district. See App. 66 (1998 winning candidate for Vermont state auditor spent about $60,000; winning candidate for governor spent about $340,000); Opensecrets.org, The Big Picture, 2004 Cycle: Hot Races, available at http://www.opensecrets.org/bigpicture/hotraces.asp?cycle=2004 (as visited June 22, 2006, and available in Clerk of Court's case file) (U.S. Senate campaigns identified as competitive spend less per voter than U.S. House campaigns identified as competitive). Moreover, Vermont's limits, unlike Missouri's limits, apply in the same amounts to contributions made by political parties. Mo.Rev.Stat. § 130.032.4 (2000) (enacting limits on contributions from political parties to candidates 10 times higher than limits on contributions from individuals). And, as we have said, Missouri's (current) $1,275 per election limit, unlike Vermont's $200 per election limit, is indexed for inflation.

The factors we have mentioned offset any neutralizing force of population differences. At the very least, they make it difficult to treat *Shrink*'s (then) $1,075 limit as providing affirmative support for the lawfulness of Vermont's far lower levels. Cf. *Shrink* (BREYER, J., concurring) (The *Shrink* "limit … is low enough to raise … a [significant constitutional] question"). And even were that not so, Vermont's failure to index for inflation means that Vermont's levels would soon be far lower than Missouri's regardless of the method of comparison.

In sum, Act 64's contribution limits are substantially lower than both the limits we have previously upheld and comparable limits in other States. These are danger signs that Act 64's contribution limits may fall outside tolerable First Amendment limits. We consequently must examine the record independently and carefully to determine whether Act 64's contribution limits are "closely drawn" to match the State's interests.

C

Our examination of the record convinces us that, from a constitutional perspective, Act 64's contribution limits are too restrictive. We reach this conclusion based not merely on the low dollar amounts of the limits themselves, but also on the statute's effect on political parties and on volunteer activity in Vermont elections. *Taken together,* Act 64's substantial restrictions on the ability of candidates to raise the funds necessary to run a competitive election, on the ability of political parties to help their candidates get elected, and on the ability of individual citizens to volunteer their time to campaigns show that the Act is not closely drawn to meet its objectives. In particular, five factors together lead us to this decision.

First, the record suggests, though it does not conclusively prove, that Act 64's contribution limits will significantly restrict the amount of funding available for challengers to run competitive campaigns. For one thing, the petitioners' expert, Clark Bensen, conducted a race-by-race analysis of the 1998 legislative elections (the last to take place before Act 64 took effect) and concluded that Act 64's contribution limits would have reduced the funds available in 1998 to Republican challengers in competitive races in amounts ranging from 18% to 53% of their total campaign income.

For another thing, the petitioners' expert witnesses produced evidence and analysis showing that Vermont political parties (particularly the Republican Party) "target" their contributions to candidates in competitive races, that those contributions represent a significant amount of total candidate funding in such races, and that the contribution limits will cut the parties' contributions to competitive races dramatically. [S]ee, *e.g.,* Gierzynski & Breaux, *The Role of Parties in Legislative Campaign Financing,* 15 AM. REV. POLITICS 171 (1994); Thompson, Cassie, & Jewell, *A Sacred Cow or Just a Lot of Bull? Party and PAC Money in State Legislative Elections,* 47 POL. SCI. Q. 223 (1994). Their statistics showed that the party contributions accounted for a significant percentage of the total campaign income in those races. And their studies showed that Act 64's contribution limits would cut the party contributions by between 85% (for the legislature on average) and 99% (for governor).

More specifically, Bensen pointed out that in 1998, the Republican Party made contributions to 19 Senate campaigns in amounts that averaged $2,001, which on average represented 16% of the recipient campaign's total income. Act 64 would reduce these contributions to $300 per campaign, an average reduction of about 85%. The party contributed to 50 House campaigns in amounts averaging $787, which on average represented 28% of the recipient campaign's total income. Act 64 would reduce these contributions to $200 per campaign, an average reduction of 74.5%. And the party contributed $40,600 to its gubernatorial candidate, an amount that accounted for about 16% of the candidate's funding. The Act would have reduced that contribution by 99%, to $400.

Bensen added that 57% of all 1998 Senate campaigns and 30% of all House campaigns exceeded Act 64's expenditure limits, which were enacted along with the statute's contribution limits. Moreover, 27% of all Senate campaigns and 10% of all House campaigns spent more than double those limits.

The respondents did not contest these figures. Rather, they presented evidence that focused, not upon *strongly contested* campaigns, but upon the funding amounts available for the *average* campaign. The respondents' expert, Anthony Gierzynski, concluded, for example, that Act 64 would have a "minimal effect on … candidates' ability to raise funds." But he rested this conclusion upon his finding that "only a small proportion of" *all* contributions to *all* campaigns for state office "made during the last three elections would have been affected by the new limits." The lower courts similarly relied almost exclusively on averages in assessing Act 64's effect. See 118 F. Supp. 2d, at 470 ("Approximately 83% to 96% of the campaign contributions *to recent House races* were under $200" (emphasis added)); *id.*, at 478 ("Expert testimony revealed that over the last three election cycles the percentage *of all candidates' contributions* received over the contribution limits was less than 10%" (emphasis added)).

The respondents' evidence leaves the petitioners' evidence unrebutted in certain key respects. That is because the critical question concerns not simply the *average* effect of contribution limits on fundraising but, more importantly, the ability of a candidate running against an incumbent officeholder to mount an effective *challenge*. And information about *average* races, rather than *competitive* races, is only distantly related to that question, because competitive races are likely to be far more expensive than the average race. See, *e.g.*, N. Ornstein, T. Mann, & M. Malbin, VITAL STATISTICS ON CONGRESS 2001–2002, pp. 89–98 (2002) (data showing that spending in competitive elections, *i.e.*, where incumbent wins with less than 60% of vote or where incumbent loses, is far greater than in most elections, where incumbent wins with more than 60% of the vote). We concede that the record does contain some anecdotal evidence supporting the respondents' position, namely, testimony about a post-Act-64 competitive mayoral campaign in Burlington, which suggests that a challenger can "amas[s] the resources necessary for effective advocacy," *Buckley*. But the facts of that particular election are not described in sufficient detail to offer a convincing refutation of the implication arising from the petitioners' experts' studies.

Rather, the petitioners' studies, taken together with low *average* Vermont campaign expenditures and the typically higher costs that a challenger must bear to overcome the name-recognition advantage enjoyed by an incumbent, raise a reasonable inference that the contribution limits are so low that they may pose a significant obstacle to candidates in competitive elections. Cf. Ornstein, *supra* (In 2000 U.S. House and Senate elections, successful challengers spent far more than the average candidate). Information about average races does not rebut that inference. Consequently, the inference amounts to one factor (among others) that here counts against the constitutional validity of the contribution limits.

Second, Act 64's insistence that political parties abide by *exactly* the same low contribution limits that apply to other contributors threatens harm to a particularly important political right, the right to associate in a political party. See, *e.g.*, *California Democratic Party v. Jones* (describing constitutional importance of associating in political parties to elect candidates); *Timmons; Colorado I; Norman v. Reed*. Cf. *Buckley* (contribution limits constitute "only a marginal restriction" on First Amendment rights *because* contributor remains free to associate politically, *e.g.*, in a political party, and "assist personally" in the party's "efforts on behalf of candidates").

The Act applies its $200 to $400 limits-precisely the same limits it applies to an individual-to virtually all affiliates of a political party taken together as if they were a single contributor. That means, for example, that the Vermont Democratic Party, taken together with all its local affiliates, can make one contribution of at most $400 to the Democratic gubernatorial candidate, one contribution of at most $300 to a Democratic candidate for State Senate, and one contribution of at most $200 to a Democratic candidate for the State House of Representatives. The Act includes within these limits not only direct monetary contributions but also expenditures in kind: stamps, stationery, coffee, doughnuts, gasoline, campaign buttons, and so forth. Indeed, it includes all party expenditures "intended to promote the election of a specific candidate or group of candidates" as long as the candidate's campaign "facilitate[s]," "solicit [s]," or "approve[s]" them. And a party expenditure that "primarily benefits six or fewer candidates who are associated with the" party is "presumed" to count against the party's contribution limits.

In addition to the negative effect on "amassing funds" that we have described, the Act would severely limit the ability of a party to assist its candidates' campaigns by engaging in coordinated spending on advertising, candidate events, voter lists, mass mailings, even yard signs. And, to an unusual degree, it would discourage those who wish to contribute small amounts of money to a party, amounts that easily comply with individual contribution limits. Suppose that many individuals do not know Vermont legislative candidates personally, but wish to contribute, say, $20 or $40, to the State Republican Party, with the intent that the party use the money to help elect whichever candidates the party believes would best advance its ideals and interests—the basic object of a political party. Or, to take a more extreme example, imagine that 6,000 Vermont citizens each want to give $1 to the State Democratic Party because, though unfamiliar with the details of the individual races, they would like to make a small financial contribution to the goal of electing a Democratic state legislature. And further imagine that the party believes control of the legislature will depend on the outcome of three (and only three) House races. The Act forbids the party from giving $2,000 (of the $6,000) to each of its candidates in those pivotal races. Indeed, it permits the party to give no more than $200 to each candidate, thereby thwarting the aims of the 6,000 donors from making a meaningful contribution to state politics by giving a small amount of money to the party they support. Thus, the Act would severely inhibit collective political activity by preventing a political party from using contributions by small donors to provide meaningful assistance to any individual candidate.

We recognize that we have previously upheld limits on contributions from political parties to candidates, in particular the federal limits on coordinated party spending. *Colorado II.* And we also recognize that any such limit will negatively affect *to some extent* the fund-allocating party function just described. But the contribution limits at issue in *Colorado II* were far less problematic, for they were significantly higher than Act 64's limits. See *id.* (at least $67,560 in coordinated spending and $5,000 in direct cash contributions for U.S. Senate candidates, at least $33,780 in coordinated spending and $5,000 in direct cash contributions for U.S. House candidates). And they were much higher than the federal limits on contributions from individuals to candidates, thereby reflecting an effort by Congress to balance (1) the need to allow individuals to participate in the political process by contributing to political parties that help elect candidates with (2) the need to prevent the use of political parties "to circumvent contribution limits that apply to individuals." Act 64, by placing identical limits upon contributions to candidates, whether made by an individual or by a political party, gives to the former consideration *no weight at all.*

We consequently agree with the District Court that the Act's contribution limits "would reduce the voice of political parties" in Vermont to a "whisper." And we count the special party-related harms that Act 64 threatens as a further factor weighing against the constitutional validity of the contribution limits.

Third, the Act's treatment of volunteer services aggravates the problem. Like its federal statutory counterpart, the Act excludes from its definition of "contribution" all "services provided without compensation by individuals volunteering their time on behalf of a candidate." But the Act does not exclude the expenses those volunteers incur, such as travel expenses, in the course of campaign activities. The Act's broad definitions would seem to count those expenses against the volunteer's contribution limit, at least where the spending was facilitated or approved by campaign officials. And, unlike the Federal

Government's treatment of comparable requirements, the State has not (insofar as we are aware) created an exception excluding such expenses.

The absence of some such exception may matter in the present context, where contribution limits are very low. That combination, low limits and no exceptions, means that a gubernatorial campaign volunteer who makes four or five round trips driving across the State performing volunteer activities coordinated with the campaign can find that he or she is near, or has surpassed, the contribution limit. So too will a volunteer who offers a campaign the use of her house along with coffee and doughnuts for a few dozen neighbors to meet the candidate, say, two or three times during a campaign. Cf. Vt. Stat. Ann., Tit. 17, §2809(d) (2002) (excluding expenditures for such activities only up to $100). Such supporters will have to keep careful track of all miles driven, postage supplied (500 stamps equals $200), pencils and pads used, and so forth. And any carelessness in this respect can prove costly, perhaps generating a headline, "Campaign laws violated," that works serious harm to the candidate.

These sorts of problems are unlikely to affect the constitutionality of a limit that is reasonably high. But Act 64's contribution limits are so low, and its definition of "contribution" so broad, that the Act may well impede a campaign's ability effectively to use volunteers, thereby making it more difficult for individuals to associate in this way. Again, the very low limits at issue help to transform differences in degree into difference in kind. And the likelihood of unjustified interference in the present context is sufficiently great that we must consider the lack of tailoring in the Act's definition of "contribution" as an added factor counting against the constitutional validity of the contribution limits before us.

Fourth, unlike the contribution limits we upheld in *Shrink,* Act 64's contribution limits are not adjusted for inflation. Its limits decline in real value each year. Indeed, in real dollars the Act's limits have already declined by about 20% ($200 in 2006 dollars has a real value of $160.66 in 1997 dollars). A failure to index limits means that limits which are already suspiciously low will almost inevitably become too low over time. It means that future legislation will be necessary to stop that almost inevitable decline, and it thereby imposes the burden of preventing the decline upon incumbent legislators who may not diligently police the need for changes in limit levels to assure the adequate financing of electoral challenges.

Fifth, we have found nowhere in the record any special justification that might warrant a contribution limit so low or so restrictive as to bring about the serious associational and expressive problems that we have described. Rather, the basic justifications the State has advanced in support of such limits are those present in *Buckley.* The record contains no indication that, for example, corruption (or its appearance) in Vermont is significantly more serious a matter than elsewhere. Indeed, other things being equal, one might reasonably believe that a contribution of say, $250 (or $450) to a candidate's campaign was less likely to prove a corruptive force than the far larger contributions at issue in the other campaign finance cases we have considered.

These five sets of considerations, taken together, lead us to conclude that Act 64's contribution limits are not narrowly tailored. Rather, the Act burdens First Amendment interests by threatening to inhibit effective advocacy by those who seek election, particularly challengers; its contribution limits mute the voice of political parties; they hamper participation in campaigns through volunteer activities; and they are not indexed for inflation. Vermont does not point to a legitimate statutory objective that might justify these special burdens. We understand that many, though not all, campaign finance regulations impose certain of these burdens to some degree. We also understand the legitimate need for constitutional leeway in respect to legislative line-drawing. But our discussion indicates why we conclude that Act 64 in this respect nonetheless goes too far. It disproportionately burdens numerous First Amendment interests, and consequently, in our view, violates the First Amendment.

[Justice Breyer concluded that the constitutional portions of the law could not be severed from the unconstitutional portions of the law.] Given these difficulties, we believe the Vermont Legislature would have intended us to set aside the statute's contribution limits, leaving the legislature free to rewrite those provisions in light of the constitutional difficulties we have identified.

IV

We conclude that Act 64's expenditure limits violate the First Amendment as interpreted in *Buckley*. We also conclude that the specific details of Act 64's contribution limits require us to hold that those limits violate the First Amendment, for they burden First Amendment interests in a manner that is disproportionate to the public purposes they were enacted to advance. Given our holding, we need not, and do not, examine the constitutionality of the statute's presumption that certain party expenditures are coordinated with a candidate. Accordingly, the judgment of the Court of Appeals is reversed, and the cases are remanded for further proceedings.

It is so ordered.

Justice ALITO, concurring in part and concurring in the judgment.

I concur in the judgment and join in Justice BREYER's opinion except for Parts II-B-1 and II-B-2. Contrary to the suggestion of those sections, respondents' primary defense of Vermont's expenditure limits is that those limits are consistent with *Buckley*. Only as a backup argument, an afterthought almost, do respondents make a naked plea for us to "revisit *Buckley*." This is fairly incongruous, given that respondents' defense of Vermont's contribution limits rests squarely on *Buckley* and later decisions that built on *Buckley*, and yet respondents fail to explain why it would be appropriate to reexamine only one part of the holding in *Buckley*. More to the point, respondents fail to discuss the doctrine of *stare decisis* or the Court's cases elaborating on the circumstances in which it is appropriate to reconsider a prior constitutional decision. Indeed, only once in 99 pages of briefing from respondents do the words "*stare decisis*" appear, and that reference is in connection with *contribution* limits. Such an incomplete presentation is reason enough to refuse respondents' invitation to reexamine *Buckley*. See *United States v. International Business Machines Corp.*, 517 U.S. 843, 856 (1996).

Whether or not a case can be made for reexamining *Buckley* in whole or in part, what matters is that respondents do not do so here, and so I think it unnecessary to reach the issue.

[Justice Kennedy's opinion concurring in the judgment is omitted. Justice Kennedy noted that "The universe of campaign finance regulation is one this Court has in part created and in part permitted by its course of decisions. That new order may cause more problems than it solves. On a routine, operational level the present system requires us to explain why $200 is too restrictive a limit while $1,500 is not. Our own experience gives us little basis to make these judgments, and certainly no traditional or well-established body of law exists to offer guidance."]

Justice THOMAS, with whom Justice SCALIA joins, concurring in the judgment.

Although I agree with the plurality that [Act 64] is unconstitutional, I disagree with its rationale for striking down that statute. Invoking *stare decisis,* the plurality rejects the invitation to overrule *Buckley*. It then applies *Buckley* to invalidate the expenditure limitations and, less persuasively, the contribution limitations. I continue to believe that *Buckley* provides insufficient protection to political speech, the core of the First Amendment. The illegitimacy of *Buckley* is further underscored by the continuing inability of the Court (and the plurality here) to apply *Buckley* in a coherent and principled fashion. As a result, *stare decisis* should pose no bar to overruling *Buckley* and replacing it with a standard faithful to the First Amendment. Accordingly, I concur only in the judgment.

I

I adhere to my view that this Court erred in *Buckley* when it distinguished between contribution and expenditure limits, finding the former to be a less severe infringement on First Amendment rights.... Accordingly, I would overrule *Buckley* and subject both the contribution and expenditure restrictions of Act 64 to strict scrutiny, which they would fail.

II

The plurality opinion, far from making the case for *Buckley* as a rule of law, itself demonstrates that *Buckley*'s limited scrutiny of contribution limits is "insusceptible of principled application," and accordingly is not entitled to *stare decisis* effect. Indeed, "when governing decisions are unworkable or are badly reasoned, this Court has never felt constrained to follow precedent.'" *Vieth* (plurality opinion). Today's newly minted, multifactor test, particularly when read in combination with the Court's decision in *Shrink, supra,* places this Court in the position of addressing the propriety of regulations of political speech based upon little more than its *impression* of the appropriate limits....

Justice STEVENS, dissenting.

Justice BREYER and Justice SOUTER debate whether the *per curiam* decision in *Buckley* forecloses any constitutional limitations on candidate expenditures. This is plainly an issue on which reasonable minds can disagree. The *Buckley* Court never explicitly addressed whether the pernicious effects of endless fundraising can serve as a compelling state interest that justifies expenditure limits yet its silence, in light of the record before it, suggests that it implicitly treated this proposed interest insufficient. Assuming this to be true, however, I am convinced that *Buckley*'s holding on expenditure limits is wrong, and that the time has come to overrule it....

Justice SOUTER, with whom Justice GINSBURG joins, and with whom Justice STEVENS joins as to Parts II and III, dissenting.

In 1997, the Legislature of Vermont passed Act 64 after a series of public hearings persuaded legislators that rehabilitating the State's political process required campaign finance reform. A majority of the Court today decides that the expenditure and contribution limits enacted are irreconcilable with the Constitution's guarantee of free speech. I would adhere to the Court of Appeals's decision to remand for further enquiry bearing on the limitations on candidates' expenditures, and I think the contribution limits satisfy controlling precedent. I respectfully dissent.

I

Rejecting Act 64's expenditure limits as directly contravening *Buckley* is at least premature....

II

Although I would defer judgment on the merits of the expenditure limitations, I believe the Court of Appeals correctly rejected the challenge to the contribution limits. Low though they are, one cannot say that "the contribution limitation[s are] so radical in effect as to render political association ineffective, drive the sound of a candidate's voice below the level of notice, and render contributions pointless." *Shrink Missouri.*

The limits set by Vermont are not remarkable departures either from those previously upheld by this Court or from those lately adopted by other States. The plurality concedes that on a per-citizen measurement Vermont's limit for statewide elections "is slightly more generous" than the one set by the Missouri statute approved by this Court in *Shrink, supra.* Not only do those dollar amounts get more generous the smaller the district, they are consistent with limits set by the legislatures of many other States, all of them with populations larger than Vermont's, some significantly so. See, *e.g., Montana Right to Life Assn. v. Eddleman,* 343 F.3d 1085, 1088 (C.A.9 2003) (approving $400 limit for candidates filed jointly for Governor and Lieutenant Governor, since increased to $500); *Daggett v. Commission on Governmental Ethics and Election Practices,* 205 F.3d 445, 452 (C.A.1 2000) ($500 limit for gubernatorial candidates in Maine); *Minnesota Citizens Concerned for Life, Inc. v. Kelley,* 427 F.3d 1106, 1113 (C.A.8 2005) ($500 limit on contributions to legislative candidates in election years, $100 in other years); *Florida Right to Life, Inc. v. Mortham,* No. 6:98-770-CV, 2000 WL 33733256, *3 (M.D. Fla., Mar. 20, 2000) ($500 limit on contributions to any state candidate). The point is not that this Court is bound by judicial sanctions of those numbers; it is that the consistency in legislative judgment tells us that Vermont is not an eccentric party of one, and that this is a case for the judicial deference that our own precedents say we owe here. See *Shrink* (BREYER, J., concurring) ("Where a legislature has significantly greater institutional expertise, as, for example, in the field of election regulation, the Court in practice defers to empirical legislative judgments"); see also *ante* (plurality opinion) ("[O]rdinarily we have deferred to the legislature's determination of [matters related to the costs and nature of running for office]").

To place Vermont's contribution limits beyond the constitutional pale, therefore, is to forget not only the facts of *Shrink,* but also our self-admonition against second-guessing legislative judgments about the risk of corruption to which contribution limits have to be fitted. And deference here would surely not be overly complaisant. Vermont's legislators themselves testified at length about the money that gets their special attention, see Act 64, H. 28, Legislative Findings and Intent (finding that "[s]ome candidates and elected officials, particularly when time is limited, respond and give access to contributors who make large contributions in preference to those who make small or no contributions"); 382 F.3d, at 122 (testimony of Elizabeth Ready: "If I have only got an hour at night when I get home to return calls, I am much more likely to return [a donor's] call than I would [a non-donor's].... [W]hen you only have a few minutes to talk, there are certain people that get access" (alterations in original)). The record revealed the amount of money the public sees as suspiciously large, see 118 F. Supp. 2d, at 479–480 ("The limits set by the legislature ... accurately reflect the level of contribution considered suspiciously large by the Vermont public. Testimony suggested that amounts greater than the contribution limits are considered large by the Vermont public"). And testimony identified the amounts high enough to pay for effective campaigning in a State where the cost of running tends to be on the low side, see *id* ("In the context of Vermont politics,

$200, $300, and $400 donations are clearly large, as the legislature determined. Small donations are considered to be strong acts of political support in this state. William Meub testified that a contribution of $1 is meaningful because it represents a commitment by the contributor that is likely to become a vote for the candidate. Gubernatorial candidate Ruth Dwyer values the small contributions of $5 so much that she personally sends thank you notes to those donors"); *id.* ("In Vermont, many politicians have run effective and winning campaigns with very little money, and some with no money at all.... Several candidates, campaign managers, and past and present government officials testified that they will be able to raise enough money to mount effective campaigns in the system of contribution limits established by Act 64"); *id.* ("Spending in Vermont statewide elections is very low.... Vermont ranks 49th out of the 50 states in campaign spending. The majority of major party candidates for statewide office in the last three election cycles spent less than what the spending limits of Act 64 would allow.... In Vermont legislative races, low-cost methods such as door-to-door campaigning are standard and even expected by the voters").

Still, our cases do not say deference should be absolute. We can all imagine dollar limits that would be laughable, and per capita comparisons that would be meaningless because aggregated donations simply could not sustain effective campaigns. The plurality thinks that point has been reached in Vermont, and in particular that the low contribution limits threaten the ability of challengers to run effective races against incumbents. Thus, the plurality's limit of deference is substantially a function of suspicion that political incumbents in the legislature set low contribution limits because their public recognition and easy access to free publicity will effectively augment their own spending power beyond anything a challenger can muster. The suspicion is, in other words, that incumbents cannot be trusted to set fair limits, because facially neutral limits do not in fact give challengers an even break. But this received suspicion is itself a proper subject of suspicion. The petitioners offered, and the plurality invokes, no evidence that the risk of a pro-incumbent advantage has been realized; in fact, the record evidence runs the other way, as the plurality concedes. I would not discount such evidence that these low limits are fair to challengers, for the experience of the Burlington race is confirmed by recent empirical studies addressing this issue of incumbent's advantage. See, *e.g.*, Eom & Gross, *Contribution Limits and Disparity in Contributions Between Gubernatorial Candidates*, 59 POL. RESEARCH Q. 99, 99 (2006) ("Analyses of both the number of contributors and the dollar amount of contributions [to gubernatorial candidates] suggest no support for an increased bias in favor of incumbents resulting from the presence of campaign contribution limits. If anything, contribution limits can work to reduce the bias that traditionally works in favor of incumbents. Also, contribution limits do not seem to increase disparities between gubernatorial candidates in general" (emphasis deleted)); Bardwell, *Money and Challenger Emergence in Gubernatorial Primaries*, 55 POL. RESEARCH Q. 653 (2002) (finding that contribution limits favor neither incumbents nor challengers); Hogan, *The Costs of Representation in State Legislatures: Explaining Variations in Campaign Spending*, 81 SOC. SCI. Q. 941, 952 (2000) (finding that contribution limits reduce incumbent spending but have no effect on challenger or open-seat candidate spending). The Legislature of Vermont evidently tried to account for the realities of campaigning in Vermont, and I see no evidence of constitutional miscalculation sufficient to dispense with respect for its judgments....

IV

Because I would not pass upon the constitutionality of Vermont's expenditure limits prior to further enquiry into their fit with the problem of fundraising demands on candidates, and because I do not see the contribution limits as depressed to the level of political inaudibility, I respectfully dissent.

Notes and Questions

1. Both Justice Thomas and Justice Souter argue that the plurality opinion written by Justice Breyer (joined by Justice Alito and Chief Justice Roberts) is inconsistent with the Court's approach in *Shrink Missouri*. 528 U.S. 377 (200). Is that a fair criticism? If so, what explains the Court's shift from *Shrink Missouri* to *Randall*? For an argument that the shift is explained by Justice Breyer's desire to keep the two newest Justices from joining the position of Justices Thomas and Scalia, see Richard L. Hasen, *The Newer Incoherence: Competition, Social Science, and Balancing in Campaign Finance Law after* Randall v. Sorrell, 68 OHIO STATE LAW JOURNAL 775 (2007).

2. The plurality opinion notes that seven states "impose limits on contributions to candidates for statewide office at or below $500 per election." Are these statutes in danger of being struck down as unconstitutional? How should lower courts following *Randall* assess the constitutionality of these laws?

3. Justice Souter agrees that some contribution limit may be so laughably low as to be unconstitutional. How would he determine when that limit has been reached? Is a "danger signs" test better than a "laughability" test?

4. Does *Randall* signal a shift towards the "political markets"/competition approach to election law of Professors Issacharoff and Pildes, described in Chapter 12, Part III? For an argument in the negative, see Hasen, *supra*. Dissenting Justices in the *McConnell* case below and critics reviewing the case argued that the law should have been stricken as an "incumbency protection" plan. See Charles J. Cooper & Derek L. Shaffer, *What Congress "Shall Make" The Court Will Take: How* McConnell v. FEC *Betrays the First Amendment in Upholding Incumbency Protection Under the Banner of "Campaign Finance Reform,"* 3 ELECTION LAW JOURNAL 223 (2004). What role *should* a concern about incumbency protection play in evaluating the constitutionality of a campaign contribution limit?

5. What is the significance of Justice Alito's concurrence? Has he committed himself to upholding *any* campaign contribution limits in the future? Has Chief Justice Roberts?

III. The End of Soft Money and the Regulation of PACs and Other Independent Expenditure Committees

A. BCRA and the End of Soft Money

After six years of failed attempts, and with impetus from an accounting scandal involving the Enron Corporation that became a hot political issue, Congress passed the most significant campaign finance changes since 1974. The campaign finance proposals had been known as the "McCain-Feingold" and "Shays-Meehan" bills before passage (named for their primary sponsors in the Senate and House, respectively), but campaign finance practitioners now refer to the law under its official title, the Bipartisan Campaign Reform Act of 2002, Pub. L. 107-155, 116 Stat. 81, or "BCRA." The law is quite complex and a whole book could be devoted to constitutional and statutory questions related to it.[f]

BCRA did much on the spending limits side of things in relation to corporations and labor unions, in developments described in the next chapter. But it also made significant changes, considered here, to the rules related to contribution limits. Putting aside much detail, the bill increased the individual campaign contribution limit to $2,000 per election (indexed, for the first time, to inflation), keeping the $5,000 contribution limit to PACs from individuals and from PACs to candidates the same. The law also barred various practices related to the raising of "soft money." In McCONNELL v. FEC, 540 U.S. 93 (2003), the Court described the rise of soft money and the emergence of BCRA's new rules as follows:

> Under FECA, "contributions" must be made with funds that are subject to the Act's disclosure requirements and source and amount limitations. Such funds are known as "federal" or "hard" money. FECA defines the term "contribution," however, to include only the gift or advance of anything of value "made by any person for the purpose of influencing any election for *Federal* office." Donations made solely for the purpose of influencing state or local elections are therefore unaffected by FECA's requirements and prohibitions. As a result, prior to the enactment of BCRA, federal law permitted corporations and unions, as well as individuals who had already made the maximum permissible contributions to federal candidates, to contribute "nonfederal money"—also known as "soft money"—to political parties for activities intended to influence state or local elections.
>
> Shortly after *Buckley* was decided, questions arose concerning the treatment of contributions intended to influence both federal and state elections. Although a literal reading of FECA's definition of "contribution" would have required such activities to be funded with hard money, the FEC ruled that political parties could fund mixed-purpose activities—including get-out-the-vote drives and generic party advertising—in part with soft money. In 1995 the FEC concluded that the parties could also use soft money to defray the costs of "legislative advocacy media advertisements," even if the ads mentioned the name of a federal candidate, so long as they did not expressly advocate the candidate's election or defeat.
>
> As the permissible uses of soft money expanded, the amount of soft money raised and spent by the national political parties increased exponentially. Of the two major parties' total spending, soft money accounted for 5% ($21.6 million) in 1984, 11% ($45 million) in 1988, 16% ($30 million) in 1992, 30% ($272 million) in 1996, and 42% ($98 million) in 2000. The national parties transferred large amounts of their soft money to the state parties, which were allowed to use a larger percentage of soft money to finance mixed-purpose activities under FEC rules. In the year 2000, for example, the national parties diverted $ 280 million—more than half of their soft money—to state parties.

---

f. In fact, one already has. See Robert Bauer, MORE SOFT MONEY, HARD LAW: THE SECOND EDITION OF THE GUIDE TO THE NEW CAMPAIGN FINANCE LAW (2004) (offering, with good humor, a guide to the statute's intricacies).

Many contributions of soft money were dramatically larger than the contributions of hard money permitted by FECA. For example, in 1996 the top five corporate soft-money donors gave, in total, more than $9 million in nonfederal funds to the two national party committees. In the most recent election cycle the political parties raised almost $300 million—60% of their total soft-money fundraising—from just 800 donors, each of which contributed a minimum of $120,000. Moreover, the largest corporate donors often made substantial contributions to both parties. Such practices corroborate evidence indicating that many corporate contributions were motivated by a desire for access to candidates and a fear of being placed at a disadvantage in the legislative process relative to other contributors, rather than by ideological support for the candidates and parties.

Not only were such soft-money contributions often designed to gain access to federal candidates, but they were in many cases solicited by the candidates themselves. Candidates often directed potential donors to party committees and tax-exempt organizations that could legally accept soft money. For example, a federal legislator running for reelection solicited soft money from a supporter by advising him that even though he had already "contributed the legal maximum" to the campaign committee, he could still make an additional contribution to a joint program supporting federal, state, and local candidates of his party. Such solicitations were not uncommon.

The solicitation, transfer, and use of soft money thus enabled parties and candidates to circumvent FECA's limitations on the source and amount of contributions in connection with federal elections....

Title I is Congress' effort to plug the soft-money loophole. The cornerstone of Title I is new FECA §323(a), which prohibits national party committees and their agents from soliciting, receiving, directing, or spending any soft money. In short, §323(a) takes national parties out of the soft-money business.

The remaining provisions of new FECA §323 largely reinforce the restrictions in §323(a). New FECA §323(b) prevents the wholesale shift of soft-money influence from national to state party committees by prohibiting state and local party committees from using such funds for activities that affect federal elections. These "Federal election activities," defined in new FECA §301(20)(A), are almost identical to the mixed-purpose activities that have long been regulated under the FEC's pre-BCRA allocation regime. New FECA §323(d) reinforces these soft-money restrictions by prohibiting political parties from soliciting and donating funds to tax-exempt organizations that engage in electioneering activities. New FECA §323(e) restricts federal candidates and officeholders from receiving, spending, or soliciting soft money in connection with federal elections and limits their ability to do so in connection with state and local elections. Finally, new FECA §323(f) prevents circumvention of the restrictions on national, state, and local party committees by prohibiting state and local candidates from raising and spending soft money to fund advertisements and other public communications that promote or attack federal candidates.

The following table from the FEC describes current federal contribution limits that were in effect, post-BCRA, for the 2007–08 election season.

Federal Contribution Limits 2007–08					
	To each candidate or candidate committee per election	To national party committee per calendar year	To state, district & local party committee per calendar year	To any other political committee per calendar year[1]	Special Limits
Individual may give	$2,300*	$28,500*	$10,000 (combined limit)	$5,000	$108,200* overall biennial limit: • $42,700* to all candidates • $65,500* to all PACs and parties[2]
National Party Committee may give	$5,000	No limit	No limit	$5,000	$39,900* to Senate candidate per campaign[3]
State, District & Local Party Committee may give	$5,000 (combined limit)	No limit	No limit	$5,000 (combined limit)	No limit
PAC (multican-didate)[4] may give	$5,000	$15,000	$5,000 (combined limit)	$5,000	No limit
PAC (not multican-didate) may give	$2,300*	$28,500*	$10,000 (combined limit)	$5,000	No limit
Authorized Campaign Committee may give	$2,000[5]	No limit	No limit	$5,000	No limit

Source: FEC website, http://www.fec.gov/pages/brochures/contriblimits.shtml (visited Sept. 28, 2007)

* These contribution limits are increased for inflation in odd-numbered years.

1 A contribution earmarked for a candidate through a political committee counts against the original contributor's limit for that candidate. In certain circumstances, the contribution may also count against the contributor's limit to the PAC. 11 CFR 110.6. See also 11 CFR 110.1(h).

2 No more than $42,700 of this amount may be contributed to state and local party committees and PACs.

3 This limit is shared by the national committee and the Senate campaign committee.

4 A multicandidate committee is a political committee with more than 50 contributors which has been registered for at least 6 months and, with the exception of state party committees, has made contributions to 5 or more candidates for federal office. 11 CFR 100.5(e)(3).

5 A federal candidate's authorized committee(s) may contribute no more than $2,000 per election to another federal candidate's authorized committee(s). 2 U.S.C. 432(e)(3)(B).

President Bush signed BCRA into law despite expressing reservations about the constitutionality of several of its provisions. Immediately upon the President signing the bill, it was challenged in federal court, first by the National Rifle Association and then by a varied collection of groups and individuals including Senator Mitch McConnell, a leading opponent of campaign finance regulation. The cases were consolidated under the name *McConnell v. Federal Election Commission,* and heard, under expedited procedures set forth in the Act, by a three-judge district court in Washington D.C. with direct appeal to the Supreme Court. The three judges hearing the case were District Court judges Colleen Kollar-Kotelly and Richard Leon and D.C. Circuit Court judge Karen LeCraft Henderson.

The three judges on the panel issued four opinions in the case, *McConnell v. Federal Election Commission,* 251 F. Supp. 2d 176 (D.D.C. 2003), totaling an astounding 1,638 typescript pages (a mere 774 pages in the printed volume). First came a *per curiam* opinion joined by Judges Kollar-Kotelly and Leon dealing with general issues and some of the law's disclosure provisions. But the *per curiam* opinion did not address the great majority of issues, including the most controversial ones. The bulk of the court's product appeared in individual opinions by each of the three judges. In broad terms, Judge Kollar-Kotelly upheld most of BCRA, while Judge Henderson regarded much of it as unconstitutional. Judge Leon took an in-between position, so that with few exceptions, his views were decisive.

The Supreme Court issued its decision in December 2003, upholding most of the BCRA, including the soft money and issue advocacy provisions (the latter of which are discussed in the next chapter). The opinions had the largest U.S. Reports page count (279, excluding the heading and syllabus) and second largest word count (89,694) in Supreme Court history.

The Court's majority opinion was divided into three parts, with Justices Stevens and O'Connor jointly writing the opinion for the Court as to the constitutionality of challenged provisions of BCRA's Title I and Title II, the act's soft money and issue advocacy provisions. Chief Justice Rehnquist and Justice Breyer each wrote opinions for the Court on other challenged provisions.

Although the opinion was long and the issues important, *McConnell* is doctrinally not as important as the *Shrink Missouri* case, and *McConnell*'s upholding of BCRA's soft money provisions followed rather naturally from the *Shrink Missouri* case and *Colorado II. McConnell* was decided before *Randall.* Consider whether anything in *McConnell* is altered by *Randall.*

McConnell's greatest doctrinal significance came in its further relaxation of the definition of corruption. Consider Richard Briffault, McConnell v. FEC *and the Transformation of Campaign Finance Law,* 3 ELECTION LAW JOURNAL 147, 162–63 (2004):

> Although the Court had previously made clear that corruption was not limited to outright vote-buying, the Court's language of undue influence had nonetheless focused on the effects of large contributions on government decision-making. By focusing on special access, *McConnell* reframed the corruption analysis from the consideration of the impact of contributions on formal decisions to their effect on the *opportunity to influence* government actions. While surely the ultimate concern with special opportunities for influence is with the effect of such influence on legislation, regulation, and other actions, the Court treated preferential access as a problem in itself, and found that Congress could take steps to eliminate a campaign finance device that created special incentives to officeholders to give special access to donors.

Consider also Lillian R. BeVier, McConnell v. FEC: *Not Senator Buckley's First Amendment*, 3 ELECTION LAW JOURNAL 127, 136 (2004):

> The *McConnell* Court [defined] corruption even more broadly than it did in *Shrink Missouri* or *Colorado II*. It defined corruption as the exchange of *access* to office-holders for soft-money contributions, and it gave its blessing to regulating soft money contributions "[e]ven if that access did not secure actual influence, [because] it certainly gave the 'appearance of such influence.'"

> Thus, in sustaining BCRA's soft money ban the *McConnell* majority effectively discarded two aspects of *Buckley*. It discarded its premise of distrust and it discarded its implicit commitment strictly to supervise the conception of corruption that would permit Congress to restrict campaign speech.

While this book was in press, the Supreme Court struck down another provision of BCRA, Section 319, known to its friends and enemies as the "Millionaire's Amendment." *Davis v. Federal Elections Commission*, 128 S. Ct. 2759 (2008). To simplify slightly, the Millionaire's Amendment allowed candidates running against self-financed opponents to accept contributions from individuals up to three times larger than the usual contribution limits. Justice Alito, writing for the Court, likened the increased contribution limits to expenditure limits, applied strict scrutiny, and struck them down. Justices Stevens, Souter, Ginsburg, and Breyer dissented.

B. PACs, 527s, and Independent Expenditure Committees

In the wake of the BCRA and the *McConnell* decision, those corporations and unions wishing to influence the outcome of federal elections looked for new avenues. One possible avenue is the political action committee (or "PAC").[g] As we will see in the next chapter, corporations and unions cannot spend their general treasury funds on certain election-related activities. Instead, they may solicit contributions of up to $5,000 for their PACs. PACs, whether or not they are sponsored by a corporation or union, may make contributions of up to $5,000 per election to federal candidates, and spend unlimited sums supporting or opposing candidates for federal office. Corporate and union PACs are restricted on whom they may solicit.[h] *See Federal Election Commission v. National*

---

g. "PAC," or "political action committee," is not a term that appears in the FECA. Most PACs are "multicandidate political committees," which the Act defines as "a political committee which has been registered ... for a period of not less than 6 months, which has received contributions from more than 50 persons, and, except for any state political party organization, has made contributions to 5 or more candidates for Federal office." 2 U.S.C. §441a(a)(4). A committee must qualify as a multicandidate political committee in order to be eligible for the $5,000 limit on contributions to federal candidates, as opposed to the $1,000 limit that is applicable to individuals and other entities. A "separate segregated fund" of a corporation or union will ordinarily qualify as a multicandidate political committee—or, in popular language, as a PAC.

h. The provisions in Section 441b(b)(4), specifying the individuals who may be solicited by corporate and labor PACs, were added to the FECA in 1976. In a controversial opinion the previous year, the Federal Election Commission had ruled by a 4–2 vote that corporations could solicit stockholders and employees. FEC Advisory Opinion 1975–23 (Sun Oil Co.) (1975). Many Democrats and union leaders had urged that corporations be limited to soliciting stockholders. Corporate leaders and many Republicans, recognizing that employees were much more likely than stockholders to contribute to corporate PACs, strenuously argued the contrary. The 1976 statutory amendments limited corporate PACs to soliciting "executive or administrative personnel." Although on the face of it this represented

Right to Work Committee, 459 U.S. 197 (1982) (*NRWC*), upholding the constitutionality of the solicitation rules.

Labor union PACs commonly collect contributions by a "check-off" procedure, whereby members sign an authorization to have a small amount deducted from each paycheck. Suppose a union PAC uses a "reverse check-off," whereby the contribution is withheld from each member's paycheck unless the member submits a request that the contribution *not* be withheld? Is such a system constitutional? See *FEC v. National Education Association*, 457 F. Supp. 1102 (D.D.C. 1978). A Michigan statute requiring union members to reaffirm annually their desire to contribute to a union PAC was upheld in a 2–1 decision in *Michigan State AFL-CIO v. Miller*, 103 F.3d 1240 (6th Cir. 1997). Disagreeing with *Miller*, the Washington state supreme court, with three justices dissenting, struck down a state statute passed by initiative requiring public sector union members to "opt in" before the union could deduct from union member paychecks monies used for political purposes. *Washington State Public Disclosure Commission v. Washington Education Association*, 130 P.3d 352 (Wash. 2006) (en banc). The U.S. Supreme Court unanimously reversed, holding that a state does not violate the First Amendment when it requires public sector union members to opt in before their fees are spent for election-related purposes. *Davenport v. Washington Educ. Ass'n*, 127 S.Ct. 2372 (2007). Whether the ruling applies to private sector employees remains to be seen.

The restrictions on solicitation of contributions by PACs in 2 U.S.C. §441b apply to corporate and labor union PACs, which have the offsetting advantage of being able to use treasury funds of the sponsoring corporations and unions to pay their administrative expenses. This is no trivial advantage, as the administrative expenses often exceed the money received from contributors and donated to candidates.

In the 2004 election, business interests "sponsored 59 percent of all PACs. Labor PACs accounted for less than 7 percent of the PAC community, and nonconnected PACs, including ideological PACs and PACs associated with federal candidates, made up the remaining 34 percent." Paul S. Herrnson, *Financing the 2004 Congressional Elections* 149, 159, in Financing the 2004 Election (David B. Magleby, Anthony Corrado, and Kelly D. Patterson, eds. 2006). The bare numbers of PACs do not say much about political influence. "Less than 14 percent of all PACs made almost 82 percent of all contributions to congressional candidates in 2004." *Id.* Unsurprisingly, corporate PACs tended to contribute more funds to Republicans, and labor PACs more to Democrats. *Id.* at 160.

The total number of federal political action committees grew rapidly in the first decade following the 1974 amendments to the FECA, and then leveled off. At the end of 1974, 608 PACs were registered with the FEC. According to the most recent FEC data, compiled in July 2007, the number was 4,168. FEC, "Number of Federal PACs Decrease," July 10, 2007, http://www.fec.gov/press/press2007/20070710paccount.shtml.

PACs have played some role, but not a dominating role, in federal election campaigns, primarily because of the $5,000 contribution limits to PACs. Thus, PACs cannot serve as a conduit for campaign contributions of large individuals. Nor can they take general treasury funds from corporations or labor unions (except to pay for administrative expenses). Still, PACs contributed $289.1 million to congressional candidates in 2004. Herrnson, *supra*.

Some wealthy individuals, along with some corporations and labor unions, looked for post-BCRA ways to contribute sums larger than $5,000 to non-PAC organizations geared

---

a compromise, as a practical matter it was a smashing victory for corporate PACs, whose expenditures increased rapidly and dramatically. In 1976, corporate PACs spent a total of $5.8 million. Corporate PAC spending exceeded $158 million in the 1999–2000 election period.

to influence federal elections. In the 2004 election, certain groups organized under section 527 of the Internal Revenue Code began accepting large donations to make electioneering communications in connection with the 2004 federal elections. The groups claimed they were not operating as "political committees" as defined in FECA, because they made no contributions to candidates and did not expressly advocate the election or defeat of candidates for office.

Although these groups have been set up for both parties, in the 2004 election the largest were Democratic groups supporting John Kerry against George Bush. The resulting controversy was pervasively ironic, as Republicans and many former opponents of BCRA claimed that it is illegal for individuals to make large donations to these groups for these purposes. Democrats and many liberals who had supported BCRA as a means of plugging loopholes called for a narrower construction to leave the section 527 organizations unregulated. As a matter of statutory interpretation, at least some of these organizations might be considered political committees because their "major purpose" is to influence federal elections, even if they fail to engage in express advocacy. Individual donations to political committees are capped at $5,000 under the FECA.

Section 527 organizations played a major role in the 2004 election, with one estimate placing their spending at nearly $400 million in the 2004 federal elections. Steve Weissman & Ruth Hassan, *BCRA and the 527 Groups*, in THE ELECTION AFTER REFORM: MONEY, POLITICS, AND THE BIPARTISAN CAMPAIGN REFORM ACT (Michael J. Malbin, ed., 2007). George Soros topped the list of individual donors to 527s at $24 million, though labor unions in the aggregate gave about 4 times as much as Soros to pro-Democratic 527s. http://www.opensecrets.org/527s/.

Some criticized the Federal Election Commission for not regulating 527s as political committees during the 2004 election season. Treating 527s as political committees would have a number of consequences, most importantly limiting contributions *to* such committees to $5,000 per person. The former chair of the FEC and his legal counsel defended the FEC's inaction, arguing that regulation of 527s would have exceeded the FEC's authority. Allison R. Hayward & Bradley A. Smith, *Don't Shoot the Messenger: The FEC, 527 Groups, and the Scope of Administrative Authority*, 4 ELECTION LAW JOURNAL 82 (2004). After the 2004 election, the action moved to Congress, where bills were introduced in both the House and Senate to change the rules related to 527s. But no bills passed, either when Republicans or Democrats controlled Congress. Meanwhile 527s were active in the 2006 elections, but did not spend at the levels seen in 2004. See Stephen R. Weissman & Kara D. Ryan, *Soft Money in the 2006 Election and the Outlook for 2008: The Changing Nonprofits Landscape*, Campaign Finance Institute, at 3, http://cfinst.org/books_reports/pdf/NP_Soft-Money_06-08.pdf.

Reform groups sued the FEC for failing to issue rules setting forth when 527s would be treated as political committees. The FEC responded by settling with some 527 groups that failed to register as political committees, fining others, and issuing an "Explanation and Justification" explaining what factors it would take into account in deciding on a 527's political committee status. A federal district court upheld the FEC's decision to judge 527s on a case-by-case basis. *Shays v. Federal Election Commission*, 511 F. Supp. 2d 19 (D.D.C. 2007). An appeal is pending.

As the FEC begins to regulate 527 organizations, albeit on a case-by-case basis, some election-related activity is expected to shift to 501(c) organizations and newer "taxable" nonprofits. See Weissman & Ryan, *supra*, at 3. There are limits on how much election-related activity beyond "[c]ompiling and circulating lawmakers' voting records and voter guides" 501(c)(3)'s may engage in without jeopardizing their non-profit status. Miriam Galston, *Emerging Constitutional Paradigms and Justifications for Campaign Finance Regulation: The Case of 527 Groups*, 95 GEORGETOWN LAW JOURNAL 1181, 1193 (2007). Other 501(c) organizations apparently are permitted more election-related activity, though the overlay of election law and tax law makes navigating in this area exceedingly complex. Weissman & Ryan, *supra* at 6–7, explain:

> Social welfare organizations [organized under section 501(c)(4) of the tax code], labor unions [501(c)(5)s] and business associations [(501(c)(6)s] have been growing in importance in federal elections. They may get a further boost from the new FEC constraints because they primarily affect 527s. Under federal tax and election law respectively, these 501(c)s have been permitted to use unlimited soft money contributions to conduct virtually the same election activities as 527s, as long as "political campaign intervention" or "federal campaign activity" is not their "primary" activity or "major purpose." Unlike 527s, 501(c)s' contributions and expenditures are largely *undisclosed* to the public. Yet it is clear from available information that corporate and union treasuries and large donors are major financing sources.
>
> Although the new FEC enforcement regime applies to 501(c) "advocacy" groups as well as 527 political organizations, it appears the former will not be treated as federal political committees if they comply with the Internal Revenue Service's requirement that political campaign intervention be secondary to their social welfare, labor union, or trade association roles. As a result, the FEC rulings appear to leave the 501(c)s largely untouched. In theory, such groups are subject, under the Internal Revenue Code, to a 35% tax on either their political campaign expenditures or their investment income, whichever is lower. In practice, weak enforcement by the IRS and low investment income can often neutralize this constraint.

Weissman and Ryan wrote these words before the Supreme Court's decision in *Federal Election Commission v. Wisconsin Right to Life*, discussed in the next chapter. The decision may lessen the need for corporations and labor unions to use these 501(c) organizations for election-related activities in the 2008 elections.

Even if Congress or the FEC eventually decides to regulate 527s and similar organizations more aggressively, there remains the question whether such regulation is constitutional as to those groups that engage only in making *independent* expenditures. Consider the following analysis.

Richard Briffault, The 527 Problem … and the *Buckley* Problem

73 GEORGE WASHINGTON LAW REVIEW 959, 981–990, 999 (2005)

III. The Constitutional Questions Posed by Applying FECA to 527 Organizations …

D. The Limit on Individual Donations

The most serious consequence of classifying a 527 as a FECA political committee would be the application of FECA's limit on individual contributions. FECA caps individual donations to political committees other than candidate or party committees to $5000 per year. This limit, unlike the statutory ceilings on contributions to candidates and to party committees, is not adjusted for inflation and has not been increased since 1974. In the 2004 election, the principal 527s received $256 million from individuals in amounts above the $5000 cap, or about sixty-three percent of these 527s' funds. These contributions averaged around $135,000, or twenty-seven times the statutory cap. Applying the FECA individual contribution limit would dramatically limit 527 fundraising and could drastically curtail their operations.

Applying this cap also raises a difficult constitutional question — a question that also applies to the donation cap on all noncandidate, nonparty political committees that engage exclusively in independent expenditures and do not make contributions to candidates or parties, or coordinated expenditures with candidates or parties.

The difficulty emerges out of the tension within the central holding of *Buckley v. Valeo*: The First Amendment permits the government to limit campaign finance activities in order to prevent the corruption of officeholders and the appearance of the corruption of officeholders, but not to equalize the influence of different individuals or groups to affect the outcome of elections. Contributions to candidates can thus be limited because a large contribution raises the danger "of a political quid pro quo" and "public awareness of the opportunities for abuse inherent in a regime of large individual financial contributions" undermines confidence in our system of government. So too, contributions to organizations that make contributions to candidates, and expenditures that such organizations coordinate with the candidates they support, can be limited to prevent circumvention of the limit on contributions to candidates. But candidate expenditures and independent expenditures — that is, expenditures for campaign activities aimed at the voters that are not coordinated with any candidate — may not be limited because they present no danger of corruption. And the "governmental interest in equalizing the relative ability of individuals and groups to influence the outcome of elections" cannot support a limit on campaign speech. If the First Amendment prohibits any limitation on how much money an independent political committee can spend on an independent-expenditure campaign, how can it permit limits on donations to committees that make only independent expenditures? In other words, if George Soros's direct expenditure of $23 million on anti-Bush or pro-Kerry ads is constitutionally protected, how does he forfeit that protection if he combines his $23 million with $20 million from Peter Lewis and maybe another $10 million from some slightly smaller fry in a fund that takes out essentially the same ads and supports the same voter drives?

Buckley upheld FECA's limit on donations to candidates, its limit on donations by political committees to candidates, and its aggregate limit on all contributions an individual can make to candidates and political committees in a calendar year. It did not, however, specifically discuss the limits on donations to political committees. Arguably, the Court may have resolved the issue when it upheld the aggregate annual cap, because that implicitly limits total individual donations to particular committees. Buckley determined that the annual aggregate limit

> serves to prevent evasion of the $1000 contribution limitation [on individual donations to candidates] by a person who might otherwise contribute massive amounts of money to a particular candidate through the use of unearmarked contributions to political committees likely to contribute to that candidate, or huge contributions to the candidate's political party.

This analysis clearly assumes, however, that donations to political committees could be limited because such committees function as conduits passing along the donations to candidates. As a result, this statement left open the question of whether a limit can be imposed on donations to committees that are not conduits because they make only independent expenditures.

Two Supreme Court decisions provide support for the argument that if an independent expenditure does not present a danger of corrupting or appearing to corrupt officeholders, then contributions to a political committee that makes only independent expenditures cannot be limited. Five years after *Buckley*, in *California Medical Ass'n v. FEC* (*CalMed*), the Court upheld the application of FECA's limit on donations to a political committee in a case involving contributions by a trade association to its own PAC. There would seem to be little danger that a trade association could corrupt its own PAC; however, the plurality opinion by Justice Marshall emphasized that the limit on donations to political committees prevented circumvention of the limit on direct contributions to candidates. The key fifth vote was provided by Justice Blackmun, who, in a concurring opinion, agreed that the limit on donations to a political committee could be upheld "as a means of preventing evasion of the limitations on contributions to a candidate." Justice Blackmun, however, went on to suggest that "a different result would follow" if the donation cap "were applied to contributions to a political committee established for the purpose of making independent expenditures, rather than contributions to candidates," because "a committee that makes only independent expenditures poses no ... threat" of corruption or the appearance of corruption. In his view, the pooling of contributions to fund independent expenditures was constitutionally protected.

Although technically dictum in *CalMed*, Justice Blackmun's position was bolstered by another decision later that year, *Citizens Against Rent Control v. City of Berkeley* (*CARC*), in which the Court invalidated a municipal cap on contributions to committees formed to support or oppose ballot propositions. Having previously ruled that ballot proposition campaigns do not present a danger of corruption because they do not involve the election of a candidate, the Court easily struck down the limit on a contribution to a ballot proposition committee as a "significant restraint on the freedom of expression of groups and those individuals who wish to express their views through committees" unjustified by the interest in preventing corruption.

CARC is significant in underscoring the connection between contribution limits and the prevention of corruption. One strand of *Buckley* emphasized that limits on contributions are to receive less exacting judicial scrutiny than limits on expenditures because contributions are a lower order of speech than expenditures. An expenditure aimed at the voters directly involves the communication of political ideas, whereas a contribution to a candidate "serves as a general expression of support for the candidate and his views, but does not communicate the underlying basis for the support." In other words, the critical political expression conveyed by the contribution is the fact of the donor's support for a candidate. The amount contributed may be limited because that does not interfere with the "symbolic expression of support evidenced by a contribution." Nonetheless, as *CARC* confirms, contribution limits do infringe on freedom of speech and, especially, on the freedom of a donor to associate with like-minded donors in order to "pool[ ] their resources to amplify their voices." There must be some "legitimate governmental interest significant enough to justify its infringement of First Amendment rights." As the Court recently restated the test, even though strict scrutiny is not applied to contribution restrictions, "a contribution limit involving significant interference with associational rights" must still satisfy "the lesser demand of being closely drawn to match a sufficiently important interest." That interest has consistently been the prevention of corruption and the appearance of corruption.

CalMed and *CARC* together indicate that in order to avoid circumvention of the limits on contributions to candidates it is constitutional to limit the size of individual donations to political committees, including 527s, that make contributions to federal candidates or coordinate their expenditures with federal candidates and also engage in independent expenditures. This position is clearly confirmed by *McConnell*, which upheld BCRA's limits on contributions to the political parties. The First Amendment does not require that the contribution limits on donations to political committees be limited to funds that the committees will use for contributions to or coordinated expenditures with candidates. As the Supreme Court has observed, such an approach "ignores the practical difficulty of identifying and directly combating circumvention under actual political conditions." The uses of specific contributions are "very hard to trace," so that Congress may require that all funds that flow into organizations that make contributions to or coordinate expenditures with candidates are subject to dollar limits in order to avoid circumvention of the limits on donations to candidates. But if, as is the case for many if not most 527s, a political committee makes no contribution to a candidate at all, the anticircumvention argument does not apply. The Blackmun concurrence in *CalMed* and the majority decision in *CARC* together suggest that it would be unconstitutional to limit donations to a political committee whose spending does not present a danger of corruption.

To be sure, proponents of applying the individual donation limits to independent expenditure 527s and other political committees can argue that the Blackmun concurrence in *CalMed* is mere dictum, while *CARC* dealt with a ballot proposition election, and the Court has consistently held that spending in ballot proposition elections enjoys greater protection, and is less subject to restriction, than spending in candidate elections. Moreover, they can argue that a footnote in *McConnell* resolves the question.

In response to Justice Kennedy's dissenting argument that Congress can limit only contributions made directly to candidates and not contributions to parties, the *McConnell* majority returned to *Buckley*'s affirmation of FECA's limits on aggregate individual donations, cited *CalMed*, and then asserted that "[i]t is no answer to say that such limits were justified as a means of preventing individuals from using parties and political committees as pass-throughs to circumvent FECA's $1000 limit on individual contributions to candidates" because, as the Court noted, FECA's donation limits would also curtail the funds available to political committees not only for contributions to candidates, but also for independent expenditures. "If indeed the First Amendment prohibited Congress from regulating contributions to fund the latter, the otherwise-easy-to-remedy exploitation of parties as pass-throughs (e.g., a strict limit on donations that could be used to fund candidate contributions) would have provided insufficient justification for such overbroad legislation." In other words, according to the *McConnell* footnote, *Buckley* implicitly but definitively upheld the constitutionality of the limits on contributions to political committees, even if such a contribution limit is not fully supported by the anticorruption rationale.

Yet, it is not clear that even the *McConnell* footnote and its reading of *Buckley* would sustain limits on donations to committees that spend exclusively on independent expenditures. The committees at issue in *Buckley* and *CalMed* made contributions to federal candidates as well as engaged in independent expenditures. The Court might have been concerned about slippage between the two activities so that money given for independent advocacy might somehow wind up paying for contributions. As previously noted, the Court has permitted restrictions on contributions to organizations that both contribute to (or coordinate expenditures with) candidates and engage in independent expenditures because of "the practical difficulties of identifying and directly combating circumvention under actual political conditions." A cap on all donations to such an organization would advance the goal of preventing circumvention of the limits on gifts to candidates. But it is not clear that the *McConnell* footnote's reading of *Buckley* and *CalMed* resolves the question of limits on donations to committees that engage solely in independent spending.

More importantly, the *McConnell* footnote was written in the course of the Court's analysis of BCRA's application of contribution limits to the activities of political parties. Indeed, a central question in the emerging debate over 527 regulation is whether 527s can be regulated just like political parties. Much of the impetus for the regulation of 527s results from the sense that with political party soft money now largely eliminated by BCRA, the 527s have taken over the financing role formerly played by parties and, so, ought to be subject to the same rules as apply to parties. Treating 527s as comparable to parties, Senator Lott has called for limits on donations to the 527s in order to maintain a "level playing field." As Senator McCain put it, "[s]ection 527 groups need to play by the rules that candidates, political parties and all other political committees play by."

But are 527s just like political parties? Looking to their electoral purpose, Professor Foley contends that they are:

> Political committees—even those that operate independently from parties and their candidates—share an essential feature with political parties: they exist to win elections.... They are not merely ideological organizations that happen to participate in election-specific activities incidental to their ideological mission. Rather their reason for being is specifically electoral: their central mission is to secure the election or defeat of a candidate.

Professor Ortiz stresses the power 527s, even those engaging solely in independent expenditures, can exercise in elections. Quoting one of the Supreme Court's statements about parties, he notes that 527s share with parties the "'capacity to concentrate power to elect'" candidates. Their activities "can have a great impact on a candidate's election.... Nothing suggests, in fact, that 527 ... spending is much less effective than spending by the candidates and parties themselves." Professor Malbin argues that with individual donations to candidate and party committees subject to statutory limits, "big 527 donors today are positioned to garner more attention and consideration from parties and candidates." Professors Foley and Ortiz agree that, given the large and growing electoral role of the 527s and the benefits they provide to candidates, large donations to these committees will "create influence over and access to federal candidates," thereby justifying regulation in order to prevent corruption.

But 527s and other independent-expenditure political committees do differ from political parties in significant ways. As the Supreme Court explained in *McConnell*, "federal candidates and officeholders enjoy a special relationship and unity of interest" with their parties. Most federal candidates run for office on party ballot lines, and the party line itself provides the candidate with a unique electoral benefit. Members of Congress sit in party caucuses, and the Congress, including its committees, is organized on party lines. The president is a partisan who was nominated by his party, ran on a party line, and is the de facto head of his party. Prior to BCRA, candidates and officeholders were actively involved in raising party funds, explaining to potential donors how contributions to the parties could benefit candidates' campaigns. *McConnell* found that this had a direct effect on the legislative process. In raising soft money, party leaders dangled before potential contributors access to federal executive and legislative officeholders as an inducement to contribute. Moreover, as the Court found, "[t]he national committees of the two major parties are both run by, and largely composed of, federal officeholders and candidates." This "close connection and alignment of interests" between parties and candidates means that "large soft-money contributions to national parties are likely to create actual or apparent indebtedness on the part of federal officeholders, regardless of how those funds are ultimately used." So too, "the close ties between federal candidates and state party committees," reflected in national party direction of soft funds to the state parties and federal candidates fundraising for state parties, support special regulation of the federal election activities of the state parties.

The 527s, by contrast, have no comparable ties to candidates. They do not control lines on state ballots. They are not the basis for the organization of Congress. Federal candidates and officeholders do not sit on their boards. No federal candidates or officeholders were involved in 527 fundraising, and opportunities for special access to federal officials were not provided in exchange for large donations. To be sure, many of the principal organizers and leaders of the 527s have long track records of committed partisanship or ongoing business ties to current party organizations, and the 527s used their funds consistently to support the candidates of one party or the other. But that is not quite the same thing as the structural and institutional interconnection that marks the candidate-party relationship.

Ultimately, the argument that Congress may treat 527 committees like parties for the purpose of the limit on individual donations boils down to two closely related points. First, donations to 527s can be limited because 527 spending benefits candidates, the candidates are "vividly" aware of the megadonations that fund such spending, and thus, "large-dollar contributions to political committees present risks of improper influence that are essentially the same as large-dollar contributions to political parties." Second, donations to independent-expenditure political committees can be limited to prevent circumvention of the limits on donations to candidates and parties.

With respect to the first point, the Supreme Court has never said that benefit to the candidate, with the inference that the candidate will be grateful for the benefit and will be tempted to provide favors accordingly, is enough to support regulation of campaign money. Indeed, *McConnell* clearly held that benefit (even benefit followed by gratitude and temptation) is not sufficient to justify a campaign restriction. In upholding BCRA's donations to state and local parties for federal election activity, the Court gave great weight to the benefits these activities provide federal candidates. This led Chief Justice Rehnquist, in dissent, to assert that the Court's rationale would necessarily apply to "[n]ewspaper editorials and political talk shows [that] benefit federal candidates and officeholders every bit as much as a generic voter registration drive conducted by a state party." The majority, however, responded that benefit to a candidate alone could not justify campaign finance regulation: "We agree with the Chief Justice that Congress could not regulate financial contributions to political talk show hosts or newspaper editors on the sole basis that their activities conferred a benefit on the candidate." Rather, "[t]he close relationship of federal officeholders and candidates to their parties" limited the scope of the benefit principle and "answer[ed] … the Chief Justice's concerns."

The anticircumvention argument runs up against a similar difficulty. To be sure, *McConnell* significantly extended the anticircumvention rationale, picking up not only the national political parties and state and local political parties, but also political-party support for politically active tax-exempt organizations (including 527s), and expenditures of state and local candidates and officeholders on public communications that promote or oppose a clearly identified candidate for federal office. In so doing, the Court relied on the long history of candidate and donor circumvention of the restrictions on contributions to candidates and deferred to Congress's judgment concerning which organizations or individuals are likely to emerge as "the next conduits" for the soft-money funding of election-related ads.

But, as the term "conduit" implies, every single one of these measures involved transactions through the parties and thus, bearing in mind the structural connection between parties and candidates, a link to federal candidates. BCRA's provisions concerning tax-exempt organizations focused on direct party solicitation for, or donations to, the tax-exempt organizations, thereby clearly triggering the anticircumvention rationale. The state and local candidates are presumably running on the same ballot lines as their fellow partisan federal candidates, and officeholders are likely to be party members. Party membership provides the link directly connecting state candidates to federal candidates. Moreover, the BCRA restriction affects only funds used to pay for the ... public communications of state and local candidates and officeholders [that support or oppose federal candidates]. The Senate's 527 Reform Act, which does not rely on any structural connection to parties or candidates, sweeps far broader, picking up and capping all contributions, regardless of the activity funded.

Descriptively, it seems correct to say that the movement of some individual funds from party soft-money accounts to 527s was a direct response to BCRA and represents the continuing efforts of wealthy individuals to deploy their funds in federal elections. Given the absence of a direct nexus to federal candidates or to intermediary organizations connected to federal candidates, however, it is not clear that this is "circumvention" of the limits on donations to candidates and parties in the sense used in *McConnell*.

The "benefit" and anticircumvention arguments both operate on the assumption that the key factor supporting limits on donations to 527s is that the 527s' expenditures are, in Professor Foley's term, "election-focused," and thus can have an impact on the election. But *Buckley* rejected election-relatedness as a test for limiting campaign money and instead looked for a connection to candidates in order to support a finding that the donation raised a danger of corruption. To find that donations to independent committees can be limited because they have an impact on the election — and to infer the possibility of corruption from the mere fact of electoral impact with connection to a candidate — is in deep tension with *Buckley*'s rejection of spending limits for independent expenditures. The proponents of limiting individual contributions to 527 committees are no doubt right in arguing that those contributions have an impact on the election and have the potential to win the gratitude of candidates, but the same can be said for the independent spending that *Buckley* protected from limitation. The real consequences posed by megadonations to 527 committees may justify limits on individual donations, but the validation of those limits may well require a reconsideration of *Buckley*....

IV. Regulating 527s and Reconsidering *Buckley* ...

Limiting individual contributions to 527s may be just the statutory move necessary to force reconsideration of the Court's campaign finance framework. The 527s do not fit easily within *Buckley*'s anticorruption paradigm, at least as the Supreme Court has defined corruption until now. Their vice is that they enable superwealthy individuals — "the wealthiest of the wealthy," in the words of Senator McCain — to deploy massive sums in pursuit of their electoral goals. To be sure, there ought to be a place for independent contributions and expenditures, even by the superwealthy. In the last election they helped maintain spending parity among the presidential candidates and played a vital role in increasing voter turnout. With the government doing little to register, educate, and mobilize voters, the activities of these megadonors actually performed the useful public function of energizing our democracy. The current statutory cap of just $5000 on individual donations to political committees — first adopted in 1974 and not adjusted for inflation since — may very well be too low in light of the public benefits of such private spending.

But unlimited megadonations create the possibility of radically uneven wealth-based influence on elections and can undermine public belief that ours is a democratic system. The rise of the 527s is not—or not simply—an evasion of BCRA's soft money limits, because the shift from parties to independent committees reduced the role of candidates and officeholders in soliciting these funds and led to changes in both who is contributing outside FECA's limits and how much they are contributing. Rather, by enabling a handful of individuals to commit literally millions of dollars to the election campaign, the rise of the 527s is a challenge to the political equality at the heart of democracy. By the same token, the rise of the 527s is also a challenge to the Supreme Court to break with *Buckley*'s rejection of equality as a component of campaign finance law and to see that dramatic funding inequalities present a compelling problem that Congress can address.

Notes and Questions

1. For additional analyses, see Edward B. Foley, *The "Major Purpose" Test: Distinguishing Between Election Focused and Issue-Focused Groups*, 31 Northern Kentucky Law Review 341, 352 (2004); Memorandum from Professor Daniel R. Ortiz, John Allen Love Professor of Law, Univ. of Va., to Democracy 21 & the Campaign Legal Ctr. 1–2 (Mar. 7, 2005), *available at* http://www.campaignlegalcenter.org/press-1051.html; Gregg D. Polsky & Guy-Uriel E. Charles, *Regulating 527 Organizations*, 73 George Washington Law Review 1000 (2005).

2. As Professor Briffault shows, the argument from Supreme Court precedent depends upon a dictum from Justice Blackmun's opinion in *CalMed* and a rather cryptic footnote in *McConnell*. If you were the Justice deciding this issue, how much weight would you give those precedents? If you were writing on a clean slate, how would you decide the case?

3. Is Professor Briffault right that regulation of contributions to independent expenditure committees requires acceptance of a political equality rationale and the partial overruling of *Buckley*? If so, should *Buckley* be overruled on this point?

4. While this book was in press, the Fourth Circuit struck down a North Carolina law barring contributions to independent expenditure committees. *North Carolina Right to Life v. Leake*, 525 F.3d 274, 295 (4th Cir. 2008). One judge dissented.

Chapter 16

Spending Limits after *Buckley*

In *Buckley v. Valeo*, the Supreme Court struck down a number of provisions of FECA limiting campaign spending, including limits on a candidate's own spending and a $1,000 limit on independent spending by an individual supporting or opposing candidates for federal office. The Court held the independent expenditure limit violated the First Amendment because it was not necessary to prevent corruption (the Court viewed the independence requirement as preventing any *quid pro quo*) and because it imposed a heavy burden on First Amendment rights of speech and association. The Court also held that the law would not be effective because, under *Buckley*'s footnote 52, the law would apply only to spending that "expressly advocated" the election or defeat of a candidate, and not to ads that avoided those words of advocacy. Finally, the Court rejected a political equality rationale for spending limits, ruling such a rationale "wholly foreign" to the First Amendment.

After *Buckley*, the biggest question mark in the spending limits area concerned the imposition of such limits on corporations and labor unions, an issue not addressed in *Buckley*. Federal law had long imposed such limits, as had many states. As we shall see, the Supreme Court's consideration of this question has been controversial and inconsistent, alternating between periods of skepticism of such limits and deference to legislative imposition of such limits. The Roberts Court has shown signs of moving back to a period of skepticism.

I. Corporate Spending Limits in Ballot Measure Campaigns

First National Bank of Boston v. Bellotti
435 U.S. 765 (1978)

Mr. Justice POWELL delivered the opinion of the Court.

In sustaining a state criminal statute that forbids certain expenditures by banks and business corporations for the purpose of influencing the vote on referendum proposals, the Massachusetts Supreme Judicial Court held that the First Amendment rights of a corporation are limited to issues that materially affect its business, property, or assets....

I

The statute at issue, Mass. Gen. Laws Ann., ch. 55, §8, prohibits appellants, two national banking associations and three business corporations, from making contributions or expenditures "for the purpose of ... influencing or affecting the vote on any question submitted to the voters, other than one materially affecting any of the property, business or assets of the corporation." The statute further specifies that "[n]o question submitted to the voters solely concerning the taxation of the income, property or transactions of individuals shall be deemed materially to affect the property, business or assets of the corporation." ...

Appellants wanted to spend money to publicize their views on a proposed constitutional amendment that was to be submitted to the voters as a ballot question at a general election on November 2, 1976. The amendment would have permitted the legislature to impose a graduated tax on the income of individuals. [Appellants] brought this action seeking to have the statute declared unconstitutional. [The state court upheld the statute.][3] ...

III

The court below framed the principal question in this case as whether and to what extent corporations have First Amendment rights. We believe that the court posed the wrong question. The Constitution often protects interests broader than those of the party seeking their vindication. The First Amendment, in particular, serves significant societal interests. The proper question therefore is not whether corporations "have" First Amendment rights and, if so, whether they are coextensive with those of natural persons. Instead, the question must be whether §8 abridges expression that the First Amendment was meant to protect. We hold that it does.

A

The speech proposed by appellants is at the heart of the First Amendment's protection....

As the Court said in *Mills v. Alabama*, 384 U.S. 214 (1966), "there is practically universal agreement that a major purpose of [the First] Amendment was to protect the free discussion of governmental affairs." If the speakers here were not corporations, no one would suggest that the State could silence their proposed speech. It is the type of speech indispensable to decisionmaking in a democracy, and this is no less true because the speech comes from a corporation rather than an individual. The inherent worth of the speech in terms of its capacity for informing the public does not depend upon the identity of its source, whether corporation, association, union, or individual.

The court below nevertheless held that corporate speech is protected by the First Amendment only when it pertains directly to the corporation's business interests. In de-

---

3. This was not the first challenge to §8. The statute's legislative and judicial history has been a troubled one. Its successive re-enactments have been linked to the legislature's repeated submissions to the voters of a constitutional amendment that would allow the enactment of a graduated tax.

The predecessor of §8, §7 ..., did not dictate that questions concerning the taxation of individuals could not satisfy the "materially affecting" requirement. The Supreme Judicial Court construed §7 not to prohibit a corporate expenditure urging the voters to reject a proposed constitutional amendment authorizing the legislature to impose a graduated tax on corporate as well as individual income.

[T]he legislature amended §7 by adding the sentence: "No question submitted to the voters concerning the taxation of the income, property or transactions of individuals shall be deemed materially to affect the property, business or assets of the corporation." The statute was challenged in 1972 by four of the present appellants; they wanted to oppose a referendum proposal similar to the one submitted to and rejected by the voters in 1962. Again the expenditure was held to be lawful.

The most recent amendment was enacted on April 28, 1975, when the legislature further refined the second sentence of §8 to apply only to ballot questions "solely" concerning the taxation of individuals. Following this amendment, the legislature on May 7, 1975, voted to submit to the voters on November 2, 1976, the proposed constitutional amendment authorizing the imposition of a graduated personal income tax. It was this proposal that led to the case now before us.

ciding whether this novel and restrictive gloss on the First Amendment comports with the Constitution and the precedents of this Court. we need not survey the outer boundaries of the Amendment's protection of corporate speech, or address the abstract question whether corporations have the full measure of rights that individuals enjoy under the First Amendment.[13] The question in this case, simply put, is whether the corporate identity of the speaker deprives this proposed speech of what otherwise would be its clear entitlement to protection. We turn now to that question.

B

The court below found confirmation of the legislature's definition of the scope of a corporation's First Amendment rights in the language of the Fourteenth Amendment. Noting that the First Amendment is applicable to the States through the Fourteenth, and seizing upon the observation that corporations "cannot claim for themselves the liberty which the Fourteenth Amendment guarantees." *Pierce v. Society of Sisters*, 268 U.S. 510 (1925), the court concluded that a corporation's First Amendment rights must derive from its property rights under the Fourteenth.

This is an artificial mode of analysis, untenable under decisions of this Court.... Freedom of speech and the other freedoms encompassed by the First Amendment always have been viewed as fundamental components of the liberty safeguarded by the Due Process Clause, and the Court has not identified a separate source for the right when it has been asserted by corporations. In *Grosjean v. American Press Co.*, 297 U.S. 233 (1936), the Court rejected the very reasoning adopted by the Supreme Judicial Court and did not rely on the corporation's property rights under the Fourteenth Amendment in sustaining its freedom of speech.

Yet appellee suggests that First Amendment rights generally have been afforded only to corporations engaged in the communications business or through which individuals express themselves, and the court below apparently accepted the "materially affecting" theory as the conceptual common denominator between appellee's position and the precedents of this Court. It is true that the "materially affecting" requirement would have been satisfied in the Court's decisions affording protection to the speech of media corporations and corporations otherwise in the business of communication or entertainment, and to the commercial speech of business corporations. In such cases, the speech would be connected to the corporation's business almost by definition. But the effect on the business of the corporation was not the governing rationale in any of these decisions. None of them mentions, let alone attributes significance to, the fact that the subject of the challenged communication materially affected the corporation's business.

The press cases emphasize the special and constitutionally recognized role of that institution in informing and educating the public, offering criticism, and providing a forum for discussion and debate. But the press does not have a monopoly on either the First Amendment or the ability to enlighten. Similarly, the Court's decisions involving corporations in the business of communication or entertainment are based not only on the role of the First Amendment in fostering individual self-expression but also on its role in affording the public access to discussion, debate, and the dissemination of information and ideas. Even decisions seemingly based exclusively on the individual's right to express himself acknowledge that the expression may contribute to society's edification....

---

13. Nor is there any occasion to consider in this case whether, under different circumstances, a justification for a restriction on speech that would be inadequate as applied to individuals might suffice to sustain the same restriction as applied to corporations, unions, or like entities.

C

We thus find no support in the First or Fourteenth Amendment, or in the decisions of this Court, for the proposition that speech that otherwise would be within the protection of the First Amendment loses that protection simply because its source is a corporation that cannot prove, to the satisfaction of a court, a material effect on its business or property. The "materially affecting" requirement is not an identification of the boundaries of corporate speech etched by the Constitution itself. Rather, it amounts to an impermissible legislative prohibition of speech based on the identity of the interests that spokesmen may represent in public debate over controversial issues and a requirement that the speaker have a sufficiently great interest in the subject to justify communication.

Section 8 permits a corporation to communicate to the public its views on certain referendum subjects—those materially affecting its business—but not others. It also singles out one kind of ballot question—individual taxation—as a subject about which corporations may never make their ideas public. The legislature has drawn the line between permissible and impermissible speech according to whether there is a sufficient nexus, as defined by the legislature, between the issue presented to the voters and the business interests of the speaker.

In the realm of protected speech, the legislature is constitutionally disqualified from dictating the subjects about which persons may speak and the speakers who may address a public issue. *Police Dept. of Chicago v. Mosley*, 408 U.S. 92 (1972). If a legislature may direct business corporations to "stick to business," it also may limit other corporations—religious, charitable, or civic—to their respective "business" when addressing the public. Such power in government to channel the expression of views is unacceptable under the First Amendment. Especially where, as here, the legislature's suppression of speech suggests an attempt to give one side of a debatable public question an advantage in expressing its views to the people, the First Amendment is plainly offended. Yet the State contends that its action is necessitated by governmental interests of the highest order. We next consider these asserted interests.

IV ...

The Supreme Judicial Court did not subject §8 to "the critical scrutiny demanded under accepted First Amendment and equal protection principles," *Buckley*, because of its view that the First Amendment does not apply to appellants' proposed speech. For this reason the court did not even discuss the State's interests in considering appellants' First Amendment argument. The court adverted to the conceivable interests served by §8 only in rejecting appellants' equal protection claim. Appellee nevertheless advances two principal justifications for the prohibition of corporate speech. The first is the State's interest in sustaining the active role of the individual citizen in the electoral process and thereby preventing diminution of the citizen's confidence in government. The second is the interest in protecting the rights of shareholders whose views differ from those expressed by management on behalf of the corporation. However weighty these interests may be in the context of partisan candidate elections,[26] they either are not implicated in this case or are not served at all, or in other than a random manner, by the prohibition in §8.

---

26. In addition to prohibiting corporate contributions and expenditures for the purpose of influencing the vote on a ballot question submitted to the voters, §8 also proscribes corporate contributions or expenditures "for the purpose of aiding, promoting or preventing the nomination or election of any person to public office, or aiding, promoting, or antagonizing the interests of any political party." In this respect, the statute is not unlike many other state and federal laws regulating corporate participation in partisan candidate elections. Appellants do not challenge the constitutionality of laws prohibiting or limiting corporate contributions to political candidates or committees, or other means of influencing candidate elections. About half of these laws, including the federal law, 2 U.S.C.

A

Preserving the integrity of the electoral process, preventing corruption, and "sustain[ing] the active, alert responsibility of the individual citizen in a democracy for the wise conduct of government" are interests of the highest importance. *Buckley*; *United States v. United Automobile Workers*, 352 U.S. 567 (1957). Preservation of the individual citizen's confidence in government is equally important. *Buckley*.

Appellee advances a number of arguments in support of his view that these interests are endangered by corporate participation in discussion of a referendum issue. They hinge upon the assumption that such participation would exert an undue influence on the outcome of a referendum vote, and—in the end—destroy the confidence of the people in the democratic process and the integrity of government. According to appellee, corporations are wealthy and powerful and their views may drown out other points of view. If appellee's arguments were supported by record or legislative findings that corporate advocacy threatened imminently to undermine democratic processes, thereby denigrating rather than serving First Amendment interests, these arguments would merit our consideration. *Red Lion Broadcasting Co. v. FCC*, 395 U.S. 367 (1969). But there has been no showing that the relative voice of corporations has been overwhelming or even significant in influencing referenda in Massachusetts,[28] or that there has been any threat to the confidence of the citizenry in government.

Nor are appellee's arguments inherently persuasive or supported by the precedents of this Court. Referenda are held on issues, not candidates for public office. The risk of corruption perceived in cases involving candidate elections simply is not present in a popular vote on a public issue. To be sure, corporate advertising may influence the outcome of the vote; this would be its purpose. But the fact that advocacy may persuade the electorate is hardly a reason to suppress it: The Constitution "protects expression which is eloquent no less than that which is unconvincing." *Kingsley Int'l Pictures Corp. v. Regents*, 360 U.S. 684 (1959). We

---

§441b (originally enacted as the Federal Corrupt Practices Act), by their terms do not apply to referendum votes. Several of the others proscribe or limit spending for "political" purposes, which may or may not cover referenda. The overriding concern behind the enactment of statutes such as the Federal Corrupt Practices Act was the problem of corruption of elected representatives through the creation of political debts. The importance of the governmental interest in preventing this occurrence has never been doubted. The case before us presents no comparable problem, and our consideration of a corporation's right to speak on issues of general public interest implies no comparable right in the quite different context of participation in a political campaign for election to public office. Congress might well be able to demonstrate the existence of a danger of real or apparent corruption in independent expenditures by corporations to influence candidate elections.

28. In his dissenting opinion, Mr. Justice WHITE relies on incomplete facts with respect to expenditures in the 1972 referendum election, in support of his perception as to the "domination of the electoral process by corporate wealth." The record shows only the extent of corporate and individual contributions to the two committees that were organized to support and oppose, respectively, the constitutional amendment. It does show that three of the appellants each contributed $3,000 to the "opposition" committee. The dissenting opinion makes no reference to the fact that amounts of money expended independently of organized committees need not be reported under Massachusetts law, and therefore remain unknown.

Even if viewed as material, any inference that corporate contributions "dominated" the electoral process on this issue is refuted by the 1976 election. There the voters again rejected the proposed constitutional amendment even in the absence of any corporate spending, which had been forbidden by the decision below.

[Although corporate spending was prohibited, opponents of the 1976 proposal outspent supporters by about $115,000 to $10,000. See John S. Shockley, *Money in Politics: Judicial Roadblocks to Campaign Finance Reform*, 10 Hastings Constitutional Law Quarterly 679, 703 n.117 (1983). Does this fact support or detract from Justice Powell's position?—Eds.]

noted only recently that "the concept that government may restrict the speech of some elements of our society in order to enhance the relative voice of others is wholly foreign to the First Amendment...." *Buckley*. Moreover, the people in our democracy are entrusted with the responsibility for judging and evaluating the relative merits of conflicting arguments.[31] They may consider, in making their judgment, the source and credibility of the advocate.[32] But if there be any danger that the people cannot evaluate the information and arguments advanced by appellants, it is a danger contemplated by the Framers of the First Amendment. In sum, "[a] restriction so destructive of the right of public discussion [as §8], without greater or more imminent danger to the public interest than existed in this case, is incompatible with the freedoms secured by the First Amendment." *Thomas v. Collins*, 323 U.S. 516 (1945).

B

Finally, appellee argues that §8 protects corporate shareholders, an interest that is both legitimate and traditionally within the province of state law. *Cort v. Ash*, 422 U.S. 66 (1975). The statute is said to serve this interest by preventing the use of corporate resources in furtherance of views with which some shareholders may disagree. This purpose is belied, however, by the provisions of the statute, which are both underinclusive and overinclusive.

The underinclusiveness of the statute is self-evident. Corporate expenditures with respect to a referendum are prohibited, while corporate activity with respect to the passage or defeat of legislation is permitted, even though corporations may engage in lobbying more often than they take positions on ballot questions submitted to the voters. Nor does §8 prohibit a corporation from expressing its views, by the expenditure of corporate funds, on any public issue until it becomes the subject of a referendum, though the displeasure of disapproving shareholders is unlikely to be any less.

The fact that a particular kind of ballot question has been singled out for special treatment undermines the likelihood of a genuine state interest in protecting shareholders. It suggests instead that the legislature may have been concerned with silencing corporations on a particular subject. Indeed, appellee has conceded that "the legislative and judicial history of the statute indicates ... that the second crime was 'tailor-made' to prohibit corporate campaign contributions to oppose a graduated income tax amendment."

Nor is the fact that §8 is limited to banks and business corporations without relevance. Excluded from its provisions and criminal sanctions are entities or organized groups in which numbers of persons may hold an interest or membership, and which often have resources comparable to those of large corporations. Minorities in such groups or entities

---

31. The State's paternalism evidenced by this statute is illustrated by the fact that Massachusetts does not prohibit lobbying by corporations, which are free to exert as much influence on the people's representatives as their resources and inclinations permit. Presumably the legislature thought its members competent to resist the pressures and blandishments of lobbying, but had markedly less confidence in the electorate. If the First Amendment protects the right of corporations to petition legislative and administrative bodies, see *California Motor Transp. Co. v. Trucking Unlimited*, 404 U.S. 508 (1972); *Eastern Railroad Presidents Conf. v. Noerr Motor Freight, Inc.*, 365 U.S. 127 (1961), there hardly can be less reason for allowing corporate views to be presented openly to the people when they are to take action in their sovereign capacity.

32. Corporate advertising, unlike some methods of participation in political campaigns, is likely to be highly visible. Identification of the source of advertising may be required as a means of disclosure, so that the people will be able to evaluate the arguments to which they are being subjected. See *Buckley*; *United States v. Harriss*, 347 U.S. 612, 625–626 (1954). In addition, we emphasized in *Buckley* the prophylactic effect of requiring that the source of communication be disclosed.

may have interests with respect to institutional speech quite comparable to those of minority shareholders in a corporation. Thus the exclusion of Massachusetts business trusts, real estate investment trusts, labor unions, and other associations undermines the plausibility of the State's purported concern for the persons who happen to be shareholders in the banks and corporations covered by §8.

The overinclusiveness of the statute is demonstrated by the fact that §8 would prohibit a corporation from supporting or opposing a referendum proposal even if its shareholders unanimously authorized the contribution or expenditure. Ultimately shareholders may decide, through the procedures of corporate democracy, whether their corporation should engage in debate on public issues.[34] Acting through their power to elect the board of directors or to insist upon protective provisions in the corporation's charter, shareholders normally are presumed competent to protect their own interests. In addition to intracorporate remedies, minority shareholders generally have access to the judicial remedy of a derivative suit to challenge corporate disbursements alleged to have been made for improper corporate purposes or merely to further the personal interests of management.

Assuming, *arguendo*, that protection of shareholders is a "compelling" interest under the circumstances of this case, we find "no substantially relevant correlation between the governmental interest asserted and the State's effort" to prohibit appellants from speaking. *Shelton v. Tucker*, 364 U.S. 479 (1960).

---

34. Appellee does not explain why the dissenting shareholder's wishes are entitled to such greater solicitude in this context than in many others where equally important and controversial corporate decisions are made by management or by a predetermined percentage of the shareholders. Mr. Justice WHITE's repeatedly expressed concern for corporate shareholders who may be "coerced" into supporting "causes with which they disagree" apparently is not shared by appellants' shareholders. Not a single shareholder has joined appellee in defending the Massachusetts statute or, so far as the record shows, has interposed any objection to the right asserted by the corporations to make the proscribed expenditures.

The dissent of Mr. Justice WHITE relies heavily on *Abood v. Detroit Board of Education*, 431 U.S. 209 (1977), and *International Assn. of Machinists v. Street*, 367 U.S. 740 (1961). These decisions involved the First Amendment rights of employees in closed or agency shops not to be compelled, as a condition of employment, to support with financial contributions the political activities of other union members with which the dissenters disagreed.

Street and *Abood* are irrelevant to the question presented in this case. In those cases employees were required, either by state law or by agreement between the employer and the union, to pay dues or a "service fee" to the exclusive bargaining representative. To the extent that these funds were used by the union in furtherance of political goals, unrelated to collective bargaining, they were held to be unconstitutional because they compelled the dissenting union member "'to furnish contributions of money for the propagation of opinions which he disbelieves....'" *Abood*.

The critical distinction here is that no shareholder has been "compelled" to contribute anything. Apart from the fact, noted by the dissent, that compulsion by the State is wholly absent, the shareholder invests in a corporation of his own volition and is free to withdraw his investment at any time and for any reason. A more relevant analogy, therefore, is to the situation where an employee voluntarily joins a union, or an individual voluntarily joins an association, and later finds himself in disagreement with its stance on a political issue. The *Street* and *Abood* Courts did not address the question whether, in such a situation, the union or association must refund a portion of the dissenter's dues or, more drastically, refrain from expressing the majority's views. In addition, even apart from the substantive differences between compelled membership in a union and voluntary investment in a corporation or voluntary participation in any collective organization, it is by no means an automatic step from the remedy in *Abood*, which honored the interests of the minority without infringing the majority's rights, to the position adopted by the dissent which would completely silence the majority because a hypothetical minority might object.

V

Because that portion of §8 challenged by appellants prohibits protected speech in a manner unjustified by a compelling state interest, it must be invalidated. The judgment of the Supreme Judicial Court is

Reversed.[a]

Mr. Justice WHITE, with whom Mr. Justice BRENNAN and Mr. Justice MARSHALL join, dissenting....

I

There is now little doubt that corporate communications come within the scope of the First Amendment. This, however, is merely the starting point of analysis, because an examination of the First Amendment values that corporate expression furthers and the threat to the functioning of a free society it is capable of posing reveals that it is not fungible with communications emanating from individuals and is subject to restrictions which individual expression is not. Indeed, what some have considered to be the principal function of the First Amendment, the use of communication as a means of self-expression, self-realization, and self-fulfillment, is not at all furthered by corporate speech. It is clear that the communications of profitmaking corporations are not "an integral part of the development of ideas, of mental exploration and of the affirmation of self."[4] They do not represent a manifestation of individual freedom or choice. Undoubtedly, as this Court has recognized, see *NAACP v. Button*, 371 U.S. 415 (1963), there are some corporations formed for the express purpose of advancing certain ideological causes shared by all their members, or, as in the case of the press, of disseminating information and ideas. Under such circumstances, association in a corporate form may be viewed as merely a means of achieving effective self-expression. But this is hardly the case generally with corporations operated for the purpose of making profits. Shareholders in such entities do not share a common set of political or social views, and they certainly have not invested their money for the purpose of advancing political or social causes or in an enterprise engaged in the business of disseminating news and opinion. In fact, as discussed *infra*, the government has a strong interest in assuring that investment decisions are not predicated upon agreement or disagreement with the activities of corporations in the political arena.

Of course, it may be assumed that corporate investors are united by a desire to make money, for the value of their investment to increase. Since even communications which have no purpose other than that of enriching the communicator have some First Amendment protection, activities such as advertising and other communications integrally related to the operation of the corporation's business may be viewed as a means of furthering the desires of individual shareholders. This unanimity of purpose breaks down, however, when corporations make expenditures or undertake activities designed to influence the opinion or votes of the general public on political and social issues that have no material connection with or effect upon their business, property, or assets. Although it is arguable that corporations make such expenditures because their managers believe that it is in the corporations' economic interest to do so, there is no basis whatsoever for concluding that these views are expressive of the heterogeneous beliefs of their shareholders whose convictions on many political issues are undoubtedly shaped by considerations other than a desire to endorse any electoral or ideological cause which would tend to in-

---

a. A concurring opinion by Chief Justice Burger is omitted.
4. T. Emerson, Toward a General Theory of the First Amendment 5 (1966).

crease the value of a particular corporate investment. This is particularly true where, as in this case, whatever the belief of the corporate managers may be, they have not been able to demonstrate that the issue involved has any material connection with the corporate business. Thus when a profitmaking corporation contributes to a political candidate this does not further the self-expression or self-fulfillment of its shareholders in the way that expenditures from them as individuals would.

The self-expression of the communicator is not the only value encompassed by the First Amendment. One of its functions, often referred to as the right to hear or receive information, is to protect the interchange of ideas. Any communication of ideas, and consequently any expenditure of funds which makes the communication of ideas possible, it can be argued, furthers the purposes of the First Amendment. This proposition does not establish, however, that the right of the general public to receive communications financed by means of corporate expenditures is of the same dimension as that to hear other forms of expression. In the first place, as discussed *supra*, corporate expenditures designed to further political causes lack the connection with individual self-expression which is one of the principal justifications for the constitutional protection of speech provided by the First Amendment. Ideas which are not a product of individual choice are entitled to less First Amendment protection. Secondly, the restriction of corporate speech concerned with political matters impinges much less severely upon the availability of ideas to the general public than do restrictions upon individual speech. Even the complete curtailment of corporate communications concerning political or ideological questions not integral to day-to-day business functions would leave individuals, including corporate shareholders, employees, and customers, free to communicate their thoughts. Moreover, it is unlikely that any significant communication would be lost by such a prohibition. These individuals would remain perfectly free to communicate any ideas which could be conveyed by means of the corporate form. Indeed, such individuals could even form associations for the very purpose of promoting political or ideological causes....

It bears emphasis here that the Massachusetts statute forbids the expenditure of corporate funds in connection with referenda but in no way forbids the board of directors of a corporation from formulating and making public what it represents as the views of the corporation even though the subject addressed has no material effect whatsoever on the business of the corporation. These views could be publicized at the individual expense of the officers, directors, stockholders, or anyone else interested in circulating the corporate view on matters irrelevant to its business.

The governmental interest in regulating corporate political communications, especially those relating to electoral matters, also raises considerations which differ significantly from those governing the regulation of individual speech. Corporations are artificial entities created by law for the purpose of furthering certain economic goals. In order to facilitate the achievement of such ends, special rules relating to such matters as limited liability, perpetual life, and the accumulation, distribution, and taxation of assets are normally applied to them. States have provided corporations with such attributes in order to increase their economic viability and thus strengthen the economy generally. It has long been recognized however, that the special status of corporations has placed them in a position to control vast amounts of economic power which may, if not regulated, dominate not only the economy but also the very heart of our democracy, the electoral process. Although *Buckley* provides support for the position that the desire to equalize the financial resources available to candidates does not justify the limitation upon the expression of support which a restriction upon individual contributions entails, the interest of Massachusetts and the many other States which have restricted corporate political activity is quite different. It is not one of equalizing the resources of opposing candidates or opposing positions, but rather of preventing institutions which have been permitted to amass wealth as a result of special advantages extended by the State for certain economic purposes from using that wealth to acquire an unfair advantage in the political process, especially where, as here, the issue involved has no material connection with the business of the corporation. The State need not permit its own creation to consume it. Massachusetts could permissibly conclude that not to impose limits upon the political activities of corporations would have placed it in a position of departing from neutrality and indirectly assisting the propagation of corporate views because of the advantages its laws give to the corporate acquisition of funds to finance such activities. Such expenditures may be viewed as seriously threatening the role of the First Amendment as a guarantor of a free marketplace of ideas. Ordinarily, the expenditure of funds to promote political causes may be assumed to bear some relation to the fervency with which they are held. Corporate political expression, however, is not only divorced from the convictions of individual corporate shareholders, but also, because of the ease with which corporations are permitted to accumulate capital, bears no relation to the conviction with which the ideas expressed are held by the communicator.

The Court's opinion appears to recognize at least the possibility that fear of corporate domination of the electoral process would justify restrictions upon corporate expenditures and contributions in connection with referenda but brushes this interest aside by asserting that "there has been no showing that the relative voice of corporations has been overwhelming or even significant in influencing referenda in Massachusetts," and by suggesting that the statute in issue represents an attempt to give an unfair advantage to those who hold views in opposition to positions which would otherwise be financed by corporations. It fails even to allude to the fact, however, that Massachusetts' most recent experience with unrestrained corporate expenditures in connection with ballot questions establishes precisely the contrary. In 1972, a proposed amendment to the Massachusetts Constitution which would have authorized the imposition of a graduated income tax on both individuals and corporations was put to the voters. The Committee for Jobs and Government Economy, an organized political committee, raised and expended approximately $120,000 to oppose the proposed amendment, the bulk of it raised through large corporate contributions. Three of the present appellant corporations each contributed $3,000 to this committee. In contrast, the Coalition for Tax Reform, Inc., the only political committee organized to support the 1972 amendment, was able to raise and expend only approximately $7,000. Perhaps these figures reflect the Court's view of the appropriate role which corporations should play in the Massachusetts electoral process, but it nowhere explains why it is entitled to substitute its judgment for that of Massachusetts and other States, as well as the United States, which have acted to correct or prevent similar domination of the electoral process by corporate wealth.

This Nation has for many years recognized the need for measures designed to prevent corporate domination of the political process. The Corrupt Practices Act, first enacted in 1907, has consistently barred corporate contributions in connection with federal elections. This Court has repeatedly recognized that one of the principal purposes of this prohibition is "to avoid the deleterious influences on federal elections resulting from the use of money by those who exercise control over large aggregations of capital." *United States v. Automobile Workers*, 352 U.S. 567 (1957). Although this Court has never adjudicated the constitutionality of the Act, there is no suggestion in its cases construing it ... that this purpose is in any sense illegitimate or deserving of other than the utmost respect; indeed, the thrust of its opinions, until today, has been to the contrary.

There is an additional overriding interest related to the prevention of corporate domination which is substantially advanced by Massachusetts' restrictions upon corporate contributions: assuring that shareholders are not compelled to support and financially further beliefs with which they disagree where, as is the case here, the issue involved does not materially affect the business, property, or other affairs of the corporation....

Mr. Justice REHNQUIST, dissenting.

This Court decided at an early date, with neither argument nor discussion, that a business corporation is a "person" entitled to the protection of the Equal Protection Clause of the Fourteenth Amendment. Likewise, it soon became accepted that the property of a corporation was protected under the Due Process Clause of that same Amendment. Nevertheless, we concluded soon thereafter that the liberty protected by that Amendment "is the liberty of natural, not artificial persons." *Northwestern Nat. Life Ins. Co. v. Riggs*, 203 U.S. 243 (1906). Before today, our only considered and explicit departures from that holding have been that a corporation engaged in the business of publishing or broadcasting enjoys the same liberty of the press as is enjoyed by natural persons, *Grosjean v. American Press Co.*, 297 U.S. 233 (1936), and that a nonprofit membership corporation organized for the purpose of "achieving ... equality of treatment by all government, federal, state and local, for the members of the Negro community" enjoys certain liberties of political expression. *NAACP v. Button*, 371 U.S. 415 (1963).

The question presented today, whether business corporations have a constitutionally protected liberty to engage in political activities, has never been squarely addressed by any previous decision of this Court. However, the General Court of the Commonwealth of Massachusetts, the Congress of the United States, and the legislatures of 30 other States of this Republic have considered the matter, and have concluded that restrictions upon the political activity of business corporations are both politically desirable and constitutionally permissible. The judgment of such a broad consensus of governmental bodies expressed over a period of many decades is entitled to considerable deference from this Court. I think it quite probable that their judgment may properly be reconciled with our controlling precedents, but I am certain that under my views of the limited application of the First Amendment to the States, which I share with the two immediately preceding occupants of my seat on the Court, but not with my present colleagues, the judgment of the Supreme Judicial Court of Massachusetts should be affirmed.

Early in our history, Mr. Chief Justice Marshall described the status of a corporation in the eyes of federal law:

> A corporation is an artificial being, invisible, intangible, and existing only in contemplation of law. Being the mere creature of law, it possesses only those properties which the charter of creation confers upon it, either expressly, or as incidental to its very existence. These are such as are supposed best calculated to effect the object for which it was created.

Dartmouth College v. Woodward, 4 Wheat. 518, 636 (1819). The appellants herein either were created by the Commonwealth or were admitted into the Commonwealth only for the limited purposes described in their charters and regulated by state law. Since it cannot be disputed that the mere creation of a corporation does not invest it with all the liberties enjoyed by natural persons, our inquiry must seek to determine which constitutional protections are "incidental to its very existence." *Dartmouth College.*

There can be little doubt that when a State creates a corporation with the power to acquire and utilize property, it necessarily and implicitly guarantees that the corporation will not be deprived of that property absent due process of law. Likewise, when a State charters a corporation for the purpose of publishing a newspaper, it necessarily assumes that the corporation is entitled to the liberty of the press essential to the conduct of its business. *Grosjean* so held, and our subsequent cases have so assumed. Until recently, it was not thought that any persons, natural or artificial, had any protected right to engage in commercial speech. Although the Court has never explicitly recognized a corporation's right of commercial speech, such a right might be considered necessarily incidental to the business of a commercial corporation.

It cannot be so readily concluded that the right of political expression is equally necessary to carry out the functions of a corporation organized for commercial purposes. A State grants to a business corporation the blessings of potentially perpetual life and limited liability to enhance its efficiency as an economic entity. It might reasonably be concluded that those properties, so beneficial in the economic sphere, pose special dangers in the political sphere. Furthermore, it might be argued that liberties of political expression are not at all necessary to effectuate the purposes for which States permit commercial corporations to exist. So long as the Judicial Branches of the State and Federal Governments remain open to protect the corporation's interest in its property, it has no need, though it may have the desire, to petition the political branches for similar protection. Indeed, the States might reasonably fear that the corporation would use its economic power to obtain further benefits beyond those already bestowed.[6] I would think that any particular form of organization upon which the State confers special privileges or immunities different from those of natural persons would be subject to like regulation, whether the organization is a labor union, a partnership, a trade association, or a corporation.

One need not adopt such a restrictive view of the political liberties of business corporations to affirm the judgment of the Supreme Judicial Court in this case. That court reasoned that this Court's decisions entitling the property of a corporation to constitu-

---

6. The question of whether [restrictions such as §8] are politically desirable is exclusively for decision by the political branches of the Federal Government and by the States, and may not be reviewed here. My Brother WHITE, in his dissenting opinion, puts the legislative determination in its most appealing light when he says:

"[T]he interest of Massachusetts and the many other States which have restricted corporate political activity ... is not one of equalizing the resources of opposing candidates or opposing positions, but rather of preventing institutions which have been permitted to amass wealth as a result of special advantages extended by the State for certain economic purposes from using that wealth to acquire an unfair advantage in the political process ..."

As I indicate in the text, I agree that this is a rational basis for sustaining the legislation here in question. But I cannot agree with my Brother WHITE's intimation that this is in fact the reason that the Massachusetts General Court enacted this legislation. If inquiry into legislative motives were to determine the outcome of cases such as this, I think a very persuasive argument could be made that the General Court, desiring to impose a personal income tax but more than once defeated in that desire by the combination of the Commonwealth's referendum provision and corporate expenditures in opposition to such a tax, simply decided to muzzle corporations on this sort of issue so that it could succeed in its desire.

If one believes, as my Brother WHITE apparently does, that a function of the First Amendment is to protect the interchange of ideas, he cannot readily subscribe to the idea that, if the desire to muzzle corporations played a part in the enactment of this legislation, the General Court was simply engaged in deciding which First Amendment values to promote....

But I think the Supreme Judicial Court was correct in concluding that, whatever may have been the motive of the General Court, the law thus challenged did not violate the United States Constitution.

tional protection should be construed as recognizing the liberty of a corporation to express itself on political matters concerning that property. Thus, the Court construed the statute in question not to forbid political expression by a corporation "when a general political issue materially affects a corporation's business, property or assets."

I can see no basis for concluding that the liberty of a corporation to engage in political activity with regard to matters having no material effect on its business is necessarily incidental to the purposes for which the Commonwealth permitted these corporations to be organized or admitted within its boundaries. Nor can I disagree with the Supreme Judicial Court's factual finding that no such effect has been shown by these appellants. Because the statute as construed provides at least as much protection as the Fourteenth Amendment requires, I believe it is constitutionally valid.

It is true, as the Court points out, that recent decisions of this Court have emphasized the interest of the public in receiving the information offered by the speaker seeking protection. The free flow of information is in no way diminished by the Commonwealth's decision to permit the operation of business corporations with limited rights of political expression. All natural persons, who owe their existence to a higher sovereign than the Commonwealth, remain as free as before to engage in political activity.

I would affirm the judgment of the Supreme Judicial Court.

Notes and Questions

1. Justice Powell wrote in *Bellotti*, "The Constitution 'protects expression which is eloquent no less than that which is unconvincing.'" Is eloquence in campaign speech equivalent to persuasiveness, as Justice Powell seems to assume? Consider the following anecdote, described by Arthur Samish, the most powerful lobbyist in California in the 1930s and 40s.

Samish placed an initiative proposal on the ballot to give a tax break to the bus and truck industry, which he represented. He tried to "educate the voting public on the need for standard taxation for buses, pointing out that 1,700 small communities had no other public transportation besides buses." But railroad companies succeeded in defeating the initiative with a large advertising campaign.

The next election, Samish tried again. He hired "a well-known cartoonist named Johnny Argens to draw a picture of a big, fat, ugly pig." The pig was placed on billboards throughout California with the slogan:

DRIVE THE HOG FROM THE ROAD! VOTE YES ON PROPOSITION NUMBER 2

Samish also distributed millions of handbills containing the pig and the same slogan. He points out that he always spelled out the word "Number." If he used the abbreviation "No. 2," "the voter might get confused and think he should vote 'No.'" Samish reports that his plan worked.

> Boy, did it work! Nobody likes a roadhog, and the voters flocked to the polls and passed the constitutional amendment by 700,000!

> All because the voters thought they were voting against roadhogs. That had nothing to do with it.

See Arthur H. Samish & Bob Thomas, THE SECRET BOSS OF CALIFORNIA 37–38 (1971).

Was Samish's campaign literature in favor of "Proposition Number 2" eloquent? Was it persuasive? Was it the kind of speech that merits the full protection of the First Amendment?

2. Justice Powell's opinion contains the statement that if "appellee's arguments were supported by record or legislative findings that corporate advocacy threatened imminently to undermine democratic processes, thereby denigrating rather than serving First Amendment interests, these arguments would merit our consideration." Is it possible, then, that in a different case a ban on corporate financial resources being used in ballot measure campaigns would be upheld? What kind of record evidence or legislative findings, if any, would lead to such a result? Would Samish's anecdote in the previous note be relevant? Would evidence that corporations often achieved electoral success by such tactics be sufficient? See generally John S. Shockley, *Direct Democracy, Campaign Finance, and the Courts: Can Corruption, Undue Influence and Declining Voter Confidence be Found?*, 39 UNIVERSITY OF MIAMI LAW REVIEW 377 (1985). Shockley writes, at 389–90:

> The Court's distinction between domination and legitimate persuasion probably hinges on *perception*. In other words, only if voters perceive big money as dominating the process, thereby alienating citizens, reducing voter turnout, and undermining the democratic process, should campaign finance reform curb such influence. Requiring a public perception of domination adds a second stage to the process, complicating the matter considerably. If the public were to recognize the overwhelming impact of campaign funds on direct democracy, would money simultaneously become less influential, as in a self-negating prophecy? What if the public does not perceive money as being dominant, but it is? Or, less likely, what if the public perceives money as being dominant, but the public is wrong? On this question of perception, is it not relevant that so many states and municipalities — often through direct voter approval of the specific laws — have tried to limit money in ballot proposition campaigns? Is this an indication that the public already perceives and understands the power of money to dominate the electoral process? For what other purposes would these states enact such laws? Unfortunately, the Court has chosen not to answer these questions.

Consider the following more recent statistics:

> Public opinion polls conducted in California shed some light on the perception question. In 2004, 48% of respondents to a Field poll believed that statewide ballot proposition elections come out the way "a few organized special interests want" rather than "the way most people want." Only one-third believed that the initiative elections came out the way most people want (10% were mixed and 9% had no opinion). The "Special Interest" response was up five percentage points over the 1999 survey, and the "Most People Want" response was down nine percentage points. More negatively, a February 2001 survey by the Public Policy Institute found that 52% of Californians believe the initiative process was controlled "a lot" by special interests, and another 44% thought it was controlled "somewhat" by them. Some of this skepticism translates into support for campaign finance reform of ballot measure campaigns. In a 1997 Field poll study, 77% of voters favored limits on the amount of money that can be spent by supporters and opponents of statewide ballot measure campaigns. These statistics appear to show that a large number of voters (though not necessarily a majority) are concerned about the role of money in the initiative process.

> These statistics do not, however, tell the full story. By large majorities, Californians approve of statewide ballot measure elections. In 2004, 68% of Cali-

fornians thought statewide ballot proposition elections were a "good thing" and another 17% had a "mixed" opinion while only 5% saw them as a bad thing. The "good thing" figure is down from a high of 83% in 1979, but is higher than the low of 62% in 1999. When asked in 2004 whether the voting public or elected representatives could be better trusted to make decisions in the public interest, respondents favored the voting public over the legislature 56% to 35%. In addition, 67% of respondents thought elected representatives were more easily influenced and manipulated by special interest groups, compared to 24% who thought the public was more easily influenced and manipulated.

Richard L. Hasen, *Rethinking the Unconstitutionality of Contribution and Expenditure Limits in Ballot Measure Campaigns*, 78 SOUTHERN CALIFORNIA LAW REVIEW 885, 911–912 (2005).

3. *Bellotti* bars expenditure limits in ballot measure campaigns. As we saw in the last chapter, in *Citizens Against Rent Control v. City of Berkeley*, 454 U.S. 290 (1981) (*CARC*), the Court struck down a $250 limit on contributions to committees formed to support or oppose municipal ballot measures. The Court relied heavily on *Bellotti* and on the First Amendment right of association.

4. Given *Buckley* (not to mention *Bellotti* and *CARC*), it is clear that a state may not limit total spending for or against ballot propositions. For a decision so holding, see *Citizens for Jobs and Energy v. Fair Political Practices Commission*, 547 P.2d 1386 (Cal. 1976).

5. Bellotti *as a corporations case*. Although we have considered *Bellotti* primarily for what it says about regulating the financing of ballot measure elections, it also has great significance for the law governing the regulation of campaign finance activities by corporations and other targeted entities. In *Bellotti*, Justice Powell avoided direct consideration whether corporations have first amendment rights by stating that the significant issue was the right of the public to hear the speech that issues from corporations. Justice Powell's analysis is criticized in Carl E. Schneider, *Free Speech and Corporate Freedom: A Comment on First National Bank of Boston v. Bellotti*, 59 SOUTHERN CALIFORNIA LAW REVIEW 1227, 1235 (1986):

> On its face, this approach to the first amendment is a little incongruous. By its terms, the amendment protects "freedom of speech," not freedom to hear. The Court, of course, reasoned that the latter freedom is necessarily implied by the former. But in the *Bellotti* situation that reasoning seems circular: whether the corporation has a right to speak depends on the listener's right to receive; but a listener presumably has a right to receive only what the speaker has a right to say. Moreover, the incongruity of *Bellotti's* theory is intensified by its distance from the general public's understanding of law and rights: in everyday language, rights protect people, not corporations; in everyday thought, the first amendment is needed for the unpopular few, not the powerful many.

> The incongruity also may be understood in a somewhat different way. "The people," acting through their government, have prohibited certain entities from speaking about certain questions. Does the first amendment prevent the people from doing so? Ordinarily, the answer would be simple, because all people have a right to speak, either as part of their right to govern or as part of their right of self-expression. But here the would-be speaker is not a person and cannot benefit from the right to speak because it has no right to govern and needs no right of self-expression. The Court's argument is that a right resides in the people to have the information they need to govern. Yet in the statute

at issue "the people" expressly decided not only that this information is not needed to govern, but that allowing the corporation to speak corrupts the electoral process and thus interferes with the people's effective exercise of their right to govern.

6. Suppose Ann is an elderly individual who purchased shares of XYZ Corporation shortly after World War II, before the enormous growth in the economy that has since occurred. Since then the value of the stock has increased greatly, and for Ann to sell her XYZ stock would have disastrous tax consequences for Ann and her children.

Suppose Bill is a state employee. The state withholds a portion of Bill's salary each month and deposits it in his behalf into the state retirement system, the investments of which include stock in XYZ Corporation. The salary withholding is mandatory and Bill has no control over the retirement system's investments.

Suppose Carol last year purchased "letter stock" in XYZ Corporation. Carol purchased this stock from XYZ in a private placement, and Carol entered into a binding agreement not to sell the stock for a two-year period.

Now suppose XYZ Corporation proposes to contribute $500,000 to the chief committee opposing Proposition W, a ballot measure that is strongly supported by Ann, Bill, and Carol. Can Ann, Bill, or Carol enjoin XYZ from making the contribution, or obtain any other relief against XYZ? See footnote 34 of the Court's opinion in *Bellotti*.

7. Does the Court's opinion leave open the possibility of a statute that would require advance stockholder approval of a corporation's political contributions? See generally Francis H. Fox, *Corporate Political Speech: The Effect of First National Bank of Boston v. Bellotti Upon Statutory Limitations on Corporate Referendum Spending*, 67 KENTUCKY LAW JOURNAL 75, 96–101 (1978–79); Victor Brudney, *Business Corporations and Stockholders' Rights Under the First Amendment*, 91 YALE LAW JOURNAL 235 (1981).

If so, and if State *A* wanted to enact such a statute, could the state make the statute applicable to participation in elections conducted in State *A* by foreign corporations (i.e., by corporations that are incorporated in another state)? For example, according to a footnote (not reprinted above) in Justice Rehnquist's opinion, one of the appellants, Digital Equipment Corporation (DEC), was incorporated in Massachusetts, but another, Gillette, was incorporated in Delaware. Would it satisfy Massachusetts' purposes if an advance stockholder approval requirement effectively prevented contributions by DEC, but was inapplicable to Gillette? What would be the effect of such applicability in litigation challenging the constitutionality of the statute? See generally Jill E. Fisch, *Frankenstein's Monster Hits the Campaign Trail: An Approach to Regulation of Corporate Political Expenditures*, 32 WILLIAM & MARY LAW REVIEW 587, 599 n.69 (1991).

Such questions prompted the following comments by Daniel Hays Lowenstein, *A Patternless Mosaic: Campaign Finance and the First Amendment After Austin*, 21 CAPITAL UNIVERSITY LAW REVIEW 381, 408–9 (1992):

> In reality, the concern for dissenting shareholders is ancillary to concerns regarding the electoral process, and the consequences of inserting such regulations into corporation laws would be untenable....
>
> This is not to say that the problem of the dissenting shareholder is completely irrelevant. The fact that corporate management is speaking with other people's money, whether or not the "owners" agree with the speech, care about it, or even are aware of it, is a relevant consideration that reduces to some degree the force behind claims for First Amendment protection for corporate participation in

election campaigns. Corporations have a weak claim, if any, to protection, to the extent freedom of speech is based on principles such as autonomy or self-realization. Justice Powell's majority opinion in *Bellotti* utterly fails to recognize the relevance of these considerations, and that failure helps to account for the perception of many that his opinion is one-sided and unsatisfactory. But if *Bellotti* is unbalanced, it is not wrong in noticing that there are instrumental values that underlie the First Amendment. The fact that when corporations speak, their managers speak with other people's money, like the fact that corporations are creatures of the state favored by certain legal advantages, is a relevant background fact, but it is no more than that.

II. Limiting Spending by Corporations, Labor Unions, and Others in Candidate Elections

Bellotti involved a state law limiting expenditures by corporations in ballot measure campaigns. At the federal level (where there are no ballot measure elections), the earliest campaign finance restriction targeted contributions by corporations. Such contributions were prohibited, and during the World War II period the prohibition was extended to labor unions. For a detailed historical account, see Robert E. Mutch, CAMPAIGNS, CONGRESS, AND COURTS (1988); see also Robert E. Mutch, *Before and After* Bellotti: *The Corporate Political Contribution Cases*, 5 ELECTION LAW JOURNAL 293 (2006). In the 1970s, the Federal Corrupt Practices Act, which contained these prohibitions, was merged into the Federal Election Campaign Act. It is now located at 2 U.S.C. §441b.

Prior to the adoption of the FECA, the Corrupt Practices Act was rarely enforced. Most of the few cases that were prosecuted were brought against labor unions. Three of these cases reached the Supreme Court, and in each instance the union in question challenged the constitutionality of a ban on union contributions. In each case, the Court either interpreted the law so as not to apply to the alleged conduct or otherwise avoided deciding the constitutional issue. See *United States v. CIO*, 335 U.S. 106 (1948); *United States v. United Automobile Workers*, 352 U.S. 567 (1957); *Pipefitters Local Union No. 562 v. United States*, 407 U.S. 385 (1972). In *UAW*, in particular, the Court seemed to stretch very hard to avoid adjudicating the constitutional question.[b]

When the ban on corporate and labor contributions was reenacted as part of the original FECA, adopted in 1971, it was qualified by express provisions authorizing corporations and unions to use their funds to pay administrative expenses of "separate segregated funds"—now almost universally referred to as PACs (discussed more fully in Chapter 15, Part III.B)—which in turn could contribute to federal candidates out of voluntary contributions they received from individuals. Many unions and some corporations had been using PACs, but their legality had been questionable. In *Pipefitters, supra*, the Supreme Court finally ruled that under the prior law PACs were permissible, but by that time Congress, in the FECA, had adopted rules legalizing and governing PACs.

The Supreme Court considered the constitutionality of one aspect of FECA related to PACs in FEDERAL ELECTION COMMISSION V. NATIONAL CONSERVATIVE PO-

---

b. *UAW*, written by Justice Frankfurter, is also noteworthy for its account of the history of federal campaign finance regulation.

LITICAL ACTION COMMITTEE, 470 U.S. 480 (1985) (*NCPAC*). Section 9012(f) of the Presidential Election Campaign Fund Act, 26 U.S.C. §9001 *et seq.* makes it a criminal offense for independent PACs to spend more than $1,000 to further the election of a presidential candidate who has opted into the public financing system. Although limits on independent expenditures were declared unconstitutional in *Buckley*, this particular provision had not been challenged by the *Buckley* plaintiffs and therefore had not been struck down specifically. In *NCPAC*, the FEC hoped concern over PACs would induce the Supreme Court to carve out an exception. But the Court struck down Section 9012(f), making these points:

> There can be no doubt that the expenditures at issue in this case produce speech at the core of the First Amendment....

> The PACs in this case, of course, are not lone pamphleteers or street corner orators in the Tom Paine mold; they spend substantial amounts of money in order to communicate their political ideas through sophisticated media advertisements. And of course the criminal sanction in question is applied to the expenditure of money to propagate political views, rather than to the propagation of those views unaccompanied by the expenditure of money. But for purposes of presenting political views in connection with a nationwide Presidential election, allowing the presentation of views while forbidding the expenditure of more than $1,000 to present them is much like allowing a speaker in a public hall to express his views while denying him the use of an amplifying system. [*Buckley.*]

> We also reject the notion that the PACs' form of organization or method of solicitation diminishes their entitlement to First Amendment protection. The First Amendment freedom of association is squarely implicated in these cases. NCPAC and FCM are mechanisms by which large numbers of individuals of modest means can join together in organizations which serve to "amplif[y] the voice of their adherents." *Buckley*; *CARC*. It is significant that in 1979–1980 approximately 101,000 people contributed an average of $75 each to NCPAC and in 1980 approximately 100,000 people contributed an average of $25 each to FCM.

> The FEC urges that these contributions do not constitute individual speech, but merely "speech by proxy," see *California Medical Assn. v. FEC* (MARSHALL, J.) (plurality opinion), because the contributors do not control or decide upon the use of the funds by the PACs or the specific content of the PACs' advertisements and other speech. The plurality emphasized in that case, however, that nothing in the statutory provision in question "limits the amount [an unincorporated association] or any of its members may independently expend in order to advocate political views," but only the amount it may contribute to a multicandidate political committee. Unlike *California Medical Assn.*, the present cases involve limitations on expenditures by PACs, not on the contributions they receive; and in any event these contributions are predominantly small and thus do not raise the same concerns as the sizable contributions involved in *California Medical Assn.*

> Another reason the "proxy speech" approach is not useful in this case is that the contributors obviously like the message they are hearing from these organizations and want to add their voices to that message; otherwise they would not part with their money. To say that their collective action in pooling their resources to amplify their voices is not entitled to full First Amendment protection

would subordinate the voices of those of modest means as opposed to those sufficiently wealthy to be able to buy expensive media ads with their own resources.

Our decision in *NRWC* is not to the contrary. That case turned on the special treatment historically accorded corporations.... Like the National Right to Work Committee, NCPAC and FCM are also formally incorporated; however, these are not "corporations" cases because §9012(f) applies not just to corporations but to any "committee, association, or organization (whether or not incorporated)" that accepts contributions or makes expenditures in connection with electoral campaigns. The terms of §9012(f)'s prohibition apply equally to an informal neighborhood group that solicits contributions and spends money on a Presidential election as to the wealthy and professionally managed PACs involved in these cases.

The Court then held that the government could not advance a sufficient interest to justify section 9012(f):

We held in *Buckley* and reaffirmed in *Citizens Against Rent Control* that preventing corruption or the appearance of corruption are the only legitimate and compelling government interests thus far identified for restricting campaign finances. In *Buckley* we struck down the FECA's limitation on individuals' independent expenditures because we found no tendency in such expenditures, uncoordinated with the candidate or his campaign, to corrupt or to give the appearance of corruption. For similar reasons, we also find §9012(f)'s limitation on independent expenditures by political committees to be constitutionally infirm.

Corruption is a subversion of the political process. Elected officials are influenced to act contrary to their obligations of office by the prospect of financial gain to themselves or infusions of money into their campaigns. The hallmark of corruption is the financial *quid pro quo*: dollars for political favors. But here the conduct proscribed is not contributions to the candidate, but independent expenditures in support of the candidate. The amounts given to the PACs are overwhelmingly small contributions, well under the $1,000 limit on contributions upheld in *Buckley*; and the contributions are by definition not coordinated with the campaign of the candidate ... It is contended that, because the PACs may by the breadth of their organizations spend larger amounts than the individuals in *Buckley*, the potential for corruption is greater. But precisely what the "corruption" may consist of we are never told with assurance. The fact that candidates and elected officials may alter or reaffirm their own positions on issues in response to political messages paid for by the PACs can hardly be called corruption, for one of the essential features of democracy is the presentation to the electorate of varying points of view. It is of course hypothetically possible here, as in the case of the independent expenditures forbidden in *Buckley*, that candidates may take notice of and reward those responsible for PAC expenditures by giving official favors to the latter in exchange for the supporting messages. But here, as in *Buckley*, the absence of prearrangement and coordination undermines the value of the expenditure to the candidate, and thereby alleviates the danger that expenditures will be given as a *quid pro quo* for improper commitments from the candidate. On this record, such an exchange of political favors for uncoordinated expenditures remains a hypothetical possibility and nothing more.

Even were we to determine that the large pooling of financial resources by NCPAC and FCM did pose a potential for corruption or the appearance of corruption, §9012(f) is a fatally overbroad response to that evil. It is not limited to multimillion dollar war chests; its terms apply equally to informal discussion groups that solicit neighborhood contributions to publicize their views about a particular Presidential candidate.

Finally, the Court refused to defer to congressional "expertise" on campaign finance and corrupting influences:

Here, however, the groups and associations in question, designed expressly to participate in political debate, are quite different from the traditional corporations organized for economic gain. In *NRWC* we rightly concluded that Congress might include, along with labor unions and corporations traditionally prohibited from making contributions to political candidates, membership corporations, though contributions by the latter might not exhibit all of the evil that contributions by traditional economically organized corporations exhibit. But this proper deference to a congressional determination of the need for a prophylactic rule where the evil of potential corruption had long been recognized does not suffice to establish the validity of §9012(f), which indiscriminately lumps with corporations any "committee, association or organization." ...

While in *NRWC* we held that the compelling governmental interest in preventing corruption supported the restriction of the influence of political war chests funneled through the corporate form, in the present cases we do not believe that a similar finding is supportable: when the First Amendment is involved, our standard of review is "rigorous," *Buckley*, and the effort to link either corruption or the appearance of corruption to independent expenditures by PACs, whether large or small, simply does not pass this standard of review. Even assuming that Congress could fairly conclude that large-scale PACs have a sufficient tendency to corrupt, the overbreadth of §9012(f) in these cases is so great that the section may not be upheld. We are not quibbling over fine-tuning of prophylactic limitations, but are concerned about wholesale restriction of clearly protected conduct.

Justice White dissented, disagreeing with much of the majority's First Amendment analysis. He also raised an additional justification for the provision:

Because it is an indispensable component of the public funding scheme, §9012(f) is supported by governmental interests absent in *Buckley*. Rather than forcing Congress to abandon public financing because it is unworkable without constitutionally prohibited restrictions on independent spending, I would hold that §9012(f) is permissible precisely because it is a necessary, narrowly drawn means to a constitutional end. The need to make public financing, with its attendant benefits, workable is a constitutionally sufficient additional justification for the burden on First Amendment rights.

The existence of the public financing scheme changes the picture in other ways as well. First, it heightens the danger of corruption discounted by the majority. If a candidate accepts public financing, private contributions are limited to zero. Where there are no contributions being made directly to the candidate or his committee, and no expenditures of private funds subject to his direct control, "independent" expenditures are thrown into much starker relief. If those are the only private expenditures, their independence is little assurance that they will not be noticed, appreciated, and, perhaps, repaid.

On the "strikingly different" tone of the Supreme Court in *NCPAC* compared to *NRWC*, see Marlene Arnold Nicholson, *The Supreme Court's Meandering Path in Campaign Finance Regulation and What it Portends for Future Reform*, 3 JOURNAL OF LAW & POLITICS 509, 529–32 (1987).

Does *NCPAC* rule out all limitations on independent expenditures under all circumstances? The Court first suggested an answer in FEDERAL ELECTION COMMISSION V. MASSACHUSETTS CITIZENS FOR LIFE, 479 U.S. 238 (1986). In that case, an incorporated anti-abortion group published a special edition of its newsletter

> prior to the September 1978 primary elections [for Congress]. While the May 1978 newsletter had been mailed to 2,109 people and the October 1978 newsletter to 3,119 people, more than 100,000 copies of the "Special Edition" were printed for distribution. The front page of the publication was headlined "EVERYTHING YOU NEED TO KNOW TO VOTE PRO-LIFE," and readers were admonished that "[n]o pro-life candidate can win in November without your vote in September." "VOTE PRO-LIFE" was printed in large bold-faced letters on the back page, and a coupon was provided to be clipped and taken to the polls to remind voters of the name of the "pro-life" candidates. Next to the exhortation to vote "pro-life" was a disclaimer: "This special election edition does not represent an endorsement of any particular candidate."
>
> To aid the reader in selecting candidates, the flyer listed the candidates for each state and federal office in every voting district in Massachusetts, and identified each one as either supporting or opposing what MCFL regarded as the correct position on three issues. A "y" indicated that a candidate supported the MCFL view on a particular issue and an "n" indicated that the candidate opposed it. An asterisk was placed next to the names of those incumbents who had made a "special contribution to the unborn in maintaining a 100% pro-life voting record in the state house by actively supporting MCFL legislation." While some 400 candidates were running for office in the primary, the "Special Edition" featured the photographs of only 13. These 13 had received a triple "y" rating, or were identified either as having a 100% favorable voting record or as having stated a position consistent with that of MCFL. No candidate whose photograph was featured had received even one "n" rating.

A complaint was filed alleging that *MCFL* violated section 441b by spending corporate treasury funds on the newsletter. The case eventually reached the Supreme Court.

The Court rejected MCFL's argument that it did not violate section 441b because its newsletter contained no express advocacy or because it should be entitled to an exemption from section 441b as a press entity:

> [Appellee] argues that the definition of an expenditure under §441b necessarily incorporates the requirement that a communication "expressly advocate" the election of candidates, and that its "Special Edition" does not constitute express advocacy. The argument relies on the portion of *Buckley* that upheld the disclosure requirement for expenditures by individuals other than candidates and by groups other than political committees. There, in order to avoid problems of overbreadth, the Court held that the term "expenditure" encompassed "only funds used for communications that expressly advocate the election or defeat of a clearly identified candidate." ...
>
> We agree with appellee that [the rationale for the *Buckley* ruling] requires a similar construction of the more intrusive provision that directly regulates in-

dependent spending. We therefore hold that an expenditure must constitute "express advocacy" in order to be subject to the prohibition of §441b. We also hold, however, that the publication of the "Special Edition" constitutes "express advocacy."

Buckley adopted the "express advocacy" requirement to distinguish discussion of issues and candidates from more pointed exhortations to vote for particular persons. We therefore concluded in that case that a finding of "express advocacy" depended upon the use of language such as "vote for," "elect," "support," etc. Just such an exhortation appears in the "Special Edition." The publication not only urges voters to vote for "pro-life" candidates, but also identifies and provides photographs of specific candidates fitting that description. The Edition cannot be regarded as a mere discussion of public issues that by their nature raise the names of certain politicians. Rather, it provides in effect an explicit directive: vote for these (named) candidates. The fact that this message is marginally less direct than "Vote for Smith" does not change its essential nature. The Edition goes beyond issue discussion to express electoral advocacy. The disclaimer of endorsement cannot negate this fact. The "Special Edition" thus falls squarely within §441b, for it represents express advocacy of the election of particular candidates distributed to members of the general public.

Finally, MCFL argues that it is entitled to the press exemption under 2 U.S.C. §431(9)(B)(i) reserved for "any news story, commentary, or editorial distributed through the facilities of any ... newspaper, magazine, or other periodical publication, unless such facilities are owned or controlled by any political party, political committee, or candidate."

MCFL maintains that its regular newsletter is a "periodical publication" within this definition, and that the "Special Edition" should be regarded as just another issue in the continuing newsletter series. The legislative history on the press exemption is sparse; the House of Representatives' Report on this section states merely that the exemption was designed to

> make it plain that it is not the intent of Congress in the present legislation to limit or burden in any way the first amendment freedoms of the press or of association. [The exemption] assures the unfettered right of the newspapers, TV networks, and other media to cover and comment on political campaigns.

We need not decide whether the regular MCFL newsletter is exempt under this provision, because, even assuming that it is, the "Special Edition" cannot be considered comparable to any single issue of the newsletter. It was not published through the facilities of the regular newsletter, but by a staff which prepared no previous or subsequent newsletters. It was not distributed to the newsletter's regular audience, but to a group 20 times the size of that audience, most of whom were members of the public who had never received the newsletter. No characteristic of the Edition associated it in any way with the normal MCFL publication. The MCFL masthead did not appear on the flyer, and, despite an apparent belated attempt to make it appear otherwise, the Edition contained no volume and issue number identifying it as one in a continuing series of issues.

MCFL protests that determining the scope of the press exemption by reference to such factors inappropriately focuses on superficial considerations of form. However, it is precisely such factors that in combination permit the distinction of campaign flyers from regular publications. We regard such an inquiry as essential, since we cannot accept the notion that the distribution of such flyers by entities that happen to publish newsletters automatically entitles such organizations to the press exemption. A contrary position would open the door for those corporations and unions with in-house publications to engage in unlimited spending directly from their treasuries to distribute campaign material to the general public, thereby eviscerating §441b's prohibition.[5]

The Court then considered whether it would be constitutional to limit independent spending by corporations, suggesting in dicta that the corporate limit ordinarily would be constitutional as applied to for-profit corporations, but holding that the rules could not be applied against an ideological corporation such as MCFL:

> When a statutory provision burdens First Amendment rights, it must be justified by a compelling state interest. The FEC first insists that justification for §441b's expenditure restriction is provided by this Court's acknowledgment that "the special characteristics of the corporate structure require particularly careful regulation." *NRWC.* The Commission thus relies on the long history of regulation of corporate political activity as support for the application of §441b to MCFL. Evaluation of the Commission's argument requires close examination of the underlying rationale for this longstanding regulation.

> We have described that rationale in recent opinions as the need to restrict "the influence of political war chests funneled through the corporate form," *NCPAC*; to "eliminate the effect of aggregated wealth on federal elections," *Pipefitters*; to curb the political influence of "those who exercise control over large aggregations of capital," *Automobile Workers*; and to regulate the "substantial aggregations of wealth amassed by the special advantages which go with the corporate form of organization," *NRWC.*

> This concern over the corrosive influence of concentrated corporate wealth reflects the conviction that it is important to protect the integrity of the marketplace of political ideas. It acknowledges the wisdom of Justice Holmes' observation that "the ultimate good desired is better reached by free trade in ideas—that the best test of truth is the power of the thought to get itself accepted in the competition of the market...." *Abrams v. United States*, 250 U.S. 616, 630 (1919) (Holmes, J., joined by Brandeis, J., dissenting).

> Direct corporate spending on political activity raises the prospect that resources amassed in the economic marketplace may be used to provide an unfair advantage in the political marketplace. Political "free trade" does not necessarily require that all who participate in the political marketplace do so with exactly equal resources. See *NCPAC*; *Buckley*. Relative availability of funds is after all a rough barometer of public support. The resources in the treasury of a business corporation, however, are not an indication of popular support for the corporation's political ideas. They reflect instead the economically motivated decisions of investors and customers. The availability of these resources may make a corporation a formidable political presence, even though the power of the corporation may be no reflection of the power of its ideas.

---

5. Nor do we find the "Special Edition" akin to the normal business activity of a press entity deemed by some lower courts to fall within the exemption, such as the distribution of a letter soliciting subscriptions, see *FEC v. Phillips Publishing Co.*, 517 F.Supp. 1308, 1313 (DC 1981), or the dissemination of publicity, see *Reader's Digest Assn. v. FEC*, 509 F.Supp. 1210 (SDNY 1981).

By requiring that corporate independent expenditures be financed through a political committee expressly established to engage in campaign spending, §441b seeks to prevent this threat to the political marketplace. The resources available to *this* fund, as opposed to the corporate treasury, in fact reflect popular support for the political positions of the committee.[11] The expenditure restrictions of §441b are thus meant to ensure that competition among actors in the political arena is truly competition among ideas.

Regulation of corporate political activity thus has reflected concern not about use of the corporate form *per se*, but about the potential for unfair deployment of wealth for political purposes.[12] Groups such as MCFL, however, do not pose that danger of corruption. MCFL was formed to disseminate political ideas, not to amass capital. The resources it has available are not a function of its success in the economic marketplace, but its popularity in the political marketplace. While MCFL may derive some advantages from its corporate form, those are advantages that redound to its benefit as a political organization, not as a profit-making enterprise. In short, MCFL is not the type of "traditional corporatio[n] organized for economic gain," *NCPAC*, that has been the focus of regulation of corporate political activity.

The Court then summarized the features of MCFL relevant to its ability to gain an exemption from section 441b:

> In particular, MCFL has three features essential to our holding that it may not constitutionally be bound by §441b's restriction on independent spending. *First*, it was formed for the express purpose of promoting political ideas, and cannot engage in business activities. If political fundraising events are expressly denominated as requests for contributions that will be used for political purposes, including direct expenditures, these events cannot be considered business activities. This ensures that political resources reflect political support. *Second*, it has no shareholders or other persons affiliated so as to have a claim on its assets or earnings. This ensures that persons connected with the organization will have no economic disincentive for disassociating with it if they disagree with its political activity. *Third*, MCFL was not established by a business corporation or a labor union, and it is its policy not to accept contributions from such entities. This prevents such corporations from serving as conduits for the type of direct spending that creates a threat to the political marketplace.

A few years after *MCFL*, the Court considered the constitutionality of campaign spending limits in candidate campaigns applied against corporations not entitled to the *MCFL* exemption.

---

11. While business corporations may not represent the only organizations that pose this danger, they are by far the most prominent example of entities that enjoy legal advantages enhancing their ability to accumulate wealth. That Congress does not at present seek to regulate every possible type of firm fitting this description does not undermine its justification for regulating corporations. Rather, Congress' decision represents the "careful legislative adjustment of the federal electoral laws, in a 'cautious advance, step by step,'" to which we have said we owe considerable deference. *NRWC*.

12. The regulation imposed as a result of this concern is of course distinguishable from the complete foreclosure of any opportunity for political speech that we invalidated in the state referendum context in *Bellotti*.

Austin v. Michigan Chamber of Commerce
494 U.S. 652 (1990)

Justice MARSHALL delivered the opinion of the Court.

In this appeal, we must determine whether §54(1) of the Michigan Campaign Finance Act violates either the First or the Fourteenth Amendment to the Constitution. Section 54(1) prohibits corporations from using corporate treasury funds for independent expenditures in support of, or in opposition to, any candidate in elections for state office. Mich.Comp. Laws §169.254(1) (1979). Corporations are allowed, however, to make such expenditures from segregated funds used solely for political purposes. §169.255(1). In response to a challenge brought by the Michigan State Chamber of Commerce (Chamber), the Sixth Circuit held that §54(1) could not be applied to the Chamber, a Michigan nonprofit corporation, without violating the First Amendment. 856 F.2d 783 (1988). Although we agree that expressive rights are implicated in this case, we hold that application of §54(1) to the Chamber is constitutional because the provision is narrowly tailored to serve a compelling state interest. Accordingly, we reverse the judgment of the Court of Appeals.

I

Section 54(1) of the Michigan Campaign Finance Act prohibits corporations from making contributions and independent expenditures in connection with state candidate elections.[1] The issue before us is only the constitutionality of the State's ban on independent expenditures.... The Act exempts from this general prohibition against corporate political spending any expenditure made from a segregated fund. §169.255(1). A corporation may solicit contributions to its political fund only from an enumerated list of persons associated with the corporation. See §§169.255(2),(3).

The Chamber, a nonprofit Michigan corporation, challenges the constitutionality of this statutory scheme. The Chamber comprises more than 8,000 members, three-quarters of whom are for-profit corporations. The Chamber's general treasury is funded through annual dues required of all members. Its purposes, as set out in the bylaws, are to promote economic conditions favorable to private enterprise; to analyze, compile, and disseminate information about laws of interest to the business community and to publicize to the government the views of the business community on such matters; to train and educate its members; to foster ethical business practices; to collect data on, and investigate matters of, social, civic, and economic importance to the State; to receive contributions and to make expenditures for political purposes and to perform any other lawful political activity; and to coordinate activities with other similar organizations.

In June 1985 Michigan scheduled a special election to fill a vacancy in the Michigan House of Representatives. Although the Chamber had established and funded a separate political fund, it sought to use its general treasury funds to place in a local newspaper an advertisement supporting a specific candidate. As the Act made such an expenditure punishable as a felony, see §169.254(5), the Chamber brought suit in District Court for injunctive relief against enforcement of the Act, arguing that the restriction on expenditures is unconstitutional under both the First and the Fourteenth Amendments....

---

1. Section 54(1) is modeled on a provision of the Federal Election Campaign Act of 1971 that requires corporations and labor unions to use segregated funds to finance independent expenditures made in federal elections. 2 U.S.C. §441b.

II

To determine whether Michigan's restriction on corporate political expenditures may constitutionally be applied to the Chamber, we must ascertain whether it burdens the exercise of political speech and, if it does, whether it is narrowly tailored to serve a compelling state interest....

A

This Court concluded in *MCFL* that a federal statute requiring corporations to make independent political expenditures only through special segregated funds burdens corporate freedom of expression. The Court reasoned that the small nonprofit corporation in that case would face certain organizational and financial hurdles in establishing and administering a segregated political fund. For example, the statute required the corporation to appoint a treasurer for its segregated fund, keep records of all contributions, file a statement of organization containing information about the fund, and update that statement periodically. In addition, the corporation was permitted to solicit contributions to its segregated fund only from "members," which did not include persons who merely contributed to or indicated support for the organization. These hurdles "impose[d] administrative costs that many small entities [might] be unable to bear" and "create[d] a disincentive for such organizations to engage in political speech."

Despite the Chamber's success in administering its separate political fund ([the] Chamber expected to have over $140,000 in its segregated fund available for use in the 1986 elections), Michigan's segregated fund requirement still burdens the Chamber's exercise of expression because "the corporation is not free to use its general funds for campaign advocacy purposes." *MCFL* (plurality opinion). The Act imposes requirements similar to those in the federal statute involved in *MCFL*: a segregated fund must have a treasurer, §169.221; and its administrators must keep detailed accounts of contributions, §169.224, and file with state officials a statement of organization, *ibid*. In addition, a nonprofit corporation like the Chamber may solicit contributions to its political fund only from members, stockholders of members, officers or directors of members, and the spouses of any of these persons. §169.255. Although these requirements do not stifle corporate speech entirely, they do burden expressive activity. See *MCFL*. Thus, they must be justified by a compelling state interest.

B

The State contends that the unique legal and economic characteristics of corporations necessitate some regulation of their political expenditures to avoid corruption or the appearance of corruption. See *NCPAC* ("[P]reventing corruption or the appearance of corruption are the only legitimate and compelling government interests thus far identified for restricting campaign finances"). State law grants corporations special advantages—such as limited liability, perpetual life, and favorable treatment of the accumulation and distribution of assets—that enhance their ability to attract capital and to deploy their resources in ways that maximize the return on their shareholders' investments. These state-created advantages not only allow corporations to play a dominant role in the Nation's economy, but also permit them to use "resources amassed in the economic marketplace" to obtain "an unfair advantage in the political marketplace." *MCFL*. As the Court explained in *MCFL*, the political advantage of corporations is unfair because

> [t]he resources in the treasury of a business corporation ... are not an indication of popular support for the corporation's political ideas. They reflect in-

stead the economically motivated decisions of investors and customers. The availability of these resources may make a corporation a formidable political presence, even though the power of the corporation may be no reflection of the power of its ideas.

We therefore have recognized that "the compelling governmental interest in preventing corruption support[s] the restriction of the influence of political war chests funneled through the corporate form." *NCPAC*.

The Chamber argues that this concern about corporate domination of the political process is insufficient to justify a restriction on independent expenditures. Although this Court has distinguished these expenditures from direct contributions in the context of federal laws regulating individual donors, *Buckley*, it has also recognized that a legislature might demonstrate a danger of real or apparent corruption posed by such expenditures when made by corporations to influence candidate elections, *Bellotti*. Regardless of whether this danger of "financial *quid pro quo*" corruption, see *NCPAC*, may be sufficient to justify a restriction on independent expenditures, Michigan's regulation aims at a different type of corruption in the political arena: the corrosive and distorting effects of immense aggregations of wealth that are accumulated with the help of the corporate form and that have little or no correlation to the public's support for the corporation's political ideas. The Act does not attempt "to equalize the relative influence of speakers on elections," *post* (KENNEDY, J., dissenting); rather, it ensures that expenditures reflect actual public support for the political ideas espoused by corporations. We emphasize that the mere fact that corporations may accumulate large amounts of wealth is not the justification for §54; rather, the unique state-conferred corporate structure that facilitates the amassing of large treasuries warrants the limit on independent expenditures. Corporate wealth can unfairly influence elections when it is deployed in the form of independent expenditures, just as it can when it assumes the guise of political contributions. We therefore hold that the State has articulated a sufficiently compelling rationale to support its restriction on independent expenditures by corporations.

C

We next turn to the question whether the Act is sufficiently narrowly tailored to achieve its goal. We find that the Act is precisely targeted to eliminate the distortion caused by corporate spending while also allowing corporations to express their political views. Contrary to the dissents' critical assumptions, the Act does not impose an *absolute* ban on all forms of corporate political spending but permits corporations to make independent political expenditures through separate segregated funds. Because persons contributing to such funds understand that their money will be used solely for political purposes, the speech generated accurately reflects contributors' support for the corporation's political views. See *MCFL*.

The Chamber argues that §54(1) is substantially overinclusive, because it includes within its scope closely held corporations that do not possess vast reservoirs of capital. We rejected a similar argument in *NRWC*, in the context of federal restrictions on the persons from whom corporations could solicit contributions to their segregated funds.... Although some closely held corporations, just as some publicly held ones, may not have accumulated significant amounts of wealth, they receive from the State the special benefits conferred by the corporate structure and present the potential for distorting the political process. This potential for distortion justifies §54(1)'s general applicability to all corporations. The section therefore is not substantially overbroad.

III

The Chamber contends that even if the Campaign Finance Act is constitutional with respect to for-profit corporations, it nonetheless cannot be applied to a nonprofit ideological corporation like a chamber of commerce. In *MCFL*, we held that the nonprofit organization there had "features more akin to voluntary political associations than business firms, and therefore should not have to bear burdens on independent spending solely because of [its] incorporated status." In reaching that conclusion, we enumerated three characteristics of the corporation that were "essential" to our holding. Because the Chamber does not share these crucial features, the Constitution does not require that it be exempted from the generally applicable provisions of §54(1).

The first characteristic of Massachusetts Citizens for Life, Inc., that distinguished it from ordinary business corporations was that the organization "was formed for the express purpose of promoting political ideas, and cannot engage in business activities." ... MCFL's narrow political focus thus "ensure[d] that [its] political resources reflect[ed] political support."

In contrast, the Chamber's bylaws set forth more varied purposes, several of which are not inherently political. For instance, the Chamber compiles and disseminates information relating to social, civic, and economic conditions, trains and educates its members, and promotes ethical business practices. Unlike MCFL's, the Chamber's educational activities are not expressly tied to political goals; many of its seminars, conventions, and publications are politically neutral and focus on business and economic issues. The Chamber's president and chief executive officer stated that one of the corporation's main purposes is to provide "service to [its] membership that includes everything from group insurance to educational seminars, and ... litigation activities on behalf of the business community." Deposition of E. James Barrett. The Chamber's nonpolitical activities therefore suffice to distinguish it from MCFL in the context of this characteristic.

We described the second feature of MCFL as the absence of "shareholders or other persons affiliated so as to have a claim on its assets or earnings. This ensures that persons connected with the organization will have no economic disincentive for disassociating with it if they disagree with its political activity." Although the Chamber also lacks shareholders, many of its members may be similarly reluctant to withdraw as members even if they disagree with the Chamber's political expression, because they wish to benefit from the Chamber's nonpolitical programs and to establish contacts with other members of the business community. The Chamber's political agenda is sufficiently distinct from its educational and outreach programs that members who disagree with the former may continue to pay dues to participate in the latter. Justice KENNEDY ignores these disincentives for withdrawing as a member of the Chamber, stating only that "[o]ne need not become a member ... to earn a living." Certainly, members would be disinclined to terminate their involvement with the organization on the basis of less extreme disincentives than the loss of employment. Thus, we are persuaded that the Chamber's members are more similar to shareholders of a business corporation than to the members of MCFL in this respect.

The final characteristic upon which we relied in *MCFL* was the organization's independence from the influence of business corporations. On this score, the Chamber differs most greatly from the Massachusetts organization. MCFL was not established by, and had a policy of not accepting contributions from, business corporations. Thus it could not "serv[e] as [a] condui[t] for the type of direct spending that creates a threat to the political marketplace." In striking contrast, more than three-quarters of the Chamber's members are business corporations, whose political contributions and expenditures can constitutionally be regulated by the State. As we read the Act, a corporation's payments into the Chamber's general treasury would not be considered payments to influence an election, so they would not be "contributions" or "expenditures," and would not be subject to the Act's limitations. Business corporations therefore could circumvent the Act's restriction by funneling money through the Chamber's general treasury. Because the Chamber accepts money from for-profit corporations, it could, absent application of §54(1), serve as a conduit for corporate political spending. In sum, the Chamber does not possess the features that would compel the State to exempt it from restriction on independent political expenditures.

IV

The Chamber also attacks §54(1) as underinclusive because it does not regulate the independent expenditures of unincorporated labor unions. Whereas unincorporated unions, and indeed individuals, may be able to amass large treasuries, they do so without the significant state-conferred advantages of the corporate structure; corporations are "by far the most prominent example of entities that enjoy legal advantages enhancing their ability to accumulate wealth." *MCFL*. The desire to counterbalance those advantages unique to the corporate form is the State's compelling interest in this case; thus, excluding from the statute's coverage unincorporated entities that also have the capacity to accumulate wealth "does not undermine its justification for regulating corporations." *Ibid*.

Moreover, labor unions differ from corporations in that union members who disagree with a union's political activities need not give up full membership in the organization to avoid supporting its political activities. Although a union and an employer may require that all bargaining unit employees become union members, a union may not compel those employees to support financially "union activities beyond those germane to collective bargaining, contract administration, and grievance adjustment." *Communications Workers v. Beck*, 487 U.S. 735, 745 (1988). See also *Abood* (holding that compelling non-member employees to contribute to union's political activities infringes employees' First Amendment rights). An employee who objects to a union's political activities thus can decline to contribute to those activities, while continuing to enjoy the benefits derived from the union's performance of its duties as the exclusive representative of the bargaining unit on labor-management issues. As a result, the funds available for a union's political activities more accurately reflect[] members' support for the organization's political views than does a corporation's general treasury. Michigan's decision to exclude unincorporated labor unions from the scope of §54(1) is therefore justified by the crucial differences between unions and corporations.

V

Because we hold that §54(1) does not violate the First Amendment, we must address the Chamber's contention that the provision infringes its rights under the Fourteenth Amendment. The Chamber argues that the statute treats similarly situated entities unequally. Specifically, it contends that the State should also restrict the independent expenditures of unincorporated associations with the ability to accumulate large treasuries and of corporations engaged in the media business.

Because the right to engage in political expression is fundamental to our constitutional system, statutory classifications impinging upon that right must be narrowly tailored to serve a compelling governmental interest. *Police Department of Chicago v. Mosley*, 408 U.S. 92, 101 (1972). We find that, even under such strict scrutiny, the statute's classifications pass muster under the Equal Protection Clause. As we explained in the context of our discussions of whether the statute was overinclusive or underinclusive, the State's decision to regulate only corporations is precisely tailored to serve the compelling state interest of eliminating from the political process the corrosive effect of political "war chests" amassed with the aid of the legal advantages given to corporations.

Similarly, we find that the Act's exemption of media corporations from the expenditure restriction does not render the statute unconstitutional....

Although all corporations enjoy the same state-conferred benefits inherent in the corporate form, media corporations differ significantly from other corporations in that their resources are devoted to the collection of information and its dissemination to the public. We have consistently recognized the unique role that the press plays in "informing and educating the public, offering criticism, and providing a forum for discussion and debate." *Bellotti.* See also *Mills v. Alabama*, 384 U.S. 214, 219 (1966) ("[T]he press serves and was designed to serve as a powerful antidote to any abuses of power by governmental officials and as a constitutionally chosen means for keeping officials elected by the people responsible to all the people whom they were selected to serve").... The media exception ensures that the Act does not hinder or prevent the institutional press from reporting on, and publishing editorials about, newsworthy events. A valid distinction thus exists between corporations that are part of the media industry and other corporations that are not involved in the regular business of imparting news to the public. Although the press' unique societal role may not entitle the press to greater protection under the Constitution, *Bellotti*, it does provide a compelling reason for the State to exempt media corporations from the scope of political expenditure limitations. We therefore hold that the Act does not violate the Equal Protection Clause.

VI

Michigan identified as a serious danger the significant possibility that corporate political expenditures will undermine the integrity of the political process, and it has implemented a narrowly tailored solution to that problem. By requiring corporations to make all independent political expenditures through a separate fund made up of money solicited expressly for political purposes, the Michigan Campaign Finance Act reduces the threat that huge corporate treasuries amassed with the aid of favorable state laws will be used to influence unfairly the outcome of elections. The Michigan Chamber of Commerce does not exhibit the characteristics identified in *MCFL* that would require the State to exempt it from a generally applicable restriction on independent corporate expenditures. We therefore reverse the decision of the Court of Appeals.

It is so ordered.[c]

Justice STEVENS, concurring.

In my opinion the distinction between individual expenditures and individual contributions that the Court identified in *Buckley* should have little, if any, weight in reviewing corporate participation in candidate elections. In that context, I believe the danger of either the fact, or the appearance, of *quid pro quo* relationships provides an adequate

---

c. Justice Brennan's concurring opinion, consisting largely of a rebuttal to the dissents, is omitted.

justification for state regulation of both expenditures and contributions.... Accordingly, I join the Court's opinion and judgment.

Justice SCALIA, dissenting.

"Attention all citizens. To assure the fairness of elections by preventing disproportionate expression of the views of any single powerful group, your Government has decided that the following associations of persons shall be prohibited from speaking or writing in support of any candidate: _____." In permitting Michigan to make private corporations the first object of this Orwellian announcement, the Court today endorses the principle that too much speech is an evil that the democratic majority can proscribe. I dissent because that principle is contrary to our case law and incompatible with the absolutely central truth of the First Amendment: that government cannot be trusted to assure, through censorship, the "fairness" of political debate.

I
A

The Court's opinion says that political speech of corporations can be regulated because "[s]tate law grants [them] special advantages" and because this "unique state-conferred corporate structure ... facilitates the amassing of large treasuries." This analysis seeks to create one good argument by combining two bad ones. Those individuals who form that type of voluntary association known as a corporation are, to be sure, given special advantages—notably, the immunization of their personal fortunes from liability for the actions of the association—that the State is under no obligation to confer. But so are other associations and private individuals given all sorts of special advantages that the State need not confer, ranging from tax breaks to contract awards to public employment to outright cash subsidies. It is rudimentary that the State cannot exact as the price of those special advantages the forfeiture of First Amendment rights. See *Pickering v. Board of Education*, 391 U.S. 563 (1968); *Speiser v. Randall*, 357 U.S. 513 (1958). The categorical suspension of the right of any person, or of any association of persons, to speak out on political matters must be justified by a compelling state need. See *Buckley*. That is why the Court puts forward its second bad argument, the fact that corporations "amas[s] large treasuries." But that alone is also not sufficient justification for the suppression of political speech, unless one thinks it would be lawful to prohibit men and women whose net worth is above a certain figure from endorsing political candidates. Neither of these two flawed arguments is improved by combining them and saying, as the Court in effect does, that "since the State gives special advantages to these voluntary associations, and since they thereby amass vast wealth, they may be required to abandon their right of political speech."[1]

---

1. The Court's assertion that the Michigan law "does not impose an *absolute* ban on all forms of corporate political spending," (emphasis added) is true only in a respect that is irrelevant for purposes of First Amendment analysis. A corporation is absolutely prohibited from spending its own funds on this form of political speech, and would be guilty of misrepresentation if it asserted that a particular candidate was supported or opposed by the corporation. This is to say that the corporation *as a corporation* is prohibited from speaking. What the Michigan law permits the corporation to do is to serve as the founder and treasurer of a different association of individuals that can endorse or oppose political candidates. The equivalent, where an individual rather than an association is concerned, would be to prohibit John D. Rockefeller from making political endorsements, but to permit him to form an association to which others (though not he himself) can contribute for the purpose of making political endorsements. Just as political speech by that association is not speech by John D.

The Court's extensive reliance upon the fact that the objects of this speech restriction, corporations, receive "special advantages" is in stark contrast to our opinion issued just six years ago in *FCC v. League of Women Voters of California*, 468 U.S. 364 (1984). In that decision, striking down a congressionally imposed ban upon editorializing by noncommercial broadcasting stations that receive federal funds, the *only* respect in which we considered the receipt of that "special advantage" relevant was in determining whether the speech limitation could be justified under Congress' spending power, as a means of assuring that the subsidy was devoted only to the purposes Congress intended, which did not include political editorializing. We held it could not be justified on that basis, since "a noncommercial educational station that receives only 1% of its overall income from [federal] grants is barred absolutely from all editorializing.... The station has no way of limiting the use of its federal funds to all noneditorializing activities, and, more importantly, it is barred from using even wholly private funds to finance its editorial activity." Of course the same is true here, even assuming that tax exemptions and other benefits accorded to incorporated associations constitute an exercise of the spending power. It is not just that portion of the corporation's assets attributable to the gratuitously conferred "special advantages" that is prohibited from being used for political endorsements, but *all* of the corporation's assets. I am at a loss to explain the vast difference between the treatment of the present case and *League of Women Voters*. Commercial corporations may not have a public *persona* as sympathetic as that of public broadcasters, but they are no less entitled to this Court's concern.

As for the second part of the Court's argumentation, the fact that corporations (or at least some of them) possess "massive wealth": Certain uses of "massive wealth" in the electoral process—whether or not the wealth is the result of "special advantages" conferred by the State—pose a substantial risk of corruption which constitutes a compelling need for the regulation of speech. Such a risk plainly exists when the wealth is given directly to the political candidate, to be used under his direction and control. We held in *Buckley*, however, that independent expenditures to express the political views of individuals and associations do not raise a sufficient threat of corruption to justify prohibition. Neither the Court's opinion nor either of the concurrences makes any effort to distinguish that case—except, perhaps, by misdescribing the case as involving "federal laws regulating individual donors," or as involving "individual expenditures," (STEVENS, J., concurring). Section 608(e)(1) of the Federal Election Campaign Act of 1971, which we found unconstitutional in *Buckley*, was directed, like the Michigan law before us here, to expenditures made for the purpose of advocating the election or defeat of a particular candidate. It limited to $1,000 (a *lesser* restriction than the absolute prohibition at issue here) such expenditures not merely by "individuals," but by "persons," specifically defined to include corporations. The plaintiffs in the case included corporations, and we specifically discussed §608(e)(1) as a restriction addressed not just to individuals but to "individuals and groups," "persons and groups," "persons and organizations," "person[s] [and] association[s]." ... In support of our determination that the restriction was "wholly at odds with the guarantees of the First Amendment" we cited *Miami Herald Publishing Co. v. Tornillo*, 418 U.S. 241 (1974), which involved limitations upon a corporation. Of course, if §608(e)(1) had been unconstitutional only as applied to individuals and not as applied to corporations, we might nonetheless have invalidated it *in toto* for substantial overbreadth, see *Broadrick v. Oklahoma*, 413 U.S. 601, 611–613 (1973), but there is not a hint of that doctrine in our opinion. Our First Amendment law is much less certain than I

Rockefeller, so also speech by a corporate PAC that the Michigan law allows is not speech by the corporation itself.

had thought it to be if we are free to recharacterize each clear holding as a disguised "overbreadth" determination.

Buckley should not be overruled, because it is entirely correct. The contention that prohibiting overt advocacy for or against a political candidate satisfies a "compelling need" to avoid "corruption" is easily dismissed. As we said in *Buckley*, "[i]t would naively underestimate the ingenuity and resourcefulness of persons and groups desiring to buy influence to believe that they would have much difficulty devising expenditures that skirted the restriction on express advocacy of election or defeat but nevertheless benefited the candidate's campaign." Independent advocacy, moreover, unlike contributions, "may well provide little assistance to the candidate's campaign and indeed may prove counterproductive," thus reducing the danger that it will be exchanged "as a *quid pro quo* for improper commitments from the candidate." The latter point seems even more plainly true with respect to corporate advocates than it is with respect to individuals. I expect I could count on the fingers of one hand the candidates who would generally welcome, much less negotiate for, a formal endorsement by AT & T or General Motors. The advocacy of such entities that have "amassed great wealth" will be effective only to the extent that it brings to the people's attention *ideas* which—despite the invariably self-interested and probably uncongenial source—strike them as true.

The Court does not try to defend the proposition that independent advocacy poses a substantial risk of political "corruption," as English speakers understand that term. Rather, it asserts that that concept (which it defines as "'financial *quid pro quo*' corruption,") is really just a narrow subspecies of a hitherto unrecognized genus of political corruption. "Michigan's regulation," we are told, "aims at a different type of corruption in the political arena: the corrosive and distorting effects of immense aggregations of wealth that are accumulated with the help of the corporate form and that have little or no correlation to the public's support for the corporation's political ideas." Under this mode of analysis, virtually anything the Court deems politically undesirable can be turned into political corruption—by simply describing its effects as politically "corrosive," which is close enough to "corruptive" to qualify. It is sad to think that the First Amendment will ultimately be brought down not by brute force but by poetic metaphor.

The Court's opinion ultimately rests upon that proposition whose violation constitutes the "New Corruption": Expenditures must "reflect actual public support for the political ideas espoused." This illiberal free-speech principle of "one man, one minute" was proposed and soundly rejected in *Buckley*:

> It is argued, however, that the ancillary governmental interest in equalizing the relative ability of individuals and groups to influence the outcome of elections serves to justify the limitation on express advocacy of the election or defeat of candidates imposed by §608(e)(1)'s expenditure ceiling. But the concept that government may restrict the speech of some elements of our society in order to enhance the relative voice of others is wholly foreign to the First Amendment, which was designed "to secure 'the widest possible dissemination of information from diverse and antagonistic sources,'" and "to assure unfettered interchange of ideas for the bringing about of political and social changes desired by the people."

But it can be said that I have not accurately quoted today's decision. It does not endorse the proposition that government may ensure that expenditures "reflect actual public support for the political ideas espoused," but only the more limited proposition that government may ensure that expenditures "reflect actual public support for the political ideas espoused by corporations." The limitation is of course entirely irrational. Why is it perfectly all right if advocacy by an individual billionaire is out of proportion with "actual public support" for his positions? There is no explanation, except the effort I described at the outset of this discussion to make one valid proposition out of two invalid ones: When the vessel labeled "corruption" begins to founder under weight too great to be logically sustained, the argumentation jumps to the good ship "special privilege"; and when that in turn begins to go down, it returns to "corruption." Thus hopping back and forth between the two, the argumentation may survive but makes no headway towards port, where its conclusion waits in vain....

C

[The Court finds §54(1) narrowly tailored to serve a compelling state interest] for the following reason:

> As we explained in the context of our discussions of whether the statute was overinclusive or underinclusive, the State's decision to regulate only corporations is precisely tailored to serve the compelling state interest of eliminating from the political process the corrosive effect of political "war chests" amassed with the aid of the legal advantages given to corporations.

That state interest (assuming it is compelling) does indeed explain why the State chose to silence "only corporations" rather than wealthy individuals as well. But it does not explain (what "narrow tailoring" pertains to) why the State chose to silence *all* corporations, rather than just those that possess great wealth. If narrow tailoring means anything, surely it must mean that action taken to counter the effect of amassed "war chests" must be targeted, if possible, at amassed "war chests." And surely such targeting is possible—either in the manner accomplished by the provision that we invalidated in *Buckley*, *i.e.*, by limiting the prohibition to independent expenditures above a certain amount, or in some other manner, *e.g.*, by limiting the expenditures of only those corporations with more than a certain amount of net worth or annual profit....

D

Finally, a few words are in order concerning the Court's approval of the Michigan law's exception for "media corporations." This is all right, we are told, because of "the unique role that the press plays in 'informing and educating the public, offering criticism, and providing a forum for discussion and debate.'" But if one believes in the Court's rationale of "compelling state need" to prevent amassed corporate wealth from skewing the political debate, surely that "unique role" of the press does not give Michigan justification for *excluding* media corporations from coverage, but provides especially strong reason to include them. Amassed corporate wealth that regularly sits astride the ordinary channels of information is much more likely to produce the New Corruption (too much of one point of view) than amassed corporate wealth that is generally busy making money elsewhere. Such media corporations not only have vastly greater power to perpetrate the evil of overinforming, they also have vastly greater opportunity. General Motors, after all, will risk a stockholder suit if it makes a political endorsement that is not plausibly tied to its ability to make money for its shareholders. But media corporations make money *by* making political commentary, including endorsements. For them, unlike any other corporations, the whole world of politics and ideology is fair game. Yet the Court tells us that it is reasonable to *exclude* media corporations, rather than target them specially.

Members of the institutional press, despite the Court's approval of their illogical exemption from the Michigan law, will find little reason for comfort in today's decision. The theory of New Corruption it espouses is a dagger at their throats. The Court today holds merely that media corporations *may* be excluded from the Michigan law, not that they *must* be. We have consistently rejected the proposition that the institutional press has any constitutional privilege beyond that of other speakers. See *Bellotti*. Thus, the Court's holding on this point must be put in the following unencouraging form: "Although the press' unique societal role may not entitle the press to greater protection under the Constitution, *Bellotti*, it does provide a compelling reason for the State to exempt media corporations from the scope of political expenditure limitations." One must hope, I suppose, that Michigan will continue to provide this generous and voluntary exemption.

II

I would not do justice to the significance of today's decision to discuss only its lapses from case precedent and logic. Infinitely more important than that is its departure from long-accepted premises of our political system regarding the benevolence that can be expected of government in managing the arena of public debate, and the danger that is to be anticipated from powerful private institutions that compete with government, and with one another, within that arena.

Perhaps the Michigan law before us here has an unqualifiedly noble objective — to "equalize" the political debate by preventing disproportionate expression of corporations' points of view. But governmental abridgment of liberty is always undertaken with the very best of announced objectives (dictators promise to bring order, not tyranny), and often with the very best of genuinely intended objectives (zealous policemen conduct unlawful searches in order to put dangerous felons behind bars). The premise of our Bill of Rights, however, is that there are some things — even some seemingly *desirable* things — that government cannot be trusted to do. The very first of these is establishing the restrictions upon speech that will assure "fair" political debate. The incumbent politician who says he welcomes full and fair debate is no more to be believed than the entrenched monopolist who says he welcomes full and fair competition. Perhaps the Michigan Legislature was genuinely trying to assure a "balanced" presentation of political views; on the other hand, perhaps it was trying to give unincorporated unions (a not insubstantial force in Michigan) political advantage over major employers. Or perhaps it was trying to assure a "balanced" presentation because it knows that with evenly balanced speech incumbent officeholders generally win. The fundamental approach of the First Amendment, I had always thought, was to assume the worst, and to rule the regulation of political speech "for fairness' sake" simply out of bounds.

I doubt that those who framed and adopted the First Amendment would agree that avoiding the New Corruption, that is, calibrating political speech to the degree of public opinion that supports it, is even a *desirable* objective, much less one that is important enough to qualify as a compelling state interest. Those Founders designed, of course, a system in which popular ideas would ultimately prevail; but also, through the First Amendment, a system in which true ideas could readily become popular. For the latter purpose, the calibration that the Court today endorses is precisely backwards: To the extent a valid proposition has scant public support, it should have wider rather than narrower public circulation. I am confident, in other words, that Jefferson and Madison would not have sat at these controls; but if they did, they would have turned them in the opposite direction.

Ah, but then there is the special element of corporate wealth: What would the Founders have thought of that? They would have endorsed, I think, what Tocqueville wrote in 1835:

> When the members of an aristocratic community adopt a new opinion or conceive a new sentiment, they give it a station, as it were, beside themselves, upon the lofty platform where they stand; and opinions or sentiments so conspicuous to the eyes of the multitude are easily introduced into the minds or hearts of all around. In democratic countries the governing power alone is naturally in a condition to act in this manner; but it is easy to see that its action is always inadequate, and often dangerous.... No sooner does a government attempt to go beyond its political sphere and to enter upon this new track than it exercises, even unintentionally, an insupportable tyranny.... Worse still will be the case if the government really believes itself interested in preventing all circulation of ideas; it will then stand motionless and oppressed by the heaviness of voluntary torpor. Governments, therefore, should not be the only active powers; associations ought, in democratic nations, to stand in lieu of those powerful private individuals whom the equality of conditions has swept away.

2 A. de Tocqueville, Democracy in America 109 (P. Bradley ed. 1948). While Tocqueville was discussing "circulation of ideas" in general, what he wrote is also true of candidate endorsements in particular. To eliminate voluntary associations—not only including powerful ones, but *especially* including powerful ones—from the public debate is either to augment the always dominant power of government or to impoverish the public debate. The case at hand is a good enough example. Why should the Michigan voters in the 93d House District be deprived of the information that private associations owning and operating a vast percentage of the industry of the State, and employing a large number of its citizens, believe that the election of a particular candidate is important to their prosperity? Contrary to the Court's suggestion, the same point cannot effectively be made through corporate PACs to which individuals may voluntarily contribute. It is important to the message that it represents the views of Michigan's leading corporations *as corporations*, occupying the "lofty platform" that they do within the economic life of the State— not just the views of some *other* voluntary associations to which some of the corporations' shareholders belong.

Despite all the talk about "corruption and the appearance of corruption"—evils that are not significantly implicated and that can be avoided in many other ways—it is entirely obvious that the object of the law we have approved today is not to prevent wrongdoing but to prevent speech. Since those private associations known as corporations have so much money, they will speak so much more, and their views will be given inordinate prominence in election campaigns. This is not an argument that our democratic traditions allow—neither with respect to individuals associated in corporations nor with respect to other categories of individuals whose speech may be "unduly" extensive (because they are rich) or "unduly" persuasive (because they are movie stars) or "unduly" respected (because they are clergymen). The premise of our system is that there is no such thing as too much speech—that the people are not foolish but intelligent, and will separate the wheat from the chaff. As conceded in Lincoln's aphorism about fooling "all of the people some of the time," that premise will not invariably accord with reality; but it will assuredly do so much more frequently than the premise the Court today embraces: that a healthy democratic system can survive the legislative power to prescribe how much political speech is too much, who may speak, and who may not.

III.

Because today's decision is inconsistent with unrepudiated legal judgments of our Court, but even more because it is incompatible with the unrepealable political wisdom of our First Amendment, I dissent.

Justice KENNEDY, with whom Justice O'CONNOR and Justice SCALIA join, dissenting.

... By using distinctions based upon both the speech and the speaker, the Act engages in the rawest form of censorship: the State censors what a particular segment of the political community might say with regard to candidates who stand for election. The Court's holding cannot be reconciled with the principle that "legislative restrictions on advocacy of the election or defeat of political candidates are wholly at odds with the guarantees of the First Amendment." *Meyer v. Grant.*

... The Court draws support for its discrimination among nonprofit corporate speakers from portions of our opinion in *MCFL*. It must be acknowledged that certain language in *MCFL*, in particular the discussion which pointed to the express purpose of the organization to promote political ideas, lends support to the majority's test. That language, however, contravenes fundamental principles of neutrality for all political speech. It should not stand in the way of giving full force to the essential and vital holding of *MCFL*, which is that a nonprofit corporation engaged in political discussion of candidates and elections has the full protection of the First Amendment.

... The majority almost admits that, in the case of independent expenditures, the danger of a political *quid pro quo* is insufficient to justify a restriction of this kind. Since the specter of corruption, which had been "the only legitimate and compelling government interest[s] thus far identified for restricting campaign finances," *NCPAC*, is missing in this case, the majority invents a new interest: combating the "corrosive and distorting effects of immense aggregations of wealth," accumulated in corporate form without shareholder or public support. The majority styles this novel interest as simply a different kind of corruption, but has no support for its assertion. While it is questionable whether such imprecision would suffice to justify restricting political speech by for-profit corporations, it is certain that it does not apply to nonprofit entities.

The evil of political corruption has been defined in more precise terms. We have said: "Corruption is a subversion of the political process" whereby "[e]lected officials are influenced to act contrary to their obligations of office by the prospect of financial gain...." *NCPAC*. In contrast, the interest touted by the majority is the impermissible one of altering political debate by muting the impact of certain speakers....

Notes and Questions

1. *Austin*'s recognition that corporate spending could be limited to prevent "the corrosive and distorting effects of immense aggregations of wealth that are accumulated with the help of the corporate form and that have little or no correlation to the public's support for the corporation's political ideas" was presaged in the *MCFL* opinion. Justice Scalia and Justice O'Connor joined that part of *MCFL* but dissented in *Austin*. What, if anything, changed from 1986 to 1990? As we will see Justice O'Connor reversed her position again on this issue in the *McConnell* case.

2. In *NCPAC*, the Court stated:

Corruption is a subversion of the political process. Elected officials are influenced to act contrary to their obligations of office by the prospect of financial gain to themselves or infusions of money into their campaigns. The hallmark of corruption is the financial *quid pro quo*: dollars for political favors

In *NRWC* the Court upheld the ban on corporate contributions in part because the ban

> ensure[d] that substantial aggregations of wealth amassed by the special advantages which go with the corporate form of organization should not be converted into political "war chests" which could be used to incur political debts from legislators who are aided by the contributions.

In *MCFL*, is the Court addressing the same state interest as in these passages from *NCPAC* and *NRWC*? Consider Marlene Arnold Nicholson, *Basic Principles or Theoretical Tangles: Analyzing the Constitutionality of Government Regulation of Campaign Finance*, 38 Case Western Reserve Law Review 589, 599 (1988):

> [In *MCFL*], the Court not only expanded its definition of corruption, beyond that articulated in *National Conservative Political Action Committee*, but in doing so it seemed to adopt a version of the much maligned equalization rationale as part of its new definition. In *Massachusetts Citizens for Life* the "corrosive effect of concentrated wealth" to which the Court referred is the effect on the electoral process, not the effect on office holders.

Is the *Austin/MCFL* "corrosion" rationale consistent with *Buckley*'s rejection of the equality rationale for limiting campaign spending?

3. In *Austin, w*hy does Justice Marshall emphasize the advantages given to corporations by state laws? Is it because of the pressure originating from Justice Scalia's argument that the fact that corporations may derive their wealth from sources unrelated to their political views does very little to differentiate corporations from many other organizations and from wealthy individuals? If so, does Justice Marshall's reliance on state-created advantages salvage his position? Is the fact that corporations receive certain advantages relevant to the extent to which they should be permitted to participate financially in electoral politics?

Bellotti was criticized by some for failing to give sufficient weight to the advantages conferred on corporations by the state. See William Patton & Randall Bartlett, *Corporate "Persons" and Freedom of Speech: The Political Impact of Legal Mythology*, 1981 Wisconsin Law Review 494, 496. Writing after *Austin*, another commentator acknowledged Justice Scalia's argument that the receipt of legal advantages is not unique to the corporation, but responded that "there are differences of degree, and the Court might properly make distinctions based on them." Julian N. Eule, *Promoting Speaker Diversity: Austin and Metro Broadcasting*, 1990 Supreme Court Review 105, 115. A variant on this view is expressed in Daniel Hays Lowenstein, *A Patternless Mosaic: Campaign Finance and the First Amendment After* Austin, 21 Capital Law Review 381, 407–08 (1992):

> [T]he question should be whether the advantages given to the corporation by the state are related to the regulation in question in a way that lends justification to the regulation. In the present context, the only apparent relation between advantages provided to corporations and regulation of their financial participation in election campaigns is that the advantages facilitate the accumulation of large amounts of capital within the corporation. Accordingly, the legal advantages enjoyed by corporations may to a degree reinforce arguments based on their ability to accumulate capital, but the legal advantages do not provide an independent justification for regulation of corporate political activity.

4. When Justice Scalia asks why it is "perfectly all right if advocacy by an individual billionaire is out of proportion with 'actual public support' for his positions," might one

response be that it is *not* all right, and that the inconsistency should be resolved by overruling *Buckley*'s strong protection of independent expenditures? But is there necessarily an inconsistency? Consider Marlene Arnold Nicholson, *Basic Principles or Theoretical Tangles: Analyzing the Constitutionality of Government Regulation of Campaign Finance*, 38 CASE WESTERN RESERVE LAW REVIEW 589, 606 (1988):

> Corporate expression does not reflect the self-realization of actual people. [She adds, in a footnote, "It probably reflects only someone's determination of what will be most profitable for the corporation, which may or may not correspond with anyone's view of good political policy."] Perhaps we must be willing to tolerate the possibility of a coercive influence of concentrated wealth when it represents someone's self-fulfillment, but we need not do so when that element is missing.

Nicholson adds that although this would be a "principled conclusion," she would reject it because the self-realization interest should be considered together with other pertinent values. All would be accommodated, she suggests, "if very generous limitations were applied to independent expenditures, the use of candidate wealth and contributions in ballot measure elections."

5. Justice Marshall attempts to rebut the dissenters' characterization of the Michigan statute as an absolute ban on corporate political spending on the ground that the statute "permits corporations to make independent political expenditures through separate segregated funds," i.e., PACs. If the use of corporate funds to pay the administrative expenses of a PAC were prohibited, would the law be constitutional? Are the dissenters correct that the corporation's ability to create and pay the expenses of a PAC is an inadequate substitute, because there is distinctive value in the speech originating from the corporation itself? For arguments supporting the dissenters on this issue, see David Shelledy, *Autonomy, Debate, and Corporate Speech*, 18 HASTINGS CONSTITUTIONAL LAW QUARTERLY 541, 569–73 (1991).

6. Is *Austin* consistent with *Bellotti*? In *Michigan State Chamber of Commerce v. Austin*, 832 F.2d 947 (6th Cir. 1987), a different case involving some of the same parties, the Court of Appeals struck down a Michigan statute that limited corporate contributions to committees supporting or opposing a ballot measure to $40,000. The court relied on the statement in *Bellotti* that "Referenda are held on issues, not candidates for political office. The risk of corruption perceived in cases involving candidate elections, simply is not present in a popular vote on a public issue." Is this statement in *Bellotti* valid given the conception of "corruption" accepted by the Supreme Court majority in *MCFL* and *Austin*? Given these two decisions, should a statute similar to the Michigan law struck down by the 6th Circuit be upheld? *MCFL* was decided nearly a year before the 6th Circuit decision in *Michigan State Chamber of Commerce*, but is not cited in the court's opinion and may not have been known to the court.

In *Montana Chamber of Commerce v. Argenbright*, 28 F.Supp.2d 593 (D. Mont. 1998), a federal district court struck down a Montana initiative preventing corporations from making contributions or expenditures in connection with ballot campaigns. The Ninth Circuit affirmed: "Even if *Austin* plausibly may be read as undermining *Bellotti*, this is for the Supreme Court, not us to say." 226 F.3d 1049, 1057 (9th Cir. 2000), cert. denied 534 U.S. 817 (2001). For a discussion of *Bellotti*'s continued viability after *Austin* and of the *Argenbright* case, see Adam Winkler, *Beyond* Bellotti, 32 LOYOLA OF LOS ANGELES LAW REVIEW (1998).

7. Has the Supreme Court changed its views regarding the First Amendment rights of corporations to engage in electoral activities? Consider *Federal Election Commission v. Beaumont*, 539 U.S. 146 (2003), a case that held corporate contributions to candidates could

be prohibited, even if the corporation is entitled to an *MCFL* exemption from the ban on independent expenditures. In particular, consider the relevance, if any, of *Beaumont*'s footnote 8:

> Within the realm of contributions generally, corporate contributions are furthest from the core of political expression, since corporations' First Amendment speech and association interests are derived largely from those of their members, see, *e.g., NAACP v. Alabama*, and of the public in receiving information, see, *e.g., Bellotti.* A ban on direct corporate contributions leaves individual members of corporations free to make their own contributions and deprives the public of little or no material information.

Might a ban on corporate *expenditures* be said to "leave individual members of corporations free to make their own contributions [and expenditures] and deprive[] the public of little or no material information"? If so, what is left of *Bellotti*? If not, what is the difference between corporate contributions and expenditures under *Beaumont*'s view of the First Amendment?

8. Given the distinction drawn in *MCFL* and *Austin* between two types of corporations, did the Court reach the right result regarding the Michigan Chamber of Commerce? If MCFL added to its political activities a program of educating pregnant women regarding pre-natal care, and if it entered into arrangements with a bank and an insurance company to provide attractive discounts on credit cards and life insurance to contributors to MCFL, would it then be constitutional to ban MCFL from making independent expenditures? If your answer is no, is it because of Justice Marshall's third point, that MCFL still would not be receiving contributions or membership payments from business corporations? See *Minnesota Citizens Concerned for Life v. FEC*, 113 F.3d 129 (8th Cir. 1997) (striking down FEC regulation providing that in order to be eligible for *MCFL* exemption, the corporation must engage in no business activities, must offer no member incentives such as credit cards, insurance policies, or savings plans, and must accept no donations from business corporations or unions).

Suppose the Michigan Chamber of Commerce continued to receive payments from corporate members but abandoned all aspects of its program other than pursuing its political agenda. Would it be entitled to an exemption from the independent expenditure ban? If not, would it be fair to say that Justice Marshall really is applying a one-part rather than a three-part test? See *FEC v. Survival Education Fund, Inc.*, 65 F.3d 285, 292 (2d. Cir. 1995). To take advantage of the *MCFL* exception, must a not-for-profit organization refuse to accept even a small amount of corporate contributions? See *Federal Election Commission v. National Rifle Association*, 254 F.3d 173 (D.C. Cir. 2001).

9. In Part IV of his opinion, Justice Marshall holds that extending the ban on independent expenditures to corporations but not to labor unions does not result in unconstitutional discrimination. Federal law extends the ban to both unions and corporations. Is the federal ban on independent expenditures by unions constitutional under the reasoning of *MCFL* and *Austin*? The Court apparently decided the question in the affirmative in *McConnell*, as discussed below.

10. CEOs of two major corporations wish to use substantial corporate resources to elect candidates they prefer for federal office. One CEO is media mogul Rupert Murdoch; the other is the CEO of General Motors. The FECA prevents the General Motors CEO from directly using corporate resources for contributions to or independent expenditures for federal candidates. 2 U.S.C. §441b. *Austin* is authority that this prohibition is constitutional. But the FECA, like the Michigan statute at issue in *Austin*, contains an exception

to the definition of expenditure for "any news story, commentary, or editorial distributed through the facilities of any broadcasting station, newspaper, magazine, or other periodical publication, unless such facilities are owned or controlled by any political party, political committee, or candidate." 2 U.S.C. §431(9)(B)(i). So Rupert Murdoch could publish editorial after editorial in his newspapers and magazines urging the election or defeat of candidates for federal office. *Austin* held that the different treatment of media corporations did not render the ban on non-media corporate independent expenditures in candidate campaigns unconstitutional. Nonetheless, some scholars have argued that there is no good reason to treat media corporations more generously under the First Amendment than others. For an argument that this "Rupert Murdoch problem" should cause courts to strike down all contribution and expenditure limits, see Arthur N. Eisenberg, Buckley, *Rupert Murdoch, and the Pursuit of Equality in the Conduct of Elections,* 1996 ANNUAL SURVEY OF AMERICAN LAW 451, 460. For an argument that equality requires regulating all corporations *including* media corporations under applicable campaign finance laws, see Richard L. Hasen, *Campaign Finance Laws and the Rupert Murdoch Problem,* 77 TEXAS LAW REVIEW 1627 (1999). On what basis did Justice Marshall uphold the different treatment? Are you convinced that the press plays the role that Marshall describes? Hasen notes that media endorsements of candidates are not randomly distributed; they favor incumbents and Republican presidential candidates. He advocates regulation of newspaper endorsements, but not news stories. Conservative organizations have presented evidence that the "working press" — reporters who write news articles on politics — are far more Democratic and liberal than the general public. Is it possible to distinguish between newspaper endorsements and news stories? Is such regulation constitutional? The Supreme Court has never held that the institutional press must receive extra or special constitutional protection. Should it?

11. If the *New York Times* is exempt from expenditure limitations when it endorses a candidate, what about the newspaper's website? What happens to the media exception in the Internet era? In *MCFL*, the Court held that a "Special Edition" of a newsletter that listed "pro-life" candidates did not qualify for the media exemption because "[i]t was not published through the facilities of a regular newspaper, but by a staff which prepared no previous or subsequent newsletter." In addition, it was distributed to an audience 20 times the size of the audience of its regular newsletter, and to many nonmembers.

The question of what happens to the media exemption in the "Internet Era" landed at the Federal Election Commission in 2005. Following the passage of BCRA, the FEC passed a series of implementing regulations, including a regulation that exempted communications over the Internet from coverage under the "public communications" portions of BCRA. 11 C.F.R. § 100.26. Congressional sponsors of BCRA brought suit challenging a number of the FEC's regulations implementing BCRA, including the Internet exemption. A federal district court struck down the exemption as inconsistent with Congressional intent and ordered the FEC to write new regulations *Shays v. FEC,* 337 F.Supp.2d 28, 65–70 (D.D.C. 2004). After a protracted process in which the FEC was lobbied heavily to keep Internet-based political activity as unregulated as possible, the FEC wrote new regulations granting a very wide exemption for most Internet-based election activity, aside from paid political advertising. The final rules, along with an explanation and justification for them, appear at 71 FEDERAL REGISTER 18589 (Apr. 12, 2006). The regulations were widely applauded by both supporters and opponents of campaign finance regulation. Does this open up a new "loophole" from regulation, or does it appropriately protect First Amendment rights of speech and association? What is different about Internet-based political activity that might justify a different set of rules?

12. Corporations and unions are not the only entities targeted for special regulation. For example, federal law prohibits contributions in *any* election—federal, state or local— by national banks and corporations specially chartered by acts of Congress (2 U.S.C. §441b); in any election or for *any political purpose* by federal contractors (2 U.S.C. §441c); and in any *candidate* election by foreign nationals (2 U.S.C. §441e). The foreign national provision took on greatly heightened salience shortly before the 1996 general election. According to news reports, supporters of President Clinton's reelection campaign, especially at the Democratic National Committee (DNC), had aggressively solicited contributions from overseas sources, especially in Indonesia and China. Congressional committees and the Justice Department investigated, leading to a number of prosecutions and a few convictions, but little evidence of a concerted effort by any foreign government to influence the outcome of the election. For one case arising out of the scandals, see *United States v. Kanchanalak*, 192 F.3d 1037 (D.C. Cir. 1999).

Section 441e does not prohibit permanent resident aliens from contributing to campaigns. See 2 U.S.C. §441e(b)(2) (defining a "foreign national" as, "an individual who is not a citizen of the United States and who is not lawfully admitted for permanent residence …").[d] In the aftermath of the 1996 scandals, both Democrats and Republicans called for section 441e to be amended to prevent permanent resident aliens from making contributions. See Jessica S. Horrocks, Note, *Campaigns, Contributions and Citizenship: The First Amendment Right of Resident Aliens to Finance Federal Elections*, 38 BOSTON COLLEGE LAW REVIEW 771, 772 (1997). Should Congress change the law in this manner? Both the student note cited above and Bruce D. Brown, *Alien Donors: The Participation of Non-Citizens in the U.S. Campaign Finance System*, 15 YALE LAW & POLICY REVIEW 503, 542–47 (1997), argue that depriving aliens of the right to make campaign contributions would run afoul of *Buckley*. Brown's argument depends upon his contention that aliens in the United States are fully protected by the First Amendment. *Id.* at 529–42. Given the Supreme Court's deference to the executive and legislative branches regarding matters of foreign policy and immigration, it seems unlikely that section 441e, even amended in the manner proposed, would be declared unconstitutional. Should Section 441e be repealed? Should it be limited to contributions from foreign governments? Should it be limited to contributions to federal candidates? What purposes are served by Section 441e?

13. Lobbyists are individuals who are employed to influence governmental decisions in the executive and, especially, the legislative branch. Not surprisingly, lobbyists often desire to or are pressured to make campaign contributions. Some states have attempted to place special restrictions on contributions by lobbyists. In one sense, such restrictions are more precisely targeted than restrictions on corporations, unions, or PACs, because, by definition, lobbyists are employed to influence public officials. But lobbyists are individuals, not organizations, and as individuals they enjoy the same constitutional rights as anyone else. Are restrictions directed at lobbyists' contributions constitutional? *See North Carolina Right to Life, Inc. v. Bartlett*, 168 F.3d 705 (4th Cir. 1999), cert. denied 528 U.S. 1153 (2000), where the court, applying strict scrutiny, upheld a North Carolina law prohibiting a lobbyist, a lobbyist's agent, or a political committee that employs a lobbyist from contributing to a member of or candidate for the North Carolina General Assembly or Council of State (an advisory body) while the General Assembly is in session. The law also prohibited candidates or incumbents from soliciting lobbyists or political

---

d. American subsidiaries of foreign corporations also appear to be outside of the section 441e prohibition. See Note,"*Foreign" Campaign Contributions and the First Amendment*, 110 HARVARD LAW REVIEW 1886 (1997).

committees that employ them during the session. Note that this provision applies to both lobbyists and to political committees that employ lobbyists. As to political committees, is the prohibition constitutional under *NCPAC*?

Would the North Carolina prohibition on contributions by lobbyists be constitutional if it applied at all times, not only during legislative sessions? In *Fair Political Practices Commission v. Superior Court*, 599 P.2d 46 (Cal. 1979), cert. denied 444 U.S. 1049 (1980), the California Supreme Court struck down California Government Code §86202, which made it unlawful:

> for a lobbyist to make a contribution, or to act as an agent or intermediary in the making of any contribution, or to arrange for the making of any contribution by himself or by another person.

The court reasoned as follows:

> The claimed state interest is to rid the political system of both apparent and actual corruption and improper influence. Under *Buckley* such a purpose justifies closely drawn restrictions. However, it does not appear that total prohibition of contributions by any lobbyist is a closely drawn restriction.
>
> First, the prohibition applies to contributions to any and all candidates even though the lobbyist may never have occasion to lobby the candidate. Secondly, the definition of lobbyist is extremely broad, to include persons who appear regularly before administrative agencies seeking to influence administrative determinations in favor of their clients. Thirdly, the statute does not discriminate between small and large but prohibits all contribution. Thus, it is not narrowly directed to the aspects of political association where potential corruption might be identified.
>
> While either apparent or actual political corruption might warrant some restriction of lobbyist associational freedom, it does not warrant total prohibition of all contributions by all lobbyists to all candidates.

How significant is the first of the court's objections, that the ban applies to all candidates for state office, even those the lobbyist may never try to influence? As of 1979, there were 127 state elective offices. 120 of these were seats in the legislature. Of the remaining seven, the Governor had the power to sign or veto bills and the Lieutenant Governor had that power when the Governor was absent from the state. At most, then, there would be five elective offices that a legislative lobbyist might be unconcerned with.

The court's second objection to the statute was that the ban applied to some lobbyists who lobbied only executive agencies. In a comment to one of its regulations, 2 Cal. Code of Regulations §18600, the FPPC made these points:

> The influence of legislative officials and elected state officers extends throughout state government, there being no precise limits of their jurisdiction. Administrative agency officials know that members of the Legislature and the constitutional officers chosen directly by the people play a role in (1) defining the agency's powers; (2) adopting legislation bearing on the work of the agency; (3) determining the budget of the agency; (4) making or confirming appointments to the agency; and (5) considering future appointments to other governmental posts for the incumbent agency officials. In addition to these factors is the prestige of these elected officials which may give their communications with and urgings upon administrative agency officials special weight.

Whatever their merits, the court's first two objections could be satisfied fairly easily by a slightly more narrowly drawn statute. The third objection is that the statute bans contributions by lobbyists rather than limiting their size. Is this objection undermined by *NRWC*?

In 2000, the California Legislature proposed and the voters approved a new campaign finance regulation including a ban on contributions by lobbyists, modified as suggested above. That is, the first two objections in *FPPC v. Superior Court* were obviated by a provision limiting the prohibition to lobbyists who were registered to lobby before the official's or candidate's agency, such as the legislature or the Attorney General's office. In addition, administrative regulations adopted since *FPPC v. Superior Court* was decided had narrowed the definition of lobbyist in some respects. But the new prohibition, like the old one, was an absolute ban, with no exceptions for small contributions or contributions made when the legislature was out of session. Is the new prohibition constitutional? See *Institute of Governmental Advocates v. Fair Political Practices Commission*, 164 F.Supp.2d 1183 (E.D. Cal. 2001).

14. Some targeted prohibitions of contributions have been upheld by state courts, including a ban on contributions by officers and "key employees" of casinos in *Petition of Soto*, 565 A.2d 1088 (N.J.Super. 1989), cert. denied, 496 U.S. 937 (1990), and by liquor licensees in *Schiller Park Colonial Inn v. Berz*, 349 N.E.2d 61 (Ill. 1976). The Louisiana Supreme Court reached a result contrary to *Soto* in *Penn v. State*, 751 So.2d 823 (La. 1999), cert. denied, 429 U.S. 1109 (2000). The court there struck down a state statute prohibiting some in the video poker gaming industry from making campaign contributions to state and local candidates and their committees. The court pointed to the fact that the ban applied only to some persons in the gaming industry and also maintained that the ban was unnecessary, given generally applicable campaign contribution limits. But the main problem for the majority appeared to be that "[t]his absolute ban on political contributions by a particular segment of society goes far beyond what *Buckley* endorsed. The First Amendment simply does not allow the State to target groups and exclude them from the political process"(Johnson, J., concurring). Citing Louisiana's rich history of corruption associated with the gaming industry, two dissenting justices would have upheld the provision as narrowly tailored to prevent corruption and the appearance of corruption. In *Casino Association of Louisiana v. State*, 820 So.2d 494 (La. 2002), cert. denied *sub nom. Casino Association of Louisiana v. Louisiana*, 123 S.Ct. 1252 (2003), the Louisiana Supreme Court upheld a law barring campaign contributions by casinos. The court both distinguished and questioned the reasoning of its earlier *Penn* decision.

Some might predict that gaming industry employees are more likely than lobbyists to corrupt the political process (or create the appearance of corruption) through the giving of campaign contributions, but others might expect the opposite. How would you bet?

III. Regulating Corporate and Union "Issue Advocacy:" The End of Spending Limits?

Part III.A of the last chapter discussed the enactment of the Bipartisan Campaign Reform Act of 2002 (BCRA) and the major challenge to the legislation in the Supreme Court case of *McConnell v. FEC*, 540 U.S. 93 (2003). There, we focused on the "soft money" provisions, the core of which limited *contributions* to political parties made by corporations, labor unions, and others. We turn now to BCRA's issue advocacy provisions.

In the 1974 FECA amendments, Congress sought to impose limits on any spending "relative to a clearly identified candidate [in federal elections]" and to require "'[e]very person ... who makes contributions or expenditures' ... 'for the purpose of ... influencing' the nomination or election of candidates for federal office" to disclose the source of such contributions and expenditures. The Supreme Court in *Buckley* viewed both of these statutes as presenting problems of unconstitutional vagueness; people engaging in political speech might well not know if the statutes cover their conduct.

In order to save both statutes from unconstitutional vagueness, the Court construed them as reaching only "communications that in express terms advocate the election or defeat of a clearly identified candidate." The Court explained that such *express advocacy* required explicit words "of advocacy of election or defeat, such as 'vote for,' 'elect,' 'support,' 'cast your ballot for,' 'Smith for Congress,' 'vote against,' 'defeat,' [or] 'reject.'" So construed, the Court still struck down the spending limits as violating the First Amendment, but it upheld the disclosure requirements (as discussed in Chapter 18).

The upshot of this part of *Buckley* is that advertisements intended to or likely to influence the outcome of an election but lacking words of express advocacy were unregulated by FECA. Such advertisements became known as "issue advocacy," even though the prime issue at stake in many of these advertisements was the election or defeat of a candidate. Thus, an advertisement lacking express advocacy but criticizing Senator Smith in the weeks before the election was not subject to disclosure under FECA, and could be paid for with corporate or union funds, and is subject to no contribution limits. The conduct escapes FECA because the advertisement ends with something like, "Call Smith and tell her what you think of her Medicare plan" rather than "Defeat Smith."

Issue advocacy exploded on the federal election scene in 1996. Individuals, political parties, interest groups, labor unions, and corporations spent as much as $150 million that year on such advertisements,[e] and the figure climbed to at least $275 million during the 1998 election.[f] The number reached $509 million for the 2000 election cycle.[g]

BCRA sought to regulate this activity through a new "electioneering communications" test. Under BCRA, corporations and unions may not spend general treasury funds (but may spend PAC funds) on "electioneering communications." An electioneering communication "encompasses any broadcast, cable or satellite communication that refers to a candidate for federal office and that is aired within 30 days of a primary election or 60 days of a federal election in the jurisdiction in which that candidate is running for office." Thus, under section 203 of BCRA, a corporation or union could not use treasury funds to pay for a television advertisement broadcast shortly before the election criticizing Senator Smith by name for her lousy Medicare plan.

By a 5–4 vote in *McConnell*, the Supreme Court upheld section 203 of BCRA. Eight of the nine Supreme Court justices rejected any constitutionally significant distinction between express advocacy and issue advocacy. Indeed, as the excerpts from *McConnell's* disclosure discussion in Chapter 18 detail, eight Justices voted to uphold BCRA's main disclosure provisions, requiring that anyone who spends enough money on "electioneering communications" must disclose such spending as well as most contributions funding that spending. (Only Justice Thomas disagreed on these points.) Thus, eight Justices

---

e. DEBORAH BECK ET AL., ISSUE ADVOCACY DURING THE 1996 CAMPAIGN 3 (Annenberg Pub. Policy Ctr. Report Series No. 16, 1997), *available at* http://www.appc.penn.org/pub.htm.

f. Jeffrey D. Stanger & Douglas G. Rivlin, *Issue Advocacy Advertising During the 1997–1998 Election Cycle, at* http://appcpenn.org/issueads/report. htm.

g. See *Issue Advocacy in the 1999–2000 Election Cycle, at* http://www.appcpenn.org/issueads/1999-2000issueadvocacy.pdf, at 4. See also *McConnell*, 540 U.S. at 127 n.20.

agreed that the presence of express words of advocacy did not limit the universe of election-related advertising that legislatures may constitutionally regulate.

That determination called *Austin* directly into question because, without a meaningful distinction between express advocacy and issue advocacy, the ban on independent spending by corporations and unions, upheld in *Austin,* was far more extensive than at the time *Austin* was decided. Furthermore, the only way to attack the electioneering provision was to attack the constitutionality of limits on *express* advocacy by corporations and unions. Thus, the focus shifted to the constitutionality of preventing corporations and unions from engaging in unlimited independent expenditures (whether containing words of express advocacy or not) mentioning candidates for federal office.

Recall that *Austin* was a 6–3 decision. Justices Kennedy, O'Connor, and Scalia dissented in *Austin*, and of the six-member majority, only Justice Stevens and Chief Justice Rehnquist remained on the Court. In *McConnell*, Chief Justice Rehnquist changed his vote, concurring with Justice Kennedy that *Austin* was wrongly decided and should be overruled. And Justice Thomas's vote against *Austin* was unsurprising, given his dissents in earlier campaign finance cases. What saved *Austin* and indeed led to its ringing affirmation in *McConnell* was the switch in position by Justice O'Connor, who joined with Justices Breyer, Ginsburg, Souter, and Stevens in the majority opinion on Title II. This was not the first time that Justice O'Connor had changed her vote on this question. Recall her vote in *MCFL*.

McConnell is also significant in extending the PAC requirement to labor unions. The *Austin* Court did not have before it a separate fund requirement for unions; indeed, the *Austin* Court held it was permissible to restrict corporations without mentioning the requirement for unions. Without any explicit discussion, the *McConnell* Court upheld the treatment of unions under the *Austin* rationale. Do unions obtain "immense aggregations of wealth" in the same manner as corporations? In light of *Abood*, do union members need the same protections as corporate shareholders? Should this matter for the constitutionality of requiring labor unions to use PACs for election-related activities? See Richard L. Hasen, *Justice Souter: Campaign Finance Law's Emerging Egalitarian*, 1 ALBANY GOVERNMENT LAW REVIEW 169 (2008), arguing that some egalitarians may oppose spending limits on unions and support them for corporations.

McConnell was a ringing endorsement of the deferential approach the Court had taken to campaign finance regulation beginning with *Shrink Missouri*. The *Election Law Journal*, Volume 3, Issue 2 (2004) features a symposium issue on the *McConnell* case, with lead articles by Lillian BeVier, Richard Briffault, and Michael Malbin, as well as commentaries by Senators, public officials (including the Chair and Vice Chair of the Federal Election Commission), lawyers who participated in the case, and a host of academic and other commentators.

But *McConnell* was not the Court's last word on the question of spending limits for corporations and unions. As of this writing, the most recent word appears in the *Wisconsin Right to Life* case (*WRTL*) below. Here's the relevant background: BCRA's electioneering communications test solved the FECA vagueness problem noted in *Buckley* (the test is easy to apply and does not involve any guesswork), but it introduced a potential problem of overbreadth. An advertisement might not be intended or likely to affect the outcome of the election, and still the advertisement would fall within the bright line electioneering communications test of BCRA section 203. Thus, a television advertisement that a corporation would like to run shortly before the election urging the President running for reelection to intervene in a labor dispute could not be paid for with general treasury funds.

In *McConnell v. FEC*, plaintiffs argued (among many other arguments) that section 203 was unconstitutionally overbroad because it captured too much so-called "genuine issue advocacy." The three lower court judges hearing *McConnell* devoted many pages and considerable effort to this question and focused particularly on two social science studies (the "Buying Time" studies[h]) examining the question. Judge Leon found that between 14.7% and 17% of the ads run before the 1998 and 2000 elections were genuine issue advertisements. Judge Kollar-Kotelly disagreed with both the 17% figure and its significance for the overbreadth analysis. Judge Henderson believed the figure was anywhere from 11.38% to 50.5% and, in any case, that the law was overbroad.

The Supreme Court majority opinion in *McConnell* devoted only a single paragraph to this issue. In language that later proved to be key to the *WRTL* case below, the Court explained why BCRA's electioneering communications test could constitutionally cover corporate and union advertisements that lacked words of express advocacy:

> This argument [that the government's compelling interest in regulating issue advocacy does not apply to "electioneering communications"] fails to the extent that the issue ads broadcast during the 30- and 60-day periods preceding federal primary and general elections are the functional equivalent of express advocacy. The justifications for the regulation of express advocacy apply equally to ads aired during those periods if the ads are intended to influence the voters' decisions and have that effect. The precise percentage of issue ads that clearly identified a candidate and were aired during those relatively brief preelection time spans but had no electioneering purpose is a matter of dispute between the parties and among the judges on the District Court. Nevertheless, the vast majority of ads clearly had such a purpose. Moreover, whatever the precise percentage may have been in the past, in the future corporations and unions may finance genuine issue ads during those timeframes by simply avoiding any specific reference to federal candidates, or in doubtful cases by paying for the ad from a segregated fund.

McConnell left open the question whether a corporation or union could bring an "as applied" challenge to BCRA section 203 by proving that a broadcast advertisement the entity wished to pay for from its general treasury funds was a "genuine issue advertisement" and therefore not subject to BCRA's restrictions. It was this issue that arose in the next case.

Federal Election Commission v. Wisconsin Right to Life, Inc.
127 S.Ct. 2652 (2007)

CHIEF JUSTICE ROBERTS announced the judgment of the Court and delivered the opinion of the Court with respect to Parts I and II, and an opinion with respect to Parts III and IV, in which JUSTICE ALITO joins.

Section 203 of the Bipartisan Campaign Reform Act of 2002 (BCRA) makes it a federal crime for any corporation to broadcast, shortly before an election, any communication that names a federal candidate for elected office and is targeted to the electorate. In *McConnell v. Federal Election Comm'n,* this Court considered whether §203 was facially overbroad under the First Amendment because it captured within its reach not only campaign speech, or "express advocacy," but also speech about public issues more generally,

---

h. CRAIG B. HOLMAN & LUKE P. MCLOUGHLIN, BRENNAN CENTER FOR JUSTICE, BUYING TIME 2000: TELEVISION ADVERTISEMENTS IN THE 2000 FEDERAL ELECTIONS (2001); JONATHAN S. KRASNO & DANIEL E. SELTZ, BRENNAN CTR. FOR JUSTICE, BUYING TIME 1998: TELEVISION ADVERTISING IN THE 1998 CONGRESSIONAL ELECTIONS (2000).

or "issue advocacy," that mentions a candidate for federal office. The Court concluded that there was no overbreadth concern to the extent the speech in question was the "functional equivalent" of express campaign speech. On the other hand, the Court "assume[d]" that the interests it had found to "justify the regulation of campaign speech might not apply to the regulation of genuine issue ads." The Court nonetheless determined that §203 was not facially overbroad. Even assuming §203 "inhibit[ed] some constitutionally protected corporate and union speech," the Court concluded that those challenging the law on its face had failed to carry their "heavy burden" of establishing that *all* enforcement of the law should therefore be prohibited.

Last Term, we reversed a lower court ruling, arising in the same litigation before us now, that our decision in *McConnell* left "no room" for as-applied challenges to §203. We held on the contrary that "[i]n upholding §203 against a facial challenge, we did not purport to resolve future as-applied challenges." *Wisconsin Right to Life, Inc. v. Federal Election Comm'n*, 546 U.S. 410, 411–412, (2006) (*per curiam*) (*WRTL I*).

We now confront such an as-applied challenge. Resolving it requires us first to determine whether the speech at issue is the "functional equivalent" of speech expressly advocating the election or defeat of a candidate for federal office, or instead a "genuine issue a[d]." *McConnell*. We have long recognized that the distinction between campaign advocacy and issue advocacy "may often dissolve in practical application. Candidates, especially incumbents, are intimately tied to public issues involving legislative proposals and governmental actions." *Buckley*. Our development of the law in this area requires us, however, to draw such a line, because we have recognized that the interests held to justify the regulation of campaign speech and its "functional equivalent" "might not apply" to the regulation of issue advocacy. *McConnell*.

In drawing that line, the First Amendment requires us to err on the side of protecting political speech rather than suppressing it. We conclude that the speech at issue in this as-applied challenge is not the "functional equivalent" of express campaign speech. We further conclude that the interests held to justify restricting corporate campaign speech or its functional equivalent do not justify restricting issue advocacy, and accordingly we hold that BCRA §203 is unconstitutional as applied to the advertisements at issue in these cases.

I

Prior to BCRA, corporations were free under federal law to use independent expenditures to engage in political speech so long as that speech did not expressly advocate the election or defeat of a clearly identified federal candidate. See *MCFL*; *Buckley*; 2 U.S.C. §441b(a), (b)(2).

BCRA significantly cut back on corporations' ability to engage in political speech. BCRA §203, at issue in these cases, makes it a crime for any labor union or incorporated entity—whether the United Steelworkers, the American Civil Liberties Union, or General Motors—to use its general treasury funds to pay for any "electioneering communication." BCRA's definition of "electioneering communication" is clear and expansive. It encompasses any broadcast, cable, or satellite communication that refers to a candidate for federal office and that is aired within 30 days of a federal primary election or 60 days of a federal general election in the jurisdiction in which that candidate is running for office.

Appellee Wisconsin Right to Life, Inc. (WRTL), is a nonprofit, nonstock, ideological advocacy corporation recognized by the Internal Revenue Service as tax exempt under §501(c)(4) of the Internal Revenue Code. On July 26, 2004, as part of what it calls a "grassroots lobbying campaign," WRTL began broadcasting a radio advertisement entitled "Wedding." The transcript of "Wedding" reads as follows:

"'PASTOR: And who gives this woman to be married to this man?

"'BRIDE'S FATHER: Well, as father of the bride, I certainly could. But instead, I'd like to share a few tips on how to properly install drywall. Now you put the drywall up ...

"'VOICE-OVER: Sometimes it's just not fair to delay an important decision.

"'But in Washington it's happening. A group of Senators is using the filibuster delay tactic to block federal judicial nominees from a simple "yes" or "no" vote. So qualified candidates don't get a chance to serve.

"'It's politics at work, causing gridlock and backing up some of our courts to a state of emergency.

"'Contact Senators Feingold and Kohl and tell them to oppose the filibuster.

"'Visit: BeFair.org

"'Paid for by Wisconsin Right to Life (befair.org), which is responsible for the content of this advertising and not authorized by any candidate or candidate's committee.'"

On the same day, WRTL aired a similar radio ad entitled "Loan." It had also invested treasury funds in producing a television ad entitled "Waiting," which is similar in substance and format to "Wedding" and "Loan."

WRTL planned on running "Wedding," "Waiting," and "Loan" throughout August 2004 and financing the ads with funds from its general treasury. It recognized, however, that as of August 15, 30 days prior to the Wisconsin primary, the ads would be illegal "electioneering communication[s]" under BCRA §203.

Believing that it nonetheless possessed a First Amendment right to broadcast these ads, WRTL filed suit against the Federal Election Commission (FEC) on July 28, 2004, seeking declaratory and injunctive relief before a three-judge District Court. WRTL alleged that BCRA's prohibition on the use of corporate treasury funds for "electioneering communication[s]" as defined in the Act is unconstitutional as applied to "Wedding," "Loan," and "Waiting," as well as any materially similar ads it might seek to run in the future.

Just before the BCRA blackout period was to begin, the District Court denied a preliminary injunction, concluding that "the reasoning of the *McConnell* Court leaves no room for the kind of 'as applied' challenge WRTL propounds before us." In response to this ruling, WRTL did not run its ads during the blackout period. The District Court subsequently dismissed WRTL's complaint. On appeal, we vacated the District Court's judgment, holding that *McConnell* "did not purport to resolve future as-applied challenges" to BCRA §203, and remanded "for the District Court to consider the merits of WRTL's as-applied challenge in the first instance." *WRTL I*.

On remand ... [after holding the case not moot], the court began by noting that under *McConnell*, BCRA could constitutionally proscribe "express advocacy — defined as ads that expressly advocate the election or defeat of a candidate for federal office — and the "functional equivalent" of such advocacy. Stating that it was limiting its inquiry to "language within the four corners" of the ads, the District Court concluded that the ads were *not* express advocacy or its functional equivalent, but instead "genuine issue ads." Then, reaching a question "left open in *McConnell*," the court held that no compelling interest justified BCRA's regulation of genuine issue ads such as those WRTL sought to run.

One judge dissented, contending that the majority's "plain facial analysis of the text in WRTL's 2004 advertisements" ignored "the context in which the text was developed." In that judge's view, a contextual analysis of the ads revealed "deep factual rifts between the parties concerning the purpose and intended effects of the ads" such that neither side was entitled to summary judgment.

The FEC and intervenors filed separate notices of appeal and jurisdictional statements. We consolidated the two appeals and set the matter for briefing and argument, postponing further consideration of jurisdiction to the hearing on the merits.

II

[The Court held the case is not moot.] …

III

WRTL rightly concedes that its ads are prohibited by BCRA §203. Each ad clearly identifies Senator Feingold, who was running (unopposed) in the Wisconsin Democratic primary on September 14, 2004, and each ad would have been "targeted to the relevant electorate" during the BCRA blackout period. WRTL further concedes that its ads do not fit under any of BCRA's exceptions to the term "electioneering communication." The only question, then, is whether it is consistent with the First Amendment for BCRA §203 to prohibit WRTL from running these three ads.

A

Appellants contend that WRTL should be required to demonstrate that BCRA is unconstitutional as applied to the ads. After all, appellants reason, *McConnell* already held that BCRA §203 was facially valid. These cases, however, present the separate question whether §203 may constitutionally be applied to these specific ads. Because BCRA §203 burdens political speech, it is subject to strict scrutiny. See *McConnell*; *Austin*; *MCFL* (plurality opinion); *Bellotti*; *Buckley*. Under strict scrutiny, the *Government* must prove that applying BCRA to WRTL's ads furthers a compelling interest and is narrowly tailored to achieve that interest. See *Bellotti*.

The strict scrutiny analysis is, of course, informed by our precedents. This Court has already ruled that BCRA survives strict scrutiny to the extent it regulates express advocacy or its functional equivalent. *McConnell*. So to the extent the ads in these cases fit this description, the FEC's burden is not onerous; all it need do is point to *McConnell* and explain why it applies here. If, on the other hand, WRTL's ads are *not* express advocacy or its equivalent, the Government's task is more formidable. It must then demonstrate that banning such ads during the blackout periods is narrowly tailored to serve a compelling interest. No precedent of this Court has yet reached that conclusion.

B

The FEC, intervenors, and the dissent below contend that *McConnell* already established the constitutional test for determining if an ad is the functional equivalent of express advocacy: whether the ad is intended to influence elections and has that effect. Here is the relevant portion of our opinion in *McConnell*:

> [P]laintiffs argue that the justifications that adequately support the regulation of express advocacy do not apply to significant quantities of speech encompassed by the definition of electioneering communications.

This argument fails to the extent that the issue ads broadcast during the 30- and 60-day periods preceding federal primary and general elections are the functional equivalent of express advocacy. The justifications for the regulation of express advocacy apply equally to ads aired during those periods if the ads are intended to influence the voters' decisions and have that effect.

WRTL and the District Court majority, on the other hand, claim that *McConnell* did not adopt any test as the standard for future as-applied challenges. We agree. *McConnell's* analysis was grounded in the evidentiary record before the Court. Two key studies in the *McConnell* record constituted "the central piece of evidence marshaled by defenders of BCRA's electioneering communication provisions in support of their constitutional validity." *McConnell v. FEC*, 251 F.Supp.2d 176, 307, 308 (DC 2003) (opinion of Henderson, J.) (internal quotation marks and brackets omitted). Those studies asked "student coders" to separate ads based on whether the students thought the "purpose" of the ad was "to provide information about or urge action on a bill or issue," or "to generate support or opposition for a particular candidate." *Id.* The studies concluded "'that BCRA's definition of Electioneering Communications accurately captures those ads that *have the purpose or effect of supporting candidates for election to office.*" *Ibid.* (emphasis in original).

When the *McConnell* Court considered the possible facial overbreadth of §203, it looked to the studies in the record analyzing ads broadcast during the blackout periods, and those studies had classified the ads in terms of intent and effect. The Court's assessment was accordingly phrased in the same terms, which the Court regarded as sufficient to conclude, on the record before it, that the plaintiffs had not "carried their heavy burden of proving" that §203 was facially overbroad and could not be enforced in *any* circumstances. The Court did not explain that it was adopting a particular test for determining what constituted the "functional equivalent" of express advocacy. The fact that the student coders who helped develop the evidentiary record before the Court in *McConnell* looked to intent and effect in doing so, and that the Court dealt with the record on that basis in deciding the facial overbreadth claim, neither compels nor warrants accepting that same standard as the constitutional test for separating, in an as-applied challenge, political speech protected under the First Amendment from that which may be banned.[4]

More importantly, this Court in *Buckley* had already rejected an intent-and-effect test for distinguishing between discussions of issues and candidates. After noting the difficulty of distinguishing between discussion of issues on the one hand and advocacy of election or defeat of candidates on the other, the *Buckley* Court explained that analyzing the question in terms "'of intent and of effect'" would afford "'no security for free discussion.'" It therefore rejected such an approach, and *McConnell* did not purport to overrule *Buckley* on this point—or even address what *Buckley* had to say on the subject.

For the reasons regarded as sufficient in *Buckley*, we decline to adopt a test for as-applied challenges turning on the speaker's intent to affect an election. The test to distinguish constitutionally protected political speech from speech that BCRA may proscribe

---

4. This is particularly true given that the methodology, data, and conclusions of the two studies were the subject of serious dispute among the District Court judges. Compare *McConnell v. FEC* (opinion of Henderson, J.) (stating that the studies were flawed and of limited evidentiary value), with *id.*, at 585, 583–588 (opinion of Kollar-Kotelly, J.) (finding the studies generally credible, but stating that "I am troubled by the fact that coders in both studies were asked questions regarding their own perceptions of the advertisements' purposes, and that [some of] these perceptions were later recoded" by study supervisors). Nothing in this Court's opinion in *McConnell* suggests it was resolving the sharp disagreements about the evidentiary record in this respect.

should provide a safe harbor for those who wish to exercise First Amendment rights. The test should also "reflec[t] our 'profound national commitment to the principle that debate on public issues should be uninhibited, robust, and wide-open.'" *Buckley*. A test turning on the intent of the speaker does not remotely fit the bill.

Far from serving the values the First Amendment is meant to protect, an intent-based test would chill core political speech by opening the door to a trial on every ad within the terms of §203, on the theory that the speaker actually intended to affect an election, no matter how compelling the indications that the ad concerned a pending legislative or policy issue. No reasonable speaker would choose to run an ad covered by BCRA if its only defense to a criminal prosecution would be that its motives were pure. An intent-based standard "blankets with uncertainty whatever may be said," and "offers no security for free discussion." *Buckley*. The FEC does not disagree. In its brief filed in the first appeal in this litigation, it argued that a "constitutional standard that turned on the subjective sincerity of a speaker's message would likely be incapable of workable application; at a minimum, it would invite costly, fact-dependent litigation."[5]

A test focused on the speaker's intent could lead to the bizarre result that identical ads aired at the same time could be protected speech for one speaker, while leading to criminal penalties for another. See M. Redish, Money Talks: Speech, Economic Power, and the Values of Democracy 91 (2001) ("[U]nder well-accepted First Amendment doctrine, a speaker's motivation is entirely irrelevant to the question of constitutional protection"). "First Amendment freedoms need breathing space to survive." *NAACP v. Button*, 371 U.S. 415, 433 (1963). An intent test provides none.

Buckley also explains the flaws of a test based on the actual effect speech will have on an election or on a particular segment of the target audience. Such a test "'puts the speaker ... wholly at the mercy of the varied understanding of his hearers.'" 424 U.S., at 43. It would also typically lead to a burdensome, expert-driven inquiry, with an indeterminate result. Litigation on such a standard may or may not accurately predict electoral effects, but it will unquestionably chill a substantial amount of political speech.

C

"The freedom of speech ... guaranteed by the Constitution embraces at the least the liberty to discuss publicly and truthfully all matters of public concern without previous restraint or fear of subsequent punishment." *Bellotti*. See *Consolidated Edison Co. of N.Y. v. Public Serv. Comm'n of N. Y.*, 447 U.S. 530, 534 (1980). To safeguard this liberty, the proper standard for an as-applied challenge to BCRA §203 must be objective, focusing on the substance of the communication rather than amorphous considerations of intent and effect. See *Buckley*. It must entail minimal if any discovery, to allow parties to resolve disputes quickly without chilling speech through the threat of burdensome litigation. See *Virginia v. Hicks*, 539 U.S. 113, 119 (2003). And it must eschew "the open-ended rough-and-tumble of factors," which "invit[es] complex argument in a trial court and a virtually inevitable appeal." *Jerome B. Grubart, Inc. v.*

---

5. Consider what happened in these cases. The District Court permitted extensive discovery on the assumption that WRTL's intent was relevant. As a result, the defendants deposed WRTL's executive director, its legislative director, its political action committee director, its lead communications consultant, and one of its fundraisers. WRTL also had to turn over many documents related to its operations, plans, and finances. Such litigation constitutes a severe burden on political speech.

Great Lakes Dredge & Dock Co., 513 U.S. 527, 547 (1995). In short, it must give the benefit of any doubt to protecting rather than stifling speech. See *New York Times Co. v. Sullivan*.

In light of these considerations, a court should find that an ad is the functional equivalent of express advocacy only if the ad is susceptible of no reasonable interpretation other than as an appeal to vote for or against a specific candidate. Under this test, WRTL's three ads are plainly not the functional equivalent of express advocacy. First, their content is consistent with that of a genuine issue ad: The ads focus on a legislative issue, take a position on the issue, exhort the public to adopt that position, and urge the public to contact public officials with respect to the matter. Second, their content lacks indicia of express advocacy: The ads do not mention an election, candidacy, political party, or challenger; and they do not take a position on a candidate's character, qualifications, or fitness for office.

Despite these characteristics, appellants assert that the content of WRTL's ads alone betrays their electioneering nature. Indeed, the FEC suggests that *any* ad covered by §203 that includes "an appeal to citizens to contact their elected representative" is the "functional equivalent" of an ad saying defeat or elect that candidate. We do not agree. To take just one example, during a blackout period the House considered the proposed Universal National Service Act. There would be no reason to regard an ad supporting or opposing that Act, and urging citizens to contact their Representative about it, as the equivalent of an ad saying vote for or against the Representative. Issue advocacy conveys information and educates. An issue ad's impact on an election, if it exists at all, will come only after the voters hear the information and choose—uninvited by the ad—to factor it into their voting decisions.[6]

The FEC and intervenors try to turn this difference to their advantage, citing *McConnell's* statements "that the most effective campaign ads, like the most effective commercials for products ... avoid the [*Buckley*] magic words [expressly advocating the election or defeat of a candidate]," and that advertisers "would seldom choose to use such words even if permitted," *id.* An expert for the FEC in these cases relied on those observations to argue that WRTL's ads are especially effective electioneering ads because they are "subtl[e]," focusing on issues rather than simply exhorting the electorate to vote against Senator Feingold. Rephrased a bit, the argument perversely maintains that the *less* an issue ad resembles express advocacy, the more likely it is to be the functional equivalent of express advocacy. This "heads I win, tails you lose" approach cannot be correct. It would effectively eliminate First Amendment protection for genuine issue ads, contrary to our conclusion in *WRTL I* that as-applied challenges to §203 are available, and our assumption in *McConnell* that "the interests that justify the regulation of campaign speech might not apply to the regulation of genuine issue ads." Under appellants' view, there can

---

6. For these reasons, we cannot agree with JUSTICE SOUTER's assertion that "anyone who heard the Feingold ads ... would know that WRTL's message was to vote against Feingold." The dissent supports this assertion by likening WRTL's ads to the "Jane Doe" example identified in *McConnell*. But that ad "condemned Jane Doe's record on a particular issue." WRTL's ads do not do so; they instead take a position on the filibuster issue and exhort constituents to contact Senators Feingold and Kohl to advance that position. Indeed, one would not even know from the ads whether Senator Feingold supported or opposed filibusters. JUSTICE SOUTER is confident Wisconsinites independently knew Senator Feingold's position on filibusters, but we think that confidence misplaced. A prominent study found, for example, that during the 2000 election cycle, 85 percent of respondents to a survey were not even able to name at least one candidate for the House of Representatives in their own district. See Inter-university Consortium for Political and Social Research, American National Election Study, 2000: Pre- and Post-Election Survey 243 (N. Burns et al. eds.2002) online at http://www.icpsr.umich.edu/cocoon/ICPSR/STUDY/03131.xml.

be no such thing as a genuine issue ad during the blackout period—it is simply a very effective electioneering ad.

Looking beyond the content of WRTL's ads, the FEC and intervenors argue that several "contextual" factors prove that the ads are the equivalent of express advocacy. First, appellants cite evidence that during the same election cycle, WRTL and its Political Action Committee (PAC) actively opposed Senator Feingold's reelection and identified filibusters as a campaign issue. This evidence goes to WRTL's subjective intent in running the ads, and we have already explained that WRTL's intent is irrelevant in an as-applied challenge. Evidence of this sort is therefore beside the point, as it should be—WRTL does not forfeit its right to speak on issues simply because in other aspects of its work it also opposes candidates who are involved with those issues.

Next, the FEC and intervenors seize on the timing of WRTL's ads. They observe that the ads were to be aired near elections but not near actual Senate votes on judicial nominees, and that WRTL did not run the ads after the elections. To the extent this evidence goes to WRTL's subjective intent, it is again irrelevant. To the extent it nonetheless suggests that the ads should be interpreted as express advocacy, it falls short. That the ads were run close to an election is unremarkable in a challenge like this. *Every* ad covered by BCRA §203 will by definition air just before a primary or general election. If this were enough to prove that an ad is the functional equivalent of express advocacy, then BCRA would be constitutional in all of its applications. This Court unanimously rejected this contention in *WRTL I*.

That the ads were run shortly after the Senate had recessed is likewise unpersuasive. Members of Congress often return to their districts during recess, precisely to determine the views of their constituents; an ad run at that time may succeed in getting more constituents to contact the Representative while he or she is back home. In any event, a group can certainly choose to run an issue ad to coincide with public interest rather than a floor vote. Finally, WRTL did not resume running its ads after the BCRA blackout period because, as it explains, the debate had changed. The focus of the Senate was on whether a majority would vote to change the Senate rules to eliminate the filibuster—not whether individual Senators would continue filibustering. Given this change, WRTL's decision not to continue running its ads after the blackout period does not support an inference that the ads were the functional equivalent of electioneering.

The last piece of contextual evidence the FEC and intervenors highlight is the ads' "specific and repeated cross-reference" to a website. In the middle of the website's homepage, in large type, were the addresses, phone numbers, fax numbers, and email addresses of Senators Feingold and Kohl. Wisconsinites who viewed "Wedding," "Loan," or "Waiting" and wished to contact their Senators—as the ads requested—would be able to obtain the pertinent contact information immediately upon visiting the website. This is fully consistent with viewing WRTL's ads as genuine issue ads. The website also stated both Wisconsin Senators' positions on judicial filibusters, and allowed visitors to sign up for "e-alerts," some of which contained exhortations to vote against Senator Feingold. These details lend the electioneering interpretation of the ads more credence, but again, WRTL's participation in express advocacy in other aspects of its work is not a justification for censoring its issue-related speech. Any express advocacy on the website, already one step removed from the text of the ads themselves, certainly does not render an interpretation of the ads as genuine issue ads unreasonable.

Given the standard we have adopted for determining whether an ad is the "functional equivalent" of express advocacy, contextual factors of the sort invoked by appellants should seldom play a significant role in the inquiry. Courts need not ignore basic background information that may be necessary to put an ad in context—such as whether an ad "describes a legislative issue that is either currently the subject of legislative scrutiny or likely to be the subject of such scrutiny in the near future," but the need to consider such background should not become an excuse for discovery or a broader inquiry of the sort we have just noted raises First Amendment concerns.

At best, appellants have shown what we have acknowledged at least since *Buckley*: that "the distinction between discussion of issues and candidates and advocacy of election or defeat of candidates may often dissolve in practical application." Under the test set forth above, that is not enough to establish that the ads can only reasonably be viewed as advocating or opposing a candidate in a federal election. "Freedom of discussion, if it would fulfill its historic function in this nation, must embrace all issues about which information is needed or appropriate to enable the members of society to cope with the exigencies of their period." *Thornhill v. Alabama*, 310 U.S. 88, 102 (1940). Discussion of issues cannot be suppressed simply because the issues may also be pertinent in an election. Where the First Amendment is implicated, the tie goes to the speaker, not the censor.[7] ...

Because WRTL's ads may reasonably be interpreted as something other than as an appeal to vote for or against a specific candidate, we hold they are not the functional equivalent of express advocacy, and therefore fall outside the scope of *McConnell's* holding.[8]

IV

BCRA §203 can be constitutionally applied to WRTL's ads only if it is narrowly tailored to further a compelling interest. *McConnell*; *Bellotti*; *Buckley*. This Court has never recognized a compelling interest in regulating ads, like WRTL's, that are neither express advocacy nor its functional equivalent. The District Court below considered interests that

---

7. JUSTICE SCALIA thinks our test impermissibly vague. As should be evident, we agree with JUSTICE SCALIA on the imperative for clarity in this area; that is why our test affords protection unless an ad is susceptible of *no reasonable interpretation* other than as an appeal to vote for or against a specific candidate. It is why we emphasize that (1) there can be no free-ranging intent-and-effect test; (2) there generally should be no discovery or inquiry into the sort of "contextual" factors highlighted by the FEC and intervenors; (3) discussion of issues cannot be banned merely because the issues might be relevant to an election; and (4) in a debatable case, the tie is resolved in favor of protecting speech. And keep in mind this test is only triggered if the speech meets the brightline requirements of BCRA §203 in the first place. JUSTICE SCALIA's criticism of our test is all the more confusing because he accepts WRTL's proposed three-prong test as "clear." We do not think our test any vaguer than WRTL's, and it is more protective of political speech....

8. Nothing in *McConnell's* statement that the "vast majority" of issue ads broadcast in the periods preceding federal elections had an "electioneering purpose" forecloses this conclusion. Courts do not resolve unspecified as-applied challenges in the course of resolving a facial attack, so *McConnell* could not have settled the issue we address today. Indeed, *WRTL I* confirmed as much. By the same token, in deciding this as-applied challenge, we have no occasion to revisit *McConnell's* conclusion that the statute is not facially overbroad.

The "vast majority" language, moreover, is beside the point. The *McConnell* Court did not find that a "vast majority" of the issue ads considered were the functional equivalent of direct advocacy. Rather, it found that such ads had an "electioneering purpose." For the reasons we have explained, "purpose" is not the appropriate test for distinguishing between genuine issue ads and the functional equivalent of express campaign advocacy. In addition, the "vast majority" statement was not necessary to the Court's facial holding in *McConnell*. The standard required for a statute to survive an overbreadth challenge is not that the "vast majority" of a statute's applications be legitimate. "[B]road language ... unnecessary to the Court's decision ... cannot be considered binding authority." *Kastigar v. United States*, 406 U.S. 441 (1972).

might justify regulating WRTL's ads here, and found none sufficiently compelling. We reach the same conclusion.[9]

At the outset, we reject the contention that issue advocacy may be regulated because express election advocacy may be, and "the speech involved in so-called issue advocacy is [not] any more core political speech than are words of express advocacy." *McConnell*. This greater-includes-the-lesser approach is not how strict scrutiny works. A corporate ad expressing support for the local football team could not be regulated on the ground that such speech is less "core" than corporate speech about an election, which we have held may be restricted. A court applying strict scrutiny must ensure that a compelling interest supports *each application* of a statute restricting speech. That a compelling interest justifies restrictions on express advocacy tells us little about whether a compelling interest justifies restrictions on issue advocacy; the *McConnell* Court itself made just that point. Such a greater-includes-the-lesser argument would dictate that virtually *all* corporate speech can be suppressed, since few kinds of speech can lay claim to being as central to the First Amendment as campaign speech. That conclusion is clearly foreclosed by our precedent. See, *e.g., Bellotti*.

This Court has long recognized "the governmental interest in preventing corruption and the appearance of corruption" in election campaigns. *Buckley*. This interest has been invoked as a reason for upholding *contribution* limits. As *Buckley* explained, "[t]o the extent that large contributions are given to secure a political *quid pro quo* from current and potential office holders, the integrity of our system of representative democracy is undermined." We have suggested that this interest might also justify limits on electioneering *expenditures* because it may be that, in some circumstances, "large independent expenditures pose the same dangers of actual or apparent *quid pro quo* arrangements as do large contributions." *Id.*

McConnell arguably applied this interest—which this Court had only assumed could justify regulation of express advocacy—to ads that were the "functional equivalent" of express advocacy. But to justify regulation of WRTL's ads, this interest must be stretched yet another step to ads that are *not* the functional equivalent of express advocacy. Enough is enough. Issue ads like WRTL's are by no means equivalent to contributions, and the *quid-pro-quo* corruption interest cannot justify regulating them. To equate WRTL's ads with contributions is to ignore their value as political speech.

---

9. The dissent stresses a number of points that, while not central to our decision, nevertheless merit a response. First, the dissent overstates its case when it asserts that the "PAC alternative" gives corporations a constitutionally sufficient outlet to speak. PACs impose well-documented and onerous burdens, particularly on small nonprofits. See *MCFL* (plurality opinion). *McConnell* did conclude that segregated funds "provid[e] corporations and unions with a constitutionally sufficient opportunity to engage in express advocacy" and its functional equivalent, but that holding did not extend beyond functional equivalents—and if it did, the PAC option would justify regulation of all corporate speech, a proposition we have rejected, see *Bellotti*. [Did *Bellotti* so hold?—EDS.] Second, the response that a speaker should just take out a newspaper ad, or use a website, rather than complain that it cannot speak through a broadcast communication is too glib. Even assuming for the sake of argument that the possibility of using a different medium of communication has relevance in determining the permissibility of a limitation on speech, newspaper ads and websites are not reasonable alternatives to broadcast speech in terms of impact and effectiveness. Third, we disagree with the dissent's view that corporations can still speak by changing what they say to avoid mentioning candidates. That argument is akin to telling Cohen that he cannot wear his jacket because he is free to wear one that says "I disagree with the draft," cf. *Cohen v. California*, 403 U.S. 15 (1971), or telling 44 Liquormart that it can advertise so long as it avoids mentioning prices, cf. *44 Liquormart, Inc. v. Rhode Island*, 517 U.S. 484 (1996). Such notions run afoul of "the fundamental rule of protection under the First Amendment, that a speaker has the autonomy to choose the content of his own message." *Hurley v. Irish-American Gay, Lesbian and Bisexual Group of Boston, Inc.*, 515 U.S. 557, 573 (1995).

Appellants argue that an expansive definition of "functional equivalent" is needed to en-sure that issue advocacy does not circumvent the rule against express advocacy, which in turn helps protect against circumvention of the rule against contributions. Cf. *McConnell*. But such a prophylaxis-upon-prophylaxis approach to regulating expression is not consistent with strict scrutiny. "[T]he desire for a bright-line rule … hardly constitutes the *compelling* state interest necessary to justify any infringement on First Amendment freedom." *MCFL*.

A second possible compelling interest recognized by this Court lies in addressing a "different type of corruption in the political arena: the corrosive and distorting effects of immense aggregations of wealth that are accumulated with the help of the corporate form and that have little or no correlation to the public's support for the corporation's politi-cal ideas." *Austin*. *Austin* invoked this interest to uphold a state statute making it a felony for corporations to use treasury funds for independent expenditures on express election advocacy. *Id*. *McConnell* also relied on this interest in upholding regulation not just of express advocacy, but also its "functional equivalent."

These cases did not suggest, however, that the interest in combating "a different type of corruption" extended beyond campaign speech. Quite the contrary. Two of the Jus-tices who joined the 6-to-3 majority in *Austin* relied, in upholding the constitutionality of the ban on campaign speech, on the fact that corporations retained freedom to speak on issues as distinct from election campaigns. See (Brennan, J., concurring) (describing fact that campaign speech ban "does not regulate corporate expenditures in referenda or other corporate expression" as "reflect [ing] the requirements of our decisions"); (STEVENS, J., concurring) ("[T]here is a vast difference between lobbying and debating public issues on the one hand, and political campaigns for election to public office on the other"). The *McConnell* Court similarly was willing to "assume that the interests that justify the regu-lation of campaign speech might not apply to the regulation of genuine issue ads." And our decision in *WRTL I* reinforced the validity of that assumption by holding that BCRA §203 is susceptible to as-applied challenges.

Accepting the notion that a ban on campaign speech could also embrace issue advo-cacy would call into question our holding in *Bellotti* that the corporate identity of a speaker does not strip corporations of all free speech rights. It would be a constitutional "bait and switch" to conclude that corporate campaign speech may be banned in part *because* corporate issue advocacy is not, and then assert that corporate issue advocacy may be banned as well, pursuant to the same asserted compelling interest, through a broad con-ception of what constitutes the functional equivalent of campaign speech, or by relying on the inability to distinguish campaign speech from issue advocacy.

The FEC and intervenors do not argue that the *Austin* interest justifies regulating gen-uine issue ads. Instead, they focus on establishing that WRTL's ads are the functional equivalent of express advocacy—a contention we have already rejected. We hold that the interest recognized in *Austin* as justifying regulation of corporate campaign speech and extended in *McConnell* to the functional equivalent of such speech has no application to issue advocacy of the sort engaged in by WRTL.[10]

---

10. The interest recognized in *Austin* stems from a concern that "'[t]he resources in the treasury of a business corporation … are not an indication of popular support for the corporation's political ideas.'" *Austin*. Some of WRTL's *amici* contend that this interest is not implicated here because of WRTL's status as a nonprofit advocacy organization. They assert that "[s]peech by nonprofit advocacy groups on behalf of their members does not 'corrupt' candidates or 'distort' the political marketplace," and that "[n]onprofit advocacy groups funded by individuals are readily distinguished from for-profit corporations funded by general treasuries." We do not pass on this argument in this as-applied chal-lenge because WRTL's funds for its ads were not derived solely from individual contributions.

Because WRTL's ads are not express advocacy or its functional equivalent, and because appellants identify no interest sufficiently compelling to justify burdening WRTL's speech, we hold that BCRA §203 is unconstitutional as applied to WRTL's "Wedding," "Loan," and "Waiting" ads.

* * *

These cases are about political speech. The importance of the cases to speech and debate on public policy issues is reflected in the number of diverse organizations that have joined in supporting WRTL before this Court: the American Civil Liberties Union, the National Rifle Association, the American Federation of Labor and Congress of Industrial Organizations, the Chamber of Commerce of the United States of America, Focus on the Family, the Coalition of Public Charities, the Cato Institute, and many others.

Yet, as is often the case in this Court's First Amendment opinions, we have gotten this far in the analysis without quoting the Amendment itself: "Congress shall make no law ... abridging the freedom of speech." The Framers' actual words put these cases in proper perspective. Our jurisprudence over the past 216 years has rejected an absolutist interpretation of those words, but when it comes to drawing difficult lines in the area of pure political speech — between what is protected and what the Government may ban — it is worth recalling the language we are applying. *McConnell* held that express advocacy of a candidate or his opponent by a corporation shortly before an election may be prohibited, along with the functional equivalent of such express advocacy. We have no occasion to revisit that determination today. But when it comes to defining what speech qualifies as the functional equivalent of express advocacy subject to such a ban — the issue we *do* have to decide — we give the benefit of the doubt to speech, not censorship. The First Amendment's command that "Congress shall make no law ... abridging the freedom of speech" demands at least that.

The judgment of the United States District Court for the District of Columbia is affirmed.

It is so ordered.

Justice Alito, concurring.

I join the principal opinion because I conclude (a) that §203, as applied, cannot constitutionally ban any advertisement that may reasonably be interpreted as anything other than an appeal to vote for or against a candidate, (b) that the ads at issue here may reasonably be interpreted as something other than such an appeal, and (c) that because §203 is unconstitutional as applied to the advertisements before us, it is unnecessary to go further and decide whether §203 is unconstitutional on its face. If it turns out that the implementation of the as-applied standard set out in the principal opinion impermissibly chills political speech, see (Scalia, J., joined by Kennedy, and Thomas, JJ., concurring in part and concurring in judgment), we will presumably be asked in a future case to reconsider the holding in *McConnell*, that §203 is facially constitutional.

Justice Scalia, with whom Justice Kennedy and Justice Thomas join, concurring in part and concurring in the judgment. ...

Austin was a significant departure from ancient First Amendment principles. In my view, it was wrongly decided. The flawed rationale upon which it is based is examined at length elsewhere, including in a dissenting opinion in *Austin* that a Member of the 5-to-4 *McConnell* majority had joined. But at least *Austin* was limited to express advocacy, and *nonexpress* advocacy was presumed to remain protected under *Buckley* and *Bellotti*, even when engaged in by corporations.

Three Terms ago the Court extended *Austin's* flawed rationale to cover an even broader class of speech. In *McConnell,* the Court rejected a facial overbreadth challenge to BCRA §203's restrictions on corporate and union advertising, which were not limited to express advocacy but covered vast amounts of nonexpress advocacy (embraced within the term "electioneering communications")....

III

The question is whether WRTL meets the standard for prevailing in an as-applied challenge to BCRA §203. Answering that question obviously requires the Court to articulate the standard. The most obvious one, and the one suggested by the Federal Election Commission (FEC) and intervenors, is the standard set forth in *McConnell* itself: whether the advertisement is the "functional equivalent of express advocacy." *McConnell.* Intervenors flesh out the standard somewhat further: "[C]ourts should ask whether the ad's audience would reasonably understand the ad, in the context of the campaign, to promote or attack the candidate." The District Court instead articulated a five-factor test that looks to whether the ad under review "(1) describes a legislative issue that is either currently the subject of legislative scrutiny or likely to be the subject of such scrutiny in the near future; (2) refers to the prior voting record or current position of the named candidate on the issue described; (3) exhorts the listener to do anything other than contact the candidate about the described issue; (4) promotes, attacks, supports, or opposes the named candidate; and (5) refers to the upcoming election, candidacy, and/or political party of the candidate." The backup definition of "electioneering communications" contained in BCRA itself offers another possibility. It covers any communication that "promotes or supports a candidate for that office ... (regardless of whether the communication expressly advocates a vote for or against a candidate) and which also is suggestive of no plausible meaning other than an exhortation to vote for or against a specific candidate." And the principal opinion in this case offers a variation of its own (one bearing a strong likeness to BCRA's backup definition): whether "the ad is susceptible of no reasonable interpretation other than as an appeal to vote for or against a specific candidate."

There is a fundamental and inescapable problem with all of these various tests. Each of them (and every other test that is tied to the public perception, or a court's perception, of the import, the intent, or the effect of the ad) is impermissibly vague and thus ineffective to vindicate the fundamental First Amendment rights of the large segment of society to which §203 applies. Consider the application of these tests to WRTL's ads: There is not the slightest doubt that these ads had an issue-advocacy component. They explicitly urged lobbying on the pending legislative issue of appellate-judge filibusters. The question before us is whether something about them caused them to be the "functional equivalent" of express advocacy, and thus constitutionally subject to BCRA's criminal penalty. Does any of the tests suggested above answer this question with the degree of clarity necessary to avoid the chilling of fundamental political discourse? I think not.

The "functional equivalent" test does nothing more than restate the question (and make clear that the electoral advocacy need not be express). The test which asks how the ad's audience "would reasonably understand the ad" provides ample room for debate and uncertainty. The District Court's five-factor test does not (and could not possibly) specify how much weight is to be given to each factor—and includes the inherently vague factor of whether the ad "promotes, attacks, supports, or opposes the named candidate." (Does attacking the king's position attack the king?) The tests which look to whether the ad is "susceptible of no plausible meaning" or "susceptible of no reasonable interpretation" other than an exhortation to vote for or against a specific candidate seem tighter. They ultimately depend, however, upon a judicial judgment (or is it—worse still—a jury judgment?) concerning "reasonable" or "plausible" import that is far from certain, that rests upon consideration of innumerable surrounding circumstances which the speaker may not even be aware of, and that lends itself to distortion by reason of the decisionmaker's subjective evaluation of the importance or unimportance of the challenged speech. In this critical area of political discourse, the speaker cannot be compelled to risk felony prosecution with no more assurance of impunity than his prediction that what he says will be found susceptible of some "reasonable interpretation other than as an appeal to vote for or against a specific candidate." Under these circumstances, "[m]any persons, rather than undertake the considerable burden (and sometimes risk) of vindicating their rights through case-by-case litigation, will choose simply to abstain from protected speech-harming not only themselves but society as a whole, which is deprived of an uninhibited marketplace of ideas." *Virginia v. Hicks.*

It will not do to say that this burden must be accepted — that WRTL's antifilibustering, constitutionally protected speech can be constrained — in the necessary pursuit of electoral "corruption." ...

Buckley itself compels the conclusion that these tests fall short of the clarity that the First Amendment demands....

If a permissible test short of the magic-words test existed, *Buckley* would surely have adopted it. Especially since a consequence of the express-advocacy interpretation was the invalidation of the entire limitation on independent expenditures, in part because the statute (as thus narrowed) could not be an effective limitation on expenditures for electoral advocacy. (It would be "naiv[e]," *Buckley* said, to pretend that persons and groups would have difficulty "devising expenditures that skirted the restriction on express advocacy of election or defeat but nevertheless benefited the candidate's campaign." Why did *Buckley* employ such a "highly strained" reading of the statute, *McConnell* (opinion of THOMAS, J.), when broader readings, more faithful to the text, were available that might not have resulted in such underinclusiveness? In particular, after going to the trouble of narrowing the statute to cover "advocacy of [the] election or defeat of a candidat[e]," why not do what the principal opinion in these cases does, which is essentially to preface that phrase with the phrase "susceptible of no reasonable interpretation other than as"? There is only one plausible explanation: The Court eschewed narrowing constructions that would have been more faithful to the text and more effective at capturing campaign speech *because those tests were all too vague.* We cannot now adopt a standard held to be facially vague on the theory that it is somehow clear enough for constitutional as-applied challenges. If *Buckley* foreclosed such vagueness in a statutory test, it also must foreclose such vagueness in an as-applied test.

Though the principal opinion purports to recognize the "imperative for clarity" in this area of First Amendment law, its attempt to distinguish its test from the test found to be vague in *Buckley* falls far short. It claims to be "not so sure" that *Buckley* rejected its test because *Buckley's* holding did not concern "what the constitutional standard was in the abstract, divorced from specific statutory language." Forget about abstractions: The specific statutory language at issue in *Buckley* was interpreted to mean "'advocating the election or defeat of a candidate,'" and that is materially identical to the operative language in the principal opinion's test. The principal opinion's protestation that *Buckley's* vagueness holding "d[id] not dictate a constitutional test," is utterly compromised by the fact that the principal opinion itself relies on the very same vagueness holding to reject an intent-and-effect test in this case. It is the *same* vagueness holding, and the principal opinion cannot invoke it on page 13 of its opinion and disclaim it on page 22....[5]

---

5. Justice ALITO's concurrence at least hints that the principal opinion's test *may* impermissibly chill speech, and offers to reconsider *McConnell's* holding "*[i]f* it turns out that the implementation

What, then, is to be done? We could adopt WRTL's proposed test, under which §203 may not be applied to any ad (1) that "focuses on a current legislative branch matter, takes a position on the matter, and urges the public to ask a legislator to take a particular position or action with respect to the matter," and (2) that "does not mention any election, candidacy, political party, or challenger, or the official's character, qualifications, or fitness for office," (3) whether or not it "say[s] that the public official is wrong or right on the issue," so long as it does not expressly say he is "wrong for [the] office." Brief for Appellee 56–57 (footnote omitted). Or we could of course adopt the *Buckley* test of express advocacy. The problem is that, although these tests are clear, they are incompatible with *McConnell's* holding that §203 is facially constitutional, which was premised on the finding that a vast majority of ads proscribed by §203 are "sham issue ads" that fall outside the First Amendment's protection. Indeed, *any* clear rule that would protect all genuine issue ads would cover such a substantial number of ads prohibited by §203 that §203 would be rendered substantially overbroad. The Government claims that even the amorphous test adopted by the District Court "call[s] into question a substantial percentage of the statute's applications,"[7] and that *any* test providing relief to WRTL is incompatible with *McConnell's* facial holding because WRTL's ads are in the "heartland" of what Congress meant to prohibit. If that is so, then *McConnell* cannot be sustained.

Like the *Buckley* Court and the parties to these cases, I recognize the practical reality that corporations can evade the express-advocacy standard. I share the instinct that "[w]hat separates issue advocacy and political advocacy is a line in the sand drawn on a windy day." See *McConnell*. But the way to indulge that instinct consistently with the First Amendment is either to eliminate restrictions on independent expenditures altogether or to *confine* them to one side of the *traditional* line — the express — advocacy line, set in concrete on a calm day by *Buckley*, several decades ago. Section 203's line is bright, but it bans vast amounts of political advocacy indistinguishable from hitherto protected speech.

The foregoing analysis shows that *McConnell* was mistaken in its belief that as-applied challenges could eliminate the unconstitutional applications of §203. They can do so only if a test is adopted which contradicts the holding of *McConnell* — that §203 is facially valid because the vast majority of pre-election issue ads can constitutionally be proscribed. In light of the weakness in *Austin's* rationale, and in light of the longstanding acceptance of the clarity of *Buckley's* express-advocacy line, it was adventurous for *McConnell* to extend *Austin* beyond corporate speech constituting express advocacy.

---

of the as-applied standard set out in the [principal opinion] impermissibly chills political speech." The wait-and-see approach makes no sense and finds no support in our cases. How will we know that would-be speakers have been chilled and have not spoken? If a tree *does not* fall in the forest, can we hear the sound it would have made had it fallen? Our normal practice is to assess *ex ante* the risk that a standard will have an impermissible chilling effect on First Amendment protected speech …

7. The same must be said, I think, of the test proposed by the principal opinion. While its coverage is not entirely clear, it would apparently protect even *McConnell's* paradigmatic example of the functional equivalent of express advocacy — the so-called "Jane Doe ad," which "condemned Jane Doe's record on a particular issue before exhorting viewers to 'call Jane Doe and tell her what you think,'" Indeed, it at least arguably protects the most "striking" example of a so-called sham issue ad in the *McConnell* record, the notorious "Yellowtail ad," which accused Bill Yellowtail of striking his wife and then urged listeners to call him and "[t]ell him to support family values." The claim that §203 on its face does not reach a substantial amount of speech protected under the principal opinion's test — and that the test is therefore compatible with *McConnell* — seems to me indefensible. Indeed, the principal opinion's attempt at distinguishing *McConnell* is unpersuasive enough, and the change in the law it works is substantial enough, that seven Justices of this Court, having widely divergent views concerning the constitutionality of the restrictions at issue, agree that the opinion effectively overrules *McConnell* without saying so. This faux judicial restraint is judicial obfuscation.

Today's cases make it apparent that the adventure is a flop, and that *McConnell's* holding concerning § 203 was wrong.

IV

Which brings me to the question of *stare decisis*. "*Stare decisis* is not an inexorable command" or "'a mechanical formula of adherence to the latest decision.'" *Payne v. Tennessee,* 501 U.S. 808, 828 (1991). It is instead "'a principle of policy,'" *Payne,* and this Court has a "considered practice" not to apply that principle of policy "as rigidly in constitutional as in nonconstitutional cases." *Glidden Co. v. Zdanok,* 370 U.S. 530 (1962) ...

Of particular relevance to the *stare decisis* question in these cases is the impracticability of the regime created by *McConnell.* *Stare decisis* considerations carry little weight when an erroneous "governing decisio[n]" has created an "unworkable" legal regime. *Payne.* As described above, the *McConnell* regime is unworkable because of the inability of any acceptable as-applied test to validate the facial constitutionality of §203—that is, its inability to sustain proscription of the vast majority of issue ads. We could render the regime workable only by effectively overruling *McConnell* without saying so—adopting a clear as-applied rule protective of speech in the "heartland" of what Congress prohibited. The promise of an administrable as-applied rule that is both effective in the vindication of First Amendment rights and consistent with *McConnell's* holding is illusory....

I would overrule that part of the Court's decision in *McConnell* upholding § 203(a) of BCRA. Accordingly, I join Parts I and II of today's principal opinion and otherwise concur only in the judgment.

JUSTICE SOUTER, with whom JUSTICE STEVENS, JUSTICE GINSBURG, and JUSTICE BREYER join, dissenting.

The significance and effect of today's judgment, from which I respectfully dissent, turn on three things: the demand for campaign money in huge amounts from large contributors, whose power has produced a cynical electorate; the congressional recognition of the ensuing threat to democratic integrity as reflected in a century of legislation restricting the electoral leverage of concentrations of money in corporate and union treasuries; and *McConnell,* declaring the facial validity of the most recent Act of Congress in that tradition, a decision that is effectively, and unjustifiably, overruled today....

In sum, Congress in 1907 prohibited corporate contributions to candidates and in 1943 applied the same ban to unions. In 1947, Congress extended the complete ban from contributions to expenditures "in connection with" an election, a phrase so vague that in 1986 we held it must be confined to instances of express advocacy using magic words. Congress determined, in 2002, that corporate and union expenditures for fake issue ads devoid of magic words should be regulated using a narrow definition of "electioneering communication" to reach only broadcast ads that were the practical equivalents of express advocacy. In 2003, this Court found the provision free from vagueness and justified by the concern that drove its enactment.

This century-long tradition of legislation and judicial precedent rests on facing undeniable facts and testifies to an equally undeniable value. Campaign finance reform has been a series of reactions to documented threats to electoral integrity obvious to any voter, posed by large sums of money from corporate or union treasuries, with no redolence of "grassroots" about them. Neither Congress's decisions nor our own have understood the corrupting influence of money in politics as being limited to outright bribery or discrete *quid pro quo;* campaign finance reform has instead consistently focused on the more pervasive distortion of electoral institutions by concentrated wealth, on the special access and guaranteed favor that sap the representative integrity of American government and defy public confidence in its institutions. From early in the 20th century through the decision in *McConnell,* we have acknowledged that the value of democratic integrity justifies a realistic response when corporations and labor organizations commit the concentrated moneys in their treasuries to electioneering.

IV …

Throughout the 2004 senatorial campaign, WRTL made no secret of its views about who should win the election and explicitly tied its position to the filibuster issue. Its PAC issued at least two press releases saying that its "Top Election Priorities" were to "Re-elect George W. Bush" and "Send Feingold Packing!" In one of these, the Chair of WRTL's PAC was quoted as saying, "'We do not want Russ Feingold to continue to have the ability to thwart President Bush's judicial nominees.'" The Spring 2004 issue of the WRTL PAC's quarterly magazine ran an article headlined "Radically Pro-Abortion Feingold Must Go!", which reported that "Feingold has been active in his opposition to Bush's judicial nominees" and said that "the defeat of Feingold must be uppermost in the minds of Wisconsin's pro-life community in the 2004 elections."

It was under these circumstances that WRTL ran the three television and radio ads in question. The bills for them were not paid by WRTL's PAC, but out of the general treasury with its substantial proportion of corporate contributions; in fact, corporations earmarked more than $50,000 specifically to pay for the ads. Each one criticized an unnamed "group of Senators" for "using the filibuster delay tactic to block federal judicial nominees from a simple 'yes' or 'no' vote," and described the Senators' actions as "politics at work, causing gridlock and backing up some of our courts to a state of emergency." They exhorted viewers and listeners to "[c]ontact Senators Feingold and Kohl and tell them to oppose the filibuster," but instead of providing a phone number or e-mail address, they told the audience to go to BeFair.org, a website set up by WRTL. A visit to this website would erase any doubt a listener or viewer might have as to whether Senators Feingold and Kohl were part of the "group" condemned in the ads: it displayed a document that criticized the two Senators for voting to filibuster "16 out of 16 times" and accused them of "putting politics into the court system, creating gridlock, and costing taxpayers money."

WRTL's planned airing of the ads had no apparent relation to any Senate filibuster vote but was keyed to the timing of the senatorial election. WRTL began broadcasting the ads on July 26, 2004, four days after the Senate recessed for the summer, and although the filibuster controversy raged on through 2005, WRTL did not resume running the ads after the election. During the campaign period that the ads did cover, Senator Feingold's support of the filibusters was a prominent issue. His position was well known, and his Republican opponents, who vocally opposed the filibusters, made the issue a major talking point in their campaigns against him.

In sum, any Wisconsin voter who paid attention would have known that Democratic Senator Feingold supported filibusters against Republican presidential judicial nominees, that the propriety of the filibusters was a major issue in the senatorial campaign, and that WRTL along with the Senator's Republican challengers opposed his reelection because of his position on filibusters. Any alert voters who heard or saw WRTL's ads would have understood that WRTL was telling them that the Senator's position on the filibusters should be grounds to vote against him.

Given these facts, it is beyond all reasonable debate that the ads are constitutionally subject to regulation under *McConnell.* There, we noted that BCRA was meant to remedy the problem of "[s]o-called issue ads" being used "to advocate the election or defeat of clearly identified federal candidates." We then gave a paradigmatic example of these election-eering ads subject to regulation, saying that "[l]ittle difference existed … between an ad that urged viewers to 'vote against Jane Doe' and one that condemned Jane Doe's record on a particular issue before exhorting viewers to 'call Jane Doe and tell her what you think.'"

The WRTL ads were indistinguishable from the Jane Doe ad; they "condemned [Senator Feingold's] record on a particular issue" and exhorted the public to contact him and "tell [him] what you think." And just as anyone who heard the Jane Doe ad would understand that the point was to defeat Doe, anyone who heard the Feingold ads (let alone anyone who went to the website they named) would know that WRTL's message was to vote against Feingold. If it is now unconstitutional to restrict WRTL's Feingold ads, then it follows that §203 can no longer be applied constitutionally to *McConnell's* Jane Doe paradigm.

McConnell's holding that §203 is facially constitutional is overruled. By what steps does the principal opinion reach this unacknowledged result less than four years after *McConnell* was decided?

A

First, it lays down a new test to identify a severely limited class of ads that may constitutionally be regulated as electioneering communications, a test that is flatly contrary to *McConnell*. An ad is the equivalent of express advocacy and subject to regulation, the opinion says, only if it is "susceptible of no reasonable interpretation other than as an appeal to vote for or against a specific candidate." Since the Feingold ads could, in isolation, be read as at least including calls to communicate views on filibusters to the two Senators, those ads cannot be treated as the functional equivalent of express advocacy to elect or defeat anyone, and therefore may not constitutionally be regulated at all.

But the same could have been said of the hypothetical Jane Doe ad. Its spoken message ended with the instruction to tell Doe what the voter thinks. The same could also have been said of the actual Yellowtail ad. Yet in *McConnell*, we gave the Jane Doe ad as the paradigm of a broadcast message that could be constitutionally regulated as election conduct, and we explicitly described the Yellowtail ad as a "striking example" of one that was "clearly intended to influence the election," *McConnell*.

The principal opinion, in other words, simply inverts what we said in *McConnell*. While we left open the possibility of a "genuine" or "pure" issue ad that might not be open to regulation under §203, *id.*, we meant that an issue ad without campaign advocacy could escape the restriction. The implication of the adjectives "genuine" and "pure" is unmistakable: if an ad is reasonably understood as going beyond a discussion of issues (that is, if it can be understood as electoral advocacy), then by definition it is not "genuine" or "pure." But the principal opinion inexplicably wrings the opposite conclusion from those words: if an ad is susceptible to any "reasonable interpretation other than as an appeal to vote for or against a specific candidate," then it must be a "pure" or "genuine" issue ad. This stands *McConnell* on its head, and on this reasoning it is possible that even some ads with magic words could not be regulated.

B

Second, the principal opinion seems to defend this inversion of *McConnell* as a necessary alternative to an unadministrable subjective test for the equivalence of express (and regulable) electioneering advocacy. The principal opinion acknowledges, of course, that in *McConnell* we said that "[t]he justifications for the regulation of express advocacy apply equally to ads aired during [the period shortly before an election] if the ads are intended to influence the voters' decisions and have that effect." But THE CHIEF JUSTICE says that statement in *McConnell* cannot be accepted at face value because we could not, consistent with precedent, have focused our First Amendment enquiry on whether "the speaker actually intended to affect an election." THE CHIEF JUSTICE suggests it is more likely that the *McConnell* opinion inadvertently borrowed the language of "intended ... effect[s]," from academic studies in the record of viewers' perceptions of the ads' purposes.

If THE CHIEF JUSTICE were correct that *McConnell* made the constitutional application of § 203 contingent on whether a corporation's "motives were pure," or its issue advocacy "subjective[ly] sincer[e]," then I, too, might be inclined to reconsider *McConnell's* language. But *McConnell* did not do that. It did not purport to draw constitutional lines based on the subjective motivations of corporations (or their principals) sponsoring political ads, but merely described our test for equivalence to express advocacy as resting on the ads' "electioneering purpose," which will be objectively apparent from those ads' content and context (as these cases and the examples cited in *McConnell* readily show). We therefore held that §203 was not substantially overbroad because "the vast majority of ads clearly had such a purpose," and consequently could be regulated consistent with the First Amendment.

For that matter, if the studies to which THE CHIEF JUSTICE refers were now to inform our reading of *McConnell,* they would merely underscore the objective character of the proper way to determine whether §203 is constitutional as applied to a given ad. The authors of those studies did not conduct discovery of the "actua[l] inten[tions]," behind any ads; nor, to my knowledge, were the sponsors of campaign ads summoned before researchers to explain their motivations. The studies merely confirmed that "reasonable people are ... able to discern between ads whose primary purpose is to support a candidate and those intended to provide information about a policy issue." J. Krasno & D. Seltz, Buying Time: Television Advertising in the 1998 Congressional Elections 9 (2000). To be clear, I am not endorsing the precise methodology of those studies (and THE CHIEF JUSTICE is correct that we did not do so in *McConnell*); the point is only that the studies relied on a "reasonable" person's understanding of the ads' apparent purpose, and thus were no less objective than THE CHIEF JUSTICE's own approach.

A similarly mistaken fear of an unadministrable and speech-chilling subjective regime seems to underlie THE CHIEF JUSTICE's unwillingness to acknowledge the part that consideration of an ad's context necessarily plays in any realistic assessment of its meaning. A reasonable Wisconsinite watching or listening to WRTL's ads would likely ask and answer some obvious questions about their circumstances. Is the group that sponsors these ads the same one publicly campaigning against Senator Feingold's reelection? THE CHIEF JUSTICE says that this information is "beside the point" because WRTL's history of overt electioneering only "goes to [its] subjective intent." Did these "issue" ads begin appearing on the air during the election season, rather than at the time the filibuster "issue" was in fact being debated in the Senate? This, too, is said to be irrelevant. And does the website to which WRTL's ads direct viewers contain material expressly advocating Senator Feingold's defeat? This enquiry is dismissed as being "one step removed from the text of the ads themselves." But these questions are central to the meaning of the ads, and any reasonable person would take account of circumstances in coming to understand the object of WRTL's ad. And why not? Each of the contextual facts here can be established by an objective look at a public record; none requires a voter (or a litigant) to engage in discovery of evidence about WRTL's operations or internal communications, and none goes to a hidden state of mind....

D

In sum, *McConnell* does not graft a subjective standard onto campaign regulation, the context of campaign advertising cannot sensibly be ignored, and §203 is not a ban on speech. What cannot be gainsaid, in any event, is that in treating these subjects as it does, the operative opinion produces the result of overruling *McConnell's* holding on §203, less than four years in the Reports....

After today, the ban on contributions by corporations and unions and the limitation on their corrosive spending when they enter the political arena are open to easy circumvention, and the possibilities for regulating corporate and union campaign money are unclear. The ban on contributions will mean nothing much, now that companies and unions can save candidates the expense of advertising directly, simply by running "issue ads" without express advocacy, or by funneling the money through an independent corporation like WRTL.

But the understanding of the voters and the Congress that this kind of corporate and union spending seriously jeopardizes the integrity of democratic government will remain. The facts are too powerful to be ignored, and further efforts at campaign finance reform will come. It is only the legal landscape that now is altered, and it may be that today's departure from precedent will drive further reexamination of the constitutional analysis: of the distinction between contributions and expenditures, or the relation between spending and speech, which have given structure to our thinking since *Buckley* itself was decided.

I cannot tell what the future will force upon us, but I respectfully dissent from this judgment today.

Notes and Questions

1. Chief Justice Roberts' opinion (joined in its significant parts only by Justice Alito) is the controlling opinion because it is narrower than the opinion of Justice Scalia (joined by Justices Thomas and Kennedy). What is the holding of the case? Under the "no reasonable interpretation" test of the controlling opinion, how is a court to determine when an advertisement funded by a corporation or union is subject to section 203? What evidence may a court consider?

As you ponder this question, ask yourself whether you believe the "Jane Doe" advertisement or the "Bill Yellowtail" advertisement (see footnote 7 of Justice Scalia's opinion) would be subject to section 203's PAC requirement under the controlling opinion. What if the "Bill Yellowtail" ad attacked Yellowtail for his stand on tax cuts, rather than on the question whether he beat his wife? Would WRTL's own ads be subject to the section 203 if the ads mentioned the upcoming election?

2. *Faux judicial restraint*? According to footnote 7 of Justice Scalia's concurring opinion, seven Justices on the Supreme Court believe that the effect of the controlling opinion and Justice Scalia's concurring opinion is to overrule *McConnell's* upholding of section 203. Do you agree? If so, why did Chief Justice Roberts not say so? If you disagree, can you state clearly what remains of section 203?

3. *"Enough is Enough."* As important as the holding of *WRTL* is, it is perhaps equally significant for its tone. Gone is the deferential language of cases like *Shrink Missouri* and

McConnell, replaced by language much more sympathetic with the First Amendment arguments. Consider Richard L. Hasen, *Beyond Incoherence: The Roberts Court's Deregulatory Turn in* FEC v. Wisconsin Right to Life, 92 MINNESOTA LAW REVIEW 1064 (2008):

> The tone of the principal opinion in *WRTL* is the polar opposite of *McConnell*. There is no nod to legislative deference or recognition of Congress's need to react to the "hydraulic" effect of money. Rather than talk of a PAC alternative, the *WRTL* principal opinion mentions a free speech "ban" (or variations on the word "ban") 12 times and a speech "blackout" 17 times, and it refers to corporate election broadcasting paid for from treasury funds as a "crime" twice. Contrast *McConnell*'s treatment of the PAC requirement: "Because corporations can still fund electioneering communications with PAC money, it is 'simply wrong' to view the provision as a 'complete ban' on expression rather than a regulation."
>
> The *WRTL* principal opinion makes no mention of Congressional deference (nor does it use the term "loophole," a term appearing 10 times in the *McConnell* joint majority opinion), but the term "First Amendment" appears 18 times and variations on the word "censor" three times. In contrast, the *McConnell*'s joint majority opinion's discussion of section 203 mentioned the First Amendment merely three times, and never to celebrate the free speech principles behind the Amendment. Describing the First Amendment principles, the *WRTL* principal opinion states that "the First Amendment requires us to err on the side of protecting political speech rather than suppressing it[;]" that "[w]here the First Amendment is implicated, the tie goes to the speaker, not the censor[;]" and that the Court must "give the benefit of the doubt to speech, not censorship. The First Amendment's command that 'Congress shall make no law ... abridging the freedom of speech' demands at least that." The principal opinion and Justice Alito's separate concurrence also stressed that *McConnell*'s holding itself could well be reexamined in a future case if it insufficiently protects the First Amendment.

Note also that Justice Alito concurred separately to invite facial attacks on existing Supreme Court precedents in both *Randall* and *WRTL*.

4. Bellotti *Lives*, Austin *Dies*? The controlling opinion treats *Bellotti*'s holding on corporate First Amendment rights quite favorably. Does the opinion deal with the tension between *Austin* and *Bellotti*? Is *Austin* still good law? If you were a lower court judge deciding a First Amendment challenge to a state law barring spending of corporate treasury funds on *express advocacy* in candidate elections, how would you rule?

As this book went to press, the Supreme Court decided *Davis v. Federal Election Commission*, discussed more fully on page 795. In *Davis*, five Justices emphatically reiterated *Buckley*'s rejection of the equality rationale for campaign finance regulation, citing Justice Kennedy's *Austin* dissent. Four dissenters in *Davis* argued that *Austin*'s rationale for limiting spending should apply to cases of large aggregations of "individual wealth" as well.

5. In Note 4 after the *Randall* case in the last chapter, we asked you to consider what role a concern about incumbency protection should play in evaluating the constitutionality of a campaign finance law. Did this concern play any role in the Court's decision in *WRTL*? Should it have?

6. *The Future of Corporate and Union Spending on Election-Related Advertising.* BCRA seemed to have a larger immediate effect on corporations than unions. Of corporations giving more than $100,000 in soft money in both 2000 and 2002, the amount of spend-

ing from corporate treasury funds fell in 2004 from $113.2 million (in soft money) in 2000 to $6.1 million (given to "527" organizations). Robert G. Boatright et al., *Interest Group and Advocacy Organizations After BCRA*, in THE ELECTION AFTER REFORM: MONEY, POLITICS, AND THE BIPARTISAN CAMPAIGN REFORM ACT 112, 118 (Michael J. Malbin, ed. 2006). As for labor unions in the 2004 elections, "the flow of treasury funds to political parties was also halted, but most of the dollars appear to have been spent elsewhere, either directly or in the form of contributions to Democratic-leaning 527s." Thomas E. Mann, *Lessons for Reformers*, in FINANCING THE 2004 ELECTION 241, 249 (David B. Magleby et al., eds. 2006). Is *WRTL* likely to affect corporate and union contributions and spending?

The finding of Boatwright et al. that BCRA greatly reduced campaign-related spending by the corporate sector has been challenged by Susan Clark Muntean, who documents large contributions to Section 527 organizations by corporate managers and insiders, such as George Soros. Clark Muntean concludes that BCRA's major influence was not to shift campaign spending out of the corporate sector but to shift spending within that sector, from broadly owned corporations to closely held firms. See Susan Clark Muntean, *Corporate Contributions after the Bipartisan Campaign Reform Act*, 7 ELECTION LAW JOURNAL 233 (2008).

Chapter 17

Public Financing

For many reformers, public financing is the *sine qua non* of campaign finance reform. The logic supporting public financing is simple. Many Americans willingly contribute modest amounts to campaigns for such reasons as ideology, party, or the candidate's leadership abilities, without expecting the contribution to exert any particular pressure on the recipient. But experience shows that contributions of this type do not consistently meet the need of candidates and parties for funds in amounts sufficient to bring their messages home to voters and to allow for vigorous electoral competition. Sometimes this gap is not filled, as is often the case for challengers in House and state legislative races. In other cases—especially for incumbents in the same races—the gap is filled by contributors who hope to apply pressure or, perhaps, are pressured into making contributions. Public financing, according to supporters, is the only way to reduce or eliminate this gap so that informative, competitive campaigns can be run, while reducing campaign financing as a source of undue pressure and influence.

Some reformers also support public financing on grounds it promotes political equality. Consider Richard Briffault's argument:

> It is not possible to truly equalize influence over elections. Indeed, given the value of robust and uninhibited political participation and the extensive regulation it would take to assure total equality, assuring absolutely equal influence over elections is not even desirable. Nevertheless, dramatically unequal campaign spending that reflects underlying inequalities of wealth is in sharp tension with the one person, one vote principle enshrined in our civil culture and our constitutional law. Public funding is necessary to bring our campaign finance system more in line with our central value of political equality. In privately funded systems, donors and independent spenders can have a bigger impact on the election than those who neither contribute nor spend, and big donors and spenders can have a bigger impact than smaller financial participants. Contribution and expenditure caps could ameliorate this, but at the cost of cutting into the ability of candidates to campaign effectively and possibly reinforcing the advantages of incumbents. Public funding can break the tie between private wealth and electoral influence while simultaneously supplementing campaign resources. Money from the public fisc comes from everyone and, thus, from no one in particular. No one gains influence over the election through public funding. The more the funds for election campaigns come from the public treasury, the more evenly is financial influence over election outcomes spread across the populace.

Richard Briffault, *Public Funding and Democratic Elections*, 148 University of Pennsylvania Law Review 563, 577–78 (1999).

Other reformers support public financing not for its own merits, but because they believe it is important to have some form or other of spending limits. Under *Buckley v. Valeo*, such limitations generally cannot be imposed except as a voluntary condition of accepting a public benefit that is offered in exchange. Ordinarily that benefit is public funding, though we shall see in Part II of this chapter that there have been some efforts to fashion incentives for the acceptance of spending limits other than public funding. Whether these will pass constitutional muster is not yet clear, but as will be briefly noted, their prospects were dampened by a Supreme Court decision issued as this book was in press.

The opposition to public financing is as vigorous as the support. In part it reflects a general opposition to new or expanded government programs. Opponents of public financing argue that in a time of fiscal pressure in which many vital programs are competing for funds, a new appropriation for political campaigns is objectionable. Furthermore, they contend taxes should not be used for the propagation of political views that the taxpayers may disagree with or even find offensive. In addition, some people oppose public funding because they believe such programs would be accompanied by contribution and/or spending limits, which are themselves objectionable. See, e.g., Bradley A. Smith, *Some Problems with Taxpayer-Funded Political Campaigns*, 148 University of Pennsylvania Law Review 591, 628 (1999) (contending that "[g]overnment subsidies of political campaigns, if not tied to bans on private contributions and spending limits, may indeed have certain benefits for political life[,]" but that "[g]overnment financing plans which include limits on contributions and spending, whether deemed 'voluntary' or not, are doomed to failure").

Perhaps the most telling argument against public financing is that it would endanger the autonomy of the political process from the state. Even laws that merely regulate the flow of money in campaigns are often enacted and implemented with political advantage—partisan or personal—in mind. To make candidates and parties dependent on public funds and the strings that are or might be attached to them would greatly magnify the danger of abuse, according to opponents of public funding. See Roy A. Schotland, *Demythologizing Public Funding*, Georgetown Journal of Law & Ethics (forthcoming 2008).

Whatever may be the force of this last argument, there can be little doubt that partisanship and calculation of advantage have been central to the politics of public financing. In general and with a number of exceptions, Democrats have supported public financing and Republicans have opposed it. Part of the reason, of course, is that some of the ideological arguments against public financing are likely to appeal more to Republicans than to Democrats. In addition, both Republicans and Democrats may believe that in the long run, Republicans—with their affinity to the corporate sector—have a natural advantage over Democrats in a privately financed campaign system. Probably a third reason, less frequently mentioned, is that most of the public financing schemes that have been proposed and debated in the last couple of decades have been fashioned by Democrats and therefore have been more attuned to the needs of Democrats than Republicans.

The debate on public financing is complicated not merely because of the competing pro and con arguments and the political cross-currents that surround it, but because "public financing" is not a single concept. Following are only a handful of the options that must be considered in fashioning any public financing plan:

- Who will be eligible for public financing? All major party candidates? If so, will public financing be available in primaries? If so, on what terms? Or will eligibility be determined by other standards? The most common method proposed is that candidates be required to raise a threshold amount in private contributions. If this method is used, what will be the terms and conditions?

- How much should the candidates receive? Will all eligible candidates for the same office receive the same amount? Or will public funds match, on a dollar-for-dollar or other basis, private contributions the candidates receive?

- Will funds be paid directly from the public treasury? More commonly, a special "fund" is created. Individuals, when they pay their federal or state income taxes, are permitted to "check off" one or a few dollars of their taxes to go into the fund. This device is intended to deflect criticism that taxpayers' funds are used to support propagation of views to which they object. But many regard this device as deceptive, because the taxpayer who checks the box on a tax return pays no additional tax for doing so. To say that the taxes of individuals who decline to check the box are not being used is thus a dubious proposition.

- Should public funding take the form of cash grants that can be used for any campaign purpose, or should it consist of "in-kind" benefits, such as reduced postage rates or free or discounted radio and television advertising?

- What additional rules and regulations should control campaign financing to complement public funding?

Supporters of public financing are by no means agreed on the answers to these and many other questions. Take the last one, for example. As we have seen, some people support public financing solely or primarily because they must do so in order to advocate spending limits. But there are other supporters of public financing who oppose spending limits. This single disagreement may be sufficient to create deep division within any coalition for public financing, and it is only one of a large number of disagreements.

Part I of this chapter surveys public financing as it presently exists on both the state and local level and through the presidential public financing system. Part II of this chapter considers in depth an issue the Supreme Court dealt with only cryptically in *Buckley*: what constraints, such as expenditure limits, may be placed upon candidates running for public office who agree to accept public financing of their campaigns? In Part III, we review various novel methods that scholars have proposed for doling out public funds for campaigns.

I. Existing Public Financing Systems

A. In the States

Kenneth Mayer, Timothy Werner, and Amanda Williams, *Do Public Funding Programs Enhance Electoral Competition?*

in The Marketplace of Democracy 245–67
(Michael P. McDonald and John Samples eds. 2006)

Advocates of public funding offer four main arguments about the consequences of taxpayer-financed elections. First, public funding can help potential candidates overcome the barriers that might deter them from running. In a vicious cycle, potential candidates who lack the ability to raise campaign funds are not taken seriously, and candidates who are not taken seriously cannot raise campaign funds. The cost of a campaign, even at the state legislative level, prevents potentially qualified candidates from even entering. A system of public grants can give candidates the seed money necessary to launch broader fundraising efforts, or even provide them all the resources they need to run credible campaigns. By reducing the campaign funding barrier, public funding systems might encourage candidates to emerge. Grants can be especially crucial for challengers, who face particularly daunting prospects in taking on an incumbent.

A corollary advantage to public financing is that it can encourage the emergence of candidates who lack substantial personal resources. Because campaigning is so expensive, candidates (especially challengers) routinely put thousands of dollars of their own money—sometimes millions—into their campaigns. Candidates without deep pockets have more difficulty persuading potential contributors (and political parties) to take them seriously. Public funding lowers this barrier, and therefore might increase the ideological and demographic diversity of candidates, as well as the range of policy positions that are put before the electorate.

Second, public grants can make elections more competitive. By reducing the fundraising advantages that, in particular, incumbents have over challengers, public funding systems can "level the playing field" and reduce the number of landslide victories.

Third, public funding can reduce the influence of private contributions on both candidates and officeholders. By replacing individual, corporate, labor, or political action committee contributions with public funds not tied to any particular interest, public funding can, in theory, refocus attention away from parochial concerns to those of the broader public.

A fourth argument put forth by advocates is that public financing can control campaign costs. Since candidates who accept public grants must, as a general rule, agree to abide by spending limits, higher participation in public funding programs can prevent further escalation in the spiral of campaign spending.

Does public financing achieve any of these goals? The short answer is that nobody knows because there has been no comprehensive evaluation of public finance systems to identify what conditions and program elements lead to successful outcomes. The conventional wisdom is based on either a limited amount of data or anecdotal impression. Consequently, the elements of clean elections programs—funding amounts, eligibility rules, spending limits, and other regulations—are based more on guesswork than on solid evidence. The clean elections movement is in part motivated by axioms about the political process: that the need to raise funds deters many candidates from emerging; that candidates need protection against independent expenditures and issue ads; and that incumbents are as a rule unbeatable. While these are reasonable conclusions, they have not been subjected to rigorous analysis and testing. "The justifications normally offered for public funding," wrote Michael Malbin and Thomas Gais, "all rest on long strings of difficult assumptions."[2]

The question was also uninteresting, since only a handful of states had public funding programs. That changed, though, when Arizona and Maine adopted full public funding (dubbed "clean elections" by proponents) beginning with the 2000 cycle. For the first time, public grants would pay the full cost of a state legislative campaign. Hawaii changed its public funding law in 1995, raising grant size from what had been a trivial amount ($50 for State House candidates) to several thousand dollars, depending on the number of registered voters in each district. New York City changed its public funding program for city council candidates to a four-to-one matching formula, in which each $1 raised

---

2. [Michael J. Malbin & Thomas L. Gais, THE DAY AFTER REFORM: SOBERING CAMPAIGN FINANCE LESSONS FROM THE AMERICAN STATES 70 (1998).]

in qualifying contributions is matched by a public grant of $4 (in December 2004, the city council raised the maximum matching rate to six-to-one). We summarize provisions of the state legislative programs in table [17-1].

This combination of major change and continuity presents an unusually favorable opportunity to see if public funding has made any difference or achieved the goals that it was intended to achieve. We are particularly interested in how public funding affects legislative elections. With legislatures, because multiple elections occur at precisely the same time, we have a much larger set of races to analyze (than, for example, after a single gubernatorial or attorney general election). We also believe a plausible case can be made that public funding is more likely to affect legislative elections, since statewide races are more likely to attract well-known and experienced candidates who may be less influenced by the existence of a public funding program. For legislative candidates, especially first-time challengers, public funding is more likely to make a difference in their decision to run.

There has been some research on the consequences of these reforms, but these initial evaluations are incomplete. Some reports, especially those produced by advocacy groups that strongly support public funding, overstate the effect of the new law and ignore other factors, such as term limits or redistricting, that have without question shaped outcomes.[4] Others, including the General Accounting Office's evaluation of the Maine and Arizona programs, understate the reforms' impact.[5] We will navigate between these two edges and make an effort to specify the conditional nature of our conclusions, which can be summarized as follows:

— Public funding programs increase the pool of candidates willing and able to run for state legislative office. This effect is most pronounced for challengers, who were far more likely than incumbents to accept public funding.

— Public funding increases the likelihood that an incumbent will have a competitive race.

— Public funding has reduced the incumbency reelection rates in Arizona and Maine, although the effects are marginal. We can say with certainty, though, that public funding has *not* made incumbents safer. Fears that public funding would amount to an incumbency protection act are unfounded.

— Public funding programs have a threshold effect: if grants sizes and spending limits do not have a realistic connection to what candidates actually need, programs will have no effect.

In the end, we conclude that public funding programs-particularly the full "clean elections" systems in Arizona and Maine-increase the competitiveness of state legislative elections....

Does It Work? The GAO Report and Beyond

Past work on public funding has come to a mixed result: some studies find evidence that grant programs increase election competitiveness, while others find no effect. As we noted earlier, the significant recent changes in Arizona and Maine make another round of investigation worthwhile. Until recently, any analysis of public funding was confined to a comparison of Wisconsin and Minnesota, since Hawaii's program offered only trivial grants to candidates until 1996.... In one of the few studies to even attempt

---

4. [Clean Elections Institute. http://www.azclean.org/; Breslow, Gorat, and Saba. 2002. Revitalizing Democracy: Clean Election Reform Shows the Way Forward. January 2002. http://www.neaction.org/revitalizingdemocracy.pdf.]

5. [General Accounting Office. 2003. *Campaign Finance Reform: Early Experiences of Two States That Offer Full Public Funding for Political Candidates.* GAO-03-453, May 2003.] http://www.gao.gov/htext/d03453.html.

Table 17-1. Characteristics of Public Funding Programs in Five States

Characteristic	State and date effective				
	Arizona 2000	Maine 2000	Wisconsin 1978	Minnesota 1976	Hawaii 1996
Qualification	Raise $1,050 in qualifying contributions ($5 each)	Raise $250 (House) or $750 (Senate) in qualifying contributions ($5 each)	Win primary with at least 6 percent of total vote for office. Raise threshold amount in $100 contributions ($1,725 for Assembly, $3,450 for Senate)	Raise $1,500 (House) or $3,000 (Senate) in qualifying contributions ($100 each)	Raise $1,500 (House) or $2,500 (Senate)
Maximum grant	Up to spending limit. Bonus provisions against privately funded candidates and independent expenditures	Up to spending limit. Bonus provisions against privately funded candidates and independent expenditures	$15,525 for Senate (2002); $7,763 for Assembly (2002). Grants for general election only	Up to 50 percent of spending limit. Small contribution refund program reimburses individuals up to $50 for contribution to participating candidate	Amount of grant restricted to 15 percent of spending limit
Spending limit (2004)	$28,300 for primary/ general in House and Senate elections	$4,406 for primary/ general in House. $23,278 for primary/ general in Senate	$17,250 for Assembly. $34,500 for Senate. Limits unchanged since 1986	$34,100 for House (2004). $64,866 for Senate (2002). Separate spending limits for election and non-election years	$1.40 x number of registered voters in district 2004 ranges (approx.): House: $14,000–19,000. Senate: $23,000–45,000
Special conditions	Unopposed candidates not eligible for public funds beyond qualifying contributions	Nonparticipating candidates face additional reporting requirements	Spending limits apply only if all candidates accept public funds	Spending limits increase by 10 percent for first-time candidates and by 20 percent for candidates running in competitive primary. Spending limits waived when nonparticipating opponent exceeds threshold expenditures	

Source: Compiled by authors.

to measure the impact, across states, of public funding on competitiveness, Malbin and Gais concluded that "there is no evidence to support the claim that programs combining public funding with spending limits have leveled the playing field, countered the effects of incumbency, and made elections more competitive."[19] However, this study, of necessity, was again limited to a focus on Wisconsin and Minnesota; other research has concluded that public funding can indeed make a difference.[20] More recent work has begun to challenge the efficacy of New York City's public funding program, noting that it has not done much to make municipal elections more competitive.[21] Through the 2000 election cycle, public funding did not have a good track record in creating competitive electoral environments, and a comprehensive study of state-level programs concluded that "full-blown public funding programs with spending limits do not *seem* to do much for competition.[22]

Section *310* of the Bipartisan Campaign Reform Act (BCRA) — more commonly known as McCain-Feingold — directed the General Accounting Office to study the Maine and Arizona public funding systems in the 2000 and 2002 election cycles. The GAO's cautious May 2003 report offered some support for the clean elections programs, but concluded that "it is too soon to determine the extent to which the goals of Maine's and Arizona's public financing programs are being met." The report found that more candidates in both states were running and winning with public funding, and that funding differences between incumbents and challengers had narrowed. But it also found no evidence that elections had become more competitive, or that interest group influence had diminished.

The GAO report received scant press attention, with no major mentions in the national media, perhaps in part because of its tentative nature (a LexisNexis search did not result in a single mention in any national newspaper). The reform group Public Campaign, which supports public funding, criticized the report as "too cautious in [its] analysis" and argued that the GAO's own evidence could have supported stronger conclusions. The publisher of the trade newsletter *Political Finance* argued that the authorizing language resulted in a report that intentionally overstated the impact of the clean elections law, attributing to public funding outcomes that actually resulted from term limits.

A review of the GAO's methods reveals that the office did significantly underestimate most measures of electoral competitiveness, in large part because the authors performed many of their calculations using unorthodox measures....

We now turn to our own analysis of electoral competition, which offers a somewhat clearer picture of the impact of the Maine and Arizona reforms.

Data on Electoral Competition

To measure the extent to which public funding has affected electoral competition, we calculated the following indicators, from 1990–2004, for elections to the lower house in the state legislatures in Arizona, Hawaii, Maine, Minnesota, and Wisconsin:

— the percentage of incumbents who faced a major-party opponent (contestedness)

— the percentage of incumbents who were in a competitive race, defined as one in which the winner received less than 60 percent of the two-party vote (competitiveness)

---

19. Malbin and Gais (1998, p. 137).

20. [Mayer, Kenneth R. 1998. *Public Financing and Electoral Competition in Minnesota and Wisconsin.* Citizens' Research Foundation, University of Southern California (April).]

21. [Kraus, Jeffrey. 2006. "Campaign Finance Reform Reconsidered: New York City's Public Finance Program after Fifteen Years." *The Forum 3 (4).* http://www.bepress.com/forum/vol3/iss4/art6/.]

22. Malbin and Gais (1998, p. 158).

—the percentage of incumbents who ran for and were reelected to office (reelection rate)

For the first and third indicators, we controlled for the presence of paired incumbents in the 2002 elections. We did not count a race as contested if the two (or more) major-party candidates were paired through redistricting, and we removed losing paired incumbents from our calculations of incumbent reelection rates. For comparison, we also calculated these figures for states that do not offer public funding.

Assessing the effect of the clean elections law in Arizona is more difficult since its implementation coincided with two other significant changes to state election law. In 1992, Arizona enacted term limits for state legislators, limiting them to four consecutive terms. The 2000 elections were the first in which members were "termed out," and fifteen legislators (nine representatives and six senators) were ineligible for reelection in 2002. Second, in 2000 voters opted to conduct the decennial reapportionment process using an Independent Redistricting Commission (IRC), rather than allow state legislators to draw district lines. Advocates of the independent commission approach hoped that the new approach would produce districts less tied to incumbent interests (indeed, the law prohibited the commission from identifying or taking into account incumbents' residency when drawing the new districts). The near simultaneous effects of these three major reforms — public funding, term limits, and a new approach to redistricting — produced significant turnover in both chambers, and it is not immediately apparent how the effects should be allocated.

In addition, the 2004 election cycle was unusually tumultuous because of legal disputes surrounding the new legislative districts that the IRC created for the 2002 elections. In January 2004, a state court rejected the redistricting plan in a lawsuit challenging the constitutionality of the proposed districts. Holding that the commission did not comply with the constitutional language requiring it to create competitive districts, a State Superior Court judge ordered the IRC to draw up a new plan for the 2004 elections. The commission complied, and in April 2004 submitted a map to the U.S. Department of Justice for preclearance under section 5 of the "Voting Rights Act." But the filing deadline for state office passed before the DOJ had approved the new plan, so state officials were forced to use a version of the 2002 plan for the upcoming 2004 elections. The uncertainty over the district maps meant that some prospective candidates had no idea which district they lived in, and some of these may have chosen to stay out of the ring until 2006.

A final problem is that Arizona's House elects its members from multimember districts, which do not translate into head-to-head campaigns. We address some of these methodological difficulties, and describe our application of an existing method of measuring competitiveness in multicandidate systems, in the appendix.

In figure 17-1, we report contestedness from 1990 to 2004. The key to this and subsequent figures is the change in the period 2000–04 in Maine and Arizona, when the full public funding system was in place. Several patterns emerge from this graph. Arizona experienced a significant jump in the number of contested races in 2002 and 2004, increasing from under 40 percent in 2000 to over 50 percent in 2002 and 2004. This increase was not only large; it also reversed the previous trend of uniformly fewer contested elections between 1994 and 2000. While we cannot attribute this shift entirely to public funding (which was also in place in 2000), it is likely to have played a key role. Of the twenty-five major-party challengers who took on an incumbent in the general election in 2002, twelve were publicly funded. Given that these races present poor electoral odds for the challenger — incumbents are difficult to beat except in unusual circumstances — it is a defensible inference that some of these candidates would have stayed away without the existence of public funding.

Figure 17-1. Incumbents Facing Major-Party Challengers in General State House/Assembly Elections, Excluding Incumbent Pairings, 1990–2004[a]

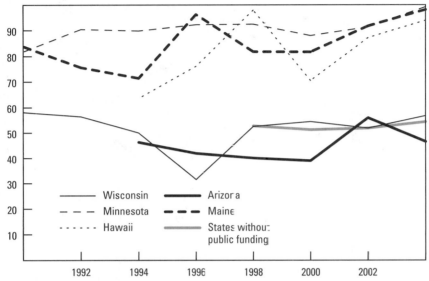

Percent incumbents in contested races

a. Incumbent pairings refer to incumbents running against each other.
Reprinted with permission. © 2006, the Brookings Institution

The patterns for Maine and Hawaii are murkier, though in the expected direction. Both saw the percentage of contested incumbents increase in 2002, and again in 2004. Maine's contested rate in 2004 (98 percent) was higher than it was at any point since 1990.

Wisconsin and Minnesota show a continuation of patterns that existed throughout the 1990s. Minnesota's public funding program, which combines direct grants with refunds of small individual contributions, is generally regarded as effective in both encouraging candidate participation and in fostering a competitive environment. Wisconsin, which provides grants that have not changed since 1986, is at the other end of the spectrum, with low candidate participation rates and a program generally considered close to irrelevant. In Minnesota, uncontested House elections are rare, with contested rates almost always higher than 90 percent. In Wisconsin, uncontested incumbents are almost the norm, with just over half of incumbents facing a major-party opponent.

For comparison, we also show the contested rate for states that do not have public funding programs, using data from the Institute on Money in State Politics (IMSP). In these states, incumbents face major-party challenges about 50 percent of the time; that figure changed little from 1998 through 2004.

In figure 17-2 we report on the competitiveness of an election when an incumbent is running. We defined a competitive race as one in which the incumbent received less than 60 percent of the two-party vote. This is not a universally accepted threshold—many political professionals would consider a 60–40 race something of a blowout—but we regard it as an acceptable minimum baseline of competitiveness, especially given the advantages that incumbents have in these low-visibility races.

Figure 17-2 shows that the percentage of competitive races went up in Hawaii, Maine, and Minnesota between 1998 and 2004. In Maine, 64 percent of incumbents were in competitive races in 2004, nearly double the 1998 rate (35 percent), and higher than the

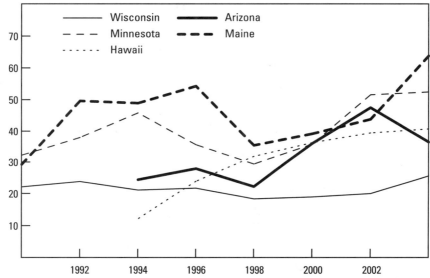

**Figure 17-2. Incumbents in Competitive Races
Assembly/House Elections, 1990–2004[a]**

Percent incumbents in contested races

a. A competitive race is defined here as one in which the winner received less than 60 percent of the two-party vote.

Reprinted with permission. © 2006, the Brookings Institution

rate in Minnesota. The increase in Hawaii was much more modest, with only a slight improvement over the 2002 and 2000 rates.

AZ ↓

The 2004 Arizona House elections proved something of a disappointment to campaign finance reformers: the percentage of incumbents in competitive races in 2004 was the same as it was in 2000 (about 36 percent), declining from a post-1990 record of 47 percent in 2002. At the same time, in Arizona this measure of competition remained higher than it had been during the pre-public-funding era (1998 and earlier).

In 2004, Minnesota continued its pattern of close races, with over half of its House incumbents facing competitive challengers. Wisconsin trails the pack, with only one incumbent in four having faced a competitive race in 2004.

Figure 17-3 shows the incumbent reelection rate—that is, the percentage of incumbents who run and are reelected to another term. This represents what many would consider to be the payoff measure. Opponents of public funding often argue that it is nothing but an incumbent protection act: since incumbents have formidable advantages in name recognition, experience, and ability to mobilize supporters, the spending limits that always accompany public grants could, in this view, simply institutionalize the inability of challenges to overcome the incumbency advantage. But this has not happened. In Arizona, the incumbent reelection rate dropped from a Congresslike 98 percent in 1998 to 75 percent in 2002 (even after controlling for incumbency pairings), and remained low in 2004, at 83 percent. In comparison with 1998, incumbent reelection rates in 2004 were also lower in Maine, Hawaii, and Minnesota. The changes in these states, though, appear to be within normal limits and are not radically different from levels that existed throughout the 1990s.

Figure 17-3. Incumbent Reelection Rates in the State Assembly/House, Excluding Incumbent Pairings

Percent incumbents who run and win

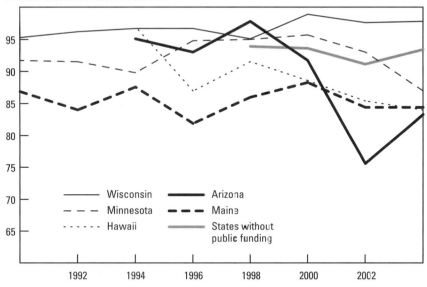

Source: Wisconsin Campaign Finance Project.

Reprinted with permission. © 2006, the Brookings Institution

Wisconsin, making a three-for-three sweep, again holds the record for the least competitive elections. Ninety-eight percent of unpaired incumbents won reelection in 2004 (eighty-eight out of ninety won).

We also include a measure of incumbency reelection for the states that do not have public funding, again using IMSP data. These data are not fully comparable to the lines for publicly funded states, both because they do not control for pairings and because they consider as incumbents lower House members running for Senate seats. This is one reason why the incumbency reelection rate dipped in 2002, after redistricting had occurred in most states. However, we calculated reelection rates using several different methods, and all were within a percentage point of the others. In the states without public funding, the incumbency reelection rate has remained stable, at about 93 percent.

What accounts for these results? Obviously, they cannot be attributed entirely to changes in campaign finance law, but all of the trends are in the expected direction. The dramatic changes in Arizona cannot be attributed to term limits, since we are focusing on incumbents who are running for reelection; nor can the Maine results be the result of redistricting, since the state did not begin the process until 2003. And the stark lack of electoral competition in Wisconsin clearly sets it apart from the other states in this group—even from Hawaii, which has been dominated by the Democratic Party for decades.

One difference among these states is the varying amounts of money available to candidates through the public funding programs. We can distinguish between the full public funding systems (Arizona and Maine), those that provide multiple sources of public grants (Minnesota), and those that provide relatively small grants (Hawaii and Wisconsin)....

These data suggest a clear explanation for why public funding has apparently made so little difference in Wisconsin, as public grants make up only a tiny and shrinking share of

More public funds = greater fluidity + competition

overall campaign spending. During the 1980s, public funds made up as much as one-third of candidate spending. But in 1986, grant levels and spending limits were fixed and have not changed since then. When a candidate has to raise $80,000 or more to run a competitive Assembly campaign, and $250,000 or more for the Senate, the maximum grants—$15,525 for a Senate candidate, $7,763 for the Assembly—are hardly worth the bother.

The data also confirm that public funding could not possibly have had any effect in Hawaii, since grants continue to make up only a trivial fraction of overall campaign spending. This is a limiting case which shows that campaign finance is not the only factor that affects election competition.

Hawaii's experience with public funding—minimal grants, but a trend toward increased electoral competitiveness—highlights some of the limits of public funding as a comprehensive reform strategy. Although the evidence from Maine and Arizona, in particular, point to a significant improvement in electoral competition, even dramatic changes in campaign finance practices do not by themselves uproot electoral systems or produce fundamental rearrangements of political influence (at least none that we can detect so far). More to the point, when the political context does change, it may be the result of broader political forces, or even idiosyncratic events.

Although Hawaii was considered a Republican state in its early years of statehood, the Democratic Party ascended in the early 1960s to dominate state politics, with a coalition of labor unions and minority groups organized into a powerful majority by skilled politicians like Daniel Inouye and John Burns.

But the Democratic hold on state elections began to waver in the mid-1990s in response to because of a combination of stagnant economic growth, ethics scandals, and efforts to organize in response to a 1993 state Supreme Court decision opening the door to same-sex marriages. Republicans held only seven of fifty-one State House seats in 1995, but won nineteen of fifty-one in the 2000 elections (Democrats now have a 41–10 majority). And although the state GOP has failed to cut into the Democratic legislative lock, in 2002 Hawaii elected its first Republican governor since 1962, and was considered competitive—for a time, at least—during the 2004 presidential election.

Conclusion: Does Public Funding Make Elections More Competitive?

We are left with something of a mixed picture. There is compelling evidence that Arizona and Maine have become much more competitive states in the wake of the 1998 clean elections programs. The fact that indicators of competitiveness in Arizona remained stable through the 2002 and 2004 cycles is evidence that the electoral dynamic has indeed changed. We have revised our view of the impact of Maine's program: based on the 2002 elections, we concluded that it was too early to tell whether public funding had changed the electoral landscape. With the 2004 results in hand, we can say that public funding appears to have significantly increased the competitiveness of State House elections, based on the percentage of incumbents who face major-party opponents and run in reasonably close races. Minnesota's program continues to show a high degree of efficacy.

Not everyone agrees with our conclusions. Elsewhere in this volume [see note 2 below—Eds.], Primo, Milyo, and Groseclose argue that "the jury is still very much out on clean elections laws," observing that the changes we noted here may be fleeting. In particular, they note that the decline in incumbency reelection rates may be the result of a culling effect, in which the best and most experienced incumbents are the first to be forced out by term limits. The incumbents who are left are, by definition, the ones with less experience. It is possible, then, that the incumbents we are observing in 2002 and 2004—that is, post-reform—are less experienced and of lower quality than those who stayed in office before term limits. If this is true, these incumbents would have wound up in closer races (because they are less experienced and skilled, or because term limits reduced the incumbency advantage in some other way) even without clean elections.

It is of course possible that the effects we have observed will ebb. Everyone who studies elections will concede that the environment is complex, with many interactions, simultaneous relationships, and causal chains that are hard to pin down. Even so, we are confident in our results, because while we cannot claim to have controlled for every possible alternative explanation, we have eliminated the most obvious ones. Moreover, a growing literature suggests that term limits may *decrease* electoral competition by giving potential challengers a reason to bide their time until a seat opens up. In any case, we expect that a few more election cycles will clear up disagreement over the public funding effect.[37]

Hawaii and Wisconsin are states with ineffective programs; the key characteristic in both states is that public funds make up only a fraction of what candidates raise and spend. Although there is some evidence from Hawaii that elections have become slightly more competitive, this has more to do with long-term changes in the political composition of the electorate than with campaign finance law (and in any event, Hawaii Republicans have yet to seriously challenge the Democratic Party's hold on the legislature, even as they have achieved some statewide successes).

One significant inference that we draw is that there is no merit in the argument that public funding programs amount to an incumbent protection act. The fear that spending limits would put challengers in an impossible strategic situation and make incumbents even more unbeatable has simply not been realized.

[handwritten margin note: Not incumbent protection]

There are limits to what these data can tell us, in any event. We do not yet have evidence that public funding has altered roll-call voting patterns or legislative coalitions, as might be expected if interest group influence or party influence has declined as legislators utilize their newfound independence. But the evidence points strongly to the conclusion that, under the right set of circumstances, public grants can significantly increase the level of election competition.

Notes and Questions

1. As the authors note, unfortunately there has been no "comprehensive evaluation" of recently-enacted state and local public financing systems. Research by these authors and others is beginning to fill in considerable empirical gaps in our understanding of campaign finance systems. This set of notes briefly reviews some of the recent literature.

2. *Competition.* How much do "clean election"-style public financing systems stimulate political competition?

> To my eye, the changes [in competitiveness described in the Mayer, Werner, and Williams article] are noteworthy enough to make good political science

---

37. Early data from 2006, while not definitive, are consistent with our argument. In Maine, 321 candidates have filed for the 151 House seats, with 81 percent stating an intention to accept public funding. One hundred forty-six of the 151 seats are contested. In the Senate, all thirty-five seats are contested by the major parties, with 71 percent of candidates accepting public funding. These figures will change, since Maine ballot laws are flexible. But they suggest that the competitive effects observed have not yet dissipated. See Maine Commission on Governmental Ethics and Election Practices (www.state.me.us/ethics/candidate-list.htm).

but hardly enough to qualitatively improve the electoral system, even if one indulges the assumption that a more competitive system would be a major improvement.

For example, the reelection rate for incumbents in Maine declined by about five percent from the high 80s from 2000 to 2004. But the 2004 figure was still not quite as low as in 1996, before "clean elections" went into effect, and the rate in all the years from 2000 to 2004 was within the normal range defined in the previous decade. Arizona saw a much sharper decline of about 20 percentage points in the incumbency reelection rate between 1998 and 2002, but the rate bounced up about ten percentage points in 2004.

Daniel H. Lowenstein, *Competition and Competitiveness in American Elections*, 6 ELECTION LAW JOURNAL 278, 292 (2007) (reviewing THE MARKETPLACE OF DEMOCRACY).

Another recent study found that "[b]efore the institution of clean elections in Maine and Arizona, only 14% of challengers won in general elections; after the program was in place, 22% of challengers did." Dorie E. Apollonio & Raymond J. LaRaja, "Incumbent Spending under Clean Election Laws," paper presented to Western Political Science Association (2005). Should this count as a qualitative difference in levels of competition? If so, does it make you more likely to favor this system of public financing? Using different methodology and focusing on competitiveness of gubernatorial elections, Primo, Milyo and Groseclose conclude that "[p]ublic funding has only a modest and statistically insignificant effect on winning margins." David M. Primo, Jeffrey Milyo, & Tim Groseclose, *State Campaign Finance Reform, Competitiveness, and Party Advantage in Gubernatorial Elections*, 268, 278, in THE MARKETPLACE OF DEMOCRACY, *supra*. Perhaps public financing is more helpful to legislative challengers than gubernatorial candidates.

3. *Who Participates?* "The conventional wisdom holds that public funding programs should be especially advantageous for candidates who are not part of existing recruitment efforts or lack access to key political elites. According to this line of thought, women and challengers—two categories of candidates traditionally shut out from established political networks—will benefit from this alternative source of campaign funds." Timothy Werner & Kenneth R. Mayer, *Public Election Funding, Competition, and Candidate Gender*, 40 PS: POLITICAL SCIENCE & POLITICS 661, 661 (2007). Looking at the results in Maine and Arizona, the authors conclude that "female candidates are substantially more likely than male candidates to accept public funding in races for the state house ... At the same time, this effect disappears in state senate races." *Id.* at 666. The authors suggest that this difference between state houses might be due to the fact that state senate candidates are less likely to be entry-level candidates, and therefore that public financing helps non-traditional candidates most at the entry level.

4. *Strategic Responses to the Matching Funds Aspect of "Clean Elections" Programs.* Candidates who accept full public financing in Maine and Arizona are entitled to additional funding beyond the initial allocation when their opponents engage in large amounts of spending or when someone runs a major independent expenditure campaign against the candidate. This feature apparently has led to some strategic timing of campaign spending. Michael Miller, examining the new Arizona public financing program, found that "traditionally-funded candidates try to maximize the competitive effect of the money that they do spend by releasing funds at the last moment, giving the Clean Elections candidate little time to react." Michael Miller, *Gaming Arizona: Public Money and Shifting Candidate Strategies*, 41 PS: POLITICAL SCIENCE & POLITICS 527 (2008). Is there anything that could be done to prevent this strategic behavior? If so, *should* anything be done?

5. *Full Public Financing versus Partial Public Financing Programs.* The literature cited above has focused on the new Maine and Arizona programs, which provide full public financing. Older programs, such as those in Minnesota and Wisconsin, provide only partial public financing, and, as suggested in the excerpt above, the evaluation of the effects of these programs has been less positive. See Herbert Alexander, Reform and Reality: The Financing of State and Local Campaigns 44–46 (1991); Michael J. Malbin & Thomas L. Gais, The Day After Reform: Sobering Campaign Finance Lessons from the American States 71–72, 137 (1998).

B. In Presidential Elections

The laws governing the Presidential Election Campaign Fund are described in detail prior to the segment of *Buckley v. Valeo* reprinted in Chapter 10 of this book. A more general discussion will suffice here.

Public financing is available to presidential candidates in both primaries and general elections, but the system works differently before and after the parties have chosen their nominees. In presidential primaries, partial public financing is provided on a matching basis. In the general election, the campaigns are entirely funded from public funds. At least that was the original conception. As Chapter 15 explained, much of the controversy that surrounds the presidential public financing system relates to the private funds that continue to influence presidential elections.

In primaries, candidates become eligible for public funding by raising $5,000 or more in contributions of $250 or less in at least twenty states. Candidates who accept public financing are subject to campaign spending limits. The nationwide spending limit for presidential primaries is adjusted for changes in the cost of living, starting from $10 million in base year 1974. In addition to this basic limit, candidates may spend an additional twenty percent in fundraising costs. For the 2008 election, the nationwide spending limit including the allowance for fundraising was estimated to be about $55.8 million. Campaign Finance Institute, Presidential Public Financing Spending Limits, 1974–2008, http://www.cfinst.org/president/PECF_SpendingLimits.aspx.

In addition to the nationwide limit, there is a spending limit for each state. The state-by-state limit serves no apparent purpose. It was initially explained as assuring "that relatively unknown candidates would have an opportunity to compete effectively against better-known or better-financed candidates in individual states."[a] If that was a plausible expectation in 1974, the information regarding incumbency and campaign spending in Chapter 14 of this book suggests that, if anything, lesser-known candidates may have a greater need than their better-known opponents to spend large amounts. As it is, the state-by-state limit interferes for no clear reason with the strategies of candidates who wish to spend disproportionate amounts in states with crucial caucuses or primaries. In practice, this means Iowa and New Hampshire, which are usually the only states in which the state-by-state limits are a factor. In the past, some have evaded the limits. For example, staffers in the New Hampshire campaign would be lodged across the border in neighboring states, with the costs attributed to those states. Many candidates simply violated the limits, with no consequence beyond having to repay modest

---

a. See Anthony Corrado, Paying for Presidents: Public Financing in National Elections 6 (1993).

amounts of public financing after audits conducted long after the election year was over.[b] Prior to the 1992 election, the Federal Election Commission adopted revised accounting rules that make it possible for virtually any campaign to avoid the state-by-state spending limits legally.

Candidates who agree to the spending limits and who receive contributions sufficient to satisfy the threshold amounts described above get public funds for their campaigns equal in amount to the contributions they receive from individuals in amounts up to $250. The maximum amount a candidate can receive in public funds is half the nationwide spending limit. However, some of the money candidates raise, such as amounts over $250 and contributions from PACs, is not eligible for matching. On average, public funding amounts to about a third of major candidates' money in presidential primaries.

After the primaries, the major parties receive flat grants to pay the costs of their national nominating conventions. The parties are not permitted to raise private funds to add to the public funds they receive.

In the general election, the major party candidates receive a flat grant, which is equal to the spending limit. In other words, presidential candidates who accept public funding cannot spend any private funds in the general election campaign. The amounts of the grant are adjusted for changes in the cost of living, based on $20 million for the base year, 1974. In 2004, the amount for each major party candidate was $74.6 million. Each national party also received $14.9 million for nominating conventions.

Candidate acceptance of public funding was nearly universal in the early years of the program. In 1980, Republican John Connolly became the first eligible major party candidate to decline public funding in the primaries. Later, Steve Forbes declined public funding in the 1996 Republican primaries and both Forbes and now-President George W. Bush declined the money in the Republican primaries leading up to the 2000 election. Unlike Connolly and Forbes, who drew on their own private funds, Bush relied primarily on fundraising. By June 2000, he had raised an impressive $94.5 million under the FECA rules limiting contributions to federal candidates to $1,000 from individuals and $5,000 from PACs, over $91 million in individual contributions. Nonetheless, Bush agreed to accept public financing for the general election as the Republican party nominee. Until 2008, no major party candidate declined public funding in the general election. (Primaries and the general are treated as separate elections, but all the presidential primaries are treated as one for purposes of the contribution limits.)

Both President Bush and Democratic candidate John Kerry decided to decline public financing in the primaries leading to the 2004 election. Bush raised $269.6 million and Senator Kerry raised $234.6 million. Additionally, a number of independent but Democratic-leaning "527 organizations" (discussed in Chapter 15) raised and spent tens of millions of dollars during the primary period. Both Bush and Kerry opted for public funding in the general election. Should presidential candidates be able to opt into public financing for the primary season but not the general election? In the 2008 election, many of the leading major party primary candidates have declined to take public financing in the primary season. Although Democratic nominee Barack Obama had pledged to accept public funds in the general election if the Republican nominee did likewise, he broke precedent and declined public financing when he concluded he could raise more money on his own, within the contribution limits.

---

b. See Anthony Corrado, CREATIVE CAMPAIGNING: PACs AND THE PRESIDENTIAL SELECTION PROCESS 37–40 (1992).

The public money is paid out of the Presidential Election Campaign Fund. Money is deposited into the Fund at the behest of taxpayers, who are permitted to "check off" an amount to go into the fund out of their taxes each year. Until 1993, each individual taxpayer could designate one dollar to go into the fund. Two dollars could be designated on a joint tax return. However, the Fund was barely adequate to cover the claims of candidates in 1992, and projections made it clear that the Fund would be inadequate in 1996. Accordingly, Congress in 1993 raised the check-off amount to $3 for individual returns and $6 for joint returns.

The main reason the amount in the Fund became inadequate was that the check-off was fixed at one dollar, whereas the amounts candidates could collect were raised with the cost of living. Thus, in 1976, the total amount paid out of the Fund to candidates and parties was $72.3 million. In 2004, that amount was $207.5 million.

A lesser reason was that taxpayer use of the check-off appears to have declined. One reason may be that only people who have tax liability are eligible for the check-off, and the percentage of individuals who file tax returns but have no tax liability increased after the 1986 Tax Reform Act. Another reason was probably heightened disenchantment with government and politics. A major point of contention is whether the decline reflected disapproval of the public financing system itself and whether, indeed, most taxpayers understand the system, whether or not they use the check-off. Unfortunately, poor record-keeping by the Internal Revenue Service makes it impossible to be sure of the extent of the decline, and even less is understood of its causes.[c]

It is also difficult to estimate the extent of participation in any given year. Figures released by the Federal Election Commission, based on information received from the Internal Revenue Service, indicate a high of 28.7 percent participation in 1981, with a decline to 12.4 percent in 1997. However, although the rate of participation has steadily declined since 1981, the actual number of participants has not. The decline is due at least in part to an increase in the number of individual tax returns filed each year.

Public funding worked well until the last few elections to accomplish many of the objectives of campaign finance regulation. As Anthony Corrado wrote:

> [T]he matching funds program has proven to be an extremely popular form of campaign finance and an important source of revenue. It has been widely accepted by candidates and has encouraged them to solicit small contributions instead of large gifts and PAC donations. The program has been especially helpful to lesser-known aspirants who lack broad bases of financial support and to candidates who lack ready access to substantial numbers of large donors. By providing such candidates with the funds needed to introduce themselves to voters, public funding has increased the choices available to the electorate and enhanced the competitiveness of nomination contests.... At the same time, it has served to diminish the role of special interest money in presidential campaigns. Because PAC contributions are not eligible for matching funds, candidates can raise more money by soliciting small contributions than PAC contributions.... The law thus gives candidates a strong incentive to choose small private gifts over PAC money. This incentive, as well as the practice of many PACs to forego making contributions in processes that select

---

c. For a careful analysis of these issues, see Corrado, PAYING FOR PRESIDENTS, at 16–36. For prospective consideration of the need to keep the Fund solvent, see Joseph Michael Pace, *Public Funding of Presidential Campaigns and Elections: Is There a Viable Future?*, 24 PRESIDENTIAL STUDIES QUARTERLY 139 (1994).

major party candidates, has led to a system in which PAC contributions play an insignificant role. On average, only two to four percent of the total monies raised by presidential aspirants comes from PACs, as compared to congressional campaigns, which often rely on PACs for 30 to 40 percent of their total revenue.[d]

Recent controversy surrounding the presidential public funding system has centered on the increasingly inadequate amounts that discourage candidates from participating and the spending limitations, which critics believe have become so riddled with loopholes that many of the objectives of the system are frustrated. Initially, it was independent spending that created this concern. *Buckley* and *NCPAC* prevented the regulation of independent-spending PACs and for a time it was feared that the activities of such groups would distort or even dwarf the publicly funded campaigns of the candidates. However, independent PAC spending in presidential elections declined after the 1984 election. As we saw in Chapters 15 and 16, public attention then shifted to the very large amounts of "soft money" and "issue advocacy" affecting the outcome of presidential and congressional races, though these phenomena did not achieve major proportions until the 1996 election year. Post-*McConnell*, attention has shifted to independent 527 organizations spending money supporting or opposing presidential candidates. Have these factors eroded the value of public financing in presidential elections so that public financing is no longer worthwhile? Consider Corrado's more recent view of the topic:

> Although both major party nominees opted for public funding in the [2004] general election, this source functioned as more of a floor rather than a ceiling in spending on the presidential race. Despite the limitations on the amounts directly spent by the candidates, the parties and their allied groups were able to supplement these resources in significant ways.
>
> The public funds received by candidates constituted less than a third of the money spent to influence the outcome of the presidential race....
>
> Above all, the [2004] presidential general election campaign, like the pre-nomination campaigns, raised important questions about the equity and adequacy of the public funding program. In 2004, the incentives to participate in public funding were still strong enough to persuade both candidates to accept the general election grant. But whether these incentives will continue to encourage candidate participation is uncertain.... The public funding system has reached its tipping point. In future elections, candidate will view private financing as a realistic alternative to the public funding option.

Anthony Corrado, *Financing the 2004 Presidential General Election* 126, 142–44 in Financing the 2004 Election (David B. Magleby, Anthony Corrado & Kelly D. Patterson, eds. 2006).

With many of the major candidates opting out of public financing in the 2008 election cycle, and declining participation in the check-off system, should the existing system be scrapped? Strengthened? For a report considering these questions and arguing that the system should be strengthened, see Campaign Finance Institute, Task Force on Financing Presidential Nominations, *So the Voters May Choose ... Reviving the Presidential Matching Fund System* (2005), http://cfinst.org/president/pdf/VotersChoose.pdf.

---

d. Corrado, *supra*, at 38, 44–45.

II. Public Financing: Voluntary or Coercive?

In footnote 65 of *Buckley v. Valeo*, the Supreme Court wrote:

> For the reasons discussed in Part III, *infra*, Congress may engage in public financing of election campaigns and may condition acceptance of public funds on an agreement by the candidate to abide by specified expenditure limitations. Just as a candidate may voluntarily limit the size of the contributions he chooses to accept, he may decide to forgo private fundraising and accept public funding.

In Part III of its opinion the Court does give reasons for the permissibility of public financing, but contrary to the statement in footnote 65, there is no explanation in Part III or elsewhere in *Buckley* why Congress may "condition acceptance of public funds on an agreement by the candidate to abide by ... expenditure limitations."

Critics of public financing conditioned on the acceptance of spending limits point out that the simultaneous enactment of contribution limits may put considerable pressure on candidates to accept the public financing/spending limits package. The argument is made cogently by Brice M. Clagett & John R. Bolton, Buckley v. Valeo, *Its Aftermath, and Its Prospects: The Constitutionality of Government Restraints on Campaign Financing*, 29 VANDERBILT LAW REVIEW 1327, 1336–37 (1976):

> [T]he candidate is presented with a particularly invidious form of the twentieth century "Catch 22" which threatens to reduce the private sector to adjuncts and servants of the state: government imposes restrictions upon, and by taxation or otherwise dries up funds formerly available to, a private activity; government then offers public funds to subsidize the activity it itself has crippled; the courts then hold that by virtue of the regulation and the subsidies the formerly private activity has become "state action" and thus subject to even greater governmental control. When this process involves a virtually coerced surrender of first amendment rights in an area going to the heart of the political process, it is difficult to see how the Court's unexplained result can be sustained if the issue is brought before it and fully analyzed.

Judge Leventhal, one of the members of the Court of Appeals panel in *Buckley*, was friendlier to FECA and therefore found footnote 65 not anomalous but evidence that despite its rhetoric, the Court regarded spending limits as "substantially and significantly less restrictive than content prohibitions." Harold Leventhal, *Courts and Political Thickets*, 77 COLUMBIA LAW REVIEW 345, 361 (1977). Professor Daniel D. Polsby, Buckley v. Valeo: *The Special Nature of Political Speech*, 1976 SUPREME COURT REVIEW 1, 30–31, took a similar but less approving view:

> [T]he Court made a mistake in allowing expenditure ceilings to ride in on the coattails of public financing. There is no good reason for the Court to allow this restraint, especially when it takes the strong position on expenditure ceilings that it does. The Court's failure even to allude to this issue has the flavor of a tacit agreement among the Justices that expenditures of private money in elections is a bad thing for which there exists no obviously constitutional remedy. Hence, expenditure limits are to be cursed with the tongue but blessed with the hand, an understandable political compromise, not dismissible out-of-hand as bad policy, but unconvincing as law and contrary to the fundamental logic of the bulk of the decision.

If, as Polsby is willing to concede, spending limits tied to public financing may be good policy, then why is a ruling that the policy is constitutionally permissible "unconvincing as law"? There are some campaign finance reformers who are less than enthusiastic about spending limits but who strongly favor public financing of campaigns and either favor or are willing to tolerate spending limits so long as they are accompanied by public financing. Is it possible that some or all of the *Buckley* majority were of this mind and that they hoped or expected that the result of the *Buckley* decision would be to induce Congress to extend public financing to congressional elections? If so, would such considerations be proper influences on a Supreme Court decision? Whether or not they existed or were proper, any such hopes or expectations on the part of the Justices have failed to come to fruition. Continuous efforts to extend public financing to congressional campaigns have consistently failed over a period of 30 years.

Whatever the merits of Clagett and Bolton's criticism of footnote 65, their prediction that the footnote would fail to withstand further scrutiny has turned out to be incorrect. The issue was presented more concretely in *Republican National Committee v. Federal Election Commission*, 487 F.Supp. 280 (S.D.N.Y.) summarily aff'd, 445 U.S. 955 (1980). That case was a challenge to 26 U.S.C. §9003(b), which requires major party presidential candidates to certify, as a condition of receiving public funding, that they will not "incur qualified campaign expenses in excess of the aggregate payments to which they will be entitled," and that no private contributions will be accepted unless necessary to make up the difference in the event that the amount available in the government's "Presidential Election Campaign Fund" should fall short of the amount candidates are entitled to receive.

Plaintiffs in *RNC* contended that as a practical matter, candidates had no choice but to accept the public funding and that in any event, the conditioning of public funding on the waiver of First Amendment rights constituted an unconstitutional condition. The District Court regarded the contention that candidates had no choice but to accept public funding as unproved. Relying on *Buckley*'s footnote 65 and on other decisions applying the "unconstitutional conditions" doctrine, the District Court held that "the fact that a statute requires an individual to choose between two methods of exercising the same constitutional right does not render the law invalid, provided the statute does not diminish a protected right or, where there is such a diminution, the burden is justified by a compelling state interest." The District Court did not think the conditions attached to presidential public funding infringed on First Amendment rights, and in any event, it found a compelling state interest in assuring that candidates who receive public funding should be "relieved of the burdens of soliciting private contributions and of avoiding unhealthy obligations to private contributors." The Supreme Court's summary affirmance (i.e., without issuing its own opinion) is an authoritative reaffirmation that expenditure limits may be imposed as a condition on public funding, but it is no indication whether the Supreme Court relied on any or all of the reasons given by the District Court.

The question whether particular public financing laws are voluntary or coercive continues to be litigated as jurisdictions pass new laws conditioning the receipt of public financing on a candidate agreeing to give up certain fundraising techniques the law otherwise would allow. One additional issue appearing in the more recent cases is whether public financing laws may infringe upon the First Amendment rights of anyone besides candidates, such as individuals who wish to make independent expenditures urging the election or defeat of a candidate. Consider the following case.

Daggett v. Commission on Governmental
Ethics and Election Practices

205 F.3d 445 (1st Cir. 2000)

COFFIN, Senior Circuit Judge.

This case involves a challenge to Maine's attempt to reconcile the state's interest in curbing the power of money in politics with the sweeping strictures of the First Amendment. In 1996, Maine voters passed via referendum An Act to Reform Campaign Finance, creating the Maine Clean Election Act, 21-A M.R.S.A. §§1121–1128, which introduced a public funding alternative to private fundraising for candidates for elective offices, and lowering the ceiling on campaign contributions.

Plaintiffs-appellants — legislative candidates, campaign contributors, political action committees (PACs), and the Maine Libertarian Party — challenged both the Act, asserting that the public funding mechanism unconstitutionally coerced candidates to participate, and the contribution limits, arguing that they infringed on the First Amendment rights of candidates as well as donors. The district court upheld the constitutionality of the public funding system and the contribution limits. Under the principles set forth by the United States Supreme Court in *Buckley v. Valeo*, as recently applied in *Nixon v. Shrink Missouri Government PAC*, we conclude that the statutes are constitutionally sound. We therefore affirm.

I. *Factual Background*

Maine voters, pursuant to their authority under Part First, §1, and Part Third, §18, of Article IV of the Maine Constitution enacted the Maine Clean Election Act (MCEA) in November 1996 to take effect on January 1, 1999. The Act creates a system of optional public funding for qualifying candidates in state legislative and gubernatorial campaigns, both in primaries and the general election. It establishes public funding beginning with the 2000 elections, and requires candidates to complete qualifying actions by March 16, 2000.

In order to qualify for public funding, a candidate must fulfill several requirements during the qualifying period. The candidate must file a declaration of intent that he is seeking certification. The candidate must seek "seed money contributions" in amounts not greater than $100, limited to an aggregate amount that varies depending on the office sought: gubernatorial candidates are limited to $50,000, Senate candidates to $1,500, and House of Representatives candidates to $500. With that seed money, candidates seek out "qualifying contributions," $5 donations in the form of a check or money order payable to the Maine Clean Election Fund ("Fund") in support of their candidacy from registered voters in their district. Again, the requisite number of qualifying contributions depends on the type of seat sought: gubernatorial candidates must collect 2,500 contributions, Senate candidates 150 contributions, and House candidates 50 contributions.

Once certified as a "participating candidate" by the Maine Commission on Governmental Ethics and Election Practices, a candidate must agree not to accept any private contributions and not to make expenditures except from disbursements made to him from the Fund. The candidate transfers all unspent seed money to the Fund and receives an initial disbursement from the Fund.

The amount of the initial distribution is the average amount of campaign expenditures in the prior two election cycles for the particular office, although for the 2000 elections that amount has been discounted by 25% in order to ensure the availability of adequate funds. For the 2000 elections, participating Senate candidates will receive an initial distribution of $4,334 for the primary ($1,785 if uncontested) and $12,910 for the general election; House candidates will receive $1,141 for the primary ($511 if uncontested) and $3,252 for the general election. Participating candidates face both civil and criminal penalties for violation of the participation rules.

In addition to the initial disbursement, a participating candidate receives a dollar-for-dollar match of any monies raised by a non-participating opponent after the opponent raises more than the initial disbursement allotted to the participating candidate. Matching funds are also provided to correspond to "independent expenditures," outlays made by an independent entity endorsing the participant's defeat or the non-participating opponent's election. Once the participating candidate has received double the initial distribution in matching funds, however, the matching funds cease. No matter how much additional fundraising the participant's non-participating opponent undertakes, the participant's matching funding is capped at two times the initial distribution.

Reduced limits on contributions by individuals and groups to political candidates were enacted simultaneously with the Act by the voter referendum and effectively apply only to non-participating candidates. The limit on contributions made by an individual to a candidate in an election was reduced to $500 for gubernatorial candidates and $250 for all other candidates; the limit on contributions to a candidate by a political committee, other committee, corporation, or association in a single election was reduced to $500 for gubernatorial candidates and $250 for all other candidates. In addition, a pre-existing disclosure statute requiring reporting of independent expenditures aggregating more than $50 in any election was adapted to conform to the Act.

The Daggett appellants are candidates who sought legislative office in 1998 and plan to seek office again in 2000, the Libertarian Party of Maine, and an individual campaign contributor. Their major complaint about the public funding system is that as a whole it is coercive in its efforts to encourage candidates to become publicly funded and therefore unconstitutionally burdens the First Amendment rights of candidates. The Stearns appellants are an individual and two political action committees, the Maine Right to Life Committee Political Action Committee State Candidate Fund and the National Right to Life Political Action Committee State Fund, which have made contributions to and expenditures on behalf of political candidates. They challenge in particular the constitutionality of providing matching funds for independent expenditures, arguing that it violates their political speech and associational rights. Both sets of appellants contest the constitutionality of the reduced contribution limits.

II. *Contribution Limits*

[The court held the contribution limits were constitutional under *Buckley* and *Shrink Missouri*.]

III. *The Maine Clean Election Act: Matching Funds for Independent Expenditures*

A. *Matching Funds*

The Stearns appellants challenge the *per se* constitutionality of that part of the matching funds provision, also known as a "trigger," that grants funds to participating candidates based on independent expenditures made either against their candidacy or on behalf of their non-participating opponent. Appellants contend that this practice violates the First Amendment rights of non-participating candidates and those who wish to make independent expenditures by chilling as well as penalizing their speech. Essentially, their argument boils down to a claim of a First Amendment right to outraise and outspend an opponent, a right that they complain is burdened by the matching funds clause.

Appellants further argue that independent expenditures should not be treated as campaign contributions by the statute because independent expenditures have traditionally been afforded broader protection. Appellants also maintain that their freedom of association is eclipsed by this provision because it forces them to be associated with candidates they oppose by in effect facilitating their speech. They urge that even if the Act is found constitutional on whole, this particular provision should be struck.

We review the challenged provision of the statute to determine whether it burdens First Amendment rights, and if it does, whether it is narrowly tailored to serve a compelling state interest.

Direct limitations on independent expenditures have been found impermissibly to burden constitutional rights of free expression. *See Buckley; New Hampshire Right to Life Political Action Comm. v. Gardner*, 99 F.3d 8, 18–19 (1st Cir.1996) (invalidating New Hampshire statute limiting independent expenditures to $1,000 per election). Such cases are of limited application, however, because they involve direct monetary restrictions on independent expenditures, which inherently burden such speech, while the Maine statute creates no direct restriction.

Moreover, the provision of matching funds does not indirectly burden donors' speech and associational rights. Appellants misconstrue the meaning of the First Amendment's protection of their speech. They have no right to speak free from response—the purpose of the First Amendment is to "secure the 'widest possible dissemination of information from diverse and antagonistic sources.'" *Buckley*. The public funding system in no way limits the quantity of speech one can engage in or the amount of money one can spend engaging in political speech, nor does it threaten censure or penalty for such expenditures. These facts allow us comfortably to conclude that the provision of matching funds based on independent expenditures does not create a burden on speakers' First Amendment rights.

Appellants rely heavily on *Day v. Holahan*, 34 F.3d 1356 (8th Cir.1994), in which the Eighth Circuit invalidated Minnesota's campaign finance statute, which increased a participating candidate's expenditure limit based on independent expenditures made against her or for her major party opponent and under some circumstances matched such independent expenditures. The court held that "[t]o the extent that a candidate's campaign is enhanced by the operation of the statute, the political speech of the individual or group who made the independent expenditure 'against' her (or in favor of her opponent) is impaired." We cannot adopt the logic of *Day*, which equates responsive speech with an impairment to the initial speaker.

Further, merely because the Fund provides funds to match both campaign donations and independent expenditures made on behalf of the candidate does not mean that the statute equates the two. Finally, appellants' freedom of association is not burdened because their names and messages are not associated—in any way indicative of support—with the candidate they oppose.

B. *Reporting Requirements*

[The court upheld the reporting requirements under that portion of *Buckley* reprinted in Chapter 18.]

IV. *Public Financing System*

Throughout this litigation, the Daggett appellants' overarching argument has been that the public funding scheme embodied in the Maine Clean Election Act is unconstitutional because it is impermissibly coercive — that is, it provides so many incentives to participate and so many detriments to foregoing participation that it leaves a candidate with no reasonable alternative but to seek qualification as a publicly funded candidate. We have already addressed the independent constitutionality of contribution limits and matching funds for independent expenditures, and now turn to consider whether the elements of the system, considered as a whole, create a situation where it is so beneficial to join up and so detrimental to eschew public funding that it creates coercion and renders a candidate's choice to pursue public funding essentially involuntary. Because the parties present only issues of law, we review the district court's judgment *de novo*. *See Vote Choice v. DiStefano*, 4 F.3d 26, 38 (1st Cir. 1993).

The Supreme Court established conclusively in *Buckley* that "Congress may engage in public financing of election campaigns and may condition acceptance of public funds on an agreement by the candidate to abide by specific expenditure limitations." *Buckley*, n. 65.

Although public financing is not inherently unconstitutional, it may be so if it "burdens the exercise of political speech" but is not "narrowly tailored to serve a compelling state interest." *See Austin*; *Vote Choice*. Thus, we determine in the first instance whether appellants' First Amendment rights are burdened.

In *Vote Choice*, this court's primary public funding case, we indicated that the appropriate benchmark of whether candidates' First Amendment rights are burdened by a public funding system is whether the system allows candidates to make a "voluntary" choice about whether to pursue public funding. *See Vote Choice* ("[V]oluntariness has proven to be an important factor in judicial ratification of government-sponsored campaign financing schemes."). We explained that the government may create incentives for candidates to participate in a public funding system in exchange for their agreement not to rely on private contributions. *See Vote Choice*.

A law providing public funding for political campaigns is valid if it achieves "a rough proportionality between the advantages available to complying candidates ... and the restrictions that such candidates must accept to receive these advantages." *Id*. "[A]s long as the candidate remains free to engage in unlimited private funding and spending instead of limited public funding, the law does not violate the First Amendment rights of the candidate or supporters." *RNC*.

Appellants argue that Maine's public financing system is involuntary because it not only deprives non-participants of the benefits of participation, but also penalizes them for not participating. They contend that the balance is weighted too heavily in favor of encouraging participation, and that, in practice, it provides no meaningful choice. Appellants highlight the matching funds provision and the potential labeling of participating candidates as "clean" by the Commission as particular elements of the public funding scheme that are too beneficial for publicly funded candidates.[28] Appellants also argue that the funding formula will leave

---

28. Appellants ... complain that the amount of the subsidy for a participating candidate does not reflect his popularity. It is not a requirement of public funding, however, that it be equated to "popularity." Correspondingly, the amount of speech undertaken by a privately funded candidate is not reflective of her popularity. Campaign contributions are symbolic of support, *see Buckley*, but do not correspond dollar-for-dollar with popularity level, and large contributions as well as the candidate's use of personal funds skew the speech-equals-popularity equation. [Assuming there is no constitutional requirement that public funds be tied to a candidate's popularity, is it a good idea? — EDS.]

participating candidates with funding that is woefully inadequate, stating that it is "barely sufficient to run an unsuccessful—much less competitive—campaign in the great majority of
cases." They assail us with statistics as to the average amount spent by various gubernatorial and legislative candidates over the last decade, in comparison with what they claim are
the paltry sums disbursed to participating candidates. This line of reasoning, however, cuts
strongly against appellants' argument that the statute is coercive because if the sums are unreasonably low, they will not attract, much less coerce, participation. We look at the provisions highlighted as problematic by appellants first, then evaluate the statute as a whole.

A. *Matching Funds*

... We now address appellants' claim that the matching funds provision penalizes non-
participating candidates for raising money beyond that amount initially distributed to
their participating opponents and allows participants to effectively bypass the spending
limitation that is the only significant burden of participation.

Appellants argue that the matching funds provision is intended to thwart attempts by
non-participating candidates to outspend their participating opponents. Appellants contend that non-participating candidates are unlikely to receive as many direct contributions because donors will not wish to give, knowing that their donations could result in
additional funding for the participating opponent....

Appellants also claim that, in the context of the scheme as a whole, allocating matching funds to correspond to independent expenditures is unfair because the participating
candidate, by receiving funds to correspond to expenditures over which the non-participating opponent has no control, effectively procures a larger pool of funds to work with
than the non-participating opponent. They allege that this provision will result in fewer
independent expenditures on behalf of non-participating opponents.[29]

We cannot say, however, that the matching funds create an exceptional benefit for the
participating candidate. Maine's Act does not provide an unlimited release of the expenditure ceiling—it allocates matching funds for the participating candidate of only two
times the initial disbursement. Thus, a non-participating candidate retains the ability to
outraise and outspend her participating opponent with abandon after that limit is reached.
Further, the non-participating candidate holds the key as to how much and at what time
the participant receives matching funds.

The appellants' expert on campaign strategy, Jay Hibbard, revealed a downside of the
matching funds bonus. He attested that "[c]ontributions and spending can be easily timed
to avoid the effective release of matching funds, and therefore, thwart the objectives of the
MCEA." Indeed, he added, heavy expenditures take place in the last ten days of a campaign. This is when attack ads occur and direct mail is timed to preclude a response before election. Moreover, the participating candidate, not having any way of foreseeing
the timing or amounts of any matching funds, is unable to budget, to commit time for

---

29. Although appellants contend that it is inequitable not to deduct independent expenditures
made on behalf of the participating candidate from the initial disbursement, the regulations require
that the sum of independent expenditures made expressly advocating the defeat of the non-participating opponent or the election of the certified candidate be deducted from the participating candidate's disbursement of matching funds. *See* Commission on Governmental Ethics and Election Practices,
Regulations Regarding Maine Clean Election Act and Related Provisions, ch. 3, §6.3.B(2). Although
independent expenditures made on behalf of a participating candidate or against his opponent are not
counted against him until his opponent raises funds in excess of his initial disbursement, this is necessary to prevent a participating candidate's already modest initial disbursement from being substantially diminished or even obliterated by independent expenditures.

radio or television, or to plan, produce, or distribute printed material. Although we may deem an overstatement Hibbard's opinion that "the matching fund mechanism has been rendered meaningless," we can acknowledge the diminished utility of a belated trigger. Finally, in view of the initial moderate allowance, without the matching funds, even though they are limited in amount, candidates would be much less likely to participate because of the obvious likelihood of massive outspending by a non-participating opponent. As the State explained, the matching funds provision allows it to effectively dispense limited resources while allowing participating candidates to respond in races where the most debate is generated.

Although no two public funding schemes are identical, and thus no two evaluations of such systems are alike, we derive at least general support from other courts' evaluations of trigger provisions. In *Gable v. Patton*, 142 F.3d 940 (6th Cir. 1998), the Sixth Circuit upheld a Kentucky statute that was clearly more beneficial than Maine's—participating candidates received a two-for-one match for private contributions raised, without any limitation. Moreover, the Kentucky statute released a slate of publicly financed gubernatorial candidates from both expenditure limitations and a ban on accepting contributions within twenty-eight days of an election if non-participating opponents raised more than the initial expenditure limit for the participating candidates. Even though the trigger provision provided a "substantial advantage" for publicly funded candidates, the court concluded that it did not rise to the level of coerciveness.

Other systems include trigger provisions that waive a participating candidate's expenditure limit once her non-participating opponent reaches a given threshold of contributions or expenditures, but allow the candidate to seek private funding rather than disbursing additional public funding. In *Rosenstiel*, the Eighth Circuit characterized the waiver of the expenditure limit in Minnesota's campaign finance law as "simply an attempt by the State to avert a powerful disincentive for participation in its public financing scheme: namely, a concern of being grossly outspent by a privately financed opponent with no expenditure limit." The court determined that the trigger provision was not coercive because it allowed a non-participating candidate to control his participating opponent's funding in a sense because it enabled him to raise funds up to a certain level before the matching funds were triggered....

With regard to matching funds corresponding to independent expenditures, we think that this contributes to any alleged coerciveness in only a minuscule way—that is, it will not play a measurable role in a candidate's decision to seek public funding because it is of such minimal proportion to the other aspects of the system. Further, if the state structured public funding with a blind eye to independent expenditures, such expenditures would be capable of defeating the state's goal of distributing roughly proportionate funding, albeit with a limit, to publicly funded candidates.

B. *Labeling*

Next, appellants prophesy that the Commission will label participating candidates as "clean," thereby creating an impermissible government endorsement that skews electoral dialogue by violating a principle of neutrality. They argue that the plain language of the statute requires the Commission to certify a candidate as a "Maine Clean Election Act candidate," and they declare that the labeling of participating candidates as "clean" is the most "ominous" aspect of the system.

Our review of the statute clarifies that it does not require the Commission, or anyone else, to classify candidates as "clean," and in fact, it refers to candidates as "participating" and "non-participating." The statute merely requires that a candidate be "certified," presumably either as a "Maine Clean Election Act candidate" or a "participating candidate," and further, the Commission has attested that it does not intend to tout participating candidates as "clean." Others may use pejorative labels for non-participating candidates, and they may just as easily use derogatory terms for participating candidates; on the other hand, participating candidates might call themselves "clean candidates." Be that as it may, such labeling is not required or sanctioned by the statute nor within the authority of the statute to control. For these reasons, any labeling performed by the Commission will not serve as a substantial benefit to participating candidates.

C. *Cumulative Effect: Coerciveness*

We now step back and look at the Maine public funding/matching funds/contribution limits system as a whole to see if the cumulative effect can be said to be impermissibly coercive. We have previously expressed that a "state need not be completely neutral on the matter of public financing of elections" and that a public funding scheme need not achieve an "exact balance" between benefits and detriments. *See Vote Choice* ("[W]e suspect that very few campaign financing schemes ever achieve perfect equipoise."). In fact, "a voluntary campaign finance scheme must rely on incentives for participation, which, by definition, means structuring the scheme so that participation is usually the rational choice." *Gable*. Nevertheless, "there is a point at which regulatory incentives stray beyond the pale, creating disparities so profound that they become impermissibly coercive." *Vote Choice*. The question before us is whether the "tilt" rises to the level of a coercive penalty.

In determining whether the net advantage to a participating candidate is so great as to be impermissibly coercive, we look both to cases where coerciveness has been found and those where the funding and contribution limits system has been upheld. In *Wilkinson v. Jones*, 876 F.Supp. 916 (W.D. Ky. 1995), a district court enjoined the enforcement of contribution limits that were lower, by a ratio of five-to-one, for non-participating candidates than participating candidates because the limits were so low for non-participating candidates that they constituted an unacceptable penalty for foregoing public financing.[33] In *Shrink Missouri Government PAC v. Maupin*, 71 F.3d 1422 (8th Cir. 1995), the Eighth Circuit held that a ban on contributions from political action committees and other organizations to privately funded candidates was unconstitutional because it prevented privately funded candidates from gaining access to funding sources to which they would be entitled but for the choice to eschew public funding and its expenditure limitations. The statutes at issue in both of these cases, however, created much harsher repercussions for non-participating candidates than the MCEA.

On the other hand, statutes creating an array of benefits even more enticing to candidates than the MCEA have been upheld. In *Vote Choice*, Rhode Island's public funding system was upheld when it disbursed matching funds for private donations up to a given ceiling, it waived the expenditure ceiling to the extent that a non-participating candidate exceeded it, it allowed a participant to raise donations in increments double that allowed for a non-participant, and it granted a participant free air time on community television stations. In *Gable*, the court upheld Kentucky's arrangement, which granted participants

---

33. The court remarked that, in application, the $100/$500 disparity between the contribution limits for participating and non-participating candidates translated into a 15-to-1 ratio between participants and non-participants because participants received a 2-to-1 match for every dollar raised; in other words, a participant would raise the same amount with 1,200 donors giving the maximum that a non-participant would with 18,000 donors.

a two-to-one match for all private dollars raised up to a certain expenditure limit and released the limit and continued to match funds at the two-to-one ratio after non-participating opponents collected more than the expenditure limit. In *Rosenstiel*, the Eighth Circuit upheld Minnesota's public funding system, which disbursed public subsidies for up to half of the expenditure ceiling, allowed taxpayer refunds of up to $50 for donations to participating candidates but not for donations to non-participating candidates, and completely released participants from expenditure limits after a non-participating opponent raised more than a certain percentage of the limit.

Turning to Maine's system, we first observe that the benefits for a participating candidate are accompanied by significant burdens. The benefits to the candidate include the release from the rigors of fundraising, the assurance that contributors will not have an opportunity to seek special access, and the avoidance of any appearance of corruption. More peripheral benefits include the ability to bypass a small number of additional reporting requirements and the opportunity to be free of the reduced contribution limits imposed on private contributions.

In order to gain these benefits, however, the candidate must go through the paces of demonstrating public support by obtaining seed money contributions as well as a substantial number of $5 qualifying contributions. Additional detriments include the limited amount of public funding granted in the initial disbursement; the uncertainty of whether and when additional funds will be received based on an opponent's fundraising; the ultimate cap on matching funds; and the foreclosure of the option of pursuing any private campaign funding or spending any monies above those disbursed by the Commission.

With regard to the contribution limits, we do not believe that they serve as a coercive penalty for non-participating candidates. Until the privately funded candidate reaches the funding level equivalent to the initial disbursement granted to his participating opponent, the contribution limits may serve to the disadvantage of the privately funded candidate. Nevertheless, once the privately funded candidate exceeds that initial disbursement level of his opponent and until he reaches the level at which his opponent's matching funds run out, the contribution limits work to the detriment of both candidates because the less the privately funded candidate raises the less his participating opponent receives in matching funds.

In conclusion, the incentives for a Maine candidate, as the district court characterized them, are "hardly overwhelming." Despite appellants' contention that a participating candidate cedes nothing in exchange for public funding, there are in fact significant encumbrances on participating candidates. The constraints on a publicly funded candidate, we think, would give significant pause to a candidate considering his options. In fact, appellant Representative Elaine Fuller has attested that she will not seek certification and appellant Senator Beverly Daggett has not yet decided. We also take note of the Commission figures that, as of February 8, halfway through the qualifying period, 27.5% of 142 legislative candidates have filed declarations of intent to seek public funding; on the other hand, at least 38, or roughly 26.7%, of the candidates have received contributions or made expenditures in excess of seed money limitations, signaling a desire not to seek certification. Thus, we hold that Maine's public financing scheme provides a roughly proportionate mix of benefits and detriments to candidates seeking public funding, such that it does not burden the First Amendment rights of candidates or contributors.

We add a final call for vigilant monitoring. In this case we necessarily regard appellants' claims as facial challenges to the public funding system and contribution limits. Although we indicate no opinion as to the success that an as-applied challenge would meet in the future, that door remains open. Experience, after all, will be our best teacher....

Affirmed.

Notes and Questions

1. Congress and state legislatures have often been more receptive to spending limits than to public financing. If you were a staff assistant to a legislator seeking a means of obtaining spending limits without public funding, how would you answer these questions?

(a) Is it permissible under footnote 65 and cases like *RNC* and *Daggett* to impose a $1,000 contribution limit on candidates, but to increase that limit to $5,000 for candidates who agree not to exceed a specified spending limit?

(b) If not, would it be permissible to impose a $1,000 contribution limit, but to increase that limit to $5,000 for a candidate whose opponent declines to agree to a specified spending limit?

2. Consider in this regard *Shrink Missouri Government PAC v. Maupin*, 71 F.3d 1422 (8th Cir. 1995), cert. denied 518 U.S. 1033, 1424 (1996), distinguished by the First Circuit in *Daggett*:

> The statute at issue in this case requires candidates for elected public office in Missouri to file an affidavit stating whether they will comply with spending limits that vary depending on the office sought. The affidavit must be filed with the candidate's declaration of candidacy. Candidates who choose not to comply with the spending limits may accept contributions from individuals only and must refuse contributions from PACs, political parties, labor unions, corporations, etc. Non-complying candidates also must submit daily disclosure reports once they exceed the spending limits. No such restrictions or requirements are placed on candidates who swear to abide by the limits, though they are penalized if they spend more than the applicable limit.

The Eighth Circuit found these provisions unconstitutional. Compare the court's reasoning with the First Circuit's reasoning in *Daggett*:

> The spending limits adopted by the Missouri legislature differ substantially from the scenario described in footnote 65 of *Buckley*, and are thus distinguishable. The Senate Bill 650 limits are not voluntary because they provide only penalties for noncompliance rather than an incentive for voluntary compliance. Therefore the state's reliance on the dicta in footnote 65 of *Buckley* is misplaced.
>
> In the hypothetical set out in footnote 65, a candidate agreeing to limit his or her expenditures receives the benefit of public funding. Candidates who do not so agree do not receive public funding, but are not penalized for their reliance on private funding. Under Senate Bill 650, however, a candidate agreeing to abide by the spending limits receives no benefit other than the state's blessing to seek the private funding he or she would be free to seek in any event. At the same time, candidates who do not agree to abide by the spending limits are penalized in two ways: (1) the state makes it unlawful to seek important sources of private funding that otherwise they would be free to seek; and (2) the state requires daily reporting of expenditures. These penalties make the limits coercive, not voluntary. The state, however, does not believe that it is withdrawing an otherwise available source of funding; it characterizes the

availability of organizational funding as the incentive that it offers to candidates to agree to abide by the spending limits. We disagree with the state's characterization.

From the state's perspective, it is providing complying candidates with a substantial benefit by "allowing" PACs, political parties, labor unions, corporations, and other organizations to make campaign contributions. The state's argument, however, assumes that it properly could ban such organizations from making any contributions to candidates running for state office. This assumption is incorrect. We believe it is clear that a ban on campaign contributions by organizations would not survive a constitutional challenge. *See, e.g., MCFL; Day....* Thus the state's argument that it offers an incentive by allowing candidates to accept such contributions is disingenuous. Organizational contributions are constitutionally protected irrespective of any agreement by a candidate to abide by the state-imposed expenditure limits. No candidate would voluntarily agree to comply with the expenditure limits in exchange for access to sources of funding to which he or she already has a constitutional right of access. Rather, Senate Bill 650 forces compliance by imposing substantial penalties for non-compliance. The purported benefit is illusory, and the statute is coercive.

Given the last paragraph of the above excerpt, was it necessary for the issue to be cast in terms of the "voluntary" spending limits and footnote 65 of *Buckley*? Could not the court simply have ruled that each of the restrictions imposed on candidates declining the spending limit was itself unconstitutional and therefore could not be imposed? In that case, the spending limit would truly be voluntary, for candidates who accepted it would do so without any legal incentive at all. Would *Maupin* be a useful precedent for a plaintiff attacking the statutes described above in Note 1?

3. In 1996, California voters passed an initiative, Proposition 208, that imposed $100–$500 limits on individual contributions to candidates for state and local office, but candidates who agreed to specified expenditure limits were subject to doubled contribution limits, from $200–$1000. The initiative did not provide for public financing. A federal district court issued a preliminary injunction striking down the lower limits. *California Prolife Council Political Action Committee v. Scully*, 989 F.Supp. 1282, 1296 (E.D. Ca. 1998). The court held that the presence of the higher contribution limits accompanying the voluntary candidate expenditure limits indicated that the lower contribution limits were not narrowly drawn to prevent corruption: "Put another way, the adoption of the variable limits reflects a conclusion on the part of the voters that the $200 limit [doubled from $100 when the candidate agreed to expenditure limits] suffices to address the issue of corruption even if it is not the lowest amount which would do so." *Id.* The court then struck down the higher limits on grounds they were unconstitutionally too low. The Court reached this result before the Supreme Court decided the *Shrink Missouri* case and *Randall v. Sorrell*, described in Chapter 15. How would a district court facing these issues decide the question today? The issue was mooted in California by a later ballot measure.

4. Some jurisdictions condition receipt of public funding upon candidates' agreement to debate their opponents. New Jersey's election commission, described below, recently proposed that publicly funded gubernatorial candidates participate in three debates. Is such a condition constitutional?

5. Arizona's public financing system, enacted by initiative in 1998, is partially funded by a 10% surcharge on criminal and civil fines. A fined motorist challenged the sur-

charge on First Amendment and other grounds. The Arizona Supreme Court rejected the challenge in *May v. McNally*, 55 P.3d 768 (Ariz. 2002). Candidates who opt into Arizona's campaign financing system and then spend over the amount they promise to spend face the sanction of removal from office. The Arizona Supreme Court upheld that sanction against a candidate who spent 17 percent more than permitted by Arizona's election law. *Smith v. Arizona Citizens Clean Elections Comm'n*, 132 P.3d 1187 (Ariz. 2006).

6. When this book was in press, the Supreme Court decided *Davis v. Federal Elections Commission*, described on page 795. *Davis* calls into question any contribution limit regime that allows one candidate a higher limit than an opponent. Variable contribution limits, as described in Note 3, and extra matching funds for participants in voluntary public financing systems, like those in Maine and Arizona, may come under challenge in light of *Davis*.

III. Proposals for Reform

Typically, as we saw in *Daggett*, public financing plans are accompanied by a *lowering* of contribution limits. For an argument that contribution limits should be *increased* in races where some candidates use public financing so as to limit money flowing to independent expenditures, see Joel E. Fleishman & Pope McCorkle, *Level-Up Rather Than Level-Down: Towards a New Theory of Campaign Finance Reform*, 1 Journal of Law and Politics 211 (1984). Does the Fleishman and McCorkle plan solve the problems identified by those favoring campaign finance regulation? How well does it address concerns of corruption or equality? Consider Marlene Arnold Nicholson, *The Supreme Court's Meandering Path in Campaign Finance Regulation and What it Portends for Future Reform*, 3 Journal of Law & Politics 509, 561, 563 (1987):

> Fleishman and McCorkle suggest increasing contribution limitations and removing overall campaign expenditure limitations in subsidized races in order to siphon off some of the funds which would otherwise find their way into independent expenditures. Although this might help decrease independent expenditures, these devices would create other problems which might be greater than those posed by the independent expenditures themselves. The potential for corruption from contributions is not disputed. Fleishman and McCorkle's approach would increase that danger in order to prevent independent expenditures, which at worst are somewhat less corrupting than contributions....
>
> Fleishman's suggestions that individual contributions should be increased to counter the influence of PACs is less convincing than his argument in favor of loosening contribution limitations applicable to parties. Such an approach would merely allow those who control PAC contributions to augment their financial investment through PACs with large individual contributions. It has been suggested that PAC contributions can be viewed as "old wine in new bottles," because large contributions usually emanate from special interest sources, whether they be individuals or PACs.

Is the Fleishman and McCorkle proposal adequate to counter the role of private money in politics? Consider Daniel Hays Lowenstein, *On Campaign Finance Reform: The Root of All Evil Is Deeply Rooted*, 18 Hofstra Law Review 301, 365–66 (1989):

Fleishman and McCorkle show that [the "level-up" theory] has many attractive features. But ... the campaign finance problem is too deeply rooted, too intertwined with a host of values and interests, to be resolved by any theory that looks at the problem from only one angle. Fleishman and McCorkle provide some unwitting empirical confirmation of this, for their good theory leads them to a bad proposal. The core of their proposal is to provide an amount of public financing in a range of $50,000 to $75,000 to each major party candidate for the House and to increase the contribution limit for individuals from $1,000 to $5,000.

The grants they would give are hardly more than tokens compared with what it takes to run a competitive campaign for the House. Their grants would yield a marginal increase in the quantity of campaign debate, but no other benefits. Any increase in competitiveness would be barely noticeable. This is because the greatest share of the money they would give away would go either to safe incumbents with no need for it, or to hopeless challengers. The increase in the individual contribution limit would simply aggravate existing problems of corruption and inequality.[e]

Fleishman and McCorkle offer a proposed reform working within the context of existing public financing plans, plans that typically give money or matching funds to candidates who opt into the system. But money may be distributed in other ways as well. Two ideas receiving some attention (at least from two-thirds of the authors of this casebook!) are financing through legislative party committees and campaign finance vouchers.

On the former, consider, Lowenstein, *supra*:

[I]t has been widely supposed that an insoluble conflict exists between the anti-corruption goal of campaign finance reform and the value of maintaining (or restoring) vigorous competition in legislative elections. The dilemma arises from the following elements:

1. To accomplish the anti-corruption goal, candidates' demand for special interest contributions must be reduced drastically. This may take the form of limits on the size of contributions, limits on the aggregate amount of special interest money that may be accepted, or expenditure limits consented to as a condition of accepting public financing.

2. Small contributions from individuals do not come close to providing the amount needed for competitive campaigns. Therefore, limits alone, regardless of their form if sufficient to substantially limit the element of corruption in the finance system, would so reduce the flow of funds that challengers, for whom the absolute amounts they can spend are more important than their spending relative to incumbents, would find their hopes of victory seriously impaired.

3. Public financing is proposed to close the gap between what candidates need to spend and what they can raise in "clean" money. As a practical matter, however, the gap is too large for public financing to fill. If a flat amount is given to major-party candidates in each district, most of the money will be wasted on races that have little prospect of being competitive. If public financing is given

---

e. Lowenstein's more recent writing reflects somewhat more agreement with the Fleishman-McCorkle approach in general, though not necessarily to the specific proposal criticized in this passage.

on a matching basis, raising the private contributions eligible for matching may be difficult. As a result the matching of public funds makes private contributions more valuable, and may, to some extent, subsidize the efforts of contributors following a legislative strategy. The size of the gap and the practical limits on the amount of public financing that can be made available assure that a compromise between the goals of restricting special interest money and permitting competitive races will end up accomplishing neither. In Gary Jacobson's words, "enough" money for a challenger to run a competitive campaign is likely to be "too much" money to be compatible with reform goals.

The dilemma that is assumed to exist turns on the assumption that public funds cannot be allocated to particular races in differing amounts other than through the matching device, which is an imperfect measure of the true competitiveness of an election and which tends to undercut the goals of reform. No one is likely to propose that government officials should make judgments as to which are the competitive races and allocate funds accordingly.

This dilemma can be solved by recognizing that the political parties constitute an excellent conduit for the allocation of public funds. By and large, the parties can be expected to place the funds where they will do the most good. Public financing, then, can provide the greater part of the funds needed in competitive elections, obviating the need for private funds in amounts that come only from special interests. Public financing that is sufficient to fill the gap between what is needed and what can be raised in "clean" money need not be prohibitively expensive, because the parties will avoid wasting money in hopeless districts. The package proposed in this Article is not a cheap one, but it is no Rolls Royce....

Consider the following criticism of Lowenstein's proposal:

[T]here are two major problems with [Lowenstein's] package. On the technical side, it ignores third parties (or independent candidates) and primary elections. Like most students of congressional elections, I do not take third parties very seriously; most of the time they are of no consequence. Nonetheless, at a few historically critical moments, third parties have been very important. Dams are designed to withstand the hundred-year flood; a campaign finance system should also be able to handle rare but momentous events. [R]egulation should not impose a permanent status quo but afford individuals the right to a continuing choice.

The third-party problem can presumably be solved through further tinkering with Lowenstein's proposal. Primary elections are another matter. Lowenstein says nothing about how, or under what restrictions, primaries are to be financed. Rather, he merely acknowledges in a footnote that, "[a]s should be clear from the nature of the proposals, they are not adaptable to primary elections." He was, no doubt, wise to ignore primaries because they introduce so many thorny complications. Not only do primaries vary widely in degree of competition and decisiveness (in some districts, the primary *is* the election), they are also spread out over seven months (early March or early October), and timing governs their relationship to the general election. Lowenstein's dilemma—reducing special interest contributions drastically while supplying sufficient money for serious competition and not wasting money in lopsided races—reappears in primary elections. However, Lowenstein's solution of party leaders deploying funds is not available.

The point is not that Lowenstein has slipped here, but that a major, perhaps intractable problem for any regulatory scheme of the kind he proposes is the diversity of circumstances to which it must be adapted. It is one thing to design a system of mixed public and private financing for a single office such as the presidency; it is quite another to design a system that does not have perverse consequences in primary or general elections in any of 435 districts and 50 states.

The other problem with Lowenstein's package is its politics. He does a reasonable job of sketching the advantages of the proposal to Democrats and Republicans, egalitarians and libertarians, incumbents and challengers. Indeed, he may even understate the attractiveness to incumbents, assuming they continue to regard fund raising as a "disgusting, degrading, demeaning experience." [The reference is to a comment once made by Hubert Humphrey.— Eds.] Lowenstein, however, is wisely modest about the short-term prospects for such a package. Without the stimulus of a major scandal, it is difficult to envision partisans overcoming their mutual suspicions and differences; partial public funding of presidential campaigns would have fallen to a presidential veto but for Watergate. Furthermore, the concentration of financial authority in legislative party leaders, congenial as it is to political scientists, will be hard to sell to a Congress composed of politicians whose career strategies are predicated on autonomy.

The more important political difficulty, however, is public opinion. Considering [the flak] members of Congress took over a proposed 51% pay raise in 1989, it is not hard to guess how the public would view spending more than three times as much ($90 million compared to about $25 million per year for the pay raise) to finance their election campaigns. Americans are disdainful of campaigning already, and excessive spending heads the list of complaints. Misguided as this view is, it is understandable to people at the receiving end of most contemporary campaigns. That Congress was willing to give up honoraria in return for a pay raise made no difference to the public. Similarly, the anticipated benefits of weakening "special interests" are unlikely to carry the day against an even deeper invasion of taxpayers' pockets. Of course, a sufficiently egregious scandal might move popular majorities to support public funds for congressional campaigns; but public opinion would probably insist upon perniciously low spending limits as part of the package.

Gary C. Jacobson, *Campaign Finance and Democratic Control: Comments on Gottlieb and Lowenstein's Papers*, 18 Hofstra Law Review 369, 380–82 (1989). Under Jacobson's view, when, if ever, is public financing justified?

Another proposal currently in circulation, at least among academics, is a voucher plan. Consider Richard L. Hasen, *Clipping Coupons for Democracy: An Egalitarian/Public Choice Defense of Campaign Finance Vouchers*, 84 California Law Review 1 (1996):

Generally, campaign finance reform plans either seek to "level-up," by increasing the ability of those shut out of the political system to participate, or to "level-down," by decreasing the ability of those with disproportionate political capital to exercise greater influence over the political system. A voluntary public financing system, which allows candidates either to accept public funds or solicit private contributions, is a classic level-up program; it amplifies the voice of the poor but does not limit the influence of the rich. A law limiting the amount an individual or PAC can contribute to a candidate is a classic level-down program.

Past proposals to use publicly funded vouchers have been of the level-up variety only. For example, in 1967, Senator Lee Metcalf proposed a plan under which taxpayers would receive campaign vouchers from the government, but politicians could accept private money as well.

Recently, however, Bruce Ackerman and I independently have proposed publicly financed voucher systems which both level-up and level-down.[1] These voucher plans level-up in the sense that all voters, even those voters who have never made campaign contributions before, are given vouchers to contribute to candidates for federal office. Vouchers facilitate the representation of groups which lack a voice in the current system. But these vouchers also level-down by prohibiting all other sources of campaign money; the rich can no longer exercise greater influence through private contributions and independent expenditures.

Here are the key elements of my voucher plan. The government provides every voter with a voucher for each bi-annual federal election.... Voters may donate their voucher dollars either directly to candidates, to licensed interest groups, or to political parties. The groups may serve whatever goals they please, whether ideological or economic. Thus, the NRA, NOW, and other ideological groups will compete for voucher dollars with the Beef Industry Council, the AFL-CIO, and other economic groups.

All campaign contributions and independent expenditures in support of or in opposition to a candidate must be made with voucher dollars. Candidates and elected officials cannot receive any other direct donations, honoraria, soft money benefits, in-kind contributions, or other donations....

Independent expenditure campaigns must be financed only through collected vouchers; with limited exceptions, no private funds may be used. Individuals like Ross Perot, Herbert Kohl, and Michael Huffington could not bankroll their own campaigns. Corporations (other than licensed interest groups) could not donate money to candidates or make independent expenditures for or against a candidate. However, political activity not directly endorsing or opposing a candidate would not be subject to any limits.

Only licensed interest groups could collect voucher dollars from others to run independent expenditure campaigns supporting candidates, and only those groups and the voters themselves could contribute vouchers to candidates. Any voter could register for a license to create an interest group, and the license would

1. I proposed a voucher plan originally in my unpublished dissertation. Bruce Ackerman then independently proposed a voucher plan in a short article in the journal *American Prospect*. *See* Bruce Ackerman, *Crediting the Voters: A New Beginning for Campaign Finance*, 13 AMERICAN PROSPECT 71 (1993). He has not had occasion to provide a scholarly treatment of his plan. Edward Foley discussed Ackerman's voucher plan in an article arguing for "equal-dollars-per-voter" as a matter of constitutional principle. Edward B. Foley, *Equal-Dollars-Per-Voter: A Constitutional Principle of Campaign Finance*, 94 COLUMBIA LAW REVIEW 1204, 1208–13 (1994) [a portion of which is reprinted in Chapter 14—EDS.]. Smurzynski hinted at a voucher plan in his discussion of campaign finance reforms. Kenneth C. Smurzynski, Note, *Modeling Campaign Contributions: The Market for Access and Its Implications for Regulation*, 80 GEORGETOWN LAW JOURNAL 1891, 1911 (1992) (suggesting that public financing could be done through the "intermediary" of interest groups). This Article is the first published scholarly look at the efficacy and fairness of a post-voucher political system. [We discuss Ackerman's recent ideas with Ian Ayres to combine vouchers with mandatory donor anonymity in the next chapter.—EDS.]

be free. An independent federal agency would process license requests. The agency could not turn down a group's licensing request for ideological reasons.

It seems likely that a voucher plan *supplementing* private financing of campaigns would be as constitutional as other public financing plans, such as the Maine system upheld by the First Circuit in the *Daggett* case above. What advantages and disadvantages do you see from use of vouchers to dole out public financing of campaigns?

Consider Daniel H. Lowenstein, *Voting with Votes*, 116 HARVARD LAW REVIEW 1971, 1989–90 (2003) (book review):

> The advantage of vouchers is not ... that they bring about a marketlike solution, but rather that they provide an alternative to the formulaic distribution of public funds among congressional candidates. Unfortunately, the alternative that vouchers provide is far from perfect. Citizens situated in the collective action problem that vouchers would create are not likely to have the desire or the ability to figure out which races are the most competitive, in which their vouchers could be put to the best use. Even if they could overcome this problem, collectively they would face a difficult coordination problem in achieving a distribution of voucher funds reasonably well-calibrated along a spectrum of the most to the least competitive races. The only way these problems could be solved, or at least mitigated, would be if citizens were to contribute a large percentage of their congressional vouchers to parties or political organizations.
>
> If vouchers were the only public financing alternative to formulaic distribution, I would embrace them warmly. But they are not. Political parties are better situated than individual citizens to distribute campaign funds for maximum competitive effect. I have proposed a public financing scheme built around grants to the Democratic and Republican campaign committees in the House and Senate, to be distributed to candidates as the committees see fit. To be sure, there are drawbacks to parties' distributing public funds, but this is not the place for an extended argument for the superiority of my plan over [a recent voucher proposal by Bruce] Ackerman and [Ian] Ayres. Much will depend on whether one accepts my criticism of the voting-with-dollars concept.
>
> In that respect, this is an appropriate place to revisit briefly the citizenship effect that Ackerman and Ayres claim will result from vouchers. They contend that the ability to make voucher contributions will stimulate citizens to take a new interest in federal campaigns and to perceive that they have a new stake in the political system. The existence of vouchers would likely stimulate some discussion and participation. But Ackerman and Ayres give no reason for us to believe that the stimulation will be greater than (or even as great as) the level provided by elections generally, or by other forms of participation, such as signing petitions. Indeed, it may be instructive to consider the means by which signatures are obtained in the states that allow statutes and constitutional amendments to be placed on the ballot by initiative petitions. In many such states, notably California, companies have arisen whose business it is to qualify initiatives for the ballot. The circulators paid by these companies to obtain signatures can perform their function virtually without regard to the content of the petitions. A significant percentage of people will sign petitions simply because they are asked. Whether similar techniques would work for obtaining voucher contributions under Ackerman and Ayres' system is hard to say. It may be that the logistics of getting a citizen to swipe a credit card or ATM card through a machine are suf-

ficiently different from the efforts required to obtain a signature that individuals would be somewhat more attentive to what they were doing. However that may be, it seems inevitable that under the Ackerman and Ayres plan, solicitors would obtain voucher contributions through mass marketing techniques comparable to those used for signature collection, mass fundraising, and electioneering. This circumstance is not necessarily bad, but it means that vouchers are not likely to produce much of a citizenship effect. Moreover, the voucher system is likely to frustrate many reformers—though not necessarily Ackerman and Ayres—who believe deep down that election campaigns ought to be run like college seminars.

Is a voucher plan *supplanting* public financing of campaigns constitutional? Consider the following criticism of Hasen:

> Hasen constructs a system that is hardly comforting to those whose primary concern is free speech. In order to make the voucher system work, Hasen would restrict all direct and indirect political donations, organizational money, in-kind contributions, honoraria, and expenses from whatever source other than government-provided vouchers. In order to participate in politics, interest groups of whatever kind would need to be licensed by a special federal agency, which would also maintain and investigatory antifraud unit...

> There should be no obfuscation of what Professor Hasen [is] proposing: to ban most existing partisan, political activity by citizens in the United States beyond a minimal expenditure allowance that each citizen obtains from the federal government.

Bradley A. Smith, *Money Talks: Speech, Corruption, Equality, and Campaign Finance*, 86 GEORGETOWN LAW JOURNAL 45, 77–78 (1997). Does the Hasen plan "ban most existing partisan, political activity"?

One alternative somewhat similar to vouchers is a tax credit for campaign contributions. See Richard P. Conlon, *The Declining Role of Individual Contributions in Financing Congressional Campaigns*, 3 JOURNAL OF LAW & POLITICS 467, 469–70, 482–86 (1987). Conlon states "[a] 100 percent tax credit (up to $100) for contributions to congressional candidates would make it easier to raise small contributions by, in effect, giving every taxpayer $100 which he or she could use for only one purpose—to support a candidate or candidates for the House or Senate." Consider this criticism from Daniel Hays Lowenstein, *On Campaign Finance Reform: The Root of All Evil Is Deeply Rooted*, 18 HOFSTRA LAW REVIEW 301, 364, 365 n.272 (1989):

> No one knows to what extent tax credits induce increased contributions. One thing that is clear is that tax credits represent an extremely inefficient method of publicly financing election campaigns. We know from current experience that a number of people do make contributions in the absence of tax credits. If tax credits are reinstated, a significant percentage of the lost revenues—possibly almost all of them—will be paid not for new campaign funds but as a gratuitous tax benefit. In short, tax credits are not worth it....

> A 100% tax credit would waste twice as much in tax relief for people who would make contributions in the absence of tax incentives. It might induce more contributions than the 50% credit did, but to the extent it succeeded, its cost in lost revenues would soar. It is sometimes proposed to deal with this problem by limiting the credit to those who contribute to federal elections. This would only exacerbate the problem of campaign finance at the state and local levels, where

the problem is sometimes at least as serious as in federal elections. Tax credits are a bad idea, but if they are adopted, they ought to be applicable to all federal, state and local elections, including ballot measure elections.

Do these same or similar arguments apply against campaign finance vouchers?

Chapter 18

Campaign Finance Disclosure

We turn now to campaign finance disclosure. Those who favor broad campaign finance regulation champion disclosure as well. For example, the web sites of two reform organizations, Common Cause, <www.commoncause.org>, and the Center for Responsive Politics, <www.opensecrets.org>, allow searches of federal contribution and expenditure databases so that interested parties can "follow the money." Many opponents of contribution and expenditure limits also favor disclosure, seeing it as a more narrowly tailored solution to the problem of money in politics. Larry J. Sabato & Glenn R. Simpson, DIRTY LITTLE SECRETS 330–36 (1996); Kathleen M. Sullivan, *Political Money and Freedom of Speech*, 30 U.C. DAVIS LAW REVIEW 1663, 668–69 (1997); *Nixon v. Shrink Missouri Government PAC*, 528 U.S. 377, 430 (2000) (Thomas J., dissenting) ("States are free to enact laws that directly punish those engaged in corruption and require the disclosure of large contributions, but they are not free to enact generalized laws that suppress a tremendous amount of protected speech along with the targeted corruption.").

As we shall see, the Supreme Court in *Buckley v. Valeo* recognized three government interests in disclosure:

(1) *Disclosure deters corruption* (the "anti-corruption" interest). Disclosure allows interested parties to look for connections between campaign contributors or spenders and the candidates who benefit from those contributions or spending.

(2) *Disclosure provides information helpful to voters* (the "information" interest). Chapter 2 demonstrated that voters often are rationally ignorant regarding details about the candidates or issues on the ballot. Disclosure provides information helpful to voters. For example, a voter knowing that the insurance industry or the Sierra Club backs a particular ballot measure may use that information as a proxy for whether the measure is in the voter's interest.

(3) *Disclosure aids in the enforcement of other campaign finance laws* (the "enforcement" interest). For example, without disclosure, contributors could evade contribution laws more easily.

Disclosure, however, has drawbacks that implicate the First Amendment. Consider the case of the Ohio Socialist Workers Party. The FBI harassed leaders and members of the party. For example, the FBI visited potential landlords of SWP members and suggested that the landlords not rent to them. Party leaders also were victims of violence. See *Brown v. Socialist Workers '74 Campaign Committee*, 459 U.S. 87 (1982). Those individuals who otherwise might contribute to the SWP could be deterred by disclosure of their identities. Should the state be allowed to compel SWP contributors to disclose their identities? More broadly, is there a constitutional right to engage in anonymous political speech? Recall that many famous political documents at the time of the American Revolution were penned anonymously. Should that history be relevant? See Justice Scalia's dissenting opinion in the *McIntyre* case below.

The Supreme Court first addressed this conflict between the state's three interests in disclosure of campaign finance information and First Amendment claims of a right to anonymity in a portion of *Buckley v. Valeo* reprinted below. *Buckley* upheld the disclosure provisions of the FECA. The Court has revisited the disclosure issue in subsequent cases, most importantly in the *McIntyre* case reprinted immediately after the *Buckley* excerpt. *McIntyre* struck down an Ohio law preventing a lone pamphleteer from distributing anonymously a pamphlet advocating the defeat of a local ballot proposition. As you read the two cases together, consider which factor or factors led the Court to different results in the two cases. What are the current rules regarding the ability of the state to compel disclosure of information related to campaign communications?

Buckley v. Valeo
424 U.S. 1, 60–84 (1976)

PER CURIAM ...

II. REPORTING AND DISCLOSURE REQUIREMENTS

Unlike the limitations on contributions and expenditures imposed by 18 U.S.C. §608,[a] the disclosure requirements of the Act, 2 U.S.C. §431 *et seq.* are not challenged by appellants as *per se* unconstitutional restrictions on the exercise of First Amendment freedoms of speech and association. Indeed, appellants argue that "narrowly drawn disclosure requirements are the proper solution to virtually all of the evils Congress sought to remedy." The particular requirements embodied in the Act are attacked as overbroad—both in their application to minor-party and independent candidates and in their extension to contributions as small as $11 or $101. Appellants also challenge the provision for disclosure by those who make independent contributions and expenditures, §434(e). The Court of Appeals found no constitutional infirmities in the provisions challenged here. We affirm the determination on overbreadth and hold that §434(e), if narrowly construed, also is within constitutional bounds.

[The Court described earlier federal disclosure requirements, dating back to 1910. These had contained various loopholes and were "widely circumvented."]

The Act presently under review replaced all prior disclosure laws. Its primary disclosure provisions impose reporting obligations on "political committees" and candidates. "Political committee" is defined in §431(d) as a group of persons that receives "contributions" or makes "expenditures" of over $1,000 in a calendar year. "Contributions" and "expenditures" are defined in lengthy parallel provisions similar to those in Title 18, discussed above. Both definitions focus on the use of money or other objects of value "for the purpose of ... influencing" the nomination or election of any person to federal office.

Each political committee is required to register with the Commission, §433, and to keep detailed records of both contributions and expenditures, §432(c), (d). These records must include the name and address of everyone making a contribution in excess of $10, along with the date and amount of the contribution. If a person's contributions aggregate more than $100, his occupation and principal place of business are also to be included. §432(c)(2). These files are subject to periodic audits and field investigations by the Commission. §438(a)(8).

---

a. Chapter 15 reprints the portion of *Buckley* reviewing the constitutionality of contribution and expenditure limits. — EDS.

Each committee and each candidate also is required to file quarterly reports. §434(a). The reports are to contain detailed financial information, including the full name, mailing address, occupation, and principal place of business of each person who has contributed over $100 in a calendar year, as well as the amount and date of the contributions. §434(b). They are to be made available by the Commission "for public inspection and copying." §438(a)(4). Every candidate for federal office is required to designate a "principal campaign committee," which is to receive reports of contributions and expenditures made on the candidate's behalf from other political committees and to compile and file these reports, together with its own statements, with the Commission. §432(f).

Every individual or group, other than a political committee or candidate, who makes "contributions" or "expenditures" of over $100 in a calendar year "other than by contribution to a political committee or candidate" is required to file a statement with the Commission. §434(e). Any violation of these record-keeping and reporting provisions is punishable by a fine of not more than $1,000 or a prison term of not more than a year, or both. §441(a).

A. General Principles

Unlike the overall limitations on contributions and expenditures, the disclosure requirements impose no ceiling on campaign-related activities. But we have repeatedly found that compelled disclosure, in itself, can seriously infringe on privacy of association and belief guaranteed by the First Amendment. *E. g., Gibson v. Florida Legislative Comm.*, 372 U.S. 539 (1963); *NAACP v. Button*, 371 U.S. 415 (1963); *Shelton v. Tucker*, 364 U.S. 479 (1960); *Bates v. Little Rock*, 361 U.S. 516 (1960); *NAACP v. Alabama*, 357 U.S. 449 (1958).

We long have recognized that significant encroachments on First Amendment rights of the sort that compelled disclosure imposes cannot be justified by a mere showing of some legitimate governmental interest. Since *NAACP v. Alabama* we have required that the subordinating interests of the State must survive exacting scrutiny. We also have insisted that there be a "relevant correlation" or "substantial relation" between the governmental interest and the information required to be disclosed. This type of scrutiny is necessary even if any deterrent effect on the exercise of First Amendment rights arises, not through direct government action, but indirectly as an unintended but inevitable result of the government's conduct in requiring disclosure.

Appellees argue that the disclosure requirements of the Act differ significantly from those at issue in *NAACP v. Alabama* and its progeny because the Act only requires disclosure of the names of contributors and does not compel political organizations to submit the names of their members.

[T]he invasion of privacy of belief may be as great when the information sought concerns the giving and spending of money as when it concerns the joining of organizations, for "[f]inancial transactions can reveal much about a person's activities, associations, and beliefs." *California Bankers Assn v. Shultz*, 416 U.S. 21, 78–79 (1974) (POWELL, J., concurring). Our past decisions have not drawn fine lines between contributors and members but have treated them interchangeably. In *Bates*, for example, we applied the principles of *NAACP v. Alabama* and reversed convictions for failure to comply with a city ordinance that required the disclosure of "dues, assessments, and contributions paid, by whom and when paid."

The strict test established by *NAACP v. Alabama* is necessary because compelled disclosure has the potential for substantially infringing the exercise of First Amendment rights. But we have acknowledged that there are governmental interests sufficiently important to outweigh the possibility of infringement, particularly when the "free functioning of our national institutions" is involved. *Communist Party v. Subversive Activities Control Bd.*, 367 U.S. 1, 97 (1961).

The governmental interests sought to be vindicated by the disclosure requirements are of this magnitude. They fall into three categories. First, disclosure provides the electorate with information "as to where political campaign money comes from and how it is spent by the candidate" in order to aid the voters in evaluating those who seek federal office. It allows voters to place each candidate in the political spectrum more precisely than is often possible solely on the basis of party labels and campaign speeches. The sources of a candidate's financial support also alert the voter to the interests to which a candidate is most likely to be responsive and thus facilitate predictions of future performance in office.

Second, disclosure requirements deter actual corruption and avoid the appearance of corruption by exposing large contributions and expenditures to the light of publicity. This exposure may discourage those who would use money for improper purposes either before or after the election. A public armed with information about a candidate's most generous supporters is better able to detect any post-election special favors that may be given in return. And, as we recognized in *Burroughs v. United States*, 290 U.S. 534 (1934), Congress could reasonably conclude that full disclosure during an election campaign tends "to prevent the corrupt use of money to affect elections." In enacting these requirements it may have been mindful of Mr. Justice Brandeis' advice:

> Publicity is justly commended as a remedy for social and industrial diseases. Sunlight is said to be the best of disinfectants; electric light the most efficient policeman.[80]

Third, and not least significant, recordkeeping, reporting, and disclosure requirements are an essential means of gathering the data necessary to detect violations of the contribution limitations described above.

The disclosure requirements, as a general matter, directly serve substantial governmental interests. In determining whether these interests are sufficient to justify the requirements we must look to the extent of the burden that they place on individual rights.

It is undoubtedly true that public disclosure of contributions to candidates and political parties will deter some individuals who otherwise might contribute. In some instances, disclosure may even expose contributors to harassment or retaliation. These are not insignificant burdens on individual rights, and they must be weighed carefully against the interests which Congress has sought to promote by this legislation. In this process, we note and agree with appellants' concession that disclosure requirements—certainly in most applications—appear to be the least restrictive means of curbing the evils of campaign ignorance and corruption that Congress found to exist.[82] Appellants argue, however, that the balance tips against disclosure when it is required of contributors to certain parties and candidates. We turn now to this contention.

---

80. L. Brandeis, OTHER PEOPLE'S MONEY 62 (National Home Library Foundation ed. 1933).

82. Post-election disclosure by successful candidates is suggested as a less restrictive way of preventing corrupt pressures on officeholders. Delayed disclosure of this sort would not serve the equally important informational function played by pre-election reporting. Moreover, the public interest in sources of campaign funds is likely to be at its peak during the campaign period; that is the time when improper influences are most likely to be brought to light.

B. Application to Minor Parties and Independents

Appellants contend that the Act's requirements are overbroad insofar as they apply to contributions to minor parties and independent candidates because the governmental interest in this information is minimal and the danger of significant infringement on First Amendment rights is greatly increased.

1. Requisite Factual Showing

In *NAACP v. Alabama* the organization had "made an uncontroverted showing that on past occasions revelation of the identity of its rank-and-file members [had] exposed these members to economic reprisal, loss of employment, threat of physical coercion, and other manifestations of public hostility," and the State was unable to show that the disclosure it sought had a "substantial bearing" on the issues it sought to clarify. Under those circumstances, the Court held that "whatever interest the State may have in [disclosure] has not been shown to be sufficient to overcome petitioner's constitutional objections."

The Court of Appeals rejected appellants' suggestion that this case fits into the *NAACP v. Alabama* mold. It concluded that substantial governmental interests in "informing the electorate and preventing the corruption of the political process" were furthered by requiring disclosure of minor parties and independent candidates, and therefore found no "tenable rationale for assuming that the public interest in minority party disclosure of contributions above a reasonable cutoff point is uniformly outweighed by potential contributors' associational rights." The court left open the question of the application of the disclosure requirements to candidates (and parties) who could demonstrate injury of the sort at stake in *NAACP v. Alabama*. No record of harassment on a similar scale was found in this case. We agree with the Court of Appeals' conclusion that *NAACP v. Alabama* is inapposite where, as here, any serious infringement on First Amendment rights brought about by the compelled disclosure of contributors is highly speculative.

It is true that the governmental interest in disclosure is diminished when the contribution in question is made to a minor party with little chance of winning an election. As minor parties usually represent definite and publicized viewpoints, there may be less need to inform the voters of the interests that specific candidates represent. Major parties encompass candidates of greater diversity. In many situations the label "Republican" or "Democrat" tells a voter little. The candidate who bears it may be supported by funds from the far right, the far left, or any place in between on the political spectrum. It is less likely that a candidate of, say, the Socialist Labor Party will represent interests that cannot be discerned from the party's ideological position.

The Government's interest in deterring the "buying" of elections and the undue influence of large contributors on officeholders also may be reduced where contributions to a minor party or an independent candidate are concerned, for it is less likely that the candidate will be victorious. But a minor party sometimes can play a significant role in an election. Even when a minor-party candidate has little or no chance of winning, he may be encouraged by major-party interests in order to divert votes from other major-party contenders.

We are not unmindful that the damage done by disclosure to the associational interests of the minor parties and their members and to supporters of independents could be significant. These movements are less likely to have a sound financial base and thus are more vulnerable to falloffs in contributions. In some instances fears of reprisal may deter contributions to the point where the movement cannot survive. The public interest also suffers if that result comes to pass, for there is a consequent reduction in the free circulation of ideas both within and without the political arena.

There could well be a case, similar to those before the Court in *NAACP v. Alabama* and *Bates*, where the threat to the exercise of First Amendment rights is so serious and the state interest furthered by disclosure so insubstantial that the Act's requirements cannot be constitutionally applied. But no appellant in this case has tendered record evidence of the sort proffered in *NAACP v. Alabama*. Instead, appellants primarily rely on "the clearly articulated fears of individuals, well experienced in the political process." At best they offer the testimony of several minor-party officials that one or two persons refused to make contributions because of the possibility of disclosure. On this record, the substantial public interest in disclosure identified by the legislative history of this Act outweighs the harm generally alleged.

2. Blanket Exemption

Appellants agree that "the record here does not reflect the kind of focused and insistent harassment of contributors and members that existed in the NAACP cases." They argue, however, that a blanket exemption for minor parties is necessary lest irreparable injury be done before the required evidence can be gathered....

We recognize that unduly strict requirements of proof could impose a heavy burden, but it does not follow that a blanket exemption for minor parties is necessary. Minor parties must be allowed sufficient flexibility in the proof of injury to assure a fair consideration of their claim. The evidence offered need show only a reasonable probability that the compelled disclosure of a party's contributors' names will subject them to threats, harassment, or reprisals from either Government officials or private parties. The proof may include, for example, specific evidence of past or present harassment of members due to their associational ties, or of harassment directed against the organization itself. A pattern of threats or specific manifestations of public hostility may be sufficient. New parties that have no history upon which to draw may be able to offer evidence of reprisals and threats directed against individuals or organizations holding similar views.

Where it exists the type of chill and harassment identified in *NAACP v. Alabama* can be shown. We cannot assume that courts will be insensitive to similar showings when made in future cases. We therefore conclude that a blanket exemption is not required.

C. Section 434(e)

Section 434(e) requires "[e]very person (other than a political committee or candidate) who makes contributions or expenditures" aggregating over $100 in a calendar year "other than by contribution to a political committee or candidate" to file a statement with the Commission. Unlike the other disclosure provisions, this section does not seek the contribution list of any association. Instead, it requires direct disclosure of what an individual or group contributes or spends.

In considering this provision we must apply the same strict standard of scrutiny....

Appellants attack §434(e) as a direct intrusion on privacy of belief, in violation of *Talley v. California*, 362 U.S. 60 (1960), and as imposing "very real, practical burdens ... certain to deter individuals from making expenditures for their independent political speech" analogous to those held to be impermissible in *Thomas v. Collins*, 323 U.S. 516 (1945).

1. The Role of §434(e)

... Section 434(e) is part of Congress' effort to achieve "total disclosure" by reaching "every kind of political activity"[97] in order to insure that the voters are fully informed and to achieve through publicity the maximum deterrence to corruption and undue in-

---

97. S. Rep. No. 92-229, p. 57 (1971).

fluence possible. The provision is responsive to the legitimate fear that efforts would be made, as they had been in the past, to avoid the disclosure requirements by routing financial support of candidates through avenues not explicitly covered by the general provisions of the Act.

2. Vagueness Problems

In its effort to be all-inclusive, however, the provision raises serious problems of vagueness, particularly treacherous where, as here, the violation of its terms carries criminal penalties and fear of incurring these sanctions may deter those who seek to exercise protected First Amendment rights.

Section 434(e) applies to "(e)very person ... who makes contributions or expenditures." "Contributions" and "expenditures" are defined in parallel provisions in terms of the use of money or other valuable assets "for the purpose of ... influencing" the nomination or election of candidates for federal office. It is the ambiguity of this phrase that poses constitutional problems.

Due process requires that a criminal statute provide adequate notice to a person of ordinary intelligence that his contemplated conduct is illegal, for "no man shall be held criminally responsible for conduct which he could not reasonably understand to be proscribed." *United States v. Harriss*, 347 U.S. 612 (1954). Where First Amendment rights are involved, an even "greater degree of specificity" is required.

There is no legislative history to guide us in determining the scope of the critical phrase "for the purpose of ... influencing." It appears to have been adopted without comment from earlier disclosure Acts.... Where the constitutional requirement of definiteness is at stake, we have the further obligation to construe the statute, if that can be done consistent with the legislature's purpose, to avoid the shoals of vagueness.

In enacting the legislation under review Congress addressed broadly the problem of political campaign financing. It wished to promote full disclosure of campaign-oriented spending to insure both the reality and the appearance of the purity and openness of the federal election process. Our task is to construe "for the purpose of ... influencing," incorporated in §434(e) through the definitions of "contributions" and "expenditures," in a manner that precisely furthers this goal.

In Part I we discussed what constituted a "contribution" for purposes of the contribution limitations set forth in 18 U.S.C. §608(b). We construed that term to include not only contributions made directly or indirectly to a candidate, political party, or campaign committee, and contributions made to other organizations or individuals but earmarked for political purposes, but also all expenditures placed in cooperation with or with the consent of a candidate, his agents, or an authorized committee of the candidate. The definition of "contribution" in §431(e) for disclosure purposes parallels the definition in Title 18 almost word for word, and we construe the former provision as we have the latter. So defined, "contributions" have a sufficiently close relationship to the goals of the Act, for they are connected with a candidate or his campaign.

When we attempt to define "expenditure" in a similarly narrow way we encounter line-drawing problems of the sort we faced in 18 U.S.C. §608(e)(1). Although the phrase, "for the purpose of ... influencing" an election or nomination, differs from the language used in §608(e)(1), it shares the same potential for encompassing both issue discussion and advocacy of a political result. The general requirement that "political committees" and candidates disclose their expenditures could raise similar vagueness problems, for "political committee" is defined only in terms of amount of annual "contributions" and "expenditures," and could be interpreted to reach groups engaged purely in issue discussion. The lower courts have construed the words "political committee" more narrowly. To fulfil the purposes of the Act they need only encompass organizations that are under the control of a candidate or the major purpose of which is the nomination or election of a candidate. Expenditures of candidates and of "political committees" so construed can be assumed to fall within the core area sought to be addressed by Congress. They are, by definition, campaign related.

But when the maker of the expenditure is not within these categories—when it is an individual other than a candidate or a group other than a "political committee"—the relation of the information sought to the purposes of the Act may be too remote. To insure that the reach of §434(e) is not impermissibly broad, we construe "expenditure" for purposes of that section in the same way we construed the terms of §608(e) to reach only funds used for communications that expressly advocate[108] the election or defeat of a clearly identified candidate. This reading is directed precisely to that spending that is unambiguously related to the campaign of a particular federal candidate.

In summary, §434(e), as construed, imposes independent reporting requirements on individuals and groups that are not candidates or political committees only in the following circumstances: (1) when they make contributions earmarked for political purposes or authorized or requested by a candidate or his agent, to some person other than a candidate or political committee, and (2) when they make expenditures for communications that expressly advocate the election or defeat of a clearly identified candidate.

[I]t is not fatal that §434(e) encompasses purely independent expenditures uncoordinated with a particular candidate or his agent. The corruption potential of these expenditures may be significantly different, but the informational interest can be as strong as it is in coordinated spending, for disclosure helps voters to define more of the candidates' constituencies.

Section 434(e), as we have construed it, does not contain the infirmities of the provisions before the Court in *Talley v. California* and *Thomas v. Collins*. The ordinance found wanting in *Talley* forbade all distribution of handbills that did not contain the name of the printer, author, or manufacturer, and the name of the distributor. The city urged that the ordinance was aimed at identifying those responsible for fraud, false advertising, and libel, but the Court found that it was "in no manner so limited." Here, as we have seen, the disclosure requirement is narrowly limited to those situations where the information sought has a substantial connection with the governmental interests sought to be advanced. *Thomas* held unconstitutional a prior restraint in the form of a registration requirement for labor organizers. The Court found the State's interest insufficient to justify the restrictive effect of the statute. The burden imposed by §434(e) is no prior restraint, but a reasonable and minimally restrictive method of furthering First Amendment values by opening the basic processes of our federal election system to public view.[109]

D. Thresholds

Appellants' third contention, based on alleged overbreadth, is that the monetary thresholds in the record-keeping and reporting provisions lack a substantial nexus with the

---

108. See n. 52, *supra*.

109. Of course, independent contributions and expenditures made in support of the campaigns of candidates of parties that have been found to be exempt from the general disclosure requirements because of the possibility of consequent chill and harassment would be exempt from the requirements of §434(e).

claimed governmental interests, for the amounts involved are too low even to attract the attention of the candidate, much less have a corrupting influence.

The provisions contain two thresholds. Records are to be kept by political committees of the names and addresses of those who make contributions in excess of $10, §432(c)(2), and these records are subject to Commission audit, §438(a)(8). If a person's contributions to a committee or candidate aggregate more than $100, his name and address, as well as his occupation and principal place of business, are to be included in reports filed by committees and candidates with the Commission, §434(b)(2), and made available for public inspection, §438(a)(4)....

The $10 and $100 thresholds are indeed low. Contributors of relatively small amounts are likely to be especially sensitive to recording or disclosure of their political preferences. These strict requirements may well discourage participation by some citizens in the political process, a result that Congress hardly could have intended. Indeed, there is little in the legislative history to indicate that Congress focused carefully on the appropriate level at which to require recording and disclosure. Rather, it seems merely to have adopted the thresholds existing in similar disclosure laws since 1910. But we cannot require Congress to establish that it has chosen the highest reasonable threshold. The line is necessarily a judgmental decision, best left in the context of this complex legislation to congressional discretion. We cannot say, on this bare record, that the limits designated are wholly without rationality.

We are mindful that disclosure serves informational functions, as well as the prevention of corruption and the enforcement of the contribution limitations. Congress is not required to set a threshold that is tailored only to the latter goals. In addition, the enforcement goal can never be well served if the threshold is so high that disclosure becomes equivalent to admitting violation of the contribution limitations.

The $10 recordkeeping threshold, in a somewhat similar fashion, facilitates the enforcement of the disclosure provisions by making it relatively difficult to aggregate secret contributions in amounts that surpass the $100 limit We agree with the Court of Appeals that there is no warrant for assuming that public disclosure of contributions between $10 and $100 is authorized by the Act. Accordingly, we do not reach the question whether information concerning gifts of this size can be made available to the public without trespassing impermissibly on First Amendment rights.

In summary, we find no constitutional infirmities in the recordkeeping reporting, and disclosure provisions of the Act.

McIntyre v. Ohio Elections Commission
514 U.S. 334 (1995)

Justice STEVENS delivered the opinion of the Court.

The question presented is whether an Ohio statute that prohibits the distribution of anonymous campaign literature is a "law ... abridging the freedom of speech" within the meaning of the First Amendment.

I

On April 27, 1988, Margaret McIntyre distributed leaflets to persons attending a public meeting at the Blendon Middle School in Westerville, Ohio. At this meeting, the superintendent of schools planned to discuss an imminent referendum on a proposed school tax levy. The leaflets expressed Mrs. McIntyre's opposition to the levy.[2] There is no suggestion that the text of her message was false, misleading, or libelous. She had composed and printed it on her home computer and had paid a professional printer to make additional copies. Some of the handbills identified her as the author; others merely purported to express the views of "CONCERNED PARENTS AND TAX PAYERS." Except for the help provided by her son and a friend, who placed some of the leaflets on car windshields in the school parking lot, Mrs. McIntyre acted independently.

While Mrs. McIntyre distributed her handbills, an official of the school district, who supported the tax proposal, advised her that the unsigned leaflets did not conform to the Ohio election laws. Undeterred, Mrs. McIntyre appeared at another meeting on the next evening and handed out more of the handbills.

The proposed school levy was defeated at the next two elections, but it finally passed on its third try in November 1988. Five months later, the same school official filed a complaint with the Ohio Elections Commission charging that Mrs. McIntyre's distribution of unsigned leaflets violated §3599.09(A) of the Ohio Code.[3] The commission agreed and imposed a fine of $100....

------

2. The following is one of Mrs. McIntyre's leaflets, in its original typeface:

<u>VOTE NO</u>
<u>ISSUE 19 SCHOOL TAX LEVY</u>

Last election Westerville Schools, asked us to vote yes for new buildings and expansions programs. We gave them what they asked. We knew there was crowded conditions and new growth in the district.

Now we find out there is a 4 million dollar deficit—WHY?

We are told the 3 middle schools must be split because of over-crowding, and yet we are told 3 schools are being closed—WHY?

A magnet school is not a full operating school, but a specials school.

Residents were asked to work on a 20 member commission to help formulate the new boundaries. For 4 weeks they worked long and hard and came up with a very workable plan. Their plan was totally disregarded—WHY?

WASTE of tax payers dollars must be stopped. Our children's education and welfare must come first. <u>WASTE CAN NO LONGER BE TOLERATED</u>.

PLEASE VOTE NO
ISSUE 19

THANK YOU.
CONCERNED PARENTS

3. Ohio Rev.Code Ann. §3599.09(A) (1988) provides:

"No person shall write, print, post, or distribute, or cause to be written, printed, posted, or distributed, a notice, placard, dodger, advertisement, sample ballot, or any other form of general publication which is designed to promote the nomination or election or defeat of a candidate, or to promote the adoption or defeat of any issue, or to influence the voters in any election, or make an expenditure for the purpose of financing political communications through newspapers, magazines, outdoor advertising facilities, direct mailings, or other similar types of general public political advertising, or through flyers, handbills, or other nonperiodical printed matter, unless there appears on such form of publication in a conspicuous place or is contained within said statement the name and residence or business address of the chairman, treasurer, or secretary of the organization issuing the same, or the person who issues, makes, or is responsible therefor. The disclaimer 'paid political advertisement' is not sufficient to meet the requirements of this division. When such publication is issued by the regularly constituted central or executive committee of a political party, organized as provided in Chapter 3517. of the Revised Code, it shall be sufficiently identified if it bears the name of the committee and its chairman or treasurer. No person, firm, or corporation shall print or reproduce any notice, placard, dodger, advertisement, sample ballot, or any other form of publication in violation of this section. This section does not apply to the transmittal of personal correspondence that is not reproduced by machine for

Mrs. McIntyre passed away during the pendency of this litigation. Even though the amount in controversy is only $100, petitioner, as the executor of her estate, has pursued her claim in this Court. Our grant of certiorari reflects our agreement with his appraisal of the importance of the question presented.

II

Ohio maintains that the statute under review is a reasonable regulation of the electoral process. The State does not suggest that all anonymous publications are pernicious or that a statute totally excluding them from the marketplace of ideas would be valid. This is a wise (albeit implicit) concession, for the anonymity of an author is not ordinarily a sufficient reason to exclude her work product from the protections of the First Amendment.

"Anonymous pamphlets, leaflets, brochures and even books have played an important role in the progress of mankind." *Talley v. California,* 362 U.S. 60 (1960). Great works of literature have frequently been produced by authors writing under assumed names. Despite readers' curiosity and the public's interest in identifying the creator of a work of art, an author generally is free to decide whether or not to disclose his or her true identity. The decision in favor of anonymity may be motivated by fear of economic or official retaliation, by concern about social ostracism, or merely by a desire to preserve as much of one's privacy as possible. Whatever the motivation may be, at least in the field of literary endeavor, the interest in having anonymous works enter the marketplace of ideas unquestionably outweighs any public interest in requiring disclosure as a condition of entry.[5] Accordingly, an author's decision to remain anonymous, like other decisions concerning omissions or additions to the content of a publication, is an aspect of the freedom of speech protected by the First Amendment.

The freedom to publish anonymously extends beyond the literary realm. In *Talley,* the Court held that the First Amendment protects the distribution of unsigned handbills urging readers to boycott certain Los Angeles merchants who were allegedly engaging in discriminatory employment practices. Writing for the Court, Justice Black noted that "[p]ersecuted groups and sects from time to time throughout history have been able to criticize oppressive practices and laws either anonymously or not at all." Justice Black recalled England's abusive press licensing laws and seditious libel prosecutions, and he reminded us that even the arguments favoring the ratification of the Constitution advanced

---

general distribution.

"The secretary of state may, by rule, exempt, from the requirements of this division, printed matter and certain other kinds of printed communications such as campaign buttons, balloons, pencils, or like items, the size or nature of which makes it unreasonable to add an identification or disclaimer. The disclaimer or identification, when paid for by a campaign committee, shall be identified by the words 'paid for by' followed by the name and address of the campaign committee and the appropriate officer of the committee, identified by name and title."

Section 3599.09(B) contains a comparable prohibition against unidentified communications uttered over the broadcasting facilities of any radio or television station. No question concerning that provision is raised in this case. Our opinion, therefore, discusses only written communications and, particularly, leaflets of the kind Mrs. McIntyre distributed....

5. Though such a requirement might provide assistance to critics in evaluating the quality and significance of the writing, it is not indispensable. To draw an analogy from a nonliterary context, the now-pervasive practice of grading law school examination papers "blindly" (*i.e.,* under a system in which the professor does not know whose paper she is grading) indicates that such evaluations are possible—indeed, perhaps more reliable—when any bias associated with the author's identity is prescinded. [How persuasive is the analogy between grading exams on an anonymous basis (or anonymous literature) and voting on the basis of anonymous campaign literature?—EDS.]

in the Federalist Papers were published under fictitious names. On occasion, quite apart from any threat of persecution, an advocate may believe her ideas will be more persuasive if her readers are unaware of her identity. Anonymity thereby provides a way for a writer who may be personally unpopular to ensure that readers will not prejudge her message simply because they do not like its proponent. Thus, even in the field of political rhetoric, where "the identity of the speaker is an important component of many attempts to persuade," *City of Ladue v. Gilleo*, 512 U.S. 43, 56 (1994) (footnote omitted), the most effective advocates have sometimes opted for anonymity. The specific holding in *Talley* related to advocacy of an economic boycott, but the Court's reasoning embraced a respected tradition of anonymity in the advocacy of political causes. This tradition is perhaps best exemplified by the secret ballot, the hard-won right to vote one's conscience without fear of retaliation.

III

California had defended the Los Angeles ordinance at issue in *Talley* as a law "aimed at providing a way to identify those responsible for fraud, false advertising and libel." We rejected that argument because nothing in the text or legislative history of the ordinance limited its application to those evils. We then made clear that we did "not pass on the validity of an ordinance limited to prevent these or any other supposed evils." The Ohio statute likewise contains no language limiting its application to fraudulent, false, or libelous statements; to the extent, therefore, that Ohio seeks to justify §3599.09(A) as a means to prevent the dissemination of untruths, its defense must fail for the same reason given in *Talley*. As the facts of this case demonstrate, the ordinance plainly applies even when there is no hint of falsity or libel.

Ohio's statute does, however, contain a different limitation: It applies only to unsigned documents designed to influence voters in an election. In contrast, the Los Angeles ordinance prohibited all anonymous handbilling "in any place under any circumstances." For that reason, Ohio correctly argues that *Talley* does not necessarily control the disposition of this case. We must, therefore, decide whether and to what extent the First Amendment's protection of anonymity encompasses documents intended to influence the electoral process.

Ohio places its principal reliance on cases such as *Anderson v. Celebrezze*, 460 U.S. 780 (1983); *Storer v. Brown*, 415 U.S. 724 (1974); and *Burdick v. Takushi*, 504 U.S. 428 (1992), in which we reviewed election code provisions governing the voting process itself. See *Anderson*, (filing deadlines); *Storer* (ballot access); *Burdick* (write-in voting); see also *Tashjian v. Republican Party of Conn.*, 479 U.S. 208 (1986) (eligibility of independent voters to vote in party primaries). In those cases we refused to adopt "any 'litmus-paper test' that will separate valid from invalid restrictions." *Anderson*, quoting *Storer*. Instead, we pursued an analytical process comparable to that used by courts "in ordinary litigation": We considered the relative interests of the State and the injured voters, and we evaluated the extent to which the State's interests necessitated the contested restrictions. Applying similar reasoning in this case, the Ohio Supreme Court upheld §3599.09(A) as a "*reasonable*" and "*nondiscriminatory*" burden on the rights of voters.

The "ordinary litigation" test does not apply here. Unlike the statutory provisions challenged in *Storer* and *Anderson*, §3599.09(A) of the Ohio Code does not control the mechanics of the electoral process. It is a regulation of pure speech. Moreover, even though this provision applies evenhandedly to advocates of differing viewpoints,[8] it is a direct

---

8. Arguably, the disclosure requirement places a more significant burden on advocates of unpopular causes than on defenders of the status quo. For purposes of our analysis, however, we as-

regulation of the content of speech. Every written document covered by the statute must contain "the name and residence or business address of the chairman, treasurer, or secretary of the organization issuing the same, or the person who issues, makes, or is responsible therefor." §3599.09(A). Furthermore, the category of covered documents is defined by their content—only those publications containing speech designed to influence the voters in an election need bear the required markings. Consequently, we are not faced with an ordinary election restriction; this case "involves a limitation on political expression subject to exacting scrutiny." *Meyer v. Grant.*

Indeed, as we have explained on many prior occasions, the category of speech regulated by the Ohio statute occupies the core of the protection afforded by the First Amendment....

Of course, core political speech need not center on a candidate for office. The principles enunciated in *Buckley* extend equally to issue-based elections such as the school tax referendum that Mrs. McIntyre sought to influence through her handbills. See *Bellotti*. Indeed, the speech in which Mrs. McIntyre engaged—handing out leaflets in the advocacy of a politically controversial viewpoint—is the essence of First Amendment expression. That this advocacy occurred in the heat of a controversial referendum vote only strengthens the protection afforded to Mrs. McIntyre's expression: Urgent, important, and effective speech can be no less protected than impotent speech, lest the right to speak be relegated to those instances when it is least needed. No form of speech is entitled to greater constitutional protection than Mrs. McIntyre's.

When a law burdens core political speech, we apply "exacting scrutiny," and we uphold the restriction only if it is narrowly tailored to serve an overriding state interest. Our precedents thus make abundantly clear that the Ohio Supreme Court applied a significantly more lenient standard than is appropriate in a case of this kind.

IV

Nevertheless, the State argues that, even under the strictest standard of review, the disclosure requirement in §3599.09(A) is justified by two important and legitimate state interests. Ohio judges its interest in preventing fraudulent and libelous statements and its interest in providing the electorate with relevant information to be sufficiently compelling to justify the anonymous speech ban. These two interests necessarily overlap to some extent, but it is useful to discuss them separately.

Insofar as the interest in informing the electorate means nothing more than the provision of additional information that may either buttress or undermine the argument in a document, we think the identity of the speaker is no different from other components of the document's content that the author is free to include or exclude.[11] We have already held that the State may not compel a newspaper that prints editorials critical of a partic-

---

sume the statute evenhandedly burdens all speakers who have a legitimate interest in remaining anonymous.

11. "Of course, the identity of the source is helpful in evaluating ideas. But 'the best test of truth is the power of the thought to get itself accepted in the competition of the market' (*Abrams v. United States,* [250 U.S. 616, 630 (1919) (Holmes, J., dissenting)]). Don't underestimate the common man. People are intelligent enough to evaluate the source of an anonymous writing. They can see it is anonymous. They know it is anonymous. They can evaluate its anonymity along with its message, as long as they are permitted, as they must be, to read that message. And then, once they have done so, it is for them to decide what is 'responsible', what is valuable, and what is truth." *New York v. Duryea,* 351 N.Y.S.2d 978, 996 (1974) (striking down similar New York statute as overbroad).

ular candidate to provide space for a reply by the candidate. *Miami Herald Publishing Co. v. Tornillo*, 418 U.S. 241 (1974). The simple interest in providing voters with additional relevant information does not justify a state requirement that a writer make statements or disclosures she would otherwise omit. Moreover, in the case of a handbill written by a private citizen who is not known to the recipient, the name and address of the author add little, if anything, to the reader's ability to evaluate the document's message. Thus, Ohio's informational interest is plainly insufficient to support the constitutionality of its disclosure requirement.

The state interest in preventing fraud and libel stands on a different footing. We agree with Ohio's submission that this interest carries special weight during election campaigns when false statements, if credited, may have serious adverse consequences for the public at large. Ohio does not, however, rely solely on §3599.09(A) to protect that interest. Its Election Code includes detailed and specific prohibitions against making or disseminating false statements during political campaigns. Ohio Rev. Code Ann. §§3599.09.1(B), 3599.09.2(B) (1988). These regulations apply both to candidate elections and to issue-driven ballot measures. Thus, Ohio's prohibition of anonymous leaflets plainly is not its principal weapon against fraud. Rather, it serves as an aid to enforcement of the specific prohibitions and as a deterrent to the making of false statements by unscrupulous prevaricators. Although these ancillary benefits are assuredly legitimate, we are not persuaded that they justify §3599.09(A)'s extremely broad prohibition.

As this case demonstrates, the prohibition encompasses documents that are not even arguably false or misleading. It applies not only to the activities of candidates and their organized supporters, but also to individuals acting independently and using only their own modest resources. It applies not only to elections of public officers, but also to ballot issues that present neither a substantial risk of libel nor any potential appearance of corrupt advantage. It applies not only to leaflets distributed on the eve of an election, when the opportunity for reply is limited, but also to those distributed months in advance. It applies no matter what the character or strength of the author's interest in anonymity. Moreover, as this case also demonstrates, the absence of the author's name on a document does not necessarily protect either that person or a distributor of a forbidden document from being held responsible for compliance with the Election Code. Nor has the State explained why it can more easily enforce the direct bans on disseminating false documents against anonymous authors and distributors than against wrongdoers who might use false names and addresses in an attempt to avoid detection. We recognize that a State's enforcement interest might justify a more limited identification requirement, but Ohio has shown scant cause for inhibiting the leafletting at issue here.

V

Finally, Ohio vigorously argues that our opinions in *Bellotti* and *Buckley v. Valeo* amply support the constitutionality of its disclosure requirement. Neither case is controlling: The former concerned the scope of First Amendment protection afforded to corporations; The relevant portion of the latter concerned mandatory disclosure of campaign-related expenditures. Neither case involved a prohibition of anonymous campaign literature.

In *Bellotti* ... we noted that the "inherent worth of the speech in terms of its capacity for informing the public does not depend upon the identity of its source, whether corporation, association, union, or individual." We also made it perfectly clear that we were not deciding whether the First Amendment's protection of corporate speech is coextensive with the protection it affords to individuals. Accordingly, although we commented in dicta on the prophylactic effect of requiring identification of the source of corporate advertising,[18] that footnote did not necessarily apply to independent communications by an individual like Mrs. McIntyre.

Our reference in [*Bellotti*] to the "prophylactic effect" of disclosure requirements cited a portion of our earlier opinion in *Buckley*, in which we stressed the importance of providing "the electorate with information 'as to where political campaign money comes from and how it is spent by the candidate.'" We observed that the "sources of a candidate's financial support also alert the voter to the interests to which a candidate is most likely to be responsive and thus facilitate predictions of future performance in office." Those comments concerned contributions to the candidate or expenditures authorized by the candidate or his responsible agent. They had no reference to the kind of independent activity pursued by Mrs. McIntyre. Required disclosures about the level of financial support a candidate has received from various sources are supported by an interest in avoiding the appearance of corruption that has no application to this case.

True, in another portion of the *Buckley* opinion we expressed approval of a requirement that even "independent expenditures" in excess of a threshold level be reported to the Federal Election Commission. But that requirement entailed nothing more than an identification to the Commission of the amount and use of money expended in support of a candidate. Though such mandatory reporting undeniably impedes protected First Amendment activity, the intrusion is a far cry from compelled self-identification on all election-related writings. A written election-related document — particularly a leaflet — is often a personally crafted statement of a political viewpoint. Mrs. McIntyre's handbills surely fit that description. As such, identification of the author against her will is particularly intrusive; it reveals unmistakably the content of her thoughts on a controversial issue. Disclosure of an expenditure and its use, without more, reveals far less information. It may be information that a person prefers to keep secret, and undoubtedly it often gives away something about the spender's political views. Nonetheless, even though money may "talk," its speech is less specific, less personal, and less provocative than a handbill — and as a result, when money supports an unpopular viewpoint it is less likely to precipitate retaliation.

Not only is the Ohio statute's infringement on speech more intrusive than the *Buckley* disclosure requirement, but it rests on different and less powerful state interests. The Federal Election Campaign Act of 1971, at issue in *Buckley*, regulates only candidate elections, not referenda or other issue-based ballot measures; and we construed "independent expenditures" to mean only those expenditures that "expressly advocate the election or defeat of a clearly identified candidate." In candidate elections, the Government can identify a compelling state interest in avoiding the corruption that might result from campaign expenditures. Disclosure of expenditures lessens the risk that individuals will spend money to support a candidate as a *quid pro quo* for special treatment after the candidate is in office. Curriers of favor will be deterred by the knowledge that all expenditures will be scrutinized by the Federal Election Commission and by the public for just this sort of abuse.[20] Moreover, the federal Act contains numerous legitimate disclosure requirements for cam-

18. "Corporate advertising, unlike some methods of participation in political campaigns, is likely to be highly visible. Identification of the source of advertising may be required as a means of disclosure, so that the people will be able to evaluate the arguments to which they are being subjected. See *Buckley*; *United States v. Harriss*, 347 U.S. 612, 625–626 (1954). In addition, we emphasized in *Buckley* the prophylactic effect of requiring that the source of communication be disclosed." *Bellotti*.

20. This interest also serves to distinguish *United States v. Harriss* in which we upheld limited disclosure requirements for lobbyists. The activities of lobbyists who have direct access to elected representatives, if undisclosed, may well present the appearance of corruption.

paign organizations; the similar requirements for independent expenditures serve to ensure that a campaign organization will not seek to evade disclosure by routing its expenditures through individual supporters. See *Buckley*. In short, although *Buckley* may permit a more narrowly drawn statute, it surely is not authority for upholding Ohio's open-ended provision.

VI

Under our Constitution, anonymous pamphleteering is not a pernicious, fraudulent practice, but an honorable tradition of advocacy and of dissent. Anonymity is a shield from the tyranny of the majority. See generally J. Mill, On Liberty and Considerations on Representative Government 1, 3–4 (R. McCallum ed. 1947). It thus exemplifies the purpose behind the Bill of Rights, and of the First Amendment in particular: to protect unpopular individuals from retaliation—and their ideas from suppression—at the hand of an intolerant society. The right to remain anonymous may be abused when it shields fraudulent conduct. But political speech by its nature will sometimes have unpalatable consequences, and, in general, our society accords greater weight to the value of free speech than to the dangers of its misuse. Ohio has not shown that its interest in preventing the misuse of anonymous election-related speech justifies a prohibition of all uses of that speech. The State may, and does, punish fraud directly. But it cannot seek to punish fraud indirectly by indiscriminately outlawing a category of speech, based on its content, with no necessary relationship to the danger sought to be prevented. One would be hard pressed to think of a better example of the pitfalls of Ohio's blunderbuss approach than the facts of the case before us.

The judgment of the Ohio Supreme Court is reversed.

It is so ordered.

JUSTICE GINSBURG, concurring.

The dissent is stirring in its appreciation of democratic values. But I do not see the Court's opinion as unguided by "bedrock principle," tradition, or our case law. Margaret McIntyre's case, it seems to me, bears a marked resemblance to Margaret Gilleo's case[1] and Mary Grace's.[2] All three decisions, I believe, are sound, and hardly sensational, applications of our First Amendment jurisprudence.

In for a calf is not always in for a cow. The Court's decision finds unnecessary, overintrusive, and inconsistent with American ideals the State's imposition of a fine on an individual leafleteer who, within her local community, spoke her mind, but sometimes not her name. We do not thereby hold that the State may not in other, larger circumstances require the speaker to disclose its interest by disclosing its identity. Appropriately leaving open matters not presented by McIntyre's handbills, the Court recognizes that a State's interest in protecting an election process "might justify a more limited identification requirement." But the Court has convincingly explained why Ohio lacks "cause for inhibiting the leafletting at issue here."

JUSTICE THOMAS, concurring in the judgment.

I agree with the majority's conclusion that Ohio's election law, §3599.09(A), is inconsistent with the First Amendment. I would apply, however, a different methodology to this

---

1. See *City of Ladue v. Gilleo*, in which we held that the city of Ladue could not prohibit homeowner Gilleo's display of a small sign, on her lawn or in a window, opposing war in the Persian Gulf.

2. Grace was the "lone picketer" who stood on the sidewalk in front of this Court with a sign containing the text of the First Amendment, prompting us to exclude public sidewalks from the statutory ban on display of a "flag, banner, or device" on Court grounds. *United States v. Grace*, 461 U.S. 171, 183 (1983).

case. Instead of asking whether "an honorable tradition" of anonymous speech has existed throughout American history, or what the "value" of anonymous speech might be, we should determine whether the phrase "freedom of speech, or of the press," as originally understood, protected anonymous political leafletting. I believe that it did. [The remainder of Justice Thomas's opinion examining the historical evidence regarding the Framers' understanding of the First Amendment is omitted.]

JUSTICE SCALIA, with whom THE CHIEF JUSTICE joins, dissenting.

At a time when both political branches of Government and both political parties reflect a popular desire to leave more decisionmaking authority to the States, today's decision moves in the opposite direction, adding to the legacy of inflexible central mandates (irrevocable even by Congress) imposed by this Court's constitutional jurisprudence. In an opinion which reads as though it is addressing some peculiar law like the Los Angeles municipal ordinance at issue in *Talley*, the Court invalidates a species of protection for the election process that exists, in a variety of forms, in every State except California, and that has a pedigree dating back to the end of the 19th century. Preferring the views of the English utilitarian philosopher John Stuart Mill to the considered judgment of the American people's elected representatives from coast to coast, the Court discovers a hitherto unknown right-to-be-unknown while engaging in electoral politics. I dissent from this imposition of free-speech imperatives that are demonstrably not those of the American people today, and that there is inadequate reason to believe were those of the society that begat the First Amendment or the Fourteenth.

I

The question posed by the present case is not the easiest sort to answer for those who adhere to the Court's (and the society's) traditional view that the Constitution bears its original meaning and is unchanging. Under that view, "[o]n every question of construction, [we should] carry ourselves back to the time when the Constitution was adopted; recollect the spirit manifested in the debates; and instead of trying [to find] what meaning may be squeezed out of the text, or invented against it, conform to the probable one in which it was passed." T. Jefferson, Letter to William Johnson (June 12, 1823), in 15 Writings of Thomas Jefferson 439, 449 (A. Lipscomb ed. 1904). That technique is simple of application when government conduct that is claimed to violate the Bill of Rights or the Fourteenth Amendment is shown, upon investigation, to have been engaged in without objection at the very time the Bill of Rights or the Fourteenth Amendment was adopted. There is no doubt, for example, that laws against libel and obscenity do not violate "the freedom of speech" to which the First Amendment refers; they existed and were universally approved in 1791. Application of the principle of an unchanging Constitution is also simple enough at the other extreme, where the government conduct at issue was *not* engaged in at the time of adoption, and there is ample evidence that the *reason* it was not engaged in is that it was thought to violate the right embodied in the constitutional guarantee. Racks and thumbscrews, well-known instruments for inflicting pain, were not in use because they were regarded as cruel punishments.

The present case lies between those two extremes. Anonymous electioneering was not prohibited by law in 1791 or in 1868. In fact, it was widely practiced at the earlier date, an understandable legacy of the revolutionary era in which political dissent could produce governmental reprisal. I need not dwell upon the evidence of that, since it is described at length in today's concurrence. See *ante* (THOMAS, J., concurring in judgment). The practice of anonymous electioneering may have been less general in 1868, when the Fourteenth Amendment was adopted, but at least as late as 1837 it was respectable enough to be engaged in by Abraham Lincoln. See 1 A. Beveridge, ABRAHAM LINCOLN 1809–1858, pp. 215–216 (1928); 1 UNCOLLECTED WORKS OF ABRAHAM LINCOLN 155–161 (R. Wilson ed. 1947).

But to prove that anonymous electioneering was used frequently is not to establish that it is a constitutional right. Quite obviously, not every restriction upon expression that did not exist in 1791 or in 1868 is *ipso facto* unconstitutional, or else modern election laws such as those involved in *Burson v. Freeman*, 504 U.S. 191 (1992), and *Buckley v. Valeo*, would be prohibited, as would (to mention only a few other categories) modern antinoise regulation of the sort involved in *Kovacs v. Cooper*, 336 U.S. 77 (1949), and *Ward v. Rock Against Racism*, 491 U.S. 781 (1989), and modern parade-permitting regulation of the sort involved in *Cox v. New Hampshire*, 312 U.S. 569 (1941).

Evidence that anonymous electioneering was regarded as a constitutional right is sparse, and as far as I am aware evidence that it was *generally* regarded as such is nonexistent.

[T]he sum total of the historical evidence marshaled by the concurrence for the principle of *constitutional entitlement* to anonymous electioneering is partisan claims in the debate on ratification (which was *almost* like an election) that a viewpoint-based restriction on anonymity by newspaper editors violates freedom of speech. This absence of historical testimony concerning the point before us is hardly remarkable. The issue of a governmental prohibition upon anonymous electioneering in particular (as opposed to a government prohibition upon anonymous publication in general) simply never arose. Indeed, there probably never arose even the abstract question whether electoral openness and regularity was worth such a governmental restriction upon the normal right to anonymous speech. The idea of close government regulation of the electoral process is a more modern phenomenon, arriving in this country in the late 1800's.

What we have, then, is the most difficult case for determining the meaning of the Constitution. No accepted existence of governmental restrictions of the sort at issue here demonstrates their constitutionality, but neither can their nonexistence clearly be attributed to constitutional objections. In such a case, constitutional adjudication necessarily involves not just history but judgment: judgment as to whether the government action under challenge is consonant with the concept of the protected freedom (in this case, the freedom of speech and of the press) that existed when the constitutional protection was accorded. In the present case, *absent other indication*, I would be inclined to agree with the concurrence that a society which used anonymous political debate so regularly would not regard as constitutional even moderate restrictions made to improve the election process. (I would, however, want further evidence of common practice in 1868, since I doubt that the Fourteenth Amendment time-warped the post-Civil War States back to the Revolution.)

But there *is* other indication, of the most weighty sort: the widespread and longstanding traditions of our people. Principles of liberty fundamental enough to have been embodied within constitutional guarantees are not readily erased from the Nation's consciousness. A governmental practice that has become general throughout the United States, and particularly one that has the validation of long, accepted usage, bears a strong presumption of constitutionality. And that is what we have before us here. Ohio Rev. Code Ann. §3599.09(A) (1988) was enacted by the General Assembly of the State of Ohio almost 80 years ago. Even at the time of its adoption, there was nothing unique or extraordinary about it. The earliest statute of this sort was adopted by Massachusetts in 1890, little more than 20 years after the Fourteenth Amendment was ratified. No less than 24 States had similar laws by the end of World War I, and today every State of the Union except California has one, as does the District of Columbia, and as does the Federal Government where advertising relating to candidates for federal office is concerned, see 2 U.S.C. §441d(a). Such a universal and long-established American legislative practice must be given precedence, I think, over historical and academic speculation regarding a restriction that assuredly does not go to the heart of free speech.

It can be said that we ignored a tradition as old, and almost as widespread, in *Texas v. Johnson*, 491 U.S. 397 (1989), where we held unconstitutional a state law prohibiting desecration of the United States flag. See also *United States v. Eichman*, 496 U.S. 310 (1990). But those cases merely stand for the proposition that postadoption tradition cannot alter the core meaning of a constitutional guarantee. As we said in *Johnson*, "[i]f there is a bedrock principle underlying the First Amendment, it is that the government may not prohibit the expression of an idea simply because society finds the idea itself offensive or disagreeable." Prohibition of expression of contempt for the flag, whether by contemptuous words, see *Street v. New York*, 394 U.S. 576 (1969), or by burning the flag, came, we said, within that "bedrock principle." The law at issue here, by contrast, forbids the expression of no idea, but merely requires identification of the speaker when the idea is uttered in the electoral context. It is at the periphery of the First Amendment, like the law at issue in *Burson*, where we took guidance from tradition in upholding against constitutional attack restrictions upon electioneering in the vicinity of polling places.

II

The foregoing analysis suffices to decide this case for me. Where the meaning of a constitutional text (such as "the freedom of speech") is unclear, the widespread and long-accepted practices of the American people are the best indication of what fundamental beliefs it was intended to enshrine. Even if I were to close my eyes to practice, however, and were to be guided exclusively by deductive analysis from our case law, I would reach the same result.

Three basic questions must be answered to decide this case. Two of them are readily answered by our precedents; the third is readily answered by common sense and by a decent regard for the practical judgment of those more familiar with elections than we are. The first question is whether protection of the election process justifies limitations upon speech that cannot constitutionally be imposed generally. (If not, *Talley v. California*, which invalidated a flat ban on *all* anonymous leafletting, controls the decision here.) Our cases plainly answer that question in the affirmative—indeed, they suggest that no justification for regulation is more compelling than protection of the electoral process....

The second question relevant to our decision is whether a "right to anonymity" is such a prominent value in our constitutional system that even protection of the electoral process cannot be purchased at its expense. The answer, again, is clear: no. Several of our cases have held that *in peculiar circumstances* the compelled disclosure of a person's identity would unconstitutionally deter the exercise of First Amendment associational rights. See, e.g., *Brown v. Socialist Workers '74 Campaign Comm. (Ohio)*, 459 U.S. 87 (1982); *Bates v. Little Rock*, 361 U.S. 516 (1960); *NAACP v. Alabama*. But those cases did not acknowledge any general right to anonymity, or even any right on the part of *all* citizens to ignore the particular laws under challenge. Rather, they recognized a right to an *exemption* from otherwise valid disclosure requirements on the part of someone who could show a "reasonable probability" that the compelled disclosure would result in "threats, harassment, or reprisals from either Government officials or private parties." This last quotation is from *Buckley v. Valeo*, which prescribed the safety valve of a similar exemption in upholding the disclosure requirements of the Federal Election Campaign Act. That is the answer our case law provides to the Court's fear about the "tyranny of the majority," and to its concern that "'[p]ersecuted groups and sects from time to time throughout history have been able to criticize oppressive practices and laws either anonymously or not at all." Anonymity can still be enjoyed by those who require it, without utterly destroying useful disclosure laws. The record in this case contains not even a hint that Mrs. McIntyre feared "threats, harassment, or reprisals"; indeed, she placed her name on some of her fliers and meant to place it on all of them.

The existence of a generalized right of anonymity in speech was rejected by this Court in *Lewis Publishing Co. v. Morgan*, 229 U.S. 288 (1913), which held that newspapers desiring the privilege of second-class postage could be required to provide to the Postmaster General, and to publish, a statement of the names and addresses of their editors, publishers, business managers, and owners. We rejected the argument that the First Amendment forbade the requirement of such disclosure. The provision that gave rise to that case still exists, see 39 U.S.C. §3685, and is still enforced by the Postal Service. It is one of several federal laws seemingly invalidated by today's opinion.

The Court's unprecedented protection for anonymous speech does not even have the virtue of establishing a clear (albeit erroneous) rule of law. For after having announced that this statute, because it "burdens core political speech," requires "exacting scrutiny" and must be "narrowly tailored to serve an overriding state interest," (ordinarily the kiss of death), the opinion goes on to proclaim soothingly (and unhelpfully) that "a State's enforcement interest might justify a more limited identification requirement." See also *ante* (GINSBURG, J., concurring) ("We do not ... hold that the State may not in other, larger circumstances require the speaker to disclose its interest by disclosing its identity"). Perhaps, then, not *all* the state statutes I have alluded to are invalid, but just *some* of them; or indeed maybe *all* of them remain valid in "larger circumstances"! It may take decades to work out the shape of this newly expanded right-to-speak-incognito, even in the elections field. And in other areas, of course, a whole new boutique of wonderful First Amendment litigation opens its doors. Must a parade permit, for example, be issued to a group that refuses to provide its identity, or that agrees to do so only under assurance that the identity will not be made public? Must a municipally owned theater that is leased for private productions book anonymously sponsored presentations? Must a government periodical that has a "letters to the editor" column disavow the policy that most newspapers have against the publication of anonymous letters? Must a public university that makes its facilities available for a speech by Louis Farrakhan or David Duke refuse to disclose the on-campus or off-campus group that has sponsored or paid for the speech? Must a municipal "public-access" cable channel permit anonymous (and masked) performers? The silliness that follows upon a generalized right to anonymous speech has no end.

The third and last question relevant to our decision is whether the prohibition of anonymous campaigning is effective in protecting and enhancing democratic elections. In answering this question no, the Justices of the majority set their own views—on a practical matter that bears closely upon the real-life experience of elected politicians and *not* upon that of unelected judges—up against the views of 49 (and perhaps all 50) state legislatures and the Federal Congress. We might also add to the list on the other side the legislatures of foreign democracies: Australia, Canada, and England, for example, all have prohibitions upon anonymous campaigning. How is it, one must wonder, that all of these elected legislators, from around the country and around the world, could not see what six Justices of this Court see so clearly that they are willing to require the entire Nation to act upon it: that requiring identification of the source of campaign literature does not improve the quality of the campaign?

The Court says that the State has not explained "why it can more easily enforce the direct bans on disseminating false documents against anonymous authors and distributors than against wrongdoers who might use false names and addresses in an attempt to avoid detection." I am not sure what this complicated comparison means. I am sure, however, that (1) a person who is required to put his name to a document is much less likely to lie than one who can lie anonymously, and (2) the distributor of a leaflet which is unlawful because it is anonymous runs much more risk of immediate detection and punishment than the distributor of a leaflet which is unlawful because it is false. Thus, people will be more likely to observe a signing requirement than a naked "no falsity" requirement; and, having observed that requirement, will then be significantly less likely to lie in what they have signed.

But the usefulness of a signing requirement lies not only in promoting observance of the law against campaign falsehoods (though that alone is enough to sustain it). It lies also in promoting a civil and dignified level of campaign debate—which the State has no power to command, but ample power to encourage by such undemanding measures as a signature requirement. Observers of the past few national elections have expressed concern about the increase of character assassination—"mudslinging" is the colloquial term— engaged in by political candidates and their supporters to the detriment of the democratic process. Not all of this, in fact not much of it, consists of actionable untruth; most is innuendo, or demeaning characterization, or mere disclosure of items of personal life that have no bearing upon suitability for office. Imagine how much all of this would increase if it could be done anonymously. The principal impediment against it is the reluctance of most individuals and organizations to be publicly associated with uncharitable and uncivil expression. Consider, moreover, the increased potential for "dirty tricks." It is not unheard-of for campaign operatives to circulate material over the name of their opponents or their opponents' supporters (a violation of election laws) in order to attract or alienate certain interest groups. See, *e.g.*, B. Felknor, POLITICAL MISCHIEF: SMEAR, SABOTAGE, AND REFORM IN U.S. ELECTIONS 111–112 (1992) (fake United Mine Workers' newspaper assembled by the National Republican Congressional Committee); *New York v. Duryea*, 351 N.Y.S.2d 978 (Sup. 1974) (letters purporting to be from the "Action Committee for the Liberal Party" sent by Republicans). How much easier—and sanction free!—it would be to circulate anonymous material (for example, a *really* tasteless, though not actionably false, attack upon one's own candidate) with the hope and expectation that it will be attributed to, and held against, the other side.

The Court contends that demanding the disclosure of the pamphleteer's identity is no different from requiring the disclosure of any other information that may reduce the persuasiveness of the pamphlet's message. It cites *Miami Herald Publishing Co. v. Tornillo*, which held it unconstitutional to require a newspaper that had published an editorial critical of a particular candidate to furnish space for that candidate to reply. But it is not *usual* for a speaker to put forward the best arguments against himself, and it is a great imposition upon free speech to make him do so. Whereas it is quite usual—it is expected—for a speaker to *identify* himself, and requiring that is (at least when there are no special circumstances present) virtually no imposition at all.

We have approved much more onerous disclosure requirements in the name of fair elections. In *Buckley*, we upheld provisions of the Federal Election Campaign Act that required private individuals to report to the Federal Election Commission independent expenditures made for communications advocating the election or defeat of a candidate for federal office. Our primary rationale for upholding this provision was that it served an "informational interest" by "increas[ing] the fund of information concerning those who support the candidates." The provision before us here serves the same informational interest, as well as more important interests, which I have discussed above. The Court's attempt to distinguish *Buckley* would be unconvincing, even if it were accurate in its statement that the disclosure requirement there at issue "reveals far less information" than requiring disclosure of the identity of the author of a specific campaign statement. That happens not to be accurate, since the provision there at issue required not merely "[d]isclosure of an expenditure and its use, without more." It required, among other things:

> the identification of *each person to whom expenditures have been made* . . . within the calendar year in an aggregate amount or value in excess of $100, the amount, date, *and purpose of each such expenditure* and the name and address of, and office sought by, *each candidate on whose behalf* such expenditure was made. 2 U.S.C. §434(b)(9) (emphasis added).

See also 2 U.S.C. §434(e). Surely in many if not most cases, this information will readily permit identification of the particular message that the would-be-anonymous campaigner sponsored. Besides which the burden of complying with this provision, which includes the filing of quarterly reports, is infinitely more onerous than Ohio's simple requirement for signature of campaign literature. If *Buckley* remains the law, this is an easy case.

* * *

I do not know where the Court derives its perception that "anonymous pamphleteering is not a pernicious, fraudulent practice, but an honorable tradition of advocacy and of dissent." I can imagine no reason why an anonymous leaflet is any more honorable, as a general matter, than an anonymous phone call or an anonymous letter. It facilitates wrong by eliminating accountability, which is ordinarily the very purpose of the anonymity. There are of course exceptions, and where anonymity is needed to avoid "threats, harassment, or reprisals" the First Amendment will require an exemption from the Ohio law. Cf. *NAACP v. Alabama*. But to strike down the Ohio law in its general application—and similar laws of 49 other States and the Federal Government—on the ground that all anonymous communication is in our society traditionally sacrosanct, seems to me a distortion of the past that will lead to a coarsening of the future.

I respectfully dissent.

Notes and Questions

1. The Court in *Buckley* recognized an exception to the FECA's disclosure requirements when a minor party shows "a reasonable probability that the compelled disclosure of a party's contributors' names will subject them to threats, harassment, or reprisals from either Government officials or private parties." Under the facts related to the Ohio Socialist Workers' Party discussed in the introduction to this chapter, the Court held in *Brown v. Socialist Workers '74 Campaign Comm.*, 459 U.S. 87 (1982), that the party was entitled to such an exemption. Three Justices agreed that the evidence showed the SWP deserved an exemption as to campaign *contributors*, but disagreed that the evidence showed that those who received *expenditures* from the SWP were reasonably likely to be subject to threats, harassment, or reprisals.

2. *Buckley* recognized three interests served by disclosure, as outlined in the introduction to this chapter: the anti-corruption interest, the information interest, and the enforcement interest. In *McIntyre*, the Court held that the anti-corruption interest could not be invoked to support the Ohio disclosure law. Citing *Buckley*, the Court wrote that "[d]isclosure of expenditures [in candidate elections] lessens the risk that individuals will

spend money to support a candidate as a *quid pro quo* for special treatment after the candidate is in office." Could the Court have reached a different result in *McIntyre* if it relied upon the broader definitions of corruption in *MCFL*, *Austin*, or *Shrink Missouri*? Ohio could not rely upon the anti-enforcement interest in *McIntyre* as the federal government did in *Buckley* because disclosure was unnecessary to support any other Ohio campaign finance regulation. That left only the information interest, which the Court held was inadequate in McIntyre's case.

Following *McIntyre*, is the information interest standing alone ever adequate grounds for disclosure in a campaign finance case? If not, it would be unconstitutional to require disclosure of contributions and expenditures in any ballot measure campaign, where the anti-corruption interest (at least in the sense of *quid pro quo* corruption) is irrelevant because there is no candidate to corrupt, and the enforcement interest is inapplicable because existing precedent (such as *Bellotti* and *CARC*) prevents contribution and expenditure limits in ballot campaigns. For a case upholding the ability of the state to require disclosure of express advocacy in ballot measure elections, see *California Pro-Life Council, Inc. v. Getman*, 328 F.3d 1088 (9th Cir. 2003).

3. Contrary to the suggestion of the last note, certainly not all the Justices would agree that the information interest standing alone is inadequate to support campaign finance regulation in *all* cases. Justice Ginsburg, for example, distinguished "other, larger circumstances" where disclosure could be required[b] and two Justices dissented in *McIntyre*. The majority itself made frequent references to the fact that McIntyre was a lone pamphleteer. Consider the following hypothetical situations involving ballot measures and decide whether disclosure could be constitutionally required:

a. Same facts as *McIntyre*, except McIntyre, CEO of a Fortune 500 corporation, spends corporate funds, in the same amount as McIntyre spent in the actual case, to oppose the initiative anonymously.

b. Same facts as the first hypothetical, except the CEO spent $1 million for direct mail and newspaper ads opposing the initiative under the pseudonym "Citizens for Responsible Government."

c. Same facts as *McIntyre*, except McIntyre is president of a large grass-roots organization opposed to the initiative, Citizens for Responsible Government, whose members wish to remain anonymous.

For an expansive reading of Justice Ginsburg's "larger circumstances" comment, see Malcolm A. Heinicke, Note, *A Political Reformer's Guide to* McIntyre *and Source Disclosure Laws for Political Advertising*, 8 STANFORD LAW & POLICY REVIEW 133, 140–41 (1997); Compare *Volle v. Webster*, 69 F.Supp.2d 171, 174 (D. Me. 1999) (holding that Supreme Court precedent amounts to "an unequivocal declaration" that "a public filing requirement in an issue-only election is not wholly prohibited") with *Yes for Life Political Action Committee v. Webster*, 74 F.Supp.2d 37, 42 (D. Me. 1999) (stating that "a determination ... cannot be made from the text of" *McIntyre* whether the Court meant to distinguish between individuals and other entities like corporations, but holding that an anti-abortion political group is more like an individual entitled to anonymity than a corporation). *Volle* and *Yes for Life Political Action Committee* were authored by the same district court judge.

---

b. Consider also *Buckley v. American Constitutional Law Foundation*, 525 U.S. 182, 202–203 (1999), in which Justice Ginsburg, writing for a Court majority, said in a dictum that "[d]isclosure of the names of initiative sponsors, and the amounts they have spent gathering support for their initiatives," responds to the "substantial state interest" in "control[ling] or check[ing] ... the domination of the initiative process by affluent special interest groups."

4. The last two notes suggest two ways to distinguish *Buckley* and *McIntyre*. The first difference is that *McIntyre* involved a ballot measure election and *Buckley* involved candidate elections, where, in addition to the information interest, the anti-corruption interest is always present and the enforcement interest may be present. The second difference is that *Buckley* involved federal elections, which are among the most expensive and salient elections, while *McIntyre* involved a "lone pamphleteer" in a small local election. What of the lone pamphleteer in a candidate election? Suppose, for example, that a lone pamphleteer passed out leaflets urging a vote for her favorite candidate for Congress. If she spent more than $100 she must file a report with the FEC. See 2 U.S.C. §434(e). Does *Buckley* foreclose an argument that, under *McIntyre*, FEC-mandated disclosure as applied to the lone pamphleteer in a candidate election is unconstitutional?

5. *Buckley* and *McIntyre* are different in one other important way. *Buckley* required disclosure in documents filed with a government agency after the expenditure or contribution, while *McIntyre* required disclosure on the face of the document itself. Indeed, the Court in *McIntyre* distinguished *Buckley* and *Bellotti* on grounds that "[n]either case involved a prohibition of anonymous campaign literature." Should the time and place of disclosure matter? Consider the following case. California law requires individuals and political committees sending mass mailings in elections to identify themselves on the face of the document. A candidate for local office sends out a mass mailing using a fictitious name attacking his opponent. In such a case, the information and anti-corruption interests are present, but disclosure is required on the face of the document itself. What result? See *Griset v. Fair Political Practices Commission*, 23 P.3d 43 (Cal. 2001). For a case holding that the time and place of disclosure matters even in candidate elections, see *Arkansas Right to Life State Political Action Committee v. Butler*, 29 F.Supp.2d 540, 550 (W.D. Ark. 1998).

A more recent U.S. Supreme Court case sent mixed signals on the question whether the time and place of disclosure matter. In *Buckley v. American Constitutional Law Foundation*, 525 U.S. 182 (1999), the Justices unanimously agreed that it was unconstitutional for Colorado to require paid initiative petition circulators to wear an identification badge displaying their names.

> [T]he restraint on speech in this case is more severe than was the restraint in *McIntyre*. Petition circulation is the less fleeting encounter, for the circulator must endeavor to persuade electors to sign the petition.... The injury to speech is heightened for the petition circulator because the badge requirement compels personal name identification at the precise moment when the circulator's interest in anonymity is the greatest.

Id. at 199. This holding suggests that the time and place of disclosure do matter. However, the *ACLF* Court in a footnote distinguished the case (and *Meyer v. Grant*, see Chapter 8) from campaign finance disclosure cases. "[T]oday's decision ... like *Meyer*, separates petition circulators from the proponents and financial backers of ballot initiatives."

By a 6–3 vote, the *ACLF* Court also struck down a requirement that initiative proponents file disclosure reports listing paid circulators and their income from circulation. Thus, the time and place of disclosure apparently were not dispositive to the six Justices in the *ACLF* majority. That holding, however, appeared to turn at least in part on the fact that initiative circulators already disclosed their names and addresses on affidavits accompanying initiative petitions filed for public inspection—thus, the additional challenged disclosure requirement was unnecessary. A Ninth Circuit court recently struck down a similar disclosure report requirement in Washington, despite the absence in Washington of an affidavit requirement similar to Colorado's. *Washington Initiatives Now v. Rippie*, 213 F.3d 1132 (9th Cir. 2000). Thus, initiative circulators in Washington can retain complete anonymity, at least until the state adopts a regulation like Colorado's affidavit requirement. Under the reasoning of *Washington Initiatives Now*, it is difficult to see how the affidavit requirement itself would survive constitutional scrutiny.

The highest criminal court in Texas struck down as violating *McIntyre* a state statute requiring one who has contracted to print or publish a political advertisement—in this case, as in *Griset*, a bulk mailing opposing a candidate in a candidate election—to identify himself in the advertisement. *Doe v. State*, 112 S.W.3d 532 (Tex. Crim. App. 2003) The dissenting judge believed the case was closer to *Buckley* than *McIntyre*.

In 2002, the U.S. Supreme Court decided another case on the right to anonymity, *Watchtower Bible and Tract Society of New York v. Village of Stratton*, 536 U.S. 150 (2002). The Court struck down on First Amendment grounds a local village's law requiring anyone who wished to go door-to-door to advocate for a political cause to first obtain a permit and display that permit to a resident on demand. The case had potentially important implications for campaign finance disclosure laws because the petitioners relied upon *McIntyre* and *ACLF* in arguing for the law's unconstitutionality.

The Court in *Watchtower* characterized *McIntyre* as a case "involving distribution of unsigned handbills." It added a dictum that a government "may well be justified" in requiring the identity of persons canvassing door-to-door based on "the special state interest in protecting the integrity of a ballot-initiative process." *Watchtower*, 536 U.S. at 167. What is the "special state interest" in this context? Is it the informational interest that *McIntyre* appeared to downplay or some other interest?

6. Does government-required disclosure of information on the face of documents (or through spoken words on radio or superimposed words on television broadcasts) violate first amendment prohibitions against compelled speech? California passed a series of provisions requiring publishers of "slate mailers" advocating the election or defeat of several candidates or ballot measures to include certain information on the face of the mailers. For example, slate mailers making a recommendation contrary to the "official endorsement" of a party "which the mailer appears by representation or indicia to represent" had to include a statement that the recommendation was "NOT THE POSITION" of the party in question. This requirement was void under the general principle that "a statute compelling speech, like a statute forbidding speech, falls within the purview of the First Amendment." See *Levine v. Fair Political Practices Commission*, 222 F.Supp.2d 1182 (E.D.Cal. 2002). An earlier decision struck down a requirement that three dollar signs accompany the publication of an endorsement of a candidate or proposition when someone paid the publisher to cover some of the cost of the mailing. The court relied upon *McIntyre's* statement that the state's information interest did "not justify a requirement that a writer make statements or disclosures she would otherwise omit." *California Prolife Council Political Action Committee v. Scully*, No. Civ. S-96-1965 LKK/DAD (E.D. Cal. Mar. 1, 2001). (The unpublished opinion may be downloaded from http://www.law.ucla.edu/faculty/bios/lowenste/slatemailorder.pdf.)[c] If the government cannot require disclosure on the face of slate mailers, can it require that a radio or television communication governed by federal campaign law include "in a clearly spoken manner, the following audio statement: '_____ is responsible for the content of this advertising.' (with the blank to be filled in with the

---

c. For more information on California's peculiar institution of slate mailers, see Shanto Iyengar, Daniel H. Lowenstein & Seth Masket, *The Stealth Campaign: Experimental Studies of Slate Mail in California*, 17 JOURNAL OF LAW & POLITICS 295 (2001).

name of the political committee or other person paying for the communication and the name of any connected organization of the payor.)"? See BCRA, §311, upheld by the Supreme Court in *McConnell v. Federal Election Commission*, and imposing a similar requirement.

7. The Sixth Circuit characterized *Buckley* and *McIntyre* as "two points on a continuum." *Kentucky Right to Life, Inc. v. Terry*, 108 F.3d 637, 647 (6th Cir.), cert. denied sub nom. *Kentucky Right to Life v. Stengel*, 522 U.S. 860 (1997). In fact, the analysis above shows three potential important distinctions between *Buckley* and *McIntyre*, leading to the eight permutations of the relevant criteria shown by tables 19A and 19B. The Court has filled in only two of the eight boxes, leaving the remainder of these issues to percolate in the lower courts.

Table 19A   Candidate elections

	lone pamphleteer	"larger circumstances"
Later-filed report	?	disclosure allowed (*Buckley*)
disclosure accompanying communication	?	? (*Griset*)

Table 19B   Ballot measure elections

	lone pamphleteer	"larger circumstances"
Later-filed report	?	? (*Bellotti*)
disclosure accompanying communication	disclosure unconstitutional (*McIntyre*)	?

Are courts to craft different rules for each of the other six categories? Should the *type* of information to be disclosed be relevant to the constitutional inquiry as well?

8. Justice Stevens ends the Court's opinion in *McIntyre* with the comment that "[o]ne would be hard pressed to think of a better example of the pitfalls of Ohio's blunderbuss approach than the facts of the case before us." The Ohio Elections Commission displayed remarkably poor judgment in levying a fine in the *McIntyre* case. Unfortunately, poor judgment in enforcement proceedings is far from rare. For example, an agency in Massachusetts interpreted the campaign laws of that state to make it illegal for candidates in the Republican primary for governor and lieutenant governor to run together as a "ticket," sharing expenses for buttons, bumper stickers, signs and the like. The agency did not bother to explain how barring such joint expenditures could conceivably be thought to advance any of the purposes of the campaign laws. The candidates had to go all the way to the Massachusetts Supreme Judicial Court to get this stupid interpretation overturned. See *Weld for Governor v. Director of the Office of Campaign and Political Finance*, 556 N.E.2d 21 (Mass. 1990).

Another example occurred in Wisconsin. As is universally the case, statutes in Wisconsin exclude certain volunteer services from the definition of "contribution." Volunteer services are not perceived as giving rise to problems associated with campaign contributions, and they are excluded from the definition so volunteers will not be entangled in disclosure and other requirements. The Wisconsin legislature enacted a ban on gifts from lobbyists to elected officials and candidates, but made an exception for campaign contributions. The Wisconsin Ethics Board ruled that lobbyists could not provide volunteer services to candidates, because those services were not "contributions," and therefore were not within the exception to the ban on gifts. This mindlessly literal juxtaposition of the two statutes to ban volunteer services was perverse. The legislature could not have intended the exception for services from the definition of "contribution" to be negated when the exception for contributions to the ban on gifts was enacted. The whole point was to insulate volunteer services from such regulatory burdens. As in Massachusetts, it took judicial intervention to overturn this foolishness. See *Barker v. Wisconsin Ethics Board*, 841 F.Supp. 255 (W.D. Wis. 1993).

We do not suggest that administrators always do the wrong thing. After all, one of the editors of this volume once chaired a state commission that administered campaign laws. It is possible that some readers of this book will serve in a similar capacity. If so, we urge you not to check your common sense at the door. Meanwhile, consider whether the possibility of malign or (more commonly, we think) inept performance by administrators bears on the desirability of the regulations we have considered in this book.

9. With all of this talk about disclosure, might there be a virtue in *mandatory* donor anonymity? The secrecy of the voting booth is sometimes defended as a way of preventing the corruption of voters; might a secret "donation booth" prevent the corruption of candidates and elected officials? See Bruce Ackerman and Ian Ayres, VOTING WITH DOLLARS: A NEW PARADIGM FOR CAMPAIGN FINANCE (2002), arguing for a combination of mandatory anonymity of donations and campaign finance vouchers. The book has received an extraordinary amount of scholarly commentary, including two symposia and a number of other reviews. Volume 91, Issue 3 (May 2003) of the CALIFORNIA LAW REVIEW features commentaries on the book by Richard Briffault, John Ferejohn, Pamela S. Karlan, and David Strauss (with a rejoinder by Ackerman and Ayres). Volume 37, Number 4 (May 2003) of the UNIVERSITY OF RICHMOND LAW REVIEW features commentaries on the book by Kathryn Abrams, Bruce E. Cain, Daniel A. Farber, Elizabeth Garrett, Richard L. Hasen, Kenneth R. Mayer, and Fred Wertheimer & Alexandra T.V. Edsall (with a response by Ackerman and Ayres). See also Lillian R. BeVier, *What Ails Us?* (Book Review), 112 YALE LAW JOURNAL 1135 (2003); Guy-Uriel E. Charles, *Mixing Metaphors: Voting, Dollars and Campaign Finance Reform* (Book Review), 2 ELECTION LAW JOURNAL 271 (2003); and Daniel H. Lowenstein, *Voting with Votes* (Book Review), 116 HARVARD LAW REVIEW 1971 (2003).

10. How does the ease of obtaining disclosure information on the Internet bear on the question of a right to anonymous political activity? See William McGeveran, *Mrs. McIntyre's Checkbook: Privacy Costs of Political Contribution Disclosure*, 6 UNIVERSITY OF PENNSYLVANIA JOURNAL OF CONSTITUTIONAL LAW 1 (2003).

11. For Part One of a symposium on campaign finance disclosure issues, see Volume 4, Number 4 (2005) of the ELECTION LAW JOURNAL. Part Two appeared in Volume 6, No. 1 (2007). Particularly noteworthy is the contribution by Democratic campaign lawyer Robert F. Bauer, who argues against campaign finance disclosure on grounds that it is a "gateway" for expanded regulation. Robert F. Bauer, *Not Just a Private Matter: The Purposes of Disclosure in an Expanded Regulatory System*, 6 ELECTION LAW JOURNAL 38 (2007).

12. In 2003, the Supreme Court decided a major campaign finance case, *McConnell v. Federal Election Commission*. Part of the case involved disclosure questions surrounding

"issue advocacy," a concept discussed in detail in Chapter 16. Be sure to review that chapter's discussion of issue advocacy before reading the excerpt below.

McConnell v. Federal Election Commission
540 U.S. 93 (2003)

JUSTICE STEVENS and JUSTICE O'CONNOR delivered the opinion of the Court with respect to BCRA [Title II.*]

IV

[The Court began this section of the opinion by upholding BCRA §201's definition of electioneering communications. "[A] plain reading of *Buckley* makes clear that the express advocacy limitation, in both the expenditure and the disclosure contexts, was the product of statutory interpretation rather than a constitutional command."]

[T]he constitutional objection that persuaded the Court in *Buckley* to limit FECA's reach to express advocacy is simply inapposite here.

BCRA §201's Disclosure Requirements

Having rejected the notion that the First Amendment requires Congress to treat so-called issue advocacy differently from express advocacy, we turn to plaintiffs' other concerns about the use of the term "electioneering communication" in amended FECA §304's disclosure provisions. Under those provisions, whenever any person makes disbursements totaling more than $10,000 during any calendar year for the direct costs of producing and airing electioneering communications, he must file a statement with the FEC identifying the pertinent elections and all persons sharing the costs of the disbursements. If the disbursements are made from a corporation's or labor union's segregated account, or by a single individual who has collected contributions from others, the statement must identify all persons who contributed $1,000 or more to the account or the individual during the calendar year. The statement must be filed within 24 hours of each "disclosure date"—a term defined to include the first date and all subsequent dates on which a person's aggregate undisclosed expenses for electioneering communications exceed $10,000 for that calendar year. Another subsection further provides that the execution of a contract to make a disbursement is itself treated as a disbursement for purposes of FECA's disclosure requirements.

In addition to the failed argument that BCRA's amendments to FECA §304 improperly extend to both express and issue advocacy, plaintiffs challenge amended FECA §304's disclosure requirements as unnecessarily (1) requiring disclosure of the names of persons who contributed $1,000 or more to the individual or group that paid for a communication, and (2) mandating disclosure of executory contracts for communications that have not yet aired. The District Court rejected the former submission but accepted the latter, finding invalid new FECA §304(f)(5), which governs executory contracts. Relying on BCRA's severability provision, the court held that invalidation of the executory contracts subsection did not render the balance of BCRA's amendments to FECA §304 unconstitutional.

We agree with the District Court that the important state interests that prompted the *Buckley* Court to uphold FECA's disclosure requirements—providing the electorate with

---

* JUSTICE SOUTER, JUSTICE GINSBURG, and JUSTICE BREYER join this opinion in its entirety.

information, deterring actual corruption and avoiding any appearance thereof, and gathering the data necessary to enforce more substantive electioneering restrictions—apply in full to BCRA. Accordingly, *Buckley* amply supports application of FECA §304's disclosure requirements to the entire range of "electioneering communications." As the authors of the District Court's *per curiam* opinion concluded after reviewing evidence concerning the use of purported "issue ads" to influence federal elections:

> The factual record demonstrates that the abuse of the present law not only permits corporations and labor unions to fund broadcast advertisements designed to influence federal elections, but permits them to do so while concealing their identities from the public. BCRA's disclosure provisions require these organizations to reveal their identities so that the public is able to identify the source of the funding behind broadcast advertisements influencing certain elections. Plaintiffs' disdain for BCRA's disclosure provisions is nothing short of surprising. Plaintiffs challenge BCRA's restrictions on electioneering communications on the premise that they should be permitted to spend corporate and labor union general treasury funds in the sixty days before the federal elections on broadcast advertisements, which refer to federal candidates, because speech needs to be 'uninhibited, robust, and wide-open.' McConnell Br. (quoting *New York Times Co. v. Sullivan*). Curiously, Plaintiffs want to preserve the ability to run these advertisements while hiding behind dubious and misleading names like: 'The Coalition-Americans Working for Real Change' (funded by business organizations opposed to organized labor), 'Citizens for Better Medicare' (funded by the pharmaceutical industry), 'Republicans for Clean Air' (funded by brothers Charles and Sam Wyly). Given these tactics, Plaintiffs never satisfactorily answer the question of how 'uninhibited, robust, and wide-open' speech can occur when organizations hide themselves from the scrutiny of the voting public. Plaintiffs' argument for striking down BCRA's disclosure provisions does not reinforce the precious First Amendment values that Plaintiffs argue are trampled by BCRA, but ignores the competing First Amendment interests of individual citizens seeking to make informed choices in the political marketplace.

The District Court was also correct that *Buckley* forecloses a facial attack on the new provision in §304 that requires disclosure of the names of persons contributing $1,000 or more to segregated funds or individuals that spend more than $10,000 in a calendar year on electioneering communications. Like our earlier decision in *NAACP v. Alabama ex rel. Patterson*, 357 U.S. 449 (1958), *Buckley* recognized that compelled disclosures may impose an unconstitutional burden on the freedom to associate in support of a particular cause. Nevertheless, *Buckley* rejected the contention that FECA's disclosure requirements could not constitutionally be applied to minor parties and independent candidates because the Government's interest in obtaining information from such parties was minimal and the danger of infringing their rights substantial. In *Buckley*, unlike *NAACP*, we found no evidence that any party had been exposed to economic reprisals or physical threats as a result of the compelled disclosures. We acknowledged that such a case might arise in the future, however, and addressed the standard of proof that would then apply:

> We recognize that unduly strict requirements of proof could impose a heavy burden, but it does not follow that a blanket exemption for minor parties is necessary. Minor parties must be allowed sufficient flexibility in the proof of injury to assure a fair consideration of their claim. The evidence offered need show only a reasonable probability that the compelled disclosure of a party's contributors' names will subject them to threats, harassment, or reprisals from either Government officials or private parties.

A few years later we used that standard to resolve a minor party's challenge to the constitutionality of the State of Ohio's disclosure requirements. We held that the First Amendment prohibits States from compelling disclosures that would subject identified persons to "threats, harassment, and reprisals," and that the District Court's findings had established a "reasonable probability" of such a result. *Brown v. Socialist Workers '74 Campaign Comm.*

In this litigation the District Court applied *Buckley*'s evidentiary standard and found—consistent with our conclusion in *Buckley*, and in contrast to that in *Brown*—that the evidence did not establish the requisite "reasonable probability" of harm to any plaintiff group or its members. The District Court noted that some parties had expressed such concerns, but it found a "lack of specific evidence about the basis for these concerns." We agree, but we note that, like our refusal to recognize a blanket exception for minor parties in *Buckley*, our rejection of plaintiffs' facial challenge to the requirement to disclose individual donors does not foreclose possible future challenges to particular applications of that requirement.

We also are unpersuaded by plaintiffs' challenge to new FECA §304(f)(5), which requires disclosure of executory contracts for electioneering communications.... In our view, this provision serves an important purpose the District Court did not advance. BCRA's amendments to FECA §304 mandate disclosure only if and when a person makes disbursements totaling more than $10,000 in any calendar year to pay for electioneering communications. Plaintiffs do not take issue with the use of a dollar amount, rather than the number or dates of the ads, to identify the time when a person paying for electioneering communications must make disclosures to the FEC. Nor do they question the need to make the contents of parties' disclosure statements available to curious voters in advance of elections. Given the relatively short time frames in which electioneering communications are made, the interest in assuring that disclosures are made promptly and in time to provide relevant information to voters is unquestionably significant. Yet fixing the deadline for filing disclosure statements based on the date when aggregate disbursements exceed $10,000 would open a significant loophole if advertisers were not required to disclose executory contracts. In the absence of that requirement, political supporters could avoid preelection disclosures concerning ads slated to run during the final week of a campaign simply by making a preelection down payment of less than $10,000, with the balance payable after the election. Indeed, if the advertiser waited to pay that balance until the next calendar year then, as long as the balance did not itself exceed $10,000, the advertiser might avoid the disclosure requirements completely.

The record contains little evidence identifying any harm that might flow from the enforcement of §304(f)(5)'s "advance" disclosure requirement. The District Court speculated that disclosing information about contracts "that have not been performed, and may never be performed, may lead to confusion and an unclear record upon which the public will evaluate the forces operating in the political marketplace." Without evidence relating to the frequency of nonperformance of executed contracts, such speculation cannot outweigh the public interest in ensuring full disclosure before an election actually takes place. It is no doubt true that §304(f)(5) will sometimes require the filing of disclosure statements in advance of the actual broadcast of an advertisement.[84] But the same would be true in the absence of an advance disclosure requirement, if a television station in-

---

84. We cannot judge the likelihood that this will occur, as the record contains little if any description of the contractual provisions that commonly govern payments for electioneering communications. Nor does the record contain any evidence relating to JUSTICE KENNEDY's speculation that advance disclosure may disadvantage an advertiser.

sisted on advance payment for all of the ads covered by a contract. Thus, the possibility that amended §304 may sometimes require disclosures prior to the airing of an ad is as much a function of the use of disbursements (rather than the date of an ad) to trigger the disclosure requirement as it is a function of §304(f)(5)'s treatment of executory contracts.

As the District Court observed, amended FECA §304's disclosure requirements are constitutional because they "d[o] not prevent anyone from speaking." Moreover, the required disclosures "would not have to reveal the specific content of the advertisements, yet they would perform an important function in informing the public about various candidates' supporters *before* election day." Accordingly, we affirm the judgment of the District Court insofar as it upheld the disclosure requirements in amended FECA §304 and rejected the facial attack on the provisions relating to donors of $1,000 or more, and reverse that judgment insofar as it invalidated FECA §304(f)(5).

JUSTICE THOMAS [concurring in the judgment in part and dissenting in part with respect to BCRA Title II.]

II.

[In a portion of Justice Thomas's dissent not reprinted here, he disagreed with the majority's position that the line between express advocacy and issue advocacy was constitutionally insignificant under *Buckley*.]

C

I must now address an issue on which I differ from all of my colleagues: the disclosure provisions in BCRA §201, now contained in new FECA §304(f). The "historical evidence indicates that Founding-era Americans opposed attempts to require that anonymous authors reveal their identities on the ground that forced disclosure violated the 'freedom of the press.'" *McIntyre* (THOMAS, J., concurring). Indeed, this Court has explicitly recognized that "the interest in having anonymous works enter the marketplace of ideas unquestionably outweighs any public interest in requiring disclosure as a condition of entry," and thus that "an author's decision to remain anonymous ... is an aspect of the freedom of speech protected by the First Amendment." *Id.* The Court now backs away from this principle, allowing the established right to anonymous speech to be stripped away based on the flimsiest of justifications.

The only plausible interest asserted by the defendants to justify the disclosure provisions is the interest in providing "information" about the speaker to the public. But we have already held that "[t]he simple interest in providing voters with additional relevant information does not justify a state requirement that a writer make statements or disclosures she would otherwise omit." *Id.* Of course, *Buckley* upheld the disclosure requirement on expenditures for communications using words of express advocacy based on this informational interest. And admittedly, *McIntyre* purported to distinguish *Buckley*. But the two ways *McIntyre* distinguished *Buckley*—one, that the disclosure of "an expenditure and its use, without more, reveals far less information [than a forced identification of the author of a pamphlet,];" and two, that in candidate elections, the "Government can identify a compelling state interest in avoiding the corruption that might result from campaign expenditures,"—are inherently implausible. The first is simply wrong. The revelation of one's political expenditures for independent communications about candidates can be just as revealing as the revelation of one's name on a pamphlet for a noncandidate election. See also *id.* (SCALIA, J., dissenting). The second was outright rejected in *Buckley* itself, where the Court concluded that independent expenditures did not create any substantial risk of real or apparent corruption. Hence, the only reading of *McIntyre* that remains consistent with the principles it contains is that it overturned *Buckley* to the extent that *Buckley* upheld a disclosure requirement solely based on the governmental interest in providing information to the voters.

The right to anonymous speech cannot be abridged based on the interests asserted by the defendants. I would thus hold that the disclosure requirements of BCRA §201 are unconstitutional. Because of this conclusion, the so-called advance disclosure requirement of §201 necessarily falls as well.[10]

JUSTICE KENNEDY, concurring in the judgment in part and dissenting in part with respect to BCRA [Title II.*]

II. TITLE II PROVISIONS
A. Disclosure Provisions

BCRA §201, which requires disclosure of electioneering communications, including those coordinated with the party but independent of the candidate, does not substantially relate to a valid interest in gathering data about compliance with contribution limits or in deterring corruption. As the above analysis of Title I demonstrates, Congress has no valid interest in regulating soft money contributions that do not pose *quid pro quo* corruption potential. In the absence of a valid basis for imposing such limits the effort here to ensure compliance with them and to deter their allegedly corrupting effects cannot justify disclosure. The regulation does substantially relate to the other interest the majority details, however. This assures its constitutionality. For that reason, I agree with the Court's judgment upholding the disclosure provisions contained in §201 of Title II, with one exception.

Section 201's advance disclosure requirement — the aspect of the provision requiring those who have contracted to speak to disclose their speech in advance — is, in my view, unconstitutional. Advance disclosure imposes real burdens on political speech that *post hoc* disclosure does not. It forces disclosure of political strategy by revealing where ads are to be run and what their content is likely to be (based on who is running the ad). It also provides an opportunity for the ad buyer's opponents to dissuade broadcasters from running ads. Against those tangible additional burdens, the Government identifies no additional interest uniquely served by advance disclosure. If Congress intended to ensure that advertisers could not flout these disclosure laws by running an ad before the election, but paying for it afterwards, then Congress should simply have required the disclosure upon the running of the ad. Burdening the First Amendment further by requiring advance dis-

---

10. BCRA §212(a) is also unconstitutional. Although the plaintiffs only challenge the advance disclosure requirement of §212(a), by requiring disclosure of communications using express advocacy, the entire reporting requirement is unconstitutional for the same reasons that §201 is unconstitutional. Consequently, it follows that the advance disclosure provision is unconstitutional.

BCRA §§311 and 504 also violate the First Amendment. By requiring any television or radio advertisement that satisfies the definition of "electioneering communication" to include the identity of the sponsor, and even a "full-screen view of a representative of the political committee or other person making the statement" in the case of a television advertisement, new FECA §318, §311 is a virtual carbon copy of the law at issue in *McIntyre* (the only difference being the irrelevant distinction between a printed pamphlet and a television or radio advertisement). And §504 not only has the precise flaws of §201, but also sweeps broadly as well, covering any "message relating to any political matter of national importance, including ... a national legislative issue of public importance." Hence, both §§311 and 504 should be struck down.

* [Chief Justice Rehnquist and Justice Scalia joined in this portion of Justice Kennedy's opinion.]

closure is not a constitutionally acceptable alternative. To the extent §201 requires advance disclosure, it finds no justification in its subordinating interests and imposes greater burdens than the First Amendment permits....

Notes and Questions

1. *Other BCRA disclosure provisions.* The majority also upheld BCRA §212 (adding a new disclosure requirement for those making independent expenditures of $1,000 or more during the 20-day period immediately preceding an election); BCRA §311 (requiring that certain communications authorized by a candidate or his committee clearly identify the candidate or committee, or, if not so authorized, identify the payor and announce the lack of authorization); and BCRA section 504 (amending the Communications Act of 1934 to require broadcasters to keep records of requests to broadcast certain advertisements by candidates and others). Section 504's "issue request" requirement is broadest of all, requiring broadcasters to keep records of requests made by anyone to broadcast "message[s]" related to a "national legislative issue of public importance" or "otherwise relating to a political matter of national importance."

Writing for a Court majority of five (Breyer, Ginsburg, O'Connor, Souter, and Stevens), Justice Breyer gave a number of reasons for the recordkeeping requirements, including that "recordkeeping can help both the regulatory agencies and the public evaluate broadcast fairness, and determine the amount of money that individuals or groups, supporters or opponents, intend to spend to help elect a particular candidate." He recognized that the "issue request" requirements could impose an administrative burden, and left open a challenge to FCC implementing regulations in the future. Chief Justice Rehnquist, joined by Justices Kennedy and Scalia (Justice Thomas dissented separately) dissented on the constitutionality of section 504. On the "issue request" provisions, the Chief Justice wrote that the requirement "is a far cry from the Government interests endorsed in *Buckley*, which were limited to evaluating and preventing corruption of federal candidates. See also *McIntyre*."

2. *The questionable vitality of* McIntyre. Justice Thomas' view of *McIntyre* is that it *sub silentio* overruled *Buckley* on the question whether the informational interest is ever sufficient to justify government-compelled disclosure of spending on election-related communications. Might it be said that *McConnell sub silentio* overruled *McIntyre*, so as to allow the informational interest alone to prevail? *McIntyre* is barely mentioned in the majority opinions. Footnote 88 in the Stevens/O'Connor majority opinion (not reprinted here) tersely distinguished the interests underlying BCRA from the interests in the *McIntyre* and *Bellotti* cases.

Justice Kennedy, joined by the Chief Justice and Justice Scalia, endorse the informational interest alone, as a sufficient basis for requiring disclosure of spending on electioneering communications. (Note, however, that Justice Kennedy fails to even mention the interest by name: "The regulation does substantially relate to the other interest the majority details, however.") Why does Justice Kennedy not consider whether the regulation is substantially overbroad as to disclosure? Why does Chief Justice Rehnquist not view the informational interest as sufficient to uphold BCRA §504?

3. As we saw in Chapter 16, the limits on corporate and union "electioneering communications" upheld in *McConnell* recently have been called into question by the Supreme Court's more recent ruling in *Wisconsin Right to Life v. FEC*. Following the issuance of the *WRTL* opinion, the Federal Election Commission engaged in a rulemaking to implement

the decision for the 2008 election. The FEC considered, but rejected, an exemption from BCRA's disclosure requirements for electioneering communications that may be paid for with corporate and union funds under the *WRTL* case. See Explanation and Justification for Regulations on Electioneering Communications, 72 Fed. Register 72899 (Dec. 26, 2007), http://www.fec.gov/law/cfr/ej_compilation/2007/notice_2007-26.pdf. The issue of the constitutionality of requiring disclosure of the funding of electioneering communications in light of *WRTL* is likely to be resolved by the courts.

4. To what extent does *McConnell* (assuming it remains good law on disclosure) resolve the other constitutional questions raised by the conflicts between *Buckley* and *McIntyre*? Consider Richard L. Hasen, *The Surprisingly Easy Case for Disclosure of Contributions and Expenditures Funding Sham Issue Advocacy*, 3 ELECTION LAW JOURNAL 251 (2004):

> *McConnell* unfortunately left open many other important questions concerning conflicts between [*Buckley* and *McIntyre*]. Even after *McConnell*, the constitutionality of disclosure rules in three important areas remains unclear: (1) To what extent may the government compel disclosure of a speaker's identity in face-to-face election-related communications or compel the disclosure of the funder of communications on the face of election-related documents? (2) To what extent may the government compel disclosure of expenditures by those using modest resources? (3) To what extent may the government compel disclosure of contributions and expenditures in ballot measure campaigns? Answers to these questions will await cases post-*McConnell*.

For an argument that *McConnell* "is good news for those who support disclosure regulations ... in both candidate and issue elections," see Elizabeth Garrett, McConnell v. FEC *and Disclosure*, 3 ELECTION LAW JOURNAL 237, 244 (2004).

5. In *Majors v. Abell*, 361 F.3d 349 (7th Cir. 2004), the Seventh Circuit, in an opinion by Judge Richard A. Posner, upheld an Indiana statute requiring political advertising that "expressly advocat[es] the election or defeat of a clearly identified candidate" to contain "a disclaimer that appears and is presented in a clear and conspicuous manner to give the reader or observer adequate notice of the identity of persons who paid for ... the communication." After surveying the confused precedent, including *McConnell*, the Court upheld the provision:

> As an original matter it could be objected that speech and the press would no longer be free if the government could insist that every speaker and every writer add to his message information that the government deems useful to the intended audience for the message, and that it is arbitrary for the government to single out the identity of the writer or speaker and decree that that information, though no other that potential voters might value as much or more, must be disclosed. But the Supreme Court crossed that Rubicon in *McConnell*. Reluctant, without clearer guidance from the Court, to interfere with state experimentation in the baffling and conflicted field of campaign finance law without guidance from authoritative precedent, we hold that the Indiana statute is constitutional. *Id.* at 355.

Judge Frank Easterbrook issued a separate opinion *dubitante* (expressing doubt, but not dissenting):

> [T]he Justices' failure [in *McConnell*] to discuss *McIntyre*, or even to cite *Talley*, *American Constitutional Law Foundation*, or *Watchtower*, makes it impossible for courts at our level to make an informed decision—for the Supreme Court has not told us what principle to apply. Does *McConnell* apply to all electioneering? All speakers? To primary communications (as opposed to notices sent

to agencies)? The Supreme Court wrote that [BCRA] §304 is valid because it is (in the view of five Justices) a wise balance among competing interests. Yet the function of the first amendment is to put the regulation of speech off limits to government *even if* regulation is deemed wise. For the judiciary to say that a law is valid to the extent that it is good is to operate as a council of revision and to deny the power of a written constitution to constrain contemporary legislation supported by the social class from which judges are drawn. And when, as in *McConnell*, the judgment is supported by a one-vote margin, any Justice's conclusion that a particular extension is unwise will reverse the constitutional outcome. How can legislators or the judges of other courts determine what is apt to tip the balance? *Id.* at 356.

In *American Civil Liberties Union of Nevada v. Heller*, 378 F.3d 979 (9th Cir. 2004), the Ninth Circuit struck down a Nevada statute requiring certain groups or entities publishing material or information related to a candidate or any question on a ballot to reveal on the publication the names and addresses of the publication's sponsors. Part of the court's decision striking down the statute depended upon a right to engage in anonymous speech recognized in *McIntyre*, and part depended upon problems specific to the Nevada statutory scheme. Despite the holding, the court noted that "[a]n on-publication identification requirement carefully tailored to further a state's campaign finance laws, or to prevent corruption of public officials, could well pass constitutional muster." The Ninth Circuit upheld Alaska's campaign finance regulations, including regulations requiring disclosure of "electioneering communications" modeled after BCRA. *Alaska Right to Life v. Miles*, 441 F.3d 773 (9th Cir. 2006). More recently, in *California Pro-Life Council v. Randolph*, 507 F.3d 1172 (9th Cir. 2007), a different panel of Ninth Circuit judges applied strict scrutiny and struck down California laws requiring certain non-profit organizations engaging in election-related activities to file detailed reports with the state's campaign finance agency.

At this point, given the confusion in the lower courts, students may wish to ask their instructors the following question: If smart judges like Judges Posner and Easterbrook cannot make sense out of the Supreme Court's campaign finance precedent, how do you expect us to do it?

Appendix

Election Law Research Guide

By Sara A. Sampson[a]

I. Introduction

Researching in the area of election law can be much more complicated than expected. One reason is that the search terms used to find cases and statutes on election law are frequently terms used in other legal areas in which elections occur. For example, even a well-written electronic database search to find cases concerning the proper procedure for counting ballots may return cases about corporate, church, or union elections as well as state, federal, and municipal government elections. Sometimes there is no way to avoid having to examine each case to determine its germaneness to your topic.

When writing a scholarly paper or doing in-depth research, it is important to find as many relevant sources as possible. Many of the resources described below allow searching by subject, as opposed to by particular words. Terms & connectors (also called "key word") searching merely finds a specific combination of words in a particular document. Terminology can vary across jurisdictions and over time. Overlooking a few key words or their synonyms may generate results that miss important articles, cases, or statutory provisions.

One way to avoid these problems is to search by subject. When conducting a subject search for cases, use West's topic and key number system or Lexis' Headnote searching. The topic of Elections is broken down into very discrete key numbers that allow a researcher to generate more precise results.

When doing a subject search for election law statutes, whether state or federal, it is important to use the index to find all of the relevant material. Relevant laws may be scattered throughout the code, even though an election law title or chapter exists. Furthermore, the code may use antiquated or local terminology Always consult the jurisdiction's election official's Web page as there may be directives, regulations and even letters to local election officials that affect the law at issue. For example, Ohio's Secretary of State's web page has links to directives that interpret Ohio election law provisions. These directives won't be found in a typical Westlaw or Lexis search.

You may also need to look outside of legal publications. Political science, sociology, history, economics, psychology and other disciplines may provide the support

---

a. Sara A. Sampson is the Head of Reference at the Georgetown University Law Library. The casebook authors thank Ms. Sampson for preparing this Appendix for inclusion in the casebook.

you need. For example, if you are advocating a change to the presidential elections from a weekday to the weekend to increase voter turnout, you may turn to sociology to determine how to predict group behavior, psychology to look at how to motivate individuals to vote, or world history to compare turnout and voting schedules in other jurisdictions.

When searching for law review articles, it is important to use an online index in addition to conducting key word searching in full text databases, such as Westlaw, Lexis, or HeinOnline. The index allows for subject searching and, therefore, ensures that all articles on a particular topic are found. Westlaw and Lexis provide the full-text of many articles, but both online services begin coverage for virtually all law journals in the early 1980s. HeinOnline, a subscription database, begins coverage for most journals with the first volume.

The next section lists election law resources by topic. Students in search of topics for papers will find that journals, blogs and websites of advocacy and interest groups are especially helpful places to find a topic on which to write. Note that your library may not have access to all of the resources described below. If you are not sure whether you have access or have trouble using a particular source or research technique (such as subject searching), consult your law librarian.

II. Election Law Resources

A. General Resources

Books & Journals

There is no currently updated general treatise on election law. A legal encyclopedia, such as *American Jurisprudence*, provides a general overview of most election law related topics as well as citations to important primary sources. To locate books on election law, searching your library's online catalog using the Library of Congress Subject Heading will provide precise search results. Possible subject headings are: Election law—United States, Voting research—United States, and Elections—United States. To browse your library's collection, be sure to visit the collection near JK 1800–2300 (which may include materials on the right to vote, voter behavior, election and campaign reform, money and politics, corruption, and political parties) and KF 4900 (which deals with all aspects of election law). If you have access to a large university library, be sure to explore their collection as well. To find materials your library does not have, you can search all library catalogs simultaneously via WorldCat (www.worldcat.org) and request materials via inter-library loan (ILL).

Congressional Quarterly's Guide to U.S. Elections provides extensive information about America's electoral system and political parties as well as statistics and summaries of presidential, congressional, and gubernatorial elections. Use the list of tables and figures at the beginning of each volume to quickly find compilations of statistics.

Election Law Journal started publication in 2002. Currently, this journal is available on Westlaw, but not on Lexis. Each issue has articles, book reviews, and reprints of important election law documents that may be difficult to find. The journal covers

United States and foreign election law topics. The journal is edited by Professors Lowenstein and Hasen.

Online Resources

CQ Voting and Elections Collection is the online version of many of CQ's popular publications. It has a wealth of statistical data and information on presidential, congressional, and gubernatorial elections, campaigns and elections political parties, voters and demographics. A subscription is required to access this database.

Ballot Access News, www.ballot-access.org, written by Richard Winger, covers a variety of election law developments, especially in relation to third parties and independent candidacies.

Electionline.org (www.pewcenteronthestates.org/initiatives_detail.aspx?initiativeID=34044) is a non-partisan organization dedicated to monitoring election reform news and analysis. They also publish in-depth reports on election administration subjects such as the Help America Vote Act.

Election Law Blog (http://electionlawblog.org), written by Professor Hasen, provides a way to stay up to date with election law news and developments. The search box allows for finding links to current election law controversies and issues.

Equal Vote (http://moritzlaw.osu.edu/blogs/tokaji) written by Professor Tokaji, discusses "election reform, the Voting Rights Act, the Help America Vote Act, and related topics—with special attention to the voting rights of people of color, non-English proficient citizens, and people with disabilities."

The Brennan Center for Justice at NYU School of Law (www.brennancenter.org) litigates cases and writes reports on various election law topics. The reports and case documents are available on its website.

The Campaign Legal Center (www.campaignlegalcenter.org) focuses on campaign finance and elections, political communication, and government ethics. It brings together information from the many government agencies responsible for campaign finance regulation.

Center for Competitive Politics (http://www.campaignfreedom.org/) seeks to educate the public on the actual effects of money in politics, and the results of a more free and competitive electoral process. Its web site contains a blog and various studies.

Demos' Democracy Program (http://www.demos.org/page13.cfm) focuses on election issues and publishes reports on issues such as campaign finance, Election Day registration, and election administration. Demos is carrying on the work of the National Voting Rights Initiative, which has archived information online (http://www.nvri.org).

Election Law @ Moritz (http://moritzlaw.osu.edu/electionlaw/index.php) provides analysis and updates on current election law issues. It follows approximately 30 pending election law cases and archives case documents.

Election Updates (http://electionupdates.caltech.edu/blog.html), written primarily by Professors Alvarez, Gronke, and Hall, focuses on election reform and election administration issues such as voting technology.

Votelaw (www.votelaw.com/blog), written by election law practitioner Ed Still, covers politics and law, including many election law topics.

B. Regulation of Campaign Finance and Campaign Speech

Books & Journals

To find materials on campaign finance topics in your library, do a subject search in the catalog for Campaign funds—Law and legislation—United States or browse near call numbers JK 1990 and KF 4920. Finding materials on free speech and campaign regulation is a bit more difficult because there is not a specific category for this topic in your library. Instead, you can do a key word search in the library catalog or combine these subjects Campaign funds—Law and legislation—United States and Freedom of speech— United States.

American Law Reports (ALR) also has many annotations on campaign finance topics. ALR annotations give a general overview of a topic along with a survey of the laws in many, if not all, United States jurisdictions. For example, *Validity, Construction, and Application of Campaign Finance Laws—Supreme Court Cases,* 12 A.L.R. Fed. 2d 1 (2007) provides a summary of the Supreme Court's jurisprudence in this area. These annotations will also provide references to relevant topic and keynumbers, law review articles, and ALR annotations on closely related topics. ALR annotations are available in print and on Westlaw.

Money & Politics Report (BNA, daily) focuses on campaign finance and lobbying issues at both the state and federal levels. It is available on Westlaw and Lexis.

Federal Election Campaign Financing Guide (CCH, updated regularly) is a looseleaf compilation of all statutes limiting the amount of contributions to candidates for federal office and expenditures from these campaigns. All FEC rules, regulations, proposed regulations, advisory opinion requests and issued advisory opinions are also included. There is also a compilation of forms required by the FEC.

Bipartisan Campaign Reform Act of 2002: Law and Explanation (CCH 2002) is an in-depth explanation of the Act and reproduces some legislative history documents.

Corporate Political Activities: Complying with Campaign Finance, Lobbying & Ethics Laws (PLI, currently published annually) is a compilation of handouts from a continuing education program on corporate political activities. While the content may vary each year, it usually provides an overview of current law and controversies.

Lobbying, PACs, and Campaign Finance: 50 State Handbook (Thomson West, published annually) surveys state legal requirements affecting lobbying and campaign finance. Some editions are available on Westlaw.

Online Resources

The FEC's website (www.fec.gov) contains the laws and regulations relating to federal campaigns, agency actions, and a disclosure database. The database is searchable by contributor information (name, city, state, zip code, principal place of business, date, and amount), candidate, or committee.

The Brookings Institution has a page devoted to campaign finance (www.brookings.edu/topics/campaign-finance.aspx).

The Campaign Finance Institute (www.cfinst.org) studies the policy of campaign finance. The institutes issues reports and analyzes FEC reports.

National Institute on Money in State Politics tracks campaign contributions at the state level and makes the information available on its website www.followthemoney.org.

Blogs: More Soft Money Hard Law (http://moresoftmoneyhardlaw.com), written by campaign finance lawyer Bob Bauer, and Skeptic's Eye (www.skepticseye.com/), written by Professor Allison Hayward, focus on campaign finance topics.

C. Election Administration

Because this topic concerns both federal and state law, be sure to search both federal and state case law using subject searching such as Westlaw's topic and key numbers as well as federal and state statutes.

Books & Journals

To find books on this topic, do a keyword search in the library catalog for the particular issue. Be sure to browse both the JK 1800-2300 area of your library as well as near KF 4900.

American Law Reports (ALR) also has many annotations on election administration topics. These annotations provide a general overview of a topic along with a survey of the laws in many, if not all, United States jurisdictions. For example, *Elections: Validity of State or Local Legislative Ban on Write-in Votes*, 69 A.L.R.4th 948 (1989) provides a nationwide summary of such bans and cases challenging their legality. While the annotation was published in 1989, it is kept current online and new cases are added as they become available on Westlaw. These annotations will also provide references to relevant topic and keynumbers, law review articles, and closely related ALR annotations. ALR annotations are available in print and on Westlaw.

Online Resources

The Election Assistance Commission (www.eac.gov) was created by the Help America Vote Act of 2002 and is charged with running the federal voting system certification program and issuing guidance to states about HAVA (including best practices guidance to state election officials). The EAC collects reports and statistics on all election administration issues such as turnout, alternative voting methods, voting systems, voting machines, and registration.

Election Law @ Moritz (http://moritzlaw.osu.edu/electionlaw) has many resources on election administration issues. In 2007, they released a study of five Midwestern states' voting systems. It is available online (http://moritzlaw.osu.edu/electionlaw/joyce/index.php) and in print form as Steven F. Huefner et al., *From Registration to Recounts* (2007).

D. Voting Rights Act & Reapportionment

Books & Journals

The Voting Rights Act is available at 42 U.S.C. §§ 1973 et seq. Peruse the annotations of the code and use subject searching in case law databases to find relevant cases. The regulations implementing the act are available in Title 51, parts 51 and 55 of the Code of Federal Regulations.

There have been many books and articles published on this topic. *The Voting Rights Act of 1965: A Selected Annotated Bibliography,* 98 Law Lib. J. 663 (2006) lists major books, articles, and online resources about the history and provisions of the Act, voting rights litigation, and the impact of the Act and its reauthorization. To find books about the Act, use the following subject headings in your library's catalog: United States—Voting Rights Act of 1965, United States Voting Rights Act, African Americans—Suffrage, and Minorities—Suffrage—United States, or browse near KF 4905. To find books and reports specifically about reapportionment, search your library's catalog with these subject headings: Apportionment (Election law)—United States, Election districts—United States, and Gerrymandering—United States or browse the library stacks near JK 1920 and KF 4890.

Online Resources

United States Department of Justice, Civil Rights Division, Voting Section (www.usdoj.gov/crt/voting) is charged with enforcing the Voting Rights Act. The website includes links to the text of the law, litigation brought by the section, and an introduction to federal voting rights legislation.

Purdue University (www.lib.purdue.edu/govdocs/redistricting.html) maintains a list of links to state redistricting websites.

E. Ballot Propositions

Books & Journals

These direct democracy tools are available at the state and local (but not federal) level, so be sure to search both federal and state case law and statutes. To find books about ballot propositions use the following subject headings in your library's catalog: Referendum or Initiative, Right of and browse near JF494 and KF 4800.

Exploring Initiative and Referendum Law (Haworth 2008) has a general overview of the topic and a state by state guide to the process, lists of general and state specific resources, and research tips.

The Initiative and Referendum Almanac (Carolina Academic Press 2003) provides a general overview of the topic and a step-by-step guide to using them. This text is not updated, so verify the text by reviewing state codes and case law. Some of this information is available online at the Initiative & Referendum Institute (www.iandrinstitute.org).

Direct Democracy in Europe: A Comprehensive Reference Guide to the Initiative and Referendum Process in Europe (Carolina Academic Press 2004) explores the initiative and referendum process in 32 European countries.

F. Violations of Election Law & Political Corruption

Books & Journals

American Jurisprudence has an overview of this area in *Elections* §§ 449–461. It includes bribery, illegal voting, intimidation of voters and offenses by election officials and campaign related offenses. In addition to a summary of the law and references to primary authority, *American Jurisprudence* identifies relevant topic and key numbers that can be used to find cases on the topic in a particular jurisdiction.

To find books related to this topic, search your library's catalog for the following subjects: Bribery and Political Corruption. For other topics, a key word search will be necessary.

G. Political Parties

Books & Journals

To find books, reports and other information about political parties, use the Political Parties—United States subject headings in your library's catalog and browse near JK 2260.

National Party Conventions (CQ, updated every four years) includes information on the conventions, including a narrative summary and a table of key votes, back to 1831.

Online Resources

Party websites often provide the party's platform and rules that govern the selection of party candidates. The Republican National Committee's website is available at www.rnc.org and the Democratic National Committee's online presence is at www.dnc.org.

H. Election Statistics

Books & Journals

There are many compilations of election statistics. To find books in your library, browse near call numbers JK 518–524 for presidential elections, JK 1010–1041 for congressional elections, and JK 1965–67 for general election related statistics.

America Votes (CQ Press, published annually) provides voting statistics by state for presidential, gubernatorial, and Congressional elections. It breaks some vote counts down by county, city or town.

The Almanac of State Legislative Elections: Voting Patterns and Demographics 2000–2006 (CQ) uses detailed demographic data to analyze voting behavior of all 6,744 state legislative districts.

Almanac of American Politics (National Journal, published biennially) has election results for state and national races, as well as astute analysis of the politics of every state and congressional district.

America at the Polls. (CQ, updated every 4 years) is a comprehensive analysis of presidential elections back to 1916.

Vital Statistics on American Politics (CQ, updated annually) included statistics on all types of political issues, including elections; specifically campaign finance, districting, minority elected officials, public opinion, results of national elections, term limits, turnout, voting equipment, and voting rights. Some statistical compilations and tables go back to 1789.

Online Resources

ANES (American National Election Studies) (www.electionstudies.org) produces statistics, data sets, and reports on voting, public opinion, and political participation in the United States. It also maintains a list of similar programs in other countries.

The United States Census Bureau provides data on voting and registration, some back to 1964 (www.census.gov/population/www/socdemo/voting.html) and provides the datasets used in redistricting (www.census.gov/clo/www/redistricting.html).

LexisNexis Statistical provides statistical data, including election information, from government and private sources. This subscription database is separate from the Lexis.com product most law students are familiar with.

I. Politics and Current Election News

CQpolitics.com (cqpolitics.com) provides breaking news coverage of political events as well as analysis of current political issues.

Political Wire (www.politicalwire.com) keeps up on the latest national political news.

Politico (www.politico.com) covers political news with a focus on national politics, Congress, Capitol Hill, lobbying, and advocacy. It also allows the reader to create an online profile that is similar to Facebook that allows readers to interact with each other in political chat rooms and blogs.

TheHill.com (www.TheHill.com) is the website for *The Hill*, which primarily focuses on the political side of Congress. It covers the Congressional calendar for upcoming legislation and unique editorials of the potential impact of pending legislation.

III. Conducting Interdisciplinary Research

Looking beyond legal topics can help support your arguments. Finding policy reasons that the law should be different or that one interpretation of a law or regulation is better can make an argument more persuasive. The resources described below can supply these policy arguments as well as support factual assertions with statistics, historical facts and news accounts of events.

CRS Reports are written for members of Congress by the Congressional Research Service (a division of the Library of Congress). The reports can analyze the policy, economic, and legal issues surrounding potential legislation, current issues, or any other topic requested by a member of Congress. The reports occasionally provide a statistical analysis of a current or proposed government program. There is no one database of these timely reports, but there are several compilations online. LLRX.com maintains a list of these compilations (www.llrx.com/features/crsreports.htm).

EconLit indexes worldwide economic scholarship. Because this is an index, full-text searching is not possible. Only the title, author, abstract, and subjects can be searched, so simple and broad searches will work well. This database can also lead to statistical reports. It is available through Westlaw.

Google Scholar uses the Google search functionality to search scholarly databases that are not included in Google. Unlike Google, the results are not always part of the free web and unless your library has a subscription to the database, you may have to purchase access to particular results. To make sure that you get the full benefit of your library's resources, set your Google Scholar preferences to include your school. Google Scholar searches HeinOnline's collection of law reviews but not the databases on Lexis or Westlaw. It can also be a good starting point in your policy or interdisciplinary research.

PAIS indexes scholarship and other publications in public policy, social policy and the social sciences. Because this is an index, full-text searching is not possible. Only the title, author, abstract, and descriptors can be searched, so simple and broad searches will work well. This database can also lead to statistical reports. This database is available through Westlaw.

PsychInfo is the leading index to worldwide psychology scholarship. It includes psychology's relationship to areas such as law, medical fields, sociology, education, and business. A law library is unlikely to have a subscription to this database. If your law school is affiliated with a University, you are likely to have access to the database through the University library.

Polling the Nations is a database of over 12,000 polls conducted by many groups around the world. There are polls relating to elections and voting and it is possible to search for polls by election year and location.

Social Science Research Network (SSRN) is a collection of working and forthcoming papers in a variety of social science disciplines, including accounting, finance, law, management, negotiations, and political science. It is the first place that many journal articles appear. The site's search feature searches just the abstract, title, keywords and author, so broad searches work best. Most papers can be downloaded from SSRN without a charge.

Social Sciences Citation Index is a citator (like Shepard's or KeyCite) for social science literature. If you have a relevant journal article or book, you can use it to find other sources from a variety of disciplines that cite the journal article or book and, presumably, are on the same topic. This database is sometimes called Web of Knowledge and is a subscription database.

Sociological Abstracts indexes international scholarship on sociology and other social and behavior sciences. Because this is an index, full-text searching is not possible. Only the title, author, abstract, and descriptors can be searched, so simple and broad searches will work well. This database can also lead to statistical reports. A law library is unlikely to have a subscription to this database. If your law school is affiliated with a University, you are likely to have access to the database through the University library.

Table of Cases

Page numbers in **bold** identify principal items. Page numbers in *italics* identify extended discussion or quotation. Only the first pages of these items are indicated. Subsequent histories of cases are omitted in this table.

United States v. Anderson, 509 F.2d 312 (D.C.Cir. 1974) 654

United States v. Arthur, 544 F.2d 730 (4th Cir. 1976) *652*

United States v. Brewster, 408 U.S. 501 (1972) *654*

United States v. Brewster, 506 F.2d 62 (D.C.Cir. 1974) 654

United States v. Carolene Products, 304 U.S. 144 (1938) 46

United States v. Carpenter, 961 F.2d 824 (9th Cir. 1992) 664

United States v. CIO, 335 U.S. 106 (1948) 680, 823

United States v. Classic, 313 U.S. 299 (1941) 437

United States v. Coyne, 4 F.3d 100 (2d Cir. 1993) 664

United States v. Gillock, 445 U.S. 360 (1980) 654

United States v. Hairston, 46 F.3d 361 (4th Cir. 1995) 664

United States v. Helstoski, 442 U.S. 477 (1979) 654

United States v. Isaacs, 493 F.2d 1124 (7th Cir. 1974) *651*

United States v. Kanchanalak 192 F.3d 1037 (D.C. Cir. 1999) 848

United States v. L'Hoste, 609 F.2d 796 (5th Cir. 1980) *652*

United States v. McCranie, 169 F.3d 723 (11th Cir. 1999) *346*

United States v. McDade, 827 F.Supp. 1153 (E.D. Pa. 1993) 662

United States v. Mokol, 957 F.2d 1410 (7th Cir. 1992) 663

United States v. Montoya, 945 F.2d 1068 (9th Cir. 1991) *661*

United States v. Sun-Diamond Growers of California, 526 U.S. 398 (1999) **666**

United States v. Torcasio, 959 F.2d 503 (4th Cir. 1992) 661

United States v. United Automobile Workers, 352 U.S. 567 (1957) 823

Upham v. Seamon, 456 U.S. 37 (1982) 104

Vander Jagt v. O'Neill, 699 F.2d 1166 (D.C.Cir. 1983) 447

Vander Linden v. Hodges, 193 F.3d 268 (4th Cir. 1999) 85

VanNatta v. Keisling, 151 F.3d 1215 (9th Cir. 1998) 770

Vieth v. Jubelirer, 541 U.S. 267 (2004) **257**

Vieth v. Pennsylvania, 188 F.Supp.2d 532 (M.D. Pa. 2002) 75

Vieth v. Pennsylvania, 195 F.Supp.2d 672 (M.D. Pa. 2002) 75

Voinovich v. Quilter, 507 U.S. 146 (1993) 73, 170

Volle v. Webster, 69 F. Supp. 2d 171 (D. Me. 1999) 935

Voting Rights Coalition v. Wilson, 60 F.3d 1411 (9th Cir. 1995) 341

Washington Federation of State Employees v. State, 901 P.2d 1028 (Wash. 1995) 382

Washington Initiatives Now v. Rippie, 213 F.3d 1132 (9th Cir. 2000) 937

Washington State Public Disclosure Commission v. Washington Education Association, 130 P.3d 352 (Wash. 2006) 796

Washington State Grange v. Washington State Republican Party, 128 S.Ct. 1184 (2008) 474, 514

Washington v. Seattle School District No. 1, 458 U.S. 457 (1982) 366

Watchtower Bible and Tract Society of New York v. Village of Stratton, 536 U.S. 150 (2002) 937

Weber v. Shelley, 347 F.3d 1101 (9th Cir. 2003) 312

Weber v. Smathers, 338 So.2d 819 (Fla. 1976) 384

Weld for Governor v. Director of the Office of Campaign and Political Finance, 556 N.E. 2d 21 (Mass. 1990) 938

Wells v. Edwards, 409 U.S. 1095 (1973) 86

Wesberry v. Sanders, 376 U.S. 1 (1964) *66*

Westwego Citizens for Better Government v. City of Westwego, 872 F.2d 1201 (5th Cir. 1989) 164

Table of Authorities

Page numbers in **bold** identify principal items. Page numbers in *italics* identify extended discussion or quotation. Only the first pages of these items are indicated.

viant" Voting and Redistricting Cases, 13 Journal of Contemporary Law 31 (1987) 98

Altman, Micah, The Computational Complexity of Automated Redistricting: Is Automation the Answer? 23 Rutgers Computer & Technology Law Journal 81 (1997) 251

Alvarez, R. Michael & Thad E. Hall, Electronic Elections: The Perils and Promise of Digital Democracy (2008) 307

Alvarez, R. Michael & Thad E. Hall, Point Click and Vote: The Future of Internet Voting (2004) 346, 348

Alvarez, R. Michael, Betsy Sinclair, & Richard L. Hasen, How Much is Enough? The "Ballot Order Effect" and the Use of Social Science Research in Election Law Disputes, 5 Election Law Journal 40 (2006) 553

Amy, Douglas J., Real Choices/New Voices: The Case for Proportional Representation Elections in the United States (1993) 175

Anderson, Eric S., Comment, Campaign Finance in Wisconsin After Buckley, 1976 Wisconsin Law Review 816 770

Anderson, John B. & Jeffrey L. Freeman, Taking the First Steps Towards a Multiparty System in the United States, 21 Fletcher Forum of World Affairs 73 (1997) 537

Anechiaricho, Frank & James B. Jacobs, The Pursuit of Absolute Integrity: How Corruption Control Makes Government Ineffective (1996) 669

Ansolabehere, Stephen, et al., Does Attack Advertising Demobilize the Electorate?, 88 American Political Science Review 829 (1994) 338

Ansolabehere, Stephen, David W. Brady & Morris Fiorina, The Vanishing Marginals and Electoral Responsiveness, 22 British Journal of Political Science 21 (1992) 597

Ansolabehere, Stephen & Alan Gerber, Incumbency Advantage and the Persistence of Legislative Majorities, 22 Legislative Studies Quarterly 161 (1997) 597

Ansolabehere, Stephen, Alan Gerber & James M. Snyder, Jr., Equal Votes, Equal Money: Court-Ordered Redistricting and the Distribution of Public Expenditures in the American States, 96 American Political Science Review 767 (2002) 72

Ansolabehere, Stephen, John M. de Figueiredo & James M. Snyder Jr., Why Is There So Little Money in U.S. Politics?, 17 Journal of Economic Perspectives 105 (2003) 714

Ansolabehere, Stephen & Shanto Iyengar, Going Negative: How Political Advertisements Shrink and Polarize the Electorate (1995) 551, 553

Ansolabehere, Stephen, James M. Snyder Jr. & Michiko Ueda, Did Firms Profit From Soft Money?, 3 Election Law Journal 193 (2004) 714

Ansolabehere, Stephen & James M. Snyder, The Incumbency Advantage in U.S. House Election: An Analysis of State and Federal Offices, 1942-2000, 1 Election Law Journal 315 (2002) 597

Apollonio, Dire E. & Raymond J. LaRaja, Incumbent Spending under Clean Election Laws, Western Political Science Association Annual Meeting (March 2005) 888

Arax, Mark & Rick Wartzman, The King of California: J.G. Boswell and the Making of a Secret American Empire (2003) 101

Arnold, R. Douglas, Can Inattentive Citizens Control Their Elected Representatives? in Congress Reconsidered (Lawrence C. Dodd & Bruce I. Oppenheimer, eds., 5th ed., 1993) 13

Arnold, R. Douglas, The Logic of Congressional Action (1990) 584

Askin, Frank, Political Money and Freedom of Speech: Kathleen Sullivan's Seven Deadly Sins—An Antitoxin, 31 U.C. Davis Law Review 1065 (1998) 733

Atwater, Lee, Altered States: Redistricting Law and Politics in the 1990s, 6 Journal of Law & Politics 661 (1990) 596

Auerbach, Carl A., The Reapportionment Cases: One Person, One Vote—One Vote, One Value, 1964 Supreme Court Review 252 (1964) 71

Backstrom, Charles, et al., Establishing a Statewide Effects Baseline, in Political Gerrymandering and the Courts (B. Grofman, ed., 1990) 144

Baker, C. Edwin, Campaign Expenditures and Free Speech, 33 Harvard Civil Rights-Civil Liberties Law Review 1 (1998) 734

Baker, Gordon E., Judicial Determination of Political Gerrymandering: A "Totality of Circumstances" Approach, 3 Journal of Law & Politics 1 (1986) 245

Baker, Lynn, Direct Democracy and Discrimination: A Public Choice Perspective, 67 Chicago-Kent Law Review 707 (1991) *404*

Baker, Lynn A., Preferences, Priorities, and Plebiscites, 13 Journal of Contemporary Legal Issues 313 (2004) 365

Balkin, Jack, Bush v. Gore and the Boundary Between Law and Politics, 110 Yale Law Journal 1407 (2001) 306

Banducci, Susan A., Direct Legislation: When Is It Used and When Does It Pass?, in Citizens as Legislators: Direct Democracy in the United States (Shaun Bowler, Todd Donovan & Caroline J. Tolbert, eds., 1998) 396

Banks, Christopher P. et al., eds., The Final Arbiter: The Consequences of Bush v. Gore for Law and Politics (2005) 305

Barone, Michael & Grant Ujifusa, The Almanac of American Politics 1994 (1993) 196, 217

Barone, Michael with Richard E. Cohen & Grant Ujifusa, The Almanac of American Politics 2004 (2003) 473

Baroni, Jr., Bill, Administrative Unfeasibility: The Torricelli Replacement Case and the Creation of a New Election Standard, 27 Seton Hall Legislative Journal 53 (2003) 399

Bartels, Larry M., Partisanship and Voting Behavior, 1952-1996, 44 American Journal of Political Science 35 (2000) 426

Basehart, Harry & John Comer, Redistricting and Incumbent Reelection Success in Five State Legislatures, 23 American Politics Quarterly 241 (1995) 251

Bauer, Monica & John R. Hibbing, Which Incumbents Lose in House Elections: A Response to Jacobson's "The Marginals Never Vanished," 33 American Journal of Political Science 262 (1989) 589

Bauer, Robert F., Not Just a Private Matter: The Purposes of Disclosure in an Expanded Regulatory System, 6 Election Law Journal 38 (2007) 939

Bauer, Robert, More Soft Money, Hard Law: The Second Edition of the Guide of the New Campaign Finance Law (2004) 791

Beck, Deborah, et al., Issue Advocacy During the 1996 Campaign (1997) 851

Bell, Jr., Derrick A., The Referendum: Democracy's Barrier to Racial Equality, 54 Washington Law Review 1 (1978) *366, 368*

Bennett, Robert W., Should Parents Be Given Extra Votes on Account of their Children? Toward a Conversational Understanding of American Democracy, 94 Northwestern University Law Review 503 (2000) 73

Bennett, Robert W., Taming the Electoral College (2006) 457

Benson, Jocelyn Friedrichs, Su Voto Es Su Voz: Incorporating Voters of Limited English Proficiency Into American Democracy, 48 Boston College Law Review 251 (2007) 340

Berinsky, Adam J. et al., Who Votes By Mail? A Dynamic Model of the Individual-Level Consequences of Vote-By-Mail Systems, 65 Public Opinion Quarterly 178 (2001) 346

Burke, Edmund, Speech to the Electors of Bristol, 1 Burke's Works (1854) 11

Burnham, Walter Dean, Critical Elections and the Mainsprings of American Politics (1970) 591

Burns, James MacGregor, The Deadlock of Democracy (1963) 419

Butler, David & Austin Ranney, Conclusion, in Referendums around the World (1994) 350

Butler, David & Bruce Cain, Congressional Redistricting: Comparative and Theoretical Perspectives (1992) 250

Butler, Katharine Inglis, Affirmative Racial Gerrymandering: Fair Representation for Minorities or a Dangerous Recognition of Group Rights?, 20 Rutgers Law Journal 595 (1995) 210

Butler, Katharine Inglis, Affirmative Racial Gerrymandering: Rhetoric and Reality, 26 Cumberland Law Review 313 (1996) 227

Butler, Katharine Inglis, Reapportionment, the Courts and the Voting Rights Act: A Resegregation of the Political Process?, 56 University of Colorado Law Review 1 (1984) 104, *119*

Bybee, Keith J., Mistaken Identity: The Supreme Court and the Politics of Minority Representation (1998) 182

Cain, Bruce E., Election Law as a Field: A Political Scientist's Perspective, 32 Loyola of Los Angeles Law Review 1105 (1999) *71*

Cain, Bruce E., Flaws Everywhere: A Review of a Badly Flawed Election, 2 Election Law Journal 525 (2003) 305

Cain, Bruce, Garrett's Temptation, 85 Virginia Law Review 1589 (1999) 619

Cain, Bruce E., Party Autonomy and Two Party Electoral Competition, 149 University of Pennsylvania Law Review 793 (2001) *472*

Cain, Bruce E., Moralism and Realism in Campaign Finance Reform, 1995 University of Chicago Legal Forum 111 722

Cain, Bruce E., The Reapportionment Puzzle (1984) 103, 248, 249

Cain, Bruce E. & Elizabeth R. Gerber, eds., Voting at the Political Fault Line: California's Experiment with the Blanket Primary (2001) 473

Cain, Bruce, John Ferejohn & Morris Fiorina, The Personal Vote: Constituency Service and Electoral Independence (1987) 593

Cain, Bruce E. & Kenneth P. Miller, The Populist Legacy: Initiatives and the Undermining of Representative Government, in Dangerous Democracy? The Battle over Ballot Initiatives in America (Larry J. Sabato, Howard R. Ernst & Bruce A. Larson, eds., 2001) 363

Calabresi, Steven G., Some Structural Consequences of the Increased Use of Ethics Probes as Political Weapons, 11 Journal Of Law & Politics 521 (1995) 669

Calhoun, John C., A Disquisition on Government (1993) [1853] 10, 360

California Commission on Campaign Financing, Democracy By Initiative (1992) *411*, 741, 744

California Commission on Campaign Financing, The New Gold Rush: Financing California's Legislative Campaigns (1985) 770

Cameron, Charles, David Epstein & Sharyn O'Halloran, Do Majority-Minority Districts Maximize Substantive Black Representation in Congress?, 90 American Political Science Association 794 (1996) *168, 184*

Campbell, Anne, In the Eye of the Beholder: The Single Subject Rule for Ballot Initiatives, in The Battle Over Citizen Lawmaking (M. Dane Waters, ed., 2001) *392*

Canon, David T., Race, Redistricting, and Representation: The Unintended Consequences of Black Majority Districts (1999) *177, 213*

Canon, David T., Renewing the Voting Rights Act: Retrogression, Influence, and the "Georgia v. Ashcroft Fix," 7 Election Law Journal 1 (2008) 139

Carvin, Michael A. & Louis K. Fisher, "A Legislative Task": Why Four Types of Redistricting Challenges are Not, or Should Not Be, Recognized by Courts, 4 Election Law Journal 2 (2005) 275

Charlow, Robin, Judicial Review, Equal Protection and the Problem with Plebiscites, 79 Cornell Law Review 527 (1994) *404*

Charles, Guy-Uriel E., Mixing Metaphors: Voting, Dollars and Campaign Finance Reform, 2 Election Law Journal 271 (2003) (Book Review) 939

Charles, Guy-Uriel & Luis Fuentes-Rohwer, Challenges to Racial Redistricting in the New Millennium: Hunt v. Cromartie as a Case Study, 58 Washington and Lee Law Review 227 (2001) 231

Chemerinsky, Erwin, Bush v. Gore Was Not Justiciable, 76 Notre Dame Law Review 1093 (2001) 306

Chemerinsky, Erwin, Protecting the Democratic Process: Voter Standing to Challenge Abuses of Incumbency, 49 Ohio State Law Journal 773 (1988) *609*

Chiles, Lawton, PAC's: Congress on the Auction Block, 11 Journal of Legislation 193 (1984) 770

Chin, Gabriel J., Reconstruction, Felon Disenfranchisement and the Right to Vote: Did the Fifteenth Amendment Repeal Section 2 of the Fourteenth Amendment?, 92 Georgetown Law Journal 249 (2004) 52

Choper, Jesse H., Observations on the Guarantee Clause—As Thoughtfully Addressed by Justice Linde and Professor Eule, 65 University of Colorado Law Review 741 (1994) 395

Citrin, Jack, Who's The Boss? Direct Democracy and Popular Control of Government, in Broken Contract? Changing Relationships Between Americans and Their Government (Stephen C. Craig, ed., 1996) 362

Clagett, Brice M. & John R. Bolton, Buckley v. Valeo, Its Aftermath, and Its Prospects: The Constitutionality of Government Restraints on Political Campaign Financing, 29 Vanderbilt Law Review 1327 (1976) 705, 708, *893*

Clark, Sherman J., The Character of Direct Democracy, 13 Journal of Contemporary Legal Issues 341 (2004) 365

Clark, Sherman J., A Populist Critique of Direct Democracy, 112 Harvard Law Review 434 (1998) 365

Coffee, John C., Modern Mail Fraud: The Restoration of the Public/Private Distinction, 35 American Criminal Law Review 427 (1998) 657

Cohen, Marty, David Karol, Hans Noel & John Zaller, Beating Reform: The Resurgence of Parties in Presidential Nominations (2001) 425

Collie, Melissa P., Incumbency, Electoral Safety, and Turnover in the House of Representatives, 1952-76, 75 American Political Science Review 119 (1981) 590

Comment, Judicial Intervention in Political Party Disputes: The Political Thicket Reconsidered, 22 UCLA Law Review 622 (1975) 435

Committee on Political Parties of the American Political Science Association, Toward a More Responsible Two Party System (reprinted as a supplement to 44 American Political Science Review No. 3, Part 2 (1950)) 420

Conlon, Richard P., The Declining Role of Individual Contributions in Financing Congressional Campaigns, 3 Journal of Law & Politics 467 (1987) 911

Cooper, Charles J. & Derek L. Shaffer, What Congress "Shall Make" The Court Will Take: How McConnell v. FEC Betrays the First Amendment in Upholding Incumbency Protection Under the Banner of "Campaign Finance Reform," 3 Election Law Journal 223 (2004) 790

Corrado, Anthony, Creative Campaigning: PACs and the Presidential Selection Process (1992) 890

Corrado, Anthony, Financing the 2004 Presidential General Election in Fi-

Eule, Julian N., Judicial Review of Direct Democracy, 99 Yale Law Journal 1503 (1990) *403*

Eule, Julian N., Promoting Speaker Diversity: Austin and Metro Broadcasting, 1990 Supreme Court Review 105 844

Eule, Julian N., Representative Government: The People's Choice, 67 Chicago-Kent Law Review 777 (1991) 404

Evseev, Dmitri, A Second Look at Third Parties: Correcting the Supreme Court's Understanding of Elections, 85 Boston University Law Review 1277 (2005) 514

Fair Political Practices Commission, Campaign Contributions and Spending Report, November 7, 1978 General Election 744

Farber, Daniel A. & John E. Nowak, The Misleading Nature of Public Forum Analysis: Content and Context in First Amendment Adjudication, 70 Virginia Law Review 1219 (1984) 539

Farber, Daniel A. & Philip P. Frickey, Law and Public Choice: A Critical Introduction (1991) 22

Farber, Daniel A., The Outmoded Debate Over Affirmative Action, 82 California Law Review 893 (1994) 179

Farnsworth, Ward, "To Do a Great Right, Do a Little Wrong": A User's Guide to Judicial Lawlessness, 86 Minnesota Law Review 227 (2001) 302

Fenno, Jr., Richard F., Congressmen in Committees (1973) 583

Fenno, Jr., Richard F., Home Style: House Members in Their Districts (1978) 593, 594

Fenster, Mark J., The Impact of Allowing Day of Registration Voting on Turnout in U.S. Elections from 1960 to 1992, 22 American Politics Research 74 (1994) 345

Ferejohn, John A., On the Decline of Competition in Congressional Elections, 71 American Political Science Review 166 (1977) 591

Fienberg, Stephen E., The New York City Census Adjustment Trial: Witness for the Plaintiffs, 34 Jurimetrics 65 (1993) 78

Fiorina, Morris P., Congress: Keystone of the Washington Establishment (2d ed. 1989) 428, 645

Fiorina, Morris P., The Decline of Collective Responsibility in American Politics 109 Daedalus 25 (1980) **421**

Fiorina, Morris P., Divided Government (1992) 433

Fiorina, Morris P., An Era of Divided Government, in Developments in American Politics (Gillian Peele et al., eds., 1992) 432, 596

Fiorina, Morris P., Retrospective Voting in American National Elections (1981) 423

Fisch, Jill E., Frankenstein's Monster Hits the Campaign Trail: An Approach to Regulation of Corporate Political Expenditures, 32 William & Mary Law Review 587 (1991) 822

Fiss, Owen M., Free Speech and Social Structure, 71 Iowa Law Review 1405 (1986) *702*

Fitts, Michael A., Look Before You Leap: Some Cautionary Notes on Civic Republicanism, 97 Yale Law Journal 1651 (1988) *23*

Fitts, Michael A., The Vices of Virtue: A Political Party Perspective on Civic Virtue Reforms of the Legislative Process, 136 University of Pennsylvania Law Review 1567 (1988) 23

Fitts, Michael & Robert Inman, Controlling Congress: Presidential Influence in Domestic Fiscal Policy, 80 Georgetown Law Journal 1737 (1992) 14

Flanders, Chad, Bush v. Gore and the Uses of "Limiting," 116 Yale Law Journal 1159 (2007) 306

Fleishman, Joel L., The 1974 Federal Election Campaign Act Amendments: The Shortcomings of Good Intentions, 1975 Duke Law Journal 851 *527*

Fleishman, Joel L. & Pope McCorkle, Level-Up Rather Than Level-Down:

Martinez, Michael D. & David Hill, Did Motor Voter Work?, 27 American Politics Quarterly 296 (1999) 342

Matsusaka, John G., Direct Democracy and Social Issues (unpublished paper, May 2007) 363

Matsusaka, John G, For the Many or for the Few (2004) 363

Mayer, Kenneth, Timothy Werner & Amanda Williams, Do Public Funding Programs Enhance Electoral Competition?, in The Marketplace of Democracy (Michael P. McDonald & John Samples, eds., 2006) 877

Mayer, William & Andrew E. Busch, The Front-Loading Problem in Presidential Elections (2004) 450

Mayhew, David R., Congress: The Electoral Connection (1974) 582

Mayhew, David R., Congressional Elections: The Case of the Vanishing Marginals, 6 Polity 295 (1974) 587

Mayhew, David R., Divided We Govern: Party Control, Lawmaking and Investigations, 1946-1990 (1990) 433, 596

Mazmanian, Daniel A., Third Parties in Presidential Elections (1974) 528

Mazur, Diane H., The Bullying of America: A Cautionary Tale about Military Voting and Civil-Military Relations, 4 Election Law Journal 105 (2005) 306

McAdams, John C. & John R. Johannes, Congressmen, Perquisites, and Elections, 50 Journal of Politics 412 (1988) 593

McCrary, Peyton, Bringing Equality to Power: How the Federal Courts Transformed the Electoral Structure of Southern Politics 1960-1965, 5 University of Pennsylvania Journal of Constitutional Law 665 (2003) 37

McCrary, Peyton, Christopher Seaman & Richard Valelly, The Law of Preclearance Enforcing Section 5, in David Epstein et al., eds. The Future of the Voting Rights Act (2006) 131

McDonald, Michael P., Portable Voter Registration, 30 Political Behavior ___ (2008) 345

McDonald, Michael P. & Samuel L. Popkin, The Myth of the Vanishing Voter, 95 American Political Science Review 963 (2001) 334

McDonald, Michael & John Samples, The Marketplace of Democracy: Normative and Empirical Issues, in The Marketplace of Democracy: Electoral Competition and American Politics (Michael McDonald & John Samples, eds., 2006) 620

McDowell, James L., "One Person, One Vote" and the Decline of Community, 23 Legal Studies Forum 131 (1999) 75

McFarland, Andrew S., Neopluralism (2004) 20

McGeveran, William, Mrs. McIntyre's Checkbook: Privacy Cost of Political Contribution Disclosure, 6 University of Pennsylvania Journal of Constitutional Law 1 (2003) 939

Meier, Kenneth J. & Thomas M. Holbrook, "I Seen My Opportunities and I Took 'Em:" Political Corruption in the American States, 54 Journal of Politics 135 (1992) 656

Melinkoff, David, Melinkoff's Dictionary of American Legal Usage (1992) 651

Mercurio, Bryan, Democracy in Decline: Can Internet Voting Save the Electoral Process?, 22 John Marshall Journal of Computer and Information Law 409 (2004) 348

Michael, Douglas, Comment, Judicial Review of Initiative Constitutional Amendments, 14 UC Davis Law Review 461 (1980) 402

Michelman, Frank I., Conceptions of Democracy in American Constitutional Argument: Voting Rights, 41 Florida Law Review 443 (1989) 50, 98

Michelman, Frank, Political Markets and Community Self-Determination: Competing Judicial Models for Local Government Legitimacy, 53 Indiana Law Journal 145 (1977-78) 98

Michelman, Frank, Political Truth and the Rule of Law, 8 Tel Aviv University Studies in Law 281 (1988) 704

Note, Freedom of Association and Selection of Delegates to National Political Conventions, 56 Cornell Law Review 148 (1970) 453

Note, Governmental Referendum Advocacy: An Emerging Free Speech Problem, 29 Case Western Reserve Law Review 886 (1979) 611

Note, The Future of Majority-Minority Districts in Light of Declining Racially Polarized Voting, 116 Harvard Law Review 2208 (2003) 165

Note, The Supreme Court, 1985 Term, 100 Harvard Law Review 100 (1986) 255

O'Rourke, Timothy G., The 1982 Amendments and the Voting Rights Paradox, in The Voting Rights Act: A Brief History, in Controversies in Minority Voting (Bernard Grofman & Chandler Davidson, eds., 1992) 119, 179

O'Rourke, Timothy G., The Impact of Reapportionment (1980) 72

Oakland, William H., Proposition 13: Genesis and Consequences, in The Property Tax Revolt: The Case of Proposition 13 (1981) 378

Olson, Mancur, the Logic of Collective Action (1965) 19

Oppenheimer, Bruce J., Deep Red and Blue Congressional Districts, in Lawrence C. Dodd & Bruce I. Oppenheimer, eds., Congress Reconsidered (8th ed. 2005) 587, 592

Orr, Graeme, A Politician's Word: The Legal (Un)enforceability of Political Deals, 5 Constitutional Law & Policy Review 1 (2002) 434

Ortiz, Daniel R., The Democratic Paradox of Campaign Finance Reform, 50 Stanford Law Review 893 (1998) 735

Ortiz, Daniel R., Water, Water Everywhere, 77 Texas Law Review 1739 (1999) 735

Overton, Spencer, But Some Are More Equal: Race, Exclusion, and Campaign Finance, 80 Texas Law Review 987 (2002) 733

Overton, Spencer A., Mistaken Identity: Unveiling the Property Characteristics of Political Money, 53 Vanderbilt Law Review 1235 (2000) 768

Overton, Spencer A., Rules, Standards and Bush v. Gore: Forms and the Law of Democracy, 37 Harvard Civil Rights-Civil Liberties Law Review 65 (2002) 306

Overton, Spencer, Stealing Democracy: The New Politics of Voter Suppression (2006) 340

Overton, Spencer, The Donor Class: Campaign Finance, Democracy, and Participation, 153 University of Pennsylvania Law Review 73 (2004) 733

Overton, Spencer A., Voter Identification, 105 Michigan Law Review 621 (2007) 331

Owens, John R. & Larry L. Wade, Campaign Spending on California Ballot Propositions, 1924-1984: Trends and Voting Effects, 39 Western Political Quarterly 675 (1986) 741

Pace, Joseph Michael, Public Funding of Presidential Campaigns and Elections: Is There a Viable Future?, 24 Presidential Studies Quarterly 139 (1994) 891

Parker, Frank R., The Constitutionality of Racial Redistricting: A Critique of Shaw v. Reno, 3 District of Columbia Law Review 1 (1995) 216

Parson, E. Earl & Monique McLaughlin, The Persistence of Racial Bias in Voting: Voter ID, the New Battleground for Pretextual Race Neutrality, 8 Journal of Law in Society 75 (2007) 330

Patterson, Kelly D., Spending in the 2004 Election, in Financing the 2004 Elections (David B. Magleby, Anthony Corrado & Kelly D. Patterson, eds., 2006) 678

Patterson, Thomas E., Out of Order (1994) 551

Patton, William & Randall Bartlett, Corporate "Persons" and Freedom of Speech: The Political Impact of Legal Mythology, 1981 Wisconsin Law Review 494 844

Peacock, Anthony, Reconstructing the Republic: Voting Rights, the Supreme Court, and the Founders' Republicanism Reconsidered (2008)

Peltason, Jack W., Constitutional Law for Political Parties, in On Parties: Essays Honoring Austin Ranney (Nelson W. Polsby & Raymond F. Wolfinger, eds., 1999) 434

Pennock, J. Roland, Democratic Theory (1979) 3

Pennock, J. Roland, Responsiveness, Responsibility and Majority Rule, 46 American Political Science Review 790 (1952) 420

Persily, Nathaniel, Candidates v. Parties: The Constitutional Constraints on Primary Ballot Access Laws, 89 Georgetown Law Journal 2181 (2002) 517

Persily, Nathaniel, Color by Numbers: Race, Redistricting, and the 2000 Census, 85 Minnesota Law Review 899 (2001) 78

Persily, Nathaniel, In Defense of Foxes Guarding Henhouses: The Case for Judicial Acquiescence to Incumbent-Protecting Gerrymanders, 116 Harvard Law Review 649 (2002) 252, 620

Persily, Nathaniel A., The Peculiar Geography of Direct Democracy: Why the Initiative, Referendum and Recall Developed in the American West, 2 Michigan Law & Policy Review 11 (1997) 349

Persily, Nathaniel, The Promise and Pitfalls of the New Voting Rights Act, 117 Yale Law Journal 174 (2007) 140

Persily, Nathaniel, The Right to Be Counted, 53 Stanford Law Review 1077 (2001) 78

Persily, Nathaniel, Toward a Functional Defense of Political Party Autonomy, 76 New York University Law Review 750 (2001) 473

Persily, Nathaniel & Kelli Lammie, Perceptions of Corruption and Campaign Finance: When Public Opinion Determines Constitutional Law, 153 University of Pennsylvania Law Review 119 (2004) 715

Petrocik, John R., Divided Government: Is It All in the Campaigns?, in The Politics of Divided Government (Gary W. Cox & Samuel Kernell, eds., 1991) 432

Pildes, Richard H., Foreword: The Constitutionalization of Democratic Politics, 118 Harvard Law Review 28 (2004) 301

Pildes, Richard H., The Theory of Political Competition, 85 Virginia Law Review 1605 (1999) 619

Pildes, Richard H., Is Voting-Rights Law Now at War With Itself? Social Science and Voting Rights in the 2000's, 80 North Carolina Law Review 1517 (2002) 139

Pildes, Richard H., Political Avoidance, Constitutional Theory, and the VRA, 117 Yale Law Journal Pocket Part 148 (2007) 141

Pildes, Richard H., The Theory of Political Competition, 85 Virginia Law Review 1605 (1999) 619

Pildes, Richard H., Why Rights are Not Trumps: Social Meanings, Expressive Harms, and Constitutionalism, 27 Journal of Legal Studies 725 (1998) 46

Pildes, Richard H. & Richard G. Niemi, Expressive Harms, "Bizarre Districts," and Voting Rights: Evaluating Election-District Appearances After Shaw v. Reno, 92 Michigan Law Review 483 (1993) 161, 211

Pinto-Duschinsky, Michael, A Reply to the Critics, 36 Representation 148 (1999) 175

Pinto-Duschinsky, Michael, Send the Rascals Packing: Defects of Proportional Representation and the Virtues of the Westminster Model, 36 Representation 117 (1999) 175

Pitkin, Hanna, The Concept of Representation (1967) 13

Pitts, Michael J., Let's Not Call the Whole Thing Off Just Yet: A Response

Ranney, Austin, The Doctrine of Responsible Party Government (1954) 419

Raskin, Jamin B., The Debate Gerrymander, 77 Texas Law Review 1943 (1999) *546, 548*

Raskin, Jamin B., Legal Aliens, Local Citizens: The Historical, Constitutional and Theoretical Meanings of Alien Suffrage, 141 University of Pennsylvania Law Review 1391 (1993) *53*

Raskin, Jamin & John Bonifaz, The Constitutional Imperative and Practical Superiority of Democratically Financed Elections, 94 Columbia Law Review 1160 (1994) 733

Rawls, John, Political Liberalism 362 (1993) 704

Rawls, John, A Theory of Justice 60 (1971) 3

Reader, Scot A., One Person, One Vote Revisited: Choosing a Population Basis to Form Political Districts, 17 Harvard Journal of Law & Public Policy 521 (1994) 73

Reichley, James A., The Rise of National Parties, in The New Direction in American Politics (J. Chubb & P. Peterson, eds., 1985) 417

Riker, William H., Democracy and Representation: A Reconciliation of Ball v. James and Reynolds v. Sims, 1 Supreme Court Economic Review 39 (1982) *97*

Riker, William H., The Number of Political Parties: A Reexamination of Duverger's Law, 9 Comparative Politics 93 (1976) 503

Rogowski, Ronald, Representation in Political Theory and in Law, 91 Ethics 395 (1981) 247

Rosberg, Gerald M., Aliens and Equal Protection: Why Not the Right to Vote?, 75 Michigan Law Review 1092 (1977) 50

Rose-Ackerman, Susan, Corruption: A Study in Political Economy (1978) 631

Rosenkranz, E. Joshua, Faulty Assumptions in "Faulty Assumptions": A Response to Professor Smith's Critiques of Campaign Finance Reform 30 Connecticut Law Review 867 (1998) 733

Rosenstone, Steven J., Roy L. Behr & Edward H. Lazarus, Third Parties in America (2d ed. 1996) *504*

Ross, Tara, Enlightened Democracy: The Case for the Electoral College (2004) 457

Rotunda, Ronald D., Constitutional and Statutory Restrictions on Political Parties in the Wake of Cousins v. Wigoda, 53 Texas Law Review 935 (1975) 439, 453

Rush, Mark E, The Hidden Costs of Electoral Reform, in Mark E. Rush & Richard L. Engstrom, Fair and Effective Representation? Debating Electoral Reform and Minority Rights (2001) 175

Rush, Mark E., Making the House More Representative: Hidden Costs and Unintended Consequences, in The U.S. House of Representatives: Reform or Rebuild? (Joseph F. Zimmerman & Wilma Rule, eds., 2000) 175

Rutherford, Thomas, The People Drunk or the People Sober? Direct Democracy Meets the Supreme Court of Florida, 15 St. Thomas Law Review 61 (2002) 384

Sabato, Larry J., The Party's Just Begun: Shaping Political Parties for America's Future (1988) 591

Sabato, Larry J. & Glenn R. Simpson, Dirty Little Secrets (1996) 913

Samish, Arthur H. & Bob Thomas, The Secret Boss of California (1971) *819*

Saphire, Richard B. & Paul Moke, Litigating Bush v. Gore in the States: Dual Voting Systems and the Fourteenth Amendment, 51 Villanova Law Review 229 (2006) 307

Saunders, Melissa L., A Cautionary Tale: Hunt v. Cromartie and the Next Generation of Shaw Litigation, 1 Election Law Journal 173 (2002) 231

Saunders, Melissa L., The Dirty Little Secrets of Shaw, 24 Harvard Journal of Law and Public Policy 141 (2000) 210

Saunders, Melissa L., Reconsidering Shaw: The Miranda of Race-Conscious Districting, 109 Yale Law Journal 1603 (2000) 211

Scarrow, Howard A., Duverger's Law, Fusion, and the Decline of American "Third" Parties, 39 Western Political Quarterly 634 (1986) 528

Schattschneider, E.E., Party Government (1942) *503*

Schauer, Frederick, Judicial Review of the Devices of Democracy, 94 Columbia Law Review 1326 (1994) 712

Schlesinger, Joseph, On the Theory of Party Organizations, 46 Journal of Politics 369 (1984) 419

Schlozman, Kay Lehman & John T. Tierney, Organized Interests and American Democracy (1986) 714

Schneider, Carl E., Free Speech and Corporate Freedom: A Comment on First National Bank of Boston v. Bellotti, 59 Southern California Law Review 1227 (1986) *821*

Schotland, Roy A., Act I: BCRA Wins In Congress. Act II: BCRA Wins Big at the Court. Act III: BCRA Loses to Reality, 3 Election Law Journal 335 (2004) 768

Schotland, Roy A., Demythologizing Public Funding, Georgetown Journal of Law and Ethics (forthcoming 2008) 876

Schotland, Roy A., Financing Judicial Elections, 2000: Change and Challenge, 2001 Law Review of Michigan State University Detroit College of Law 849 769

Schotland, Roy A., In Bush v. Gore: Whatever Happened to the Due Process Ground?, 34 Loyola University of Chicago Law Journal 211 (2002) 301

Schotland, Roy A., Proposals for Campaign Finance Reform: An Article Dedicated to Being Less Dull Than Its Title, 21 Capital University Law Review 429 (1992) 733

Schrag, Peter, Paradise Lost: California's Experience, America's Future (1998) 360

Schuck, Peter H., Against (and For) Madison: An Essay in Praise of Factions, 15 Yale Law & Policy Review 553 (1997) 8

Schuck, Peter H., The Thickest Thicket: Partisan Gerrymandering and Judicial Regulation of Politics, 87 Columbia Law Review 1325 (1987) 247, 254

Schultz, David, Less than Fundamental: The Myth of Voter Fraud and the Coming of the Second Great Disenfranchisement, 34 William Mitchell Law Review 438 (2008) 330

Schuman, David, The Origin of State Constitutional Direct Democracy: William Simon U'Ren and "The Oregon System," 67 Temple Law Review 947 (1994) 349

Schumpeter, Capitalism, Socialism and Democracy (1942) 419

Schwartzchild, Maimon, Popular Initiatives and American Federalism, Or, Putting Direct Democracy In Its Place, 13 Journal of Contemporary Legal Issues 531 (2004) 361

Shafer, Byron E., Quiet Revolution: The Struggle for the Democratic Party and the Shaping of Post-Reform Politics (1983) 449

Shambon, Leonard, Implementing the Help America Vote Act, 3 Election Law Journal 424 (2004) 342

Shambon, Leonard & Keith Abouchar, Trapped by Precincts? The Help America Vote Act's Provisional Ballots and the Problem of Precincts, 10 N.Y.U. Journal of Legislation & Public Policy 133 (2006-2007) 343

Shapiro, David L., Mr. Justice Rehnquist: A Preliminary View, 90 Harvard Law Review 293 (1976) 52

Shapiro, Martin, Corruption, Freedom and Equality in Campaign Financing, 18 Hofstra Law Review 385 (1989) *721*

Shapiro, Martin, Gerrymandering, Unfairness, and the Supreme Court, 33 UCLA Law Review 227 (1985) *244,* 247

56 Vanderbilt Law Review 395 (2003) 362

Stedman Murray S., & Herbert Sonthoff, Party Responsibility—A Critical Inquiry, 4 Western Political Quarterly 454 (1951) 420

Stein, Robert M. et al., Voting Technology, Election Administration, and Voter Performance, 7 Election Law Journal 123 (2008) 307

Steinberg, Jonathan H. and Aimee Dudovitz, Branch v. Smith - Election Law Federalism After Bush v. Gore - Are State Courts Unconstitutional Interlopers in Congressional Redistricting?, 2 Election Law Journal 91 (2003) 114

Stewart, Charles, Residual Vote in the 2004 Election, 5 Election Law Journal 158 (2006) 307

Stratmann, Thomas, Ballot Access Restrictions and Candidate Entry in elections, 21 European Journal of Political Economy 59 (2005) 517

Strauss, David A., What is the Goal of Campaign Finance Reform?, 1995 University of Chicago Legal Forum 141 *722*

Sullivan, Kathleen M., Political Money and Freedom of Speech, 30 U.C. Davis Law Review 663 (1997) 702, 722, 733, 734, 913

Sundquist, James L., Needed: A Political Theory for the New Era of Coalition Government in the United States, 103 Political Science Quarterly 613 (1988) 432, 596

Sunstein, Cass R., Beyond the Republican Revival, 97 Yale Law Journal 1539 (1988) *22*

Sunstein, Cass R., Political Equality and Unintended Consequences, 94 Columbia Law Review 1390 (1994) *703, 734, 735*

Sunstein, Cass R. & Richard A. Epstein, eds., The Vote: Bush, Gore and the Supreme Court, (2001) 305

Swain, Carol M., Black Faces, Black Interests (1993) *178, 183*

Symposium: Baker v. Carr: A Commemorative Symposium, 80 North Carolina Law Review 1103 (2002) 66

Symposium: The Bill of Rights vs. the Ballot Box: Constitutional Implications of Anti-Gay Ballot Initiatives, 55 Ohio State Law Journal 491 (1994) 367

Symposium, Election Law as Its Own Field of Study, 32 Loyola of Los Angeles Law Review 1095 (1999) 24

Symposium, National Summit on Improving Judicial Selection: Call to Action, 34 Loyola of Los Angeles Law Review 1353 (2001) 769

Taormina, Rosanna M., Comment, Defying One-Person, One-Vote: Prisoners and the "Usual Residence" Principle, 152 University of Pennsylvania Law Review 431 (2003) 53

Teixeira, Ruy A., The Disappearing American Voter 9 (1992) 333

Thernstrom, Abigail M., Whose Votes Count? (1987) *177*

Thomas, Scott J., Do Incumbent Campaign Expenditures Matter?, 51 Journal of Politics 965 (1989) 716

Thompson, Dennis F., Mediated Corruption: The Case of the Keating Five, 87 American Political Science Review 369 (1993) *663, 674*

Tocqueville, Alexis de, Democracy in America (Phillips Bradley, ed., 1945) *335*, 360

Tokaji, Daniel P., The Birth and Rebirth of Election Administration, 6 Election Law Journal 118 (2007) (Book Review) 281, 331

Tokaji, Daniel P., Early Returns on Election Reform: Discretion, Disenfranchisement, and the Help America Vote Act, 73 George Washington Law Review 1206 (2005) 304, 342

Tokaji, Daniel P., First Amendment Equal Protection, 101 Michigan Law Review 2409 (2003) 301

Tokaji, Daniel P., Intent and Its Alternatives: Defending the New Voting

Rights Act, 58 Alabama Law Review 349 (2006) 341

Tokaji, Daniel P., Judicial Review of Election Administration, 156 University of Pennsylvania Law Review PENNumbra 379 (2008) 331

Tokaji, Daniel P., Leave It to the Lower Courts: On Judicial Intervention in Election Administration, 60 Ohio State Law Journal 1065 (2007) 331

Tokaji, Daniel P., The Paperless Chase: Electronic Voting and Democratic Values, 73 Fordham Law Review 1712 (2005) 307, 312

Tokaji, Daniel P., The New Vote Denial: Where Election Reform Meets the Voting Rights Act, 57 South Carolina Law Review 689 (2006) 332

Tomz, Michael & Robert P. Van Houweling, How Does Voting Equipment Affect the Racial Gap in Voided Ballots? 47 American Journal of Political Science 46 (2003) 307

Traugott, Michael W., Why Electoral Reform Has Failed: If You Build It, Will They Come?, on Rethinking the Vote: The Politics and Prospects of American Election Reform (Ann N. Crigler, Marion R. Just & Edward J. McCaffery, eds., 2004) *347*

Tribe, Laurence H., American Constitutional Law (2d ed. 1988) 52, 98, 255, 515, 539, 704

Tribe, Laurence H., roG v. hsuB and Its Disguises: Freeing Bush v. Gore From Its Hall of Mirrors, 115 Harvard Law Review 170 (2001) 306

Tucker, James Thomas, The Battle over "Bilingual Ballots" Shifts to the Courts: A Post-Boerne Assessment of Section 203 of the Voting Rights Act, 45 Harvard Journal on Legislation 507 (forthcoming 2008) 341

Tucker, James Thomas, Enfranchising Language Minority Citizens: The Bilingual Election Provisions of the Voting Rights Act, 10 N.Y.U. Journal of Legislation and Public Policy 195 (2006/2007) 340

Tucker, James Thomas, The Politics of Persuasion: Passage of the Voting Rights Act Reauthorization of 2006, 33 Journal of Legislation 205 (2007) 140

Tucker, James Thomas & Rodolfo Espino, Government Effectiveness and Efficiency? The Minority Language Assistance Provisions of the VRA, 12 Texas Journal on Civil Liberties & Civil Rights 163 (2007) 340

Tushnet, Mark, Darkness on the Edge of Town: The Contributions of John Hart Ely to Constitutional Theory, 89 Yale Law Journal 1037 (1980) 63

Tushnet, Mark, Renormalizing Bush v. Gore: An Anticipatory Intellectual History, 90 Georgetown Law Journal 113 (2001) 306

Uelmen, Gerald, Handling Hot Potatoes: Judicial Review of California Initiatives after Senate v. Jones, 41 Santa Clara Law Review 999 (2001) 391

Uslaner, Eric M. & M. Margaret Conway, The Responsible Congressional Electorate: Watergate, the Economy, and Vote Choice in 1974, 79 American Political Science Review 788 (1985) 595

Volokh, Eugene, Freedom of Speech and Speech about Political Candidates: The Unintended Consequences of Three Proposals, 24 Harvard Journal of Law and Public Policy 47 (2000) 709, 768

Weeks, Joseph R., Bribes, Gratuities and the Congress: The Institutionalized Corruption of the Political Process, the Impotence of Criminal Law to Reach It, and a Proposal for Change, 13 Journal of Legislation 123 (1986) *655*

Weissman, Steve & Ruth Hassan, BCRA and the 527 Groups, in The Election After Reform: Money, Politics and the Bipartisan Campaign Reform Act (Michael J. Malbin, ed., 2007) 797

Weissman, Steven R. & Kara D. Ryan, Soft Money in the 2006 Election and

Index

Page numbers in **bold** identify principal discussion. Page numbers in *italics* identify extended discussion or quotation. Only the first pages of these items are indicated.